Publications by the same author

HISTORICAL

Gold in Dean Forest. Transactions of the Bristol and Gloucestershire Archaeological Society. 1944. (7 pp).
The Extent and Boundaries of the Forest of Dean and Hundred of St. Briavels. John Bellows. Gloucester. 1947. (70 pp).
The Verderers and Speech-Court of the Forest of Dean. John Bellows. Gloucester. 1950. (70 pp).
The Commoners of Dean Forest. British Publishing Company. Gloucester. First Edition, 1951. (179 pp).
Laws of Dean. British Publishing Company. Gloucester. 1952. (25 pp).
The Free Miners of the Royal Forest of Dean and Hundred of St. Briavels. British Publishing Company. Gloucester. First Edition, 1953. (527 pp).
The Dean Forest Eyre of 1282. MA Thesis. Bristol University. 1955. (405 pp).
Lord Bledisloe of Lydney. The Forest of Dean Newspapers Ltd. 1957. (76 pp).
'101 Not Out': The Story of Lydney Cricket Club. The Forest of Dean Newspapers Ltd. 1963. (68 pp).
Watts of Lydney. The Forest of Dean Newspapers Ltd. 1965. (72 pp).
Royal Forest: A History of Dean's Woods as Producers of Timber. Oxford University Press. 1966. (367 pp).
Archaeology in Dean: A Tribute to Dr C. Scott-Garrett, MBE. John Bellows. Gloucester. 1967. (68 pp).
The Industrial History of Dean. David & Charles. Newton Abbot. 1971. (466 pp).
The Verderers and Forest Laws of Dean. David & Charles. Newton Abbot. 1971. (240 pp).
Coleford: The History of a West Gloucestershire Forest Town. Alan Sutton Publishing. 1983. (573 pp).
The Regard of the Forest of Dene in 1282. 1987. (70 pp).
The Forest of Dean: New History. 1550-1818. Alan Sutton Publishing. 1995. (330 pp).
Between Severn and Wye in the Year 1000: A Prelude to the Norman Forest of Dene. Alan Sutton Publishing. 2000. (138 pp).
The Commoners of Dean Forest. Second Edition. Lightmoor Press. 2002. (272 pp.)

FORESTRY

Practical Forestry for the Agent and Surveyor. The Estates Gazette Ltd. 1967. Third Edition. Alan Sutton Publishing. 1995. (658 pp). Latest reprint 2002.
British Trees in Colour. Michael Joseph Ltd. 1974. (64 pp). Also Paperback Edition published 1986 by Michael Joseph Ltd for Mermaid Books.
English-French, French-English: A Handbook of Forestry and Woodland Terms. (L'Exploitation Forestière: Guide Pratique des Termes) (with J. W. A. Newhouse, Hazelholt Farm, Bishops Waltham). (47 pp).
Forestry in Europe. A Report for the Committee on Agriculture of the Council of Europe: Strasbourg. March 1979 (45 pp).
Effect of Taxation on Forest Management and Roundwood Supply. A Report for United Nations, ECE & FAO. Geneva. September 1980. (119 pp).
Taxation of Woodlands. 7 Editions, the last in 1986.
Private Woodlands: A Guide to British Timber Prices and Forestry Costings. 7 Editions, the last in 1987.
Alternative Silvicultural Systems to Clear Cutting in Britain: A Review. Bulletin 115 of the Forestry Commission. HMSO. 1995.

THE FREE MINERS

of the

Royal Forest of Dean

and

Hundred of St. Briavels

'An Ancient Free Miner' (a brass in Newland Church).

THE FREE MINERS

of the
Royal Forest of Dean
and
Hundred of St. Briavels

Second Edition: 2002

With emendations to the First Edition 1953,
and an update of the whole to 2002

by

CYRIL HART

OBE, MA, MSc (Oxon), PhD, FRICS, FICFor
Chartered Land Agent/Surveyor; Chartered Forester

H.M. Senior Verderer of the Forest of Dean

LIGHTMOOR PRESS, 2002

First published in the United Kingdom in 1953
The British Publishing Company Ltd, Gloucester

This Edition 2002
Lightmoor Press
47-49 High Street, Lydney, Gloucestershire

British Library Cataloguing in Publication Data

A catalogue record for this book is available from the British Library.

ISBN 1 899 889 10 8

FOREWORD TO THE FIRST EDITION, 1953

by

Rev. F. W. POTTO-HICKS, MA

THERE is no doubt about the relevance of the story of the Dean free miners to the present general concern with coal mining. Sentiment is not enough to regulate industrial relationships, and the free miners' history will help to make us more sagacious therein.

The author was born in the Forest which contains the coalfield of which he writes; he has always been in happy contact with those interested in all aspects of the life of the Forest of Dean, and is desirous of serving the free miners by making available for them, and also for others, the history of their craft. By his long years of research on the Forest and his position as one of its ancient and honourable body of Verderers I know of no one better able to produce a trustworthy volume on the subject of the free miners.

Our old mining communities of Dean are more than fossils in the social strata, and the Forest is the home of many industrious people quite capable of seeing that as long as coal remains under their feet they do not become mere relics of a defunct industrial organisation. Many, but by no means all, of these inhabitants have, besides their mining, ancient privileges which they wish to continue enjoying. Almost without exception they have an unbounded affection for a corner of England which has to a peculiar degree kept its gracious greenness and quietude. But they are not blind to the fact that, although they enjoy certain exemptions under recent mining Acts, there is a danger of the institution of the free miner becoming little more than an interesting vestige of ancient industrial practice. As during the centuries mining in the Forest has ebbed and flowed outsiders have entered the field and claimed privileges therein without the slightest justification. The want of vigilance on the part of the genuine free miners has suffered their privileges to be eroded and attenuated so that today they are of less worth than formerly, and thus a stalwart company of favourably-placed industrious persons has almost lost its identity in the general body of mine-workers.

Two matters in this connection called for clear and sustained consideration: the history of the free miners, and the elucidation for the free miners and others of the causes of the tendency of the Dean miners to lose their identity. With both these prime matters Mr. Hart has ably dealt. His painstaking work has meant the printing of many records and those who will read these records attentively will find in them many elements of great value to students of social conditions.

Mr. Hart reminds me that when he was engaged on the research for the present work I wrote to him: 'Your work will be a valuable historical document and a memorial to the folly of the free miners! What a fine bit of socialism in the best sense they blew to smithereens!' Yes, in the spontaneity of a friendly letter I did so write. But after reading this volume I believe my words though hasty yet not harsh.

The author has done an immense service to those whose present concern is with coal-getting and coal-using, and also to those who in the not-distant future will need to know the history of an industry then replaced by another providing the community's industrial and domestic energy.

F. W. Potto-Hicks.

Elkstone Rectory,
Cheltenham.
15 May, 1953.

IN MEMORIAM

of Doris

who shared with me
the First Edition

CONTENTS

CHAPTER PAGE

List of Plates xi
Preface xiii
Abbreviations xx
Introduction xxi

PART ONE: PRE-1831

I. The Free Miners 3
(a) The Customs of the Free Miners 3
(b) The Origin of the Customs 11
(c) Military Services rendered by the Miners 19
(d) Ancient Miners' Tools, Equipment and Workings 22

II. The Dean Miners' 'Laws and Privileges' 31
III. Gavellers and Deputy Gavellers 45
IV. The Mine Law Court 59
V. To 1667: Mining and Smelting 141
VI. 1668-1830: Acts of 1668 and 1808 195

Appendices to PART ONE: PRE-1831

1 Emendations to the First Edition, 1953 231
2 Early 'Custodians of the Gawle' (later termed Gavellers) 235
3 Estreat Roll: Forest of Dean 1469-1470: Glos.R.O. D6177/1, 2 237
4 The miners' fight against the Terringham family and others: 1635, 1637, 1667-8 239
5 The (So-called) 'Book of Dennis' 241
6 Mine Law Court Records: 1706-1777: Glos.R.O. D9096, F26/1 243
7 Minutes of the Mine Law Court: 7 February 1730 245
8 A Return from the Commissioners of Woods, 1818 247

continued over

CONTENTS (continued)

PART TWO: 1831-2002

VII. 1831-1841: Fourth Report (1835); Act of 1838; Awards of 1841 251
VIII. 1842-1873: Committees of 1848 and 1854; and Acts of 1861 and 1871 ... 321
IX. 1874-1883: The Committee and Bill of 1874 359
X. 1884-1937: Bills of 1884 and 1889; Acts of 1904, 1906, and 1919 419
XI. 1938-2001: Acts of 1938, 1946, 1969, and 1994 471
XII. The Present Day (AD 2002) 495

Appendices to PART TWO: 1831-2002

A Free Miners' Rights in Private Property ('Excepted Lands') 513
B Gales of coal amalgamated, sub-divided, or rearranged by the Dean Forest (Mines) Act 1904 532
C Gales of coal vested in the NCB: 9 September 1948 534
D Agreement between the Forestry Commission and the Coal Authority: 26 February 1997 536
E The gaveller and deputy gaveller 538
F Gales of iron ore and coal 540
G Deposits of mining records in Glos.R.O. by the Forestry Commission in 1989-98: D5947 and D7920 544
H PRO: Additional mining records relating to the Forest of Dean 545
I Foreword by Cyril Hart to the reprint in 2000 of James G. Wood's *The Laws of the Dean Forest and Hundred of St. Briavels* (1878) 546
J The Cyril Hart Dean Mining Collection donated in 2002 to the Forestry Commission, Coleford 549

Glossary 551
Bibliography 561
Index of Subjects 565
Index of Personal Names 583
Index of Place Names 596

LIST OF PLATES

'An Ancient Free Miner' (a brass in Newland Church) .... *Frontispiece*

PLATE PAGE

I. The Forest of Dean Region 2

II. Ancient miners' and smiths' tools depicted in Abenhall Church 23

III. 'The Miners Lawes and Privilledges': 1673 transcript 33

IV. A Mine Law Court Order of 1728 114

V. The statutory Forest of Dean 142

VI. The Hundred of St. Briavels 143

VII. Geological Plan of the Forest of Dean 250

VIII. Edward Machen, deputy surveyor 1808-1854 322

IX. James G. Wood, a 19th century distinguished barrister, often consulted on freemining 420

X. Trustees of the Free Miners for the 'Deep Coal Gales': *c.*1906 468

XI. Distribution of 'Gale Money' in 1951 474

XII. Typical mid-twentieth century free miners and their coal 'Level' ... 478

XIII. Richard Davies, a Chartered Land Agent/Surveyor, area land agent for the Forestry Commission, who attends to stone quarries in the statutory Forest 484

XIV. Roy Piggott, deputy gaveller 1994-1997, a Chartered Mining Engineer and Chartered Minerals Surveyor, who took an important balanced view of the 1994 Act 484

XV. John Harvey, deputy gaveller 1997- , a Chartered Mining Engineer, who administers freemining on behalf of the Forestry Commission per the Dean Forest Mines enactments 484

XVI. Free Miners Association officials, 2002 504

XVII. A free miner in 2001: Gerald Haynes at his Hayners Bailey coal mine (now renamed Monument mine, of Ray Ashley and Mark Bradley, free miners). 509

PLEASE NOTE

Throughout the text monetary sums are given in the old imperial coinage; they have not been converted to decimal coinage as used in the United Kingdom after 1971.

d. = penny
s. = shilling
£ = pound

12d. = 1s.
20s. = £1 (one pound)
£1 1s. = one guinea

Decimal equivalents
1s. =5p
£1 = 100p

PREFACE

THE Forest of Dean between the lower mighty Severn and the meandering Wye in south-west Gloucestershire – and one-time partly in south Herefordshire – was and remains part of the domain of the Crown, administered by its officers under rules and regulations. Currently it is managed by the Forestry Commission through its deputy surveyor and its minerals through its deputy gaveller. This volume is devoted to one of the Forest's ancient customs – the right of freemining of coal, iron ore, and stone.

During the almost half century which has elapsed since the First Edition in 1953, much has occurred of relevance to mining in the Forest and the substantially larger and not fully co-terminous Hundred of St. Briavels of which the Crown owns only a portion.[1] In 1946 the UK coalfields including that of the Forest were nationalised though without harming the free miners' rights; iron ore mining virtually ceased; and deep mining of coal was abandoned in 1965. Many sections of relevant Acts have been repealed or amended. Further research has produced additional documents and other information. The First Edition, researched during 1949-52 and written in 1952-3,[2] was undertaken with a view to considering and recording the history of the ancient unique mining privileges in the interesting but comparatively unknown part of England – the Forest and hundred. Underlying the once ancient and royal Forest are a relatively small coalfield and an iron ore field, as well as significant stone deposits, mostly covered and surrounded by woodland. No such mineral field, worked for at least two millennia, has more distinct characteristics, peculiarities, and interests.

In Dean are many places of great beauty, and there are few districts more attractive and richer in history. Here kings and poets, statesmen and labourers have found pleasure, peace and solitude – though never was a part of England often so little understood and at times so inadequately managed. It was the first National Forest Park to be constituted in England (1938).

Until recent decades, few books have extolled the Forest and few poets have sung its praises. In 1878 Sir John Maclean, once of English Bicknor, a great lover of the Forest and its past, wrote[3] that its early days were 'an obscure page of Gloucestershire history which deserves to be cleared up'. The few early books that have been written are now scarce, copies being found only in public libraries or jealously and proudly held in a few households

---

1 The Hundred of St. Briavels (so named from *c.*1154) comprises the whole of the now statutory Forest as well as the surrounding parishes of Hewelsfield, St. Briavels, Newland, Staunton, English Bicknor, Ruardean, Mitcheldean, Abenhall, Flaxley, and Littledean.

2 Early in May 1953 the printed proof pages accompanied me in R.M.S. *Queen Mary* purposefully to utilise the five-day voyage from Southampton to New York, thereby enabling me to prepare a limited Index. On my arrival in New York the Index was posted to my publishers in England. Following my first tour of forests on the west coast of America, I returned to England to learn that the book including the Index was published.

3 *Trans. B.&G.A.S.*, vol. iii, p. 367.

within the locality. My First Edition was an attempt partly to fill that gap.

Many readers may not have heard of the ancient miners of coal, iron ore, and stone possessing exclusive privileges which were consolidated by the Dean Forest (Mines) Act 1838 to achieve the status of 'Free', a right retained to this day. They are a people apart – as unique as their ancient laws and privileges, and as engaging as the Forest itself. During and around the Roman Period local miners won iron ore, and to a lesser extent coal, when and wherever they desired, and without let or hindrance of anyone – generally working the relatively easily mined outcrops. Today a registered free miner is a male person born and abiding within the Hundred of St. Briavels, of the age of 21 years and upwards, who has worked a year and a day in a coal or iron ore mine (or a stone quarry) within the hundred. Their customs and privileges are documented from *c.*1244, and confirmed in 1282. The earliest transcript of their 'Laws and Privileges' is one of 1612. The lengthy Orders and Minutes of their Mine Law Court – a self-regulating court with jury – documented from 1469 are herein transcribed; and they remain the only coal miners in the Kingdom who are called 'Free'.

I record my indebtedness to the late James G. Wood (Plate IX), a nineteenth century distinguished barrister, once of Chepstow, whose book *The Laws of the Dean Forest and Hundred of St. Briavels* written in 1878[1] proved invaluable to the mining community of the district. His book – to which in 1952 I had the pleasure of writing a modest supplement, *Laws of Dean* – having been prepared from a statutory viewpoint, included a most useful collection of Acts, Awards and Reports; but omitted much of the interesting and informative ancient records, depositions, minutes of evidence, etc., connected with these and other aspects of the mining history. Many of the records likewise were unavailable to the Rev. H. G. Nicholls for his three otherwise valuable 'pioneer' books on the history of the Forest written in 1858, 1863, and 1868 (see list of abbreviations on p. xx).

In writing the First Edition, 1953, the relative customs in Dean proved a productive field for study and speculation. I first sought information to enrich my knowledge of the Forest – my birthplace and sylvan home. Later I became anxious to communicate it to others. When I first set upon my task I was little aware of the time and attention that would be required to accomplish it. The more closely I investigated the subject the wider the field expanded to my view. For instance, I had scarcely commenced my labours when I found it was necessary to direct my attention to a study of ancient forest law – a most fruitful and interesting exercise. The same had to be done with other aspects of my task; and the results of some of my contemporary research were published in earlier books.[2] The First Edition appeared to have been well received: today copies are scarce.

* * *

[1] Fortunately I came into possession of James G. Wood's personal copy of his book containing his emendations and extra notes. [Donated in 2002 to the Forestry Commission Office, Coleford in The Cyril Hart Dean Mining Collection.] In 2000, Wood's book was reprinted, together with a Foreword by the present author – see Appendix I, and Plate IX.

[2] *The Extent and Boundaries of the Forest of Dean and Hundred of St. Briavels* (1947); *The Verderers and Speech-Court of the Forest of Dean* (1950); *The Commoners of Dean Forest* (1951); and *Laws of Dean* (1952). Most of the source material for my earlier and later Dean books and articles are available thus: (a) In Gloucestershire Record Office: D3921: The Cyril Hart Dean Collection (deposited 1980 onwards); (b) In the Forestry Commission Office, Coleford: The Cyril Hart Dean Forestry Collection (donated in 1999); and The Cyril Hart Dean Mining Collection (donated in 2002).

I have now thought it useful and prudent to enhance my earlier history of freemining by way of emendations to 1953 – see Appendix 1 – as well as to update the history to 2002. The timing is also appropriate because by 2002, opposition by the free miners to some proposals of the Coal Authority, made from 1994, which might harm freemining has been debated. This Second Edition is divided into Part One: Pre-1831 and Part Two: 1831-2002 – being the appropriate text division to record the ancient and unique history of the free miners, and 1838 being the year in which the Dean Forest (Mines) Act replaced their relevant 'laws and privileges' by statutorily defined rights and regulations. That statute has been followed by others of relevance, mainly in 1861, 1871, 1904, and 1906 – the whole, as amended, now referred to as the Dean Forest Mines enactments, allegedly somewhat incompatible with the Coal Industry Act 1994 discussed in Chapters XI and XII. Superimposed on the foregoing is much recent legislation relating to town and country planning, environment, Health & Safety, and mining subsidence damage regulations.

The cycle of events of freemining is briefly noted later in this Preface. Much debate has ensued as to whether from early times any royal approval of the miners' privileges was simply toleration of an economically valuable operation, or whether they were specifically favoured and 'protected'. Without approval and encouragement there would have been no mineral revenue for the Monarch or his assigns. Although the miners from time to time have referred to a charter or some other official endorsement (perhaps related to their known splendid military and other services) no authentication or verification of such from any king or from any other high source has been discovered.

As noted earlier, the miners' privileges are documented from *c.* 1244, and confirmed in 1282. From about 1435 the king granted the mining dues from the miners to successive subjects 'by his grace and favour' – a sinecure office termed 'custodian of the king's *Goale minarum* (*c.* 1464)' and later becoming known as 'gaveller'. Eventually the beneficial office was split between 'the custodian of the gale Above the Wood' (the west part of the hundred) and 'the custodian of the gale Below the Wood' (the east part of the hundred). The custodial beneficiaries may or may not have resided in or near the Forest; each would have employed someone locally to collect the dues from the miners – leading to the office of 'deputy gaveller'. [Hence has continued to this day the long connection between gaveller, deputy gaveller, and miners as noted particularly in Chapter III and in Appendix E.]

The foregoing mining situation continued to about 1611 when James I granted to William, earl of Pembroke, 'the Forest of Dean including mines and quarries' for 40 years; and in 1614 a like grant of 'the iron ore and coal found in the Forest'. The first grant led in 1612 to the earliest known challenge to the miners' customs and privileges. In response they produced the earliest transcript of their 'Laws and Privileges', a rewrite in 1612 of an earlier parchment, called 'The Inquisition', which also included the regulations of their own self-regulating Mine Law Court. The earl eventually allowed the miners 'out of grace, not of right' to continue to mine, and then only to supply his nominees – mostly ironmasters of 'the King's Ironworks'. There followed a period of supplying iron ore, and a little coal, to the early increasingly voracious furnaces. At the Dean Forest Eyre of 1634 the miners did not attempt to claim their privileges (at that time they were not considered to be a corporation), which probably led in 1635 and later to claims against them made by the Terringham family (see Appendix 4) but successfully opposed by the miners.

The Dean Forest (Reafforestation) Act 1668 S.XI briefly referred to 'the miners and persons using the trade of digging for iron ore, coal and ochre' but did not define their privileges. However, it was of utmost importance to the miners. The ownership of the minerals remained in the Monarch with a deputy gaveller to liaise with the miners and to collect their dues. (Later the privileges extended to millstones and grindstones, but eventually related to the Forest only, not to the hundred.) In 1675-6, the miners successfully pursued a 'case' against a challenge raised by a man surnamed 'Dennis' (see Appendix 5).

Although the miners may have claimed themselves 'Free' as early as the thirteenth century, they were first recorded as such in a Report of 1788 and repeated in an Act of 1831. In the Dean Forest (Mines) Act 1838 their rights were statutorily verified. Thereafter the Crown was represented by the Office of Woods and Forests. Although in 1874-5 and 1884-8 the Government attempted to promote Parliamentary Bills which, if enacted, would have harmed freemining, the rights continued unchallenged up to and after the appointment in 1919 of the Forestry Commission who, as gaveller from 1924, benefited directly through its deputy gaveller's collection of dues from miners. Up until the 1938 Coal Act the rents and royalties from coal, iron ore and stone accrued to the Forestry Commission; thereafter the revenues from coal went to the Coal Commission, but iron ore and stone revenues remained (and remain) to the Forestry Commission. A statutory 'challenge' of some alarm made in 1994 by the Coal Authority in regard to coal, but not to iron ore and stone, is noted later in this Preface.

Freemining may have arisen either by a process of 'custom', or 'prescription', or most unlikely, 'lost grant'. In about 1244 (and sometimes claimed by the miners to be 'from before the Conquest', 1066), the king and his nine foresters-of-fee, each a custodian of a bailiwick within the Forest, permitted the miners (then generally termed 'diggers', 'workers' and 'pioneers' together with 'carriers') to continue to win iron ore (then termed 'mine') and coal (then termed 'sea-cole') subject to cash and other dues rendered either to the king or to his assigns. This arrangement and co-operation continued to at least 1282 as recorded in the Dean Forest Eyre and Regard of that year. In and around the fourteenth century the dues were collected by officials on behalf of the king's Receiver and paid by him either into the Exchequer or to a grantee or lessee of the king. The cycle of events of freemining in brief has been:

- Initially, sporadic mining of iron ore, followed later by modest quantities of coal (both mined chiefly from outcrops – relatively easily worked surface deposits and seams) in order to 'eke out a livelihood' and for personal gain. Apparently encouraged or demanded by persons needing the ore for smelting in primitive small furnaces and later for production in forges.
- From as early as about 1244, and confirmed in 1282, increased mining, still mainly of iron ore, to sustain the rising demand of improved 'ironworks'. Again, as a livelihood and for personal gain. A contemporary modest increase in coal mining. A self-regulating Mine Law Court was extant from at least 1469.
- From the 1600s, a further increase in iron ore mining to sustain early increasingly voracious furnaces, fuelled by charcoal, of the ironmasters, usually those leased from the king. Such employment was welcome. A contemporary increase in coal mining.

- Increasing iron ore mining to sustain local ironworks, also those on the fringe of the Forest; as well as some for export. Employment and personal gain were again the driving forces. (The last Mine Law Court was held in 1777.) Increasing coal mining, especially as wage workers in the employ of wealthy 'foreigners', continuing to the end of the nineteenth century. The coal industry had passed largely into the hands of 'foreigners'. A great gulf remained between them (virtually supported by the Crown) and the free miners. Unsuccessful attempts were made by Government in 1874, 1884, and 1889 to extinguish or weaken freemining.
- From 1904, greatly increased coal mining, but reducing iron ore mining. Welcome employment as wage workers in deep coal mines owned by large companies (as well as receiving a modest payment per ton for the cost of coal gales transferred).
- From 1946, continuing employment in deep coal mines under the National Coal Board (later British Coal Corporation), ending in 1965.
- Thereafter, a reversion to private individual or partnership small coal mining enterprises – some successful, others not – in modest-sized units, levels/adits and dipples. Many small sized coal gales changed hands by sale, lease, gift, or bequest (and continues at present).
- Several small opencast coal mining enterprises were undertaken, including in 1980-2 a large area, providing only modest local employment for a few years.

[Incidentally, mining and commoning in the Forest are not related, but some miners have been commoners (until 2001 they needed few qualifications). Mining, from 1838, is a statutory right, whereas commoning is a sufferance. Usually miners when required added their weight to the interests of commoners, and *vice versa*.]

Throughout the centuries, following the gradual dwindling of apparent 'protection' by the reigning monarchs and their assigns, the great drawback in the presentation of the miners' case, and the guarding of their customary privileges, has been lack of substantial backing, lack of unity, and lack of adequate presentation.

However, since the advent of the locally alarming Coal Industry Act 1994, renewed efforts to safeguard their rights have been made by several of the few dozen profoundly interested free miners, as discussed in Chapters XI and XII. The compatibility or otherwise of that Act and the Dean Forest Mines enactments has caused considerable concern – to the Forestry Commission, as gaveller, the Coal Authority, and more particularly to the free miners who are now involved in a dual licensing scenario (i.e. gale and licence) with all the implications and financial costs thereof. The incongruity between the two sets of legislation has for almost a decade been actively pursued by the free miners with the relative Government departments. The Coal Authority stance (enlarged upon in Chapter XI) appears to be that whilst acknowledging freemining rights under the amended enactments, the 1994 Act is equally cogent, with its relationship with the Forestry Commission being that set out in their Agreement of 1997 (see Appendix D). This scenario appears to have induced much frustration to the few working, and some politically motivated, free miners, thereby making the prospects of active freemining seemingly unnecessarily uncertain, fragile and speculative. Acting under a strong sense of principle, and alarmed at what they consider an impingement of their rights, the situation has generated in the free miners a resurgence, reinvigoration and strengthening of their endeavours to safeguard their ancient customs and heritage. It remains to be seen whether their discontent will be satisfactorily abated (see p. 495).

Already the Coal Authority has made some concessions, chiefly by reducing its licence fee to £50, and increasing its licensing extraction limit from 500 to 1,500 tonnes per annum.

Uncertainties relate to the resolution of two separate factors. First, the achievement of the essential qualification of birth within the Hundred of St. Briavels, there now being no Maternity Hospital therein. Second, obtaining the qualification of working for a year and a day in a local mine, there now being relatively few active workings.

The present day situation and potential of freemining are discussed in Chapter XII. Currently the rights of the free miners are as set out in the Dean Forest Mines enactments (1838 to 1906, as amended). Their heirs and assigns – as galees – have no right of a grant of a gale, but they do possess all the other rights, and can, paradoxically, be either male or female: several females today hold coal gales, both dormant and active, but themselves take no part in the working. Today, the total number of free miners on the Register is 4,345; most are deceased. About eight are operators of small coal mines, and one is extracting a small amount of ochre from an iron ore mine. Four miners, not free miners but galees, are operating small coal mines under licence. The rights continue to this day, though slightly modified, and are jealously guarded, so far as the statutes allow. The present free miners remember with a certain amount of pride the hard struggles that their predecessors experienced in retaining their rights, and hold tenaciously to them. Though most gales are now of small monetary value, the history of the free miners continues as of unusual interest. They have played a great part in the economic development of the district.

From time immemorial, minerals have been extracted from the Forest region (and precisely since *c.*1154 from the Hundred of St. Briavels). Commencing with the extraction of iron ore in pre-Roman times, the relatively thick deposits became commercially largely exhausted by the turn of the twentieth century, with the last significant mining ceasing at the end of the Second World War. By AD 2002, only small token amounts of ochre in abandoned iron ore workings are infrequently extracted. During the last millennium, significant developments in coal mining came about, culminating in the closure of the last deep shaft mining in 1965. In parallel with the iron ore and coal extraction, stone was also extracted, latterly on a significant scale, which still persists, for road-stone use throughout the country. Over at least two millennia, and throughout the many overlapping but different extraction phases, mining and quarrying have produced an immense benefit to the local economy by providing many livelihoods and, at the same time, a significant input into the economy of the country. Whilst the statutory rights of free miners had their genesis out of these many years and phases of mineral extraction, in more recent years, following much progress as well as many vicissitudes, freemining has constricted to limited local economic value, generating only a somewhat precarious livelihood for about a dozen of the populace.

I would like to comment that all who have the interests of the Forest at heart, may well appreciate that (a) the Coal Act 1938 (which nationalised all UK coal, and vested it in the State under the aegis of the Coal Commission) saved the rights of freemining; and (b) the Coal Industry Nationalisation Act 1946 (which nationalised both the UK coal and coal mines, and vested them under the aegis of the National Coal Board) again saved the rights of freemining. Also, incidentally, that an Act of 1981 decrees, again uniquely, that, of all the Forestry Commission's forests, only Dean cannot be sold.[1] (This exception being in addition to an Act of 1971 abrogating forest law, the only exception being that therein is saved 'the appointment and functions of verderers', and that, again uniquely, 'verderers in the Forest of Dean shall continue to be elected and hold office as at the passing of this Act'.)[2] All four enactments were unique benefits to the Forest and are noteworthy and appreciated.

In the Preface to the First Edition, 1953, I expressed warm thanks to the Rev. F. W. Potto-Hicks MA, a knowledgeable helpful friend (once of Cinderford) with a profound love of the Forest, also to W. D. Meredith (then secretary to the free miners), Ralph Harper (of the gaveller's office), W. D. Jenkins, and Tom Bright. I repeat those thanks in this Second Edition, 2002, in which I am likewise pleased to acknowledge helpful comments on portions of Part Two received from two accomplished deputy gavellers – Roy Piggott and John Harvey – each possessing a profound knowledge of the Forest's coalfield – and Richard Davies, area land agent of the Forestry Commission; however, any errors of commission or omission are of course my own. Also I thank Rob Guest, the current distinguished deputy surveyor of the Forest for Forest Enterprise, as well as several other individuals, including free miners and galees, with whom the research for this Second Edition has brought me into touch. My warm thanks are likewise recorded to the staff of the Public Record Office, the British Library, the deputy surveyor's staff in Coleford, the Gloucestershire Record Office, the Gloucester County and City Libraries, the Dean Heritage Centre, and the Forest of Dean Local History Society. Also to my friend Vernon Daykin. Without the help and co-operation received this Edition would not have been so comprehensive and rewarding to me. My grateful thanks are expressed to Ian Pope my publisher, himself an authority on the history of the Forest. Finally I record my gratitude to my two children, Judith and Anthony, who with several mutual friends have provided an encouraging and helpful family environmental background during my researches and writings.

The pleasure and satisfaction I have derived from the preparation of this book, and from meetings I have had with people interested in the Forest of Dean, have amply repaid my labours. If this Second Edition proves of interest and usefulness to the free miners together with readers seeking knowledge of them, and in some small measure assists them to understand and appreciate their ancient rights, then I shall be adequately satisfied.

CYRIL HART
Chenies
Coleford
Forest of Dean
Gloucestershire GL16 8DS
26 April 2002

---

1 Notes of the present author's modest contribution with Lord McNair and the Forest of Dean District Council to obtain the 1981 concession are deposited in Glos.R.O., Hart Dean Collection, D3921, II 25, 26 (Access. 7366). To commemorate Lord McNair's services, three oaks were planted in 1981 in the northwest corner of the Speech House field.

2 Notes of the present author's modest contribution to the Law Commission in their drafting of the 1971 Act are deposited in Glos.R.O., Hart Dean Collection, D3921, II 25, 26 (Access. 7366).

ABBREVIATIONS USED IN FOOTNOTES

Br. Liby.	British Library, London
Cal.	*Calendar*
Cal.Pat.Roll	*Calendar of Patent Rolls*
Cal.SPD	*Calender of State Papers Domestic*
Cal.Treas.Books	*Calendar of Treasury Books*
Cal.Treas.Books and Papers	*Calendar of Treasury Books and Papers*
Coms.	Commissioners and/or Commissions
DTI	Department of Trade and Industry
Exch. Deps. by Coms.	Exchequer Depositions by Commissions
Glos.R.O.	Gloucestershire Record Office
Glouc.Liby.	Gloucester Library
H.M.C.	*Historical Manuscripts Commission*
Harl.MSS	British Library, Harleian Manuscripts
I.P.M.	*Inquisitiones Post Mortem*
Lansd.MSS	British Library, Lansdowne Manuscripts
NCB	National Coal Board (later British Coal Corporation)
NH	Rev. H. G. Nicholls: *The Forest of Dean: An Historical and Descriptive Account* (1858)
NI	Rev. H. G. Nicholls: *Iron Making in the Olden Times: As instanced in the ancient mines, forges and furnaces of the Forest of Dean* (1866)
NP	Rev. H. G. Nicholls: *The Personalities of the Forest of Dean* (1863)
Procs. C.N.F.C.	Proceedings of the Cotswold Naturalists Field Club
PRO	Public Record Office, Kew
Rawl.MSS	Bodleian, Rawlinson Manuscripts
Rpt.	Report
SP	State Papers
Trans. B.&G.A.S.	*Transactions of the Bristol and Gloucestershire Archaeological Society*
Wood	James G. Wood: *The Laws of the Dean Forest and Hundred of St. Briavels* (1878)
3rd Rpt. of 1788	Third Report of the Commissioners appointed to inquire into the State and Condition of the Woods, Forests, and Land Revenues of the Crown (London), 3 June 1788

Most documents, unless stated otherwise, are in the Public Record Office, Kew.

INTRODUCTION

'Here, queen of forests all, that West of Severn lye,
Her broad and bushy top Dean holdeth up so high,
The lesser are not seen, she is so tall and large,
And standing in such state upon the winding marge. …
So fruitful in her woods, and wealthy in her mines.' [1]

THE Forest of Dean and the substantially larger Hundred of St. Briavels,[2] not fully co-terminous, lie in the lower part of the triangle formed by the rivers Severn and Wye, in south-west Gloucestershire. Dean is one of the ancient royal forests of England, which, besides holding a wealth of timber, contains extensive (but now depleted) seams of coal and deposits of iron ore (including small quantities of ochre), and much high quality stone.[3] The coalfield extends over about fifty-four square miles. At one time the Forest included almost the whole district lying between the two rivers south of a line running approximately from Gloucester *via* Newent to Ross-on-Wye, but throughout the centuries it has been reduced in area[4] until at the present time the statutory Forest comprises a district of just about 8,200 hectares (20,254 acres) in the central portion of its former extent. Dean is distinctive in both its scenery and the life of its inhabitants, and contains much of antiquarian interest. Within it are combined the charms of a landscape one would expect in a forest and the features of a now rehabilitated mining district. Thankfully, kind nature and wise management by the Forestry Commission since 1919 have clothed the majority of the old spoil tips and workings with bracken, birch and other trees including pines, while woodlands screen the few small coal mines which are still working.

Dean is different from other forests in having been from early times a mining district. Many of its inhabitants were miners with customs and manners of their own,[5] living in an area for centuries largely reserved for royal hunting and the supply of venison to royal larders; and later for timber supplies. Iron and timber were for many centuries its

1 Michael Drayton. 1613. Poly-Olbion, Song 7.

2 For a consideration of the Hundred of St. Briavels (named from *c.*1154) see Hart, *The Extent and Boundaries of the Forest of Dean and Hundred of St. Briavels* (1947). Also see Glossary and Plates V and VI.

3 For the general history of Dean's mining, see Hart, *Industrial History* (1971), pp. 216-52 and Plate VII (iron ore), 253-95 and Plate VII (coal), and 296-315 (stone quarrying).

4 By deforestation, sales, grants and encroachments. The encroachments have since been confirmed to their possessors and are now no longer vested in the Crown.

5 For some light on the characteristics of the inhabitants of Dean Forest, see *No Quarter* by Mayne Reid (1888); *Dene Forest Sketches* by S. M. Crawley-Boevey (1887 and 1889); *The Life of Warren James* by A Resident Forester (1831), and *Sixty-two years of the Life of a Forest of Dean Collier* by Timothy Mountjoy (1887).

two key industries, and the story of Dean as a forest has been largely one of conflict between these two industrial interests.[1] Dean's isolation was not only geographical, it was political and social as well. The government in London must have appeared a tremendous distance away. Being a royal forest with officers and courts of its own, only in troublesome times did the county and country officials have much to do with it. The inhabitants had little dealing with outsiders; strangers (locally termed 'foreigners') visited the district at their peril. Attacks on their time-honoured customs were immediately resisted. Any attempt by the Monarch to assign or inclose portions of the Forest, was sufficient to cause a serious riot, and the fences, hedges, walls, and gates might be quickly destroyed. Most disturbances were related to the privilege of commoning.[2] Lacking adequate education, organisation, and the means to present their case to numerous commissions and committees, the inhabitants' discontent at decisions adversely affecting their customs found its expression in obstruction. There is no doubt, however, that in the majority of cases the inhabitants were sincere in their belief that the privileges they enjoyed were their legal due. They certainly tried their hardest to retain them and resist intruders.[3]

To comprehend adequately the rich and ancient history of the Forest one should become acquainted with some of the forest laws. These begin with the code attributed by the Normans to King Cnut, and said to have been promulgated by him in 1016, but modern criticism has declared them at least in part a forgery, perhaps adapted by the Normans to gain legal authority for their own practices. The first genuine code of forest laws is the Assize of Woodstock (1184) in Henry II's reign; then came the *Magna Carta* of John (1215) and the *Carta de Foresta* of Henry III (1217).[4] The last code ended the arbitrary extensions of the royal *forests*,[5] cancelling the post-Conquest enlargements, and mitigating the harsh penalties previously enforced against those who harmed the king's deer.[6] In common with other royal forests (except the New Forest demarcated by William I in 1079) no information exists as to the first demarcation of Dean Forest (first so named in 1086). It has, however, been heavily wooded land

1 Hart, *Royal Forest* (1966).

2 Hart, *The Commoners of Dean Forest*, 1st Edn. (1951) and 2nd Edn. (2002). In 1981 the sufferance of commoning was regulated by the Forestry Commission in an Agreement under the Byelaws, with the Forest of Dean Commoners Association. Following an outbreak of Foot and Mouth Disease in 2001, the Forest was closed from 28 February to 14 July, and about 4,500 roaming sheep were culled, some having been infected. A new Agreement with the Commoners Association was made on 17 December 2001.

3 A summing up of the characteristics of the inhabitants and the administration of the Forest in the seventeenth century is given by W. B. Willcox, *Gloucestershire: A Study in Local Government,* 1590-1640 (Yale Univ. Press, 1940).

4 The reader who desires to pursue forest law further is referred to: Manwood, J., *A Treatise and Discourse of the Laws of the Forest* (1598, 1615, 1665 and 1717); Coke's Fourth Part of the Institutes (Jurisdiction of Courts): 1648, pp. 289-320; Turner, G. J., *Select Pleas of the Forest* (1901) (Selden Society); Cox, J. C., *Royal Forests of England* (1905); Petit-Dutaillis, C., *The Forest: Studies and Notes Supplementary to Stubbs Constitutional History, II* (1915: Univ. Press, Manchester); Lewis, P., *Historical Inquiries concerning Forests and Forest Laws, etc.* (1811); and Bazeley, M. L., see Bibliography.

5 The extension of a royal forest did not mean the covering of the additional area with trees, but only that the area was brought under the jurisdiction of *forest law* and the freedom of the inhabitants curtailed accordingly.

6 Article 10 reads: 'No man from henceforth shall lose either life or member for killing our deer, but if any man be taken therewith and convicted for taking of our venison he shall make grevious fine, if he hath anything whereof to make fine; and if he hath nothing to leese, he shall be imprisoned a year and a day, and after the year and a day expired (if he can find sufficient sureties) he shall be delivered, and, if not, he shall abjure the realm.'

from time immemorial, particularly following the end of the last Ice Age more than some 10,000 years ago.

Abundant evidence is available as proof of the occupation of the district – including mining – previous to and during the Roman occupation.[1] Domesday (1086) incidentally refers to 'the forest' at the time of Edward the Confessor (1042 to 1066), three thegns holding land in the district 'free from geld (tax) for the service of guarding the forest'.[2] It was one of the hunting grounds of our Norman and Angevin kings and a valued provider of venison for their larders; it received occasional visits from them.[3]

From the twelfth century the Forest was administered on behalf of the Monarch by the constable of St. Briavels castle (built *c.*1130) who was also warden of the Forest. The prestige and hunting benefits of the Forest were perhaps more acceptable to the king than the profit of its minerals.[4] Its timber was increasingly used for mining purposes but mainly made into charcoal for the smelting of iron ore; some was used for ship-building, some for royal alms for building and repairing religious houses and churches, and much for other donations. The privileges of common and pannage were claimed by the king's subjects in the district, but along with others they were continually disputed throughout the centuries either by the king directly or by those enjoying grants under him. Successive Decrees or Acts of Parliament have been necessary to provide working arrangements tolerable to all parties.[5] The ancient 'Courts of the Forest', while they lasted, had a great influence on the administration and on the inhabitants of the Forest. These Courts were: the Justice Seat in Eyre, the Swanimote Court and the Court of Attachment or Verderers' Court.[6] They were in addition to the miners' own self-regulated Mine Law Court, the Court of the Hundred of St. Briavels and the Court of the Manor of St. Briavels,[7] as well as the later Court of Requests.[8] Superimposed on all the foregoing history were the mining privileges (rights from 1838) of the Dean miners of coal, iron ore, and stone.

The Forest's iron industry flourished until it was gradually reduced by the destruction of trees available for smelting purposes, and by the rivalry of other districts more suitably placed in consequence of improved transport facilities and the use of coking coal for smelting. At the same time, the Forest became one of the chief sources of

---

1 Hart, *Archaeology in Dean* (1967); *Report on Excavations in Lydney Park* by R. E. M. and T. V. Wheeler: (Report of Res. Com. Soc. Antiq. of London, IX, 1932); *Roman Mining in Britain* by G. C. Whittick, MA (Trans. Newcomen Society, vol. xii, 1931-2, pp. 57-84). For the Anglo-Saxon period, see Hart, *Between Severn and Wye in the year 1000* (2000), pp 20, 54, 56, 62, 63.

2 *Domesday*, Glos 167b; Hart, *Between Severn and Wye in the year 1000* (2000), p 82.

3 William the Conqueror visited the Forest in 1069; Henry I at some time before 1107; Henry II in 1158, 1164-5, and 1179; John in 1200, 1207, 1209, 1212, 1213, 1214; Henry III in 1226, 1229, 1232, 1256.

4 Even in later centuries the Forest was well stocked with deer. They were removed in 1850, but there is now a herd (fallow) of around 300, and another in the adjoining High Meadow Woods. See Hart, *The Verderers and Forest Laws of Dean* (1971).

5 Hart, *The Commoners of Dean Forest* 1st Edn. (1951) and 2nd Edn. (2002), and *New History* (1995).

6 Hart, *The Verderers and Speech-Court of the Forest of Dean* (1950) and *The Verderers and Forest Laws of Dean* (1971).

7 The two last courts appear to have been a combination of the courts leet and baron of the manor of St. Briavels and also the court of the not fully co-terminous hundred; See E134/16 Chas. I/M/38 and Willcox, *op. cit.*, pp. 187, 290, 291.

8 Only the Verderers' Court now remains – held four times each year at the Speech House in the centre of the Forest. The present verderers are Dr C. E. Hart, OBE, A. M. R. Watts, OBE, R. W. Jenkins and R. Wright. The steward is K. P. Griffin.

supply of timber in the country, its oak being especially valued for ship-building. So important was this national storehouse of naval timber in the sixteenth century that, according to John Evelyn and others,[1] one of the orders given to the commander of the Spanish Armada in 1588 was to the effect that on landing he was to endeavour to destroy the Forest's timber trees (an enormous task) in order to cripple their enemy's naval activities, though research has shed some uncertainty on this matter.[2]

The mining of iron ore, and its smelting using charcoal, had such a disastrous effect on the timber resources that in and after 1668 the Monarch and Government became seriously alarmed, generating various schemes for conserving and increasing timber trees in the Forest. These were in part successful. Iron magnates had not been the only offenders: other men, high and low, were responsible for much of the loss, and the Government did not stop them. It was even less possible to cope with the inroads of lesser folk attracted to the Forest by the iron industry: there was not enough employment to go round. Stealing of timber was resorted to, the thefts being converted into materials for boats, coopers' wares and other articles. Furthermore, the deer always posed a temptation.

Until 1668 the Forest passed through a period of almost unbroken mismanagement through being 'farmed out' from time to time by the Monarch to court favourites, 'farmers', and others, either by way of reward, or favour, or for revenue. In 1705 it came under the jurisdiction of the surveyor-general of the Royal Forests, and certain improvements occurred, although even after seventy years under the new management, Commissioners reporting in 1788 disclosed many adverse conditions. Subsequent to their Report the Forest timber was, on the whole, well cared for. Various replantings took place and in spite of many conflicts in the eighteenth and nineteenth centuries between local and government interests which gave rise to departmental troubles, and several Inquisitions and Commissions, the Forest became once again a national storehouse of naval timber, as in past years.[3] The adjacent High Meadow Estate, about 8,014 hectares (19,796 acres), mainly woodland, was purchased from Viscount Gage in 1817. From 1834 the Forest was controlled by the Commissioners of Woods, Forests and Land Revenues of the Crown,[4] until in 1924 it was transferred to the Forestry Commission (formed in 1919) by an Order in Council dated 21 March 1924, under the Forestry (Transfer of Woods) Act, 1923.[5] A notable local School of Forestry was

---

1 John Evelyn recorded: 'I have heard, that in the great expedition of 1588, it was expressly enjoined the Spanish commanders of that signal Armada, that if, when they landed, they should not be able to subdue our nation, and make good their conquest, they should yet be sure not to leave a tree standing in the Forest of Dean' (John Evelyn, *Silva*: 1662; p. 564 of 1776 Edn.). *Cf.* another version in S. Hartlib, *His Legacie* (2nd Edn. 1652, p. 88) – 'The Spaniard sent an Ambassador purposely to get this wood destroyed.'

2 Documents of an Elizabethan era spy – Dr John Dee – in Richard Deacon: *John Dee*, (Frederick Muller) 1968, pp. 6-11; and Maurice Broadbent, 'An Elizabethan James Bond' (*Gloucester and Avon Life*, June 1975, pp. 32, 33).

3 The last great 'fall' of naval timber took place in 1853. See Hart, *Royal Forest* (1966), p. 221.

4 Referred to throughout this volume as the 'Commissioners of Woods'. The controlling body was frequently referred to as the 'Office of Woods'. Under the Act 50 Geo. III, c. 65, 1810, the Commissioners of Woods were first appointed in lieu of Surveyors-General. From 1 January 1925, pursuant to an Order in Council dated 8 December 1924, the Commissioners of Woods were designated Commissioners of Crown Lands.

5 The woods of Highmeadow Estate are now managed by the Forestry Commission in conjunction with Dean Forest.

instituted in 1904.[1] In 1938 the Forest's many attributes were recognised, by establishment as a National Forest Park, the first to be constituted in England. The Forest's timber resources, as well as its valuable minerals, proved of immense value during the two world wars. Thereafter the felled areas were soon replanted and the woodlands rehabilitated.

At the present time coal is practically the only mineral mined underground in the Forest but the resource is minimal, although there are three significant stone quarries, each with a production capacity of up to one million tonnes per annum. It was necessary, for the economic stability of the inhabitants, to attract new industries to the district; hence there are many new industrial developments side by side with the great national multiple-use forest policy in which Dean is playing a major role.

The Forest and several extensive neighbouring woodlands are in the charge of the Forestry Commission's deputy surveyor, Rob Guest, a professional forester and keen conservationist. He is also steward of the Crown manors[2] and 'an inspector of railways' within the Forest. Some fifty people find direct or indirect employment in the woods, which are run on multiple-use silvicultural lines.[3]

The Crown via the Forestry Commission is free to enclose most of the Forest for the purpose of the growth of timber,[4] but such area must not at any time exceed 4,451 hectares (11,000 acres); if a new area is 'taken in' some areas may be 'thrown open', regulated by Inclosure Commissioners appointed by the Crown. The four verderers also hold an interested co-operative brief. The inclosures are freed from the privilege of common so long as enclosed, and the same applies to the rights of the free miners. The Open Forest, which includes all forest land not for the time being enclosed, is subject by custom to privileges of common and pannage, and is grazed by the sheep of the commoners of whom about 60 commoners now exist.[5] [Since an Act of 1668 the inhabitants have had no right to estovers;[6] and the former privileges of the Crown workmen to free grazing, firewood, etc., were later commuted.]

The relationships with the free miners and the mineral estate management of the mines are now carried out on behalf of the Forestry Commission (as gaveller) by a deputy gaveller who until 1969 by statute had to be a person skilled in mining. The office is of ancient origin, shown in the text including Appendix E. The present holder is John Harvey, a chartered mining engineer with an office at Coleford, who collects and updates his records from the plans of each of the coal and iron ore mines provided by the galees.[7] Under the provisions of the Coal Act, 1938, which vested all unworked coal in the Coal Commission, the royalties on coal were from 1942 to 1946 collected from the free miners, or galees holding gales under them, for that Commission by the

---

1 W. Thompson, *The Dean Forest School of Forestry* (Procs. C.N.F.C., 1912, XVIII, pp. 63-5); Geoff Waygood, 'The Dean Forester Training School', *The New Regard*, 17, 2002, pp. 35-40.

2 The Crown manors are now St. Briavels, English Bicknor, Staunton and Newland.

3 The deputy surveyor also has jurisdiction over the woods of Highmeadow Estate, Tintern, Chepstow Park and Sedbury.

4 By the Dean Forest (Reafforestation) Act, 1668 [now repealed], and the Dean Forest (Timber) Act 1808.

5 Hart, *The Commoners of Dean Forest*, 1st Edn. (1951) and 2nd Edn. (2002), *Royal Forest* (1966) and *New History* (1995).

6 This exclusion does not apply to the Hudnalls at St. Briavels.

7 Currently it is a statutory duty of a mine operator to appoint a qualified mine surveyor to prepare the plans. See also the 1997 Forestry Commission and Coal Authority Agreement (Appendix D).

deputy gaveller, the management and administration being as hitherto. The rights of the Dean free miners were not usurped by the Coal Industry Nationalisation Act 1946, and coal gales continue to be granted and worked. The rights were saved and the Dean free miners were the only coal miners not 'nationalised' in the whole of the British Isles. Nevertheless, certain aspects of the rights received some alarm from the Coal Industry Act 1994 as discussed in Chapters XI and XII.

For countless years Dean provided for the hunter and the hunted. Later it yielded substantial quantities of iron ore, coal, and stone, much at the expense of its abundance of trees. Its woods and beasts gave sport and food to kings and courtiers; people in the neighbourhood obtained necessary wood, pasture, pannage, and agricultural land. It furnished timber and iron to build and maintain upon the high seas a fleet that brought the nation through perils, that carried her trade and her colonists to the farthest corners of the earth, and that wrought the downfall of the Napoleonic empire. During two world wars it gave strength and sustenance to endure the strains of warfare on sea and land. Throughout two millennia, the Forest's iron ore, coal, and stone have been appropriately exploited creating many diverse industries. Signs of the latter, and of the scars left by the extraction of the minerals, have now largely disappeared beneath the renewed tree cover.

Dean continues to be a working Forest which produces an annual sustainable yield of timber of many qualities and dimensions. At the same time it provides a sustainable sylvan landscape, comprising healthy trees of a variety of species and age classes, shared almost equally between broadleaves and conifers. It is also a very special environmental region, with abundant wildlife, notably deer, water features, and important conservation interests. It offers substantial outdoor recreational facilities for walking, leisurely cycling and horse riding, picnicking, and camping – the whole being a valuable part of the lung of the nation.

PART ONE : PRE-1831

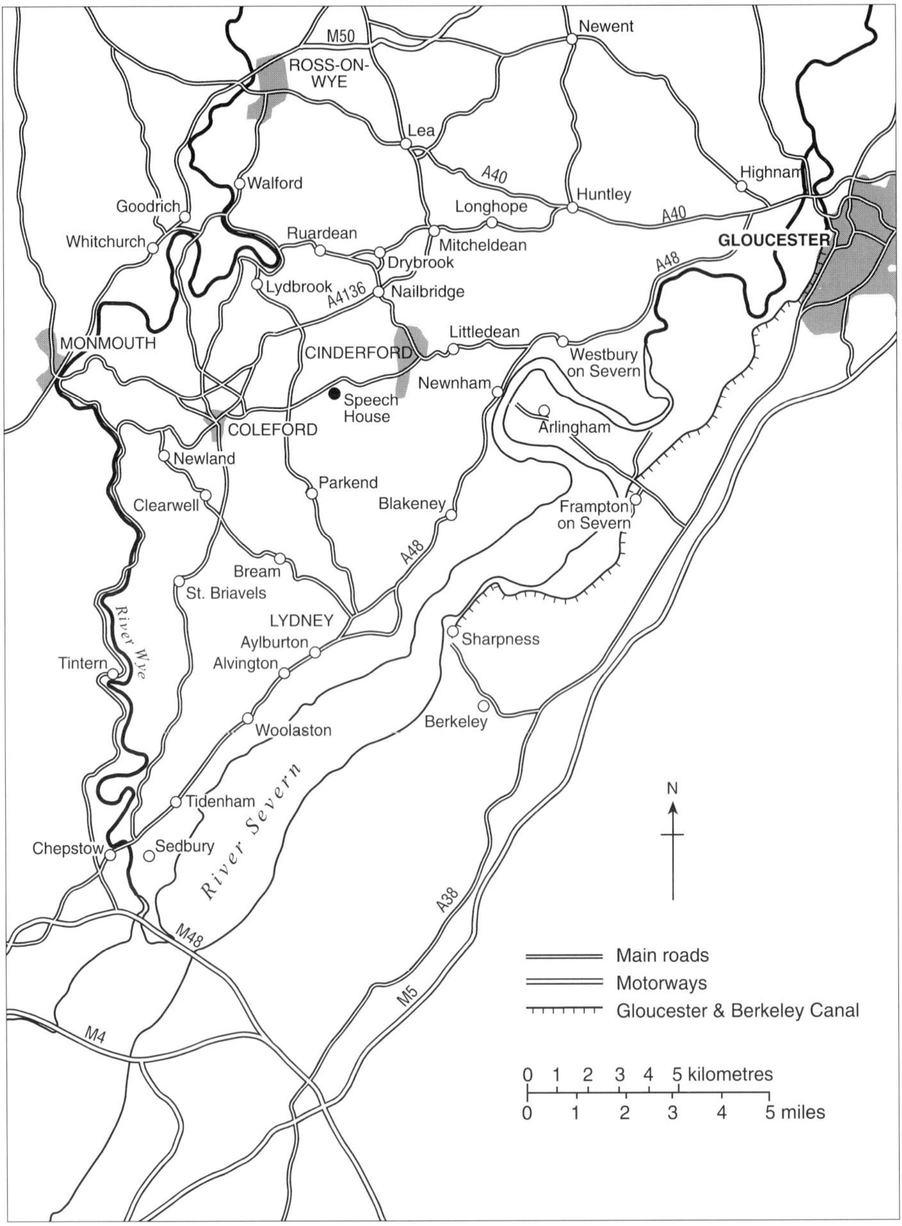

Plate I. *The Forest of Dean Region.*

CHAPTER I

THE FREE MINERS

'Have there not been always within the Forest of Dean and Hundred of the Castle of St. Briavels certain persons called and accompted free miners there; who, time out of mind, have enjoyed without interruption the liberty of entering, digging and working in the mines of coal and iron ore to their own proper use, and have they not been called always the King's miners?' [1675][1]

'Is there not and hath there not always, time whereof the memory of man is not to the contrary, been this custom there used: That any man born within that part of the Hundred of the Castle of St. Briavels as lyeth within the perambulation of the Forest of Dean and bred and brought up in the mystery or craft of mining, after he hath wrought in his own proper person one whole year and a day in some mine within the Forest, is and hath always been accompted and taken for a free miner, and might lawfully and hath been accustomed at his will and liking, by himself or other partners being also free miners, to enter into any place, as well of the King's waste soil or ground of the Forest, as of the several lands of any of his subjects or tenants within the Forest (except gardens, orchards and curtilages) there to dig for the finding of minerals of iron and coal; and the same so found to cast up, take, carry away and convert to his or their own proper use?' [1675][2]

(*a*) THE CUSTOMS OF THE FREE MINERS

THE immemorial usages and customs which have governed the working of the mines of the Forest of Dean and the Hundred of St. Briavels are of unusual interest, and few such subjects are so obscure as the special position and privileges of the free miners[3] and the relation in which those miners have stood to the rest of the community through the centuries. Although somewhat similar privileges, as we shall see, applied to the lead and tin mining industries, the Forest of Dean is the only known district in Great Britain where coal mining and iron ore mining were ever directly subject to such customs.

1 E134. Exch. Deps. by Coms. 27 Chas. II, 1675, Mich. No. 28. Extract from Interr. No. V on behalf of the defendants. Witnesses answered in the affirmative.

2 *Ibid.*, Interr. No. VI. Witnesses answered in the affirmative.

3 The body of free miners are referred to at various times as 'The King's Miners', 'The Company of Miners', 'Pyoneers' or 'The Fellowship of Miners'. Certain of the miners were referred to as 'Master-miners' in the Pipe Roll 20 Edw. III, m. 8.

The Dean free miners exercised their customary privileges under royal protection and their code of 'Laws and Privileges', given in full in Chapter II, refers in several places to regulations being enforced 'by the strength of the king'.[1] Their operations were carried on in an atmosphere of remoteness and secrecy. Thus we find approaching strangers being warned to 'come by the noise of the horn or the cry'[2] and the stipulation that no stranger should 'come within the mine to see and know the privities' of the same.[3] To become 'free' a miner must have been born in and living in the Hundred of St. Briavels and the Forest of Dean,[4] and to have worked at least a year and a day[5] in a coal or iron ore mine within the hundred. In the seventeenth and eighteenth centuries the miners themselves amended the rules of membership and made regulations regarding apprentices. They also made regulations regarding the loading and carrying of their minerals.[7]

Each free miner, subject to the approval of the king's gaveller[8] and payment of

1 Clauses 13, 18, 21, 31 and 32 of the miners' 'Laws and Privileges'.

2 *Ibid.*, clause 2.

3 *Ibid.*, clause 30.

4 The earliest extant transcripts (from 1612) of the miners' 'Laws and Privileges' give the bounds as: 'First between Chepstow Bridge and Gloucester Bridge, the half dole of Newent, Ross Ash, Monmouth Bridge, and so far into the Seassoames as the Blast of a horn or the voice of a man may be heard. 'Seassoames' is possibly a misreading of 'Saeferne' (AS Severn). 'These bounds approximately agree with those defined by Perambulations of 1228 and 1282. (See Hart, *The Extent and Boundaries of the Forest of Dean and Hundred of St. Briavels.* 1947)

5 The period 'a year and a day' was a common one in the Middle Ages (see, e.g., Art. 10 of *Carta de Foresta,* 1217). Order No. 16 (1741) of the Mine Law Court *infra* stipulated that an applicant must 'prove by the oath of two or more credible witnesses his lawfully working at coal or ore a year and a day'.

6 Order No. 1 (1668) of the Mine Law Court stipulated that no young man, whether born in the Hundred of St. Briavels or not, should be allowed to work on his own account iron ore or coal unless he had already worked a year and a day, and paid the king's dues, 'except he be bound apprentice under a free miner and lawfully serve him as an apprentice for the term of six years'; also 'no person whatsoever that was born upon the waste soil of the Forest as a cabbiner shall work at any ore or coal or shall or may transport or carry the same with any manner of carriage unless he hath lawfully worked for the space of seven years'. Order No. 4 (1680) decreed that the apprenticeship should be for five years, and that the applicant for free minership should be at least 21 years of age; this was confirmed by Order No. 5 (1682). Order No. 15 (1737) stipulated that no 'foreigner's' son should become a free miner until he had been apprenticed for seven years to a free miner. It was stated in 1637 that it was also usual for an applicant for free minership to 'bestow a dinner on the Company' (E134. Exch. Deps. by Coms. 13/14 Chas. I, Hil. 16). The Dean Forest (Mines) Act, 1838, recognised and confirmed the period of a year and a day in all cases.

7 Order No. 1 (1668) decreed that no 'foreigner' should carry ore or coal unless first carried to them outside the Hundred of St. Briavels by a free miner; also no free miner was to load any 'foreigners' carriage; no person 'born upon the waste soil of the forest as a cabbiner' was to haul ore or coal unless he had served 7 years under a free miner, and 'no young man shall carry any ore or coal except he possesseth a house of himself'. Order No. 2 (1674) allowed 'foreigners' to carry for their own use only, but inhabitants of the Forest were to be supplied first. Order No. 4 (1680) stipulated that inhabitants of the Hundred of St. Briavels were to be supplied before 'foreigners', while Order No. 5 (1682) confirmed that no young man should be allowed to transport ore or coal unless he 'keep house of himself' or rented sufficient land on which to keep his horses. Order No. 7 (1687) decreed that inhabitants of the Forest should be served first before the miners themselves loaded their own carriages for transport. Further stipulations were imposed by Orders Nos. 13 (1719), 14 (1728). and 15 (1737).

8 The king's gaveller who, through his deputies, collected the dues on behalf of the king. He officially recognised or disallowed a new mine, and allocated a right of way. There were usually two deputy gavellers – one in charge of 'Above the Wood' and the other of 'Below the Wood'. (See Chap. III.)

certain weekly and quarterly dues to the king, shared the exclusive right of his 'Fellowship' to dig for iron ore, coal and ochre[1] where he pleased within the bounds of the Forest, whether on the royal demesne or on the lands of private persons.[2] The king received a share in any newly opened mine by being allowed to put in a workman, known as the 'king's man', without having to bear any of the expenses of sinking or maintenance.[3] In the case of private lands the lord of the soil, as well as the king received a share, by being allowed to put in a workman, known as the 'lord's man'[4].[5]

Certain of the inhabitants of the Forest obtained a right by prescription to quarry and work stone. This right was, however, originally distinct from the rights of the free miners.

Among other privileges of the free miner were the grant of free timber for mining purposes,[6] rights of way to and from the mines,[7] the right to distrain for debt[8] and to try cases affecting the mines in the miners' own Mine Law Court (*infra*), and power to exclude 'foreigners'.[9] When a free miner wished to open a new mine he chose a spot from his local knowledge of the minerals underground and commenced working without asking the consent of the gaveller or the owner of the ground. According to early

---

1 There is no indication of the free miners being connected with copper mining in the Forest nor with the few attempts at gold mining in the district.

2 'The miners may mine in any place that they will as well without the bounds as within, without the forbodement of any man;' (Clause 4 of the miners' 'Laws and Privileges'); 'The miner hath such franchises to inquire the mine in every soil of the king's of which it may be named and also of all other folk without withsaying of any man.' *(Ibid.,* Clause 12). At a later period gardens, orchards and curtilages were excepted (E134. Exch. Deps. by Coms. 27 Chas. II, Hil. 21) and, since 1668, certain areas for the time they remain enclosed (Act 19 & 20 Chas. II, c. 8). Their rights have been disputed in some private properties, especially in the 'Excepted Lands' referred to in Appendix A of this volume.

3 'At all times the king's man shall come into the mine without any cost asking of him and shall be the third better man of the Fellowship' (Clause 15 of the miners' 'Laws and Privileges').

4 'The lord of the soil... shall have a dole without paying anything at his first coming and shall be the last man of the Fellowship' *(Ibid.,* Clause 14).

5 The king is often referred to as 'the fifth man of the Fellowship', and the lord as 'the sixth man of the Fellowship', but no early documentary reason has been found for this. How often in early times advantage was taken of this right by the king and the lord is uncertain. but in 1625 Anthony Callowe deposed that he had put a workman in for himself (E134. Exch. Deps. by Coms. 22 James I, Easter, 8); and in 1637 Thomas Sternehold deposed that 'the miners have digged in his freehold lands, and he might have had a share of the benefit of the pit sank in his grounds, but permitted his tenant to take the same' *(Ibid.,* 13/14 Chas. I, Hil. 16). In later years, in any case, it was rarely exercised: The Coms. of 1831 stated that no instance of a 'fifth man' being put in by the Crown had occurred within the memory of witnesses examined by them (4th Rpt. of 1835), but one witness (Davis) deposed: 'I have known the lord put in his man. The lord's tenant put in a sixth man on me in the Five Acres.'

6 'The Constable... shall deliver the miners... sufficient timber to maintain the king's advantages and profit as also for the salvation of his miners' (Clause 26 of the miners' 'Laws and Privileges'). Naturally, the king was only too willing to allow free timber, as, unless the mine was sunk and maintained, ore would not be forthcoming and his own man could not be 'put in'. *Cf.* the Regard of 1282: 'the foresters take the top and lop of the trees delivered to the miners to timber their mines, and make thereof their profit out of them' (F.P.T.R. No. 31).

7 'With a convenient way next stretching to the king's highway' (Clause 13 of the miners' 'Laws and Privileges'). See also deposition of Nicholas Brownrick of Coleford in 1637: 'their cattle keeping the appointed way into such pit' (E134. Exch. Deps. by Coms. 13/14 Chas. I, Hil. 16).

8 See Clause 7 of the miners' 'Laws and Privileges'.

9 People in the hundred or Forest whose fathers were not 'free', and people outside the hundred.

seventeenth-century evidence,[1] after the miner had 'digged the pit three steps deep' he gave notice to the gaveller and paid him 1d. for himself and 1d. for each other workman 'for entering of his name and the name of the pit'.[2] The earliest documentation of the miners' privileges is in 1244, and confirmed in 1282 (see pp. 11-14)

The dues paid by the miners have varied from time to time. In the thirteenth century the usual payment was 1d. per week from each miner, besides which the miners had to supply the king with 'Law ore' at fixed rates. The rates varied in the different bailiwicks[3]; the arrangement in the year 1282 in the bailiwick of Great Dene is the most enlightening[4]:

> 'The lord the King has the ore in Great Dene bailiwick and takes of each worker who seeks pay three seams of ore 1d. a week, and when at first the ore is found the Lord the King shall have one man working with the other workers at the ore and will hire (control) him for 2d. a day and will give as pay as much as falls to one worker. Item, the Lord the King will have ore weekly, six semes of ore which are called 'Law ore' and will give for this to the workers 6d. a week.'

The above is the earliest mention of 'Law ore' and seems to imply that it was an obligation in return for which the king protected the miners' 'law' or mining privileges. From later evidence we learn that a 'seam' or 'seme' was 'one seameinge or man's bearing on land of iron or coal'.[5] The miners' 'Laws and Privileges' lays down that '... The King's man nor the Lord's man ought not to enter into the Mine till the pit be gavelled (that is to say) for every dole one penny to the King... of the which Mine of every miner travelling within the said Mine the King shall have every week a penny if so be that the miner win three seames of mine [ore]'.[6] Also, 'The King shall have every quarter of a year of every miner travelling within the Mine a seam of mine which is called Lawe ore...'.[7] By the first quarter of the seventeenth century the Dean

---

1 Deposition by Chris. Tucker, deputy gaveller, in 1625 (E134. Exch. Deps. by Coms. 22 Jas. I, Easter, Glos. 8).

2 The procedure had changed somewhat by the early nineteenth century, for Wm. Morgan informed the Coms. of 1831: 'The gaveller attends and delivers the spot of ground to the miner. He then cuts two sticks and a turf, putting the turf upon the sticks. The gaveller asks if there are any partners, and how many, if any; he cuts notches [presumably in one of the sticks before placing under the turf: the Coms. stated that the stick was forked down by two other sticks] to designate the number, and enters the names in a book. The gale-mark being made, the gaveller asks what vein of coal it is to; the miner names one, two or three veins, or as many as he pleases and pays 5s. for each vein for entry.' According to A. L. Poole (*From Domesday Book to Magna Carta:* 1087-1216, p. 412), the conveyancing of land was generally accompanied by a symbolic transference of some material object and 'in Anglo-Saxon times this might be a turf of the ground to be conveyed'. (For examples see Birch, *Cartularium Saxonicum,* nos. 107, 291, 840, 842-3. See also F. M. Stenton in *Essays in Honour of James Tait.* p. 317.): 'After the Conquest, a knife was commonly used, perhaps the knife which was supposed to have cut the sod.' For the present-day method of granting a gale, see Chap. IX.

3 In some cases the foresters-of-fee of the bailiwicks received dues from the miners.

4 F.P.T.R. No. 31.

5 E134. Exch. Deps. by Coms. 27 Chas. II. Mich. 28. Nicholls considered 'six semes' to be eight bushels (N.I. p. 22); David Mushet thought a 'seam' meant 'bag' *(Papers on Iron and Steel* 1840, p. 396). Another meaning of 'seam' has been given as 'a horse load' (J. J. Watson: *A Compendium of British Mining,* 1843).

6 Clause 15.

7 Clause 16.

miners were still paying 1d. per week ('provided he gained in that week as much as 9d.') and supplying the king with one seam of coal or iron-ore per quarter (or 3d. per quarter in lieu thereof).[1] The king still retained his right to put in a workman. 'Law ore' was still being paid[2] and was soon afterwards being utilised for expenses of their Mine Law Court (*infra*). In the early days the king's dues were collected by the gaveller or his deputies each Tuesday 'between Matins and Mass'.[3] On many occasions the king farmed his entitlement of dues, as for example in 1282 when he did so for £46.[4] In the seventeenth century certain of the deputy gavellers commuted with the miners for lump sums to be paid annually to obviate the trouble in collecting the customary dues.[5] In the eighteenth century, owing to slack administration and the difficulties of collection, the Crown's portion was commuted by the gaveller, and a few shillings were paid every year for each vein or seam worked.[6] The commutation was supposed to be based on the king's right to put in a workman. The amounts increased early in the nineteenth century[7] and were soon stepped-up to varying amounts, in some cases as much as several hundred pounds, merging into royalties of from 2d. to 1s. per ton.[8] These

1 E134. Exch. Deps. by Coms. 22 Jas. I, Easter, Glos. 8.

2 In 1637 Thomas Whitson of Clearwell, miner, aged 76, deposed: "He has often quarterly paid to H.M.'s use a seam of ore or coal, commonly called 'Mynelawe ore', and sometimes in lieu thereof 3d. in silver and has paid the same to the Gaoler for the time being." (E134. Exch. Deps. by Coms. 13/14 Chas. I, Hil. 16).

3 In the nineteenth century the gale rents and royalties were paid periodically at the Speech House; on such occasions the Crown gave what were known as 'gale dinners' (see Chap. X). Payments were subsequently made at the Gaveller's Office, Coleford.

4 F.P.T.R. No. 31.

5 E134. Exch. Deps. by Coms. In 1637 Nicholas Brownrick of Coleford deposed that he has known 'Thomas Duninge stop £15 due to Sturley Kedgin, one of the miners, for and on behalf of John Tipper, gent. then deputy gaoler for lawe ore and gaole due to his Majesty'. (*Ibid.,* 13/14 Chas. I, Hil. No. 16) Thomas Wellington of Littledean, deposed that he had paid to the then deputy gaveller, Chris. Tucker, 'in Law Ore to the value of £16 (in money and ore). About 3 years ago he and his co-partners John Vere and Wm. Nicholls compounded with Tucker to pay him £5 yearly in lieu of Myne Law Ore during the time of his office for his Majesty's use'. (*Ibid.*) Thomas Mawswell, of English Bicknor, said he compounded with Chris. Worgan, deputy gaveller, 'to pay him 4 nobles [gold coins of value of 6s. 8d. or 1/2 a mark] per annum for and in lieu of the penny to be weekly paid and the quarterly payment of Mine Law Ore and for and in lieu of his Majesty's part out of one pit which was sunk by himself and his co-partner miners being 3 or 4 in number which annual sum of 4 nobles likewise paid to the said deputy gaveller during the time of 3 years'. (*Ibid.*) In 1675 John Brinkworth of Littledean, one-time deputy gaveller, deposed that instead of collecting the usual dues from the miners he 'has usually compounded for 5s. a year for each pit'. He had also collected 3s. 4d. a year for each quarry (E134. Exch. Deps. by Coms. 27/28 Chas. II, Hil. No. 21. Glouc.).

6 Deposition by the gaveller in 1788 (Chap. VI). A witness (Meek) deposed before the Coms. of 1831 that until about 20 years previously he had paid sums of 8s., 9s., and 10s. per seam per year.

7 See deposition by Wm. Morgan before the Coms. of 1831: 'The yearly rent agreed to be paid to the King has been two guineas for each vein. When the miner gets to the vein he pays the gaveller in advance in proportion to the coal got. Such advance should be proportioned to the King's share, one-fifth; and if the gaveller and miner cannot agree, the crown and the miner are left to their respective rights, which rights have never been exercised within my memory. I never paid any composition per ton, but composition generally: I do not consider that any custom of paying composition per ton exists or ever existed. The highest sum I ever paid was eight guineas, and that for two pits worked at the same time at Young Colliers. If the gaveller and I could not agree, I should give him notice to put in his fifth man, and take his share.'

8 There is no wonder that a witness (Thomas Philips) before the Coms. of 1831 (4th Rpt. of 1835, pp. 35-37), referring to the way in which the dues paid by the miners had increased throughout the centuries, stated: 'In old times nothing was claimed; the march of intellect is very expensive.' Actually, something was claimed, but, even so, his statement is of interest.

royalties were, during the period 1838 to 1904, subject to adjustment every twenty-one years.[1]

The partners in the application for, and working of, a mine were known as 'verns'.[2] The concession granted to the partners by the gaveller was known as a 'gale'[3] and each partner's share was termed his 'dole'. The free miners always claimed the right to sell or bequeath their doles or gales.[4] Their right in any particular gale lapsed unless, during the year and a day after granting, they worked at least one day on that gale and at least one day in each subsequent year and a day.[5]

As mentioned earlier, the free miners received free timber for their works. No doubt the king was quite willing for this, for otherwise the mines could not be sunk and maintained, and supplies of ore and coal would not be forthcoming. In later centuries the miners obtained their timber from the keeper of the Walk in which their mine was situated. A small fee[6] was paid to the clerk of the Court of Attachment who issued the order[7] on behalf of the verderers for cutting in a suitable place The miners did the cutting, and the keeper received the lop and top as an addition to his salary. Later chapters will show from official reports how the arrangement was abused both by the miners and the crown officials. The first curtailment of the custom took place after a Justice Seat in Eyre held in 1634, and again after the passing of the Dean Forest (Reafforestation) Act of 1668. Nevertheless the custom of taking timber dwindled until finally it was abolished by S.30 of the Dean Forest (Mines) Act, 1838.[8]

The miners' own Mine Law Court – a self-regulating court with jury – is fully dealt with in Chapter IV where it will be seen that especially in the seventeenth and eighteenth centuries the free miners, though many could not so much as sign their names, were a businesslike if somewhat crude fellowship. By their various Orders they fixed prices for coal and iron ore and charges for haulage of the same;

---

1 Since 1904 adjustments are to be made every 63 years.

2 Probably from the A.-S. 'fere', a companion, the initial letter being hardened; the plural would be 'feren'; taken for a singular this would be made plural in 's'. I have in my possession a letter of 1831 written by one of the Coms. of that year to the Rev. I. Webb of Ross, asking, *inter alia,* for information on the origin and meaning of 'vern'. See E146/30. *re 'socij' (verns)* being fined for not filling in pits.

3 Simply, a 'gale' is now a grant to work or 'win' coal, iron ore, ochre or stone from a tract of land. A tract when granted is said to be 'galed'. However, the modern use of the word 'gale' is secondary, for it originally implied 'tax' due to the king. The payment of 'gale' was recognition of the king's possession of the soil.

4 'Every miner in his last days and at all times may bequeath and give his dole of the mine to whom he will as his own chattle, and if he do not the dole shall descend to his heirs' (Clause 24 of the miners' 'Laws and Privileges'). This right was confirmed by statute in 1838. As early as 1656 a widow sued her late husband's partners in the Mine Law Court for non-compliance with a bequest to her of a share in a mine (Chap. IV). In 1637 William Morgan deposed that he "has seen divers precidents of such sales and gifts written and kept in a book" (E134. Exch. Deps. by Coms. 13 Chas I, Mich. 42).

5 New regulations have been in force since 1838, see Chap. VII.

6 The 4th Rpt. of 1835 states that the fee was 1s. and that until within about the last ten years a fee of 2s. was also paid to the keeper.

7 A copy of a warrant is given in Chap. IV.

8 Previous to this Act there had been a stipulation in the Acts of 49 Geo. III. cc. 158 & 159 (Local and Personal) that no one claiming or taking timber for mining purposes under the then existing custom should use the tramways (from Cinderford Bridge to Churchway and from Lydney and Lydbrook to Churchway).

appointed 'bargainers' to arrange sales of coal and iron ore; and made regulations regarding qualifications for entrance to their 'fraternity'. They also made rules regarding measures,[1] distances between pits or levels,[2] and the fencing of pits.[3] The usual penalty for breaking the regulations was 'one hundred dozen[4] of good and sufficient ore or coal, one-half to the King's Majesty and one-half to the miner that shall sue for the same in the Mine Law Court'.[5] The miners were, therefore, encouraged to be their own 'watchdogs' over their interests.[6] They also levied on themselves sums to form a fund to defend at law their customary rights,[7] and to afford monetary help to members of their fellowship who might be injured at their

1 The measure for coal and iron ore was to be the Winchester bushel, three such bushels to a barrel (Order No. 2 of 1674). Every 'dozen' was to comprise 12 bushels 'the one heaped as long as any will lie on from the level without handing it, and the other struck to the wood and not by any other or greater measure' (Order No. 4 of 1680). Order No. 9 of 1694 confirmed the use of the lawful bushels, to be used 'without handing, thrusting, kicking or knocking the bushels'. Order No. 10 of 1701 stipulated that at every coal pit Below the Wood there should be a pair of scales, and 'each ton to contain 21 cwts. and no more'. Clause 31 of the miners' 'Laws and Privileges' had laid down that only the measure called 'Belleyes' should be used.

2 Clause 34 of the miners' 'Laws and Privileges' states: 'The pit shall have such liberties and franchises that no man shall come within so much space that the miner may stand and cast redding and stones so far from him with a bale as the manner is, and shall have his marks pertaining to his said pit.' Order No. 2 of 1674 stipulated that no surffe should be within 100 yards of another. This was amended to 300 yards by Order No. 8 of 1693. to 500 yards by Order No. 14 of 1728, and to 1,000 yards by Order No. 17 of 1754. The last two distances applied only to the mines 'Beneath the Wood'. The Coms. of 1831 (4th Rpt. of 1835) state that at that time regulations as to distances with respect to levels were 1,000 yards to the land side (without limitation to the deep) and, with respect to a water pit, a radius of 12 yards from the centre of the pit.

3 Order No. 5 of 1682 states: 'Whensoever any colliers have fully wrought out a coal pit through which the "Goutwater" must necessarily run for draining of the work, the said colliers shall secure the pit by setting up strong and sufficient posts and rails round the pit.' Order No. 7 of 1687 states: 'all coal pits and dangerous mine pits which are not in working or which hereafter, shall not be brought in for one whole month together shall be sufficiently secured by a wall of stone or by railing the same with posts and rails placed about two feet distant from the mouth of such pits by the proprietors thereof, and likewise all pits left open for a "goutway" upon pain of l0s. to be forfeited for every omission and neglect.' By Order No. 11 of 1707 proprietors of dangerous pits who did not securely fence the same after ten days' notice, were to he fined 20s.

4 A 'dozen' was 12 bushels and was considered to be equal to 21 cwts.

5 In some cases, e.g., Order No. 4 (1680), in addition, the offending miner was to 'be expelled the fellowship of the mine and lose his freedom for ever'.

6 Records of a Mine Law Court held in 1656 give several instances of miners suing for the customary reward (Chap. IV).

7 By Order No. 3 of 1675 all free miners of 15 years and over and all widows of free miners that kept horses for carriage were to pay 6d. per quarter per horse; and all persons working in mines, of 15 years and over, were also to pay 6d. quarterly. Six collectors were appointed, each to receive a commission of 1s. in the £. Order No. 4 of 1680 levied further dues (the commission in this case being 1s. 6d. in the £). Order No. 5 of 1682 levied on all miners of the age of 13 years and over, 6d. each and 6d. for each of their working horses, 'besides the 2d. quarterly imposed by a former Order'. Order No. 6 of 1685 stipulated that similar levies could be made at any time by any jury, but such jury should consist of half colliers and half iron ore miners. Order No. 7 of 1687 levied 2s. on every miner and 2s. for each working horse, while Order No. 8 of 1693 made levies of 1s. in each case. Order No. 10 of 1701 made further provisions, while Order No. 11 of 1707 and Order No. 12 of 1717 made levies of 1s. and 6d. respectively. Rudder, *A New History of Gloucestershire*. p. 33. writing in 1779 says: 'They are said to be able to raise about £40 at 6d. per head'; this would mean about 1600 payments.

work.[1] The usual penalty for non-payment of these sums was a fine of double the amount due, and one-half was to be allowed to the miner prosecuting. Treasurers were appointed to collect the levy and were allowed a commission on their receipts; if they defaulted they were 'henceforth never to be entrusted with anything relating to the public concern of the miners'.[2] A member of the fellowship convicted of perjury was 'for ever to lose and totally forfeit his freedom as touching the mines and be utterly expelled out of the same, and all his working tools and habit to be burnt before his face, and he never afterwards to be a witness or to be believed in any matter whatsoever'.[3]

The main purpose of the Mine Law Court (see Chapter IV) was the settling of disputes between the gaveller (on behalf of the king) and the miners, between the freehold lord and the miners, between miner and miner and between miners and the carriers of their ore and coal. Here the gaveller, or his deputies, sued for non-payment of dues, etc.,[4] and miner sued miner for breach of their customs and regulations, thus claiming the customary reward.[5] The miners were not allowed to sue regarding iron ore or coal in any other court.[6] The records of the Mine Law Court show, too, that the miners knew something of diplomacy, or graft. In 1674[7] the miners altered certain of their regulations as a favour to the constable of St. Briavels, 'in thankful acknowledgement of his constant favours from time to time expressed to the said miners in vouchsafing to be their patron and defender of their ancient privileges'. By the same Order they appealed to the constable 'to be pleased to continue his patronage of them and to vouchsafe them the honour to be one of their Society'. The deputy constable was likewise made a honorary free miner. The following year[8] they stipulated that the deputy constables, most important officials with whom to keep on good terms, should have the benefit of always being supplied first at the pits; this was stated to be 'as a thankful acknowledgement of the many favours received from them in holding their courts and in maintaining their privileges and customs'. The granting of honorary membership was a breach of custom, and is most significant, being one of the first symptoms of the decay of the system.

On several later occasions the miners also granted entrance to their fellowship to other constables and deputy constables and also to important local personages as well as deputy gavellers, castle clerks and deputy surveyors, 'out of the due and great respect,

---

1 'For the relief and help of such poor miners who shall happen to be maimed or hurt underground in the getting or ore, coal or ochre' [Order No 3. of 1675].

2 Order No. 3 of 1675.

3 Order No. 7 of 1687. In 1680 the Mine Law Court stipulated that all miners of 21 years and over should enter into 'an obligation of the penalty of £10 for the true observing, fulfilling and keeping the several Orders and Ordinances' [Order No. 4 of 1680].

4 As early as 1656 a deputy gaveller sued a miner for a horse distrained for non-payment of coal dues (Chap. IV).

5 For examples see Chap. IV.

6 See Chap. IV.

7 Order No. 2.

8 Order No. 3 of 1675.

honour, and esteem borne towards them'.[1] The underlying aim of the free miners was no doubt to obtain influential 'backing' in the struggle to retain exclusively their customary privileges.[2] The Crown officials connived at, and in some cases joined in, this breach of custom. Later they also connived at the custom of free miners obtaining gales and then leasing or selling them to 'foreigners' who were sometimes extraneous capitalists. In 1652[3] a deputy gaveller acquiesced in the lease of both the Crown's and the miners' share in a mine to a 'foreigner', while in 1751[4] the then gaveller held a personal interest in a gale; a deputy gaveller, John Robinson, held a similar interest some years later.

(*b*) THE ORIGIN OF THE CUSTOMS

A necessary adjunct to numerous iron forges operating in Dean throughout the twelfth and thirteenth centuries was a vigorous mining community, and it is with this community that we are chiefly concerned. There are indications of the existence of miners in Dean at least as early as the time of the Romans.[5] Under what terms they worked we do not know, but it is reasonable to assume that the Romans, bent on exploiting Dean's mineral wealth to the full, would be willing to allow the native miners to continue their operations, and would no doubt encourage and 'protect' them. The same would be the case in later centuries, the various kings being anxious to ensure a supply of iron-ore for their forges. In addition, the fact that in times of emergency the miners were highly valuable as 'engineers' and 'specialist troops', would be sufficient to encourage the king to treat them as a privileged class of operatives.[6]

By the first half of the thirteenth century the Dean miners for some reason were considered as emancipated and allowed to mine on their own account, subject to certain restrictions imposed by the king. Until that time it is difficult to find direct and specific mention in private or public records of Forest of Dean mines or miners, though indirect references are quite frequent. By about the year 1244 iron ore was worked in the Dean bailiwicks of English Bicknor, Staunton, Abenhall, Bearse and elsewhere in the Forest. Sea-coal[7] was worked in the bailiwicks of Blakeney, Staunton and Abenhall. The

---

1 As a comparison to the granting of honorary membership, it is interesting to note that in the nineteenth century Robert Forester Mushet, son of the famous David Mushet, worked out his freedom as a free miner in Dean Forest iron mines; 'this he did by fair work for a year and a day as custom required, being the only gentleman who had done so, except Mr. Charles Edwin an ancestor of the Dunraven family': *Something about Coleford and the Old Chapel* (1877), p. 28. A year and a day was sufficient under the Act of 1838, even though his father was not free.

2 Nicholls' referring to these practices, stated: 'We need not call in question the truthfulness of such protestations; but doubtless, had these worthy miners perceived the inconsistency of such admissions, they would not have so readily dispensed with the ancient regulation which restricted the fellowship of the mine to those who had worked therein. They were well intended at the time, but long afterwards weakened in a legal point of view the free miners' rights.'

3 Chap. IV.

4 Chap. VI.

5 See p. 24.

6 See p. 19.

7 'Sea-coal' was used for the word 'coal' at this time.

custodians of the bailiwicks were foresters-of-fee. The relevant decipherable portions of the mutilated document supplying this information are given below[1]:

'[*Concerning sea-coal found, &c.*] They [the jurors] say that when it is found in the bailiwick of Blakeney all the men who dig the coal... ... ...to the Constable of St. Briavels 2s. a year. And to Thomas of Blakeney, forester, 2s. a year. And besides... ... ...each week a halfpenny. And they say that when it is found in the bailiwick of Staunton each one who digs coal gives to the Constable... ... ...and to Richard of Staunton, forester, a halfpenny each one for himself. And they say that when it is found in the bailiwicks of Abenhall and... ... ...each week for each horse one penny but they give nothing to the Constable, and they do not know by what warrant.

[*Concerning iron ore*] They say that when iron ore is found in the bailiwick of William Joce [Bearse], forester of St. Briavels... ... ...and from each man in each week who works in a mine if he makes a profit of three loads (*summas*) he shall have a halfpenny... ... ...[Nigel] Hathewy in some part but they know not by what warrant. The same Nigel has in the bailiwick of Staunton... ... ...The same has the forester of Bicknor in his bailiwick. The same has Gilbert Talbot in the bailiwick of Lea... ... ...in his bailiwick. The same has the forester of Abenhall in his bailiwick. And the knights and free tenants... ... ...have in their woods; but the lord king when he has forges wandering about takes in his demesne woods and... ... ...free ore each load (*summam*) for one penny where others give two pence for each load ... ... he takes a halfpenny for each load which is carried into Wales except the ore which is carried into the land... ... ...which is carried into the land of lord John of Monmouth whence the return of that ore annually 30 marks.'

It is possible therefore to confirm that by this time (*c.* 1244) the Dean miners were allowed to mine for iron ore and coal subject to certain payments either to the forester-of-fee of the bailiwick or to the constable of St. Briavels on behalf of the king. The next relevant document is one which from internal evidence appears to be of the date 1279-82.[2] Its main contents are claims made by various foresters-of-fee and sergeants-of-fee, probably for presentation at the Justice Seat of 1282. Walter of Aston, custodian of the bailiwick of Blakeney, claimed sea-coal and iron ore if they were found in his bailiwick. Ralph of Abenhall, custodian of the bailiwick of Abenhall, claimed the same if found in his bailiwick. Thomas Walding 'Lord of Staunton in the bailiwick of Staunton' claimed sea-coal found in his land.[3] In 1282 Regarders reported as follows in regard to iron ore[4]:

'They say that Ralph of Abenhall has the ore in the bailiwick of Abenhall, and the lord the King has nothing thereof except six semes of ore per week, and he gives because of this to the workers 6d.

---

1 E146. For. Proc. K. R. bdl. 1 No. 25 (c. 1244). See also Hale MS. XLV, No. 5 (Lincoln's Inn Library); and Hart, 'The Verdict of the Three Foreign Hundreds' *The New Regard*, 2000, pp. 65, 66.

2 F.P.T.R. No. 32. A mixture of French and Latin.

3 It seems that the King claimed the iron ore, and the coal in the remainder of this bailiwick.

4 F.P.T.R. No. 31. Part printed in *Trans. B.&G.A.S.*, vol. 14, Pt. II (1889-90), pp. 368-9. A full transcription is in Hart, *The Regard of the Forest of Dean in 1282*, (1987) pp. 54, 55.

Cecilia of Muchegros has the ore in the bailiwick of Bicknor if it should be found.
Walter of Aston claims the ore in the bailiwick of Blakeney if it should be found.

The Lord the King has the ore in Great Dene bailiwick and takes of each worker who seeks pay three semes of ore 1d. a week, and when at first the ore is found the lord the King shall have one man working with the other workers at the ore and will hire (control) him for 2d. a day and will give as pay as much as falls to one worker.

Item, the lord the King will have ore weekly, six semes of ore which are called "Law ore" and will give for this to the workers 6d. a week.

The lord the King has in the bailiwick of Bearse, because there is more ore there than in the bailiwick of Dene, all things as in the bailiwick of Dene, excepting this, that he has thereof weekly twenty-four semes of ore, which are called "Law ore" and gives for this to the workers weekly 2s.

The lord the King has in Staunton bailiwick the ore and takes thereof all things as in Great Dene bailiwick, except this, that the lord the King will have of every worker who seeks pay weekly three semes of ore ½d. a week and not more.

Item, if the lord the King has an itinerant forge the aforesaid miners will find him ore to sustain the aforesaid forge and the lord the King will give them for every load 1d.

Item, the lord the King will have of every seme of ore which will be taken beyond the Forest ½d. and all things which the lord the King takes of ore is placed at farm for £46.[1]

Item, in Lacu[2] bailiwick is ore and Sir Richard Talebatt[3] has it but it is not known by what warrant, and the lord the King takes nothing thereof.

Item, the Earl of Warwick[4] has the ore in his wood of Lideneye and the lord the King takes nothing thereof, except of the mine [ore] which is carried without the Forest ½d. (per load).'

Thus in 1282 the foresters-of-fee of the bailiwicks of Abenhall, Bicknor and Blakeney claimed the ore in their respective bailiwicks, and the king received nothing except that in the first bailiwick he had six loads per week for which he paid the workers 6d. The forester-of-fee of The Lea claimed the ore there, but it was not known by what warrant. The Earl of Warwick claimed the same in his land at Lydney, the king receiving only a due of ½d. on each load of ore taken out of the Forest. The king held the ore in the bailiwicks of Great Dene, Bearse and Staunton but seems to have let the miners seek for it and win it at their will subject to certain conditions. In the case of Great Dene he received three loads of ore weekly from each worker, for which he paid 1d. per week, and also had a man ('the king's man') working with the other miners, for whom he paid 2d. a day; he also received six loads of ore weekly known as 'Law ore' for which he paid the miners 6d. As previously stated this 'Law ore' would seem to imply that it was an obligation to the king in return for which he protected their 'Law' or privileges of mining, or was possibly compensation for withholding his man. In Bearse the king had the same as in Great Dene except that he had four times as much 'Law ore'

---

1 See account rendered for Dean Forest by Ralph of Sandwich: Mins. Accts. bdle 850, No. 19, 8-9 Edw. I.

2 The Lea.

3 Sir Richard Talbot of Goodrich Castle.

4 In 1293/4 John of Auste was his 'receiver of the issues of his mine of iron and sea-coal' at Lydney – probably Bream Grove or Old Park (Exchequer of Pleas 15-20 Edw. I, No. 19, m. 67).

(the reason being that there was more ore in Bearse than in Great Dene) for which he paid 2s. weekly. In Staunton the king again had the same as in Great Dene except that he had of every worker three loads of ore weekly for which he paid $^1/_2$d. In addition the miners had to supply the king with ore for his itinerant forges, for which he paid 1d. a load. He also levied a custom of $^1/_2$d. a load on all ore taken out of the Forest. Instead of being troubled with the collection and payment of the many petty items involved, the king was content to farm out the whole for £46 each year. As to coal, the Regarders of 1282 reported as follows[1]:

> '*Concerning sea-coal*:
> Ralph of Abenhall has a sea-coal pit in his bailiwick of Abenhall and takes coal thence. And the King takes nothing thence.
> The Lady Cecilia of Muchegros claims to take in the same way in the bailiwick of Bicknor.
> The custodian of the bailiwick of Staunton takes in the same way in the bailiwick of Staunton.
> Walter of Aston takes in the same way in his bailiwick of Blakeney.
> Nicholas of Lea claims to take in the same way in the bailiwick of Lea.
> The Earl of Warwick takes likewise sea-coal in his wood of Lydney.
> [In all these cases] It is not known by what warrant.
> The Lord King takes sea-coal if it is found in his bailiwicks of Bearse, Ruardean, Great Dene and Little Dene.'

Thus the foresters-of-fee of the bailiwicks of Abenhall, Bicknor, Staunton and Blakeney took the coal found in their bailiwicks, the king exacting nothing. The forester-of-fee of the bailiwick of Lea claimed to take in the same way. The Earl of Warwick took coal found in his wood of Lydney. In all these cases it was 'not known by what warrant'. The king took coal found in the bailiwicks of Bearse, Ruardean, Great Dene and Little Dene. Another reference to coal in the last document is the mention of a 'ride', stated to be near '*Secolepyttes*' (sea-coal pits) in Staunton bailiwick near '*Wartokesay Juxta Newernehey*' [Cannop]. Another interesting statement made by the Regarders was that 'the foresters-of-fee take the lop and top of the trees delivered to the miners to timber their mines and make thereof their profit out of them'.[2] It will have been noted that there is no mention of iron ore in Ruardean, Littledean, Abbot's Wood or 'Bleyth's' bailiwick. The reason for this may be due to the fact that the monks of Flaxley had the ore in Abbot's Wood[3] and the probability that there was no known or workable ore in the three other places. Nor is there mention of ore in Moseley Green, Saintlow, Cannop, Whitemead, Whiteley Green, 'Oldefolde', Kensley, Crump Meadow and Walmore, all of which are mentioned in the document as being pasture lands owned in the Forest by the king. In connection with the above, the names of the bailiwicks are, according to Dr. Grundy,[4] misleading. Dr. Grundy confirmed that no portion of

---

1 See Hart, *The Regard of the Forest of Dean in 1282*, p. 82

2 This was still going on in 1788 – *vide* 3rd Rpt. of the Commissioners.

3 It appears from an Inquisition of 1287 that as early as 1265-72 the monks claimed the ore in their lands at Flaxley.

4 *Trans. B.&G.A.S.*, vol. 58 (1936), pp. 65-154, *The Ancient Woodland of Gloucestershire.*

Staunton is in Staunton bailiwick[1] and not as much as one-tenth of Ruardean is in the bailiwick of that name. Again, with the exception of The Lea, the open lands of the Forest region were not included in the bailiwicks. The bailiwick of Great Dene consisted of a narrow belt of woodland winding in and out between the bailiwicks of Ruardean and Abenhall.

It will have been seen that by the thirteenth century there is proof of the existence in the Forest of Dean of a specially privileged class of mining operatives. However, Dean was not an isolated case in this respect, and in our quest for knowledge as to the origin of the customs it is instructive first to examine in its main outlines the origin and development of English mining law in the light of the growth of mineral law elsewhere in Europe. Early mining law in Europe has been so thoroughly dealt with by G. R. Lewis,[2] Prof. J. U. Nef[3] and others, that it would be but repetition to attempt an account here. Suffice it to say that in Germany, at least in the twelfth century, miners were given freedom to discover and win ore where they pleased on application to the mine-master.[4] Such application might not be refused except by reason of conflicting claims, in which case the concession would be granted to the first applicant. Similar customs apply equally to the Forest of Dean. Again, as in Dean, the interest of the concessionary was permanent, assignable and transmissible. Obligations were imposed of continual working payments of a fixed proportion of the product and a small fixed quarterly rent. A mine deserted by its occupants was declared vacant, and the lapse of a year without working *ipso facto* discharged the miners' rights.[5] According to Lewis[6] 'the share of the product which the lord reserved for his own use amounted originally to a half or a third of the whole, but in the course of time this fell by degrees to a tenth and even less, so that from the sixteenth to the eighteenth century the lord's income was probably equal only to that of one of the mine partners. The miners, like the ordinary farm tenants, at first subject to eviction at caprice, gradually through custom acquired an interest in their holdings which their superiors found difficult to shake off.'

In many respects the mining customs of Dean Forest provide a striking resemblance to those above described.

Early mining was carried on under local custom in other parts of England. In the lead mining district comprising the wapentake of Wirksworth and seven small liberties in the High Peak, in Derbyshire, one might dig for lead in another's soil 'so far as the party may throw his mattock'. Here the crown was represented by 'bar-masters' who granted a concession or 'meer', a portion of the seam 29 yards in length, to miners on their discovering ore.[7] The king was entitled to the adjoining half-meer. As in Dean Forest, the mining customs included the right of access to the highway, and the right to

1 However the mention in the document of 1279-82 of 'Staunton in the bailiwick of Staunton' would tend to disprove this theory. See Hart, *The Regard of the Forest of Dean in 1282*, (1987) p. 32

2 *The Stannaries* (Harvard Univ. Press, 1924), pp. 64-84; see also Vict. C.H. Glouc. ii, pp. 222-3.

3 *Camb. Econ. Hist. of Europe,* vol. II, chap. vii.

4 Lewis, *op. cit.* p. 69. Lewis gives the provisions of an interesting mine charter of 1185.

5 *Ibid.*, p. 70.

6 *Ibid.*, pp. 70, 71.

7 *Ibid.*, p. 81; Vict. C.H. Derbyshire. ii, p. 325; Roy. Com. on Mining Royalties, 3rd Rpt.; James Mander: *Derbyshire Miners' Laws and Customs* (1824).

take Crown wood for shafts, etc. There was a special miners' court to try offences. Similar customs were in operation in the Hope manor in Flintshire and several neighbouring manors.[1] On Alston Moor in Cumberland, we find the lead miners possessing as early as the thirteenth century certain liberties under the king's protection, and having their own 'court of the mines'.[2] Again, in Cornwall, tin mining was allowed on wastes and demesne lands, and in Devon on enclosed lands as well, subject to a payment of a portion of the products to the lord of the manor.[3] Mining laws for the Stannaries of Devon and Cornwall were made by 'Convocations' or 'Parliaments of Tinners'. Parallel customs existed over the Mendip lead-mining district in Somerset where miners had the privilege of digging for lead subject to a payment of every tenth pound of lead to the lord of the soil.[4] A code of privileges was drawn up in 1470,[5] and two courts were held each year at the instance of the lord.

It has already been noted that the Forest of Dean is the only known district in England where coal mining and iron ore mining were ever subject to such special privileges. Likewise there is no other instance in Great Britain of special mining courts in connection with the coal and iron ore industry. Although certain of the customary privileges of the Dean miners can be gathered from the documents of *c.* 1244 and 1282 already cited, one is obliged in order to obtain a connected view of them to have resort to two transcripts, one of 1612 and the other of 1673, containing the code of customary law which regulated the exercise of mining rights within the district. These transcripts are of a memorandum 'what the Customes and ffranchises hath beene that were granted tyme out of Minde and after in tyme of the Excellent and Redoubted Prince King Edward[6] unto ye Miners of the fforrest of Deane and the Castle of St. Briavels and the bounds of the fforrest'. The code is known as the Dean miners' 'Laws and Privileges' and since the nineteenth century has wrongly been referred to as the 'Book of Dennis' instead of the 'Book against Dennis'. A copy is given in Chapter II, and see Plate III.

The early references to the English miners' privileges give the impression of unwritten customary law, rather than of rights formally conferred by charter. In Derbyshire the customs rested upon immemorial usage, which Edward I merely confirmed in 1288.[7] The Alston miners received similar confirmation of ancient privileges by a charter from Henry V.[8] Similarly the privileges of the Devon and Cornwall tinners seem for the most part to have relied upon tradition, their liberties

1 Exch. T.R. Misc. Bks. vol. 297, ff. 42 *sq.*

2 Lewis, *op. cit.,* p. 80.

3 *Ibid.,* Roy. Com. on Mining Royalties, Final Rpt., pp. 25-29; Thomas Pearce: *The Laws and Customs of the Stannaries in the Counties of Cornwall and Devon* (1752); Edward Smirke: *The case of Vice against Thomas* (1843).

4 *Ibid.,* p. 80; V.C.H. Somerset, ii, pp. 362, *sq.*; J. W. Gough: *The Mines of Mendip* (1930); Lord Choke's *Laws of Mendip.*

5 Printed in Final Rpt. of Roy. Com. on Mining Royalties, p. 82, and Thomas Houghton: *The Compleat Miner,* Pt. III (1688); see also Trans. Roy. Geol. Soc. Cornw., vi, pp. 327-33.

6 See p. 17 for consideration of which King Edward this might be.

7 Exch. Enr. Accounts, 16 Edw. I, No. 34.

8 Pat. R. 4 Hen. V, m. 8.

later being embodied in a royal charter of 1201[1] and added to in 1305.[2] No trace of a charter or like grant to the miners of Dean is to be found. In any case it is not easy to see in what form one could have been issued, seeing that the miners were not a corporate body with responsible heads,[3] although we have seen that similar grants had been confirmed in the thirteenth century to miners of certain other districts in England. Nicholls[4] thought it probable that during one of the visits to the district made by William the Conqueror between 1066 and 1069, the Forest miners applied for and obtained confirmation of their 'customs and franchises' and that the king may have agreed to this as compensation for the demands made upon the citizens of Gloucester for a yearly supply of iron[5] for the navy. In any case the Conqueror, like the kings after him, would no doubt be anxious to enable the miners to continue the necessary supply of ore from the Forest and would, therefore, protect them against third parties so long as they worked the mines to his advantage. Nicholls also considered that many of the points and clauses in the miners' 'Laws and Privileges' when the rights were first committed to writings were inspired by the Saxons and were of Germanic origin.

There is a tradition that the Dean miners were granted confirmation of their customary privileges by Edward I, II or III for their useful military services especially in connection with the Scottish wars, and in particular the sieges of Berwick.[6] No records are available of such services during the reign of Edward I (1272-1307); during the reign of Edward II (1307-27) we have records of Dean miners being sent to Berwick-on-Tweed in 1310 and to Newcastle-upon-Tyne in 1319; during the reign of Edward III (1327-77) Dean miners were sent to Portsmouth in 1346, to Newcastle-upon-Tyne in 1355, and elsewhere in 1359. Even if the tradition is based on fact it is uncertain to which Edward we can ascribe the confirmation of the miners' customs.[7] The earliest extant transcript (1612) of the Dean miners' 'Laws and Privileges' gives 'Edward III' but the next extant transcript (1673) refers to 'the Excellent and Redoubted Prince King Edward', without implying which King Edward this might be. However, the first printed copy (1687) based on the 1673 transcript adds 'III'. In 1614[8] certain of the Dean miners asserted to the Exchequer Court that their 'liberties and franchises have been by ancient usages, customs and prescriptions time out of mind ratified and confirmed, and as they will manifestly prove has been allowed before the Justice in Eyre and also at the Courts of Justice holden in King Edward the Third's time'.

1 Chart. R. 36. Hen. III. m. 18.

2 *Ibid.*, 33 Edw. I, m. 40, 41.

3 A return to a commission of enquiry concerning the Forest, dated 5 March 1671, drew attention to this question of the miners not being a corporation.

4 N.H. p. 7

5 In this connection see Domesday, 1, 162a (36 dacres of iron and 100 bars of iron suitable for making nails). Giraldus in his *Itinerary* speaks of the 'noble Forest of Deane... which amply supplies Gloucester with iron and venison' (Trans. Hoare, i, 102).

6 See p. 20.

7 The area over which the rights were exercised seems to be that defined by the perambulations of 1228 and 1282, which rules out the reign of Edward II (1307-27) and Edward III (1327-37) seeing that in these two reigns the forest was defined by the reduced area given in the perambulations of 1300.

8 E112/83/411, m.3.

Further uncertainty is raised by the statement in 1625 of Christopher Tucker of Littledean, aged thirty-eight, miner and deputy gaveller to Thomas Cachmayne, Esq., that he had 'seen an ancient deed dated in the reign of King Edward the Second testifying the liberty and privilege of the miners within the Forest'.[1] Again there was at Whitemead Park a second, mutilated, copy of the miners' laws and customs which reads 'Edward III'.[2]

Nevertheless, it has been seen that the customary privileges were exercised before the reign of even Edward I at least as early as *c.* 1244. It is quite possible however that the hall-mark of a royal confirmation may have followed faithful service at the wars. The mention in 1282 of 'Law ore' is significant, and falls within the reign of Edward I.

It is reasonable to assume that the privileges and customs were first put into writing at some date not earlier than *c.* 1244; otherwise the document of that year, or the report of the Regarders of 1282 already cited, would presumably have referred to such a grant or confirmation, or to a relevant document. As further weight to this assumption, the mention in the 'Laws and Privileges' (Clause 6) of 'St. Briavells gate' would date this code after 1131, about which year the castle was built, and 'Litele Deane' (Clause 6) points to a date after 1220, about which time Dene manor was divided. To what extent the earliest (1612) transcript of the miners' 'Laws and Privileges' compares with the wording of any possible confirmation or grant in the thirteenth to sixteenth centuries is uncertain, but a perusal will induce a strong conviction in any reader acquainted with the legal phraseology of the Middle Ages that part at least was originally drawn up in Latin, though the English translation may be far older than the seventeenth century. It is considered, however, that the translation was done before the Reformation, as the use of certain ecclesiastical terms[3] would suggest, and possibly much earlier at a time when the extended boundaries of the Forest, reduced in 1300, had not been forgotten; these boundaries are given in the early extant transcripts as the area over which the customs of the free miners extend, there being no limitation, as in later times, to the Hundred of St. Briavels.

There is another theory regarding the interesting question as to when and by whom the privileges of the miners were granted or confirmed. A witness in 1637[4] deposed that he was son and heir of John Morgan, deceased, steward for many years of the Mine Law Court, and that 'after his father's death he found in his father's study a copy of an ancient Inquisition written in French having relation, as he, this deponent conceiveth, to a charter granted or to be granted from John, Duke of Bedford to the miners of the said hundred for service done by the said miners in France, which said copy of Inquisition he, this deponent, delivered to one Edward Keare a miner then held most ancient and of most credit amongst them for the benefit of the miners'. The French wars with which the Duke was concerned occurred in the first quarter of the fifteenth century,[5] and there is a

---

1 E134. Exch. Deps. by Coms. 22 James I (1625), Easter, 8.

2 Now in Glos.R.O. D9096, F16/19.

3 *E.g.*, 'Between Matins and Mass' (Clause 18).

4 E134. Exch. Deps. by Coms. 13 Chas. I (1637), Mich. 42.

5 John, Duke of Bedford (1389-1435) was the third son of Henry IV.

record of Dean miners being sent to France in 1419. Such a charter would no doubt have been confirmation of the customs which had operated from at least the first half of the thirteenth century; it might too have been confirmation of a charter granted by one of the Kings Edward. However, no charter has been found.[1]

(*c*) MILITARY SERVICES RENDERED BY THE MINERS[2]

The miners of Dean, being men of a sturdy race, skilled in their own craft, were frequently summoned to assist the kings in their wars, being apparently treated as 'specialist troops' or engineers.[3] The expenses of forty miners sent to London by the king's orders appear on the constable of St. Briavels' account in 1222.[4] Possibly they had been employed in the siege of Bytham the year before. In 1223 the accounts showed the sum of £3 11s. 2d. as expenses of twenty miners despatched to Montgomery[5] 'for the work of the castle being built there'.[6] Dean miners were again employed in 1224 in the siege of Bedford, as the constable's accounts for 8 and 9 Henry III include 'expenses of 30 miners sent from Hereford to Bedford for 9 days at 2 pence a day each, 20 shillings... and John the Miner with 10 other miners, at 3d. a day each, for 4 days going to London, 11 shillings'.[7] John the Miner and certain of his fellow miners later received favours from the king, for in the same year[8] the constable was ordered to assign to 'John de Standon our miner (*mineatori nostro*) 12 acres of land near "Sitegave", and likewise 8 acres to his three companions – Hugh son of Wulwin, Walter son of Walding and Neel le Bret'. However, it seems that the constable attempted to charge seven marks for the land, and also molested the miners. He was ordered by the king, in no uncertain manner, to remedy this.[9]

On 13 March 1225[10] the king again needed the services of Dean miners, and the constable was ordered to send John the Miner with ten other miners to London 'to

---

1 See added comments to Appendix 8.

2 No full account is given here of the many occasions on which men of the Forest of Dean rendered military service in the ordinary ways such as soldiers (footmen and horse), archers, etc. See also Fourth Report, 1835, p. 4.

3 The Commissioners of 1831 (4th Rpt. of 1835) stated: 'Traces of the existence of the Forest of Dean miners are certainly to be found in early history. It appears that they were summoned to attend the royal armies in the reigns of Edward I and II, and there is a tradition in the Forest that exclusive privileges were given to them in consequence of their services at the siege of Berwick. It is uncertain to which siege of Berwick this tradition refers, but the writs stated in the margin show that they were frequently required in the Scotch Wars. In the reign of Edward III they were summoned to attend the camp near Berwick, and in Guthrie's *History of England* it is stated that "Sir Edward Manny bringing engineers out of the Forest of Dean, and Edward investing the place with a prodigious army, the Scots capitulated" They were also ordered by the same king to join his army at Portsmouth in the years 1346 and 1359.'

4 P.R., 6 Hen. III.

5 *Ibid.*, 7 Hen. III; *Rot. Litt. Claus.* I, p. 565.

6 C.R., 7 Hen. III, m. 1.

7 P.R., 9 Hen. III.

8 *Rot. Litt. Claus,* vol. i, 8 Hen. III, m. 6. p. 617.

9 *Ibid.* vol. ii, 9 Hen. III, m. 8, p. 23.

10 *Ibid.*, p. 23b.

go in our service where we shall order them'. The constable was to find them money for their expenses to London, namely 3d. a day each. On 23 April the same year[1] the king instructed the Treasurer to pay the miners 22s. for the return expenses. John appears to have been killed soon after, for the Pipe Roll of 10 Hen. III contains an entry of 12d. as rent paid by Maciane, widow of John the Miner, killed in the king's service at Bedford. On 17 August 1233[2] the constable was ordered to send ten miners (*minitores*) from his bailiwick to demolish the house of Gilbert Basset at Festerne co. Wilts, and to cause them to have their expenses thither. The sheriff of Wiltshire was instructed to pay them 3d. a day while there, and to find them implements. On 20 July 1245[3] the sheriff of Hereford was commanded 'to cause twelve miners of the Forest of Dean, well skilled in their art, to come to the king at Chester; and to make 4 iron hammers for breaking rock, and 6 crows (*crowas*) for raising it up, and send them to Chester to the king'.

The miners also served overseas, for in 1253[4] twenty of the best to be found were summoned to accompany the king on his expedition to Gascony. In a writ[5] dated 2 August 1310 the constable was commanded to select 100 archers and 12 miners and conduct them to Berwick-on-Tweed, while on 26 March 1319[6] twelve miners were ordered to be sent to work the iron mines of Hugh le Despenser the younger in Glamorgan. Another writ,[7] dated 7 June the same year (1319), demanded twenty of the strongest miners and their instruments to be sent to Newcastle-upon-Tyne for the Scottish War; the following year[8] the constable of St. Briavels petitioned for the wages for fifteen days of 4 master *(magistri)* miners at 4d. per day and 16 other miners at 3d. per day. This came to £4, and in addition the carriage of their mining instruments to Newcastle-upon-Tyne was 10s. Another writ,[9] dated 8 December 1355, mentions a demand for forty miners to be sent to the same place. On 1 April 1346[10] Guy de Brian was ordered to choose forty miners including four master (*magistri*) miners, to be sent to Portsmouth. It is uncertain whether these are included in the sixty miners, including six master miners, who were sent in 1346 to Portsmouth by Guy de Brian.[11] For the five days' journey the master miners were paid 4d. per day each, and the other miners 3d. per day. Reasonable allowances were also made for the six horses which bore their mining instruments. The whole sum spent was £4 5s. No doubt the miners were used in the campaign of Crecy in that year. On 1 February 1359[12] Edward III wrote to de Brian, 'or his deputy, and to John atte Hale, Wm. del Mulle, Philip Hok and Richard White, miners in the said Forest: Know you that we have commissioned you... to choose...

1 *Rot. Litt. Claus,* vol. i, 8 Hen. III, m. 15, p. 33.
2 *Cal.* Liberate Rolls, Hen. III, 1226-40, p. 228.
3 *Ibid.,* vol. ii, p. 316.
4 C.R., 37 Hen. III, m. 7.
5 *Rot. Scotiae,* vol. i, p. 91.
6 C.R., 12 Edw. II, m. 13d.
7 *Rot. Scotiae,* vol. i, p. 195b; Exch. Var. Accts. E101, bdl. 15, No. 21, m. 1.
8 Exch. Var. Accts. E101, bdl 15, No. 21, m. 2.
9 *Rot. Scotiae,* vol. i, p. 784.
10 *Rot. Franc.,* 20 Edw. III, Pt. I, m. 22; Rymer *'Fœdera'*, vol. iii, Pt. I, p. 78.
11 P.R., 20 Edw. III, m. 8.
12 *Rot. Franc.,* 33 Edw. III, Pt. I, m. 2; Rymer, *op. cit.,* p. 417.

four smiths (*fabros*) and forty miners (*minearios*) of the best and ablest... to go in our following'.

In 1365[1] John de Monmouth was instructed to send twelve Dean miners to Wales. On 26 May 1372[2] John of Gaunt instructed his receiver of Monmouth that he was sending John Joce to select sixteen Dean miners and one smith to accompany him on his next voyage, while in 1375[3] John Joce and Thomas Bray were ordered to send twelve more to Edward le Despenser. On 29 August 1419[4] a commission was issued to Thomas Gernoun 'to take twenty miners in the Forest of Dean to serve the king on his works in Normandy'. This may have been one of the occasions following which John, Duke of Bedford, may have confirmed or granted the rights of the Dean miners.[5]

The various kings occasionally acknowledged the services rendered by the miners of the Forest of Dean and showed them favours. The preferential treatment of John the Miner and his companions in 1224 has already been recorded. Eight years earlier[6] the king had granted twelve acres of land near 'Redebroc' (Redbrook) to another miner, John son of Wulewy. On 1 August 1363[7] Edward III granted a pardon to Adam atte Mulle 'Mynour' of the Forest of Dean who killed Thomas Thomas of Lynton in self defence; this was on account of his 'good service in France and elsewhere'. Again, on 15 November 1383[8] Richard II granted 'at the supplication of the bishop of Llandaff' to William Robert, miner in the Forest of Dean, the release of his goods to the value of 20 marks which had been seized because he had been convicted of arson. This royal favour is stated to be on account of 'his service in the war in the late reign'. The same king, on 11 April 1390,[9] granted in the Forest of Dean, the office of one of the king's rangers. In 1522 the demand for Dean miners was renewed and three hundred were ordered to be at Dover on 31 July.[10] In 1577 twelve more were called for to accompany Captain Martin Frobisher in his search for the North-West Passage.[11]

On considering all the above, one feels that during at least the period 1221 to 1365 the Dean miners were on many occasions well to the fore in the thoughts of the king and his council. The reigning kings during the period were Henry III, Edward I, II and III, any of whom might have confirmed or protected their customary privileges. In any case it is certain that the miners were treated as a specialised class of operatives, and no doubt 'protected' both in view of the nation's need of ore and for their skill in times of emergency.

---

1 *Rot. Vascon.,* 39 Edw. III. m. 11; Rymer, *op. cit.* Pt. II, p. 762.
2 John of Gaunt's Register (Roy. Hist. Soc.), Pt. I, p. 50, No. 71.
3 *Rot. Franc.*, 48 Edward III. Rymer, *op. cit.* Pt. II, p. 1021.
4 *Cal.Pat.Roll.*, 7 Hen. V, m. 26d, p. 269.
5 See p. 18.
6 *Rott. Litt. Claus* I, p. 285.
7 *Ibid.,* 37 Edw. III, m. 29, Pt. II, p.403. Confirmed on 13 February 1364 (Cal. Pat. R., 38 Edw. III, m. 40, Pt. I, p. 467).
8 *Ibid.,* 7 Rich. II m. 1, Pt. I, p. 346.
9 *Ibid.,* 13 Rich. II, m. 22, Pt. II, p. 236.
10 *Cal.* L. & P. Hen. VIII, vol. iii, Pt. I, p. 1005, No. 2374.
11 Acts of the Privy Council, 1575-7, p. 335.

(d) ANCIENT MINERS' TOOLS, EQUIPMENT AND WORKINGS[1]

Our earliest guide to the mining tools used by the ancient miners of Dean is given by the short, sharp incisions from 2 to 12 inches in length found in the clay-like 'clod' in the old iron ore mine which was discovered in Lydney Park in 1932.[2] These point to the use of short pick-hammers, presumably, from the nature of the marks and the limited space available for manipulation, a pointed single-pronged pick. No actual pick has yet been found at Lydney although many examples have been found in the Roman iron mines of Spain. However an iron toy-model of typical form was found at Lydney amongst other Roman material in the occupational layer of the floor of a third century hut adjoining the iron mine. Another discovery was an iron hoe used possibly in agriculture but perhaps alternatively for removing debris from a mine shaft.

We are given an idea of the equipment of a seventeenth or eighteenth century miner in the heraldic crest on a brass[3] measuring 12 inches by 7¾ inches on the floor of the Clearwell (Greyndour) Chapel of Newland Church (see Frontispiece). He wears a cap or 'wooff', and carries a candlestick between his teeth, the candle to be fixed to the stick by a lump of clay. This latter characteristic continued even into the middle of the nineteenth century, a piece of clay being used to fix the candlestick into a suitable position when working. In his right hand is a small pick[4] with which to loosen the mineral earth in the cavity in which he worked, or else to detach the ore lining its sides. A light wooden billy or mine-hod hangs at his back from a shoulder-strap fastened to his belt. He is clothed in what appears to be a thin flannel jacket, and his short leather breeches are tied with thongs below the knee. Although in this representation his feet are concealed, many shoe-footed marks have been discovered on the moist beds of some of the old excavations. Several mattock heads exactly resembling the one which this miner is holding have also been discovered, as well as oak shovels for collecting the ore and putting it into the mine-hods.

The British Association Report of 1856[5] gives a description of an ancient miner's axe found at an iron mine near Lambsquay, and the Proceedings of the Society of Antiquaries[6] of wooden and iron implements found in the Westbury Brook Iron Mines. The former description is by Robert Mushet, and the latter by John Irving.

On the octagonal font of local sandstone in Abenhall church (Plate II) are carved on one face six iron-miners' picks and two shovels, and on another face two horseshoes between smiths' tongs. The font, which is of date of *c.* 1450, is also enriched with other shields charged with coats of arms, and is considered to have been the gift of the free miners and free smiths of the Forest. Another set of tools was carved on the outer

1 'Are there not within the said grounds, or some of them, apparent notes of pits where anciently there hath been digging for the same.' (E134. Interr. No. 1: Exch. Deps. by Coms. 22 Jas. I (1623-4)).

2 Report on Excavations in Lydney Park: R. E. M. and T. V. Wheeler: Report of Res. Com. Soc. Antiq. of London IX 1932 pp. 18-22.

3 Believed by Nicholls and others to be of the fifteenth century, whereas it may be of much later date (*Trans. B.&G.A.S.* vol. 7, 1882-3, pp. 121-2; *Ibid.*, vol. 55, 1933, p. 218).

4 The pick or mattock seems modelled on the horn tine which was used in primitive mining.

5 pp. 71, 72.

6 11 April 1861, and 14 January 1864. See also *Notes on Ancient mining tools found in the Forest of Dean* by T. Forster Brown, deputy gaveller: *Trans. B.&G.A.S.* (1895-6), xx, 155-60, 1 plate.

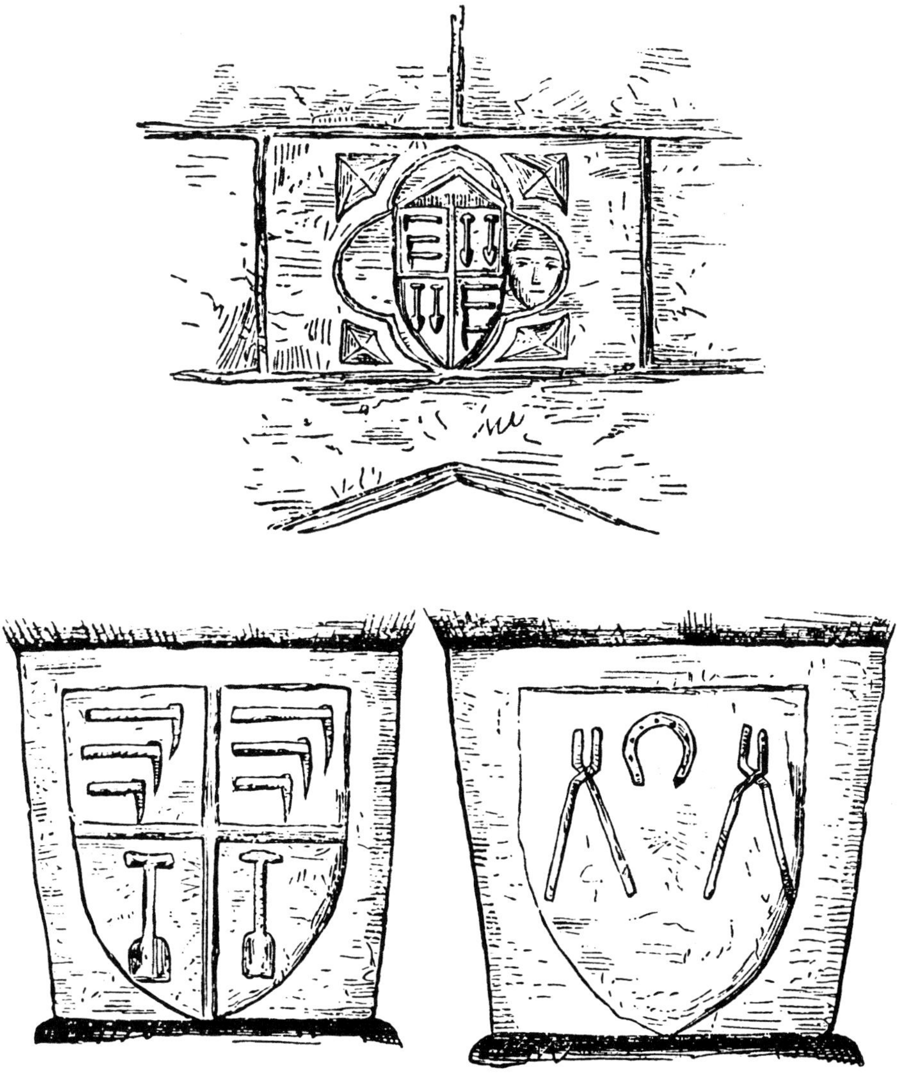

Plate II. *Ancient miners' and smiths' tools depicted in Abenhall Church.*
Top*: on west face of tower*
Bottom*: on font.*

face of the west wall of the tower, but they are no longer visible. They were set on a carved shield as follows: Quarterly, 1st and 4th, three miners' picks in pale, 2nd and 3rd, two shovels in fess, handles upwards. On one side of the shield appeared a human head wearing a miner's cap. It is not known whether the shields and devices in any way represent the armorial bearings or 'coats of arms' of the guilds or fraternities of free miners and free smiths. It is unlikely they were ever confirmed by the College of Arms, and they may be more properly called trade-marks with a semblance of heraldry.[1]

It is almost certain that the iron ore deposits in the region were worked by the early Britons, particularly the Silures. In any case ample evidence is forthcoming that the Romans knew of the deposits and worked them,[2] even though the actual labouring was done by the subjugated Dean miners. How far the pre-Roman population of the region subsisted upon the winning and trafficking of the local iron ore, we cannot say. But at any rate with the coming of the Romans the local mineral wealth was exploited on a considerable scale with all the knowledge that Roman mining-engineering could bring to bear. During the second and third centuries A.D. a Romano-British population, engaged to some extent upon organised iron mining, occupied a 'promontory fort' or small embanked hill-town at Lydney established in or shortly before the first century B.C. In clearing away the floor of one of the Roman huts in 1932[3] a shaft of an iron mine, not later than the third century A.D., was laid bare. This is the first British iron mine which can, on conclusive evidence, be assigned to the Roman period. It conforms in general type to the better-known Roman iron mines of Spain. The open end of the shaft is about 18 ft. long and from 3 ft. to 4 ft. wide, and is cut into the rock to a depth of about 5 ft. At a distance of about 18 ft. from its outer end begins the rock-cut tunnel of the shaft itself. There is abundant evidence of this mine being of Roman or pre-Roman times. The lower part of the open end of the cutting was filled with debris left by the miners among which was a piece of a Roman roofing-tile and a fragment of a grey cooking-pot. The soil above the debris contained an *antoninianus* of Carausius (A.D. 287-93) and other Roman items. The floor of a Roman hut, known to have been in use at the end of the third century, lay above this, which in turn was covered with occupation-debris and humus which contained minute Roman potsherds and thirty-seven Roman coins of dates between A.D. 253 and 361. The whole was completely covered by the structure of a post-Roman rampart. In determining the earlier limit for the cutting of the mine, the Report states[4]:

> 'That the mine was Roman may be inferred, not merely from its character, but from the fact that it had been cut through the prehistoric rampart. The only object found in the working-levels was the Roman roof-tile mentioned above. All that can be said, therefore, as to the actual date of the mine is that it was cut during the first two and a half centuries of the Roman occupation. It may be suggested that the absence of debris in the opening prior to the

1 See *Trans. B.&G.A.S.*, vol. iii (1878-9), pp. 302-4; and vol. xl (1917), pp. 43-5. See also Hart, *Archaeology in Dean* (1967).

2 The late Rhys Jenkins considered that the Romans found the industry in existence, although no doubt it was developed considerably in their time.

3 Report on Excavations in Lydney Park: R. E. M. and T. V. Wheeler: (Report of Res. Com. Soc. Antiq. of London, IX) 1932, pp. 18-22.

4 *Ibid.*, p. 19

late third-century filling points to an initial date not long anterior to that filling. Moreover, the coinage indicates a marked general influx of wealth on to the promontory in the same period. On these two grounds, it seems likely that the mine was cut during a period of enhanced industrial activity in the middle or latter half of the third century.'

Dr. P. G. North, Keeper of Geology in the National Museum of Wales, assisted in the exploration of the tunnel or shaft, and reported as follows[1]:

'The mine is a narrow passage cut in dolomite rock of the Carboniferous Limestone series, and it follows one of the joints that affect the rocks of the area, striking in a north-easterly direction and descending nearly vertically from the surface. The passage is about 18 to 24 in. wide; one side (that on the south-east) is formed by the relatively smooth wall of one side of the joint, and the other (on the north-west) presents the rough surface resulting from the removal of the stone.

The roof, and where they are seen, the sides of the passage, are intact, but the present floor is formed of debris – blocks of rock with much friable red loamy material. The debris does not present material that fell from the roof and sides subsequent to the working of the mine, because the tool marks, to which reference will be made later, indicate that no falls of roof have occurred since the passage was cut. On the other hand, the present height of the passage near the entrance (only 3¹/₄ ft.) is such as to indicate that the floor-debris is not the material dislodged during the cutting of the passage, for the space is too small to permit the manipulation of picks and wedges. From this it appears that the floor near the entrance is made up of debris thrown in after the abandonment of the passage, from which it follows that the original floor is covered by an unknown thickness of loose material.

Although the roof maintains a uniform descent of about 20 degrees from the horizontal, excavations made in it by the original miners about 17 ft. from the entrance make it possible to stand erect in the passage, but beyond that the debris approaches nearer to the roof and the open channel becomes too small to be traversed.[2]

The passage was evidently an exploratory road cut along a joint-plane in search of ore, and as is often the case with such joints, the rocky sides were separated by a layer, 6 in. or so in thickness, of ferruginous marl. This material is purplish-red in colour, and when damp is somewhat plastic and easily kneaded: it is called *clod* by local miners of the present age, following long usage, although neither in character nor mode of occurrence does it resemble the clod of the coal mineral. In some of the Forest of Dean mines clod is sufficiently abundant and rich enough in iron to have been regarded as an ore, but in the present instance it does not appear to have been sufficiently thick for the passage to have been made expressly for its extraction.

The miners were evidently following the band of ferruginous marl with the not unreasonable hope of being led by it to an ore body. The exploratory character of the passage is indicated by the trial holes that had been made in the roof: these are situated near the present penetrable limit of the passage, and of them, one goes forward and upward with a rapidly decreasing

1 Report on Excavations in Lydney Park: R. E. M. and T. V. Wheeler: (Report of Res. Com. Soc. Antiq. of London, IX) 1932, pp. 20-21.

2 Subsequent exploration has revealed the inlet of the mine on the adjacent hillside. Within this inlet, the beginning of a further small shaft, extending apparently northwards, was found but could not be followed.

diameter for about 5 or 6 ft. – the maximum distance that could conveniently be reached by means of a bar manipulated from the main passage, while the other goes backwards and upwards for a smaller distance.

Between the trial hole going forwards and the main channel which continues to go downwards, the undisturbed material is continuous across the end of the passage, and the layer of 'clod' can be seen between the two opposing rock faces.

In addition to the general character of the opening with its possibility of proper exploration, a specially interesting feature is the preservation of the marks made by tools – presumably, from the nature of the marks and the limited space available for manipulation, a pointed single pronged pick similar to those used throughout the history of mining for removing relatively soft material.

It is to the presence of the clay-like clod that the preservation of the pick marks is due. In the vertical band of that material where the main passage diverges from the forward projecting trial hole there are many vertical furrows made by the tools, and similar marks are to be seen on the roof, especially around the trial holes and, also on the thin clayey film that lines the smooth side of the passage. On the opposite side of the passage where the surface is produced by the removal of blocks of the much jointed stone, such marks are less likely to have been made and relatively few can be detected.'

There are also indications of a mine under the south-western part of the Roman guest-house, and the Report states[1]:

'For the rest, it may be assumed that some at least of the other ancient mining shafts which may be seen on the Lydney promontory and, indeed, throughout the Forest of Dean justify their popular ascription to the Romans. It has already been observed that almost the whole of the northern half of the Lydney Camp is honeycombed with the hollows which represent blocked mine shafts. These hollows are now on the average only 1 ft. deep in the centre and from 12 to 20 ft. in diameter. One of these was excavated in 1929... The earthen filling extended to a depth of about 7 ft. and contained nothing but Roman relics... Below 7 ft., the rock-cut shaft of the mine tunnelled downwards in a south-easterly direction. It was largely choked with broken rock and was not further cleared. The presence of the Roman relics in the blocking is not, of course, conclusive as to the Roman date of the mine, since the whole of the surface of the promontory is riddled with Roman remains. All that we can say is that the whole of the evidence is consistent with a Roman origin of the shaft.'

A small hoard of Roman coins was also found at the ancient iron mines a mile to the north-east of the promontory.[2] Furthermore, during recent excavations in the fields known as 'The Chesters' at Severnside, close to the now dried-up Woolaston Pill, where a Romano-British villa was discovered,[3] a heap of outcrop coal was found by the side of one of the furnaces on the site as well as some spent clinker. The coal, which was of a shaley nature, was believed to be from the Forest of

1 pp. 21-2.

2 p. 14. See also Hart, *Archaeology in Dean* (1967).

3 *Chesters Roman Villa, Woolaston* by Dr. C. Scott-Garrett assisted by F. H. Harris; *Arch. Cambrensis,* vol. xciii, 1938, pp. 93-125; and see *Glevum* by L. E. W. O. Fullbrook-Leggatt, *Trans B.&G.A.S.*, vol. lv (1933).

Dean as it was very similar to Forest outcrop coal.[1] Frank Harris says[2] that the area of the villa was covered with iron slag and one of the roadways to the main gate of the courtyard was made of the same material. It would seem that the site was an export point on the Severn for the iron of the Forest, and by the size of the villa (about thirty rooms have been discovered and one large wing not yet opened) it may have been the headquarters of a Roman official in charge of the Forest iron mines. Mr. Harris also found plenty of iron slag mingled with Roman pottery when the building site on the Holm Farm at Lydney was developed.

Many remains of ancient roadways are to be found in the Forest, probably constructed to facilitate the transport of iron ore. The best example is the portion near Blackpool Bridge which retains its original paving, bounded by kerb-stones. In tracing and excavating 'The Dean Road' from Lydney to Mitcheldean in 1932-5, A. W. Trotter and Arthur Hicks found many signs of an ancient iron industry. Mr. Trotter[3] records:

> 'Metalliferous nodules, presumably produced in the smelting of iron ore, are to be found at nearly all points along the course of the Dean Road, including places on the probable course over the fields from Billing's Barn to Highfield. On the average, these nodules would be about equal in bulk to one and a half to two and a half inch cubes. A number, however, are very much larger, one weighing twenty-eight pounds, being found on the Dean Road in the lane at Abinghall. Judging from its appearance, it is probable that when in a molten state this specimen had been run into a hollow made in the ground. It is roughly circular, the diameter being about 8½ inches and the thickness 3½ inches. One side is comparatively smooth, whilst the other is rough, somewhat porous, and has several pebbles adhering to it. Most of the nodules do not seem to be dross or residue left after smelting, being very dense, of black iron-like appearance, smooth of surface and almost non-porous. Occasionally porous nodules, obviously residual, are met with and these are usually much larger, and one piece between three and four feet in length, lies half buried in the earth and vegetation about midway along the Abinghall lane at the eastern side. Many of the non-porous nodules have been found on the surface of the Dean Road paving at places where the road has long since been abandoned, and at a depth of 6 to 8 inches below the present ground level. The weight and appearance of the latter type of nodules suggest that they represent an intermediate stage in the process of ancient iron-making and that they were transported in large quantities over the Dean Road for final treatment elsewhere.'

The ancient and mediaeval mining in the Forest of Dean was naturally of a primitive character, open-cast workings being sufficient in the case of the shallower deposits of iron ore along the outcrop of the 'crease' limestone.[4] Instances of old workings of this type are to be seen in many parts of the Forest, as at Bream,[5]

---

1 *Arch. Cambrensis,* vol. xciii (1938), pp. 103 and 113.

2 In a letter to the present author, 27 March 1944.

3 *The Old Dean Road,* 1936; pp. 53, 54.

4 Kendal, *Iron Ores of Great Britain*, p. 364.

5 For a description, see *The Forest of Dean* by A. O. Cooke (1913), pp. 215-16.

Dean Pool,[1] Noxon and Perry Grove Wood.[2] They are known locally as 'scowles',[3] and are usually winding passages open at the surface. In many cases they are now rendered weirdly picturesque by the growth of mosses, ferns, beeches and gnarled yews which have sprung up from the red soil or rock.

The deeper deposits of ore are found in 'churns' or chambers. Some are quite small, but others have ranged to a capacity of 50,000 or 60,000 tons of ore.[4] To reach these deposits, bell or beehive-pits were sunk, a small pit being driven through the surface cover and widened below. The working was left as soon as all the ore had been taken that could safely be removed, and a fresh pit opened up beside it.[5] This method of working was especially useful in dealing with the irregular deposits of iron ore connected by 'strings' or 'leads' which are characteristic of the Forest of Dean formations. The ore had, in the first instance, to be simply dug out at the surface, but as the excavations became deeper it had to be carried up. This was done in shallow, oval boxes or trays called 'billies' which were slung over the shoulder, held in position by a crooked stick, and carried by boys. According to W. H. Fryer[6]:

> 'the primitive way of getting the hard ore was by lighting fires against it, and, when hot, throwing water over it, thus causing it to crack. A later method would seem to have been to ram unslaked lime into the crevices, or into holes bored for the purpose, and then plug them up, when the damp would gradually slake the lime, and thus break down the ore. Old wood ashes and lime, which would appear to have been the result of these operations, have sometimes been found mixed with refuse ore in the "old men's' workings".'

Besides the places already mentioned, there are some 'scowleholes' in Abbot's Wood, where 'some are mere shallow pits of conical or basin shape; others extend far down into deep workings long disused'.[7] West of Coleford is a hamlet called The Scowles – named after the old workings in the area. On the High Meadow Estate, which adjoins the Forest, are other signs of ancient mining, for example Lady Park Cave which is an old iron mine running 300 yards or more into the rock from the cliff face, with high roofed chambers in places. On the other side of the Wye, on the Doward Estate near Biblings Lodge, iron was worked up to about 1870 by the then owner of the mansion of Wyaston Leys, which stands above the Wye a mile below the Lodge.[8] Other ancient workings are to be found at Crabtree Hill, where many Roman coins were found in 1839.[9]

Writing of the ancient workings in 1780, George Wyrral,[10] an authority in his day on the Dean iron industry, stated:

---

1 *The Forest of Dean* by A. O. Cooke (1913), pp. 244-7

2 'Puzzle Wood', B. F. Watkins, *Dean Forest Guardian,* 9 August 1935.

3 A corruption, perhaps, of the British word 'crowll' meaning cave.

4 *Vict. C.H.* Glos., vol. ii, p. 219.

5 Galloway, *Annals of Coal Mining,* i, p. 32.

6 *Trans. B.&G.A.S.*, vol. 29, 1906, pp. 313-4.

7 Cooke, *op. cit.* p. 102.

8 *Ibid.*, pp. 272-5.

9 *Trans. B.&G.A.S.*, vol. vi, 1881, p. 108.

10 Of Bicknor Court. A copy of his work is included in *Trans. B.&G.A.S.*, vol. ii, pp. 216-34.

> 'There are, deep in the earth, vast caverns scooped out by men's hands, and large as the aisles of churches: and on its surface are extensive labyrinths, worked among the rocks, and now long since overgrown with woods; which whoever traces them must see with astonishment, and incline to believe them to have been the work of armies rather than of private labourers. They certainly were the work of many centuries, and this, perhaps, before they thought of searching in the bowels of the earth for their ore – whither, however, they at length naturally pursued the veins, as they found them to be exhausted nearer the surface.'

Interesting descriptions are also given by Dr. T. A. Ryder in a Paper entitled 'Notes on the "Scowles"' written in 1929.[1]

The old workings have the appearance either of quarries, as at the 'Devil's Chapel' near Bream, or of spacious caves, as at Lydney[2] and on the High Meadow and Doward Estates, or of steep-sided, irregular, passages left by the removal of the earth, rocks and ore. One of the deeper workings occurs on Lining Hill Wood, above Mitcheldean. In several places the workings cover large areas and consist of tree-covered, irregular, broken ground, clefts, fissures and holes. Nicholls[3] states:

> 'The shallower but more capacious mine holes appear with greater frequency on the south and west sides of the Forest, where, too, they were nearer to the water carriage of the Severn and the Wye... Occasionally they are found adorned with beautiful incrustations of the purest white, formed by springs of carbonate of lime, originating in the rocky walls of the limestone around. Sometimes, after proceeding for a considerable distance closely confined in height and width, they suddenly open out into spacious vaults, fifteen feet each way, – the site, probably, of some valuable "pocket" or "churn" of ore; and then, again, where the supply was less abundant, narrowing into a width hardly sufficient to admit the human body. Now and then, the passage divides and unites again, or abruptly stops, turning off at a sharp angle, or, changing its level, shows rude steps cut in the rock, by which the old miners ascended or descended.'

Many of the features of the old workings have become weathered into fantastic shapes. At Bream, one structure resembling a canopied pulpit is known as the 'Devil's Chapel'; a horizontal cleft in the rock nearby as the 'Devil's Larder' (or 'Pantry'), and, underneath it, a small vertical fissure known as the 'Devil's Well'.[4] B. F. Watkins,[5] who made a study of the Forest iron industry, gives an interesting

---

1 *Trans. Woolhope Nat. Field Club*, 1929.

2 See Report of Lydney Excavations (*op. cit.* p. 26). *Cf.* also Rudge (vol. ii, p. 122) who, writing in 1803, stated in referring to Lydney: 'In the wood above the mansion house is a cavern, called the Scowles, to which the entrance is between long unwrought stones, serving as pillars to support a rocky roof. Within, it is about 18 feet long and 9 feet wide. This was unquestionably an old mine.' (Both Dr. Wheeler and Frank Harris are of opinion that this was *not* a mine.)

3 N.I., pp. 4, 5.

4 There are also some old iron ore workings which form a long, deep chasm known as the 'Devil's Ditch' in Lydney Park Woods, half a mile south-east of Chelfridge.

5 'Forest Iron Ore Industry', article in *Dean Forest Guardian,* 9 August 1935.

description of the old workings in Perry Grove Wood,[1] which, he says:

> 'affords an amazing example of the extent of the old surface workings. Millions of tons of ore must have been gotten from this area; wherever the ore has run between the rocks, the ancient miners have removed it, working to considerable depths, over, through and under the rocks, leaving a veritable labyrinth of dingles, passages, ravines, caves and stupendous masses of rocks, standing still as a majestic monument to the miners of long ago. Slowly throughout the centuries nature has beautified this spot, shrouding each and every rock with moss of softest green, converting this one-time wilderness into an emerald isle, where sway tall trees, old oaks and ancient yews cast their shadows.'

Visiting this area, one is struck by a sense of weirdness and awe, and it is quite understandable that superstitious people in the past have associated these ancient iron ore workings with spirits, both good and bad. The area is symbolic of the ancient history of the Forest: on the one hand the works of the ancient miners, and on the other hand the gnarled yews so valued in their earlier years for the making of bows.

1 Approximately half of this wood is known locally as 'Pain's Wood' or 'Puzzle Wood', – and the other half as 'Turner's Wood' or 'Watkins' Wood'. The whole totals about 40 acres, and a large area has been laid out with paths, bridges, arbours, steps and seats, for the convenience of visitors. Over 3,000 Roman coins were found in the area in 1848.

CHAPTER II

THE DEAN MINERS' 'LAWS AND PRIVILEGES'

'*This deponent* [in 1625] *deposed that he has seen an ancient deed dated in the reign of King Edward the Second testifying the liberty and privilege of the miners within the Forest.*' [1]

'*This deponent* [in 1625] *produced several ancient instruments in writing expressing their customs within the Forest.*' [2]

'*This deponent* [in 1637] *deposed that after his father's death he found in his father's study a copy of an ancient Inquisition written in French having relation as he conceived to a Charter granted or to be granted from John, Duke of Bedford to the miners of the said Hundred of St. Briavels for service done by the said miners in France, which copy of Inquisition he delivered to one Edward Keare a miner then held most ancient and of most credit amongst them for the benefit of the miners.*'[3]

'*This deponent* [in 1675] *sayeth that he hath not only read the same in a certain writing now owned by the miners, called the Miners' Inquisition, setting forth their custom, but also in a certain ancient writing in parchment being a memorandum or declaration concerning and setting forth the custom and usage of the miners within the Forest for digging and gaining of the myne [ore].*'[4]

THE oldest extant documents containing the Dean miners' 'Laws and Privileges' are several copies of a transcript dated 16 April 1612. The copy in the Public Record Office, among the Knole-Sackville MSS (Cranfield Papers), No. 1444, comprises one large sheet and another sheet one-eighth the size of the large one. The small sheet has writing on both sides. The date 'April 16, 1612' appears on the larger sheet where the documents are joined with string. At the head is 'Ao.dm.1612'. The document is headed in a later hand: '1612: Forest of Dean: Regulations in it: Very curious'. Contemporary copies of the 1612 document are in the Centre for Kentish Studies, Maidstone (Ref. U269/1-E232), and another in the Gavellers' Office, Coleford.[5] The transcripts refer to 'Edward the Third' [1327-1377].

---

1 E134 Exch. Deps. by Coms. 22 James I (1625), Easter 8. Deposition by Christopher Tucker, a deputy gaveller.

2 *Ibid.*, Deposition by James Keare, miner.

3 *Ibid.*, 13 Chas. I (1637), Mich. 42. Deposition by William Morgan, miner.

4 *Ibid.*, 27 Chas. 11 (1675), Mich. 28. Deposition by John West, miner.

5 Photocopies of each of the various transcripts of 1612 are in The Cyril Hart Dean Mining Collection donated in 2002 to the Forestry Commission, Coleford.

They were sometimes referred to by the earlier miners as 'The Inquisition'. They are obviously a copy of an earlier written transcript, possibly prepared by the miners in support of their opposition, not wholly successful, to challenges made to their mining customs by William, Earl of Pembroke during 1611-12 (see Chapter V).

The next oldest extant transcript is on parchment and dated 7 January 1673 (see Plate III) – almost the same wording as the 1612 transcript except that it refers simply to 'King Edward' and omits the names of some of the miners that 'took this Inquisition'. A postscript states: 'Written out of the parchmt roll now in ye hands of Richard Morse [a deputy gaveller] of Clowerwall, 7 January 1673'. It is signed in a different hand, 'Tho. Davies'.[1] The manuscript, headed 'The Miners Lawes & Privilledges', consists of ten pages, each measuring 12½ inches by 15½ inches, and has been backed with linen. [It was held in about 1858 by John Atkinson, deputy gaveller, at Coleford; in 1953 it was with the deputy surveyor in Whitemead Park. Another copy there was unfortunately mutilated, and is thought to be of a later date (it refers to 'Edward III').] The original parchment roll copy is now in the Gloucestershire Records Office, Ref. D9096, F16/18, 19. It was probably amongst the 'ancient instruments in writing' produced by James Keare, miner, in 1625 (*supra*) and is doubtless that referred to by John West, miner, in 1675 (*supra*).[2]

In addition to the various copies noted above, others of later date are to be found in the Bodleian Library,[3] the British Library,[4] and Gloucester Public Library.[5] The insertions made by the 'editors' in the printed version (*infra*) and by Nicholls are collations of the later manuscripts with an earlier more nearly corresponding to the 1612 transcript. In the printed versions (*infra*) there are some emendations and misreadings which are suspected to be simplifications of then unfamiliar terms. Many of the words italicised in some versions are emendations, often quite unnecessary.

A copy of 'The Miners' Lawes & Privilledges' based on the 1673 parchment transcript (see Plate III) first appeared in print in 1687 under the title of *The Laws and Customs of the Miners of the Forest of Dean*; it was printed for 'William Cooper at the Pellican, in Little Britain' (London). Only three copies of the first edition of the booklet have been found: one in the British Library (Ref. 445a. 25(2)), a second in the University Library, Cambridge, and a third in the Gloucester Public Library. The booklet, totalling twenty-two small pages, was in some instances printed and bound with a modest general mining collection edited by 'S. Houghton', which included 'An Explanation of the Miners' Terms of Art used in this Book', also 'The Orders and Rules of the Court of St. Briavels ... as they are to be seen in the same Court, 1687'. In 1800, one hundred copies were printed for Thomas Philips by O. Tudor of Monmouth,[6] and another edition

1 Thomas Davies was an official at St. Briavels Castle. As deputy castle clerk he attended several of the Mine Law Courts. He was one-time Collector for the Aids of the Forest of Dean (*Cal.Treas.Bks*., vol. iii, 1669-72, p. 1300), while in 1675 he deposed that he had been bailiff to the farmer of the Forest or farmer himself for 12 years (E134 Exch. Deps. by Coms. 27/28 Chas. II, Glos., Hilary, No. 21).

2 A photocopy of part of the 1673 parchment is shown in Plate III. A photocopy of the whole parchment is in The Cyril Hart Dean Mining Collection, donated in 2002 to the Forestry Commission, Coleford.

3 Bodleian, Rawl. MS C.798, fol. 58v to 70v.

4 British Library, Add. MS 6683, p. 577.

5 Glos. P. Library, L.5.2.

6 Evidence before Coms, of 1831 in 4th Rpt., Evidence, p. 37. Copy in Glos.R.O., D5947.

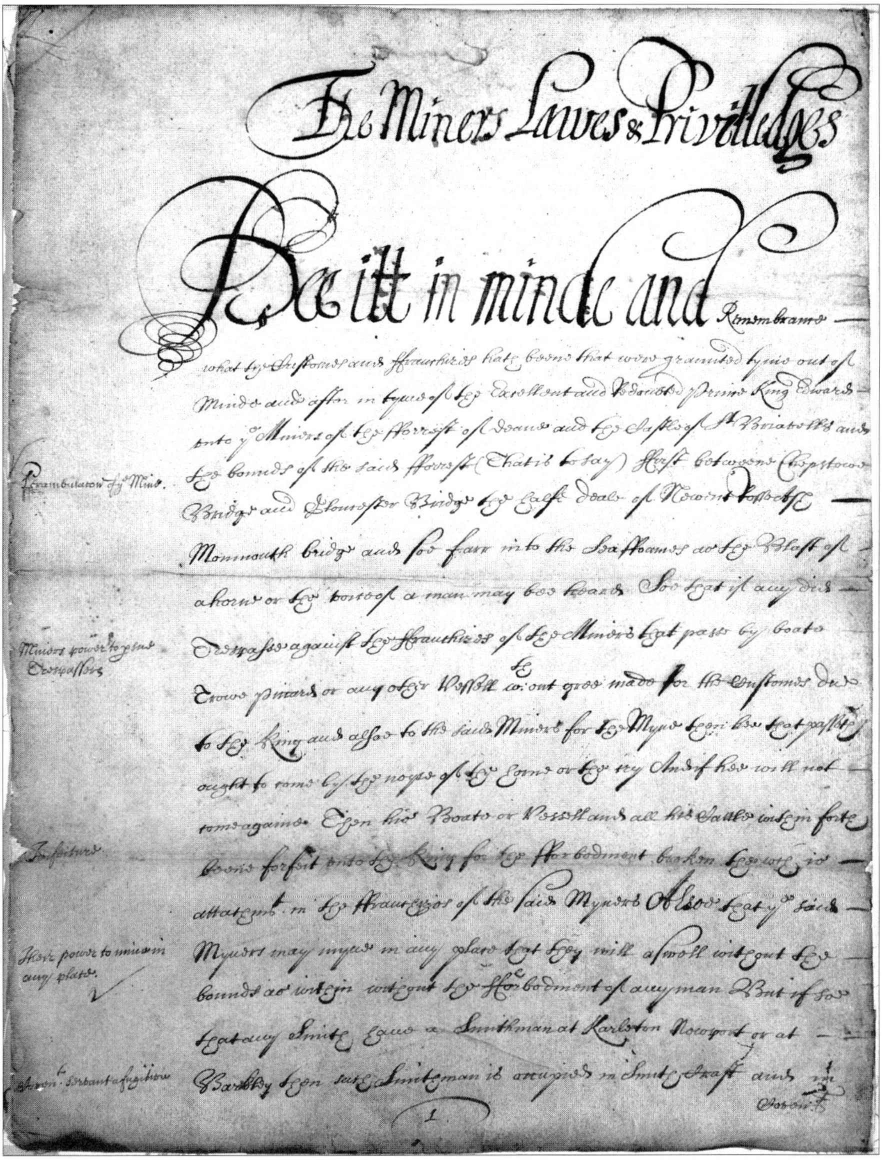

Plate III. *'The Miners Lawes & Privilledges': first page of the 1673 transcript.* *(See text p. 35.)*

was printed by Charles Heath of Monmouth in 1830. In 1866, Nicholls,[1] with the help of Mr. E. Smirke, Judge of the Stannaries of Cornwall, checked the printed version against the 1673 transcript, and in publishing a more accurate copy of the transcript, records: 'Although its early date, and one or two forms of expression may seem to indicate that it was first of all written in Latin, yet so many of its words and phrases, together with its concluding signatures, are so thoroughly old English, as to show that it was most probably composed in our own language. There are no paragraphs or punctuations.'

By the nineteenth century the booklet copy of 'The Miners' Lawes & Privilledges' became known (wrongly) as the 'Book of Dennis'. In 1840 David Mushet referred to 'an old book called "Dennis" being a reprint in the year 1668 [meant for 1687] of "the Miners' Customs of the Forest of Dean"'.[2] Nicholls repeated the error in 1866.[3] John Bellows in 1899 refers to 'Denys',[4] while in 1906 W. H. Fryer refers to 'Dennys'.[5] None of the booklets mention 'Dennis'. The explanation is as follows. In about 1675-6, the miners had a 'Contest' in the Exchequer Court with a Mr Dennis (probably of Clearwell) whose lands were the first that the miners ever carried their coalmining to outside the Forest. However, no Decree was ever made of this 'Cause', and Dennis 'gave up the Contest as being too weighty for him'.[6] In opposition to Dennis the miners probably used their transcript of 1673. A printed copy of it was not made until 1687, in booklet form, and although no reference then or since was made to it as the 'Book of Dennis', the miners later loosely referred to it by that name. Any relevant reference to it should have been made to 'The Book Against Dennis' or to the 'Book Printed Against Dennis'. (See Appendix 5).

Somewhat similar codes of mining law to that in the Forest and hundred were drawn up at different times in other mining districts. The Lord of Hope manor in Flintshire had a code of 'laws and customs of the Minorie', set forth in a document of 1353 which apparently applied also to several neighbouring manors, and which corresponded closely with a code of laws in operation in Derbyshire.[7] In 1470 a code of privileges was drawn up for the Mendip miners,[8] while in 1752 an old code was re-enacted for the Stannaries of Cornwall.[9] The interesting German mining charter of 1185 has already been alluded to.[10] It is not known whether the Dean miners had any knowledge of the mining laws or mining conditions in other parts of the country. However, although, for example, no Cornish names appear in the long lists of Forest of Dean miners, etc. in the Plea Rolls, the village of Ruspidge may have been named by a Cornish miner after the Respeygh in co. Cornwall.[11]

---

1 N.I., pp. 71-82.

2 D. Mushet *Papers on Iron and Steel,* p. 395.

3 N.I., p. 65.

4 Proc. American Antiq. Soc., 1899.

5 *Trans. B.&G.A.S.*, vol. xxix, Pt. II, 1906, p. 316.

6 Hart, 'The (So-called) Book of Dennis', *The New Regard*, 1999, p. 30. See Appendix 5

7 Exch. T. R. Misc. Bks., vol. ccxcvii, ff. 42 *sq.*; J. U. Nef: *The Rise of the British Coal Industry,* vol. i, p. 276.

8 Printed in Thomas Houghton: *The Compleat Miner,* Pt. iii (1688); see also Trans. Roy. Geol. Soc. Cornw., vi, pp. 327-333.

9 Printed in Thos. Pearce: *The Laws and Customs of the Stannaries in the Counties of Cornwall and Devon* (1752).

10 p. 15. n. 4.

11 W. St. Clair Baddeley: *Place Names of Gloucestershire,* p. 131.

A complete copy of the Dean miners' 'Laws and Privileges' is given below.[1] It is based mainly on the 1673 transcript (Glos.R.O. D9096, F16/18, and see Plate III). Comments and annotations have been added after a thorough study of the various written transcripts and the printed versions.

'THE MINERS LAWES & PRIVILLEDGES

Bee itt in minde and Remembrance what the Customes and ffranchises hath beene that were grannted tyme out of Minde and after in tyme of the Excellent and Redoubted Prince King Edward[2] unto ye Miners of the fforrest of Deane and the Castle of St. Briavells and the bounds of the said fforrest, (That is to say)

Perambulation of ye Mine.

(1) ffirst betweene Chepstowe Bridge and Gloucester Bridge the halfe dole of Newent Ross Ash[3] Monmouth Bridge and soe farr into the Seassoames[4] as the Blast of a horne or the voice of a man may bee heard

Miners' power to prevent Trespassers

(2) Soe that if any did Trespasse against the ffranchises of the Miners that pass by boate, Trowe, piccard[5] or any other Vessell without gree[6] made for the Customes due to the King, and alsoe to the said Miners for the Myne, then hee that passeth ought to come by the noyse of the horne or the cry[7]

Forfeiture.

(3) And if he will not come againe Then his Boate or Vessell and all his Chatel within forth beene forfeit unto the King for the fforbodment[8] broken the which is attachmet in the ffranchises of the said Myners

Power to mine in any place.

(4) Also that ye said Myners may myne in any place that they will as well without the bounds as within, without the fforebodment of any man.[9]

---

1 The numbering of the paragraphs has been made to conform with the old printed versions for ease of reference.

2 For consideration of which King Edward this might be, see p. 17. Edward III in 1612

3 James G. Wood (*Trans. Woolhope Nat. Field Club*, 1900-1, p. 209). says: 'I have no doubt that "Rosse Ashe" mentioned here is the Ash at the Ashwell named in the Perambulation of 1300 at the head of the Bishop's Brook which runs into the Wye between Kerne Bridge and Lydbrook.'

4 Possibly a misreading of 'Seaverne' (see *Men and Armour for Glos.*: 1608, p. 205) or 'Saefern(e)' (Anglo-Saxon). A mutilated copy once at Whitemead Park gave the spelling as 'Sea forme'. Another suggestion is that it is a misreading of 'leasowe' (meadow-land) from the A.-S. 'Leeswe' (pasture). As to the area over which privileges extended, note there is no limitation, as in later times, to the Hundred of St. Briavels. It was the Dean Forest (Mines) Act of 1838 which first limited the rights as to mines to the Hundred of St. Briavels and as to quarries to the Forest perambulation. The area given conforms with the area of the Forest delineated by Perambulations of 1228 and 1282, and not the reduced area comprised in a Perambulation of 1300 (see Hart, *The Extent and Boundaries of The Forest of Dean and Hundred of St. Briavels,* 1947).

5 Printed as 'pichard' or 'pickard'. Perhaps referring to the Wye coracle. (The MS. copy in the Bodleian Library also reads 'piccard'.)

6 Satisfaction.

7 The laws of Wihtred, King of the Kentish men in the seventh or eighth century, provided (s. 28) that 'If a man from afar, or a stranger, goes off the road, and neither shouts nor blows a horn, he shall be reputed a thief, to be slain or put to ransom'.

8 This word and its variations is technical, and is nearly equivalent to a prohibition or injunction. Injunctions under the name of 'forbids' were granted and damages recovered for breaches of the laws and customs.

9 For consideration of this general liberty of mining without restriction, see Appendix A. Several instances are there given of how this liberty has been disputed by certain landlords.

Covenant servant a fugitive

(5) But if soe that any Smith[1] have a Smithman at Karleton,[2] Newport or at Barkley[3] then such Smithman is occupied in Smith Craft and in Covenant with a Smith holder within the said Bounds, Then the Smith holder within shall goe to the said Townes to prove his Covenant and after his proffe he may not have his Smithman, Then ye Smith holder shall forbidd all the Myne that ought to be carryed of the said strainger that occupieth the said Smithman unto the tyme that hee answereth as right is. Then the Smith holder within shall not forbidd the Myne of noe other but only of him that occupieth the said Smithman

Gavellor is Bayliffe of the Mine.

(6) Alsoe in the said manner if any Smithman bee in Monmouth or Trelliche, Then the Smith holder within shall come to St. Briavells gate and there with three handes[4] shall prove his Smithman and the prooffe made a precept shall bee delivered by the Constable to the Gavellor the which is Bayliffe of the said Myne to forbidd the Myne of him that occupieth the said Smithman till hee bee restored and only of him and noe other

Miners and Bayliffes; may arrest chatel for their debts.

(7) Also the Myners have such libertyes and ffranchises that for chatel to them due for their Myne that they beene Bayliffes to take the Chatel of their debtors and to arrest them without the leave of any man till gree bee made if hee bee within the bounds aforesaid, And if the debtor bee without the bounds in what place that hee bee, Then the Miner shall forbidd all the Myne that ought to bee carryed to the place in wch the debtor bee abiding till Gree bee made to the Myner And after the forbodment if any carry to the place aforesaid against the forbodd the Carrier shall bee accomptable and debtor to the Miner as the principall was And alsoe the beastes that carry the Myne shall be forfeit to the King for the forbodd broken

Forebode for debt due without the mine.

Distreyning a horse: Hue and Crye.

(8) And if a Smith holder or any other bee debtor for the Myne unto a Myner the wch Smith holder or other bee within Then the Myner is Bayliffe in every place (Except his owne close) to take the horse of the said debtor if hee bee sadled of a work saddle and of noe other saddle bee it that the horse bee halfe within the door of the Smith soe that the Myner may take the tayle of the horse The debtor shall deliver the horse to the Myner And if hee doe not the Myner shall leavy and make huy and cry agt. the horse and then the horse shall bee forfeit to the King for the hue and Cry made and leavyed And yet ye Miner shall present the debtor in the Mine-Lawe the wch is court for the Myne

Holly sticke and Sweare his debt. Amerciandt.

(9) And there the debtor before the Constable and his Clarke the Gavellor and the Myners and none other ffolke to plead right, but only the Myners shall bee there, and hold a sticke of holly and then the said Myner demanding the debt shall putt his hand upon the sticke and none others with him and shall sweare upon his ffaith that the said debt is to him due, and the prove

1 In early times the smith ranked very high among artificers and was honoured in proportion (see replicas of smith's tools in Abenhall Church, Plate II).

2 Caerleon

3 Berkeley

4 Three witnesses.

made the debtor in the same place shall pay the Myner all the debt proved or els hee shall be brought to the Castle of St. Briavells till gree bee made and also hee shall be amercied to the King in twoe shillings

Distresse.

(10) and the same manner Myner to Myner and Myner to all other ffolke Also if a distresse bee taken in like manner as aforesaid And the Debtor lett the distresse dye or bee impaired within ye ward of the Myner for fraud or for malice and after the Myner shall distreyne and take more distresse if any bee till Gree bee made

Horse girth and halter.

(11) And bee it that the distress dye or bee impaired within the ward of the Myner the debtor shall not have right to implead the Miner neither noe right to grieve him for the Trespasse done But at all tymes the Myner have right to take other distresse till Gree bee made Also for the Myne of an horse as is aforesayd the Miner shall take the foregirth for three halfe pence and for one penny the halter

To dig in ye King's soyle or any othere.

(12) Also the Myner hath such ffranchises to inquire the Myne[1] in every Soyle of the King's of which it may be named and alsoe of all other ffolke without withsaying of any man[2]

Wayes to ye pitte.

(13) and also if any bee that denyeth any soyle whatsoever hit bee, bee hit sowed or noe or what degree hit may be named, Then the Gavellor by the strength of the King shall deliver the soyle to the Myners with a convenient way next stretching to the King's highway by the wch Myne may be carried to all places and waters that beene convenient to the sayd Myne without withsaying of any man

The Lord of ye Soyles pte.

(14) ffor the wch Soyle in wch the myne is within found The Lord of the Soyle at the first time if hee will enter into the said myne ffreely hee shall and shall have a dole[3] without paying anything at his first comeing and shall be the last man of the ffellowship, but moreover hee shall doe coste as the ffellowship doth And if after it please the Lord to voyde he may well and if after that hit please him to come againe he may well. But hee shall make Gree for the coste done in the meanetyme for his pte as the ffellowship can prove at the pitt's mouth afterwards as another

Kingsman. Pitt Gavelled. King's Duty.

(15) And at all tymes the King's Man shall come into ye Myne without any coste asking of him and shall bee the third better man of the ffellowship in mayntenance and in helping of the Myne and of the ffellowship But the King's Man nor the Lord's man ought not to enter into the Myne till the pitt be Gavelled (That is to say) ffor every dole one penny to the King at the first and after if the ffellowship doe make a new Dole after the ffirst Gavelling without the King's Leave wherefore for every Dole soe delivered the King shall have another Dole of the wch Mine of every Miner travelling within the said Mine the King shall have every weeke a penny if soe bee that the

---

1 E. Smirke considered the phrase 'to inquire the Myne' to be of Latin origin – '*liberatem inquirendi mineam*' – in which language he thought the whole of the document was probably first composed (N.I., p. 75).

2 See Appendix A.

3 A partner's share

Myner winn three Seames[1] of Myne measured by the Standard of the King of old tyme used at the least and bee it the King shall have noe more

Gavellor's duty in receiving ye King's Customes.

(16) Also the King shall have every Quarter of a yeare of every Miner travelling within the Myne a Seame of Mine the wch is called Lawe oare[2] And every weeke the gavellor shall visitt the Tuesday the whole Mine or at least within two weeks to receive the Customes due to the King aforesaid And if not the Miner for the said tyme shall not bee accomptable But if the Gavellor come in the quarter to visit the Mine as is aforesaid and finde not the Miner at that tyme the Gavellor shall receive soe much of Mine as is due to the King without leave of any

(17) Also if the Gavellor come in due tyme to receive the Customes aforesaid and the debtor will not at that time pay Then the Gavellor shall forbode soe much of myne there as hitt is due to the King by witnesse of the Miners and underneath hee shall putt a sticke of holly and after the Miner carry the said Mine without gree made to the King then the Miner shall be amercied in twoe shillings and also shall make Gree to the King for the Debt, and if any such Mine bee forbad for Lawe Oare Then the Miner shall measure soe much of the Mine that is due to the King to make Gree, and the Remnant they shall carry at their owne pleasures and that by the witnesse of another Miner, and if hee doth not hee shall have the pennance aforesaid

A forsworne Miner.

(18) And if the Gavellor come in due time to visitt the mine (That is to say) Betweene Mattens and Masse and finde not there the Miner at the end of twoe weekes (that is to say) the Tuesday in his workeing place as the manner is The Gavellor shall take him that as is due, And if hee bee not there present or any other for him and at what tyme the Gavellor cometh to prove if the Miner beene ready to pay the Customes aforesaid or noe and they deny Then the Gavellor by the strength of the King shall make the Miner swear. by his ffaith And if the Miner bee found by his fellowship forsworne then the Miner shall be attaint against the King and shall never bee believed more agt. any man and after if hee bee found with Mine within the Mine in his Cloathes pertaining to the Mine every weeke hee shall pay to the King one penny

Beneath the Wood.[3]

(19) And the Miners of the Beneath the Wood (that is to say) Mitcheldeane Littledeane and Ruardeane every weeke the which the Miner travelleth in the Mine hee shall pay unto the King Twelve charges of Mine by a certaine measure if they have soe much gotten by the weeke And the Gavellor shall pay the Miners there Twelve pence

Constable to keepe Courts on Tuesdaye. No forreigner to be present.

(20) Alsoe the Constable shall bee attendant by the reason of his office for Twoe weekes (that is to say) the Tuesday to hold the Court that is called Myne Lawe and there to heare and trye the right of our Soveraigne Lord the King and of Miners and of pty and pty if any bee, And at ye same Mine Lawe shall not bee more sitting with the Constable but himself

[1] See p. 6.
[2] *Ibid.*
[3] See p. 46.

the Gavellor and the Castle Clarke and the Miners before being and noe other. But if soe bee any other have to doe in the said Mine Lawe, and in the said Mine Lawe noe man shall plead neither mayntaine noe cause but only the Miners But if soe any bee attached to answere in the said Mine Lawe hee shall answere for himself and shall be judged by the Miners of all things touching the Mine and in noe other Courte, and then hee that is found guilty Miner to Miner or any other man shall be amercied to the King in two shillings

Pleading in no other Court.

(21) And bee it if any will plead with any Miner for a thing touching the Mine in any other Court before a Justice or any other Man whatsoever hee bee Then the Constable by the strength of the King shall require and bring the plaint into the Mine Lawe and there hit shall be tryed by the Constable and the Miners and then the pty guilty shall be amercied to the King as aforesaid

Manner of Tryall by Juryes by 3 degrees.[1]

(22) And if any plaint bee in the Myne Lawe, at the first day hit shall be put upon twelve Miners the wch shall give ye prove ye first day, The second day upon ffower and Twenty and ye third day upon eight and forty wch eight and forty shall give judgment the wch shall be affirmed firme and stable without calling againe for evermore

Miner forsworne.

(23) And if any Miner bee found forsworne by his faith as hit is aforesaid in the proofe against any Man in the Mine Lawe, Miner to Miner or Miner against any other man and the said Eight and fforty have given for judgmt that hee is forsworne then the guilty shall be attaint against the King and shall have the pennance aforesaid and shall restore the other of all his coste in all points and never prove more

Miner may sell or bequeath his dole.[2]

(24) Alsoe every Miner in his last dayes and at all tymes may bequeath and give his dole of the Mine to whom hee will as his own chatel, And if hee doe not the dole shall descend to his heire

(25) And if hee to whom the dole is soe bequeathed or given by Testamt eyther otherwise hath need to prove his dole in ye Mine Lawe he shall come there and shew ye Testamt and bring wth him twoe witnesses to testifie the will of the Miner and then as right is hee shall bee delivered without any coste made or asked

Timber for ye Pitts and manner of having it.

(26) Also for the Customes that ye Miners done to the King, the Constable that is for the time shall deliver the Miners in six weekes at the Speech that is the Court for the wood[3] before the Verderers by the woodwards that keepeth the place (that is to say) Sufficient of Tymber to mayntayne the King's advantages and proffitt as also for the Salvacon of his Miners as they did in

1 Resembles the process of reversing a verdict of 12 jurors by a verdict of 24 by the Old Writ of Attaint (see Blackst. Com., vol. iii; N.I., p. 78, n.).

2 This is still legal; many widows, for example, hold shares in gales. It is not clear whether anciently a gale bequeathed or sold to a 'foreigner' was allowed to be worked by him or whether he had to dispose of it to a free miner for the purpose of having it worked.

3 The Verderers' Court of Attachment, held at the Speech House from (about) 1680, and previously at 'Kenesley House' (see Hart, *The Verderers and Speech-Court of the Forest of Dean.*)

tyme out of minde without hurt or attachmt made of the King's Officers (that is to say) ffree the fforest unto ye Miners[1]

(27) And also bee it that ye Miner carry tymber from the woods into his place or into any other the wch tymber is made and cut for the boothes[2] for the Mine That for that noe attachment shall be made of any man

(28) And if the Constable will deliver noe tymber as aforesaid and the Miner of his owne authority fetch tymber in ye fforrest for the Mine and carry hit to ye Mine and after that ye Tymber bee in theyr place that is called Gavell place the wch is knowne by the old Custome Then is the Tymber as their owne chatel and none attachment shall be made for that

Sea Cole.

(29) Alsoe the Sea Cole Mine is as free in all points as the Oare Mine But if the ffellowship Mine by ye week three charges the King shall have of every of ye ffellowshipp a penny

A strainger not to pry.

(30) Alsoe noe Stranger of what degree soever hee bee but only that beene borne and abideing within the Castle of St. Brevills and the bounds of the fforrest as is aforesaid shall come within the Mine to see and knowe ye privities of our Sou'aigne Lord the King in his said Mine

Cart nor Wayne. Measure.

(31) Alsoe that noe Smith holder neither Myner neither any other shall make carriage of the said Myne neither by Cart nor by waine but only by the measure called Belleyes[3] by ye wch the Custome of ye King bee measured Soe that the Gavellor may knowe and soe that the King have right in every pointe And if any such unreasonable measure shall be found then the Miner by the strength of the King is Bayliffe to arrest the Beaste and whereof ye beaste shall be forfeit to ye King and ye measure burnt

(32) And bee it that the Miners for duty or for wretchlessnesse will such wrong suffer and alsoe ye Gavellor for his owne Lucre Then the Constable by ye reason of his office shall pursue by ye strength of the King to take and to doe as is aforesaid

(33) Alsoe that noe Smith holder after hee holdeth Smith or become partner to hold Smithy hee shall not have none of ye ffranchises aforesaid within a yeare and a day

Lodges for pitts. Bounds of pitt. Marks.

(34) Also by the ffranchises aforesaid the Constable shall deliver Tymber to the Miners sufficient to make a lodge upon their pitt to keepe and to save the pitt of the King and ye Miners And the pitt shall have such liberties and ffranchises that noe man shall come within so much space[4] that ye Miner may stand and cast redding[5] and stones soe farr from him with a Bale as the manner is[6] And shall have his marks perteyning to his said Pitt

---

1 PRO F20/1 (17) This custom was abolished in 1838 by Sect. 30 of the Dean Forest (Mines) Act.

2 Perhaps 'casks for the ore'. The Bodleian MS. copy reads 'botthells'.

3 *Cf.* the terms 'billy boy' and 'billies' employed with regard to hod-carriers in the Dean iron mines. The Bodleian MS. copy reads 'Belyn'.

4 The distance altered materially during the following centuries.

5 The surface material to be removed before the minerals were reached.

6 Similar to the 'throw of the hache (or hacke)' of the Mendip miners (*The Ancient Laws of the Miners of Mendip,* 1687, p. 4). Also suggests, what we otherwise know to have existed, the opencast and bell-pit systems of working. In Bohemia the arrow flight fixed the limits of the concession (N.I., p. 80).

(35) Also shall have a Bold place in the wch the Miner make and performe the tymber to build the said pitt

(36) And if any other come to travayle and to worke within the place aforesaid hee shall be forbode of ye ffellowship of the pitt

(37) And if after hee come again hee shall loose to ye King two shillings

(38) Alsoe ye pitt shall have a windeway[1] soe farr from him as is aforesaid perteyning to the said pitt

(39) Also the Ptie that is amercied in twoe shillings shall avoyd the place by the Law of the Miners

Drulling a pitt.

(40) Also if a pitt bee made and upon adventure cometh another up another way within the ground and drulleth[2] to ye said pitt at what tyme hee drulleth to ye said pitt he shall abide till the other ffellowshipp of the said pitt bee present at wch tyme if the other ffellowship will not receive him he shall returne again by the forbode and by the Lawe of the Mine But if he drulleth to the said pitt in a certaine Myne then the said Mine shall bee free to both pties which hit dureth and afterwards each one shall come agen to his owne place Saving to each one ye place of others and after if one or the other doe hurt to ye other he shall restore again soe much to him if hee dig and make ye pitt fall he shall build it again and if hee distrouble the other soe that he may not travaile to win his proffitt and the Customes of the King hee shall restore all the lost of the king and the Miner

Wrong forbode.

(41) Alsoe if any bee wrongfully forbode by the Miner or by any other Then hee that is forbode shall come to ye pitt and shall bring with him his Instruments perteyning to ye Mine with his light as another of ye ffellowshipp and there hee shall abide so long as the ffellowshipp and then by ye judgement of eight and forty hee shall receive so much as any other of the ffellowship etc.

The Miners' names yt tooke this Inq^{ton}:

John Garren, Stephen Preest, John Clarke, Thomas Wytt, Thomas Norton, John Hathway, Thomas Michill, John Michill, John Smith, John Lambert, Nicholas Orle, John Barton, Richard Haynes, John Arminger, Walter Rogers, Richard Hathen, Walter Smith, William Miller, Thomas Cromhall, Walter Dau, Richard Timber, William Baker, Thomas With, John Baker, Phillip Dolewyre, John Adys, William Hynd, William Tallowe, John Brute, John Mitchill, Richard Hopkins, Thomas Baster, John Lawrence, Thomas Tyler, Walter Dolett, William Callowe, Richard Hold, Walter Warr, John Robert, Henry Doler, John Parsons, William Holder, Thomas Clarke.

Bee it knowne to all men that shall see or heare this writing that the Inquest of fforty and eight Miners witnesseth and confirmeth all the Laws comprized in ye said Roll. In witnesse whereof they have put their Seales.

Written out of a parchmt roll now in ye hands of Richard Morse of Clowerwall

7 Jany 1673

[*Signed in a different hand*] Tho. Davies.'

---

1 This either refers to an area round the pit which might be utilised for tipping soil and stone, or to a hole or shaft for ventilation purposes.

2 Perhaps an original or local word connected with drilling a hole. The sense is clear.

It will be seen that the names of the miners, using only those in the 1673 transcript, are forty-three in number; thus five are missing. The manuscript copy in the Bodleian Library reads:

'The names of the Jury being forty and eight myners that confirmed this law: John Garon, Stephen Priest, John Clarke, Thomas Witt, Thomas Norton, John Hathley, Thomas Michell, John Michell, John Smith, John Lumbard, Nicholas Orle, John Barron, Richard Haynes, John Myning, Walter Rogers, Richard Heth, Walter Smith, Thomas Crumhall, Walter Dull, John Loofe, Roger Skinner, Harry Norton, John Backstar, John Laurence, Thomas Tyler, Walter Davies, William Calnoe, Richard Holte, Walter Warre, John Roberte, Harry Dorrett, John Parson, William Holder Be it knowne unto all men that shall heare and see this writting that the Inquest of XLVIII mynors wittnesseth and confirmeth all the Lawes comprised in the said Rowle. In witnesse of which they have putt theire seales.'

Alongside the names and in the right-hand margin are added:

'Thomas Forthy, Walter Wilks, Richard Tinker, William Baker, Thomas Wath, John Baker, Phillip Dolwy, John Addis, William Hadd, William Tallow, John Drutt, John Michell, John Hopkin, Thomas Clarke.'

This makes a total of forty-seven, still leaving one missing, possibly 'William Miller'. Allowing for errors in transcription, forty-two of the names in the Bodleian manuscript agree approximately with the forty-two (i.e. all excluding 'William Miller') in the 1673 transcript, leaving unaccounted: 'John Loofe, Roger Skinner, Harry Norton, Thomas Forthy, Walter Wilks.' Thus it seems that the forty-eight free miners comprised the forty-three in the 1673 transcript plus the five mentioned in the last sentence. This is also somewhat confirmed by the fragmentary copy once at Whitemead Park and the 1612 transcript.

It is suggested that the sequence of the handing down of the customary code of laws might be as follows. The parchment roll referred to in the 1612 transcript and held by Richard Morse in 1673 was the record of an earlier 'Inquisition' taken by forty-eight free miners ('The Miners' names yt tooke this Inq^{ton}'). The purpose of this 'Inquisition' was to co-ordinate all the then known details of the customary privileges which had previously been based either on custom or on some earlier code or grant. The 'Inquisition' commences: 'Bee itt in minde and Remembrance what the Customes and ffranchises hath beene that were granted tyme out of Minde.' It ends by saying 'Bee it knowne to all men that shall see or heare this writing that the Inquest of fforty and eight Miners witnesseth and confirmeth all the Laws comprized in ye said Roll'. The 1612 and 1673 documents are simply transcripts or copies of the Roll. The year in which the above-named forty-eight miners took the Inquisition has remained unsolved. All we know with certainty is that it was before 1612. Likely sources such as muster rolls and wills do not reveal comparative names to enable us to settle this interesting point. In 1683,[1] witnesses in a lawsuit were asked: 'Do the quarrymen and miners derive their customs from an ancient Inquisition or from any and what other authority

1 E134 35 Chas. II, M. 40, 1683. Becke *v* Cowles, and *v* Terringham. See Appendix 4.

have you seen the same or a copy thereof; is the copy now produced to you a true copy of such Inquisition?' John Symonds of Clearwell, aged twenty-five years, deposed that he had 'seen a writing which some of the inhabitants have called the copy of an Inquisition'. Trestram Tresteed of Newland, aged ninety years, said he had 'heard the same read, and the same is of great antiquity of three hundred years standing as he hath heard'. William Probyn of Newland, aged sixty-two years, had similarly 'heretofore seen a parchment or paper writing called by the miners an Inquisition'. Henry Hooper of Clearwell, aged eighty-nine years, asserted that 'the miners do ground their customs upon a certain writing commonly called an Inquisition, which writing he hath heard, and begins in these or the like words (*viz.*): "Be it remembered that these are the laws and customs of the miners of the Forest of Dean."'

It is to be regretted that some of the ancient documents of the miners are not extant. There is no trace of any original charter, if there ever was one, or of the parchment roll held by Richard Morse as late as 1673. Certain papers referred to by Nicholls as dating from 30 April 1706[1] are also missing. Fortunately transcripts of the parchment roll remain though differing in some respects from each other. Also available are the originals of seventeen Orders of the Mine Law Court.[2] In addition, certain gale books are available from 1788 onwards.[3] Whom can we blame for the disappearance of the other documents? James Keare possessed certain records in 1625,[4] Richard Morse the parchment roll and transcript[5] in 1673. Order No. 10 (of 1701) of the Mine Law Court directed that certain collectors should 'take care to get and collect all the writings and papers belonging to the miners that were made use of at the last hearing in the Exchequer out of the hands of all such persons as now have any of them in their custodies, and shall put them together with all other the Orders and Records of the Mine Law Courts into the chest prepared to keep them and safely lock them up therein and leave the said chest in the custody of Francis Wyndham, Esq. one of the Society of the Miners who is humbly desired to keep the same for the use and benefit of the miners'. It seems that the order was not complied with, for Order No. 11 (of 1707) recites similar provisions. An index was to be made of the documents, and the Orders were to be copied out into a book provided for that purpose. Again it seems that nothing materialised for in 1719 (Order No. 13) it was ordered 'that all former Orders relating to the Miners, in whose custody soever they now are, be delivered to William James Esq., to be by him kept in the Miners' Chest then at the Speech House, and also that Mr. William Davies do

1 N.H., p. 236.

2 These have been fully transcribed by the present author, and are included *in extenso* in Chap. IV. Also Glos.R.O. D9096, F26/1 – many cases of 'miner against miner' 1706-1777.

3 Gaveller's Office, Coletord, *viz.:*

An unlettered Gale Receipt Book 1788—1793.
Gale Book lettered 'A' 1793-1800.
" " " 'B' 1800-1804.
" " " 'C' 1804-1807.
" " " 'D' 1807-1812.
" " " 'E' 1812-1821.
There was also an old record book showing Gale Dinner expenses.

4 E134 Exch. Deps. by Coms. 22 Jas. I, Easter, 8.

5 This was in the hands of John Atkinson, deputy gaveller, during Nicholls' time.

deliver unto the said William James, Esq., all the records, writings, and papers in his custody or possession relating to this Court to be kept in the said Miners' Chest'. By Order No. 15 (of 1737) William Davies was again required to release records in his possession. He was to receive three guineas 'upon condition that he delivers up all records and papers in his custody or procurement relating to the mines'. How far this order was complied with is not known.

Later, Thomas Davies, one of the witnesses before the Commissioners of 1831, deposed that he believed the Mine Law Court 'was given up because somebody took all the papers away from the Speech House and they were considered to be stolen. The deputy gaveller, John Robinson, was a partner in the Fire Engine Mine, and was supposed on that account to have taken them away'. About the same time, Thomas Tovey, deputy gaveller, said, 'I have heard that the records were removed and came into the possession of Colonel Hopkinson' (gaveller). Another witness, Philip Robinson, junior,[1] assistant to Thomas Tovey, handed in certain gale books, etc.,[2] and deposed: 'My grandfather, John Robinson, was clerk to the magistrates and perhaps in that way he got possession of the Mine Law Court records now produced. I do not recollect the Mine Law Courts being held; I have some of the records'.

In a Memorial of 1833 to the same Commissioners, David Mushet deposed[3] that after the conclusion of the last Court 'some person or persons broke open the chest at the Speech House and removed the documents'. It will be seen later that several documents and records came to light during the investigations of the Commissioners of 1831. However, some which would have been of great interest at the present time are still unaccounted for.[4]

1 His father and grandfather had been deputy gavellers.

2 4th Rpt. (25 August 1835), pp. 33 and 39.

3 *Ibid.*, pp. 44-5.

4 Several relevant documents are now in Glos.R.O. D9096, F16/1-17, and F26/1. See also Appendices 6, 7, E, F, G, H, and J.

CHAPTER III

GAVELLERS AND DEPUTY GAVELLERS

'Are there not and have there not been time out of mind two officers within the Forest of Dean called the King's Galors or Gavellors, the one called the Galor or Gavellor Above the Wood, the other the Galor or Gaveller Beneath the Wood; and have they not always been made and authorised by Letters Patents under the Great Seal of England or the Exchequer Seal? [1675][1]

Are they not appointed and have they not been always used and accustomed time out of mind to collect and gather within their respective precincts all duties and dues of our Lord the King or Queen for the time being unto them from time to time arising and coming out of the mines of coal, iron and ochre found or gained by the miners or workmen labouring within the mines in the Forest? [1675][2]

THE ancient office of gaveller[3] in Dean Forest is of unique interest and has been handed down unbroken to the present day. The main duty of the office has been the collection from the Dean miners of the king's dues in respect of coal, iron ore, ochre and stone and the general supervision of the mining customs of the Forest. (Some miners were recruited as deputy gavellers.)

The gaveller was the king's representative; he, through his deputies, took the gavel or due on behalf of the king[4] and officially recognised or disallowed a new mine or

---

1 E134 Exch. Deps. by Coms. 27 Chas. II (1675). Mich. 28. Interr. No. IV on behalf of the defendants. Witnesses answered in the affirmative.

2 *Ibid.*, Interr. No. V. Witnesses answered in the affirmative.

3 'Gaveller' is sometimes pronounced 'gawler' in the Forest. It is also spelt in old documents either as 'Gailor', 'Gaoler', 'Gaoller' or 'Galor'. 'Gaveller' is derived from 'Gale' which, although now used (especially in Ireland) as a synonym for rent, had originally the meaning of tribute or service. It was the Saxon 'gafol' hence 'Gavelherte', or 'Gavelerth', the duty of ploughing so much land for the lord, and 'Gavelrep', the duty of reaping for him *(Cf.* also 'Gavelking' and 'Landgable'). A 'Gawlgate' is mentioned in a Flaxley Charter, and there is a place named 'Gaulet' south of Abenhall. Referring to 'Gaulet', Baddeley *(Place Names of Gloucestershire.* 1913, p. 68) writes: 'In the Forest of Dean, S. of Abenhall. *Gawlet. The Gawle* (1510). *Gale. Gauly.* The Bog-myrtle (*myrica*) A.S. Gagel (E. Gale) appears as 'Gaul' and 'gawil' in Prompt: Parv: 189 (Stratmann-Bradley). It may be that the ground so-called was held with his office by the *Gawler* of the Forest: i.e. 'gaveller'. A recent deputy gaveller (R. I. Treharne Rees, Esq.) thought 'gale' may have been derived from the Welsh 'gafael' meaning a holding. For some 'local colour' on deputy gavellers *(c.* 1688) see 'A Silver Token', being pp. 181-236 of *Dene Forest Sketches,* 2nd Series, by S. M. Crawley-Boevey (1899).

4 'The office of the King's gailor in the Forest is to gather and receive the duties aforesaid to his Majesty's use from the diggers and getters of iron stone and iron ore, and to attend the Myne Lawe Courte and the business apertaining to the same' (E134 Exch. Deps. by Coms. 22 Jas. 1 (1625), Easter 8: deposition by Whittington to Interr. No. IV on behalf of the plaintiffs). The deputy gavellers had 'power by testimony of two miners to discharge and forbid any miners to work any further in the pits if default is made in dues paid quarterly. Whether the miners gain or lose by their labours, his Majesty is to be fully paid' (*ibid.*, 13/14 Chas. I, 1637-8, Hil. 16: deposition of Thomas Wellington).

gale.[1] The deputy gavellers were responsible for allotting a right of way from the mines to the king's highway, and had to decide, or help to decide, disputes between miner and miner, and had power to sue in the Mine Law Court, which they always attended.

Gavellers were appointed by the king by Letters Patent. It was a sinecure office.[2] Their deputies were supposed to collect the king's dues each Tuesday 'between Matins and Mass'. On some occasions in the seventeenth century deputy gavellers commuted with the miners for lump sums to be paid annually to obviate the trouble of collecting the customary dues. For some centuries there were two deputy gavellers – one in charge of 'Above the Wood' and the other of 'Beneath the Wood'. The division of the Forest mining district into 'Above the Wood' and 'Beneath the Wood' is of considerable antiquity. As early as the fifteenth century there was a 'Custodian of the Gawle Above the Wood' and a 'Custodian of the Gawle Beneath the Wood'. However, apart from being told that 'Above the Wood' lay 'towards Newland' we have to wait until the seventeenth century for an explanation as to what areas were comprised in each division. The 1673 transcript of the miners' 'Laws and Privileges' mentions only 'Beneath the Wood' and says it comprised Mitcheldean, Littledean and Ruardean, while in the Rules of St. Briavels Court,[3] said to have been drawn up in 1663 and which were printed in 1687, we come across the terms 'on this side of the Wood' and 'beyond the Wood'. However, in 1675 we find an explanation by a witness in a lawsuit of that year who deposed:[4] 'The parishes of St. Briavels, Newland, Staunton and Bicknor are within the precincts of the Gaoler Above the Wood, and all the parishes of Ruardean, Mitcheldean, Flaxley, Littledean, part of Awre and part of the Lea, within the precincts of the Gaoler Below the Wood.' Thus as late as the seventeenth century there was a gaveller or deputy gaveller for each of the two districts.[5] In 1741 the division was clearly defined by Order No. 16 (of 1741) of the Mine Law Court:

> 'Whereas the mines of this Forest have time out of mind been divided into two parts and called or known by the several names of the Mines Above the Wood and the Mines Beneath the Wood, and the ancient bounds of the said parts we conceive to be, and we do hereby order and ordain that the bounds or limits between the said two parts of the

1 The method of galing a mine is explained later. But note also the deposition of Hooper (E134 Exch. Deps. by Coms. 22 Jas. I (1625), Easter 8: to Interr. No. IV on behalf of the plaintiffs): 'It is *not* the office of the King's Gailors to assign and appoint the places where any ore shall be gotten or digged within the Forest, but that at the first opening of the work the workman or workmen go to the Gailor and acquaint him therewith, whereupon the Gailor comes to the ground and gaileth the pit, and the several workmen give unto the Gailor a penny apiece, and after the Gailor gathereth and receiveth the duties aforesaid to his Majesty's use; and is to attend upon the Myne Lawe Courte and the business apertaining to the same.' Other witnesses deposed on similar lines.

2 The office of gaveller required little or no work but yielded an income after paying the deputies. They had no active participation with the miners, and may never have visited the Forest.

3 See p. 32.

4 E134 Exch. Deps. by Coms. 27 Chas. II (1675), March 28. Deposition of William Hawkins of Coleford. Confirmed by PRO F20/1 (17) in 1662.

5 James G. Wood *(op. cit.,* p. 134) erred in stating: 'The duties of the keeper of the Gawle-above-the-Wood extended to the area within the forest perambulation; those of the keeper of the Gawle-below-the-Wood to that part of the Hundred (of St. Briavels) which lies without that perambulation.'

Mines shall remain, continue and be as followeth (that is to say) Beginning at the river Wye at Lydbrook, where the brook there leading from the forges falls into the said river, and so up the said brook or stream unto a place in the said Forest called Mirey Stock, and from thence along a wayn way at the bottom of a place called Sally Vellet, and so along the same way between the two old enclosures that did belong to Ruardean and Littledean Walks, unto Cannop Bridge, and from thence along the road or highway to the Speech House, and from thence along the said highway to Foxes Bridge, and from thence down Blackpool Brook to Blakeney.'[1]

The division approximately corresponds with that laid down in 1842 as the division between East and West Dean.[2] The same Order ruled that 'where a free miner shall occupy coal works in both the said parts of the Mine at the same time such free miner shall serve on juries for that part wherein he inhabiteth, but all other persons shall serve on the jury for that part of the Mines wherein his works doth lie'. It is shown by the Orders of the Mine Law Court that certain mining regulations which applied to Above the Wood did not apply to Beneath the Wood, and *vice versa*.[3] The ancient division also seems on occasions to have been the deciding factor regarding markets, for by Order No. 10 (of 1701) and No. 13 (of 1719) miners Above the Wood were prohibited from supplying coal for carriage by river above Welsh Bicknor, while No. 16 (of 1741) prohibited miners Beneath the Wood supplying coal for carriage on the Wye below Lydbrook.

The first intimation of the office of gaveller in Dean is in the account of the king's Receiver of the Forest for 1435-6[4] where we learn that 'the mines under "le Wode" as for the portion of the Lord called "le Gravell"' had been demised to Henry Deane and John Cromehale for ten years. This seems to imply the commencement of the system of gavellership, the lessees corresponding to the later gavellers and having deputy gavellers to collect the dues from the miners. From that time the issues or 'gale' of the king's portions of the mines were granted as favours or rewards to various of the king's subjects. This is clear from the grant made to Robert Hyett on 5 December 1464, which reads:[5]

'The King [Edw. IV] to all to whom the present writing shall come, greeting. Know ye that we by consideration of the good and faithfull service which our humble and faithful undersaid

1 'Provided always that certain coal works near Lydbrook called or known by the name of Wyrrall Hill that now are or hereafter shall be carried on in the said Hill, and also another coalwork called or known by the name of Dowlers Chambers, and likewise another coalworks called Speedwell near Tresser Mill, shall each and every of them be deemed, accepted, reputed and taken to be in that part of the Mines called Beneath the Wood although they do not lie within the boundaries thereof as above described.'

2 The division given by The Dean Forest (Poor) Act, 1842 is: 'along the centre of the turnpike road which enters the Forest at or near Viney Hill along to Deadman's Cross, then following a line drawn lengthways along the centre of the road from Deadman's Cross to Blackpool Bridge, then following the Blackpool Brook to Fox's Bridge, then following a line drawn lengthways along the centre of the turnpike road to the Severn and Wye Railroad near Cannop Bridge, then following a line drawn along the eastern boundary of the said railroad to where it quits the Forest near Lydbrook.'

3 Nos. 1, 10, 13, 14 and 16.

4 E101/141/I. John, Duke of Bedford at this time held the Forest and St. Briavels Castle by gift of the king.

5 Pat. R., 4 Edw. IV, m. 25 (Cal. Pt. II, p. 361). C.66/509/m. 25. See Appendix 2 (1464).

Robert Hyett has before now paid to us and in future will pay we have given and granted to him the Gale of our mines *(Gaole minarum)* within our Forest of Dean in the county of Gloucester, which Gale indeed a certain Thomas Wodeward lately had and occupied, with the custody of our park of Whitemead in our said Forest, to have and to occupy the said Gale with the custody of the same park for himself or for his sufficient deputy during the life of the aforesaid Robert, with all fees, profits and conveniences belonging to the said Gale and park and from of old time due and customarily received from the issues, profits, and reversions of our said Forest coming forth by the hand of the Receiver there for the time being whereby the express mention of the true annual value of the said Gale fees, profits, and conveniences stands here made at the least or by any statute, act, ordinance, provision or restriction thence to the contrary made, ordained or provided notwithstanding. In testimony whereof witnesseth the king himself at Westminster the fifth day of December by writ of privy seal and on the above date etc. [1464].'

No trace has been found of the grant to the above-named Thomas Wodeward. Hyett was followed by John Grenehill 'the king's servant and one of the yeomen of the crown' who on 8 October 1481[1] received a grant for life 'of 6d. daily for his fee of the crown from the issues of "le gawleship" of the king's mines in the Forest of Dean, as Robert Hyett, late occupier there, had'.

On 17 September 1484[2] the same John Grenehill received a grant for life 'of the custody of "le gawle" of Great and Little Dene, *alias* "le gawle byneth the wodde", with all profits as Robert Hyett had'. The issues of the mines 'Above the Wood' were granted separately on 24 September 1485[3] to Thomas Moton who was made keeper 'of "le gawle" called "le gawle above the wode" within the Forest, for life, with the profits, fees, rewards and emoluments arising therefrom without account'.[4] John Moton took over the office held by Grenehill on 9 October 1485 being granted for life 'the office of keeping of the "goal" ("gawle") of Great Dene and Little Dene, otherwise called the "gaol under the wode"'.[5] According to Rudder[6] the grant to 'Thomas Motten' was of 'the mines of Newland for life, without rent'; he adds: 'As lately as 4 Henry VII (1489) William Llewellyn, the king's Receiver, accounted for the mines of Newland and Le Gawle, and other the king's mines in the Forest, a copy of whose account I have by me.'

On 17 November 1492 Henry VII made a grant for life to Sir Robert Johns, 'one of the sewers of the king's chamber, of le gale under the wood, which has come to the king's hands by the death of John Motton, king's servant'.[7] Johns was succeeded

1 Pat. R., 21 Edw. IV. m. 1 (*Cal.* Pt. II, p. 287).

2 *Ibid.,* 2 Rich. III, m. 22 (*Cal.* Pt. II, p. 516).

3 *Ibid.,* 1 Hen. VII. m. 9 (*Cal.* Pt. I, p. 5). This grant is confirmed in *Rot. Parl.* (vol. vi, p. 376) which mentions 'the Keeping of the Gaoll there, called the Gaoll above the Wode'.

4 Thomas Moton was granted at the same time 'the office of porter of the castle of St. Briavels within the Forest of Dean with the office of bedel of the said Forest, by himself or deputy, for life, with the ancient accustomed wages by the hands of the receiver, farmer, bailiff, or other occupiers of that Forest'. PRO F20/1/19.

5 *Cal.Pat.Roll*, 1 Hen. VII, m. 19, Pt. I, p. 18. This grant is confirmed in *Rot. Parl.* vol. 6, p. 347 (1 Hen. VII – 1485), which mentions 'the Keeping of the Goale within our forest of Deane, called the Goale Beneath the Wood'.

6 *History of Gloucestershire* (1779), p. 30.

7 *Cal.Pat.Roll*, 8 Hen. VII, m. 13 (8), Pt. I, p. 406. See also Mem. Roll, 29 Hen. VIII, m. 5d.

by David Morgan on 5 November 1520,[1] who in turn was succeeded by Ralph Johnson on 2 February 1529.[2] On 24 December 1493 a grant was made for life to Thomas Bassh 'one of the yeomen of the crown, of the "gaol Above the Woode" in as ample a manner as Robert Hyett, deceased, had it'.[3] He was succeeded on 21 July 1509 by Philip Cachemay,[4] who in turn was succeeded by Richard Longe on 15 May 1533.[5] Longe was succeeded by Henry Brayne on 4 February 1535.[6] Two years later Brayne was granted 'the wood under the Gall'[7] – presumably 'Beneath the Wood'.

In 1553 a Commission ordered to enquire into the king's revenue throughout the land reported that Brayne rented 'the mine of the king called "Gale", in Great and Little Dene, and that he was allowed £12 yearly as a deduction out of his rent'. It also reported that Ralph Johnson rented 'the mine of Newland' and was allowed a deduction of £9 yearly, and that both these 'mines' [i.e. iron ore] were part and parcel of the manor of St. Briavels.[8] On 15 July 1558 we find the following grant[9]:

> 'Philip and Mary, by grace of God King and Queen of England, Scotland and France, Defenders of the Faith, to all whom the present document comes, greeting. Be it known that we give and grant to our noble and well-beloved Thomas Baynham 'le Gale' of our Forest of Dean in the county of Gloucester, to be owned, held, occupied and enjoyed by the said 'le Gale', forenamed Thomas Baynham, or by a proper deputy, for the duration of his life, with all debts, advantages, and other conveniences, which are customary or observed for the benefit of the said 'Gale' instead of Ralph Johnson, or any other person.'

Hence by this time there is evidence of the derivation of gaveller from a person entitled to receive the revenues from the mines to an official of that title.[10] Some of the grants of gaveller in the thirteenth and fourteenth centuries also included that of riding forester, custodian of Whitemead Park and aleconner within the Forest.

By 1625 Thomas Cachmaye was gaveller, with Christopher Tucker and Christopher Worgan his deputies.[11] Interrogatories and depositions in a lawsuit of 1637[12] supply additional information showing the duties of the deputy gavellers at that time:

---

1 *Cal.* L. & P. Hen. VIII, vol. iii, Pt. I, No. G.1081 (5). p. 395. See also Mem. Roll, 29 Hen. VIII, m. 5d.
2 Mem. Roll, 29 Hen. VIII, m. 5d. E368/311, m. 5d.
3 *Cal.Pat.Roll*, 8 Hen. VII, m. 7 (15), Pt. II. p. 421. See also Mem. Roll 28 Hen. VIII, m. 2d.
4 *Cal.* L. & P. Hen. VIII, vol. i, Pt. I, No. 132 (68), p. 67 (Pat. I. Hen. VIII, p. 1,. m. 13). See also Mem. Roll, 28 Hen. VIII, m. 2d. The grant was again confirmed in 1510 with effect from 21 July 1509 (Cal. L. & P. Hen. VIII, vol. i, Pt. I. No. 587 (12), p. 337: Pat. 2 Hen. VIII, p. 2, m. 6).
5 *Cal.* L. & P. Hen. VIII. vol. 6, No. G. 578 (33). See also Mem. Roll, 28 Hen. VIII, m. 2d. Longe was 'one of the esquires of the king's stables'.
6 *Cal.* L. & P. Hen. VIII, vol. 8, No. G. 291 (8), p. 118. See also Mem. Roll, 28 Hen. VIII. m. 2d. PRO F20/1/17. See also Appendix 2.
7 *Hilarii Recorda*, 28 Hen. VIII, *rot.* 2, and *Trin. Rec.* 29 Hen. VIII, *rot.* 5d; See Jones's Index to the Memoranda Rolls. vol. ii.
8 Fosbrooke, *op. cit.* i, p. 113. See Appendix 2.
9 The original grant is in Glouc.Liby (ref.: 3004.L.5.7). See also *Cal.Pat.Roll.* 5 & 6 Philip and Mary, 15 July 1558, m. 30, p. 423 – '*Le Gale subtus le Wode*'.
10 PRO F20 (1) 17, p. 10, 1662.
11 E134 Exch. Deps. by Coms. 22 James I, Easter 8. Tucker owned mines himself – *vide* Drew's deposition.
12 *Ibid.*, 13 Chas. I, Mich. 42 (1637).

'Interrogatories ... on behalf of the defendants':

'III.' 'What officer or officers have you known during all your remembrance to be appointed and serve over the miners within the Forest; Whether hath there been during the uttermost of your knowledge and remembrance a certain officer called a gaoler or gaveller for the time being who hath always accustomed on the behalf of his Majesty and his predecessors to put or appoint a workman in each pit or mine there to work and gain a part for his Majesty or his predecessors after such time as the pit or mine is sunk and perfected at the labour and charge of the miner or miners; And whether have the freeholders also, upon whose soil any such pit, pits or mines have been sunk or digged, used and accustomed to have a like workman in the same pit or mine of ore and coal?'

The substance of this interrogatory was answered in the affirmative by Edward Worgan, William Morgan, Thomas Phelpotte and Thomas Browne.

'VII.' 'Do you know or believe that the custom now is, and for the time whereof the memory of man is not to the contrary hath been, that the gaveller may by vertue of such his office visit the mines of the Forest once every fortnight (if he so please) and to gather and collect, for his Majesty's use, of the miners the dues and customs before mentioned; and in case any miner there hath refused to make payment thereof, hath the gaveller had power and authority (by the testimony of one miner or more) may seize and take to his Majesty's use out of such mines iron ore or coal his Majesty's part; and in case such miner hath not enough ore or coal to give his Majesty ample satisfaction, hath not the custom been time out of mind that the gaveller may sue and implead such miner or miners for his Majesty's dues and customs in his Majesty's Mine Law Court, and there receive the same?'

The substance of the interrogatory was corroborated by Edward Worgan and Thomas Browne.

'XII.' 'Did not you heretofore, or now do, execute the office of deputy gaveller within the Forest of Dean: and whether were you so deputed Above the Wood or Beneath the Wood; and what did you by vertue of your office ? Did not you by vertue of your office from time to time collect and receive of the miners of iron ore and coal inhabiting within the Hundred of St. Briavels and Forest of Dean divers dues, customs and rents from the miners belonging unto his Majesty out of the miners' gettings of iron ore and coal, and what sums of money or mine of ore and coal did the miners answer and pay to you for his Majesty's use or his progenitors; and have not you for non-payment thereof sued such miner or miners as have not paid the same in his Majesty's Mine Law Court, and have not such miner or miners for not paying his dues aforesaid been fined in the Mine Law Court? And do you know or credibly have heard that his Majesty that is and divers of his noble progenitors have made and created the office of gaoler by divers and sundry grants and Letters Patent giving power thereby to make any deputy or deputies for execution of the said office? And were not you or now are a lawful deputy gaveller for the receiving of the king's dues Above the Wood or Beneath the Wood; and what yearly rent do you know or have heard that the chief gaveller have answered and paid to his Majesty or his progenitors for the custom and dues arising from the miners of the Forest of Dean? Declare in particular to your knowledge or remembrance what person or persons by name have been heretofore or now is seised or possessed of the office of gaveller by vertue of the king's Majesty's Letters Patents or of his progenitors. And also what power, privilege and authority the gaveller have by vertue of his office; and what rent did you pay or satisfy to the chief gaveller for his profit and advantage arising by vertue of his office from the mines?'

Christopher Worgan, of St. Briavels, aged forty-eight years, deposed:

'He did execute the office of deputy gaveller within the Forest of Dean Above the Wood about the space of five or six years which were expired in 1628; and during the time of his office he collected and gathered of the miners such rents, dues and customs due and belonging to his Majesty out of the miners' gettings of ore and coal; and according to the tenor of his office he respectively collected and received of every particular miner one penny a week if so it did appear that he got nine pence the week by his labour. And did also receive quarterly of every such miner certain ore or coal called Mine Law order or three pence in lieu thereof of every particular miner. And he from time to time according to his office hath duly paid all such rents, profits and customs which he hath at any time received of the miners to his Majesty's use and hath received divers particular acquittances under the hands of the chief gaveller and of others to his use, of which acquittances he knoweth to be the handwriting of Thomas Catchmay, Esq., being then chief gaveller which are ready to be shown forth in this honourable Court at the hearing. And by vertue of his office and in discharge thereof he hath at certain Mine Law Courts sued the miners which have made default in payment of the goale money who at the beginning of every particular suit have satisfied their dues to him, otherwise by the power of their Mine Law Court they were liable to certain amerciaments, and upon satisfaction thereof he hath released the suit. He hath seen an old Patent under the great seal granted in the reign of Queen Mary [1558] to one Thomas Baynham, Esq., late of Clearwell, deceased, and one other Patent under the great seal granted by King James to Thomas Catchmay, Esq., and hath seen a copy of another Patent granted to Mr. John Gibbons whereby the gaveller was created and authorised to execute the office in manner and sort aforesaid; And that the gaveller has also power thereby to appoint his deputy under him to execute the same.'

Christopher Tucker, of Littledean, miner, aged fifty-one years, deposed:

'He hath hitherto executed the office of a deputy gaveller Below the Wood in the Hundred of St. Briavels and in the Forest of Dean by vertue of a deption to him granted by Thomas Catchmay, Esq., who had Letters Patent from the late King James as he believeth. And by virtue of his office he received the king's dues from the iron mines but not the full dues of his Majesty out of the coal pits. And he hath sued some miners in the Mine Law Court for non-payment of his Majesty's dues for ore, and hath recovered against them in the said court, but did never sue any there for the king's dues for coal. He is now deputy gaveller under the deption of Mr. [John] Gibbons who hath a grant of being chief gaveller by vertue of his Majesty's grant which now is. And during the time of his office he hath well and truly collected and paid all such rents, customs and demands whereunto he was liable by vertue of his several deptions.'

Interrogatories Nos. XIII and XIV also dealt with the office of gaveller but the information therein is covered by the deposition of Morgan, given above. Witnesses in the continuation of the lawsuit in 1638[1] named other deputy gavellers. One witness, Thomas Sternhold, aged sixty-four years, deposed that the first deputy gaveller he had known was 'Edward Keare, after him his son, then Richard Yerworth, Thomas Hooper and Christopher Worgan besides divers others whose names he doth not now remember'. A second witness, Nicholas Brownrick, aged thirty-nine years, said he had known John Typper, one-time deputy gaveller,[2] while a third witness, Thomas Wellington, aged fifty-two years, deposed that he had known 'divers deputy gavellers – Thomas Rock, George Bennys and Thomas Mungey' and that the present deputy gaveller 'Beneath the Wood' was Christopher Tucker. A fourth witness, William Yearworth, believed Sturley Kedgwin also held office – presumably 'Above the Wood'. In 1656[3] there were three deputy gavellers, acting it seems on behalf of the Protector. They were Sturley Kedgwin, James Weysom and Christopher Tucker. All three attended the Mine Law Court held that year.

In 1660, Sir Baynham Throckmorton, junior, of Clearwell, whose father and grandfather had clashed with the free miners in 1625, was appointed 'Keeper of the Gawle Above the Wood'.[4] He was also deputy constable at that time. His deputy gaveller was John Williams.[5] The deputy gavellers in 1668[6] were Richard Morse, Nicholas Kedgwin, Robert Woods and William Adams. Richard Morse still held office in 1673.[7] Throckmorton held office until at least 1680.[8] His deputies in 1674,[9] 1673[10] and 1680[11] were George Arundel[12] and William Adams. The deputy gavellers in 1682,[13] 1685,[14] 1693[15] and 1694[16] were Richard Worgan the younger and William Adams. In 1687[17] Richard Jelfe and John Knight held the offices.

It seems that in the early part of the seventeenth century William, Earl of Pembroke, and John Gibbons[18] received the issues of the office of gaveller, as did

1 E134 Exch. Deps. by Coms. 13/14 Chas. I, Hil. 16.

2 Brownrick had 'known Thomas Dunninge stop £15 which was due to Sturley Kedgin one of the miners for and on behalf of John Typper, gent, then deputy gaolor for law ore and gaole due to his Majesty' [*ibid*].

3 Proceedings of the Mine Law Court, 20 May 1656.

4 C.S.P.D. Chas. II. 1660-1, vol. xxiv, p. 431; also 2 Pars. Orig. 12 Chas. II. *rot.* 81 – '*Baynham Throgmorton, Jun. Militi, concessio officii de le Gawle vocati le Gawle* Above the Wood'. PRO F20/1/17, p. 13. He held this office along with that of 'Riding Forester and Aleconner'.

5 E134 Exch. Deps. by Coms. 27,28 Chas. II, Hil. 21.

6 Order No. 1 of the Mine Law Court.

7 The parchment roll containing the miners' 'Laws and Privileges' was transcribed for him that year.

8 Order No. 4 of the Mine Law Court.

9 *Ibid.*, No. 2.

10 *Ibid.*, No. 3.

11 *Ibid.*, No. 4.

12 Referred to elsewhere as George Arnold (E134 Exch. Deps. by Coms. 27 Chas. II, Mich. 28 – deposition of John West).

13 Order No. 5 of the Mine Law Court.

14 *Ibid.*, No. 6.

15 *Ibid.*, No. 8.

16 *Ibid.*, No. 9.

17 *Ibid.*, No. 7.

18 Eustace Hardwicke deposed in 1675-6 that about the year 1647 he was deputy gaveller by grant of John Gibbons who held the office of gaveller by Patent of Chas. II (E134 Exch. Deps. by Coms. 27/28 Chas. II, Hil. 21). In the same lawsuit, John Brinkworth deposed that he had been a deputy gaveller.

William Wolseley[1] and Charles, Marquis of Worcester,[2] later in the century.[3] This is confirmed by the following grant made on 14 June 1692[4]:

> 'Royal Warrant, under the Queen's [Mary] sign manual, to the attorney-general for a great seal for a grant to Phillip Ryley (surveyor-general of Woods South of Trent) of the office of Keeper of the Gawle called the Gawle Above the Wood in Dean Forest, and of one of the riding foresters and of the Aleconner in the said Forest, and of Keeper of the Gawle under the Wood there: all as amply, etc. as William, Earl of Pembroke & Montgomery, John Gibbon, Thomas Catchmay, Sir Baynham Throgmorton, William Wolseley or Charles, Marquis of Worcester, or any other predecessor therein: with all the profits thereof accrued since 13th February, 1689.'

In 1702 John Howe was made 'Keeper of the Gawle Above the Wood'.[5] The deputy gavellers in 1701[6] were Richard Worgan and William Hatton; in 1707[7] Richard Priest and Robert Wood; in 1717,[8] 1719,[9] 1728,[10] 1737,[11] and 1741[12] George James. On 19 February 1727 William Jelf was appointed 'Keeper of the Gawle Above and Beneath the Wood'.[13] He was succeeded on 20 May 1737 by Thomas Wyndham, junior, who was appointed by Treasury Letters Patent 'Keeper of the Gawle Above the Wood in Dean Forest, and Keeper of the Gawle under the Wood there, and also one of the Riding Foresters and Aleconners'.[14] In 1748[15] Christopher Bond was gaveller on behalf of Augustus, Earl of Berkeley,[16] Philip

---

1 In Dec. 1681 he was granted the offices of Keeper of the Gawle Above and Beneath the Wood (C.S.P.D. Chas II, 1680-1, p. 600).

2 On 17 Dec. 1685 he was made Keeper of the Gawle Above and Beneath the Wood, also Riding Forester and Aleconner (Cal. Pat. Rolls, Jas. II, Press H/34).

3 The two last were also Constables of St. Briavels Castle and Wardens of the Forest of Dean.

4 C.T.B., vol. ix, 1689-92, Pt. IV, p. 1682; see also *Orig.* 4 Will. and Mary, *rot.* 59.

5 1 *Pars. Orig.* 1 Anne. *rot.* 10. C.T.B. vol. xvii, p. 380.

6 Order No. 10 of the Mine Law Court.

7 *Ibid.,* No. 11.

8 *Ibid.,* No. 12.

9 *Ibid.,* No. 13.

10 *Ibid.,* No. 14.

11 *Ibid.,* No. 15.

12 *Ibid.,* No. 16.

13 *Cal. Treas.Books and Papers*, vol. iii (1735-8), p. 454.

14 *Ibid.*

15 Proceedings of the Mine Law Court, 13 Dec. 1748.

16 It does not appear that the Lords Berkeley were entitled to the Crown's issues of the mines and minerals in their position as lessees of the castle and manor of St. Briavels, although Charles, Earl of Berkeley, besides being styled 'Lord High Steward of her Majesty's Court of Pleas, Courts Leet and Mine Law Courts within the Forest' was also appointed '*Custos omnium Ferarum et Boscorum infra predictam forestam durante bene placito, – feodum* 40 *li. per annum*', i.e. 'Keeper of all Beasts and Wood within the aforesaid forest during pleasure, – fee £40 per annum' (Pat. R. 2 Anne [1703], Pt. I, roll 10; and *Trans. B & G.A.S.*, vol. iii, p. 348). See also 1 *Pars. Orig.* 9 Will. & Mary, *rot.* 8 ('*Concessio Officii Constabularii Castri S. Briavelli et Custodis Ferrarum et Boscorum, infra Forestâ de Deane*') and *ibid.*, 2 Anne, *rot.* 8 ('*Carolo Berkeley Comiti, Regina concessit officia custodiendi et tenendi Curias Placitorum et Curias Letas pro Hundredo de Mine-Law-Court in foresta de Deane*'); also Pat. R., 11 Anne, 1712 – Viscount Weymouth '*custodis Ferrarum et Boscorum*'.

Elly being deputy gaveller.[1] Elly was also deputy gaveller in 1754.[2] It seems that a Mr. Cooke and a Captain Gough were either gavellers or deputy gavellers at some time prior to 1776.[3]

In 1775[4] we learn that 'the place of gaveller within the Forest of Dean is held by Patent from the Crown, and by vertue of his office the gaveller has a right to put a man to work in every coal work or work for iron mine within the limits of the Forest, or within any private person's property in the Hundred of St. Briavels (but not in any stone quarry that is belonging to Lord Berkeley). This right the gaveller never makes use of by setting his man to work in the mine pit or coalwork, but lets it out to the partners of the work at such price as he can agree for, which is from twenty shillings to three pounds a work.'

John Robinson was deputy gaveller from at least 1775 to 1777,[5] and in midsummer 1793.[6] George Caesar Hopkinson was gaveller from 4 June 1782 to 1808.[7] In his deposition to the Commissioners who reported in 1788[8] he explained that by Letters Patent dated 4 June 1782 he was granted 'the office and offices of Keeper of the Gawles above and under the Wood, Riding Forester, and Ale Conner in the Forest of Dean (but commonly called gaveller of Dean Forest) to hold the same during his Majesty's pleasure, together with all wages, fees, profits, rewards, perquisites, allowances, dues, commodities, advantages, liberties and emoluments whatsoever, to the said offices respectively belonging'. He asserted that at one time the gaveller had six deputies or assistants for collecting the dues. He had 'no salary for the exercise of the offices, or either of them, but that as gaveller he received and took to his own use, as his predecessors had always done, all the fines, fees or compositions paid by the miners or colliers, without rendering any account thereof, the gaveller paying or allowing to his deputy such certain salary, or such share of the said fees and compositions, as he thinks fit'. By agreement with his late deputy, Philip Robinson, he received £100 annually, his deputy being allowed to retain the balance.

About 1808[9] 'the office of gaveller [but not of deputy gaveller] was abolished, and the then gaveller received a compensation, and the office was vested in the surveyor-general of Woods, without emolument; the produce of the mines, after paying a compensation to the late gaveller and the persons who executed the office of gaveller, was carried to the general account of the Forest'. James Davies (Machen) was a deputy gaveller about this time, as well as being deputy surveyor. His son, Edward Tomkins Machen,[10] also held both offices at a later date. Thomas

---

1 Proceedings of the Mine Law Court, 13 Dec. 1748. In the 4th Rpt. of 1835 he is referred to as deputy gaveller (App. I, p. 35) and also as 'Crier of the Mine Law Court' in 1741 (App. I, p. 45).

2 Order No. 17 of the Mine Law Court.

3 4th Rpt. of 1835, App. I. p. 45.

4 N.H., pp. 285-6.

5 4th Rpt. of 1835, App. I, p. 32

6 They held the office for some time, jointly renting it from the Crown (4th Rpt. of 1835, App. I, p. 32).

7 Evidence of Edward Machen before the 'Duncan Committee' of 1849.

8 3rd Rpt. of 1788, App. XXV, p. 91.

9 Evidence of Alexander Milne (one of the Coms, of Woods) before the 'Duncan Committee' of 1849. The Dean Forest (Gale Rents) Act 1819, see page 248, applies.

10 We know from a lawsuit of 1751 that an ancestor of the same christian names and surname was interested in a gale. He was made an 'honorary free miner' in 1741. In 1717 Richard Machen also received the honour.

Tovey of Newnham was deputy gaveller from Midsummer 1793 to at least 20 February 1832.[1] He was assisted by Philip Robinson, senior, and later by Philip Robinson, junior.[2] From 1820 until 1832 James Court was 'deputy gaveller for stone quarries', his father having previously held the office.[3]

In 1832 Thomas Philips informed the Commissioners of 1831[4] that 'the office of gaveller was at this time [about 1800] a sort of pension; the deputy collected about £240 a year in small sums, of from £1 to £2 and £3 a year for the king's right, supposed to be permanent and paid £100 to his principal, but nothing was paid to the Crown'. In 1838 it was enacted that[5] 'the office of Keeper of the Gawle Above the Wood within the Forest of Dean, and also the office of Keeper of the Gawle Under the Wood within the Forest, and which office or offices are now known or designated as the office of gaveller, is hereby vested in the First Commissioner for the time being of her Majesty's Woods'.[6] Provision was also made[7] that the deputy or deputies appointed by the First Commissioner for executing the duties of the gaveller, should be a person or persons skilled in mining. The same 1838 Act declared[8] that it shall be lawful for the gaveller and his deputy 'at all reasonable times to enter into and upon any gale, pit, level, work or quarry' within the Hundred of St. Briavels, 'and to inspect the state and workings of every part thereof, and to make a plan thereof', and that all proper facilities and information should be furnished by the owner.[9] Provision was made[10] for the granting of a salary to the deputy gaveller, and the payment by him to the Commissioners of Woods of all fees received, to be carried to the account of the annual income of the Forest. Rules drawn up in 1841 by the Dean Forest Mining Commissioners empowered the gaveller or his deputy to settle any disputes as to boundaries.

John Atkinson was deputy gaveller from July 1838 to 1864,[11] sharing the office from 1838 to 1854 with Edward Tomkins Machen (deputy surveyor), and from 1854 to 1864 with Sir James Campbell who succeeded Mr. Machen on 11 November 1854. W. W. Smyth acted in conjunction with Mr. Atkinson for a short period from 1 January 1853.[12] Edward Tomkins Machen in giving evidence before the 'Duncan

1 He possibly relinquished the office in or prior to 1835 for in that year he is referred to as the late deputy gaveller (4th Rpt. of 1835, p. 1).

2 *Ibid.*, App. I, pp. 18 and 32.

3 Except in the case of the bailiwick of Blakeney in which certain rights were claimed by a Mr. Ambrose (5th Rpt. of 1835, App. II, p. 70).

4 4th Rpt. of 1835, p. 36.

5 Dean Forest (Mines) Act, 1838, S. 13. (Repealed by the Act of 1969, *infra.*)

6 The first holder of the office under this section was Viscount Morpeth.

7 Dean Forest (Mines) Act, 1838, S. 13. Thereafter Edward Machen and John Atkinson as joint deputy gavellers continued to collect 'Gawle Rents'. An Act of 1969 (*infra*) cancelled the requirement for a deputy gaveller to be skilled in mining.

8 *Ibid.*, S. 53

9 The provisions of this section were repeated as Rule No. 17 in the Second Schedule of the Coal and Iron Awards of 1841.

10 Dean Forest (Mines) Act, 1838, S.88 (Repealed by the Act of 1969, *infra.*)

11 The 41st Rpt. (1865) of the Coms. of Woods includes an item of £281 10s. 2d. being 'salary and allowances of deputy gavellers from 1st April to 23rd October, 1864'.

12 31st Rpt. (1853). App. XIII (A.C.). pp. 342-7.

Committee' of 1849 stated that his own duty as deputy gaveller was 'to assign to the miners places where they should open their works and to receive the gale rents'; Mr. Atkinson's duty was 'to visit the works, and to keep correct plans of all workings'. The salaries of the deputy gavellers for the eight years 1842-3 to 1849-50 amounted to £350 per annum, and for the two following years £500 per annum.[1] Of this latter amount, Mr. Atkinson received £400 and Mr. Machen £100.

Following the Woods and Forests (Amendment) Act of 1851, T. F. Kennedy, one of the two Commissioners of Woods, was assigned the duty of gaveller. In 1852 an Act[2] was passed which included provision to obviate a legal discrepancy in the vesting of the office of gaveller.[3] The following year there seems to have been additional trouble regarding the legal position.[4] On 12 May 1854 Mr. Kennedy was succeeded by the Hon. Charles Gore who in turn was succeeded on 31 March 1855 by the Hon. J. K. Howard.

An Act of 1861[5] empowered the gaveller to sue in the county court for any rent, royalty or other payments due, not exceeding £50; also to alter, with consent of owners, the boundaries of any adjoining gales, and to license the working and disposal of coal in any barrier. In the same year a house and premises were purchased at Coleford as an office for the deputy gaveller, the price being £800.[6]

John Atkinson was succeeded as deputy gaveller in March 1865 by Thomas Forster Brown who held the office until 1 June 1903. For some time his assistant was T. Llewellyn. On 3 June 1884 George Culley of the Office of Woods was appointed gaveller. Westgarth Forster Brown succeeded his father as deputy gaveller on 1 June 1903 and held the office until his death in 1943.[7] The next holder of the office was R. I. Treharne Rees who was appointed on 1 September 1943. He died in May 1946, and was succeeded in office on 1 July of that year by A. R. Thomlinson. Major H. P. Herdman[8] was appointed after the death of Mr. Thomlinson in June 1950. The foregoing deputy gavellers were all distinguished professionals.

1 31st Rpt. of Coms. of Woods (1853], App. XIII (Y), p. 339.

2 Woods and Forests (Amendment) Act, 1852.

3 31st Rpt. of Coms. of Woods (1853), pp. 140-2 and 336-47.

4 *Ibid.*, App XIII (A.C.), pp. 342-7.

5 Dean Forest (Amendment) Act, 1861. An Act of ten years later empowered the gaveller to accept surrender or part of a gale [Dean Forest (Mines) Act, 1871. S.33].

6 39th Rpt. of Coms. of Woods (1861), App. A.A. No. 36, p. 159. Part of the premises not immediately required were let the following year to Messrs. Hartland & Co. on behalf of the Glos. Banking Coy. for £50 per annum (40th Rpt. of Coms, of Woods, 1862, App. V, p. 109).

7 He held many important posts, being chief mineral adviser to the Coms. of Crown Lands, a member of the Board of Governors of the Imperial Institute and of the Institute's Advisory Committee on minerals. From 1 June 1942 he was Estates Manager under the Coal Commission for the Northern and Southern Regions. He gave evidence before a Committee of the House of Commons in connection with the Dean Forest (Mines) Act, 1904.

8 He was for many years in practice as a mining engineer and mineral agent in Cardiff acting on behalf of many large estates in South Wales, England and Scotland. He was a member of the Institution of Mining Engineers and the South Wales Institute of Engineers. He had a considerable knowledge of the Forest of Dean, as during his period of private practice he was mining adviser to a colliery company operating in the Forest, and also had various other interests in the district. In 1942 he was appointed Regional Estates Manager in the Coal Commission, and upon the advent of the nationalisation of the coal industry he was appointed Estates Manager for the South Western Division of the National Coal Board. He was a Justice of the Peace for the County of Glamorgan.

So too were the subsequent ones noted in a later chapter.

In 1924 the office of gaveller was vested in the Forestry Commission (appointed in 1919), but under the provisions of the Coal Act, 1938, the interests of the Forestry Commission in unworked coal and in certain associated minerals were acquired by the Coal Commission on 1 July 1942. This did not affect the status and duties of the deputy gaveller. Currently the office of gaveller is held by the Forestry Commission in respect of coal and iron ore but not of stone.

In summary, the cycle of events of gaveller and deputy gaveller has been the derivation from a person entitled by the Monarch in the thirteenth century to receive the dues from the miners, to an official as noted in Appendix E. In 1808 the office was vested in the surveyor-general of woods. In 1924 it was vested in the Forestry Commission, and continues at the present time. All gavellers appointed their deputies.

Today, the deputy gaveller is the Forestry Commission's representative in connection with the coal and iron ore of the Forest. His headquarters is 'The Gaveller's Office' at Coleford. He is responsible for granting gales and seeing that they are worked according to statutory regulations set out in the Dean Forest Mines enactments. He also collects galeage rents and royalties. Plans of the gales and mines, and records of output, royalties, etc., are held in his office where he keeps up to date the plans submitted by galees of their collieries and iron mines, noted in greater detail in Appendix E of Part Two. As to stone quarries, see page 476 and Appendix F.

As completion of this chapter, following is a list of gavellers, each being a 'custodian of the Gawle [Gale]' either of Above the Wood or Below the Wood, or of both. Each gaveller, favoured by Letters Patent of the kings, appointed one or two deputy gavellers. The office, a sinecure – a position that required little or no work but yielded income – often included the office of riding forester, aleconner of the Forest, and custodian of Whitemead Park:

Henry Deane	1435
John Cromehale	1435
Thomas Wodeward	1463
Robert Hyett	1464
John Grenehill	1481-1484
John and Thomas Moton	1485-1491
Sir John Johns	1492
Thomas Bassh	1493
Philip Cachemay	1495
David Morgan	1520
Richard Longe	1533
Henry Brayne	1535-1537
Ralph Johnson	1537
Thomas Baynham	1558
William, Earl of Pembroke	*c.*1612
Thomas Catchmay	1625
John Gibbons	1625-1647
The Protector (Oliver Cromwell)	1656

continued

List of gavellers, continued

Sir Baynham Throckmorton	1660
William Wolseley	*c.*1681
Charles, Marquis of Worcester	*c.*1685
Philip Ryley	1692
John Howe	1702
William Jelf	1727
Thomas Wyndham junior	1737
Christopher Bond	1748
George Caesar Hopkinson	1782-1808

The custodians (gavellers) took no active participation with the miners, and most may never have visited the Forest. Dealing with the miners was left to their deputy gavellers who collected the fees etc. and passed the net receipts, after deducting their salary and expenses, to the gaveller. Previous to about 1808, the deputies, often being recruited from miners, were probably skilled in local mining and conditions. Thereafter they were mainly highly skilled professional mining engineers and the like (*infra*).

In 1808 the office of gaveller was vested in the Crown's surveyor-general of Woods and Forests. Since 1924 it has been vested in the Forestry Commission, who appoint their deputy gavellers (See Appendix E), namely J. R. Tallis, A. E. Howell, Roy Piggott and John Harvey.

CHAPTER IV

THE MINE LAW COURT

'Miner against Miner, and Miners against all other men' [1697][1]

'Do you know that his Majesty's "Pyoners" and Miners within the Forest have for their better government a Court called the Miners' Court; how long have they had such a court; what businesses, ordinances or constitutions are there handled or made; who are the principal officers belonging to the same Court; and how hath the usage been thereof time out of mind, as you know or have heard, and of what authority or power; and what are the officers and ministers belonging to that Court; and how do you know the same to be true'? [1625][2]

MINERS' courts for settling disputes in the lead and tin mining industries were common in medieval England.[3] They were necessary to overcome the technical difficulties abounding in mining lawsuits. However, Dean is the only record of such a court in connection with local coal and iron ore mining industries. Some account of the functions of the Dean miners' Mine Law Court – a self-regulating court with jury – has been given in Chapter I.

Commissioners of 1788 and 1831 erroneously stated that the Court is first mentioned in the claim made by Philip, Earl of Pembroke, at the Justice Seat in Eyre held at Gloucester in 1634, when the Earl claimed to be constable of St. Briavels and warden of the Forest, and in view of those offices to be chief judge of the Mine Law Court.[4] Exchequer Depositions by Commissions provide earlier mentions, and it is certain that the Court was in existence by 1469.[5] Certain Dean miners in 1614[6] asserted to the Exchequer Court that there was and had been 'within the bounds of the Forest of Dean time out of mind a Court holden and kept for myne laws to try matters touching the myne and ore before the constable of the Forest and the clarke of the Courte of the Castle of St. Brevells and the gaylor or the King's bayliff, and if the plaintiffe or defendant be convicted an amercement of two shillings is imposed and due to the

1 Inscription on sword once owned by Sir John Palmer, Bt. The inscription continues: 'Eustace Hardwick, Esq., Free Miner of Ye Forest of Deane, 1697'.

2 E134 Exch. Deps. by Coms. 22 James 1(1625), Easter 8: Interr. No. V on behalf of the defendants.

3 Lewis, *op. cit.*, pp. 79-81, 88.

4 The Coms. of 1788 stated (p. 12): 'This is the first mention which we have anywhere found of a Mine Law Court'. Both they, and the Coms. of 1831, appear to have been unaware of the most interesting and informative E134 Exch. Deps. by Coms.

5 At 'Hyll Pit' 1469-70 (Jury of 12 and 48 miners), see Appendix 3.

6 E112/83/411, m. 3.

King's Majestie and ought to be paid to the said gaylor or bayliffe for the King's use, and every Myner ought to pay for the said myne law in every quarter of a year a seame of ore worth threepence called 'law ore' and among profits due to his Majesty out of the said Court do arise touching the proceeding therein as by ancient evidence yet remayninge in the defendants hands yet doth appear'.

Additional relevant information is given in depositions of witnesses in lawsuits of the seventeenth century. Thus, a witness, Anthony Callowe, deposed in 1625[1] to the Interrogatory given at the commencement of this chapter:

> 'He doth know and remember for these thirty years past, there has been a "Myne Lawe Courte" kept at several times as occasion has required, which was for the most part for settling of peace between the miners or pioneers themselves or betwixt them and the Lords of such grounds as they are working in, and sometimes for matter of difference between the "gailor" and miners and pioneers as also betwixt the miners and carriers of their ore or mine; and this Court has been usually kept in some open place of the Forest, for that there is no house or certain place appointed for the same; and the officers of this Court are the constable of the Forest, the "gailor" and steward; and he knows of no particular fee that any of these officers have for the keeping of the said Mine Court, and this Court hath had continuance for thirty years to this deponent's own remembrance and for longer time it has had continuance as he has credibly heard.'[2]

Another witness, James Keere, in the same lawsuit deposed:

> 'The officers belonging to the "Myne Lawe Courte" are distinguished by the names following, viz.: The constable of the Forest for the time being, the Castle clerk of the manor of St. Briavels who is steward of the "Myne Courte", and the two "gailors" who hold the "Courte upon the Myne" within the Forest, not in any certain place or house but as occasion is offered, sometimes under a tree or under a hedge, or, if there be a house upon the "Myne", then in the house. And these Courts be commonly called by the "gailors" at any time there be three actions to be tried and as necessity shall require... and the Court has continued by the space of forty years to this deponent's own knowledge and as he has heard by his father and others a long time before.'

This deposition was confirmed by other witnesses, while Callowe added:

> 'There is a steward of the "Myne Courte" who receives 33s. 4d. yearly for the keeping of the said "Myne Courte", the Castle Court of St. Briavels and "Speeche Court" and he, this deponent, hath heretofore (being his Majesty's "bailiffe" in the Forest) paid the fee to the steward for the time being forth the profits and rents of the Forest, which fee he verily thinketh was for the keeping of the aforesaid Courts.'

A lawsuit of 1636-7[3] produced additional information. Interrogatories included:

---

1 E134 Exch. Deps. by Coms. 22 James I (1625), Easter 8.

2 Similar depositions were made by three other witnesses.

3 E134 Exch. Deps. by Coms. 13 Chas. I, Mich. 42 (1637).

'V.' 'Hath there been as you know or believe, the time whereof the memory of man is not to the contrary, a certain court holden within the Forest before the constable and castle clerk or steward of St. Briavels, or any other officer and officers, for the well ordering and government of the mines and miners, and also to try and determine titles and differences touching any matter or contract arising or growing within the Forest concerning iron ore and coal as well between the king's Majesty and his predecessors and the miners there as between miner and miner or any other touching the mines; And have not every such miner as aforesaid during all your remembrance, usually accustomed every quarter of the year to pay unto his Majesty's use for the time being one seame of ore or coal or else in lieu thereof three pence in money in respect of the same court; and have not such ore and coal during all your remembrance been commonly called Law Ore? And who by name have been judges, stewards, gavellers and other officers there?'

The substance of this interrogatory was affirmed by Edward Worgan, of Woolaston, aged sixty years, William Morgan, of Chappell Hill, co. Monmouth, aged sixty years, and Thomas Browne, of Clearwell, aged eighty-four years. Worgan added that he remembered one John Morgan late of Bream who was steward of the court. Another interrogatory was:

'X.' 'Did not you heretofore execute the office of deputy constable in the Forest of Dean for his Majesty that now is or his noble progenitors; and how long time did you so execute the office; and from whom or under whom were you deputed and authorised for execution of the office; and did not you by vertue of the office keep a certain court holden within the Hundred of St. Briavels and within the Forest called the Mine Law Court, for trial of actions, suits and controversies arising between the king's Majesty or his noble progenitors and the miners, and between miner and miner of iron ore and coal; and were not you the Chief Judge or officer of the Court by vertue of the said office for the trial and determination of all actions and pleas in that Court; and what other officers were attendant or belonging unto the court with you; and was not there a jury sworn and impannelled for trial of such actions and causes as were there depending; and how many did the same jury consist of; and have not you several and sundry times received their verdict upon trial of such actions and causes and did not you thereupon give judgement; and did not you convey that such verdicts were legal and authentical and according to the ancient laws, rights and privileges of the court; and at whose instance or requirement was the court holden; and how many times in the year was the same court holden and kept?'

Thomas Morgan, of Hurst, aged forty years, deposed:

'He hath heretofore executed the office of a deputy constable in the Forest of Dean for his Majesty which now is and for the late King James, and William, late Earl of Pembroke deceased, chief constable of the Forest, during the space of four years; and by vertue of his office kept divers courts at several times within the said four years in the Hundred of St. Briavels, commonly called the Mine Law Court, for trial of actions, suits and controversies happening betwixt his Majesty and the miners, and also betwixt miner and miner, touching ore and coal within the Forest. And as he can conceive he was by vertue of his office for the time then being Chief Judge of the Mine Law Court; and he hath impannelled divers several juries, some of them consisting of the number of twelve miners, sometimes of twenty-four miners and sometimes of forty-eight miners, according to the ancient custom and use of the court; and hath also received the jurors' verdicts, and gave judgement and granted execution thereupon, which he conceiveth was lawful by the ancient customs of the court so to do; and such courts have been kept by him at the request and notice of the miners and gaveller, and for the ordering of the differences betwixt them; and there was a clerk of the court, two gavellers and a beadle, under-officers accustomed to attend him in court during the execution of his office there.'

Interrogatory No. 'XI' was similar to No. 'X' above and elicited the following deposition from James Kirle, of Walford, aged forty-five years:

'He hath and doth execute the office of a deputy constable in the Forest of Dean for his Majesty in the Mine Law Court, for trial and determination of actions arising betwixt his Majesty and the miners, and between miner and miner; and such actions have been tried before him in the court by a jury, whereof at some times there have been thirteen, sometimes more, and sometimes sixteen, impannelled on the jury, which juries have at several courts there holden also delivered up their verdicts in a legal way to himself as he conceiveth; and the chief officer which attendeth the court is the gaveller; and such miners which have not attended the court and done their service there, or otherwise done any injury to his Majesty in detaining his Majesty's rents or other dues from him, have been there also fined and amerced; and also paid their fines and amerciaments as he knoweth, for the certainty whereof he referreth himself to the rolls of the Mine Law Court.'

Another interrogatory was:

'XV.' 'Are not you at this present time and so for divers years last past have been steward of divers courts as well for his Majesty as also for his noble progenitors within the Hundred of St. Briavels and Forest of Dean, and amongst which have not you for divers years last past kept and holden for his Majesty and his progenitors a certain court within the Forest called the Mine Law Court; and have there not been divers actions, pleas and suits depending between his Majesty and the miners of the Forest, and between miner and miner there; and have there not been a jury sworn and impannelled for trial of such actions and suits; and have not you by vertue of your office received divers and several verdicts from the jury as well on the behalf of his Majesty and the miners as also between miner and miner; and have you not made records for the same; and what exactions, process, warrants or mandates have you by vertue of your office awarded out of the court; and against what person or persons have you so awarded the same and at whose suit and prosecution as you now remember; and who are the officers attendant and belonging unto the Mine Law Court; and do you believe that the Mine Law Court hath been holden within the Hundred of St. Briavels

> for and on his Majesty's behalf and his noble progenitors time out of mind for trial of actions between the king and the miners and between miner and miner; and have not you divers records and writings to manifest the same; and hath not the court been holden for the benefit and advantage of his Majesty in case any miner shall make default of payment of his Majesty's dues and customs, and also for the well ordering and government of the said mines of coal and iron ore within the Forest?'

Thomas Phelpotte, of Goodrich, aged thirty-three years, deposed:

> 'He, as servant to William Carpenter who was steward of the Mine Law Court was present at the holding of the court and knoweth that at such courts there hath been divers actions brought as well by the gavellers on his Majesty's behalf against the miners, as also by one miner against another; and that upon such actions and trials verdicts have been had and obtained in the court against the party and parties offending his Majesty or touching any other for legal proceeding and trial; whereof a jury hath (according to their custom) been impannelled, and there have been also received in the court divers verdicts from the jurors so impannelled, and records thereupon entered and judgement given, and thereupon also executions granted, but against what person or persons such judgement was given and executions granted he doth not know and remember, but for the more certainty of his knowledge he referreth himself to the records of the court. And the officers belonging to the court are the constable, court clerk or steward, two gavellers and the janitor or beadle of the castle of St. Briavels; and he doth believe that the court hath been holden for his Majesty's benefit.'

John Maddock, of Mitcheldean, aged fifty years, deposed:

> 'He is and hath been one of the clerks in the Mine Law Court for divers years past in the Hundred of St. Briavels in the Forest of Dean and hath there attended the constable at divers courts and entered divers plaints and actions depending betwixt his Majesty's gavellers and miner and miner in the court, where the gaveller hath declared his action on the king's behalf against the miners, and miner also declared against miner according to their usage and custom there used; and jurors there impannelled have been sworn according to the usage there, and have delivered up their verdicts according to their custom then used; and the officers are the constable and his clerk, and two gavellers one Beneath the Wood and another Above the Wood, belonging to the court; and he believeth that Mine Law Courts have been kept in the Hundred of St. Briavels time out of mind; and he hath kept a Register of such plaints, actions and proceedings in the court which have happened or been during the time of his office; and the holding and keeping of the Mine Law Court hath been reputed to be for the benefit of the king and for the well ordering and governing of the mines and miners in the hundred and Forest.'

During the continuation of the same lawsuit in another term[1] Thomas Sternhold of the parish of Dixton, co. Monmouth, aged sixty-four years, deposed that 'he hath known

1 E134 Exch. Deps. by Coms. 13/14 Chas. I, Hil. 16 (1637-8).

Edmond Berrow, Esq. to be deputy constable of the Forest who hath kept the Mine Law Court, and hath known William Carpenter, John Probin and John Maddock, clerks of the Mine Law Court'. Thomas Wellington of Littledean, miner, aged fifty-two years, said he 'has served upon divers juries and likewise done as other jurors have accustomed for the time being in maintaining their ancient laws and customs'. Thomas Whitson of Clearwell, miner, aged seventy-six years, likewise deposed that he had been a juror, while John Adeane of Awre, one of the regarders of the Forest, aged forty-one years, said he 'was at the court within the space of ten years where he saw and heard the orders of the court'.

Somewhat similar depositions are to be found in other lawsuits. In 1675[1] John West deposed that once he had officiated as steward of the Court as deputy to William Rowles, while Rowles deposed that he had been steward of the Court for about twenty years. In 1683[2] John Symonds declared that he 'has known several trials and controversies heard and determined in the Mine Law Court, but none relating to quarries'. He had been clerk to William Rowles, steward of the Court. William Staden of Coleford deposed that about eighteen months ago he was 'sued in the Mine Law Court upon an action for slanderous words supposed to be spoken by his wife against one Tyler although he never was a miner, and it was so proceeded in the said suit that Tyler received against him 40s. damages which was afterwards abated to 20s., upon which he was arrested to be imprisoned; but before he was brought there he paid the 20s. and 3s. or 4s. more for charges demanded of him by the officers that arrested him'. Henry Hooper deposed that he had been a juror at the courts and that 'quarryers are not concerned in the Mine Law Courts, neither have those courts jurisdiction over them as quarryers'. William Probyn had also attended the courts.

The Mine Law Court seems to have been in some sense a moot of miners similar to the 'Parliament of Tinners' of Cornwall and Devon, and capable not merely of declaring the Forest mining customs, but of framing new rules and regulations for the maintenance of the miners' privileges. The Stannaries of Devon and Cornwall had their 'Convocations' or 'Parliaments of Tinners'. The Lordship of Hope in Flintshire had a yearly 'Court of the Minorie'.[3] Similar courts to try offences were held in the lead districts of Derbyshire; here they were held by the bar-master whose other duties included the overseeing of bounds and the detection of infractions of the law; he also had to act as general executive head of administration.[4] A miner if convicted a third time for theft of ore in Derbyshire had the palm of his right hand pierced with a knife and pinned to the uprights of his windlass.[5] In Flintshire, a miner if convicted a third time for bloodshed, received the same punishment except that the hand was pinned to the stocks 'until he either die or tear himself away'.[6] In the Mendips, two courts were held each year, at the

1 E134 Exch. Deps. by Coms. 27 Chas. II, Mich. 28 (1675).

2 *Ibid.*, 35 Chas. II, M. 40.

3 Exch.T.R. Misc. Bks., vol. ccxcvii, f. 42.

4 Lewis, *op. cit.* p. 81.

5 L. F. Salzman: *English Industries of the Middle Ages,* pp. 44-6.

6 Exch. T. R. Misc. Bks., vol. ccxcvii. ff. 42 *sq.* Nef., *op. cit.* vol. i. p. 277.

instance of the lord of the soil, in which a jury of twelve miners presented infractions of their customary law, but usually civil suits and many mine offences were tried either on the manor or in the courts of common law.[1] The manor of Chewton in the Mendips also had a 'minery court'.[2]

The lead miners of Alston Moor in Cumberland had their own 'court of the mines' which 'took cognizance of all pleas of felonies, trespasses, injuries, debts, accounts, contracts and personal actions in respect to the miners and their servants, as well as any others in the moor. The miners elected from their number a coroner and a bailiff, known as the King's sergeant. They were entitled to all fines and amerciaments before the coroner and all waifs and strays found upon the moor. No bailiff of the King nor any other officer might serve a summons or a process within the liberties, unless by default of the miners on their own bailiff to do the same.'[3] Mine courts were also in existence on the continent, in Germany,[4] France[5] and Belgium.[6]

Two Chancery bills of the fifteenth century contain references to an ancient court held at St. Briavels castle. In the first of these,[7] dated about 1433, John Luke of Gloucester complained of the arrest of goods and merchandise to the value of £20 at Mitcheldean by Thomas and Harry White, who carried them to St. Briavels castle, where they were withheld from the owner until he 'had found sufficient surety to appear in his proper person in the court holden there from "iij wokes to iij wokes"', while by 'favour of the court he was denied the right to make attornay, in no wise, which is against the law'. About fifty years later[8] there is a record of a similar court where 'they daily make new laws at their wills and call them from thenceforth customs', and where no challenge of the jury was permitted. It is doubtful whether the Dean miners had any connection with this court, but the references to the denial of an attorney, the making of new 'laws', and the fact that no challenge of the jury was permitted, point to that possibility.

The main function of the Dean miners' Mine Law Court up to 1777 was the settling of disputes (*a*) between the gaveller or deputy gavellers (on behalf of the king) and the miners, (*b*) between miner and miner, (*c*) between the miners and any private landlord, and (*d*) between the miners and the carriers of their iron ore and coal. Here the gaveller or his deputies sued for non-payment of dues, miners sued for debt,[9] and miner sued miner for breach of their customs and regulations, thus claiming the customary reward (*infra*). The miners were not allowed to sue

---

1 Lewis, *op. cit.* p. 80.

2 Star Chamber Proc., James I, 153/17.

3 Lewis, *op. cit.* p. 80.

4 Trans. Roy. Geol Soc. Cornw., vi, 160.

5 *Ibid.*, 252, 257.

6 Jars: *Voyages Métallurgiques,* i, pp. 371-2. At Liége there was in the fourteenth century a coal miners' court called the *Voir Jurés des Charbonnages.*

7 Early Chanc. Proc. bdl. 12, No. 41.

8 *Ibid.,* 60, No. 200.

9 'The miner shall present the debtor in the Mine Law the which is Court for the Mine' (part of Clause 8 of the miners' 'Laws and Privileges'). Numerous cases are recorded in 1706-1777; Glos.R.O. D9096, 26/1. See Appendix 6.

regarding iron ore or coal in any other court.[1]

Another function of the Court was to draw up orders and regulations fixing prices of coal and iron ore, appointing bargainers for sales, determined weights and measures, qualifications for membership, minimum distances between pits or levels, and the fencing of pits. The Court was also used for levying sums on the miners for legal aid in defending their customary rights, and to afford monetary help to members of their fellowship who might be injured at their work. Treasurers were appointed to collect the sums levied. The Court also fixed regulations regarding loading and carrying, and in later years granted honorary freeminerships to many influential persons, – a serious breach of tradition.

Up to the middle of the seventeenth century the Courts do not seem to have been held in any set place, but in some open area of the Forest – sometimes under a tree or under a hedge, or if there happened to be a convenient house, then in that house. Later the Courts were held at the Speech House, at Coleford, Clearwell and elsewhere; there is one instance of a session taking place at St. Briavels castle.

The chief officers of the Court were the constable of St. Briavels or his deputy,[2] the castle clerk or steward, and the deputy gavellers. In addition, at times, there was a court crier.[3] No particular fees appear to have been attached to these offices, except in the case of the steward who received 33s. 4d. for holding this and other courts.[4] In addition to the officers there was a jury 'sworn and impannelled' consisting of twelve, twenty-four, or forty-eight free miners. None but the officers and free miners were allowed to attend Court,[5] and the verdict of the jury was 'firm and stable', no appeal being allowed.[6] No one was allowed to appear in defence of any accused.

The Courts were convened by the gavellers or their deputies 'at any time there be three actions to be tried and as necessity shall require'. Concerning this, clause 20 of the miners' 'Laws and Privileges' states:

---

1 'And be it if any will plead with any miner for a thing touching the miner in any other court before a justice or any other man whatsoever he be, then the constable by the strength of the King shall require and bring the plaint into the Mine Law and there it shall be tried by the constable and the miners and then the party guilty shall be amerced to the King as aforesaid' (*ibid.*, Clause 21). Order No. 1 of 1668 states: 'No miner or miners whatsoever nor any person or persons shall or may sue in any court for ore or coal except it be in the Mine Law Court, under the penalty as aforesaid, so as the person to be sued live within the liberty of the Mine.' Order No. 12 of 1717 states: 'If any free miner shall sue another free miner in any other court other than the Mine Law Court for or concerning any matter or thing relating to the mine, the miner so suing in any foreign court shall forfeit the sum of £30, the one half to the King and one-half to the miner that shall sue for the same in the Mine Law Court.'

2 Fosbrooke, *op. cit.* I, p. 115 says there were six deputies 'who presided alternatively at the Court of Free Miners'.

3 Order No. 15 of 1737.

4 *Ibid.*: £13 17s. was allowed to the steward who had 'for the space of 9 years attended our Courts as a clerk to enter the proceedings, and also hath drawn several warrants, Orders and other writings relating to the mines'.

5 In 1656 there is a record of the widow of a free miner attending the Court (see p. 71).

6 'If any plaint be in the Mine Law, at the first day it shall be put upon 12 miners the which shall give the proof the first day; the second day upon 24 and the third day upon 48, which 48 shall give judgement the which shall be affirmed firm and stable without calling again for evermore' (Clause 22 of the miners' 'Laws and Privileges').

'The constable shall be attendant by the reason of his office for two weeks (that is to say) the Tuesday to hold the Court that is called Mine Law, and there to hear and try the right of our Sovereign Lord the King and of miners and of party and party if any bee, and at the same Mine Law shall not be more sitting with the constable but himself, the gaveller and the castle clerk and the miners before being and no other. But if so be any other have to do in the said Mine Law, and in the said Mine Law no man shall plead neither maintain no cause but only the miners. But if so any be attached to answer in the said Mine Law he shall answer for himself and shall be judged by the miners of all things touching the mine and in no other court, and then he that is found guilty miner to miner or any other man shall be amerced to the King in two shillings.'

The miners were encouraged to be their own 'watchdogs' over their customary rights for they were entitled to one-half of the customary penalty if they successfully sued one of their members for breach of custom or regulations. The usual penalty for breaking the regulations was 'one hundred dozen of good and sufficient ore or coal, one-half to the King's Majesty and one-half to the miner that shall sue for the same in the Mine Law Court'. In some cases monetary penalties were imposed; there are several instances of the sum being £5, and one instance of £30. In the case of non-payment of levies for legal aid, the fine was usually double the amount due. In all cases, one-half was payable to the miner who sued for the same.

It is not known how long each session of the Court lasted, but in later years they seem to have been of considerable duration. For instance the session held in 1682 commenced on 19 September 'and from thence continued by several adjournments' until 28 November.[1] Again, the session held in 1707 commenced on 1 July at Mitcheldean 'and from that day and place continued by several adjournments until 12 August at Coleford'.[2] In what way the sessions were convened by the gaveller it is impossible to say. Possibly the dates were made known by the deputy gavellers on their collecting visits, or perhaps there were special messengers. The free miners may have had set rallying or meeting places, and perhaps the stone known as Gattle's Cross at Scar, near Milkwall, was one such place. One need only dwell for a short while on the state of travel in those far-away days, the long walks or rides involved, and the lack of roads, to realise the great difficulties of convening such a Court and of attending the same. Consider for instance a free miner of Mitcheldean or Littledean having to attend a Court at Clearwell.

Some idea of the procedure at the Court is obtained from Clause 9 of the miners' 'Laws and Privileges' which reads:

'There the debtor before the constable and his clerk, the gaveller and the miners and none other folk to plead right, but only the miners shall be there, and hold a stick of holly and then the said miner demanding the debt shall put his hand upon the stick and none others with him and shall swear upon his faith that the said debt is to him due, and the prove made the debtor in the same place shall pay the miner all the debt proved or else he shall be brought to the Castle of St. Briavels till gree be made and also he shall be amerced to the King in two shillings.'

---

1 Similar adjournments were made in the sessions of the Courts held in 1685, 1687, 1693, 1694, 1701, 1707, 1717 and 1754.

2 Order No. 11.

The custom of using a stick of holly is most interesting. In this connection, Sir Robert Atkins, writing in 1712,[1] states: 'Every miner is to be sworn touching the bible with a holly stick that they may not defile holy writ with unclean hands, and they are to wear a particular cap when they are to give evidence'. Fosbrooke[2] asserts that the parties and witnesses were sworn upon a Bible, into which a stick of holly was put, and were obliged to wear their working cap, or 'wooff', on their heads during the examination. Sir Charles Dilke, Bt.,[3] has suggested that the usage of the oath taken 'touching a holly-wand' was possibly of pre-Roman or Celtic origin,[4] while Nicholls[5] says the same stick was usually employed, being considered by long usage as consecrated to the purpose. The custom seems to have died out by the nineteenth century, for Thomas Davis, an eighty-year-old free miner of Five Acres, giving evidence before the Commissioners of 1831, stated: 'We were sworn as at other courts by taking the testament in hand. I never saw or heard of a holly stick in Court.' However, John Bellows[6] stated in 1899: 'This custom survived down to our own times, for Kedgwin H. Fryer, the late town clerk of Gloucester, once told me he had often seen a miner sworn in the Court touching the bible with a holly stick.' Additional information on the procedure of the Court is obtained from Order No. 9 of 1694, which includes:

> 'That for the better regulating the proceedings and trials in this Court for the future, and preventing the odious sin of perjury, no person be permitted to swear in his own cause nor prove any debt upon his own oath unless it be for or concerning a matter transacted under ground, or where it was difficult to have any witnesses of which cases the constable and the rest of the officers of the Court then present are to be judges, and that no Bargain shall be binding except the same shall be proved by two witnesses at least.
>
> That all causes where the debt or damages demanded in the plea do amount to 40s. shall be tried by a Jury of twelve miners, and the witnesses on both sides openly heard in Court. And thereupon the Jury do give their Verdict according to the method and usage of other Courts of Law; and all causes under that value shall upon hearing such proof as shall be produced on either side be determined by the constable then holding the Court according to the ordinary and usual proceedings of the Court.
>
> That all persons summoned to this Court to answer any action shall have 24 hours notice at least given before the Court to the end they may be provided with such witnesses as they shall think fit to produce, who shall have 12d. apiece paid them for their day's work by the person on whose behalf they are produced.
>
> That no greater or other fees be allowed to any officer of the Court than what have been formerly paid and allowed time out of mind.
>
> To prevent vexatious suits the plaintiff if the cause goes against him or he become non-suited shall pay to the defendant the usual costs of the Court as well for his own day's work as for his witnesses (if he hath any) for which costs the usual process of the Court shall issue.'

---

1 *The Ancient and Present State of Gloucestershire,* 2nd Edn., 1768. pp. 200-1.

2 *Op. cit.* I, p. 107.

3 Vict. C.H. Glouc., ii. p. 221.

4 'A stick of holly' was used too for another purpose (see Clause 17 of the miners' 'Laws and Privileges'). See also PRO F20/1 (17), p. 13.

5 N.I., p. 66

6 Proc. American Antiquarian Soc., 1899.

Whether or not the sessions of the Court were orderly is not known but in 1656 and 1718 miners were fined for disorderly conduct in the Court. Again, it must have been particularly hard for as many as forty-eight Dean miners to have agreed amongst themselves. It is known that the Court was held over a period of more than three hundred years[1] during which time at least seventeen Orders were made.

The earliest session of the Court of which a record of the proceedings is extant took place in 1469-70, see Appendix 3. Another session was held on 20 May 1656, at Littledean,[2] of which the manuscript reads as follows (gaps and undecipherable passages in the manuscript are indicated by an asterisk):

> 'Littledeane. At ye Myne Law Court there houlden the 20th day of May. 1656. Before Thomas Hodges. Esq., deputy constable, Sturley Kedgyn, James Weysom, Christopher Tucker, deputy gavellers.
>
> The names of ye Jury

Edward Hoop,	Richard Morse,	Sworn
Oliver Worgan,	William Vaughan,	
Nicholas Kedgyn,	William Yemm,	
Henry Phelpott,	John Weare,	
John Ranells of Berry Hill,	Wm. Nicholls,	
Henry Worgan,	James Heane.	

> (I): Christopher Tucker complayneth against Solomon Symms of Newnham. The plaintiff doe demand, being deputy gavelor under His Highness the Lord Protector his Broad Seal of England, one gray shoed horse late goods of Rich. Gowstanne of the parish of Westbury, which was resined out of the plaintiff's hands for money due for coale from the said Rich. Gowstanne to the plaintiff for coale delivered out of ye Gaule Beneath the Wood. Which horse the plaintiff conceives to be worth 20s., and this he put to the word of * .[3]
>
> (II): Sturley Kedgyn complayneth against James Clement al. Soop.
> I doe complaine against James Clement al. Soop for saying that I took a false oath this day three weeks in this house and at ye Parke end, did say that I did take a false oath, which I will prove of witnesses. And ye mynors would not reckon nor pay me my due which is due to me being deputy gavelor to his highness Lord Protector nor shall not travell ye myne till I have freed myself of ye oath to the damage of 100s. And this I put to the word of * . The defendant aske the plaint abated for a good cause why Christopher Bond * witness I never said that Sturley Kedgyn took a false oath at the Parke end or elsewhere in my life, and I put to ye word of * . [The verdict is given later.]
>
> (III): Sturley Kedgyn complayneth against Richard James. Agreed.

1 The Court was discontinued during part of the Commonwealth although there is a record of a session in 1656.

2 Glos. City Liby. Ref. 2937, L.F.I.I. The earliest record of a Court found by Nicholls and the Coms. of 1831 and 1838 was that of 1668.

3 This indecipherable word occurs on numerous occasions; it may possibly be meant for 'Cross', but appears to be written 'Ceasse', and often 'Proofe'.

(IV): John Phillipps complayneth against Henry Eddy of Ruardeane. Agreed.

(V): John Taylor complayneth against John Wellington al. Francis.

(VI): Richard Humphries complayneth against John Voyce.
I doe claime 6s. of money due for labour of John Voyce and his company for hauling of water, and so I put to ye word of * . The defendand aske the plaint abated because he oweth him nothing what was due to him. I paid him, and so I refered that to ye word of * .

(VII): John Voyce complayneth against Richard Humphries.
I do complain against Richard Humphries for getting coale of myne and my vearnes Beneath the Wood if my Lord Protector's myne which did belong to a pitt called by ye name of Crabtree pitt, which was conditioned by him that I and my vearnes should have to my damage 40s. by ye coale which he got from me and my vearnes which in his Highness myne and about his mine, and so I refer that to ye word of * .

The defendand aske the plaint abated because I gott none of his coale but what belonged to my owne pitt for there was a later bargaine made that should goe till the * did meete so I put to ye word of * .

(VIII): Christopher Tucker complayneth against Thomas Korb the * and demandeth of him 10s. for damages which he did assume and promises to pay to ye said plaintiff if he did not sinke the deepe pitt within the Gaule of oake pitt in Aywood neere to ye way that goeth from the meene to Aylloe hill, in consideration that I should work a pitt that John Heane did give me freely all but one parte so as I did work that pitt he did engage to pay me all my damages that I should sustain if he did not go on with that worke according to ye agreement so soone as he saw the plaintiff's worke come to perfection he never worked ye pitt to coale according to his promise and Agreement which thing I ought to have according to ye franchises and liberty of ye mynores to have his proof in this Court. The defendant gave out words that I should not have benefit of my proofe in this Court. The reason why I should have that or any plaints because that if any man should swear by his faith in this Court before and the Wopp. constable and the Gavelor here he ought to have an attainte against him and shall have no more to doe in the mine and shall make restitution to him that is damnified by that oath for manifesting of this, here is John Weare, and John Heane, they shall prove that my declaration is truth and that in sinking of this pitt which he never went to coale which he told his Company if he did not goe down with that pitt he should forfeit 10s. to ye plaintiff which words he said to John Humfries this was within the Gaule Beneath ye wood within His Highness ye Lord Protector's myne. *John Heane sworn as witness.*

The Defendant asked the plaint abated, this oake pitt was coaled and worked out which the plaintiff declareth against and was answered and proved here in this Court the laste Court here held, and their deepe pitt was sinked as deepe as I could possible worke for water. And so I leave it to ye word of * .[1]

(IX): Thomas Ellis complayneth against Richard Worgan the elder.
I do complaine against Richard Worgan for bearing iron oare to Lydinies Pill with mare and

---

1 This 'case' is stated in Hart, *New History*, (1995), pp. 146, 147.

mare foale contrary to an order made by 48 men which was measured of his myne to the value of 80 doz. after the six bargainers was chosen and it was not delivered uppon no former bargain, for after ye 300 doz. was measured wich will be proved by witness he solde his myne contrary to order and received money for it without ye consent of six men which were chosen by ye Fellowship of Mynors to bargain and sell. For so doing he is liable to ye forfeit of ye order which is 100 doz. of sufficient mine which in his Highness' myne about ye mynor's mine. And so I put it to ye word of * .

The defendand aske ye plaint abated with a good cause why, for I brought in ye greatest part of this myne upon ye bargaine of 300 doz. and the rest had layen upon my lands 2 years and upwards there where two of the bargayner was consented to put it of as well as their own. And so I put it to ye word of * , *Thomas Preece sworn as witness.*

(X): George Church amerced iis. for uncivil carriages in Court.

(XI): John Watkins amerced iis. for uncivil carriages in Court.

(XII): William Morgan complayneth against John Watkins.
I doe complayne against John Watkins that carried iron mine to Longhope (Thomas Weale) which mare and mare foal contrary to an order made by 48 men in the forfeit of 100 doz. of ore, which that he did confess himself that he had a bargayne and he had carried all in saving 8 seames of ore which he have carried a great dele more than ye 8 seames. I will bring witness to prove it within my Lord Protector's mine. And therefore I put it to the word of * .
Thomas Sybranco sworn witness.

The defendant aske the plaint abated and say that he have bargayned nor carried any contrary to ye order. And therefore I put it to ye word of * . *Richard Weale sworn witness.*

(XIII): Joane Parry[1] complaineth against George Church and Mathew Davis.
I doe demand of Mathew Davis and George Church who were partners with my husband in a coal pitt in a gauile [gale] Above ye Wood called by ye name of Hopewell. After the death of my husband they compounded with me to pay me 1s. 6d. every week and one seame of coale so long as the pitt did last and they and * together according to ye jamling [? gavelling] of ye pitt but of purpose to deprive the plaintiff of her right have found some other way to take ye coale out of that Gauile place or pitt of purpose to deceive the plaintiff to the damage of 11s. And so I put to ye word of * . *James Baddam and Robert Coole sworn witnesses.*

The defendant Mathew Davis asked the plaint abated a good cause why the plaintiff had a parte in Hopewell. We partners did agree with her to pay her 1s. 6d. by ye week for long as that we did worke there and have paid and caused to be paid to her her full due so long as we did work there and hew coale too.

(XIV): George Fox complayneth against Edward Care.
I complaine against Edward Care for bearing iron mine to Lydnies Pill with mare and mare foal, likewise to Longhope, which was contrary to the last order sealed by 48 men that no one should bear any mine to Lydnies Pill but what was those that bargained for 300 doz. He bore iron mine thither without consent of ye six bargayners, which was the forfeit of 100

---

1 The only instance found of a female attending the Court.

doz. of iron mine and so I put it to the word of the * . *Thomas Preece sworn witness.*

The defendant aske the plaint abated for a good cause why I carried no iron mine to Lydneyes pill, but what I was allowed by one of ye bargayners. And I was the first man that measured of ye 300 doz. that was bargained for and that I will prove of witness. And if the plaintiff can prove that I carried any more to Longhope than I have bargained for let him * that, for I put it to ye word of * .

(XV): Christopher Baddam complaineth against George Church.
I doe complayne against George Church for 100 doz. of good and sufficient fire coal for making a breach of the order, which was made of the last 48 men for the hiring and employing forriners [foreigners] in his work, and that I will prove of witness, in his Highnesses mine and without the mine, and that I put to ye word of * . *James Baddam and Robert Coole sworn witnesses.*

The defendant aske ye plaint abated for a good cause why because I have made no breach since the last agreement and also agreed with Sturly Kedgin, Gavelor, and witness to prove, and so put to ye word of * .

(XVI): Thomas Ellis complaineth against Christopher Thorne.
I doe complain against Christopher Thorne for bearing iron mine to Lydnies pill with mare and mare foal contrary to an order made by 48 men, and sold it without the consent of the six bargayners the sum of 10 doz. which is liable to ye breach of order, which is 100 doz. of sufficient mine, which he measured and delivered after ye 300 doz. was delivered within His Highness's mine and without the mine. And that I put to ye word of * . The defendant aske ye plainte abated for a good cause why because I carried no mine to Lydnies pill, but what was consented with ye bargayners, and so I put to ye word of * .

(XVII): John Morgan complains against Morgan ap. Morgan.
I complain against Morgan ap Morgan for 50 doz. of good lawful coale to the said Slads at Wyeside at 2s. 8d. per doz. in the mine and about the mine, and so I put that to ye word of * .

(XVIII): This is our fardile. Edward Hoop. Oliver Worgan, Nicholas Kedgyn, Henry Phelpot, John Ranells of Berry Hill, Henry Worgan, Richard Morse, William Vaughan, William Yemm, John Weare, W. Nicholls, James Heane.

We of the jury intreate Sir Sturly Kedgyn in ye behalf of James Clement to be favourable and merciful to this poor man. He is hearty sorrowful for what he has spoken, and pray that you will show favour to him as you hope to find favour.

The defendant doth submit and is sorry for his offence and is forgiven for the offence by the plaintiff and is adjudged by the constable and becometh prisoner to ye castle of St. Briavels for * and no longer pay his fees.'

The next recorded session is that of 18 March 1668, held at Clearwell, and fortunately the Order (No. 1) made at this Court is extant. It is given in full[1]:

---

[1] There were seventeen Orders at Whitemead Park, and by courtesy of a one-time deputy surveyor (A. D. Hopkinson, Esq.) I transcribed them fully for the first time. Nicholls made brief extracts in the nineteenth century as did also the Dean Forest Mining Commissioners in 1831. Both made several errors in the dates etc. of the Orders (see pages following). The Orders are now in Glos.R.O. D9096, F16 (1-17). An Order of 1730 recently found is now in Glos.R.O. – see Appendix 7.

ORDER NO. 1 (18 MARCH 1668)[1]

'Forest of Dean } At the Myne Law Court holden at Clowerwall the 18th March in the 21st year of the reign of our Sovereign Lord Charles the Second by the grace of God of England Scotland France and Ireland King, Defender of the Faith, anno domini 1668 [*sic*]

The juries of forty-eight mynors whose names are hereunto subscribed then and there appointed and sworn before Sir Baynham Throckmorton Knight and Baronet deputy constable to the Right Honble Henry Lord Herbert Marquis of Worcester Constable to our lord the King of his manor and castle of St. Briavels and Forest of Deane, and William Rowles Gent the Clerk or Steward of the Castle aforesaid and Richard Morse, Nicholas Kedgwin, Robt. Woods and William Adams, deputy Gavillers of the Myne aforesaid, do order and ordain as follows, viz:–

Imprimis we do order and ordain that no foreigner living out of this hundred (or elsewhere) shall or may at any time hereafter transfer or carry any iron ore or coal contrary to our customs except it be carried and delivered unto them by a free miner out of the hundred[2] under the penalty of one hundred dozen of good sufficient ore or coal, the one half to be forfeited to the King's Majesty and the other half to the miner that will sue for the same.[3]

And we do order and ordain that no free miner shall or may hereafter load any foreigner with mine [ore] or coal with any manner of carriage whatsoever under the penalty aforesaid.

Item, we do order and ordain that no young man shall or may hereafter work at mine or coal (although he be born within this hundred) if he hath not worked lawfully twelve months and one day already and paie the king's rent except he be bound apprentice unto a free miner and lawfully serve him as an apprentice for the term of six years under the penalty as is in the former Article expressed.[4]

Item, we do order and ordain that there shall be six men (being free miners) chosen by the Company of miners to be bargainers for iron ore. And that none of the said six men shall hereafter make any bargain for any iron miner without it be with the consent of the said six Bargainers or the majority of them. Notwithstanding the Company of miners (if they find just cause) with mutual consent may alter or change the said Bargainers at their wills and pleasures. And if any miner or miners whatsoever do or shall bargain for any Iron mine [ore] except those six bargainers aforesaid such miner or miners shall forfeit one hundred dozen of good sufficient iron mine or coal the one half &c.

Item, we do order and ordain that if the said bargainers or the majority of them as aforesaid shall make any Bargain with any Iron master or Iron master's Clerk for any quantity of Iron myne, all free miners shall and may lawfully carry until the said Bargain be fully carried in, And that they may measure the said mine all at the same time and receive their money all at the same time and not otherwise. And if the said Bargainers shall think that the said bargain be carried in to any furnace or place whatsoever where they have so bargained as aforesaid.

1 Nicholls (N.H., p. 45) is in error in giving this date as 1663.
2 By Order No. 2 of 1674 these restrictions were cancelled.
3 In the pages following the penalty is curtailed to save space.
4 Order No. 4 of 1680 confirmed this regulation, while Order No. 15 of 1737 laid down a term of 7 years in the case of the son of a 'foreigner'. The Dean Forest (Mines) Act, 1838, confirmed the period in all cases as 'a year and a day'.

And if the said Bargainers do or shall give notice to the company of Carriers that the said bargain is fully carried in as aforesaid, If any miner shall carry after such notice given as aforesaid such miner or miners shall forfeit one hundred dozen of good sufficient iron mine or coal the one half &c.

Item, we do order and ordain that any free miner may carry 'Lyme Coale' to the Slad called the Lyme Slad at the rate of 3/- ye dozen or upwards and not otherwise, And that they may measure the same Lime Coal by the same measure there as fire coale and other mine is measured by, And that the said rate be measured and received by the owners thereof, and not otherwise, And if any miner or miners do or shall carry any Lime Coal to the place aforesaid and contrary to the bargain measure as aforesaid, shall forfeit &c. ..., provided always that if any free miner or miners hath bargained for any iron ore, coal or lime coal before the eleventh day of this instant March it shall and may be lawful for the said miner or miners to carry in the same according to his bargain (if he can prove the said bargain by oath and not otherwise).

Item, we do order and ordain that any free miner shall or may carry Lime Coal to the top of Little Dower [Doward] at the rate of 5/6d. ye dozen And at the other Kills [Kilns] belonging to the said Little Dower at the rate of 5/4d. And at the Blackstones 6/-. and at the weir beyond Wye at the rate of 4/- And at the said weir on this side the River of Wye at the rate of 3/6d ye dozen, And at Coldwall at the rate of 3/6d, And to Monmouth lime coal at the rate of 5/6d ye dozen or upwards. And if any miner or miners do or shall carry any lime coal to the several places aforesaid under the rates aforesaid and contrary to the measure as aforesaid shall forfeit &c. ...[1]

Item, we do order and ordain that no miner or miners whatsoever nor any person or persons shall or may sue in any Court for mine or coal except it be in the Myne Lawe Court under the penalty as aforesaid, so as the person to be sued live within the liberty of the Myne.

Item, we do order and ordain that no person whatsoever that was born upon the waste soil of the Forest as a cabbiner[2] shall work at mine or coal or shall or may transport or carry the same with any manner of carriage unless he hath lawfully worked for the space of seven years already under the penalty as aforesaid.

Item, we do order and ordain that no free miner shall or may carry mine or coal with more than four horses mares nor mare foals in number under the penalty as aforesaid.

Item, we do order and ordain no young man shall carry or transport any mine or coal with any manner of carriage whatsoever except he [? possesseth] a house of himself under the penalty to be forfeited as aforesaid.

Item, we do order and ordain that no free miner shall carry any Lime Coal to a place near Lydbrook called the Boxbush under the rate of 3/- ye dozen according to the measure aforesaid nor to Redbrook under the rate of 4/4 of the measure aforesaid upon pain of forfeiting one hundred dozen of cole as aforesaid.

Provided that nothing herein contained shall bind the miners Beneath the Wood but that they may carry their coal to Mitcheldeane, Littledean, Westbury, and Newnham as formerly they have used, and of right ought to do, so as no fforreynor be permitted to be laden by them within the hundred.

---

1 The regulations fixing prices for delivery and sale of coal and iron ore were dispensed with by Order No. 7 of 1687.

2 Sometimes known as 'squatters'.

Memorial that all the interlining erasures herein above made was done before the signing hereof by the eight and forty whose names are hereunto subscribed.'

There follow forty-eight names in the same hand, mostly illegible, and a few have marks appended to them. Among the names that can be deciphered are Edward and Hendry Hoop, Edmond Bannister, Thomas Silbrance, Thomas Raynells, John Bennett and George Chrisham. In addition are the following genuine signatures:

'B. Throckmorton
deputy constable.

Richard Morse
Nicholas Kedgoing[1]
....
..............................[2]
} Deputy Gavillers.'

The Orders continue as follows:

ORDER NO. 2 (8 SEPTEMBER 1674)[3]

'Forrest of Deane { *At* the Court of Myne and Myners of the said Forest holden at Clowerwalle within the said Forest on Tuesday the 8th September in the 26th year of the reign of our most gracious Sovereign Lord Charles the Second by the grace of God of England, Scotland, France and Ireland King, Defender of the faith &c. Before Sir Baynham Throckmorton Knight and Baronet, Deputy to most Honble. Henry Marquesse of Worcester, Baron of Chepstoll and Gower, Lord President of his Majesty's Counsel within his Principality and Marches of Wales. Knight of the most Noble Order of the Garter. One of his Majesty's most Honble Privy Council. Lord Warden of His Majesty's said Forest of Dean and Constable of his Castle of St. Briavels within the same Forest of Dean, and William Rowles, Gent., Clerk of the Castle aforesaid, And George Arundell and William Adams deputy gavellers of the Mine within the same Forest. The Jury then and there sworn consisting of 48 miners did order and ordain as followeth, viz:-

Whereas at a Mine Law Court at Clowerwall the 18th day of March in the 21st year of the said Majesty's reign before the said Sir Baynham Throckmorton deputy constable, and the said William Rowles Clerk of the Castle of St. Briavels aforesaid and Richard Morse, Nicholas Kedgwin, Robert Wood and William Adams, deputy gavellers of the Myne aforesaid, the Jury of 48 miners then and there impannelled and sworn, for the better ordering and government of the said Mine and miners did (amongst divers other orders therein mentioned) order and ordain that no foreigner living out of the hundred shall or may at any time hereafter

1 Meant for Kedgwin; he signed 'N.K.', the full names being written in as the 48 others. (No seals are attached to this Order.)

2 The two other deputy gavellers did not sign.

3 Nicholls (N.H., p. 49) and the Dean Forest Mining Commissioners are wrong in stating this as Order No. 3. They also give the dates wrongly.

transport or carry any iron ore or coal contrary to the custom except it be carried and delivered unto them by a free miner out of the hundred, under the penalty of 100 dozen of good sufficient ore or coal, the one half &c.

And that no free miner shall or may hereafter load any foreigner with mine or coal with any manner of carriage whatsoever under the penalty as aforesaid. Which orders have proved prejudicial to the said Lord Constable of the said Castle of St. Briavels and to several of his Lordship's friends and tenants living within the counties of Monmouth and Hereford who usually make use of the coal of this forest both for fire for their houses, and lime for their husbandry, without which they cannot well subsist. In thankful acknowledgement therefore of his Honourable's constant favours from time to time expressed to the said miners in vouchsaying to be their great Patron and Defender of their ancient privileges they the said miners being as aforesaid a full Jury of 48 do wholly repeal, revoke, make void and null, the said Order as the same in manner and form is above expressed. And as concerning the same, they being very willing and ready to comply with the conveniency of his Lordship's friends and tenants of the aforesaid counties and all other their neighbours do now order and ordain that whensoever any foreigner not being a free miner shall repair to any the coalpits of the said miners for fire coal or lime coal it shall and may be lawful to and for every such foreigner to have and carry any such coal as aforesaid for their own proper use and expense not carrying the same to sell to others nor upon hire, without being troubled or questioned for the same as fully as a free miner may or ought to do.

Provided always that the inhabitants within the perambulation of the forest of Dean for their own use and expense from time to time be first served and supplied upon the place. And they the said Jury do further order and ordain that all and every other the Orders and Ordinances mentioned and contained in the said former Order of the said former Jury be confirmed and accordingly they do ratify and confirm the same and every of them and do order that they be inviolably observed and kept under the pains penalties and forfeitures therein mentioned and expressed.

And the Jury aforesaid do further order and ordain that the constant future measure of iron ore and coal shall be according to the Winchester bushel (as by law is directed) and not otherwise (three of such bushels shall be a barrel). And that if any person shall presume to measure the same by any other measure, such person or persons shall forfeit one hundred dozen one-half &c. And that no fire coal be sold by any miner under 4d. the said barrel under the penalties aforesaid.

And further the said Jury as the utmost (though poor) testimony of their gratitude that they are able to make to his Lordship for his many noble favours to the said miners do humbly beseech his most Noble Lordship to be pleased to continue his patronage of them, and to vouchsafe them the honour to be one of their Society. And accordingly they do order and ordain that the said Right Honorable Henry Lord Marquis of Worcester be and shall be a free miner within the said forest of Dean to all intents and purposes whatsoever and shall have and enjoy all and every the liberties, privileges and immunities whatsoever as fully and amply as any free miner doth may or might have and enjoy.

And further the said Jury do order and ordain that the aforesaid Sir Baynham Throckmorton be a free miner to all intents and purposes whatsoever and shall and may have and enjoy all and singular privileges and advantages as fully and amply as any free miner doth may or might have and enjoy.

And whereas the miners within the forest are at a very great charge to make surffes for the draining of their pits to get coal, which when they have finished, others sink pits so near them that they are deprived of the benefit of their labour and charge to their very great loss and damage, for remedy whereof it is now ordered that after a surffe is made no miner shall come to work within 100 yards of that surffe to the prejudice of the undertakers without their consents and without being contributory to the making of the said surffe, upon pain of forfeiting one hundred dozen of good fire coal, one half &c.

And lastly the said Jury in pursuance of the said Order do nominate and appoint Richard Morse, Thomas Skynn, James Yerworth, Richard Priest, George Churchay and William Adams to be the present six bargainers mentioned in the said former order to make bargains on the behalf of the whole Society with iron Masters and their Clerks, for the sale and carriage of iron ore to their respective ironworks and to the Rivers of Severn and Wye at the best rates and prizes[1] they can agree for, which shall be binding to the whole Society. And if any miner shall make any bargain of himself without the said bargainers or four of them at the least, or shall carry for any lower rates and prizes[1] than they shall agree for and appoint, such miner shall forfeit for every such offence as in the said former order is mentioned one hundred dozen of iron ore the one moiety to the King's Majesty, and the other to the miner that will sue for the same. Notwithstanding the said six bargainers or any of them may or shall be changed and altered by the consent of the company of miners at the Mine Law Court as there shall be occasion. *In witness* whereof the said deputy constable, Castle Clerk, gavellers and jurors have subscribed their names and set their seals in open Court the day and year above written.[2]

B. Throckmorton,
deputy constable.
Willm. Rowles,
Castle Clerk.
George Arundell,
Wm. Adams,
deputy gavellers[3]

George Churchay
William Boseley
John Watkins
Thomas Jones Jnr.
Richard Priest
William Ambrey
John Moore
William Pitchard
Richard Morse
Edmond Banister
David Griffiths
Gyles Yerworth
Richard Robins
Henry Hooper
James Priest
Thomas Wallon
Richard Bond
Edward Bray
Richard James
John Yem
Nichas. Mowsall
Thomas Wysham
William Trigge
Richard Lewis

Nichas. Kedgwin
Thomas Kedgwin
William Keare
Henry Wilcox
Giles Powell
Richard Smyth
William Cooke
William Rocke
Edward Keare
John Philpott
William Humfreys
William Callowe
Thomas Skyn senr.
William Whetston
Richard Elly
Thomas Manning
Henry Morgan
John Dowle
Edward Sibranco
Thomas Skyn
John Smyth
Richard Nelmes
Thomas Mountjoy
Thomas Wood'[4]

1 Written thus, but obviously meant to be 'prices'.

2 Red seals are placed against each of the following miners' names. The same is the case in all the Orders except the first one.

3 All genuine signatures except Adams who made his mark.

4 All the above signatures are written in the same hand but marks are attached to each.

ORDER NO. 3 (9 MARCH 1675)[1]

'Foresta de Deane
in Com. Glouc.
At His Maties Court of Myne and Myners within the said forest holden at Clowerwall on Tuesday the 9th day of March in the seven and twentieth year of the reign of our Sovereign Lord Charles the Second by the Grace of God of England Scotland France and Ireland King Defender of the Faith, before Sir George Probert Knight deputy to the Right Honble Henry Lord Marquis of Worcester constable in his Maties Castle of St. Briavells within the said forest and Warden of the same forest, And George Arundell and William Adams deputy gavellers of the Mynes within the said forest And William Rowles Gent. Clarke of the said Castle of St. Briavells.

Whereas the ancient rights privileges and customs of His Maties Myners of the said forest of Deane have of late been much invaded and still are threatened, and several suits in the same have been lately commenced and are now depending concerning the same, for the just and necessary defence and preservation whereof in a legal way, there will be occasion for the raising of money as well at the present as for time to come from the several miners of the said forest in the most equal and proportionable way according to each miners profit and getting in the said Art or "Mistery of Myning" To which end and purpose We the jury of forty-eight miners at this court now impannelled and sworn, according to the custom there used for all the time whereof the memory of man is not to the contrary by and with the consent and approbation of the said deputy constable, gavellers, and Castle Clerk do agree consent ordain and order as followeth viz: That every free miner within the liberty of the said forest being of the age of fifteen years and upwards and the widows of all free miners that now do or hereafter shall keep any horses or mares for the carriage and transportation of iron ore, coal or ochre to any place whatsoever shall hereafter pay six pence every quarter of a year for every such horse or mare so kept by him or them for carriage and transportation as aforesaid unto the treasurers or receivers hereinafter named or to be named and appointed at the four most usual quarter days of payment the first payment thereof to be made and begin upon the five and twentieth day of March the four and twentieth day of June the nine and twentieth day of September and the five and twentieth day of December yearly and other person being of the age of fifteen years and upwards that shall work at myne [ore] coal or ochre shall in like manner pay for every quarter of a year wherein they or any of them shall labour in the said art or mystery of mining (be it much or little) the like sum of sixpence, the same to be paid at the four quarterly days of payment in the year before-mentioned unto the receivers or treasurers aforesaid. The said several payment to remain and continue as long as there shall be occasion for the same and until the same shall be revoked and otherwise determined by order of a jury of 48 miners to be impannelled and sworn as aforesaid. Which said money so raised and to be raised shall from time to time (when occasion shall require) shall be laid out and expended by the said treasurers or receivers in and about the just and legal defence of the rights customs and privileges of the said miners and allow for the relief and help of such poor miners who shall happen to be maimed or hurt underground in the getting of ore, coal or ochre aforesaid.

And the jury aforesaid do further order and ordain that if any free miner or carryer or their children or servants aforesaid or any of them shall neglect or refuse to make payment of the money aforesaid unto the treasurers or receivers aforesaid by the space of fourteen days next

1 Nicholls (N.H., p. 47) and the Dean Forest Mining Commissioners are wrong in stating this as Order No. 2. They also give the dates wrongly.

after any of the said quarter days of payment in the year aforesaid whereon the same ought to be paid as aforesaid every such person or persons shall forfeit the sum of two shillings for every neglect or default, the one half to the King's Majesty and the other half to the miner that will sue for the same in the Mine Law Court.

And to the end that a true and just account may be had and made of the monies so to be raised and expended as aforesaid, the jury aforesaid do order and ordain that the said treasurers or receivers for the time being shall yield up their account in writing upon oath in open court every half year (that is to say) at the first Mine Law Court that shall happen to be holden after Michaelmas and our Lady Day yearly unto the deputy constable of the said Castle of St. Briavels for the time being and other officers then holding the said courts of all the monies by them and every of them received and disbursed particularly and distinctly being examined and allowed by the said constable under his hand shall be a discharge to the said treasurers or receivers. And if the said treasurers or receivers or any of them shall refuse or neglect to give an account at the times and in such manner as aforesaid, or shall give an unjust and false account, every such treasurer or receiver shall forfeit the sum of five pounds for every default, to be received in the Mine Law Court, the one half thereof to the use of the King's Majesty and the other half to the miner that will sue for the same. And such treasurer or receiver shall thenceforth never be entrusted with anything relating to the public concerns of the miners.

And the jury aforesaid do hereby name and appoint Richard Worgan the younger of Clearwell, Thomas Danniel of Coleford, William Adams, John Bennett, William Wyseham and Richard Morgan of Esbach to be the present treasurers and receivers of the said monies to be raised as aforesaid who for the collection and disposal of the said monies and giving an account thereof as aforesaid shall have allowed to each of them twelve pence in the pound for every quarter of a year they shall remain and be in that employment. And that upon the death, neglect or infirmity or otherwise of any one of them the deputy constable and officers of the Mine Law Court aforesaid with the consent of the jury then sworn may alter, change, put out and remove any such treasurer or receiver and put in another in his room and place as they shall think fit, who shall execute do and perform and be subject to the pains and penalties as are before-mentioned. *And* the jury aforesaid as a thankful acknowledgement of the many favours received by them from the deputy constables aforesaid in holding their courts and maintaining their privileges and customs do order and ordain that when any of the deputy constables aforesaid for the time being shall send their own horses or mares to any of the coalpits of the said miners for coal the miners shall presently seame and load them before any other person whatsoever, any useage or custom to the contrary notwithstanding. In witness whereof the said deputy constable, gavellers, castle clerk and eight and forty jurors have hereunto set their hands and seals the day and year first above written.

George Arundell	Rich. Griffith		
William Adams	Giles Powell		
deputy gavellers	Edw. Brayne		
	Ja. Gething	Rich. Morse	
	Jo. Bennett	Ri. Banister	
	Jo. Godding	An. Smart	Jo. Westerd
	Geo. Banister	Thos. Jones	Ri. Nelmes
	Rich. Smyth	Edw. Smart	Henry Griffiths
	Thom. Rannell	Wm. Wyseham	Hen. Meredith
	Jo. Morse		
	Tho. Cassel	Ri. Mathews	Tho. Skyn Jnr.

continued

continued	Tho. Elly	Ri. Worgan	Ni. Mowsall
	Wm. Boseley	Edw. Tyler	Geo. Whetson
	Edw. Keare	James Parish	Tho. Bond
	Jo. Moore	Ri. Worgan	Wm. Vaughan
	Will. Byrt	Edw. Griffith	Waltr. Howell
	Arthur Hynam	John Davis	Jo. Keare
	An. Andrews	Tho. Skyn	John Phillpott
	Chr. Godding	Tho. Watten	Win. Humfry
	Geo. Church		

George Probert. [Sir]'[1]

Before continuing with the remaining Orders of the Mine Law Court it is necessary chronologically to include copies of extant records of seven sessions or adjournments of the Court held between 18 January 1676 and 26 June 1677. They are as follows:

(I) 18 January 1676[2]

'The Forest of Dean in ye County of Gloucester. } Att the Court of Myne and Myners of our Sovereign Lord the King within his Forest aforesaid holden at Coleford the 18th day of January in the 27th year of the reign of our Sovereign Lord Charles II &c., Before Sir George Probert, Kt., Deputy to the most Honble. Henry Marquis of Worcester, Constable of our said Lord the King of his Castle of St. Briavells, George Arundell and William Adams, deputy gavellers of the Myne, and William Rowles, Gent., Clarke of the said Castle.

Nomina Juratorum

Edward Hooper	Richard Lewis
John Jane	William Hewett
Richard Bond	Anthony Andrews
John Smyth	William Whetson
Oliver Worgan	William Rocke
Thomas Bond	George Lodge

John Philpott for default of appearance 2s.

We doth give the Plaintiff his profe.

James Jones agt. James Wade Deft, and his vernes.

We find for the Plaintiff James Jones for one pte. in this pitt.

I complayne agt. James Wade and his vernes for a part in a cole pitt called Hopewell and another pitt wch. was adriving wch. the gaveller galed wch. they denyes us our part to the damage of £10 and keepes all our tooles so that we cannot enter upon our ptes. We profferred our money for driving but they would not receive it wch. we shall go to tryal with them for now or else put it to the 48 [miners] wch. we paid for galing the pitt and this we will prove in the King's Myne &c.

I ask his plaint abated &c. Because we never denied the Plaintiff his part if

1 All the above signatures are written in the same hand, except Sir George Probert which is a genuine signature. He was the deputy constable.

2 Glos.R.O. Probyn Papers D23, 657 (2); there is an imperfect copy on 657 (1). Numerous other 'cases' are in Glos.R.O. D9096, F26/1 (1700-1777).

he had brought in his money. He denied it himself, he being at Staunton did say that if the pitt were worth anything he would have a part but if it were not he would not meddle with it and being askt. again for his money he said if he did not bring it by a day about a fortnight after we should sell the pte. or do what we would with it. And he did not bring his money by that day whereby we suffered above £20 damage. And then he denies disposal of the pte. of the pit to him, and that we will prove by witnesses to the King.

John Taylor agt. David Griffith.

We give the Plaintiff his profe upon defalt.

Recovered.

I complain agt. David Griffith for [carrying iron] myne with mare and marefoale to Redbrook furnace contrary to an Order whereby my Lord Marquis and Sir Baynham Throckmorton were made Free Myners. In so doing he hath forfeited 100 dozen of lawful iron myne, the one half to the King and the other half to the Informer. And this I will prove within &c.

John Tyler agt. John Blunt.

We give the Plaintiff his profe.

Recovered.

I complayne agt. John Blunt for carrying iron myne with mare and marefoale to Redbrook furnace contrary to an Order that do make my Lord Marquis and Sir Baynham Free Myners. In so doing he hath forfeited 100 dozen of good iron myne, the one half to the King's Majesty and the other half to the Informer. And this I will prove in the King's Myne &c.
I ask his plaint abated. I have not bargained in any place nor carried but where the six bargainers intrusted for the whole Company have bargained and carried. In &c.

William Worgan agt. Gyles Hynam als. Symons.

We give the Plaintiff his profe according to his ple.
Def:
Recovered.

I complayne agt. him for carrying myne with mare and marefoales to Brockweare and Gunpill to the breach of an Order, to the forfeit of 100 dozen of iron myne wch. I will prove by myself and by witness. The one half to His Majesty and the other half to the Complainant. Within &c.

John Tyler agt. Geo. Banister.

We give the Plaintiff his profe.

Recovered.

I complayne for carrying iron myne with mare and marefoale to Redbrook furnace contrary to an Order that do make my Lord Marquis and Sir Baynam Throckmorton Free Myners. In so doing he hath forfeited 100 dozen of good iron myne, the one half to the King and the other to the Complainant, and this I will prove within &c.
I ask &c. I have not carried any myne contrary to our Inquisition nor to our Law and Custom, In ye King's Myne &c.

Richard Elly agt. Thom. Rannell and his pledge.

We give the Plaintiff his profe.

I complaine agt. Thomas Rannell and John Mowsall his pledge for 7s. which is due to the King and this the Gavellor will prove within &c.
I ask his plaint abated &c. *Nil dicit.*

William Adams [deputy gaveller] agt. William Cowley als. ...

Condemned by defalt.

Defalt.

I complain agt. Wm. Cowley for 6s. 6d. for Law and Gale wch. he past for, for James Good to pay at Christmas last and this I will prove by myself and witnesses within &c.

John Jones agt. Richard Hayes.

We give the Plaintiff his profe according to his plee.

Recovery.

Def:

I complayne agt. him for carrying and transporting Smyth Coale not having lawfully wrought according to our Custom whereby he hath forfeited 100 dozen of Smith Coale, the one half to the King and the other to the Complainant and this I will prove by myself and witnesses within the King's Myne &c.

We give the Plaintiff his profe.

Recovered.

Def:

William Davis agt. Thomas Howe,

I complayne agt. Thomas Howe for 19s. for wages and this I can prove within &c.

William Milson agt. John Watkins.

We give the Plaintiff his profe.

Recovered.

Def:

I complayne agt. John Watkins (6s.) for not bringing and paying his money to the Treasurers according to the last Order whereby he hath forfeited 2s., the one half to the King and the other half to the Plaintiff. Within the King's Myne &c.

We give the Plaintiff his profe.

Def:

Recovered.

William Milson agt. Giles Hynam als. Symons.

I complayne agt. Gyles Hynam for not bringing and paying 6s. unto ye Treasurers according to ye last Order, whereby he hath forfeited 2s.

William Milsom agt. Richard Nelmes.

Def:

Recovered.

I complaine agt. him for not paying to the Treasurers 6s. according to the last Order whereby he hath forfeited 2s. the one half to the King and the other to the Complainant, and this I shall prove within &c.

The same agt. Tho. Davis of St. Briavells.

Def:

Recovered.

For not paying 6s. according &c.

The same agt. Thomas Gilbert.

Def:

Recovered.

For not paying 4s. according &c.

The same agt. Henry Hooper, Senior.

Def:

Recovered.

For not paying 6s. according &c.

The same agt. Henry Hooper, Junior.

Def:

Recovered.

For not paying 6s. according &c.

The same agt. Chr. Thorne.

Def: Recovered. For not paying 4s. according &c..

The same agt. William Keare.

Def: Recovered. For not paying 8s. according &c.

William Worgan agt. James Gething.

Recovered. For 6d. due according to the last Order and for not paying the same 2s. &c.

The same agt. Thomas Sibrance.

Recovered. For 4s. due &c. and for not paying the same 2s. &c.

William Byrt 2s. for disturbance in ye Court.'

(II) 1 February 1676[1]

'The Forest of Deane in the County of Glouc. } Att ye Court of Myne and Mynors of our Sovereign Lord the King within his Forest aforesaid holden at Clowerwall upon Tuesday the first day of February in the 28th year of the reign of our Sovereign Lord Charles II &c. Before Sir George Probert Kt., Deputy to the most Honble. Henry Marquis of Worcester, Constable of His Majesty's Castle of St. Briavells, and George Arundell and William Adams, deputy gavellers of the Myne within the said Forest, and William Rowles, Gent., Clarke of the said Castle.

Nomina Juratorum

John Worgan	Henry Hooper, Junior
Edmond Banister	John Dowle
Henry Griffith	Thomas Montjoy
William Annesley	Anthony Smart
Richard Hayward	John Andrewes
Anthony Workman	William John

Richard Mathews 2s.
Peter Bray 2s. } For not appearing to serve on the jury.

John Smyth agt. John Philpott.

We do give the Plaintiff his profe. I complayne agt. him for carrying iron myne to Brockweare and Cunpill with mare and marefoale contrary to an Order made by 48 Myners, by doing whereof he hath forfeited 100 dozen of Myne, the one half to the King and the other half to him that doth sue for the same, And this I shall prove &c. In &c.

Recovered upon the Plaintiff's profe. I ask &c. I carried no oare to Brockweare nor Cunpill but what the bargainers had bargained for as by the Order is directed and carried with them. In the King's Myne &c.

[1] Glos.R.O., D23, Probyn Papers, m. 6 and 7.

George Lodge agt. Wm. Adams [deputy gaveller].

We do give the Plaintiff his profe. Recovered.

Paid in Court..

I complayne agt. him for 3 seames of cole 1s. 6d. that his horses his profe. fetched from my work and my vernes. And that I will prove &c.
I ask his plaint &c. It is unknown to me whether I had the cole. I never sent to him for any. If my son did fetch any cole with my horses, if the plantiff had asked me for it, he should have it.

William Adams [deputy gaveller] agt. Thomas Haynes.

Recovered by default.

For 5s. 10d. for a year's Law and Gale which is due unto me. And this I will prove In the King's Myne &c.

William Adams [deputy gaveller] agt. George Lodge.

We do give the Plaintiff his profe. Recovered 2s. by default. Paid the Amercement in Court and the debt.

I complayne agt. him for a quarter's Law and Gale due unto me at our Lady Day last being 18d. And this I will prove &c.
I ask &c. I did not make sale of any cole nor did get cole to the value of a weeke but if he had demanded any Law and Gale he might have had it for the time I did work in the King's Myne &c.

William Adams [deputy gaveller] agt. John Davis.

Recovered by defalt.

I complayne agt. him for 6s. that he received of John Daw being my money as being due to the King for taking a horse upon the forfeiture mentioned in an Order. This John Davis doth not deny the money but promised to pay it. And this I will prove &c. In &c.

John Jones agt. William Cooke.

Recovered by defalt.

I complayne agt. him for 10s. in money which he promised to pay unto me before this day. And this I will prove by witness, by which I am damnified 2s. in the King &c.'

(III) 15 February 1676[1]

'Forest of Deane. } Att the Court of Myne and Myners of our Sovereign Lord the King holden at Coleford upon Tuesday the 15th day of February in the 28th year of the reign of our Sovereign Lord Charles II &c. Before Sir George Probert Kt., Deputy to the most Honble. Henry Marquis of Worcester, Constable of His Majesty's Castle of St. Briavells, and George Arundell and William Adams, deputy Gavellors of the Mynes within the said Forest, and William Rowles, Gent., Clerke of the said Castle of St. Briavells.

Nomina Juratorum

Stirley Kedgwyn	Thomas Sibrance
Geo. Banister	John Godwin

continued

1 Glos.R.O., D23, Probyn Papers, m. 8, 9, 10.

continued

Henry Hooper	William Nicholas
Richard Keare	Richard Priest
Thomas Skynn, Senior	Richard Griffith
Nicholas Mowsall	Thomas Kedgwin
Thomas Skynn, Junior	William Trigge
Edward Sibrance	Thomas Jones
Richard Nelmes	Geo. Malden
William Boseley	George Whitson
Richard Hawkins	William Cooper
William Byrt	William Cooke

Richard Wood 2s.	Geo. Church, Senior 2s.	Amerced for not appearing to serve on the Jury.
John Brayne 2s.	Wm. Godwin 2s.	
John Moore 2s.	John Kedwellen 2s.	
Walter Howell 2s.		

This is non-suited.

William Parler agt. William Hughes.
I complayne agt. him being a Forreyner for carrying firecole with mare and marefoale upon breach of an Order and against the Custom which I can prove upon oath whereby I do serve my Recovery in the King's Myne &c. I ask his plaint abated. The defendant Hughes is not guilty in the King's Myne &c.

This is non-suited.

William Parler agt. Rob. Hobbs.
I complayne agt. Robt. Hobbs for carrying and transporting Smyth Cole with mare and marefoales which I can prove upon oath by his own confession upon breach of an Order and contrary to our Custom. In ye King's Myne &c.
I ask his plaint abated. The defendant Rob. Hobbs is not guilty. He never carried any Smyth Cole but lived in Gloucester this 8 years, and since that time he never carried any cole &c.

Richard Morse agt. Thomas Sibrance.
I complayne agt. Thomas Sibrance of Coleford for an action of trespass on the case for speaking three words following, That Richard Morse took a false oath against me in the Myne Law Court meaning the said Thomas Sibrance to the damage of £40. It hath cost me above 50s. in money which I shall prove by my own oath, and for the fact I shall prove by witnesses in the King's Mine &c.

This plaint is non-suited.

I ask &c. I do confess that I did say the words in the Plaintiff's plea mentioned and will prove it in the King's Myne &c.

We do give the Plaintiff his prooffe. Recovery. Defalt.

John Morgan agt. William Parler.
I complayne agt. him for 10s. which he promised me for the arresting of Robt. Hobbs which I did do according to my office, and this I will prove by witnesses and by myself, In &c.

William Adams [deputy gaveller] agt. Geo. Lodge.
I complayne agt. him for 3 quarters of customary Law and Gale being 4s. and this I will refer to the Inquisition and the Jury in the King's &c.
I ask &c. I did not work at Cole but since about 3 weeks before Christmas, and that I tendered him, and this I will prove, In &c.

We do give the Plaintiff his prooffe according to his plea.

William Adams [deputy gaveller] agt. Geo. Lodge.
I complayne for taking an oath against me (a prooffe) whereby he proved 18d. due to him whereas there was but 16d. his due. He proved 3 seames of firecole whereas one of them was Smythcole, and I do usually give to the partners of that pitt but 6d. a seame for firecole and 4d. for Smythcole &c. And this I will prove by witnesses &c.
I ask &c. I did not name which cole he had of me... of firecole, which Wm. Trigg received of other people for the same quantity of Coale, and this I will prove by William Trigg's oath, In &c.

We do give the Plaintiff his prooffe according to the Inquisition.

William Adams [deputy gaveller] agt. Geo. Lodge.
I complayne agt. him for following two professions and callings, a Myner and Collyer and a quarryman contrary to our Law and Custom. By so doing he forfeits £5 and this I leave to the Inquisition &c.
I ask &c. I confess that I do follow sometimes one Calling and sometimes the other calling as other men do and is not contrary to the Custome &c.

This is non-suited.

Will. John 2s. for disturbance in the Court.
Jo. Philpott 2s. for the same.

Att this Court 12 out of the 48 Jurymen whose names are undernamed have been elected and chosen to consider of such Orders as have heretofore been made for the better ordering and management of the concerns of the Myners, and to consider which of them are fit to be made void and revoked and what Orders are fit to be continued and remain. And that the said Jury of 48 Myners impannelled and sworne at this Court do present the same Orders and what they have considered concerning the same at the house of Susan Arundell in Clowerwall on Tuesday next by ten of the clock in the forenoon payne of 5s. each making defalt. To which time and place this present Jury and the Court is now adjourned. And it is further ordered that the said 12 men do often consult with the residue of the Jury concerning the said Orders that may be made for the best advantage of the Myners.

The names of the 12 Myners:

Edward Hooper	Stirley Kedgwin
John Smyth	Geo. Banister
Richard Bond	Henry Cooper
John Worgan	Richard Keare
Edmond Banister	Tho. Skynn
Henry Griffith	Thomas Montjoy

Richard Tresteed 2s. for disturbance.
Geo. Fox for the like.'

(IV) 28 March 1676[1]

'This Court called over and adjourned to Tuesday the 23rd day of May next at the house of H. Tovey in Coleford by ten of the clock in the forenoon. That the Treasurers do bring in their accompts and money at the next Court and that Mr. Davies do prepare their accompt for them against that day.'

(V) 23 May 1676[2]

'This day the Court was called and Jury called and then adjourned to this day fortnight at the house of [blank] in [blank] by ten of the clock in the forenoon. And that the Treasurers do bring in the money they have received and their Accompts of whom the same have been received.'

(VI) 21 November 1676[3]

'Forest of Dean in the County of Gloucester. } At the Court of Mine and Miners of the said Forest holden at Clowerwall within the said Forest on Tuesday the 21st day of November in the 28th year of the reign of our most gracious Sovereign Lord Charles the Second by the Grace of God &c before Sir Baynham Throckmorton Kt and Bt, Deputy to the most Honourable Henry Marquis of Worcester &c Lord Warden of His Majesty's Forest of Dean and Constable of St. Briavels, And William Rowles, gent. Clerk of the Castle aforesaid, And George Arundell and William Adams, Gavellors of the Myne within the same Forest, and thence adjourned by several adjournments until Tuesday the 16th day of January in the said 28th year.[4]

Whereas several suits, controversies and contentions have of late years happened and arisen amongst the said Miners of this Forest of Dean and likewise with and amongst their neighbours touching their rights, privileges and customs within the same, for prevention whereof for the future and for the better reducing of the said customs of the said Miners to a certainty as heretofore the same have been. The Jury of 48 Myners at this Court now impannelled and sworn according to the customs thereof for all the time whereof the memory of man is not to the contrary, do order and ordain as followeth:

And first they do ordain, order and agree that all and every the matters, clauses, articles and things mentioned, expressed and contained in a certain writing called an Inquisition being a summary collection of the customs of the Myners within this Forest of Deane used long before the time of William the Conqueror King of England, and which was made and reduced into writing not long after the reign of the most famous Edward the third King of England and subscribed by a Jury of 48 Myners at that time impannelled and sworn, shall in all things remain, stand and continue and be in full force and effect and shall be inviolably observed and kept by and among all the said Myners within the said Forest.

And to that end and purpose they have caused the said Inquisition to be now verified and ingrossed in parchment and have set their hands and seals unto the same. And do declare that the same do contain the ancient rights, customs and privileges of the said Myners.

---

1 Glos.R.O., D23, Probyn Papers 658.

2 *Ibid.*

3 *Ibid.* This document has been considerably altered in places; the dates are unreliable.

4 This would appear to be an error; it should be 29th year.

And whereas at a Mine Law Court holden at Clowerwall the 18th day of March in the 21st year of His Majesty's reign before Sir Baynham Throckmorton Kt. and Bt., deputy constable to the said Right Honourable Henry Marquis of Worcester &c and the said William Rowles clerk of the Castle of St. Briavels aforesaid and Richard Morse, Nicholas Kedgwin, Robert ? Wood and William Adams, deputy gavellors of the Myne aforesaid.[1]

The Jury of 48 miners then and there impannelled and sworn did make divers orders touching their customs, and touching the carriage and transportation of iron ore and coal, and constituting of Bargainers for the same and setting rates and prices upon the same and prohibiting Foreigners from carriage of coal for their own private use and benefit, which orders have been the occasion of much trouble, strife and contention amongst the said miners and have proved not only very prejudicial to themselves but also to the said Lord Constable of the said Castle of St. Briavels and to several of his Lordship's friends and tenants living within the counties of Monmouth and Hereford who usually make use of the coal of this Forest both for fire for their houses and lime for their husbandry without which they cannot well subsist [In thankful acknowledgement therefore of this Honor's constant favours from time to time expressed to the said miners in vouchsafing to be their great patron and defender of their ancient privileges[2]] Therefore they the said miners being as aforesaid a full jury of 48 do now wholly repeal and revoke, make void and null all and every the said order made at the said Mine Law Court and every matter, Article, Clause and thing therein contained as if the same had never been made.

And in thankful and humble acknowledgement of his Honor's constant favours expressed to the said miners by vouchsafing to be their great Patron and Defender of their Ancient Privileges, and being very willing and ready to comply with the conveniences of his Lordship's friends and tenants of the aforesaid countries and other their neighbours, do now order and ordain that the Order made at the Mine Law Court holden at Clowerwall on Tuesday the 8th day of September in the ? 21st or 22nd year of His Majesty's reign before the said Sir Baynham Throckmorton by the then Jury of 48 miners impannelled and sworn for these words following that is to say, That whensoever any person or person (not being Free Miners) shall repair to any the coalpits of the said miners for fire-coal or lime-coal it shall and maybe lawful to and for every such person or persons to have and carry away such coal as aforesaid for his and their own use and expense, not carrying the same to sell to others nor upon hire, without being troubled or questioned for the same. Provided always that the inhabitants within the perambulation of this Forest of Dean for their own use and expense from time to time be first served and supplied upon the place: shall remain continue and stand firm, and accordingly this present Jury do ratify and confirm the same, they paying the rates and prices at the pits as those who are not Free Miners do pay, and no more.

Likewise the said Jury do ratify and confirm one other Order made at the said Mine Law Court holden the 8th day of September, whereby the said Right Honourable the Lord Marquis of Worcester is made a Free Miner, as also one other Order made at the same Court whereby the aforesaid Sir Baynham Throckmorton is made a Free Miner within the said Forest.

Likewise the said Jury do ratify and confirm one other Order made at the said Court prohibiting the miners from coming within 100 yards of any surffe that shall be brought up by any of them to the prejudice of the undertakers thereof.

---

1 The foregoing paragraph has been struck through.

2 The portion in square brackets has been struck through.

And the said Jury do wholly repeal and revoke an Order made at the said Court whereby six bargainers are named and appointed for making bargains for the whole Society and every Clause and article in the same contained, it having been the occasion of much contention amongst the miners and proved very prejudicial to them.

And whereas several suits are now depending in His Majesty's Courts at Westminster against the miners and colliers of this Forest concerning their rights and customs for the just and necessary defence whereof they are put to great expense and charge of which those that are not Free Miners and have no right (though they have almost an equal benefit) yet bear no part of it, therefore, as also for that the said miners and colliers are now prohibited and restrained from having and taking wood out of His Majesty's said Forest for the support of their pits, (which time out of mind they have constantly had and hope to prove to be their just rights to take) though at present they are forced to buy the same at great rates and prices and can hardly have it for their money and that they do buy they are forced to fetch many miles from their pits, The colliers Above the Wood are inforced to raise the price of their coal at their respective pits (as the colliers Beneath the Wood have long time done at theirs) from 4d a seame for fire coal to 6d a seame, and from 12d a dozen for lime-coal to 18d a dozen, And therefore the Jury aforesaid do order and ordain that if any collier Above the Wood from and after the 24th day of June instant for the space of two years from thence next ensuing shall directly or indirectly sell, offer, dispose or load to any person or persons whatsoever (other than a Free Miner or a deputy constable of this Forest for the time being) any fire-coal or lime-coal for or at any lower or lesser rate and price than 6d a seame or barrell for fire-coal and 18d a dozen for lime-coal, every such miner or collier for every such offence shall forfeit one hundred dozen of such coal as shall be sold and disposed under the rate aforesaid to be recovered or the value thereof in the Mine Law Court, the one half to the King's Majesty and the other half to the miner that shall sue for the same.

And whereas at a Mine Law Court holden at Clowerhall on Tuesday the 9th day of March in the 27th year of His Majesty's reign [1675] before Sir George Probert, Knt, deputy constable, and the said deputy gavellers and Castle Clerk and Order was made for the raising of money for the just and necessary defence of the customs, rights and privileges of the said miners in a legal way by taxing and charging every miner and carrier with a quarterly sum of money which is found to be the most equal, certain and speedy way of raising of money which is as aforesaid, and therefore the Jury aforesaid do hereby fully ratify and confirm the said order and every matter and thing therein contained for the space of two years from the 26th day of December last and no longer.'

(VII) 26 June 1677[1]

'Foresta de Deane } At the Court of Myne and Myners of our Soveraigne Lord the King holden at Coleford within the said Forest upon Tuesday the xxvith day of June in the xxixth yeare of the Reigne of our Soveraigne Lord King Charles the Second now King of England etc. Before Henry Milborne Esqr. deputy unto the Right honble. Henry Marquesse of Worcester Constable of our said Soveraigne Lord the King of his Castle of St. Briavells and Warden of the said Forest of deane, And George Arundell and William Adams deputy Gavellors of the Mynes within the same Forest And Thomas Davies deputy clerke of the said Castle of St. Briavells.

[1] Glos.R.O., D23, Probyn Papers, 659.

Nomina I ur' ad triand' exit' inter p'tes.

Richard Davies alias Evans	Thomas Raynell
Edmond Griffith	Thomas Byrt
Thomas Kedgwin	Tho: Montjoy
Wm. Boseley	Stephen Yemm
William Byrt	Wm. Cooper
John Davis	Phillip Evans

Wm. Veare made default of appearance and is amerced 2s.

Christopher Godwin agt. Owen Thomas.

We give the defender his Ricought with witness If thay will prove him free bornd In the honered of saint breveles and work lanes full according to our custome proves him borne in a house under Symons Yate wherein he now lives

I complayne against Owen Thomas for working in the Art of myning and carrying not being a freemyner borne according to our Custome for which hee hath forfeited 100 dozen of firecole In the Kings Myne &c.

Wm. Worgan pleaded

I aske his plaint abated that 8 yeares agoe or thereaboutes I was proved to be a free Myner before Sr. Duncombe Colchester at the Myne Lawe Court holden at Mitchel-Deane as being borne within the hundred of St. Briavelles and this I shall likewise prove by witnesses at this court, In &c.

The defendant by Wm. Browne Wm. Gardner and George Godwyn proves the house to bee within the Perambulacion and by Wm. Worgan to have pd. Lawe and Gales and to have wrought 40 yeares at tymes. And therefore by the Court he is adjudged a freeman

James Gethins against John Coster: Agreed

James Wade agt. John Lewellen: Agreed

George Arundell [deputy gaveller] agt. James Good and Roger Skinner.

Condemned by default

I complayne agt. them for 5s. for Law and Gale due to his Majesty for his part which they owe and this I will prove by witnesse In the Kings Myne

George Arundell [deputy gaveller] agt. William Cowley.

I complayne against him for 5s. due to me for Law and Gale which he agreed to pay and this I will prove In &c.

The defendant condemned by Confession in Court.

John Jones agt. John Andrewes.

Will wee give the Plaintive his aprove According to his plee

I complayne against him for tymber and Rayles of a Pitt called Hopewell which cost mee £20 which Pitt he refuseth to lett me have, though it bee myne, and I have wrought in it though not of late, which tymber hee this Complaynant claymeth and now sueth for, and this I will prove In &c.

The tymber Recovered by default,

William Pitcher agt. Wm. Clement.

Recovered by default

I complayne against Wm. Clement alias Soper for not paying unto the Treasurer 3s. due upon the money order at our Lady day last past for the defence of our Rightes, whereby hee hath forfeited 2s. the one moyety to the Kings Majusty and the other to the Complainant And this I will prove.

The same agt. John Lowe alias Watkins.

We give the plant. his proufe According to his pleae

I complaine against him for 4s. due upon the money order at our Lady day last past for non payment whereof hee hath forfeited 2s. the one moyety to his Majesty and the other moyety to the Complainant And this I will prove by witnesse
I owe nothing not carryed in that quarter at all, And this I put to the Awards of Craft &c.
Recovered 2s. for one quarter at our Lady day and comitted in Court.

William Godwyn agt. Christopher Godwyn and his wife.

Wee will give the plainte. his proufe acording to his pleas

I complaine against him for fowerteene pence which is due unto mee and my vernes for oare sold and delivered after the Rate of 2s. 4d. a dozen for 20 dozen for which shee paid us part of the money and this is yet unpaid. And this I will prove By which I am damnified 20s. for the Kings Myne &c. I aske &c. Wee neither bargained with the plaintiff for any oare, nor had any of him, But my wife made a bargaine with Jone Tresteed for 20 dozen of oare in the Blakes and fully paid her for it And this I will prove In &c.
Recovered 14d. in this Court.
Richard Elly fined for disorder 2s. in the Courte
John Tresteed 2s.
Chr. Godwyn 2s.
Wm. Godwyn 2s.

At this Court came Christopher Godwin in his proper person and complayned against Owen Thomas in these words I complayne against Owen Thomas for working in the Art of Myning and carrying, not being a free Myner borne according to our Custome, for which hee hath forfeited 100 dozen of fire coale, the one half to the Kinges Majesty and the other halfe to mee the Complaynant who now sueth for the same And this I will prove In the Kings Myne and Anunt the Kings Myne And so I refer it to the Award of Craft etc. Whereunto the said Owen by William Worgan his Atturney appeared and craved the said Playnt might be abated &c. And for a good cause why &c. Because that 8 yeares agoe or thereaboutes hee the said Owen was proved to bee a free Myner before Sr. Duncombe Colchester Knt. one of the deputy Constables of this Forest of Deane at a Myne Law Court holden at M. Deane as being borne within the hundred of St. Briavells and wrought lawfully according to the Custome And the same hee is now ready to prove by witnesses at this Court In the Kings Myne &c. And soe hee likewise puts it to the Award of Craft &c. As the said Christopher before hathe done &c. And there upon it is comaunded to the Gavellors of the Myne that they have here imediately twelve free Myners who &c. to try the Said issue joyned as aforesaid who then and there returned Richard Davis alias Evans Edmond Griffith Thomas Kedgwin William Boseley William Byrt John Davis Thomas Rannell Thomas Byrt

Thomas Montjoy Stephen Yemm William Cooper and Phillip Evans twelve good and lawfull free myners who &c. being And the said Jurats appeared and charged, and being sworne to try the said issue having duely considered of the same doe give the defendant Owen Thomas his prooffe by witnesses according to his plea. And thereupon the said Owen produced herein Court these witnesses following (that is to say) Elizabeth Jenkins of the parish of English Bickner spinster aged about 60 yeares who being duely sworne and examined upon her oath did depose and sweare that the said Owen was borne under Symons Yatt not far from the River Wye in a house which is now downe and decayed wherein the Father and Mother of the said Owen formerly lived and sold ale which she beleeves is scituate within the hundred of St. Briavells for that it hath ever beene in her tyme so reputed. Alsoe William Browne of English Bickner gent. one of the Regarders of the said Forest who being sworne and examined did depose and sweare that hee did knowe the said house wherein the said Owen Thomas was born. And that hee haveing made severall perambulacions of the said Forest of Deane (as being one of the Regarders thereof) the said house was alwayes in his tyme reputed to bee, and accordingly was taken into the hundred of St. Briavells and Forest of Deane by the space of about 8 yards by measure. Also William Gardner the elder of English Bickner aforesaid gent. who being likewise sworne and examined did depose that hee knewe the said house wherein the said Owen was born and knoweth that the same is situate within the hundred of St. Briavells, for that hee hath beene upon severall prosessions of the boundes of the parish of English Bickner aforesaid upon which the said house was taken into the said parish about the space of 8 yards which hee hath measured.

Also George Godwyn of English Bickner aforesaid yeoman who being sworne and examined deposed the same which William Gardner last before named.

Also William Worgan of Coleford who being likewise sworne and examined deposed that the said Owen Thomas hath wrought in the Art of Myning at severall tymes about 40 years last past, and that hee paid Lawe and Gale and Rented the Kinges part and the Gale or some part thereof heretofor, in the tyme of Stirley Kegwin and John Willim being Galers of the Mynes. All which prooffes being openly heard and duely considered by the Court They doe adjudge the said Owen Thomas to bee a Free myner within the said Forest, and to have and enjoy all rightes and privelledges which to a free Myner doth belong according to the Custome, And that the said Owen bee here without day &c.

William Pitcher complaines against these severall persons under named for non payment of the money set at their respective names due at our Lady day last upon the money order and the same have receaved by default videlicet

William Clement alias Soper	3s.	Recovered by default.
Richard Robyns	2s.	
Trestnam Tresteed	4s.	
Richard Bond sen.	12d.	
John Philpott	3s.	
Mary Tyler	12d.	
Thomas Ellis jun.	12d.	
James Preist	3s.	
John Smith	18d.	
Ralph Stevens	2s.	
Henry Worgan jun.	2s.	
Oliver Worgan jun.	18d.	
Mary Evans	3s.	

Amercied for agreement.

William Whitson agt. Thomas Walden jun.	2s.
Thomas Walden jun. agt. William Whitson	2s.
William Whitson agt. Thomas Haymes	2s.
The same agt. Joseph Rocke	2s.
Thomas Brinkworth agt. Richard Knight	2s.
Richard Knight agt. Thomas Brinkworth	2s.
James Gething agt. John Coster gent.	2s.
Chr. Tench agt. Mathew Parry	2s.
James Wade agt. John Lewellen	2s.
Chr. Tench agt. Thomas Wyteham	2s.
Thomas Skyn agt. William Pitcher	2s. '

[In 1676-1677 there was an 'Order and Ordinance of a Jury of Miners at a Court of Mine and Miners held at Clearwell'[1]]

The Orders continue:

ORDER NO. 4 (27 APRIL 1680)

'Forest of Dean } *At* the Court of Mine and Miners of the said forest holden at the Speech House within the said forest the 27th day of April in the 32nd year of the reign of ... Charles the Second..., Before Sir Baynham Throckmorton ...[2] and William Rowles, gent. Clerk of the Castle aforesaid, And George Arundell and William Adams, deputy gavellers of the mine within the same forest, the Jury then and there sworn and consisting of 48 miners do order and ordain as followeth, viz:

For that the miners and colliers of this forest have of late been very much impoverished by the exceeding low rates and prizes to which their ore and coal is brought, occasioned for want of a certain known rate and prize to be set at each place to which the same is carried, for certifying and ascertaining therefore of the said rates and prizes thereof so as both Getters and Carriers may gain a comfortable subsistance for themselves and family and the Iron Masters may likewise have reasonable profit thereby, it is now fully and unanimously agreed by the present Jury and so by them ordered, established and ordained that no miner or collier or carrier whatsoever within this forest shall henceforth directly or indirectly sell, utter, carry, dispose or deliver iron ore to any the ironworks or other places of laying down the same hereafter particularly named at and for any lower rate or prize than is hereafter particularly mentioned (that is to say) to St. Wannards[3] furnace in the county of Hereford the sum of 10s a dozen, to Whitchurch furnace in the same county the sum of 7s a dozen, to Bishopswood furnace in the same county the sum of 7s a dozen, to Linton furnace in the same county the sum of 9s a dozen, to Longhope furnace in the county of Gloucester the sum of 9s/– a dozen, to Flaxley furnace in the same county the sum of 8s a dozen, to Gunsmills furnace in the same county (if the same shall be rebuilt again) the sum of 7s a dozen, to

1 PRO F20/1/21
2 As Order No. 2.
3 St. Weonards

Blakney furnace in the same county the sum of 6s a dozen, to Lidney furnace in the same county the sum of 6s a dozen, to the furnaces within the forest lately demolished (if they shall be rebuilt again) the prizes and rates given at each of them in the year 1668, to Redbrooke furnace in the same county the sum of 4s/6d a dozen, to Abby[1] furnace in the county of Monmouth the sum of 9s a dozen, to Brockweare the sum of 6s/6d. a dozen, to Redbrooke passage the sum of 5s/6d. a dozen, to Gunspill [Conpill] the sum of 7s a dozen, every dozen to contain twelve bushels the one heap't as long as any will lie on from the level without handing it, and the other struck to the wood and not by any other or greater measure; And to be all measured at one time without preferring one man before another, and to be paid at the time of measuring of the ore upon pain for every offence against this order to forfeit one hundred dozen of good iron ore, one half &c, And also the offender to forfeit his freedom and to be utterly expelled out of the Mine.

Provided that this order shall not extend to make void one bargain lately made by James Yerworth and others for the delivery of about 450 dozen of ore to Linton furnace aforesaid to make up that which is already at the said furnace 600 dozen, and two other bargains made by Richard Keare and others for the delivery of 600 dozen of ore to Flaxley furnace and 600 dozen of ore to Bishopswood furnace, but that the said three bargains may be carried in and delivered at the rates agreed for (this order notwithstanding)

And it is further agreed, ordered and ordained that the gaveller of the Mine or one of his deputies shall give public notice to the miners when in his or their judgement the said three bargains shall be fully carried in and delivered, after which time of notice or forbode if any miner shall carry or deliver any ore at any of the three furnaces aforenamed under the rates above set down such miner shall forfeit the mine or ore by him carried and delivered and also one hundred dozen of good ore, the one half &c.

And it is also further agreed and ordained that when any bargain shall be hereafter made for the delivery of any ore to any furnace or place of delivery there shall be public notice given by the clerk, stocktaker, or other person concerned when the bargain of ore contracted for is in his or their judgement brought in and delivered, after which notice or forbode if any miner shall carry or deliver any ore at that place every such miner shall forfeit as in the last precedent Article is mentioned.

And for the discharging of such debts and sums of money as the late suits with Mr. Terringham and others have contracted and for which many of the colliers stand engaged by bonds, it is now agreed that the sums of money set upon every Getter and carrier and comprised in the rate now made and agreed upon by the Jury aforesaid and subscribed by the foreman in the name of the most and approved by the said deputy constable and gavellers of the Mine and subscribed by them, be paid by every of them, the one half forthright and the other before Michaelmas day next in full discharge of the said debts and other charges and in case of non-payment of the same with 24 hours after demand by George Arundell and William Adams, deputy gavellors, and Jno. Bennet of Ruardean who are hereby made Receivers thereof, and to have in every pound, for their pains eighteen pence, Then every miner named in the said rate shall forfeit 4s the one half &c. And not any of the said money be paid without the direction of the said Sir Baynham in writing under his hand.

And in consideration of the said rate the jury aforesaid do fully agree that one Order[2] made

1 Tintern Abbey.

2 No. 3 of 1675.

by a former jury of 48 miners bearing date the 9th day of March 1675 and in the 27th year of his now Majesty's reign concerning the raising of money for carrying on the said suits and other expenses and every matter clause and thing contained therein be from this day repealed and made void.

And it is further ordered and ordained that no miner shall hereafter make any bargain with any Iron Master or Clerk or any other person for any iron ore without binding and obliging the person with whom he makes such bargain at the same time, in a penalty of double the value of the ore contracted for, to make full payment at the time of the measuring thereof to all and every the miner and miners that shall bring in any ore upon and in part of the said bargain. Then such miner or miners that shall not take such obligation as aforesaid shall forfeit one hundred dozen of good and sufficient ore, one-half &c.

And further it is ordered and ordained that if any miner or miners for lucre or deceit do make any bargain with any person or persons for iron ore, and shall not declare the effect of bargain to the Fellowship of the Mines, or shall directly or indirectly hinder or cause to be hindered or debarred any free miner from carrying in part of his bargain or of part of the three bargains before mentioned to Linton, Flaxley and Bishopswood or shall by deceit and collusion measure any part of his ore before the rest that have likewise carried part of the said bargain do also measure, or shall receive any money before the rest, every such miner shall forfeit for every offence contrary to this order, one hundred dozen of good and sufficient ore, one-half, &c.

And further the said Jury for the better reforming and preventing the inconveniences happening amongst the said miners by the men young men and boys that contrary to former usage have of late times set up for themselves to work at and carry mine and coal, not renting land and keeping house as by the Custom they ought, do now order and ordain that no person shall be reputed or taken to be a free miner within the precincts thereof or shall keep horses for carrying any ore or coal, until every such person shall have lawfully served in the art or mystery of Mining by the space of five years as an Apprentice to be bound by Indenture to his father (being a free miner) or to some other person that is a free miner. And shall attain to and be of the full age of one and twenty years, before he be free to keep horses, and to transport, upon pain to forfeit upon every default one hundred dozen of good iron ore or fire coal, one-half &c.

And it is further consented unto and agreed that all and every the inhabitants of the hundred of St. Briavels when they shall bring or send their horses for any sort of coal to any pit or pits shall be seamed and laden by the coalminers belonging to such pit before any foreigners whatsoever although they came after such foreigner upon pain every person doing contrary to this order ten dozen of good fire coal, one-half &c.

And for reforming the great mischiefs happening to the miners and colliers by the carriage and delivery of coal at the Lymeslades in Maylescott at such low prices that the same coal is sold by retail at Monmouth and parts adjacent at cheaper rates than the miners and colliers can carry and deliver the same there, it is ordered, agreed and consented unto and ordained, that if any miner or collier shall hereafter sell, utter, dispose or deliver any fire coal, smith coal or lime coal at any place or places upon the banks of the River of Wye between Monmouth Bridge and Huntsham ferry for any lower rate and prize than 8s a dozen for fire coal, and smith coal 8s a dozen, and for lime coal 4s/6d. a dozen according to the Winchester bushel, three of which make a barrel, every such miner and collier shall forfeit for every offence contrary to this order one hundred dozen of good fire coal, one-half &c. and be expelled the fellowship of the mine and lose his freedom for ever. And if any miner or coalminer shall sell and deliver any lime coal or other coal at any place upon the banks of the said River of Wye between Huntsham Ferry and Wilton Bridge under the rate of 3s. 6d. a dozen according to the measure above mentioned every such miner and collier shall forfeit as in the last precedent article is mentioned.

And lastly it is agreed that every miner within the forest of the age of one and twenty years shall before Midsummer day next enter into an obligation of the penalty of £10 for the true observing, fulfilling and keeping the several Orders and Ordinances before in these presents contained according to the true intent and meaning thereof. In witness whereof as well the said deputy constable and the deputy gavellers of the Mine, as the said 48 miners now sworn have hereunto set their hands and seals the day and year first above written.'

The following Order consists of three membranes joined together. On the back of one membrane is:

'At the Court at the Speech House 3rd August 1680 }

Whereas a bargain was heretofore made by George Banister and James Yerworth for the carriage of 600 dozen of ore to St. Wannards Furnace at 6s. 6d. a dozen to be delivered, *viz*: 300 dozen at Mich. next and 300 dozen the next year, which bargain was intended to be comprised and excepted in this Order but that the said George Banister was at Bristol at the time of the sealing thereof; Therefore it is now agreed that the said bargain shall be allowed to be carried in by them (and all the rest of the miners to have a share of the carriage) this order notwithstanding.

B. Throckmorton.[1]

B. Throckmorton	Rich. Wysham	Richard Griffiths	Thos. Griffiths
	Tho. Casway	Thos. Mowsall	Richard Keare
Wm. Adams	Thos. Kedgwin	Anthony Smart	George Elly
Geo. Arundell	William Cooper	William Humphreys	Richard Worgan
deputy	Richard Priest	Thomas Silbrance	John Watkins
gavellers[2]	Giles Yerworth	Rich. (?)	John Smith
	Jo. Philpott	G. Harries	Thomas Mountjoy
	Tho. Walden	John Adams	Henry Worgan
	John Worgan	George Banister	Rich. Elsome
	Rich. Smyth	James Gething	Henry Smith
	Rich. Yorke	Thomas Wysam	Wm. Wisham
	W. Morse	Edmond Banister	Wm. Palmer
	Edward Keare	Thos. Kedgwin	Thos. Skin
	Chris. Davis	Wm. Rooke	Geo. Whetson
	Evan Morgan	Joseph Rooke	Anthony Andrews
	Edward Smart	Wm. Trig	Rich. Nelmes'[3]

1 A genuine signature.
2 Genuine signatures.
3 About fifteen signed, the others making their marks.

ORDER NO. 5 (19 SEPTEMBER 1682)

'Forest of Dean } At the Court of Mine and Miners of our sovereign Lord the King within the said forest holden at Clowerwall upon Tuesday the 19th September in 34th year of the reign of our sovereign lord Charles the second … and before Henry Milbourne and William Wolseley Esqs, Deputies unto the most honourable Henry Lord Marquis of Worcester constable of his Majesty's Castle of St. Briavels within the said forest and Richard Worgan the younger and William Adams, deputy gavellers of the Mines there and Thomas Davies, deputy clerk of the said Castle and from thence continued by several adjournments until Tuesday the 28th November then next following, the Jury then and there impannelled and sworn consisting of 48 miners, by and with the consent of the said deputy constables, deputy gavellers and deputy clerk do order and ordain as followeth (viz):

Imprimis that for raising of a present sum of money for the urgent occasions of the said miners every miner of the age of 13 years and upwards within the said Mine do forthwith pay unto one of the said gavellers the sum of 6 pence for himself and 6 pence more for every working horse kept by any miner for carriage (besides the 2 pence quarterly imposed by a former order) upon pain every person making default by the space of six days after demand to forfeit one dozen of fire coal or two dozen of iron ore, one-half &c. And they further ordain that the said former order for the payment of 2 pence quarterly be confirmed and continued and the money thereupon now due be presently collected by the said deputy gavellers for the use of the said miners and that a due accompt of both monies be given at the next Mine Law Court.

And for that it hath been found by experience that the binding forth of boys to the art of mining according to many former orders have been of great advantage to the miners the Jury aforesaid do now ordain that all the said former orders for binding young boys to the art of mining for the space of five years be punctually observed for the future by all persons concerned. And that henceforth every boy when he shall be of the age of twelve years or upwards shall be bound forth apprentice to his father, if a free miner, or to a free miner that is of sufficient ability to take such apprentice, and their indentures to be entered at the next Mine Law Court that shall happen to be holden after such binding, to the end the Court may judge of the fitness, both of the miner and the apprentice and that there may be no fraud or deceit used, under the penalties and forfeitures in the said former orders contained.

That from henceforth no young man that keep not house of themselves and rent sufficient land shall keep horses to carry ore or coal being contrary to former orders in this behalf made upon pain to forfeit for every default one hundred dozen of good iron ore or fire coal one-half etc.

And whereas some miners do underhand carry and transport lime coal into Hereford and Monmouth shires at lower rates than heretofore have been set and agreed upon to the prejudice of the rest of the miners, therefore it is now ordained no miner shall henceforth sell any lime coal into those counties before a bargain be first made by the four Bargainers named in the former order for the ore or any three of them at such rates and prizes as they shall agree for, for the performance of which bargains they shall take security and in all other things do and perform as they are injoyned and directed by the said order and under the same penalties as fully as if the lime coal had been therein particularly mentioned and expressed.

And lastly it is agreed and ordained that whensoever any colliers have fully wrought out a coal pit through which the 'Goutwater' must necessarily run for draining of the work, in such case the said colliers shall secure the said pit by setting up strong and sufficient posts and rails round the said pit upon pain to forfeiture one hundred dozen of good fire coal one-half, etc.

In witness whereof the said deputy constable, gavellers, Castle Clerk and Jurors have hereunto set their hands and seals the said 28th day of November in the 34th year above said.

Win. Wolseley	Kedgwin Hoskin	Thomas Worgan (?)	Henr. Morgan
Richard Worgan	John Berrow		Christor Godwin
William Adams	Chr. Vowle	John James	Ri. Nelmes
Tho. Davis[1]	Edw. Sibranco	Hen. Morgan	James Gething
	Ed. Tyler	Tho. Elly	Jo. Wilcox
	Edmond Symons	John Bennet	Ri. Mathews
	Rich. Boughton	William Adams	Tho. Walden
	Wm. Triggs	Wm. Whetston	Hen. Sibranco
	Ri. Smith	Jo. Yem	Geo. Banister
	John Way	Ri. Lewis	William Palmer
	Richard Keare	John Smyth	Richard Priest
	John Westwood	Thomas Keare	John Wade
	Richard Bannister	Rich. Boughton	Henry Hooper
	Jo. Keare	Jo. Philpott	Ri. Keare
	Wm. Morse	John Tyler	Anthony Smart
	Richard Hayward	Tho. Teague	Wm. Moorfield'[2]

ORDER NO. 6 (8 DECEMBER 1685)

'Foresta de Deane } At the Court of Mine and Miners of our Sovereign Lord the King within the said forest holden at Clowerwall within the same forest on Tuesday 8th December in the 1st year of the reign of our most gracious Sovereign Lord James the second &c. Before William Wolseley, Esq., Deputy to the most Noble Henry Duke of Beaufort constable of his Majesty's Castle of St. Briavels within the said forest And Richard Worgan and William Adams deputy gavellors of the said Mines and Thomas Davies gent deputy Clerk of the said Castle, and continued by several Adjournments unto the 9th February then next following, the Jury consisting of 48 miners then and there impannelled and sworn according to the custom there used for all the time whereof the memory of man is not to the contrary, did order and ordain as followeth, viz:–

Imprimis the Jury aforesaid for the raising of money as well for the discharge and payment of the debts which the late suit in his Majesty's Court of Exchequer with Mr. Becke and others concerning the rights and privileges of the said miners hath occasioned and contracted, as for the future defence thereof and other necessary occasions of the said miners from time to time. do now agree, order and ordain that the rate and tax set upon every miner within the liberty of the mine at the Mine Law Court holden at Clowerwall the 13th January last past,[3] be and is hereby confirmed and ratified And that the said miners who have not already paid the said money imposed on them in and by the said rate do pay the same within ten days now next ensuing upon pain of forfeiting double the sum of money therein imposed on them respectively to be recovered in the Mine Law Court by any miner that will sue for the same, the one half &c.

1 All genuine signatures except Adams who made his mark.

2 About fourteen signed, the others making their marks.

3 There is no record of this session.

And for the raising of a speedy sum of money for the present occasions of the said miners, the said Jury have now consented unto and agreed on a rate upon every miner within the said mines and have reduced the same into writing and the same is subscribed by this Jury and is allowed and subscribed by the deputy constable aforesaid and the gavellers of the said mines; The said money in the said rate contained to be paid within ten days now next ensuing the passing and signing of this order; And if any miner in the said rate named shall neglect or refuse to pay the sum whereat he or she is therein rated, such miner shall forfeit double the sum whereat he or she is rated therein, to be recovered in the said Mine Law Court by any miner that will sue for the same, the one moiety &c.

And they do further order agree and ordain that it shall and may be lawful to and for any Jury that shall hereafter be impannelled and sworne at any Mine Law Court to rate, tax and assess upon every miner within the liberty of the said mine any sum or sums of money not exceeding 10s on each miner at one time as shall be by them thought necessary for the occasion then requiring the same; which rate and tax being reduced into writing and allowed and subscribed by the deputy constable then holden such Court and the deputy gavellors of the said mine and the said Jury shall be obliging and binding to every miner therein named to make payment thereof within such time and in such manner as in the said rate shall be ordered and appointed; And if any miner in the said rate named shall neglect or refuse to pay the money rated and taxed upon him in manner as aforesaid, he or she shall forfeit double such money the miner shall be therein rated, to be recovered in the Mine Law Court by any miner one-half etc.

And it is further ordered and agreed that when any such Jury shall be impannelled for the raising of money as aforesaid the one half of them shall be coal miners and the other half miners of iron ore, and that the monies so to be raised presently be paid unto the gavellers of the mines until such Jury shall order otherwise.

In witness whereof the said deputy constables, gavellers and jurors have hereunto set their hands and seals the day and year first above written.

Wm. Wolseley	Tho. Worgan	Geo. Banister	John Barrow
	Hen. Worgan	Rich. Keare	Hen. Hooper
Rich. Worgan	Hen. Morgan	Ri. Priest	Tho. Evans
William Adams	Edw. Bray	Thomas Mowsall	Richard Keare
deputy	William Godding	Thomas Westwood	Wm. Pitcher
gavellers[1]	Richard Morgan	Anthony Smart	Ant. Andrews
	Tho. Walden	Anthony Reynolds	Joseph Hart
Tho. Davies	Jo. Yem	Jos. Montjoy	Cha. Jones
	Jo. Worgan	Thomas Reynols	Richd. Griffiths
	Tho. Keare	Rich. ?	Jo. Davis
	Ri. Hayward	James Gething	Ja. Preece
	William Humfreys	Jno. Griffith	Jno. Wilce
	Tho. Kedgwin	Geo. Banister Jnr.	Wm. Worgan
	Jno. Tyler	John Worgan	Thom. Wisham
	John ?	Richard Nelmes	Geo. Elly
	Ri. Linch	Wm. Yem	James Good'[2]

1 All genuine signatures except Adams who made his mark.

2 The whole of this Order, including the names of the jurors, is in the handwriting of Thomas Davies, deputy clerk. There are no 'marks' against the signatures.

ORDER NO. 7 (11 JANUARY 1687)

'Foresta de Deane } At the Court of Mine and Miners of our Sovereign Lord the King holden for his said forest at Clowerwall within the same forest upon Tuesday the 11th January in the second year of the reign of our Sovereign Lord James the second &c. Before William Wolseley Esq. Deputy to the Most Noble Henry Duke of Beaufort Constable of his Majesty's Castle of St. Briavels within the said forest and Richard Jelfe and John Knight deputy gavellers of the said mines and Thomas Davies deputy clerk of the said Castle, And from that day continued by several adjournments until Tuesday 5th April in the third year of the reign of the said Majesty that now is, the Jury of 48 miners then and there impannelled and sworn according to the Custom of the said miners for all the time whereof the memory of man is not to the contrary there used and approved do now order establish and ordain by and with the approbation and consent of the said deputy constable in manner and form following, that is to say:

Imprimis for the final discharge and payment of the debts yet remaining due and unpaid from the said miners and which were occasioned and contracted by reason of the late suits in the Exchequer and otherwise, the said Jury have agreed and accordingly do now order and ordain that there shall be forthwith paid the sum of 2s by and from every miner that traveleth in the mine and the like sum of 2s for every working horse and mare kept for carriage of mine, coal or ochre, the same money to be duly paid unto Thomas Worgan and Richard Jelfe, Collectors made thereof and appointed in this behalf, who are to give an accompt upon oath at the Mine Law Court when required, and to have such allowance for their pains therein as by the same Court shall be thought convenient; And if any miner chargeable by this Order shall neglect or refuse to pay the sum justly due from him or her by the space of 14 days after demand such miner shall forfeit double the sum he or she ought to have paid, the one half &c.

Item it is further ordered and ordained that all coal pits and dangerous minepits which are not in working or which hereafter shall not be wrought in for one whole month together shall be sufficiently secured by a wall of stone or by railing the same with posts and rails placed about two feet distant from the mouth of such pit by the proprietors thereof And likewise all pits left open for a 'goutway' upon pain of 10s. to be forfeited for every omission and neglect, the one half &c.

Item it is further ordered and ordained that for the restraining of that pernicious and abominable sin of perjury, too much used in these licentious times, every miner convicted by a Jury of 48 miners in the said Court shall for ever lose and totally forfeit his freedom as touching the mines and be utterly expelled out of the same, and all his working tools and habit be burnt before his face, and he never afterwards to be a witness or to be believed in any matter whatsoever.

Item whereas complaint hath been made that the inhabitants of the Hundred of St. Briavels cannot have their horses and other carriages laden with fire coal for their own private uses at the several coalpits within the same hundred until the colliers belonging to the said pit have first laden their own horses with coal to transport and carry away the same out of the said hundred, whereby the horses and other carriages of the said inhabitants are many times forced to stay at the said pit all day and sometimes to come home again unladen to the great prejudice of the said inhabitants, for prevention whereof for the future it is now agreed and ordered that the horses and other carriages belonging to the said inhabitants shall henceforth be laden with fire coal at the said several pits before any colliers horses belonging to such pits that do carry and transport the same out of the said hundred upon pain of forfeiting by every person doing contrary to this Order one hundred dozen of good firecoal, the one moiety &c.

Item whereas several Ordinances and Orders have heretofore been made for setting and ascertaining the rates and prizes of ore at and to the several furnaces and places of carriage within and adjoining unto this forest, and also of lime coal sold into the counties of Monmouth and Hereford and other places near the said forest And appointing bargainers to contract for the same, which said Orders have not had the good effects designed by them, the Jury aforesaid do therefore now agree, and accordingly do order and ordain that all Ordinances and Orders made since the happy restoration of his late Majesty King Charles the second of ever blessed memory that do any way relate unto the setting of rates and prizes of ore and lime coal to any furnaces or other places whatsoever or that do nominate and appoint Bargainers for the same, be from henceforth totally repealed and made void and of none effect to all intents and purposes as if the same had never been made; And that all miners be left at liberty to sell carry and deliver their ore and coal to whom where and at what rates and prizes they can best agree for without incurring any penalty or forfeiture for so doing.

Item the Jury aforesaid do further ordain that no working horses shall be hereafter kept to transport or travaile within the mine except such miner have land of his own or shall rent lands sufficient to maintain such number of horses kept by such miner or shall keep them at 'tacke'[1] upon pain that such miner shall be debarred from transporting with his horses until such miner shall have or rent lands to keep the said horses and to forfeit 5s/– a day to be recovered as aforesaid; This Order not to take effect until after the 11th November next ensuing.

In witness whereof the said deputy constable, gavellers, castle clerk and Jurors have hereunto set their hands and seals the day and year first above written.

Wm. Wolseley	Thomas Wisham	Richard Preest	Tho. Monjoy
	Richard Nelmes	Henry Hooper	William Keare
Richard Jelfe	Richard Keare	John Tyler	William Davis
John Knight	Edwd. Rocke	Paul Hobbs	Geo. Morgan
Tho. Davies[2]	John Worgan	Rich. Keare	Rich. Robins
	Thom. Nash	Tho. Sibranco	Jo. Preest
	Wm. Goding	Wm. Morse	John Trigge
	John Andrews	John Ward	Steph. Trigge
	Geo. Bannister	Thom. Skyn	Thomas Kedgwin
	Edmond Griffiths	Thomas Kedgwin	Tho. Sibrance
	Edm. Symons	Owen Thomas	Richard Hayward
	John Watkins	John Banister	Rich. Mowsall
	Jo. Philpot	John Watkins	John Worgan Jnr.
	John Beach	Willm. Adams	Joseph Rooke
	Franc. Wood	Chr. Davis	John Meeke, snr.
	Hen. Embrey	Richd. Probert	Wm. Trigge'[3]

1 Local term for short lease.
2 The above four signatures are genuine.
3 About fourteen signed, the others making their marks.

ORDER NO. 8 (17 JANUARY 1693)[1]

'Forest of Dean } At the Court of Mine and Miners of our Sovereign Lord and Lady the King and Queen holden at Clowerwall within the said forest on Tuesday 17th January in the 4th year of the reign of our Sovereign Lord and Lady William and Mary &c. before Tracy Catchmay, John Higford and George Bond, Esquires, Deputies to the Most Noble Henry Duke of Beaufort constable of their said Majesties' Castle of St. Briavels within the said forest and Richard Worgan and William Adams, deputy gavellers of the mines there, And Thomas Davies deputy clerk of the said Castle, and from that day continued by several adjournments to Tuesday the 14th February then next following, the Jury of 48 miners &c.

Imprimis for the full and final discharge and satisfaction of the debts yet remaining due and unpaid from the said miners which were occasioned and contracted by the late suits in law in the Court of Exchequer at Westminster and otherwise and for suing forth the decree made in the said Court upon hearing of the cause, And for getting into the custody of the said miners their writings and evidence which were produced and made use of at the said hearing and for preserving them for the future benefit of the said miners, And for raising monies for other necessary occasions, the Jury aforesaid have agreed and accordingly do now order establish and ordain that there shall be forthwith paid by and from every miner that travayleth in the said mines the sum of 12d., and the like sum of 12d. for every working horse and mare kept for carriage of iron-mine coal or ochre, the same money to be duly paid unto Richard Worgan and William Adams, Collectors elected and appointed in this behalf who are to give an accompt thereof upon oath at the Mine Law Court when required, And if any miner chargeable by this order shall neglect or refuse to pay the money wherewith he or she shall be chargeable at the next Mine Law Court that shall be holden within the said forest every such miner shall forfeit double the sum of money which he or she ought to have paid by virtue of this Order, the one half &c.

Item the Jury aforesaid do hereby ratify and confirm one Order[2] heretofore made by a Jury of 48 miners dated 8th September in the 26th year of the reign of our late Sovereign Lord King Charles the second whereby all colliers are prohibited from coming to work within 100 yards of another's work that hath brought up a gout or surffe to the prejudice of the first undertakers, which order though very beneficial to the colliers in preservation of their coal-pits from being spoiled and destroyed yet doth not so fully provide for the same as if the space and distance were 300 yards, This Jury therefore do now order establish and ordain that the said space or distance be now settled at 300 yards, And whosoever shall offend shall incur the penalty in the said Order contained.

Item the Jury aforesaid for divers weighty reasons inducing then hereunto do order, establish and ordain that from henceforth no iron ore or mine shall be sold and delivered at any place or places upon or near the Rivers of Severn or Wye by any miner whatsoever to be thence transported into the Kingdom or Ireland under the rate and price of 6s. 6d. for every dozen [Forest measure] the same to be fully paid for at the time of the measuring or delivery

1 Nicholls (N.H., p. 56) is in error in giving the year as 1692. The Dean Forest Mining Commissioners are in error in quoting this Order as No. 9 and in giving the year as 1697.

2 Order No. 2.

thereof by the buyer thereof, All that all miners that please shall have liberty to carry and deliver a share thereof without any manner of contradiction, And if any miner shall sell or deliver any iron ore or mine contrary to this Order or shall interrupt any miner in the carrying and delivery of any part of the Bargains that shall at any time hereafter be made for any iron ore or mine to be transported into Ireland as aforesaid, every such miner shall forfeit one hundred dozen of good iron ore, the one half etc.

In Witness whereof the said deputy constables, gavellers, castle clerk and 48 miners have hereunto set their hands and seals the aforesaid 14th February in the year above written.

T. Catchmay	George Banister	Edw. White	Tho. Kidgwin
John Higford	John Tresteed	Ni. Mowsall	James ?
Geo. Bond	Tho. Walden	John Jones	Fran. Meeke
Rich. Worgan	Thomas Wisham	Sturly Kedgwin	Rich. Preest
Will. Adams	Rich. Beach	Ma. Ambrose	Geo. Whetson
Tho. Davies[1]	Anthony Reynolds	Anthony Smart	Ri. Watkins
	Edw. Palmer	Tho. Palmer	George Whetstone
	James Yearoth	Thomas Lodge	Henry Worgan
	Rich. Lewis	John Davis	John Preest
	Chri. Davis	Fr. Keare	Thomas Keare
	Jno. Cooke	Ralph ?	Tho. ?
	Hen. Jordan	Tho. Wood	Will Morse
	Henry Wilcox	Fran. Wood	Thomas Montjoy
	?	John Yem	?
	?	? Wysham Snr.	John Meeke
	Tho. Haynes	Thomas Walden	Richard Haynes'

ORDER NO. 9 (23 APRIL 1694)[2]

'Forest of Dean { At the Court of Mine and Miners of our Sovereign Lord and Lady William and Mary &c. holden and begun at Clowerwall within the said forest upon Tuesday the 23rd April in the 6th year of their said Majesties' reign before John Higford and George Bond, Esquires Deputies to the Most Noble Henry Duke of Beaufort, constable of their said Majesties' Castle of St. Briavels within the said forest of Dean, And Richard Worgan and William Adams, deputy gavellers of the mines within the said forest, and Thomas Davies, gent. deputy clarke of the said Castle, and continued by several adjournments until Tuesday the 3rd July next in the year abovesaid, the Jury of 48 miners &c.

1. Imprimis – That for the better regulating the proceedings and trials in this Court for the future, and preventing the odious sin of perjury, no person be permitted to swear in his own cause nor prove any debt upon his own oath unless it be for or concerning a matter transacted under ground, or where it was difficult to have any witnesses of which cases the Constable and the rest of the officers of the Court then present are to be judges, And that no Bargain shall be binding except the same shall be proved by two witnesses at least.

1 All genuine signatures except Adams who made his mark.

2 The Dean Forest Mining Commissioners are in error in quoting this Order as No. 8.

2. That all causes where the debt or damages demanded in the plea do amount to 40s. shall be tried by a Jury of twelve miners, and the witnesses on both sides openly heard in Court, And thereupon the Jury do give their Verdict according to the method and usage of other Courts of Law; And all causes under that value shall upon hearing such proof as shall be produced on either side be determined by the Constable then holding the Court according to the ordinary and usual proceedings of the Court.

3. That all persons summoned to this Court to answer any action shall have 24 hours notice at least given before the Court to the end they may be provided with such witnesses as they shall think fit to produce, who shall have 12d. apiece paid them for their day's work by the person on whose behalf they are produced.

4. That no greater or other fees be allowed to any officer of the Court than what have been formerly paid and allowed time out of mind.

5. To prevent vexatious suits the plaintiff if the cause goes against him or he become non-suited shall pay to the defendant the usual costs of the Court as well for his own day's work as for his witnesses (if he hath any) for which costs the usual process of the Court shall issue.

6. And whereas by the last Order made the 17th January in the 4th year of their present Majesties' reign it was (amongst other things) agreed and ordained that the rate of all iron ore or mine carried to any place or places to be thence transported into Ireland should be 6s. 6d. per dozen, which order having proved very prejudicial to the miners, it is now ordered and ordained that the future price of all ore to be transported into Ireland and pitched at Brockweir shall be 5s/– a dozen and that pitched at Wyes Greene shall be 4s a dozen and not under. And that a fifth part of all such ore so to be transported shall be laid down and pitched at Wyes Green aforesaid, And that all Bargains henceforth to be made for such ore shall be made by Thomas Wysham the younger of Stanton, George Banister the younger of Clowerwall and Richard Preest of Breeme and by no other person or persons whatsoever, On pain to forfeit one hundred dozen of iron ore to be recovered as other penalties as are usually done in this Court.

7. That the price of fire coal to the Copper Works[1] shall be henceforth (after all Bargains in writing already made shall be fulfilled and made good) 8s per dozen and not under and Smith coal 6s per dozen and not under, and charking[2] at 8s per dozen and not under, on pain to forfeit one hundred dozen of fire coal to be recovered in this Court after the usual manner; And that Richd. Elly and Sturley Kedgwin be Bargainers, and also William Milson.

8. That all laws, ordinances and orders heretofore made for the punishment of the abominable sin of perjury be confirmed and put in effectual execution against the offenders.

9. That no miner do hereafter measure any iron mine at any furnace or other place but by the usual accustomed and lawful bushels without handing, thrusting, kicking or knocking the bushels, on pain of forfeiting one hundred dozen of iron mine to be recovered as aforesaid.

That all Bargains made for coal to either of the Copper works by any person whatsoever since the said 23rd day of April shall be absolutely void and of none effect.

In testimony whereof the said deputy Constables and other officers and the said Jury of 48 miners have hereto set their hands and seals the day and year first above written.

---

1 At Redbrook.

2 Chark – to make charcoal.

John Higford	Will. Milson	Henry Bannister	John Davy
Geo. Bond	Thomas Kedgwin	J... Higgins	John Tyler
Richard Worgan	Jo. Thomas	Em. Bennett	Thom. Montjoy
Wm. Adams	Wm. Cowmeadow	Tho. Nelmes	Tho. Palmer
Tho. Davies[1]	Geo. Bannister	John Lewis	?
	Anthony Symons	Henry Keare	Thom. Nash
	Ric. Voyce	Wm. Rocke	Step. Adams
	Wm. Lewis	Tho. Stephens	Richard Preest
	Richard Lewis	John Bannister	Rich. Powell
	Jo. Morgan	And. Jones	John Bannister
	Thom. Reynold	Henry Hooper	John Dukes Jnr.
	Henry Morgan	John Beach	John Jordan
	Tho. Adams	George Stephens	Jno. Wood
	An. Andrews	Nich. Annatts	An. Reynolds
	James Preest	Will Jelfe	Willm. Davis
	Richd. ?	Thomas Wysham	Richard Wysham'[2]

Although no detailed records can be found, it appears that sessions were also held on 12 March 1699 and 7 November 1700 (at Ruardean) for Order No. 10 of 1701, which follows, refers to certain temporary Orders made on these two dates.

ORDER NO. 10 (27 JANUARY 1701)

'Forest of Deane : The Court of Mine and Miners of our Sovereign Lord the King holden for the said forest at Clowerwall upon Tuesday the 27th January in the 13th year of the reign of our Sovereign Lord William the Third etc. Before William Powlett Serjt. at Law and George Bond Esq. Deputies to the Right Honble Charles Earl of Berkley Constable of the Castle of St. Briavels within the same forest. And Richard Worgan and Philip Hatton deputy gavellers of the Mines, and Thomas Davies deputy clerk of the said Castle, And by divers adjournments continued unto the 10th March then next following, the Jury of 48 miners etc.

6d. stamp

6d. stamp

Whereas the Jury of 48 miners by their Order bearing date the 12th March which was in the year of our Lord 1699, and in the 12th year of His Majesty's reign that now is, did establish, order, ordain and prohibit the loading of foreigners' horses, carts and carriages at their respective coalpits and coalworks with any sort of coal in other manner than in the said Order is contained, and did likewise prohibit the sending down the River Wye any sort of coal to any place whatsoever upon the said River below Welsh Bicknor under the several penalties and forfeitures for every of the said offences as in the said Order is particularly mentioned and expressed, and although the said Order hath been and is of very great advantage and benefit to the said miners in relation to their coal; Yet the same being a temporary order and to continue in force but to a certain day which is elapsed and past, The said miners have suffered and may be very much prejudiced by the expiration and noncontinuance thereof, *Therefore* this present Jury of 48 miners having duly considered the same and the consequents thereof do hereby fully and unanimously agree, order, ordain and establish, That the aforesaid Order and every clause, sentence, matter and thing therein contained as well touching and concerning the said coal as the raising of money for payments of the debts of the miners and

1 All genuine signatures except Adams who made his mark.

2 About eighteen signed, the others making their marks.

securing their Records and Writings and making free the deputy constables and other persons therein named and all other things therein contained and mentioned be henceforth made perpetual and the same is hereby made perpetual and is fully ratified and confirmed in every particular thereof to all intents, constructions and purposes whatsoever as if the same were herein particularly recited and expressed, *And* the Jury aforesaid do hereby declare, that if any miner shall presume to break the same Order (until it shall in due form be altered or repealed by a future Jury of 48 miners according to their custom) or shall offend in any of the matters therein mentioned, he shall suffer and pay the penalties therein contained to the utmost severity[1] according to the customs of the said miners.

And the Jury aforesaid do also order, establish and ordain that when the monies aforesaid in the said recited order mentioned and intended to be raised, shall be levied and received, the Collectors therein named (to whom Thomas Kedgwin the younger is hereby added and appointed as one) shall take care to get and collect all the writings and papers belonging to the said miners that were made use of at the last hearing in the Exchequer out of the hands of all such persons as now have any of them in their custodies, and shall put them together with all other the Orders and Records of the Mine Law Courts into the chest prepared to keep them and safely lock them up therein and leave the said chest in the custody of Francis Wyndham, Esq.[2] one of the Society of the Miners who is humbly desired to keep the same for the use and benefit of the miners, And that likewise the said Collectors do take care that the decree made upon the aforesaid hearing in the Exchequer be drawn up and entered on record in the said Court, and a copy thereof obtained and kept for the use of the miners, And that they do likewise upon payment of any of the debts mentioned in the said Order take legal discharges in full from the persons to whom they pay the same that so the miners may at length be wholly discharged therefrom.

And they do further order, establish and ordain that Richard Worgan the [deputy] gaveller, Richard Keare, William Yerworth, Jmm. Higgins and James Worgan be and they are hereby appointed bargainers for all ore that shall be sold and transported to Ireland in the room and place of Richard Preest and George Banister junior (who are hereby discharged therefrom) And they or any three or more of them are to act do and perform all such matters and things and in such manner as in and by an Order made by 48 miners bearing date the 23rd April, and in the year of our Lord Christ 1696[3] is directed and appointed. And that the said Richard Worgan, Richard Keare, William Yerworth, Jmm. Higgins and James Worgan and every of them be indemnified by this Court for what they or any of them have already done therein since and pursuant to the Order of the Mine Law Court held at Ruardean the 7th November last, And that henceforth it shall and may be lawful for the deputy constable or steward holding any Mine Law Court with the consent of the Jury then sworn to alter change and remove all or any of the said last named bargainers and to put others in their room and so from time to time henceforth without the formality of an Order made by 48 miners, anything in their Custom contained to the contrary thereof in anywise notwithstanding.

And the Jury aforesaid do hereby further ratify and confirm another Order made at the same time as the first mentioned whereby the before-named Francis Wyndham is made and constituted a free miner.

---

1 Nicholls (N.H., p. 62) refers, in error, to a jury 'of utmost seventy'.

2 Chosen no doubt for his good character. He was interested in the Society for the Promotion of Christian Knowledge.

3 Presumably refers to Order No. 9 of 1694.

And further the Jury aforesaid do hereby order, establish and ordain that no collier or miner shall henceforth carry any lime coal or other coal whatsoever to any place or places within or without the liberty of the Mine to the intent that the same shall be sent down the River of Wye by boat to or for the use of John Hopkins of Monmouth, limeburner, or any other person or persons whatsoever, on pain to forfeit for every offence contrary to this Order one hundred dozen of the same sort of coal so carried to be sent down the said River of Wye as aforesaid, the one half &c. Notwithstanding any miner or collier may carry and deliver any lime coal to any the kiln or kilns of the said John Hopkins or to his use by and upon any horses or marefoals at the rate and price of 7s. a dozen and not at any other or lower rate, upon pain of forfeiting one hundred dozen of lime coal to be sued for and recovered in the Mine Law Court as abovesaid, And that we do order and ordain Jmm. Higgings and Richard Wysham to be and they are hereby appointed bargainers for all coal carried to the use of the said John Hopkins and Walter Williams.

And the Jury aforesaid do hereby order, establish and ordain that every miner Below the Wood shall henceforth keep a pair of Scales at their several coalpits to weigh their coal withall, And that no coal shall be sent or delivered away unweighed to foreigners from any of their coalpits, each ton to contain twentyone hundred [weight] and no more, And the price of coal at the coalpits Below the Wood shall not exceed 5s. a ton to the inhabitants of this Hundred, and shall not be less than 6s. a ton to foreigners upon pain that every person offending herein contrary to this Order shall forfeit one hundred dozen of such coal as he or they do so load away unweighed or above the weight abovesaid or the value thereof in money, the one half etc.

And the Jury aforesaid do further order and ordain that any miner or collier Above the Wood shall not carry any sort of coal by water above Welsh Bicknor upon the penalty aforesaid.

In testimony whereof the said deputy Constables, deputy gavellers of the Mines, deputy Castle Clerk and 48 miners have to this Order, written upon parchment having the two sixpenny stamps hereon, set their hands and seals the day and year first above written.

Wm. Powlett	Sturly Kedgwin	Richard Keare	Thomas Kedgwin
Geo. Bond	James Keare	Jmm. Higins	Richard Martin
Rich. Worgan	Henry Griffith	George Marshall	Hen. Foden
Philip Hatton	John Forden	Richd. Thomas	John Thomas
Tho: Davies[1]	Samuel Cooke	Richard Tombe	Cha. Trested
	Robert Badham	Willm. Yemm	Henry Worgan
	Rich. Wysham	Geo. White	Hen. Wallding
	Thomas Nelmes	Willm. Mathews	Richd. Morefeild
	Henry Hooper	Tho. Wysham	Will. Keare
	Jo: Worgan	? Tresteed	James Worgan
	Willm. Bangham	Thomas Kedgwin Snr.	William Lewis
	Joseph Dukes	Henry Smyth	Chr. Dowle
	Rich. Worgan	William Bond	Thomas Hooper
	Thomas Bond	John Jordan	Rich. Symons
	Edw. Trested Snr.	Arthur Symons	Will. Wysham
	Will. Jelfe	John Jones	Nicholas Annetts'[2]

1 All genuine signatures except Hatton who made his mark.

2 About eighteen signed, the others making their marks.

ORDER NO. 11 (1 JULY 1707)

'Forest of Deane. At the Court of Mine and Miners of our Sovereing Lady the Queen holden for the said forest at Mitcheldeane upon Tuesday the 1st July in the 6th year of the reign of our Sovereign Lady Anne etc. Before George Bond, Esq., Roynon Jones, Esq., Deputies to the Right Honble Charles Earl of Berkly, Viscount Dursley, Baron Berkly of Berkely Castle Lord Chief Steward of Her Majesty's Court Leets, Courts of Pleas and of the Mine Law Courts within the said forest etc., And Richard Preest and Robert Wood, deputy gavellers of the said Mines, And Thomas Davies, deputy Clerk of the said Court of Mine Law, And from that day and place continued by several adjournments until Tuesday the 12th August then next following at Coleford, the Jury of 48 free miners &c.

6d. stamp

6d. stamp

Whereas for the better preservation and maintenance of the ancient Rights and privileges of the said miners according to their said Custom it is very necessary that all their Records, writings and papers especially those that were made use of at the last Trial in the Court of Exchequer should be speedily collected together and carefully laid up and kept in the chest heretofore provided for that purpose, And that all the debts that are now remaining unpaid from the said miners should (at last) be fully satisfied and paid which hath been proposed but hath hitherto been neglected, this Jury doth therefore now Order and ordain that the said Records, writings and papers shall be forthwith collected together by the said deputy gavellers and clerks of the said Miners and safely put into and locked up in the said chest and an index made of them and all the Orders of the said miners are to be copied out into a book to be provided for that purpose which is to be produced by the Clerk of the said Court at every of the said Mine Law Courts (if required) which chest this Jury doth humbly pray Francis Wyndham Esq. one of the Society of the said Miners to keep for the use and benefit of the said miners upon all occasions, And that there be forthwith levied, raised and paid by every miner that travaileth in the said mines or hath so done at any time since the 8th March which was in the year of our Lord 1706, the sum of 1/–s quarterly for and from Midsummer last past, And the like sum of ls/– quarterly for every horse mare or marefoal used and employed in the carriage of iron ore, ochre or coal within the time aforesaid to be likewise paid, unto Richard Keare, Henry Hooper, Thomas Wysham, George Mason, Jmm. Higgins, Richard Wyesham, John Bennett, William Mathews, Giles Lockyer, George Eddy, William Yerroth, John Watkins (for one year as aforesaid the first payment to begin at Michnelmas next) or to any of them being Collectors chosen and appointed for this purpose who are to gather the same forthwith upon pain of paying the same (if any shall neglect or refuse) And the same so collected to pay or cause to be paid unto the said Francis Wyndham or to whom he shall appoint, And the said Collectors are to give a true accompt of all the monies by them received at the next Mine Law Court that shall be holden after Michaelmas next; And, the said Collectors are to have 6d. in the £ for their pain in collecting the same; And if any miner shall neglect or refuse to pay the sum of money wherewith he or she shall be charged pursuant to this Order by the space of ten days after demand thereof, every such miner shall forfeit and pay double the sum charged pursuant to this Order, to be recovered in the Mine Law Court by any one of the said Collectors in the said Court and the usual cost, which said monies shall not be diverted or employed to any other use than the payment of the said debts due from the said miners and defense of their Rights and privileges; And the surplusage of the said money (if any be) shall be expended and laid out to and for such uses and in such manner as by any two deputy Stewards of the said Courts by and with the consent of the Jury then sworn at such Court shall be directed and appointed; Or by the said Collectors or the major part of them.

And this Jury doth further order and ordain, that if any miner or other person shall find him or themselves agrieved by the leaving open of any dangerous coalpit or minepit, such miner or other person shall give ten days' notice at the least thereof to the proprietors or last workers in such pit to fill or sufficiently secure the same in some reasonable time; And in case of the neglect or refusal of such proprietor or last worker to do the same, then he or they shall forfeit the sum of 20s. to be recovered in the Mine Law Court after the usual manner. Provided nevertheless, and it is further ordered, that if it shall appear that the sums of money hereby ordered to be raised for the purposes aforesaid shall be more than sufficient for these ends, that then it shall and may be lawful for any Constable holding any Mine Law Court with the consent of the Jury then sworn to put a stop to and to discharge the further payment of any more money in pursuance of this Order.

In witness whereof as well the said deputy stewards as the said Jury and other officers above named have hereunto set their hands and seals the day and year above written.

George Bond	George Banister	Sturly Kedgwin	Jmm. Higins
Roy Jones	Francis Keare	Tho: Wysham	Richard Keare
Richard Preest	Henry Banister	John Watkins	George E ?
Rob. Wood	Chr. Davis	Henry Dubberly	Wm. Mathews
Tho: Davies[1]	Tho: Wysham Snr.	Henry Worgan	John Banister
	Rich. Wysham	E. White Snr.	Tho: Skin, Snr.
	Ri. Hawkins	Phillip Elly	Richard ?
	Richard Benett	Thos. Meeke	Giles Lockier
	Henry Hooper	Richard Lewis	Geo. Mason
	Andr. Jones	Edm. Symons	Arthur Symons
	Tho: Nash	John Worgan	John ?
	William Symons	William ?	Tho: Monsell
	John Beach	Danl. Elsmore	Wm. Elsmore
	Tho: Palmer	? Mathews	Fran. Meeke
	John Bennett	Henry Edy	John Jones
	Aaron Hale	Jer. Meeke	Edri. Jordan'[2]

ORDER NO. 12 (7 JANUARY 1718)

'Forest of Dean. 6d. stamp 6d. stamp 6d. stamp

At the Court of Mine and Miners of our Sovereign Lord the King holden at the Speech House within the said forest on Tuesday the 7th January last in the 4th year of the Reign of our Sovereign Lord George [I] &c. Before Richard Machen and William James. Esqs., Deputies of the Right Honble James Earl of Berkeley &c. And George James deputy gaveller of the Mines there, And William Davies, Gent, clerk of the said Castle, And from that day continued by adjournments to Tuesday the 4th February then next following, The Jury of 48 miners &c.

1 The above five signatures are genuine.
2 About nineteen signed, the others making their marks.

Imprimis for raising monies for defending as well the free miners of the forest as also the deputy Constables of the said Castle of St. Briavels from all Actions and Suits which now are or hereafter may be brought against them or any or either of them in any of His Majesty's Courts at Westminster for or concerning anything relating to the mines or miners or touching their privileges of the said Court of Mines or Miners or to any proceedings in the Law Courts, And for the prosecuting or defending any *Certiorari Recordari* or other Writ which shall at any time be brought to Remove any Action out of this Court,[1] The Jury aforesaid have agreed and do accordingly now order, establish and ordain, that for defending any such Action or Actions and Suits now depending or which hereafter shall be brought against any freeminer or any deputy constable of the said Castle of St. Briavels for or concerning anything relating to the Mines or Miners or to the privileges or proceedings of the said Court of Mine or Miners, And for prosecuting and defending all and every *Certiorari Recordari* or other Writs which hereafter shall be brought for removing any Action out of this Court, there shall be forthwith paid by and from every miner that travailleth in the said Mines the sum of 6d, and the like sum of 6d for every working horse and mare kept for carriage of iron mine, coal or ochre, the said money to be duly paid unto Edward Mousall and Arthur Symons for Clowerwall, Charles Goodwin and Will. White for Coleford and Staunton, Thomas Roberts for English Bicknor, John Morse for Bream, John Morefield and John Morse for Ruardean and Mitcheldean, Thomas Waldin for Littledean, Collectors elected and appointed in this behalf who are to give an accompt thereof upon oath at a Mine Law Court when required; And if any miner chargeable by this Order shall neglect or refuse to pay the money wherewith he or she shall be chargeable at the next Mine Law Court that shall be holden within the said forest every such miner shall forfeit double the sum of money which he or she ought to have paid by virtue of this Order, the one-half &c.; And when any Action or Suit shall hereafter be brought against any free miner or any deputy constable in any other court for and touching or concerning any the matters or things aforesaid or when any *Certiorari Recordari* or other Writ shall be brought for removing any Action out of this Court. And if the sums so to be raised shall not be sufficient for the purposes aforesaid, then twelve miners at any Mine Law Court by the approbation and consent of the deputy Constables may from time to time as there shall be occasion order the raising and paying the like sum or sums of money for the purposes aforesaid.

Item. Out of the due and great respect, honour and esteem we sincerely bear to the Honble. Mathew Ducie Morton, Esq., Thomas Gage, Esq., John Wyndham, Esq., Richard Machen, Esq., William James, Esq., Christopher Bond, Esq., and Thomas Pyrke, Esq., we do hereby unanimously constitute, ordain, confirm and make the said Mathew Ducie Morton, Thomas Gage, John Wyndham, Richard Machen, William James, Christopher Bond and Thomas Pyrke and every of them free miners of the said forest of Dean to all intents and purposes whatsoever, and to have take and enjoy all and singular the privileges, benefits and advantages whatsoever touching and relating to the Mine and Miners in as full ample and beneficial manner as any other free miner or miners within the said forest doth, can, may, might or ought to have and enjoy and same.

Item. We do further order, establish and ordain that if any free miner shall sue another free miner in any other court other than the Mine Law Court for or concerning any matter or thing relating to the mine, the miner so suing in any foreign court shall forfeit the sum of £30, one-half etc.

1 See 'case' against George Gardner in Berkeley Castle Muniments.

In witness whereof etc.

Richard Machen	Thomas Mousall	Thomas Palmer	Thomas Godwin
William James	Danl. Elsmore	John Worgan	Edwd. Tresteed
Geo. James	Richd. Keare	Wm. Elsmore	John Morfield
Wm. Davies[1]	Wm. Mathews	Wm. Williams	Joseph Montjoy
	Andrew Jones	Arthur Symons	Edward Mousall
	Wm. Kedgwin	John Morse	James Gething
	Wm. White	Enoch Jones	Henry Stephens
	John Morse	Danl. Hobbs	Richd. Lewis
	John Morse	James ?	Mathew Parry
	John Cook	John Keare	James Mathews
	Thomas Roberts	Wm. Lewis	Chris. Griffith
	Henry Byrt	Henry Hayward	Charles Godwin
	John Worgan	Richd. Morse	Henry Roberts
	John Jows	Jon. Chapman	James Adams
	John Watkins	Tho: Waldin	Henry Edy
	Charles Waldwin	Thomas Bennett	Richd. Probert'[2]

Another session was held on 13 May 1718, for that is the date on which fines are recorded for disturbances in Court.[3]

ORDER NO. 13 (10 NOVEMBER 1719)

'Forest of Dean in the County of Gloucester } At the Court of Mine and Miners of our Sovereign Lord the King within the said Forest of Dean holden by adjournment at the Speech House within the said Forest on Tuesday, the 10th November in the 6th year of the reign of Our Sovereign Lord George &c. Before Richard Machen and William James, Esquires, Deputies to the Right Honble James Earl of Berkeley &c. and John Everett deputy clerk of the Castle aforesaid, and George James, deputy gavellor of the Mines within the said Forest, the Jury then and there sworn consisting of 48 miners, &c.

6d. stamp

6d. stamp

6d. stamp

Whereas at the Court of Mine and Miners holden at Clowerwall the 18th March in the 21st year of the reign of our late Sovereign Lord King Charles the second[4] before Sir Baynham Throckmorton Kt. and Bart., deputy constable, and William Rowles, gent, Clerks of the

1 All genuine signatures, except James who made his mark.

2 About eleven signed, the others making their marks.

3 The record reads:
'John Davis, for talking in Court .... 2s.
John Kear, for talking in Court .... 2s.
Wm. Rudge, for disturbing ye Court .... 2s.
Nich. Whitstone, for the like .... 2s.
Thomas Rudge, for the same .... 2s.
John Griffiths, for disturbing the Court.............. 2s.
Thomas Rudge, for the same offence .... 2s.
John Trigg, for the same offence .... 2s.
Griffith Cooper, for talking in Court .... 2s.
(N.H., p. 237.)

4 Order No. 1.

Castle of St. Briavels aforesaid and Richard Morse, Nicholas Kedgwin. Robert Wood and William Adams. deputy Gavellors of the Mines aforesaid, the Jury of 48 miners then and there impannelled and sworn, for the better ordering and government of the said Mine and Miners, did (amongst divers other orders therein contained) order and ordain that no foreigners living out of the Hundred of St. Briavels should or might at any time thenceafter transport or carry any iron ore or coals contrary to the custom except it was carried and delivered to them by a free miner out of the said Hundred of St. Briavels under the penalty of one hundred dozen of good sufficient ore or coal, the one half &c., And that no free miner should or might thenceafter load any foreigner with mine [ore] or coal with any manner of carriage whatsoever under the penalty aforesaid, And whereas at a Court of Mine and Miners of the said Forest holden at Clowerwall within the said Forest on Tuesday the 8th September in the 26th year of the reign of our said late Sovereign Lord Charles the second,[1] before the said Sir Baynham Throckmorton, deputy constable, and the said William Rowles, clerk of the Castle of St. Briavels aforesaid, and George Arundell and William Adams, deputy gavellors of the Mines within the said Forest, the Jury of 48 miners then and there impannelled and sworn did wholly repeal, revoke, make void and null the said Order as the same in manner and form is above expressed, And did then order and ordain that whensoever any foreigner not being a free miner should repair to any the coalpits of the said miners for fire coal or lime coal, it should and might be lawful to and for every such foreigner to have and carry away such coal as aforesaid for their own proper use and expense, nor carrying the same to sell to others nor upon hire, without being troubled or questioned for the same as fully as a free miner might or ought to do. *And whereas* great abuses are dayly committed by foreigners living in the counties of Hereford and Monmouth who upon pretence of carrying coal for their own use do transport great quantities of coal selling the same to others and also carrying upon hire contrary to the intent of the last recited Order to the great damage of the free miners of the said Forest, for remedy whereof it is hereby ordered and ordained and the said Jury of 48 miners now sworn and impannelled do hereby order and ordain that no foreigner living out of the said Hundred of St. Briavels other than such as live in that part of Gloucestershire called the Forest Division containing the Hundreds of Blideslow, Westbury, Botloe and the Duchy of Lancaster shall or may at any time hereafter transport or carry away any coal contrary to the custom of the said Mine and Miners of the said Forest of Dean except it be carried and delivered to them by a free miner without the said Hundred of St. Briavels, upon pain of forfeiting one hundred dozen of good and sufficient fire coal the one-half &c., And that no free miner shall or may hereafter load any foreigner living out of the said Hundred of St. Briavels other than such as live within that part of Gloucestershire called the Forest Division with mine or coal with any manner of carriage whatsoever, upon the like penalty to be recoverable as aforesaid, Provided always and we do hereby allow that foreigners living within the said Hundreds of Blideslow, Westbury, Botloe and the Duchy of Lancaster may lawfully have and carry away such coal as aforesaid for their own proper use and expense not carrying the same to sell to others or upon hire or gift, nor hauling above twenty hundred weight at a load and paying 4d. for every hundred weight Beneath the Wood.

And it is hereby further ordered and ordained that no person or persons whatsoever shall carry or transport with any carriage whatsoever any mine [ore] or coal until he shall attain his full age of 21 years, upon pain of forfeiting the sum of £5, the one-half, etc.

1 Order No. 2.

And it is hereby further ordered and ordained that no person living Above the Wood shall carry any coal by water upon the River Wye higher than the parish church of Welsh Bicknor, And that no person living Beneath the Wood shall carry any coal by water upon the River Wye lower than the parish church of Welsh Bicknor aforesaid, And that no coal shall be pitched on any place on the bank of the River Wye between the said parish church of Welsh Bicknor and Monmouth Bridge, And if any person whatsoever shall offend in any the kind aforesaid such person shall forfeit for every such offence one hundred dozen of good and sufficient fire coal, the one-half &c.

And it is hereby further ordered and ordained that three Bargainers shall be made choice of living within the three parishes of Newland, English Bicknor and Staunton to bargain for all coal to be delivered for the use of the lime kilns at Monmouth on both sides the River Wye, And that Henry Griffith of Coleford, Yem Higgins of Staunton and Richard Wysham of English Bicknor be the present Bargainers, And that a Jury of twelve free miners with the approbation of two deputy Constables may from time to time appoint new Bargainers as there shall be occasion, and that the prices shall be 9s for every dozen barrells of fire coal, the sum of 8s for every dozen barrells of Smith coal and 5s. 6d. for every dozen barrells of lime coal delivered at Monmouth lime kilns aforesaid.

And it is further ordered and ordained that no free miner shall sell more than 36 bushels of lime coal for a dozen barrells nor shall sell any fire coal between Lidbrooke and Bishops Wood to send up the River Wye under 8s a ton, nor Smith coal there under 6s for every dozen barrells, nor any lime coal there under the rate of 3s for every dozen barrells, upon pain to forfeit one hundred dozen of good and sufficient coal, the one-half etc.; And also that no free miner Beneath the Wood upon the penalty aforesaid shall sell to another free miner any fire coal under the rate of 3s for every ton Beneath the Wood, And shall not sell above 21 hundred [weight] to the ton, and may weigh the same if they think fit.

And further the said Jury do order and ordain that Roynon Jones, Esq., and Edmund Probyn, Esq.,[1] be free miners within the said Forest to all intents and purposes whatsoever, and shall and may have and enjoy all and singular privileges and advantages as fully and amply as any free miner within the said Forest doth or may have and enjoy.

And lastly the Jury aforesaid do order that all former Orders relating to the said Miners, in whose custody soever they now are, be delivered to the above named William James, Esq., to be by him kept in the Miners' Chest now at the Speech House, And also that Mr. William Davies do deliver unto the said William James. Esq., all the records, writings, and papers in his custody or possession relating to this Court to be kept in the said Miners' Chest.

In testimony whereof etc.

Richd. Machen	Richard Godwin	John Worgan	James Worgan
Will. James	John Watkins	Edwd. Wilcox	John ?
John Everett	Isaac Morgan	James White	Rich. Bennett
Geo. James[2]	James Mutley	William Stephens	Jonathan Chapman
	John Trusted	Geo. Reynolds	John Griffith
	Wm. Lewis	Chr. Griffith	Phil. Youre
	John Hayward	Phil. Elly	Giles Brayne

continued

1 Grandfather of John Probyn, one of the Dean Forest Mining Commissioners.

2 All genuine signatures except James who made his mark. See Plate IV.

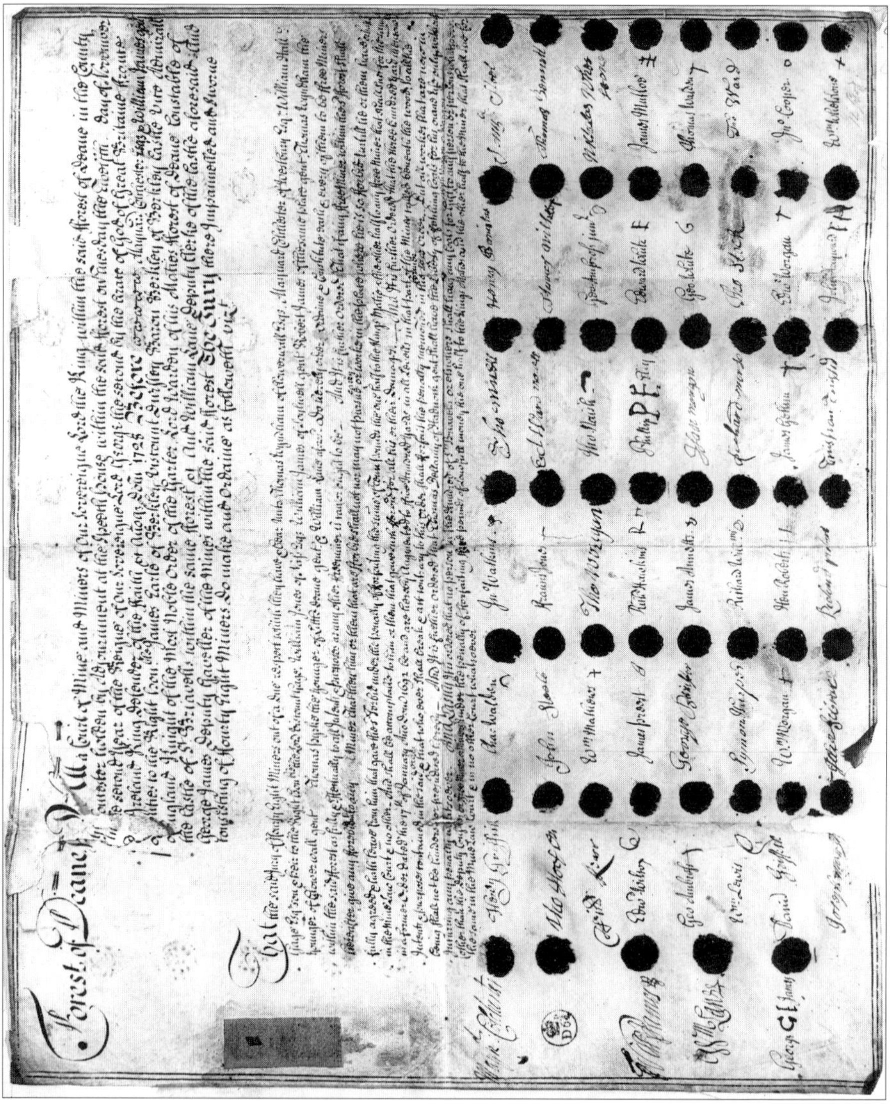

Plate IV. *A Mine Law Court Order of 1728.* *(See text pp. 115, 116.)*

continued	Richd. Bradley	Richd. Probert	John Meeke
	Jmm. Higins	Tho: Wysham	Hen. Griffith
	Charles Godwin	John Symons	Richd. Keare
	Arthur Symons	Edward Mousel	George Banister
	John Morse	Richd. Morse	Samuel Morse
	Richard Williams	Wm. Birt	Mathew Powell
	Hugh Powell	Chr. Davis	James ?
	Jeremiah Meeke	Henry Stephens	Charles Walding
	Walter Meeke	John Morse	John Grifflth'[1]

ORDER NO. 14 (12 NOVEMBER 1728)

'Forest of Deane. At a Court of Mine and Miners of Our Sovereign Lord the King within the said Forest of Dean in the County of Gloucester holden by adjournment at the Speech House within the said forest on Tuesday, the 12th November in the 2nd year of the reign of Our Sovereign Lord George the second etc. A.D. 1728. Before Maynard Colchester Esq. and William James gent, Deputies to the Right Honble. James Earl of Berkley etc., and William Lane deputy clerk of the Castle aforesaid, and George James deputy gaveller of the Mines with the said forest, the Jury there impannelled and sworn consisting of 48 miners etc.

6d. stamp

6d. stamp

That the said Jury of 48 miners out of a due respect which they have and bear unto Thomas Wyndham of Clowerwall, Esq., Maynard Colchester of Westbury, Esq., William Hall Gage, Esq., son and heir to the Right Honble the Lord Viscount Gage, William Jones of Nass, Esq., William James of Soylewell, gent., Robert James of the same place, gent, Thomas Wyndham the Younger of Clowerwall, gent, Thomas Pyrke the Younger of Little Deane, gent., Robert and William Lane aforesaid, do hereby order, ordain and constitute each and every of them to be free miners within the said forest as fully and effectually to all intents and purposes as any other free miner is, can and ought to be. And it is further ordered that if any free miner within the said forest shall hereafter give any forbidment to any Miner, that they, him or them that are forbid shall not nor may not pursue, carry on work in the place where his is so forbid until he or them have or hath fully agreed and hath leave from him that gave this Forbid under penalty of forfeiting the sum of £10, the one-half etc, And shall be accomptable to him or them that gave such forbid for all his or their damages. And it is further ordered that the 300 yards mentioned in a former Order dated the 17th January 1692[2] be and are hereby augmented to 500 yards in all levels in that part of the Mine called Beneath the Wood, to all the intents and purposes contained in the said Order, and that whoever shall break and act contrary to this Order shall forfeit the penalty mentioned in the former Order. But all works that are now in being shall not be hindered or prejudiced hereby. And it is further ordered that Thomas Bellamy of Hadnock, gent., shall have the liberty of fetching coals for his own use only without incurring any penalty whatsoever. And lastly it is ordered that no person in the Hundred of St. Briavels or elsewhere shall haul any coal for gift with waggon or waggons to any person or persons whatsoever (other than the deputy Constables or free miner or miners) under the penalty of forfeiting £5 of lawful money, the one-half etc.

1 About nineteen signed, the others making their marks.
2 Meant for 1693 (Order No. 8).

Maynd. Colchester	Henry Griffith	Tho. Hooper	Will. Keare
Will. James	Edwd. Wilcox	Geo. Ambrose	Wm. Lewis
Wm. Lane	David Griffith	Joseph Marshall	Cha. Walden
George James[1]	John Steele	Wm. Mathews	James Preest
	George Banister	Symon Harper	Wm. Worgan
	John Sibranco	Jno. Watkins	Francis Jones
	Tho. Worgan	Richd. Hawkins	James Annetts
	Richard Williams	Hen. Roberts	Richard Probert
	Tho. Mansel	Edward Mourall	Tho. Naish
	Philip Elly	John Morgan	Richard Morse
	James Gethin	Tristram Tingle	Henry Banister
	Thomas Wilkes	Geo. Ambrose	Edwin White
	Geo. White	Tho. Stock	Edwd. Worgan
	John Hayward	? Steel	Thomas Bennett
	Nicholas Whetstone	James Mutloe	Thomas Walden
	Tho. Ward	Jno. Cooper	Wm. Whetstone'[2]

A Court Record of 7 February 1730 has recently been discovered.[3]

ORDER NO. 15 (6 DECEMBER 1737)

'Deane Forest. *At a Court* of Mine and Miners of our Sovereign Lord the King within the Forest of Dean in the County of Gloucester holden by adjournment at the

6d. stamp

Speech House in the said Forest on Tuesday the 6th Dec. in the 11th year of the reign of our Sovereign Lord George the second etc. 1737, *Before* William Jones, Esq., deputy to the Right Honble Augustus Earl of Berkeley, constable of the Castle of St. Briavels etc. and William Lane, deputy clerk of the said

6d. stamp

Castle, and George James deputy gaveller of the Mines in the said Forest, The Jury there impannelled and sworn consisting of 48 free miners &c.

Whereas great abuses have of late been committed by loading of waggons and other carriages belonging to foreigners living in the counties of Hereford and Monmouth, who upon pretence of carrying of coals for their own use do transport or carry out of the said Forest into the said counties great quantities of coal, selling the same to others, and carrying upon hire to the great damage of the Miners of the said Forest, and is contrary to the Customs and to several Orders formerly made for the prohibiting any such foreigners being loaded with coals in the said Forest or within the limits thereof, for remedy therefore of the like abuses for the future *It is ordered* and ordained and the said Jury of 48 free miners do hereby order and ordain that no waggon or other carriage whatsoever, horses or other beasts belonging to any person or persons inhabiting in the counties of Hereford or Monmouth or of either of them shall after the day of the date hereof be loaded with any sort of coals or myne [ore] within the limits of the Hundred of St. Briavels aforesaid.

And that if any free miner or other person working at the mines within the said Hundred shall presume to load or permit and suffer any waggon or other carriage, horses or other beasts belonging to such foreigners as aforesaid to be loaded with his or their coals or mine

1 All genuine signatures except James who made his mark.

2 About twenty-two signed, the others making their marks.

3 See Appendix 7.

[ore], the person or persons so loading or permitting to load such foreigners' carriages, horses, or beasts as aforesaid within the limits of the said Hundred shall each of them forfeit and pay the sum of £5 of good and lawful money of this Kingdom the one-half thereof to the use of His Majesty his heirs and successors and the remaining half to the free miner who shall sue for the same in the Mine Law Court, where the said forfeiture shall be sued for and recovered and by an execution levied upon the goods and chattells of the person or persons respectively who shall by convicted at the said Court of the offences aforesaid. And if any person convicted as aforesaid of the said offence shall not have sufficient goods and chattells whereon to levy the said forfeiture, that then such offender shall be order of the said Court be committed to the Castle of St. Briavels aforesaid there to remain as a prisoner for the space of twelve months until the said forfeiture and the charges of committment shall be well and truly satisfied and paid, And that it shall and may be lawful to retain any such offender convicted of the said offence in custody until a Return be made of such Execution against the said offender's goods so that the same be made within the space of three days next after the Court where such conviction shall be made, to the end that if there cannot be found sufficient goods to satisfy the said forfeiture, the said offender may be committed in manner as aforesaid.

And for the more effectual distraining and prosecuting the persons who shall be guilty of loading foreigners' carriages or horses as aforesaid *It is further ordered* and ordained by the said Jury that if any verne or partner or person working for hire at any coal works within the said Hundred shall know and be privy to the loading of any such foreigners' carriages or horses in manner as aforesaid, and shall not within the space of three days next after such loading give notice thereof to the deputy gaveller of the Mines of the said Forest, and also give evidence of the same at the next Court to be held for the said Mines, that then all and every such person and persons being sued and convicted at a Mine Law Court of knowing of the said offence, and not discovering the same according to the true intent and meaning of this our Order shall forfeit and pay the same penalty or suffer imprisonment in like manner as for the actual loading of any such foreigners' carriages or horses. *Provided* always that whereas it hath been ordered by former Juries consisting of 48 free miners that John Vaughan of Courtfield, Esq., and Thomas Bellamy of Hadnock, yeo., both of the county of Monmouth should have the liberty of fetching coals out of the said Hundred of St. Briavels for their own use only notwithstanding any Law or Custom to the contrary, which said former Orders and grants made to the said John Vaughan and Thomas Bellamy we do hereby ratify and confirm, *And* we do hereby further order and grant the same liberty and privilege unto Herbert Westphaling of Rudhall in the county of Hereford, Esq., of fetching or causing to be fetched all such coals as shall be for his own use only, this or any former Order to the contrary therein anywise notwithstanding.

And whereas the above named William Lane hath for the space of nine years last past attended our Courts as a Clerk to enter the proceedings, and also hath drawn several Warrants, Orders and other writings relating to the Mines, and it appearing unto us by an accompt stated of the monies raised by the miners of this Forest in the year 1730 that the sum of £13 17s. do remain now in the hands of the said William Lane, *It is therefore* hereby *Ordered* that the said sum of £13 17s. be allowed unto the said William Lane for his services aforesaid And it is further ordered that for the future the Clerk attending the said Courts shall have and take 6d. of the plaintiff for entering every Action there and the like sum of every defendant for entering his plea, which said fees are and shall be in full satisfaction for the said Clerks attending the said Courts. But when any Order or other extraordinary writings are to be made the Clerk shall have reasonable satisfaction for the same. And we do further order that the sum of three guineas be paid unto William Davies. gent., in consideration of his being formerly Clerk of our Courts, upon condition that he delivers up all records and papers in his custody or procurement relating to the said Mines unto our Clerk or the deputy gaveller. And we do hereby make, ordain and constitute the following gentlemen to be free miners, and to have and enjoy all the rights and privileges of free miners within the said Forest and the liberties thereof (that is to say) The Honble Thomas Gage, Esq., Christopher Bond the Younger, Esq., Thomas Crawley, Esq., James Rooke, Esq., Thomas James, gent., Thomas Barron, gent. and Thomas Marshall of the parish of English Bicknor, yeoman.

And we do also give and grant unto Phillip Elly the Cryer of our Court all the liberties and privileges of a free miner excepting only that of carrying and transporting of coals out of the Hundred of St. Briavels or elsewhere.

And we do further order that no foreigner's son though born within the Hundred of St. Briavels shall hereafter be permitted to be a free miner unless he shall be bound as an apprentice for the term of seven years[1] to a free miner and do accordingly serve the said seven years in working at the mines, and to prevent any frauds the said Indentures shall be entered in the records of the Mine Law Court. *And* further we do order that any free miner shall have the liberty of carrying of coals for his own fire with one horse at any time whilst the four other horses are employed in carrying or transporting of coals elsewhere.

And likewise we do order that no person whatsoever shall be sued or prosecuted for loading or permitting any foreigner's waggons, or carriages to be loaded by virtue of any former Order made for that purpose. *And* we do agree that John Wade of the Tything of Clowerwall shall be made free on his working a year and a day according to the usual Custom. *And* further we do also give and grant unto Thomas Lilly of Hunsham, William Morgan of Coleford and Richard Bound of Labou [?] to have the liberty of fetching of coals for their own use and that that said William Morgan may sell the lime he makes of the coal he so fetches.

Willm. Jones	Thomas Palmer	William Thomas	Joseph Preest
Wm Lane	George Preest	William Beach	John Davies
George James[2]	John Symons	Hen. Hayward	Thomas Rudage
	William Trigge	John Steel	John M ?
	George Den	James Mathews	James Corry
	Anthony Worgan	Saml. Gething	Tristram Tingle
	John Godwin	Thomas Jenkins	Richard Wood
	William Tingle	James Bennett	John Bennett
	Tho: Monsell	Richd. Worgan	Jno. Hayward
	Wm. Aubry	George Churchay	George Ambrose
	John Cook	Peter James	Thomas Barrow
	James Gething	Richard Morse	Wm. Lewis
	Richd. Portimer	?	Thomas Gilbert
	Saml. Steel	Richd. Bradly	Thomas Morgan
	Richard Wheatstone	John Meek	Anth. Jones
	Richard Probert	Willm. Cowmeadow	John Elsmore'[3]

1 *Cf.* Orders Nos. 1 and 4.

2 All genuine signatures except James who made his mark.

3 About twenty-five signed, the others making their marks.

ORDER NO. 16 (2 MARCH 1741)

'Forest of Dean. At a Court of Mine and Miners of Our Sovereign Lord the King within the Forest of Dean in the county of Gloucester holden by adjournment at the Speech House within the said forest on 2nd March in the 15th year of the reign of our Sovereign Lord George the second &c., 1741, Before Edward Tomkins Machen, Esq., Deputy to the Right Honourable Augustus Earl of Berkeley &c, William Lane, deputy clark of the said Castle, and George James, deputy gaveller of the Mines within the said forest, the Jurors there impannelled and sworn consisting of 48 free miners &c.

Whereas the Mines of this Forest have time out of mind been divided into two parts and called or known by the several names of the Mines Above the Wood and the Mines Beneath the Wood, and the ancient bounds of the said parts we conceive to be, and we do hereby order and ordain that the bounds or limits between the said two parts of the Mines shall remain, continue and be as followeth (that is to say) Beginning at the River Wye at Lidbrooke, where the brook there leading from the forges falls into the said River, and so up the said brook or stream unto a place in the said forest called Moyery Stock, and from thence along a Wayn Way at the bottom of a place called the Sally Vellet, and so along the same way between the two old Enclosures that did belong to Rewardean and Little Deane Walks, unto Cannops Brook, and down the said brook to Cannops Bridge, and from thence along the road or highway to the Speech House, and from thence along the said highway to Foxes Bridge, and from thence down Blackpoole Brook to Blackney. *Provided* always that certain coal works near Lydbrooke aforesaid called or known by the name of Wyrrall Hill that now are or hereafter shall be carried on in the said Hill, and also another coal work called or known by the name of Dowlers Chambers, and likewise the coal works called Speedwell near Tresser Mill, shall each and every of them be deemed, accepted, reputed and taken to be in that part of the Mines called Beneath the Wood although they do not lie within the boundaries thereof as above described. *And* it is further ordered that where a free miner shall occupy coal works in both the said parts of the Mine at the same time such free miner shall serve on Juries for that part wherein he inhabiteth, but all other persons shall serve on the Jury for that part of the Mines wherein his works doth lie.

And we do likewise order and ordain that no miner belonging to or occupying any coal works in that part called Above the Wood shall hereafter sell any coals to any person or persons whatsoever that shall carry or cause, permit or suffer the same to be carried in any Barge or other Vessell on the River Wye between the city of Hereford and the town of Monmouth, neither shall any such miner send or carry himself, or permit or suffer, any of their coals to be so carried or water-borne on the said River between Hereford and Monmouth aforesaid, *And* that if any of the said miners shall break this Order in either of the said cases that each of them so offending shall forfeit and pay the sum of £5 of lawful money of this Kingdom, the one-half &c.

Provided always that it shall and may be lawful to pitch lime coal on the banks of the River Wye and carry the same by water for the use of certain lime kilns at a place called Baddhams Lays situate in the parish of Gannerew in the county of Hereford and now in the occupation of Phillip Price, upon condition that 4s for each dozen of the said lime coal delivered at New Weare Foard be well and truly paid, and that no more than 20 dozen of such coal be pitched at or near the said River at any one time, And likewise that Bargainers be always appointed for selling the said coals and delivering the same in manner as aforesaid. *And* we do hereby appoint George Dew and William Ambury to be the present Bargainers for that purpose, And do also order that it shall be in the power of a Jury of 12 free miners at any Mine Law Court to appoint new Bargainers from time to time as there shall be occasion.

And we do likewise order and ordain that no miner belonging to or occupying any coal work in that part called Beneath the Wood shall hereafter sell any coals to any person or persons whatsoever that shall carry or cause, permit or suffer the same to be carried in any Barge or other Vessell on the River Wye below an island in the said River over against Courtfield House near Lidbrooke aforesaid, neither shall any such miner send or carry himself or cause, permit or suffer any of their coals to be so carried or water-borne on the said River below the said island, *And* if any of the said miners shall break this our said Order in either of the said cases that each of them so offending shall forfeit and pay the sum of £5 of like lawful money to be sued for recovered and divided in manner as aforesaid.

And it is further hereby ordered that if any Barge or other Vessel shall be found with any coals on board at any place on the River Wye between Lydbrooke and Monmouth and the owner or master of the said Vessel shall not give or cause or procure to be given a true account upon oath at the next Mine Law Court of the name or names of the person or persons who sold or delivered the said coals being thereunto required by any free miner, that then and in such case it shall and may be lawful for any free miner to give a forbid to all other free miners or the whole Fellowship that none of them do load or permit or suffer the said vessel or any other belonging to the same owner to be loaded with coals for the future.

And for the better explaining some former Orders made in this Court, we do hereby order and establish that if any person or persons inhabiting within the liberties of the miners of that part of Gloucestershire called the Forest Division who is not duly admitted a free miner shall hereafter haul or carry any mine [ore] or coal (got or raised within the liberties of this forest) with any cart or other carriage or with any horse, mare, mule, ass or other beast but only for their own private use or uses or to or for the use of any deputy constable, all and every such person or persons so hauling or carrying for gift or for hire shall forfeit and pay the sum of £5 of lawful money to be divided, sued for and recovered in manner as aforesaid.

And we do further order that no person whatsoever shall for the future be admitted a free miner unless he can prove by the oath of two or more credible witnesses his lawfully working at coal or mine [ore] a year and a day.

And we do further order that no free miner that brings coal to the River Wye shall refuse any free miner who keep a Barge any sort of coal at the usual rates to be paid for in one month after it is bargained for, and if the free miner or Barge owner cannot meet with the proprietor of the said coal to bargain for it he shall leave word at the place of his abode that he designs to buy his coal and likewise what day he will load it in his Barge, and if the proprietor denyeth the said free miner or Barge owner he shall be guilty of breaking this our Order and forfeits the penalty above mentioned. *And* if any foreigner is suspected to sell coal to any of the inhabitants of the city of Hereford or the suburbs of the same under the price of 13s. per ton, any free miner shall summons him or his haulier to the next Mine Law Court to give satisfaction to the said Court, And if they refuse to obey the summons of the said free miner he shall have liberty to forbid the whole miners from loading any vessel belonging to the said foreigner any more, and if the said foreigner obey the said summons and cleareth himself the free miner that sued him shall pay the charges according to custom of the Court.

And whereas it may sometimes happen that more coals are brought to the said pitching places at Wye than can be disposed of at Hereford and the other usual places of selling coals, for remedying whereof it is hereby ordered that when and as often as complaint shall be made within the space of two years next ensuing at a Mine Law Court that it would be for the interest of the miners to stop the getting and carrying of coals to the said pitching places for some short time by six or more of such miners who have shares in such works so to be stopped (that is to say) three of the said miners having shares in the Hill Works near unto Rewardean and three other miners having shares in the Works near unto Serridge, that then and in such case only it shall be in the power of such Mine Law Court to make an order to stop the getting and carrying of any coals to the said River from all the coalworks from whence coal is usually carried to the pitching places at or near Lidbrooke for so long time as the said Court shall think proper – not exceeding three weeks at any one time, nor more times than twice in one year (that is to say) for three weeks between Michaelmas and Christmas and for other three weeks between Christmas and Ladyday, And if any person shall get or carry coal to the said River during the time the said Works are ordered to be stopped in manner aforesaid such coal so got or carried shall not be accepted or taken by any Barge owner, anything herein before to the contrary thereof in anywise notwithstanding. And such getter or carrier that shall break such order made at a Mine Law Court shall also forfeit and pay the sum of £5 of lawful money to be sued for, divided and recovered in manner as aforesaid.

Provided always that the Barge owners shall and do employ all such men as shall be stopped in their work by order of Court as aforesaid in hauling their Barges and allowing them the usual wages for so doing. And if any such man who is able to haul shall offer his services to a Barge owner for that purpose, and the said Barge owner shall not employ him or cause or procure him to be employed the said Barge owner shall forfeit and pay to the man so refused the same wages as shall be given to other men hauling Barges at the same time, and to be sued for and recovered in the Mine Law Court.

And we do likewise order that if any Barge owner whatsoever shall after the 25th day of March next coming sell or otherwise dispose of any fire coals at the city of Hereford under the rate of price of 13s. for each ton, that then and in such case it shall be in the power of any free miner to give a forbid to all the rest of the miners and owners of coals not to load the Barges or other Vessels of such owner that shall sell their coals there for a lesser price.

And it is hereby further ordered and ordained that all the getters and owners of coals in that part called Beneath the Wood shall allow two hundreds and one quarter wt. of coals for each Horse Seam and at the price of 6d. at the pit, and that no more weight shall be carried upon any horse or other beast to the River Wye or any other place for the use of foreigners, and that ten such seams pitched at Wye shall be accepted and taken for a ton of coals, And the buyer or seller to weigh the said coals there if either of them think fit, And if any seller of coal shall refuse to deliver such weight of coals for 6d. or shall not provide sufficient scales and weights for the weighing of it when required, shall forfeit and pay for each time the sum of 2s. 6d. to the said buyer to be sued for and recovered in the Mine Law Court. No free miner living Beneath the Wood shall sell no more fire coal than one hundred weight for 4d. and no more than three bushels of Smith coal for 5d. and lime coal for 1d. a bushel at the coalpit to any person living out of the Hundred of St. Briavels, nor shall load any more than two hundred weight upon one horse, mare, mule, ass or other beast, nor more than twentyone hundred in any team or carriage belonging to any person living out of the Hundred aforesaid, the deputy constable only excepted, And to weigh the said coal at the pit into any waggon, wayn or other carriage it shall be loaded into, And whatever free miner refuseth to obey this Order shall forfeit the sum of £5 to be sued for and recovered and divided in manner as aforesaid.

No person living Above the Wood shall deliver any more than twentyone hundred weight of fire coal for 7s/6d. weighed and delivered at Lidney Pill or at Pyrton Pill or at Gatcomb under the penalty of £5 to be sued for and recovered in the Mine Law Court in manner as aforesaid.

The vearns belonging to the levels which are between Drybrooke and Cannops Bridge and between Seridge and Rewardean Town shall get coal out of not more than two pits at one time belonging to one level till the said two pits are worked quite out, And those who keep two pits in work or one level shall not sink any other new pit till the old ones are quite worked out and done with for the use of getting coal, under the penalty of £5 to be sued for, recovered and divided as aforesaid.

And we do further order and ordain that no free miner in that part called Above the Wood shall carry any more than three bushels of coals (Winchester measure) upon one horse or other beast to the Copper works at Read Brooke, the town of Monmouth or to any lime kilns, and shall carry no more than two hundreds and one quarter of coal to any foreign teams on any horse or other beast, And if any person shall load or carry more than three bushels as aforesaid shall each of them forfeit the sum of 2s. 6d., And any person carrying more than two hundreds and one quarter weight on any horse or other beast to foreign teams as aforesaid shall forfeit the said sum of 2s. 6d. to be sued for. recovered and divided in manner as aforesaid.

And it is also ordered that all the miners Above the Wood shall have the same liberty of carrying with horses or other beasts so much fire coal, Smith coal and stone coal charks that shall be wanted at either of the Copper Works at Red Brooke and shall all and every of them have and receive the prices following for the coals respectively at the said Copper Works (that is to say) for fire coal and stone coal charks 7s. for each dozen, and for Smith coal 5s. 6d. for each dozen, And if any miner shall sell or deliver any coals at the said works at any other or lower prices he or she shall forfeit and pay the sum of £5 of lawful money to be sued for, recovered and divided as aforesaid, And it is hereby further ordered that if any good and merchantable coals of any or either of the sorts above mentioned shall be refused by the proprietors or agents belonging to the Copper works aforesaid that then the owner of the coal so refused shall and may forthwith give a forebid to all other miners for delivering any coals to the said works until the coals so refused are first taken and accepted of at the prices above mentioned.

And we further order that no free miner Above the Wood or Beneath the Wood shall hereafter carry on any new coalworks or get any coal for any person who is not a free miner, upon the penalty of forfeiting and paying the sum of £5 of lawful money to be sued for, recovered and divided in manner as aforesaid, but this Order shall not prejudice the owners or proprietors of any works that is now in being though they are not free miners.

And it is further ordered that if any of the free miners above said shall happen to bring less than three bushels of coal on each horse or beast to the said Copper works that then they shall be allowed and paid in proportion to the rate above mentioned for what coal they have or bring.

And we the said Jury of 48 free miners do hereby request and desire that Richard Clarke and Edward Tomkins Machen, Esquires, two of the Judges of this Court, that they will be pleased to accept of being admitted into our Society of Free Miners, and we do accordingly order that the said Richard Clarke and Edward Tomkins Machen be and are hereby declared to be free miners to all intents and purposes, and also that the said Richard Clarke shall and may have full and free liberty of fetching coals with waggons or other carriages for his own horses use, notwithstanding any former Order to the contrary heretofore.

We do also order that the Articles left in Thomas Terret's hands of Rewardean be void and of none effect.

It is likewise ordered that if any free miner liveth Above the Wood and occupieth or is an owner of any share in a coalwork Beneath the Wood, he shall have the privilege of carrying and selling the coal gotten at the works Beneath the Wood to Lidbrooke or any other pitching place Beneath the Wood.

Edwd. Tomkins Machen
George James[1]

George Dene
George White
Henry Willcox
James Mullen
Anthony Worgan
William Lewis
William Fox
Thomas Drinkwater
William Webb
Richard Hawkins
George White
Thomas Worgan
John Teynolds
Thomas Beach
Robert Cowmeadow
James Bennett
Thomas Trested
William White
Richard Elley
William Webb
Samuel Gething
John Dukes
Thomas Evans
Samuel Brinworth

Charles Godding
John Godin
William White
William Tingle
William Biby
Samuel Trigge
James Drew
Samuel Trigge Jnr.
William Phillips
John Elsmore
Henry Heane
James Morgan
John Sladen
Richard Reynolds
Thomas Mounjoy
Jesiah Williams
William Worgan
John Phillips
William Webb
William Mousell
Thos. Higgins
Richard Wood
Geo. Williams
Thomas Lewis'[2]

Numerous cases of 'miner against miner', 1706-1777, are extant.[3] The next recorded session, although no Order was made at it, was held at the Speech House on 13 December 1748. The manuscript[4] reads as follows:

1 Machen signed, but James made his mark.
2 About eighteen signed, the others making their marks.
3 Glos.R.O. D9096, F26/1
4 N.H., pp. 283-4.

'Forest of Deane to witt.	At a Court of Mine and Miners of Our Sovereign Lord the King, held at the Speech-House in and for the Forest of Dean, on Tuesday, the 13th December, in the year of Our Lord 1748, before Christopher Bond Esq., and Thomas James, gentleman, deputies to the Right Honourable Augustus, Earl of Berkeley, Constable of the Castle of St. Briavels, in the County of Gloucester, Christopher Bond, Esq., gaveller of the said mines, and Philip Elly, deputy gaveller of the said mines.

The names of the Jury – Richard Powell, Simon Bannister, George Thomas, Frances Dutheridge, William Kerr, Richard Hawkins. Joseph Cooper, Samuel Kerr, Henry Roberts, William Meeke, Richard Tingle, James Teague.

William Gagg otherwise Smith, and his Vearns, against James Bennett and his Vearns:
I complain against William Gagge and his Vearns for hindering our level and doing of us wilful trespass, whereby we have sustained great damage, at a stone (lime) coal work called Churchway, otherwise Turnbrooke, in the Hundred of Saint Briavels, (as this,) they hindered the level and deepwall they would not bring forward to our new pit that was then just down. I asked them the reason, and they told me it was to make coal scarce and men plenty; they went back sixteen or eighteen weeks into their scale, contrary to the rule and custom of all free miners Beneath the Wood with us; and likewise before, they hindered the level in their new deep pit. And wilfully more they cut up to their land gutter, and took in the water by a single sticken gutter in their backer deep pit, and turned it across the bottom of our deep pit into our air gutter, which we prepared for ourselves and them, whereby our lamping the charks was swelled down, and have destroyed the air, and filled our gateway with water and sludge, and very likely to destroy the levels, and put us by getting a scale of coal there. And by their so doing, I and my vearnes are damnified £30. All this I will prove myself and by evidence in the King's mine.'

We leave this to the best proof and the order.

It would appear that a further session was held on or about 20 January 1753 for a lawsuit, mentioned later,[1] is recorded under that date.

ORDER NO. 17 (22 OCTOBER 1754)

'Forest of Dean	*At* the Court of Mine and Miners of Our Sovereign Lord the King holden at the Speech House within the said forest on Tuesday the 22nd October last past in the 28th year of the reign of our Sovereign Lord George the second &c. Before Maynard Colchester and Thomas James Esquires. Deputies to the Right Hon. Augustus, Earl of Berkeley &c. And Thomas Baron the Younger, gentleman, clerk of the said Castle and Phillip Elly deputy gaveller of the Mines there, And from that day continued by several adjourments at the Speech House aforesaid to Tuesday this 19th November in the said Year of our Lord 1754 and then held before the said Maynard Colchester, Thomas James, Thomas Baron and Phillip Elly, The Jury of 48 free miners &c.
6d. stamp 6d. stamp 6d. stamp	

[1] See p. 128.

Imprimis. The jury aforesaid do unanimously constitute, order, ordain, admit and make The Rt. Hon. George Augustus Lord Dursley, Charles Wyndham of Clowerwall, Esquire, The Reverend Roynon Jones of Monmouth, Clerk, John Probyn of Newland Esquire, Edmund Probyn Esquire, son of the said John Probyn, Maynard Colchester the Younger, Esquire. Roynon Jones the Younger of Nass Esquire, Kedgwin Webley of London, Gentleman, Kedgwin Hoskins the Elder of Clowerwall, Gentleman, William Probyn the Younger of Newland, Gentleman, Mr. Kedgwin Hoskins the Younger of Clowerwall, Mr. Edmund Probyn the Younger son of the said William Probyn, Mr. Thomas James the Younger, Mr. Thomas Baron the Younger son of Mr. Thomas Baron of Colford, Herbert Rudhall Westfaling of Rudhall in the county of Hereford, Esquire, John Clark of the Hill in the said county of Hereford, Esquire, Thomas Foley the Elder of Stoke Eddy in the said county of Hereford, Esquire, Thomas Foley the Younger of the same, Esquire, and John Symons of the Meen in the said county of Hereford, Esquire, and each and every of them, free miners of the said forest of Dean to all intents and purposes whatsoever, *And the said Jury* do also as much as in them lie resolve, ordain, order and agree that they the said Lord Dursley, Charles Wyndham, Roynon Jones, Clerk, John Probyn, Edmund Probyn, Maynard Colchester the Younger, Roynon Jones the Younger, Kedgwin Webley, Kedgwin Hoskins the Elder, William Probyn, Kedgwin Hoskins the Younger, Edmund Probyn the Younger, Thomas James the Younger, Thomas Baron, Herbert Rudhall Westfaling, John Clarke, Thomas Foley the Elder, Thomas Foley the Younger, and John Symons and each and every of them shall and may from henceforth have, use, occupy and enjoy all and all manner of rights, liberties, privileges, franchises and advantages whatsoever of and belonging to the Mine and Miners therein, in as full, large, ample and beneficial manner and form as any other free miner or free miners within the said forest doth or do or can may or shall or might could should or ought to have and enjoy the same.

And the said Jury do also as much as in them lie further resolve, order, ordain and agree that they the said Herbert Rudhall Westfaling, John Clarke, Thomas Foley the Elder, Thomas Foley the Younger and John Symons and each and every of them shall have liberty to fetch (with their own teams only and not otherwise) fire coal or lime coal out of the said Forest of Dean for their and each and every of their own private use and benefit only without any let, suit, trouble or denial to them or any or either of them or to any other free miner or free miners loading or permitting them or any or either of them to load or carry away such fire coal or lime coal, any law, custom or usage of the said free miners heretofore made to the contrary thereof in anywise notwithstanding.

Item. The Jury aforesaid do also further resolve, ordain, order and agree to make John Yate of Arlingham in the county of Gloucester Esq., William Lane of King Standley in the said county of Gloucester, gentleman, and Barrow Laurence of Breems Lodge in the said county, gentleman, and each and every of them be free miners of the said Forest of Dean to all intents and purposes whatsoever. John Vaughan of Courtfield in the county of Monmouth, Esq., to fetch coal for his own use only. *Whereas* William Philips of the Lea in the said county and George Dew of Huntsome and John Bennett of Ruardean (for the use of his house and labour in barn and lime kilns) and each and every of them to fetch coals for their own use only.

And the said Jury do further order and ordain that no free miner or miners shall or may sink any water pit and get coal out of it Above and Beneath the Wood within the limits or bounds of 1,000 yards of any free miner's level to prejudice that level; if they do they shall forfeit the penalty of the Order which is £5, one-half etc.

And it is further ordered and agreed upon by the authority aforesaid that the Water Wheel Ingine[1] at the Orling Green near Broadmoor in the said forest of Dean be taken to be and is hereby deemed and declared to be a level to all intents and purposes and liable to the same laws and restrictions as other levels brought up from the Grass Moore. *And we do also agree* that Mr. Woodward of the Hill in the county of Monmouth shall have leave to fetch coal for his own use only.

Mayn. Colchester	Edn. Mousel Jnr.	John Banister	John Morse
Thos: James	Thos. Keare	Jno. Rannels	William Phillips
Phill. Elly[2]	Symon Banister	William Skinn	John Bennett
	James Bennett	Wm. Howell	Thomas Mountjoy
	Thomas Barrow	John Ward	John Tyler
	Thos. Mansell	Richard Wilcocks	William Dukes
	James Elsmore	John Morse Jnr.	John Cradock
	John Davis	William Moore	John Eddy
	Samuel Steel	Wm. Ambery	Wm. Bennett
	Richard James	William Tingle	Samuel Gethin
	John Court	Richard Hawkins	Thomas Gething
	John Rannells	William Watkins	William Collins
	George Wintle	Wm. Thomas	Henry Tyler
	Richard Jones	William Manning	John Stephens
	Thomas Wilce	Christofer Davis	Richard Probert
	John Knight	William Turner	Anth. Andrews'[3]

This was the last recorded Order made by the Mine Law Court. However, a session of the Court seems to have taken place in 1775 for David Mushet in a Memorial dated 12 April 1833[4] refers to 'resolutions passed in 1775' in which the connection of persons not free miners 'with the mines is fully and clearly established, as well as the right of the free miner to sell or bequeath his property in the mines to any persons he may think proper; which facts may be gathered from the four following clauses in that general resolution:

'8. Every miner or collier may give his mine or coal works to any person that he will, but if he does give it by will, that person, if required, shall bring the testament, and show it to the Court, but if it is a verbal will, he shall bring two witnesses to testify the will of the miner.

16. Foreigners having any mine or coal work carried on in the Hundred of St. Briavels, shall sell it to some free miner by private contract if they can, or otherwise expose it to sale by auction, by the Mine Law Court.

1 Galed to 'foreigners', but subsequently conveyed to them at different times in shares to various persons, including the gaveller by whom the first fire-engine was put up in 1777. The 4th Rpt. (dated 25 August 1835) gives the date of galing as 1766. The machine was evidently the first of its kind erected in the Forest, as was also the steam-engine which superseded it, each manifesting the improvements in the method of working the mines.

2 All genuine signatures.

3 More than half signed, the others making their marks.

4 4th Rpt. of 1835. pp. 44-5. Unfortunately it has not been possible to find a full copy of the resolutions.

17. If a free miner dies and leaves his mine or coal works by will or testament to a foreigner, or it come to him by heirship or marriage, he shall sell it as aforesaid, or hire free miners to work it for him.
18. If any free miner sells any mine or coal work to a foreigner, he shall be liable to a penalty of £20, to be recovered in the Mine Law Court.'

A Memorial presented to the Commissioners of 1831 by the free miners on 24 September 1834[1] refers (wrongly) to the above session of the Court as being held in September 1775 'which was the last year in which the Mine Law Courts met'. The Memorial continues:

> 'The foreigners finding the Mine Law Courts an unsuperable obstacle to their success, and more particularly that by the orders last quoted of 1775, there was no chance of their being permitted to work in the mines, found that the only means by which they could hope for success was to destroy the Mine Law Courts.
> The documents of this Court were always kept in the Speech House, but that after the conclusion of the last Court in 1777 some person or persons broke open the chest in which they were contained and removed them.
> The free miners from that period to the present have made repeated applications to the wardens and the gavellers respecting these orders and documents, but that the wardens and gavellers, while they declared that they could not hold the Mine Law Courts as usual without these documents, at the same time denied all knowledge of their existence.
> The free miners themselves, in fact, never heard of these documents again till the present inquiry before your Honourable Board, when Mr. Tovey, the King's gaveller, produced them to your Honourable Board.'

The last session of the Mine Law Court was held on the 25 August 1777.[2] A memorandum with which its last minute was endorsed reads: 'Mine Law Court, 25 August 1777. There has been no Court holden for the miners since this day, which is a great loss to the gaveller, and causes various disputes amongst the colliers, which is owing to the neglect of the Deputy Constables.' Various reasons have been given for the discontinuance of the Mine Law Courts. The free miners failed to agree in their verdicts, and the gentlemen of the neighbourhood refused to attend owing to the violent quarrels and disputes which arose between the free miners themselves and between them and 'foreigners'. It is also reported that the decisions of the Court were often not observed, no Act of Parliament having been passed to make them valid. The quarrels were an unfortunate feature. No coalfield or iron ore field offered such a chance of ideal conditions as Dean, yet the stupidity and disputes of the miners buckled the chance. In any case, gradually common law was bound to oust mine law. In evidence before the Commissioners of 1788, the then gaveller, George Caesar Hopkinson, stated[3]:

1 4th Rpt. of 1835, pp. 44-5.
2 Glos.R.O. D9096, F26/1: 1706-1777. See Appendix 6.
3 3rd Rpt. of 1788, App. XXV, p. 91.

'That a court called the Mine Law Court was formerly held at the Speech House in the Forest, by the deputy wardens and deputy constables of the Forest, for the regulation of all matters relating to the mines and for settling disputes and questions between the miners, at which court the gaveller or his deputy used to attend to receive all fines imposed for any offences cognizable by the court, and all other profits due to the king; but that for some years past the deputy wardens and deputy constables have discontinued holding the court, but for what reason this examinant knoweth not. That while the Mine Law Court continued to be held the payment of the dues and compositions were enforced in a speedy and effectual manner but since the court had been discontinued the gaveller had been put to great trouble and expense in bringing actions for recovering the same.'

Other relevant evidence was given to the Commissioners. Maynard Colchester stated[1] that the office of deputy warden and deputy constable 'is to preside at the Miners' or Mine Law Court, to try all offences committed against the miners' laws and to enforce due obedience to them by all those who are amenable thereto', while Joseph Pyrke deposed:[2] 'The place of deputy constable of the Forest of Dean, was in the first institution, to hold courts, in order to settle disputes between the miners; but no Act of Parliament having ever passed to render the decisions valid, they are seldom adhered to; and of late years the courts have been discontinued. The place has no perquisite, fee, or salary, no tenement belonging to it, or any Walk; it is held at pleasure under Lord Berkeley.'[3]

Examples are given below of (I) a Mine lawsuit of 1753. (II) a Mining Agreement of 1754, (III) a Mining 'Forbid' of 1775, and (IV) a Warrant for Timber of 1784:

(I) Mine Law Suit, dated 20 January 1753[4]:

'William Dukes and his vernes, plaintiffs, against William Keare and his vernes, defendants. We complain against William Keare and his vernes for wrongfully forbidding us out of a stone coal work, called the Gentlemen Colliers, within the Hundred of St. Briavels, that we should not get any coal of the deep side of our former work, which coal our level drains, and ours being the most ancient level. We have attended the place, and burned our light, according to our laws and customs, and through this wrong forbid we are damnified £5. And whereas several forbids have been given before, we, the aforesaid plaintiffs and defendants, left the same to the determination of Charles Godwin and Richard James, and we the said plaintiffs have duly observed the said determination, and that the said defendants have gone contrary to an order made by 48 free miners in getting of coal that our level would have drained, and have damnified our level, whereby they have forfeited the penalty of the said Order. And this we will prove by evidence, and the damages in getting coal we will leave to the Order in Ct.

We leave this to the best evidence.

We deny the forbid given to him or his vernes. We forbid them in getting any coal betwixt our work and theirs, except their level could dry it fairly. There was an agreement betwixt us, and they went contrary to the agreement, and this we will prove ourselves and by witnesses.'

1 3rd Rpt. of 1788. App. XVII

2 *Ibid.*, App. XX.

3 Charles, Earl of Berkeley, an ancestor of the then Lord Berkeley, was, in 1703, granted 'the offices of holding and keeping of the Mine Law Court' (C.S.P.D. Anne 1703-4, p. 465).

4 N.H., p. 284.

(II) Copy of an Agreement[1] (1754) (resembling that mentioned above):

'August the 8th. – In the year of our Lord 1754. An award, or an Agreement, made by Richard Powell, John Jenkins, Wm. Thomas, Thos. Worgan, and James Elsemore, betwixt James Bennet and his vearns, belonging to a coal work called by the name of Upper Rockey, and Robert Tingle and his vearnes, belonging to the Inging Coale Work near the Nail Bridge, within the Hundred of Saint Bravewells; and we have farther agreed that the fore said James Bennet and his vearns shall have the liberty of getting what coal their leavel will dry without being interrupted, but they shall not get coal by the strength of hauling or laveing of water within the bounds of Robert Tingle and his vearns, except to drowl their work, under the forfet of the sum of £5; and we do farther agree that Robert Tingle and his vearns shall come in at any time to see if they do carry on their work in a proper manner without trespassing them; and if the fore-said James Bennet and his vearns do interrupt them for coming in to see their work, they shall forfeit the sum of £5.
And we do order the parties to stand to their expenses share share alike, and the viewers to be paid between both parties, which is fifteen shillings.

The mark of Richd. Powell.
The mark of John Jenkins.
The mark of James Elsmore.
The mark of Wm. Thomas.
The mark of Thos. Worgan.'

(III) Specimen of an official 'Forbid'[2] (1775):

'Thomas Hobbs. I do hereby, in his Majesty King George the Third's name, being owner and chief gaveller of his Majesty's Forest of Dean, in the county of Gloucester, and of the coal and mines therein, forbid you, your verns, your servants, agents, or workmen, for getting, digging, or raising any more stone coal out of any fire pitt or pitts, or water pitt or pitts, a deep the Majors [Wade's] suff level gutter in the said Forest, or to permit or suffer any stone coal to be got, dug, or raised out of any such pitt or pitts, until you have satisfied and paid me his Majesty's gale and dues for working and getting coal in such pitts for two years last past, and until you agree with me for the gale and dues of such pitt and pitts for the future. If you break this forbid, you will incur the penalty of an Order made by forty-eight free miners.

Dated this 22nd day of May, 1775 { John Robinson, &c., deputy gaveller.'

(IV) Copy of a Warrant or Order for the Delivery of Timber to a Coal Miner in Dean Forest[3] (1784):

'Forest of Dean { AT the Court of Attachments, holden at the Speech House the 25th Day of Sept[r] 1784, came *Phil Hatton,* and demanded Timber for himself and Verns, for the Use of their Coal Works called *Young Colliers* in *Ruardean* Walk, within the said Forest, according to custom.

Jno. MATTHEWS, Stew[d].

1 N.H., pp. 284-5
2 *Ibid.*, p. 285. As to 'forbids', see Order No. 14, p. 115.
3 App. XXXVI to 3rd Rpt. of 1788 (p. 105).

To Mr. John Bradley, keeper of the said Walk, by Certificate.
Some Timber to be delivered fit for sinking.'
Indorsed '4 Oakes'.[1]

As a further example of litigation, the following is given: in 1751, Maynard Colchester, William Jones and Thomas James were selected as Arbitrators in a mining lawsuit respecting a coal level called 'The Windmill'. The case was rendered peculiarly embarrassing by the position of the parties at issue, as will be seen from their 'award' given below[2]:

'Whereas, upon the Evidence of the Plaintiffs, Willm. Philips and his Vearnes & Edward Tomkins Machen. Esq.,[3] Defendant in an Action brought here by the Parties the last Court and agreed to be referred to us. – We do think and are of opinion that the Plaintiffs by Ancient Custom have an undoubted right to the Worke in question there being no Gale or Worke prior theirs. But in as much as the Defendant, some time before this Worke was Galed to the Plaintiffs, demanded the Gale of it to himself, which the gaveller neglected to do & at the same time gave Assurances to the Defendant that he would Gale the same to no other Person or Persons. We are of opinion his Gavelling it to others afterwards is a hardship on the owner and appears to be done by surprise since he the gaveller has a share and is interested in these worke, had not yet been the fact the Award must have been in favour of the Plaintiff but We apprehend the Defendant would have had it Galed to him had it not been through the omission of the gaveller,We see no reason he should suffer by such neglect, We do therefore Award in and for the Defendant, – Provided always if the said Defendant does not make use of the Worke or carry the same into Execution then the Miners at large are at Liberty to have the same Galed to him and work the same. Given under our hands this 17th of December.

Maynd. Colchester.
Wm. Jones.
Thos. James.'

Of course this Award was not satisfactory to the plaintiffs, but what further steps were taken, if any, do not appear.

It is interesting to note the procedure adopted in the conferring of 'honorary free minerships'. That in connection with Mr. William Jones of Naas and others was mentioned in the *Gloucester Journal* of 2 November 1728 as follows:

'They write from Coleford of the first instant that at a Mine Law Court holden at the Speech House in the Forest of Dean, on Tuesday last, it was unanimously resolved by a Jury of 48 Free Miners, that at their next meeting which will be the 12th instant, they will Complement

---

1 Edmund Probyn stated to the Coms, of 1788: 'The number of trees delivered to the miners, to carry on their coal and mine works, are annually returned on oath by the keepers to the verderers at Swanimote Court, and recorded by the steward of the court. The keepers always receive orders at the court to fell no more trees than are absolutely for the mine works.' (3rd Rpt. of 1788. App. XVIII, dated 7 June 1787). For a discussion as to free timber, see PRO F20/1 (17).

2 N.P., p. 75.

3 He was made an honorary free miner in 1741.

the following gentlemen with their Freedom, viz., The Hon. Thos. Wyndham, Esq., and his son, Maynard Colchester, Esq., the eldest son[1] of Roynon Jones Esq., and Mr. William James, Clerk of the Peace; which piece of Honour is to be granted to them in Consideration of the manifold Services which these Gentlemen's Predecessors have done for the Fraternity of Free Miners. And its not to be doubted, but the Parliament of Free Miners will be all Gentlemen on this Occasion.'

On 12 November William Jones was duly elected, the following being a copy of the manuscript in which the event is recorded:[2]

'Forest of Deane, &c. Att a Court of Mine and Miners of our Sovereigne Lord the King within the said fforest of Deane in the County of Gloucester holden by adjournment att the Speech House within the said fforest on Tuesday the Twelfth day of November in the Second Year of the Reigne of our Sovereigne Lord George the Second by the Grace of God of Great Britaine, ffrance and Ireland King defender of the ffaith, &c., ano. Dom. 1728. BEFORE Maynard Colchester Esq. & William James Gent, deputies to the Right honble. James Earle of Berkeley &c., &c., Lord Warden of his Maties fforest of Deane, constable of St. Briavell's Castle within the same fforest &c., and William Lane deputy clarke of the Castle aforesaid. And George James deputy gaveller of the Mines within the said fforest. The JURY there Impannelled and sworne consisting of ffourty eight Miners Do make and ordaine as followeth viz:–

THAT the said Jury of ffourty eight Miners out of a due Respect which they have and bear unto WILLIAM JONES gent son and Heir apparent unto Roynon Jones of Nass Esq. one of the deputy constables of the said Castle of St. Briavells doe humbly pray him the said William Jones to do the said Miners the honour of being one of their Society. AND they do accordingly Order, Ordaine and establish hereby that the said William Jones be constituted and made a Free Miner within the said fforest as fully and effectually to all intents and purposes as any other ffree Miner within the said fforest is can or ought to be.

IN WITNESS whereof the said deputy constable, gaveller and castle clerke and also the said ffourty eight Miners have hereunto sett their hands and seals in open Court holden at the time and place above mentioned.'[3]

It will have been seen that the meeting places of the thirty-two recorded sessions of the Mine Law Court were as follows:

Clearwell:	1668, 1674, 1675, 1676 (twice), 1682, 1685 (twice). 1687, 1693, 1694, 1701.
The Speech House:	1680, 1717, 1719, 1728, 1737, 1741, 1748, 1754.
Mitcheldean:	1707 (adjourned to Coleford).
Coleford:	1676 (twice), 1677, 1707 (an adjournment of the one held at Mitcheldean).
Littledean:	1656.
Ruardean:	1700.
Place unknown:	1698, 1699, 1718, 1753, 1775, 1777.

1 William Jones.

2 Nicholls (N.P., p. 77) states that the parchment existed in the family archives.

3 Here followed their signatures, forty-eight in number.

The names of those who presided over the various sessions are given as follows (in those years marked with an asterisk (*) the office was shared):

George Bond (of Redbrook): 1693,* 1694,* 1701,* 1707.*
Tracy Catchmay (of Bigsweir): 1693.*
Col. Maynard Colchester (of Westbury): 1728,* 1754.*
John Higford (of Alvington): 1693,* 1694.*
William James (of Soylewell[1]): 1717,.* 1719,* 1728.*
Thomas James (of Soylewell): 1748,* 1754.*
Roynon Jones (of Nass): 1707.*
William Jones (of Nass): 1737.
Richard Machen (of English Bicknor): 1717,* 1719.*
Edward Tomkins Machen (of English Bicknor): 1741.
Henry Milbourne: 1677, 1682.*
Sir Baynham Throckmorton, Jnr. (of Clearwell): 1668, 1674, 1676, 1680.
Christopher Bond: 1748.*[2]
Thomas Hodges: 1656.
Sir George Probert: 1675, 1676 (thrice).
William Wolseley: 1682,* 1685, 1687.
William Powlett: 1701.*

The person or persons who presided in 1698, 1699, 1700, 1718, 1753, 1775 and 1777 are not known.

The total number of recorded honorary free miners is 53, namely:

1674: Henry, Marquis of Worcester (constable); Sir Baynham Throckmorton, Jnr. (deputy constable).
1701: Francis Wyndham (of Clearwell).
1717: The Hon. Matthew Ducie Morton; Thomas Gage; John Wyndham; Richard Machen; William James; Christopher Bond; Thomas Pyrke.
1719: Roynon Jones; Edmund Probyn.
1728: Thomas Wyndham (of Clearwell); Col. Maynard Colchester (of Westbury); William Hall Gage (of Highmeadow); William Jones (of Nass); William James (of Soylewell); Robert James (of Soylewell); Thomas Wyndham the younger (of Clearwell); Thomas Pyrke the younger (of Littledean); William Lane (deputy clerk).
1737: The Hon. Thomas Gage (of Highmeadow); Christopher Bond the younger; Thomas Crawley; James Rooke; Thomas James; Thomas Barron; Thomas Marshall (of English Bicknor); Phillip Elly (Court Crier).
1741: Richard Clarke; Edward Tomkins Machen (of English Bicknor).
1754: The Rt. Hon. George Augustus Lord Dursley; Charles Wyndham (of

1 Sully or Soilwell.
2 Appointed in 1737 as an honorary free miner (Glos.R.O. D2026, F18) Appointed 1746 as gaveller by the Earl of Berkeley (*Ibid.*, F.21)

Clearwell); Rev. Roynon Jones (of Monmouth); John Probyn (of Newland); Edmund Probyn (of Newland); Maynard Colchester the younger; Roynon Jones the younger (of Nass); Kedgwin Webley (of London); Kedgwin Hoskins the elder (of Clearwell); William Probyn the younger (of Newland); Kedgwin Hoskins the younger (of Clearwell); Edmund Probyn the younger (of Newland); Thomas James the younger (of Soylewell); Thomas Baron the younger (of Coleford); Herbert Rudhall Westfaling (of Rudhall in Herefordshire); John Clarke (of 'The Hill' in Herefordshire); Thomas Foley the elder (of Stoke Edith in Herefordshire); Thomas Foley the younger (of Stoke Edith in Herefordshire): John Symons (of Mine in Herefordshire); John Yate (of Arlingham); William Lane (of King Stanley in Gloucestershire); Barrow Laurence (of Breems Lodge).

It will be seen that the list includes, in addition to deputy constables, holders of the offices of deputy gaveller, deputy surveyor, deputy clerk and court crier. Of the above, Edward Tomkins Machen is the only one who is known to have directly held an interest in a gale. The lapsing of the Mine Law Courts in 1777 ended the conferring of honorary memberships, and in any case this practice was made illegal by the Dean Forest (Mines) Act of 1838.

In 1807 the free miners held a meeting at which a resolution[1] was passed earnestly requesting the Warden of the Forest to hold a Mine Law Court as soon as possible with a view to regulating the levels, pits and engines. Nothing, however, appears to have been done about the matter. Within the next quarter of a century things became worse, and an unsettled state of feeling existed in the minds of foresters with regard both to rights of common and mining rights, and to the fact that the various works were fast passing from the hands of the native free miners into those of 'foreigners'. Many of the grievances were set forth in a periodical called *The Forester,* published at Newnham, while May 1831 saw the riotous destruction committed on the fences and banks of the inclosures by a large number of foresters.[2] The result was the appointment of a Commission to investigate the whole position. This Commission is referred to in other chapters and there are some interesting remarks regarding the Mine Law Court in the depositions of the witnesses.[3] From the following depositions it will be seen that the majority of the witnesses in 1832 favoured the restoration of the Courts, and also there was a divergence of opinion as to why the sessions of the Courts had been discontinued:

Wm. Morgan of Worrall Hill, free miner, aged seventy deposed:
'I have known Mine Law Courts held once or twice but was never at one. I think it would be very useful to have the Courts restored, but I cannot tell in what manner.'

---

1 See *The Life of Warren James* by A Resident Forester (1831).

2 See Hart, *The Commoners of Dean Forest* 1st Edn. (1951).

3 In their 1st Report (of 17 June 1839) the Coms. stated that a copy of the Mine Law Court records had been handed to them by the Board of Woods. They prepared a digest (a copy accompanied by their Report). The digest was read at a public meeting of the Mining Coms. at Coleford. 'Copies of the entire documents were lodged with the deputy gaveller for the inspection of the free miners.' Now see Glos.R.O. D9096, F16 (1-19) and F26/1.

Thomas Meek of Ruardean, free miner, aged sixty-seven:
'I think a re-establishment of Mine Law Courts would be of great advantage to the miners, because it would enable them to try causes there, which they are now obliged to try at Gloucester.'

James Trigg of Littledean, free miner, aged eighty-one:
'I have been to several Mine Law Courts held at the Speech House.'

Richard James of Whitecroft, free miner, aged fifty-three:
'I am very anxious for the Mine Law Courts in order to regulate as to foreigners, whose numbers would, I think, be diminished; and to restrict the sale of mines by free miners, as by the laws of the Mine Law Courts there was a fine for such selling.'

John White, free miner and keeper, aged seventy-four:
'I have known many Mine Law Courts held but I do not know how their verdicts were enforced nor how or in what manner witnesses were sworn.'

Peter Teague of Coleford, free miner, aged forty-five:
'I think it would be a great advantage to get the Mine Law Courts re-established to enable miners to try causes instead of going to Gloucester where mine causes are not understood and generally referred.'

James Machen, aged ninety:
'I believe the Mine Law Courts dropped because the miners behaved badly, and there was always so much confusion that the gentlemen would not attend; the miners quarrelled amongst themselves and created disturbances.'

Thomas Davis of Five Acres, free miner, aged eighty:
'I have been at Mine Law Courts; while they lasted no foreigner ever thought of having refuge in the Forest. The Court was given up because of a dispute between free miners and foreigners whom we did not consider fit to carry on the works. The workers of the Broadmoor Engine were cast[1] twice at a Mine Law Court. The 48 (jurors) were only to make laws between miner and miner, and try forbids. I do not recollect that it was a court to try debts; I never knew a man in prison for disobeying the order of the court. We were sworn as at other courts, by taking the Testament in hand; I never saw or heard of a holly stick in the court. A miner was allowed to plead his own cause, and had a cap on his head while pleading. While the Mine Law Courts lasted I never knew a foreigner to hold a work on lease; they sometimes lent money to carry on, but the free miner conducted it; our laws never forbid a free miner having money from any quarter, but there was no appearance of the lender if a foreigner. If four verns were in partnership, each might have 4 horses, and put in what men were necessary; if each vern did not do what he ought, we could put in a man for him. I have known many a man fined for loading a foreigner's waggon; if the foreigner got his coal away, very well, but if the free miner who loaded was found out, then he was fined.

I believe the Court was given up because somebody took all the papers away from the

[1] Perhaps 'thrown out of Court'.

Speech House, and they were considered to be stolen. The gaveller, one John Robinson, was a partner in the Fire Engine, and was supposed on that account to have taken them away. The Mine Law Courts gave damages for injury to any cattle injured by a pit being left open, and if there were 4 verns the damage was paid as the person injured could get it. I believe Mine Law Courts were held after the Broadmoor Engine was erected.'

Thomas Tovey, deputy gaveller:
'The Mine Law Court was before my time. If any advantage is to be obtained by the revival of the Mine Law Court, it must, in my opinion, be revived with extended powers. I think adding to the St. Briavels Court, so as to have but one court, would be most likely to be beneficial. I have heard, as the reason for the Mine Law Courts being dropped that the gentlemen could not manage the miners or keep order at the trials. I have heard that the records were removed and came into the possession of Colonel Hopkinson, but I never heard that that was the reason of the court being dropped, and I do not believe it was so, but that the reason is as I before stated.'

John Worgan of Five Acres, free miner, aged fifty-seven:
'I think the Mine Law Courts would enable us to tell who was free and who was not; it would prevent foreigners managing everything their own way.'

Philip Robinson, Junior, aged forty-six (he assisted the deputy gaveller Thos. Tovey; his grandfather and father had been joint deputy gavellers):
'My grandfather was clerk to the magistrates, and perhaps in that way he got possession of the Mine Law Courts records now produced. I do not recollect the Mine Law Courts being held; I have some of the records. I believe the deputy gaveller always had a right to be at the Mine Law Courts; but I am not aware that he acted as a judge or officer of the court. I produce certain records of the court of 1744 and other dates. I have heard my father often converse with free miners, and tell them it was their own fault the Mine Law Court dropped, and arose from their own supineness.'

William Collins, aged seventy-seven:
'I remember the Mine Law Court as well as I know where I am now; I was 18 years of age when the courts were held at the Speech House. I can remember my father was obliged to hide for 6 weeks for fear of the court, because he drove coal to Monmouth and had never worked his freedom. None but free miners could keep horses.'

Thomas Philips wanted 'The Mine Law Courts to be resumed, and held 4 times a year by a Commission'.

William Williams of Coleford, a free miner 'at least seventy-four years of age': 'I recollect several of the Mine Law Courts being held, and they were very particular then in their admissions [of people claiming to be free miners].'

James Morgan, aged seventy-nine, deposed that at the two Mine Law Courts he had attended there was never any such claim examined by the Court and added: 'The business done was suing one another.'

Stephen Jones of Hoarthorns, 'over eighty-two':
'I have attended the Mine Law Court at the Speech House. I was not one of the jury of 48; I was not old enough. All the 48 were free miners; they were chosen by the judges of the court in the open court, out of the miners present. There was always a large congregation of miners present at every court. After I worked a year and a day I was called to the court to prove my freedom; I was obliged by custom to bring those who worked with me to prove it, and I had to give them a free dinner.'

In a Memorial[1] given in full in Chapter V, the free miners requested the Commissioners:

'To take into their consideration the distress to which they have been reduced by the disuse of the Mine Law Courts, by which their rights and privileges were formerly protected, and which they have repeatedly solicited to have restored; the consequences of which disuse have been, that foreigners, who had originally no right to enter the mines, have gradually possessed themselves of property therein, and again sold the same to other foreigners, to the exclusion of the free miners themselves; that the free miners have not been able to obtain redress, owing to there being no tribunal except the Mine Courts which could legally investigate their claims; that in many instances they have been arbitrarily despoiled of their possessions by foreigners, and altogether, from the numbers of strange workmen and others introduced into the Forest, and employed in the hauling of mine, coal and ore, the free miners have been deprived of work, and themselves and their families reduced to the utmost distress.'

The free miners also included the following in their Statement of Claims,[2] given in full in Chapter V:

'That the ancient Mine Law Courts which formerly and from time immemorial used to be held at the Speech House for the adjudication of all disputes arising between the free miners, should be immediately revived for the purpose of ascertaining what persons have usurped the privileges of the free miners, and of awarding redress.

That the constable of the Castle of St. Briavels be the chief judge of the said court, and that the deputy wardens of the castle are the deputies of the said constable, and should preside in the said court.

That the free miners have sundry other rights and privileges which are laid down in the books and documents relative to the ancient Mine Law Court, and which they claim to have restored to them.'

Having given the reader an idea of the proceedings and Orders of the Court of Mine Law, the following interesting extracts from Thomas Sopwith's Preface to the earlier edition of the Awards of 1841 are now included:

'In ancient times, the practices of the Free Miners as regards the opening and working of mines, and the carrying of coal or iron ore, was regulated by a court or jury of Free Miners who met at the

---

1 4th. Report (dated 25 August 1835), p. 20.

2 *Ibid.*, p. 20-1

Speech House[1] in the centre of the forest, and adjudicated on all such matters. Some records of this Court of Free Miners are preserved in the Office of Woods, and furnish much authentic and valuable testimony as to the nature and operation of the mining laws and customs of Dean Forest.

These documents are seventeen in number; the earliest of them bears date in 1668, and the latest in 1754. The period of time included is therefore from 86 to 172 years ago, and the practices of the Free Miners are thus illustrated for a period of 86 years.

Whether these are the only Mine Law Orders made during the period of 86 years does not appear, but from the circumstance that no reference is made,[2] except to such as are in this series, it is probable that they comprise the whole of the Mine Law Orders made during the period above described. If this be correct, it follows that the Mine Law Orders were not made at any regular times of meeting, but at various periods; thus the number of years which intervened between the several Mine Law Orders now referred to were 6, 2, 4, 2, 3, 2, 7, 3, 4, 6, 10, 2, 9, 9, 4, and 13 years.[3]

As these Orders throw much light on the former usages of the forest, and form an interesting illustration of the history of mining in this country, the following condensed epitome of them, comprising all the leading points of information they contain, forms an appropriate accompaniment and introduction to the award and regulations of the Dean Forest Mining Commission, and for the sake of clearness, this abridgment is arranged under the following heads:

1. Right of Free-minership.
2. Regulations of Free Miners.
3. Raising of Money.
4. Apprentices.
5. Working of Mines.
6. Protection.
7. Penalties.

1. Right of Free-minership. – The first of this series of Orders gives to the Free Miners the sole privilege of carrying ore and coal according to the custom. No foreigners (i.e. persons not Free Miners) were to be allowed to carry ore and coal. Eight[4] years afterwards, viz., in 1676,[5] this privilege was abandoned. The Order No. 5,[6] states that the prohibiting foreigners from carrying ore and coal had proved prejudicial to the constable of St. Briavels, and to several of his lordship's friends and tenants in the counties of Monmouth and Hereford. The Order was therefore "wholly repealed, revoked, and made null and void", they being very ready to comply with the conveniency of his lordship's friends and tenants. The foreigners were therefore allowed to carry coal "not being to sell to others or for hire"; but the Free Miners were to have a preference in being loaded at the pit. The Free Miners at that time were subject to regulations fixing the prices at which they were to carry ore and coal until 1687, when by Order No.7, they were declared to be at liberty to sell, carry, and deliver their coal and ore to whom, where, and at what rates and prices they could best agree for, without incurring any penalty or forfeiture

1 Only after 1680.
2 Reference *is* made in 1701 to other orders.
3 Some errors.
4 The corrections would make this 15 years.
5 The date should be 1674.
6 Actually it is No. 3.

for so doing. From this it evidently appears that the rights of the Free Miners were not fixed upon any firm and definite basis, but were matter of discussion, and were changed from time to time as circumstances rendered most convenient. The mode of conferring the rights of free-minership appears to have varied at different times as regards the time of servitude in the mines, which is alluded to as being respectively "a twelve-month and a day", five years, and seven years. These rights were also conferred at various times by these Orders on Gentlemen who had not worked in the mines, and amongst these, in an Order dated 10th November, 1719, is the name of Edmund Probyn, the grandfather of Mr. John Probyn, one of the Dean Forest Mining Commissioners.

2. Regulations of Free Miners. – These chiefly relate to the time and mode of serving apprenticeships, to the renting of land, and keeping house as essential to the privilege to work or carry ore or coal. They were to be subject to bargains made by six persons called bargainers, appointed by the Mine Law Court, to use not more than four horses for carrying; they were not to undersell ore or coal, and were required to deposit ten pounds as a security for obedience to the regulations, nor were they to sue in any court but the Mine Law Court.

3. Raising of Money. – In one of the Orders, dated 1674, it appears that the ancient rights, privileges, and customs had been much infringed, and several suits in the law commenced. For the defence and preservation of such rights, the Order states that "there will be occasion for the raising of money, as well at the present as for time to come, from the several miners in the most equal and proportionable way, according to each miner's profits and gettings in the said art or mystery of mining". It then provided that all Free Miners of Fifteen years old and upwards, and widows of Free Miners that keep any horses or mares for carrying iron ore, coal, or ochre, shall pay 6d. every quarter of a year for every such horse or mare. Every Free Miner, and all servants and children above fifteen years of age to pay 6d. quarterly on the 25th March, the 24th June, 29th September and 25th December. The moneys thus raised were to be spent in legal defence of the privileges, and for the relief of miners who were maimed or hurt in the mines.

Another Order for raising money "for the urgent occasions of the miners" was made in 1682, and the next Order, made in 1685, related entirely to the raising of money to defray legal expenses.

4. Apprentices – By the first Order, dated in 1668, it is ordered, that no young man, although he be born within the hundred, shall work at coal or mine if he hath not worked twelve months and a day already, except he be bound apprentice to a miner and serve five years.

5. Working of Mines – There are very few allusions in these Orders to the actual working of mines. The only matters bearing on it are, that old pits when abandoned shall be secured by railing or walls on the surface and the limits within which another work was not to be begun, and which is commonly known amongst the forest miners as "protection".

6. Protection. – In an Order made in 1676,[1] it is stated, that when the Free Miners have at great cost made 'surffes' for the draining of their pits to get coal, which, when they have finished, others sink pits so near them that they are deprived of the benefit of their labour and charge, to their very great loss and damage; it is therefore ordered, that after a surffe is made, no miner shall come within 100 yards of that surffe, on penalty of 100 dozen of coal. It does not define any particulars as to being on the land side, etc. Twenty-one years[2] after this last Order, the distance was extended by an Order[3] to 300 yards; it recites that the last Order had been "very beneficial to the colliers in preservation of their coal pits from being spoiled and destroyed, yet it doth not so fully provide for the same as if the

[1] Meant for 1674.
[2] Fourteen years.
[3] No. 8 of 1693.

space and distance were 300 yards".

This distance continued in force thirty years,[1] and we then find an Order in 1728 to augment the distance from 300 to 500 yards. It is important here to observe, that a reservation is made that, "all works now in being shall not be injured or prejudiced thereby", which shows that a hasty or arbitrary interference with existing works was not contemplated by the change.

Twenty seven years afterwards it is ordered, that no free miner shall sink a water pit within the limits or bounds of 1,000 yards of any Free Miner's level, to prejudice that level; and in the same Order, dated 22nd October 1754 it is ordered, that the waterwheel engine at the Oiling-green near Broadmoor shall be taken to be, and is hereby deemed, a level to all intents and purposes, and liable to the same laws and restrictions as other levels brought up from the Grass-moor.

7. Penalties. – In all the regulations with respect to carrying, the penalty is 100 dozen of good and sufficient ore or coals, one half is invariably to be paid to the king, and the other half to the miner who will sue for the same.

Underselling was to be punished by expulsion from the fellowship, and perjury by the loss of freedom, with the burning of the habit and tools of the offender before his face. Some other penalties, as lesser quantities of coal, or various sums of money, occur, but in most instances no second penalty is mentioned for a repetition of the offence, and some of them which relate to the sinking of pits are clearly inadequate as a means of prevention.

From these documents, it is evident that the Free Miners, by an act of their Mine Law Court, were compelled to abandon the restrictions on foreigners carrying coal or ore, and to abandon also a system of prices which had doubtless thrown their carrying trade into the hands of foreigners. It appears also that the renting of land and keeping house were essential before a Free Miner could work or carry coal, and even then he was limited to four horses; all which shows the petty and trifling nature of the work then carried on, and also shows that extensive works were not contemplated. From the contributions raised in 1674, 1682, and 1685, and probably also in the intervals of these times, to defray expenses In the Court of Exchequer, it is evident that neither "the strength of the custom", nor the influence of the Mine Law Court, were sufficient to maintain peace and order, but that a ruinous and expensive litigation was constantly going on. The Customs of the Forest, by the showing of these Orders, appear not to have been steadily and definitely fixed, but were subject to continual change and innovation to meet each particular exigency. Even the protection granted to works appears to have been fixed so late as 164 years ago, at the very limited extent of 100 yards, than which nothing can more strongly show that the custom in its origin, and up to that period, merely contemplated the working of small pits, and this limitation to small works is further indicated by the restriction to use only four horses by each free miner. Twenty-one[2] years afterwards this distance was extended to 300 yards. In thirty[3] years after this last extension, the distance was fixed at 500 yards, and in twenty-seven years afterwards, the distance was fixed at 1,000 yards. This was in 1754, so that in seventy-eight years the protection was increased from 100 to 1,000 yards. This shows at once that the Mine Law Court was fully sensible of the necessity of giving greater limits to the works, and that under its government, the forest mines were gradually becoming of greater extent and importance. In the period of eighty-six years, which has since elapsed, there has been no extension of the custom by any Mine Law Order, (at least so far as this series of them goes) but it appears highly probable, that if that jurisdiction had continued, the metes and

1 Thirty-six years.
2 Fourteen years.
3 Thirty-six years.

bounds would have been settled, and limits assigned to water-pits as well as levels. The Order of October 22nd 1754, recognises the waterwheel engine to be a level to all intents and purposes, and this looks very like an intention on the part of the Mine Law Court to abolish the distinction between a level and a water pit. Whether, however, this case was for some particular reason made an exception to the general custom, or whether it was meant as a recognition of a water-pit being entitled to the privilege of a level, admits of some doubt. The water-wheel engine-work having been attended with considerable expense, and being liable to be injured by a water-pit sunk at the very limited distance of twelve or fourteen yards, the Mine Law Court saw that such a work ought to have further protection, and therefore, by their Order, virtually abandoned the old custom of only allowing ten or twelve yards radius to a water-pit. This much, however, appears evident, from the series of Mine Law Orders now referred to:–

1. That the customs were liable to numerous and very considerable changes.
2. That frequent and expensive litigation ensued from the mode of working the mines.
3. That the customs, especially as regards foreigners having coal to carry from the pits, gave way to the convenience of the public of the adjoining counties.
4. That the working of a year and a day was virtually abandoned, and an apprenticeship of five years substituted for a Free Miner, and of seven years for a foreigner's son born in the hundred.
5. That the whole spirit of the proceedings and regulations points only to the carrying on of land works of very limited depth, and were totally inapplicable to the deep coal of the Forest.
6. That the spoliation and destruction of each other's coal was a frequent occurrence.
7. That the powers of the Mine Law Court were totally inadequate to the proper regulation of the Forest mines.
8. That the regulations of the Free Miners, as regards obtaining their free minership, the privilege of carrying coal, the extent of their mines and other privileges, were subject to alteration and amendment, and were never stationary, as has been the case since the Mine Law Court fell into disuse.
   And,
9. That judging from the progressive nature of the Orders, from their having been adapted from time to time to suit public convenience, from the great and rapid extension of the limits assigned to works, there seems every reason to believe that if the Mine Law Court had been continued it would have aimed at regulations and metes and bounds, similar to those which it has been the especial object of the Dean Forest Mining Commission to establish.

Eventually the Mine Law Court became wholly inadequate for the regulation and control of the Forest mines, and therefore fell into disuse. Subsequently for a long period the coal and iron mines of the Forest were under the control of persons not conversant with practical mining, and hence much inconvenience arose. The old customs were always referred to as the general rule by which the agents of the Crown, as well as the Free Miners were to be guided; but from the very vague and indefinite nature of these customs, as developed in the Mine Law Orders, they were altered from time to time to suit particular circumstances, as the exigency of the case required; consequently, as the mines became deeper and more expensive to work, a corresponding alteration of the customs would doubtless have been made, if the Mine Law Court had been continued. Such, however, was not the case; and the greatest practical inconvenience, loss and injury arose from the customs, as usually recognised, becoming altogether inapplicable to the working of deep and extensive mines.'

CHAPTER V

TO 1667: MINING AND SMELTING

'I now advert to the Forest of Dean – that very fine possession of the crown.'[1]

THE Forest of Dean has been wooded land from time immemorial and abundant evidence is available as proof of the working of its minerals during and after the Roman Occupation. It is not certain at what date it became part of the ancient hereditary estates of the Crown, but as early as the eleventh century various lands and privileges in the Forest were granted by the king, either for revenue, or as reward or favour. At the time of Domesday (1086) various thegns held manors in the district; for example Earl Godwin held Staunton, William de Ow held Wygate (and Ralph de Limesi before him), while William fitzNorman held 'Tatinton'. The last also held 'Dene' which had been held in the time of Edward the Confessor by three thegns (Godric, Elric, and Ernui) 'free from tax for the service of guarding the forest'.[2] The forest referred to could not have been other than Dean.

At some time before 1130[3] the financial responsibility for the Forest passed into the hands of the fitzNorman family, while, in the later years of Stephen, William of Dene who had come into some at least of William fitzNorman's lands was confirmed in his 'ministry of the Forest of Dene'. About 1140, the Empress Matilda (Maud) bestowed on Earl Milo[4] of Gloucester, the castle of St. Briavels and the whole of the Forest of Dean.[5] It is doubtful whether Stephen (1135-54) ever recognized this grant, but it is reputed that he granted the Forest to the daughter of fitzWalter on her marriage with Herbert fitzHerbert. However, it is known that Henry II (1154-89) reserved the castle and Forest to himself[6] when confirming the various possessions inherited by Milo's son, Roger.[7] From that time on, the ownership of the Forest remained vested in the Crown, although it was usually 'sub-let' or 'farmed' with ill effects, as will be seen in later pages. Nigel fitzArthur seems to have been in charge of the Forest in 1156,[8] Roger of Powis in 1158,[9]

---

1 T. F. Kennedy, Commissioner of Woods (30th Rpt., 1852).

2 *Glos. Domesday,* 167b. See Hart *Between Severn and Wye... in the Year 1000* (2000).

3 In 1130, Hugh, son of William fitzNorman, accounted for £13, the profits on the Forest of Dean and the Hayes of Hereford (P.R. 31 Hen. I).

4 Slain in 1143 by a chance arrow shot at a deer.

5 J. H. Round, *Geoffrey de Mandeville*, p. 56.

6 *Cart. Flax. Abb.*, p.8 and Report on Dignity of a Peer, v, App. V.

7 Died 1155. He granted Hayes, or Wood of Ross, to the See of Hereford.

8 P.R., 2 Hen. II. p. 48.

9 *Ibid.*, 4 Hen. II, p. 168.

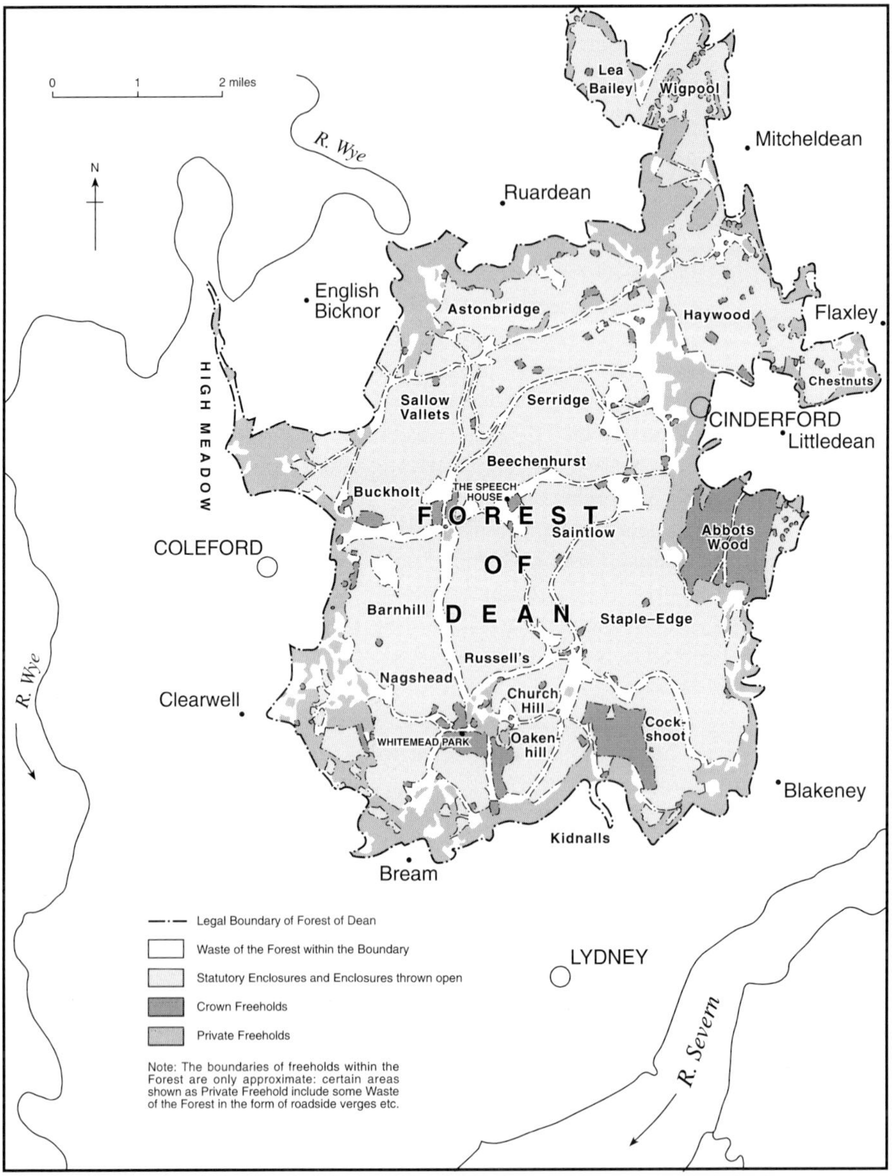

Plate V. *The Statutory Forest of Dean (named from* c.*1080). Substantially smaller than the Hundred of St. Briavels and not fully coterminous with it.*

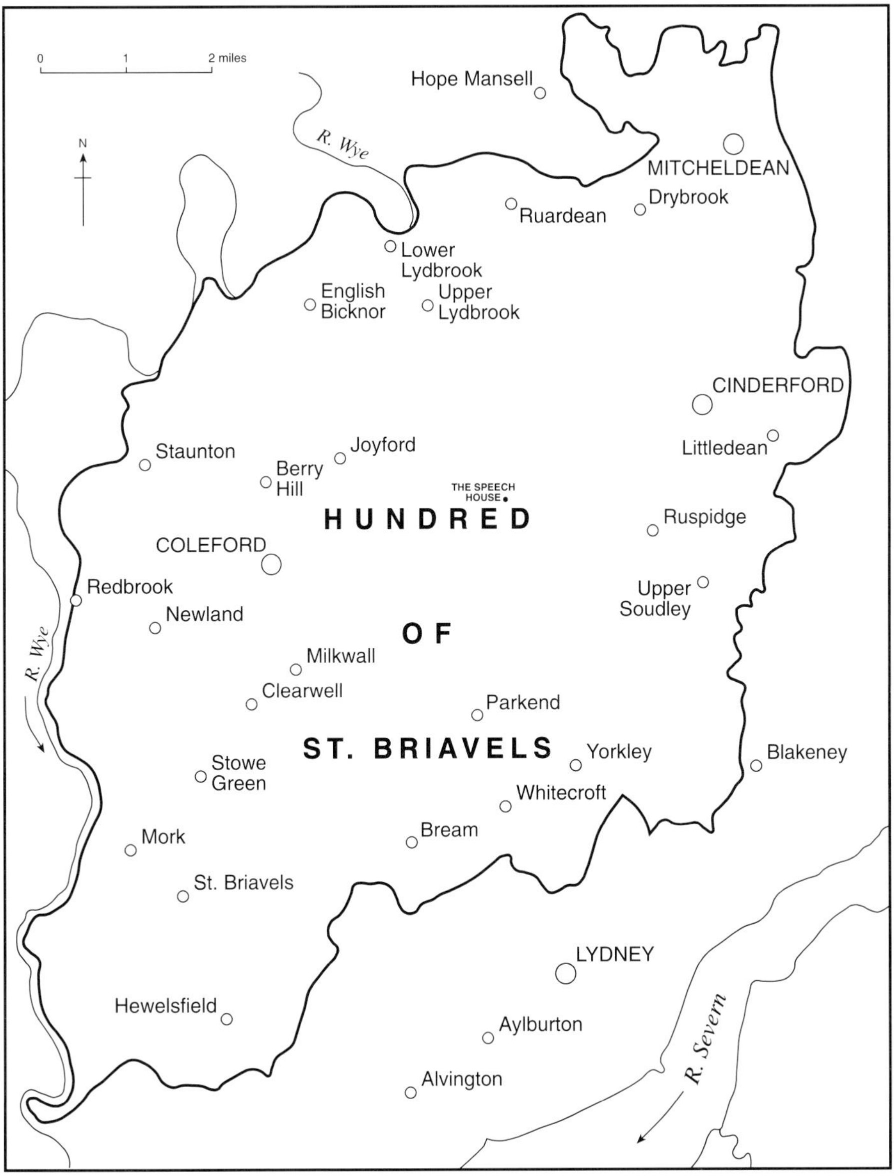

Plate VI. *The Hundred of St. Briavels (named from* c.*1154). Substantially larger than the Statutory Forest of Dean and not fully coterminous with it.*

William de Neville in 1164[1] and[2] William Marshall in 1195.[3] It is not until early in the thirteenth century that we find an adequate administrative system, although there were already Justices of the Forest.[4] At that time Dean came under the general supervision of the Justice of the Forest south of Trent. Below him was the warden of the Forest and his deputies; he was frequently also the constable, with his deputy constable, of St. Briavels Castle.[5] In addition there were verderers (four), regarders, rangers, foresters-in-fee (nine), sergeants-in-fee, riding foresters and ordinary foresters. There were also woodwards, beadles, custodians of the gawle (gavellers) and aleconners.[6] The 'Courts of the Forest' have been dealt with in another volume.[7] In 1266 the castle and Forest were granted to Edward the king's son, and his heirs, 'so that they be not separated from the Crown of England'.[8] This does not seem to have affected the administration of the Forest.

The history of Dean Forest involves the history of St. Briavels Castle which is said to have been built by Milo, Earl of Gloucester, in Henry I's reign. This castle was the ancient administrative centre of the royal hunting ground, and its constableship was usually associated with the office of warden of the Forest.[9] Some of the constables and wardens held office under a fixed annual payment, others rendered all their receipts into the Exchequer. Later the various duties with which the Forest representatives of the Crown were charged came to be assigned to different officials, and often fulfilled by one or more deputies. Thus, whilst some nobleman was nominally constable of St. Briavels Castle, another person of little more than local fame acted for him on the spot.

The Cistercian Abbey of Flaxley[10] has also played an important part in the history of the Forest. It was founded by Roger[11] eldest son of Earl Milo[12] of Gloucester during the reign of Stephen between the years 1148 and 1154. As formally notified in a charter of Richard I, it was considered to be specially under the protection of the sovereign, and all its more important rights and privileges were derived from the favour of the Crown. The forest privileges granted to the 'monks of Dene' brought them into frequent conflict with the authorities who were under the control of the constable of St. Briavels

1 P.R., 12 Hen. II, p. 77.

2 John de Albemarle accounted for the Forest in 1180 (P.R., 26 Hen. II). In 1189 we learn that Robert de Albemara owes £4 3s. l0d. by the king's amercement for the Forest. Further, that Lawrence Mallore rendered account of 8s. 4d. by the king's amercement for the Forest, and that Richard Bule owes 6s. 8d. for bad custody of the same (P.R., 1 Rich. I; *N.P.*, p. 11).

3 P.R., 10 Rich. I.

4 E.g., Geoffrey de Dangel and Alan de Neville.

5 The offices of warden and constable were granted together except in two cases. For a list of wardens and their deputies in the thirteenth century, see Bazeley, *op. cit.*, pp. 177, 182 and 183. For a list covering other centuries, see *Trans. B.&G.A.S.*, vol. iii, 1878-9, pp. 325-67.

6 In later centuries there were overseers, conservators or supervisors, keepers and underkeepers.

7 Hart, *The Verderers and Speech-Court of the Forest of Dean.* (1950) and *The Verderers and Forest Laws of Dean.* (1971).

8 Pat. R., 50 Hen. III, m.30; see also Cat. of Ancient Deeds, vol.1, p. 107, A.910.

9 The Constable of St. Briavels Act, 1836 (6 Will. IV, c.3) vested the office of constable in the First Commissioner of Woods. For an account of the history of the castle see *Trans. B.&G.A.S.*, vol. iii, 1878-9, pp. 325-67.

10 Dedicated to St. Mary. See Baden Watkins, *The Story of Flaxley Abbey*, (1985).

11 Died 1155.

12 Killed while hunting in Dean Forest, Christmas Eve, 1143.

Castle, and the sovereign was often invoked to protect and enforce the privileges of the Flaxley monks.[1] Much the same was true of other convents having forest privileges. Henry II confirmed to the 'monks of Dene' the grant of the valley of Castiard, where the Abbey was founded, and all the donations of Roger, Earl of Hereford, besides all easements in the Forest, namely common of pasture, tithes of chestnuts, a movable forge at Erdland, and as much wood and timber as they required.[2] At the time of the foundation of the Abbey the Forest and its adjacent parts were a deanery in the diocese of Hereford until the establishment of the See of Gloucester in 1540. In 1255 two 'dry oaks' in the Forest were granted to the abbot weekly, and this continued until 1258 when a large tract of the Forest now known as 'Abbot's Wood'[3] was granted by Henry III in lieu of the grant. As the forge was a movable one it had been difficult for the Forest officials to supervise its consumption of wood; the grant had therefore been an unpopular one and the officials had frequently been ordered by the king to observe it.[4]

The abbot and convent of Tintern enjoyed the right to take iron ore from the Forest for their forge without payment.[5] The bishop of Llandaff, too, was a beneficiary at the expense of the mineral revenue of the Forest, receiving certain tithes connected with iron ore.[6]

During most of the twelfth century and the first quarter of the thirteenth century, the annual 'firm' paid to the king by the warden or 'farmer' of the Forest was £10.[7] In some years payment was excused for certain reasons, such as for guarding the castle of St. Briavels. Any 'profit' received by the warden or 'farmer' over and above his 'firm' appears to have been his own entitlement. Further sums payable to the king were revenue derived from sales of produce, profits in kind, and fines. From 1232 the annual amount of the 'firm' varied. In that year it was £20,[8] £40 in 1236,[9] £50 in 1237,[10] £60 in 1241,[11] £166 13s. 4d. in 1247,[12] £170 in 1248,[13] £140 in 1255,[14] £100 in 1272,[15] £140 in 1281,[16] and £160 in 1287.[17] The position of the warden or 'farmer' is

1 *Flax. Cart.*, iii.

2 F.P.T.R. No. 31, etc.

3 Charter Rolls 42 Hen. III, m.2; *Flax Cart.*, p. 109. The wood is situated between Littledean, Soudley and Cinderford.

4 Following the first dissolution of the monasteries, the Abbot's Wood was granted to Sir William Kingston in 1537 (L. & P. Hen. VIII, 1537, vol. xii, Pt. I, p. 353). Two centuries later the estate was held by the Crawley-Boevey family. Sir Thomas Crawley-Boevey sold it to William Crawshay in 1836. In 1870 Henry Crawshay secured an Award by Act of Parliament (33 & 34 Vict. c.8) disafforesting the estate, and discharging it of commoners' rights, for which compensation was made. The Crown received £12,162 which had been fixed by arbitration and also reserved (as it had always done) the minerals. In 1899 the Crown repurchased from Messrs. Crawshay & Co. (then owners) 666 acres of the 800 odd granted to the Abbey.

5 Exch. Rec. 29.

6 Rhys Jenkins, *op. cit.*, etc.

7 See. e.g., P.R. 31 Hen. I and 4 Hen. II.

8 P.R. 17 Hen. III.

9 *Ibid.*, 20 Hen. III.

10 *Ibid.*, 21.

11 *Ibid.*, 29.

12 *Ibid.*, 33.

13 *Ibid.*, 33. The same sum was paid for the seven following years (Inq. 15 Edw. III, No. 75).

14 *Ibid.*, 40.

15 F.P.T.R. No. 30, m.30.

16 P.R. 13 Edw. I.

17 *Ibid.*, 15.

made clear in the appointment, on 17 November 1255, of Robert Walerand[1]:

> '... to keep the castle and manor of St. Briavels and the Forest of Dean for five years from Michaelmas last, so that he have the issues and profits of the king's demesnes, of the yearly rent, and of the King's weirs, of the said manor, and also of the foreign great mines, the foreign forges and the sea-coal of the said forest and the custom of sea-coal brought over the Severn, the cheminage through the same forest to Gloucester, the herbage, wind-fallen wood, loppings (*cooperonum*) of oaks given away by the King or felled to his use and of the timber (*lignorum*) thrown down by the wind; pannage, ashes, nuts and chestnuts in the said forest; and the perquisites of the forest; and the issues of the halmote of St. Briavels and of the ropers (*cordariis*) and sievemakers (*sievemakers*) of the said forest; Rendering £140 yearly at the Exchequer and keeping the castle and forest at his own cost, and so that there remain to the King the King's great forge of the said forest to dispose of as he will.'

Domesday (1086) made no mention of the mineral wealth of the Forest of Dean and the first direct documentary evidence of the use of Dean minerals is found in the twelfth and thirteenth century records of forges in the district and the despatch of iron to various destinations.[2] Some of the forges belonged to the king, others were in private hands, held either under royal licence, or by doubtful right.[3] In an undated document[4] of the reign of Henry III and of about the middle of the thirteenth century, an estimate is given of the value of the various sources of revenue. Some of the items are given below and are compared with those from the extant accounts for the six other years in which the profits were paid direct into the Exchequer[5]:

	Estimate: 1247(?)-1256	1246-7	*Jan.-Nov.* 1255[6]	1275-6	1276-7	1277-8	1279-80
Severn custom on coal and ore	£24. 0. 0[7]	£23. 6. 8		£26.16.3	£26. 2. 0	£24. 12. 0	£23. 0. 0
Chiminage	£1. 0. 0	£-.13. 4		£3. 0.0	£3. 6. 8	£3. 6. 8	£2.16. 6
Ore & coal leased	£10.16. 0	£3. 0. 0					
			£23. 1. 4	£23.16.9½	£23.18.11	£24. 6. 0	£23.19.0[8]
Great ore	£17. 0. 0						
Rent of foreign forges	£9. 2. 0	£8.18. 0	£8. 4. 6	£11. 1. 4	£13. 6. 1½	£14.10.0	£12. 0.0
Cinders	£-. 6. 8			£5.15.0	£6.18.9		
King's great forge	£50. 0. 0	£24. 0. 0	£22.10. 0				
Other forges			£4. 9. 3				

1 *Cal.Pat.Roll* 40 Hen. III, m.21, p. 450.
2 F.P.T.R. 30, 31.
3 *Ibid.*
4 F.P.K.R. bdl. 1, No. 26. The document is headed '*Exitus annuus foreste de S. Breavello*'.
5 Bazeley, *op. cit.* p. 222, based on P.R. 33, 40 Hen. III and 4, 6, 9 Edw. I.
6 These figures agree with those in the account of James Freysil for the year 1256-7 (Inq. 15 Edw. III, No. 75). K.R. Mem. Roll, E159/117.
7 Farmed to Payn of Lydney for £24.
8 Ministers A/cs 850/19, 9 Edw. 1, 1281. Accounts for '£23 19s. of great and little minerals, iron with sea coal sold'. Also £12 of rent of smithies (*fabricarum*) in the Forest of Dean.

The foregoing Estimate explains the first item as ½d. on every load of sea-coal taken beyond the Severn, while for the year 1246-7 it is referred to as 'from a certain water custom for taking ore into Wales'. The second item in the Estimate is referred to as 'chiminage through the Forest towards Gloucester' but it is not certain whether the toll levied on transport by land was only in connection with ore or on loads of all sort. The revenue derived from ore and sea-coal is entered under two headings in the Estimate: 'foreign (*forinsecus*)[1] mine and sea-coal'; secondly, 'great mines'. In 1246-7 £3 appears as the 'profits of the mines'; from 1255 the revenue in question is described as the 'issues of the great and lesser mines and sea-coal'.

In 1276[2] it is recorded that 'the Forest of St. Briavels belongs to the king and is worth by the year with perquisites of mines, pannage and herbage and other appurtenances £37'. This is much lower than in some of the previous years, while the revenue from mines alone was farmed in 1282 for £46.[3] Miss Bazeley[4] thinks it possible that all the revenue derived from private forges passed through the hands of the justices in eyre in the form of fines. She points out that in the reigns of Henry II and John occasional payment '*pro saisina fabrice*' or simply '*pro fabrica*', ranging from one to ten marks, appear among the Forest pleas,[5] and that it is not clear whether they were made in addition to, or instead of, an annual rent. If the latter, such payments must have been usually included under some general head. The half-dozen entries relating expressly to forges during the reigns of Henry II and John cannot possibly represent the whole amount raised in this period, for over twenty forges are referred to at a later date as in existence at this time.[6] In 1287 we learn that some fifteen to twenty years earlier the monks of Flaxley forbid mining in their lands as appears from the following[7]:

> 'At the time when Thomas Clare[8] was custodian of the Forest of Dean there came William de Abbenhale, Walter Page and Elys Page, miners, and first when digging in the land of the Abbot of Flaxley at Ardlonde they found metal there. And the Abbot hearing of this immediately removed the miners and filled up the ditch of the mine with stones and earth, so that before the Abbot did this Jordan la Ware, Constable of the said Thomas, came and took 4d. only of the issues of the mine. The said Jordan, by a writ of the King obtained by the said Abbot, caused an enquiry to be made whether the said mine belonged to the King or not, and by the said inquisition he learnt that it did not belong to the King but to the Abbot and convent of Flaxley. And then the miners ceased to work there until the coming of Grimbald Pauncefot, Keeper of the Forest, who again began to work there with certain of his miners, the Abbot being unwilling. And he took of the issues in his time for his own use £6. And William de Staure took the gift of the said Grimbald 10s. And William Hathewy of the gift

---

1 It is not known whether this meant mines outside the Forest or Hundred of St. Briavels, or mines other than those of the King.

2 Hundred Rolls (4 Edw. I), vol. i, p. 176.

3 F.P.T.R. No. 31.

4 *Op. cit.* p. 225.

5 *Cf.* P.R. 31 Hen. II; 1 and 10 John, Glouc.

6 *Cf.* Vict. C.H. Glouc., ii, p. 216.

7 Chanc. Inq. p.m. 15 Edw. I, No. 67; Glos. I.P.M., vol. iv, p. 144.

8 Thomas Clare was appointed keeper in 1265 (*Cal.Pat.Roll* 49 Hen. III, m. 17). He was replaced in 1272 (F.P.T.R. No. 30, m. 30).

of the same, 10s. And Walter, son of Nicholas, Walter Holt, Walter Page, John Kinggot, Alexander Burgeis, Alexander Hok, John Jordan and Gilbert Cameron, miners of the time of Grimbald of the profit, £4 – *viz.* each of them 10s. And William Hathewy, Keeper of the Forest, continuing the working of the said Grimbald, took therefor from the time of the death of the said Grimbald up to now 7s. 7d. and against the will of the Abbot. As to the estimation of the value of the mine by the year they say that it cannot be estimated because the metal is found casually and more often fails.'

Meanwhile, as recorded in Chapter I, the Dean miners were being called on many occasions to assist in military operations. Their value in times of emergency, and the king's need to ensure a supply of ore for his forges, caused them to be treated as a specialised class of operatives, and to be favoured with the king's 'protection'. The dues paid by the miners were not an important consideration, and in any case in 1317 we find Edward II willing to grant a tithe of his mining profits to the Bishop of Llandaff.[1] The annual value of the king's mines and forges was given in 1341 as £34.[2] Thirty years later doubt had arisen as to who was entitled to the issues of the mines, and on 8 October 1371 the following was addressed to the Treasurer and Barons of the Exchequer[3]:

> 'Order, if assured that the King's toll of the mines in the Forest of Dean is parcel of the issues and profits of the Forest and ought to pertain to Guy de Brienne by reason of his keeping the same, that he received of Peter de la Mare a sum of £21 12s. as parcel of the said issues and profits, and that the said toll used heretofore to be allowed to the said Guy and other the keepers of the Forest in their farm thereof as parcel of the same, to stay their demand made by the Exchequer summons upon the said Guy for life the keeping of the Castle of St. Briavels and of the said Forest with all issues and profits thereof arising from a set yearly farm; and now on behalf of the said Guy and Peter, the King has learned that, although from the date of that grant the said Guy has taken the said toll as parcel of his farm, and the said Peter has paid him £21 12s. of that toll as parcel of the said issues and profits, the treasurer and the barons are unlawfully distraining them to account for that sum by colour of an inquisition lately taken before William de Wykeham late keeper of the King's forest this side Trent, whereupon the said Peter was indicted for six years' detenue of the said toll amounting to the said sum, Wherefore the said Guy and Peter have prayed for remedy.'[4]

[1] Tithes to the value of £10 were granted [C.R. 10 Edw. II]. On 15 Nov. 1320 Edw. II ordered the keeper of the Forest 'to cause a tithe of the profits of the King's iron ore in the Forest within the parish of the bishop of Llandaff's Church of *Nova Terra* (Newland) to be paid to the said Church hereafter, the King having granted such tithe in response to the petition of J. bishop of Llandaff, although it appears by the Exchequer certificate that tithe of such profit has not been paid hitherto and that no recompense has been made in place of such tithe' (C.C.R. 14 Edw. II, m. 14, pp. 278-9). A similar order was sent on 9 June 1328, the keeper having refused or neglected to render the tithe *(ibid.* 2 Edw. III, m. 23, p. 296). Similar instructions were issued to Robert de Sapy on 26 Feb. 1332 *(ibid.* 6 Edw. III, m. 33, p. 443); again on 26 Nov. 1356 (*Cal.Pat.Roll* 7 Rich II, m. 14, Pt. II, p. 395) and on 15 March 1384 (*ibid.*).

[2] *Cal.Pat.Roll* 14 Edw. III, Pt. I, m. 14d; *ibid.*, 15 Edw. III, Pt. I, m. 9; Inq. of 15 Edw. III (1342).

[3] Cal. C.R. Edw. III, 1371, m. 12, p. 258.

[4] As to Guy de Brienne's claim for a reduction in his 'firm', see C.R. 11 Edw. III. Pt. I, m. 33; Pat. R. 14 Edw. III, Pt. I, m. 14d. and 15 Edw. III. Pt. 1. m. 9; *Cal.Pat.Roll* Edw. III, 1348-50, p. 428.

In 1375 there was proof that those engaged in mining and iron making (which were distinct crafts) did not always agree. In consequence of some dispute the iron workers had set about raising ore themselves, and a Commission was issued to Guy de Brienne (warden of the Forest), Robert Cole, John Joce and Thomas Athewy 'to make inquisition in the county of Gloucester touching an information that, by occasion of certain debates and dissensions which have arisen between the miners of the Forest and the ironworkers there, the ironworkers to vent their malice against the miners have taken away the ore of the Forest, and daily do so'.[1]

Meanwhile the reigning kings were bestowing the Forest on certain of their relatives, and in 1391 we find it in the hands of Thomas, Duke of Gloucester, having been granted to him that year by Richard II.[2] He was followed by John, Duke of Gloucester.[3] Later Henry IV granted the Forest to John, Duke of Bedford,[4] who also held it during the reign of Henry V (1413-22).[5] Following his death his widow, Jacquetta, was granted, *inter alia*, the profits of '*carbonum*, pannage, agistments, etc. in Dean Forest, as well as the pasture of Walmore'.[6]

About this period we find a note which shows that the spiritual needs of the miners were not neglected, for John Chinn on his death in 1416 endowed a chapel in Newland Church that a priest might celebrate 'at the altar of our Lady and be bound to go from one smithy to another and from one mining pit to another twice a week to say them Gospels'.[7]

In 1430 we have an indication of lawlessness in the Forest. In that year the men of Tewkesbury petitioned Parliament in respect of damage and loss they had suffered when sending shipping down the Severn. The culprits were stated to be the inhabitants of the Forest and the hundreds of Bledisloe and Westbury who 'will not obey any ministry of the law, nor the execution thereof, but at their own lust; nor the officers nor the ministers of the law of the same shire in any wise do come within the said Forest to execute any matter or process of law against the will and

---

1 *Cal.Pat.Roll* 49 Edw. III, Pt. I, m. 12d. p.155.

2 *Cal.Pat.Roll* 14 Rich. II; Parl. R. II, 278b. According to Manwood *(op. cit.* 1717 Edn.) 'King Richard II granted to Thomas, Duke of Gloucester, the castle of St. Briowell, and the Forest of Dean, in special tail; and it was afterwards enacted by the Parliament that the Duke should hold the said Forest as a forest, with power to constitute such Justices and Officers &c. as are incident and belonging to a forest'.

3 N.P., p. 23.

4 *Cal.Pat.Roll* Hen. IV, 1399-1401. p. 159.

5 Exch. 14 Hen. VI.

6 *Inq. p.m.*15 Hen. VI, No.76 (1437).

7 In March 1704 the Treasury made an endowment to the town of Coleford of £12 yearly for repair of their chapel wherein sermons were preached which tended to help 'the edification of the miners and colliers of the said town and their children' (C.T.B., vol. xix, p. 167). In later years several Dean colliers stand out as exponents of religious teaching in the district: see (a) *A Brief and Authentic Statement of the origin of an Established Church and National Day School in His Majesty's Forest of Dean ... and ... a Memoir of the late Thomas Morgan, Collier, who was eminently useful in promoting the above design,* by P. M. Proctor (1819); (b) 'The Petition of the Methodist Society of Colliers in the Forest of Dean', *Wesleyan Methodist Magazine,* 3rd series, vol. iii: the Petition, signed by Robert Meredith, is addressed 'To the Methodist Ministers in Conference Assembled', and prays that a regular preacher may be sent to Dean Forest; (c) *Sixty-two years in the Life of a Forest of Dean Collier*, by Timothy Mountjoy (1887).

entent of the commoners of the same Forest and hundreds'.[1] Legislation was passed to mitigate this nuisance.

To revert to the management of the Forest. Each holder had his appointed receiver, and in the year 1435-6[2] we find our first indication that the King, or those holding the Forest under his grant, had commenced to farm out the issues of the mines. In an account for that year, Hugh Cromhale (receiver for John, Duke of Bedford) rendered account of '£22 of the farm of the mines Under "le Wode" as for the portion of the Lord called "le Gravell" so demised to Henry Deane and John Cromehale for the term of ten years'.[3] Henry Beauchamp, Duke of Warwick, held the Forest in 1446 at a rent of £100 per annum,[4] followed on 4 September 1464 by George, Duke of Clarence.[5] Later the holder was Richard, Duke of Gloucester.[6]

Records concerning the mines and miners of Dean Forest in the fifteenth and sixteenth centuries are scanty. We know, however that 300 'pioneers' were sent from the district to Dover in 1522,[7] and twelve miners were impressed to assist Martin Frobisher in 1577.[8] In 1531 Forest ironworkers were sent to Glamorgan to assist in the iron industry there.[9] Detailed records of the appointments of 'Custodians of the Gawle' (gavellers) are available,[10] besides the usual constables, wardens, rangers, beadles, riding foresters, aleconners, etc. It is also known that the Mine Law Courts were held in 1469-70.[11] Musters were common throughout the period and excellent records of these are available.[12] As to the behaviour of the inhabitants during these centuries, we find them continuing to resist intruders,[13] and it is certain that strangers entered the district at their peril. Encroachments were made at the expense of the Forest, and the stealing of game continued. In 1533 we hear of 'an inquisition of wastes done by divers persons in the King's Forest of Dean'.[14,15] We have a report that in 1540 the Forest was 'fruitful of iron mines, and divers forges be there to make iron'.[16] Again, in 1566, we find Sir William Cecil being informed that 'the Forest of Dean contains plenty of

1 Pet. in Parl. 8 Hen. VI; Parl. R. iv. 345.

2 E101/141/1.

3 The same receiver stated that there had been no unlawful carrying of minerals within the Forest, and rendered 'nothing here of issues of cinders within the Forest this year, nevertheless in the 15th year past at 20s. and before at greater sums, because none were sold'.

4 *Cal.Pat.Roll* 24, Hen. VI.

5 *Cal.Pat.Roll* 4 Edw. IV, m. 14, Pt. I. p. 329: 'Grant for life to the King's brother George, Duke of Clarence, of the castle, lordship and town of St. Briavels and the Forest of Dean with all lands, mills, rents, services, woods, fees, franchises, liberties, etc., rendering to the King nearly £40 yearly.'

6 Harl. MSS. 433; Fosbrooke, *op. cit.* I, p. 103.

7 P. 24.

8 *Ibid.*

9 L. & P. Hen. VIII, R.J.

10 Chap. III.

11 Chap IV and see Appendix 3.

12 C.S.P.D. various.

13 Glos. Corp. Rec., 1500, fol. 279; Lansd. MS. 76, No. 47. fol. 105-105v.

14 L. &. P. Hen. VIII. 1533, vol. vi, p. 134.

15 In 1519-20 there was a dispute between inhabitants of the east of Dean and the west of Dean. From the large numbers of 'Smyth holders' who signed acceptance of an arbitration award it seems that the dispute arose from the iron industry. PRO Star Chamber Proceedings, Hen. VIII, bdle 17, m. 24; Hart, *Royal Forest* (1966) p. 74 and Hart, *Industrial History* (1971), p. 7.

16 *Trans. B.&G.A.S.* vol. xiv, Pt. II, pp. 221-84.

good iron'.[1] Nevertheless lack of consistent policy on the part of the Crown towards the owners of forges must have caused great fluctuations in the fortunes of the Dean miners. At times, in order to increase revenue, the iron industry would be encouraged, while at other times the need for growth and conservation of timber for shipbuilding would be a detriment to the industry. The year 1588 brings us to the eclipse of the Armada and the often-asserted Spanish aim to destroy the Forest. It has been suggested that the would-be invaders had the suppression of the ironworks as much in mind as the spoliation of the timber.

Although it is not possible to ascertain the number of miners existing in Dean Forest during the centuries, we are fortunate in having a record of many of the 'mynors', 'collyers' and smiths in 1608. In that year a list was compiled by John Smith[2] of 'all the able and sufficient men in body fit for his Majesty's service in the wars', for the county of Gloucester. The following extracts are taken from the printed copy of the list[3]:

	'Mynors'	*'Collyers'*	*Smiths*	*'Naylors'*	*'Sundry'*
Hundred of St. Briavels:					
Micheldean:	–	–	1	2	–
Littledean:	11	1	1	17	–
Abenhall:	1	–	3 and 2 apprentices	–	–
Staunton:	4	–	3	–	–
Coleford:	6	–	–	2	2 'Grindstone hewers'
Clearwell:	3	–	2	1	2 'Grindstone hewers'
Bream:	2	–	1	1	–
St. Briavels:	2	–	1	–	–
Churchends Beame:	–	1	2	–	2 'Milstone hewers'
Flaxley:	–	1	–	–	–
English Bicknor:	1	–	1	–	1 'Iron workman' 1 'Dyer'
Ruardean:	–	1	6	6	2 'Lyme burners'
Lea:	–	–	2	–	–
Northwood:	–	–	1	–	1 'Mettleman'
Hundred of Westbury:					
Netherley & Overley:	–	–	2	–	–
Newnham:	–	–	2	–	1 'Wyer drawer'
Tidenham:	–	–	1	2	1 'Wyer drawer'
Bulley:	–	–	1	–	–
Hundred of Bledisloe:					
Lydney:	–	–	1	1	–
Aylburton:	–	–	2	1	1 'Ironfounder'
Allaston:	–	–	1	–	–
Etloe:	–	–	1	–	–
Blakeney:	–	1	2	6	2 'Grindstone hewers'
Duchy of Lancaster:					
Longhope:	–	3	3	–	–
Minsterworth:	–	–	4	–	–
Huntley:	–	4	1	–	–
Tibberton:	–	–	(3)	–	–
Rodley:	–	–	2	–	–
Adset:	–	–	1	–	–

1 C.S.P.D. Eliz., vol. xl, p. 275, No. 17.
2 Of North Nibley (1567-1641): Smith's MSS. 3 books in folio, acquired by Lord Sherborne.
3 *Men and Armour for Gloucestershire in 1608*, pp. 31-76 (printed 1902).

Several influential people had by this time recognised the value of the mineral deposits in Dean and sought and obtained concessions in the Forest. Amongst them we find Lord Lisle and Sir Francis Bacon (who had wire works at Tintern and Whitebrook), Sir Edward Winter (who had ironworks at Lydney)[1] and Henry Lord Herbert of Raglan. The effect of the iron industry on the woodlands had now become serious. Nevertheless in 1611 sales of large supplies of cordwood were arranged by the Crown with Giles Bridges[2] for ironworks; he was also empowered to take iron ore, cinders, coal and marl.[3] The agreement was for ten years but in 1611-12 it was superseded by a grant of virtually the whole of the minerals and wood (excluding ship timber) of the Forest to William, Earl of Pembroke.[4] The Earl was granted liberty to take iron ore, cinders, coal, etc., necessary for his ironworks, 'no person or persons whatever other than the said Earl ... to take or carry out of the Forest any wood, timber, mine ore or cinders without the consent of the Earl'. The monopoly, which only lasted for three years, was strongly objected to by the miners. Previous to this time they had exercised their custom without 'interruption or denial'. They rioted[5] and also continued at their customary work without the Earl's consent. In consequence, an Information was filed against them by the attorney-general. As a result, the following Order, dated 28 January 1613, was made by the Exchequer Court and was a severe blow to the miners[6]:

> 'Whereas the 25th of May, in Easter term last, the court was informed by His Majesty's attorney General, that the King's Majesty by his letters patent under the great seal of England, had granted to the Right Hon. the Earl of Pembrooke (amongst other things) the mine, ore and cinders, to be found out and gotten within the forest of Dean in the county of Gloucester for 21 years, for the yearly rent of £2,433 6s. 8d. and that to the prejudice of His Majesty's said farmer, one Thomas Monjoye the elder, Thomas Monjoye the younger, John Hill, and

1 In 1617, he was sued for misappropriation of timber [E134 Exch. Deps. by Coms. 14 James I, Hilary, No. 8, Glouc.].

2 ? Lord Chandos of Sudeley Castle.

3 Lands. M.S. 166, £365 (Br. Liby.).

4 *Ibid.* The grant of the Forest, Castle and Minerals was dated 13 June 1611, and the grant of timber supplies 17 February 1612 (E112/83/411). In 1608 he succeeded Sir Edward Winter as constable of St. Briavels Castle. He was Governor of the Corporation of the Mineral and Battery Works, a company that was drawing iron wire by power at Tintern under a patent granted to Humfry and Shutz in 1565. See Hart, *Royal Forest* (1966) pp. 89-93.

5 C.S.P.D. James I, vol. lxx, p. 144, No. 49: 14 Aug. 1612: 'Earl of Northampton to Earl of Rochester regarding riots in Dean Forest on occasion of cutting down of wood for the Earl of Pembroke, who is much disliked.' The Earl's men tried to avoid trouble by cutting and cording his wood while the people were at church. However, 'some fifteen desperate knaves set it on fire, ... and dancing about the fire cried "God save the King!" They still walk about the woods with weapons, and as I hear with shot; they call their neighbours cowards for not assisting them.... The justices hath given order for their apprehension, but the country favour them.' The privy council called upon the sheriff, the J.P.s, the lord and deputy lieutenants, to aid in suppressing and apprehending the 'seditious rogues'. 'Had the matter been put into the hand of the gentlemen who could have tempered the wild humours of those Robin Hoods, things had been carried in a better fashion. But the Earl is extremely odious, and with attributes that concern himself will put other matters in distemper.' A letter dated six days later says: 'Glad the King approves the course taken about riots in Dean Forest' (*Ibid.*, p. 145. No. 55(I)).

6 E126/1, fol. 270 – Hil. Term 10 James I, 28 Jan. 1613; also printed, with some errors, in Rudder's *New History of Gloucestershire,* (Appendix).

others, mine diggers and carriers of mine and cinders within the said forest, do daily dig and carry away out of the said forest the mine and ore there gotten; whereupon it was then ordered, that His Majesty's writ of injunction under the seal of this court should be awarded to the said parties, commanding them and every of them, upon pain of £500 not to carry nor transport any of the mine and cinders to be digged or gotten in the said forest, except they should show good cause to this court by or before the first Saturday of Trinity Term then ensuing, and thereupon the court would then take other order, as by the said recited order it plainly appears; whereupon the said Monjoye and other the said parties before mentioned came, and by Mr. Estcourte of their counsel learned, informing this court that they were poor labouring men, and were wholly sustained, with their wives and families, with digging and carrying of such mine, ore, and cinders; acknowledging, as well by their answer to the said information as by the counsel at the bar, the soil to be His Majesty's, and that they had no interest therein, humbly praying they might be permitted to continue their digging and carrying the said mine, ore, and cinders, as they had been accustomed, having no means to relieve their poor estates; whereof the court taking due consideration, and upon the humble submission of the said parties for their offences formerly past, and considering also that His Majesty's farmer of the said iron work, paying a great rent, should not be furnished of matter to keep his forges in work if the said ore and cinders should be carried away; it pleased the court to move that the said parties before named, and such others as have been accustomed to dig and get mine, ore, and cinders, in the said forest, of charity and grace, and not of right, might be permitted, for the maintenance of their wives and children, who might by the means of their labour live, to continue to dig for the said mine, ore, and cinders, to be carried to His Majesty's forge and iron works within the said forest, and not to any other place; and being paid for the same according to such rates as they have been accustomed to sell to other men before His Majesty leased the same; to which motion His Majesty's said attorney-general, in commiseration of the poor men's estates, did assent, it being as good for His Majesty's farmer to employ those that are always exercised in the said works as others; and thereupon it was then ordered by such consent as aforesaid that the said parties above named and such others as have been accustomed to dig and get mine, ore, and cinders in the said forest, should, of charity and grace, and not of right, be permitted to continue the digging and getting of the said ore and cinders, so as they carry or cause the same to be carried to His Majesty's iron works and forges, receiving for the same such rateable price as they had been usually accustomed to sell to other men before His Majesty leased the same, until such time as the cause now depending by English Bill brought in the name of divers [of] the inhabitants of the said forest by way of petition, touching their claims in the said forest shall be heard and decreed, and thereupon this court will take other order:

And for the better performance of the said order, it was then also further ordered by the court, that His Majesty's writ of injunction should be awarded to the said parties aforenamed, and to Thomas Maddock, John Gwyll'm, John Fryes, and to all other the inhabitants, diggers, miners and workmen in the said forest, for the due observing and performing of the said order, upon pain of £100 to be levied upon him that should break the same.

Now, upon the motion of Mr. Attorney General this day in court, shewing, that notwithstanding that said former order and injunction, divers persons inhabiting within the said forest, have, since the said order, carried out of the said forest great quantities of cinder and mine ore unto other places, and not unto the king's works within the said forest, as by the affidavit of William Whitefoote, of the parish of Chappell Hill, in the county of Monmouth, wiredrawer, made the 28th of October, in Michaelmas term last past, and this day read in court, appeareth; and that thereupon process of attachment being awarded against some of the said persons for the said contempts, some of them have appeared this term in person, the court again entering into consideration of some course to be taken for the immoderate carrying away of the said mine, ore, and cinders, from the king's works in the said forest, to other places out of the said forest, and yet having regard to the poverty of the said inhabitants, who receive most part of their maintenance and relief thereby, for the better establishing of the said matter hereafter, have thought fit, and it is this day so ordered, that the inhabitants of the said forest which have heretofore used to dig and carry mine, ore, and cinders; shall be permitted, of favour and grace, and not of right, to continue the same until the hearing of the said cause now depending by the English bill as aforesaid, so as they carry the same, or offer it, to the king's works; and if the same shall be refused by the farmers or other officers of His Majesty's works then the said diggers and carriers of mine and cinders may sell the same to any other works within and near about the said forest for the service of such works; and further that no new diggers or carriers of mine and cinder, whereof the court is informed there are very many, shall hereafter be allowed, but only such poor men as are inhabitants of the said forest:

And it is further ordered, that a Commission shall be drawn, with articles to be thereunto annexed, by such as follow for the king, and the same to be shewed to the defendant's counsel; upon which, if they cannot agree, then the barons will consider thereof, as also of the Commissioners to be therein nominated, which Commissioners shall have power to appoint what number of new diggers and carriers shall be allowed, and to consider of their estate, quality and condition, and of what rate they and all other the diggers and carriers of mine, ore, and cinders, shall sell the same to the king's works, consideration being had of the distance of place where the cinders and ore are digged, and the king's works to which they shall be carried, and to set down such prices for the said ore, mine, and cinders, as shall be thought fitting in respect of their labour therein; and also when and in what manner they shall be paid for the same.

And, as touching the two defendants, Randall Marks and William Sybberus, now appearing upon the aforesaid attachments, it is ordered that they may in the meantime till the commission be executed carry their ore and cinders to the king's works, at such rates and prices as have been heretofore most usually paid to them for the like, to be paid unto them every two months, when the same shall be measured, and the rest of the said inhabitants which have used to dig and carry mine, ore, and cinders as aforesaid are in the like manner permitted to do the like;

And if the farmer of the king's works refuse to give the said rates as is above mentioned, and such other further rates as shall be appointed by the aforesaid Commissioners then they are left at liberty to carry the same elsewhere at their pleasures to other works within and near about the said forest for the service of such other works: And touching the contempts of them, and all the other said persons, the court is pleased to suspend them till the hearing of the said cause.'

Commissioners who reported on the Forest in 1788 were in error in thinking that all proceedings were stayed and that all parties acquiesced.[1] They added: 'It is conjectured, not without probability, that from this Order, by which the inhabitants only who had

1 3rd Rpt.of 1788, pp. 11, 12.

been accustomed to work in the mines were permitted to dig for ore, they have since considered that restriction as an establishment of their right, and a record in their favour, and have from that time called themselves free miners.'[1] On the contrary, the miners would not compromise their rights for the future by succumbing to the above-mentioned Order, and renewed litigation ensued in the Exchequer Court in 1613-14.[2] Relevant extracts from documents relating to the case are given below:

The Earl of Pembroke's Bill of Complaint to the Chancellor of the Exchequer, the Chief Baron, &c.

'Most humblie complaining sheweth unto your honours your suppliant William Earl of Pembroke being His Majesty's farmer of the Forest of Dean. ... That whereas our most gracious &c King James [I] was lawfully siesed in his demesne as of fee in right of his crown of England of the Castle, Town and Manor of St. Brevells in the sd co. and of the sd. Forest and of a great quantity of waste ground and other grounds parcel of the sd. Forest in which grounds there is great quantity of iron myne and ore and similar fit to be converted into iron, and divers open mines wherein the same myne and ore is to be digged and gotten and hath heretofore been digged and gotten. And our sovereign Lord so being seised of the premises the 13th day of June in the 9th year of His Majesty's reign [1611] by his highness letters patents sealed. ... Did demise grant and lett unto your suppliant the sd. Castle, Town, Manor, Forest ground and ore, myne and synders (excepting all woods and trees thereupon growing) for the term of 40 years from then and next following yielding and paying therefore yearly the yrly rent of four score seaven pounds and five shillings of lawful money of England And the King's Majesty by his Indenture sealed and bearing date the 17th day of February in the sd. 9th year of his majesty's reign did grant and sell unto your sd. suppliant 1200 cords of wood yearly [etc. see Pembroke's grant] The first year's rent or sum of two thousand four hundred thirty three pounds six shillings eight pence as afsd to be paid at the feast of St. Michael the Archangel which day be in the yr of our Lord God 1613 as in and by the sd Indenture at large appeareth. By virtue of which several grants to your Suppliant made, your Suppliant was and is lawfully possessed of the premises and hath bestowed and disbursed great somes of money amounting to £3000 and above in making and erecting of iron works, furnaces and forges and cutting and coaling of the sd. wood and digging and getting of the sd. myne, sinders and ore and in other necessary provisions for the renting and spending of the sd. woods whereby to raise the said great yrly rent.... But now so it is may it please your Lordships that one William Hall, gent, John Morgan, gent, Thomas Phillipp, John Harper, Henry Willcocks, John Kedgin, James Burt, Richard Birt, William Yeme, Christopher Skyn, William Morse, Thomas Kedgin, John Burt, Thomas Whitson, William Siberance, Henry Tyler, Edward Wheler *als* Partridge, Edward Keere, Richard Keere, George Plummer, Thomas Price the elder, Thomas Price the Younger, Christopher Dowle, Richard Dowle, Thomas Monsell, Randall Mark, Henry Dowle, John Fox, Henry Morton, William Tomlyne, Kedgin Hoiskins, Thomas Fryer, Thomas Madock, and Mathew Morse and divers other persons to your Suppliant as yet unknown who have heretofore by pretence of title of comon and of Estovers in the sd. Forest taken libertie to themselves to fell cut down, waste and spoil his Majesty's wood growing in the sd. Forest at their wills and pleasures and therefore intending

1 3rd Rpt.of 1788, p. 12.
2 E112/83/411 (Exch. K.R.'s Bills and Answers 11 Jas. I).

to hinder his Majesty to make any benefit or profit of his sd. woods, to the end they may continue their said spoils have sithence the sd. several grants made to your Suppliant combined and confederated together and bound themselves by oaths, bonds, covenants and promises and otherwise to digg myne and get into their hands all the myne, iron ore and sinders being within the sd. Forest and the same to carry and convey in the Palatine of Ireland and to other ironworks and places from your Suppliant's sd. works and utterly to take away all the myne, iron ore, sinders and other matter wherewith your Suppliant shd make Iron with the same woods &c. and thereby to disable not only your suppliant to pay the sd. yrly Rent &c. And for the effecting of their sd. confederacy and combination they the said William Hall, gent, John Morgan [as above] and the sd. other persons unknown have at divers times [since beginning of Pembroke's grant] wrongfully entered the sd. Forest and they have unlawfully digged the grounds and soils of the sd. Forest and have there digged and gotten great store of iron mynes, ore and sinders amounting to six thousand cartloads of iron myne and ore, every load being well worth thirty shillings and 6000 cartloads of sinders every load thereof being well worth fifteen shillings and all the same Iron myne, ore and sinders have taken and carried to the rivers of Severn and Wye to be transported into the realm of Ireland and to divers ironworks and other places without the licence or consent of your Suppliant and against his will and there have sold and converted the same to their own uses and the said [names as above] and other persons unknown not therewise satisfied have utterly refused and denied and still do refuse and deny to bring any of the sd. Iron myne ore and sinders being by them gotten as afsd to your Suppliant's factors and servants although they would and will give as much as any other for the same.... Since about Trinity term now last past granted and awarded out of his Majesty's Court of Exchequer and directed to the said [names as above] and all the other inhabitants of the sd. Forest thereby forbidding them and every of them to carry away Iron Myne, ore and sinders out of the sd. Forest to any place but only to your Suppliant's sd. works and to and for yr Suppliant's use, which Injunction was duly published and made known to all and every the sd. persons and inhabitants, yet they the sd. William Hall [&c. as above] being inhabitants of the sd. Forest at the time of the awarding of the sd. Injunction and ever since thence and well knowing of the sd. Injuncton have continued their sd. wrongful digging, getting, carrying, selling and controlling of the sd. Iron myne ore and sinders to the sd. Rivers and other places.... [This being contrary to the grant]... In tender consideration whereof ... [asks for writs of suppoena to be directed to all the named men to make them appear in the Court of Exchequer].'

'*The joint and several answers of James Burte, Edward Kyn, John Burte, Thomas Whitson, Henry Tyler, Edward Partridge, Thomas ..., John Smyth, James Keere, Richard Whoper, Thomas Whoper, George Keere, Thomas Keere, William ..., John White, William Worgan, Thomas Morse, John Williams ..., Symon Griffiths, Giles Cassell, James Elley, defendants. to the Bill of Complaint of the Right Honourable William Earl of Pembroke*:

Those defendants saving unto them and every of them all advantage and benefit of exception to the substantie and insufficiency of the said Bill of Complaint hereafter to be by them or any of them for answer ... true it is for ought these defendants know that the King is lawfully seized of his demenses of fee in the right of the crown of England of the customs, town and manor of St. Brevells and of the sd. Forest and of a great quantity of waste ground and of wooded ground in the sd. Forest. [They recognised the grant that Pembroke has from the

King as it appears in the Bill of Complaint] And those defendants do not hold it such interest right and title of and in the premises which do belong unto the King's most excellent Majesty or his patent but doth crave the favour of his honourable Court that all such liberties and franchises and privileges as doth belong to those defendants and to the rest of the Mynors, within the sd. Forest may be allowed unto them and therefore those defendants for further answer doth say and every of them sayeth as followeth: that by all the time whereof the memory of man is not to the contrary there hath been and now are certain men the number of whom hath been and now is uncertain who hath been trained up to dig and work in the myne and myne Pitts within the Forest of Dean and the liberties of the castle of St. Brevells within the assart lands adjoining the sd. Forest, and other ancient demenes lands lying near the sd. Forest for Iron ore, which men hath byn tyme out of mind of man called Mynors of the Forest of Dean and ought by ancient custom to be borne within the liberties of the Forest of Dean as those defendants hope they shall manifestly prove, and they hope likewise to manifest by good proofs to this honorable court that the King's Majesties most noble progenitors, Kings of this Realm of England granted the liberties, franchises, customs and privileges hereafter following and mentioned to the sd. Mynors which liberties and franchises have been by ancient usages, customs and prescriptions tyme out of mind ratified and confirmed, and as those defendants to the further satisfaction of this honorable Court will manifestly prove has been allowed before the Justice in Eyre and also at the Courts of Justice holden in King Edward the Thirds tyme before the Constable of the sd. Forest and Steward of the castle of St. Brevells and gaylor thereof and kept within the limits of the sd. Forest upon the Myne which is called the Myne Lawe by and signed by 48 Mynors sworn, those customs hereafter specified were by their verdict affirmed and confirmed as by ancient evidence it doth appear ready to be shown to this honorable Court to the which former certainty they do refer themselves, which liberties and franchises be as followeth: that the Mynors of the sd. Forest may dig within the King's soil within the sd. Forest of Dean for myne of Iron and ore, and convert the same to their own uses and behalf yielding to the King's Majesty the profit and benefit hereafter mentioned, *viz*: for the ore that after the sd. Mynors have or any of them hath, made and digged a myne pytt to digge ore the sd. pytt ought to be gayled, and marked, and of every partner in the sd. pitt one penny ought to be pd to the King's bayliff or gayler called the gaile penny; after the Pytt is gayled and the parties thereof divided, the gaylor which is the King's bayliff for the Mynors may and used to appoint one of the mynors of the sd. Forest of Dean skylful in the sd. trade of myninge to enter freely without charge into the sd. myne pitt and digg and get ore for the King: the profit thereof is answered to the sd. Gaylor or to the King's Majesties Bayliff who is and ought to be accountable to the King's Majesty for the same. And also every Mynor within the sd. Forest for every week that he worketh, hath used and ought to pay to the sd. Gaylor or the King's Bayliff a penny. And also within the bounds of the sd. Forest of Dean tyme out of minde a Court hath been used to be holden and kept for myne laws to try matters touching the sd. myne and ore before the Constable of the sd. Forest of Dean and the clarke of the Courte of the castle of St. Brevells and the Gaylor or the King's Bayliff and if the plaintiffe or defendant be convicted an amerciament of two shillings is imposed and due to the King's Majestie and ought to be paid to the sd. Gaylor or Bayliffe for the King's use and every Mynor ought to pay for the sd. myne law in every quarter of a yeare a seame of ore worth threepence called 'lawe ore' and among profits due to his Majestie out of the sd. Courte doe arise touching the proceeding therein as by ancient evidence yet remayninge in the defendants' hands yet doth appear and the sd. Mynors tyme out of mynde have used to have timber and wood within the sd. Forest for working and preserving their Myne Pitt to be allotted unto them either at the Speech Court or by the Woodward freely without paying anything for the same over which payment and condition the sd. Mynors and their ancestors, and other Mynors that are dead from time out of mind have enjoyed the same liberties and franchises in and or concerning the sd. Mynes without any interruption and denial until an injunction granted upon an order dated the 25th day of May in the 10th yr. [1612] of his Majesties reign of England. The sd. Mynors were prohibited and injoyned under payne of £100 apiece not to carry or transport any of the sd. Myne or ore digged in the sd. Forest contrary as the defendants do take it under favour of this honourable Court to the customs and privileges affore alleged, in consideration whereof they humbly submit to the Judgement of the Judges of this honorable Court with this that they hope to prove that his Majestie in or about 5 years sithence by his letters Patent under the great seal of England dated in or about the tyme aforesaid did licence one William ? Chorval (Cheinall), Merchant of London and his assignes for and during the term and tyme of Eleaven yeares next ensueing the date hereof at their will and pleasures to ship, load and carry from any parte of England or Wales into Ireland all manner or ore, sinder and myne, for the making of iron without any manner of lett, interuption or disturbance, of which covenants and bondes the sd. Mynors are likewise forfeit if by order of this Honorable Courte they be estranged and prohibited to dig and carry the same in performance of these sd. Contracts duringe the tyme aforesd. ... These defendants have heard and veryly thinketh ytt be true that by this transportinge of ore and making of iron in Ireland, many parties of the sd. country being unpeopled before are now planted and increased thereby ... and his Majesty's customes hereby much advanced and augmented, there arising to the King for the custom inward and outward of the sd. iron 14s. upon every ton, and for the custom of the iron ore outward 1 1/2d. upon every ton whereas it will be evidently proved and manifested as these defendants are informed that there is transported into the sd. realm of Ireland out of the sd. Forest of Deane and the liberties thereof 1400 tons or iron yearly or thereabouts.

And there is made of the sd. iron ore in the Realm of Ireland six hundred ton or thereabouts of Iron the greater part whereof is yrly conveyed again into the realm of England.... [They hoped the King or Court will find for the Miners] ... the said defendants at danger of their lives doe gett a poore living thereby [and the King gets some of it] ... these defendants or the greater part of them have been trayned up in the same trade of Myne and borne within the precints of the sd. Forest [they had dug pits &c. in the Forest, made all the payments required &c., taken timber to keep their pits in order, but only] by the appointment of the sd. Speeche Courte or Woodward of the sd. Forest. [Some of them were freeholders or farmers in Newnham parish and claim that they shd have Firebot, Housebot, Estovers and they have had some tops of trees. The defendants] have not digged nor carried away above 300 loads or thereabouts, every load whereof they have not nor could not sell for above 7s. a load and without that the defendants have digged any synder ... [they had not carried to the Wye except as customary; they had not] ... refused and denied any of the Iron Myne and ore by them digged to the complainants workes or to sell the same to his servants. [but they had brought in almost a year's supply with the other; in fact] divers of the defendants after Candlemas term then laste carryed in divers horse loades of myne and ore to the sd. Complainants workes and his agents and servants did refuse to accept of the same and willed the defendants or some of them to do with ytt what they would. [The miners wd starve if they were to rely only on the custom of Pembroke's works] ... these defendants and the rest of the mynors are able by their labours to gett sufficient iron ore and myne for the complainant's works within half a year which the complainant's forges and mills will hardly spende and work out within one year after as the other half year your defendants and the rest of the mynors shall be voyde of worke and thereby have not means to maintain themselves and their charges ... [they had not taken away any ore out of the Forest to sell but had mined outside the forest and sold that].'

'*The joynt and several answers of John Kedgen, Henrie Wilkcoke, ? William Yeme, Thomas Kedgyn, ? William Sibrance, John Worgan, Richard Bewte, William Morse defendants*:

'These defendants sayinge unto them ... as followeth [The King's claim is rightful; the grant to Pembroke is in order; they beg to have the established privileges etc. retained ... William ?Charval was granted permission to take to Ireland without] interruption or disturbance of any person or persons whatsoever or to the same effect for certaintie thereof these defendants do refer themselves to the said letters patents and since the sd. licence so made from the King's most excellent Majestie as aforesd. the sd. Pattentie and his assignes being Merchants of London have contracted with divers of the sd. Fellowship of Mynors and with many of these defendants for and during the time and term of 4 years yet to come or thereabouts to dig get and carry Iron myne out of the sd. Forest and the assart lands therein and from ancient demesne lands thereunto adjoining to the banks of Wye from whence the sd. Merchants do load the same for Ireland which contract made with the sd. Merchants the sd. Mynors of the sd. Forest and many of these defendants have by their Indenture of Covenant called and delivered or by bond bound themselves to perform faithfully, and keep during the tyme of the said agreement to the persons aforesaid which covenant, bond or bonds the sd. miners are like to forfeit if by order of this honorable Court they be destroyed and prohibited to dig and carry the same to the banks of Wye in performance of the sd. Contract [They had taken to the Wye only ore as mentioned above. The agents of Pembroke after Candlemas refused more ore] and willed these defendants or some of them to do with it what they would. [The ore taken since the Injunction came from assart and ancient demesne near the Forest.]'

Although it is not possible to say with certainty the result of this litigation, undoubtedly it gave the miners great cause for alarm. They do however appear to have emerged with their customs unbroken though the first symptoms of the decay of their exclusive privileges were apparent.

On 22 November 1613[1] the Privy Council issued a warrant to 'the constable of the Forest of Dean and to George Marshall, His Majesty's servant', stating that 'upon information of much abuse and disorder in the felling and cutting of wood and timber trees within the Forest of Dean' connected with the grant to the Earl of Pembroke and 'as otherwise by the borderers and near dwellers to the Forest for their private benefit and advantage', the Council had sent George Marshall to investigate. From his report it appeared 'that the abuses and disorders are such that unless some course be taken to stay and hinder the proceedings therein, it will tend to the utter devastation and spoil of the said Forest, to the great inconvenience of the public, in such store and provision of timber as is requisite and necessary for the use of His Majesty's Navy. These are, therefore, to will and require you to make your present repair unto the said Forest, and

1 A.P.C. 1613-14, p. 279.

to give order for the stay of any further cutting or felling of any kind of wood or tree whatsoever within that Forest, until His Majesty's pleasure be further known; and likewise to forbid and inhibit, and in His Majesty's name to charge and command all timber men from any further proceeding, in felling, cutting down or clearing, any kind of timber within the said Forest, and that they so dispose of themselves, as every man may return home to his own country, without any expectation of further employment in that place; and lastly to inform yourself by all good ways and means of the disorders and abuses that have of late been committed in felling of trees in the said Forest.'

The Earl of Pembroke seems to have abused his office of Chief Constable in 1617 by having authorised his men to cut trees to which he was not entitled.[1]

In the sixteenth and seventeenth years of his reign, James I granted to sundry persons divers lands which had been taken by assart and purpresture out of the Forest; and in every such grant the mines and minerals were reserved.[2]

The Earl of Pembroke was not the only person responsible for abuses in the Forest, for Sir William Throckmorton, Challoner and Harris, and others, were convicted of misappropriation of timber, etc., during the first quarter of the century. This was partly due to the lack of correct administration of Dean which, with other forests, reflected the sleepy remote atmosphere which pervaded them all. The Crown policy, too, was remarkably inconsistent, grants of wood, and suspensions of felling, following each other at periodical intervals.

Early in the seventeenth century an urgent social problem developed in the Forest. A report of 1610[3] stated that the Forest sheltered 'such a multitude of poor creatures, as it is lamentable to think so many inhabitants shall live upon so bare provision as upon spoil of the forest woods'. Hundreds of the lesser folk were being attracted to the Forest by the iron industry. Employment was sporadic. There was not always enough employment to go around. Consequently resort was made to stealing timber, game, etc. In 1622 the more respectable inhabitants petitioned against their depredations describing the perpetrators as 'people of very lewd lives and conversations, leaving their own and other countries, and taking the place for a shelter and a cloak to their villainies'; there was no hope of them earning a legitimate livelihood. In 1640[4] it was feared that 'the poorer people would impoverish the richer sort'. Again, in 1646, regarders reported:[5] 'We are not able to suppress them. They resist us, and have often beaten and abused most of us. We have no power in our commission to require the aid

1 E178/3837 and E134/22 James I/M/42. Sound oaks were supposed to be marked for the king, and only decayed oaks given to the farmers. Royal Commissioners had been sent into the Forest to mark trees for the king's use. They had done their work sloppily, if not dishonestly, and the earl's men disregarded the little they had done. Some of his woodcutters when asked how they dared cut trees marked for the king answered 'that they had done nothing but that which, if it were to be done again, they would do it'. John Snaype, a woodcutter to the said earl, being found cutting down another marked tree, was demanded how he durst so do. Whereunto he answered 'that for two pots of ale he would cut down that tree, or any other so marked'.

2 3rd Rpt. of 1788, p. 12. (See, for example, grant by James I of certain lands to William Winter and William Bell, saving to himself and his successors all mines, 'quarries of sea-coal,' etc. – 5 Prs. Orig. 16 James I. *rot.* 3; or 13, or Prs. Orig. 16 James I. *rot.* 171, L. 172.)

3 Lansd. M.S. 166, fol. 354 (Br. Liby.).

4 E134/16-17 Chas. I/H/1.

5 E101/141/6.

or assistance of any officer or soldier whatsoever. If there be not some speedy course taken for the pulling down of the cabins, and for the punishment of these beggarly persons that are common spoilers of the timber, there will be every day more and more spoils made and committed.'

At this time many of the inhabitants depended for a livelihood on the quarrying and working of stone in the Forest. In 1622 some of them dug, and claimed a right to dig, grindstone on lands in the Forest 'farmed' by Sir Richard Catchmaid.[1] In consequence the attorney-general filed an Information in the Exchequer Court against some of them (Young, Elly and others) on Sir Richard's behalf. The Court, without decreeing the right, on account of their poverty recommended it to Sir Richard not to oppress them for so trifling an article, the stone not being worth more than the labour of raising it, and it seems they paid ten groats (3s. 4d.) each as an acknowledgement for digging.[2]

In 1627 the Earl of Pembroke again came into possession of the ironworks, subletting to Sir Basil Brooke, George Mynne and Thomas Hackett. In the same year Sir John Winter,[3] who was destined to play an important but unfortunate part in the Forest, completed an agreement with the Crown for the rental of woodlands to supply fuel for use in his ironworks at Lydney.[4] He was to follow this in 1640 with a much more important agreement which had disastrous effects upon the Forest.

Various Exchequer Depositions by Commissioners provide relevant information on the Dean mines and miners of the seventeenth century.[5] One of the most useful is in connection with a lawsuit at Gloucester in 1625.[6] The two principal points at issue were the right of the miners to mine in land in private ownership,[7] and to dispose of the iron ore as they pleased. The most useful portions of the Interrogatories and Depositions are given below:

'Interrogatories administered for the examination of witnesses on the part and behalf of Sir William Throckmorton, Kt. and Bt., and Bayneham Throckmorton, Esq., in a cause depending in his Majesty's High Court of Exchequer commonly called the Exchequer Chamber wherein the said Sir William ...and Bayneham Throckmorton are plaintiffs and Sir Thomas Coventry, Kt., the King's Majesty's attorney-general, defendant.'

'I. Do you know the freeholders' lands and tenements within the perambulation of the Forest of Dean in the County of Gloucester and the customs and usages within the freehold

1 This family name appears as Cachiman, Cachemay, Catchmay, Catchmaye, Catchmaid and even Katchmayd.

2 Fosbrooke, vol. ii, p. 112. The acknowledgement of 3s. 4d. remained as the charge for opening and working quarries until 1859, when it was amended to £1 for each quarry of 20 yards in length and 1s. for every additional yard of length (39th Rpt. of Coms. of Woods dated 28 June 1861). See also PRO E125/24/f155, 1642: Richard Elly and William Vick *v*. John Catchmay. For a 'case' re taking (illegally) grindstones, millstones and other stones from Bickshead Quarry, see Maidstone Record Office, 1622 (Cranfield Papers, U.269/1. OE 1585/5).

3 Born about 1600, d. about 1673.

4 F. H. Harris: *Wyntours of the White Cross House*, (1923), p. 42.

5 It is surprising that these Depositions were not scrutinised and referred to by the Commissioners of 1788, 1831 and 1838.

6 E134 Exch. Deps. by Coms., 22 James I (1625) Easter, 8. Certain extracts from this Dep. were included by the present author in an article in the Three Forest Newspapers, 19 January 1945.

7 In particular, Noxon Park (east of Clearwell).

lands and tenements concerning the digging and getting of iron stone and iron ore out of the same lands and the employment of the same ore; and for how long time have you known the same? Declare the truth in particular and at large upon your oath and what you have credibly heard concerning the said custom and usage before the time of your knowledge; declare the truth also upon your oath.'

To this Interrogatory, Richard Whittington of Newland, gentleman, aged sixty years, deposed:

'He doth know divers of the freeholders' lands and tenements within the perambulation of the Forest of Dean and he doth partly know the customs and usages concerning the digging and getting of iron stone and iron ore out of the lands, and the employment of the ore, and the same he has known for the space of 30 years or thereabouts, and further says that since the time of his knowledge the miners and pioneers had used and still do use to come into the grounds of any of the freeholders to dig iron mine and iron ore, and to take, carry away, and dispose thereof to their best advantage at their pleasure, without taking any leave of the owners of the ground.'

Thomas Hooper of Clearwell, miner, aged fifty-four years, deposed:

'By their custom they have entered and do usually enter into any such lands, without the leave or consent of the owners of the said lands, and set themselves on work and dig iron stone and iron ore at their pleasure, disposing thereof to their own use, and advantage, yielding to His Majesty a penny a week forth of every man's work during the time they do work, and to the gailor [gaveller] four seams of ore for the whole year, or three pence in money every quarter in lieu of every seam, and further that His Majesty may put in one workman into every mine pit so entered upon and the owner of the ground another for their own several uses, and he has never heard otherwise concerning the said customs or usages.'

Edward Skynn of Clearwell, miner, aged fifty years, Thomas Kedgewin of Clearwell, miner, aged fifty years, and Thomas Borrowe of St. Briavels, miner, aged thirty-six years, deposed on similar lines to Whittington and Hooper.

'II. Whether all and every such person or persons as have used to dig and get iron stone and iron ore from time to time on any freeholders lands within the forest have done the same by the appointment of the King's Majesty or his predecessors Kings and Queens of this Realm of England or of some of their officers, or else by the only power and right of those who have digged and gotten the said iron stone and iron ore, or for whom they have digged or gotten the same? Declare the truth upon your oath.'

Whittington deposed:

'All and every such person and persons as have so used to dig and get iron stone and iron ore from time to time in any freeholder's land have pretended to do by their custom and not by any appointment to the King's Majesty or his predecessors.'

Hooper, Skynn, Kedgewin and Borrowe deposed on similar lines.

'III. Whether hath the now King's Majesty or any his predecessors King or Queens of England had or received from time to time any other or further benefit or profit of iron stone or iron ore gotten or digged out of any freeholder's land within the said forest than only certain duties usually paid by the diggers of the said ore that is to say one penny a week from every miner or digger of iron stone or iron ore for breaking of the ground within the liberty of the King's forest and three seams of ore to be paid once every quarter, or certain sum of money in lieu thereof for the maintenance of the 'myne lawe' there for the ordering and governing of those businesses both between them and any others that they have to do with all in those businesses, and, if yea, then what sum; And liberty further for the King in respect of his Royalty of the said forest by his officer of the miners there called the 'Gaoller' to put in one workman or miner into every mine, pit or work place, that hath been before digged and made fit for getting of mine or ore by some other miners, the said workman or miner for the King to get ore out of the said place for the use and benefit of the King? Declare the truth upon your oath.'

Whittington deposed:

'He doth not know any benefit that the King's Majesty or predecessors have had or received of iron stone or iron ore gotten or digged out of any freeholder's land within the forest, than only 1d. per week from every miner or digger of iron stone or iron ore; if they do work and get the hire and liberty for the gailor to put in one workman on behalf of the King's Majesty into every mine pit.'

The other witnesses deposed on similar lines.

'V. Whether it is lawful or free by the ancient custom and usage of the said forest for any miner or digger of ore in the forest to dig and get ore in any place within the liberties of the forest without the assignment, appointment or leave of the King, his farmers or officers or any of them or of the said Gaollers of the mines in the forest, and whether may the miners and diggers of ore in the forest and those for whom they dig and get the ore according to the custom and usage of the forest carry away and dispose of the said iron stone and iron ore whither and to whomsoever they please as well within the liberty of the forest as without for their own benefit and advantage without the leave of the King, his farmers or officers or of the said Gaoler or any other of the King's officers? Declare the truth upon your oath.'

Whittington deposed:

'By the ancient custom and usage of the forest it is lawful and free for any miner or digger of any iron stone or iron ore to dig and get ore in any place within the liberties of the forest, and to dispose and sell the same to their own benefit and advantage without the assignment, appointment or leave of the King's farmers, the said Gailors or any other officers of the forest; only whether they may sell such ore out of the liberty of the forest this deponent knoweth not.'

Hooper deposed similarly, but added: '... they have sold and do usually sell such ore as well without as within the liberty of the forest.' The other witnesses deposed on lines similar to Hooper.

'VI. Whether by the custom and usage of the forest may the King or his farmers or gaolers or other officers as in the King's own right to dig or get any iron ore in any of the freeholders' lands within the liberty of the forest for the King's own use and benefit other than one workman or miner into every pit or work place as aforesaid after the said pit or work place hath been first opened by some of the miners of the forest in their own right and liberty or by the appointment of such others in the forest as have right to the said pit or workplaces? Declare the truth in particular and at large upon your oath.'

Whittington did not depose to this Interrogatory, but Hooper deposed:

'By the custom and usage of the forest neither the King's Majesty nor his farmers, gailors or other officers as in the King's own right may dig or get any ore within any of the freeholders' lands within the liberty of the forest for the King's own use and benefit other than one workman or miner in every pit or workplace as aforesaid after the said pit or workplace has been first opened by some of the miners of the forest in their own right and liberty, or by the appointment of such other miners in the forest as have right to the said pits or workplaces.'

The other witnesses deposed likewise. We now come to:

'Interrogatories administered unto the witnesses produced on the part and behalf of Sir Thomas Coventry, Kt., Defendant, His Majesty's attorney-general for and on the behalf of His Majesty at the suit of Sir Willm. Throckmorton, Kt. and Bt., and Bayneham Throckmorton, Esq., Complainants.'

'I. Do you know certain grounds and parcels of lands called the 'Thraves', 'Kingsmore', 'Chelfridge' and 'Lanquire', yea or no; if yea, in what parish do the same lie, and whether are the same within the precincts and limits of the King's Majesty's forest of Deane in the county of Gloucester, yea or no; And whether have the miners and Pyoners heretofore digged or may Pioners and miners within the forest dig in the aforesaid grounds and parcels of land and other the premises for iron ore and iron stone, 'Sea-cole' and 'Oker' by the custom of the forest, yea or no; And how do you know the same to be true; And how long have you known that it hath been so used or accustomed; And whether are there not within the said grounds or some of them apparent notes of pits where anciently there hath been digging for the same?'

Anthony Callowe of Mitcheldean, gentleman, aged sixty-five years, and Christopher Tucker of Littledean, aged thirty-eight years, miner and deputy gaveller to Thomas Cachmaye, Esq. (gaveller), did not depose to this Interrogatory. James Keere of Newland, miner, aged fifty years, deposed that the miners' custom had always been exercised in 'Thraves', 'Kingsmore', 'Chelfridge' and 'Lanquire'. Christopher Morgan the Younger of Clearwell, aged thirty-five years, deputy gaveller to Thomas Cachmaye, Esq., deposed that he knew Noxon Park and confirmed the miners' custom, except in 'Chelfridge'.

> II. Do you know of any custom or usage for the digging of iron stone and iron ore, 'Seacole' or 'Oker' within the freehold lands of any of His Majesty's subjects lying within the forest of 'Deane' for the making of iron at all times; if yea, declare the said custom and usage, and who have used to dig there, for whom and for whose profit hath the same been and what advantage hath His Majesty or any of his progenitors had out of the same; And by whose appointment have they so digged there, and how long hath the same been so used, and what is the said custom and usage and how hath the same been used for the manner of digging for the said iron stone and iron ore?'

Callowe deposed that he was a freeholder at Mitcheldean and that the miners had free access during the last forty years; and when they had entered their pit 'with a descent of three steps'[1] they called for the 'gailor'. He continued: 'The said 'Pyoners' or miners take upon them this freedom (as they say) of an ancient grant made unto them by some King or Kings of England, His Majesty's progenitors, by which they claim a custom of free digging in any man's freehold land within the perambulation of the forest, which they have used and do use until this day.' He added that he has put in one workman for himself and had the benefit thereof. Keere more or less confirmed, and mentioned that the gaveller must also grant a right of way to the mines. Tucker deposed:

> 'That he is 'Deputy gailor Beneath the Wood' and has received the duties due to His Majesty from the miners for digging and getting of mine out of the several grounds and freehold lands of Wm. Callowe and Mr. Aileway and other grounds within His Majesty's waste of 'Michel Dene', and that he hath received 12 seams of ore, by every week forth of the said several mines (be the workmen or works more or fewer) and further says that by the custom and usage of the forest it is lawful for the freeborn miners to enter upon any man's ground ... without leave of the owner. At the opening of the ground when they have digged the pit three steps deep the miner gives the 'gailor' notice thereof and gives him 1d. for himself and pence apiece for as many as shall work with him in the same pit for the entering of his name and the name of the pit, and that upon the finding of the mine [ore] it is lawful for the 'gailor' to put a man into the work for the King's Majesty, and the lord of the soil can put in another; and that if any of the said workmen who did first undertake the work do take unto themselves any one or more to help them in the work and thereby make a new 'dole' or part, then it is lawful by their custom for the 'gailor' to put in for the King one other workman into every such 'dole' or part, and that every company of colliers that draw three charges of 'cole' by the week do pay by the week to the 'gailor' for His Majesty's use a 1d. a man if they get three charges every week and a seam of 'cole' every quarter of a year that they work to the 'gailor' which he receives to His Majesty's use for their 'lawe'.'[2]

Tucker added that he had known these customs for twenty years and had heard the

---

1 Keere, in his deposition to Interrogatory No. I also confirms *re* the 'descent of three steps'; see also Tucker, *infra*.

2 Keere, in his deposition to Interrogatory No. I also mentioned this 'Lawe oare'.

same from his ancestors. Morgan deposed likewise, and it is important to note that the two deputy gavellers, who would, if anyone, know the correct customs and usages of the miners, throughout their depositions confirmed, as far as was in their power, these customs and usages.

> 'III. Whether have His Majesty or any of his progenitors or his or their officers or workmen used to dig freely in all the freehold lands within the forest for iron stone and iron ore for the making of iron or for 'Seacole' or 'Oker', yea or no; if yea, what be those officers and workmen and how are they called that have used to dig for iron stone and ore for His Majesty's use; And how long hath there been any such usage for digging; And by whose appointment have they used to dig; And what are the officers called and how are they distinguished in their several places and names that are employed therein, and how long have they continued within the forest and how ancient hath the said Custom been for digging within all the freeholders' lands of the said forest as you know or have heard?'

Callowe confirmed the miners' customs while Keere produced several 'ancient instruments in writing expressing their customs within the forest'. Tucker confirmed the custom in freehold lands and others, and added that he 'has seen an ancient deed dated in the reign of King Edward the Second testifying the liberty and privilege of the miners within the said forest'. He also confirmed the previous witnesses' comments on the Mine Law Court and its officers. Worgan confirmed Tucker's deposition.

> 'IV. Whether doth the Park or inclosed grounds of the said Sir William Throckmorton called 'Noxon Parke' lie within the precincts of the forest, yea or no; if yea, whether hath His Majesty's officers or the officers of any his progenitors or any of 'the Company of Pyoners and Minors' within the forest used to dig within the same inclosed ground called 'Noxon Parke' for iron stone and ore for the making of iron for His Majesty, yea or no; if yea, who have so used to dig there and by whose appointment have they so digged there; How hath the iron stone and ore thence coming been employed and for how long time have they so used to dig as you know or have heard and what profit hath His Majesty or any of his progenitors used to have out of the same?'

Callowe and Keere could not say for certain as regards Noxon Park, but they thought the miners' customs applied to those lands as to other places. Tucker did not depose but his colleague, Worgan, confirmed the customs as applying to Noxon Park, adding that the king received the same from mines in Noxon Park as from other lands in the Forest.

> 'VI. Do you know of any other matter of thing concerning the usage and custom of digging for iron stone and ore, 'seacole' or 'oker' for His Majesty's service as is aforesaid within the freeholders' lands within the precincts of the Forest; Have not His Majesty's officers, pioneers and miners within the Forest or some of them used to dig generally in all the lands of the freeholders for iron stone and ore as cause did require; And how hath the usage and custom thereof been in all the time of your memory, and how hath the same been formerly used as you have heard, and what are the reasons that make you so to say or affirm; declare your full and whole knowledge therein to the best of your uttermost memory; And whether do you

> know or have credibly heard that the miners or pioneers digging in any of the aforementioned grounds or any of the lands of other the freeholders within the Forest have converted or sold to their or any of their uses any of the mine [ore] so digged; if yea, to whom to your knowledge?'

This interrogatory brought forth nothing more of interest other than the confirmation by Tucker that the miners sold ore both to the king and to others, and outside as well as inside the Forest. It has not been possible to trace the result of the lawsuit, but in later years the free miners were refused the right exclusively to claim gales in Noxon Park.

In 1631 the Privy Council issued an injunction against felling any trees within three miles of the Wye or ten miles of the Severn, 'it being the usual care of the State, and of this Board in particular, to respect the preservation of timber for the upholding of navigation'.[1] During March and April of the same year serious riots took place in the Forest, particularly at Mailscot,[2] and were repeated periodically until well into 1634. The Forest and county officials were all invoked to try to keep order. One of the reasons for the disturbances was the attempt by Sir Edward Villiers to enclose certain lands at Mailscot and to open coal and iron ore mines there, under a grant received in 1625.[3] In April 1633[4] John Broughton, the first deputy surveyor for Dean, complained that 'the spoils done are so great that he will undergo excessive toil to reform abuses'. The previous year 'necessary remembrances' had been sent to the Forest officials to conserve timber, as shipbuilding supplies were at a low ebb throughout the country.[5] The position was the same in March 1634.[6]

It appears that about this time the king was seriously considering selling a large portion, or all, of the Forest. In 1633 we find Charles, Viscount Andover and James Levingston offering 4s. per acre for 8,000 acres 'which is a rate far beyond the proffer of any other person for forest lands'.[7] Should a better offer be received, they ask for preference. Later in the year they drew attention to their original offer adding: '...but then it was not thought a fit course, the Commissioners being in treaty with some persons for particular parcels of the same.' 'The King having since declared to incline that way' the petitioners pray 'that on the general disafforestation they may proceed as offerers for the parcels of land given in to the Commissioners'.[8] However, in April 1634, we hear that Sir John Winter 'having proffered to perpetuate to His Majesty and his successors £4,000 yearly from the Forest of Dean in consideration of certain grants to be made to him of the growing trees in Dean Forest and the ironworks there, after the determination of the grant therefore to the Earl of Pembroke, and having already lent the King £4,000 in part of £8,000 for two years' rent agreed to be advanced, the Lord Treasurer is to draw up a contract.[9]

---

1 MS. A.P.C., xli. 207.
2 See Hart, *The Commoners of Dean Forest*, 1st Edn. (1951).
3 C.S.P.D., Chas. I. p. 538, App.
4 *Ibid.*, 1633-4, vol. ccxxxvi. p. 20; see also *ibid.*, vol. ccli, p. 296.
5 *Ibid.*, 1631-3, vol. ccxxix, p. 491.
6 *Ibid.*, 1633-4, vol. cclxii. p. 484.
7 *Ibid.*, vol. cclvii, pp. 380-1, No. 92.
8 *Ibid.*, 1634, p. 381, No. 93.
9 *Ibid.*, 1633-4, vol. cclxvi, p. 576.

The Justice Seat in Eyre of 1634. Meanwhile preparations were being made for the holding of a Justice Seat in Eyre for the Forest[1] which proved to have far-reaching effects on the inhabitants and the various assignees of the Forest. The Eyre was held in Gloucester castle during July 1634. Here all officers of the Forest, and freeholders and others of the Hundred of St. Briavels and of the lands bordering the Forest, were entitled to put in their claims to privileges and rights, and to attempt to establish the same to the satisfaction of the Court. Those dealing with commoning are included in another volume.[2] One of the claims was by the Earl of Pembroke to be constable of St. Briavels Castle and warden of the Forest under a grant from the King, and in virtue of that appointment to be chief judge at the Mine Law Court held and used for the governing of the mines of iron ore and coal and the workmen within the Forest.[3] No claim by miners appears, the same apparently having been rejected as illegal 'they not being a Corporation'.[4] However, mention of the Mine Law Court gave credence to the miners' customs and privileges. Other claims were by Edmund Berrow, Esq., of 'all mines, seacoal and iron ore' within his bailiwick of Blakeney,[5] and by Sir Baynham Throckmorton, senior, Bart., of '16d. of profit on each [char]coal pit within the Forest'.[6] At the same Court the Government effected the enlargement of the Forest to its widest extent as in 1228 and 1282.[7] No record appears of any claim being allowed with reference to the free miners, and, if we can believe a later account,[8] 'the claim of the miners had been rejected at this Justice Seat [1634], they not being a corporation'.[9] At the same Court it was ascertained that there were only six houses in the Forest proper; the miners must therefore have lived on the fringe of the Forest.[10] In 1634 'the lieutenants and deputy constables of the castle of St. Briavels and the Forest of Dean' were given instructions 'that no man be suffered to carry any ore or cinders out of the Forest or precincts thereof to any other works than the King's own'.[11]

---

1 Numerous records of the Eyre are extant in Hart, *New History*, pp. 52-78. Officials at Justice Seats had to enquire, *inter alia,* 'if any Mine, Delf of Coal, Stone, Clay, Marle, Turf, Iron or any other Mine hath been made, and who made it, and where'. Also to inquire 'if any Mine hath been made in the Forest since the last Session, or before and hath not been presented, and to present the name or names who made it' (Manwood, *op. cit*., p. 66. See Hart, *New History,* pp. 52-82.)

2 Hart, *The Commoners of Dean Forest*, 2nd Edn., 2002, pp. 29-32.

3 F20/1(17); Hart, *Royal Forest,* pp. 111 *et seq*.

4 F20/1(17), p. 7; 3rd Rpt. of 1788, p. 125

5 Similarly on 3 August 1642 the lord of the manor of Mitcheldean professed ownership of all mines within his manor *(Trans. B.&G.A.S.,* vol. vi, 1881-2, p. 209).

6 This was in Throckmorton's capacity of chief forester; see *Cal.Pat.Roll*, 1 Edw. IV, 12 Feb. 1471, p. 296 (Robert Greyndour, chief forester, to which office 'there has belonged from time immemorial, a certain profit, to wit, in every pit of charcoal 20d. every six weeks').

7 Hart, *The Extent and Boundaries of the Forest of Dean* (1947).

8 Return of a Commission of Enquiry dated 5 March 1671 (3rd Rpt. of 1788, p. 12).

9 The Coms. of 1788, in quoting this account, assert that 'if the miners had been dissatisfied with the rejection of their claim, or had thought them well-founded, it was in their power to have sued out a Writ of Allowance (for timber, etc.), by which they would have been restored to the exercise of their rights, if the decision of the Court had been illegal; but this does not appear to have been done (3rd Rpt. of 1788. p. 12).

10 The position was the same in 1712, the six lodges built for the keepers being the only houses within the Forest, though 'there have been many cottages erected within the wastes, but they have been lately pulled down as the best means to preserve the woods and inclosures' (Sir Robert Atkyns: *The Anc. and Present State of Glouc.,* p. 348).

11 C. 99/31.

The next few years witnessed extended litigation between the various ironmasters in the Forest. After almost a quarter of a century of leases of the Crown's ironworks in the Forest, during which time frequent assaults were made directly or indirectly upon the privileges of the miners by the lessees and others, we find the position of the miners again being attacked in 1635. Sir Sackville Crowe writing to Henry, Earl of Holland, on 15 September[1] asserts that some of the inhabitants 'opposed the King's power to dispose of mines, pretending the miners' right of custom; others that the King could not grant common or enter common'. He adds: 'The summer has been spent in needless dispute.' Then on 5 December the same year Edward Terringham (or Tyringham), one of the Privy Councillors, ignored any rights the local miners might have as regards coal and made the following petition[2]:

'Concerning the coalmines in Dean Forest, it is humbly offered to your Lordships' consideration: That the farming of them will not be any way prejudicial to his Majesty either in the farming of the woods and ironworks there, or any way tends to the waste and consuming of his Majesty's woods in that Forest, which may appear as followeth:

It cannot be any prejudice to his Majesty in the farming of his woods and works, for the coalmines afford neither fuel nor any other materials to the making of iron neither hath there been any use made of them at any time heretofore by any of the farmers of his Majesty's woods and works there, being only of use to them the mines of iron ore which I seek not.

It cannot be any prejudice to his Majesty any other ways in the waste or consuming of his woods and timber, for the building of the coalpits, for whereas the colliers (which have taken the liberty to dig and dispose of these mines at their pleasure without rendering to the King any profit for it) have used and spent his Majesty's timber for the building and repairing of their coalpits (out of which his Majesty receives no benefit), I will save his Majesty that expense and waste of timber for I will not desire the allowance of any but find it at my own charge.'

The same day the Lords Commissioners of the Treasury commanded the surveyor-general to consult the auditor of co. Gloucester and to certify 'what profit do now come to his Majesty by the coalmines and what parties do now make use of the said mines and by what warrant'.[3] The surveyor-general, Charles Harbord, reported on 29 December 1635 as follows[4]:

'May it please your Lordships,

Upon this reference touching the coalmines in Dean Forest I have called the Auditor who allegeth that he hath no record in his custody touching the same and can say little thereunto; but I find that the said coalmines have yielded small or no benefit to his Majesty or the crown at any time yet there hath been some use made of them within his Majesty's soil, and that for the most part by the miners of the said Forest who pretend a custom to open and dig mines of iron ore and coal there as well within his Majesty's own soil there as elsewhere, paying his Majesty some small duty for every pit or mine so opened by the hands of an officer there called the Gawler or Gavelor of the Forest, of which custom Mr. Attorney-

1 C.S.P.D. Chas. I, 1635, vol. cccxi, p. 381, No. 45. (3 pp.).
2 *Ibid.,* vol. ccciii, p. 535, No. 61. See Appendix 4.
3 *Ibid.*, No. 61, I.
4 *Ibid.*, No. 61, II.

General hath taken consideration upon a former reference touching the same wherein I did attend him. At what time there was a claim made to the said coalmines amongst other things by the Lord Chamberlain by vertue of a lease of the said Forest granted for 40 years unto the late Earl of Pembroke, Lord Steward, deceased, whereby it was conceived that the soil and all the mines open at the making of the said lease were granted, and that no new mines may be opened either by the lessee or by any others during the said term without the licence of the lessee or his assigns.

It will be inconvenient that any of the said coalmines should be opened or used within any coppice or inclosure to be made within the said Forest, or that any of his Majesty's wood or timber should be wasted or imployed therein, which I humbly submit to your Lordships' great wisdom.'

The two following documents were attached:

'It appeared lately upon debate before Mr. Attorney-General in the presence of the 'Councell of the Mynerall men' of the Forest of Dean, that the miners could not prescribe nor make any title unto the coals as belonging unto them in respect of their 'Mynerall worke'. For that it is of another nature and no way useful or pertinent to the making of iron, but is merely a fuel. And is only in the King to grant and was never formerly granted unto any. Neither do the coal mines pass unto my Lord Chamberlain by his lease as appeareth by a case under my Lord Chief Justice's hands subscribed when he was the King's servant. Neither hath my Lord Chamberlain made use of those mines or any claim thereunto by vertue of his lease: there being now above twenty years thereof encurred.'[1]

'By these words in the King's patent – *Tradimus Concedimus et ad Firmam dimithimus Domin*[iu] *Maner – Villam et Forestade Deane et omnes Mineras eisdem vel alicui eoru spectant vel ptinent* – the lessee hath not power to dig and take coals or other things in mines that were not open or known mines at the time of the patent and grant made. For it doth plainly appear by these words *spectant et ptinent* that it was not the King's meaning to grant any other mines than those only by that were then open and known.'[2]

Terringham had to wait until 1637 before he met with success and in the meantime we find a further restriction on the miners in the form of the undermentioned warrant dated 31 March 1636[3]:

'A warrant to the deputy constables or constable of the castle of St. Briavels and to ye woodwards, foresters, keepers and all other his Majesty's officers and ministers there whom this may concern:

Whereas we are informed that notwithstanding former several restraints made against the carriage of his Majesty's mines [iron ore] and cinders out of the Forest of Dean, divers persons of late times by the connivency of the officers and foresters, and especially since ye standing still of his Majesty's works, have digged within his Majesty's soil iron mines and cinders, and the same have carried and sold to strangers' works, some within some without

1 C.S.P.D. Chas. I, 1635-6, vol. cccvii, p. 23, No. 8.
2 *Ibid.*, No. 8, I.
3 *Ibid.*, vol. cccxvii, pp. 340-1, No. 79. See Appendix 4.

ye Forest, without warrant or licence therefore had or obtained either from his Majesty or any of his officers that had power to licence ye same, and that great quantities now lie at ye River of Wye and elsewhere ready to be transported out of the Forest to foreign works, which for the present tend much to the detriment of his Majesty's farm, and in future may much lessen (if not endanger) the loss of that revenue which his Majesty may make by his iron work there. His Majesty having therefore taken into his particular consideration of what importance the restraint of the mines and cinders is and will be to his own service as also to the general good of his whole realm and resolving to restrain all such mines and cinders as within the said Forest may any way belong to his Majesty to his own work only, and such other as by his Majesty with the advice and consent of his farmers there for the time being shall be licenced to use the same. And the care of such restraint being strictly commanded us by his Majesty, now for the better effecting hereof we have thought good to will and require you (calling before you the miners of the Forest and such other as to you shall seem meet for the discovery of the truth) with what care and diligence you may to examine and certify to us what quantities of mines and cinders have lately and since the Justice Seat [1634] been digged and carried out of the Forest and employed and used in any other work but his Majesty's and by whom carried, and to what works conveyed, and by whom the same was used. And forthwith likewise to seize and take into your possession for his Majesty's use, all such mines and cinders as have been so digged at any of his Majesty's quarries within the said Forest and now lie either carried towards the waterside and laid down there or elsewhere within the Forest ready to be transported, and all such as are laid down at any stranger's furnace within the Forest not licenced by his Majesty to use and spend the same. And that you take good caution for safe custody thereof until you shall receive further order from us therein.

That you forthwith likewise call before you the miners of the said Forest or the most or chief of them and in his Majesty's name straightly require them that from henceforth neither they nor any of their company or servants presume to dig or carry any mines or cinders to or for any work but to his Majesty's work only and such as his Majesty shall from time to time licence as before to be served therewith as they will answer the contrary at their peril. And if any shall after this contemptuously cause to be digged or carried or dig or carry any of his Majesty's mines or cinders out of the said Forest to any other work, than is as before expressed, that you attach or cause to be attached all such horses as you shall find so carrying of mines and cinders. And all such diggers and carriers you shall also apprehend and commit to safe custody until they with sufficient sureties by recognizances to be taken before some Justices of the Peace next adjoining be bound to appear before us or before the Lord Treasurer and Chancellor of the Exchequer for the time being at a certain day to be limited to answer such their contempt. Before which time you shall certify us of your proceeding therein that so we may take such further course as shall be fittest for his Majesty's service. Hereby willing and requiring all Justices of Peace, Constables, foresters, woodwards, keepers and all other his Majesty's officers as well of the said Forest as otherwise whatsoever to be aiding and assisting to you herein as they tender his Majesty's service and will answer the contrary at their peril. And this shall be to you and them and every of them a sufficient warrant in that behalf. Dated at Whitehall the last of March 1636.'[1]

1 Signed by: 'Lo. ArchBpp. of Cant; Lo. Keeper; Lord Treasurer; Lord Privie Seale; Ea. of Salisbury; Ea. of Exeter; Ea. of Morton; Lo. Cottington: Lo. Newburgh; Mr. Sec. Coke; Mr. Sec. Windebanke.'

In 1637 Terringham at last received the grant for which he had petitioned. According to Nicholls[1] the grant included 'all the mines of coal and quarries of grindstone within the Forest of Dean, and in all places within the limits and perambulations thereof, as well those within his Majesty's demesne lands and the waste and soil there, as also all such as lay within the lands of any of his Majesty's subjects within the perambulation of the said Forest, to his Majesty reserved or lawfully belonging, to hold for thirty-one years, at the rent of £30'. Terringham experienced much resistance from the local miners. This appears from the following letter sent by the Privy Council on 2 April 1637[2]:

> To Sir Baynham Throckmorton, Bart., Sir Robert Coke, Kt., Charles Bridgman, Esq., Justices of the Peace for the county of Gloucester.
> Whereas his Majesty being present in Council complaint was made unto the Board by Edward Terringham, Esq. his Majesty's servant, of sundry breaches of the Peace in a high and insolent manner committed upon the persons of such servants and workmen of the said Edward Terringham used by him and employed in and about the digging of coal in his Majesty's coal mines within the Forest of Dean in the county of Gloucester, and also of grindstone in his Majesty's quarries of grindstone there, demised by his Majesty's Letters unto the plaintiff at a certain rent and under such conditions as in the said Letters Patents at large do appear; informing that some of them have been outrageously beaten and drawn out thence for dead, their works smothered and fired, and the whole business with much violence hindered and perturbed, by certain people of base and mean condition, intruding and taking unto themselves a right to dig coal and grindstone in the said mines and quarries though without colour of reason to justify their actions, amongst whom are Christopher Yearesley, Christopher Prosser, William Smith, John White, James Wisham, William Yeames, James Parry and Edward Rannall: the plaintiff humbly seeking for relief herein and that those insolences and misdemeanours might be duly punished, his Majesty taking due consideration of the premises, and finding the things complained of to be of very ill example and the consequence dangerous if such disorders and offences should be let pass with impunity, hath commanded us by express Letters from the Board to require you according to the duty of your place, as being his Majesty's Justices of the Peace for the county aforesaid, both jointly and severally to make strict inquiry of all the insolences and outrages aforesaid, and to punish the offenders according to law, particularly those persons aforenamed, if it shall appear they are guilty of the offences laid to their charge by the said Edward Terringham; and to use all dilligence to maintain and keep his Majesty's peace in the working of those aforesaid mines and quarries. In doing whereof, in case, through the refractorines and disobedience of the offenders, ordinary means to you shall not seem sufficient, you are then to bind over the offenders to answer for their several offences at this Board, and to certify unto us the recognizances together with the examinations of the parties offending to the end such further course may by us be taken as may best serve for repressing all disorders of this kind: And so not doubting of your care in a business of this consequence, we bid you, etc...'[3]

1 N.H., p. 27. I have not traced the actual grant.

2 A.P.C., MS. vol. xlvii. fos. 303-4. See Appendix 4.

3 Footnote: 'Ld. Archb. of Cant.; Lo. keeper; Lo. Trer; Lo. P. Seal; Lo. Chamblayne; Mr. Vice-Chamblayne: Mr. Secretary Windebank.'

About this time the farmers of the ironworks petitioned the King for 'a proclamation for restraint of the mines which during this dispute by the unruly multitudes are violently in all disorder, and infinite quantities carried away to strangers' works'.[1] The petition was referred to the attorney-general to prepare the necessary proclamation. The Justices of the Peace were ordered to suppress the rioters. The local miners apparently did not challenge Terringham's right to mine in the Forest but only his desire to interfere with their own concessions. However, after six months Terringham gave up working on his own account, and the same year (1637) witnessed a determined effort on the part of the Crown to decide the legality or otherwise of the miners' customary privileges. Sir John Bankes, the attorney-general, commenced a suit on behalf of Terringham against Sir John Winter and the following miners: Christopher Yarsley, Christopher Prosser, William Smith, John White, James Wisham, William Yeame, James Parry and Edward Rannal. The Interrogatories and Depositions[2] in connection with this suit supply the following items of interest:

'*Interrogatories ministered by Sir John Bankes, attorney-general, to witnesses produced against all defendants.*'[3]

'II. Were or are you a servant to any of the defendants and how long? Were you born in the Hundred of St. Briavels within the Forest of Dean? How many parishes are there in the said hundred? How long have you lived in any of them? Have you been a miner or digger of coals, and where? And what coals have you had from thence?"

Edward Worgan of Woolaston, husbandman, aged sixty:

He was born in Newland parish in the Forest, was never servant to any of the defendants, never had any benefit out of the mines of coal or ore since he was 14 years old at which time he wrought for and under his father. He has lived in the parish of Woolaston about 40 years and now lives there and expects no benefit of the said mines, ore or coal.

William Morgan of Chappell Hill, co. Monmouth, gent., aged sixty:

He was born in the Hundred of St. Briavels in the parish of Newland and has lived there sundry times about 27 years. He was never servant to any of the defendants, nor had nor expects profit from coal, etc.

Christopher Worgan of St. Briavels, yeoman, aged forty-eight:

He was born in Newland and has lived in the Hundred of St. Briavels the great part of his life. Was never servant to any of the defendants, nor worked in any pits for 35 years and only for his father's benefit before that. Although he has not worked he hopes his right and interest

1 C.S.P.D. Chas. I, 1637-8. vol. ccclxxiii, p. 18. See also E112/181/155, 1636-37.

2 E134 Exch. Deps. by Coms. 13 Chas. I, Mich. 42 (1637).

3 Although I have made a transcript of all the Interrogatories and Depositions, in order to conserve space I am including abstracts only. Note also that certain abstracts respecting the office of gaveller and the Mine Law Court are included in Chapters III and IV respectively.

thereof have not diminished.

'III. Do you know the Manor of Lydney now or sometime in the possession of Sir John Winter? Of what extent is it? Does it lie in the metes of the Forest of Dean? Do you know a woodground called Norchards in his possession? How big is it? In what lordship does it lie? What coal mines are there thereon and what coal has been dug there in the last six years and of what value?'

There were no depositions to this Interrogatory.

'IV. How long is it since coal was found in the Forest?'

Christopher Tucker of Littledean, miner, aged fifty-one:

He believes coal has been found in the Forest beyond the memory of man and certainly since his own remembrance.

John Teckall of Littledean, miner, aged fifty:

He believes coal was found in the Forest long before he was born.

'V. Do you know a coal mine in Covord [Coleford], parish of Newland? Is it in the waste of the Forest or in whose freehold, of what value and have defendants taken coal there during the last six years, and from what other mines in the Forest and of what yearly profit?'

There were no depositions to this Interrogatory.

'VII. What coal mines do you know in the parishes of St. Briavels, Newland, Staunton, Bicknor, Ruardean, Mitcheldean, Littledean, Newnham, Blakeney and Lydney, and by whom dug, etc.?'

There were no depositions to this Interrogatory.

'VIII. Do you know the manor and park of Lydney and a waste called Sneade and two other parcels near Lydney Park called 'Yarkley' [Yorkley] and Norchards? Do any of these lie within the ancient or new survey of the Forest and what coal mines have been made on such wastes?'

Tucker deposed that he knew the wastes mentioned but was uncertain whether they lay in the old or new perambulation. He knew one pit in the Norchard which had been wrought by Staffordshire men and other strangers, and not by any miners or workmen inhabiting the Forest. He did not know how much coal they obtained. Teckall deposed likewise, adding that he worked in three pits of the three wastes during the last six years as a servant of Sir John Winter and for his use, and about 200 dozen of coal was extracted during that time. Strangers also worked there.

'*Interrogatories ...on behalf of Sir John Winter.*'

'II. Did Sir Edward Winter receive the issues of the parish and manor of Lydney and are the coal mines in the Norchard parcel of the manor and parish of Lydney? Does Sir John Winter now take the issues of Lydney manor and of the coppice and coalmines and is he not reputed to be lord of that manor?'

Morgan, Henry Hooley of Lydney, yeoman, aged sixty-nine, George Taylor of Lydney, gent., aged seventy, Richard Foule of Lydney, husbandman, aged sixty-seven, and Christopher Wyntour of Lydney, yeoman, aged seventy-two, all deposed in the affirmative.

'III. Was the said manor and parish of Lydney and the said coppice out of the perambulation until the Justice Seat held in July 1634?'

Morgan deposed in the affirmative.

'*Interrogatories ... on behalf of the other defendants.*'

'II. Do you know, believe or have credibly heard that within the Forest of Dean and within the precincts and perambulation of the same, the time whereof the memory of man is not to the contrary, there hath been and yet is an ancient and approved usage and custom that any man born within the Hundred of St. Briavels may be educated and brought up as a miner within the Forest to dig for, take and carry away, iron ore and coal within the Forest, and to convert the same to his and their own use, And that for the time aforesaid any miner or miners so born and educated have without any interruption or denial used to dig for iron ore and coal within the waste grounds and soil of his Majesty and his predecessors within the Forest or in the soil of any other person or persons within the precincts of the Forest?'

Worgan confirmed in full, as did Thomas Browne of Clearwell, ex-miner, aged eighty-four, and Thomas Phelpotte of Goodrich, aged thirty-three. Morgan added that 'his reason of his knowledge is because he having lands within the precincts of the Forest in which the miners entered to dig for ore or coal, did commence a suit at the Council of the Marches of Wales against the said miners, but by reason of their ancient custom he was advised by his counsel to let fall his suit and not proceed to trial with them'.

'IV. Do you know or believe that within the Forest the usage and custom, for all the time whereof the memory of man is not to the contrary, hath been that in case any coal or ore have been discovered or found out in any the said pits or mines by the great industry, labour and charge of the miners who digged and sunk the same, that then the officer called the Gaoler or Gaveler for the time being hath always accustomed to enter and deliver to every such miner respectively his part and share of his dole or part out of the same pit, whether such pit or mine were in any of his Majesty's soil or in the soil of any other, the miners respectively paying and giving to his Majesty's officer for the time being one penny for every part so entered and delivered to the miners aforesaid, and have the miners also during all the time of your remembrance accustomed to pay unto the said Gaoler or Gaveler for his Majesty one penny out of the profits of such miners made of the said ore or coal in case such profit did amount to nine pence a week?'

The substance of this interrogatory was confirmed in full by Worgan and Phelpotte.

> 'VI. Hath the usage and custom within the Forest and precincts thereof, the time whereof the memory of man is not to the contrary, been that such workman as aforesaid working for his Majesty in any the pits or mines there, hath had free liberty of ingress, egress and degress to enter into such mine, pit or pits at his will and pleasure after the same hath or have been perfected at the labour and charge of the miners or any of them, without paying or sustaining any charges or costs in the new building or afterwards in repairing of the mine, pit or pits; And whether have the freeholders or owners of such lands wherein iron ore or coal have been gotten or found, accustomed to have such freedom without paying an equal and proportionable rate and part with other his co-partners in the mine, pit or pits when and as often as the same have been amended and repaired?'

The substance of this interrogatory was confirmed in full by Worgan and Browne.

> 'VIII. Do you know or believe that the customs used and approved within the Hundred of St. Briavels, whereof the memory of man is not to the contrary, hath been that all and every such miner and miners as aforesaid being born, brought up and educated within the same hundred might by his last will and testament give, bequeath or dispose of his part of and within any mine pit of ore or coal wherein he had a dole or part; And in case the same were not demised or disposed of by will as aforesaid, whether hath the same of right descended upon the heir at the common law of such miner?'

The substance of this interrogatory was confirmed in full by Worgan and Morgan. Morgan added that he 'has seen divers precedents of such sales and gifts written and kept in a book'.

> 'IX. Are there within the Hundred of St. Briavels a great number of families (and how many as you can say or can judge) that do depend only upon the mines for the maintenance of themselves and their families?'

Browne made the only deposition to this interrogatory: 'He believeth in his conscience that there are above a hundred families within the Hundred of St. Briavels who have no other help for their maintenance but the digging and getting of ore or coal.' The remainder of the interrogatories and depositions dealt with the office of gaveller and the Mine Law Court and are included in Chapters III and IV respectively. The interesting deposition of Morgan in connection with the ancient document found in his father's study has been given in Chapter II. The suit was continued in Hilary Term.[1] Similar Interrogatories were administered and brought further confirmation of the ancient customary privileges of the free miners. It would be but repetition to recite them at length, but among the depositions were the following[2]:

William Yearworth of Newland, yeoman, aged twenty-five:

---

1 E134 Exch. Deps. by Coms. 13/14 Chas. I. Hilary 16 (1637-8).

2 Certain of the Depositions respecting the office of gaveller and the Mine Law Court are included in Chapters III and IV respectively.

In the last six years he has known divers coalpits in several places in the Hundred of St. Briavels in the Forest; six or seven having been sunk by the defendants – some in the King's soil and three in this deponent's father's ground called Stanck. He does not know how much coal has been dug. Of coal pits dug by others than the defendants, four are in the ground of Sturley Kedgin and three or four in the lands of Sir Baynham Throckmorton, Bt. He has heard 'that persons born in the Hundred of St. Briavels after they have wrought twelve months and a day in the mine pits may, after bestowing a dinner on the Company [of Miners] be free amongst the miners and dig in any of the freeholders' grounds'.

John Teckoll of Littledean, miner:

He does not know whether the manor of Lydney is within the bounds of the Forest. There is a coal mine in Norchard owned by Sir John Winter but does not know when it was sunk.

John Typer of Aylburton, gent., aged fifty-eight:

He gave evidence as to the title of the lands held by Sir John Winter. He was of opinion that the Norchard was never a part of the Forest of Dean.

John Adeane of Awre, aged forty-one, and Warren Gough of Hewelsfield, aged thirty, both Regarders of the Forest, deposed on similar lines to Typer. Adeane also added that 'he knows there are forty families or more in the hundred depending upon the profits of iron ore or coal'. Thomas Mawswell of English Bicknor, miner, aged fifty, confirmed the customs of the miners but that 'interruption had been made by Lady Villiers or her servants'.[1] Thomas Whitson of Clearwell, miner, aged seventy-six:

'Many poor families to a far greater number than he can remember, born and educated in the said hundred which live poorly for want of exercising their labour in mining as formerly they have done are like to perish for want of maintenance.'

It has not been possible to trace the judgment in this case, but it is clear that Terringham soon tired of trying to support his coal grant. In May 1640 he surrendered his lease and it was arranged that he should be paid a 'pension' of £300 per annum for thirty-one years from Lady Day, 1640, out of the fee farm rent to be paid by Winter in connection with his lease of practically the whole of the Forest.[2] From later evidence we hear that Terringham expended £2,500 in attempting to defend his rights.[3] The suit was reopened in 1675-6 and 1683.[4]

In 1634[5] Dean was referred to as 'the famousest and best wooded forest in England, which lately hath been much cropt'. Its timber supplies had diminished through many causes, the chief ones being the smelting of iron ore and the supply

1 Presumably at Mailscot.

2 C.S.P.D. Chas. I, 1640, vol. ccccli, p. 120. Nef (*op. cit.* I, pp. 279-80) asserts that the original grant to Terringham had contained the stipulation that if he failed to derive a profit from the mines he was to receive a £300 annuity. See Appendix 4.

3 *Ibid.*

4 *Ibid.*

5 Lansd. MSS. No. 213, p. 366 (Br. Liby.). Quoted in Glos. N. & Q., vol. iii, No. 1311.

of shipbuilding timber. A survey in 1638[1] disclosed a stock of only 105,557 trees, estimated to contain 61,928 tons of timber and 153,209 cords of wood. What was more serious from the nation's point of view was the fact that only about 14,350 loads were fit for shipbuilding 'as the trees were generally decayed and passed their full growth'. The whole was valued at £120,261 2s. 2d.[2] The need for conservation of timber and of growing further supplies was great. However, any attempt to carry this out in Dean Forest necessitated the satisfying of the commoners of the district and agreeing on suitable areas to be set aside as nurseries of timber. Consequently a commission was issued to Sir Charles Harbord (Surveyor-General of Woods) and others to investigate the position and to enquire into rights in the Forest.[3] It does not appear that any claim was made by the miners on this occasion, but a great deal transpired with regard to rights of common, in connection with which an amicable agreement was reached.[4]

Unfortunately the fortunes of the Forest soon received a great reverse, for on 20 February 1640 Charles I sold to Sir John Winter[5] 18,000 acres of the Forest in consideration of £10,000 'fine', a yearly sum of £16,000 for six years, to commence from 1 April 1640, and a fee farm rent for ever of £1,950 12s. 8d.[6] The sale excluded the Lea Bailey but included all the mines of iron ore and coal, and cinders and stone quarries, together with all timber, trees, wood and underwood. The terms included the allocation to Sir Baynham Throckmorton and others of certain ironworks and supplies of wood.[7] 'The Chestnut-Wood' or 'Coppice' had previously been leased to Richard Brayne, and the woods called Snead and Kidnalls to Tristram Flower.[8]

This important sale followed several petitions from various people who desired large grants in the Forest on hearing that the king had decided to disafforest large portions.[9] Undoubtedly James I was in dire need of money, and in July 1641 we find him reminding the Treasury of 'the many great straits I am in for want of money' and commanding 'that the first (money) you can procure out of the Forest of Dean, concerning which we understand you are in treaty with Sir Baynham Throckmorton and others ... be paid in for the satisfaction of the East India Company's debt'.[10]

Winter's relations with the miners after 1640 are uncertain, but it is clear that the

---

1 3rd Rpt. of 1788, App. No. VI, p. 60. Sir Wm. Masters, Sir Rbt. Cooke, Sir Walter Pye, Nathaniel Steevens, James Kirle, Adrian May, and Henry Steevens were members of the Commission.

2 C.S.P.D. Chas. I, 1641-3, vol. ccccIxxxxi, p. 352, No. 62.

3 3rd Rpt. of 1788, p. 13 and App. No. 6, p. 60. Other members of the Commission were John George, Wm. Morgan, John Smith and Wm. Singleton.

4 See Hart, *The Commoners of Dean Forest*, 1st Edn. (1951).

5 Winter was knighted in 1624. He was lord of the manor of Lydney, and before the above grant he had made a good deal of money from coal and iron mines within his manor and from his ironworks. His unfortunate connections with the Forest are narrated in later pages and also in Hart, *New History* (1995) pp. 1-24.

6 C.S.P.D. Chas. I, 1639-40, vol. cccclxviii. p. 560. The terms did not include the constableship of St. Briavels. This was held by Philip, Earl of Pembroke together with the manor of Newland and Whitemead Park (C.S.P.D. Chas. I, 1639-40, vol. ccccIxvi. p. 498; *ibid.*, 1640, vol. ccccIv, p. 232, No. 46). See Hart, *Royal Forest* (1966) pp. 124, 157, 161, 183, and Hart, *New History* (1995) pp. 1-24.

7 Rhys. Jenkins *op. cit.*

8 Exch. L.T.R. [E367], No. 52 [1625].

9 See Hart, *The Commoners of Dean Forest*, 1st Edn. (1951).

10 C.S.P.D., Chas. I, 1641-3, vol. ccccIxxxii, p. 67.

local inhabitants were greatly dissatisfied with the position. They petitioned against the disafforestation of Dean and prayed that their ancient rights and privileges might be reserved.[1] He had never been a popular figure in the district, and later events tended to accentuate this. He too seems to have had no warm feelings for the inhabitants. In 1636 he reminded the king that he 'has been ready upon all occasions to assist his Majesty's officers, even to endangering his life', and that he was then engaged on the king's special service 'though not very pleasing to his countrymen'.[2] He was involved in much litigation and was one of the prime figures in the accusations and counter-accusations which studded the history of the Dean iron industry in the period 1620-40. However, his troubles were only a fraction of those he encountered in later years, and a good portion of his life was taken up in petitioning the king and the government on numerous occasions, and in litigation.

During the **civil wars** which soon followed, many fences which Winter had erected were thrown down by the inhabitants. Being an ardent royalist, Winter fought hard for the king's cause. In February 1642 'the Committee of the Forest of Dean' decided that Winter 'by reason of his recusancy and not performing conditions with the king, is not fit to hold his bargain any longer, especially his bargain being disadvantageous to the Commonwealth.[3] Winter seems to have been willing to surrender his patent under certain terms. Auditors were appointed to investigate his accounts. Throckmorton and his partners were allowed to continue, but in July 1642 Winter was ordered to deliver up certain of his ironworks to John Browne the king's gun-founder. For a considerable time he refused to do so, and in addition appears to have managed to hold control over at least certain portions of the Forest for a while. Following his defeat in 1644 he was deprived of the benefits of his patent and on 29 September 1645 his estate and ironworks together with wood were assigned by the House of Commons to his main opponent Major-General Massey.[4] Later his estate was vested in trustees.[5] Winter was imprisoned in the Tower but was later given a certain amount of freedom during which time he experimented with the 'calcining' of coal for fuel.[6]

It is uncertain what the fortunes of the Dean miners were during the **civil wars**[7] but it seems they were inclined towards the side of Parliament and were plundered and pillaged by the troops of both armies. It is known that Prince Rupert's men tried to increase their forces on entering the Forest, for a warrant dated 14 April 1645 and

---

1 See Hist. Mss. Com. IVth Rpt. p. 70: Lords Jnl. iv, pp. 219, 262.

2 C.S.P.D. Chas. I, 1636-7. vol. cccxxxix, p. 267, No. 93.

3 *Ibid.*, 1641-3, vol. cccclxxvix, p. 285, No. 35.

4 'Who in consideration of his good and faithful service he hath done for the Kingdom, shall have allowed him the estate of Sir John Winter (who is a delinquent to the Parliament) in the Forest of Dean; all his iron-mills, and the woods (timber trees only excepted not to be felled) with all the profits belonging to them.' Massey held the grant for only a short period.

5 'An Act for the sale of several lands and estates forfeited to the Commonwealth for treason': 16 July 1651 (Acts and Ordinances of the Interregnum, vol. ii, p. 520).

6 Rhys. Jenkins *op. cit.*

7 For information on the Civil Wars as affecting the Forest of Dean, see Mayne Reid, *No Quarter*, and *The Civil War in the Forest of Dean*, 1643-5, by Sir F. A. Hyett (*Trans. B.&G.A.S.*, vol. xviii, 1893-4). In 1643 '40 miners from the Forest of Dean were impressed to repair the artillery train in Gloucester, under siege'. Glos.R.O. D115.

addressed to 'the Constables, Tithing-men and Inhabitants of Little Dean' commanded 'that, without delay or excuse, all men betwixt the age of 16 years and 60 do come in and appear before us at Clowerwale [Clearwell] Mine the 16th of this month of April. And that they bring in all their arms with them'.[1] In the same month it was reported that Prince Rupert's men 'burnt in two or three parishes all the houses which were little better than cottages' and 'burnt some of the iron mills'. According to Hyett[2] 'so great was the panic at this time that it is said that many of the inhabitants fled from their houses and hid themselves in the mines'.

During the **Commonwealth** [1649-1660], according to later evidence,[3] 'Cromwell in his Military Parliament resumed the Forests, and reafforestated the 18,000 acres, and preserved the same by the forest law, with all the wood and trees; and expelled near 400 cabins of beggarly people living upon the waste and destruction of the wood and timber, and great numbers of goats, sheep and swine that destroyed the young wood and soil thereof.' Measures, some successful, were adopted and steadily pursued for the prevention of waste and abuses in the Forest. On 19 April 1648 an Ordinance for conservation of timber in the Forest of Dean had been made law. This read as follows[4]:

> 'The Lords and Commons in this present Parliament assembled, taking into consideration the great spoil, waste and destruction of timber made of late years throughout the whole Kingdom, and particularly in the Forest of Dean, are resolved to preserve the same by all good ways and means for time to come; and therefore do hereby restrain and prohibit the felling of any timber hereafter of oak, ash, elm or beech within the said Forest upon any pretence whatsoever; and that no person or persons whatsoever hereafter presume on any pretence whatsoever, to lop or top any of the said timber trees within the said Forest, or to do any waste or spoil in the same; and such timber as is already felled, and now there remaining upon the place, shall be disposed of and employed for the use of the navy, or as much thereof as the officers of the navy shall find fitting for that service; and the residue of the said timber is to be disposed of by the Committee of the Revenue for the best advantage, and the monies thereupon proceeding to be paid unto the Earl of Salisbury in part of the monies owing unto him according to former Ordinances of Parliament in that behalf.'

On 17 March 1649[5] a prohibition was placed on the felling of timber or carrying away any already cut. Conservation of timber was again ordered on 3 April[6] and it was directed that when wood was cut for iron smelting the copses were 'to be preserved'. All offenders were to be reported. On 6 June[7] the Council of State instructed Christopher Worgan, Andrew Horne, Thomas Berow and Arthur Rowles, 'preservators of the Forest of Dean', to examine and report on offenders who had wasted and spoiled wood and timber. The sheriffs and Justices of the Peace of Gloucestershire and Monmouthshire were commanded to assist them. A report was made on 19 December

1 Hyett, *op. cit.*, p. 104.
2 *Ibid.*
3 Sir Chas. Harbord, 1661 (3rd Rpt. of 1788, p. 14).
4 Acts and Ordinances of the Interregnum, vol. i, pp. 1125-6.
5 C.S.P.D. Interr. 1649-50, vol. i. p. 42.
6 *Ibid.*, p.67, No. 35; see also *ibid.*, p. 69.
7 *Ibid.*, vol. ii, p. 176.

by Col. J. Brownwick and Capt. George Bishop of spoils in the Forest.[1] Upwards of 50,000 trees had been destroyed since 1641, 'some of which were of the best of an ell and a half square'. The chief destroyers were Col. Kerle and Captains Pury, Gifford, Braine and Phillips, as well as the 'Preservators of the Forest' who are proved to have destroyed almost 16,000 timber trees and 237 tons, besides other trees. Government orders had been disobeyed and cutters encouraged to break the law. To this end 'the honest officers are put out, and knaves put in, ... trees are cropped that they may rot, valuable timber put amongst stub-wood. ... Holes were made in trees and fire put in to kill them'. After enumerating other abuses[2] they stated that the country had been defrauded of at least £2,000 besides the destruction of so much timber 'and the goodliest forest in England'. If the ironworks were not stopped immediately the whole Forest would be destroyed.

In 1650[3] the Committee ordered all ironworks to be suppressed and demolished. This was thoroughly done, but in 1653 the government reversed its policy in this respect. Major John Wade was directed to build a new furnace and repair another one for production of guns and shot for the navy.

A digression is made here to record a lawsuit[4] in 1652, which is of particular interest in that it is the first record of the lease by free miners of their interests 'seized to them and their heirs' in a gale.[5] It seems that six miners, Christopher Tucker,[6] John Veare, John Brinckworth, Thomas Wellington, William Nicholls and Fortune Wood, arranged to lease to a John Brayne Esq., 'their several shares or parts in the mine or 'okerpitt'[7] called Maplepitt[8] or Yellowshroft[9] and all the profits to be issuing thereout, and their right, title and interest therein, and the several liberties and privileges which they claim therein or to be thereunto belonging by reason of any custom or mine law time out of mind used within the said Forest, and the working part of the gaveller or galor within the said pit'. The term agreed for the lease was twenty-one years, and the rent £70 per annum – £20 to be paid to Christopher Tucker, £10 of which was applicable to himself as a miner and the other £10 being the amount of the king's share for which he as deputy gaveller was the collector, and £10 to each of the other five miners. Brayne was to secure the miners against certain covenants entered into by them before February 1650 with John Brett and Peter Vowell, merchants of London, possibly for delivery of ochre.

The miners failed to deliver up to Brayne's lawyer the covenants entered into with the London merchants. Nevertheless Brayne drew up a lease of the pit and this was signed by Nicholls and Wood. The other four miners, however, refused to sign it, their reasons being that Brayne had not secured them against the covenant to the London

1 *Ibid.*, vol. iii, p. 443. No. 102.
2 See Hart, *The Commoners of Dean Forest*, 1st Edn. (1951).
3 Report by 'Preservators of the Forest'.
4 'Brayne v. Tucker and ors. (Exch. Decree, 13 May 1652: E126, vol. v, fol. 274).
5 Nef, *op. cit.*, vol 1, p. 279, thinks this is proof that 'already in the days of the Commonwealth more money was needed to start a colliery than poor miners could muster'. He was, however, in error in referring to this as a coal mine.
6 The, or one of the deputy gavellers.
7 It is uncertain whether the pit was worked primarily for ochre, but the name 'Yellowshroft' would imply this. Iron ore would also have been mined.
8 A 'Maple Iron Mine' Gale was among those awarded in 1841.
9 The meaning of 'shroft' is uncertain, but *cf.* modern 'Buckshraft'.

merchants and had not given security for the rent nor paid the half-year's rent due in advance; also Stephen Willcox, an agent, had the deeds of covenant and they could not be produced. Consequently Brayne brought an English Bill into the Exchequer Court against Tucker, Veare, Brinckworth and Wellington, stating 'the great hindrance and damage' he had suffered having made 'provision of workmen and materials' to work the pit. The case was argued and on 13 May 1652 the Court ordered (*a*) the miners to produce and show the complainant the covenant, (*b*) the lease to be made to Brayne commencing Michaelmas next and a half-year's rent to be paid by him, (*c*) Brayne to give to the defendants double the bond stipulated in the covenant to Brett and Vowell, (*d*) a clause to be inserted that if the defendants are damnified by breach of covenant by Brayne, the lease to be void, (*e*) Brayne to give security for payment of rent, and (*f*) the miners to be bound in £200 apiece for due performance of their part of the lease. This case is extraordinary in the fact that here we find a deputy gaveller agreeing to commute the king's expected annual receipts from a gale to a lump sum over a period of twenty-one years, and the miners agreeing to lease their customary rights in the same way. This was certainly a new interpretation of custom.[1]

On 22 November 1653[2] the Forest of Dean was expressly excluded from the provisions of 'An Act for the Deafforestation, Sale and Improvement of the Forests, etc.' In December of the same year the inhabitants of the Forest petitioned against the sale of Whitemead Park.[3] They also petitioned[4] for allowance of their rights of common, housebote and firebote; also for the continued suppression of the ironworks, and for the appointment of a constable[5] and verderers[6] to keep the forest courts and the Hundred Court.

The following year, on 29 November, Cromwell showed his personal interest in the Forest when he wrote the following letter to the Justices of the Peace of Gloucestershire[7]:

> 'Oliver P
>
> Trusted and well beloved we greet you well. Forasmuch as we are given to understand that there hath been very great waste and spoils committed upon the Forest of Dean, to the prejudice of the Commonwealth, and that no provision hath of late years been made for the preservation and growth of the timber and trees within the said Forest, the due care whereof hath been ever esteemed of special concernment to the public interest of the nation. Now for preventing the like spoils and inconvenience for the future, and that there may be a timely provision made for the growth and preservation of the woods and timber for the public use and service of the Commonwealth, we have thought fit to authorize and empower, and accordingly do hereby authorize and empower you, or any three or more of you, to put in execution the laws in force made for encopsing the common woods within the said Forest,

1 The Coms. of 1831 were apparently unaware of this early breach of custom.

2 Acts and Ordinances of the Interregnum, vol. ii, p. 811.

3 See Hart, *The Commoners of Dean Forest,* 1st Edn. (1951).

4 C.S.P.D. Interr. 1653-4, vol. xlii, p. 326, No. 96. Glos.R.O. D2026, X.20.

5 'The office of the constable of the Forest hath ever been a place of honour for he is the chief of the Hundred Court, the Speech Court, and the Mine Court without whom neither of the said Courts can be held. His fee is nine or ten pounds per annum with fee bucks and does, and certain trees of oak and beech. Upon the acknowledging of a fine (of lands sold within the hundred) his fee is six or seven shillings. It being a place more looked at for the title than the profit thereof.'

6 'The said verderers were usually chosen to the whole 'country', a writ being sent down to that purpose.'

7 Rawl. Mss. A. 261, f. 29 (Bodleian Library).

and do make such proceedure therein as that the present season may be improved for the present, taking in of so much of the said Forest for the uses aforementioned as the laws in that behalf do allow and permit, and as may be most for the behoof and benefit of the public service. And so we bid you heartily farewell. From Whitehall the 29th of November, 1654.

To our trusted and well beloved Thomas Hodges, John Stephens, Christopher Guise, Silvanus Wood, William Cooke, William Webley, John Wade, Esqs., Justices of the Peace in our county of Gloucester, and Richard Machin, Gent., or any three or more of them.'

About 1655[1] the inhabitants again petitioned the Protector for the appointment of a constable of the Forest for the conservation of timber; also, for the holding of forest courts to allow 'their rights of estovers, pasture and pannage'. In July of the following year, 1656,[2] records of the 1634 Justice Seat were ordered to be sent down to the Forest; the holding of forest courts was planned. In November 1656[3] Major John Wade was confirmed in charge of the Forest and was instructed to conserve timber and prevent spoils. He had also to supervise the shipbuilding and timber industries in the Forest, and was assisted by Daniel Furzer and Augustine Aldridge.

The Justice Seat in Eyre of June 1656. In 1656 the Council of State and the Office of Lord Protector, Oliver Cromwell, planned the holding of a Justice Seat in Eyre for the Forest (incidentally, the last to be held for the Forest). Major John Wade, supervisor of the Forest, was much involved.[4] The Eyre, started as a Swanimote Court, began at Mitcheldean on 9 June 1656. Many records of the Court are available.[5] The only matter recorded relating to mining was:[6] 'The colliers Beneath the Wood [i.e. in the east of the Forest] have unreasonably and extraordinarily enhanced the price of their coal, to the great oppression and grief of the country.'

On 9 June 1657 an Act[7] was passed by the Commonwealth mitigating the rigour of forest law in the Forest.[8] The Act reads as follows:

'Whereas the forest laws have seemed to be grievous and burdensome to the good people of this Commonwealth inhabiting within the Forest of Dean, in the county of Gloucester, by reason of the rigorous execution thereof, in things nearly concerning their particular estates and properties; for the mitigation therefore of the rigour of the said laws, and for the establishing of the rights, liberties and privileges of the said people, endeavoured to be violated and taken from them in the reign of the late King Charles by Sir John Winter, Kt., and others, Be it enacted by his Highness the Lord Protector and this present Parliament and by the authority thereof, that from henceforth it shall and may be lawful, to and for all and every the owners, tenants and occupiers of all and every the lands and

1 C.S.P.D. Interr., 1655-6, vol. cii, p. 83, No. 185 (113 signatures).
2 *Ibid.*, 1656-7, vol. cxxix, p.2, No.3. The records were bulky and the Keeper of the Tower would not entrust them to anyone. He requested £50 and three horses and would then deliver them to the Forest himself (*ibid.*, p. 33).
3 *Ibid.*, vol. cxxx, pp.155-6. See Hart, *New History* (1995), pp. 126-49.
4 Hart, *New History* (1995), pp. 126-47.
5 *Ibid.*, pp. 103-25.
6 *Ibid.*, p. 123.
7 *Acts and Ordinances of the Interregnum*, vol. ii, pp. 1114-15.
8 Hart, *The Free Miners*, 1st Edn., pp. 201-3, and *Royal Forest*, pp. 98, 124, contain a copy of the Act.

tenements which remain and are within the metes, limits and bounds of the said Forest, to cut down and dispose of any the timber trees, woods and underwoods growing in and upon all and every their several and respective lands and tenements at their own will and pleasure without licence of any Justice in the Eyre or his deputy, and without the licence or view of any officer of the said Forest whatsoever; And also to manure and improve their said several lands and tenements, by ploughing, assarting, digging, inclosing and fencing the same at their will and pleasure, and to keep their dogs unexpeditated, any statute, act, ordinance, assize or law of the forest to the contrary thereof in any wise notwithstanding.

And that all and every person and persons whatsoever shall and may henceforth have and enjoy all and every such their lawful rights, liberties and privileges within the said Forest, according to the assize and law of the Forest, as he or they might or ought lawfully to have had and enjoyed; Any grants, charters or letters patents granted or made to the said Sir John Winter, John Gibbon, John Mansel, Ambrose Babin, or any other person or persons by the said late King, or any act or ordinance of Parliament to the contrary thereof in any wise notwithstanding.

And be it further enacted by the authority aforesaid, that all and every bargains, articles, covenants and grants of or concerning the demesne wastes and woods of the said Forest of Dean, or any part or parcel thereof, or of the wood and timber thereupon being, or of any mines, of other things therein made and granted by the said late King to the said Sir John Winter, John Gibbon, John Mansel and Ambrose Babin, or either of them, and all letters patents and charters made or granted thereupon or in pursuance thereof, by the said late King, for the sale, destruction or dissolution of the said Forest, shall be and are hereby declared and enacted to be henceforth repealed, annulled and void, and of no force nor effect in the law; and that the said demesne woods and wastes shall henceforth be and remain in the same state and form and condition, as they were in the twentieth year of the reign of the late King James to all intents and purposes whatsoever; And that the same from henceforth shall be and remain, and are hereby enacted to be and remain in the real and actual possession and seizin of his Highness the Lord Protector and his successors for ever to the use of the Commonwealth; any grant, charter, letters patents, act or ordinance of Parliament to the contrary thereof in any wise not withstanding. And it is declared and enacted by the authority aforesaid, that it shall and may be lawful to and for his Highness the Lord Protector and his successors, from time to time, to encoppice and inclose such part of the said demesne wastes of the said Forest as by reason of the growth and thriving of young wood, there shall be thought fit and most convenient, for and toward the raising and preserving of wood and timber, so as there be not inclosed and incoppiced above one third part of the said demesne wastes at any one time, but that from time to time, upon any new enclosing or incoppicing, whereby more that a third part shall come to be inclosed and incoppiced at any one time, so much of the former inclosure as shall be best grown, and freest from the danger of spoil by cattle, shall be, by convenient gaps and ways made in the fences and mounds thereof, left open, whereby all such person or persons as lawfully claim any rights, liberties and privileges therein as aforesaid, may have and enjoy the same, according to the law and assize of the Forest as aforesaid.

Provided always, and it is hereby further enacted by the authority aforesaid, that the inclosure of such third part of the said Forest, or any parcel of the same third part, shall not be continued above the space of twelve years, to be accounted from the time of such inclosure as aforesaid.

And it is lastly enacted and ordained by the authority aforesaid, that the Court of the Manor and Hundred of St. Briavels, usually held on Monday every three weeks before the Constable of the castle of St. Briavels within the said Forest of Dean, or his deputy, shall from and after the 24th June 1657 be held on the Tuesday every three weeks, any law, custom or usage to the contrary in any wise notwithstanding.'

Thereafter abuses still continued in the Forest and on 8 April 1659[1] Major Wade wrote to the Admiralty Commissioners:

'It were well if a Justice in Eyre were resolved upon and empowered: never more needed, when horrid offenders can so impudently appear with petitions in their hands, calling that to be right which is against all law and justice. One of those petitioners has come down, making great brags of what great favour their petitions receive, and that all the inclosures shall be put open, and the whole rabble put in their cattle of all sorts; there are boasts of what great promises some members of the House have made, that all things shall be granted that is desired; out of the encouragement they receive by letters from London, they speak strangely, and act worse, for the Forest in the chief coppices has been set on fire in 20 places. The chief of these petitioners is named Stallard, and is now in London; he was heretofore a Cavalier, and for offences done in the prime part of the Forest was fined at the last Justice Seat nearly £300, but it was mercifully mitigated to £20. Lord Desborow knows him well and so does Serjeant Seise.

Some conference should be had about it, but if it be the Parliament's pleasure, or any others, that the Forest shall be left at the pleasure of the people, let me know it, and I shall as willingly turn my back upon it as ever I came from school. It were acting the part of a schoolboy to make complaints, but I have cause, as last Monday some of the officers were set upon in performance of their duty, one being knocked down; but the next day I sent some more, who met with no opposition.'

On 11 May the same year[2] Col. White reported to the House of Commons the information of Major Wade that 'upon the third day of this instant month, divers people, in tumultuous way, in the Forest of Dean, did break down the fences and cut and carry away the gates of certain coppices inclosed for the preservation of timber, turned in their cattle, and set divers places of the said Forest on fire, to the great destruction of the young growing wood'. It was ordered that the matter 'be referred to the sheriff and the Justices of the Peace of Gloucester to take especial care to suppress and prevent all tumults and riotous meetings within the Forest of Dean'. Also a Committee of twenty-two members of the House was appointed 'to take care of the preservation of the timber and woods of the Commonwealth in the Forest of Dean and all other forests of the Commonwealth'. The outrages are referred to in a letter dated 4 June[3] which states: 'There were risen in the Forest of Dean 800 men at the first meeting who declared for nothing but their forest privileges, which they say have been extremely violated.' Another letter dated 24 August the same year[4] mentions that "Col. [John] Okey was sent down to suppress those that met in the Forest of Dean'. Other than for an Order in

1 C.S.P.D. Interr. 1658-9, vol. ccii, p. 328, No. 70. See Hart, *New History* (1995) pp. 126-149.

2 *Glos. Notes and Queries*, vol. v, Pt. III, New Series.

3 Hist. MSS. Com. Bath MSS., vol. i, p. 132.

4 *Ibid.*, p. 136.

Parliament on 9 July 1659,[1] Wade appears to have found it impossible to obtain any substantial help, and we find him again writing to the Admiralty Commissioners on 13 April 1660[2] as follows:

> 'I have already informed you of the throwing open of the enclosures and coppices, and of the horrid wastes and spoils committed, and by whom the people were instigated; all of which availing nothing, nor procuring any redress, it put a stop to my further troubling you in a business of such nature.
>
> The master-builder, seeing the horrid destruction that was committed by daily burning and cutting down of young and old trees, and carrying them away, together with such timber as he had prepared for building the frigate, as also that cut by the State for the use of the ironworks, made a journey to London to wait upon you therein; but I hear of no coercial power to punish what is already done, or to prevent further mischief.
>
> My humble entreaty is that my account may be taken and I discharged, for it eats my very heart and mind to see the barbarous dealings that are done in this forlorn, disowned piece of ground so much talked of, and so little cared for in reality. It lies at such a pass now that it is dealt with by the inhabitants as if proclamation were made: 'Let all the waste, spoil, and destruction be done and committed upon the Forest of Dean that the hearts of wicked people can invent or imagine to do.' It had been better that the State had given £10,000, and I dare say twice told, than that the same law that preserved should have been forborne to be executed, which has been the cause of all the ruin that has followed.'

Following the Restoration [1660] the Acts made during the Commonwealth were declared void. Winter, who was in royal favour on account of his record in the civil war, claimed possession of a large portion of the Forest under his patent. However, he was still unpopular with the inhabitants and as soon as he began to repair his enclosures he met with renewed opposition. The inhabitants represented to the government that the continuance of Winter's grant would be harmful to both them and to the nation. Winter was prepared to surrender his patent provided he was financially compensated. This was arranged and the question of the ironworks settled.[3]

On 5 March 1661[4] a Commission was issued to Lord Herbert, constable and warden, and others to enquire into the state and condition of the Forest.[5] During its investigations Sir Charles Harbord, surveyor-general of Woods, made various representations to the government. On 28 December 1661 he reported[6]:

> 'His Majesty has been pleased to be present with my Lord Chancellor and Lord Treasurer, etc., at the hearing of this business (of the Forest) and hath given order that a Commission … enquire into the state of the Forest; intending upon the Return of the said Commission to acquaint Parliament with the true state of the business, and to recommend it to their wisdom to provide that the said Forest may be restored to his Majesty's demesne and reafforested, and improved by enclosures for a future supply of wood, for a constant support of the

1 C.S.P.D. Interr. 1659-60. vol. cciii, p. 14.

2 *Ibid.*, vol. ccxx, pp. 413-14, No. 79.

3 C.T.B., vol. vii, pp. 1531-2, 2 March 1661. See Hart, *New History* (1995), pp. 1-24.

4 The Commissioners reported their findings on 12 April 1662 (see next page).

5 C.T.B., vol. i, p. 58.

6 3rd Rpt.of 1788, p. 14.

ironworks there, producing the best iron in Europe for many years, and for the produce of timber for the navy and other uses in time to come, which might be of great use for defence of this nation, the old trees there standing being of above 300 years' growth, and yet as good timber as any in the world; and the ground so apt to produce and so strong to nourish and preserve timber, especially oaks, that within a hundred years there may be sufficient provision there found to maintain the royal navy for ever.'

The Commissioners were presented by the inhabitants with an important memorial.[1] They claimed 'as enjoyed for divers hundred of years': 'Liberty to dig and get mine [iron ore] and coal in all places within the Forest at their pleasure, and liberty also to have and take sufficient timber with the said woods for their necessary support and building of their mines and coalworks according to their ancient usage and customed rents and duties to his Majesty for the same.' They offered to forgo their claim to wood and timber provided the king would suspend the ironworks and the cutting of the Forest, and would secure to them their other rights and privileges. They prayed that they might be freed of forest law and that Winter's grant of the 18,000 acres should be made void. About the same time, Aubrey Earl of Oxford petitioned 'for a grant of great sums of money due to the Crown by insufferable abuses in the Forest of Dean, with power to prosecute for, and recover, same'.[2] The petition was referred to the Lord Treasurer but no other action can be traced. The Commission reported their findings to the Exchequer on 12 April 1662.[3] They estimated the Forest to contain 30,233 trees equivalent to 11,335 tons 30 feet of ship timber. Also 72,786¾ long cords of cordwood. The following are extracts from their Return:

'(8) We also viewed the several mines and quarries within the said Forest and find that there is in one coppice called Lynnards and the Wallsringes containing near 500 acres formerly granted by Hen. VI to the abbot of Flaxley and now in the possession of one Abraham Clark, gent., the said king reserving to himself his heirs and successors all the game, herbage, mines and quarries of stone, and red and yellow ochre pits, and although by reason of the miners' specious pretences hitherto no profit hath accrued to the Crown out of it, yet their claim having already been rejected at a Justice Seat held by Henry Earl of Holland 10 Charles [1634], by reason of their not being a corporation or body pollitique it was declared to be against law and their claim not allowed, A revenue might certainly be raised out of it by laying an imposition on every barrel exported, for this is found to exceed all other so far as the merchants as we were informed do adulterate a coarser sort by colouring of it with this, and lest these miners should clog the market pay them not to dig forty pounds per annum amongst eight of them. And upon what computation we can make by the several informations were given us, it may arise to near £250 per annum, perhaps more.

We also viewed the several coal works and the surfe, and although the ordinary pits be liable to water and the miners could only dig in the summer, yet the surfe hath made such a passage for the water as they dig the whole year and get a vast quantity of good coal, their presences being as inconsiderable as the former received the same judgement, and if any imposition were laid on this by degrees would raise a good yearly revenue. But it must be

1 The author has had sight of a nineteenth century MS. copy of the same. See also PRO F20/1/(17), 9, 10.
2 C.S.P.D. Chas. II, 1661-2, vol 1, p. 280.
3 Harl. MSS. 6839. fol. 332 (Br. Liby.).

raised proportionable to the rent and not great at first, and by the best informations we could receive we compute that being well and directly managed might yield per annum £500.

There are several quarries of stone as grindstone fit for the navy, paving tyle slade excellent for building and some millstone, but by reason never as yet any yearly advantage accrued by it we cannot set any positive value.

There is also mine of ore, on which it would be convenient to lay an imposition at 6d. at first for fifteen bushells and we were informed that there is carried out yearly at least 4,000 dozen, and there is now lying at Newnham a small vessel to transport some for Ireland.

There must needs be a prohibition to carry out of the Forest any cinders lest his Majesty's own works should need them in time.'

The Commission also enquired as to 'cabins' built in the Forest and were informed 'that in or about the year 1653 there were near 400 cabins and cottages then standing, but the person [John Wade] then instructed with the supervisorship of the Forest and wastes ejected them by due course of law'. They added that they found 'not above 5 now standing'. As to what damage they occasion to the wood and timber, 'they erect their cabins and cottages with the king's timber, breed great store of swine, burn the offal wood, committing many other wastes'. The Commissioners recommended 'the same course as formerly must be used to prevent their increase'. The Commission gave recommendations as to the setting apart of 4,000 acres for the use of commoners, and also advised that the king should take the ironworks into his own hands. They ended their Return thus:

'We have endeavoured with all exactness to answer to the best of our judgements all the foregoing Articles of our Instruction and this later commanding our opinion upon the whole state of the Forest together with our advice for its preservation thereof towards an increase of wood and timber, we humbly conceive it very necessary for his Majesty to reasume all grants and to take the whole unto his own hands, giving such other satisfaction to the grantees as in his Majesty's gracious judgement may seem meet, or else in our opinion it will be almost impossible to preserve the whole for a future nursery by reason of the country's obstinancies and the inconveniences that will happen by a division; As also that present care be taken for encopsing it, ... And for as much as former allowances of perquisites to the respective officers of the Forest did conduce much to the destruction of the timber and wood, we humbly conceive it necessary upon a reafforestation to retrench them and reduce them to moderate and certain salaries.'

On 30 July 1662[1] the government saw fit to make a new agreement with Winter.

[1] Pepys, under date 20 June 1662, records: 'Up by 4 or 5 o'clock, and to the office, and there drew up the agreement between the King and Sir John Winter about the Forest of Deane; and having done it, he come himself, whom I observed to be a man of fine parts; and we read it, and both liked it well. That done, I turned to the Forest of Deane, in Speedes's Mapps, and there he showed me how it lies; and the Lea-bayley with the great charge of carrying it to Lydney, and many other things worth knowing.' Again, in August of the same year, Pepys mentions that he meets Winter 'a very worthy man, and good discourse, most of which was concerning the Forest of Deane, and the timber there, and iron workes with their great antiquity, and the vast heaps of cinders which they find, and are now of great value, being necessary for the making of iron at this day: and without which they cannot work'. Pepys thought it 'a fine thing ... to see myself come to the condition of being received by persons of this rank'. Other entries connected with the Forest were made on 15 March and 30 April 1667. See Hart, *New History* (1995), pp. 1-24.

In consequence his former grant was surrendered, and a grant of the ironworks was made on Winter's nomination to Francis Finch and Robert Clayton. Winter reserved to himself the woods called Snead and Kidnalls, while his lessees were allowed to use the timber in the Forest except the 11,335 tons of ship-timber for which Winter had still to account to the king.[1] It has not been possible to trace the actual agreement but some of the terms are suggested from a proposal made by Sir Baynham Throckmorton on 7 July, 1662[2] 'to pay the £30,000 allowance to Sir John Winter by his Majesty for surrender of his grant of the Forest of Dean, thereby to obtain some advantage to the king, and satisfaction to himself, for his interest in the woods'.[3] Meanwhile restrictions on the local coal miners are apparent from the following warrant of 1661[4]:

> 'For as much as I am informed by Sir Charles Harbord Kt. his Majesty's Surveyor-General that Edmond Haynes, Thomas Haynes and other colliers of the Forest of Dean have of late presumed to enter upon the soil and to dig coal and sink pits near unto his Majesty's surffe and coal works [Aywood] there in contempt of the warrant and authority given by Mr. Surveyor to John Witt to whose care and management the said surffe and coal work was committed by my order, These are in his Majesty's name to will and require you to give present warning to the said Edmond, Thomas Haynes and all other colliers and workmen who have entered upon the soil of the said Forest to sink any pits or dig any coals there or to affront the said John Witt in the execution of the said warrant immediately to forbear the same, and in case they shall persist therein then forthwith to inform me of the names and places of abode of all the said colliers and workmen by certificate thereof under your hand and seal that I may take such order for their punishment as shall be agreeable to justice and also to cause them to be apprehended by the constables of the places where they inhabit to be carried by them before Sir Baynham Throgmorton Kt. or some other of his Majesty's Justices of the Peace of the said county to find sufficient surety for their good behaviour and to appear at the next general assizes and quarter sessions to answer their offences and to be proceeded against according to the course of justice. Hereby willing and requiring all constables and other his Majesty's officers of the said Forest and county to be aiding and assisting unto you in the execution hereof upon request in that behalf. Given &c. at Southampton House the 8th day of February 1661.
>
> T. SOUTHAMPTON.
> [Treasurer]
>
> To Major John Wade and all his
> Majesty's verderers and regarders of the
> said Forest and to every of them.'

A sidelight on the Dean miners of this period is furnished by the following letter, of unknown date, written by Sir Baynham Throckmorton to Henry Lord Percy[5]:

---

1 They were also granted the trees in Whitemead Park (3 *Pars. Orig.* 14 Chas. II).
2 C.S.P.D. Chas. II, 1661-2, vol. lvii, p. 430.
3 See also Rudder, 1779, p. 31 and Eng. Hist. Rev., vol. xxi, 1906, p. 450.
4 C.T.B., vol. i, p. 361, Glos.R.O. D2026 Bund. 1755, X.20.
5 Rawl.MS. D.395, fol. 196 (Bodleian Library). The date is believed to be before 1659.

'My Lord,

Last night the miners were here and this morning most of them are gone home without ever acquainting me with it (notwithstanding my strict command to them to the contrary); four are here, but of the most ignorant of them; and therefore I do forbear to send them to your Lordship; I have already now sent away servants of my own with strict warrants and commands to bring them and more with them presently hither, and have sent strict orders both to some horse and foot that I have in that county, to bring them away by force, and not neglect a minute of an hour in it day and night; and I am confident by tomorrow noon here will be some reasonable number of them, and they shall instantly be brought to your Lordship; I beseech you, my Lord, judge charitably of this unhappy accident, for never man had such rogues to deal with; but I have given order to my officers to burn the houses of those that resist or refuse instantly to come with them.'

It has not been possible to trace the circumstances of this letter nor whether its author was Sir Baynham Throckmorton senior, or his son of the same name.

Although Winter had lost a great deal of his hold on the Forest, he seems to have assisted his nominees, Finch and Clayton, to obtain large quantities of timber. New complaints were soon made to the House of Commons of the serious inroads into the stocks of timber. In consequence a committee was appointed to take the whole matter into consideration, and from this committee Sir Charles Harbord reported to the House[1] 'that Sir John Winter had 500 cutters of wood employed in Dean Forest, and that all the timber would be destroyed if care should not be speedily taken to prevent it'.[2] The House made an order prohibiting further felling of timber, and a Bill was afterwards brought in 'for settling the Forest' and increasing and conserving its timber.[3] Parliament prorogued before the Bill could pass, and so the House recommended to the Lord Treasurer and the Chancellor of the Exchequer to take care for the conservation and improvement of the Forest. Moreover, the inhabitants continued attempting to persuade the government of the necessity of putting a stop to the destruction of their Forest. They intimated their willingness to comply with whatever should be thought best for the improvement of the Forest and for the conservation of timber. In 1663 they presented the following **Proposals** to the Committee[4]:

'Proposals by and on the behalf of the freeholders, inhabitants and commoners within the Forest of Dean, for the preservation and improvement of the growth of timber there.

Imprimis, that 11,000 acres of the waste soil in the Forest of Dean, whereof the Lea Baily and Cannopp to be part of the said waste, may be enclosed by his Majesty, and discharged for ever from all manner of pasture, estovers and pannage; and if ever his Majesty or his

1 Journals of H. of C., 13 April 1663.

2 A great storm on 18 Feb. 1662 had considerably added to the devastation. A storm comparable to this had taken place on 11 Oct. 1634: C.S.P.D. Chas. I, 1634, p. 237.

3 About this time John Evelyn projected new ideas of silviculture (*vide* his book *Sylva,* 1662) and his Diary contains the following entry for 5 Nov. 1662: 'The Council of the Royal Society met to amend the Statutes, then dined together; afterwards meeting at Gressham College, where was a discourse suggested by me, concerning planting his Majesty's Forest of Dean with oak, now so much exhausted of the choicest ship-timber in the world.' (1819 Edn., p. 354.)

4 3rd Rpt. of 1788, p. 15.

successors shall think fit to lay open any part of the said 11,000 acres, then to take in so much elsewhere, so as the whole enclosure exceed not at any one time 11,000 acres.

That all the wood or timber which shall hereafter grow upon the remaining 13,000 acres shall absolutely belong to his Majesty, discharged from all estovers[1] for ever, and pannage for twenty years next ensuing. That the whole waste soil be reafforested and subject to the forest laws; but that the severity of the forest laws be taken off from the lands in several, belonging to the freeholders and inhabitants within the said Forest, they themselves being contented to serve his Majesty, according to their several offices and places, as formerly at the forest courts.

That the deer to be kept on the said waste soil may not exceed 800 at any one time,[2] and the fees which belong to the particular officers touching venison may be preserved to them, as to venison only, and not to wood and trees.

That it is consented to that the winter heyning and fence month, according to the forest law, being such times wherein no kind of cattle be permitted to abide in any part of the said waste, may be understood to be from Saint Martin's day in the winter to Saint George's day in April; and afterwards, from fifteen days before Midsummer to fifteen days after.

That all grants of any part of the waste soil of the said Forest be re-assumed and made void; and that no part of the said waste or soil be aliened for ever from the Crown, or farmed to any particular person or persons, by lease or otherwise.

And that this may be settled by Act of Parliament.

(*Signed*) HEN. HALL. DUN. COLCHESTER
WM. PROBIN. JO. WITT.'

These '**Proposals**' had far-reaching effects at a later date,[3] but for the present the Forest was not in any way settled despite several attempts to find a solution. On the one hand Winter and his nominees would not stop their operations in the district, while on the other hand the overseers and other officials would not agree to the Forest being mis-managed and despoiled. In addition, Sir Baynham Throckmorton was anxious to oust Winter, possibly for the good of the Forest, possibly for his own advancement. In February 1664[4] we find William Harbord (son of the Surveyor-General) being paid for services rendered in making several surveys and estimates of the value of the wood and timber in Dean, and in making an improvement of a great part of the waste in the Forest. In July 1665[5] a warrant was issued to Sir George Charnock (serjeant-at-arms) and Thomas Agar (one of the surveyors of woods) to survey Dean Forest which the king had resolved to conserve as a nursery for ship-timber. They were commanded to report on the present state of the timber, the best method of enclosure, etc., 'and

1 Since the resultant Act of 1668, the inhabitants have been unable to claim wood or timber, either for firewood or repairs to their buildings.

2 On 7 Sept. 1666 Sir Christopher Gyse (Guise), of Brockworth, wrote to the Editor of the *Gazette* saying that he 'hears that the king is resolved to destroy the deer in the Forest of Dean', and begging some breeding deer for his park (C.S.P.D. Chas. II, vol. clxx, p. 106).

3 The Commissioners of 1788 informed the descendants of those gentlemen who signed the document that they had thereby lost all claim to any perquisite in the way of bark and windfalls; observing also that the important resultant act of 1668 was approved by and obtained at the desire of the freeholders, inhabitants and commoners then living.

4 C.T.B., vol. i, p. 584.

5 *Ibid*., p. 673.

particularly to inform themselves on conference with the freeholders of the several parishes concerning their discontent at the award made formerly by Sir Charles Harbord and others by way of composition for their pretended rights of common therein'.

On 21 December 1665[1] the Treasury commanded Kettford Brayne and Thomas Creed 'to take special care to prevent the spoils which are daily committed in the underwood and cover of Dean Forest'. On the same day we hear that 'the whole scheme for the improvement of the Forest as a nursery for timber is to be committed to Winter's hands'.[2] This must have come as a great disappointment to the inhabitants and officials. Winter was to have a grant of 8,000 acres, and the remaining 10,000 acres were to be managed by him as a nursery for timber. On 28 January 1666[3] a warrant was issued for confirmation of the arrangement. Winter attended before the Treasury on 1 July 1667[4] and notes of the meeting include the following:

> 'His warrant from the King read and the articles produced. Consider how the King shall be secured for performance of his covenants. Winter says that if his own 8,000 acres be not obliged to make up the fences by the present articles he is willing it should be so; as also a proportionable part of it for ever for maintaining the fences. The first article of the return read, *viz*: that no freeboard be left on the highways but each two miles or mile and that he has 8 or 10 acres to be left for a house on one side only, and that the highways should be 60 feet broad. Attorney-general and Surveyor-General of Lands to consider whether the whole land is obliged to make the fences and part to keep them up. A new commission to go out.'

On 3 July 1667[5] the attorney-general reported that Winter's articles 'do oblige the land, which he is to have, to make the fences, and part to make them good'. The Treasury ordered Winter's agreement to be made good, and on 5 July[6] it was decided to allow Winter 180 acres in lieu of the 'freeboard' mentioned above.[7] A warrant for confirmation under the Great Seal of Winter's articles of indenture was issued on 26 July.[8] It appears that Winter's powers did not supersede the duties of the various forest officials. In August 1667[9] the king dealt direct with the Marquis of Worcester who was constable of St. Briavels and warden of the Forest. He drew attention to the fact that the late king had issued a commission to Sir Charles Harbord and others for the improvement of the wastes of Dean Forest, and that those inhabitants who assented to the improvement had been freed from the jurisdiction of forest law. The forest courts had been discontinued 'to the great destruction of timber and retardment of its future growth'. The king now ordered the courts to be revived and the forest laws obeyed – 'excepting therefrom only those freeholders who assented'. The same month, Mr. Horne,

1 C.T.B., vol. i, p. 699, R.P. MS., p. 19
2 *Ibid.*
3 C.S.P.D. Chas. II, 1665-6, vol. cxlvi, p. 222.
4 C.T.B., vol. ii, p. 23. See Hart, *New History* (1995), pp. 1-24.
5 *Ibid.*, p. 26.
6 *Ibid.*, p. 29.
7 On 5 Nov. 1667 the Treasury ordered the Commissioners 'to allow foreboard on those parts of the nurseries that adjoin the enclosures of the adjacent freeholders: all in order to prevent trespass through the fences of other persons' (*ibid.*, p. 200).
8 C.S.P.D. Chas. II, 1667, vol. ccxi, p. 330.
9 *Ibid.*, vol. ccxii, p. 368.

woodward of Dean Forest, was commanded to inform the Treasury from time to time 'what abuses were presented at every three weeks' court'.[1]

Meanwhile there was some trouble over the question of the 11,335 tons of timber which Winter, under one of his former grants, had been obliged to reserve for the king.[2] Although Winter went to great pains to deny it, it appears that he had appropriated far more timber, etc., than he had the right to do. A survey in 1667 disclosed that of 30,233 trees sold to him there remained only about 200 in the Forest; and of the 11,335 tons of ship-timber reserved to the king only 1,000 tons had been delivered and about 500 tons only were lying squared in the Forest.[3] Navy surveyors were ordered to mark out all the timber they found fit for shipbuilding, and Winter was to be charged for the discrepancy at the rate of 15s. per ton. Winter petitioned in this connection in July 1667.[4]

New commissions were issued in August 1667 to Sir Baynham Throckmorton, junior, Sir Charles Harbord and others, for a survey of the Forest and for setting out the 10,000 acres which under Winter's new agreement were to be reserved for timber.[5] Returns were made to the Treasury on 7[6] and 14[7] October the same year, and it seems that Winter was in disagreement with the Commission regarding the profits of the Forest. On 21 November[8] a warrant was issued to stay further proceedings of the Commission, and Throckmorton and the Marquis of Worcester attended before the Treasury on the 29th.[9] The Marquis informed the Treasury that they could 'improve the business of timber and yet satisfy the country as to their right of common, for by Sir John Winter's grant the king is to have but 10,000 acres, Winter 8,000 acres, and the commoners 4,000 acres. As to this, the country would be willing the forest law were set up again in the Forest, and would consent to what further is necessary for the common good. As to the great occasion of the destruction of wood (*viz,* the right of the commoners to estboot [estover] or cutting of wood for their own use, and pannage or the swines' going to eat acorns) these two the country are willing to part with, provided always one-third of the Forest shall lie in inclosure, and as any of the wood opens then liberty to the king to enclose as much more.' He believed 'the enclosure of a third of the Forest may be done for £1,000, but the commoners desire the forest lands may be taken off their own hands. The king may have presently £2,000 per annum out of the underwoods and £4,000 per annum out of them after six years.'

On 17 December[10] we hear that 'the whole business of the Forest of Dean is before Parliament'. The main difficulty seems to have been the unpopularity of the grant to Winter, the inadvisability of such a grant in view of the questionable way in which Winter had executed commitments in the past, and the endeavour of the commoners, while wishing to agree to anything for the good of the district and the nation, to ensure that their customary rights were respected and that they were allocated a reasonable

1 C.T.B., vol. ii, p. 39.
2 *Ibid.*, p. 54.
3 *Ibid.*, p. 149; Harl. MSS. 6839, fol. 356; 3rd Rpt. of 1788, p. 14.
4 *Ibid.*, p. 169.
5 *Ibid.*, p. 174.
6 *Ibid.*, p. 102.
7 *Ibid.*, p. 107.
8 *Ibid.*, p. 123.
9 *Ibid.*, p. 131.
10 *Ibid.*, p. 151

amount of suitable common.

In March the following year (1668)[1] another attempt was made to settle the question of Winter's deficiency of timber, and he, together with one of his nominees, Clayton, was called before the Treasury. Clayton 'refused to join in the security and would rather stay till the king's debts be satisfied', while Winter, hopefully, prayed 'for any overplus that may remain after satisfaction of this debt'. A few days later[2] a warrant was issued to seize Winter's stock of iron and charcoal, while the ironworks were to continue. Lawrence Bathurst, Daniel Furzer and John May, Overseer, acted promptly. However, Winter and Clayton appealed and on reference to the attorney-general it was found that the seizures were, after all, illegal.[3] Consequently the forest officers were told to remit the seizure 'but not to suffer any more wood to be converted into charcoal, and to continue the seizure of the forges'.

Nevertheless on 30 June 1668 we find Winter being granted a 'Release' of £6,692 6s. 'due to the King for 8,921 tons 25 feet of ship-timber; also of his covenants concerning the improvement of the waste soil in Dean Forest and of his recognisance of £2,000 entered into in pursuance of the same'. Thus almost ended Winter's long but unfortunate connection with the Forest.[4] He was without doubt one of the main reasons for discontent in the district over a long period, a period which saw the timber supplies dwindle to a low ebb. Among other causes of depletion, though comparatively small, were the two great storms previously mentioned, and the use of timber by the miners. Doubtful rights to 'fee trees' had also had an adverse effect, while the local inhabitants' instinctive 'love of acquisition' of whatever timber and wood they required, whether legally entitled to it or not, helped to deplenish stocks.[5] Shipbuilding, too, made great inroads into the timber of the Forest. Large quantities of wood and timber had been wastefully used for the smelting of iron, under the system periodically adopted for farming the Forest, for it was obviously to the advantage of each farmer to obtain all the iron ore, cinders, coal and wood that he could while his lease lasted.

Fortunately a new Act in 1668, under Charles II, dealt with in Chapter VI, started a new era in the development of the Forest. It is possible that if the process of depletion had not been arrested the course of British history would have been changed, for the oak necessary to build the ships for the great naval battles of the eighteenth and early nineteenth centuries would probably not have been forthcoming.

---

1 C.T.B., vol. ii, pp. 269-70.

2 *Ibid.*, p. 535. Winter's debt is stated to be £6,691 6s. 1d.

3 *Ibid.*, pp. 288, 543 and 581.

4 Winter tried hard to vindicate himself. In 1673 he published an answer to 'a pretended paper, lately published, wherein divers things are most falsely charged on his grants in the Forest of Deane, reflecting very much on the integrity of divers of his Majesty's officers, and several other persons of great worth and reputation' (Gough's *British Topography).* See *A True Narrative &c.* [Br. Liby. 726. e. 1(2)]. After Winter had given up, in 1669, his post as Secretary to the Queen Mother he made an attempt to work a colliery near Coventry ('the famous Coal Delfe' at Bedworth and Grieff) aided by finance from the city of Coventry [C.S.P.D. 1671-2, pp. 159, 181;. see also Dict. Nat. Biog.]. He was unsuccessful. By 1676 he was of 'mean and low estate' [C.T.B. vol. iv, p. 169]. His descendants were still holding several hundred acres in the Forest in 1719 [C. T. Papers, vol. v, pp. 457, 461, 473]. See Hart, *New History* (1995), pp. 1-24.

5 Regarding the prohibition of miners taking free timber see PRO F20/1(17), 12.

CHAPTER VI

1668-1830: Acts of 1668 and 1808

THE ***Dean Forest (Reafforestation) Act 1668***.[1] This followed and embodied the **Proposals** referred to in Chapter V, starting a new era in the history of the Forest. In the Act the privileges of the miners received their first statutory notice, but no explanation was given to show what rights, if any, were valid.[2] The main purpose of the Act was to increase and conserve timber in the Forest, and its clauses were drawn up in a manner which would satisfy both the Crown and the inhabitants. Section XI saved 'unto the miners and persons using the trade of digging for iron ore, coal and ochre in the Forest their lawful rights and privileges in all lands and grounds lying within the perambulation and regard of the Forest, other than the inclosures for the time being they shall continue inclosed, as fully and absolutely as if this Act had not been had or made'. This section was of the utmost importance to the miners. Section XVII provided that 'any lease or leases made or to be made by his Majesty, his heirs or successors, to any person or persons whatsoever for any term or term of years not exceeding the terms of thirty-one years in possession of the coal mines and quarries of grindstone in the Forest or any part thereof, shall be of like force as if this Act had never been made, except of such coal mines as are or shall be in any part of the 11,000 acres allotted for his Majesty's inclosure and as shall continue inclosed'.[3] This section was meant to cover a lease of coal mines and quarries to Captain Francis Terringham which the attorney-general had been instructed to prepare on 21 November 1667.[4]

Following the Act, the miners were made to pay for the timber they required for their works,[5] but it was not long before they again demanded such supplies for nothing, as a right.[6] According to Commissioners of 1788[7] a Return to a Commission of Inquiry

1 19 and 20 Chas. II, c.8. Copy in Hart, *Royal Forest* (1966), pp. 291-5.

2 Definition and confirmation of the miners' rights had to await the passing of the Dean Forest (Mines) Act, 1838.

3 Wood (*op. cit.*, p. 34) points out that there is an obvious error in the last sentence and suggests the probable meaning was: 'in any part of the 11,000 acres allotted for his Majesty's inclosure so long as the same shall continue inclosed.'

4 See this Chapter p. 196 and Appendix 4.

5 In 1669 John May was ordered by the Treasury 'not to suffer the colliers to have any wood unless they buy it, this being cut off by the Act' (C.T.B., vol. iii, pp. 112-13; p. 262). However, on 27 January 1673 he was instructed 'to forbid all colliers and miners to cut any beech, birch, ash, hazel or other underwood upon the wastes of the said forest or late forest of Dean other than as to what right is saved to them by the Act of 20 Chas. II' (*ibid.* vol. iv. p. 48). See also PRO F20/1/17.

6 3rd Rpt. of 1788, pp. 16, 17: 'Immediately after the passing of this Act, the colliers, who, it is said, now pretend to have a right to whatever timber they find necessary for carrying on their works in the Forest, without paying anything for it, then purchased it from the Crown.'

7 *Ibid.*, p. 12. See Hart, *New History* (1995), pp. 52-82, and *The Verderers and Forest Laws of Dean* (1971).

concerning the Forest, dated 5 March 1671, stated that the claims of the miners had been rejected at the Justice Seat of 1634, 'they not being a corporation'. No confirmation of this has been found.

About this time certain administrative changes were made in the Forest. A new 'Speech House'[1] was arranged to be built to replace the old court-room at 'Kenesley'; a supervisor was appointed at a salary of £100, and six keepers at salaries of £20 – each in charge of a 'Walk'. It was arranged that £30 per annum should be allowed for repair of gates and fences, and it was recommended that the ironworks should be demolished and their materials used in building lodges for the keepers. The Admiralty continued to take an interest in the Forest with an eye to ship-timber supplies, and we find Samuel Pepys and others paying a three-day visit in July 1671.[2] A watchful eye was however kept by the Treasury and forest officials to see that only the minimum of timber was taken from the Forest. Conservation was the order of the day. Nevertheless certain of the inhabitants appear to have given much trouble to those responsible for the new policy in the Forest.[3] Besides the breaking into inclosures already mentioned, fires were ruthlessly started[4] and hedges pulled down.[5]

On 3 June 1673[6] the Treasury gave instructions for a commission to be issued to the Marquis of Worcester, Sir Baynham Throckmorton, Bart., and others 'to view and perambulate Dean Forest'. Among other matters they were to enquire as to the ironworks and the inclosures; also 'as to coal pits taken into inclosures which might conveniently be left out (without prejudice to the young wood) for the benefit of the country'. In February of the following year[7] the Treasury referred to the Lord Chief Baron the question of prosecuting those guilty of offences in the Forest.[8] They also decided to advise the King to demolish the ironworks, and agreed that the timber in the Lea Bailey should be sold. The sale of the Lea Bailey timber was effected and the ironworks were sold for demolition to Paul Foley for £500.[9] The demolition was done so thoroughly that before long the demand for iron ore came mainly from outside the Forest. Therefore, from this period on through the eighteenth century, coal works were constantly on the increase, so as eventually to throw the mining of iron ore into the shade.

The year 1675 introduced a suit[10] between Katherine Terringham, widow of the son of Edward Terringham to whom a grant of coal mines and quarries had been made in 1637, and certain miners and quarrymen. The records of this suit throw further light on the free miners. They commence with:

---

1 See Hart, *The Verderers and Speech-Court of the Forest of Dean* (1950).

2 C.S.P.D., Chas. II, 1671, p. 369.

3 The Marquis of Worcester and Sir Baynham Throckmorton endeavoured to carry out the intentions of the Act of 1668, although it seems that they were at times at variance. They were assisted by John May (overseer), while Mr. Agar (surveyor-general of woods) also took an active interest.

4 C.T.B., vol. iii, pp. 112-13, and 1065.

5 *Ibid.*, p. 457.

6 *Ibid.*, vol. iv, p. 150.

7 *Ibid.*, vol. iii, pp. 227-8.

8 Misappropriation of timber was also occurring in 1676 (*ibid.*, pp. 51, 59, 203).

9 Rhys Jenkins *op. cit.* etc.

10 E134 Exch. Deps. by Coms. 27 Chas. II, Mich. 28, 1675. (Terringham v. Yarworth etc.). Copy in Glos.R.O. D3921, I/7, Hart Collection. See Appendix 4.

'Interrogatories administered to witnesses on behalf of Katherine Terringham.'

'II. Did you at any time heretofore and when know Edward Terringham Esq. deceased father of the said Francis Terringham; do you know believe or have heard that he the said Edward Terringham was in his lifetime, and when, in possession of the coal mines and quarries of grindstones or any other mines or quarries; and what mines in the Forest of Dean; in what part of the Forest were such mines, how long was he in possession thereof; how, when and in what manner and for what cause did he leave the possession thereof; was it by composition with Sir John Winter for his interest therein, or by reason of the breaking out of the late wars, or what was the cause thereof as he so left the possession? Declare the truth herein as you know, believe or have creditably heard what profit or rent might he have made thereof if he had peaceably enjoyed the same as you believe in your conscience.'

Henry Mathon, of Howle, Herefordshire, 'coalminer aged about 58 years', deposed:

'That about 35 years since the said Edward Terringham was in possession of the mines of coal in the Forest of Dean by virtue of a patent to him thereof granted by his late Majesty as this deponent believes for that he hath seen a Patent for that purpose as he hath beene told, and being so possessed did employ this deponent with several others to sink a mine for coals in the same Forest which they accordingly did, and this deponent did help to sink a mine for the said Mr. Terringham in a place called Aywood part of the Forest of Dean and within the Hundred of St. Brevills, which work went on without any interruption, and Mr. Terringham enjoyed the advantage thereof for about six months and might as yet as this deponent conceiveth; and this deponent believeth that the sole reason why Mr. Terringham did not go on with the work was for that coal was not of so great value neither did the work turn to so great account as now it doth, and no other reason.'

John Drew of Littledean, 'Free miner, aged about 50 years', deposed:

'That about 30 years since Edward Terringham, Esq., was by virtue of a patent to him granted by his late Majesty (as this deponent hath heard and believeth) in possession of two mines of coal in the Forest of Dean and did employ several Free Miners to work under him whereof this deponent was one and one Henry Mathon another and did drive up a surfe for the better carrying on his work which to this day is called 'Tyrringham's Surfe' and continued in possession thereof for about the space of six months without any interruption and shortly after the war broke out which was the only reason the said Mr. Terringham left the works as this deponent believeth. And this deponent further saith that one Christopher Tucker did for many years after by himself and his servants to the number of twenty and more, whereof this deponent was one, work in the said mines under colour or pretence that he had a title from Mr. Terringham without any interruption.'

George Brayne of Littledean, 'Free miner aged 63 years or thereabouts', deposed:

'That about 40 years he first knew Edward Terringham Esq. and that the said Mr. Terringham sometime before the wars was in possession of some coal mines in Aywood by virtue of a patent from his late Majesty as this deponent hath heard, and did employ several workmen to work there for some time without interruption, and this deponent doth conceive that the sole reason why Mr. Terringham left the possession thereof, was for that the same works were not then of so great value or worth as now they prove to be and for want of money to carry it on.'

'III. Do you know or have you heard that long before the late wars there was a "decretall" Order or Injunction out of his Majesty's Court of Exchequer against all or most part of the Colliers and quarrymen of that Forest that none should get, sell or dispose of any of the sale coal; and for the quieting the possession thereof either in his Majesty that then was, or in the said Edward Terringham?"

No witness deposed to this Interrogatory.

'IV. Do you know the mines of coal or how many coal mines do you know that lie within the limits and perambulation of the same Forest of Dean as well those that lie within the demesne land of his Majesty as the waste soil thereof as also all such as are and lie in the lands of any of his Majesty's subjects within the perambulation of the Forest, that are now open, or may be opened; if yea, how much may the said mines be worth by the year to be let and set, how much coal and to what value has been gotten and disposed of the last seven years past within the waste soil of the said Forest and the lands adjacent within the perambulation thereof?'

Mathon deposed:

'That there are many coal mines in the Forest of Dean and Hundred of St. Brevills but how many this deponent knoweth not; but this deponent believeth that the same might now be worth if enjoyed without interruption £500 per annum besides all charges of managing the same.'

Drew deposed:

'That he knoweth most of the mines now in the perambulation of the Forest of Dean and hath known them for many years past, and doth believe that the coal there gotten may be worth for the seven last years past Fifty pounds per annum above all charges.'

George Brayne deposed that he knew the coal mines but not the value of them.

'VI. What customs, rights or privileges are justly due to the miners of coal and quarrymen within the Forest or perambulation thereof: declare the particulars thereof and how long the miners did so hold and enjoy the same without interruption; by whom were they interrupted, and when and upon what occasion? Are there not now several persons that by themselves or servants get coal which were never born within the hundred of St. Brevills nor brought up as a miner ?'[1]

Drew was the only witness to reply to this Interrogatory, his deposition being:

'That there are several customs claimed by the miners of coal and quarries of grindstone in the Forest of Dean but what is justly due to them this deponent doth not well know, but doth very well remember that Mr. Terringham hath several times interrupted them therein since his having the works.'

1 An early hint of the intrusion of so-termed 'foreigners'.

'VII. Were you born within the Hundred of St. Brevills or where were you born; are you now or were you at any time heretofore allowed, owned or reputed as a miner or having right to work in any of the mines or quarries of stone lying within the Forest of Dean or perambulation thereof? If yea, what mines or quarries did or do you now claim a right or interest in, and by what title or custom? Do you know the pretended title and custom of the miners? If so, how long is it since you so understood and knew the same? Have not the miners to your own particular knowledge or hearing within these few years broken and altered many of their pretended ancient customs? If yea, in what have they so broken them, and how many years is it since they have broken the same?'

There were no depositions to this Interrogatory.

'VIII. Do you know, believe or have heard that Sir John Winter, Kt., did surrender up the Patent to him made of the mines of coal and quarries of grindstone amongst other things and for what consideration and to what end; and whether Sir John Winter did by the continuance of such his grant until such surrender pay or cause to be paid to Edward Terringham father of the complainant's husband the annuity of £300 therein reserved or how much thereof? Do you know, believe or have heard that the complainant Katherine Terringham hath since her husband's decease taken out Letters of Administration?'

William Brayne of Littledean, 'gent., aged 36 years or thereabouts', was the only witness to reply to this Interrogatory, his deposition being:

'That Sir John Winter, Kt., had a grant of the quarries and coal mines together with the greatest part of the waste of that Forest and that he made [– – – *illegible* – – –] upon composition with his now Majesty, but remembers not the particular agreements.'

There followed:

'*Interrogatories administered ... on the part of James Yerworth, John Dowle, John Ambrey, and John Jones* alias *Philips, four of the Defendants.*'

'I. Do you know the parties, plaintiff and defendants, and which of them do you know and how long have you known them?"

William Hawkins of Coleford, shoemaker, aged 77, deposed:

'He knoweth not Katherine Terringham the complainant but he very well knows the defendants James Yerworth, John Dowle and John Ambrey.'

John West, 'Gent., aged 51 years or thereabouts', deposed[1]:

'He doth not know the complainant but he knows the defendants James Yerworth and John Dowle.'

1 He was 'one of his Majesty's Suitors' at St. Briavels Castle, and 'foreman of the Regard of the Forest' (Deposition to Interr. Nos. II and III).

'V. Have there not always within the Forest and hundred of the castle of St. Briavells certain persons called and accompted free miners there; who time out of mind have enjoyed without interruption the liberty of entering, digging and working in the mines of coal and iron to their own proper use, and have they not been called always the King's miners?'

Hawkins deposed:

'There have been for the space of three score years last past to this deponent's knowledge certain persons called and accompted free miners within the Forest which have entered and digged within the mines of the Forest to their own use.'

'VI. What is and hath been the custom of the mine and miners within the Forest? Is there not and hath there not always, time whereof the memory of man is not to the contrary, been this custom there used? That any man borne within that part of the hundred of the castle of St. Briavells as lies within the perambulation of the Forest of Dean, and bred and brought up in the mystery or craft of mining, after he hath wrought in his own proper person one whole year and a day in some mine within the Forest, is and hath always been accompted and taken for a free miner; and might lawfully and hath been accustomed at his will and liking, by himself or other partners being also free miners, to enter into any place, as well of the King's waste soil or ground of the Forest as of the several lands of any of his subjects or tenants within the Forest (except gardens, orchards and curtilages) there to dig for the finding of minerals of iron and coal? And the same so found to cast up, take, carry away and convert to his or their own proper use.'

Hawkins deposed:

'That there is and hath been always, time whereof the memory of man is not to the contrary as this deponent believeth for he hath known it for 60 years past, this custom used in the Forest of Dean. That any man born within the part of the hundred of the castle of St. Briavells as lies within the perambulation of the Forest and bred and brought up in the mystery or craft of mining, after he hath wrought in his own proper person one whole year and a day in some mine within the Forest, is and hath always been accompted and taken for a free miner and might lawfully and hath been accustomed at his will and liking by himself or other partners being also free miners to enter into any place as well of the King's waste soil or ground of the Forest as of the several lands of any of his subjects or tenants within the Forest (except gardens, orchards and curtilages) there to dig for the finding of minerals of iron and coal, and the same so found, to take, cast up, carry away and convert to his or their own proper use.'

West deposed:

'That for 30 years last past or thereabouts this deponent doth know that there are within the Forest of Dean certain persons called free miners who have time out of mind, as this deponent verily believeth, used and accustomed to get myne of coal and iron to their own use within the Forest, as well in his Majesty's waste soil there as in the several lands of his Majesty's subjects and tenants within the perambulation of the Forest and hundred of St. Briavells, and the reason that this deponent believeth that the said miners have used so to dig and get myne of coal and iron within the Forest time out of mind is for that he, this deponent, hath not only read the same in a certain writing now owned by the miners, called the Miners Inquisition, setting forth their custom, but also in a certain ancient writing in parchment being a memorandum or declaration concerning and setting forth the custom and usage of the miners within the Forest for digging and gaining of the myne And this deponent sayeth that the free miners have several times heretofore, and within few years last past, digged and gained considerable quantities of iron myne in the lands in the possession of this deponent within the Forest and hundred, which he, this deponent, would not willingly have suffered could he have found any legal way to hinder them.'

'VII. What recompense or satisfaction have such free miner or miners used been accustomed to give and allow unto the King's Majesty for their liberty of digging or getting coal within his Majesty's waste soil? Doth not such miner or miners after they have been at the whole charge of working and coming unto any mine of iron and coal used to allow, and hath not he or they time out of mind used to allow and ought to allow unto the King's Majesty so much mine of coal or iron as can or might be gotten or gained by one workman or miner, to be appointed there to dig and work freely (without paying anything) in such mine by the Galer in whose precincts such works shall happen to be? And is not and hath not such workman so put in been always called the Kings man? And are not such miner or miners so working and digging for the finding of coal and iron mine put many times to very great charge before they come unto or find any such coal or iron mine?'

Only Hawkins deposed to this Interrogatory, his deposition being:

'That the officer called the King's Gaolor, time whereof the memory of man is not to the contrary as this deponent believeth for he hath known it 60 years, hath used to put in a man called the King's man into every pit of iron or myne within the Forest after a certain fraternity of the free miners and their partners within the Forest have been at a very great charge, sometimes forty shillings, sometimes ten or twenty pounds, to drive or dig the pit or myne from the surface of the earth till they come to the myne of coal or iron. And the man so put in and appointed by his Majesty's officer is to work and gain myne of iron and coal to the use of the King without contributing anything to the charge of driving and digging the pit or myne. And if there be any stoppage in the myne the King's man is obliged to work no longer than there is myne [ore] current, and then he comes in again at his pleasure.'

'VIII. What other recompense or satisfaction have such free miner or miners been used to allow to the use of the King's Majesty after the finding and coming to coal or iron mine within the waste soil or ground of his Forest of Dean? Hath not the custom been always such: that every such miner hath always paid and ought to pay unto the said Galor to the use of the King's Majesty 1d. for every such miner labouring in the mine, when the Galor comes to gale the pit? As also one seame of coal or iron mine every quarter of a year. And also 1d. for each miner weekly so long as any mine of coal or iron shall be found or gained within any such pit?'

Hawkins deposed:

'That every such free miner and miners hath also been used to allow to the use of the King's Majesty, after the finding or coming to coal or iron myne within the waste soil or ground of his Forest of Dean, and every miner hath always paid and ought to pay unto the officer called the Gaoler to the use of the King's Majesty 1d. for every such miner labouring in the said myne when the Gaoler comes to gale the pit. And also one seameinge or man's bearing on land of iron and coal every quarter of a year that they work in the mine, and also 1d. for every miner weekly so long as any myne of coal or iron shall be found or gained within any such pit.'

'IX. What is the custom in case any coal or iron mine be found in any the several lands of his Majesty's subjects or tenants within the Forest of Dean? Hath not such free miner or miners over and besides such workman allowed to the King and other allowances as aforesaid, been used to and accustomed and ought to allow to the proprietor and owner of the soil so much mine of coal or iron oare, as may be gained by one other workman to be put in by such owner or proprietor, to have and dispose of to his own use. And is not and hath not such other workman been always called the Lord's man?'

Hawkins deposed:

'That in case any coal or iron myne be found within any of the several lands of his Majesty's subjects or tenants within the Forest, the said free miners so finding the said myne over and besides such workman allowed to the King and other allowances as aforesaid, have been used and accustomed to allow to the proprietor and owner of the soil so much myne of coal or iron oare as may be gained by one other workman to be put in by such owner or proprietor, to have and dispose of to his own use, which workman is usually called the Lord's man.'

'X. What is meant by galing a mine pit or coal pit? Is not the custom this: when the miner hath come unto or found any coal mine or iron mine, doth not the King's Gaylor repair to the pit upon notice thereof and there agree on the name of the pit, and enter into his book how many partners or shares there are therein, that he may know how much to demand for the King's use? And in case it shall happen any such pit so sunk or digged to be in the several lands of any his Majesty's subjects or tenants, doth not the said Galer make out a way to the next highway or common or waste ground from the pit? And hath not the miners or partners working in such pit been used to hedge in the said way that so the owner of the land may receive as little damage as may be by the passing and repassing of horses and other carriages to the work?'

Hawkins confirmed the custom explained in the Interrogatory in identical terms adding: 'This is called Gaoleing the pit.'

'XI. Were not the defendants every of them born within the hundred of the castle of St. Briavells and also within the perambulation of his Majesty's Forest of Dean – that is to say James Yerworth and John Dowle at the parish of Newland, John Ambrey at the parish of Staunton, and John Phillips *alias* Jones at the parish of Ruardean? And were not every of them the defendants bred up in the craft or mystery of mining? And have not they and every of them worked a year and a day in the mine in their own proper persons? And are they not free miners within his Majesty's Forest of Dean? And have been so accompted for many years past?'

Hawkins deposed:

'That he knoweth that the defendants James Yerworth and John Dowle were born at the parish of Newland, and John Ambrey at the parish of Staunton, all within the hundred of the castle of St. Briavells and within the perambulation of his Majesty's Forest, and were bred up in the craft or mystery of mining and have worked many years in their own proper persons and are free miners of the Forest of Dean and so accompted.'

'XIII. What benefit and advantage are you to enjoy or hath the plaintiff promised you, or anyone on his behalf promised you, that you shall have and enjoy for being a witness in this cause or in case the complainant shall obtain a Decree for the coal mines and quarries or either of them?'

No deposition was made.

George Brayne of Littledean, 'free miner aged 63 years or thereabouts', who earlier had been examined on the part of the complainant was then cross-examined on the part of the defendants. He deposed:

'That there are in the Forest of Dean and hundred of St. Briavels two officers called the King's Gaolers or gavellers, whose office within the Forest is to gather the dues and duties of the King or Queen for the time being arising out of the mines of coal and iron found and gained by the free miners within the Forest and hundred. And the free miners have used always for this 50 years last past to this deponent's knowledge and time out of mind as this deponent hath heard from his ancestors and other ancient men to get mine of coal, iron and oaker within the Forest to their own proper use and behalf without any interruption except some suits of law brought against them by one Mr. Terringham. And these persons using their custom have been always called the King's miners for that they pay the King a certain duty or yearly revenue called Gale money.

That one Mr. George [Edward] Terringham about 40 years ago came into the Forest of Dean and claimed an interest or title in the mines of coal and iron, who employed this deponent with five other persons to take possession of some coal pits in the Forest near Coleford, and this deponent and the five other persons were beaten off by the miners belonging to the pits.'

The suit was continued in Hilary Term 1675-76[1] and similar Interrogatories were used. The witnesses were William Rowles of Newnham, 'gent. aged 59', Eustace Hardwick[2] of Littledean, 'gent. aged 68', John Brinkworth of Littledean, weaver aged 70, James Yem of Staunton, house-carpenter aged 80, Henry Davis of Newland, narrow-weaver aged 72, Thomas Davies of Clearwell, 'gent. aged 40', William Crosse of

1 E134 Exch. Deps. by Coms. 27/28 Chas. II, Hilary, 21 (1675-6): Terringham *v.* Yarworth.

2 See p. 59 n.l.

Mitcheldean, 'yeoman aged 51', John Stephens of Ruardean, basketmaker aged 83, Thomas Creede of Ruardean, 'gent. aged 60', John Williams of Clearwell, 'yeoman aged 71', and Thomas Palmer of Coleford, blacksmith aged 74. It would be repetition to include the substance of their depositions as they tended to confirm the customary privileges of the miners and quarrymen on similar lines to those already mentioned.[1] The suit was re-opened in 1683 but was adjourned.

It appears that about this time, people other than free miners were attempting to 'cash-in' on the rights of the latter, for in 1675 several gentlemen and freeholders of the parish of Newland presented a Petition to the Treasury, in which they set forth[2]:

> 'That there had been, and then was, great store of coal in several Men's lands in the said Parish, and in the adjoining waste; that the free miners opened and dug pits at their pleasure, as well in his Majesty's waste, as in the lands of private men; and did then take considerable quantities of his Majesty's wood, for support of their coal works, as of right appertaining to their custom; that the inhabitants of the adjacent country were supplied from thence with coal for firing, without which great spoils would be inevitably committed in his Majesty's woods, and also for lime coal, without which there would be little tillage; that the Petitioners finding the free miners to abuse the country, by lessening the former measures of coal, and to make daily consumption of his Majesty's woods, had, without the least prospect of gain, in hopes of putting a stop to those mischiefs, and for the better accommodation of themselves and neighbours, agreed together to try for, and carry on, digging of coal for both uses, at a place called Milkwall, near to the works of those free miners in his Majesty's waste, but not within the Inclosures, for the support of which they did not intend to claim or use any of his Majesty's woods, but to buy in the country, although they had equal Pretence of Right, as well to wood, as to the Liberty of digging; but that having been obliged to make the end of their level for draining their pits a little within the Inclosure of the Forest (without the least prejudice thereto) they found that by the extreme hardness of the rock they could not, without excessive charge, compass their level, unless they might have leave to turn into the Hill within the Inclosures, not exceeding 5 or 6 acres at most (wherein there was no wood) to carry through the said level. Praying, therefore, that for a work of such Public Advantage they might be allowed to alter that part of the Inclosure, and to carry in the ditch so much further as to exclude the said 6 acres, doing the same at their own cost.'

Sir Charles Harbord, reporting on the Petition, stated[3]:

> 'That he had seriously considered the Petition, and perused the Act of Parliament [1668], wherein it is expressly provided that the Inclosures should remain in severalty, in the actual possession of the Crown, for ever, freed and discharged from all right, title and pretence whatsoever, and should be made and reputed a nursery for wood and timber only; in consideration whereof, and of the 7th Clause in the said Act, he could not advise any warrant for breaking into the Inclosures, without Mr. Attorney's opinion; and that the claims, as to

[1] The present author has made a transcript of the whole of the Interrogatories and Depositions (Glos.R.O. D3921. Hart Collection). Certain of the Depositions dealing with the office of gaveller and the Mine Law Court are in Chapters III and IV respectively.

[2] 3rd Rpt. of 1788, p. 17.

[3] *Ibid.*, pp. 17-18.

the Mines and Quarries, did not seem to be legal or justifiable in point of right, though they had been long permitted; and as to the coal works, there never was any such claim to his remembrance, much less to any liberty of cutting his Majesty's woods for the support thereof; and the same ought to be totally suppressed, and would be so by a good officer, as Colonel [John] Wade was in the time of the Usurpation, and that only by the Forest Law, and the authority of a Justice of Peace; and that nothing was more necessary than the preservation of the Inclosures from spoil and harm, and the rest of the growing wood upon the wastes without the Inclosures from unlawful pretences and destruction, which might well be done by the Forest Law, if the same were duly executed, as it ought to be.'

The Petition was rejected for the reasons suggested by Sir Charles Harbord, even though Sir Baynham Throckmorton, who had been one of the Commissioners first appointed for carrying the Act of 1668 into execution, gave it as his opinion that agreement to the Petition would tend to the preservation of the woods, and the convenience and advantage of the country. In August 1679[1] a commission was ordered to be issued to the Marquis of Worcester and others to report on the state of the Forest. They were to inquire *inter alia* what abuses and spoils had taken place; also as to illegal commoning, what 'digging for mine, earth, tile, cinder or stone' had taken place, and what wood had been delivered to the colliers and miners and by what right. Their Return dated 23 April 1680 contained a description of the Inclosures which had been made in consequence of the Act of 1668, and the state of the fences and woods, both within and without the Inclosures. The Return states, *inter alia*:

"That the colliers and miners have had some birch and orle [alder] delivered to them for the support of their pits, of the value of £6 or £7, and without paying for the same of late years, which they pretend an ancient right to by prescription.

That they were of opinion that the most likely way to render the Forest Courts effectual, and to compel the Officers of Inheritance to be diligent and faithful in the discharge of their several duties, for the preservation of the Forest, would be to procure a Justice Seat once a year, for six or seven years, to be held in the Long Vacation within the Forest, or not remote from it.

That there were remaining about thirty cabins[2] in several parts of the Forest inhabited by about 100 poor people, many of whom had been born in the Forest and never lived out of it; and that they had taken care to demolish the cabins and the inclosures about them, but that it would require some little longer time for the effectual removal and legal settlement of them in other places.'

In 1683[3] the rights of the quarrymen and, to a lesser extent, the free miners, were once again challenged. The suit particularly concerned the quarrying rights in the Forest

1 C.T.B., vol. vi, pp. 145, 196, 482.

2 The cabins (crude houses) are believed to have consisted of a turf-covered roof resting on four dry stone walls with a low door but no windows. There was no doubt a rough fireplace and chimney, and the floor may have been paved with rough stones. There are remains of some of these cabins in 2002. An old collier, writing in 1905 states: 'I have seen some of those cabin houses on bits of ground stolen from the Crown; when the door was shut there was no light inside except what came down a low squat of a chimney; no tax nor vote'. (Letter dated 25 January 1905, once in the office of deputy surveyor.)

3 E134 Exch. Deps. by Coms. 35 Chas. II, Mich. 40. Thomas Becke *v.* Cowles and certain other quarrymen.

and very little transpired regarding the free miners except that it was asserted that their rights did not extend to stone. Depositions were made implying that 'the quarrymen were not governed by the laws and customs of the miners', and that 'the quarryers were not concerned in the Mine Law Courts, neither had those courts jurisdiction over them as quarryers'. An interesting deposition was that of Trestram Tresteed of Newland, aged ninety years, who said: 'He hath not contributed to the charge of the suit but he is concerned in defence of the rights of the miners and hath contributed to the defence of former suits brought against the miners 40 years ago and since, and the same hath cost him at least £10; and he will be still ready and will always contribute his share in defending any suits that shall be brought against them.'

In June 1683 a proposal similar to the one ten years before was made by Sir John Ernle, junior, supervisor and conservator of the Forest, to the Treasury 'on their encouragement' for raising a constant revenue out of the Forest by the making of iron.[1] This proposal was referred to a Commission, consisting of William Harbord, Mr. Agar and the forest officials, appointed in November 1683.[2] It was rejected,[3] on account of the need to conserve timber, although large quantities were cut in the following years for the navy and for various iron masters, in particular Paul Foley.

Abuses and spoils continued to exercise much of the time of the forest officials.[4] Certain of the officials themselves were proved in later years to have been far from innocent in this connection. In 1688, during a period of national discontent, some of the inhabitants pulled down Worcester Lodge and York Lodge, besides damaging the Speech House.[5] Large quantities of timber were destroyed, and fences and mounds thrown down. These outrages were probably connected with the unpopularity of James II. Thus much of the good work done following the Act of 1668 had been undone. Later, other efforts were made to make amends. Philip Ryley, the new surveyor of the Forest, made determined efforts, while in November 1690[6] Sir John Guise made an offer to carry out a policy of silviculture in connection with the young growth in the Forest. This proposal was among the items to be considered by a new commission issued on 18 May 1691 to Henry, Duke of Bedford, warden of the Forest, and others.[7] The Commission received detailed Articles of Instruction, by which they were ordered to enquire, *inter alia*[8]:

(*a*) Whether the Ironworks should be set up as formerly.
(*b*) What coalpits were taken into the Inclosures which might conveniently be left out (without prejudice to the younger woods) for the benefit of the public.
(*c*) What wastes and spoils had been committed since 13 February 1688, and who had dug

1 C.T.B., vol. vii, pp. 845, 859, 963.
2 *Ibid.*, vol. ii, pp. 962-4.
3 3rd Rpt. of 1788, p. 19.
4 C.T.B., vol. viii, pp. 1254-5.
5 *Ibid.*, p. 586. The estimated cost of making good the damage was stated in 1692 as £219 10s.
6 *Ibid.*, vol. viii, p. 901.
7 *Ibid.*, vol. ix, pp. 1156-7.
8 App. VIII to the 3rd Rpt. of 1788 contains a full copy of the Commission's Deed of Appointment, and their Return to the same. A MS. copy of the Return once held at Whitemead Park, had been presented by W. H. Fryer in 1902.

'any mines, coal, tiles or cinders within the Forest'.

(*d*) Who have dug or left open any sort of pits or quarries of stone and built lime kilns, and burnt lime, and by what pretence of right.

The Commission in their Return in 1692[1] to the Court of Exchequer estimated that there were 615,500 short cords on 9,025 acres in the Forest, worth, at 4s. 10d. per cord, £148,745 16s. 8d. This was excluding the larger timber. They advised against any large grant of timber in the Forest, in view of the Act of 1668, and drew attention to the fact that similar proposals in 1662 and 1674 had been rejected. They set forth the same reasons against any new ironworks, and pointed out that the cordwood was now saleable at a price 1s. 8d. each long cord more than the value in 1662 and 1674. They added:

'It may be taken notice of also, the great difficulty with which the many Freeholders that had Right of Common, and other Privileges, were prevailed with in the year 1665 to submit the same to the Crown for inclosing the Forest, according to the Statute 20th Chas. II [1668], many of the same persons are yet living, and would doubtless be concerned to see the profit of it in any private hands, when they have freely parted with theirs for the Public Utility; and we are credibly informed, that if any such Grant pass, the Freeholders do intend to prefer a Petition to be restored to the Rights of Estovers enjoyed by them before the making of the Statute.'

The Commissioners also reported:

(*a*) 'There are but six coal pits within all or any of their Majesty's Inclosures, and of those places, the Inclosures being generally down, and not necessary to be repaired, the Wood therein being of a growth past danger, the country are not incommoded or prejudiced in that respect.'

(*b*) 'The colliers of this Forest have, time out of mind, had an allowance of wood for support of their pits, which allowance hath been usually made unto them by Order of the Verderers, and taken by view of a woodward or keeper; but the allowance having been stopped for some time, upon a question of their rights thereunto, they have taken the same without such Order or View, by which great wastes are daily committed: For prevention whereof, and that the Colliers may be duly supplied, as we are humbly of opinion, they ought, we propose it as expedient, that the allowance may be made to them by the Order of the Verderers at the Attachment or Swanimoot Courts, and taken by the view of a woodward or keeper as formerly.'

(*c*) If their main recommendations are adopted 'the vain hopes that some Persons have given to many and daring Offenders about this Forest, that the same shall be made a free Chace, and consequently be destroyed, and they exempted from punishment, will be utterly defeated and disappointed.'

The Return was signed by 'Wm. Cooke, R. Pyndar, Wm. Boevey, J. Viney, Jo. Kyrle, and Ph. Ryley'. Following the Return, the Treasury issued a warrant on 17

[1] (See p. 208 n. 1.)

February 1692[1] for raising £20,000 by wood sales in Dean over a period of seven years.[2] They also instructed Ryley that 'the allowance of wood to the colliers is to be continued by order of the verderers and to be taken by view of the woodward or keeper as formerly'.[3] Large quantities of cordwood were sold to Messrs. Paul and Thomas Foley, Jnr., John Wheeler and Richard Avenant, and to Mrs. Boevey, Lady Winter and a Mr. White – all of whom had ironworks in or near the Forest. In addition, large sales of cinders were now being effected in the Forest, whereas it seems they had before been used without payment. About this time little copper ore may have been mined in the Forest but it was usually imported.[4] There is no indication that the free miners of the Forest were in any way connected with this industry, neither is there any trace of them being connected with the few attempts at gold mining which took place in the district.[5]

Although in 1706 many of the inhabitants petitioned[6] against an official plan to enclose the Forest, on the grounds that it would adversely affect rights of common, a counter petition[7] was made by 'a number of poor inhabitants employed in the service of the iron manufacturers, praying that the plan of inclosure might be persisted in, for the increase of underwood, by the cutting of which they gained their livelihood'. The scheme proceeded, the produce being sold in the main to the ironmasters.

A relevant and interesting lawsuit of the year 1752[8] is given below:

> 'In Easter Term, 1752, the Governor and Company of Copper Mines in England commenced an action in the Court of King's Bench against Thomas Philips and others for breaking and entering their closes, etc., to which defendants pleaded their custom that all persons born within the Hundred of St. Briavels, within the Forest and having worked in any of the mines within the hundred for the space of one year and one day, there called free miners or the King's miners, and abiding within the hundred, have entered when and as often as they please, as well into the lands and soil of the king, as of any other person within the hundred, to search for, dig up, and get coal there, and carry away the same to their own use, paying to the king certain dues and duties; and issue was joined thereupon, but afterwards, by leave of the court, they amended their plea, and added "by the licence and consent of a certain officer of the king called the king's gaveller for the time being, or his deputy, entered, etc." The cause was tried at Gloucester Assizes before Mr. Justice Birch, and the custom was found by the jury, but no further proceedings appear to have been had upon it. In or about the same

1 C.T.B., vol. ix, pp. 1495-7.

2 Additional authorisations for sales were made soon after.

3 Confirmed again on 8 April 1692 (C.T.B., vol. ix, pp. 1583). The Coms. of 1788 state that during the reigns of William and Anne the miners seem to have been suffered to take wood for the use of their works, but not timber (3rd Rpt. of 1788, p. 19).

4 Rhys Jenkins: 'The Copper Works at Redbrook and at Bristol' (*Trans. B.&G.A.S.*, vol. lxiii, 1942, pp. 145-67): 'Eric Odelstierna, writing in 1692, stated that recently a company had begun to work some mines in the Forest of Dean, and that a small quantity of copper had been smelted. Six years later Thomas Cletscher wrote that the Forest copper mines were quite exhausted.' The smelting industry was then carried on at Redbrook using ore brought by sea from Cornwall to Chepstow, and then up the Wye.

5 See Hart, 'The History of Gold Mining in the Forest of Dean' (*Trans. B.&G.A.S.*, vol., 65, 1944, pp. 98-104).

6 3rd Rpt. of 1788, p. 19 (14 Jan. 1706).

7 *Ibid.*, 10 Feb. 1706.

8 4th Rpt. of Coms. of 1831.

year one Francis Jones commenced an action in the Court of King's Bench against Philips and others for breaking and entering his stables and closes, and taking, driving away, detaining, and selling three mares; to which defendants pleaded that in the Forest of Dean there had been immemorially divers mines of iron, coal, and other minerals of the king and his predecessors and divers persons employed in the working of the mines called free miners; and there had been immemorially in the Forest a certain court of record of our Lord the king, being the court of the mine and miners of our lord the king, called the Mine Law Court, which immemorially had been and of right ought to be holden before the constable of the castle of St. Briavels, steward of our lord the king of the said court or his deputy; and that the defendants did recover in action brought in the said court £10, and prosecuted and sued out a precept upon which the mares, etc., were levied, etc. upon which the said Jones sued out a writ of error, to which a return was made and errors assigned, but in consequence, as is alleged, of some dissensions arising between the members of the Copper Company who caused the said suit to be commenced the errors were never argued.'

Abuses continued in the Forest. On 27 September 1707[1] Mr. Wilcox, the surveyor-general, reported that the bark of twenty oaks had been stripped three or four feet above the ground, and others just within the ground, to kill them so that they might be taken as dead trees. In 1711 a Bill was filed in the Exchequer by the attorney-general against William Parry, John Reynolds, and other colliers, for cutting down trees and wood in the Forest. However before a decision was reached in the suit all proceedings ceased owing to the death of Queen Anne (1714).[2] Acts of a riotous nature occurred in 1735.[3] The same year, on 18 March, the surveyor-general complained that 'a practice has prevailed among the colliers of boring large holes in trees, that they may become dotard and decayed, and as such may be delivered to them for the use of their collieries'.[4] Consequently directions were given that 'in order to prevent such pernicious and destructive practices, such bored trees as appear to be dead and spoiled shall be felled, taking care that none be cut down that may be of use to the navy.'[5] A letter dated 30 May 1769[6] asserts that 'great abuses are committed by the colliers ... who annually cut down great numbers of oak trees under a right they claim to timber for the use of their coal pits, and are guilty of many unwarrantable practices, which tend to destroy the growth'. Another letter of the same year[7] reads:

1 C.T.B., iii. p. 537, No. 140.

2 The Coms. of 1788 (3rd Rpt. of 1788, p. 20) commented: 'We do not find that any process has been instituted by the Crown lawyers since that time for the prevention or punishment of abuses in this Forest'.

3 See Hart, *The Commoners of Dean Forest* (1951).

4 Warrant 18 March 1735 (Third Rpt. of 1788, p. 22).

5 3rd Rpt. of 1788, p. 22. The Commissioners state: 'Not a word is said about endeavouring to discover the offenders that they may be punished, or recommending more attention and care to the officers of the Forest ... it not only shows the slight attention then paid by the Government to this subject ... but it is necessary to mark that from this paper it appears that the colliers, who now frequently obtain from the keepers the best trees in the Forest, did not at that time think themselves entitled to have any that were not dotard and decayed.'

6 *Eighteenth Century Documents Relating To The Royal Forests, The Sheriffs and Smuggling* (selected from the Shelburne Manuscripts in the William L. Clements Library), by A. L. Cross (Macmillan Company, New York, 1928), p. 105.

7 *Ibid.*, pp. 103-4 (15 May 1769).

'I beg leave to acquaint you with some remarks I have made in His Majesty's Forest of Dean, respecting the timber, and to offer some reasons why so much of it is annually destroyed and why there is not more young Timber coming up. The Colliers (of which there is a great number,) who formerly were accustomed to make use of decayed Beech, Ash, Birch, or other Offal Timber, that grew in the Forest, have for some years past claimed a right to Oak Timber for their Works, and I have been well informed that they had one year, thirteen hundred trees and oftentimes more, but seldom less than from Seven Hundred to a Thousand every year, which Trees are delivered to them by the keepers, by a Warrant which the Colliers obtain from the steward of the Swanimote Court; a Court held by the Verderers of the Forest, who are chosen by the Freeholders of the County. This Court ought to he held by any two at least of the Verderers annually on the 25th Day of September where the keepers are to deliver an Account upon Oath of all the Timber delivered to the Colliers within the year past, and of all the Deer killed that comes within their knowledge either by Warrant or otherwise. But this Court I am told is not regularly held nor any proper Register nor Entry of the Proceedings in it kept. The Colliers most of them have houses on the Verge of the Forest, and in order to procure Grass for their Horses, often set fire to the Goss or Furze, and by that means the Bushes are destroyed, which would otherwise defend the Young Trees from the Cattle and encourage the Growth of them, but there are many Acres of the Forest from that cause now wholly destitute of Trees, which was formerly covered with Timber. They also often take in part of the Forest for Garden Ground, and keep a great number of Hogs to run in the Forest, & I have been informed great Numbers are also sent there by other Persons, oftentimes to the amount of three, four, five or six Thousand, and it is said by some Persons that the keepers themselves, whose business it is to prevent any Hogs from coming into the Forest, are paid by the Owners of them for their running there, which I apprehend to be as great a Prejudice as any to the Forest. For they grub up the Roots of the Fern, and by that means also destroy many Acorns [*sic.*] that fall from the Trees, which would naturally grow to be Timber, if not destroyed by this means, it being evident that there are many Acres, in different parts of the Forest so broken up by the Hogs, that the Ground appears as if it had been ploughed and harrowed or rather like a Summer fallow. Though a Conservator is appointed by the Lords of the Treasury, and paid one hundred Pounds a year to inspect the Forest and see that no Incroachments are made, and to pull down and lay waste all Cottages erected or Ground taken in for Gardens: Yet to all Appearances no notice is taken of these Nuisances as they are daily increasing.

I also beg leave further to observe that there is a Company at Bristol, who have lately erected a forge in the Forest near Lydbrooke who as I have been well informed have had a least five Hundred loads of Timber for that building, and a Water Wheel, under Sanction of one or two of the Colliers who call themselves free Miners and claim a right to Timber, and they are now employing a great Number of them to dig for Cinders or Slagg, left formerly by the Ancient Bloomerys in many parts of the Forest, and I am told propose to enlarge their works, by which means a much larger Quantity of Timber will be destroyed if not timely prevented.

The Soil in general in this Forest is so suited for the growth of Timber that the great Increase of the Trees growing thereon is almost incredible, and I am humbly of the Opinion if proper care is taken to preserve the present Trees and inclosures made for a succession, this Forest would supply great part of the Timber wanted for the service of His Majesty's Yard at Plymouth.'

In a third letter, dated 30 April 1777, the writer comments[1]:

'Dean Forest is going to wrack and ruin. The depredations made therein by the colliers and country people are incredible: especially at the late Election. One of the witnesses now in town on the Contested Election, told a gentleman of my acquaintance that he met no less than eleven teams of horses loaded with large timber stolen out of the Forest by Mr. [Earl] Berkeley's Tenants, and winked at by him, he being Lord Warden. ... Mr. Andrews the purveyor in Dean Forest told me some years ago that things were got to such a pass, he durst not speak his mind there, and even take notice of these depredations; if he had he would have been murdered; he further said that a Regiment of Soldiers would scarce effect a reformation.'

A fourth letter, dated 28 February 1780, continues the sorry tale[2]:

'For some years it has been the custom with the people in the Forest to steal the body of the tree in the night, and cut it into cooper's ware, leaving the top part on the spot, which the keepers take as their perquisite. At this time large trees are conveyed every spring tide to Bristol. When I was at Gatcomb, in one day there were five or six teams came with timber, plank and knees (winter felled), and other timber, among which were several useful pieces for ships of 64 and 50 guns. I am therefore humbly of opinion, unless some method is found to prevent such depredations, in a few years the whole Forest must be destroyed.'

Between the years 1771 and 1786 John Pitt, surveyor-general of Woods, made various representations to the Treasury relative to abuses and depredations committed in the Forest by the miners, timber stealers, and others.[3] Various means were tried to prevent the abuses, such as introducing checks on the delivery of the timber to the miners, and offering rewards for the discovery and conviction of offenders. However, 'the little success which followed these well-intended measures, shows how useless it is to attempt an improvement in this Forest, while the resident officers derive advantages from the continuance of the abuses.[4] In spite of the endeavours of the surveyor-general, the quantity of the timber delivered to the miners has increased every year; and the inclosures which were made on his recommendation, were very soon suffered, by those who had the charge of them to go to ruin.'[5]

Dean was not the only Forest that had fallen into such an unsatisfactory position, and eventually Commissioners were appointed in 1780 to enquire into the state of the Woods, Forests and Land Revenues of the Crown. They went thoroughly into the

1 *Eighteenth Century Documents Relating To The Royal Forests, The Sheriffs and Smuggling,* p. 141 (Rt. Gregson to Lord Shelburne).

2 *Ibid.*, p. 110 (Bn. Slade, one of the King's purveyors, to the Navy Board).

3 In 1786 Warrants were issued for raising £2,000 from timber sales in Dean Forest towards building a gaol. It was stated: 'One of the Houses of Correction is to be erected within our Forest of Dean ... and ... it is probable our rights in the said Forest will be much benefited by a House of Correction and Confinement being erected therein' (App. XXXV to 3rd Rpt. of 1788). 1,690 trees were viewed and marked by J. Pyrke and T. Crawley-Boevey.

4 App. No. XXXVIII to 3rd Rpt. of 1788 discloses that in the seven years to Mich. 1787, 247 persons were convicted of timber stealing and other offences, fines amounting to £727 9s. 6d. imposed, and £540 paid as rewards by the deputy surveyor.

5 *Ibid.*

question of all the Crown Forests and issued seventeen most useful Reports. Their Third Report,[1] rendered on 3 June 1788, dealt almost exclusively with Dean Forest. It is a most important record comprising about 150 folio pages, containing much interesting information. Nicholls drew heavily upon it, and the same source has been used for some portions of the present work. From the Report,[2] we learn that the officers of the Forest were:

(*a*) The surveyor-general of the Woods and Forests.
(*b*) The Lord Warden of the Forest and constable of St. Briavels Castle. The office was held by Frederick Augustus, Earl of Berkeley, during the king's pleasure, and it was stated: 'No Salary is paid for the exercise of that office but an annual sum of £210 is issued to the Lord Warden from the Exchequer, by quarterly payments, for the wages of the conservator and six keepers; and a further sum of £40 per annum is allowed for wages of the keepers out of the rent reserved on a lease of the Manor and Hundred of St. Briavels, held by Lord Berkeley under the Crown.[3] The Lord Warden being Judge of the Court called the Mine Law Court, … the deputy wardens are appointed by the Lord Warden to execute that part of his office; but no Mine Law Court has been held for several years past'.
(*c*) One deputy surveyor (and an assistant).
(*d*) One conservator.[4]
(*e*) One gaveller.
(*f*) Six deputy wardens.
(*g*) Four verderers.
(*h*) One steward of the Swanimote Court.
(*i*) Nine foresters-of-fee (of which one is Chief Forester and Bowbearer).[5]
(*j*) Seven woodwards.
(*k*) Three deputy woodwards.
(*l*) Six keepers.
(*m*) No regarders (but there should be twelve).
(*n*) One watchman.[6]

The Report mentions the fees and perquisites received by the Forest officers in addition to their salaries. In the case of the deputy-surveyor, these were:

(*a*) 'The tops of all naval timber, refused by the Purveyor of the Navy as unfit for naval use';
(*b*) 'The tops of all stolen timber';
(*c*) 'All trees felled by wood-stealers, if found before they are cut into Kibbles,[7] or conveyed away';

---

1 Signed by Charles Middleton, John Call, and John Fordyce.
2 Pp. 26, 27 and App. No. XIV.
3 The Lease was of 'The Manor, Lordship, Township, and Castle of St. Briavels, the Manor of Newland, and Whitemead Park'. It was dated 19 Nov. 1777 and expired on 13 Jan. 1808.
4 As to this office see App. XXI to 3rd Rpt. of 1788.
5 *Ibid*., App. XXII to 3rd Rpt. of 1788.
6 *Ibid*., App. XXVII to 3rd Rpt. of 1788.
7 When cut into lengths and pieces for the use of cask-makers and wheelwrights.

(*d*) 'Moiety of cordwood,[1] made from the offal wood of timber delivered to the miners, and of stolen timber';
(*e*) 'In some Walks of the Forest 4d., and in others 6d., for every tree felled for the use of the miners';

besides certain other fees and perquisites.[2] The then deputy surveyor believed that he received £300 to £500 per annum from the above during the first few years of his appointment but only £50 during the last year. The keepers received the following in their respective Walks:

(*a*) 'One shilling on every Order for delivery of timber to the miners';
(*b*) 'Moiety of all cordwood of stolen timber';
(*c*) 'All Kibbles of stolen timber';
(*d*) 'Bark of the timber delivered to miners, and of all stolen timber found';
(*e*) 'Certain fees for cattle trespassing on the Forest in the fence month and winter haining'; besides certain fees regarding deer.

In such circumstances, how can the full blame for abuses in the Forest be attached to the local people, as sometimes has been alleged? George Caesar Hopkinson, gaveller of the Forest of Dean, was examined by the Commissioners on 4 April 1788, and deposed as follows[3]:

> 'This examinant saith, that His present Majesty, by Letters Patent bearing date the Fourth Day of June, in the Twenty-second Year of His Reign [1782], gave and granted unto this examinant the Office and Offices of Keeper of the Gawles Above and Under the Wood, riding forester, and ale conner within His Majesty's Forest of Dean in the County of Gloucester (but commonly called gaveller of Dean Forest) to hold the same during His Majesty's pleasure, together with all wages, fees, profits, rewards, perquisites, allowances, dues, commodities, advantages, liberties and emoluments whatsoever, to the said offices respectively belonging: That the duty of the said Office of gaveller is to preserve His Majesty's rights in the mines of coal, and other mines within the Forest, and to receive His Majesty's share of the iron ore and coal raised from such mines, or the compositions paid by the miners in lieu thereof: That this examinant hath been informed, and believes, that His Majesty is entitled to one fifth part of all the iron ore or coal raised within the Forest, or to put a sixth man into every pit or work carried on there, and to have a proportionable share of the produce of such work free from all expenses whatever, which share this examinant is informed was formerly taken in kind, and that the gaveller then had six deputies or assistants for collecting the same; but that for many years past the miners and colliers have paid an annual acknowledgement or composition in money for such share, the gaveller or his deputy agreeing with them as to the sum to be paid on that account: That upon marking or gavelling the ground, for a free miner to begin a new pit or level, the miner pays to the gaveller for his attendance, and for entering

1 The cordwood (a cord at that time measuring 8ft. 8in. long, 4ft. 4in. high and 2ft. 2in. wide) was made into charcoal in the Forest for the use of iron furnaces, forges, and manufactories of the district.

2 The abuses etc. connected with the measure and sale of timber by the deputy surveyors as disclosed by the Commissioners, are almost unbelievable of public officers.

3 App. No. XXV (p. 91) to 3rd Rpt. of 1788.

the same, a fee of five shillings, over and besides the annual compositions aforesaid: That a court called the Mine Law Court was formerly held at the Speech House in the Forest, by the deputy wardens and deputy constables of the Forest, for the regulation of all matters relating to the mines, and for settling disputes and questions between the miners, at which Court the gaveller or his deputy used to attend to receive all fines imposed for any offences cognizable by the said Court, and all other profits due to the King; but that for some years past the deputy wardens and deputy constables have discontinued holding the said Court, but for what reason this examinant knoweth not: That this examinant hath no salary for the exercise of the said Offices, or either of them, but that as gaveller he receives and takes to his own use, as his predecessors have always done, all the fines, fees, or compositions paid by the miners or colliers as aforesaid, without rendering any account thereof, the gaveller paying or allowing to his deputy such certain salary, or such share of the said fees and compositions, as he thinks fit: That this examinant received, by agreement with his late deputy, Philip Robinson, the annual sum of one hundred pounds, and allowed him to retain to his own use the residue of the said fees, compositions, and other profits, for assisting him in executing the said Office: That, according to an account made out in August last, by the said Philip Robinson, there were then within the Forest of Dean 121 coal pits (thirty-one of which were not actually in working) which pits produced 1,816 tons of coal per week: That there were 662 free miners concerned and employed therein; and that the annual compositions paid by them amounted to £215 8s. or thereabouts: That there is no regular iron mine work now carried on in the Forest, but, according to the account of Philip Robinson, there were about twenty-two poor men, who, at times when they had no other work to do, employed themselves in searching for and getting iron mine or ore in the old holes or pits in the Forest, which have been worked over many years; and that they annually pay to the gaveller four shillings per man, amounting to the yearly sum of four pounds eight shillings, which, with the aforesaid annual compositions of £215 8s. paid by the colliers, make together £219 16s. per annum; and that the fees paid to the gaveller, upon marking or gavelling ground for beginning new pits or levels, have amounted, one year with another, to about forty shillings a year: That many of the miners and colliers are so poor that no money can be collected from them; and there are great arrears of compositions due to this examinant, and some incurred in the times of his predecessors, and still remaining unpaid: That while the Mine Law Court continued to be held, the payment of the said dues and compositions was enforced in a speedy and effectual manner; but since the said Court hath been discontinued the gaveller hath been put to great trouble and expense in bringing actions for recovering the same: That this examinant hath always understood, and believes, that the Crown is entitled to all the mines of iron and coal within the whole perambulations of the Forest, whether the lands in which such mines are found be freehold, and in cultivation, or otherwise: and that there are at this time in working two pits, called True Blue and Windrells, not within the lands belonging to the Crown in the Forest, but within the perambulation thereof, for which pits this examinant receives the customary Gale Duty or composition.'

Appendix No. 10 to the 1788 Report is an abstract of an account received from John Matthews, steward of the Swanimote and Attachment Courts, of 'Timber delivered to the Coal Miners from 25/9/1780 to 25/9/1787', in the respective six Walks. From this we learn that 2,930 Orders were issued, and 7,486 oaks, 494 beech and 749 various trees known to have been delivered. In addition, 460 of the Orders were not returned correctly endorsed with the number of trees delivered, and the steward estimated these as 1,620, making a total of 10,349 trees. Appendix No. 24 is an 'Abstract of the Examinations of the six keepers of the Forest', taken on oath in 1788. The six keepers were:

(1) Thomas Harvey of Speech House Walk.
(2) William Stephens of Blakeney Walk.
(3) Richard Bennett of Worcester Walk.
(4) John Brett of Latimer Walk.
(5) Robert East of Parkend Walk.
(6) Richard Bradley of Ruardean or Herbert's Walk.

Their relevant depositions are summarised below:

(*a*) 'Fees on delivery of timber to miners':
Keeper No. (1) received 6d. per *tree* on 'executing every order or delivery of timber to miners or colliers'. The other keepers received 1s. per *order.*

(*b*) 'Perquisites from the offal wood, and bark of miners' timber and stolen timber':
All the keepers took to their 'own use the half of all offal wood of miners, and stolen timber, and the lengths or pieces of trespass or stolen timber, called Kibbles', together with all the bark of the foregoing.

(*c*) 'Profit from bark of miners' and stolen timber'[1]:
No. (1) – About £135 and £10 respectively, per annum.
No. (2) – About £30 per annum.
No. (3) – About £35 per annum.
No. (4) – About £21 12s. and £5 respectively, per annum.
No. (5) – About £53 and £5 respectively, per annum.
No. (6) – About £122 10s. per annum.

(*d*) 'Number of Coal pits and colliers' within their respective Walks:
No. (1) – 7 coal pits, employing 13 free miners, 8 boys 'who are working their freedom' and 2 women.
No. (2) – 7 coal pits; employees not known.
No. (3) – 17 coal pits, employing 81 free miners, and 17 boys 'who are working their freedom'.
No. (4) – 8 coal pits, employing 44 free miners, and 27 boys 'who are working their freedom'.
No. (5) – 8 iron mines, employing about 20 free miners and 3 boys 'who are working their freedom'; also 39 coal pits, employing 91 free miners; and 22 boys 'who are working their freedom'.
No. (6) – 28 coal pits, employing 133 free miners and boys, and 4 women.

(*e*) 'Mode of delivery of timber to miners':
All the keepers agreed that when the miners supplied from their Walks 'are in want of timber for the use of their works, they apply to the keeper, who thereupon views such works; and when satisfied that timber is wanted for such works, he certifies the same to

1 In addition to offal wood and kibbles.

the steward of the Swanimote Court, who issues an Order for the delivery of such timber. That the Orders are brought by the respective miners to the keeper, who, with the deputy surveyor or his agent, attended by the miners, mark and deliver the timber accordingly. That the Orders are returned to the Swanimote Court on the 25th Sept. in every year, each Order indorsed with the number of oak or beech trees delivered by virtue thereof.'[1]

(*f*) 'Trees delivered':

No. (1) – 'In general he delivers 4 trees on each Order, and that the trees by him usually delivered contain, on an average, 35 feet each'.

No. (2) – 'He delivers 2, 3 or 4 trees on each Order, which amounts to about 100 trees annually'.

No. (3) – 'In general he delivers 3 trees on each Order, which never exceed a ton each'.

No. (4) – 'Usually delivered 2, 3 or 4 trees on every Order, which trees, on an average, might contain the quantity of 3 tons or thereabouts on every Order'.

No. (5) – 'Does not exceed 2 tons on every Order'.

No. (6) – 4 trees on every Order, but 5 if the trees are on the small side, 'which may contain from 5 to 8 loads or tons on each Order'.

None of the keepers delivered any timber fit for the Navy 'except when the miners were sinking new pits, and taking up old pits, when it was necessary for them to have good cleft timber'.

(*g*) 'Misapplication of timber by colliers':

No. (1) – had 'reason to believe that part of the timber delivered to the miners for the use of their works had often been misapplied, and Informations had been exhibited against some of them, and the offenders punished for such abuse; and in particular, about 3 years since he delivered oak timber to one Jas. Tingle, a free miner, and his verns (partners) at a coal work called the Fire Engine, and a suspicion arising that part of such timber was converted and secreted by such miners, an Information was made and a Search Warrant obtained, when a large quantity of vessel heading and staves for casks, containing about 4 tons, was found in the possession of the said Tingle, but for want of sufficient evidence of the conversion of such timber the Miners were only compelled to pay the costs of the proceedings, and enter into bond for their future good conduct; which heading and staves were divided between himself, the deputy surveyor, and his assistants, as perquisites of office'.

No. (2) – had 'at times had great reason to suspect the colliers misapplying part of the timber delivered to them, by having found vessel timber for coopers ware hid near their works, which he had taken away; but as he could not prove that it was from such timber, he had never been able to convict any miner for such offence'.

No. (3) – No deposition.

No. (4) – 'has frequent reason to believe that the miners had misapplied part of the timber delivered to them for the use of their works, and particularly, about 9 years since, he saw one Wm. Wheatstone load 4 horses with part of the timber by him delivered, for the use of a Coal Work called the Tail Levell, for which an Indictment was preferred against Wheatstone, who was convicted and found £5 for such abuse'.

No. (5) – 'Believed that part of the timber had been frequently misapplied, he having

---

1 A typical Order is given in Chapter IV, p. 129.

several times found fresh oak timber converted into spokes for wheels and staves for vessels, hid and secreted in and about several coal works within his Walk, and for such misapplication the miners so offending had been refused timber for a considerable time afterwards; which spokes and staves, when found, he had taken to his own use as a perquisite of office; and the quantity he had so taken within the last 10 years may have amounted in the whole to one ton or thereabouts'.

No. (6) – 'Had heard, and believed, the miners have frequently misapplied a part of their timber, by the disposing of the same for board, quarter and other purposes for building, and he had taken from divers persons at different times a quantity of vessel staves hewn up for the purpose of making casks, which is now in his possession. That timber is delivered from his Walk to two pits, called True Blue and Windrells, out of the limits of the Forest, but within the Hundred of St. Briavell's, paying Gale to the gaveller of the Forest.'

Appendix No. 23 of the document under review is the report of the examination of Thomas Blunt, deputy surveyor since September 1780. He deposed:

'That, upon every application for timber by the miners, for the use of their works, the keeper of the Walk in which the mine is situated informs the steward of the Swanimote Court, that timber is wanted for such a work, who issues his Order for the allowance thereof, directed to the keeper, which timber is then delivered to the applicant; and he believes that within the time of his knowledge there has been about 1000 loads of oak timber annually felled for the use of the miners, of which at least one-fifth part has been fit for naval purposes; and that the great waste, spoil, and destruction of the timber and wood on the Forest is and hath been occasioned by an improper application of the timber delivered to the miners for the use of their works, as he apprehends and believes that one moiety or half part of the timber which they have had delivered to them would have been more than sufficient to have answered every needful purpose to which it ought to have been appropriated; and the abuses which have existed, and do now exist, in the Forest, are principally owing to the great increase of coal works, the not holding regular Courts at the Speech House as usual for the trial of offenders, the depasturing a greater number of horses, sheep and swine on the Forest than were formerly permitted, the officers of the Forest being suffered to accept fees and perquisites, the insufficiency of the Forest Laws, and the lenity shewn by the Justices to wood stealers, by a mitigation of their penalties when convicted: That, under the authority and direction of the surveyor-general, he hath frequently seized large quantities of offal timber, and such other timber as the miners could not use in their works; and in particular, that on or about the 28th day of January 1783, he seized and took 586 feet of oak timber, and more than 200 cleft pieces of oak, called Kibbles, which were found on the grounds of one George Martin, who, after such seizure, acknowledged that the same had been unlawfully taken and hauled away from off the said Forest, and that the same was the property of His Majesty: He also seized, at the Fire Engine on the Forest, between two and three waggon loads of timber, hewn up and converted by the colliers into coopers wares for market: That he divided and applied such seizures agreeable to the instructions he received from Mr. Pitt; and, by the sale of 96 loads and 19 feet of timber so seized, he caused a house to be built in Staplidge Inclosure, for the preservation of that inclosure, which cost forty-three pounds or thereabouts and the balance of the timber sold still remains to be accounted for by this examinant: That for preventing, as much as possible, the like abuse in future, he hath taken divers bonds and other securities, in large penalties, to be forfeited by the obligors, in case they should ever after be detected in the stealing of wood and timber from the Forest, or misapplying the timber supplied to them for the use of their works.'

Blunt also deposed that among the customary fees or perquisites of office received by him, exclusive of his salary, was 'one half part of the cordwood made from the offal wood of the miners; and fourpence or sixpence for every tree felled for the use of the miners'. Appendix No. 26 is an extract of a letter written by him dealing with the price of coal. Appendix No. 39 is the report of the examination of Miles Hartland, assistant for the last six years to the deputy surveyor. Among his depositions was the following:

'He does not know, nor ever made any calculation, what quantity of timber is annually delivered to the miners. The sorts of wood or timber delivered to them are oak and beech, and none other; chiefly oak in the summer, more pits being sunk in the summer than in the winter, and the keepers having the bark; more beech is allowed in the winter than oak; But oak timber is necessary, and is always allowed for sinking the pits, and for making what the miners call the gateway or gangway from the body of coal to the pit, and also for the gutters in the levels for draining off the water: but beech, birch, orle [alder], holly, or any other kind of wood, would serve for the purpose of getting coal, and supporting the earth after the coal is taken away, but none is ever delivered to them but oak and beech. He believes that much of the timber delivered to the miners for their works is misapplied. He has frequently found oak timber in the possession of the colliers, converted into staves and spokes for coopers and wheelwrights: And it is extremely difficult to prevent such misapplications: for if the colliers are detected in doing it, the Justices will not fine them, or take cognizance of it as an offence, unless the officer will swear that the timber is the King's property, which it is very difficult to ascertain, after it has been cut up and converted by the colliers. The only method of punishing them for such misapplication, at present, is by refusing to deliver any more timber to them, which has frequently been done after such detection. If timber were to be refused entirely, he believes the colliers would take it by force.'

On pages 34 and 35 of their 1788 Report, the Commissioners state:

'The next source of waste and abuse that we shall take notice of, is that of the delivery of timber to the miners and colliers, for the use of their mines and coal works; and this is the more necessary to be attended to, because they pretend to claim a prescriptive right, not only to work the mines and coal pits, when opened, but to be supplied with timber for their works. Instead of using arguments against this claim, or stating our opinion on a question which may come before a court of law, we have judged it proper to bring into view such extracts from the grants and other documents which we have met with in the course of our enquiry, as may enable the legislature to form some judgment of this claim, and of the propriety of making such an arrangement with the colliers and miners as we shall venture to suggest; but in this part of our Report we mean only to point out the advantages which the different officers of the Forest derive from this waste of timber, and to explain the division made between them and the colliers and miners of the trees cut for this purpose. The colliers and miners themselves admit that the consent of the officer of the Crown, called the gaveller, is necessary, before they can break the King's soil, in his demesne lands, or begin to dig for ore or coal, where they are the property of the Crown. When, therefore, a collier or miner proposes to open a new work in the Forest, he applies to the gaveller for his permission; for which, as we before have observed, he pays a fee of 5s. and he enters, at the same time, into an agreement with the gaveller, to pay a certain sum annually, in proportion to the number of men he is to employ in such works, as a composition for the share of the coal or ore due to the Crown, which was formerly taken in kind. Having paid the gaveller his fee, made an agreement for the annual composition, and obtained his permission to begin the work, he applies to the keeper of the Walk, and represents to him the occasion he has for timber for the work he proposes to carry on; which the keeper certifies to the clerk of the Swanimote Court; and upon receiving that certificate, with a fee of one shilling, the clerk gives a Warrant to the collier for delivering the timber required, but without specifying any quantity or number of trees; This Warrant the collier carries back to the keeper, who, with the deputy surveyor, or his agent, mark such trees as they think proper for the purpose. – No verderer or Justice of the Peace ever attends on such occasions, and even the appearance of their viewing the trees is not thought to be necessary. The keeper receives a fee of 1s. on every Warrant; and the trees being then cut down are divided in the following manner:– the miner has the body of the trees; the deputy surveyor one half of the cordwood, and 4d. or 6d. for every tree felled: the keeper gets the other half of the cordwood, together with the bark; and if the collier be detected in misapplying the timber, the keeper seizes it for his own benefit. In sinking a pit oak timber is deemed necessary; for other uses within the pits it is admitted that other wood may answer; but as the bark is now one of the perquisites of the keeper, and as the bark of no tree, except the oak, is of any value for sale, it is not surprising that though formerly only a few beech or orle trees were given to the colliers and miners, they now get chiefly oak, especially in the spring and summer; and as the deputy surveyor and keepers receive so great a share of the value of the tree, it cannot be matter of wonder that the colliers are most liberally supplied. It appears from the evidence of several of those who have been examined, that at least 1000 loads of oak timber have been, one year with another, delivered to the colliers; and as the country improves, and the demand for coal increases, unless the system of management be altered in this particular, and a stop put to this profuse disposition of the timber, at present left to the direction of those who derive a profit from it in proportion to the waste, the property of the coal and ore, instead of producing a revenue, as it formerly did, and ought now to do, will in a very few years occasion the consumption of all the remaining timber, and complete the destruction of the Forest.'

The Commissioners of 1788 referred to the many encroachments and other abuses 'in consequence of the general relaxation in the management of the Forest, which has prevailed during the greater part of the present century', and added[1]:

'It is obvious that the different fees, perquisites, and emoluments which we have enumerated, are so many premiums for the encouragement of waste in the felling, measurement, and sale of the timber, of extravagance in the expenditure of the produce, and of the profusion in the

1 Pp. 38-9.

delivery of timber to the miners, while they tend to the destruction of the inclosures, and the prevention of the growth of wood in succession; and the neglect of the officers adds force, on the ground of prescription, to the claims of those who work the mines, or have made encroachments; nor can it be matter of wonder if all these circumstances have had their full effect in the general devastation of the Forest. ... The great want of information, from official books, papers, and documents, during the present century has made it impossible to ascertain at what time, or under what administration, the present abuses were first introduced; but it is not to be supposed that a system of management so absurd and ruinous was the contrivance of any administration. Errors and abuses have, without observation, crept gradually into practice; and all that can be justly imputed to Government is the having so long suffered them to prevail, without that kind of check or inquiry which could lead to an effectual remedy; neither must it be understood that such destructive practices have been introduced by those who now hold, or have lately held, offices in this Forest: many of them we know to be of an older date, and the late or present officers have, perhaps, only continued to take those advantages which were received by their predecessors. Under such circumstances, where so many were doing the same thing, and where Government interposed no check, it was not to be expected that the temptation would be resisted, or that the resident officers of the Forest would point out the true causes of the devastation, from which their advantages arose.'

The Commissioners pointed out that Dean Forest was not alone in the question of neglect and abuses, stating[1]:

'In almost every forest belonging to the Crown, as well as in this, we have found circumstances to shew the necessity there was for such an Enquiry as that in which we have been employed; and have seen many strong proofs that the public has suffered by its having been so long delayed.'

To overcome the disgraceful state of affairs, the Commissioners made detailed recommendations, among which were the following[2]:

'Power should be given to the same Commissioners to enquire into the claims of the miners and colliers, and to make a final arrangement and settlement with them; and we apprehend it will not be found to be very difficult: For supposing that they could succeed in establishing their right to dig for ore and coal, and to be supplied with such wood or timber as may really be necessary for their works, yet even on that supposition it appears from the Collection of Laws of the Free Miners, or Constitutions of their Mine Law Court, as well as by the information of the gaveller, and late deputy gaveller, that the Crown is entitled to, and it is said did formerly take, so considerable a share of the ore or coal dug up, as would pay well for any quantity of wood or timber that they could possibly have occasion for in carrying on their works.

We will not presume to point out the particulars of the arrangement that should be made with the miners and colliers; but in our humble opinion all the fees paid to the steward of the

1 P. 39.
2 Pp. 41-5.

Swanimote Court, and keepers, should be abolished, and such moderate compositions only should be paid by the colliers and miners as the Commissioners shall think fit to establish, for the purpose of preserving the right of the Crown to the mines; and the colliers and miners should not, afterwards, be allowed to have wood or timber from the Forest, but by fair purchase; and although, from being obliged to pay for the wood and timber which they are at present supplied with gratuitiously, it may become necessary for them to make some small advance in the price of coal, yet this will prove no real loss to the colliers, nor will they be in any danger of losing the market in consequence of it.

From the accounts of the quantity of coal raised in the Forest, given by the gaveller; from the accounts of the steward of the Swanimote Court, deputy surveyor, and others, of the quantity of timber and wood delivered to the colliers; and from the information which we have received respecting the price of coal dug in the Forest, and of coal brought into that country from other parts, we have all the circumstances before us which are necessary to enable us to form an opinion on this subject. The quantity of coal raised in the Forest, according to the weekly average stated by the gaveller, is about 94,432 tons in the year; the average price of the different kinds is 3s. 3d. per ton at the pit: from the price of imported coal, which is 14s. per ton at Newnham, in the neighbourhood of the Forest, and from all the information we have been able to procure, it appears certain that no coal, imported from other parts, can be supplied in that neighbourhood as near so low a rate as from the Forest. The timber delivered to the colliers has been from 1,000 to 1,500 tons annually, of which much has been misapplied by them; and the value of the kinds which they have been supplied with is about 25s. per ton: supposing, therefore, this whole quantity to be really necessary for their use, it would cost them only £1,875; but as the fees they now pay to the steward and keepers are proposed to be abolished, a deduction must be made on that account from the value of the timber to be purchased by the colliers, which would probably reduce the expense to less than £1,500 and that sum would be amply compensated by an addition of not more than 4d. per ton on the quantity annually sold from the Forest, which would raise £1,573; so that the colliers could suffer no detriment by purchasing the timber necessary for their works, nor incur any danger of losing the market; and as the country round the Forest would even then, be furnished with coal at a very cheap rate, and free from any tax, it cannot surely be thought reasonable that Government should furnish timber to the colliers from the Forest for nothing, solely to enable them to supply that part of the country with coal on still lower terms. …

The arrangement and settlement with the colliers and miners would also be of great benefit to the public, and probably in the end of no disadvantage to the miners and colliers themselves: At present they are supplied with timber by means of fraudulent and collusive practices, in conjunction with the resident Forest officers; they are liable to punishment on detection, and at all times to demands of fees or gratuities; they probably make but a small profit of the wood and timber improperly allotted to them, and keep but for a short time the little they so acquire. Upon a regular settlement with them, they would be altogether independent of the Forest Officers; they would buy such wood and timber only as their works should really require; and as that would be chiefly what is dotard or decayed, and of kinds unfit for shipbuilding, they would be supplied with it on moderate terms; and there being no other place from which the neighbouring country can be supplied with coal at so cheap a rate as from the Forest, the demand for the Forest coal would continue, and the colliers would obtain from the consumer a fair price, to make up for the additional expense occasioned by the purchase of wood and timber for their works.

The benefit to the public is obvious:– it would put an end to the greatest source of waste and destruction of useful timber, and of temptations to corruption in the Officers, that exists in the Forest; it would create a demand for such trees as are dotard or decayed, and of kinds unfit for ship-building, so as to derive from them some revenue; and at the same time thin the woods, and gradually give room to the best trees to grow and become timber.

Those who have built cottages, and inclosed small pieces of land (which are distinguished in the Plan of the Forest by the red colour) are the next about whom it is necessary to form some determination. Different examples have been given in this Report of the expulsion of similar intruders from the Forest:– Once in the time of the Protector Cromwell, when 400 cottages were pulled down, and the inclosures destroyed; again, after passing the Act 20th Charles II [1668] when about thirty, the remains of a greater number, were in the same manner demolished, and the Forest cleared; and we have shewn, on the authority of Sir Robert Atkins, whose book was published in 1712, that when he wrote there were no houses in the Forest, except the six lodges of the keepers.

In general, those cottagers are represented to us as living on the spoil of the Forest; and the conservator and all the keepers declare, that the encroachments have been made in defiance of all the opposition they could give, and have been supported and renewed, in spite of all their endeavours to destroy them. There are, indeed, so many inducements to build there, and the intrusions have of late increased so rapidly, that for the preservation of the Forest some vigorous measures must be speedily taken.

The Forest being extra-parochial, the inhabitants are free from all kinds of rates or taxes; and they have the advantage of unlimited pasture for horses, cows, or sheep, and of acorns and beech mast for their swine, besides the access to the wood and timber; for all which they pay nothing, unless perhaps some gratuities to the keepers, to prevent them from disturbing their possession.

The same Commissioners should have powers and instructions similar to those which were given to the Marquis of Worcester and others, after the passing of the Act of the 20th Charles II [1668], to remove the cottagers, and reclaim the encroachments: But discretionary powers should at the same time be given to them, to shew indulgence to any of those intruders who have been born in the Forest, and had long uninterrupted possession, and whose cottages are not so situated as to interrupt the plan of inclosures; or to make some allowance to such of them as have been long established, under the like circumstances, within the parts necessary to be inclosed.

We would humbly propose that powers should also be given to the same Commissioners, to determine what roads are necessary to be made and kept in repair at the expense of the Forest, and what roads are to be considered as public roads, necessary for the country, to be afterwards made and kept in repair by turnpikes or otherwise, but not at the sole expense of the Forest. If any timber shall be carried through the gates on the public roads, toll must be paid for it; and checks might be easily formed, by means of such turnpikes, which would prove a great security against the stealing of timber; and at the same time put an end to a great and fruitful source of unnecessary expense, and shameful imposition.

As the execution of all that has been proposed will be attended with considerable expense, the following is humbly suggested as the best mode that occurs to us for providing an adequate fund to defray it.

There are several detached pieces of land belonging to the Forest, containing about 440 acres: the Commissioners should be impowered to sell all or any of those detached parts, under such restrictions as the legislature may judge it proper to appoint, or to exchange or allot any of them, as an equivalent for any of the rights admitted and enjoyed in the Forest, by the parishes having Right of Common, or by the Officers of Inheritance, and in case further sums should be necessary for defraying the expense that may be incurred in the execution of what is proposed, the same Commissioners should be empowered to sell, or direct the sale, of such dotard and decayed trees, or trees not fit or likely to become fit for naval use, as they shall think proper to be felled, in order to supply the deficiency.

No prejudice to the public interest will attend either of these measures. The detached pieces of land last mentioned are of so small extent, that the inclosure and protection of them would be very expensive if kept by the Crown; and the clearing the Forest of dotard and decayed trees at the time of inclosing, would not only be of use in giving room for the young spring of wood to grow, but would prevent for some time the damage to the inclosures and young wood, by frequent cuttings.'

After this important Report of 1788 it is surprising to find that no legislation of a serious character ensued, except that in 1795 an Act (36 Geo. III, c. 131) was passed for making new roads, and improving existing roads, through the Forest, which was part of the Commission's recommendations. Lord Nelson himself tried to draw attention to the unsatisfactory state of affairs. In a Memorandum[1] written about 1803 he explained the poor state of the Forest, and gave amongst the reasons that of official inattention. He went so far as to suggest a suitable plan. Amongst his comments he mentions – 'Vast droves of hogs are allowed to go into the woods in the autumn, and if any fortunate acorn escapes their search, and takes root, then flocks of sheep are allowed to go into the Forest, and they bite off the tender shoot'. Again – 'There is also another cause of failure of timber; a set of people called Forest Free Miners, who consider themselves as having a right to dig for coal in any part they please'.

About this time, improvements in communication were planned and a system of tramroads was soon in operation. These were superseded to a large extent in later years by the modern railways. In 1808, it became necessary to pass the **Dean Forest (Timber) Act** (48 Geo. III, c. 72) to confirm, explain and amend the Act of 1668.[2] Its chief object was to increase and preserve timber, and it confirmed the power to enclose 11,000 acres. In 1810, an important departure was made by the Act George II, c. 65, in the mode of government and management of the Crown lands and revenues. This was the appointment of Commissioners of Woods, Forest and Land Revenues of the Crown, in lieu of the surveyor-general of Woods and Forests and the surveyor-general of Land Revenues, which offices had been established in the reign of Charles I. Henry Somerset, Duke of Beaufort, held the grant of the Forest in 1804 and held office until succeeded by the Commissioners of Woods in 1838.

In 1812 a case[3] was decided at the Gloucester Lent Assizes which has an interesting bearing on this present work; the following is taken from Peake's record:

1 30th Rpt. of Coms. of Woods (1852), App. XVI, Pp. 223-4.

2 A copy of the 1808 Act is in Hart, *Royal Forest* (1966) pp. 315-17.

3 *Doe dem Thomson* and Others *v*. Pearce (Peake's *Nisi Prius* Cases, vol. ii, 1795-1812, pp. 242-4).

'In this case the lessors of the Plaintiff claimed as devisees in remainder named in the will of William Thomson; the Defendant claimed as a purchaser, under Sarah, the widow and executrix of William Thomson; so that the only question in the cause was, whether the property in question was freehold, subject to the limitations of the will, or whether it went to the executrix as a chattel interest.

The property in dispute consisted of a share of a coal mine in the Forest of Dean, within the Hundred of St. Briavels; and it appeared that (the land within the Forest belonging to the Crown) it had from time immemorial been the custom for persons of a certain description, called free-miners (*viz.* those who, being born within the hundred, had worked as miners for a year and a day), to apply to the gaveller of the hundred, or his deputy, to allot them a particular spot of land for a coal-pit; that the work was generally undertaken by a number of persons as partners, and when the spot was agreed upon, the servant of the gaveller cut a turf, and having cut a stick, so many notches were cut in it as there were to be partners in the intended work, and also one for the King and one for the gaveller; that the stick was fastened down with pegs on the spot where the turf had been pared away, and the turf laid down again; after which the spot was considered appropriated, and no other person took possession of it. The present deputy-gaveller said, that during his time there had always been paid a small annual rent until they began to find coal, as a compensation for the timber allowed out of the Forest for the work, and as soon as coal was procured a rate was set, which was also an annual money payment for the King's share of the coal; that he had never known any other than a money payment, but he had heard from his predecessor, and other old people now dead, that in former times, when they could not agree, a man used to be put in to work on the part of the King, and take his share of the coal gotten from the pit; that sometimes the work would be abandoned, and if that happened for a year and a day the King took possession and the payment ceased. It was also proved that the general reputation of the hundred was that this was freehold property, and that it went to the eldest son on the death of the first adventurer, and many instances were adduced of its having so descended, but some instances were also shown of the widow having taken possession and sold to others, even where there were children. One old witness stated that he remembered courts being formerly holden within the hundred, at which twelve free-miners attended as a jury, and the steward presided; but no very distinct account was given of the constitution of the court, no records appeared to be in existence, nor did it appear that any written admissions or grants of the right in question had ever been made. It was also proved that till of late years the only mode of transfer known was delivery of the possession of the windlass, but that a practice had since prevailed of conveying by feoffment, lease and release, passing fines, &c.

On this evidence the Counsel for the lessor of the Plaintiff contended that this was freehold; but the Defendant's Counsel, on the contrary, submitted that if there was any right at all it was a mere chattel; but that in fact it was nothing more than a licence, and conveyed no right whatever.

Wood, B. adjudged "I think that this is clearly freehold; it is the same kind of right that exists among the miners in the Peak in Derbyshire, which has been always so considered; and therefore it must be liable to the same limitations as any other freehold property."'

On 15 May 1817, the adjacent Highmeadow Estate was purchased by the Government from Viscount Gage. The whole property contained 4,257 acres and, including all the timber and underwood, with certain forges, mills, limekilns, iron and tin works, was valued by the referees at £155,863 3s. 2d., the timber being priced at £61,264 4s. The agreement was confirmed by the Act of 57 Geo. II, c. 97. The corn-mill, two forge-houses with appendages, the tolls of the Coleford Market-house, and about 423 acres of land, were later sold for the most part at higher prices than were given for them. This estate, originally Crown property, had been at some remote period detached from the Forest, as appears by the perambulation of 28 Edward I. It constituted part of one of the ten bailiwicks of the Forest as early as 10 Edward I (1282) when it was held by John Walding, called John de Staunton. After passing through the families of Baynham, Brain, Winter, and Hall, it became, by marriage, the property of Sir Thomas Gage. H. C. Hill, when reporting[1] on the area in 1897, stated that at the time of the purchase by the Government it comprised 2,229 acres of wood and 696 of other lands, which were retained and planted up, making a total of 2,025 acres. The Crown is absolute proprietor, and the property is free from common rights and free miners'[2] rights.

The Act of 1810, with some later Acts relating to the Commissioners, was repealed and consolidated by the Act 10 Geo. IV, c. 50 (1829) which repealed quite a number of Acts dealing with the Crown estates and allocated the revenues to the consolidated fund. The most important clause as regards Dean Forest was No. 34, which empowered the Commissioners to sell absolutely parcels of land, and to resume the many encroachments made, and, where they thought proper, to give compensation to those disturbed, and to allow others to remain where it would not be likely to interfere with the growing timber. The Act also made it unlawful for anyone to appropriate gravel, sand, ashes, etc.; the 'right' to do this had long been exercised by the inhabitants without any legal grounds.

The next Act of relevant interest was the **Dean Forest (Gale Rents) Act**, 1819[3], 'for the better collection and recovery of the Gale Rents in the Forest of Dean' which provided that 'the person who now does and who shall be appointed to and hold the office of gaveller or Keeper of the Gawle, called the Gawle Above the Wood, within the Forest of Dean' may distrain for gale rents or gawle rents due to the Crown, and may institute proceedings to recover arrears, etc.[4]

About this time certain difficulties were arising in connection with the working of the Dean mines. This is clear from the following Memorial presented to the two joint deputy gavellers, Thomas Tovey and Edward Machen (Plate VIII), on 27 April 1825[5]:

> 'We the undersigned Free Miners, proprietors and occupiers of Collieries in His Majesty's Forest of Dean, present the following Memorial to Thomas Tovey Esq. and Edward Machen, Esq., gavellers of the said Forest, upon the subject of that part of the Custom which relates to the Galing of Engine Pits in relation to previously existing Levels.
>
> In the first place your Memorialists consider that Mines worked under a custom, should be regulated more by a spirit of equitable decision, than by a rigid adherence to usages, established at a time when mining in this district was in its infancy; customs at the time

1 Working Plan Report for the High Meadow Woods (1897), p. 7.

2 See Grindell's Petition (p. 518) where he attempted to dispute this.

3 The 1819 Act was the result of a Return to the House of Commons in 1818, see Appendix 8, and comments added thereto.

4 The Dean Forest (Mines) Act, 1871, S. 36 extended this to the recovery of any galeage, dead or certain rent, royalty or tonnage accruing to the Crown.

5 The original Memorial was once at Whitemead Park.

competent to the protection of the capital and property as it then existed, but quite inadequate to protect the large investments of the present times.

That your Memorialists in referring to the decisions of the Mine Law Courts, which formerly regulated the working of the mines, uniformly perceive this equitable spirit in operation during the succession of Courts from and after the period of the Restoration [1660] till the time when these Courts were, from some cause unknown to your Memorialists, discontinued [1777] to be held, to the great prejudice of the interests of your Memorialists.

In the year 1676 the Mine Law Court passed its first Resolution as to the protection of Levels, and declared it to be the custom "that after a Surf (Level) made, no miner should work within 100 yards of such Surf to the prejudice of undertakers, without their consent, and being contributory to making the said Surf a forfeiture of 100 dozen of good fire coal".

This regulation appears to have been sufficient for the working of the earliest Levels for the space of 23 years. As these became exhausted and as new and more expensive ones were brought in, the Mine Law Court acting with that spirit of equity, so essential to a beneficial enjoyment of mines worked under a custom, in the year 1697 passed another Resolution for the protection of Levels in the following words: "That the Order of 8 September, 16 Charles II (1676) as to collieries working within 100 yards of other works be confirmed, and that the distance be settled at 300 yards under the penalty of former Order" – so that in the short space of 23 years our ancestors thought it just and wise to enlarge the boundaries and consequently the protection afforded by a Level, to three times the extent of the original custom.

At a more advanced period, we see the same liberal spirit in full operation, retaining the rule of 1697, as applicable to certain situations Above the Wood, and framing a new law for the protection of Levels Beneath the Wood.

On 12th November 1728 the Mine Law Court in its 14th Resolution resolved "That the distance of 300 yards mentioned in Order of 17 January 1697 be augmented to 500 yards in all levels Beneath the Wood on penalty mentioned in said Order but that all works then in being should not be hindered or prejudiced".

In the absence of more minute information your Memorialists are obliged to infer that local difficulties existed Beneath the Wood such as longer levels, driven through stone, or levels driven under the coal and against the measures requiring larger sums of money and consequently a proportionate share of protection than was deemed necessary to be extended to those levels or undertakings carried on Above the Wood. In these different regulations your Memorialists see a constant regard on the part of the Mine Law Court to the interests of existing levels and an equitable distinction in favour of situations and circumstances where a greater investment of capital was necessary to complete an undertaking.

Your Memorialists more particularly request your attention to that part of the present resolution which protects all works then in being from the operation of the new law, plainly indicating that the security of the existing levels was at all times a principal consideration with the miners, who framed these various regulations, and that the custom was altered from time to time to extend a protection adequate to the expanse of the undertakings of the day.

This fact is again most strikingly illustrated and confirmed by the seventeenth, and, as your Memorialists believe, the last perfect resolution of the Mine Law Court and which contains the first and, in consequence of the discontinuance of these Courts, the only order for the protection of levels against Water Pits, Water Wheels and Engines.

In this last resolution passed in 1755, it was made law as follows: "That no free miner or miners sink any Water Pit Above or Beneath the Wood within the distance of 1,000 yards of any free miner's level, to the prejudice of his level, on penalty of £5". Now whether the expression "any free miner's level" relates to the tail or commencement of the level, or to the head or farthest progress the level has made in the coal or mine is the subject now at issue.

Your Memorialists contend that the head of the work is here intended to be meant, which opinion is corroborated by another law generally agreed upon, that no miner has a right to pump or throw water within 1,000 yards of the head of another man's level. That situations probably may occur wherein it would be necessary to drive a level 1,000 yards in the stone before it reached the coal and where the gale of a Water Pit or Engine would not leave such level one yard of coal. And above all upon the great probability that those who framed this law, being proprietors of levels at the time, would make that protection as ample against Water Pits as possible.

Your Memorialists further contend that it is only of late years, in consequence of the great influx of capital arising from the establishment of the Rail Roads, that a contrary opinion has been held by those who wished to open Engines to the injury of levels. Whatever opinions however may have been held upon this subject as to the strict definition of the phrase "any free miner's level" your Memorialists submit ought not to be altogether the subject matter for your consideration, but more especially what is just and equitable to existing levels, in the present day, some of which, at the expense of several thousand pounds, have been carried to a distance of 700 and 800 yards through solid rock.

The propriety and necessity of a liberal protection becomes the more reasonable, particularly against Engines, when we consider that from the year 1676 to the year 1755, a period of 80 years, the Mine Law Court deemed it expedient to enlarge the protection due to levels from 100 to 1,000 yards, whereas from the year 1755 to the present time, a period of 70 years, not only no increased protection has been awarded to levels, but, in the opinion of many, amongst whom are your Memorialists, the Water Pit or Engine has, as far as it respects Levels, in some instances encroached upon the liberties of the same.

Your Memorialists however beg to observe that they have been informed and believe a series of resolutions were signed by 47 free miners in or about the year 1775 extending the protection to levels against Engines or Water Pits, and that one of such resolutions was in the following words: "That no person shall sink any Water Pit within 1,500 yards of any person's level in work under the penalty of £5", since which other attempts have been made with liberal spirit of extension. And it appears that at a meeting held at the Speech House on 8 December 1807, a series of resolutions were passed and signed by 48 free miners, whereby the 1,500 yards as above is expressly recognised.

Your Memorialists therefore hope that by drawing your attention to this subject and to the changes that have from time to time taken place in the custom, proceeding regularly upon an acknowledged principle of protection, commensurate to the magnitude of the existing works, and more particularly in consequence of the great expense of the present levels, compared with those of 1755, when the protection of 1,000 yards was first granted, you will feel the justice and necessity of concurring with us in the opinions now expressed, and in your practice as gavellers unite with us in having it declared to be custom that no Water Pit or Water Wheel or Engine Pit shall be galed or sunk or worked or coal or iron ore obtained or gotten from the same or either of them within at least 1,000 yards of the head of another free miner's level or work.'

The 1825 Memorial, signed by sixty-one free miners and by fourteen other proprietors of mines, contains some errors as to date but this does not invalidate its arguments. Nevertheless no action appears to have been taken by the deputy gavellers. However, changes were imminent, as is discussed in Chapter VII.

APPENDICES TO PART ONE : PRE-1831

Appendix 1

EMENDATIONS TO THE FIRST EDITION, 1953

Page number in First Edition	
ix	For '1610' read '1612'.
xi	PRO documents subsequently transferred from London to Kew.
xix	Grazing is a privilege not a right (see Byelaws).
4	As to grant of free timber for mining purposes: Glos.R.O. Bond MSS D2026 (3), pp. 17, 18, of 1565, is the earliest confirmation for both iron ore and coal: 'And the jurors say that the myners of the said Forest as well for the ore [iron ore] myne as for the cole [coal] myne to be there found and gotten from the time whereof the memory of man is not to the contrary have always and ought to have from time to time by the old ancient use and custom of the same Forest sufficient timber to be taken in the said Forest for the same and safe building of their myne pittes under the early homage of a great (?) deponer. As well for the safety of the persons of the said myners as to the C… and conditions to land of the Queen's [Elizabeth] myne.'
10	As to disputes between miner and miner. For numerous cases see Glos.R.O. D9096, F26/1, 1706-1777 (the last Mine Law Court). See Appendix 6.
12, 13, 14, 15	Here, 'forester' means 'forester-of-fee' of a bailiwick.
18	For '1610' read '1612'.
18	For 'Book of Dennis' read 'Book against Dennis'. See Appendix 5.
19	For 'Whitemead Park' read Glos.R.O. D9096, F16/18, 19.
19, 23, 24	No charter has been found or authenticated.
30	Add 'Noxon' and 'Puzzle Wood'.
33	Add 'Puzzle Wood'.
34 n.4	Add 'see also Cranfield MSS U269/l.E232, Maidstone, 1612'.
35	Add 'Inquisition, 1327-1377' and Glos.R.O. D9096, F16/18, 19.
35	For 'Book of Dennis' read 'Book against Dennis'. See Appendix 5.
35	For 'Coleford' read Glos.R.O. D9096, F16/18.
36	For 'Book of Dennis' read 'Book against Dennis'. See Appendix 5.
36	Add: see also British Library 445. a, 25(2) and Glos.R.O. D5947 (1800).
37	For 'Whitemead Park' read Glos.R.O. D9096, 16/18, 19.
38, 39, 42	For 'cattle' read 'chatel'.
42	As to 'Sufficient of Tymber' see PRO F20/1(17).
43	For 'cattle' read 'chatel'.
45	For 'Whitemead Park' read Glos.R.O. D9096, F16/18, 19.
46	For '1610' read '1612'.

46, 47, 48 Many of the lost documents have since been discovered, including Glos.R.O. D9096, F26/1: 1706-1777, F16/1-17, 18, 19.

49-61 For derivation of 'gaveller' from a person entitled to the revenue to an officer of that title, see PRO F20/1 (17), p. 10, 1662; and Appendix E.

49-61 Here note the definitions of 'Above the wood' and 'Beneath the wood'. And see Glossary. See also Glos.R.O. D6177 (1, 2); PRO F20/1 (17); C66/509, m 25.

54 For 'mines' read 'iron ore'.

54 n.6 For 'equerries' read 'esquires'.

62 Add to 'Act', 1838.

63 Add to '1924', Transfer of Woods, Order.

64 After 'minerals' add: 'other than stone'.

65 For 'sixteenth' read 'fifteenth'. The earliest record of a Mine Law Court is in 1469-1470, Glos.R.O. D6177/1 (12 miners), /2 (48 miners). See Appendix 3.

67 To 'Morgan' add 'John'.

69 To 'Phelpotte' add 'Thomas of Goodrich'.

72 As to disputes between miner and miner. For numerous cases see Glos.R.O. D9096, F26/1 (1706-1777). See Appendix 6.

73 As to St. Briavels Castle, a Mine Law Court was held there on 1 Sept. 1719 (Glos.R.O. D9096, F26/1).

Plate III For 'Whitemead Park' now read 'Glos.R.O.'.

75, 76 As to 'a stick of holly' see also PRO F20(1)17, p. 13.

77 The earliest record of a Mine Law Court is in 1469-1470 (Glos.R.O. D6177/1). See Appendix 3.

77 The missing word is probably 'prooffe'.

78 As to 'VIII', see Hart, *New History*, pp. 146, 147.

79 For 'about' read 'above'.

89 For numerous additional 'cases' see Glos.R.O. D9096, F26/1 (1706-1777). See Appendix 6.

90, 91, 93, 94, 95 Adams was a deputy gaveller.

96 Two copies of (VI) are in PRO F20/1.

96 For 'infrossed' read 'ingrossed'.

98 For 'pets' read 'pits'.

98 For 'Proberty' read 'Probert'.

99 Arundel was a deputy gaveller.

102 Here should be noted a newly found Order and Ordinance of 1676-1677 held at Clearwell (PRO F20/1/21).

103 For 'Gunspill' read 'Conpill'.

120 See Berkeley Castle Muniments re case against George Gardner.

124 n.2 Add: See Plate IV.

125 For 'Radnock' read 'Hadnock'.

126 At top insert newly found Mine Law Court Minutes of 7 February 1730 (Gaveller's Office, Coleford). See Appendix 7. The Miners' 'Chest at The Speech House' has never been found.

132 For 'Read Brooke' read 'Redbrook'.

135 For 'Nas' read 'Nass'.

137 As to 26 August 1777, see Glos.R.O. D9096, F26/1. See Appendix 6.

140 As to Majors suff, see Hart, *New History*, p. 235.
145 n.2 Now Glos.R.O. D9096, F16/1-19 and F26/1.
148 As to the 17 documents, see Glos.R.O. D9096, F16/1-19 and F26/1.
158 For '1675-6' read '1275-6'.
158, 159 For additional details of 'holders of the Forest of Dean etc.' see Inquisition 15 Edward III, 1341, No. 75 and Glos. *I.P.M's* V. p. 287-289.
163 For other 'proceedings' and 'orders' see emendations and additions above.
166 An additional reference is PRO F20/1(17).
184 To 'this Justice Seat' add '1634'.
184, 186, 188, 189, 194 As to the Terringham family see Appendix 4.
185 To '25 December' add 1635.
197 As to the Civil War, in 1643 '40 miners from the Forest of Dean were impressed to repair the artillery train in Gloucester (under siege)', Glos.R.O. D115.
198 For 'Brame' read 'Brain'.
199 As to ochre, see Hart, *New History*.
200 As to '22 November 1635 Act' see Glos.R.O. D2026 X.20.
201 As to John Wade, see Hart, *New History*.
201 A Justice Seat was held at Mitcheldean in 1656, see Hart, *New History*.
203, 204 As to John Wade, see Hart, *New History*. (1995)
204 n.6 }
206 n.2 } A copy is in PRO 20/1(17) 9, 10, 11.
206 For 'Flaxand' read 'Flaxley'.
209 Delete 'was'.
211 For 'with' read 'within'.
212 To '3 July' add '1667'.
215 To 'new Act' add '1668'.
218-225 The depositions were made in 1675.
226 n.3 The transcripts are in Glos.R.O. D3921, The Hart Collection.
251 The Act of 1819 followed a Report in 1818 to the House of Commons, See Appendix 8.
261 For 'compensation' read 'composition'.
264 The names and residences of each free miner in 1835 are recorded.
267 The dates of the two lawsuits are 1829 and 1830.
268 Thomas Tovey was a deputy gaveller.
277 Thomas Phillips was a member of The Copper Company.
308 For a discussion on 'timber for mines' see PRO F20/1(17).
313 For 'riun' read 'ruin'.
356 As to early cases of 'subsidence', see Glos.R.O. D9096, F26/5, 6, 8, 9, 11.
424 For 'Howard' read 'Horace'.
434 A supplement to James G. Wood's *The Laws of The Dean Forest and Hundred of St. Briavels* (1878) is Hart, *Laws of Dean* (1952).
435 n.1 Copy in Glos.R.O. D9096, F26/19, 20, 21, 23, 24.
480 On 17 March 1903 W. Forster Brown, deputy gaveller made to the Commissioners of Woods a Report of Proposals re the Deep Mines. PRO F26/26.
481 n.1 For '116' read '156'. A copy of the Dean Forest (Mines) Act is in Hart, *Laws of Dean*, (1952).
483 For '66' read '156'.

486 See Plate VII.

487 In 1930 there was a Resolution from Free Miners to the Government to reopen iron mining (Hart, *Industrial History*, pp. 338-40). J. Riley Brown was chairman, and William Pace secretary.

488 The Coal Act 1938 nationalised the coal but not the mining companies nor the free miners' 'holdings'/rights.

488 n.1 The valuation was under S12(3) of the Coal Industry Nationalisation Act 1946.

490 The Coal Industry Nationalisation Act 1946, S63(2), nationalised the mining companies but not the free miners' 'holdings'/rights.

492 See Plate VII.

493 From 1838 to 31 December 1991, 4,302 free miners were registered, but about 75% were then deceased. Total applications were 127,643, many later cancelled.

504 As to Lydney Park Estate, see PRO F26/3.

514 'Wellington' was the old name of 'Newland'.

521,End Add 'i.e. the Hundred of St. Briavels'.

423 INDEX. As stated, this was a limited Index prepared under somewhat difficult conditions on board the R.M.S. *Queen Mary* between Southampton and New York, May 1953. The Index has since been prepared *in extenso* and a copy deposited in Glos.R.O. and in 'The Gaveller's Office', Coleford.

Appendix 2

EARLY 'CUSTODIANS OF THE GAWLE' (later termed GAVELLERS)

1. *Grant in 1464 of 'The Gaole' of the King's mines in the Forest of Dean* (PRO Patent Roll 4 Edw. IV pt. 2, m.25: C66/509 m.25)

The King to all whom the present writing shall come, Greeting. Know ye that by consideration of the good and faithful service which our humble and faithful undersaid man Robert Hyett has before now paid to us, and in future will pay, we have given and granted to him *the Gaole of our mines (Gaole minarum) within our Forest of Dean* in co. Glouc, which Gaole indeed a certain Thomas Wodeward lately had and occupied with the custody of our park of Whitemead in our said Forest, to have and to occupy the said Gaole with the custody of the said park for himself and for his sufficient deputy during the life of the said Robert with all fees, profits and conveniences belonging to the said Gaole and park, and from of old time due and customarily received from the issues, profits and reversions of our aforesaid Forest coming forth by the hand of the Receiver there for the time being whereby the express mention of the true annual value of the said Gaole fees, profits and conveniences stands here made at the least or by any statute, act, ordinance, provision or restriction thence to the contrary made, ordained or provided notwithstanding. In testimony whereof witnesseth the King himself at Westminster the fifth day of December [1464], by writ of Privy Seal and on the above date etc.

2. *Grant in 1536 of the custody of 'The Gawle above the Wood' within the Forest of Dean* (Memoranda roll, Exchequer, Lord Treasurer's Remembrancer: 28 Hen. VIII, PRO E368/310, Hilary Term 28 Hen. VIII, m.2d)

Grant to Henry Brayne of the custody of 'The Gawle above the Wood' within the Forest of Dean. Henry VIII, etc., to all to whom these present Letters shall come, Greeting. Know that whereas we by our Letters Patent dated 15 May 25 Hen. VIII [1533] of our especial grace, certain knowledge and mere motion, as well as in consideration of the true and faithful services done to us by our servant Richard Longe, gent., one of the esquires of our stables, have given and granted to him as well *the custody of the Gawle called 'the Gawle above the Wood' within our Forest of Dean,* then by the death of Philip Cachemay vacant and the office of a riding forester and the aleconner within Dean Forest then in our gift and disposition to have and to hold and occupy as well the said custody as the said office and each of them to the said Richard Longe and his assigns from the death of the said Philip during the life of Richard Longe, with all wages, fees, profits and emoluments as well as the said custody of the Gawle as of the said office and all thereunto appertaining and belonging in as ample manner and form as the said Philip or any other custodian of the said office before had and took for exercising the same, etc.

And without any account to be rendered to us or our heirs as by our Letters Patent more fully may appear. And whereas the said Richard Longe has returned the said Letters Patent into our Chancery to be cancelled with the intention that other Letters Patent more fully may appear. And whereas might be issued, we have granted the same to our servant Henry Brayne to hold the said Gawle above the Wood within our Forest, as well as the said office of riding forester and of aleconner within Dean Forest now being in our gift and disposition, to have, hold and occupy both the aforesaid custody and office and any of them as the said Henry Brayne and his assigns from the time of the cancellation of the said Letters Patent in the abovesaid form during the life of the said Henry Brayne, with all wages, fees and profits of the regard of the emoluments etc. appertaining to the said custody and office, taking and receiving the same at the usual terms, without rendering any account, etc. So that express mention, etc. In witness we have caused these Letters to be made Patent. Witness myself at Westminster 4 February 26 Henry VIII [1534-5]. By writ of Privy Seal and date aforesaid by authority of Parliament.

3. *Grant in 1537 of 'The Gawle below the Wood' in the Forest of Dean*
(Memoranda Roll, Exchequer, Lord Treasurer's Remembrancer 28-29 Henry VIII, PRO E368/311, Trinity Term, 29 Hen. VIII, m.5d)

Grant in 1537 to Ralph Johnson of 'The Gawle below the Wood' within the Forest of Dean, co. Glouc. Henry VIII, etc. to all to whom these present Letters shall come, Greeting. Whereas, etc. we by our Letters Patent which are dated at Westminster 5 November, 12 Hen. VIII [1520] of our especial grace, certain knowledge and mere motion, have given and granted to David Morgan the Gale below the Wood of our Forest of Dean, to have and to occupy and enjoy the same Gale to the same David, by himself or his sufficient deputy during his life with all wages and rights, dues, conveniences and other advantages to the same Gale in any manner accustomed or belonging in as ample manner and form as Robert Johns, Knt. had and took in and by the same and in like manner as before was used as in the same Letters is contained. And now the said David being in will to return to us our said Letters Patent to be cancelled in our Chancery with the intention that we may grant other Letters Patent to our servant Ralph Johnson, we considering the premises and the good and acceptable service which the said Ralph Johnson has before this time given us, of our especial grace, certain knowledge and mere motion have given and granted and by these presents give and grant to the said Ralph Johnson *the Gale below the Wood of our Forest* to have and occupy and enjoy the same Gale to the same Ralph Johnson, by himself or his sufficient deputy for life with all wages, rights, dues, conveniences and other advantages to the same Gale in any way accustomed or belonging and in as ample wise and form as the aforesaid Robert Johns or any other person or persons heretofore was used to do. So that express mention of certain premises or any statute, act, ordinance, provision or restriction thereof to the contrary had, made or ordained or any other thing, cause or matter whatsoever in anything notwithstanding. In witness whereof these our Letters we have caused to be made Patent. Witness myself at Westminster 2 February 20 Henry VIII [1528-9].

Appendix 3

ESTREAT ROLL: FOREST OF DEAN 1469-1470: Glos.R.O. D6177/1, 2

This document of 1469-70 (the 9th and 10th years of Edward IV) is the earliest record of the Mine Law Court.

(*1*) *Estreat roll of Forest of Dean Miner's Court, 1469, 1470: Glos.R.O. D6177/1*

Hyll Pytt

Estreats of the Court of 12 miners held there on Tuesday, 5 December, 9 Edward IV (1469):
2s. from John Haukyns for licence to imparl with Robert Fortey; 2s. from Thomas Dey for abandoning his suit against Joan Sheyare; 2s. from John Mylle for non-appearance to reply to John Raulyns; 2s. from Richard Portyngale for non-appearance to reply to John Raulyns. Total: 8 shillings.

Hyll Pytt, Above the Wood

Estreats of the Court of 12 miners held there on Tuesday next after the Purification of the Virgin Mary 9 Edward IV (7 February, 1470):
2s. from Thomas Reynolds of Lydney for non-appearance to reply to Philip Slye of the same place; 2s. from Richard Norton of Stanton [Staunton] for non-appearance to reply to Philip Carpynter; fine 2s. from William Hanys for the penalty incurred at the inquiry against John Raulyns from whom he received 3 dozen of ore at le den'; 2s. from John Carpynter of Coll' [Coleford] for non-appearance to reply to Thomas Tomsett; 2s. from Richard Sutton for non-appearance to reply to William Morgan; 2s. from John Myll of Clor' [Clearwell] for non-appearance to reply to John Raulyns of Clor' [Clearwell]; 2s. from John Twety for abandoning his suit against Henry Byrley; fine 2s. from Richard More *alias* Portyngale for non-appearance against John Raulyns of Clor' [Clearwell] from whom he received 8 seams of ore at lamsq' [Lambsquay] and on that account he is fined. Total: 16 shillings.

Hyll Pytt, Above the Wood

Estreats of the Mine Court of 12 miners held there on Tuesday, June 5, 10 Edward IV (1470):
2s. from James Bufford for abandoning his suit against John Keare; 2s. from John Keare of Clor' [Clearwell] for abandoning his suit against Henry Bele; 2s. from William Keare for non-appearance to reply to Richard Hamond; 2s. from William Hop' of Hanford for non-appearance to reply to Thomas Berowe; fine 2s. from John Myller of Clor' [Clearwell] for non-appearance to reply to John Raulyns from whom he received 6 seams of ore from Seynt Colas pytt and on that account he is fined; 2s. from

Philip Slye of Lydney for abandoning his suit against Thomas Reynolds; 2s. from Richard Norton of Stanton [Staunton] for non-appearance to reply to Philip Carpynter; 2s. from John Carpynter of Coll' [Coleford] smytholder for non-appearance to reply to Thomas Tomsett; 2s. from Richard Sutton of Lydney for non-appearance to reply to William Morgan. Total: 18 shillings.

(2) *Estreat roll of Forest of Dean Miner's Court, 1470: Glos.R.O. D6177/2*

Hyll Pytt, Above the Wood

Estreats of the Court of 48 miners held there on Tuesday, July 3, 10 Edward IV (1470): 2s. from Richard Ocle for abandoning his suit against James Bryte; fine 2s. from Richard Sutton of Lydney because he acknowledged a debt in a plea with William Morgan from whom he received 3 weys and 4 seams of sea coal and on that account he is fined; fine 2s. from Robert Skyme for the penalty incurred at the enquiry against John Raulyns from whom he received 2 seams of ore at le deen and on that account he is fined; fine 2s. from John Raulyns for the penalty incurred at the enquiry against Robert Skynne from whom he received one stone axe and on that account he is fined; 2s. from John Carpynter for non-appearance to reply to Henry Hall and Thomas Day; fine 2s. from Richard Ocle for the penalty incurred at the enquiry against James Byrt from whom he received 15d. and on that account he is fined; fine 2s. from John Carpynter because he incurred a penalty at the enquiry against Thomas Tomsett from whom he received 13s 4d. and on that account he is fined; fine 2s. from William Keare because he incurred a penalty at the enquiry against Richard Hammond from whom he received 12d. and on that account he is fined; 2s. from Thomas Dey senior for abandoning his suit against William Knyght; 2s. from Robert Myllyng for abandoning his suit against William Knyght; 2s. from Philip Bond for abandoning his suit against Henry Hall, John Parsons and Thomas Dey.

Comment: The two documents show that the Courts were held before 12 miners; on one occasion before 48. They took place at Hyll Pit 'Above the Wood', i.e. somewhere in the west part of the Forest. The jury for three of the sessions comprised 12 miners; in the other session it comprised 48. The main discussions, decisions and adjudications concerned offences or complaints between individual named miners; one dispute was between a miner and a smithman in Coleford. Items in dispute related to: 3 dozen of ore at le den' (a location unknown); 8 seams of ore at Lambsquay [south of Coleford]; 6 seams of ore from Seynt Colas pitt (location unknown); 3 weys and 4 seams of sea coal (i.e. mineral coal); and two seams of ore at le deen. Only one item related to coal; the remainder related to iron ore. The fine in each case was 2s. These estreats are thought to have been paid to the Receiver of the Forest as benefits either to the king [Edward IV] directly or to beneficiaries under his gift. A seame was 'one seameigne or man's bearing on land of iron ore or coal'. A dozen comprised '12 bushels and was considered to be equal to 31 cwts'. 'Above the Wood' included Clearwell, Coleford, Lambsquay, Newland, and Staunton.

Appendix 4

THE MINERS' FIGHT AGAINST THE TERRINGHAM FAMILY AND OTHERS: 1635, 1637, 1667-8

On 5 December 1635, Edward Terringham, one of Charles I's Privy Councillors, applied to him for grant of the coal and stone resources in the Forest of Dean, asserting that the king received little revenue from them, yet allowing free timber to the workers. Terringham had to wait until 1637 before he received the grant of 'all the mines of coal and quarries of grindstone for 31 years, at a rent of £30'. After attempting to work 'Aywood' coal mine and 'Terringham's Surfe' for six months, Terringham soon experienced much opposition from the local miners and quarrymen who challenged his right to interfere with their customs and interests. Within the year, 1637, the attorney-general commenced a suit in conjunction with Terringham against certain named miners.[1] The interrogatories administered and the depositions to them are extant.[2] However, no judgement or Decree was forthcoming. Terringham tired of trying to support his grant; he had expended £2,500; he surrendered his lease, and instead was granted (under the terms of a sale of the Forest to Sir John Winter in 1640) an annuity of £300 for 31 years.

During the Civil Wars, Major John Wade, administrator of Dean for the Commonwealth, worked the 'Aywood mine', probably 'Oake Pit'.[3]

Following the Restoration, Captain Francis Terringham applied for a re-grant of his father's lease. On 21 November 1667, the attorney-general was instructed to prepare a lease of the coal mines and quarries. The Dean Forest (Reafforestation) Act 1668, S.17, provided for such a grant. The re-grant to the Terringham family in 1667 soon experienced renewed opposition from the miners and quarrymen. In 1675, Katherine Terringham, widow and administratrix of Francis Terringham, brought a suit in the Exchequer Court against certain named miners and quarrymen.[4] The interrogatories and the depositions to them are extant.[5] The suit was continued in Hilary term 1675-6[6] and similar interrogatories were used: these, and the depositions to them are extant.[7] The situation is summed up in a document[8] which records: 'About this time [*c.* 1675-6] the miners had a Contest in the Exchequer Court with the widow and administratrix of Francis Terringham, lessee of the Crown of the coal mines and quarries of grindstone; and also some few years later with Mr. Dennis whose lands were the first the miners

---

1 PRO E134 13 Chas. I, Mich. 42, 1637, and Hil. 16.

2 Copies in Glos.R.O., Hart: Dean Collection D3921.

3 Hart, *New History* (1995), pp. 146, 147.

4 PRO E134 27 Chas. II, Mich. 28, 1675: Katherine Terringham v. Yarworth etc. In this suit, on 27 September 1675, the interrogatories and the depositions were taken before a Commission appointed by the Exchequer Court at the house of Thomas Luker in Littledean.

5 Copies in Glos.R.O., Hart: Dean Collection D3921.

6 PRO E134 27/28 Chas. II, Hil. 21, 1675-6: Katherine Terringham v. Yarworth etc. In this suit, on 3 January 1676, the interrogatories and depositions were taken before a Commission appointed by the Exchequer Court at the house of Stephen (?) Dovye, innholder, in Coleford.

7 Copies in Glos.R.O., Hart: Dean Collection D3921.

8 Hart MSS, p. 22.

ever carried their coalworks into out of the Forest. But no Decree was ever made in either of these Causes for it is probable the widow grew sick of the expense as Dennis, who gave up the Contest as being too weighty for him.'

The suit was reopened in 1683.[1] The interrogatories and the depositions to them are extant.[2] Trestram Trusteed of Newland, aged 90 years stated: 'He hath not contributed to the charge of the suit but he is concerned in defence of the rights of the miners and hath contributed to the defence of further suits brought against the miners 40 years ago and since, and the same hath cost him at least £10; and he will be still ready and will always contribute his share in defending any suits that shall be brought against them'. No settlement was reached; the two relevant 'Decree documents'[3] simply record this, also the need for a new hearing to be arranged; one did not occur. The situation is summed up in a document which records[4]: 'The Miners also, in James II's reign, had a Contest with [Thomas] Beck(e) but it never came to a Decree or Judgement.' The opposition of the miners (financed by levies made on themselves in their Mine Law Court) appears to have been successful. No evidence is available that the Terringham family received any further recompense for their intolerable grant, nor of any further action against the miners by 'Mr Dennis' (see Appendix 5) or by Thomas Beck(e).

Although the foregoing actions of the Exchequer Court were directed against certain named coalminers and quarrymen, and usually concerned the Terringham claims, they were a direct challenge to the miners' interests. Hence the miners' levies were recorded as being 'for the just and necessary defence and preservation in a legal way of the ancient rights, privileges and customs of His Majesty's miners of the Forest of Dean'. To this end they were supported by the deputy constable and clerk of St. Briavels Castle, and the two deputy gavellers.

A connection with the Terringham family's short tenure of coalworks in 'Aywood' (modern Haywood, north of Cinderford and east of Bilson) remains in the fact that since 1861 some 7 acres of woodland there (replanted in that year, with oak and larch) has been designated as 'Crown Freehold'.[5] Furthermore, the 'Terringham Enclosure' is recorded in 1912.[6]

1 PRO E134 35 Chas. II, Mich. 40, 1683: Thomas Beck(e) *v.* Cowles etc. quarrymen re Terringham. In this suit, on 11 September 1683, the interrogatories and depositions were taken before a Commission appointed by the Exchequer Court at the house of Jonathan (?)Lough called 'The Sign of the Kings Head' in Ross-on-Wye.

2 Glos.R.O., Hart: Dean Collection D3921.

3 PRO E126. Vol 12, 28 Chas. II, fol. 302 (English Bill 12 Jan.) and 326 (English Bill 13 Jan.), Terringham v. Yarworth etc. The solicitors acting for each party are named.

4 Hart MSS, p. 22; and see Hart, *The Free Miners*, 1st Edn. (1953) p. 108.

5 H. C. Hill's Forestry Report and Plan, 1897.

6 Glos.R.O. D9096, F3/1343, file 1864.

Appendix 5

THE (SO-CALLED) 'BOOK OF DENNIS'

The code of customary law of the Forest of Dean Miners' 'Laws and Privileges' since the 19th century has been referred to occasionally as *The Book of Dennis*. The title never appears in the miners's documents. It was first recorded in 1840, when David Mushet[1] refers to an old book called *Dennis* being a reprint in 1664 [believed to be an error for 1687] of *The Miners' Customs of the Forest of Dean* (copied from a 1673 transcript).[2] In 1866 the Rev. H. G. Nicholls[3] continued the use of the title, stating that 'The miners invariably refer to *The Book of Dennis*'.

The earliest known handwritten transcript of the 'Laws and Privileges' is in 1612. It was copied, again as a transcript, in 1673,[4] from which in 1687 it was first printed for 'William Cooper at the Pellican, in Little Britain, London'. Reprintings followed in various modes. A recently discovered document[5] states: 'About this time [c.1675-6] the miners had a Contest in the Exchequer Court with the widow and administratrix of Francis Terringham, lessee of the Crown of the coal mines and quarries of grindstone;[6] and also some few years later with Mr. Dennis whose lands were the first the miners ever carried their coalworks into out of the Forest. But no Decree was ever made in either of these Causes for it is probable the widow grew sick of the expense as Dennis, who gave up the Contest as being too weighty for him.' Opposition by the miners (financed by levies made on themselves at their Mine Law Court) appears to have been successful. The relevant levying of sums of money on the miners is recorded in 1675, 1675-6, and 1680.

Who was 'Mr. Dennis'? The foregoing information indicates that in 1675-6 he was suing the miners for apparently working coal and possibly grindstone in his private property outside the Crown Forest (although possibly within the Hundred of St. Briavels). It is believed that he was a member of the Dennis family of Clearwell connected with the mining industry. Yet the first printed copy of the miners' 'Laws and Privileges' did not appear until 1687, and it would not have been in *his* interests to publicise them.

A similar suit was reopened in the Exchequer Court in 1683[7] on behalf of the Terringham family (Appendix 4) but 'Mr. Dennis' does not appear in the relevant records. Again, opposition by the miners (likewise financed by levies made on themselves at their Mine Law Court) appears to have been successful.

Although the foregoing actions in the Exchequer Court were directed against certain named coalminers and quarrymen, and usually concerned the Terringham claims, they were a direct challenge to the miners' interests. Hence the miners' levies were recorded

---

1 Mushet, D., *Papers on Iron and Steel* (1840), p. 395.
2 Glos.R.O. D9096, F16/18, 19.
3 Nicholls, H. G. *Iron Making* (1866), pp. 65, 57, 69.
4 Glos.R.O. D9096, F16/18, 19.
5 Hart MSS, p. 22.
6 See Appendix 4.
7 PRO E134 35 Chas. II, Mich. 40, 1683: Beck(e) v. Cowles etc. re Terringham.

as being 'for the just and necessary defence and preservation in a legal way of the ancient rights, privileges and customs of His Majesty's miners of the Forest of Dean'. To this end they were supported by the deputy constable and clerk of St. Briavels Castle, and the two deputy gavellers.

In Summary

There never existed a *Book of Dennis.* Any relevant references should have been made to the 'Book Against Dennis' or to the 'Book Printed Against Dennis'.

Appendix 6

MINE LAW COURT RECORDS: 1706-1777: Glos.R.O. D9096, F26/1

The records comprise over fifty 'cases' of 'miner(s) against miner(s)'. The first court was held at Littledean 20 April 1706. The last court was held 26 August 1777 (venue not stated). The 'cases' were spread throughout that period. The venue was mainly the Speech House, but also Littledean, the Market House in Coleford, Clowerwall in the house of John Morse, and in St. Briavels Castle. Deputy constables of St. Briavels were usually present. As examples, the first six courts were in brief:

1. At Littledean 20 April 1706 before Maynard Colchester and Roynon Jones, etc., Thomas Davies clerk of the Court; and 12 (named) jurors:
   Anthony Prichett proved his freedom;
   George Bannister against Alexander Philips.

   Adjourned to the house of John Morse in Clowerwell 14 May 1706 before George Bond etc., Thomas Davies deputy clerk of the Court, and 12 (named) jurors:
   Edward Tyler against Thos. Skin, etc.

   Adjourned to the Market Place in Coleford 28 May 1706 before George Bond etc., Thos. Davies clerk of the Court, and 12 (named) jurors:
   John James against George Ambrose and his verns, etc.

   Adjourned to the Speech House 25 June 1706 before Francis Wyndham and George Bond, etc., and before Richard Preest and Robert Wood, deputy gavellers, Thos. Davies deputy clerk, and 12 (named) jurors:
   George Bannister against Alexander Philips, etc.

2. At St. Briavels Castle 1 September 1719 before William James, etc. and 12 (named) jurors:
   Thos. Wilcox against Richard Keere and verns, etc.

3. At the Speech House 17 January 1720 before Richard Machen, etc. and 6 (named) jurors:
   Richard Hewlett against John Morgan and verns, etc.

4. At the Speech House 31 January 1720 before Richard Machen, etc. and 12 (named) jurors:
   William Matthews against Nicholas Whetstone, etc.

5. At the Speech House 17 May 1720 before William James, etc. and 12 (named) jurors.

6. At the Speech House 8 November 1720.

25 August 1777: John Watkins and his verns against William Braine and his verns.

continued

I complain against William Braine and his verns for working at a Stone Coalpitt called by the name of Little Rockey in the Hundred of St. Briavels. By his so doing I am damnified six pounds by his working at the pitt. I will prove … and the damage I will prove myself by evidence in the King's name: Judgment for the plaintiff. Verdict to his damage £4. 14s. 6d. Cost: 6s. 10d.

> It is ordered that Thos. Nicholas be and is hereby amerced two shillings for disturbing the Court.
> It is ordered by this court that George Bradley be and is hereby amerced two shillings for disturbing the Court.

[In a later hand] *Mine Law Court 25 August 1777*: There has been no Court holden for the Miners since this day which is a great loss to the gaveller and causes various disputes amongst the colliers, which is owing to the neglect of the deputy constables [of St. Briavels Castle].

Appendix 7

MINUTES OF THE MINE LAW COURT: 7 FEBRUARY 1730[1]

Whereas an Order was made by 48 Freeminers with the consent of two deputy constables on the 7th day of January in the 4th yr of the reign of King George I [1718], wherein amongst other things it is there ordained that for the defending of all actions and suits, that then were or which should thereafter be brought in the Courts at Westminster concerning the Mine, and for the prosecuting and defending any Certiorari, Recordari or other writ to be brought to remove any Action of proceeding in the Miners Court – All miners travelling in the Mine, Coal or Oaker should pay six pence, and for every horse and mare kept and used for carriage of the same to pay also six pence to certain Collectors therein named – And if such sums were not sufficient for those purposes, it should be in the power of a jury of 12 miners with the consent of two Deputy Constables at any time to raise the said sums on all Freeminers and on their horses and mares used for carriage as aforesaid – And that if any person did refuse to pay the said sums, that then such Freeminers should forfeit double the sum so due, to be sued for and recovered in the Mine Law Court, as by the same Order doth and may more at large appear. And whereas other certain actions from the Court of Westminster have been brought against divers miners for matters and things concerning the Mine, And the liberties and privileges of all the miners are in danger to be subverted and destroyed if proper methods are not speedily taken for preventing the same – In consideration whereof we the deputy constables and Jury of 12 miners whose names are hereunto subscribed do hereby (in pursuance and by virtue of the same recited Order) direct, order and appoint that every miner travelling in the Mine, Coal or Oaker as aforesaid shall pay the sum of six pence of lawful money. And also that for every horse or mare kept or used for the carriage of Mine, Coal or Oaker the like sum of sixpence shall be also paid by the owner of such horse or mare unto the respective Collectors hereinafter named, And that if any person or persons shall refuse or neglect to pay the same sum or sums of money hereby ordered to be raised and paid by them respectively within six days after demand made, that then and in such case, all such person or persons shall be sued and prosecuted at the next Mine Law Court for the penalty and forfeiture mentioned in the said recited Order. And we do further order and direct that when the said monies shall be raised and paid, the same shall be applied in the most effectual manner in the defending of any such Actions that are already, or shall be brought against any free miner for and concerning the Mines or the rights and privileges thereof. And that all such sums of money as shall not be so expended shall be applied for and towards the collecting of all the Charters, Records and other writings relating to the Mines and Miners, And if upon a strict search and enquiry to be made for such Charters etc. it shall appear that the said Charters are lost, or not be recovered, that then what money shall remain unexpended shall be applied for and towards the searching for and suing out such Charters and Records formerly granted for establishing and supporting the Rights and privileges of the said Mines and Miners in such manner and sort as the Judges of the said Court or any two of them shall from time to time direct, order or

1 Recently discovered in 'The Gaveller's Office', Coleford

appoint And lastly we do nominate and appoint the persons following to be Collectors and Receivers of the said sums of money (viz.) George James for Bream and Blakney, Henry Banister and Thomas Hooper for Clowerwall and St. Briavels, Phillip Elly for Coleford and Newland, George Marshall and Tristram Trusteed for Staunton and Bicknor. Thomas Bennett for Ruardean and Mitcheldean, and Thomas Haynes for Littledean. And that the said Collectors do upon the receipt of a precept to them directed under the hands and seals of two or more Deputy Constables for that purpose make a true and perfect list in writing of the names of all free miners of the age of sixteen years and upwards inhabiting in the several places for which they are appointed Collectors upon the oath of such Collector and likewise of the number of horses and mares that each of the said Miners or other persons shall keep or use for carriage as aforesaid, which list so must the said Collectors are to bring to the next Court to be held for the said Mines, together with the money they shall have collected thereon by virtue of this Order, And that the said monies be there paid unto William Lane who is hereby appointed Treasurer and Receiver thereof, And that the said William Lane do keep an exact account of the same in a Book to be kept for that purpose, And the said Collectors shall have sixpence in the pound for collecting the said sums of money if they perform the same, otherwise the gaveller shall have the said six pence in the pound if he collects the same.

Thos. Pyrke [deputy constable]
Wm. Colchester [deputy constable]
Wm. James [clerk]
Wm. Lane [deputy clerk]

George Marshall
Tho. Hooper
Henry Banister
Richard Morse
Trustram Trusteed
Clifford Morse
Henry Lewis
? Jones
Thos. Mounjoy
John Steel
Thomas Haynes
William (?) Skeffington

[12 Free Miners]

Appendix 8

A RETURN FROM THE COMMISSIONERS OF WOODS, 1818

To the Orders of the House of Commons, dated the 30th day of April 1818; - for

INFORMATION RESPECTING THE MINES IN DEAN FOREST; - *VIZ*

ORDERS:	RETURN:
1st – THAT there be laid before this House, copies of the several Charters, Grants and other Documents, under which the Persons styling themselves 'The Free Miners of the Forest of *Dean*,' claim to get or consume, carry away and sell, the Coal, Ironstone, and other Minerals lying within the said Forest.	1st – WE are not in possession of any Charters, Grants, or Documents, of the nature described in this Order; nor have we ever been able to ascertain that any such Documents exist.
2nd – THAT there be laid before this House, an Account of the Number of Tons of Coal, Ironstone, and other Minerals, got and consumed, or worked up within the said Forest, by the Free Miners and other Persons in partnership with or claiming under them, from the year 1800 to 1817, both inclusive; distinguishing the Quantities raised in each Year. 3rd – THAT there be laid before this House, an Account of the Number of tons of Coal, Ironstone, and other Minerals, got and carried away, or sold, from the Mines within the Forest of Dean, by Persons calling themselves 'Free Miners', and other persons in partnership with, or claiming under them, from 1800 to 1817, both inclusive; distinguishing the quantities so sold, or carried away, in each Year.	2nd & 3rd. } AS no Tonnage is paid by the Free Miners for the Share of the Produce of the Mines to which the Crown is entitled, no accurate Account of the Number of Tons got, can be rendered; according to a conjecture formed by the principal resident Officer of the Forest, the quantity raised from 1800 to 1806, was about 70,000 Tons annually; from 1807 to 1816, about 100,000 Tons annually; and in 1807, about 13,000 Tons.

4th – THAT there be laid before this House, an account of the Rents, Royalties, or Free Share, paid or payable to the Crown, for such Coal, Ironstone, and other Minerals, and by whom the same has been paid, or is payable.

4th – THE Composition for the King's Share of the Produce of the Mines, and for the privilege of opening Mines, paid or payable in each year from 1800 to 1817, is as follows:

		£.	s.	d.
In	1800	225.	9.	9.
	1801	228.	4.	3.
	1802	235.	1.	3.
	1803	247.	16.	1.
	1804	257.	5.	0.
	1805	260.	6.	0.
	1806	258.	6.	0.
	1807	257.	8.	0.
	1808	261.	9.	9.
	1809	302.	15.	3.
	1810	349.	10.	9.
	1811	599.	17.	9.
	1812	583.	9.	0.
	1813	604.	7.	9.
	1814	626.	14.	0.
	1815	671.	16.	6.
	1816	698.	12.	3.
	1817	737.	16.	1.

5th – THAT there be laid before this House, an Account of the Duties paid or payable for Coals raised within the Forest of Dean, and conveyed from Lidney, Bullo Pill, and other Places upon the River Severn.

5th – WE have no means of furnishing the information required by this Order.

Office of Woods, &c.
29th May 1818.

W. D. ADAMS.
HENRY HAWKINS.

Comments: The 1st Return was unhelpful to the miners' interests. One result of the Return was the Dean Forest (Gale Rents) Act 1819.

PART TWO : 1831-2002

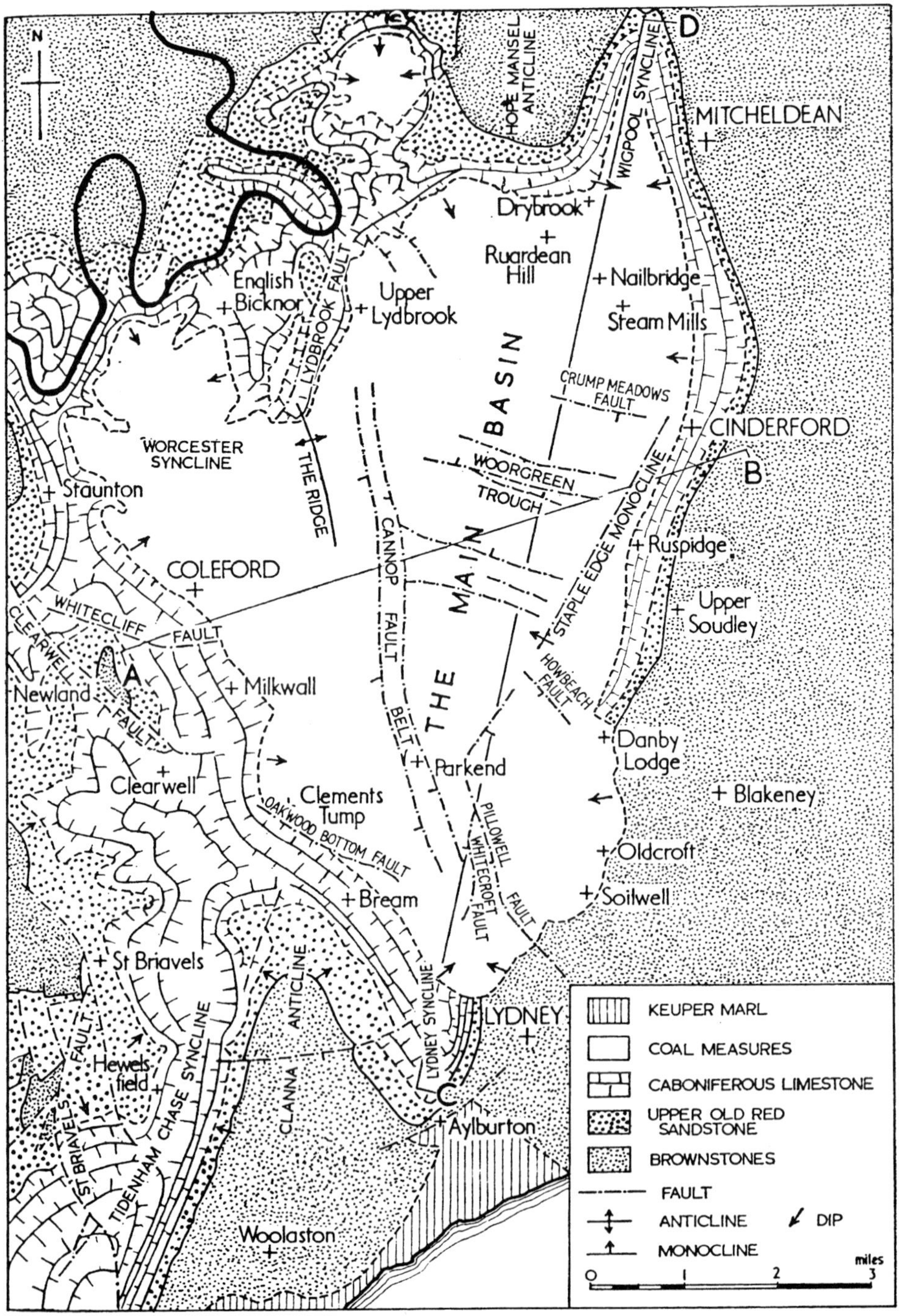

Plate VII. *Geological Plan of the Forest of Dean Coal and Iron Ore Field (1942).*

CHAPTER VII

1831-1841: Fourth Report (1835); Act of 1838; Awards of 1841.

PARTITIONING of the text here is because of the progression from 1831 to the year 1838 when the free miners' 'laws and privileges' were replaced by statutory defined rights and regulations. Previously their customs remained intact, yet ill-defined and always liable to challenges of one kind or another.

The year 1831 was particularly pertinent in the history of the Forest and hundred. For some time, certain of the inhabitants had been agitating with regard to free miners' and commoners' customs and privileges, some evincing a very strong resentment to what they considered was usurpation of their 'rights' by usually wealthy outsiders, which they termed 'foreigners'. Many of the latter had become the principal coal or iron mine owners, including such entrepreneurs as Mushet, Allaway and Protheroe. Destruction of Crown inclosure fences and hedges took place in the early part of the year, and feeling had grown so strong that in June a ringleader, Warren James, organised a substantial raid on the Office of Woods' inclosures on the west of the Forest. A periodical named *The Forester*[1] edited, printed and published at Newnham by William Birt, carried in Issue No. 11 (4 August 1831) an 'Explanation' of the incidents, setting forth 'the numerous ills the free miners have been made to suffer prior to 8 June 1831'. Among the points mentioned was that the Duke of Beaufort, as constable of St. Briavels castle, and lord chief ranger of the Forest, had been 'for nearly three years past trifling with the patience and miseries of the free miners by denying their just demands of opening their Free Miners' Courts', and that they had been 'prevented from following their Mine train [tramway] through the Enclosures (alias Game Preserves)'; also that 'foreigners' had been favoured 'who have crept in to rob us of our rights', and 'other acts equally unconstructional and oppressive'.[2] Some £1,500 worth of damage resulted.

The Dean Forest Commission Act 1831. The foregoing situation led to, or at least hastened, the appointment of the Dean Forest Commission following the passing of the Dean Forest Commission Act 1831. The members of the Commission[3] were commanded to enquire into: (1) the boundaries of the Forest; (2) encroachments; (3) the existence, origin, and particulars of the rights and privileges claimed by the persons

---

1 The first number of *The Forester*, 26 May 1831, carried the editorial promise: 'I will support the Foresters, the real Foresters, those who work and toil for their bread, in their old laws, new laws, or any laws that will fairly amend their circumstances.'

2 Accounts of the riots are given in Hart; *The Commoners of Dean Forest* 1st Edn. (1951) and 2nd Edn. (2002) and in R. Anstis, *Warren James and the Dean Forest Riots* (1986).

3 Robert Gordon, M.P., Kemble; Ebenezer Ludlow, serjeant at law; Charles Bathurst, Lydney Park; Edward Machen, Whitemead Park; Henry Clifford, Over Ross, Herefordshire; Clerk; Thomas Graham, Mitre Court, Temple; Surveyor, John Hosmer.

born within the Hundred of St. Briavels, calling themselves Freeminers; (4) the Court of Mine Law and the Court of St. Briavels, also the condition, etc., of the prison belonging to the latter Court; and (5) the expediency of amalgamating parishes (i.e. parochialising the Forest). Command number (3), showed the anxiety of the government of that time to settle the question of the free miners:

> 'We further command that you … make a report … of your opinion touching the origin of the rights and privileges claimed by the said persons calling themselves free miners as aforesaid, and touching the qualifications as to birth, occupation, or otherwise necessary to entitle any person to such rights and privileges, and that you do in like manner and form report what the nature and particulars of the said rights and privileges are as now exercised, and over what lands within the said forest or elsewhere such rights and privileges extend or are exercised, and of the variations, if any in the manner in which the said rights and privileges have at different times been exercised, and also of particulars of any former proceedings at law or in equity as in your opinion shall tend to ascertain the said rights and privileges, and also your opinion whether any such rights and privileges legally exist, and whether the manner in which the said rights and privileges are exercised is warranted by law, and whether any rights and privileges which legally exist are abused or are made the cover for illegal practices, and in what particular, if any, the exercise of the said rights and privileges departs from, exceeds, or is inconsistent with the exercise of the said rights and privileges as warranted by law, and that you do in like manner and form report your opinion as to the steps proper to be taken for settling the claims of the persons calling themselves free miners.'

Before discussing the work of the Commissioners of 1831 it is appropriate to note that in 1832 further disquietude and agitation was in play in connection with a Parliamentary Bill to empower the making of a railway or steam-carriage road from Foxes Bridge to Purton Pill. Certain 'vested interests' opposed a fourth railway in the Forest, while the free miners and the majority of the proprietors of the works and mines supported the Bill. At a meeting of free miners held at Yorkley on 5 March, the following resolutions were made[1]:

> 'That a large portion of the working class of this Forest, together with their numerous families, are great sufferers for want of employment; to which cause they ascribe entirely the recent Disturbances which took place in the Forest, and being destitute of good and profitable labour, & oppressed with hunger, the Foresters were led astray and made the dupes of a wicked artful & designing faction.
>
> That it is appalling and dismaying to see a robust & able bodied set of men (willing to work and earn an honest livelihood) driven in dispair to beggary and to obtain support by voluntary contributions: when their native soil is capable of supplying their wants, by the exercise of their own industry, and at the same time producing a benefit to the public at large.
>
> That at some of the most extensive coalworks in the Forest the labour of the workmen has been already reduced to three days per week, (although in the middle of winter) and the approaching summer is likely to impress more districts than any preceding one in consequence

[1] Glouc.Liby, ref. 2985(7).

of the want of employment.

That the whole of such Districts is to be entirely ascribed to the notorious monopoly exercised by a few individuals in the Forest, and that the public at large together with ourselves are greatly injured thereby.

That if anything was required to convince the public of the truth of this statement, this meeting would refer them to the well known fact (established by circular letters from the Coalmasters of the Forest) declaring forest coal, conveyed along the present lines of railway, at Bullo Pill and Lydney, at the extravagant and enormous price of fourteen shillings per ton, although within so short a distance of the pits' mouth.

That under such circumstances it is impossible for the Forest to secure a trade, (except in a few months of the year) as the coal from distant parts of the kingdom is brought into our native markets and sold at less than ten shillings per ton.

That nothing will open the Forest of Dean, to benefit the public and ensure permanent employ to its numerous population short of a new communication to Purton Pill: the old ancient and established shipping port of the Forest. Where, in addition to the advantage of home markets, the large vessels trading to the port of Gloucester from Ireland and other distant parts (which cannot enter the ports of Lydney and Bullo Pill) will be supplied with a back, or outward, freight of Forest produce: thus effectually securing the opening & working of our mines to the public at large, by means of the natural port.

That it is in vain for the proprietors and abettors of the existing railways to contend that the roads already formed are adequate for such purpose, or that branches extending from their main roads can be made beneficially applicable for the transit of the whole of the Forest produce. Experience has dearly taught us the contrary, and the numerous Population thrown out of Employ the greater part of the year, fully and lamentably demonstrates the fact. The present Railways do not afford constant Employment at the works situate immediately upon their main roads: and how can the produce of the Forest depend upon branches to be united with roads not calculated to convey their own immediate produce to market, except at the enormous price we have already quoted?

That copies of these Resolutions be printed and sent to His Grace the Duke of Beaufort, Lord Seagrave, and the Members of Parliament for the city and county of Gloucester and to the Members for Ireland; to Edward Sheppard, Esq., Chairman of the Woollen Manufacturers of this county; Edward Machen, Esq., of Whitemead Park, and all the neighbouring gentlemen supposed to take an interest in devising and supporting measures calculated to ensure constant and permanent employ to the numerous population of His Majesty's Forest of Dean.

Signed on behalf of the Meeting: John Davis, chairman and free miner.'

In the same year, 1832, a petition was presented to the House of Commons by the proprietors of works and mines, praying support for the Bill.[1] Reasons for supporting, or of opposing the Bill were printed and distributed, the following handbill being an interesting example.[2]

'Security & protection of forest rights by a free miner. Being extracted from the Purton Steam-carriage railway Cos. Bill now pending in Parliament.

---

1 Glouc.Liby, ref. 2985(10).

2 *Ibid.*, ref. 2985(9).

And whereas His Majesty in right of His Crown is entitled to certain gawles or rents or shares in respect of the mines and minerals of the said Forest, and various disputes have arisen in respect of the precise amounts thereof, and it is desirable that the amount of such rights should be ascertained: Be it enacted, that no coal, stone or iron ore shall be carried upon or along the said Railway or Steam-carriage Road or Branch hereby empowered to be made and maintained, or any part thereof, the produce of the said Forest from any pit mine or quarry, the owner or occupier of which, for or in respect of working such mines, does not consent to pay such sums, gawles, rents or dues as from time to time shall be appointed on behalf of His said Majesty, His heirs and successors, by the proper officer of the said Forest, provided such payment or gawles, rents, dues or tonnage shall be fixed not to exceed at and after the rate of [blank] per ton.

Now if the free miners can obtain their gawleages at [blank] per ton as stated in the above clause what more can be effected or desired. The Lydney and Bullo Pill Acts of Parliament contain no blank charges but on the contrary they are filled up with the most unprecedented and extravagant charges of tonnage and wharfage to the great injury of the miners and public at large. And notwithstanding these facts staring them in the face. These Foreigners belonging to these two Roads want to persuade the poor starving colliers that 'tis better to pay them 3 shillings per ton than two pence to the Crown.

Only look into the clauses of those Railway Acts and you will see that both the Proprietors and Landholders have taken ample care of themselves and forgot the poor miners. The Purton Railway Act when all the blanks are filled will not contain one half of the amount of tonnage which those other acts contain. What can the opponents of the Purton Road say to this?

Stinson, Printer, Coleford, 1832.'

Local opposition proved too strong and the Bill was withdrawn.

The Fourth Report: 25 August 1835. The Commissioners of 1831 held most of their sittings at the Bear Inn, Newnham, although they also sat occasionally at The Angel Hotel, Coleford, The Speech House, St. Briavels and Westbury. Of their five Reports, their Fourth (dated 25 August 1835) is so relevant to the present volume that it is included below, almost in full[1]:

'The origin of the rights and privileges of the free miners is involved in obscurity, and we cannot upon search find anything which enables us to refer to it with certainty.

There are undoubted proofs that the Romans were established in the immediate neighbourhood, and there can be little, if any, doubt that they availed themselves, as probably the Britons had done before them, of the iron ore, which, being in many places near the surface, was easily accessible.

The excavations, provincially called scowles, which exist in many parts of the Forest, have evidently been made for the purpose and in the course of getting out the ore; and the cinders, which are often found in large quantities, attest the use of bloomeries and forges in

---

1 It appears that the Commissioners of 1831 in producing their Fourth Report (1835) did not have sight of such records as the Mine Law Court 1469-70, the first transcript of the 'Lawes and Privilleges' of 1612, the true meaning of the so-called 'Book of Dennis' (from 1687), some additional Orders and Minutes, and records of 1702-1777 detailing numerous cases of 'miner against miner'.

manufacturing the iron.

Whether the coal was also used by them, or when it was first brought into use, does not clearly appear.

The Sea Coal Mine is mentioned in the 'book' [1687] of the Laws and Customs of the Miners of the Forest of Dean hereafter referred to, which would carry back a customary mode of working it at least to the time of Edward III.

Probably before, and certainly soon after the Roman Conquest, the soil was in the crown, and all the rights of a royal forest were in force. The persons by whom the mines were then worked could not have been in the first instance free tenants of the crown; it is more likely that they were in a state of servitude, and subjected in that character to perform the labour required.

The name 'free miner' by which they are and have for centuries been known, seems to refer to some right or privilege distinct from their original condition and the word 'verns' which occurs in the proceedings of the Mine Law Court, and is still occasionally used in the Forest, has been supposed to be derived from their having been in bondage to the king.

This derivation is probably erroneous; it may, however, be considered as traditionary of the former condition of the miners, and it does not appear unreasonable to suppose that certain persons at some distant period of time, either by having worked for a year and a day, or by reasons of some now unknown circumstance connected with the origin of the privilege, were considered as emancipated, and thereupon became entitled, or were allowed to work the mines upon their own adventure, concurrently with or subject to the right of the crown to a certain portion of the product.

The respective periods of a year and a day and of seven years as connected with the means of becoming free by working and by apprenticeship are well known in English Law, and both periods are in operation for this purpose among the free miners, a year and a day being the time required for working in the case of a person born in the hundred of a free parent, and seven years for the apprenticeship of the son of a person not free.'

[The Commissioners then give information regarding the military services rendered by the miners during the reigns of the first three Edwards. – See Chapter I, p. 19.]

'By the 'book' [1687] entitled "The Laws and Customs of the Miners of the Forest of Dean, in the County of Gloucester" it would appear that the customs existed before and at the time of Edward III.

Bodies of miners existed at the same time in the mineral counties of Derbyshire, Cornwall and Somerset.'

[The Commissioners then explain the information contained in the Third Report of 1788 regarding the claims of the Dean miners. – See p. 212.]

'There is, however, an express reservation of their rights and privileges in the 12th section of the 20th Chas. 2. c. 3 [1668], and the office of gaveller appears to be consistent rather with a right in the miners to some enjoyment of the mines under the crown, than with their being merely employed as labourers or servants, as the term implies the letting upon a rent or the reservation of a share of the produce. To whatever circumstances the origin may be referred, it seems to be a reasonable foundation for it that the reserving a certain share of the produce to the landlord, and giving up the remainder as the price of the labour of getting it, would be a convenient mode of having the mines worked. This appears to have prevailed also in the mines of Cornwall, Mendip, and Derbyshire, and is now very usual in working mines.

The next point is the qualification, which we consider to be that the person should be born within the Hundred of St. Briavels, should work there a year and a day in one of the mines, and should abide within the said hundred. It is, however, insisted on by many of the miners that in addition to this qualification it is necessary to be the son of a free father.

An order of the Mine Law Court, dated December 6th, 1737, declares, that "No foreigner's son, though born within the Hundred of St. Briavels, shall hereafter be admitted as a free miner unless he shall be bound as an apprentice for the term of seven years to a free miner, and do accordingly serve the said seven years in working at the mines". Hence it seems that although it was only necessary for a free miner's son to work for a year and a day, it was required that a foreigner's son should be bound an apprentice to a free miner for seven years.

It was part of the regulations of the Mine Law Court that none but free miners should be allowed to work, and no foreigner could be introduced or at least allowed to continue to work in the mines.

The free miners appear to have taken their sons to work with them, and thereby and by the occasional taking of apprentices their existence as a body was continued with a recognition amongst themselves of each individual's right.

The means of resorting to a periodical test ceased with the discontinuance of the Mine Law Court [1777], and although there is a great jealousy on the part of those who can trace their derivative title against those who have not such hereditary claim, it would be difficult if not impossible at the present time to confine the title to anything beyond birth and service, whatever may have been the original requirements.

Every free miner, duly qualified, claims the right to demand of the king's gaveller a gale, that is, a spot of ground chosen by himself for sinking a mine, and this, provided it does not interfere with the works of any other mine, the gaveller considers himself obliged to give, receiving a fee of 5s. and inserting the name of the free miner in the gale book. The limit of interfering with other works has been from time to time varied by the order of the Mine Law Court, but at present appears to be with respect to levels at the distance of 1,000 yards to the land side (without limitation to the deep), and with respect to a water pit to a radius of 12 yards from the centre of the pit. The gaveller goes to the spot selected with the free miner making the application and gives him possession with the following ceremonies:– The gaveller cuts a stick, and asking the party how many verns or partners he has, cuts a notch for every partner and one for the king; a turf is then cut and the stick forked down by two other sticks, the turf put over it, and the party galing the work is then considered to be put in full possession. The free miner thus having obtained possession is compelled to proceed with the work by working one day in the following year and day, and a day in each subsequent year and day (forfeiting the gale if he fails so to work), and to pay an annual sum of two guineas to the gaveller for each vein of coal he intends to work, till he gets at the coal, after which he agrees with him for the amount of the composition to be paid to the king in lieu of his fifth, which in case of their not agreeing must be taken in kind by the king's putting in a fifth man. Of this, however, no instance is known to have occurred within the memory of witnesses examined by us. The composition so fixed upon may be determined by either party on giving six months' notice. The right to the gale is considered by the free miners to carry with it that of timber for the use of their works; this seems to extend no farther than to the offal and soft wood, and the mode of obtaining it is for the miner to apply to the keeper of the walk in which the mine is situated for an order, which he takes to the clerk of the Swainmote court, who on receiving a fee of 1s. as a matter of course gives him another order directed to the keeper of any walk in which there is timber fit for the purpose. The miner cuts the timber when assigned, and until within about the last ten years paid a fee of 2s. to the keeper. There is no limit as to the quantity of timber if it be strictly applied for the use of the works, but free miners using the tramways are prohibited by the 49th Geo. 3 [1808], from claiming any timber.

The free miners claim a right to have land galed to them for opening mines not only in the open lands of the forest but also in all enclosed lands within the Hundred of St. Briavels, except churchyards, gardens, and orchards, and excepting also such enclosures as have been made by the crown under the statute 48th Geo. 3 [1808], for the time they shall continue enclosed. The only difference is that in the case of gales in private ground the proprietor is let in as a partner, thus making a partnership of six, as the company generally consists of four, and the king who is considered a partner. The free miners have fully exercised this right from time to time, except in Noxon Park, the property of Lord Dunraven, Kidnalls and Sneyd Woods, the property of Mr. Bathurst, and Mailscot, now the property of the crown, in which their rights have been more or less disputed.

With reference "to the variations (if any) of the manner in which the rights and privileges of the free miners have at different times been exercised" it does not appear that there has been any material variation, except that the dues payable to the crown, which were at one time almost nominal, have been gradually but very moderately increased, and that restrictions to prevent the interference of foreigners with the free miners have been established and extended by the orders of different Mine Law Courts. The incidents to the qualification of a free miner have, however, varied, at least they are differently stated by different witnesses. By some it is alleged that none but free miners could according to the ancient custom hold a mine either by transfer, descent, devise, or in partnership, while others maintain that a mine, being originally galed to a free miner, might be sold, leased devised or pass by descent to a foreigner. It appears by the 'book' of laws and customs that the free miners might bequeath their doles or shares in the mines, in default of which the doles descended to their heirs. It is not, however, clear whether a foreigner so taking or inheriting was entitled to work the mine himself, or was obliged to dispose of it to a free miner for the purpose of having it worked. The Old Fire Engine or Oiling Gin Coal Work is said to have been originally galed to foreigners in 1766, and to have been subsequently conveyed by them in shares at different times, and to different persons, free miners and others.

Transfers of mines also took place in 1774 between Thomas Neale and Thomas Crawley Boevey, both foreigners.

Since the discontinuance of the miners court in 1777, similar transfers and leases have taken place, though most commonly free miners have been named as trustees, and it has been almost the uniform practice that no foreigner's name shall be inserted in the gale book, but that a free miner's name should appear even after the interest has been transferred to a foreigner as that of the person to whom the gale apparently belongs. The king's gaveller, however, receives the annual composition in many cases from the person in possession, crediting in the gale book the amount so received to the free miner in whose name the work stands. Some few objections have been urged, especially that the names of Messrs. Hartford, Partridge, and Company, and the persons working the Gentleman's Collieries, are to be found in the gale book. A practice, however, existed of making honorary free miners, and several, if not all, the persons belonging to the Gentleman's Collieries whose names are entered in the gale book are stated to be honorary free miners.

Search has been made to discover any former proceeding at law or in equity which might aid us in ascertaining these rights and privileges, but without success. From the passing of the act 20 Charles 2, c. 3 [1668], before referred to, down to the present period, the matter has been occasionally a subject of discussion, but no judicial or other ascertainment of them seems to have taken place.'

[The Commissioners continue with the cases of the Governor and Company of Copper Mines *v.* Philips, and Francis Jones *v.* Philips. [1752] – See Chapter VI, p. 208.]

'Without further discussing the origin of the free miners' rights or the peculiarities affecting their claims of title and qualifications, it may be sufficient to observe that the enjoyment of the right was always connected with a customary mode of exercising it, whereby at once a stimulus was provided for continuing exertion and a limit assigned to the extent of the works.

The operation of getting at the coal was always carried on upwards to the land of or from the level, it was to be of a reasonable fair breadth of work, it might be carried on upwards so far as uncut coal could be found but no further, and when parties under different gales were approaching each other they might proceed until their mattocks should meet.

The reasonable breadth of the work prevented what was called under cutting by narrow headings; the limitation of ceasing the operation upon coming to cut coal stimulated each party to gain as much as he could fairly get at before his rival should have reached it.

Whenever the introduction of foreigners first took place it is beyond doubt that it has occurred from time to time for many years, but more particularly within the last thirty years, Mr. Mushet and Mr. Protheroe and others having invested large sums in several works, either alone or in conjunction with free miners.

Having thus considered the preliminary points submitted to us, we have now to express our opinion:

That certain rights of free miners for working the Forest mines by custom exist, but the manner in which such rights and privileges are at present exercised do not appear to us to be in all respects strictly conformable to the customary right, and so to be not warranted by law.

That such rights and privileges were originally personal.

That the strict custom required that the mines should be worked by companies of four persons called verns or partners, the king being considered as a fifth.

That all the verns were required to be free miners, and to proceed in driving or working the level or sinking and working the water pit by their own labour or assisted by their sons or by apprentices.

That the introduction of engines under licences granted by the crown was an inroad upon the custom and inconsistent with the ancient usages of working the mines. By the greater outlay of capital which has taken place under the new system, the custom of working by partners and apprentices has been nearly abolished, and has been succeeded by the practice of working the mines by hired labourers.

That free miners rarely, if ever, before, but frequently since the discontinuance of the Mine Law Court, have leased, mortgaged, and sold the works under their gales to foreigners, either directly or indirectly through other free miners as trustees.

That by means of sales, mortgages, assignments, transfers, and leases most of the larger works have of late years become vested either wholly or in part in foreigners, and recent instances have occurred of a free miner being employed by a foreigner to get a work galed to such free miner by name in order to transfer it at once to the foreigner, the remuneration of the free miner for his part in the ceremony being a payment of some small sum or other consideration. We consider these practises to be illegal, and that the foreigners have exercised the free miners' rights and privileges in a manner contrary to and unauthorised by ancient custom.

That during the existence of the Mine Law Court, injunctions under the name of "forbids" were granted, and damages recovered for breaches of the laws and customs.

That such laws regulated the title to and enjoyment of particular gales, the working of coal by headings of a proper breadth and level, prohibited the interference or employment of foreigners either in working or carrying coal, and exercised jurisdiction as well in recovering the rents or gales due to the crown as in settling debts and disputes between the free miners themselves.

The remaining part of our duty is to report our opinion as to the steps proper to be taken for setting the claims of persons calling themselves free miners.

The present system of working the mineral property of the crown is most defective and productive of constant disputes and expensive litigation, and taking the opinion which we have given of the rights of the free miners to be correct a very important question arises whether they can be now maintained with advantage to themselves or to the community.

The claims of the free miners to the exclusive holding of gales, and to be exclusively employed as labourers in the mines, occasion constant and never-ending jealousy and dissatisfaction on their part. The foreigners who have got into the possession of extensive works, although they in general give a fair preference to the free miners, consider themselves quite at liberty to employ, and do employ, some foreign labourers.

The free miners by lending their names and giving their assistance to foreigners in obtaining possession of coal works, and being themselves parties to the legal fraud by which such possession is maintained, cannot justly or equitably demand that these foreigners should now be deprived of their property. The crown having recognised the introduction of foreigners by receiving gale rents from them, and granting licences for steam engines, may be in a great degree barred from interference, although there can be no doubt but that as the mineral property belongs wholly to the crown, subject only to the rights of the free miners, a fraud is practised by the working of the mines by foreigners under the cover of the free miners' rights.

So long as the Mine Law Court existed the foreigners were not permitted to possess mines, and all persons possessing them were obliged to work according to the custom of the Forest, and were not permitted by narrow headings or unfair working to disturb or interfere with the rights of neighbouring miners. In the hope of effecting an arrangement various attempts have been made to induce the contending parties to acquiesce in a limitation of the coal field to be allotted to each gale, and the proposals of Mr. Mushet, a foreigner, and of certain free miners, will be found in the evidence.

Mr. Protheroe, by far the largest proprietor, complains strongly of the injustice with which he should be treated if his rights were not duly recognised, and his evidence details the circumstances of his case. Finding that there was no prospect of any satisfactory arrangement, and having no plan of the mines on which we could obtain the opinion of scientific men, we suggested the propriety of having a regular mineral survey prepared, which has been done by Mr. Sopwith, and is deposited in the office of woods and forest, an objection having been raised by Mr. Protheroe to the survey of his work being made known, except for the purpose of the act under which our commission was issued.

How far the crown, having dealt with foreigners by its agents and by granting licences, may have legalised their operations, is not now the question before us: what we wish at this time to state is that the customary mode of working has become altogether inapplicable to the present state of things. Mr. Protheroe, in particular, having taken gales and erected engines at various points, considers himself entitled to undercut by narrow headings any work to the land of any part of his district, as the only means of securing the coal he alleges he has won by draining it by means of his engines.

He claims also and exercises when occasion arises the employment of foreigners in his works, the preference which he gives to free miners being, as he says, wholly voluntary.

These circumstances lead to continual complaints at the loss of the Mine Law Courts, which, however, probably could not be renewed or made available to oust the common law jurisdiction, at least where foreigners are concerned.

Taking all the circumstances of the case into consideration, we are of opinion that the monopoly and customary workings are practically at an end, and that it is impossible to suggest any satisfactory arrangement for the working of the coal or the limitation of districts.

The right of the soil is clearly in the crown, and as against all other persons but the free miners would give the ordinary title and control as to the enjoyment; even as to the free miners, their right is rather under than against the crown, being merely a mode of working under a customary sort of tenure.

Few of the free miners are actually in possession of any subsisting work of importance. Those who happen to have large works would probably not object to become lessees of a defined district at an ascertained rent under some general arrangement giving them favourable terms; with regard to those who are not such possessors, there probably would be but little difficulty in obtaining a release of their rights, such as they are, in consideration of a sum of money or of a grant of land on lease according to such terms and qualifications as the particular circumstances of each case might require.

The whole coalfield might then be let by the crown as between landlord and tenant, defining the limits and regulating the workings.

We have had several meetings for the purpose of obtaining a register of all who claim to be free miners, and about 1,000 have been placed on the annexed lists, but we believe there are others who have not yet put in their claim.

We think that under an act of parliament the desired objects may be effected by means of commissioners acquainted with the value of mineral property, to be appointed as well by and on the part of the free miners as the crown; and considering the present state and condition of the mines and of the population and the extreme difficulty, if not absolute impossibility, of making any satisfactory regulation, we do not hesitate to submit our humble recommendation that such a course should be adopted.'[1]

1 Signed by R. Gordon, E. Ludlow, E. Machen, H. Clifford. Charles Bathurst, the other Commissioner, did not take part in this branch of the Commission, for the reason that free miners' rights were and had been, by some persons, claimed as extending to lands in his ownership.

Appendix No. II of the Fourth Report (1835) records:

'A Schedule of Persons who claimed to be considered Free Miners, showing against whom objections have been made, and the ground of objection.'

[Summary]:

	Walks					
	York	*Worcester*	*Herbert*	*Latimer*	*Danby*	*Total*
(1) Persons considered to be Free Miners	274	209	167	88	60	798
(2) Persons objected to as being Quarrymen, and not having worked in mines	55	39	28	3	18	143
(3) Persons questioned as to birth, and having worked	29	17	14	5	5	70
(4) Persons questioned as to their Fathers not being free	15	13	10	17	14	69
	373	278	219	113	97	1,080

The Commission's Minutes of Evidence run into many pages, and they contain such a wealth of information that for reasons of clarity it has been decided to treat of them by way of the following subdivisions:

(*a*) General.
(*b*) The case for the 'Foreigners'.
(*c*) Memorial by the free miners, and their case against the 'Foreigners'.
(*d*) Memorial by certain free miners objecting to others on the grounds of non-qualification.
(*e*) Timber for Mines.
(*f*) Methods of Working.
(*g*) Mine Law Court (included in Chapter IV).
(*h*) The 'Excepted Lands': Free miners' rights in private property (See Appendix A.)

(*a*) GENERAL

On 16 February 1832, John James of Tovey[1] and James, solicitors, of Newnham, delivered the following claims on behalf of the free miners:

'A free miner is defined to be a person born within the Hundred of St. Briavels, having worked his year and a day in the pits, and abiding within the hundred.

1 Thomas Tovey was at that time deputy gaveller. They had been partners since 1805.

The free miners claim to work the mines of the Forest, having first applied to the King's gaveller for his consent; having obtained such consent (which they maintain cannot be refused) they proceed to open their works, and work them according to the custom of the Forest.

They claim the power of transferring, by will or conveyance, their right in any mine which they have opened to any person, free miner or not, together with all the privileges attending the original right.

They also claim, for such of the free miners as do not use the railroads [tramroads], the use of timber for their works, in whatever way these works may be conducted, whether by the use of steam engines or otherwise.

They also claim that the Mine Law Court shall be re-established for the preservation of their rights; and the settlement of disputes between them.'

Various free miners and others then made the following depositions. William Morgan, of Worrall Hill, free miner, aged seventy,[1] deposed that 'he had known notice by the gaveller to the miner, and by miner to gaveller, that gale [fee] must be advanced or reduced, and such notice (being half a year's notice) would determine the composition.' A similar deposition was given[2] by James Trigg of Littledean, free miner, aged eighty-one, thus: 'I have given notice to lower, and had gale lowered; I have had notice to raise, and had gale raised.' Thomas Meek of Ruardean, free miner, aged sixty-seven, deposed[3] that he formerly 'paid 8s., 9s. and 10s. per vein [seam] per year; within the last twenty years it has been two guineas.' He held one gale for fifty years. 'I was dissatisfied with one gale, and gave notice to the gaveller to put in his man; he never put in a man; I continued, worked it out, and never paid any gale. I have known persons who were not free miners obtain and hold mines by will, but they did not work them after they got them; except in one instance, where a free miner's widow worked it, and then sold to a free miner.' Other depositions were made by William Cook of Whitecroft, free miner aged forty-five, James Teague of Littledean Woodside, free miner aged thirty-nine, Richard James of Whitecroft, free miner aged fifty-three, and John White, free miner and keeper, aged seventy-four. William Williams of Coleford, a free miner, 'at least seventy-four years of age',[4] deposed: 'I consider a free miner to be a male born within the hundred, and working a year and a day at the mines. My father was not a free miner, and I never heard an objection made to a free miner because the parents were not free.' Edward Teague[5] deposed:

'I think the small veins [seams] would employ more men than the large; and that if the large works were stopped more men would be employed; though certainly, if foreigners were driven away, many workmen must at present be discharged, and if large pits were stopped smaller ones would be drowned.'

John James, partner of Thomas Tovey, deputy gaveller[6]:

1 P. 11.
2 P. 13.
3 P. 12.
4 P. 21.
5 *Ibid.*
6 P. 15.

'I have received gales from free miners since 1805, and from foreigners also; I have never granted a gale, my partner did that. I have been present when my partner made compositions with foreigners for mines galed to a free miner, both in cases of foreigner being in partnership with free miner, and when alone. In all cases the name of a free miner stands on the gale book as the owner of the work, though the foreigner's name is used as owing the composition. I have known injunction obtained for trespass in the Forest of Dean, one miner against another; and where the workings have been contrary to custom, I have known injunction obtained by foreigners against free miners; by foreigners and free miners against free miners; and foreigner against foreigner.

I know where the Crown has, at the request of free miner and foreigner, by their own solicitors, Messrs. Green & Co., at the recommendation of the gavellers, obtained an injunction against free miner on behalf of such foreigner and free miner; but I know of no solemn decision as to the title which foreigners derived from free miners nor have I ever known the title disputed. I have known a free miner convey direct to a foreigner, and not through the medium of a trustee.'

Mr. James handed in 'a copy of injunction from the Court of Exchequer 10 Geo. 4 [1829], A-G, informant, John Trotter and others, plaintiffs, against George Gwynne, in which plaintiffs were foreigners, except one named Hawkins; and produced another from the Court of Chancery, Hilary vacation, 11 Geo. 4 [1830], Montague and others, plaintiffs (foreigners and free miners), Thos. Meek and others, defendants (all free miners)'. Edward Machen, one of the Commissioners and deputy surveyor, in reply to the last witness asserted[1]:

'I have known licences to erect engines leading to coal mines, originally galed to free miners, granted by the Office of Woods; they have been granted through me. In communications to the office, the attention of the Commissioners of Woods has been fully called to the facts of the original gale having been made to a free miner, and the subsequent occupation by a foreigner. I have remonstrated with foreigners for employing other workmen than free miners, and I have succeeded in limiting such employment: but I never insisted, or considered that I was entitled to insist, that they should not employ them.'

John Lewis of Lydbrook, free miner aged fifty, deposed that he had worked 'all his days in the mines' adding 'I have worked in partnership with free miners, and all in our company's work are free miners. Our company pays ten guineas for one work, and four guineas for another.' Thomas Davis of Five Acres, free miner, aged eighty, deposed [2]:

'It was always a rule between miners, that the seller and buyer (of a mine) goes to the pit, the seller takes a mattock or pick-axe, breaks a coal and gives it to the buyer, which is giving possession; they then go out of the pit, the seller takes hold of the windlass and turns it into the buyer's hand. There are generally witnesses, and a little agreement was made between themselves; they then had to go to the gavellers, who took the name of the seller out of the

1 P. 16.
2 Pp. 17-18.

book, and put in the name of the buyer. When I was young I never knew a sale of mines in any other way; never any parchment writing. We never wanted anything more between miner and miner. … If a free miner dies intestate, leaving two daughters, one marrying a free miner and one a foreigner, she marrying a free miner had the mine. …

… If a free miner has a son born within the liberty, and he goes away without working his freedom, he may come back after his father's death if he is his heir, and by working his freedom take possession of his father's mine. …

… If foreigners were excluded, I think there is capital enough amongst free miners to carry on the work. I think there is great profit to be got by working the mines. I should consider that the foreigners are making great interests of their money. What is the grief among the miners is, that foreigners should employ foreigners instead of free miners. We should not object to foreigners, if they were obliged to employ free miners to work. …

… A great many of the workmen we call foreigners, are men who have been born in the Forest, but are not free miners. I have known many free miners distressed for employment when foreigners have been in work by preference.

I think the coal is now going quicker than will be for the benefit of this country sometime hence.'

Thomas Tovey, of Newnham, deputy gaveller, aged sixty-nine, deposed[1]:

'I have executed the duty of deputy gaveller since Midsummer 1793, upwards of 38 years. I succeeded Philip Robinson: I am not certain, but I think he was engaged in coal works at that time. I do not know the reason why Mr. Robinson left the office. In the early part of my office, and for some years, he assisted me. The deputy gaveller goes with the miner to the Forest; the miner shows the spot. The gaveller sees whether it is a proper place, and if it do not interfere with another's rights, he cuts a turf from the ground and a piece of stick from a hedge. He cuts as many notches as there are partners in the work, and also a notch for the King; sometimes he has cut one for the gaveller also. He then cuts another stick which has a fork, and with that confines down the other, and then covers it over with the turf. The miner pays a fee to the deputy gaveller of 5s. which is the gaveller's own. I have always allowed the assistant gaveller to take this fee. I have many times galed in private grounds, in which case I do not cut a notch for the lord, but, as in other cases, for the number of partners, and the King, and the gaveller, or in some cases for the partners and the King only: the fee has always in my time, and I believe in Mr. Robinson's, been the same, viz. 5s. I do not think I have any option, but must gavel the ground, if required, and it be within the hundred and do not interfere with other gales, although it may be in private grounds.

Some years ago we used to receive generally one guinea a year, sometimes less; but I think it was about the time the Railways were made in the Forest. People were very anxious to get the mines, and to prevent too frequent galing, it was suggested by me that they should pay two guineas a year, to which those who afterwards took gales consented. The old gales were raised. I consider I have a right to advance the composition to meet the King's share; if the galee will not pay, and gaveller and miner cannot agree, I consider that the King has a right to put in his man.

I have had many disputes, but never went so far as to put in this man; we always came to

[1] Pp. 18, 19 and 20.

terms at last. I never heard that Mr. Robinson put in a man, though I have heard it was done formerly. If a galee disposes of his property to a free miner, I do not always change the name on the gale-book, though I have in some instances done so. I always consider the man on the book to be liable to the gale, although he may have sold his gale. I should not enter the name of any foreigner purchasing a gale as the owner of the gale, but when once a foreigner has paid me gale-money, I consider him tenant of the gale.

I do not think I have ever gone to law to recover gale: in many instances, free miners have sold their mines to foreigners. I cannot say whether it was so before Mine Law Courts dropped. I have drawn conveyances to foreigners myself. If all foreigners were removed from the Forest, I do not say it would be impossible, but it would, perhaps, be doubtful whether free miners could find capital to carry on the works; they would not, I conceive, be so extensively engaged as now.

I do not of my own knowledge know the King's share, but I have understood, from conversations with miners and with my predecessor, that the custom was for the miner to drive his level and sink his pit, and when he came to the coal, then the King was entitled to his fifth share by putting in his fifth man and paying his share of the expenses in working.

I do not know of any instance of any man being put into private lands, but I have heard of its being done; what the lord's right is has always been undefined. I believe that a fellowship in the Forest has always been considered to consist of five, the King forming the fifth. The composition was generally made in proportion to the coal got. The Mine Law Court was before my time. If any advantage is to be obtained by the revival of the Mine Law Court, it must, in my opinion, be revived with extended powers.

I think adding to the St. Briavel's Court, so as to have but one Court, would be most likely to be beneficial. The Forest of Dean is now exempt, in common with other parts of the Country, from the coast duty; I do not recollect ever galing in Mailscot. I have ever considered that a free miner was a man born and abiding within the Hundred of St. Briavels and working a year and a day. I never heard that it was necessary qualification that the father should be a free miner, and I never acted upon it. I have heard, as the reason for the Mine Law Courts being dropped, that the gentlemen could not manage the miners or keep order at the trials. I have heard that the records were removed and came into the possession of Colonel Hopkinson, but I never heard that that was the reason of the Court being dropped, and I do not believe it was so, but that the reason is as I before stated. I think the working free miners would be worse off if the foreigners were driven away. Gales since 4th September 1829, have been mostly made, under the order of the Commissioners of Woods, at two guineas a year till coal gotten, and afterwards at 2d. per ton for the coal gotten, determinable on the usual six months' notice by either party. ... There are at present collieries, mine works, and gale marks for collieries, and mine works to the number of 174, or thereabouts. ... I have been in practice for 47 years; during, I believe, all that time, certainly during 45 years, I have been in the habit of conveying gale property to persons who I believe were not free miners.

In 1786 I drew one to a person whom I believe was not a free miner: it is dated 27th October, and is of the equity of redemption in one-sixteenth of a coal work, and conveyed direct to the mortgagee. The original mortgage was £160, the interest £7, the purchase money £170, making a total of £337, I produce it: "William Howell, of Little Dean, to Philip Robinson, of the same place." It recites indentures of lease and release of the 24th and 25th December 1778, which was a mortgage in fee. It also recites, that the work passed by will, and contains a covenant to levy in St. Briavels' Court a fine to bar dower.

I believe Robinson was not a free miner, though his name is on the gale-book, but I do not know.

I produce another conveyance by lease and release: "Mr. Harvey to Thomas Fisher", both of Newnham, dated 1st and 2nd August 1788; I know that Thomas Fisher, the purchaser, was not a free miner.

The practice of selling and mortgaging collieries has been continued in my office up to the present time, and I have always treated this property as other real estate. Sometimes a name appears in the gale-book which is not a free miner's. I have generally endeavoured to keep a free miner's name on the books, to trace the original gale to a free miner. A work now called Lidbrook Water Engine, stand in the name of Harford, Partridge & Co. on the gale-book: these persons are not free miners, but I consider the original gale was Brown's Green Water Engine, and held by George Morse in 1792. I cannot tell whether he was a free miner or not.'

John Worgan of Five Acres, free miner aged fifty-seven, deposed:

'I think free miners are imposed upon very much by foreigners. They bring in their own foremen and their own foreign workmen; I was myself turned away to make room for a Bristol man, and we cannot remedy ourselves, unless our Mine Law Courts be revived. …

... I have heard that when miners sold to each other they only delivered their tile [?title]; sometimes there was an agreement, and at others not.'

Thomas Beddis of Littledean Hill, aged fifty-two, said his father and others had informed him 'that by the laws made at the Speech House no free miner was allowed to load a foreigner's team; men not free were kept to load. If a free miner did load, he was obliged to plead his cause at the Speech House, and he was fined £5, but the Court could reduce it to 40s.' On 10 April 1832, James Smith, clerk, of Coleford presented the following Memorial and Statement of Claims on behalf of the free miners:

'The Humble Memorial of the Free Miners of the Hundred of St. Briavels, in the Forest of Dean.[1]

The free miners beg leave most respectfully to offer to the consideration of the Commissioners the annexed statement in writing of the heads of their claims, and humbly to request that the Commissioners, in their Report, will be pleased to report specifically upon such heads.

The free miners most respectfully wish also the Commissioners to take into their consideration the distress to which they have been reduced by the disuse of the Mine Law Courts, by which their rights and privileges were formerly protected, and which they have repeatedly solicited to have restored; the consequences of which disuse have been, that foreigners, who had originally no right to enter the mines, have gradually possessed themselves of property therein, and again sold the same to other foreigners, to the exclusion of the free miners themselves; that the free miners have not been able to obtain redress, owing to there being no tribunal except the Mine Courts which could legally investigate their claims; that in many instances they have been arbitrarily despoiled of their possessions by foreigners, and altogether, from the numbers of strange

1 P. 20.

workmen and others introduced into the Forest, and employed in the hauling of mine, coal and ore, the free miners have been deprived of work, and themselves and their families reduced to the utmost distress.'

'Statement of the Claims of the Free Miners of the Forest of Dean.[1]

1st. That the qualifications which entitle any person to the rights and privileges of free miners of the Forest of Dean are, that the said person should be born of free miners within the Hundred of St. Briavels, within the bounds of the said Forest; that he should work a year and a day within the mines, and that he should reside within the above-described boundaries.

2nd. That the free miners alone have any right or title to hold or to work any mines, quarries or coal pits within the said Forest; all other persons being foreigners, and holding and working such mines, quarries or coal pits, wrongfully and illegally, and to the great detriment and damage of the free miners.

3rd. That the ancient Mine Law Courts which formerly and from time immemorial used to be held at the Speech House for the adjudication of all disputes arising between the free miners, should be immediately revived for the purpose of ascertaining what persons have usurped the privileges of the free miners, and of awarding redress.

4th. That the constable of the castle of St. Briavels be the chief judge of the said court, and that the deputy wardens of the castle are the deputies of the said constable, and should preside in the said court.

5th. That the free miners have a right to dig for ore or coal within any part of the boundaries of the said Forest within the Hundred of St. Briavels, on paying the dues to the King's gaveller.

6th. That the free miners have a right to the delivery of timber to them for their work.

7th. That the free miners have sundry other rights and privileges which are laid down in the books and documents relative to the ancient Mine Law Court, and which they claim to have restored to them.'

On 11 April 1832, the Commissioners attended at the Angel Hotel, Coleford, and recorded:

'A great many free miners attended; much discussion took place. The general impression seemed to be, that if foreigners had a bounty allowed for the employment of free miners in preference to foreigners, the former would be satisfied; and that the capital of the foreigner was necessary to the well being of the Forest.'

The next deposition was by John James of Lydney[2]:

'I am an iron-master; I hold iron mines and coal works which stand on the gale book in the names of free miners, who sold to me and my partners their rights for a valuable consideration, and granted leases in 1825 for 1,000 years, at 1/- rent, to two foreigners and a free miner. I have other leases more recently granted.'

---

1 Pp. 20-1.
2 P. 31.

David Mushet of Coleford, deposed[1]:

'I came from Derbyshire to settle in the Forest of Dean. I was acquainted with mines in Derbyshire, and finding they were transferable, I made enquiry about such property here, and finding they were considered freehold, I bought some, and those miners who sold to me knew I was a foreigner.

Three-fourthes of a work called the Gentleman's Colliery I bought of Giles Griffith, which was conveyed to me direct.

A work I bought of William Jerdan and — Blanch, free miners; it was conveyed to a free miner, who executed a declaration of trust that he held it for me: this is the only purchase I made which was conveyed in trust.

I have no works in my possession which were got by employing a free miner to get the gale with a view to transfer it immediately to a foreigner, but I know it has been done.

About eight years ago I bought two works from Edward Protheroe, called Howler Slade Deep Engine and Old Furnace Level; they were conveyed to Edward Protheroe by free miners for a lease of 500 years, in consideration of a small sum of money and an annual rent to each party of 5s. I had a direct conveyance from Edward Protheroe, in which the original lease was recited.

I purchased another work of a free miner named Hawkins, which was conveyed to me by lease for 500 years.

In working our mines we are occasionally obliged to run narrow headings; but I have never done it more than once, and then I was driven to it in self defence. I think instances may occur when narrow headings are fair, but in three cases out of four I think they are illegal.

I think it very advisable that limits should be fixed to all new gales, because they will be opened at much less expense than those at present existing have been opened.

I do not think it would be fair towards old works, as the proprietors have been at very great expense; the works are now proceeding according to arrangements between different parties, and any interference would upset all these arrangements. I think the depth of the pit should determine the limits or extent of coal field.

I produce articles of agreement, dated 15 April, 1776, between Robert Pyrke, of Newnham, gentleman, John Robinson, of Little Dean, Selwyn James, of Chepstow, Thomas Weaver, of Gloucester, Joseph Lloyd of Guns Mills, Thomas Crawley Boevey, of Flaxley, esquire, William Howell, of Little Dean, coal miner, as proprietors of parts or shares in the coal work called the Oiling Gin (a fire-engine), of the one part; and Thomas Hobbs, of Little Dean, Thomas Hale, of the same place, James Tingle of the same place, and Anthony Mountjoy, coal miner, of the other part; by which, in consideration of 2,100 £, twelve sixteenth shares in the said coal work were covenanted to be granted and conveyed to be held in shares.

These purchasers were free miners forming a company to work the fire-engine, and the vendors were foreigners.

The work was originally galed in 1766; the foreigners thus selling had been in partnership 10 years before they sold to the free miners.

I produce another conveyance, dated 1st June, 1766, whereby Thomas Sargent, of Mitchel Dean, baker, conveyed to Thomas Hobbs, in consideration of 120£., one-sixteenth of the

[1] Pp. 30-1.

same engine.

This was a foreigner selling to a free miner.

I produce another, dated 13th September, 1774, whereby Thomas Neele, of the parish of Westerly, Gloucester, engineer, conveyed to Thomas Crawley Boevey, esquire, in consideration of 105£., one-sixteenth in the same work; both are foreigners.

I beg to put in the following paper relative to the King's share and to the lord's, as Thomas Steel, whom I intended to produce as a witness, is dead.'

The above note of the conversation with Thomas Steel reads:

'Coleford, 19th February, 1818.

Conversed with Thomas Steel, aged 75 years and blind, worked in coal works from a boy; says that levels were always entitled to what coal they could dry in the deep side of any other level brought in within 1,000 yards in the land; that a deep level has no right to cut up or cross another man's work so long as the deep level has any coal, and even then he thinks a deep level has no right to take the coal that belongs to another man's work or level. Mendall Level, near Coleford, intended, being a deeper level, to cut across the Young Colliers' Work, but received a forbid. The proprietor then applied to the Mine Law Court, who permitted him to cut a head of 12 feet wide across the Young Colliers' Work, to enable him to lay dry a piece of 'down leap' coal, which otherwise neither Mendall nor the Young Colliers' Level would have dried, but this grant was made with the consent of the proprietors of the Young Colliers', who in return obtained a pit of coal upon the new deep work when the level came forward.

Recollects disputes in old times between the gaveller and the miners, and at Mendall, where six men were then at work, one Phillipps went to the gaveller and took the King's share, and became in consequence the seventh man in the mine; he cut his own coal, filled it, and brought it out; but soon grew tired, and in less than two months it was totally given up, and the usual money-rent agreed to by the gaveller.

A similar circumstance took place in regard to the Young Colliers', where eight men were at work, and the King's man became the ninth; he got his own coal and paid his own charges, but no dead work. He continued but a short time, and the common gale-money was resorted to.

I have known two instances of coal being worked in free land; in Pulwell Level and the Gentleman's Colliery. The lord in each case paid a ninth share of the expenses, and received a ninth share of the produce.'

Philip Robinson, of Hillhouse, near Littledean, deputy gaveller, aged forty-six, deposed[1]:

'My father and grandfather were deputy gavellers. I now assist the gaveller. I have been connected with the Forest system about 34 years.

I have never understood that the foreigners' names were put on the gale-books, though they take shares of works. We never put any other than a Miner's name on if we knew it; but at the same time we knew companies of foreigners were forming.

---

1 Pp. 32-3.

The custom of galing is 2£. 2s. at the time of galing, and a subsequent increase according to the work done.

My father was a partner in the Old Fire Engine Company, and I believe my grandfather had a share in it while they were deputy gavellers.

My grandfather was clerk to the magistrates, and perhaps in that way he got possession of the Mine Law Court records now produced.

When my grandfather and father were joint deputy gavellers they rented the gales from the Crown; they recognised other than free miners as paying gales. I do not recollect the Mine Law Court being held; I have some of the records.

I believe the deputy gaveller always had a right to be at the Mine Law Court; but I am not aware that he acted as a judge or officer of the Court.

I produce certain records of the court of 1744 and other dates.

I produce a printed notice to all colliers, miners and others, renters of gale in His Majesty's Forest of Dean, to pay arrears of gale, signed by J. and P. Robinson.

I produce an agreement, dated 15 April 1776, between Robert Pyrke, of Newnham, gentleman; John Robinson, of Little Dean; Selwyn Jones, of Chepstow; Thomas Weaver of Gloucester; Joseph Lloyd, of Gun's Mills; Thomas Crawley Boevey, of Flaxley, esq.; William Howell, of Little Dean, coal miner; as proprietors of parts or shares in the coal work, called the Oiling Gin (Fire Engine), of the one part; and Thomas Hobbs, of Little Dean; Thomas Hale, of the same place; James Tingle, of the same place; and Anthony Mountjoy, coal miner, of the other part; whereby in consideration of 2,100£. 12 sixteenth shares in the said coal work were covenanted to be granted and conveyed to held in shares.

The parties agreeing to sell were all foreigners; those buying were four free miners.

The name of the work was The Oiling Gin, otherwise Water-wheel Engine at this time, but the original names in the gale-book were different; it was the work belonging to the old fire engine company, which comprised several gales; the Major Suff formed part of it; this was originally galed in 1766 to William Whetstone, John Trigge, William Matthews, James Tingle, William Tingle, Anthony Mountjoy, Joseph Blanch, and Nicholas Annets.

I have heard my father often converse with free miners, and tell them it was their own fault the Mine Law Court dropped, and arose from their own supineness.

Three gentlemen, named Lloyds, came in as heirs-at-law of Robert Pyrke to the one fourth part of the work, which was not sold by the agreement of 1776, and it is now occupied by John Jordan as their tenant.

I have heard my father say, that the original gale was put in by William Howell for the company of gentlemen whose names appear in the agreement of 1776, and that Howell retained one sixteenth for his share, and as a remuneration; that share my father subsequently purchased, and under his will I sold it to Mr. Mountjoy, a free miner, 23 years ago.

I produce an old gale-book, in which is the following entry:

"Gentlemen Colliers Dr.

Mr. Richard Sladen, Mr. Dew, Richard Wilcox, Mr. Dutton, John Hawkins, John Sladen, Henry Wilcox, Henry Yarworth, to 10 Months' gale, due Midsummer 1766, at 4£. per annum, 3£. 6s. 8d." Thus showing that at Midsummer 1766 10 months' gale was due for the Gentlemen Collieries, the gale standing in the names of Richard Sladen, Mr. Dew, Richard Wilcox, Mr. Dutton, John Hawkins, John Sladen, Henry Wilcox, and Henry Yarworth. I produce two papers, marked respectively (A.) and (B.).

They are copies from the gale-book, in the handwriting of my grandfather, then deputy gaveller, and relate to Brown's Green Colliery, and show that the rent was in 1772 paid by Partridge, Platt & Co., who were foreigners, although the names on the gale-book for the original gale were different.

I produce the gale-book, in which it appears that Messrs. Partridge, Platt & Co., are made debtors for gale on Moorwood Coal works in 1773.'

Thomas James, aged fifty-eight, deposed[1]:

'The Rev. Mr. Davis and his sisters became possessed about 20 years ago of a share in a coal mine, called the Gentlemen's Colliery, either as devisees or heirs-at-law of Richard Sladon. Mr. Davis and his sisters are foreigners.

My father was in possession of a share in Arthurs' Folly, another work, it having been left him by will of Matthew Paul, a solicitor of Newent; it descended to me; there were several partners; some of them were free miners; I believe a man named Trusteed was one; but others were foreigners.

My father was, I believe, an honorary free miner, as I find his name in a copy of one of the mine law orders.

Within about the last 30 years I have conveyed coal works in the Forest in the same way as freehold estates.

I think I have prepared wills, I know I have seen them, under which the devisees have taken possession of the shares in these works.

I have known foreigners hold works in the Forest for many years.

Mr. Paul, one of the names in the gale-book (A.), in 1789, page 74, was not, to the best of my knowledge and belief, a free miner.

Arthur's Folly was originally galed, as appears by the gale-book, in 1774, from which the following extract is taken:

"Folley, Arthur Symons's.

William Bennett, 2 shares, Arthur Symons, Mr. Paul (Newent), Mr. Hooper, Mr. Fryer, Richard Powell, George Bond, Mr. Rogers (Usk), partners.

Galed, September 7, 1774, by I. H.: have got coal as much as this two years and a half.

November 25. – Agreed with Richard Powell, Mr. Fryer, Mr. Bennett, for the gale of Arthur's Folley, a coal work; level begun in the 30 acres, and brought up into Little Cross Hill, at 2£. 2s. per annum, from Christmas 1785."'

James Ward, of Bishop's Wood, aged forty-two, deposed[2]:

'My father was not a free miner, I am a foreigner.

I am a coal merchant and wharfinger, I have a share in the "Strip-and-at-it" Colliery, and the Cannop Bridge Level.

I bought my share in the former of John Davis, a miner. There are six proprietors; one is a lady.

---

1 P. 34.

2 *Ibid.*

In the latter I am the only foreigner; there are three other partners, who are miners, William Morgan was one until lately, John Hutton, and John Ross. I have several times paid the gaveller the gales for both at the Speech House.

My grandfather was, I believe, a free miner; he was upwards of 80 when he died. I have heard him speak of a Bristol Company, and say that they had works in the Forest.

I have heard my grandfather say, that it was part of the custom, 60 or 70 years ago, for free miners to transfer their mines to foreigners.

The company ceased to exist 40 years ago. I have known sales of mines from free miners to foreigners, and from foreigners to free miners, of recent date. I do not know one instance of an engine of any extent being worked in the Forest by free miners only, without foreigners.'

William Collins, aged seventy-seven deposed[1]:

'I can recollect the Gentlemen Colliers between 60 and 70 years. The partners in the work were John Sladon, Mrs. Dew, Richard Sladon, Mr. Dutton and John Hawkins. I worked for them for 6d. a day. I have seen Richard Sladon at the work; I never saw John Sladon or Mr. Dutton there; I have seen Mrs. Dew there. I do not know whether Mr. Dutton was a free miner or not; I believe Mr. Sladon was, as he had a pit and lived at Coleford. It was called the Gentlemen's Colliers, because they were all gentlemen who had to do with it. I might be 10 or 11 years when I worked for them, but I cannot say exactly; Richard Wilcox hauled at the top of the pit and winded it up; John Hawkins did the same.

More than 60 years ago I remember the Copper Company [of Tintern]; I cannot tell whether they were foreigners, but I dare say they were, because a free miner galed a work to them. I remember a man named Frank Jones; he was the man who galed a coal work in the Five Meadows, and gave it up to the Copper Company. The miners tried to stop the company and could only do it by cutting under and letting the company's work fall in. The Copper Company prosecuted and was beaten, when they gave it up.

Thomas Philips of the Copper Company in a letter dated 10 August 1832 to the Commissioners stated[2]:

'I was anxious to bring the question of the miners' rights before the Commissioners in the form of a legal proceeding, and made some preparation for that purpose. I had procured a gale for a level, and intended to have had it in work according to the claims of right, to avoid any confusion by the workmen, and witnesses would have been produced to give evidence, in number and manner suited to its importance, who, with their expenses, must have been paid, but could obtain no assistance, even of a small loan, from any gentleman of the neighbourhood; and having borne the expenses of these proceedings for many years, I could not at present engage to pay them. A Report against the miners' rights by this Commission will produce great public confusion, and having been the voluntary instrument of tranquillising the Forest in the scarcities of 1795 and 1801, and laid the foundation for the future, I am anxious it may continue.'

1 P.33.

2 Pp. 35-7.

He also deposed that in 1800 he had 100 copies printed and distributed of an earlier edition of the Miners' Laws. Also, that 'the office of gaveller was at this time a sort of pension; the deputy collected about £240 a year in small sums, of from £1 to £2 and £3 a year for the King's right, supposed to be permanent, and paid £100 to his principal, but nothing was paid to the Crown'. He proposed:

'No person alone or in partnership should have more than one licence for a steam-engine or one line of railroad district, the working distances limited, and narrow headings prevented, and more than one gale declared void, or at least no licence granted, and the excess will be given up, which will prevent the vexatious greedy practices complained of.

The Mine Law Courts to be resumed, and held four times a year by a Commission, and above all, a skilful coal viewer appointed gaveller. A very moderate gale rent of £1, £2 or £3, for small works would pay the expenses of both.

If great capitalists, with or without steam-engines, choose to become tenants at will to the Crown, as intimated by one deposition, still let the limitation of distance and one engine on the line be observed, and the narrow heading be prevented as to them. The miners' evidence states the manner of becoming free and the course of galing, for which nothing can be due as commutation till the pit comes into work. Whether first a guinea and then two guineas are demanded a year, in old times nothing was claimed; the march of intellect is very expensive. ... One thing is obvious, and I cannot suppress the pressing it in the court ... that a survey of the whole coal district should be made by a competent person, who should give a plan for the whole draining and working under a competent gaveller, without monopolising or regard to selfish objects.'

In a letter dated 20 August 1832 to the Commissioners, William Williams, coal miner, of Coleford, stated[1]:

'This meeting having been called for the benefit of the free miners of the Forest of Dean, with a view to re-establish their rights and old privileges, I beg to assert, from my own knowledge as a free miner, that there are at the present time hundreds of that body and their offspring in a starving state, and inevitably thrown on their respective parishes from one sole cause: that is, there are men of all classes and trades from other parts beyond the limits of our old established bounds allowed to carry coals on all occasions, and to all markets thereby depriving this great body of free miners and their families of their rights and only means of support. Gentlemen, I beg to remind you that it was ever our rule, and invariably put in force, to inflict a penalty of 5£. in every case where the getter, that is, the owner of the works, loaded or suffered to be loaded any of these people's waggons or carts who were not entitled as free miners to haul or carry coals for sale, thereby preserving our rights so far as our limits extended. There are no less than seven parishes now suffering from this infringement; therefore, gentlemen, I beg, in the name and for the sake of every free miner, you will take this as one of our great grievances into your most serious consideration, and once more forward to us the full enjoyment of our privileges, which we have so tamely and injudiciously suffered others to encroach upon. By such an act of justice you will call forth the prayers of every free miner and

1 Pp. 37-8.

their rising generations, and ever gratefully acknowledged, by, gentlemen,.

Yours most obedient and humble servant,

(signed) William Williams.'

There appears to have been a 'Test Case' as to free miners' qualifications, for the same William Williams, further deposed[1]:

> 'I recollect several of the Mine Law Courts being held, and they were very particular then in their admissions. I have had gale works galed to me at different times before Mr. Tovey's time, nearly 60 years ago: one down in the bottom by Howlett's [? Howler's] Slade, and also the Young Colliers. When I was a boy no miner could employ any but one free, by being born in the hundred, without being fined by the Mine Law Court. I was employed then, which I could not have been without I was considered free.'

Cross-examined by Mr. Clarke on behalf of certain free miners, he deposed that his father was a Welshman. He was born in the hundred but his father was never admitted a free miner. He himself was admitted and his gales were galed after the Mine Law Court was discontinued. James Morgan of Littledean Woodside, aged seventy-nine, deposed[2] that he had twice attended at Mine Law Courts, and that on those two occasions there was no claim examined about admittance of free miners. He added that 'according to the rules, if a man was born in the hundred, and worked his year and a day, that was all that was required'. Stephen Jones, of Hoarthorne, 'over eighty-two years of age', deposed[3] that he had worked for Williams, and had never known him interrupted. He added:

> 'Unless the father was born in the hundred, the son could not be put to work his freedom: but it was not necessary that the father should work his freedom as well as be born in the hundred. I have more than once known a boy sent away from working in a mine, because the father was not freeborn; but I have heard that a miner might take a foreigner's son apprenticed for 7 years, and so make him a free miner. The indentures ought to be produced to the Mine Law Court, before a foreigner's son could be admitted, as I have heard say, but I have never seen it done. If a foreigner's son served his apprenticeship, and was admitted, he was as good as any other free miner, and then his sons were entitled.'

(*b*) THE CASE FOR THE 'FOREIGNERS'

The case for the 'foreigners' consisted chiefly of a Memorial presented by David Mushet on behalf of himself and others, and a long deposition by Edward Protheroe who was the largest proprietor of coal and iron mines in the Forest. In addition, on the 22 August 1832, Hall and Hooper, solicitors, of Ross-on-Wye appeared for Thos. Trotter & Co., proprietors of Howler's Slade or Vellet's Level[4] and other

---

1 P. 52.

2 *Ibid.*

3 Pp. 52-53.

4 Originally galed, at £3 12s. per annum, to Jas. Williams, John Nicholls. Rbt. Turner. Geo. Bradley, Chas. Gibbons, Francis Meek and Thos. Nicholls.

collieries, The Strip-and-at-it[1] Company and the Cannop Bridge Company. On their behalf they claimed[2]:

'rights to be lessees and to purchase and transmit gales and mines. ... We claim under deeds of conveyance from free miners, and as in partnership with free miners. We do not claim to hold except where a free miner intervenes between us and the Crown, and we claim that the free miner has a right to sell a gale to foreigners. ... Our clients are partly free miners and partly what are called foreigners. ... Foreigners claim in all respects to treat gales thus obtained as freehold property.'

Mr. Hooper of the above firm of solicitors deposed[3]:

'I was articled to my father in 1802 or 1803, and have been admitted nearly 24 years. During the early part of my clerkship, and since I have been in practice, I think upwards of 50 conveyances by lease and release, and also by long demises from the free miners of shares or parts of collieries, have been executed to both foreigners and to free miners, and from foreigners to foreigners, by way of sale for a valuable consideration, and for various purposes of assurance, as of other freehold property. I have prepared mortgages and other securities in the nature of mortgage, both in fee and by demise, in the usual manner of such securities upon ordinary and real estates.

This has been the practice of the office long before I was articled. I have levied fines to bar dower in the Common Pleas on conveyances and mortgages, where the husbands have not been free miners as well as where they have been, and it was the custom of professional men at that time to treat these gales wholly as estates of inheritance. I never knew the rights thus to sell and mortgages questioned or disputed until this Act had passed, and many of my clients have lent heavy sums, which I certainly should not have allowed them to lend, and bought shares in collieries, which I should not have allowed them to purchase, had I considered that any doubt could exist as to title.

I have known, where monied persons have formed a company for working gales, declarations of trust have been prepared, that the free miner who had the gale should stand possessed of the work for the partners, according to the shares they had in it.

I have made and acted under wills in which the gales have been charged as free hold property, with legacies, which have been duly paid, and provisions for children, which have been duly raised.

I have never had under my cognizance a conveyance of a gale taken by a free miner at the suggestion and for the benefit expressly of a foreigner, the free miner being remunerated for the use of his name in obtaining the gale. I have heard of such things, but know nothing of them.'

Some of the free miners wanted the 'foreigners' to continue in the Forest, for example John Lewis deposed that 'the removal of foreigners would cause more evil than good to the Forest as they employ so many miners'. Again, Peter Teague asserted that 'if foreigners were prevented working, it would be a serious injury to

1 Originally galed to a free miner named Gagg.
2 P. 29.
3 Pp. 29-30.

the Forest and if the large engines were stopped the Forest would be drowned because they draw the water from other works.' He was of the opinion that 'if foreign capital were withdrawn, and the present mode of working mines put an end to, it would be wholly impossible for the free miner to work the mines; they could not find the capital, and it would ruin the Forest.' Further, the general feeling of the miners at a meeting at Coleford on 11 April 1832, was on the same lines. On 12 April the same year at the Bear Inn, Newnham, Edward Protheroe presented to the Commissioners a list of thirty gales held by him through free miners, for which he paid to the Crown £273 7s. 6d. a year plus £48 5s. for engine licences. In addition, he had two new gales and had applied for others. His depositions[1] to various questions put by the Commissioners are given below:

(*I*). *'At what time and in what manner did you become possessed of this property?* I was first connected with the Forest of Dean about the year 1809 or 1810, when my late uncle, John Protheroe, asked me to take some shares in a railway about to be formed to connect his coal works and iron furnace with the Severn. I took originally 20 £50 shares; but as subscribers could not be found to complete the undertaking, I gradually increased my number, as money was required, until I held 1500 shares, being nearly half the concern. I was privy to and present at many of the original bargains and arrangements made with the Crown and the miners for accomplishing the objects which they had in view that of the miners being to obtain cheap and quick conveyance to the great markets of the Severn and the Wye, and that of the Crown to obtain security for the Royal timber, and at the same time to create an improvement in the condition and habits of the Forest population. In long continued discussions and negotiations with the Commissioners of Woods and Forests, and the Crown Officers, it was clearly understood and acknowledged that these objects would be best obtained by the formation of railway communications, to be undertaken by the different capitalists interested in the Forest mine works, and by their friends and connections. These persons were, according to very ancient custom, either partners with free miners or lessees under them, or possessed of coal and iron mines conveyed to free miners in trust for their use.

My uncle was either partner or lessee in various works, and he was constantly purchasing additional shares either for money paid down or annuities to the free miners. About the year 1812, in conjunction with my late relative Thomas Waters, I purchased the principal part of my uncle's collieries for the sum of 20000 guineas; and after we had expended a considerable amount in their improvement, I paid to the executor of Mr. Waters £25,000 for his moiety of the Park-end works. I have since secured, in the usual manner, additional gales, and sunk additional pits connected with those works. In the year 1825 or 1826, I purchased the Great Bilson coal works of the Bullo Pill Company and I consider that the whole coal property in the Forest, now held by me, has cost not less than £200,000, and that I have myself expended in the coal works and railways more than that amount. Every transaction has taken place with the sanction of the Crown Officers, and with the general knowledge of the free miners, and without any hindrance, protest or legal objection on their part.

(*II*). *In what way has the sanction of the Crown Officers been given?* In the first place by their making the Crown a party to the different Acts of Parliament for forming railways in

[1] Pp. 22-7.

the Forest at the expense of the foreigners (as they are called), who held coal and iron mines, with whom they concerted all those clauses in the said Acts designed to give security to the Royal timber, and which have actually produced incalculable benefit to the Crown property, this security being only obtainable through our intervention.

Secondly, by their entering the various conveyances and leases of gales from free miners to or for foreigners, in the Crown books, and receiving the rents and dues from the foreigners.

Thirdly, by their granting after such transfers, licences for engines and railroads, etc. directly to such foreigners describing the mines or works as the property of the said foreigners.

Fourthly, by their lending to the foreigners so possessed of works in the Forest the protection and direct interference of the power of the Crown in suits against free miners illegally interrupting the proceedings, or injuring the property of the foreigners, as occurred in my case in the year 1824, when the attorney-general filed a bill in the Exchequer for my protection against the Churchman Company of free miners, and obtained an injunction on their proceedings, which was acquiesced in and obeyed. In that bill the whole process of galing and acquiring possession of mines by the free miner, is distinctly described, and it is declared that after such grant has been so made to any free miner, such free miner is deemed and considered to have acquired an absolute and exclusive right to dig for coal, commencing from the place so galed to him, according the laws and customs aforesaid, and to have a power of assigning such right for any number of years to any person or persons.

Fifthly, by the written explanation and declaration from Lord Lowther, when Chief Commissioner, to myself, in a letter dated 8th June 1830, written in answer to a formal enquiry on my part. His Lordship's words are "With respect to works carried on under licence from the Crown, we can have no intention of disputing a right exercised under such a licence, as that would be to quarrel with the title which we ourselves confer."

(III). In the Exchequer suit to which you allude, was not the name of the attorney-general necessarily used, pro forma, and the bill in fact filed by your own lawyers? Decidedly not. It is only in very strong cases that the local officers of the Crown recommend the Commissioners of Woods to interfere in Forest disputes, and then their protection is given in the most effectual and handsome manner. In the instance which I have mentioned, such a recommendation was given. The suit was commenced by the direction of the Commissioners, and conducted by their solicitors, the attorney-general, the solicitor-general, Mr. Roupell and Mr. Fane, being the Counsel employed, and the whole expense was born by the Crown. The bill recites that by certain deeds of assignment I had become and was then entitled to all such coal works, etc.

(IV). Are you not aware that it is contended by the free miners that no foreigner can, by the Laws of the Mine Courts, be legally possessed of, or work any Forest mine? I have never heard such opinion, except from a few disappointed men who had been unsuccessful in trying to make money by us. The most intelligent of the free miners, whose authority is considered the highest among themselves, distinctly acknowledge that they may sell their rights, or at all events lease them to a foreigner. Mr. James, their chosen solicitor for maintaining their rights and privileges upon the occasion of this commission, declares that the free miners claim the power of transferring their rights to any person, free miner or not. Mr. Lucas, another solicitor of great authority, and steward of the Court of Attachments, says, that he has been accustomed to make no distinction between the free miner and foreigner in supplying the Crown timber, and adds that his father, the most experienced solicitor,

maintained the legality of our titles. I may add, that their Mine Law Book (if any authority be attached to such a confused collection) expressly says "twenty-four. Also, every miner in his last days, and all times, may bequeath and give his dole of the mine to whom he will, as his own chattel; and if he do not, his dole shall descend to his heir." In point of actual custom and practice, no doubt or difficulty ever occurs. Conveyances, leases and mortgages, of almost all the mines in the Forest have been made to foreigners, or to free miners in trust for them, and the attempt to subvert or disturb such vested interests, would be a complete revolution in the established laws and customs of the district, without the least benefit to one individual.

(V). Do you not consider that your acquisition of the mines deprives the free miners of a beneficial interest and occupation? Far from it. The free miners have not the means of rendering the deep coal mines of the Forest available to them. Wherever the veins were sufficiently shallow to be accessible by short levels, or horse gins, there the free miners exercised their rights themselves, generally in large companies, and in some few instances they have combined to erect a steam-engine, dividing their works into small transferable shares, but even in these, foreigners have been admitted as partners when their aid was wanted. These works are confined to the crops of the mines where the cost of sinking and working is small; they do not attempt to send coal to the Severn, but principally supply the local country demand at higher prices; and I abstain, as much as possible, from interfering with them in this trade. As this shallow coal was becoming exhausted, the attention of the miners was directed to the deeper coal, which is accessible only by means of the steam-engine, and its expensive pumping and drawing machinery. The free miners took out gales by way of experimental speculation, and in the first instance bargained with strangers possessed of capital for the opening of these works on the terms of holding shares therein themselves; but it was soon found that disagreements and quarrels ensued, and the free miners were obliged to be bought out. It was also found that the expense of opening a deep colliery was so enormous, and the difficulty of establishing a new trade was so great, that the first adventures among foreigners expended their fortunes and received no return to encourage them or others to go with the system. This was the case with my uncle, who never received back one shilling for his large expenditure. Under these circumstances, he offered his works for sale, and I bought them in conjunction with Mr. Waters, upon the express condition that he should get conveyed to us all the shares of the various free miners who were concerned in the different collieries as partners with him. These shares he purchased for different considerations either in ready money or annuities, some of which I continue to pay to this day. I never heard of the least doubt or difficulty as to the right of conveying or leasing in the way before mentioned. The free miners then finding that there was no profit to induce strangers to embark their money in the objectionable mode of partnership with them, adopted the system of taking out gales in the most eligible places, and disposing of them to strangers for a small sum of money paid down, and a nominal rent for a long term of years. It is generally acknowledged that these considerations, however small, together with other advantages attending the system, have been much more beneficial to the free miners than their independent speculations. They are mostly working men, and are employed in sinking the pits, in managing the machinery, and in working the mines. It is well known that the condition of the whole population has been decidedly improved by the expenditure of our great capital in the Forest. I have myself paid to free miners about £6,000 as direct

consideration, or in annuities, and the amount of wages paid by me in the last 12 years to colliers, hauliers and labourers, is upwards of £150,000, giving constant employment of the average to from 400 to 500 individuals, full nine-tenths of whom are natives of the Forest and its neighbourhood.

(*VI*). *Though some of the free miners may thus benefit from your operations, will not others be injured, and can the free miner who may be no party to such an arrangement, have any redress from this invasion of rights claimed exclusively by them?* The whole body of free miners have the opportunity of benefiting, and in truth do benefit, by the system pursued; and we do not pretend to invade or exercise ourselves the rights exclusively belonging to them, nor would the Crown officers permit us to do so. In point of fact, all the free miners together are not possessed of capital sufficient to open and carry on one deep coal work, and all the valuable mines of the Forest would be locked up if they had not the power to assign their rights of opening and working pits galed to them. As every free miner has an equal right to take and transfer a gale, and there are situations in abundance unoccupied, it is evident that the open competition for bargains must bring the treaty between the free miner and foreigner to a fair consideration for what is conferred. I expressly deny that the free miners possess or ever claim, or have any interest in possessing or claiming the exclusive right of opening and working coal; but even if they could have substantiated such a right or claim upon the ancient system, new circumstances have arisen which would interpose serious obstacles to their obtaining any redress from the invasion of such rights. The deep coal cannot be worked without the power of steam-engines, and the Crown does not acknowledge the right of the miners to erect buildings on the surface of the ground. It has taken power by Acts of Parliament to grant leases or licences for steam-engines for a limited period, and for these an annual rent is paid, and sundry conditions and obligations are imposed on the occupier. The wording of these Acts has, I believe, crept on in adding to the authority of the Crown; but unless the free miners are prepared to contest with the Crown in law or equity, their independent right of using the surface land for the erection of all buildings and machinery required for the underground works, it is evident that they have no beneficial right which is not dependent on the discretionary will and acts of the Crown; now the Commissioners and Crown officers have, in perfect consistency with the general system adopted in the Forest, recognized and acted upon the legality of the assignments in question, and actually granted to us foreigners the leases and licences for our roads, engines and buildings. They cannot therefore grant other leases and licences for getting the same coal, nor can any free miner justly complain of the denial when he is told that the Forest lies open for his choice of gales, and that the same facilities will be afforded to him or his assigns in his fair and legal pursuits. The question after all is founded on a visionary assumption. Though there is something specious and tempting in the proposal to turn rich men out of their improved property and divide it among those that are poorer, yet the foresters in general have sense enough to understand the fable of "The Belly and the Members", and know that they would be the first victims of such an impolitic change, were it ever so easy. I need hardly add that the Crown, the railway companies, the landowners, and the whole neighbourhood, would suffer from the consequences.

(*VII*). *Do not the free miners complain of your employing strangers in your coal works?* I have sometimes heard such complaints when work is scarce, but though I strenuously set my face against any right or claim on their part to prevent my employing whom I please, yet I direct my managers to give the most decided preference to foresters. At the present period I have only about eight or nine strangers in my works, and all these have been in my employ from eight to seventeen years. The truth is, that although complaints come from the foresters of our employing strangers, it is the free miners themselves who really adopt that practice in their own collieries, as they do not scruple to engage any man who may offer, if they can save 6d. in the wages.

(*VIII*). *Is there not something collusive or deceptive in the mode of your making use of the agency of a free miner to obtain the gales for a mere nominal consideration?* I think not; no secret is made of the exact nature of the transaction, which is well known to the officers of the Crown and the whole country. In point of fact, no party whatever is either deceived or damnified. The Crown is benefited by the acquisition of payments in the shape of fees, rents and royalty, or composition, all of which would be lost but for this system. The free miners employed in taking the gales get a small sum, which is clear gain, and obtain other advantages already noticed. I maintain they obtain the full value of what they transfer, and in illustration of this, I appeal to the judgment of any surveyor or experienced miner, whether, after I have paid the free miner £5 for his day's work, and engaged to give him 5s. a year rent, and have then expended from £10,000 to £30,000 in sinking the pits and opening the coal works, I could obtain, when it was finished, the amount of my expenditure if it were offered for sale, or perhaps half that amount. The principal reason of this, is the very great expense in erecting and maintaining powerful steam-engines, owing to the extraordinary quantity of water in our Forest mines, when compared with those of rival coal districts. And this extra expense more then counterbalances the smallness of our royalty. The truth is, that the only persons who have ever ventured to open deep coal works have done it to serve their interests as railroad proprietors: at least I can answer for myself. The Crown, the free miners, the lawyers and the railway proprietors are the only persons who have ever received money from such undertakings. If the free miners had been able and willing to open collieries for the supply of the railways, I would never have interfered with them.

(*IX*). *Are you not, in point of fact, in possession of the principal part of the deep coal of the Forest, so have to have a monopoly in your hands of the hard coal trade?* There cannot be a greater mistake than such an assumption. Though the extent of my works, or rather of my actual working, is very great compared with that of others; yet it is comparatively trifling in reference to the great coal field of the Forest. Upon a rough calculation made by intelligent persons, it is estimated that the whole of my works and gales will not command more than one-tenth of the workable coal of the Forest; so that there is no pretence for a charge of monopoly nor any occasion for jealousy. Collieries of far greater extent than mine, may at this moment be obtained precisely in the same way and at much less cost than mine, since the reduction in the price of coal has led to various economical improvements in the sinking and opening of pits. I will readily undertake not to interfere with any adventurers disposed to lay out their money in this manner, and, as a proprietor in the railways, I shall rejoice to witness more spirit in such speculations.

(*X*). *What is the depth of the shafts of your coal works?* The depth of my principal pits at Park End and Bilson varies from about 150 to 200 yards. That of my new gales for which I have engine-licences, is estimated at from 250 to 300 yards. I have 12 steam-engines, varying from 12 to 140 horsepower, nine or ten of which are at work, the whole amounting to 500 horsepower; and I have licences for four more engines, two of which must be of very great power. My works have an additional importance as being connected with extensive iron works dependent on them for a supply of coal. These iron furnaces and forges have recently been erected at the cost of about £100,000 and the whole property is held under the rights and titles of foreigners. I may add too, that upon both iron and coal works so held, very large sums belonging to ladies, minors and others have been advanced and secured by mortgage, and that the whole value of the railways, in which £200,000 have been invested, would be sunk and lost by the destruction of the trade depending on our capital.

(XI). Do you not think it might be practicable to introduce some new regulations affording a partial advantage to the free miners, either in the amount of gale-rent or in some other mode when they work their own coal? I should consider such a novel attempt as unjust and impolitic, as it would be inconsistent with the present laws and customs of the Forest and the practice of the Crown officers. It would be nothing less than reverting to the barbarous and exploded system of bounties and partial privileges, which the wise policy of modern government is taking pains to abolish, besides the close competition of the coal districts of Staffordshire, Shropshire, Monmouthshire and Glamorganshire (which possess very superior advantages in the thickness and dryness of the veins of coal), cuts down our profits to the lowest degree at which we can continue to work, and we can hardly afford to pay the small composition now settled in our arrangements with the gaveller.

(XII). Should you make any objection to a fair plan of partition of the coal of the Forest, in which due regard should be had to the rights of existing works, as well as to a fixed equitable compensation for the interest of the Crown? Being under the present system, in possession of extended works, and the means of securing them according to the Forest laws and customs, I am not desirous of any experiments which might injure my comparative situation, but it is not my disposition to throw impediments in the way of any permanent regulations that may be thought desirable by this Commission for the benefit of the Crown property and the Forest population. I am apprehensive, however, of great difficulties in the settlement of any such plan; those possessed of collieries opened at a great expense, will naturally demand a corresponding extent of boundary secured against invasion or injury; and the thinness of our veins and the remarkable perviousness of the strata for the passage of water, which is so fatally abundant, would justify an extent of demand that would probably be thought unreasonable by those who have accurately investigated the expense and duration of the forest-colliery; yet if the works now opened were not invested with the privilege of obtaining all the coal that could by any means be dried by their machinery, there would be a great hazard of a total failure of supply. It matters not who might enjoy the right of opening collieries upon the allotments made to others, if a calculation of the profit to be obtained by the coal that they contain, would not show the probability of a return of four per cent., upon the necessary expenditure in sinking the pits and raising the coal. The works now open and in use are estimated to have cost £500,000, and would supply double the present demand, but there is a constant renewal of expense to be calculated upon, as the levels are continued and new draining pits are sunk. Still this expense is trifling compared with

the great and indefinite cost of establishing new works, which no prudent man would encounter in the present state of trade. It could in fact only arise from the spirit of the dog in the manger, that any one would raise an objection to another being allowed to take and use that which he himself would not venture to use if he had it given to him. Still I have heard of such absurd propositions on this point, that I am mistrustful of any reasonable adjustment. I am most ready to admit, that in one respect the plan would be most desirable. However good our titles may be for possession, we know that they are not legally marketable, unless in our own district, where the whole system is known and understood. A variety of causes may render sales of importance to us, and for one, I should be quite content to make some sacrifice of profit, but a small addition to the Crown rent in return for a clear title to a definite extent of coal property, which might be worked or not at the pleasure of the owner. I am ready at any moment to enter on a fair discussion of any plan for accomplishing these objects.

(*XIII*). *Are you prepared to submit any plan of your own for the consideration of the Commissioners?* I am not, not having turned my attention to the details of the subject.

(*XIV*). *Have you seen the suggestions communicated to the Commissioners by Mr. Mushet, and if so, what is your opinion of them?* I have only just seen the paper and cursorily perused it. Any proposition from a person of his intelligence and experience must be entitled to respectful attention, but it is quite apparent that Mr. Mushet's views are chiefly directed to collieries worked by level. Still his suggestions appear to me generally correct and fair, and I should not object to take them as the basis of a plan to be matured by free discussion.

(*XV*). *Would you object to admit the restriction proposed by Mr. Mushet on carrying on narrow headings?* According to the present Forest laws applicable to water-pits, absurdly limited as is generally thought to the protection of 24 yards round the pit, we have no available means to secure ourselves against the iniquitous spoliation, except the plan of running narrow headings; and I am quite sure that in practice the system cannot be carried to an extent beyond what is required for the just protection of deep works. I have never heard the legal right of thus cutting out questioned by any one; I have only used it against other miners as a defensive measure, and that only in one or two instances where my natural rights were invaded. The proceeding was avowed and justified in the bill filed by the attorney-general for the Crown and myself against the Churchway Company of Free Miners, and the legal right was never questioned by them. They themselves attempted to defeat my proceeding and to gain the coal by a cut out, but they were stopped by an injunction, upon the express ground that the cut out was not commenced from the level of a vein of coal according to the Forest law; still I do not at present see any objection to an equitable arrangement restricting the exercise of this power of cutting narrow headings, according to Mr. Mushet's suggestion, but it would require consideration to guard against the risk of abuse and injustice.

(*XVI*). *As you enjoy your rights under the free miners, do you not consider yourself bound to work as free miners would work, and it is stated in evidence, that narrow headings were not the custom of the Forest till* 17 *or* 18 *years ago?* Certainly, I am bound to adhere to all the legal customs of the free miners; but I am prepared to show the falsehood of the evidence mentioned, and that narrow headings are of ancient use, as they are of indispensable necessity, under their laws. No prudent man would commence a work within the limits of injury by such a mode of working, and the extent of our headings is always sufficiently known to apprise others where they are safe against being cut off. There is another effectual protection against our abuse of the right: it is our great object to secure our deep works against the land-water, and were we to run our headings up to the level of shallower works, we should have all their water thrown upon our engines, and they, our rivals, would work in dry coal.

(*XVII*). *Have you not made use of the plan of cutting back in the vein, to the injury of others works: and do you consider that plan justified by Forest laws and customs?* I am surprised to hear any doubt on the legality of cutting back, after passing through a vein, to a deeper part of that vein, provided the gale be taken from the level of another vein. The question was solemnly argued years ago before the deputy gavellers, who, after hearing the testimony of aged miners, decided in favour of such right, and have constantly granted such gales. I am not aware of ever having myself exercised the right offensively, or even defensively; but in several instances it has enabled me to double the extent of coal acquirable from a colliery, and at a very moderate expense. For instance, I have lately gained by such a cut back at my Bilson works, a new coal work, at the cost of less than £2,000, which could not otherwise have been obtained for less than probably 10 times the expense; but I have injured no one by this proceeding. There is no coal work to the deep to be robbed of any of its supply, my own gale being the next. I may say the same as to a similar cut back at Park-end; and why any persons should wish to prevent the coal being worked in the cheapest manner, I cannot conceive. When such gales are applied for, the gavellers give notice to the neighbouring coal owners, who attend and state any objections, if there be ground for them; and the gavellers are now in the habit of attending very much, not merely to the law, but to the equity of all proceedings of the kind. I can appeal to them whether I have ever persevered in any proceeding which they have discountenanced.

(*XVIII*). *Have you ever had your attention directed to the efficacy of the Mine Law Courts, and the expedience of their re-establishment?* I am too little acquainted with the construction and practice of those Courts, to hazard an opinion on their advantages. The perusal of the small book containing their laws and customs, would by no means impress me with a high opinion of their capability, as law makers or judges. Generally speaking, there is an advantage in trying questions near home, at little expense; but upon important questions relating to property, it would be highly objectionable for the decision of such courts to be without appeal; they would be peculiarly open to be influenced by prejudices and partialities, though, as referees, their mining experience might render their opinions and judgments useful and important. Probably the establishment of Courts of Arbitration, as suggested by the Lord Chancellor, or the Common Law Commissioners, would supersede the occasion for Mine Courts; but I should make no objection to the reconstruction of the latter, if adapted to the present state of property, and the new modes of working coal, provided always their judgments were open to appeal.

(*XIX*). *Do you see any objection to the division of the Forest into parishes, and the introduction of poor laws?* I cannot conceive a more unfair and uncalled for innovation than this would be. One reason for our establishing our coal and iron works in the Forest, subject to the situation is to numerous disadvantages, was, that we were there free from the operation of the poor laws. Probably we owe much of the quiet and good order among our workmen to this circumstance, and during the 22 years in which I have been connected with the district, I never heard a single complaint from a man in my employ upon the subject, or of a single case of practical hardship arising therefrom; nor have the landowners or inhabitants of the neighbouring parishes any cause for complaint. Nearly a million of my money has been expended within the last 20 years by us foreigners in the Forest of Dean; and the introduction of so much capital, with the excitement thus given to productive labour, has diffused competence and comfort throughout the neighbouring towns, villages and country. It is true, that some burthens may have accompanied these advantages, and some trouble may have been given to the magistrates; but I would beg them and the Commissioners to compare the situation of our poor with that of the poor of other districts, and to consider how remarkably exempt we have generally been from those trying scenes of violence that occur so frequently in other places among a mining manufacturing, or even an agricultural population. I think that I am not mistaken in saying, that the good sense of most of the neighbouring parishes renders them quite satisfied with things as they are, and that they would reply to any questions from the Commissioners in relation to this and any other projects, "Let us alone". Good and pious people have already built churches and established schools, so that we are not in want of the means of instruction and charity, which form an usual object for parochial divisions, and, in truth, we have an improved and improving population; and when the number and occasional distress of the labourers are considered, their quiet, and orderly conduct is very creditable. I may observe, that when work is scarce arrangements are made for dividing it, so as to give employ to as many as possible, and those who can find none emigrate to other districts; but all this would be altered if we were bound down by the ties of the poor laws; in short, I know of no one motive for wishing to introduce them, and I should resist it as an act of the greatest impolicy, as well as injustice.

(*XX*). *Have you any further information or opinion to offer in furtherance of the objects of this Commission?* I am not sure that I correctly understand those objects, since the solemn assurances given to me by the First Commissioner of Woods and the Chief Clerk, as to vested rights and interests, appear to be set aside; but I would beg leave, in the most respectful manner, to represent to the honourable Members of this Commission, the very dangerous consequences of unsettling opinions on long-established rights and usages, upon confidence in which depends the fortunes of hundreds, and the livelihood of many thousands; at the same time, I offer to them and to the Crown my cordial assistance and influence in settling, in a just, prudent and benevolent manner, all questions of doubt or difficulty affecting the rights and interests of all parties concerned in the Forest of Dean; and if, from any motives, it be desirable for the Crown to obtain possession of the mines, I am ready to give up my interests for a fair consideration, calculated either upon the cost of the works, or their present and prospective value.'

The Memorial, dated 12 April 1833, presented by David Mushet on behalf of himself and others, was[1]:

---

1 Pp. 44-5.

'The Memorial of persons not Free Miners, Proprietors and Occupiers of Coal and Iron Mines in the Hundred of St. Briavels, in His Majesty's Forest of Dean.

Setting forth,

That your memorialists have by purchase, partnership, inheritance or otherwise, become possessed of coal and iron mines as above, to which they claim to be lawfully entitled under the rights immemorially exercised by the free miners, under the sanction and authority of the Crown.

That your memorialists having been called upon by your Honourable Board to produce evidence of their claims so derived, and of the working of mines by persons not free miners in the Forest of Dean, beg leave to state in the first place that such usage is of long standing; in proof of which, they refer you to the Third Report of the Commissioners of Land Revenue, p. 17, wherein it is stated that as early as 1675, only 12 years after the re-establishment of the Mine Law Court, several gentlemen and freeholders of the Parish of Newland, not free miners, associated themselves together for the purpose of working and selling coal not for profit to themselves, but for the benefit of the public, and for the declared purpose of counteracting the effects of a monopoly in coal, then being about to be established by the free miners, under the abuses sanctioned by the Mine Law Court such an association claiming an equal right to dig and work coal with the free miner, and in the immediate vicinity of his works; nor does this claim seem to have been objected to on the part of the free miners as the resolutions of the Mine Law Court, are silent upon the subject.

Your memorialists have further to state, that upon a careful examination of the proceedings of the Mine Law Court, as seen in the various resolutions passed in that court from time to time, associations of persons, not free miners, for the purpose of working the mines, must then, as now, have been attended with great public advantage, as the tendency of its whole proceedings had little or no regard to the working and equitable administration of the mines, but to sustain an illegal monopoly as to price and carriage against the consumer in the neighbourhood, as well as in the counties of Gloucester, Hereford and Monmouth.

Your memorialists, in reference to the transactions of the Mine Law Court, and upon a careful examination of all its documentary proceedings, can find no order, or resolution calculated to prevent the working and occupation of mines by persons not free miners; on the contrary, in the resolutions passed in 1775 their connexion with the mines is fully and clearly established, as well as the right of the free miner to sell or bequeath his property in the mines to any persons he may think proper; which facts may be gathered from the four following clauses in that general resolution.

Clause 8 – "Every miner or collier may give his mine or coal works to any person that he will, but if he does give it by will, that person, if required, shall bring the testament, and show it to the court, but if it is a verbal will, he shall bring two witnesses to testify the will of the miner."

Clause 16. – "Foreigners (i.e. persons not free miners) having any mine or coal work carried on in the Hundred of St. Briavels, shall sell it to some free miner by private contract if they can, or otherwise expose it to sale by auction, by the Mine Law Court."

Clause 17. – "If a free miner dies and leaves his mine or coal works by will or testament to a foreigner, or if it come to him by heirship or marriage, he shall sell it as aforesaid, or hire free miners to work it for him."

Clause 18. – "If any free miner sells any mine or coal work to a foreigner, he shall be liable to a penalty of £20, to be recovered in the Mine Law Court."

Your Memorialists, in the further elucidation of their case and evidence, have examined the earliest gale-books that have been found, and in which, between the years 1765 and 1778, they find the entry of several gales, wherein the names of free miners with foreigners are inserted, also the names of foreigners alone, and that such gales were made when the Mine Law Court was in full operation.

That your Honourable Commission have it also in evidence from Mr. Robinson, that one of the late gavellers galed in 1766 the Arling [Oiling] Green Water Engine, Major Suff and Churchway Fire Engine, for a company of persons not free miners. That the said persons, not being free miners, continued to work the same for 10 years, allowing the free miner that galed the same a share for his management, when the greater number sold out their interest to the extent of three-fourths of the whole to free miners by direct conveyance in 1776.

That your Honourable Commission have not only had the draft of this agreement of sale laid before you, but sundry other drafts of conveyances of coal property from the year 1773 to 1778, some from free miners to foreigners, others from foreigners to free miners, and some from foreigners to foreigners; the most of which were completed before the abolition of the Mine Law Court.

Your memorialists have also laid before you the testimony of Mr. Tovey, who has been the King's gaveller for 39 years, who is intimately acquainted with the modes by which the mines of the Forest of Dean have been conveyed by free miners to foreigners, and from foreigners to each other; and who has been in the constant practice of framing conveyances for this purpose during the last 50 years. You have also the evidence of his partner, Mr. James, of Messrs. Hooper and Edwards, attornies of Ross, and Mr. James of Coleford, to the same effect, as well as the transmission of shares in the mines by foreigners as property of inheritance.

Your memorialists, in short, have laid before your Honourable Commission evidence of an uniform system of practice for upwards of 60 years, wherein mines have been leased, sold and conveyed by free miners to foreigners, who have occupied and worked the same for their own benefit.

Your memorialists beg leave further to state, that they have good grounds for supposing, that could the older gale-books, belonging to Philip Ely, who was crier of the Mine Law Court in 1741, Mr. Cooke, Captain Gough, and other gavellers, prior to 1766, be produced, they would be enabled to shew a continued working in the mines by persons not free miners, from the date of the earliest gale-book in 1765, to which they have had access, back to the year 1675, already referred to in the Report on the Land Revenues, and which would complete a chain of evidence for 157 years.

Your memorialists further crave the attention of your Honourable Commission to this most important fact, and they now solicit for the production of all such gale-books, provided the same can be found, and for all other documentary evidence bearing upon this subject, during this period of 90 years from 1675-1765.

Your memorialists further submit, that all their transactions in respect to the mines in the Forest of Dean have been open, unconcealed, entered into and carried on with the full knowledge and privity of the Crown, who under the authority of its own officer, the gaveller, has from time to time, not only granted gales to, and received rents from, persons, knowing at the time that they were not free miners, as well as having granted them licences for engines to work particular veins of coal, and to make and complete branches of railroads, but also became parties in suits in equity, at the instance of persons not free miners against free miners, wherein His Majesty's attorney-general obtained injunctions to stop the workings of the latter, the same being contrary to custom; and which injunctions, so obtained at the suit of persons not free miners, remain undissolved to this day.

Your memorialists therefore, with perfect confidence, submit, that the honour and good faith of the Crown stand pledged to them to maintain the value and integrity of the investments which they have made in the mines of Dean Forest, and that under so solemn a sanction they confidently hope and believe that for the future the same protection shall be extended to them which they have hitherto enjoyed, and that whatever regulations the Crown may think proper to introduce in respect to the mines for the future, the property of your memorialists shall remain untouched, and stand upon the same footing as that worked by free miners alone.

Your memorialists further assure your Honourable Commission, that the capital possessed by persons calling themselves free miners, is totally inadequate to the opening and working of deep and extensive mines, the construction of public tramroads to carry the produce of the same to market, and of maintaining at low prices, in the face of the Welsh, Staffordshire and Shropshire collieries, that active and unremitting competition, by which only a market can be obtained for the forest coal.

That the capital invested by persons called foreigners in mines and tramroads made under the authority of several Acts of Parliament, amounts to £700,000 and upwards, without the investment of which the mines would have remained comparatively unopened, no tramroads would have been constructed, coal to the public would have been nearly double the present price, the claims of the foresters to timber would have existed, and the Forest itself subject to the same waste and depredation which characterised it in former years, before the introduction of the capital of your memorialists.

Your memorialists, in conclusion, beg to urge upon the consideration of your Honourable Commission, that amongst others the Crown has derived the following direct and important advantages from the introduction of their capital into the Forest of Dean, viz:

An increased galeage from the mines. Fencing the plantations.

An annual ground-rent of £450 in perpetuity.

The establishment of a ready-money market for the sale of large quantities of pit-timber and cord-wood, which formerly went to satisfy the demands of the miners, but which now yield £1,000 per annum.

David Mushet, Coleford.
David Davies, Lydney.
Forest of Dean Iron Company, Park-end.
John James, Lydney.
Thomas P. James, Lydney.
William Montague, Gloucester.
William Bishop, Cinderford.
Cinderford Iron Company, Cinderford.
Montague and Church, Gloucester.
James Fraser, Gloucester.
Samuel Hewlett, Ayleford.
Richard Cox, Oxford.
James Ward, Bishopswood.
John Watkins, Drybrook.
Arabella Holt, Gloucester.
Robert Williams, Gloucester.
Thomas Rudge, Ross.
James Thomas, Winnall's Hill, near Coleford.
Nathan Atherton, Calne, Wilts.
William Whitworth, Stanley, Wilts.
Joseph Priestley, Wakefield, Yorkshire.
William Crowdey, Highworth, Wilts.
Edwin Whitehouse, Lower Redbrook.'

(*c*) MEMORIAL BY THE FREE MINERS AND THEIR CASE AGAINST THE 'FOREIGNERS', 1834.

The case for the free miners against the 'foreigners' was incorporated in the following Memorial delivered by Mr. Clarke, on behalf of the free miners, at Newnham on 24 September 1834[1]:

'To the Honourable the Commissioners of Inquiry into the Rights and Privileges of the Free Miners of the Forest of Dean [1834].

The said Free Miners, in reply to the Memorial presented 12 April 1833, to your Honourable Board, by certain persons "not being free miners, proprietors and occupiers of coal and iron mines in the Hundred of St. Briavels, in His Majesty's Forest of Dean", and which persons, as well as all other persons whatsoever who are not free miners, are known to the free miners by the name of foreigners, beg leave respectfully to state:

That the foreigners themselves assert, that the free miners have "rights", which have been immemorially exercised under the sanction and authority of the Crown.

That the fact which the foreigners thus distinctly bear witness to, is in itself a direct proof that the free miners exercised those rights to the exclusion of all others classes of His Majesty's subjects, since it is plain that the name of free miners would otherwise have been unnecessary and would not have been used.

That as the rights of the free miners, thus "immemorially exercised", have never been abolished by law, they are good, valid and upstanding at the present time; and are, in themselves, a provision against their exercise by any other persons, so long as they remain untouched by Act of Parliament.

That although the free miners cannot deny that foreigners do now possess and work mines in the Forest of Dean, yet they assert that such possession and working are in direct violation of the rights and privileges of the free miners, contrary to their custom and franchises and are acts of injustice and usurpation.

That the free miners altogether deny the truth of the statement made by the foreigners that such usage is of "long standing", affirming, on the contrary, that it commenced and grew up only since the discontinuance of the sittings of the Mine Law Courts.

That the Mine Law Courts were in active working during a period of time beginning far beyond the memory of man and extending down to the year 1777, during which their rules and regulations, under the sanction and authority of the Crown, strictly checked and prevented all intrusion into the mines by foreigners.

That a great proof of the power of the Mine Law Courts, and habitual exercise of it so long as they habitually met, is to be found in the memorials of the foreigners themselves; since, when they complain of the "monopoly" which those courts established and protected, they at least admit that such monopoly was enforced practically in favour of the free miners.

That although the foreigners pretend that foreigners were accustomed to work mines, even during the time that the Mine Law Courts were in existence, they yet complain of the "illegal monopoly" in favour of the free miners which those Mine Law Courts sanctioned and enforced; two statements plainly irreconcilable with each other, since, if foreigners were at that time in the habit of working the mines undisturbed by the Mine Law Courts, then no monopoly could have been exercised to complain of; while, if there was a monopoly

1 Pp. 46-52.

then operating against the foreigners, they clearly could not have been working the mines at all.

That the free miners claim the privilege of holding and working mines in the Forest of Dean to the exclusion of all foreigners.

That whether this monopoly has been or may be advantageous to the public or not, they do not now stop to enquire, but they deny that these privileges can be justly deemed "illegal", which were invariably exercised and enforced by the jurisdiction of the Mine Law Courts, "under the sanction and authority of the Crown", during a period of so many hundred years.

That the legality of the Mine Law Courts, and consequently the legality of their rules and regulations in all matters relating to the mines are established, and proved by the fact of their undisturbed existence, and by the exercise of their authority from times immemorial down to the year 1777, when foreigners, having obtained the discontinuance of those courts which they found to interfere with their intrusion, were enabled to invade the rights and violate the franchises of the free miners with impunity.

That your honourable Board have already in evidence before you, many facts and documents necessary to prove both the antiquity of the Mine Law Courts, and the extent and nature of their jurisdiction; and are doubtless better acquainted with the history of the case than the free miners themselves, who, in addition to their being for the most part poor and unlearned men, are labouring under the disadvantage of being deprived of the ancient records of the Mine Law Court.

That nevertheless, for the better understanding of their case, they beg the attention of your Honourable Board to the statement of such facts in support of their claims, as they are enabled to collect, humbly hoping that your honourable Board will, excuse their repetition of such as you are already in possession of, and will not suffer them to be prejudiced by the omission of such facts as your Honourable Board may be enabled to supply.

That in or about the year 1334, the customs and franchises of the free miners, which had been long previously enjoyed and exercised by them, were confirmed by King Edward 3.

That a printed copy of such franchises and customs, as then confirmed, has been already submitted to your Honourable Board, by which it will be perceived that the peculiar privileges of the free miners alone to work and to hold mines of coal and ore in the Forest of Dean, and to have all matters concerning the mine tried and adjudged before the Mine Law Court alone, and before no other court whatever, are distinctly laid down.

That the privileges of the free miners to work in the mines, and the exclusion of strangers, are to be plainly gathered from the following clauses, to which the free miners entreat the attention of your Honourable Board:

Clause 4. "That the said miners may mine in any place that they will, as well without the said bounds as within, without forbodement of any man."

Clause 30. "Also, that no stranger, of what degree soever he be, but only that been born and abiding within the castle of St. Briavels and the bounds of the Forest as is aforesaid, shall come within the mine to see and to know the privities of our Sovereign Lord the King in his said mine."

Clause 33. "Also, that no smith holder, after he holdeth smith or become partner to hold smith, he shall not have any of the franchises aforesaid within a year and a day."

Clause 12. "Also, the miner hath such franchises to inquire the mine in every soil of the King's of which it may be named, and also of all other folk, without withsaying of any man."

Clause 13. "And also, if any be that deemeth any soil, whatsoever it be, be it sowed or no, or of any degree it may be named, then the gaveller, by the strength of the King, shall deliver the soil to the miners, with a convenient way next stretching to the King's highway, by the which mine may be carried to all places and waters that is convenient to the said mine, without withsaying of any man."

Clause 14. "Further, which soil in the which the mine is within, found, the lord of the soil, at the first time, if he will enter into the said mine freely he shall, and shall have a dole without paying anything at his first coming, and shall be the last man of the fellowship, but moreover he shall do costs as the fellowship doth; and after it please the lord to void, he may well; and if after that it please him to come again, he may well, but he shall make gree for the costs done in the meanwhile for his part, as the fellowship can prove at the pit's mouth; afterwards as another."

Clause 15. "And at all times the King's man shall come into the mines without any costs asked of him, and shall be the third better of the fellowship in maintenance and helping of the mine and of the fellowship; but the King's man, neither the lord's, ought not to enter within the mine till the pit be gavelled", etc. etc.

That the privilege in the above clauses conferred on the miners, of searching for mine in any part of the Hundred of St. Briavels, whether the soil wherein they searched belonged to the King or to private individuals, can by no possibility of legal or legitimate construction be made to extend to any other persons than the miners.

That as this privilege, thus conferred by law, has, as will be proved, been constantly exercised down to the present time, it is of itself sufficient to prove the validity of the other customs detailed in the above clauses, whereby strangers are excluded from entering into the mines.

That by the 26th and 34th clauses the claims of the miners to timber, "as they had in time out of mind, without hurt or attachment of the King's officers", are especially laid down.

That these rights and privileges, which the foreigners now pretend are illegal, were, on the contrary, enjoyed and exercised under the protection and jurisdiction of the Mine Law Courts.

That these courts were presided over by the constable of the castle of St. Briavels, or his deputies, and attended by the King's gaveller, the clerk or recorder of the castle of St. Briavels, the miners, and none others.

That by the 21st clause it appears, "that if any will plead with any miner for a thing touching the mine in any other court, before a justice or any other man, whatsoever he be, then the constable, by the strength of the King, shall require and bring the plaint into the Mine Law, and there it shall be tried by the constable and the miners".

That it is now exactly 500 years ago since the above customs and franchises were confirmed by King Edw. 3; and the free miners are informed, and verily believe, that they continued to be enjoyed by the free miners in the manner therein laid down, from the time of that King until the reign of King Chas. 2, whence, as your Honourable Board are well aware, the records of the Mine Law Court now in existence commence.

That the free miners are unable to refer to any documents or proceedings of their Mine Law Court from the time of King Edw. 3 till that of King Chas. 2, although they verily believe that such were in existence, as well as many other authentic records concerning the same; but of the exercise of the privileges of the free miners in the intermediate time aforesaid they beg leave to adduce the following proof:

That in the ninth year of the reign of King Jas. 1 [1611-1612], that King who, as your Honourable Board well know, was in the habit of assuming rights of absolute dominion over the lives and properties of his subjects which he was unable to reduce into practice, made a grant to William Earl of Pembroke "of the lordship, manor, town and castle of St. Briavels, and all the Forest of Dean, etc., and all mines and quarries". etc.; and in the same year the said earl obtained a grant (among other things) "to dig for and take, within any part of the said forest, so much mine, etc.; and that no person or persons whatsoever, other than the said earl, should be permitted, during the said term, to take or carry out of the said Forest any wood, timber, mine, ore or conder without consent of the said earl".

That the miners nevertheless, in spite of the said exclusive and arbitrary grant, continued to dig for ore in the Forest as by their customs aforesaid they were used and authorised to do, whereupon an information was filed by the attorney-general against some of them.

That in Hilary Term, 10 Jas. 1 [1612], an order was made by the court, "that such miners, and such others as had been accustomed to dig for ore in the Forest (upon their humble submission for these offences, and acknowledgement that the soil was the King's, and that they had no interest therein, and upon their motion by counsel that they were poor and had no other means of support, and praying to be continued in their employment), should be permitted out of charity and grace, and not of right, to dig for mine, ore and cinder, to be carried to his Majesty's iron works and not to any other place, at the accustomed rates, etc.; but no new diggers were to be allowed, but only such poor men as were inhabitants of the said Forest."

That these circumstances are detailed in pages 11 and 12 of the Third Report of the Commissioners of Land Revenues, dated 3rd. of June 1788; and the Commissioners proceed to observe thereon, that "it is probable that all proceedings were stayed, and that all parties acquiesced; and it is conjectured, not without probability, that from this order, by which the inhabitants only were accustomed to work in the mines, were permitted to dig for ore, they have since considered that restriction as an establishment of their right, and a record in their favour, and have from that time called themselves free miners".

That the free miners fully admit the importance of the above order "as a record in their favour"; and they urge upon your Honourable Board that this arrangement was entered into with the free miners by a King so arbitrary that he never surrendered his claims unless compelled by the force of law; and that even with reference to rights which he allowed to the other classes of His Majesty's subjects, he was in the habit of allowing them only "as matter of charity and grace, and not of right", and always talked about his authority when he was compelled to abandon it the most.

That the free miners, however, cannot allow that this "order" was to be considered as the foundation of their rights, since it is clear that they were exercised previous to its being made, and the "order" only confirmed and established them.

That without disputing the King's right to the soil, your Honourable Board will not fail to notice, that the Crown hereby entered into an arrangement with the free miners to continue to them privileges which it expressly denied to all who "were not inhabitants of the Forest, and accustomed to dig in the mines"; and they submit that this is conclusive against the claim of the foreigners now set up.

That these claims and privileges did not subsequently fall into disuse, but that they were enjoyed by the free miners, and acquiesced in and acknowledged by the Crown, is clear from the fact, that in the 10 Chas. 1 [1634], at a justice-seat held for the Forest of Dean, Philip Earl of Pembroke, a descendant of the above-mentioned Earl of Pembroke, "claimed by virtue of the appointment as constable of the castle of St. Briavels, and warden of the Forest, to be chief judge of a court called the Mine Law Court, held for the regulation of the mines of iron and coal, and of the miners".

That although the Commissioners, in their said report, remark that, "this is the first mention they have anywhere found of a Mine Law Court", yet the very fact of the claim being made and allowed is a proof of its previous existence and of its sanction by the Crown.

That it appears also that at this justice-seat the miners "made a claim to be supplied with wood for the works, but that the same were not allowed, they (the free miners) not being a corporation".

That the Commissioners hereupon remark, that if the miners had been "dissatisfied with the reception of their claims, or had thought them well founded, it was in their power to have sued out a writ of allowance, by which they would have been restored to the exercise of their rights, if the decision of the court had been illegal; but this does not appear to have been done".

The free miners must hereupon observe that the inference drawn by the Commissioners that the claims of the free miners must have been ill-founded, because they did not sue out a writ of allowance for their restoration, is altogether fallacious, since, in the first place, so far from being interrupted in the exercise of their rights, the very report here quoted from and referred to admits that they did claim and receive timber as well as wood; and in the second place, as they were poor men, it was not likely nor necessary that they, not being interrupted in the exercise of their privileges, should have resorted to the tedious and expensive process of suing out a writ of allowance, even supposing them to have been acquainted with its nature and with their power so to do, a process which, had it terminated in their favour, would only have had the effect of placing upon record rights which they actually and practically enjoyed.

That in short, as it would have answered no useful purpose to have sued out a writ of allowance, it is not wonderful they should have abstained from so doing, and the free miners must on this occasion take the opportunity of protesting against the doctrine that this or any other of their claims must have been illegal because they were not enforced in other courts of law, since they were restricted from applying to the other courts of justice in the kingdom by the mine laws already referred to, and in the second place they were too poor to have recourse to such costly expedients.

That it is the great grievance of which the free miners complain, that from their poverty they have been unable to obtain, and are still prevented from obtaining, the restoration of the Mine Law Courts.

That the free miners have no evidence of the proceedings of the Mine Law Courts during the troublous times of the civil war and the government of Oliver Cromwell, but that in the reign of Chas. 2, in the year 1663, the Mine Law Courts were assembled during the constableship of Lord Herbert, the Marquis of Worcester.

That at a court held in that year an inquest was made by 48 miners, according to custom, into the rights and privileges of the free miners, when they placed upon record the customs and franchises already referred to as confirmed by King Edward 3, as the then good, valid and inalienable rights of the free miners.

That the Mine Law Courts continued to assemble, as appears by the records thereof already laid before your Honourable Board, from 1663 unto the year 1777.

That these courts not only met with no disturbance or denial of their jurisdiction by the Crown or the Parliament, but continued to meet periodically under the presidency of the constable appointed by the King, and to be attended by his deputies and by the King's Gaveller.

That if there had been anything illegal in these courts, or if the privileges which they secured to the free miners had been destructive to the country, as the foreigners of that time pretended, an excellent opportunity was afforded for determining the same rights when the Act of 20 Chas. 2, c. 3 [1668], was passed, when the Forest of Dean was regulated and apportioned.

That, on the contrary, one of the clauses of the said Act runs as follows: "Saving to the miners and persons using the trade for the digging of mine ore, coal and ochre in the said Forest, their lawful rights and privileges in all the lands and grounds lying within the perambulation and regard of the said Forest (other than the said inclosures for the time they shall continue inclosed) as full and absolutely as if this Act had never been made."

That those rights and privileges are of so strange and exclusive and important a nature, that they never would have been saved to the free miners if they had not been so established by previous laws and confirmed by custom, that the Legislature could neither honestly gainsay nor equitably abolish them.

That the free miners having now traced the history of the Mine Law Courts, and of the practice of the free miners, from the reign of King Edward 3, through the reigns of James 1, and Charles 1, to the reign of Charles 2, and having proved that the essence of these privileges consisted in the working of the Mine Law Courts and the exclusion of foreigners, now arrive at the period when the foreigners pretend in their memorial they have found a proof of their usage in working the mines as well as free miners.

That the transaction on which they rely took place only in the year 1675, and even when considered in the most favourable light to the foreigners, is but an exception, which proves the rule, and would be a solitary instance of the fact of which they do not pretend to bring forward any other proof till a period of 90 year afterwards.

That, however, the free miners contend and confidently submit that this very transaction when fairly and honestly told, not only does not prove anything in favour of the foreigners' claims, but is absolutely totally destructive of it.

That the free miners humbly request the attention of your Honourable Court to the facts detailed in the document from which they quote, instead of the garbled statement of them made in the foreigners' memorial.

"In the same year several gentlemen and freeholders of the Parish of Newland, within the Forest, presented a petition to the Treasury, in which they set forth, that there had been and then was great store of coal in several men's lands in the said Parish, and in the adjoining waste; that the free miners opened and dug pits at their pleasure, as well in His Majesty's waste as in the lands of private men, and did then take considerable quantities of His Majesty's wood for support of their coal works, as of right appertaining to their custom; that the inhabitants of the adjacent country were supplied from thence with coal for firing, without which great spoils would be inevitably committed in His Majesty's woods, and also for lime coal, without which there would be little tillage, that the petitioners, finding the free miners to abuse the country, by lessening the former measures of coal, and to make daily consumptions of His Majesty's woods, had, without the least prospect of gain, in hopes of putting a stop to those mischiefs, and for the better accommodation of themselves and neighbours, agreed together to try for and carry on digging of coal for both uses at a place called Milkwall, near to the works of those free miners in His Majesty's waste, but not within the inclosures, for the support of which they did not intend to claim or use any of His Majesty's woods, but to buy in the country, although they had equal pretence of right as well to wood as to the liberty of digging, but that, having been obliged to make the end of their level for draining these pits a little within the inclosure of the forest (without the least prejudice thereto), they found that by the extreme hardness of the rock they could not, without excessive charge, compass their level, unless they might have leave to turn into the hill within the inclosures, not exceeding five or six acres at most (wherein there was no wood), to carry through the said level."

"Praying, therefore, that for a work of such public advantage they might be allowed to alter that part of their inclosure, and to carry in the ditch so much further as to exclude the said acres; doing the same at their own cost."

"This petition was referred to Sir Charles Harbord, who, in his report thereon, says, 'That he had seriously considered the petition and perused the Act of Parliament [1668], wherein it is expressly provided that the said inclosures should remain in severality in the actual possession of the Crown for ever, freed and discharged from all right, title and pretence whatsoever, and should be made and reputed a nursery for wood and timber only, in consideration whereof, and of the seventh clause in the said Act, he could not advise any warrant for breaking into the said inclosures without Mr. Attorney's opinion, and that the claims as to the mines and quarries did not seem to be legal or justifiable in point or right, though they had been long permitted; and as to the coal works, there never was any such claim, to his remembrance, etc. etc.'"

That the free miners are informed that, according to the established laws of evidence all the allegations of an adversary are admitted as conclusive, when they are in favour of the persons whom he wishes to destroy, while they are carefully to be weighed when they are against them.

That on analysing the above transaction, it appears that there were two parties, viz, the Crown and the "Foreigners" directly interested in subverting the privileges of the free miners.

That it may therefore be assumed as an indisputable fact, from the statements in the petition, that the "free miners opened and dug pits at their pleasure, as well in His Majesty's waste as in the lands of private men, and did then take considerable quantities of His Majesty's wood for the support of their coal works, as of right appertaining to their custom."

That by the strong language in which the petitioners complain of the practices of the free miners "their abusing the country by lessening the measures" and consuming His Majesty's wood, they indirectly but incontestably admit their right to do so, for it is preposterous to suppose for a moment that these "gentlemen and free holders" united, as they pretended to be, "without the least prospect of gain, in the hopes of stopping those mischiefs, and for the better accommodation of themselves and neighbours", would not instantly have put down the monopoly and stopped the "abuses" complained of by an appeal to law, if law had afforded them the least prospect of success in their unselfish and public-spirited objects.

That these petitioners were "gentlemen and freeholders", and rich men, and therefore had not the sad excuse of the free miners for not vindicating their claims by law, if they had been well founded, and moreover, they might have relied, perhaps, upon support of the public, in behalf of whom they represent themselves to have been so disinterestedly striving and in the sympathy of the Crown, whose interest they pretend to promote.

That so far from granting the prayer of the petition to be allowed to work mines, the Crown, as already stated, peremptorily refused it.

That although the foreigners may pretend that the Crown rejected their petition simply because they thought they might damage the inclosures, the free miners observe, that if they had any pretence of right, they might have tried their fortune in other parts of the Forest, as they assert the free miners did, at their pleasure, if they had had the same right as the free miners; and the free miners observe that as the uninclosed part of the Forest exceeds 12,000 acres, such public-spirited gentlemen need not have been at a loss for some other place than Milkwall.

That in short it appears from the very fact stated, that the petitioners, pretending to have a public object in view, did not and could not enforce their claim, while the Crown and the Public, although expressly called to the consideration of the alleged evils of the monopoly and the abuses committed by the free miners, took no steps whatever to put a stop to them.

That in answer to the remark made by the memorialist that "these claims of the foreigners do not seem to have been objected to by the free miners, as the Mine Law Courts are silent of the subject", the free miners reply that the free miners, poor and unlearned persons as they are, had no means of becoming acquainted with private petitions and memorials transmitted in a private manner to a Secretary of the Treasury, and not knowing could not answer their contents; and the free miners cannot avoid noticing that the very memorial of the foreigners, to which they are now replying, might have remained equally as unanswered, and according to the reasoning of the memorialist might have been equally to be taken as a true statement of facts if it had not been for the kindness and justice of your Honourable Board in causing it to be publicly read and subsequently transmitted to them.

That, however, it is not altogether true that the resolutions of the Mine Law Courts "are silent on the subject", since by resolutions of that court, passed 9th March 1674, about the time when this attempt of the foreigners was made, it is expressly stated that "the ancient rights, privileges and customs of His Majesty's Mines of the Forest of Dean had been much invaded, and were still threatened".

That the necessity of any further or specific entry on the subject was removed by the simple fact that the Petitioners' claim was rejected by the Crown, and the projected works at Milkwall were abandoned.

That the foreigners do not pretend to adduce any other instance from 1675 to 1765 of foreigners having held or worked mines, and as the free miners have shown that it disproves the very fact which it was brought forward to support, the free miners have reduced the period of "usuage" to within the last 60 years, and subsequent to the discontinuance of the Mine Law Courts.

That the free miners need not enter into any argument to disprove the assertions that such "associations of foreigners must have been advantageous to the country", since the foreigners have failed in their proof that such associations had any existence; and with regard to the charge made against the Mine Law Courts of their sustaining an "illegal monopoly", the free miners see no reason to deny the efforts, and the successful efforts, made by the Mine Law Courts, to preserve to the free miners their exclusive rights, derived to them from such early ages, and enjoyed by them during so long a period of time.

That the free miners are nevertheless surprised to find in the very next paragraph of the memorial of the foreigners, that although they in the preceding paragraph charged the Mine Law Courts with sustaining a "monopoly" which they are pleased to term "illegal" now state that they can find in the records of that Court no order or resolution calculated to prevent the "working and occupation of mines by persons not being free miners".

The free miners, on the other hand, after requesting your Honourable Board to bear in mind that in the passages already quoted from their customs as confirmed by Edw. 3, the exclusion of foreigners is directly enforced and established; that by the terms of the compact entered into with the Crown in the reign of James I, that exclusion was maintained and allowed by the Crown, confidently refer to the whole records of the proceedings of the Mine Law Court now in existence for a series of orders and resolutions, illustrative of the said exclusive rights.

That the only orders which the foreigners venture to quote themselves are certain resolutions passed in September 1777, which was the last year in which the Mine Law Courts met.

That these resolutions can, if correctly quoted, so far from disproving, confirm the fact of the non-allowance of foreigners to work the mines.

That the eighth clause establishes the necessity of all persons whatever, deriving by gift or will, coming before the Mine Law Court to prove the will; and the free miners submit that if in this instance the custom of the free miners was binding to force the foreigners to admit the jurisdiction of the court, so also must the other resolutions of the same court be binding which restrain the working by foreigners.

That the 17th clause, even as quoted by the foreigners, proves the above statement, since it expressly states that any person who is a foreigner acquiring coal works by heirship, marriage or will, he shall sell his coal works by the Mine Law Courts, or hire free miners to work it for him; while the 11th clause, as quoted by them, inflicts a penalty of £20 on any free miner who even sells any mine or coal work to a foreigner.

But the free miners contend that the quotation made by the foreigners of the 16th of the resolutions last mentioned, is incorrect, for that resolution, when correctly given, runs thus:

"If a free miner die and leave his mine or coal work to a foreigner, or it fall by heirship, he shall have the liberty of hiring a free miner to work it for him, or sell it to a free miner, but shall not work it himself."

The free miners have thus shown that the resolutions quoted by the foreigners themselves distinctly refute the pretence they have set up; while the resolutions as really standing in the Mine Law Courts, establish the custom of the free miners and the exclusion of the foreigners, beyond the possibility of fair denial or doubt.

That the free miners positively contradict the assertion that an examination of the gale-books will prove that mines are galed by the gaveller to persons not free miners; on the contrary, they submit that, both by the evidence of the gale-books, and the verbal evidence of Mr. Tovey, no fact, throughout the long examination before your Honourable Board, was so distinctly proved by the concurring testimony of all persons, whether free miners or not, as that no mines were galed by the gavellers to foreigners.

That the free miners do not pretend to deny that such foreigners might, 60 years ago, as they do now, have had mines galed to them; but they assert that this, if done wrongfully and illegally, and the Mine Law Courts having been discontinued, the free miners had no means of redress.

That the free miners do not anywhere pretend to deny that conveyances have been made within the last 60 years from free miners to foreigners, and that foreigners have in consequence held and worked mines openly since that period; this being the very grievance and oppression which has reduced the free miners to such distress, and proved so ruinous to their country; but they contend that this practice never could have been successfully carried on had the Mine Law Courts not fallen into disuse.

That the free miners having proved that, during the sittings of the Mine Law Courts, the foreigners were precluded from holding mines, have now only to state to your Honourable

Board that the falling of the Mine Law Courts into disuse did not arise from any conduct on their part, as to give foreigners a title through the neglect of the free miners.

That a reference to the Mine Law Court rolls from 1665, when they were re-established in the reign of Charles 2, and until 1777, when they fell into disuse, proves that during that time, a period of 112 years, constant endeavours were made by the foreigners to intrude into the mines, which endeavours were defeated and baffled by the Mine Law Court.

That the foreigners finding the Mine Law Courts an unsuperable obstacle to their success, and more particularly that by the orders last quoted of 1777, there was no chance for their being permitted to work in the mines, found that the only means by which they could hope for success was to destroy the Mine Law Courts.

That the documents of this court were always kept in the Speech House in the Forest of Dean, but that after the conclusion of the last court in 1777, some person or persons broke open the chest in which they were contained and removed them.

That the free miners from that period to the present have made repeated applications to the wardens and the gavellers respecting these orders and documents, but that the wardens and gavellers, while they declared that they could not hold the Mine Law Courts as usual without these documents, at the same time denied all knowledge of their existence.

That the free miners themselves, in fact, never heard of these documents again till the present inquiry before your Honourable Board, when Mr. Tovey, the King's [deputy] gaveller, produced them to your Honourable Board.

That in proof that the free miners never abandoned their claim to have the Mine Law Courts in operation, and continually sought to have them re-established, the free miners beg to refer to a resolution passed at a meeting of free miners in the year 1807:

"Resolved, that a copy of these resolutions be sent to the wardens of the Forest, and the respective officers of the Mine Law Courts; that they be earnestly requested to hold a court as soon as possible; that the same be regularly confirmed by 48 free miners, and entered amongst the records of the said court, as the future orders by which all cases of levels or engines shall be regulated."

That your Honourable Board cannot fail to observe from these facts that the Mine Law Courts fell into disuse, not from any fault of the free miners, but from their having been wrongfully deprived of their documents connected with it, and that the applications which they have from time to time, since 1777 up to the present time, made to the proper officers to hold such courts for their behalf, were quite sufficient to remove from them all imputation of having acquiesced in the usurpation of the foreigners, or from having lost their rights from their own negligence.

They maintain, therefore, that having proved the wrongfull discontinuance of their courts in 1777, and the applications for their renewal since, their rights to have the Mine Law Courts is as good and just as that of the other inhabitants of this country to have the assizes held from year to year.

And that as their court is a legal one, so also are the orders and resolutions made at the time of its last sitting, are still good, valid and upstanding, and ought to be received as declaratory of the rights and privileges of the free miners at the present moment.

That the free miners, conceiving their claim to the Mine Law Courts to be undeniable in law, submit that they are not bound to show any grounds of expediency for their revival, they would merely observe, that the want of capital, which the foreigners impute to them, arises partly from their having been intruded upon by the foreigners precisely at the time when the mines were becoming more valuable in consequence of the increasing commerce of the country.

That if these Mine Law Courts were re-established, and their right and privileges restored to them, there would be no difficulty in finding capital for the proper working of the mines.

The free miners, therefore, most humbly entreat of your Honourable Board to recommend the restoration of their Mine Law Courts, as the mode by which they can effectually recover their other rights and privileges, and the only step which can restore the quiet of the district, and deliver them from the oppression which they have long been suffering.'

[Signed by 1,036 persons and dated 24 September, 1834.]

(*d*) MEMORIAL [1834] BY CERTAIN FREE MINERS OBJECTING TO OTHERS ON THE GROUNDS OF NON-QUALIFICATION

The following memorial dated 23 December 1834 was forwarded to the Commissioners in London, by Mr. Clarke, on behalf of certain free miners, eighty-three in number,[1] who objected to other miners on the grounds of non-qualification:

'This humble Memorial of the Free Miners, whose names are hereto subscribed and annexed: Sheweth,

That, with reference to the qualifications necessary to entitle any person to the name of a free miner, and the privileges consequent thereon, it is requisite that a free miner should be born of free miners, as well as in the Hundred of St. Briavels, and the bounds of the Forest.

That these memorialists are not anxious to dispute the title of any person who can prove his descent from a father a free miner, since they themselves can now only claim on the presumption that their own ancestors were duly admitted as free miners at the Mine Law Courts, although, owing to the loss of many of the documents thereto belonging, no direct evidence of the fact of their admission can now be produced.

That they trust, therefore, that they themselves may have the benefit of the presumption that their own ancestors were duly admitted; a presumption analogous to that which is frequently admitted in other courts of law, which will presume in many cases a grant or conveyance, although none such can be found, when there has been an uninterrupted possession for a series of years in the ancestors of the persons claiming, and no evidence of a contrary nature can be produced.

That they are willing to allow the same presumption in favour of those whose fathers were indisputably free miners, and to suppose that their ancestors were duly admitted, although the records confirming their admission are not to be found.

That they cannot however allow that the mere circumstance of birth within the hundred should now entitle persons, whose parents it has been distinctly proved were not free miners as of indefeasible right, to the rights and privileges of free miners, although they may comply with the other conditions laid down in their laws and franchises.

That the memorialists admit, that in the copy of their customs and franchises, as confirmed to them, as they verily believe, by Edward 3, in the year 1334, the words are "only that been born and abiding within the castle of St. Briavels, and the bounds of the Forest" (vide Clause 30,) and that no mention is here made of the necessity of such persons being also born of free miners.

---

1 Pp. 53-5.

That they contend, however, that the constant practice and custom were for all free miners to be admitted at the Mine Law Courts held under the jurisdiction of the King's deputy and the King's gavellers, who attended for the preservation of the rights of the Crown, and a jury of miners, who watched over the rights of the free miners; and that the omission of the description of the qualification of birth of a free miner proceeded upon the absolute certainty that no other person than one so qualified would presume to claim admission, or if claiming, would ever have been admitted.

When it is considered that the free miners claimed and possessed, and for so many years have exclusively enjoyed, the important privilege of mining at their pleasure in any place that they would (see clauses, 4, 12, 13, and 14, of their customs and franchises), it is evident that it would have been equally injurious to the King's interest, as well as to that of the free miners, to adopt a construction which would allow to all persons an indefeasible right to the same privilege, merely from their having been born within the Forest bounds,

That their "custom and franchises" apply only to the rights of those who were free miners, and not to those who were not.

That in support of this view of the case, they may refer to the arrangement which was made in the 10th year of the reign of King James the First [1612], between the King and the free miners, the records of which are to be found in the order of the Court of Exchequer of Hilary term of that date, wherein it is expressly confirmed, "that only those who were inhabitants of the Forest, and had been accustomed to dig for ore, should be allowed the privileges of free miners".

That those who now claim as pure free miners, that is, as born of free miners, as well as fulfilling the other conditions of the qualifications laid down in their customs and franchises, are either the descendants of those who in James the First's time "were accustomed to work in the Forest", or of those who since were duly admitted in the Mine Law Courts.

That on the revival of the Mine Law Courts in 1663, it is probable that persons born in the Forest were frequently admitted free miners after working a year and a day; not as a matter of right, but of favour and expediency, of which the jury of miners were good judges, as far as concerns their interests; while the deputies of the warden and the King's gavellers would doubtless watch over the admissions, to prevent any injury to the rights of the Crown.

That to prove such persons were admitted, not as a matter of right, but of favour, the free miners appeal to the order of the Mine Law Court, held 18th March 1668, before Sir Baynham Throckmorton, deputy to the Lord Herbert, which runs as follows: "We do order and ordain that no young man shall or may hereafter work at any mine or coals (although he be born within the hundred), if he hath not worked lawfully 12 months and a day already, and paid the King's rent (except he be bound apprentice unto a free miner, and lawfully serve him as an apprentice for the term of five years, under the penalty as aforesaid)."

From this order it clearly appears that although persons born within the hundred after working a year and a day had been admitted as free miners, yet the court then thought fit to order that such persons claiming on such grounds only should thenceforward serve an apprenticeship to free miners, an order which would not have been made had they possessed an indefeasible right; the distinction between a free miner and a foreigner being, that the former has an indefeasible right to admission on serving a year and a day, while the latter is subject to such restrictions as the court chose to impose.

That an order of the same date ordains, "that no person that was born upon the waste as a cabbiner should be allowed to work who had not already worked for seven years", thus tolerating all those who, born as cabbiners in Cromwell's time, had actually worked seven years, but excluding for ever all cabbiners who had not so worked, disregarding their plea of birth on the waste.

That other orders, subsequent to those already cited of 18th March 1668, subsequently passed, confirmatory of the regulations with regard to the admission of foreigners' sons, although born within the hundred, only after an apprenticeship of five years; but such orders are not now to be found.

That their existence, however, is proved by the order of 19th September 1682 (made 14 years after the last cited orders), which recites, "that the binding forth of boys to the art of mining according to many former orders hath been of great advantage to the miners", and continues with ordaining that "all the said former orders for binding boys to the art of mining for the space of five years be punctually observed; and that every boy henceforth of 12 years old shall be bound apprentice to his father, if a free miner, or to a free miner".

Another order on this subject, dated 6th December 1737, ordains, that "no foreigners' son, though born within the hundred, shall be admitted a free miner, unless he shall be bound as an apprentice for seven years to a free miner"; and to prevent any fraud, the indentures were to be registered in the Mine Law Court.

This order clearly establishes the position contended for by your memorialists; viz., that while free miners' sons were admitted, as of course, on working only a year and a day, those of foreigners, not having a similar indefeasible right, were not to be admitted until after an apprenticeship of seven years, a qualification never insisted upon with regard to the free miners' sons.

The next order on the subject of admission is dated 2nd March 1741, and orders, that "no persons whatsoever shall for the future be admitted free miner unless he can prove, by the oath of one or more credible witnesses, his lawfully working at coal or mine a year and a day".

This order does not revoke the order last quoted as to the regulations under which foreigners sons, at the discretion of the court, might be admitted after a seven year's apprenticeship, but prescribes a new regulation with regard to free miners' sons themselves, who were now for the first time called to prove their title by working a year and a day, by the oath of two persons; the regulation not establishing or conferring a right, but merely that those having a right should prove it.

Accordingly in the proceedings of the Mine Law Court subsequent to this period, are to be found entries of persons being admitted under the forms above prescribed.

That this appearing to be the law from the documents belonging to the court now in existence, so it appears equally confirmed by the oral testimony adduced before your Honourable Board.

Your memorialists especially refer to the evidence of Thomas Davies, of Five Acres, taken at one of the early meetings of your Honourable Board, and to the evidence of Stephen Jones taken on 26 day of September last.

They are aware that evidence of a contrary tendency has been given, but that such evidence has been given by persons themselves claimants as sons of foreigners, and finally they would remark that it was probably thought as unnecessary and superfluous to insert formally in the orders of the court, or in the declarations of their customs and franchises, that no foreigner's son should be entitled to the privileges of the free miners, as it was to declare that no foreigners should work or hold mines in the Forest, both being considered equally impracticable and impossible.

Your memorialists therefore respectfully contend that no person should be considered as a free miner whose birth from parents free miners cannot be proved.'

[Signed by 83 free miners].

Mr. Clarke requested that none of the names on either of the lists objected to, might be allowed to remain. No fresh evidence was intended to be offered by the miners as to the names of claimants on the list, to which no objection had before been made.

(*e*) TIMBER FOR MINES

The Commissioners considered the question of timber for the mines, and the depositions of the steward of the Court of Attachments, and of three keepers are of interest in this connection. John Lucas, solicitor of Newnham, and steward of the Court of Attachments, deposed[1]:

'The miner gets a written order from the keeper of the walk to come to me, as steward of the court, for an order for timber; I give it without inquiry as to whether the applicant be a free miner or not; and I did not consider that such inquiry was requisite, or that I had any discretion on the subject. I considered it my duty to give the order, as a matter of course. I grant and date the order as of the last court. I receive 1s./- for each order. I cannot, of my own knowledge, state whether any person, other than a free miner, has ever had timber from me. I consider mine merely an executive duty.'

John White, keeper, aged seventy-four years, deposed[2]:

'If a miner applies to me for timber, I ask him for what work, and whether he wants one or two orders. I do not always go to see the work. I generally know the applicant to be a free miner, because I know them all pretty well. I do not know that a foreigner ever applied to me. If I had known any applicant to be a foreigner, I should not have given timber. I never refused timber that I recollect, but I should have refused if I had known that it was not wanted for the work for which it was applied for. The first thing I ask an applicant, if I do not know his work to be galed, is "Is your name on the gale book?" and if I am not satisfied, I demand a note from the gaveller; if he gets this, I give him an order to go to the steward for his order, and on his bringing such order I mark timber for him as he may want it. During my time beech only was marked, never oak or ash. If a foreigner came to me with an order in the name of a free miner, I should give him timber; but I certainly would refuse a foreigner presenting an order in his own name, if I knew him to be a foreigner.'

William Harvey, keeper of Worcester Walk for sixteen years[3]:

'The miners have not of later years come frequently to me for timber; there is not much in my walk, and I have not had any applications for 12 months; when they do come I always

1 P. 13. For a discussion on timber, see PRO F20/1 [17].
2 P. 14.
3 P. 16.

know whether the applicant is a free miner or not, because I know them all from being always looking among them. I certainly should not give timber to a foreigner. I generally see the pit for which the timber is delivered, and can judge if it has been made use of there.'

Thomas Witts, keeper of Speech House Walk[1]:

'When I give timber I only look to the order, I do not see how it is applied: though when I suspect an applicant I make enquiries. The timber not being used in my walk, I leave it to the other keepers.'

(*f*) METHODS OF WORKING

Certain aspects of the working of the mines of the Forest have already been included in (*b*). Other relevant depositions are:

William Morgan[2]:

'The level is on the falling ground of a hill, a drain by which the water is taken out, so that we carry on the level until we come to the coal; and we may go on following the vein until another work meets us. We sink pits on the level; we cannot cross another work; no other gale can be marked on the hill or landside above, within 1,000 yards, but in the deep, as nearly as may be. Water pits are galed in the same way, and sunk down from the surface, according to the custom of the Forest. I consider a water pit is protected 12 yards all round from the centre of the Pit.'

Thomas Davis[3]:

'The level always has the command of the mine, waterworks (whether engine or otherwise we call waterworks) we do not think anything of, but the level is what commands the mine. A level is the mother of a mine; the bound is 1,000 yards. If the gaveller gives a gale within 800 yards, the galee has a right to cut off any water pit, if he has a level that will raise the coal.'

On 11 April 1832 Richard James presented the following proposals which had been drawn up by James Smith, clerk, at the request of about fourteen, who consider themselves to represent the body of free miners[4]:

'1st. That it is expedient to allow, for an engine-pit that exceeds 120 yards in depth, 1500 yards in length and 200 in breadth, 750 yards of length to be taken each way, to make up the 1500 in length.

2nd. That it is expedient to allow, for an engine-pit that exceeds 90 yards, and does not exceed 120 yards in depth, 1000 yards in length and 150 in breadth, 500 yards to be taken

1 P. 14.
2 P. 12.
3 P. 17.
4 P. 21.

each way, to make up the 1000 in length.

3rd. That it is expedient to allow, for an engine-pit that exceeds 60 yards and does not exceed 90 yards in length, 1000 yards in length and 100 in breadth, 500 yards to be taken each way, to make up the 1000 in length.

That the above allotments should be applicable to any vein not less than a yard in thickness.

That where the vein is less than a yard in thickness, it be permitted to work two of the same description, according to the above limitations.

That all levels shall be allowed 1000 yards in length from the end where the coal is first cut by it, and not exceeding 200 in breadth.

That the foregoing proposals are made on the supposition, that when the present levels are worked out according to the above limitations by those now holding or working them, the Parliament will not allow any foreigner to come in.

And to increase in the same proportion as you get deeper.

Where works at present at work have gone out of the limits above proposed I consider they ought to be stopped; they have had their share.'

John Lewis deposed:

'I have nothing to do with waterworks, but I think where persons have gone to great expense they ought not to be stopped at once, even if out of the limit proposed by Mr. James, because they have many men employed. I think foreigners are advantageous to the Forest.'

William Morgan said he had no objection to the proposals but asserted:

'There should be an addition when people get deeper. A pit 150 yards deep should take 1,500 in length and 300 in breadth, and so on, on the plan proposed; but I do not agree on the last proviso, as to the exclusion of foreigners; I think they are advantageous to the Forest. Above all, the working of narrow headings should be stopped; it is that which has done all the mischief.'

The following suggestions were made by David Mushet on 28 August 1832[1]:

'1st. No new gales for levels, water pits or engine pits to be made in the land of any existing work, whether the same be a level, water pit or engine work, unless at the distance of 1,000 yards from any or either of them.

2nd. All levels, water pits and engine pits to be entitled only to the coal they will respectively dry on the deep side of any previously existing work.

3rd. No narrow headings to be run up in the land from the deep of any work, for the purpose of cutting off or intercepting the coal that could be dried by any previously existing work.

4th. Levels penetrating through 600 yards of rock or shale and upwards, and going for both sides of the hill, to be entitled to 750 yards right and left, or 1,500 yards in all, along the level course of the coal.

5th. Levels of 300 yards and upwards, 600 yards right and left, or 1,200 yards in all, along

1 Pp. 38-9.

the level course.

6th. Levels under 300 yards, 500 yards right and left, or 1,000 yards in all, along the level course.

7th. Levels going in on one side of the hill, in coal, to be entitled to a length of 1,000 yards, and a regaleage when this is exhausted, provided the same would not interfere with any existing work.

8th. Levels that cross the pitching either way, whether obliquely or directly, and going for one side of the hill, to be entitled to 1,500 yards in all, along the level course, and to a regaleage when this is exhausted, provided that such regaleage did not at the time interfere with any existing work.

9th. Proprietors of land works to keep on their deep headings; and in case of neglecting to do so, upon receiving proper notice from the deep-level proprietor, they are forthwith to proceed with the same, that the boundary of the land-level coal may be known and respected.

Such notice as above to be given when the deep level has reached the extent of its boundary, but not till then.

10th. Should the land-coal proprietor, after due notice has been given, neglect to carry forward this deep heading, so as to mark out the boundary of his work, the deep-level proprietor having no guide to go by, will not be accountable for any trespass that may arise.

11th. Engine pits or water pits to be entitled to a length both ways of 1,500 yards, and to all the coal between the gale and the next land work; but in the cases of deep shafts, and a narrow breadth the land, the distance along the level course to be extended to 2,000 yards, or 1,000 yards, when the same is practicable, upon each side of the engine pit.

12th. Proprietors of engine pits to be allowed to sink other pits within their boundary, for the purpose of working and raising the coal without the same being considered as new galeages.

13th. Proprietors of levels to have the same privilege, or to make use of land levels within their own boundary or both, for the purpose of airing the works or bringing out the coal.

14th. No engine pit or water pit to be galed or sunk, or coal got or raised therefrom, within 1,000 yards of the level heading of any established level work, such distance at the time the shaft so sunk shall reach the coal.

15th. When disputes and differences arise, the same to be settled by a jury of 12 of the most intelligent coal and mine proprietors, to be summoned upon proper notice by the gaveller, a verdict given by a majority of whom shall be binding upon the parties; and in case of an equal division of opinion, the gaveller to have the casting vote.

16th. Proprietors of engine and water pits situate in the land to carry out their headings along the level course towards the limits of their boundaries, so as to form lines of division between the land and the deep works; should they neglect the same, the deep-level proprietor, as soon as he has attained the extent of his deep workings, shall give due notice to the land-coal proprietor to proceed with his deep headings; and for any trespass that may arise from a neglect of the same, the deep-coal proprietor shall not be accountable. The central district of the Forest Basin requires a separate consideration from the foregoing. Along that line the pits to the upper workable coal, such as the Park End High Delf and the Church Coal, will range from 200 to 350 yards, and to the lower coal series from 150 to 250 yards in additional depth.

Pits sunk in this situation will drain both planes of coal, as well as the rising plane in the direction of Churchway, and ought to take their respectively breadth accordingly; and this in reference to the depth of the engine pit.

The depth of this multiplied by four would perhaps furnish a proper rule to abide by, and would give to each engine work according to its depth, from 800 to 1,500 yards, or from 400 to 750 yards from each plane in breadth.

Another plan would be to except out of the general custom half a mile in breadth in each side of the central line, and divide this into prospective collieries of from 100 to 200 acres each.

These proposed arrangements are intended to apply only to a new state of things. I consider it utterly impossible to enter into any compromise in respect of existing works, or reconcile the jarring and conflicting interests of the free miners and foreigners, and the free miners with each other.

The only safeguard for the interest of all in respect to existing works, would be to declare that narrow headings for cutting off coal previously laid dry were illegal, and the gale for a water pit at 24 yards ceased to be part of the custom.'

Moses Teague, coal surveyor and engineer, sent the following letter to the Commissioners in April 1832[1]:

'I shall not at present call your attention to any observations I might be able to make in respect of the claims or rights of the free miners or any other persons to the minerals of this Forest. My object in now addressing you is to solicit your attention to the mode hitherto adopted in working the same, as I consider this subject of more importance than any other in respect thereof; for if the plan or custom (hitherto practised and laid down as a law) be persisted in, it will at no very remote period be of little or no importance to whom these mines belong, as by such mode of working they will become altogether unavailable.

The mode hitherto adopted and laid down as the Forest law, as established from time immemorial is, that when any miner has obtained his vein of coal or mine, he is at liberty to prosecute and carry on the same, by working in the said vein until he intersects or comes in contact with another person's work underneath the ground. This the mine-law terms, working towards each other until the mattocks meet, and this has hitherto been considered the only mode of ascertaining fixed bound of every work.

Now this custom when made might be perfectly reasonable and applicable to the purposes thereof, as the mines in these remote times were attainable by water levels or drains, driven in an horizontal direction from the sides of the hills, and thereby intersecting the veins of mine, and by such means drawing off and draining the water therefrom, without the use of expensive machinery or mechanical power, and it was of little consequence whether the water of the mine ran off through drains or levels A, or B, or C; also of little importance which sides of the hills the same would flow.

But in the present age, when the working of the mines are beginning to be carried into the deep of the measures; and in parts where no drain or level can be made to carry off the water, it is of the utmost importance (not only for the security of the existing works, but much more so for the protection of the mines to be worked in future ages) that so barbarous a system as working till mattocks meet, or otherwise cutting into each other's works, should be abolished, and if suffered to be persisted in must eventually inundate and destroy the deep and large

[1] P. 28.

interior of the Forest coal-field, by bringing down what is termed the land or surface water into the deep mines, so as to defy even the power of steam-engines to lift or drain the same, except at such an enormous expense as to preclude the working of these mines at anything like a marketable price. As the law or custom stand at present, one miner, who has nearly worked out and exhausted his colliery, having previously connected himself with other old works, and let in vast bodies of water, may cut into his neighbour's work, which perhaps is not half worked out, or only just begun, and by so doing might entirely destroy it, presuming (as is always the case) that no person goes to the expense of erecting a steam-engine more powerful than is necessary for his own purpose. Instances of this nature have already occurred in this Forest, and the right of working, as it is termed, till mattocks meet, has been exercised for no other purpose than that of destroying a neighbour's work, and large bodies of coal have already been lost, both to the miners, the Crown and the public in consequence thereof, and the pursuance of such a plan must eventually destroy all those deep mines of the Forest. The only plan I can suggest is, that defined meets and bounds should be fixed to each work. A law so undefined as that of cutting until mattocks meet must be bad, and must eventually end in ruin to all parties concerned therein. The mineral property of the Forest, if considered as belonging to one landlord, who has the leasing of it out to his different tenants, would soon point out an effectual way of having the same farmed in a proper manner.'

The foregoing Fourth Report (1835) had far reaching effects, as noted in the Act of 1838, *infra*.

The Dean Forest (Mines) Act 1838. The most relevant outcome of the Fourth Report (1835) was the enactment of the locally very important Dean Forest (Mines) Act 1838, which *inter alia* defined and, as so defined, confirmed, the rights of the free miners; for the first time, changing their 'laws and privileges' to rights. Its purpose was 'to regulate the opening and working of mines and quarries in the Forest of Dean and Hundred of St. Briavels'. 'The Dean Forest Mining Commissioners' appointed to carry the Act into execution were: Thomas Sopwith[1] of Newcastle-upon-Tyne (mining engineer, appointed by the Commissioners of Woods); John Probyn[2] of Manor House, Longhope, Glos. (selected by the free miners to act on their behalf); and John Buddle of Wallsend (mining engineer, as umpire or arbitrator). Thomas Graham acted as solicitor, and Henry Elsworth as clerk. The Act's most relevant provisions were[3]:

- The office of gaveller ('Keeper of the Gawle-Above-the Wood and of the Gawle-Under-the Wood') to be vested in the First Commissioner of Woods. The deputy gaveller must be a person 'skilled in mining'. S.13 [repealed in 1969].

- Qualification of free miners *as to coal and iron ore*: 'All male persons born or hereafter to be born and abiding within the Hundred of St. Briavels, of the age of twenty-one years and

1 Robert Sopwith *Thomas Sopwith Surveyor* (The Pentland Press, Edinburgh), 1994.

2 John Probyn of Gloucester was a mining engineer connected with Newland and Longhope Manor House. Unlike some members of his family, he was not made an Honorary Free Miner; his grandfather, Edmund Probyn, held such an appointment.

3 Currently available from H.M.S.O. is an Official Revised Edition of the 1838 Act (to 1 February 1978), omitting spent and repealed Sections. See also Appendix I.

upwards, who shall have worked a year and a day in a coal or iron mine within the Hundred, shall be deemed and taken to be free miners for the purposes of this Act.' [The further condition of 'free-parentage' insisted on by some of the witnesses before the Commissioners of 1831 did not receive the sanction of the legislature.] S.14.

- Qualification of free miners *as to stone quarries*: 'All male persons born or hereafter to be born and abiding within the Hundred, of the age of twenty-one years and upwards, who shall have worked a year and a day in a stone quarry within the Forest, shall for the purposes of this Act, so far as relates to having gales or leases of stone quarries within the open lands of the Forest, but not otherwise, be taken to be free miners.' [The rights of quarrying, therefore, do not extend beyond the Forest perambulation.] S.15.

- Register to be kept by the gaveller or deputy gaveller of all free miners, distinguishing such as have worked in mines and such as have worked in quarries. [The reason for this differentiation is seen from the latter part of S.23: 'Provided always, that no person registered as a free miner by reason of his having worked a year and a day in a quarry shall have a right to have any gale made to him of any mine; but that nothing herein contained shall prevent such free miners as shall be registered by reason of having worked a year and a day in a mine from having leases of quarries granted to them under the authority hereinafter contained.'] Ss. 16, 20, 21, 22.

- The gaveller or deputy gaveller may refuse to register the name of any person claiming to be a free miner, unless satisfactory evidence is produced. The right of appeal to the Dean Forest Mining Commissioners was given while acting, or, after the Commissioners have ceased to act, to the general or quarter sessions or to any court of Verderers or attachments. Ss. 17, 19.

- Registered free miners to have the exclusive right of having gales or works granted to them by the gaveller or deputy gaveller, to open *mines within the Hundred of St. Briavels,* and to have gales or leases of *quarries within the Forest of Dean.* [This is the first limitation of the rights *re* mines to the Hundred of St. Briavels and *re* quarries to the statutory Forest perambulation.] S.23.

- The Commissioners to (*a*) make an Award of gales of coal mines, iron mines and quarries, as legally possessed at the time of the passing of the Act – either to free miners or as lessees of free miners, (*b*) to prepare plans and schedule or description of such gales, pits, levels, works and quarries; (*c*) determine the extent to which and the mode in which such gales etc. shall be continued and worked; (*d*) set forth general rules, orders, and regulations under which the mines etc. shall be worked; (*e*) determine who were at the passing of the Act in possession of licences to erect buildings and machinery in the Forest for working the mines etc. and the terms thereof. Ss. 24, 27, 29.

- The Commissioners of Woods may grant leases of small portions of land for the purpose of the mining works. S.25.

- The Commissioners to allot and set out the metes and bounds of each gale or work. S.27.

- The Commissioners may unite two or more works, and award compensation. [This was only acted upon in the case of the Newcastle gale – *vide* Award as to Coal Mines 1841.] S.28.

- The Commissioners to make general rules, specifying the mode in which gales, etc. shall be worked; and, on breach of such rules, gales, etc. to be forfeited. [The Rules and Regulations were included in the second schedules respectively to the Awards of 1841.] S.29.

- Free miners' claims to timber to cease, and the value thereof to be taken into consideration in settling the galeage rent, royalty, tonnage duty, or other payments to the Crown. S.30.

- After the Award is made, 'all and every the customs respecting the said mines, minerals and quarries in the Forest of Dean and also in the Hundred of St. Briavels, and the rights and privileges of or claimed by the free miners, other than such as are or may be confirmed by this Act or any Award specifying such rules and regulations as aforesaid, shall absolutely cease'. S.31.

- Confirmation of all sales, mortgages, leases etc. of gales etc. made before the passing of the Act by any free miner or any other party. [Before the passing of the Act some free miners when selling a gale demised it for some long term of years, at a peppercorn rent, to avoid any question of forfeiture. Others dealt with gales as fee simple estates.] S.40.

- The Commissioners to fix royalties payable to the Crown for existing coal works; such royalties not to exceed 4d. per ton, and due regard being given to the relative value of the coal from each works. The Commissioners also had the right to fix a minimum or dead rent as well as a tonnage royalty. [Messrs. Morrel in a case at Gloucester Summer Assizes in 1850, and afterwards in the Court of Queen's Bench in 1851, pleaded against the payment of dead rent. The Court decided against Messrs. Morrel, Mr Justice Patteson saying that it seemed to him that the dead rent was really in lieu of the fifth man.] S.41.

- The Commissioners to fix similar royalties for iron ore works, the maximum to be 4d. ton. S.42.

- The Commissioners to fix royalties for minerals other than coal and iron, with a proviso that the total payments shall not in any case exceed 1/10th share of the value of such mineral when made marketable. S.42.

- Rents payable under licences for erecting steam engines or the formation of private railways or tramroads, to be considered in awarding future rents or royalties. S.43.

- Future rents or royalties to be deemed in lieu of the right of the Crown to put in a fifth man to work the gales, etc. and share the profit thereof. S.44.

- The Commissioners to make rules and orders for keeping accounts of the produce from gales, pits, levels, works and quarries, to enable the gaveller to ascertain the amount due for rent, royalty, etc. S.45.

- The galeage, rents, royalties, etc., to be revised every twenty-one years if the gaveller, or galee (or lessee) shall so elect. In case of dispute the amount of the new rent, etc., to be referred to arbitration, costs to be equally borne by the Crown and the party disputing. S.46.

- Gavellers and others on behalf of the Crown to have the right to enter and survey works. S.53.

- Grants of gales and transfers of gales to be entered in gaveller's books. Ss. 57, 58, 59.

- Gavellers to grant gales to free miners in the order of their applications in writing to be made from and after the passing of the Act. In the case of more than one application on the same day for the same gale, the matter to be decided by drawing lots. Ss. 60, 63.

- No free miner to be entitled to have more than three gales granted at any time. If the free miner requires a fourth he must surrender one of the three. S.61.

- Gavellers not to grant gales which may interfere with existing gales. S.62.

- Gales not to be granted in inclosed Crown lands set aside for the growth and preservation of timber, so long as the lands continue to be inclosed – 'Provided always, that this shall not extend to prevent any person from working any gales to which he may be entitled under such inclosed lands, so as no damage shall be thereby done to such inclosed lands, or the fences thereof, or to the trees within such inclosed lands.' S.64.

- The Commissioners of Woods may grant licences for air shafts in, and for railroads and tramroads across, any Crown inclosures. S.65.

- In the case of 'inclosed lands of the Hundred not within the Forest, one-half of the gale rent to be paid to the owners of the inclosed lands. [The owner of the Abbot's Wood was not entitled to share in the rents and royalties arising from mines and minerals within that estate – S.9 of the Abbot's Wood Act, 1870.] S.67.

- Free miners, or their assigns, to pay compensation to owners of inclosed lands for surface damage. [As to 'surface damage' the following extract from the judgement of the court in the case of Allaway *v.* Wagstaffe (1859) is of interest: 'The free miners have the power to open mines within the hundred, and to work mines and quarries therein, that is to say, sink shafts, raise the minerals, make heaps and roads, and to do all other acts to work mines and quarries on the land, except erecting steam-engines and dwelling-houses without leave of the owners. This working the miners may lawfully do, but there is no provision in the Act of Parliament to enable free miners to leave the soil without support so as to cause a subsidence, nor is there any clause from which such a licence could be inferred. It follows that free miners, whether working the coals under inclosed land from shafts sunk therein, or by outstroke from other lands, and causing a subsidence to the damage of the owner of the land, would be liable for this by action, for which Humphries *v.* Brogden is sufficient authority.'] S.68.

- No steam-engines or dwelling houses to be erected within inclosed lands of the hundred without previous consent and licence. S.69.

- The Commissioners of Woods may grant leases of quarries to free miners for any term not exceeding twenty-one years. [This was for leasehold interests only, as distinct from the gales of quarries confirmed by the Award of 1841 which were grants of fee simple estates. S.34 of the Dean Forest (Mines) Act, 1871, stated that renewals of quarry leases may be granted to persons not free miners.] S.83.

- Commissioners of Woods may grant leases to any person for any term not exceeding twenty-one years to get clay and sand from the open or waste lands of the Forest. S.84.

- A proviso that nothing in the Act shall prejudice the rights of the Crown and the claims of William Ambrose, lord of the manor of Blakeney, legal proceedings on which were pending.[1] S.85.

The 1838 Act was virtually the end of an era. S.31 (repealed in 1969) laid down that 'all and every the customs ... and other rights and privileges of or claimed by the free miners, other than such as are or may be confirmed by the Act shall absolutely cease'. Thomas Sopwith (one of the three Dean Forest Mining Commissioners) later added: 'The origin of the mining customs of the Forest of Dean ... is involved in much obscurity, and is now curious as a matter of antiquarian research rather than as to leading to any practical results of the mode of working the valuable minerals of this romantic district'.[2] The 1838 Act opened the way for further statutory provisions relating not only to mine working facilities in the Dean coalfield and iron ore field, but also to the necessity of plans, and to health and safety matters relating to mining. As well as setting up an overall management structure by outlining the roles of the gaveller and deputy gaveller, it set out a comprehensive licensing regime and also codified:

- rules for applying for and claiming mining and quarrying
- rules for setting out mining gales
- the making of rules of mining and quarrying

---

1 These alleged claims were decided to be unfounded and bad in law in A.-G. *v.* Mathias (see Chap. VIII, p. 345, n. 4). In compliance with S.67 of the 1838 Act, the deputy gavellers have in many cases galed minerals under freehold private lands other than 'Excepted Lands' (see Appendix A). In these cases they have collected the royalty and handed over a moiety, less 2$^{1}/_{2}$ per cent., to the freeholders. Even in the instance, for example, of a widow owning a small cottage and garden under which minerals have been extracted, the appropriate amount was computed and accounted for.

2 Strangely, Sopwith apparently knew little of ochre in the Forest. In a 'case and opinion' regarding a Report in 1857-8 on 'Paint or Colour Material in Iron Mines' (Hart MSS., 1857-8), he stated that in the Forest of Dean 'no substance' [ochre] had been brought to his notice and he was unaware of their existence there'. [Information on gales of ochre in 1873 (Hart MSS., 1873) is available for Ruardean Hill Colliery (S. Dykins) and Pluckpenny Level (J. B. Brain). For the history of mining of ochre in Dean Forest see Hart, *Industrial History*, (1971) pp. 243-9.]

- assignment of a gale on the death of a free miner, or during his lifetime
- access to unenclosed lands of the Forest [later adjusted by the Statute Law (Repeals) Act 1969 *infra*]
- requirements as to any other separate licences and permissions required (S.27)
- setting of rents and royalties [S.46, later amended by the 1969 Act *infra*]
- disputes and arbitration (Ss. 47, 48)
- records and plans (S.57)
- all other matters relating to the proper opening, working and management of gales [later amended by the Dean Forest (Amendment) Act 1861, *infra*].

[Previous to the 1838 Act, coal, iron ore, and stone were vested in the name of the Monarchy. Thereafter they were vested in the State (of which the Crown is head) under the aegis of the then Commissioners of Woods.]

Thomas Sopwith helps to show the necessity for the 1838 Act, and the difficulties at that time, in his paper on 'Mining Plans and Records' read before the British Association at Newcastle in 1838.[1] He said of the mine planning inadequacies at that time because of non-management and non-regulation:

> 'Great distrust of any interference existed, and some of the mine owners refused to allow of underground surveys being made. Numerous and conflicting parties were then working mines under customs which were totally inapplicable to the present state of mining; destructive at once to the interests of the free miners of the Forest; ruinous, as sad experience had shown, to the enterprising capitalist; and subversive of the rights of the Crown. So great was the perplexity, and so numerous and conflicting were the claims of contending parties, that the law advisers of the Board of Woods deemed it almost impossible to arrive at any satisfactory adjustment of them within the period of three years, as named in the Dean Forest Mining Act. The ruinous and unsatisfactory state of the mines must appear obvious on a slight consideration. As no plans existed, it was impossible to tell to what extent or in what direction the underground works were being carried. The crossing of mattocks, that is to say, the actual meeting of the workmen underground, was often the abrupt signal for contention; the driving of narrow headings was a means by which one coal owner might gain possession of coal which of right belonged to another; and a pit, though sunk at a cost of several thousand pounds, had no secured possession of coal beyond 12 yards round it, that is, a tract of coal 24 yards in diameter. At 40 or 50 yards from such a work another adventurer might commence a pit, and have an equal right, if right it could be called, to the coal. If a long and expensive adit was driven, another one might be commenced only a few yards deeper; and, from such a state of things, it is quite clear that great uncertainty and frequent losses inevitably ensued.'

The 1838 Act, now considerably modified, remains the most important of the Dean Forest Mines enactments. Though parts are spent or repealed by subsequent legislation (see Appendix I), it defines and confirms the right of freemining as to coal, iron ore and stone. [However, leases of stone quarries and of surfaces are now under the

1 The present author possesses a letter dated 17 March 1857 written by Thos. Sopwith to Rev. H. G. Nicholls enclosing a copy of this paper, portions of which Nicholls included in his book of 1858 (N.H.).

jurisdiction of the Forestry Commission's area land agent in liaison with their deputy gaveller – see Appendix F.]

The Dean Forest Mining Commissioners' Awards of 1841. The 1838 Act had led to the setting up of the Dean Forest Mining Commission, comprising: Thomas Sopwith for the Crown, John Buddle of Wallsend as 'umpire' or 'arbiter', and John Probyn of Longhope probably as representing the free miners. They sat from 1838 until 1841, opening their meetings on 5 September 1838 at Coleford. Their last meeting was on 20 July 1841, and the Commission closed six days later. The expenses of the Commission amounted to £10,003 12s. 0d.[1] The Commissioners issued three interim reports of their progress to the Commissioners of Woods, dated respectively 11 March 1839, 13 March 1840, and 12 March 1841. Sopwith wrote an interesting preface to the former edition of the Awards, portions of which have been included in Chapter IV, while additional relevant extracts are given below[2]:

> 'All male persons born in the Hundred of St. Briavels, and having worked a year and a day in a coal or iron mine, have been generally considered, and are now recognised by the Dean Forest Mining Act, as being Free Miners of the Forest of Dean.
>
> From time immemorial, this body of persons (of whom there are at present, 1 November, 1841, 829 registered) have enjoyed the right of working the coal and iron mines of the said Forest, subject, however, to the leave or licence of the gaveller or deputy gaveller of the Forest being first obtained, and further subject to the payment of an annual galeage rent or duty to the said gaveller or deputy gaveller, acting for and on behalf of the Crown.
>
> In default of, or in lieu of such payment, the Crown was entitled to put in a fifth man to share his work, with four other men, after the coal or iron had been won by means of a shaft or level, in the making of which the Crown's fifth man was not required to assist.
>
> If the Free Miners as a body had preserved amongst themselves the privileges of working the coal under any assumed and stationary customs, the principle of regulation and amendment would have been comparatively simple; inasmuch as the royalty might have been dealt with as belonging jointly to the Crown and to the body of Free Miners, and the mines have been worked for their joint benefit in certain portions. By this means the whole would have participated in the benefits derived from the royalty dues, and at the same time have enjoyed the same, or perhaps much greater advantages, from being employed as workmen, than they now possess. It is obvious, however, that while some individuals obtained possession of large tracts of coal, and others received considerable sums of money by selling gales, the great bulk of the Free Miners received no advantage; so that as a privilege belonging to them as a body, it became altogether unproductive of benefit except to a comparative small number of individuals. The rival operations of these parties, contending for the possession of coal and mine to which no specific limits were allotted, may readily be conceived to have produced much injury, and to have involved the loss of considerable capital, and under these inauspicious circumstances many of the mining speculations of the Forest ended in the ruin of the parties engaged in them.

1 31st Rpt. of Coms. of Woods (1853), App. 13 (Y), p. 338.

2 Wherever in the text of 'Mr. Sopwith's Preface' reference is made to the 'present work' or the 'present volume' they refer to the original edition of the Coal and Iron Awards published in 1841.

A still greater degree of perplexity was introduced into the Forest mining, by a practice of the Free Miners which appears to have been very rarely, if at all, practised during the period of the Mine Law Courts, this was the practice of Free Miners selling or assigning gales to persons not being Free Miners, and who were generally known in the Forest by the term 'foreigners', which term, for the sake of brevity, is used in the sequel. The foreigners, by introducing large capital into the Forest, were enabled to prosecute works of much greater magnitude than were contemplated by the old customs, which it has been seen were such as could only relate to workings of a comparatively limited extent. So far as the Free Miners were concerned, a few individuals reaped the advantage of these sales; but the Free Miners, as a body, had no participation therein. Indirectly however, it is evident that the expenditure of large capital in working extensive coal and iron mines, has been a fruitful source of employment to the labouring population, and the system having been so long practised and connived at by the Free Miners, and having had the collateral sanction of the officers of the Crown, could not be dealt with otherwise than with due regard to the rights of property as they now exist.

The greatest defect in the mining customs of Dean Forest was, that when a starting point was fixed for working a coal or iron mine, no other limit was assigned; it has indeed been held to be the custom, that no gale could be granted within 1,000 yards, either in advance of the level or on the land side of an existing work; the consequence was, that contiguous works not having definite boundaries, it became a matter of contention which could first obtain possession by extending their underground workings. Again, the said custom was considered to confer a title of 1,000 yards to a level, but only a circle of twelve yards radius to a water-pit; hence in sinking pits at a much greater cost than driving levels, and in working the coal by steam-engine drainage at a much greater cost than free drainage, a merely nominal, or rather in a practical point of view, no protection whatever was afforded to such water-pit mines.

By the common acceptance of the privileges conferred on Free Miners by a gale, it was commonly understood that the workings of a coal or iron mine might be carried to an indefinite extent unless interrupted by another work. This, however, as well as the other concomitants of the custom of galing was, in the very nature of things, only applicable to veins of a very limited depth and was altogether inapplicable to the working of the deep coal of the Forest; for if it had been so, the very foundation of all commercial enterprise would have been destroyed, inasmuch as the capital required for such extensive winnings would rarely have been ventured, on so slender and uncertain a chance of return as that which the custom of galing affords. Indeed, it plainly appears that deep and extensive shafts were not contemplated in the original custom, which afforded only a protection of a circle of twelve yards radius, or twenty-four yards diameter, to a water-pit.

As this limited right to work the coal by a water-pit was not in conformity with the custom as regards levels, which assigned a considerable distance in advance of the level; it is evident that the custom only contemplated water-pits of very moderate depth near the outcrop of the coal, and was not meant to apply to those veins which, from their great depth, could only be worked by means of deep shafts and extensive machinery. It is extremely probable that the distance of twelve yards radius which was acted upon as the protection to a water-pit, applied only to the erection of machinery and other uses of the surface, and had no reference to the coal. On the other hand, however, the general practice or custom acted upon was to consider the circle of twenty or twenty-four yards diameter as defining a tract of coal, which at any considerable depth was manifestly absurd.

These and other similar considerations had an important bearing on the practical operation of the 1838 Act as regards the assigning due limits to works which were so differently recognised by the old customs, and which from their number and extent had become of considerable importance to the Crown, to the owners of mines, and to the working population of the Forest.

If the ancient customs alone had been followed, the important question of the ownership of the coal would have been sufficiently definite, inasmuch as the right of the Crown to a share of the mine equivalent to the working of a fifth man has never been disputed; so far all is clear and simple, and the question of original ownership consequently becomes a matter of curiosity rather than of practical importance. The change effected by the act in this respect and the extension of privilege conceded by the Crown, is elucidated by the following considerations:

As a large portion of the coal in Dean Forest cannot be wrought except by the use of engines and machinery erected on the soil of the Forest, and as such engines and machinery could not be erected by the Free Miners under the ancient customs without the express permission of the owners of the soil it follows that this portion of the coal was inaccessible to the Free Miners, in the same manner that many extensive coal mines of the north of England can only be worked by payment of a greater or less rent to the owners of the freehold or copyhold lands in which it may be requisite to sink a pit. The privilege of access to the coal was therefore one which the Crown fully commanded previous to the passing of the Dean Forest (Mines) Act 1838, and a clear understanding of this point is of the greatest moment in considering the general operation of that Act.

In granting this privilege, as regards the surface, the Commissioners of Woods and Forests could only be guided by a discretionary power based on reasonable data, and not based upon the old custom of galing; for by the custom of galing, twenty, forty, or even a hundred gales might be granted within the scope of one reasonable tract of coal for a single work. To have granted a licence to each would have been utterly futile, since it is out of the nature of things that so many shafts would be sunk to a deep vein of coal at a cost of £5,000 or £10,000 each. If, then, the said deep vein of coal belonged to the Free Miners it was of little or no value subject to this prohibition which existed in the power of the Crown.

The Crown might refuse to grant a licence to erect an engine, and thus at once put an end to the Free Miner's access to the deep coal. Assuming that the Crown would not interpose any arbitrary or vexatious prohibition, and was even disposed to afford every facility, still the Free Miners, as a body, were very little nearer any valuable enjoyment. Numerous gales existed in situations as above described, and to work them all would have been utterly useless and ruinous. It is evident, therefore, that a great number of the gales so situated were merely vague, indefinite, and in many cases, visionary claims repugnant to every consideration of practical utility, and many of them, to all intents and purposes, utterly valueless.

The ownership of the coal, as among the Free Miners, depended chiefly on the construction that might be put upon what was called the 'protection' to a level or pit; extending, in the case of a level, to 1,000 yards, and, in a water-pit, to a circle of twenty or twenty-four yards diameter. If then, the ownership of a gale was conceded to any one part, at the distance of, say, 100 yards from another, and supposing that a water-pit was the only mode of access to each, did the ownership of each gale, under the old custom, extend to the twenty-four yards only, or to the whole intermediate space? If it extended only to the twenty-four yards, or a radius of twelve yards round each pit, to whom did the intervening coal belong? That it did not belong to the holder of either pit, as a matter of right, is clear, from the circumstance that a third party might demand a gale between them, and, in practise, might actually have sunk to and worked the coal. This state of things was inevitable so long as the ancient custom was considered as being applicable to the deep coal of the Forest. In practice, if two pits had been so sunk, the intervening coal would become the property of the first party that drove the 'narrow heading' or other working along it, and would, therefore, resolve the property or ownership of the coal into a matter of chance, and not of intrinsic right.

Another point, as to the legal ownership of the coal under the old custom, was, where a Free Miner or a foreigner, by virtue of a gale, had obtained possession of a coal vein in such a manner that he virtually commanded a very large tract of coal, by the power of extending his work, if necessary, before a pit could be sunk, and also by obtaining possession of gales near to any rival work. This is a case which resulted from the supposed reference of the custom to the deep coal, and it has been exemplified in several of the larger mines in the Forest.

These considerations strongly pointed out the importance of a clear understanding on these two points: viz., in whom, and subject to what conditions, was the ownership of the deep coal, not under gale, legally vested? and: Was the deep coal of the Forest subject to the ancient customs or not?

Now, in the first of these cases, whether it belonged to the crown or to the body of Free Miners, it is evident that no clear and distinct title could either be claimed or conferred as to any one part, with the exception of a circle of twenty-four yards in diameter. All beyond this was mere chance and this necessarily resolved itself into a prohibition to work the coal at all, or an entire and uncontrolled monopoly on the part of adventurous speculators.

In the second case, every practical consideration shows that the occupation of the deep coal, as claimed under the ancient customs, was altogether an encroachment, which was so far sanctioned that it could not afterwards be disallowed, but the irregularity was such as to render it absolutely necessary that a more clear knowledge should be arrived at as to the mode of occupying this portion of the coalfield.

An absolute necessity for some legislative enactment, therefore, existed, without which it was impossible to begin, much less to conclude, any award among the respective miners. In ordinary cases the several parties interested would have been met upon the broad principle of legal rights and of definite and distinct claims of ownership. In the Forest mines, there was, unfortunately, no such thing; if the custom was taken for a guide some of the owners of large mines in the deep coal of the Forest could at once claim a large tract of coal, and say, This is mine, because by the custom I can get at it before any rival can sink a pit; then came a host of gale owners, who having paid a guinea or two for having a gale granted, each claimed a gale, and that the gale under his gale-mark was absolutely his. Therefore, in the absence of a clear understanding as to the legal ownership of the coal, the question was so intangible, that it completely eluded every attempt to deal with it on business considerations, and the powers of an Act were requisite to confer the proper means of dealing with them.

In these remarks on the legal difficulties which impeded any attempt at adjustment under the ancient customs, no allusion has been made to the legality or illegality of the right of the foreigners; as their interests were fully recognised by the Act, so far as any interference with actual property and reasonable expectations were concerned.

In a financial point of view it became a very difficult and complicated subject to deal with existing interests in Dean Forest, inasmuch as many of the items of purchase of gales and of interruptions by faults and dislocations, etc., etc., could not be arrived at without an exact search into many pecuniary arrangements, and the awards to be made were to be based on mining as well as financial considerations. In a mining point of view, the amendment of the mining customs necessarily involved the discontinuance of several gales and applications for gales. The necessity for this existed in the very nature of the subject; there was no alternative but to perpetuate the previously existing state of things, and the following are the general principles upon which the alteration has been carried into effect under the powers of the Dean Forest (Mines) Act, 1838.

Seeing that there existed no definite legal rights to determine the boundaries of mines in the deep coal, and that the power to confer a right on the part of the Crown was subject to some uncertainty, the allotment of coal and mine to each work under the powers of the Mining Commission were necessarily based on equitable considerations.

Mr. Buddle and Mr. Sopwith, in their reports submitted to the Board of Woods and Forests, were strongly impressed with the desirableness of finding, if possible, some definite scale, some proportional dependance on the area already worked; the probable area commanded, the cost of winning, the average produce of each mine, and other points; but they found the circumstances of the mines to vary so much, the expenses so increased, and the profits so diminished in particular cases by the operation of the Forest customs; that they were not able, after the closest investigation to discover any fixed rule or principle that could be defined in terms so clear and explicit as to afford satisfaction to the owners of the several works. The rights of property, as they have for many years existed under the alleged customs of the Forest, were fully recognised, with a view to meet the reasonable expectations of the owners of large works; this was done by having respect to the particular circumstances of each mine, and chiefly to the first cost or purchase, which had varied in almost every instance; to the annual sums paid as galeage to the Crown, and payments for engine licences, and to Free Miners, etc., which also varied; to the depth of the pit or pits; to the nature of the strata sunk through; to the greater or less abundance of water in the mine; to the number, thickness, and quality of the veins of coal, which varied much in the same mine, as well as the different mines; to the contingencies arising from the overflowing of water from adjacent land workings; to the peculiar facilities or difficulties which had been experienced in each particular mine; to a retrospective view of the profits of the mine as well as its cost of working; to the area which, in all probability, would have been worked if the former customs had remained unaltered, and to the number and estimated value of the gales, pits, or works to be purchased in order to obtain possession of a fair field of coal.

Now, in all these matters there were not two mines exactly alike in the whole Forest, and this rendered it difficult to lay down or to act upon any definite rule that should apply equally to each particular case. They are all elements which, when combined, presented the means of applying as a general principle that the extent of coal to be allotted to each work ought to be proportionate to the capital expended in each mine, and to the cost of working, in order that an ample prospect of return might be afforded to those who had embarked their capital in the Forest mines.

The practical rules for laying out the future boundaries of large collieries were, therefore, in some measure, founded on the state of mining affairs under the ancient custom, which called for an alteration of one kind or another. This alteration, if it had been altogether restrictive, would have been a matter of considerable jealousy; but the Dean Forest Mining Act 1838 conferred benefits which the parties did not clearly possess previously to its being passed; such as the right of the Free Miners to a large tract of coal, which the Crown then held, as it were under lock and key, by means of the command of the surface; security to a definite tract of coal, which is another and very important advantage conferred by the Act; and, above all, the conferring of a saleable title, and an easy mode of adjusting differences, which hitherto had been most ruinous.

From these various considerations, it will be seen that the peculiarities of the Dean Forest customs were such as to preclude the application of any remedy, save that of discretionary powers based on the plain principle of common justice to the owners of the several properties, and of reasonable compensation in every case of inevitable loss or injury. Mining is, under all circumstances, a very speculative subject, as regards prospective valuations; and the peculiar and irregular practices in Dean Forest rendered it most difficult to define express rules. In most mining districts, the customs are tolerably well agreed upon: and there are, in addition, grants or leases which afford a guide in a legal point of view; the ownership is usually clear and undisputed; the financial matters are also usually well defined; the cost of sinking and working is unencumbered with indirect and doubtful payments, as in the purchase of gales, and the payment of a rent, which was rendered a minimum rent by the difficulty of applying the only remedy, viz. the putting in of a fifth man. In mining districts generally, it is usual to have definite tracts of coal, and protection from adjacent works; but in Dean Forest, all these were hitherto wanting; there were no clear legal rights to dispose of or allot, more than a mere spot, or circle of twenty-four yards in diameter of the deep coal. There were no means of establishing a colliery with an absolute certainty of a safe investment; and the want of a definite tract, the liability to encroachment, and the flowing of water from adjacent works, tended to create great confusion even in the free-drainage works, and to make the large mines comparatively valueless.

If the owners of the large mines could, as in other districts, have secured an equivalent tract of coal, the difficulty of arriving at a satisfactory conclusion would have been materially lessened. But this in practice was not so; the custom of galing, in many cases, occupied coal which might have been reasonably expected to be worked by other parties. The Mining Commissioners attentively considered the various suggestions which had been made; and after a deliberate examination of the circumstances of each case, a transition from the then impracticable customs, to a rational and provident system of mining, has been effected in the Forest of Dean.

The deep workings lie at a considerable depth from the surface of the lowest valleys, and even below the level of the sea; land or free drainage is therefore precluded. The strata abound with water, which, from so great a depth, cannot be drawn without the use of horse-gins, or manual labour; and where the mines are deep, and the quantity of water such as prevails in the mines of Dean Forest, steam-engines and machinery are indispensable.

The great expense attendant on such works rendered it necessary that tracts of coal of an extent corresponding to the outlay of capital should be awarded. After much careful deliberation, and having a due regard to the numerous, important, and complicated interests involved, the Mining Commissioners completed this service, and set forth in 1841 the Awards of Coal, Iron Mines and Quarries.'

Sopwith then gave a description[1] of the series of sixteen engraved plans of the Dean Forest mines the surveys for which he had completed in 1835. In their 'Award of Coal Mines' (8 March 1841) the Commissioners state 'the several persons hereinafter named, were, at the passing of the Dean Forest (Mines) Act, 1838 (either as free miners or as claiming through or under free miners, or as lessees of free miners) in possession of or entitled to the several hereinafter named gales, for the purpose of working the Coal Mines of the said Hundred of Saint Briavels'. Then followed Awards of 104 Coal Gales. The Commissioners then dealt with cases where free miners had after 9 April 1832 made applications in writing for gales of coal (but which applications had not been granted); and acted (or their assignees acted) upon such applications 'as if the same had been granted, and erected works and proceeded therein under such applications, at considerable expense'. The gales were awarded by the Commissioners, and described in detail in their first Schedule. The rents varied from £2 to £200 and the royalties from 1d. to 6d. a ton. The Commissioners made a similar Award of Iron Mines (20 July 1841). Twenty are named and the rents varied from £5 to £100 and the royalties from 2d. to 6d. a ton. Quarries were similarly treated, a total of 313 being awarded in the Award of Quarries (24 July 1841).

Several items of interest may be gathered from the Awards. The conditions of the Lightmoor Colliery gale included provision that the royalty should be 4d. per ton on coal for sale, but 3d. only on coal used for furnaces; that of Foxes Bridge Colliery gale – 6d. on Churchway High Delph coal, 3d. on coal from other veins. Of the large number of 'foreigners' claiming under or through free miners, some (such as Edward Protheroe – who held the largest number of gales) held the full gale, while in some cases ownership was divided, various persons having shares of one-eighth or one-quarter or one-half or even one-twentieth. Several instances are given of the leasing of gales by free miners to 'foreigners', the usual term being 1,000 years; other leases were for 99 years, 200 years and 500 years. Sometimes a free miner purchased a gale from another free miner, for example James Cowmeadow purchased the Cinderford Bridge Water Pit gale from Moses Teague. Sarah Whitehouse, widow of a free miner, sold her half-share in the Newcastle gale for £200 to Edward Protheroe.

The Awards also contain instances of wealthy 'foreigners' financing, by way of mortgage, the works of certain free miners. Instances are also given of gales purchased outright from free miners by 'foreigners' among whom were: William Crawshay of Cyfartha Castle, Glam.; Edward Protheroe, senior, and Edward Protheroe, junior, both of Newnham; Cheltenham Protector Coal Company; Anthony Hill; Sir Josiah Guest of Dowlais House, Glam.; George Elwell Jackson, ironmaster, Birmingham; and David Mushet. The following is a typical description of the coal gales granted under the Awards:

'True Blue and Newham Bottom Collieries

All that tract of coal in the Hill Delf vein, lying in the land of and drained by the True Blue Level, extending in a north-western direction as deep as the level will drain, to the line of 2 boundary stones,[2] N^{od} 1 and 2, to be set up as the north-western boundary of True Blue

[1] Included by Wood, *op. cit.*, pp. 194-8.

[2] Some boundary stones may be seen throughout the Forest to this day. They sometimes protrude from the ground up to three feet. A book at the Gaveller's Office, Coleford, once contained a full list of the situations of these boundary stones.

Colliery, and extending in a south-eastern direction, to the line of 2 other boundary stones, N^{od} 3 and 4, to be set up as the south-eastern boundary of the same colliery. And also all that further tract of coal in the same vein lying in the land of the Newham Bottom Level, up to the True Blue Level, extending in a south-eastern direction as deep as the said level will drain, from the pit A on the plan, to the line of 2 other boundary stones. N^{od} 5 and 6, to be set up as the north-western boundary of the Pluckpenny Colliery, and in a north-western direction to the line of 2 other boundary stones, N^{od} 7 and 8, to be set up as the north-western boundary of the Newham Bottom Colliery, except that at each end adjoining such boundary lines, and also adjoining the True Blue Level, a barrier of coal 20 yards in width[1] shall be left.

Rendering and paying therefore to her Majesty, her heirs and successors, up to Midsummer next, the former galeage rent, and thenceforward for all such coal as shall be brought out the sum of 2d. per ton as tonnage, such tonnage to be paid on the 24th day of June and the 25th day of December in every year. And further, so working the said colliery, as that there shall be wrought and gained in every year, from Midsummer next, a quantity of not less than 1,800 tons. Provided that if, by any reason whatsoever, in any one year no coal shall be got in respect of the said colliery, or the tonnage-rent to be paid for coal got within the year, under the aforesaid reservation, shall not amount to £15, then either the full sum of £15 or such other sum, as together with the amount paid or to be paid for tonnage-rent in respect of coal got within the year (as the case shall be) will make up the full sum of £15, shall be made up and paid to Her Majesty, her heirs and successors, on the 24th day of June in every year.'

In effect the Dean Forest Mining Commission defined the extent of all the gales – by description and plans in the 1841 Awards of coal and iron ore gales, and of stone quarries. Each Award contains a Schedule setting out the Rules and Regulations for working by the galee by imposing a personal obligation on the galee for the time being, for liability for forfeiture in default. The Rules relate to the payment of rents and royalties, management, safety of working, *bonâ fide* working, surrender, etc. For coal gales there were 23 Rules; for iron ore, 21; and for stone quarries, 8. These Rules, *inter alia,* required that galees should keep plans of the workings and mine in a fair, orderly and workmanlike manner, according to the best and most improved system for the time being of working, and not desist from *bonâ fide* working for 5 years at any one time. Much credit is due to the Commissioners for the able way in which they carried out their task: the fact that no appeal was made against any of the Awards is proof of their care and accuracy.

It seems remarkable that in a coalfield which produced at its highest less than 1% of the total U.K. coal output, so much time, effort and money were applied to sorting out the Forest coalfield's many problems which existed prior to the passing of the 1838 Act and the Awards (*supra*) which followed it.

The assignees of gales, their rights assured, and regulations made to obviate much of the earlier chaos, began to develop the works, and a profound change emerged in the reorganisation and scale of the Forest's mining.[2] Though now partly of academic interest, much of the Awards and the Rules and Regulations of 1841 (later modified or

1 The Dean Forest (Amendment) Act 1861, S.24, empowered the gaveller or deputy gaveller to grant permission for the working and disposal of coal in any barrier, under certain conditions.

2 See list in Hart, *Industrial History* (1971), pp. 270-7.

amplified by the Acts of 1861, 1871, 1904, 1938, 1946, 1969, and 1994) still apply and provide the bases of mining in the Forest and hundred.

Before closing this chapter, mention is made of the useful annual Reports of the Commissioners of Woods[1] which contain much information regarding gales, encroachments, sales, purchases and exchanges, and leases of land, stone and clay. All of importance for the present volume has been included. In all transactions the Crown reserved 'mines, minerals and quarries'.

[1] Reports Nos. 1 to 15 cover the period 1812 to 1838.

CHAPTER VIII

1842-1873: Committees of 1848 and 1854; and Acts of 1861 and 1871

THE *Duncan Committee, 1848*. A Select Committee, known as the 'Duncan Committee', was appointed in 1848 to report upon the Crown forests. In connection with the Forest of Dean, they questioned Edward Machen (Plate VIII), deputy surveyor and joint deputy gaveller; John Atkinson, joint deputy gaveller; John Langham, one of the assistant deputy surveyors, and several other people. They did not have time to report their opinion during the then session of Parliament but issued the Minutes of Evidence on 17 July 1849,[1] some of which are included in the following pages.

Edward Machen, (5 March 1849):

'Q. 2321. What are your duties as gaveller? – To assign to the miners the places where they should open their works, and to receive the gale rents; Mr. Atkinson's part is to visit the works, and keep correct plans of all workings; I do not understand mining myself.

Q. 2322. Is it your duty to receive the rents? – Yes, and I assist Mr. Atkinson upon disputed points; the Commissioners of Woods wished me to be joined with Mr. Atkinson.

Q. 2323. Will you state shortly to the Committee who the free miners of the Forest of Dean are? – They are all persons born in the Hundred of St. Briavels, and residing there, and who have worked a year and a day in one of the mines.

Q. 2324. Do they claim any rights in the Forest? – Yes, and their rights are recognised by Act of Parliament [1838]; it is to them that the gales are granted in the first instance.

Q. 2326. What is the extent of the mineral produce in the Forest of Dean, and of what does it consist? – Coal and iron ore, and the quarries pay a very small sum; the tonnage on coal varies from 2d. to 1½d. and 1d. a ton.

Q. 2330. What are the arrangements adopted with regard to the mines; what is the mode of letting out the gales? – The principle is settled by Act of Parliament; the principle is, that the Crown is supposed to have the right of putting in a fifth man to work after a mine has been opened, and it is an equivalent for that right.

Q. 2332. How are the quantities of coal upon which royalty is paid, ascertained? – They are ascertained by the return of the miners themselves, with power in the gavellers to inspect the books, but that power has not been exercised; but in the last year we have had returns from the two railway companies, and that has been checked by the miners' returns, and there

---

1 First Report of the Select Committee on the Woods, Forests, and Land Revenues of the Crown together with the Minutes of Evidence and Appendix ordered to be printed 17 July 1849 (H.M.S.O.). Index printed on 27 July 1849, combined with the Second Report. A copy of the draft printed Report, 25 July 1848, Ref. 338-III(2) House of Commons, is in Glos.R.O., Hart Dean Collection D3921.

Plate VIII. *Edward Machen, deputy surveyor 1808-1854. He died at English Bicknor in October 1862, aged 79.*

seems no reason to doubt the accuracy of them, and we have not inspected the books.

Q. 2334. Are there any arrears for the royalty, or rent of the coal-mines? – Yes there are very small arrears for the coals, and there are arrears for rents, which are called the dead rents, and considerable arrears.

Q. 2335. What is the reason of those arrears? – The parties give various reasons; they think they are too highly set; most of them were set by the [Mining] Commissioners [in 1841], and one argument that the parties bring forward is that the Commissioners set them under the idea that a steam railroad would be brought into the Forest at the time they were being set, and various circumstances have prevented that, and they seem to consider the rents too high.

Q. 2336. Do they dispute the right of collecting them? – They have memorialized, and stated it in that way, but no positive legal steps have been taken; what are called the dead rents are not wholly lost to the Crown if unpaid, because, if they were paid, the parties would have a right to deduct them out of the tonnages hereafter, when they open mines.

Q. 2337. Those dead rents were settled by the [Mining] Commissioners under the Act of Parliament [1838]? – Yes, most of them; there is a settlement of the gale-rent in the case of every new mine opened, but the principal rents were settled by the Commissioners.

Q. 2343. Can you state the amount of revenue derived from the minerals in the Forest? – It is about £4,000 a year now. (In reply to Q. 2590 and Q. 2591 he said the cost of collecting same was about £400 including Mr. Atkinson's salary.)

Q. 2345. You say it amounts to about £4,000 a year ? – Yes, at present; that was after the Mining Act; from 1837 to 1841, it averaged about £700 or £800 a year.

Q. 2346. Subsequently to that period it averaged £4,000 a year ? – It increased gradually after the Mining Act passed; for the last four years it has exceeded £4,000.

Q. 2347. Could any improvement be suggested by you with a view to facilitate the means of increasing the revenue derived from minerals in the Forest of Dean? – An improved transit would open the workings and improve the revenue, but the means of effecting that I cannot point out.

Q. 2348. Can mines be opened at present in the plantations? – No; the coals can be worked under the plantations by openings [from] outside.

Q. 2349. Why are they not allowed to be opened in the plantations? – The Act of Parliament discharged all the plantations from all rights of every kind during the time they were inclosed as nurseries of timber.

Q. 2350. Do you think an alteration in the Act in that respect would have any effect upon the mining revenue? – No, I do not think it would now; I think the state of trade hardly calls at present for many more openings than they have the means of effecting now.

Q. 2436. Will you explain to the Committee what miners' timber is? – The miners' timber is the larger part of the thinnings, and the cordwood is the smaller part.

Q. 2438. Were not the free miners in the Forest of Dean long ago entitled to a certain supply of timber for the use of their mining works ? – Yes, they claimed it, and they took it.

Q. 2439. This right was extinguished by the provisions of the Act of 1 & 2 Vict. c. 54 [1838]? – It was entirely extinguished then; it had been very much diminished before that by the Railroad Act.

Q. 2444. What is the reason of that price [10s. a cord] being put upon it ? – The reason at first was to let the miners down easily, after their having had it for nothing; then for the last two years we have given them notice to advance the price; they have memorialized the

Board [of Woods] to say that the state of trade has been bad from the want of a steam railroad, and their being subjected to new burdens. It has not been raised at present, but after the 31st of this month they have no promise of its being continued at that price.'

John Langham, assistant deputy-surveyor:

'Q. 3116. Who sets out the miners' timber? – I do, it is in my department; we cut the miners' timber in our regular thinnings and it is brought to the drives and ranked, and we have monthly sales; at Christmas I always send a circular to the coal proprietors stating that on certain days in every month I shall attend to sell them pit timber as they may want it; I accordingly attend and they attend, and it is sold in that way; they draw tickets as to the preference, who shall take up first and so on and it is delivered to them in any quantity they may want, from two to 200 cords.

Q. 3117. Are those sales by private contract? – They are.

Q. 3118. Is one lot better than the others? – It may happen if there are ten applicants, that number seven or any other number may fall in a part of their inclosure where there is a sprinkling of fir, which they do not like; we do not cut much fir excepting larch fir pit timber, therefore we cut it up to cordwood; it might happen that there might be a larger proportion of fir to any given number than in the other cases; we make no selection for the purpose of having one better than the others.

Q. 3119. Who settles the lots? – There are no decided lots; A, B and C apply for timber; A wants 10 cords, B wants 50, C wants 7, and D 70, as the case may be; No. 1, according to the tickets[1] which are drawn, goes round with me and hammers his own timber, till he has taken up his 7 cords, or 70, or whatever number he wants.

Q. 3129. What is the distinction between miners' timber sold by cord and cordwood? – The miners' timber is all the best part of the pole, cut out to certain lengths to suit the delphs of coal; 6ft. 6in., 8ft. 8in., 13ft. are generally the lengths that are wanted; then the remainder, the refuse of the pole, is cut up for cordwood.'

Langham also explained that the cordwood for mining was sold by public auction, in lots of 300 to 400 cords, twice a year. John Alford did the stacking and recording of miners' timber and cordwood, totalling 8,000 to 10,000 cords a year at 5d. a cord.

The next witness was Thomas Nicholson,[2] coal proprietor. He had been in the coal trade for twenty-eight years and was 'one of the occupying tenants of the Parkend Collieries, belonging to Edward Protheroe', and New Fancy Colliery. The previous year he had sold about 100,000 tons of coal which was about one-quarter of the whole coal trade of the Forest. His galeage rents amounted last year to about £700. Audits were held half yearly when the two deputy gavellers were present and collected the rents and royalties. As to the payment of dead rents fixed by the Dean Forest Mining Commissioners, he pointed out that new pits must be opened within five years but that this was impossible financially without better railways. He and others had objected to the Office of Woods regarding dead rents on collieries on the outskirts of the Forest. At a meeting at the Speech House he had proposed an *ad valorem* rent-charge based

1 The meeting was arranged for 10 a.m. and the tickets placed in a hat.
2 Q. 3277-3605.

on the more valuable collieries. Others would not agree as they wished the old nominal rents of pre-Award days. As they could not agree they had acted separately. He was paying £100 a year for an outlying colliery whereas £20 was its worth. He was paying £150 and £200 respectively for his two 'interior' collieries. The maximum tonnage rent by the Act of 1838 was 4d. and the deputy gaveller had fixed rents of recent gales very much lower than those fixed under the Awards. 'We do not object', he said, 'to the tonnages, we do not wish to deprive the Crown ultimately of any amount of revenue; all we object to is to our being called upon to pay so large a sum beforehand on future gales.' They did not wish 'to exclude other parties from the mines and not to pay any rents themselves for them'. He had bought his unopened colliery gale from James Brooks of Bream when the latter was in difficulties on the understanding that he could repurchase it when able to do so. Brooks, who was not a free miner, obtained the gale from a Mr. Priest of Bream, a free miner. It had been originally galed by the Crown for three or four guineas per annum, perhaps six guineas; now it was charged at £100 per annum. He was three years in arrears with his dead rent. No objection had been made at the time of the Award, because suitable railways had been expected. Mr. Buddle, one of the Dean Forest Mining Commissioners, had told him 'it is impossible things can remain as they are; you will be sure to have a railway communication'.

Mr. Nicholson said that the local officers allowed every facility for the opening and working of collieries but sometimes there was a little difficulty when wanting to open mines in inclosed parts of the Forest, although he added: 'they manage it for us as well as they can'. He thought it would be of great advantage if they could have increased facilities for residence for their workmen. Under existing legislature they must build on a thirty-one-year lease. Only a few houses existed – near the Wellington and Brunswick Collieries; many were needed at Parkend, Rose-in-Hand, near the Speech House, and Foxes Bridge Collieries. His collieries supplied 1,000 to 1,200 tons of coal per month to Parkend Furnaces. Many thousands of tons were also sold at the pit head. Farmers used to send food and drink with the waggoners for the colliers and obtained a good load! The system was not entirely abolished. There was no check in these cases from the Crown's point of view. In the case of coal sent by rail there were the truck weights; he noticed at the last audit that the deputy gaveller had a railway account before him for the first time. At his Parkend Colliery there were six seams of coal but only four were being worked. The thickest was 3-4 feet, others were 2 feet, others 14-30 inches. Sometimes as much as 3,000 tons were obtained from an acre. He agreed that colliers were much addicted to poaching, adding: 'it is a bad thing to have game in a mining district.' At the last verderers' election the coal proprietors united in an address to the candidate tendering support if he would use his influence to abolish the deer. Deer meant colliers poaching; poaching meant absence from work; absence from work meant the collier's 'company (gang) being put out of gear'.

Isaiah Teague,[1] mineral surveyor, of Blakeney, the next witness, gave the prices of coal as: about 7s. to 8s. 'at the pit's mouth', 8s. to 9s. 'for land sales at pit's mouth', and 7s. 'for soft coal'. He valued the Crown's fifth share as 2d. per ton on hard coal, 1½d. on soft and inferior coal, and thought that 2d. per ton was a fair compensation to the Crown in lieu of the right to put in a fifth man. He owned Howbeach Engine and

1 Q. 3606-3714.

High Delph Engine gales on which he owed dead rents of £550 and £275 respectively, and had signed a Memorial against the high rents. He was unwilling to pay the dead rents until the mines were opened, and was willing to forfeit his gales if necessary. Some galees had paid their dead rents and others had not. His deposition continued:

'Q. 3698. Can you give any instance in any part of England where either the dead rent or the charge for royalty of 2d. a ton, is so small in proportion to the price of coal, as it is in Dean Forest? – I cannot give an instance, but Her Majesty had never a right but to the fifth part of the works; Her Majesty had no right to put on a dead-rent, she cannot force us to work the mines, unless we wish to work them.

Q. 3699. You think that the Award the Mining Commissioners made under the Act was an illegal award? – I do; the tonnages no one can object to, but the dead rent is oppressive.

Q. 3707. Do you think that the establishment of railway communication would entitle the crown to charge more than 2d. a ton for their royalty? – I think not; 10d. a ton was an excellent price and Her Majesty had only a right to one-fifth, and that is putting the tenant's right down at 10d. a ton.

Q. 3708. But Her Majesty, as I understand you, did not participate in the expenses of working the mines, does not that make a difference? – Yes it does, but not to that extent.

Q. 3709. Do you mean to say that it would not be a much larger sum than 2d. a ton, when you come to deepen the mines? – It depends upon the quantity you get.

Q. 3711. You are now speaking of deep mines which are to be opened, and which are to be benefited by this railway communication; if a railway comes which is to benefit those deep mines, for the working of which the miners are liable to pay the whole expense, would not the Crown be entitled to an increase upon the 4d. ton royalty? – Under the circumstances I do not think they would; I consider that for any of our collieries a tenant's right of 6d. a ton is quite sufficient, and the tenant's right is now put at 10d. a ton; there is a good deal of risk in mining property, to parties who embark their capital in it, and I do not think it would be fair for the Crown to ask more than 2d. a ton.'

William Downes,[1] who had inspected the Forest on his own account, said: 'The coal raised upon this property is of immense extent, and is daily increasing.' 'There are several seams which are divided into three series, viz.: First or Highest Series are three small veins of Woorgreens which are unimportant; Second or Middle Series, Smith's Coal, Lowrey or Parkend High Delph, Rocky vein and Upper and Lower Churchway veins; these extend over an area of 7,000 acres; Third or Lowest Series, Nag's Head Coal, Whittington's Delph Coal, Coleford High Delph vein, Upper and Lower Trenchard veins; these extend over 16,000 acres. The Coleford High Delph vein is the most important; it lies at a considerable depth below the Middle or Park veins, and has not been worked to any great extent; the thickness of the veins runs from one or two to six feet, some up to eight, ten or twelve feet, but in these latter cases they are apt to be faulty.' Mr. Downes estimated that the Awards of 1841 allowed for the annual working of 391,840 tons of coal at a minimum rent of £3,171, and of 14,000 tons of iron ore at a minimum rent of £213. Adding licences for tramways, steam engines, etc., the total would come to £3,545 6s. As regards coal gales, the

[1] Q. 3785-4024.

greatest quantity named in any one lot was 30,000 tons per annum whereas he understood the Colliery working that gale (Bilson Colliery) was winning 300 tons per day, equal to 90,000 tons a year. As to the sale of cordwood to miners at 10s. per ton, he said that the cost of cutting a cord 16ft. 8in. long, 2ft. 2in. wide and 2ft. 2in. high was 2s. 4d., plus 5d. for stacking and recording. This he thought left 'but a moderate return'. He added: 'How far the legal right to this moderate charge can be maintained, I was unable to ascertain; the same rate of charge is, however, made to other parties, not claiming it as a right in virtue of their mines.' He handed in a valuation from which the following is extracted:

Annual rents of coal and iron gales, and licences for tramways, steam engines, &c., £3,545, but worth in his opinion	£7,518
Quarries and sundry encroachments	250
....	£7,768
At 20 years' purchase this would be	£155,360

He thus valued the Crown's rights in the Dean coal, iron ore and quarries at £155,360.

Thomas Sopwith,[1] one of the Mining Commissioners of 1838, then gave evidence. He said that at the time of the Awards (1841) there were the Severn and Wye Tramway, and the Bullo Pill Railway (since, more frequently called the Forest of Dean Railway) on the east side, and a part of the Severn and Wye Tramway which extended to Monmouth on the west side. He had no reason to change the amounts of the gale rents he had helped to fix in 1841. No inducement had been held out of hope of new railway communications. Although 'in the air' it had not affected the Award figures. The object of the dead rents was to prevent a large quantity of coal being locked up. He had intended the payments to be enforced or forfeiture in five years, and had no reason to change his opinion. No money was paid down at the time the gales were granted. Sopwith agreed that the office of deputy gaveller should be a full-time one,[2] but that the Office of Woods had fixed a figure for salary of £150 only and arrangements had to be made accordingly. On being asked whether Mr. Atkinson would be capable as a check-surveyor, upon entering a mine, of telling if any large quantity had been won that had not been accounted for, he replied: 'It is his duty to do so.'

Alexander Milne,[3] one of the Commissioners of Woods, confirmed that up to 1808 the gaveller received all the Crown's portion of the produce of the mines, adding: 'About 1808 the office of gaveller was abolished, and the then gaveller received a compensation, and the office was vested in the surveyor-general of woods and afterwards the Chief Commissioner for the time being, without emolument; and the produce of the mines, after paying a compensation to the late gaveller, and the persons who executed the office of gaveller, was carried to the general account of the Forest.' He stated that whereas in 1808 the Crown received no yield from the mines and minerals, the average yield for the four years to 1848 had been £4,050; this, at twenty years'

---

1 Q. 4495-4607.

2 Thomas Nicholson also pointed out this desirability.

3 Q. 4701-2 and Q. 4747-5070.

purchase, made a capital value of £81,000. Mr. Milne explained that two large coal works were about to be opened, one by Mr. Crawshay on which upwards of £20,000 had been expended, and the other belonging to Messrs. Morrells of Oxford. He said there had been very strong appeals both to the Board and to the Chief Commissioner from the year 1844 down to the present time imploring the forbearance of the Crown regarding dead rents; the reasons given were the poor state of the coal trade, lack of capital, and need of improved railway communications. In June last year letters had been sent by the Board threatening legal proceedings if the dead rents were not paid. One result was a deputation of miners who stated 'that it would be perfectly ruinous to them if the dead rents were enforced'. The miners asked time for consideration and for making some proposition. No proposition had been forthcoming, and the deputy gaveller had been urged to press for payment, short of legal proceedings. Some miners had since paid; others had not.[1]

The relevant parts of the evidence of John Atkinson, joint deputy gaveller with Edward Machen, are given below[2]:

'Q. 2793. By whom were you appointed? – By Lord Duncannon.

Q. 2794. Were you appointed in consequence of the recommendation of the Dean Forest Mining Commissioners? – I came to Dean Forest at the particular request of John Buddle, who was one of the Commissioners.

Q. 2795. What amount of money do you collect for the Crown? – The last three years the average, after all expenses of collection are paid, has been rather more than £3,500 a year; that is the average net receipt.

Q. 2796. What has been the average gross receipt? – About £4,200.

Q. 2797. What is the nature of your duties as deputy gaveller? – My duties are exceedingly various: In the first place, I examine and make surveys and keep plans of all the mines in the Forest, and also in the Hundred of St. Briavels; my duties extend considerably beyond the boundary of the Forest; the Hundred of St. Briavels comprehends several parishes under which a portion of the mines run; and where-ever the mines are to be found within the Hundred of St. Briavels, there my duties extend.

Q. 2798. Do the Crown's rights extend beyond the Forest? – Yes.

Q. 2799. Do the Crown's right of minerals extend over the whole hundred of St. Briavels? – Yes.

Q. 2800. Is the boundary of the Hundred of St. Briavels accurately defined? – It is not, to my knowledge; I know there are certain parishes within the Hundred of St. Briavels, underneath which the mineral basin extends.

Q. 2801. How do you know the district to which your duties extend? – I simply make inquiry whether such a parish is within the Hundred of St. Briavels; if it is within the Hundred of St. Briavels, there I know my duty extends.

Q. 2802. There is no doubt, is there, where the Hundred of St. Briavels extends? – I believe not.

Q. 2803. Do you act in the Forest for the Crown alone, or do you sometimes act for

1 Appendix H (p. 461) to the Report showed that the arrears of dead rents due upon coal and iron ore mines up to Christmas 1848 amounted to £8,852 0s. 8d.

2 Q. 2789-3050.

private individuals? – I act as agent for the Crown alone; but where persons want plans of their workings, or anything of that sort, they generally come to me for them; when I first came to the Forest, unfortunately, there was scarcely a plan to be found; they were all working without any aim, except that of cutting each other out, and no limits were defined: the Act of Parliament [1838], however, if it is enforced, obliges them to have plans of all their workings; no person has the same opportunity of making such plans as myself and they generally come to me for such plans of the working of their collieries.

Q. 2806. Are you paid by the private parties to whom you have referred, as well as by the Crown? – Yes; I always charge when a plan is to be made for a private party; it is no part of my official duty to make private plans for anybody; when I came to the Forest, the late Mr. Buddle, who was my patron, said, "Your duties in the Forest will, I expect, not be very serious; you will have plenty of time to do other matters; therefore", he said, "you need not be astonished if you have not a very high salary." Unfortunately it has turned out that Mr. Buddle was mistaken in his notion about the duties I had to perform; the duties have become very onerous indeed, and as to making any of these plans myself, it is out of the question, unless I have assistants to do it; I have had several pupils, teaching them mineral and land surveying, through whose assistance I have been able to do those things, and the Crown also has had the benefit of those assistants.

Q. 2808. Your salary would be rather low, as an average salary, for a person in your profession, occupying the situation and performing the duties which you do? – Very low indeed, much too low, it is scarcely half enough. My duty is also to agree with the free miners, and set out their new gales and collieries, and mine works, within the Hundred of St. Briavels, and to grant them; to collect all the rents from them and for the quarries; to issue notices of various kinds; and I am subject to be called upon by every person where there is a dispute as to boundaries, or anything of that kind; they all come to me directly, and very fortunately too, instead of going to law, which in many cases saves a great deal of expense in money. I am very often called on to settle boundary disputes, and also to enter transfers of the sale of every gale of mineral property in the Forest and Hundred of St. Briavels; they all have to be registered in our books, which are open to parties who are purchasing, to come and see whether the same property has been previously transferred.

Q. 2809. Do you keep an accurate register of all the gales set out in the Forest? – Yes, every one of them.

Q. 2816. Do you recollect the whole number of acres which your map comprises? – The total quantity is 22,522 acres, within the Forest Boundary.

Q. 2817. Can you state how much of that belongs to individuals? – About 3,190 acres.

Q. 2818. Though the land belongs to private individuals, the Crown is entitled to the mines under it? – Yes.

Q. 2819. Is it all in St. Briavels? – Yes.

Q. 2842. What system of royalties is adopted in regard to working the mines? – The Crown's royalty is two pence; in no case for coal is it more than two pence; sometimes three halfpence.

Q. 2843. When is that royalty payable? – It is payable every Midsummer and Christmas.

Q. 2844. When and by whom are the royalties settled? – By the Dean Forest Mining Commissioners appointed by Act of Parliament [1838].

Q. 2845. Who are the parties who have a right to open mines in the Forest of Dean? – The parties having right to mines are parties called free miners; those are men who have been born within the Hundred of St. Briavels, and have worked for a year and a day in a coal or iron mine; that constitutes a free miner; he is then entitled to take out a gale, as it is called; that is, to make an application in a given spot for a colliery or an iron work; those applications are entered in a book and they are dealt with in the order in which they are made; the person making the first application, of course, has the best chance, the miners and myself agree as to the terms and boundaries; that is sent up to the Commissioners for their approval and then they are granted to them.

Q. 2846. To whom is the application made in the first instance? – To Mr. Machen and myself.

Q. 2847. Are there cases of common miners coming and applying for these gales? – There are nothing but common miners; they are nearly all poor men; they cannot open them by themselves; they used to be very tenacious about foreigners coming into the Forest; these coal basins all crop out at the surface; the miners then could dibble down a certain distance, as far as their means permitted and no further; now they find it necessary that somebody else should come and therefore they sell their gales to foreigners.

Q. 2848. They have not capital to work the mines themselves? – No.

Q. 2849. When one of these free miners applies to you for a gale, what quantity of mineral do you award him? – It depends upon circumstances; we take the probable depth into consideration and the difficulties and so on; where it is close to the cropping out we award him a very small piece; where it is very deep it would amount to something like 300 acres sometimes.

Q. 2850. Do you inquire into his capacity to work it? – No, we have no business to do that, I apprehend.

Q. 2851. How much is paid for a gale? – That depends on circumstances also; upon the very small ones, a couple of pounds certain rents, perhaps; then when the man comes to work it there is also a tonnage in all cases paid.

Q. 2852. Who reports upon the value of a gale? – There is no person but myself and the free miner.

Q. 2853. Are there any large workings by companies which have capital in the Forest? – There are some very extensive ones.

Q. 2854. How have those gales been obtained? – They were obtained by free miners in the first place.

Q. 2855. What extent of minerals is held by any of those large companies? – Some of them have three to four or five hundred acres.

Q. 2856. Was that quantity of minerals granted originally to a single free miner? – No, when those large workings which are now open were granted, the free miner could only command the particular spot upon which his gale was granted; outside the radius of 12 yards another free miner could put in another application; then they might go down and undercut one another.

Q. 2857. Have not those conflicting rights been settled by the Commissioners under the Act of Parliament? – Yes.

Q. 2858. Did that Act of Parliament [1838] fix the number of acres which each free miner might have when he made application? – No it did not.

Q. 2859. It left that to the discretion of the Commissioners? – Yes; all free miners having claims at the time of the Mining Commission, put in such claims to the Mining Commissioners. The claims were discussed, and where the Commissioner, thought it right, they set out a tract of coal, and put boundary stones to it; previously to that there were no boundary stones at all used.

Q. 2860. Have you had any instances lately of companies with large capital purchasing up the rights of a number of free miners, and applying to you for a large extent of minerals, to work upon a great scale? – They could not do it in that way. What they purchase now, they know the extent of, because there is a plan of it; any person wanting to purchase, does not purchase the spot only, but the tract allotted to the applicant.

Q. 2861. First of all an allotment is made to the free miner upon his application and then he disposes of that to some one else? – Exactly so.

Q. 2862. Have you ever known large sums given to a free miner for a tract which had been allotted to him? – Not large sums; some of them get £700 or £800; I think I recollect a case some little time ago, in which two levels were sold to some parties, and I think it was £800 which was given for each of them.

Q. 2863. What has the crown received from those parties? – Not a fraction yet in tonnage; they are not opened; they pay certain rent.

Q. 2864. The crown only receives a royalty when the mine has been worked? – For a certain time after a grant is made the crown receives a certain rent; such certain rent is liquidated by the over-working of succeeding years, when the works are open.

Q. 2865. Then the free miner who is totally incapable, from the want of capital, of working properly a valuable tract of mineral, may by acquiring it, prevent its being worked efficiently for the benefit of the Crown? – There are rules and regulations in existence which compel them to open the mine within five years, otherwise it is liable to forfeiture.

Q. 2866. Every grantee must open the work within five years? – Yes or it is liable to forfeiture.

Q. 2867. May he not then turn out 20 tons a year instead of 500 after he has commenced? – There are rules and regulations also, which govern that; they oblige him to work it in a proper manner; if we saw a man shirking it in that way we should consider it the same as if he did not work it at all, and it would be liable to forfeiture.

Q. 2868. Is there any rent paid as well as royalty? – There is a certain rent.

Q. 2869. How is the quantity of coal on which the royalty is paid ascertained? – From the parties.

Q. 2870. When a forfeiture of the kind referred to takes place, do the rights of the free miner become extinct or has he any right to make a further application? – A free miner has a right to hold only three gales at one time and so long as a gale is in existence, I apprehend, whether he or anybody else hold it, he has no right to another, if that is one of his three.

Q. 2871. If it becomes worked out he can claim another? – Yes; he can.

Q. 2872. Then the right is never extinct? – No.

Q. 2873. And it is limited to three gales? – Yes.

Q. 2874. What is a gale? – It is a technical term for a tract of coal.

Q. 2875. It is not defined in quantity? – It is defined now as the grant of the gale, but it was not so before the Mining Act passed.

Q. 2876. What is the quantity which is now defined? – It depends on circumstances connected with the gale; if it be near the cropping out of the coal, it will take very little to get the coal, but if it be 300 yards deep, we put a quantity in proportion.

Q. 2877. After all, therefore, a gale is not a defined quantity, but it depends upon circumstances? – Yes.

Q. 2878. And they depend again upon the appreciation of the Commissioners? – And ourselves.

Q. 2879. Do you act as arbitrator in case of dispute? – No; if there is a dispute between a free miner and myself as to the terms of the grant, I believe an arbitrator may be called in.

Q. 2880. What average sum is paid for each gale? – I have not the amounts here; the sums are, some of them, small; under the Mining Commission the highest, I think, was £200 a year for a large tract of coal and in some cases £1 a year.

Q. 2881. Is that independently of the tonnage which is paid upon the coal when it is worked? – It is, in fact, a certain rent; they shall pay 2d. per ton, the Award says, but they shall not get less than a certain number of tons per year, which will cover say £100, perhaps; but if they work less, they shall pay for that number; then, when they work over and above that, the overworkings shall go to liquidate what they have paid by way of rent.

Q. 2882. You said that the quantity of the coal upon which the royalty was paid was ascertained from the parties themselves? – It is.

Q. 2883. How is the quantity of coal which is taken away upon the railways checked? – They have machines for the purpose.

Q. 2884. What check have you upon the quantities, in order to ascertain that the proper amount of royalty is paid? – We have only the check of the machines.

Q. 2885. Who keeps the machines? – The railway company; I sent last year to each of the companies asking them for the return for the half year and they sent it to me.

Q. 2886. How do you ascertain what quantity of coal is taken away upon the roads? – That we take from the parties.

Q. 2887. From the coal owners? – Yes.

Q. 2888. Do they weigh the coal when they put it into the carts? – Yes, they do; there are some of them who do not; in fact some of the little places are so insignificant, that it would ruin them to have to put up a weighing machine.

Q. 2889. Have you no check upon the amount which is taken from each mine? – No, but we have the liberty, if we choose to exercise it (and that they know), of requiring their books to be laid open to us.

Q. 2890. Should you, from your experience, be able to tell by looking at a mine, how much had been worked out of it? – We could do so.

Q. 2891. Did it ever strike you that any large quantity had been taken away unduly? – I have never had reason to suppose so.

Q. 2892. Do you think you have the means yourself of estimating by measurement or by computation whether the returns which are made to you are accurate or not? – I could do so if I had the slightest suspicion of anything wrong.

Q. 2894. Have you ever had any reason to suspect anything wrong? – No.

Q. 2895. And therefore you have never had any reason to check the quantity? – No.

Q. 2896. Have you ever sent to any of the railway companies for a return of the coal sent by railway before last year? – No.

Q. 2897. Had you any reason for suspicion then? – No; in fact it turned out exactly as I am telling you; the quantities agreed very nearly indeed with the colliery returns.

Q. 2898. Is there much coal which is sold otherwise than by means of the railways? – There is some sold to the country traders.

Q. 2899. Is that a trifling quantity or a considerable quantity? – Not considerable; Monmouth and Herefordshire are the principal places; there are about 4,000 inhabitants in Monmouth.

Q. 2900. The quantity of coal which is sold to the country not being considerable, all the rest is disposed of by railway? – Yes.

Q. 2901. Have you the means of informing the Committee of the amount which is carried on the railway, by reference to the books of the company? – No I do not think the company are obliged to do so, but they sent to us the accounts from their books when we asked for them.

Q. 2902. You do ask for them do you sometimes? – I asked, last year simply as a check, and their accounts agreed with ours quite satisfactorily.

Q. 2903. Should you be enabled to judge of the quantity of coal obtained, by the number of people employed in the respective pits? – It would help us in some degree; but sometimes, though, there are a couple of hundred men employed, a hundred men would work the same quantity.

Q. 2904. How many mines are there at present worked under the Dean Forest workings? – There are about 20.

Q. 2905. What is the largest of those? – Parkend Colliery is one of them.

Q. 2906. By whom is that held? – It is held by lease under Mr. Protheroe.

Q. 2907. What is the number of tons turned out of that colliery annually? – About 80,000 tons.

Q. 2908. What is the thickness of that seam of coal? – They are working several seams; the principal one is about three feet thick.

Q. 2909. Is that the thickest? – At that colliery; it is three feet in a single coal.

Q. 2910. Is there another seam of coal near to it, near the division of a band? – There is nothing within seven or eight yards of it.

Q. 2911. Is the extent of the mineral field, which those parties hold large? – At its present depth, it is nearly worked out in the best vein; but there are several acres below which are not touched; they must go deeper down to get at that.

Q. 2912. About what is the extent of the Parkend Colliery? – About 500 acres; one half of which is worked out in the principal vein, but only a small proportion of the other veins are worked.

Q. 2913. What is the nature of the dead rents? – The dead rent is a sum put upon a colliery requiring them to raise a certain number of tons, which must amount to that sum; if they do not realise that in working, they must pay that sum; if they don't work at all after the first two years of holding (they have two years for the purpose of opening the works during which they pay nothing), then they are still liable to pay this, and after the colliery is in work, whatever is worked over and above that sum, goes to liquidate what they have paid beforehand by way of certain rent.

Q. 2914. Are the dead rents regularly paid, or are there any arrear? – They are, some of them, irregularly paid; there are very few who dispute the payment; some, I believe are too poor to pay, in fact, and some will not pay; I think those are the two classes, some cannot and some will not.

Q. 2915. How long is it since they refused to pay? – I cannot say, without reference to the account; there is one case of an absolute refusal; the party supposes that the law is not stringent enough to make him pay; I have told him that I apprehend he will find himself mistaken; he is a lawyer. There are three or four whose rents come rather heavy, and their arrears are, of course, very large, they have paid nothing at all.

Q. 2916. For how long have they paid nothing at all? – The Award was signed about Midsummer 1841 and I think at Midsummer 1843 they commenced paying for those unopened works; that would leave five years at Midsummer 1848.

Q. 2917. And they have paid nothing? – Some of them have paid nothing.

Q. 2918. Can you give the Committee the names of the parties in arrears and the amount of dead rents which is uncollected? – I can.

Q. 2919. Will you do so? – I will. The amount is about £8,850.

Q. 2920. Do these parties refuse to pay the tonnages due? – No, we have had no instances of that.

Q. 2921. Those parties of whom you have been speaking have not yet opened their mines? – No.

Q. 2922. Therefore no tonnage dues have been incurred at present? – No; some of those parties who are most extensively in arrear pay their tonnages after they are written to several times, but they will not pay the certain rents.

Q. 2923. Do you mean by certain rents – the dead rents? – Yes.

Q. 2924. When the mines are opened, then they will pay the dead rents will they not? – By tonnage, but by their not being opened they are liable to forfeiture; they have five years allowed them for opening.

Q. 2925. Have you ever made any representation upon the subject of those arrears? – Many times.

Q. 2926. To whom? – To the Board.

Q. 2927. What answer have you received? – We have always been led to understand that they would be proceeded against; in fact, Mr. Gardiner has always said they were determined to enforce the payment of them.

Q. 2928. And they have security, have they not, for payment of them? – Not in the cases in which the collieries are not opened, because there is no plan yet; I believe the Act of Parliament for distraining says, that we shall seize upon the goods and chattels wherever they shall be found.

Q. 2929. Do the parties allege, as the reason for the non payment of those dead rents, the non opening of the railway through the district? – They have done so.

Q. 2930. Do you apprehend, when the railways are opened through the district, there will be a great extension of the sale of coal? – I have no doubt of it.

Q. 2931. Will it then be of their advantage to open those mines which are not now opened, supposing they are not forfeited? – Decidedly so; it must be more to their advantage to open them, than to keep paying the dead rents for nothing. It is very unfair however on those parties who are paying dead rents; either all ought to pay or none.

Q. 2932. Can you tell the Committee when the Act of Parliament for the railway in the Forest of Dean passed? – The South Wales Bill passed the year before last.

Q. 2933. When were the arrangements made with those parties for the dead rents? – With those parties who are so extensively behindhand, they were made in 1841.

Q. 2934. Was there any Act for any railway to the Forest of Dean at the time when the arrangements were made with those parties? – None except the existing tramways.

Q. 2935. Was there any in contemplation? – I contemplated better roads; the mode of transit was one of the first things I found fault with, when I went there.

Q. 2936. Were there railways in contemplation, which would have given access to the Forest at the time when those leases were granted? – None but the present tramways.

Q. 2937. Were there any in contemplation? – None that I am aware of, at least none were proposed.

Q. 2938. Does not the Forest of Dean Railway extend to Gloucester? – No.

Q. 2939. Is there any railway that extends to near Gloucester? – No.

Q. 2940. Does not it extend to the Severn? – Yes, but a long way below Gloucester, to a place called Bullo Pill.

Q. 2941. From Bullo Pill, the Severn is navigable up to Gloucester, is it not? – Yes.

Q. 2942. Is there not a great deal of the Forest of Dean coal carried along the Great Western Railway from Gloucester? – I believe not; I believe very little Forest coal is sold in Gloucester at all; there is more sold in Cheltenham than in Gloucester.

Q. 2943. Is it not carried round by the Great Western Railway? – I do not think it comes on to the Railway at all.

Q. 2944. Does the South Wales Railway extend over every part of the Forest of Dean or only through a portion of it ? – Over only a portion of it.

Q. 2945. Have you raised your dead rents or your tonnage rates since the passing of any Act of Parliament for Railways through the Dean Forest? – No, we have not.

Q. 2946. Shall you do so when the Railways are made? – We cannot; as to all that I have granted, and I think I have granted nearly all that is grantable, I have kept the certain rents lower than the Commissioners.

Q. 2947. Should any Railways be made in the Forest of Dean should you increase the rental of the coal in consequence of the establishment of those Railways? – I do not think I should; It would be very unfair to do so.

Q. 2948. I am only speaking of those rights which are to be hereafter granted not those that are granted? – There is a period coming, which is fixed by the Act of Parliament, when the royalty is to be changed if thought proper.

Q. 2949. Have you any power otherwise than recording to the Act of Parliament to change the rent? – When it is within the maximum we have; the maximum is 4d., therefore we might take it up to 4d.

Q. 2950. Have you any instances of tonnage rates being 4d. a ton at this moment? – Not for coal.

Q. 2951. Can you state what proportion of the coalfield is already let? – I may say, in round numbers, the whole of the dark coloured piece in the centre of this map [a map and a model being placed before the Committee] every piece of that is let; underneath the black patch, the coal is unlet, because it is not accessible at the present; they must go down below the upper series from 200 to 300 yards to obtain that.

Q. 2952. When you grant a right over the upper series has not the party working the upper seam the right of going down and working the lower seam also? – No, not in those cases; we mention certain coals in the grant; for instance, taking the lower seam of the upper series, we say that seam and all the seams above it.

Q. 2953. What is the price of the coal at the pit's mouth? – About 7s. 6d. a ton; but not being a coal-seller I cannot say precisely.

Q. 2954. Is that coal of a very fine quality? – Yes it is good coal.

Q. 2955. Take the other seams of the inferior coal, what do they sell for at the pit's mouth? – The Coleford High Delph is sold for something less at the pit's mouth to go to the river.

Q. 2956. The cartage has to be added to that price? – Yes.

Q. 2957. Are those mines of the best coal worked from what you call the crop, or the shafts? – By shafts.

Q. 2958. What depth are those shafts generally? – Crump Meadow Colliery is 240 yards, Parkend is about 180 yards, Bilson 160 yards.

Q. 2959. You have mentioned three mines; will you have the goodness to tell me what is the royalties paid by those three collieries? – Two pence a ton; it is the same in each case.

Q. 2960. Do you know the relative proportion of the royalty to the price of the coal in any other situation than the Dean Forest? – I do not. In considering the royalty, it must be looked at in this way: the royalty, as it appears there, appears remarkably small; but if you come to look at the circumstances, and at the right of the crown it is not quite so small; the right of the crown is to put in a fifth man, and to take the profits of the workings of the fifth man after the coal is obtained; that is the old custom. The Dean Forest Mining Commissioners were empowered to impose a royalty upon the coal in lieu of the fifth man.

Q. 2961. Two pence a ton is considered the equivalent of that? – Yes.

Q. 2962. How would you estimate the right of the crown in the way of tonnage rate, in lieu of the previous one fifth? – I followed in the steps of the Dean Forest Mining Commissioners in a great measure; they had the cutting out of the best part of the coal field decidedly, and left me the inferior.

Q. 2963. Did it never occur to you of making an estimate of the crown's right of putting in a fifth man, in order to impose the tonnage-rate or royalty upon the coal? – I do not know what estimate the Commissioners made; I made none.

Q. 2964. Did not Mr. Buddle, Mr. Sopwith, and Mr. Probyn estimate those rights, with a view of ascertaining the royalty which would be due to the crown? – Yes, I suppose so.

Q. 2965. And those gentlemen fixed a maximum of 4d.? – The Act of Parliament fixed the maximum 4d., those gentlemen never exceeded the rate of 2d. for coal.

Q. 2966. Did they fix the rate for the mines? – Yes.

Q. 2967. Are the rights of the crown over the ironstone the same as over the coal? – Yes.

Q. 2968. Is it exactly the same? – Precisely.

Q. 2969. You have stated the amount of coal in the Forest; can you state the amount of ironstone? – No I cannot; it is a total impossibility to calculate it; there is no data for such calculation.

Q. 2970. Can you state the amount of rental you receive from the iron ore? – About £1,000 a year.

Q. 2971. Is the iron ore of a fine quality? – Of a very good quality indeed, some of it.

Q. 2972. Do you think it is likely to be worked to a great extent when the railway is made? – I expect it will; I expect the railway will affect everything equally.

Q. 2973. You say you would not increase your tonnage rates even if you had a railway? – I do not see why we ought to; it would be quite unfair, I think, when parties are already holding three-fourths of the whole coalfield, to increase the tonnage rates if a railway were to come; at the end of 20 years from the date of Award they will be all subject to alteration and it would be unfair for me to step out of the ordinary course.

Q. 2974. Who acted as agent for the South Wales Railway, in the Dean Forest? – I did so myself as far as making plans and sections went.

Q. 2975. You were employed by the South Wales Railway Company? – Yes, by Mr. Brunel.

Q. 2976. Independently of the Government? – Yes, Mr. Brunel came and asked me which lines I thought would accommodate us best and I pointed out to him certain routes and he told me to get plans made, which I did.

Q. 2977. You say the South Wales Railway only goes over a portion of the Forest and not over the whole? – It embraced the whole, but they were opposed on the western side by the Severn and Wye Railway Company and the Bill was thrown out. The Severn and Wye Railway Company also opposed on the eastern side, but there was an arrangement entered into when the Bill was before the Lords, that the South Wales Railway Company should make a present to the Severn and Wye Railway Company, to induce them to withdraw their opposition, of £15,000 which was to be expended in improving that side by themselves, so that ultimately the two lines would meet.

Q. 2978. It ultimately resulted in a compromise? – Yes, which I am sorry to say there appears no probability of being carried out.

Q. 2979. You acted for the South Wales Company? – In making their plans for them. I did.

Q. 2780. Do you think the free miners, if those railways were established through the Forest would demand more money in case of their selling their portions of coal to foreigners or other parties? – I think they are getting more money now in consequence of the contemplated railways.

Q. 2981. If they were established, do you think they would be likely to get more? – Yes.

Q. 2982. Do you think, if the free miners get more, there is any reason why the Crown should not have a proportion of the increase? – I should think it would be unfair to raise the rents; I think it would be giving an unfair advantage to the people at present trading, to raise the rents of any future colliery; they are all situated in so small a space, that by raising the rent of some and not the others, you would shut them out of the benefits of the railway.

Q. 2983. Is that the mode under which a private coal owner would act under such circumstances? – I do not know.

Q. 2984. I understand you to say, that the free miners, if the railways were made, would demand more supposing they were to resell their portions of the mines in consequence of those railways? – Yes but I am not quite prepared to say that they would get more, though it is likely they would.

Q. 2985. Would railways be of any advantage to the working of the mines and in cheapening the transit of coal? – Yes, they would cheapen the transit and increase the quantity, because they would have the effect of opening fresh markets.

Q. 2986. And they would carry for less than it is carried for now? – Yes.

Q. 2987. Therefore parties offering to buy mines from the free miners, would be in a condition to give a higher price with a railway than without it? – Yes.

Q. 2988. What is the system pursued in keeping the accounts of the mineral produce? – There is no particular system except that we have ledgers in which we enter the half yearly quantities.

Q. 2989. Do you keep a cash-book? – Yes and a ledger.

Q. 2990. How often are your accounts rendered? – Every six months; we have received directions to render them every three months at present; but we cannot render ours every three months by the Award; I believe we can only ask for the returns every six months.

Q. 2991. You say, at present; is any alteration to take place? – We are in future to render our accounts every six months for the mines and every 12 months for the quarries.

Q. 2992. Have you been asked to render them oftener? – There was an order to render the surface produce accounts oftener, I believe.

Q. 2993. To whom do you render your accounts? – Directly to the Office of Woods.

Q. 2994. Do you find any security? – No I do not.

Q. 2995. Do you or Mr. Machen send up the accounts to the office? – The books and everything are kept at the office where I live in Coleford; once in 6 months I attend at the Speech House, in the centre of the Forest; we have the parties brought there by circulars; they pay the money, Mr. Machen being present, and I generally take it myself and deposit it in the bank to his credit.

Q. 2996. Is the present charge of transit high in the Forest? – It is very high.

Q. 2997. Could you suggest any mode by which it would be possible to lower it? – I know of nothing but an increased quantity which would have that effect; of course that could be only got by having railways and so giving them access to markets from which they are now shut out entirely.

Q. 2998. Do those tramways belong to private individuals? – No, to companies.

Q. 2999. Are they constructed under Act of Parliament? – Yes.

Q. 3000. There are frequently clauses in those Acts, raising the price unduly are there not? – Yes; they can charge enormously if they choose; at present the tonnages upon the

Severn and Wye Railway for what is called "Low Delph Coal" are 1/6d. a ton for the whole distance, which is five miles; that is simply the tonnage; then comes hauling and the use of the trains for the coal proprietors to find; under their Act of Parliament the Severn and Wye Railway have power to charge 3/– a ton for that distance, if they please and I think the Bullo Pill is something like the same.

Q. 3001. Is that the usual charge upon railways in other coal districts? – Certainly not.

Q. 3002. That charge of 3s. they were permitted by the Act of Parliament to impose? – Yes; but they do not feel it in their interest to impose it.

Q. 3003. How long has their Act of Parliament been passed? – Thirty years, I should think, not more.

Q. 3004. Long before you knew the Forest? – Yes.

Q. 3005. And you do not know what the cost of carriage to the same point was before the railway was made? – No.

Q. 3006. Do you know what the shareholders are receiving in the shape of dividend? – I do not.

Q. 3007. Do you know whether it is a paying concern or a losing one? – I have heard it is a paying concern, but I know nothing of my own knowledge.

Q. 3008. What is the present state of the iron and coal trade in the Forest? – The iron trade I think is about as it is in other places; it is not very dull; at present the coal trade is rather slack.

Q. 3009. Is there much litigation in the Forest about the mineral property now? – Not now.

Q. 3010. You state that the deputy gavellers have the power of arbitration? – We have not the power, except in cases of boundary disputes, but the miners all come to us.

Q. 3011. You in fact act as arbitrator? – Yes I am very frequently called.

Q. 3012. You state that you make plans for private individuals? – For any persons who wish them.

Q. 3013. Might any dispute arise with regard to those plans? – The plans themselves would show the dispute if it is a dispute respecting boundaries.

Q. 3014. Can any inconveniences arise from your making those plans for private parties? – Not the slightest.

Q. 3015. In fact yours is the only general record of the state of the mines? – It is.

Q. 3016. You make a plan for them because they request it, and you are the most competent person to do so? – Yes.

Q. 3017. Might not it be an advantage if you were employed exclusively by Government? – That I should have no objection to.

Q. 3018. Do you see any direct advantage which would result from your being so? – I do not see any direct advantage; we should still have to act always as kind of judges among them; we could not avoid it.

Q. 3019. In fact, the wish for you to act as arbitrator between two parties where there is any dispute, is rather showing deference to the opinion of the crown and its agent, than otherwise? – I think so.

Q. 3020. When people come to you to ask information, you give them that information in the shape of a map? – Yes when they request it.

Q. 3021. Have you any recommendation to make to the Committee by which you think the mineral property in the Forest of Dean might be increased in value in any way? – Getting the railway into operation would be of a great advantage; then the raisings would be increased and of course the revenue of the Crown increased.

Q. 3022. You do not see any mode of dealing with the property by the Crown itself or by Parliament by means of which the interests of the Crown could he advantaged? – No, I do not see that it could be so; nothing occurs to me; what is wanted in the Forest is a cheap mode of taking the coal out; all other good effects will follow that.

Q. 3023. And to carry the timber out too? – Yes, to carry everything out.

Q. 3024. Are you aware what the produce of the minerals was before the Act of Parliament establishing the Commission, was passed to settle the rights of the miners? – Something like £700 a year.

Q. 3025. You have now said that for the last three years it has averaged about £3,500 a year? – Three thousand, five hundred pounds, after all payments are made.

Q. 3026. Does that include the arrears which are due? – Those are the actual receipts.

Q. 3027. Would it amount to as much as £4,000 a year if the arrears were paid? – I should think it would.

Q. 3028. So that the Committee may consider the real value to be about £4,000 a year at present? – Quite that.

Q. 3029. You contemplate that it would increase in amount, if the proposed railways were completed? – If the railways were completed, I think so, inasmuch as parties now paying £200 a year, certain rent, if they could get into operation and find a market for 90,000 or 100,000 tons a year, would increase it considerably.

Q. 3030. And one result would be that they would be enabled to pay dead rents in arrear? – Decidedly.

Q. 3031. Did the Commissioners of Woods and Forests when these railways were proposed, promote them or object to them? – They promoted them.

Q. 3032. Did they enter into arrangements with the Company at the time for the price of land? – I do not know.

Q. 3033. You do not know whether any arrangement was made between the Commissioners of Woods and Forests and the promoters of the railways? – I should think not inasmuch as a person was sent to value the land after one of the Acts was passed.

Q. 3034. Do you know what value was put upon the lands? – No.

Q. 3035. Who was the person who was sent to value the lands? – There has been no valuation made in the Forest; but for the Monmouth and Hereford Railway, a portion of which was to run over the lands on the High Meadow Estate, a person of the name of Apperley was sent down, I understand.

Q. 3036. You have stated that the amount of income derived from the minerals is about £4,000 a year? – Yes.

Q. 3037. Can you state what is the cost of collecting that amount? – The cost of collecting for the last three years has been £571; the gross receipt for the last three years has been £4,234.

Q. 3038. Does that include the dead rents in arrear? – No.

Q. 3039. If the dead rents in arrear were collected would it add £500 a year more to that income? – I think it would.

Q. 3040. Am I to understand you to say, that the future gross rents, if the dead rents were collected, would amount to about £4,500 a year? – Yes but the dead rents are not at present all collected.

Q. 3042. How much is there of the open waste which is uninclosed? – Not a great deal.

Q. 3043. Can any further part of the Forest be inclosed? – No further part ought to be inclosed.

Q. 3044. If any further part were inclosed would it be injurious to the miners? – I think it would; I do not think they could inclose any more now.

Q. 3045. Do you mean to say that this is the case by Act of Parliament? – I do not think there is any space for it.

Q. 3046. Do you think there is any means for the inclosure of any further quantity? – No.

Q. 3047. Then the Crown has exercised its extreme right of inclosure? – Yes.

Q. 3048. Inclosure to a further extent would be injurious to the miners? – It would.

Q. 3049. Do you think any portion of the waste land near the mines could be sold with advantage, supposing a power were taken to sell it? – The miners themselves occupy any waste land which is in the immediate neighbourhood, with the necessary buildings and spoil-banks.

Q. 3050. Do they pay for that occupation? – Not for the spoil-banks; but in the case of any buildings which they put up, supposing they want buildings for workmen's houses, for instance, there is a clause in the Act of Parliament which gives the Commissioners power to grant not more than an acre and a half to each lease for the purpose.'

Appendix (L)[1] to the 1849 Report gives the first detailed figures of the Crown's portion of the mineral produce of the Forest. For the years 1845-6, 1846-7 and 1847-8 the figures are:

Gross receipts from minerals in Dean Forest (excluding High Meadow Estate):

	£	s.	d.
1845-6	4661	7	1
1846-7	4267	15	0
1847-8	4121	2	0

Expenditure in connection with the above:

	1845-6	1846-7	1847-8
Salaries of deputy gavellers	350 0 0	350 0 0	350 0 0
Rent of Office	–	–	10 0 0
Payments to the owners of lands, being a moiety of the tonnage duties payable in respect of coal and iron ore from under their respective lands, under the Act 1 & 2 Vict. c. 43	117 12 9½	125 3 11½	206 3 2
Labour on coal surveys	86 14 10	98 6 4	93 12 6
Stationery, implements, &c.	114 8 6	129 10 11½	143 1 9½
	£668 15 11½	£703 1 3	£802 17 5½

Previous to the 'Duncan Committee' [1848-1849] already treated of, a similar committee with Lord Duncan as Chairman had made enquiries as to Crown revenue. Nothing of interest transpired regarding Dean Forest except that it was stated that 'Viscount Morpeth was gaveller under 1 & 2 Vict. c. 43 [1838]'. The committee reported on 25 July 1848.[2] A lengthy Appendix of 755 pages was issued separately

1 P. 466.

2 Report from the Select Committee on Woods, Forests and Land Revenues of the Crown: 1848: 325 pages.

at the same time.[1] Appendix (B.7) included details of all gales of coal and iron ore granted from 1832 to 1847 inclusive and all leases of quarries for the same period. Appendix (I.I.37) gave the following details of timber supplied to the miners:

	From Dean Forest Cords	*From High Meadow Estate Cords*
1838	2348¼[2]	1165
1839	3637¼	2052¾
1840	2491¾	1645¼
1841	4641¼	534
1842	3611½	98½
1843	3264	478¾
1844	2965¼	186
1845	3952¼	547½
1846	4027½	862
1847	5959¼	399½

Appendix (K.K.) 38 mentions that the expenses incurred by the Dean Forest Commissioners regarding the Acts of 1838 and the Awards of 1841, and the carrying into effect of their recommendations, had amounted for the years 1831-44 to £19,549 16s. 1d. On 27 July 1849, the 'Duncan Committee' issued a second Report[3] but this did not refer to Dean Forest. However Appendix (L.II.) gave details of the receipts and expenses regarding the mineral produce of Dean for the year 1848-9. The 28th Report, dated 30 July 1851, of the Commissioners of Woods states [4]:

> 'In the 18th & 19th Reports, 1841 and 1842 of this Board, the proceedings which it had been found necessary to adopt in consequence of the complicated questions arising from the conflicting claims of the crown, and of certain parties who claimed rights of a peculiar description in and to the mines, minerals and quarries in Dean Forest, were detailed.
>
> In these Reports it was stated that, in pursuance of the Act 1 & 2 Vict. c. 43 [1838] for regulating the opening and working of mines and quarries in the Forest of Dean and Hundred of St. Briavels, the Commissioners appointed under the Act had published their Awards of the Coal and Iron Mines, and the Rules and Regulations for the future working thereof; and expectations were held out, that the adjustment of the various claims effected by these Awards would ultimately prove profitable to the Crown, by the increase of revenue to be derived from the minerals, and beneficial to the free miners and other adventurers, by enabling them to carry on their works freed from the litigations to which they had formerly been liable under the ill-defined and objectionable customs, or alleged customs, which had for a great length of time prevailed in the Forest and hundred.
>
> We are now enabled to state, that the anticipations referred to, so far as this Board are more immediately interested, have been borne out by result.

1 The Report and Appendix necessitated a separate Index; this was printed at the same time: 84 pages.
2 This included 640 cu. ft. of beech timber supplied free to the miners. This was the last free timber supplied to them.
3 Second Report of Select Committee on Woods, Forests and Land Revenues of the Crown together with Appendix and Index.
4 Pp. 26-8.

The average amount annually received by the crown from the mines, minerals, quarries and tram-roads within the Forest, for the 6 years preceeding the date of the Awards of Coal and Iron Mines, was £826 2s. 10½d.; and for the same length of time, ending March 31st, 1850, the revenue derived by the crown from the like sources, has amounted, on an average, to £4,281 17s. 4d. per annum, in addition to which, a considerable profit is derived every year from the sale of cordwood and timber to the miners, which, previously to the passing of the Act 1 & 2 Vict. c. 43 [1838], had been claimed by, and allowed to them as a matter of right, but which claim was by the 30th Section of the Act abolished, and the produce of the cordwood and timber, since sold to the miners, has been brought to account, and credited to the Public.

The increase here referred to, has arisen almost entirely from the Royalties or Tonnage-dues on the coal and iron ore actually raised, as considerable difficulty has been experienced in procuring payment of the minimum or Dead Rents fixed by the Mining Award; and although our attention had been constantly directed to the necessity of preventing an accumulation of any arrear on these Rents, the inexpediency of taking any active steps for their recovery during the then depressed condition of the coal trade in the Forest had been felt, more especially as the parties had the power, under the Award, of making up the short workings in any succeeding year or years.

During the latter part of the year 1849, in compliance with the urgent representations of certain owners and occupiers of Coal Mines in the western part of the Forest, to the effect that the depression in question was principally caused by the high rates of carriage charged on the Severn and Wye Railway, we concluded arrangements with that Company, the particulars of which are detailed in our 27th Report for the year 1850, for a reduction of those rates in consideration of a temporary sacrifice of the Rent payable by the said Company to the crown.

Notwithstanding these concessions, several of the Proprietors of Collieries continued to evade the demands which were made for the payment of the Dead Rents, the arrears of which had accumulated at Christmas 1850 to £12,805 8s. 2½d., and at length some of the parties in arrear, at a period when the Mining Act had been 10 years in operation, and when payment of these Rents had been made in many instances, raised a legal question as to whether or not the Mining Commissioners had not exceeded their powers under the Act 1 & 2 Vict. c. 45 [1838] in awarding any Dead Rent to be paid to the crown by the miners or parties in occupation of the Mineral Property during the time when no Coal or Mineral was raised from the Mines.

It thereupon became necessary to have recourse to legal proceedings for enforcing the Award, and having the question thus raised as to its validity judicially settled; and an action was brought in the name of the gaveller against Messrs Morrell, who were in arrear for Dead Rents to an amount of £1,239 1s. 2d.[1] in respect of certain Works claimed by them.

The action, "Lord Seymour *v.* Morrell", was tried at the Gloucester Summer Assizes, 1850, before Lord Campbell and a special jury, and a verdict was found for the Crown, subject to the opinion of the Court of Queen's Bench upon a special case. The case was thereafter stated and agreed upon, and was, at the expiration of the period embraced in this Report, waiting for argument in the Court of Queens Bench.

N.B. The Case has since been argued, and the Judgement of the Court pronounced in favour of the Crown.'

---

1 Paid on 11 November 1852.

In their 30th Report (1852) the Commissioners of Woods continue[1]:

'In conformity with this judgement, Messrs. Morrell made payment of the amount due by them; so that by the Judgement and subsequent payment by Messrs. Morrell, the subject of the Dead Rents was set at rest in all time coming, and the Rights of the Crown in this respect placed beyond question.'

They added that the arrears to Midsummer 1851 were[2]:

	Coal Mines	*Iron ore Mines*
	£ s. d.	£ s. d.
Dead Rents	10,680 18 2	321 6 2
Tonnage Duty	1,008 8 0½	107 1 0
	£11,689 6 2½	£428 7 2

A letter was sent to the several parties in arrear, demanding payment. 'Various replies were received, intimating the extreme hardship of their position, stating, in a majority of cases, their inability to pay, and stating in several cases their readiness, if required, to surrender their grants of minerals. Some payments were also made, but they amounted only to £1,084 14s. 2d., which, being deducted from the total amount due at Midsummer 1851 leaves a total arrear due at 31st March 1852, amounting to £11,032 19s. 2½d.'[3] The First Commissioner of Woods pointed out that the payments must be enforced, but that in certain cases discretion must be used in the enforcement of such payments, owing to the very peculiar circumstances of Dean Forest. He further explained the difficulties of railway communication in and to and from Dean Forest, and stated: 'I consider the interests of the Crown are deeply involved in the speedy development of a sound system of railway accommodation in the Forest. If such a system were even in certain prospect, all difficulties respecting the payment of dead rents would speedily disappear, and I entertain no doubt would be rapidly superseded by the payment of a large amount of tonnage duties, the sure and satisfactory proofs of the expenditure of capital, and of industry and prosperity within the Forest.'[4] He hoped that necessary Bills would be enacted whereby a satisfactory system of railways might be provided, adding 'that great object once attained, all other arrangements having reference to the Mineral affairs of the Forest would, I have no doubt, be speedily placed upon a satisfactory footing.'[5] On 27 February 1855 the deputy gaveller, John Atkinson, supplied the following details of arrears of dead rents and tonnage duty up to Christmas 1854[6]:

	Coal Mines	*Iron ore Mines*
	£ s. d.	£ s. d.
Dead Rents	13,796 19 6	1,842 18 7
Tonnage Duty	828 12 6	216 13 4
	£14,625 12 0	£2,059 11 11

1 P. 97.
2 App. 14, p. 222.
3 *Ibid.*, pp. 222-3.
4 P. 100.
5 P. 101.
6 34th Rpt. of Coms. of Woods (1856), pp. 94-5.

The large majority had been owing over two years. Demands for payment had been sent out on 3 March 1855 threatening legal proceedings if not paid before 24 June that year. £5,527 3s. 5d. for coal mines and £477 8s. 6d. for iron mines was received up to 29 March 1856, but old and fresh arrears still left outstanding at 31 March 1856 amounted to £10,432 0s. 8d. for coal mines and £685 14s. 4d. for iron ore mines. The First Commissioner commented:

> 'In consequence of the circulars issued on 3rd March, 1855, many communications have been received, asking for a consideration of the decision therein announced, and requesting an extension of time for the payment of arrears. In some cases these applications have been complied with, on condition that some portion of the arrears were liquidated, and in the case of gales, the opening of which was being proceeded with, on condition that the works were prosecuted with vigour. The arrears due on the Resolution and Safeguard Colliery, amounting to £1,725, were remitted, as it was found that the surface of the gale was occupied by an inclosure so as to render the opening of the gale impracticable. The rent will, under the special and very peculiar circumstances of this case, continue to be remitted year by year until the Lessees shall be enabled to work the coal comprised in their gale.'

Following the termination of office of the Dean Forest Mining Commissioners on 26 July 1841, Thomas Sopwith continued to give the Crown the benefit of his extensive mining knowledge, and £455 fees were paid to him.[1]

The 'Drummond Committee', 1854. A Select Committee of the House of Commons known as the 'Drummond Committee', similar to that of 1849, was appointed in 1854. Witnesses in connection with the Forest were Edward Machen, deputy surveyor, and T. F. Kennedy, lately one of the Commissioners of Woods. The Committee's Report,[2] dated 17 July 1854, is only of limited interest for this volume. Mr Machen was able to say that there was certainly now a very great difference in the habits of the inhabitants.[3] Their Appendix 2, being a paper handed in by Mr. Machen, contained the following figures:

Total Gross Receipts of Minerals in Dean Forest

	£	s.	d.
1845	3,163	7	7
1846	4,661	7	1
1847	4,267	15	0
1848	4,121	2	0
1849	3,569	9	7
1850	4,351	7	6
1851	4,740	1	3
1852	6,486	5	6
1853	5,605	2	11
1854	4,500	12	11
	£45,466	11	4

1 31st Rpt. of Coms. of Woods (1853), App. 13(y), p. 339.

2 Report of Select Committee on Crown Forests together with Proceedings of the Committee. Ordered to be printed 17 July 1854 (H.S.M.O.), 193 pages with index.

3 *Ibid.*, Q. 212

Then followed 'A Comparative Statement of the Value of the Crown's Interests in the Forest in 1808 and 1854', in which is recorded: 'Minerals – Gale rents increased from £800 per annum to £4,200 per annum, at 20 years' purchase = £68,000.'

In 1855, the Dean Forest, &c. (Leases), Act (18 Vict. c. 16) was passed, by which the powers of leasing given by the Woods and Forests (General Powers) Act 1829 even extended to cover all or any parts of the Forest of Dean except any portion of the Forest 'for the time being inclosed under the authority of any acts or act for the growth of timber or other trees'. But for this proviso, the powers of leasing mentioned would have extended to such lands. Meanwhile the mines and pits were drawing heavily upon the timber supplies of the Forest; but even so they were a handy outlet for crown produce which it would have been hard to have sold elsewhere. In the official reports it is only for the years 1848-9 to 1856-7 that we find any records of such timber, viz.:

'Sales of 'Miners Timber'

Year	*From Dean Forest* £	s.	d.	*From Highmeadow Estate* £	s.	d.
1848-9	2,037	5	0	655	2	6
1849-50	1,717	12	6	493	17	6
1850-1	1,380	17	6	477	12	6
1851-2	2,049	7	6	411	7	0
1852-3	2,153	12	6[1]	381	17	6[2]
1853-4	2,019	18	6	727	19	0
1854-5	2,907	18	0	867	15	6
1855-6	2,335	7	0	520	7	6
1856-7	3,287	14	0	292	8	0'

It is of interest to include at this point some legal comments made in 1858 on the rights of the free miners. The occasion was a lawsuit of that year.[3] The suit was brought to try the alleged right of the lord of the manor of Blakeney to grant gales for quarries in the bailiwick of Blakeney, and to exact rents and royalties therefor.[4] The rights of the free miners were not at issue but were discussed at some length. Mr. Justice Byles gave the following as part of his opinion:

> 'It seems to me, first, that the free miners themselves could, in point of law, have had no such right as the defendants' claim assumes them to have had. Now the claim of the free miners is to subvert the soil, and carry away the sub-stratum of stone without stint or limit of any kind. This alleged right, if it ever existed, must have reposed on one of three foundations: custom, prescription, or lost grant. The right of the free miners is incapable of being

1 4307¼ cords.

2 763¾ cords

3 A.-G. *v*. Mathias (4 K. & J., p. 579).

4 The gist of the case was this: The Fifth Report (dated 25 August 1835) of the Coms. of 1831, mentioned that 'a claim had been made by Mr. Wm. Ambrose, as lord of the manor of Blakeney, to grant gales [for quarries] and exact gale fees and rents within his bailiwick, founded upon a grant in the time of Edward III', but it did not appear to them 'that a good title can be established thereto against the crown'. S. 85 of the Dean Forest (Mines) Act, 1838, reserved the claim for decision. The suit in question was brought to try the alleged right of a Mr. Mathias (claiming through Mr. Ambrose) to grant a gale for quarries to a Mr. Morse and exact royalties therefor. The alleged right was found to be bad in law.

established by custom, however ancient, uniform and clear the exercise of custom may be. The alleged custom is a custom to enter the soil of another, and carry away portions of it. The benefit to be enjoyed is not a mere easement; it is a *profit à prendre.* Now it is an elementary rule of law that a *profit à prendre* in another's soil cannot be claimed by custom, for this reason, among other reasons, that a man's soil might thus be subject to the most grievous burdens in favour of successive multitudes of persons, like the inhabitants of a parish or other district, who could not release the right. The leading case on the subject is Gateward's Case. ... The next question is, can such a right as this be claimed even by prescription? I will assume against the fact, that there is no evidence to negative prescription. The present is a claim not only to carry away the soil of another, but to carry it away without stint or limit; it is a claim which tends to the destruction of the inheritance and which excludes the owner. A prescription to be good must be both reasonable and certain; and this alleged prescription appears to me to be neither. ... The only remaining question on this part of the case is this, – can the claim be sustained by evidence of a lost grant? Prescription presupposes a grant; and if you cannot presume a grant of an unreasonable claim before legal memory, *a fortiori* can you not presume one since. The defendants have relied on statutes of limitation; but as to that, a claim which is vicious and bad in itself cannot be substantiated by a user, however long. ... The statute of the 2 and 3 Will 4, c. 71, enacts that no claim which may be lawfully made at common law by custom, prescription or ancient grant, shall be defeated after the periods there mentioned; yet Clayton *v.* Corby shows that if the claim was not one which could lawfully be made by custom, prescription, or presumed grant, it will, however clearly proved, nevertheless be defeated. These legal objections apply to the claim of the free miners. ...'

James G. Wood,[1] though pointing out that no doubt was intended to be raised as to the point actually decided, made the following comments in regard to the position of the free miners:

'Now, on the question of a lost grant, there was, at least, according to the Fourth Report of the Commissioners of 1831, some evidence of such a grant, and the reasons for it being made. If such a right as that in question could not be founded on grant (which, however, has never been decided as an abstract proposition), then it is conceded that it could not be established by prescription, which presupposes a grant; but, with all submission, it seems to the writer, that the case on the question of prescription is not put satisfactorily; for the word "unreasonable" begs the whole question. Again, the claim of the free miner, at least so far as regards collieries and iron mines, was not "without stint", or to "exclude the owner"; for the crown's right to put in the fifth man was always admitted, and the gales were not unlimited, but fixed by the crown officer himself; and for quarries, royalties were paid to the crown. ... It is not proposed here to discuss further this abstract question of law. Suffice it to point out, that if the case is again mooted, as between the free miners and the crown, the matter cannot be treated as *res judicata* against the former; and that the opinion expressed in Attorney-General *v.* Mathias is at least apparently inconsistent with some of the decisions referred to in this note, and grounded in part on assumptions not in accordance with the facts found by the Commissioners of 1831, and stated in their reports and detailed

1 Wood, *op. cit.*, p. 138.

in the evidence before them. It does not follow that a custom is uncertain because the evidence as to it is in some particulars conflicting.'

In 1859 a case[1] was decided dealing with surface damage. In it the plaintiffs (representing the Cinderford Iron Company) sued the defendants (owners of the Cinderford Bridge Colliery), upon the award dated 28 May 1858 of the deputy gaveller, John Atkinson, to recover the sum of £60 awarded by him.[2] This was for surface damage[3] caused by the underground operations in the defendants' colliery to a miller's house, a yard and two buildings, built in 1836 situate in Abbot's Wood in Ruspidge Common on common or waste land within the Forest perambulation. There were no openings into the mines on the plaintiff's premises, the surface works of the colliery being about 200 yards therefrom. The house stood on uninclosed land, and was itself without any inclosure on three sides thereof. There was a wall round the yard, which adjoined the north-east end of the house; and the outbuildings opened into the yard. The case was first argued on demurrer[4] when the declaration was, as a matter of pleading, held sufficient. The action went to trial, and a verdict was taken for the plaintiffs. On a rule to enter the verdict for the defendants, the judgment of the court was given by Watson, B for the defendants as follows:

'It was argued, on behalf of the plaintiffs, first, that the place was within the jurisdiction of the deputy gaveller. We think it is within the Hundred of St. Briavels, and therefore it is within the limit of the jurisdiction of the deputy gaveller. Indeed, the defendant, whatever he did at the trial, did not, as we understand, contend to the contrary in the course of the argument.

But it was contended, on the part of the defendant: first, that this house and yard, standing on uninclosed land of the hundred and open on three sides of it, was not inclosed land within the meaning of the 68th section of the Act. Secondly, that this damage arising to the house and land by sinking, caused by improper working, was not within the meaning of the 68th section of the Act, and that the injury was not surface damage but permanent damage to the house and land. No doubt, a house is inclosed land in one sense, but it is difficult to say that it is so within the meaning of this Act, which gives power to open mines and work the minerals on such land.

But, without putting our decision on this point, it is sufficient to say that this matter was not within the jurisdiction of the deputy gaveller. The free miners have the power to open mines within the hundred, and work mines and quarries therein; that is to say, to sink shafts, raise the minerals, make heaps and roads, and do all other acts to work mines and quarries on the land (except erecting steam engines and dwelling houses without leave of the owner). This working the miners may lawfully do. There is no provision in the act of parliament to enable the free miners to leave the soil without support so as to cause a subsidence, nor is there any clause from which such a licence can be inferred. It follows that a free miner, whether working the coals under inclosed land from shafts sunk therein, or by outstroke

1 Allaway and Another *v*. Wagstaff (4 H. & N., pp. 681-90). Glos.R.O. D9096 F26/11.

2 Under Sect.68 of Act 1 & 2 Vict., c. 43.

3 The damage consisted of fissures in the walls of the house. There were deep cracks in the floor of the kitchen, so that a stick could be thrust between the stones to some depth into the soil.

4 Allaway *v*. Wagstaff, 4 H. & N., 307; S.C., 29 L.J., Exch. 51. Examples of subsidence awards by the deputy gaveller are in Glos.R.O. D9096 F26/5, 6, 8, 9, 11.

from other land, and causing a subsidence, to the damage of the owner of the land, would be liable to an action: *Humphries v. Brogden*.[1] We think that the 68th section is confined to the assessment of compensation for the damage done to the surface, and sinking shafts and making roads, &c. on the surface, in exercise of the powers granted, and not to enable the gaveller to try the question whether the defendant by his acts is liable to pay damages, and then to award first, the damage done to the tenant, and, secondly, the damage done to the reversioner, which is, in fact, trying the cause. No power is given to summon witnesses or to administer an oath. Contrasting that provision with the sections above referred to, where the Commissioners and the arbitrator to be appointed by the gaveller in certain cases have the power to examine witnesses and administer an oath, it would appear that he has not the means of inquiring into and deciding such a question.

The surface damage, on the other hand, that is, injury to crops or destruction of grass, is a mere matter of ocular observation and computation. The computation can be made and the amount of damage ascertained and determined by the view of the gaveller. Surface damage, again, must mean damage to the surface. The expression "surface damage" is a term well known in the north of England in the Colliery districts, it is damage to the crops by using the surface, or by the smoke coming from the colliery works, or pit heaps, in respect of which compensation is payable under leases, or reservations of coal, or where lords work coal by custom under copyhold lands. It is difficult to say that the injury to the foundations of a house extending to the walls and roof of the house, or the subsidence of the soil partially or wholly destroying the future fertility of the soil, is a surface damage; it may be damage to the house and land, but not surface damage. Again, the clause in this same section, which prevents a person who has neglected or refused to pay the compensation awarded, from continuing his working until the compensation is paid, applies more to the case of damage to the land, by working and getting the coal therein, than to injury by reason of leaving the land without support.'

James G. Wood[2] asserts that this decision must be considered to have tacitly received legislative sanction; for S.16 of the Dean Forest (Amendment) Act 1861 *infra* which made new provisions as to the manner in which compensation may be awarded, leaves untouched the questions raised in the above case, and S.15 applies only to damage done to waste or inclosed lands of the Crown, or to any mine, quarry, land or work comprised in any existing gale, lease or grant.

The Dean Forest (Amendment) Act 1861. In 1861 the Commissioners of Woods pointed out[3] that the royalties on the gales of coal mines and iron ore mines awarded in 1841 would need to be refixed in July 1862; also that about 120 gales of coal mines and 28 iron mines, besides stone quarries, had been granted since the Award and that the royalties on these likewise would have to be refixed as the statutory twenty-one years from the dates of the grants expired. The 1861 Act amended that of 1838, by making 'further provision for the management of the Forest of Dean, and of the mines and quarries therein and in the Hundred of St. Briavels'.

1 12 Q.B. 739.

2 Wood, *op. cit.*, p. 171.

3 39th Report (1861), pp. 78-9. Currently available from H.M.S.O. is an Official Revised Edition of the 1861 Act to 1 February 1978 omitting spent and repealed Sections. See also Appendix I.

The nature of the interest conferred on a galee by the grant of a gale was defined; the powers conferred by S.25 (repealed in 1969) of the 1838 Act as to leases of land for mining purposes were enlarged; the Commissioners of Woods were empowered to grant licences to sink pits, and to use and exercise other rights, easements, etc., in inclosures, and other lands in the Forest; the person in actual possession or receipt of the proceeds of a gale was made personally liable to pay the rent or royalty; the gaveller was empowered to sue in the County Court for the recovery of arrears not exceeding £50; power was given to the gaveller or deputy gaveller to refuse the registry of any transaction until the rent and royalty had been paid; and also to refuse the registry of any transaction which is imperfect; lands appropriated for cottages and buildings for woodmen and labourers, with garden attached thereto, might, on the throwing open of inclosures, remain and be held in severalty in the actual possession of the crown, freed and discharged from all right of common and other rights, titles, or claims whatsoever; and powers were given to the verderers of the Forest to proceed against persons in all cases of trespasses by cutting, taking, or carrying away turf, gravel, stone, sand, or other soil within the Forest, in addition to all other trespasses of which they were, under the powers of previous Acts, empowered to take cognizance.

S.l of the 1861 Act[1] also confirmed that the grant of a gale of coal, iron ore or stone quarry, imposed on a free miner, his heirs and assigns, a licence to work in the nature of a real estate, nevertheless conditional on the payment of rents and royalties, and the observance of the Rules and Regulations for the time being in force. S.3 confirmed the position with regard to *forfeiture* in regard to default of these obligations, and S.4 emphasised that the galee had a *personal obligation* in this regard. Another important provision was to the effect that even if rent is paid, there is no waiver of forfeiture for default of other obligations. Ss. 10 to 14 spelled out the procedure for the proper registration of assignments of gales by will or assignment, so that the original grant and assignment documents have to be properly endorsed to that effect in accordance with statutorily prescribed procedure. By S.14, all transfers of gales are void unless properly registered. Ss. 58 and 59 provided that such transfers should be registered within 3 months – otherwise the consent of at least two Commissioners is required to permit the authorisation of a gale transfer *nunc pro tunc* (i.e. 'then for now').[2]

The 1861 Act also empowered the gaveller or deputy gaveller, (*a*) with the consent of the holders, to divide a gale, or annex one of the divided parts to an existing gale; (*b*) to settle any disputes as to boundaries, and to alter, with the consent of the holders, the boundaries of any adjoining gales (gales divided only by a barrier which has been directed to be left unworked to be deemed adjoining gales); and (*c*) to license the working and disposing of the coal in the barrier. The Act also provided that the cessor

1 S.1 of the 1861 Act reads: 'The grant of a gale of coal or iron ore, or of a stone quarry, shall be deemed to have conferred and shall confer on the galee, his heirs and assigns, a licence to work the mine, vein, or pit therein comprised, and such grant shall be deemed to have conferred on the grantee, his heirs and assigns, an interest of the nature of real estate, such licence nevertheless being conditional on the payment of all the rents, royalties and other dues from time to time payable to her majesty, her heirs and successors, in respect thereof, and the observance and performance of the several enactments, provisions, rules, and regulations for the time being in force for the proper opening, working, using, and management of the gale.' This Section was repealed in 1969.

2 Only one such permit was given in recent years, by Roy Piggott, deputy gaveller.

or determination of galeage rents, royalties or tonnage duties should be, as regards gales of coal, at the end of twenty-one years from 24 June next following the date of the Award, and in the case of gales of iron ore at the end of twenty-one years from 25 December next following the date of the Award. As, according to the above-mentioned provision, the rents and duties applicable to coal gales would cease and determine from 24 June 1862, the following notice was issued on 15 February to holders of these gales.[1]

> 'Take notice that, in pursuance of the power given to me by the Acts of 1 & 2 Vict. c. 43 [1838], and the 24 & 25 Vict. c. 40 [1861], I, the undersigned James Kenneth Howard, one of the Commissioners of Her Majesty's Woods &c. and the Gaveller of the Forest of Dean, have elected, and do hereby elect, that the several galeage or dead or certain rents, and also the several royalties or tonnage duties now payable to Her Majesty, her heirs and successors, under the Award of the Dean Forest Mining Commissioners, of the 8th day of March, 1841, for or in respect of the several undermentioned gales of coal or coal mines and works, shall cease and determine from the 24th day of June, 1862.
>
> And take notice also, that upon such cessor I shall proceed to fix the amount of the new galeage rents, royalties or tonnage duties, to be paid for the 21 years then next ensuing, according to the provisions of the said Acts.
>
> Signed; James K. Howard. Dated; 15 Feb. 1862.
> Office of Woods,
> London.'

In the event of the owners of coal mines not agreeing to the new galeage rents to be proposed on behalf of the Crown, the matter was to be settled by a reference to arbitration, powers for which were provided by the recent Act. Subsequent Reports of the Commissioners of Woods contain lists of galees with whom agreements had been made under the revised rents and royalties. In some cases the galees had objected to the new charges and arbitration was in progress. The Gales of Iron ore Mines were similarly treated of, but the datum period was twenty-one years from 25 December 1862 instead of 24 June 1862 as was the case of the Coal Gales. Queries soon arose regarding 'short-workings'.[2] Rule 14 of the Rules and Regulations under the Awards of 1841 provides that galees should have the liberty of making up the short-workings of any year or years in any succeeding year or years. In several cases the galees had failed to work to the full extent provided in the gales, paying nevertheless to the Crown the reserved dead rent. Thus there had accumulated to their credit considerable sums in the name of short-workings. Some of the galees of the gales in respect of which the Rules and Regulations fixed by the Awards of 1841 had now been adjusted expressed their hope that the short-workings under the expired terms would still be allowed to them. The law officers of the Crown advised the gaveller, J. K. Howard, that this was not legal. However the gaveller reported that he had 'reason to suppose that this construction is contrary to the general belief and expectation of the galees, and would

1 40th Rpt. (1862), App. No. 13, p. 116.

2 41st Rpt. (1863) of Coms. of Woods, pp. 92-3. (An item of interest in this Report is on p. 183: 'Cost of preparing specimens of Mineral Products from Dean Forest for the International Exhibition'.)

press severely on those who have paid their dead rents most regularly, and would thus operate unfavourably on their future conduct'. He submitted the whole matter to the Treasury and he was authorised by them 'to take such steps in the allowance of short-workings ... as may appear to be advisable in each case'. The gaveller, however, informed the galees that they were clearly to understand that this allowance would be altogether exceptional, and would not be made in future.

The Walmore and Bearce Common Inclosure Act, 1866 (29 & 30 Vict. c. 70) was passed to disafforest and enclose Walmore and Bearce Commons, but the only point of relevance was a saving clause to cover 'the lawful rights of freeminers in the rest of Dean and Hundred of St. Briavel's and those claiming under them to existing or future gales of coal or iron (if any) in or under the same'.

A case[1] was decided in 1865 dealing with the working of gales in such a way as not to impede the working of other gales. The facts of the case were shortly as follows: On 8 March 1841 the Commissioners of 1841 made an award by which they confirmed the right of Edward Protheroe, under whom Messrs. Goold, the plaintiffs in the original suit, claimed to work gales in the Bilson Colliery in the upper series of coal down to and including the 'Churchway High Delph Vein', but subject to certain rules and regulations imposed by the Commissioners. In 1863 the Great Western Deep Coal Company, the defendants in the original suit, purchased gales which had been allotted in 1843 and 1852 for working the Coleford High Delph coal seam which lay about 160 yards below that part of the Churchway High Delph coal seam which had been allotted to Messrs. Goold. The company commenced sinking a shaft through the Churchway High Delph in order to reach their own vein. Messrs. Goold immediately filed a bill to restrain them and were granted an injunction to restrain the defendants from working so as to injure their mines. Messrs. Goold then drove a level from one of their old workings in such a manner as to obstruct the company's pit, and the company filed a cross bill and claimed compensation.

In the suits that followed Messrs. Goold contended that if the Coleford High Delph stone which lay just above the Coleford High Delph coal was pierced through by the company a large quantity of water would find its way from the higher levels into the Bilson Colliery, and flood their works. The company, however, produced evidence to prove that the water was not likely to rise to any dangerous extent and that it could be kept in check by pumping at a reasonable expense. The original suit was dismissed without costs, the Vice-Chancellor being of opinion that the company were entitled to sink their shaft through the Bilson Colliery, but that the damage anticipated from the water gave the plaintiffs reasonable ground for coming to Court. In the cross suit Messrs. Goold were restrained from interfering with the company's works and directed an inquiry to be made as to the injury already done by the level.

Messrs. Goold appealed against this decision, their case being as follows: Firstly, they had by ancient custom an exclusive right to work their mine without interference from any galees of the lower strata. There was nothing in the Act 1 & 2 Vict. c. 43[1838] to take away this right; the Act only ascertained and confirmed it. The Commissioners had no power to make any rules or conditions which would derogate from the appellants'

---

1 Goold *v.* The Great Western Deep Coal Company; and The Great Western Deep Coal Company *v.* Goold (De Gex Jones & Smith's Reports, vol. ii, pp. 600-12).

rights. Secondly, they contended that upon the true construction of the Act there was no reservation on the part of the crown, as owner of the soil, of any power to permit any subsequent galees to work through or otherwise interfere with appellants' colliery.

The rights of the company were expressly made subordinate to the rights of the appellants. If the construction contended for the company be correct, the Commissioners might grant any number of licences to break through the appellants' mine, which would make it practically valueless. If it had been intended that any such injury should be done, the Act would have contained a clause giving compensation to the galees of the upper strata. This is not like the case of a way of necessity, for there are other modes of getting at the lower seams beside breaking through the appellants' colliery. Thirdly, the company will cause by their pit irreparable damage to the appellants' works, by letting the water in, and they feel they are therefore entitled to an injunction.

The Great Western Deep Coal Company in stating their case pointed out that the Act of 1838 made a complete *tabula rasa* of all rights in Dean Forest acquired previously to the passing of the Act but that the appellants did not rest their title on prescription but on the Act, and the Award of 1841, and treated the regulations of the Commissioners as binding their interest. The reservation of the lower seams of coal implied a right of way of necessity, and the company thought it sufficient if they showed that the most convenient way of reaching the lower seams was through the appellants' colliery. The restriction in the regulation, as to working the lower seams without impeding the workings of the seams previously allotted, applied to the working of the coal when reached, and did not restrict the liberty of sinking shafts. The danger anticipated from the water in consequence of the working of the company's mine was merely visionary. The evidence proved that there will be no injury unless the mine is improperly worked. Until it was shown that the company was working or were intending to work their mine improperly, the Court should grant no injunction.

Before delivering judgement, Lord Chancellor Westbury asked for further details of the various workings, the number of men employed, the quantity of coal raised, the quantity of water met with by the company and the power of their steam engines. Affidavits were accordingly filed from which it appeared that actual experience of working had in the meantime proved that not more than 15 to 20 gallons per hour flowed into the deep pit of the defendants and not more than 40 to 50 gallons per hour into the other pit. The defendants' engine was capable of winding 5,400 gallons of water per hour and a new engine to be completed in a fortnight would be capable of lifting 30,000 gallons of water per hour. The Lord Chancellor in a written judgement referring to the right to sink through another's gale, commented:

> 'The Act [of 1838] of course assumes that the powers conferred on the deputy gavellers by sections 56, 60 and 62 will be exercised with discretion and care, and that liberty to sink pits will not be given to the galees of the under seams when the exercise of such right would be attended with any serious loss to the upper galee.
>
> It is true, that the Act has not provided for compensation to the upper galee for the coal that will necessarily be lost to him by the sinking through his vein: and it is possible that the legislature considered that the gaveller, whenever he gave a licence to win the under seams by working the upper, would impose as a condition on the galee of the under seams the obligation of making full compensation to the galee of the upper. Otherwise there seems a

defect in the act in this particular, for although a Court of Equity would give the upper galee an account of the coal gotten by the under galee in the process of sinking, yet this would not be the full measure of the compensation that ought to be made, for, in addition to the coal actually severed in the process of sinking, a considerable extent of a vein of coal might become unprofitable, by reason of a pit having been sunk through it. But, for the reasons already given, I cannot allow this want of an effectual remedy for his loss by the upper galee to be a ground for depriving the crown of the right to gale the under seams, with liberty to sink through the upper, or for depriving the under galee of his right to the benefit of the grant so made to him.'

Referring to the possible damage by water, he wrote:

'I cannot, therefore, but conclude, in the language of the Defendants' affidavits, that there is not, upon the facts as they now stand, any risk whatever of the Plaintiffs' mines being damaged by any water that may arise from Defendants' workings. I am also satisfied that the workings of the Defendants are being conducted upon a skilful and improved method, and that the means which they have provided in their engines and apparatus are sufficient to remove all reasonable ground of apprehension of danger to the Plaintiffs. In my judgment, therefore, the Plaintiffs' case entirely fails, and I have reluctantly been forced to the conclusion that this suit has been instituted, not so much for the legitimate purposes of relief, as in the hope of its becoming an instrument to effect a different object. I must therefore decline to interfere with the decree of the Vice-Chancellor, and I am obliged to dismiss this appeal with costs.'

In 1869 many people residing in the Forest made complaints to Col. Robert Kingscote and Samuel Marling, Members of Parliament for the Western Division of Gloucester, regarding the state of conditions there, and their relations with the Crown. A meeting that year at the Speech House was the largest ever held in the Forest, and was attended by a very large body of freeholders, miners and commoners. The following Resolution was moved by William Crawshay and seconded by Timothy Mountjoy, and carried[1]:

'That this meeting believing that the inclosure of the Forest of Dean, having due regard to the rights of all parties interested, and reserving a certain portion for public recreation grounds and cottage gardens, will be beneficial to the Crown; the county and the country request the Members of Parliament for West Gloucestershire, to endeavour by such means as may be necessary to obtain the sanction of Parliament to the inclosure and sale of the Forest, portions of it in small allotments, to suit the convenience of the working men.'

Nothing of relevance appears to have been done in this connection, the same need being stressed by witnesses before the Select Committee five years later (in 1874).

Meanwhile, in 1870 was passed the Abbot's Wood (Dean Forest) Act (33 Vict. c. 8) 'to ascertain and commute Commonable and certain other rights in the Abbot's Wood'. Sections 9 and 10 (given below) are of interest:

1 Minutes of Evidence, p. 124 of Report of Select Committee, 1874.

'9. Notwithstanding any disafforestation or inclosure of the Abbot's Wood which may take place under the provisions of this Act, the Abbot's Wood shall for all the purposes of the said Act of the first and second Vict. c. 43, and of the said Act of the twenty-fourth and twenty-fifth Vict. c. 40, as between her majesty, her heirs and successors, on the one hand, and the owner on the other, be deemed to continue uninclosed land within the Forest of Dean, and the owner and his successors in title shall not at any time become entitled under the 67th section of the former of those Acts or otherwise to one moiety or any other share of any galeage rent, royalty, or tonnage duty, or other moneys to be received by her majesty, or her successors, from or in respect of any coal or iron or other mine or minerals within or under the Abbot's Wood.

10. Nothing contained in this Act, or in the award to be made by virtue hereof, shall prejudice or affect the right of her majesty and her successors to the mines and minerals in and under the Abbot's Wood, all which mines and minerals are as between her majesty, her heirs and successors, on the one hand, and the owner on the other, by this Act reserved to the queen's most excellent majesty, nor shall anything in this Act or in such award prejudice or affect the rights (if any) reserved to or conferred upon her majesty and her successors by the hereinbefore recited Acts of the first and second Vict. c. 43. or the twenty-fourth and twenty-fifth Vict. c. 40; nor shall anything in this Act or in the said award prejudice or affect the rights of any free miners under the said Act of first and second Victoria or otherwise.'

The Dean Forest (Mines) Act 1871. This Act made 'further provision respecting the opening and working of Mines and Quarries in the Forest of Dean, and in the Hundred of St. Briavels'. It further amended parts of the Act of 1838, and, as before, did not apply to 'Excepted Lands' regarding which notices had been given by the owners.[1] The following are the main points of the Act[2]:

- Three Mining Commissioners to be appointed,[3] to (*a*) give a true interpretation of Rule 4 and Rule 14 of the Second schedule to the Awards of 1841, of which there had been doubts as to the true meaning; and (*b*) settle, by Award, all matters that may come before them under this portion of the present Act.
- Duties and powers of the Mining Commissioners to cease after the publication of the Award.
- Power given to the gaveller or deputy gaveller to (*a*) accept surrender of part of a gale; (*b*) grant renewals of leases to assignees of free miners, 'in like manner as if such person or persons so in possession were a freeminer or freeminers' (S.34).
- Minimum or dead rent to be made up to 31 December, and royalties and tonnage dues on 30 June and 31 December.

The Mining Commissioners issued the following substitute Rule 4:

1 See Appendix A.

2 Currently available from H.M.S.O. is an Official Revised Edition of the 1871 Act to 1 February 1978 omitting spent and repealed Sections. See also Appendix 1.

3 The following Commissioners were appointed: Evelyn Ashley, Alfred Buckley, and John Taylor.

'All persons now or at any time hereafter holding any unopened[1] gale or gales of coal or iron ore shall *bonâ fide* commence opening the same within the space of five years from the date of this award as regards gales now held by them, and as regards all other gales or new grants of surrendered or forfeited gales within five years from the date of the grant thereof respectively;

Provided, nevertheless, in the event of any unavoidable and unforeseen mining accident or impediment occurring, or other reasonable cause of delay being proved to the satisfaction of the gaveller, to prevent the opening of such works within the said period of five years, then the time may be extended at the discretion of the gaveller, by some writing under his hand, according to circumstances. But if any dispute shall arise between the gaveller for the time being and any person or persons entitled to any gale respecting the extension of time for the said opening, or any dispute as to whether there has been a *bonâ fide* commencement of the opening of any gale, then in such case the matter in dispute shall be referred to the decision of an arbitrator to be appointed in all respects as the arbitrator is directed to be appointed in the Acts of 1838 and 1861 relating to the Forest of Dean, in cases of dispute as to the amount of new galeage rents and royalties to be paid by galees on the cesser and determination of the old rents and royalties; and the costs of the said arbitration shall be paid in the same manner as is provided in S.37 of The Dean Forest (Mines) act, 1871.'

The Mining Commissioners also defined Rule 14 as follows:

'The galee, or other person holding through or under him, shall have the liberty of making up the short-workings of any year or years in any succeeding year or years, so long as he continues in the occupation of the gale paying the proper rents and royalties to the crown, and duly observing the conditions under which he holds; the meaning of the word "holding" not being limited to any defined period, but being co-extensive with the occupation of the gale by the galee, his heirs and assigns, until the gale is surrendered or forfeited to the crown.'

The emendation of Rules and Regulations are still of importance (especially as regards forfeiture).

In 1871, according to Timothy Mountjoy,[2] he 'and William Morgan, of Readings, and George Goode, of the same place, with 20 other good and true men, started a Union in Cinderford, which grew into a grand society called "Amalgamated Association of Miners". We had 4,500 join us in the Forest of Dean; Thos. Halliday was the President; but there was some mismanagement in Manchester, at the head, or the society would have been good today. When it dissolved, the National took us in. The Forest miners had at that time one of the best central committees that the Forest miners could produce; there was no waste of money, no cheating, no secrecy as to how things were done. William Morgan was treasurer, and every payment was made at the monthly meeting, and monthly balance sheets issued to every lodge; no embezzlement could be carried on under such management; but the extra officious ones that sought office made a disturbance, and the Fancy men gave out paying, several other lodges followed, and the society broke up.' He added[3]:

1 For definition of 'unopened' gale see lawsuit Young and Grindell, 1878, p. 4.

2 Mountjoy, *op. cit.*, p. 35.

3 *Ibid.*, p. 62.

'In 1874 (November) the Forest Colliers came out on strike against a 10% reduction.' The year 1872 saw another case[1] dealing with Dean Forest, this time in connection with the rateability of coal and iron ore mines.

The year 1873 witnessed the deciding of a case[2] by which it was confirmed that if a free miner who holds three gales, surrenders one of them on the ground that there is not coal enough in it to work it at a profit he can claim another gale. The defendant, James Davis, was a free miner who had, since the passing of the Act of 1838, had three gales granted to him, either alone or jointly with other persons. The first was made on 7 February 1843 in equal parts to Thomas Jenkins, Thomas Phipps, and the defendant, and was called the Old Forester Colliery. The second was made on 27 June 1843 to the defendant alone, and was called the Speedwell Colliery. The third was made to the defendant alone, and was called the Pluckpenny Colliery. The plaintiff, John Ellway, also a free miner, alleged that none of these three gales had been yet exhausted within S.61 of the 1838 Act. On 4 November 1868 the defendant applied to have a fourth gale granted to him of a particular pit, and on 20 July 1871 the plaintiff applied for a grant of a gale of the same pit, and subject to the right, if any, of the defendant, the claim of the plaintiff was prior to that of all other free miners of the Forest. The claim, however, of the defendant, to have such gale granted to him, was alleged by the plaintiff not to be well-founded, inasmuch as if the defendant's application were acceded to, he would become the grantee of more than three unexhausted gales at one and the same time, contrary to the provisions of the Act in that behalf. Notwithstanding that the defendant was not so entitled, the deputy gaveller had given notice that the defendant's application would be acceded to. But the plaintiff had given notice of his objection to the grant, which was thereupon deferred in order that the plaintiff might have an opportunity of asserting his rights in priority to the defendant.

The defendant alleged that he was entitled to the said grant on the ground that in the year 1859 he had surrendered the gale to work the Speedwell Colliery, after having tried it and found that there was not sufficient coal to make it worth working, and that he was consequently not now the holder of three unexhausted gales within the meaning of the Act; but the plaintiff charged that such surrender did not assist the defendant, inasmuch as the Act referred to an exhaustion of ore, and not an exhaustion of interest of the galee, and in support of this contention the plaintiff referred to the 15th Rule of the Dean Forest Mining Commissioners, whereby it was provided that should any galee be minded to give up his gale before it should be worked out or exhausted of its coal, he should only be permitted to do so on condition that he left the horse roads, and other roads and passages which might be requisite for working such coal as might remain in the several veins, in a free and open state and condition, fit for a succeeding galee. The defendant also alleged that as the gale to work the Old Forester Colliery was granted to him in conjunction with two other free miners, it was not a gale within the meaning of the 61st section of the Act. But the plaintiff contended the contrary, and charged that for the purpose

1 George Morgan and Others *v.* Henry Crawshay. (Law Reports: House of Lords, vol. v, English and Irish Appeals, pp. 304-20.)

2 Ellway *v.* Davis (Law Reports: 16 Equity, 1873, pp. 294-8.)

of reckoning the number of gales granted to a free miner it was wholly immaterial whether such grant were joint or several. The bill prayed that it might be declared that the defendant was not entitled to have any further gale granted to him by the gaveller or deputy gaveller of the Forest until one or more of the said three gales already granted to him should have been worked out or exhausted of its ore; and that the defendant might be restrained by injunction from prosecuting the application made by him on 4 November 1868 or from accepting any grant from the said gaveller or deputy gaveller in pursuance of such application. Mr. Cotton, Q.C., and Mr. Cookson, in support of the motion stated:

> 'The only question in this case is, whether the Defendant, who has had three gales granted to him in the Forest, is entitled to a fourth gale before he has completely worked out one of the three gales. We contend that, under the words of the 61st section of the Act. 1 & 2 Vict. c. 43, the mine must be exhausted; and this cannot be the case until the mine has been worked and all the coal abstracted. The Defendant had not worked the mine at all, but, finding that it would not pay for the working, he has surrendered it without working. The meaning of the Act must be that each free miner is to select such pit as he thinks best suited to him, and, having made his choice, must be bound by the grant, and cannot be allowed to give it up and select another until the first pit is exhausted; that is, he cannot have a fourth gale until one or other of the three gales granted to him shall have been worked out; and it can make no difference that one of the gales was taken by the Defendant in conjunction with other persons.'

Sir R. Malins, Vice-Chancellor, in giving judgement, said:

> 'In order that there shall be a fair distribution of the grants, it is provided by the 61st section of the Act that one man shall not engross too much of the land, and shall not be entitled to have more than three gales granted to him at one time, and should not have any other gale granted to him until one or more of the said three gales shall be exhausted. ... It appears that in 1850 the Defendant discovered that one of the gales which had been granted to him was not workable so as to yield a profit, and he consequently gave notice to the deputy gaveller that he would surrender the gale, as it was useless for the purpose of working. Then, having surrendered one of the three gales in 1850, the question is, whether he comes within the words of the 61st section. It is said he cannot have a fourth gale because he is the grantee of three gales; but he contends, on the other hand, that, as he surrendered one of the gales in 1850, he is the grantee of only two gales. The Plaintiff says, "You cannot stand in my way, because you have had three gales granted to you, none of which have been exhausted". Now has he or not exhausted one of the three mines within the meaning of the Act? In my opinion, exhausting does not mean working out every hundredweight of coal; but a mine is exhausted when there is not enough coal in it to make it worth working. The Defendant says he tried the mine, and took steps to work it by means of the Speedwell Coal Company, and there was not coal enough to make it worth working. That is, in my opinion, bringing the case within the meaning of the word "exhausted" as used in the Act; and I think it a very material point in the Defendant's favour that the deputy gaveller accepted the surrender, which he ought not to have done unless he was satisfied that the coal was worthless, or could not

> be worked at a profit. Having thus surrendered the grant, and the surrender having been accepted, I think the Defendant is at liberty to apply to have another gale granted to him on the ground that he is not now the holder of three gales. The motion therefore fails, and must be refused.'

The Crown Lands Act, 1873. This Act empowered the then Commissioners of Woods and Forests to grant leases of stone quarries for up to 21 years, apart from the rights of free miners. It also confirmed that the Commissioners could not grant mining rights for gold or silver.

CHAPTER IX

1874-1883: The Committee and Bill of 1874

THE *Select Committee of 1874*. During parts of the first half of the nineteenth century the Crown and the inhabitants had been in dispute about three main matters: the use of the land, the freemining rights, and commoning. In the second half of the century the Crown again pursued these matters, and by another series of Parliamentary Bills and Inquiries attempted to extinguish the claims the free miners possessed on the coalfield. The Crown found itself in alliance with the principal colliery owners (mainly galees). Once again the move to eliminate some rights of freemining (and of privileges of commoning) provoked profound opposition.

The first phase of the new struggle culminated in a Select Committee of the House of Commons appointed in 1874: 'To enquire into the laws and rights affecting Dean Forest, and the condition thereof, having especial regard to the social and sanitary wants of its increasing population; and further to enquire whether it is expedient that any, and if so what, legislation should take place with respect to such Forest, and the future disposition or management of the same.' Col. R. Kingscote MP was chairman of the Committee, and their Report and Minutes of Evidence,[1] known to the inhabitants of the Forest as 'The Blue Book' because of its cover, is of much interest, as many of the then local residents were called to London as witnesses, and their evidence is fully recorded. A most sorry state was disclosed as regards roads, drainage, sanitation, and housing facilities. The Committee probed these questions thoroughly, as well as others such as the advisability or otherwise of selling the whole of the Forest, compensating the free miners and commoners. They considered what share of the badly-needed amenities and utilities the Crown should properly bear, remembering that the proprietors of the coal and iron mines should also contribute. Most of the witnesses asked for better road communications, land for houses near centres of employment, and land for hospitals and schools.

A Parliamentary Bill was produced, which on the face of it represented a victory for the working men of the Forest, who had for some time been demanding, *inter alia*, the sale of Crown wasteland for house building. The Bill proposed to satisfy that demand. The Crown's programme was proposed to be to abolish freemining and commoning, and to consolidate the deep coal gales in the hands of the Crown, all to be paid for by the sale of the waste land. Nonetheless, bitter opposition to the Bill arose and the free miners, commoners, and most of the other inhabitants rallied to defend their rights and privileges. The land campaign had come from a small relatively privileged section of the working classes, who had lost touch with the traditions of the inhabitants. The Commissioners of Woods withdrew the Bill. They thought that much would be

[1] Ordered by the House of Commons to be printed 10 July 1874.

accomplished if the Crown were empowered to (*a*) grant leases of land on longer terms than the then thirty-one year term; (*b*) sell small quantities of the waste of the Forest for the inhabitants' own use, for housing or otherwise, at a small price. The Minutes of Evidence are too extensive to include at length, but in the following pages the most interesting and relevant evidence is given. Anyone attempting a study of the social and economic history of the Forest will find the Report and Evidence indispensable. Horace Watson,[1] solicitor to the Commissioners of Woods, outlined the legal position in Dean Forest, from an historical viewpoint following in a large measure the Report of 1788. Of the mines, he stated:

> 'With regard to the leases under the Mining Acts the number is 78, and the number of existing gales of coal in the Forest about 200. The number now in work is between 50 and 60. The number of existing gales of iron about 60; the number now in work is between 25 and 30. The number of quarries awarded 176, the number of leases since granted about 145. The number of registered free miners who have been registered since the passing of the Act [1838] is 1,186; which of those are dead there are no means of stating; but, of course, there are a good many. The number of free miners having leases of quarries is 243. The present net income from minerals and quarries is about £15,000.
>
> The quantity of coal annually produced, including colliery consumption, is about 900,000 tons; of iron ore about 170,000 tons, in the raw state. I believe the Commission on the Exhaustion of Coal Mines considered the probable quantity in the Dean Forest to be about three hundred million tons. I have been given to understand there is some reason to doubt, in the opinion of persons qualified to form an opinion, whether that may not be an overestimate; and it is also very likely that the quantity produced may be considerably increased in the course of a few years' time, so that the exhaustion of coal in the case of Dean Forest may take place at a much earlier period than would be arrived at if you contrast the present production with the estimated quantity given by the Coal Commission. It is impossible to form any estimate that could be relied upon in regard to iron, owing to the extreme uncertainty as to where it is to be found. It is usually found in pockets and cavities in the limestone; but there is so much uncertainty with regard to it that no possible estimate that could be relied on if the quantity could be given. As regards the surface, and with respect to the mines, there is a deputy gaveller and a registrar, who receives and makes entries of changes of proprietorship in the mines, and he has an office in Coleford. There is also a receiver of rents and royalties, payable to the Crown.'

M. F. Carter,[2] solicitor, of Newnham, coroner for the West Division of Gloucestershire, clerk to the justices at Newnham, including East Dean, and superintendent registrar of the Westbury Union, gave evidence regarding the rating of the Forest, stating that the collieries of East Dean were valued for rating purposes at £21,304 13s. 10d., the iron mines[3] not being rateable. The surface connected with the latter and the machinery upon it was rated at £1,575 10s., the iron furnaces at £4,500, and railways at £5,676. He pointed out that although there was a Mines Inspector for

---

1 Pp. 1-16.

2 Pp. 17-27.

3 If rateable, these would have been valued at about £6,000.

the district no safety rules had been formulated, stating that 'in 1871 there were 11 killed in the collieries and none in iron mines. In 1872 there were five killed in collieries, and one in an iron mine; and in 1873 there were nine killed in collieries, and no death in iron mines. I am bound to say that I think it very important that special rules should be made for the working of iron mines, and none have been made for our district up to this time. There was a case the other day, where, I think, if there had been any rules, the accident might have been prevented. It was a case where a roof fell in, which had not been inspected for several days, and probably several weeks.' On being asked as to the basis upon which the rateable value of collieries was ascertained he replied: 'The collieries were rated by Mr. Headley who has great experience in these matters, and the highest would be a shilling upon the ton [and the lowest 6d.]. In each half year we obtain from the deputy gaveller's office the number of tons obtained from each mine, and we then put a tonnage rate upon it ... varying according to the value of the mines, the number of veins, the thickness of coal, and so on.' D. J. Smith,[1] assistant overseer for West Dean, stated that for West Dean the rateable value of coal mines was £6,939; iron and tin works £1,110; plant of iron mines £913; quarries £485; railways and tramways £3,820.

James Wintle,[2] solicitor, of Newnham, steward to the verderers, and clerk to The Dean Forest Turnpike Trust and The Huntley Roads Trust, answered:

'Q. 700. You were asked as to the increased value of the Crown property consequent upon the springing up of a population which had stolen the land of the Crown some time ago; is it not a fact that the population is in a very large degree a population claiming privileges called the privileges of free miners, or something of that sort? – No, the free miners of course do live in or close to the Forest, but I think you must separate the free miner and his interest from the surface owner.

Q. 701. Free miners have had a very large share in the profit of opening mines, have they not? – I think, comparatively speaking, the free miner has had very little benefit himself, though his representative has had, no doubt.

Q. 702. It comes to very much the same thing? – There is this distinction, although the free miner has not derived great benefit and his representative has, the representative has only obtained that benefit by the introduction of a very large amount of capital into the Forest.

Q. 703. But still the free miner and his representative are the persons who have been much more largely benefited than the owner of the land, subject to the limitations to which the Crown is subject as owner? – Possibly they are.

Q. 704. So that the population of free miners have been much more largely benefited by the robbery, as the phrase goes, which took place many years ago, than the Crown has been, if the Crown has been benefited at all? – That is from the nature of the tenure upon which the two properties were held.

Q. 705. The accident has been that these free miners have been benefited by the introduction of the population? – I cannot in my own mind separate the two; the Crown cannot derive an income from the mines unless they are worked, and the mines cannot be

[1] Pp. 27-9.

[2] Pp. 33-41.

worked unless you have got a population to work them; the Crown owning so very large a surface area in the immediate neighbourhood of the works have hitherto, I think, from a desire to protect the surface, rather sacrificed and pinched the success of the mining interest.

Q. 706. Has it been possible for the Crown under the powers which they possess of selling land to do otherwise than to pinch the mining interest? – It is admitted, I believe, that they have the power to sell, but there has been such a restrictive price put upon it.

Q. 732. You have said that the commoners' interests could be so acquired that the Crown might be enabled to sell or lease for the purposes of building, is there anything in the rights of the free miners that would prevent the use of that power to sell or to lease or to build upon the land so sold or leased? – Only this, an owner of a work might possibly wish to establish further works upon the land sold to or allotted to the commoners.

Q. 733. Do I understand you to say, if the Crown sold or leased land under the provisions that you recommended, that after the sale or lease by the Crown the free miners might come upon the land so purchased and leased and prevent the use of it for building and for gardens, and so on? – I think it must be so, but then those privileges exist over the freeholds in the Forest and in the hundred, but the landowner, if his property is required by the free miner, receives compensation.

Q. 734. Practically, you think that would not be a serious difficulty? – No, I do not think it need be.'

Alfred Goold of Newnham,[1] proprietor of coal and iron mines and chairman of the Westbury Union, deposed that the coal proprietors were obliged to make their own roads leading from the turnpike roads to the collieries; his company had made and maintained for the last fifty years a mile or so of road; Mr. Crawshay had done at least as much. He employed about 700 men at Bilson Colliery and Crump Meadow Colliery. He advocated that the Crown should be empowered to offer more suitable terms for land for building purposes than the thirty-one year lease, adding: 'One of the great hardships experienced by the miners in the Forest of Dean is, that they have to walk one, two, and three miles to get to their work, not only in the summer but in the winter, through snow and rain; so that when they get to their work many of them are saturated with wet, or half stifled with snow, as the case may be.' His evidence continued:

'Q. 909. Is there any probability of the coal in the Forest of Dean being worked out? – I believe, according to the present computation, there is coal sufficient to last for 100 or 150 years,[2] certainly at the present get; I should say there is sufficient coal to last for 150 years.

Q. 910. Not more? – Not to work profitably: of course, there will be a lot of odd pieces left after that time, but I should say after 150 years the forest coal field will be in a very small compass indeed.'

Referring to the deputy gaveller residing outside the Forest, at Cardiff, Goold thought that 'the resident mining engineer might live in the Forest with great advantage, not only to the interests of the Crown, but to the interests of the mine owners. … There is an office at Coleford, but what we complain of is, that there is not a chief there; we like to deal with chiefs rather than with deputies. … At present there are many local matters

1 Pp. 45-58.

2 100 years has proved to be about right (C.H.)

that we do not wish to come up to London about; if we go to Mr. Howard we get every attention that we can possibly have; we have nothing to complain of; on the contrary, we are exceedingly well satisfied with the regulations of that office; but of course they make us pay for their good services. I would say, so far as getting attention to our requirements is concerned, we are perfectly well satisfied; but there are little matters that we do not like always to be running up to London about. What the foresters would like to see is a mining engineer's office in the Forest, where we can go and get an answer at once.' He added that the office at Coleford was one 'without any authority; plans and maps, and some details are kept there; but after all, the whole of the business is done in London.' Mr. Goold also drew attention to the fact that 'under the Mines Regulations Bill, all persons interested in a colliery, ever so remotely, are prohibited from sitting as magistrates during any inquiry in respect to any breach of the Act of Parliament; I can sit as a magistrate under no circumstances whatever, if an inquiry be going on relating to an accident, or in relation to any contravention of the Act of Parliament. Many of us think that that should not only apply to colliery proprietors, but that it should equally apply to Crown officials. We would like to see that no Crown official should act as a magistrate where there was any inquiry relating to colliery proprietors going on; I dare say that many gentlemen here present well know that colliery proprietors are not looked upon as ordinary human beings; there is a general prejudice against them; many people think they are mere brutes, and extort everything they can from their workmen without giving anything in return in every possible way; they are rather set on one side in the matters referred to, that is, magisterial and other matters. I am not the only person who thinks it, but it is generally thought that Crown officials ought not to sit as magistrates in any colliery inquiry, any more than that colliery owners should not sit on a similar inquiry. Of course, I have not the slightest objection to owners of land sitting in cases where inquiry is going on in relation to offences that have taken place in connection with the land; but I think, if I am not much mistaken, that a recent Act of Parliament has placed occupiers of land under somewhat similar restrictions as the Factory Act has placed other employers of labour, but without the restrictions in this respect applied to mine owners; although, as a rule, we do not object to the prohibition as far as regards colliery owners (in fact, I think there is something wholesome in it); yet, at the same time, we think it rather a one-sided matter.' Goold also deposed:

'Q. 997. Have you any objection to state the output of your colliery? – At the present moment it is about 120,000 tons a year; before the general strike that took place in the year 1871 we were getting 150,000 or 160,000 tons a year.

Q. 998. Your average daily output each working day would be 500 tons? – We can turn out 500 tons per day, but the average is not that; it would be about 400 tons a day, I think.

Q. 999. How many men do you employ? – We have usually about 700 men.

Q. 1000. And you say they have to come long distances, do you find that that creates difficulties in getting labour? – Yes; they always go to the nearest colliery to work.

Q. 1001. If you had better facilities for having cottages near your pit that would be an advantage to you? – Yes; and a greater advantage to the men.

Q. 1002. You would get men more easily? – Yes.

Q. 1003. Would you get a larger output per man, do you suppose? – No, I think not; I think they have decided that they will only work eight hours a day under any circumstances, and will have a certain amount of wages per day.

Q. 1004. The mode of letting the coal is peculiar to the Forest of Dean? – We let it by the ton.

Q. 1005. I want to know how this large concern of yours has grown up under the circumstances of the old forest law? – I presume you allude to the free miners' rights.

Q. 1006. I mean the difference between the ordinary way in which coal is let, and the law which prevails in the Forest of Dean. How is it that this large concern of yours has grown up? – I am sorry to say I am scarcely able to go into this matter, because I thought Mr. Watson had thoroughly explained it to the Committee. Many years ago there was a considerable difficulty as to the rights of mine owners; it is an admitted fact, I believe, that a man formerly could have certain rights and privileges.

Q. 1007. Perhaps I had better not take up the time of the Committee with this. Is the Crown a co-partner of yours, or do you pay a rent? – First of all it is set out in given acres, and it is governed chiefly by the quantity of coal; certain level roads driven underground will drain.

Q. 1008. What is set out in given acres? – What we call a coal award, and it is governed mainly by the quantity of coal that can be gotten by a level road driven in a certain direction. The Crown lays down pretty closely what a certain colliery will give under the regulations that they have set out. A free miner applies for the award; it is granted to him, and he sells it to some one else, in all probability a capitalist; the capitalist, of course, develops the mine, the free miner being given something for his interest in it.

Q. 1009. You have originally purchased a right of some kind? – Yes: of the free miner.

Q. 1010. What do you pay to the Crown? – We are supposed to pay to the Crown one-fifth of our profits, and those profits are ascertained every 21 years; the Crown is supposed to be a partner so far as to receive a fifth of the profits after we have won the coal, but instead of taking a fifth of the profits it is generally arranged every 21 years what we shall pay per ton to the Crown in lieu of the profit share.

Q. 1011. You arrange from time to time a tonnage rate as the rent to the Crown? – Yes; that is so practically.

Q. 1012. The Crown is co-partner with you in the concern? – I do not know whether the word "co-partner" will apply, but the word "partner" will apply; I do not understand the strict legal meaning of the word "co-partner", but to the extent of one-fifth the Crown is a partner with us in the colliery. The profits per ton are ascertained on an average of 21 years, and instead of paying a fifth of the profits, we pay a royalty of 2d., 3d., or 4d. a ton as the case may be.

Q. 1013. But still under that arrangement, whatever duties were incumbent upon you as coalmasters and coal-owners, it was understood that a relative proportionate share of those duties should fall also upon the Crown? – It is not so; we take all the responsibility, and the Crown takes a fifth of the profits.

Q. 1014. That is practically so; but if you take the theory under which those mines are let, would not the Crown be liable to the extent of its beneficial share in the occupation to the duties which fall upon the coal-masters? – I am very much inclined to think the Crown took sufficient care to get an Act of Parliament to exempt them from all liability, and that only an Act of Parliament can make them liable to any of the risks and dangers connected with colliery property.

Q. 1015. Whereas mining industry necessitates a large population, and therefore creates the necessity of sanitary arrangements, it seems to me, under existing circumstances the whole of that is thrown upon those who work the coal, and not upon the Crown? – It is unquestionably the case.

Q. 1044. You mentioned that you held your colliery, or part of it, under a 31 years' lease; does that apply to the surface, or to the underground workings? – Simply to the surface.

Q. 1045. Upon what terms do you hold your underground workings? – It is a freehold, subject to the right of the Crown to one-fifth share of the profit.

Q. 1046. Is it a fee simple? – Freehold.

Q. 1047. Is all that acquired by you from persons called free miners? – Yes, it is.

Q. 1048. How many free miners had you to deal with in acquiring your present colliery? – Only one, I believe, for each colliery.

Q. 1049. I suppose, from the quantity of output you have mentioned, you have a very considerable underground district? – We have about 700 acres, but those 700 acres are comprised of three or four gales or awards. Our collieries are called the Bilson and Crump Meadow Collieries. Bilson is one award, and was taken out by a free miner called A., we will say; and Crump Meadow is another, or two or three, and they were taken out by free miners called B., C., and D., we will say, and all put into one, and made a colliery.

Q. 1050. By whom put into one; by you, when you bought it? – Yes.

Q. 1051. You did not understand my question, when you said you had only to deal with one free miner? – For a given quantity of coal.

Q. 1052. For the whole quantity of your colliery how many do you say, six or seven? – I think not, but the colliery was formed when I was a very little boy, and I cannot go back into the origin of it.

Q. 1053. Is it your impression that one free miner had granted to him direct as much as 100, or 200, or 300 acres under ground? – Yes.

Q. 1054. Is the whole of your colliery comprised in what you have called Awarded gales, or had you any of a more recent date? – All Awarded, I think.

Q. 1088. What benefit does the Crown derive from Cinderford? – I have paid the Crown £1,100 a year, and my colliery is in Cinderford. Mr. Crawshay, perhaps, pays the Crown £2,000 or £3,000 a year, and his collieries are in Cinderford. Messrs. Brain pay the Crown £1,000 or £2,000 a year, and their collieries are practically at Cinderford.

Q. 1099. What are the rights that belong to colliery owners in reference to the land at their collieries? – I believe they are simply these, that the colliery owner, with a certain area of coal, can claim almost as of right, though perhaps not literally, a certain quantity of land surrounding his colliery, for the purpose of building cottages, or making any erections he may think proper, under a 31 years' lease, and that is where the difficulty arises. Give me a 99 years' lease, and I will have 50 cottages erected, so to speak, tomorrow.

Q. 1100. There is a general desire on the part of colliery owners to obtain land in connection with their collieries, for the purpose of erecting cottages? – Yes, I think so; as I have already stated, I would erect cottages immediately if I had a long lease.

Q. 1105. Take your colliery, for example; how much land do you cover with your spoil banks? – Take Crump Meadow Colliery; I daresay we cover two or three acres, if not more; to go to the outside, we do not cover more than five acres, but I should put it down at three acres; our Bilson Colliery probably covers the same acreage there, or more.'

J. T. Thomas[1] of Coleford, colliery proprietor, deposed that he employed about 200,[2] the coal output being about 2,000 tons a month. The thickness of the seam being worked averaged between 4ft. 9in. and 5ft. but that trade was very bad and his men were not working more than three days a week. He further deposed:

'Q. 1307. What is about the extent of colliery underground that you have the right to work? – I am rather puzzled; we have several old collieries which we have been working; the same family have been working collieries for the last 70 years, and some part of the coals is not worked out yet; there are other collieries that we have, but I cannot come to any exact conclusion about them.

Q. 1308. Is it 100, 200, or 300 acres? – More than that, a good deal.

Q. 1309. Five hundred? – Yes, altogether.

Q. 1310. Do you know whether all this was acquired from free miners? – Entirely purchased of free miners. First, in my grandfather's time, they leased before the Act of Parliament was passed, and since the Act of Parliament passed, in 1841, they have been purchased.

Q. 1311. Do you know from how many free miners you have purchased? – One colliery was an original gale, and we bought out the free miner, who was a partner.

Q. 1312. Do you know how many altogether your family had to deal with in order to acquire the property ? – No, I do not; we purchased of different persons.'

W. B. Brain[3] of Cinderford, a free miner and part owner of Trafalgar Colliery and other collieries in East Dean, stated that he employed about 1,000 men and boys. He confirmed other witness's appeals for better terms regarding leases of land as a means to more and better housing facilities. Some of the seams being worked were 17in., another about 2ft., and one about 3ft. His evidence continued:

'Q. 1491. Supposing the Forest were put up to auction in lots, from time to time, by the Crown, say 100 or 200 lots, and they were sold, what would be the position of the man buying those lots in regard to the free miner? – It would be something like it is in the neighbouring parishes now.

Q. 1493. Supposing our Chairman were to buy a 500 acre lot in the Forest, and I, who am not a free miner, came to him, and you, who are a free miner, came to him, and he preferred me as a tenant, would not he be obliged to take you? – No.

Q. 1494. Then the free miners' claims are not before others? – The free miner has a right to the mineral underneath; he has nothing to do with the surface. The right of the free miner is to extract the minerals that belong to him underneath. If he held a gale underneath your property he would have a right decidedly to get the minerals.

Q. 1495. He must hold the gale from the Crown? – Yes.

Q. 1497. I am supposing the Crown sold its rights such as they are by auction, and that our Chairman bought 500 acres of it; then would not you, as a free miner, have a right to go and ask him for the gale? – No.

---

1 Pp. 59-64.

2 Including quarrymen.

3 Pp. 64-74.

Q. 1498. What, then, are your rights as a free miner? – The gales would remain as they were.

Q. 1499. Supposing there were no gales affecting that purchase? – That is decided and settled already. The whole of the gales in the Forest of Dean are granted. There is no spare land under which there is coal or mineral property but what is originally granted.

Q. 1500. Many of those gales are not worked? – Some of them.

Q. 1501. Does not that stand very much in the way of the value of the Crown estate that there should be those gales existing that are not worked? – I do not think so.'

Referring to the position of rights in the case of a sale of the Forest, Brain's answers were:

'Q. 1540. I suppose the mineral holders may be dealt with in the same way as the other commoners? – But I mean the rights of working the mines; it would be impossible to destroy the rights of the free miners to open their works.

Q. 1541. If you paid them in proportion to their rights, I suppose there would be no difficulty in getting rid of those rights ? – Not if you purchased the whole of their property.

Q. 1542. What do you mean by purchasing the whole of their property; that is what I do not understand? – If I possess mineral property in the Forest of Dean, and I could not penetrate the land over it to open it, the property would be of no value.

Q. 1543. That does not answer my question. You say there are certain people who have mineral rights in the Forest of Dean, and I want to know how you would get rid of those mineral rights; I want to know whether those mineral rights could not be dispensed with? – I do not think you could dispense with them.

Q. 1544. Why not? – Because you must destroy the whole of the property to dispense with them.

Q. 1545. What is the property you would destroy? – If you stopped the means of opening it, you would destroy the coal and iron, or at least it is equivalent to destroying it if you cannot open it.

Q. 1546. Certainly not, if you are paid for that which you believe you have a right to? – Not if we were paid.

Q. 1547. That is the very question I asked you, whether you saw any difficulty in getting rid of the free miners' rights which they now have upon the property? – There would be no difficulty if their rights were purchased.

Q. 1548. And I suppose it would be also sufficiently easy to ascertain what those rights were? – I do not think it would be very easy.

Q. 1571. What extent of colliery have you the right to work under? – From 600 to about 800 acres.

Q. 1572. Part of that you acquired as a free miner yourself? – Part of it was an original grant to my father.

Q. 1573. And do you know from how many other free miners you or your father have acquired the rest? – I think my father purchased from about half-a-dozen besides. He had his own right, and he purchased the rights of about half-a-dozen others.

Q. 1574. Have you added anything to those? – I have added to them myself.

Q. 1575. From how many free miners have you added? – From two.

Q. 1576. Making altogether eight or nine? – Yes.

Q. 1577. You are yourself registered as a free miner? – Yes.

Q. 1578. Did I really understand you that all the ground in the Forest of Dean is now let, so that there is no more to be got by the free miner? – All the gales of coal are.

Q. 1579. Is the right of a free miner for any future gales worth anything? – Not much now.

Q. 1580. You say not much; but what chance has he that makes it worth anything? – Very little chance. The Crown has nearly swallowed up the rights of the free miners.

Q. 1581. Still you imply that there is a little chance; can you tell me what the little chance is? – There is this chance; supposing a gale was abandoned and given up to the Crown again, I, as a free miner, could put in an application; I have that gale granted to me.

Q. 1582. In such a case, then, the chance of getting it would depend entirely upon your early information and application? – It would depend partly upon that and partly upon the will of the deputy gaveller.

Q. 1583. He would have the right of discriminating? – I cannot define what his rights are, because the rights of the deputy gaveller have increased almost past the knowledge of free miners; we hardly know what they are now.

Q. 1584. Therefore, if you heard of one of those gales falling in, you would feel quite uncertain whether you could obtain it or not? – We should put in an application, and then trust to goodness to get it.

Q. 1585. As far as you know, someone else putting in even a subsequent application might get it? – The prior application would have the best chance.

Q. 1630. You said the Crown has swallowed up nearly the whole of the rights of the free miners. What did you mean? – I meant that the rights of the free miner used to be very much more extensive than they are now. They were not surrounded by so many restrictions. We used to buy timber for clearing purposes at 2s. 6d. a stick, and now we pay 22s. per stick. When we used to have a grant of a gale the grant was a freehold; now it is a lease of a grant, or rather a license. Once we used to pay £10; it is now £240 dead rent.

Q. 1631. Were they rights? – They were rights, I believe, by Act of Parliament.

Q. 1632. If they were rights by Act of Parliament, how is it that they have been altered? – That I cannot tell.

Q. 1633. Are you prepared to say that the Crown has acted in defiance of Act of Parliament? – I am not prepared to answer you that question.

Q. 1634. Was there any Act of Parliament which fixed the price of timber? – We believe so. We imagine that we are injured, but I am not prepared to say so positively.

Q. 1635. You are not able to state how you are injured, or in what way, you are injured; it is only in imagination? – Perhaps I have not sufficient experience myself to state the reasons, but I think you will hear them from some of the witnesses.

Q. 1636. You are aware that there is a certain power in right, if right exists? – I am aware there is a certain power vested in the deputy gaveller.

Q. 1637. Are you aware a free miner, if he has a right, can assert his right? – Yes.

Q. 1638. How is it then, if these rights existed, that they have not been asserted? – I think they have been asserted.

Q. 1639. What has been the result? – In some cases a failure, and in others a success; I do not think it has been uniform.

Q. 1640. If there has been a failure, to what was that failure due? – To the want of influence.

Q. 1641. Then it is not a court of law in which these rights have been asserted, but a court of favour; is that so? – I should not like to say.

Q. 1642. Do you really mean to say that any rights exist which by the arbitrary act of any Crown officer can be put on one side and treated as nothing? – I think that it has been partly done so.

Q. 1643. Can you mention one instance? – Yes.

Q. 1644. Will you state the facts to the Committee? – I have applied for a license myself for a railway, and I believe we have a right to do so. It has been positively refused by the deputy gaveller.

Q. 1645. If you believe you have a right, why do not you, a man of substance, take that belief into some court, and prove it? – Because of the expense of so doing it would be a very costly process for us to do so.

Q. 1646. Are you aware on what ground any right you have asserted has been refused? – I do not know of any ground on which it has been refused, except that the deputy gaveller presumed it was not desirable for us to have it.

Q. 1647. I want you to state to the Committee the ground which was alleged by the Crown officer for refusing to allow what you considered to be your right? – To the best of my recollection, there was no ground stated whatever; but the words of the letter were, "We refuse to entertain your application", and then it dropped.

Q. 1648. You consider that is a "swallowing up" of your right? – I do.

Q. 1649. It is extraordinary that you do not assert it; you stated, I think, that applications for grants were not considered in the order in which they were made? – I do not think I did. You misunderstood me.

Q. 1650. I should be glad if you would repeat what you said? – I do not think I mentioned that at all.

Q. 1651. You said the prior applicant had the better chance? – Yes, I remember I said that.

Q. 1652. That is, the man who makes the first application has the best chance? – Yes.

Q. 1653. Do you complain of that? – No.

Q. 1654. Are you aware that under any Act of Parliament, the Crown is obliged to consider applications in the order in which they are made? – I believe so.

Q. 1703. I think you said you have known land sold in the Forest possessing common rights? – I have known land sold subject to the free miners' rights; but I have not known any sold subject to the common rights.

Q. 1704. I understood you to say that, the coal being already allotted, the rights of the free miners that have not been claimed are not a matter of great importance? – Yes, that is so. That would go on the same way as it is now.

Q. 1705. As to the license that was refused, you thought the expense of fighting the Crown would be greater than the license would be worth? – I cannot say that; but we did not feel ourselves in a position then to go to the expense of what we imagined it would cost us.

Q. 1706. Did I understand you to say you thought a miner in search of work in hard times would be better off if he could leave his wife and children in a rent-free house than if he and they were turned out of it altogether? – Decidedly so.

Q. 1707. As regards buying timber, is it not the case that you are buying timber from Ireland cheaper than you can buy it from the Crown? – Yes.

Q. 1708. Is the timber as good? – Not for all purposes; but for a great portion of our work it is equally as good, and better.

Q. 1709. There is timber in the Forest which you would like to buy, and you can go into the open market and buy the same kind cheaper? – Yes.'

T. Nicholson[1] of Yorkley, colliery proprietor (who had previously given evidence before the Duncan Committee of 1849) deposed:

'Q. 1792. Can you speak to the rights of free miners, as to their being encroached upon in any way? – Yes. I know all about that; the free miners had a right to apply for a gale, and I believe the Crown had no discretion originally in the matter, but was compelled to grant to the first applicant. More recently a discretionary power has been vested in the gaveller, and he is not compelled to gale to the first applicant. He is to take all matters into consideration and act accordingly, so that the first applicant cannot always enforce the granting of the gale. There is nothing at all in the suggested difficulty with regard to the minerals in the case of selling this land. All the property in the Hundred of St. Briavels is held subject to that right, not merely the forest proper, but in all the Hundred of St. Briavels. The free miners have a right to enter a man's freehold estate, except an orchard or a garden.

Q. 1793. Or a churchyard? – Or a churchyard; they might go, perhaps, into my chapel yard.

Q. 1794. Can they go into your chapel yard? – I do not know what their legal right is, but I should not let them. Of course the minerals are reserved, and we all know that landowners are frequently disposing of the surface property, and reserving the minerals. With regard to those little freeholds, if the free miner or his lessee should do them any damage, either on the surface or underground, he must pay them compensation; there is no difficulty about that.

Q. 1795. Have you ever known cases in which compensation has been paid? – Yes, scores. A house has been undermined and thrown out of the perpendicular, and the man who has done the injury has had to pay. Sometimes the cottager has made a good thing of it, and would not object to having another cottage undermined and damaged in the same way.

Q. 1798. On Friday last I asked you if you could speak of the rights of free miners, as to their being encroached upon in any way; you answered the question, but I think you did not state all you could; tell us about what you considered to be the rights of free miners? – I thought, from what I heard on Friday, that there was a little misapprehension, and I should like to explain it. The original free miner's right was not confined to the Forest of Dean, but extended to all the parishes in the Hundred of St. Briavels as well as the Forest of Dean, and the law applicable to the encroachments would be also applicable to the land in all the parishes of the Hundred of St. Briavels. The whole of the parishes were subject to the rights of free miners. I had understood that the recent sales to the foresters would put the new purchases upon the same footing as the old freeholds, but since I have been here I have looked at several of the conveyances, and I am apprehensive that they are not put upon the same footing, though I think they ought to be. The new sales ought to be put upon the same footing as the old freeholds that were legalised some years ago by Act of Parliament.

Q. 1799. Did not some commission sit upon this question a short time since? – Not upon this question at all. The free miners had a right to take minerals, subject to a grant from the Crown; but if there was any surface damage they had to pay for it, that is, they had to pay the owners of the property for the surface damage; and I think that rule ought to apply to these purchases by the poor men now if they make purchases.

Q. 1800. You think the same rule ought to apply now as formerly? – Yes, I think so, as regards all property bought of the Crown. The gaveller has the power to determine what the

[1] Pp. 74-9.

satisfaction should be.

Q. 1801. And this is the only court that does determine it? – I suppose there might be an appeal to a higher court, but I believe there never has been.

Q. 1802. Is there anything else that you want to say? – Yes; I wanted also to explain that the free miners' rights were, in point of fact, inapplicable to the deep coal. The free miner had a right to sink a shaft or drive a level, as well as a right to a spoil bank, but he had no right to erect steam-engines or buildings; consequently the Crown or the landowner was master of the situation; nothing could be done without a voluntary arrangement. Then another point I should wish to mention is this; the free miners never had any allotment of coal; the free miner could not put his finger upon any piece of coal, and say, "That is mine"; his right was, in point of fact, a right to lay out money and fight a battle; he had no protection beyond 20 yards, and any other free miner could come at a distance of 25 yards alongside of him, and then there would be a fight for the coal.

Q. 1803. In fact, you do not think much of the rights of free miners? – Not under existing circumstances; I think the rights of the free miners, regarded apart from the importation of foreign capital and the consent of the landowner, would amount to very little with regard to deep coal.

Q. 1804. In point of fact, are any more of these free miners' rights now springing into existence? – A free miner is a man born within the Hundred of St. Briavels, who has worked a year and a day in a colliery or iron mine. I am a free miner by birth, but I never took up my freedom by working; but there are young men continually working up who can claim to be free miners.

Q. 1805. Beyond those who are now on the register, will there be any fresh names put on? – Yes, young men continually; but the coal is all awarded.

Q. 1806. That is what is meant. Practically, there could be no fresh awards to free miners? – Except in cases where collieries are abandoned, and then they may be re-galed to a new applicant, and these new men may have a chance.'

E. Crawshay[1] of Cinderford, coal and iron mine proprietor, deposed that he employed between 1,500 and 2,000 men and boys. He was owner of Abbot's Wood, and answered as follows:

'Q. 1917. Can you give any evidence as to free miners? – It would only be repetition.

Q. 1918. I mean in your own collieries; whether you have had to buy any free miners' rights? – We have always had to purchase the free miners' rights. We purchase the property from the free miners; we are necessitated to make an application for a quarry to a free miner, or we were.

Q. 1919. Are you so now? – An application now for a quarry must be made through a free miner in the first instance.

Q. 1920. After that, can you renew the lease without its going through a free miner? – Yes.

Q. 1927. You have a right to a certain quantity of timber yearly, have you not? – There is a share allotted to each colliery on certain days of timber that has been cut by the Crown previously, by payment; but you are not necessitated to take it up without you choose.

Q. 1928. You have a prior right to your share? – I believe we have, but I think since that

[1] Pp. 79-87.

right was granted I have heard something to the effect that the Crown had given some compensation for it, but what it was I really cannot say.

Q. 1929. You do not find this right, if it exists, of any great value in your own case? – No.

Q. 1930. Is it your opinion, from your observation in the Forest, that the timber there is sold to the best advantage to the Crown; or, let me put this, have you ever known it to be unsold? – Yes, I have; between Gun Mills and Little Dean I have known a great number of sticks to lie; and I believe I am within the mark in saying I have known them to lie there for two years, and they were afterwards offered to me at 1s. a foot. I believe that a quantity of it was bought by Messrs. Brain.

Q. 1931. In buying any timber other than oak for your colliery do you find it best to buy from the Crown? – They have now raised the price. It in a measure depends upon distance, because, for want of communication and roads, the hauling is very expensive. At the present time I am buying timber delivered into my works cheaper than I could buy from the Crown, if I had any distance to haul it.

Q. 1932. Have you ever bought Irish timber delivered? – I have bought French timber, and am now buying a great deal. I believe it is in the New Forest, or some such district; it is shipped at Heigh Bridge, and delivered at Lydney.

Q. 1933. This is delivered to you cheaper than you could draw the Forest timber, for want of roads? – Yes, at the present moment; the same timber that I took from the Crown last time is not, taking into account the description of timber, of the same value as that I am now buying.

Q. 1934. So that, from seeing these sticks lying for this time, and knowing that they were supposed by the Crown to have deteriorated in value, from the offer which they made to you, and from your own experience of buying, you think that the Crown are undersold in their own market by timber brought from a distance? – They were not undersold in that instance, because at a shilling a foot I don't think many residents will sell their timber; I know the present price of oak timber of the same class is two shillings.

Q. 1935. That is what I mean, their market was spoilt by want of communication; this timber belonging to the Crown could not be sold for its full value for the want of roads? – Because it was deteriorated when it was sold.

Q. 1936. It had deteriorated, I suppose, from the difficulty of hauling it? – I do not pretend to judge the Crown's reasons for not having sold it.

Q. 1957. Your works are numerous, I suppose? – I am chairman of a new company called the Great Western Coal Consumers' Company, situated near the Speech House.

Q. 1975. What do you value the rights of the free miners at, who are not in possession of coal? – I do not at present value them very highly, because the greater portion of the coal is already awarded. The free miner's right, as far as I at present can see, would only come into existence in case of any of the gales lapsing to the Crown.

Q. 1976. Is it your opinion that the rights of the free miners are of very little value in themselves, but of considerable detriment to the Crown in dealing with mineral property? – You asked me their rights relative to coal; there would be other rights of course besides coal.

Q. 1977. The other rights are ironstone mining and quarrying? – Yes.

Q. 1978. And there they end, do they not? – Yes.

Q. 1979. Keeping your attention to coal, do not you think that their rights are not very valuable individually, but of considerable detriment to the Crown property? – I do not think I have a right to give an opinion regarding that.

Q. 1980. Have you ever turned your attention to the question as to how this coal could become freehold coal, vested in the Crown, extinguishing the rights of free miners in the coal? – No. It is a point I do not see my way to enter into; a free miner has a right at any time for any period so far as I understand it, and should a piece of coal be thrown into the Crown, that is to say, should a lease of coal lapse to the Crown, he would have a right to apply for it. We cannot tell what may become workable or what may not.

Q. 1981. You have become the freeholder of the surface of Abbot's Wood by extinguishing the rights of the commoners either by an allotment of land or by money payment? – Yes.

Q. 1982. Do you think that process could be adopted towards the free miners, who are, as it were, commoners, with certain rights of working minerals under certain circumstances? – That is in my opinion a legal question with regard to which I am not capable of giving an answer.

Q. 1983. No, it is not a legal question; it is a question bearing on law, the solution of which the Committee may have to suggest? – If a child is born in the Hundred of St. Briavels he becomes a free miner, and how could his right be done away with.

Q. 1984. Let me put it this way; you have already done away with, by your own enclosures, the rights of the commoners yet unborn in Abbot's Wood; do you see any difficulty in dealing with the rights of the free miners in the same kind of way? – I do foresee a difficulty. In dealing with the rights of the commoners by handing them over their encroachments you at once leave that property to them and their families, and it becomes their actual property.

Q. 1985. I will put it to you another way; is there any compensation that could be given to the free miner to extinguish his rights in the same manner as you have dealt with the commoners, either by cash compensation or compensation in land? – It is a question I have not gone sufficiently into to be able to answer.

Q. 1986. Would the Crown have any difficulty in buying up the rights of the owners in the same way as you bought them up in Abbot's Wood? – Very little difficulty.

Q. 1987. Was that by money payment in your case? – Yes.

Q. 2013. I think you have stated there are not many free miners who have rights besides those whose gales are now taken up? – I believe I stated, as regards the coal and iron, that the greater portion is, to the best of my knowledge, already awarded.

Q. 2014. Then, as regards quarries, they are still open; but I think you stated there were not many free miners of that class who had rights? – I do not quite catch the meaning of the question.

Q. 2015. The meaning of my question is this, that most of the free miners' rights are now in occupation; but still there are some free miners who have not exercised any rights, and they are few in number? – The whole number of free miners have the same equal rights, as far as I am aware, at the present time.

Q. 2016. That is not what I mean; you stated there were some free miners who might have rights, but who claimed no rights? – There may be free miners who have no rights at present, that is to say, not holders or galees at present.

Q. 2017. I thought you said they were but very few? – As regards the coal and iron, I still state that, to the best of my knowledge, the greater portion is already taken up.

Q. 2018. Then there would be no difficulty in dealing with the rights of those few that are left? – But still they have those rights, should at any time any of those gales be given up or returned to the Crown.

Q. 2019. But their rights are prospective, and might now, perhaps, be easily dealt with? – I should think the Crown might deal with them.

Q. 2020. Having dealt with those rights, there would then only remain the people in possession? – Yes, or what relapsed; that is the difficulty I found in answering the question before. Of course, if the Crown could in any way deal with the whole of the free miners' rights, then, as a matter of course, if the gale relapsed to the Crown it would become private property.

Q. 2021. Do you see any means of arriving at that? – I can only reiterate what I have already said; but I have not gone sufficiently into the question to be able to give an absolute answer.

Q. 2022. With regard to the commoners' rights, you did deal with them so far as Abbot's Wood was concerned? – Yes.

Q. 2023. Therefore there would be no difficulty in the Crown dealing with the commoners' rights over the rest of the Forest? – I apprehend there would be very little difficulty.

Q. 2024. Having got rid of the commoners' rights, there would be nothing left but these rights, such as they are, of the free miners? – There would be this right, if there is the right still existing, namely, that colliery owners can claim a certain amount of timber; that would have to be dealt with also.

Q. 2025. Supposing the colliery owner could claim a certain right as to timber, that right could certainly be dealt with, because, taking one year with another, you would know what you have received from the Crown with regard to timber? – It comes to this, that all rights can be dealt with if an Act is obtained for so doing. It only resolves itself into a matter of compensation required by the parties.

Q. 2026. Taking your own right in regard to that, should you consider that the compensation you would ask would be large? – No.

Q. 2056. You mentioned the number of workmen you employed as being between 1,500 and 2,000? – Yes.

Q. 2057. About how many of those are employed in working coal? – Between 1,200 and 1,500.

Q. 2058. About what is the extent of your collieries? – Do you mean in area?

Q. 2059. Yes, in Dean Forest? – Between 3,000 and 4,000 acres.

Q. 2060. Is any of that under Abbot's Wood ? – No.

Q. 2061. Do you know with how many free miners you have had to deal in acquiring this extent of colliery? – We had not to deal with free miners.

Q. 2062. Did you not originally acquire it from free miners? – Yes.

Q. 2063. Do you know with how many free miners you, or those who preceded you, had to deal in acquiring this colliery? – No; I cannot tell you.

Q. 2064. Abbot's Wood is not and never has been worked as a colliery, I understand you to say? – There is no coal, I believe. I hardly think the coal touches upon Abbot's Wood. The strata only touches it on one corner.

Q. 2065. I think I understand you to say that the rights of free miners, if any, under those had not been purchased? – The whole of it has been awarded.

Q. 2066. But has not been worked? – The crop of the coal that touched Abbot's Wood has been worked.

Q. 2067. Your impression is that it is exhausted, or substantially exhausted? – Yes.

Q. 2068. In answer to an honourable member, who asked you concerning the rights of free miners, you say, at all events, they had rights to any colliery which might lapse to the Crown ? – Yes.

Q. 2069. Am I right in supposing that the colliery most likely to lapse is the colliery of the least value? – That again depends upon the power of the free miner of holding or selling; if a free miner is granted an award, I believe that the Crown has a right, should he not pay the dead rent within a certain period, to forfeit that gale; I believe there is a decision upon that point.

Q. 2070. Assuming it to be so, is it not the case that if it were a very good piece of coal it would be very unlikely that the person entitled to it would lose it by failing to pay his rent? – That in a great measure depends upon circumstances, because the Crown in the last few years have raised the dead rent of gales very much, and it would be a question whether or not a capitalist could very soon be found to raise a sufficient capital to open it.

Q. 2071. Do you know of any case within the last few years of a lapse? – No, I do not.

Q. 2072. What is the last one you remember? – I am not aware of any that have lapsed; I am entirely unaware of what takes place in the gaveller's office.'

Timothy Mountjoy[1] of Bilson Green was the next witness of relevance. A free miner, he had been a collier all his life, being latterly employed as a 'cropper',[2] while for the last year he had been agent for the local miners' union, The Amalgamated Association of Miners. His evidence reads:

'Q. 2199. Have you devoted yourself entirely to that? – Yes, since that time.

Q. 2200. Therefore you have the means of knowing the feelings of the men in that part of the country? – Yes, I have the means of knowing the feelings of 5,000 of the colliers and miners.

Q. 2247. Supposing the waste land belonging to the Crown is put up for sale, who do you think ought to be allowed to buy it; would you have any preference, or would you put it up to public auction? – The foresters decidedly object to putting it up to public auction, because they say rich capitalists come in and buy it up; and in fact, it would be making the rich richer and the poor poorer.

Q. 2248. How would you propose that it should be sold; who should have the first right or claim upon the land? – I have been holding meetings upon the subject amongst colliers and miners of late, meeting 5,000 of them at different places, and they all, with one unanimous voice, say they think the foresters who have been bred and born in Her Majesty's Forest ought to have the first refusal; that the portions to their gardens and dwellings should be sold to them first, and if there was an overplus left they would have no objection to any other ratepayer who had settled down in the Forest of Dean, and who had been working at the mines for three or four years, to come in and buy a piece separate and apart from theirs.

Q. 2261. And, therefore, you think the commoners' rights in the Forest of Dean might be very easily got over, or put on one side, by selling this waste land? – Yes, I do.

Q. 2262. Are you a free miner? – Yes.

Q. 2263. Do you know anything of the rights of free miners? – Yes.

Q. 2264. Have you sold your rights in any way to a colliery proprietor? – No; I never knew of a gale that I considered it worth my while to put in an application for. I believe

1 Pp. 92-107. This witness later wrote *Sixty-two years of the Life of a Forest of Dean Collier* (1871).

2 A superintendent 'to see that the men did not send out more than the stipulated quantity of lime and coal per cent.'

applications are in for all the profitable gales, and consequently I never put in an application for one, although I had a right to do so.

Q. 2265. There are those who possess gales that are valuable, I conclude, or are they nearly all worked out? – Nearly all the surface veins [seams] are worked out, but there are deep veins.

Q. 2266. There are ironstone gales, are there not? – Yes, there are; but they are very deep; most of the surface veins of the iron are worked on our side of the district.

Q. 2267. Supposing it were found necessary to free the Crown from these free miners' rights, do you think there would be any difficulty in getting rid of them? – I do not think the Crown could get rid of the free miners' rights to the iron ore, which they have awarded to them by the Crown.

Q. 2268. That would stand very much in the way of the Crown being able to dispose of any portion of the Forest? – No; I think not.

Q. 2269. Why not? – I think that where any proprietor has an award of so many acres of iron ore or coal, that the Crown, before selling or attempting to sell, should ask these parties who own the gale where they intended to put their plant and pits; and then I think it would only be right and fair for those who hold the award to point out to the deputy gaveller where they would like to put their plant, and that there should be so many acres left for them upon which to put their "dirt mounds", as we call them, and to erect the plant.

Q. 2270. Do you think that the free miners' rights would not interfere with the Crown in selling their property? – No, not in the least, if that precaution were taken of leaving so many acres for the plant to be erected upon.

Q. 2271. Still you would have these portions of ground over which the free miners would have their rights dotted all about the Forest, and do you not think that would prevent people purchasing and working? – No; these free miners' rights are not dotted about in that way; they are not so plentiful as that, they are scarce and far between. If I may use the expression, there are landmarks and stones put up between; they are very few and far between.

Q. 2272. You think there would be no difficulty upon the score of these free miners' rights? – There would be no difficulty if the precaution I have named were taken.

Q. 2273. You say you have attended several meetings upon the subject lately? – Yes, scores.

Q. 2274. During those meetings has it not been stated that the foresters think they have the right to ask the Crown for ground for a hospital? – Yes, they do, and they have requested me to ask for ground for a hospital.

Q. 2275. Is there an hospital in the whole Forest? – No, not in the Forest of Dean proper; there is one in the parish of Newland, I believe, built by Lady Dunraven, but it is of very small dimensions.

Q. 2276. How far have you to go to take any people hurt by accident? – When we have any accidents we have to take our men from 12 to 14 miles in a spring cart to the nearest hospital; such is the deplorable condition of our neighbourhood, that we have not a proper conveyance at our Forest pits in which to take a poor fellow to the hospital so that he can lie straight along. I have known cases where the horse has run away with him on the way to the hospital, and thrown him out upon the road.

Q. 2277. Owing to the badness of the roads, or was it the horse's fault? – I might say that a more up-and-down road than that which leads from the Forest of Dean to Gloucester, or half way to Gloucester, could scarcely be found in any part of the country.

Q. 2292. Is there anything else that you wish to state to the Committee? – As regards the house accommodation, I might say that it would be a great advantage to our Forest miners if the Crown were to sell the waste land at a reasonable price for garden and building purposes: and, what is more, it would be an inducement to our young men to save their money and buy a piece of land and cultivate it, and when they have no work at the pits it would keep them at home in our country, instead of going out to till the backwoods of America, as hundreds of them have done; and it is more than probable that they will sooner or later be called upon to fight us in case of a dispute between the country and us.

Q. 2338. You stated that you never yourself put in an application for a gale because you did not know of one that you considered worth taking up. Is it your opinion that there is likely, within any time that we can foresee, to be many applications for gales? – I believe that every gale worth applying for is already applied for and entered upon, the gaveller's books. I would not give, I was going to say, 2½d. for those that are left.

Q. 2339. Do you think no great difficulty would arise in the future if the claims of the present gale holders were not interfered with? – None whatever; I cannot see how any difficulty could arise provided the precaution was taken that I have already suggested, namely that those who already hold a gale should have so many acres apportioned off for the working of that gale. In my opinion that would remove all the difficulty.

Q. 2366. With regard to these free miners, you say that every possible gale you can contemplate is now taken up? – Yes, with the exception of stone quarries; there may be a few stone quarries.

Q. 2367. I understand you propose that there should be places set apart in any allotment of land for sale for the pits, spoil banks, and so on? – Yes; where the award is already given. Where a gentleman has already got an award on the gaveller's book, then I think that there should be that precaution taken.

Q. 2368. Can you give me any idea how far these would be apart, because I understood you to say there are not very many? what sort of distance, on an average, would they be apart? – From two to three miles.

Q. 2369. Do you consider that these galees have the right to use the land for spoil banks without making any payment for it? – I do.

Q. 2370. You consider they have a right to occupy a portion of land for a spoil bank without payment at all? – Yes, I do, because I think the royalties coming to the Crown, amounting to hundreds and thousands of pounds from the iron and coal are quite sufficient remuneration to the Crown for all spoil banks that arise.

Q. 2371. Does the Crown charge for land for spoil banks? – I have never known a case. I should be very sorry myself if I were a coal proprietor to pay for a spoil bank; I never knew a charge made for a spoil bank.

Q. 2372. That is altogether independent of the right of renting six acres, or taking a lease of six acres of land near to the collieries if the proprietors choose; that has nothing to do with spoil banks? – No; I believe the object of that is for the purpose of sawpits, engine-house, and so on.

Q. 2375. With regard to free miners, do you know how many there are on the gale book? – No.

Q. 2376. You do not know what proportion of them have gales? – I could not say how many.

Q. 2377. You valued the rights of free miners who are not in possession of gales at less than 2½d.? – I do not understand your question.

Q. 2378. Did you not say you considered the right of free miners who did not hold a gale was not worth 2½d.; that all the good gales were taken up? – I said this, I think, that I did not believe there was a gale now that could be obtainable.

Q. 2379. That you could not get a gale now that would be worth 2½d. to you; all the valuable gales are taken? – No doubt.

Q. 2380. It is only in the event of a gale falling in that the free miner has any right whatever? – I never knew a gale fall in. I do not understand the term.

Q. 2381. When I say "fall in", I mean when a gale lapses or is given up? – I should call that forfeited. If I discontinued to pay my dead rent for a certain number of years, and so forfeited my gale, if you were the first applicant for the gale that I had so forfeited you would of course get it.

Q. 2382. Do you think the chances of obtaining gales are very valuable? – Yes, they are just now.

Q. 2383. You think they are worth something; I do not think you understand the question. Let me put it this way; you do not hold a gale? – No.

Q. 2384. Do you think you have a good chance of getting a gale? – No.

Q. 2385. As what do you value your chance as a free miner of getting a gale? – I do not set it up as very valuable.

Q. 2386. If I gave you a sovereign would you give it up altogether, and say you would never ask for a gale? – I never intended to ask for one without a sovereign.

Q. 2387. Supposing I gave you a sovereign, and asked you to give up your rights and your children's rights to a gale, would you give them up? – Yes, for getting a gale.

Q. 2388. You think your chances are so small as that? – Yes.

Q. 2389. I suppose a gale includes all the veins within the acreage of the gale? – No; not all the veins.

Q. 2390. Are gales to be had of the lower veins? – Yes; there are gales that may be purchased of the lower veins, but they are already awarded to persons on the gaveller's book.

Q. 2391. The shallow veins and the deep veins in the same area are awarded to different gale holders? – Perhaps to six different parties; one gale one vein, and another gale another vein; 10 or 15 or even 30 yards between.

Q. 2392. Are the deep veins and shallow veins worked at the same time? – No.

Q. 2393. Is there any reason why they should not be? – Yes.

Q. 2394. What is the difficulty, or what is the reason, why two gale holders should not be working in the same place in different veins? – Supposing there is a pit here, and you have an award of the deep vein, and I have an award 40 yards above; if we can agree as to the sinking of that pit between us, and the putting of the plant, we may both work our two veins out of the same pit.

Q. 2395. If I have a gale of the deep vein, I can sink through the old workings of the shallow vein? – Yes; there is no difficulty about that.

Q. 2396. I shall be pumping the upper gale-holder's water? – Yes, just so; the principal veins that are being worked now in the Forest of Dean are the deep veins; but the deepest vein we know of, and what is supposed to be the best vein, is not yet touched, excepting the crop.

Q. 2397. Is it let? – It is all awarded and bought for a considerable sum of money; they sell them by the acre the same as you sell land, except that they get as many thousands as they would pence, I suppose, for land.

Q. 2398. There would be no difficulty in the way of a galeholder working a deep vein, although the upper veins may be working at the same time? – No, providing he could do it; but my impression is that no proprietor will be able to work the deep vein unless a number of proprietors go down to the same vein at the same time, because of the quantity of water coming up; there has been one company trying now, I think, for six years, who have spent I cannot say how much, perhaps £300,000 or £400,000, and they are not down yet, and I believe they never will get down.

Q. 2399. They get the whole of the water of the district? – Yes; until several gentlemen agree to put down pits in several places, so that they will be all pumping up the same water. I think the vein will never be worked.

Q. 2400. What sort of water is it? – It is not first-class water; it is what we call good water; but our doctor tells us we have no good water, because it is a mineral water; although it is clear, sweet, and good to the taste, they tell us, being a mineral water, it does affect the liver. There are very few men in our locality but what are affected with a liver disease.

Q. 2401. What is the depth of this vein from the surface? – From three to four hundred yards.

Q. 2402. You say you have been holding a good many meetings in the Forest of Dean? – Yes.

Q. 2403. Did it ever occur to you at any of these meetings to suggest that the persons who were interested in the welfare of the people should have provided some sort of convenience in cases of accident, or some means of assisting themselves in cases of troubles occurring, such as those of which you have spoken? – I have never heard any one suggest it; but I think it is a disgrace to the proprietors that they have not erected something in which to take the men away.

Q. 2404. You say it is a disgrace to the proprietors, do you include the Crown as one of the proprietors? – No, I do not.

Q. 2405. Do you not know that it is the usual thing in these large districts, where these sort of operations are carried on, for people to help themselves? – Of late years the men have begun to help themselves; but I really think, where there is a large plant, and where they are raising 700 tons of coal a day, thereby accumulating large fortunes, the least the proprietors in that case could do would be to provide every available comfort essential in cases of accident to take the men to the infirmary when crushed.

Q. 2417. As I understand you, the proprietors of coal, or the coalowners in that neighbourhood, have not done their duty towards those they employ? – We think not.

Q. 2432. I should like to know whether you think there would be any objection to the Crown buying up the interests of any galees or of any gales that might happen to fall in, or of those who might wish to sell? – I do not believe it would be very much to the interest of the Crown to buy any forfeited gale, because I feel persuaded no man would allow his gale to be forfeited if it were worth much to him.

Q. 2433. Supposing there were an opportunity afforded to the Crown to buy any property of that description, should you have any objection to their doing so? – I should, supposing anyone put in an application for it. I think if any free miner put in an application for it he should have the award granted to him as a right belonging to a free miner. I think the free miner should have the preference before the Crown.

Q. 2434. That is to say, if the Crown had an opportunity of buying up this gale you think it ought to be open to any free miner there might be, whether his name was on the list or not? – If his name were not on the list he would not of course be an applicant, but if he made an application I think the person who made the application first should be the party to whom the gale should be awarded.

Q. 2435. You might have the right, and you might wish to give up the right. Supposing that were so, should you see any objection to the Crown buying up that right, because it might happen that for a small sum of money a right might be bought up? – I should see no objection whatever if there were no other applicant.

Q. 2436. I think you have stated, so far as you are a free miner, as yet you have not applied, and you do not think your chances worth much? – No, I do not.

Q. 2437. Therefore, as regards free miners in the same position as yourself, there would be no difficulty in getting rid of the rights? – No, none whatever.

Q. 2438. The only difficulty the Crown would have in dealing with property of this description would be in the case of those who now have the gales, or those who are down, and applying for any gales? – There would be no difficulty then if the precaution were taken in the case of any gale of so many acres round the portion pointed out where the pit is to be were set aside for the spoil bank and other purposes in connection with the plant, and not to be sold to anybody.

Q. 2510. You say many of these colliers have gone to the backwoods in America? – Yes.

Q. 2511. Have you heard anything of them? – Yes.

Q. 2512. How are they going on? – I have heard of a great number of them being scorched in one pit.

Q. 2513. In a colliery? – Yes.

Q. 2514. Have you heard of any of them settling? – Yes.

Q. 2515. Are they doing well? – Some of them are doing well, and some doing ill.

Q. 2516. Have any of them come back? – Yes, some of them have come back.

Q. 2517. Have they come back to the Forest? – Yes.

Q. 2518. Did they emigrate in consequence of a strike? – No.

Q. 2519. Why did they emigrate? – They thought to go and better their condition.

Q. 2520. For want of work in the Forest? – No, not altogether so.

Q. 2521. You stated that the time might come when the nation would want these men? – Yes. I believe it will.

Q. 2522. Do you recollect the nation thirty years ago? – Yes.

Q. 2523. Has not the population trebled in that time? – Yes.

Q. 2524. How did the nation get on with the third of the population? – The same as it does now. We have been in several conflicts since then, and I have no doubt a great number of these men from the Forest of Dean have helped to fight in these conflicts. Some of them I have seen back here with medals, who were fortunate enough to come back with their lives.'

Richard Hewlett[1] of Bream, a free miner and commoner, answered:

'Q. 2636. Have you exercised any right as a free miner; have you ever sold your gale? – No; I never had one of my own; I have not seen the chance to take one out; I did apply for one, but I was a little behind time for the portion I wanted.

Q. 2637. Are you very likely to have the right of a gale, or to obtain a gale? – I do not know.

---

1 Pp. 107-8.

Q. 2638. Have you an application before the gaveller at this moment? – No.
Q. 2639. Do you consider your right as a valuable one? – Yes.
Q. 2640. Would you take a sum of money for your right? – No.
Q. 2641. No sum of money? – No, I should not sell my rights as a forester.
Q. 2642. You would like to retain your rights, although you do not think you would get anything for them? – Yes.'

John Miles[1] of Berry Hill, a free miner and commoner, deposed:

'Q. 2724. Have you ever exercised your free miner's rights? – No, I never have.
Q. 2725. Have you ever applied to have a gale? – No.
Q. 2726. Do you look upon those rights as valuable? – Yes; I have only to be registered, and if there was a chance I could gale as well as any other man.
Q. 2727. Are you likely to go and get registered? – No, not unless I could see anything worth it, I should not trouble.
Q. 2728. You never have applied to have your name upon the list? – No.
Q. 2729. Are you aware that there are not many gales left? – I do not think there are.
Q. 2730. You are in no hurry to make your demand for one? – No.
Q. 2737. As regards free miners' rights; you might have been registered as a free miner when you were 21 years? – Yes.
Q. 2738. How many years ago is that? – Thirty years ago.
Q. 2739. Unless you were registered, you could not have asked for a gale if one had fallen in? – I could not have taken a gale.
Q. 2740. According to the tables, you have 15 years longer to live; for 30 years you have not thought of being registered; during the next 15 years do you intend to be registered? – Unless I could see anything worth taking a gale out for I should not.
Q. 2741. Supposing your rights to be worth nothing for 30 years, what do you think they are worth for the 15 years to come? – The rights of common would be worth something.
Q. 2742. Are they worth anything at all? – Yes.
Q. 2743. Are they worth a sovereign? – Yes.
Q. 2744. Are they worth a shilling a week; would you rather have a shilling a week or your rights? – My rights.'

C. E. Machen[2], landed proprietor, of Staunton:

'Q. 2766. You have no land taken for the use of mines? – Yes, we have a small quantity.
Q. 2767. How was that arranged for; by agreement? – No; the gale was applied for at the Crown Office; the shaft was then sunk, and the gaveller made a valuation of the surface damage, which award was paid over to the farmer.
Q. 2768. Was the award of the gaveller in that respect satisfactory to you? – No, I cannot say it was at all.
Q. 2769. Is it generally the case that there is dissatisfaction at the price awarded? – Yes; the awards are too small, as a rule, I think; they do not take into consideration that in a few

[1] Pp. 108-9.
[2] Pp. 110-11.

years the coalpits will increase a great deal, spreading more and more over the ground.

Q. 2770. The ground was taken once for all; a limited quantity, I suppose? – They are liable to encroach if they are not looked after very sharply, when they throw up the dirt and refuse.'

Thomas Goold[1] of Newnham, solicitor and colliery proprietor:

'Q. 2775. Can you give any information as to the position of the free miners now as compared with their position immediately after the passing of the Act of the 1st & 2nd of Victoria [1838]? – Including in the term "free miners" the present colliery proprietors, I think their position is not so good by a great deal as it was immediately after the passing of the Act.

Q. 2776. What brings you to that conclusion; you say, as between the Crown and themselves, you think their position is deteriorated since that time? – Yes, I certainly think it has.

Q. 2777. How has this arisen? – It has arisen, in my opinion, from the constant attempts on the part of the Crown, some of which have been successful and some unsuccessful, to restrict our rights, and as they have called the men who took in the land before the passing of the Act encroachers, they have attempted, in my opinion, to encroach upon the rights that we had before the Act, and the rights confirmed to us by that Act.

Q. 2778. Can you give us any illustrations? – Yes, several. Before the passing of the Act of the 1st & 2nd of Victoria, the free miners and colliery owners, as representing them, were entitled to pit timber. That was found by the Commissioners in their Fourth Report, and it was confirmed by the 30th section of our first Act of Parliament, which says, "That from and after the passing of this Act, all claim or right of any free miner to timber or wood of the said forest growth shall cease: Provided always, that in fixing the galeage rent, royalty, tonnage duty, or other payment to be made to Her Majesty, her heirs and successors, the Commissioners hereby appointed shall take into consideration the value of such claim or right hereby extinguished, having regard to the provisions contained in all or any of the Acts of Parliament under the authority of which railways may have at any time heretofore been made within the said Forest, or any part thereof." At the time that Act was passed, the timber was of the value of 10s. a cord, and that value was, of course, taken into account in fixing our galeage rent. Gradually, and since then, before the first term of 21 years had expired, the Crown raised the price of our timber to 15s., 20s., 25s., 30s., and even up to 40s.

Q. 2779. What is it now? – I think it is 42s. a cord now. I should say that the cord is now a little larger, and contains a little more in quantity than the cord at the time of the passing of this Act; but irrespective of that, we now pay four times as much as we paid for the pit timber when this Act was passed.

Q. 2780. Is the position of things the same as regards the land for engine-houses, and other purposes, for the working of a colliery? – No, it is not the same. The 43rd section of that Act reads thus: "Provided always, and be it enacted, that in fixing the said galeage rent, royalty, or tonnage duty, the said Commissioners shall take into their consideration the rent or rents now payable to Her Majesty by the owner or owners of any existing gales, pits, levels, or works under leases or licenses granted for the erection of steam-engines, or the formation of private railways or tramroads, for the more convenient working of any of the

1 Pp. 111-24.

said gales, pits, levels, or works, which rent or rents now payable to Her Majesty, under or by virtue of such leases or licenses (being so taken into consideration by the said Commissioners), shall from and after the making of the said Award merge and be extinguished in the galeage rent, royalty, or tonnage duty, to be settled and awarded by the said Commissioners as payable to Her Majesty in respect of existing gales, pits, levels, or works as aforesaid." So that before the Act we had to pay for the licenses to erect engines, and so on. When our royalty was settled those rents were to cease, and all that was to be taken into consideration in the fixing of those rents, and we were, as a consequence, to have this land necessary for engines, and so on, free of expense.

Q. 2781. Is that the case now? – No; we have lately been made to take leases of all this land.

Q. 2782. Since when? – As early as 1858 the firm which I afterwards represented had been made to take leases of land for cottages in connection with the collieries, and in 1862 we were made to take leases of land expressly for the purpose of our engines. I hold a lease in my hand now made to the firm which I represented, not only for the land for machines and blacksmiths' shops, but for pumping-engine, winding-engine, weighing machine, buildings, engine-houses, and boiler seats.

Q. 2783. Everything, in fact, connected with the mines? – Yes.

Q. 2784. Does that include the spoil bank? – No, it does not include the spoil bank.

Q. 2785. What happens with regard to the spoil bank; you are not charged for spoil banks, are you? – We are not charged for spoil banks at present, but I am almost afraid, from some questions that have been asked here, and some evidence which has been given, we shall not be allowed to escape very much longer as to that if the Crown can help it.

Q. 2786. You are not charged for it at present? – No, not at present, and we are most clearly entitled to the ground for spoil banks. It is expressly mentioned in the rules and regulations attached to the Award that we should be entitled to all necessary heap or tip room.

Q. 2792. In what other respects do you consider that the Crown have endeavoured to encroach upon or restrict the rights of free miners, and to make them in effect mere tenants? – If you take our second Act of Parliament, or rather I would say the Bill as originally drawn by the Crown in 1861, that would have made us no better than tenants, and would not indeed have placed us in quite so advantageous a position.

Q. 2793. There is no Act to that effect? – No; because when we came to resist what we called these attempts to restrict our rights we succeeded in getting all the obnoxious clauses struck out.

Q. 2794. And the Bill was withdrawn? – No, it was not withdrawn, but the obnoxious clauses were struck out.

Q. 2795. There is no such Act in existence, although another Bill was brought in in 1871? – This Bill, as altered and amended, was passed in 1861. The objectionable clauses were struck out. They introduced clauses forfeiting for all manner of things. The same thing occurred again in 1871.

Q. 2796. The objectionable clauses were not passed? – We succeeded in knocking out the objectionable clauses in that instance also, but still I put it as illustrating what I said just now. The Crown have attempted successfully sometimes, and sometimes unsuccessfully, to encroach upon our rights, and to place us in a much worse position than we are entitled to be under our first Act of Parliament. If the objectionable clauses in these two Bills had passed we should have been really no better than tenants under the Crown, and in some respects in not so good a position.

Q. 2797. Although you have not attacked the Crown legally, have you had much correspondence with them? – Yes, a good deal at different times.

Q. 2798. Can you give a summary, and the result of the Lightmoor barrier correspondence? – That particular case, I think, is a very strong illustration of what I have been just now stating. A brother of mine, who died in 1866, was the manager of our collieries at that time, and for some little time after his death we could not succeed in appointing an efficient manager, and were obliged to leave it to a considerable extent to our bailiff; during that short time the barrier between us and Lightmoor, which we were bound to leave, was pierced by our men to some extent; there was a barrier of 20 or 30 yards, and they drove into it perhaps 10 or 12 yards.

Q. 2799. Unknowingly to you? – Yes; directly we knew anything about it we informed the owners of the Lightmoor Colliery about it, and also the Crown; and the Crown wrote to us stating that we had forfeited the colliery by that act, and that we were liable also to a fine, the amount of which was in their discretion. They fixed the fine at £25, and positively told us that we had forfeited the colliery, but if we would pay this fine, pay certain costs, and pay the royalty in respect of a part of the Lightmoor Colliery which was to be left in lieu of what we had taken, so as to make the barrier good, and so on, they would waive the forfeiture.

Q. 2780. What was the result? – The result was this, that after a lengthened correspondence, they sent me down a draft, which was, in fact, a covenant between ourselves and the Crown, and the owners of the Lightmoor Colliery. On the part of the Lightmoor Colliery, they consenting to leave a part of their colliery to make good the barrier, and on our part, to pay £25 for compensation to the Crown for the trespass we had committed, and to pay the costs of this deed. They recited, "That by such unlawful working, the said owners of the Crump Meadow Colliery have become liable to a forfeiture thereof". And then they set out, that, in consideration of our doing these things, they would kindly waive the forfeiture of this property. In my last letter which I addressed to the Crown upon the question (with the exception of mere formal letters), I told them in distinct terms that we never would sign any document making any admission of the kind that we had forfeited, or making any admission that they had any right to inflict a fine upon us; and ultimately the draft was settled and executed with all those clauses entirely cut out. That was another instance of an attempt on the part of the Crown to do something which they had no right to do.

Q. 2801. There the matter rests now? – Yes, there the matter rests; the deed has been executed with all those objectionable clauses cut out. This is an instance where the Crown set up a claim to forfeit a property which has been lately sold for a sum close upon £100,000, simply because inadvertently, and unintentionally, we had cut into the barrier.

Q. 2802. Has there been any alteration, to your knowledge, in the form of the grant of a gale? – I confess I am at a loss to understand the reason of any such alteration; they used to grant a gale to the free miners, but now they are in this form: "Do hereby grant a gale of a license to get the coal within"; what they mean by it I do not know.

Q. 2803. They have inserted the word "license"? – Yes.

Q. 2804. That was not so formerly? – No; and I am quite at a loss to comprehend the meaning of it.

Q. 2805. Do you know the first instance of this? – No; but I have had this one in my possession some three, four, or five years.

Q. 2806. Do you see what the difference is? – I really do not see why it should be, nor can I understand why they should have made any such alteration.

Q. 2807. Has any objection been made to the insertion of those words? – I cannot say that of my own knowledge, because I never applied for a gale myself, not being entitled to apply. I am not a free miner, and I cannot say whether anybody else has made any objection.

Q. 2808. You do not know of a case of a Mr. Brain applying for a gale? – That was under the Highmeadow Woods, I think.

Q. 2809. And does not refer to this form? – No.

Q. 2810. You do not know it of your own knowledge as to when the alteration first took place? – No.'

Mr. Goold was of opinion that as the Crown had from time immemorial taken one-fifth of the clear profits of all the collieries in the Forest without any responsibility or liability whatever, they should contribute a clear one-fifth towards the expenses of roads and drainage. He was in favour of selling the whole Forest subject to the settling of the rights of free miners and commoners. He also confirmed the inconvenience caused by the deputy gaveller residing outside the Forest and the way in which the price of Crown pit timber had been increased. He continued:

'Q. 2932. Do you think there would be any advantage in doing away with the rights of the free miners, and putting the free miners of the coal, or the holders of the coal from the free miners, in the position in which a colliery lessee usually stands in other parts of the country? – That would be an advantage, perhaps, to the Crown; but certainly not to the coal owner.

Q. 2933. You do not think it would be desired or desirable for the district that there should be any alteration in the system of free mining, and the rules under which the coal is now worked? – Not as to existing collieries, certainly.

Q. 2934. The whole of the gales, as far as they are believed now to be working, are taken? – Yes, so far as the coal gales, I believe; I am not sure that there may not be here and there a spot of coal or some tract of coal in the deep series on our side of the Forest not galed; but, speaking generally, it is the fact, no doubt, that the coal gales have been granted.

Q. 2935. Would it be practicable, in any way, to buy up the rights of the free miners? – Yes, I think so.

Q. 2936. Could you purchase the rights of the free miners, except by a purchase of their collieries? – The collieries are now in the hands of purchasers from the free miners, and in the hands of a very few individuals. The free miners are a large class of men in number, but their rights now practically are of little or no value. I confine myself now to the coal gales, because there may be some iron gales of some value not galed. The free miners' rights are practically of very little value; and really it would be almost impossible to say, with respect to them as a whole, that they were of any money value.

Q. 2937. I understand you to say, as far as the free miners, or holders of the coal from the free miners, are concerned, there is no desire to alter the present system? – No, certainly not, on the part of the holders of the coal.

Q. 2938. What I want to know is, if it were desirable on the part of the Crown, or for the general good of the district to purchase the rights of free miners, could that be done except by purchasing the collieries and all the interests connected with them, from the present holders under the free miners? – Yes; the right of the free miner is this, to have a gale granted to him that has not been already granted, and therefore in buying up the rights of free miners you would be simply buying a right on their part to have a gale granted here, or there, or any other place, if any such gale existed.

Q. 2939. There could only be advantage in taking rights conferred upon the free miners in respect of those gales that are taken; and those rights, I imagine, could only be acquired by satisfying the holders and others who hold the coal from the free miners? – That would be, practically, buying up the whole colliery property of the Forest.

Q. 2940. Would there be any other means of putting an end to the rights of free miners in the Forest? – There certainly would be another way of putting an end to the free miners' rights, because, as I said before, their rights are to put in an application for a gale, and if you destroy those rights there is an end to any future gale being granted to a free miner.

Q. 2941. As far as regards the gales that are at present taken, you would not recommend any alteration, or do not suggest any means by which the system with regard to them could be altered? – The only means by which that system could be altered, would be to let them purchase the royalties of the Crown, which would make the mine their own subject to the surface rights of the Crown.

Q. 2942. You would suggest that the free miner should buy the Crown's fifth share, and not that the Crown should buy the free miners' rights? – I think that would be the more feasible plan.

Q. 2943. You do not think that it would be necessary, or greatly desirable for the district, that the question of the coal, and the mode in which it is held, should be interfered with, or altered? – Not unless the Crown determined to sell the entire Forest. If they only determined to sell certain portions of the waste land, it would not be desirable, I think, to interfere with the present state of things, as far as the colliery proprietors are concerned; but whether or not it would be desirable to do away with the free miner's right to get another gale, is another question.'

Samuel Marling MP[1] of Stroud, who represented the Western Division:

'Q. 3054. From inquiries you have made, I believe you ascertained that there has been no complaint made by the commoners, or any attempt made by the commoners to assert their right over land sold by the Crown? – I think that no commoner has ever objected to those inclosures; with regard to the other rights of free miners, I think it will be found, if the question is carefully examined, that those free miners' rights need not be any bar at all to the inclosure.

Q. 3055. What makes you think that? – I would suggest to the Committee that they need not be at all interfered with, because those free miners' rights, as I think Mr. Goold stated, are practically of very little money value, and they interfere very little indeed with the profitable occupation of the surface; for instance, they extend over the whole of the Hundred of Saint Briavels, and I think that the larger portion of the Hundred of Saint Briavels is inclosed land, and I know that it is not uncommon in other mining districts for the surface to belong to one man, and the minerals to belong to another, which would be simply the case here; and whatever is done with the surface, or whatever is done with the miners' rights, I think it is to the interest of the Crown and nation, that the minerals should be retained in the hands of the Crown, and the free miners' rights respected. Suppose a gale were granted after

[1] Pp. 124-32.

the surface had been disposed of, the person to whom the gale was granted would have to pay compensation to the person whose land he interfered with, to enter and work the mine.

Q. 3066. Your opinion is, that the whole of the Forest ought to be sold? – Yes, within a very moderate time; I have tried, in looking into this matter, to see what interest the Crown has in keeping the Forest as it is, but I cannot see that it gets anything by it; I believe the net revenue yielded by the surface of the Forest of Dean is very trifling, and under the existing system will continue to be so.

Q. 3067. Would that be with the mineral rights or without? – No; I think you would find an enormous amount of complication if you attempted to sell the mineral rights, and I do not see any advantage in it.

Q. 3098. We have had evidence that nearly every gale of coal which is of any value has been granted in the Forest? – I cannot speak with certainty on that subject of my own knowledge, but I understand it is so.

Q. 3099. And it has been stated to the Committee that a free miners' right to obtain a gale is worth very little indeed at the present time? – Yes, very little.

Q. 3100. Do you see any objection to a provision in any Act of Parliament which would enable the Crown to buy up dormant rights, rights which have not been exercised by these free miners? – I am not lawyer enough to give a confident opinion; but as a practical man of business I do not see much advantage in it, though there may be reasons for it which I do not see.

Q. 3101. Large parts of the Forest I apprehend are granted, and the rights granted are not exercised, but lie dormant for a time? – Yes.

Q. 3102. In the event of its being thought expedient to authorise the Crown to sell the Forest, do you see any objection to granting to the Crown the power to deal with the grantees, so as to compensate them for any value there may be in their grants which they have not worked or exercised? – Certainly not, if it does not prove too costly and complicated, because your question seems to imply that they would be dealt with fairly, and if an extortionate or unreasonable price were demanded the negotiation need not go on; I apprehend you do not contemplate a compulsory commutation.

Q. 3103. No, certainly not? – Then I see no objection with the proviso I have named.

Q. 3104 What I ask you is, whether there is any objection in policy so far as the Forest is concerned, and the people who reside in it, that the Crown should be empowered to acquire on fair terms rights which have been granted and have not been exercised? – I believe the number of free miners existing is something like 1,000 or 1,100, speaking roughly from memory, and I see no objection if the legal gentlemen see their way to such a course being taken, and I think there might be advantages in it, if moderate terms, fair to all parties, could be agreed on.

Q. 3118. Broadly you say there would be no objection in the Forest, and in the interests of the population, to disafforesting it, to enclosing it, to selling the whole or such portions as might appear to be expedient, on the condition that regard was had, as a private owner would have regard, to the interests of adjoining occupiers; and also on the condition that some provision was made for recreation ground for the larger centres of population? – I should be careful in saying there would be no objection, because I believe the free miners and foresters have not a very small notion of what their rights are in the forest; I believe there would be objections, but I believe at the same time, that their best interests would be served, although they might not see it, and might not all agree to it very readily; but if an enclosure took place having due regard to the rights and interests of all concerned, all the sanitary evils of the Forest would be in a right way for correction, and the interest of the foresters and the Crown promoted.

Q. 3119. You speak of expectations of the free miners and foresters as being such as are not based on any real and proper foundation? – I certainly should say that a kindly and liberal consideration should be made to the inhabitants of the Forest, and I think that might be done with due consideration to the rights of the Crown and nation.

Q. 3120. And you think it desirable in their interests, and the interests of the public, that those impressions of a sort of community of property which exists with regard to the Forest should be dissipated? – Yes, I do certainly; I do not think they are founded in fact; but all the foresters' rights founded in law or custom should be respected, but the sale of the surface of the Forest is quite consistent with that.'

Sir James Campbell, Bt.[1], deputy surveyor since 1854:

'Q. 3237. A complaint has been made to the Committee that an alleged right of the galees to timber has been injured by the Crown raising the price of pit timber; are you aware if the galees have a legal right to timber from the forest? – No; they have no legal right at all; that was done away with by the Act 1 & 2 Victoria, cap. 43 [1838]. We sell all the timber to them, but they have no legal rights; by that Act all claims of timber were to cease.

Q. 3239. Has the price of pit timber been raised, and how much, if it has been? – The pit timber in the Forest has always been sold at an average price, and 20 years ago a great deal of it was bad, crooked timber, and limbs of old trees, and after that was used up it has been of a much better quality, and the price was naturally raised in accordance with the quality; but since then, the value has increased very much of timber of that sort, and raised again.

Q. 3241. Do you think it is an advantage to the galees to have timber at the existing rates? – Undoubtedly it is the cheapest timber they have and the best.

Q. 3242. Would they pay more elsewhere? – They do pay more elsewhere; I can give the Committee the prices that are paid, if they would like to have them. We sell the Crown's timber by the cord, which is supposed to contain about two tons five to seven cwt.[2]

Q. 3248. Do you make any rule with regard to selling it; do you sell it first come first served? – No; the coal proprietors in the Forest have agreed among themselves the proportions which each should take, according to the value of their works; that is divided into about 50 odd shares. One proprietor probably takes four shares, another three, another two, and so on, and sometimes down to even half or a quarter of a share; so that if 50 shares were applied for on any particular day, and there were 200 cords to sell, one will get 16 cords, and another perhaps 12, and so on down to half a cord.

Q. 3256-7. It has been stated to the Committee that there is a strong feeling in the neighbourhood of the Forest in favour of the Crown buying up and making compensation for rights of common, in order that the Forest may become the absolute property of the Crown, subject to the rights of galees and free miners, provision being made for certain places, as for instance near the Speech House, being set out for public recreation, and for

1 Pp. 135-44.

2 He explained that cords used to be 68 cubic feet, but were now 128 cubic feet, the price working out (at 40s. per cord) at 17s. to 17s. 9d. a ton in the wood or 23s. to 23s. 6d. at the pit's mouth.

some other public purposes. Assuming the wishes of the locality to have been accurately represented to the Committee, do you see any objection to such a scheme being proposed for the consideration of Parliament? – Yes; I believe there is pretty generally.

Q. 3259. Do you see any objection to it generally? – No, not generally. I think it will be a difficult matter to settle.

Q. 3312. Have you any memorandum of the number of tons of timber that is annually sent from the Forest to the mines? – I have not got any memorandum to that effect, but I can tell you in general terms; it is about 2,000 to 3,000 cords, and that would be from about 6,000 to 7,000 tons, a cord being about two tons and a quarter, or a little more.

Q. 3322. With regard to the free miners, I presume you know very much their feelings; do you think that a similar process might be carried out towards them, so as to extinguish their rights, that is to say, that land should be sold to them at a certain deduction from its valued price permissively, and such process being carried out, so gradually extinguishing their rights? – That is a very difficult question to answer, because you would have to do it for a long course of years. The free miners are a race of people who are continually growing in number, and you would have to extinguish them, beginning at a certain date; you must extinguish the power of making free miners before doing anything; at present, a man who is born in the Hundred of St. Briavels, and works a year and a day in a mine or quarry, becomes a free miner or free quarry man, and until you put an end to that of course the number will keep increasing; there are a great many on the register now, and a great many others might be on the register if they took the trouble to register themselves; you would have all those to deal with, and you would have to stop the increase of free miners, or the formation of free miners, so to speak, hereafter.

Q. 3323. The actual value of the free miners' rights is almost nominal? – At present it is not great, because most of the mines have been awarded or applied for; the deputy gaveller, who probably will be examined, can give you all the information upon that point, and I only know it second hand as it were.

Q. 3357. We have heard that it would be expedient to sell the whole of the Forest; that is not your opinion, I presume? – No, certainly not.

Q. 3384. Everything relating to mines being out of your province? – Yes; everything relating to underground would be out of my province, except that a lease of land for mining purposes would come through my hands.

Q. 3385. Any arrangement as to surface matters connected with mines would also be within your province? – Yes; that would also be within my province, because it might happen that any grant of that sort might interfere with timber, and therefore I should have to value it; but my duties are entirely with reference to the surface.'

Thomas Forster Brown[1], deputy gaveller since March 1865 when he succeeded Mr. Atkinson, deposed that his office was at Coleford, which he attended once each week. When first appointed it was stipulated that he should reside in the immediate vicinity of the Forest. This he did for two years, but being offered a partnership in South Wales, the matter was reconsidered by the gaveller and the stipulation was waived. He had as his assistant at Coleford a mining engineer holding a certificate under the Mines Regulation Act. His evidence continued:

[1] Pp. 145-51.

'Q. 3464. Will you describe the Dean Forest mineral field? – The Dean Forest coalfield is nearly a complete coal basin; the coal extends over about 20,000 acres in the lower measures, and the ironstone extends over about 25,000 acres. The present output of the coalfield is about 900,000 tons a year, and of iron ore about 160,000 tons. In 1853 the output of coal was about 400,000 tons. I may also state that the quantity of coal contained in the coalfield is about 265 millions of tons, of which probably 150 millions of tons will be coal of moderately good quality. Looking at the progress which has been made in the development of Dean Forest, I should be disposed to think that, probably within the next 25 years, the output from coal will be doubled.

Q. 3465. What is your opinion as to the exhaustion of the times? – I was going on to say that I think, having regard to the comparatively smaller proportion of good coal unworked, that probably the output will commence to permanently decrease in from 50 to 60 years of the present time.

Q. 3466. Can you form any opinion as to the length of time the coal will last? – No; it would be impossible to do that, because by a certain period the output will commence to permanently decrease, and the rate of the ratio of decrease it is impossible for me to state.

Q. 3467. It has been proposed to the Committee that the Crown should sell small plots of land for building miners' houses; do you agree in that? – No; I do not agree with it. If the coalfield were in the nature of a permanent property, so that the occupation for the people was permanent, then I think the objection which I have made might not be a tenable objection, or, at all events, so strong; but, having regard to the fact that the coal is exhaustible, the effect of having small plots of freehold land it appears to me would have a very unfortunate effect upon the rest of the property, when the time arrived for the coal to be exhausted or the output reduced.

Q. 3468. From your experience, can you inform the Committee if it is usual for lessees of collieries to provide cottages for the workmen? – It is usual for lessees to provide cottages for the workmen.

Q. 3469. Is it usual for them to pay for land occupied by spoil banks and tramways? – Yes. I might perhaps explain that probably I have been acting as lessor's agent in the letting of 8,000 or 10,000 acres of new mineral field in the last two to three years, and in every case the lessee pays for the land he requires for surface purposes.

Q. 3470. What proportion, in your judgment, do the royalties at the present time paid to the Crown bear to the royalties which would be paid for similar mines to an owner who held free from the customs of the Dean Forest? – I should say from a third to a half.

Q. 3471. Is it, in your opinion, reasonable that the Crown or the public should be expected to do more for the collieries in Dean Forest than an ordinary lessor would do? – No; I do not see upon what principle they should be called upon to do so. I should say I do not think at the present time that the galees in Dean Forest are paying their full proportion of one-fifth. I cannot undertake to say whether they paid the full proportion when the assessment was made at the beginning of the 21 years; but at the present time I believe it is materially below the proper proportion.

Q. 3472. Does the Act of 1 & 2 Vict., c. 43 [1838] direct the gaveller to grant gales to applicants in the order of their application, subject to the 62nd section of the Act? – Yes; there are two sections, the 56th and the 62nd sections. The 56th section states the rules to be observed in granting the gales, and the 62nd section provides that the gaveller shall not grant gales which may interfere with existing gales. The words are, "And be it enacted that the said gaveller or deputy gaveller for the time being shall not be compellable to grant any gale which he may conceive will interfere with any existing gale, pit, level, or work, or which, either from its proposed situation or extent, shall not, in the opinion of the said gaveller or deputy gaveller, be considered as adapted for obtaining the coal or other mineral in the best and most economical manner."

Q. 3473. It has been stated to the Committee that the Crown has swallowed up nearly the whole of the rights of the free miners; are you aware of any case since you have been deputy gaveller in which the rights of the Crown and the free miners have not been dealt with in accordance with the Dean Forest Acts? – I know of no case.

Q. 3474. And the awards made under those Acts? – No.

Q. 3475. Are you aware of any case in which the assertion of the rights of free miners has failed from want of influence? – No.

Q. 3476. We have had it stated to the Committee, as an instance, in which the right of a free miner has been asserted and refused, namely, a case in which an application was made for a license for a tramway and refused by you; what was the nature of that application? – Mr. Brain was perfectly correct in stating that the license was refused; but he was not correct in stating that the grounds of refusal were not distinctly stated to him in the presence of Sir James Campbell at the time. The circumstances were these, which were quite exceptional, and for which there was no precedent. Mr. Brain had a colliery called the Trafalgar Colliery, and he has a license from there to a public railway of about a mile; he then applies for a licence from that to an iron mine about two miles away, and comes forward and says, "I want a licence in respect of my colliery, commencing at a point three or four miles from my colliery, and going on from there to a public line of railway". The grounds of objection were these: that this tramway was intended to pass through a valley at the northern end of the Forest, and I should perhaps explain that the coalfield altogether is considerably elevated above the rest of the district, and there are only two outlets from the northern end, and one of those outlets would have been occupied by this tramway, and I thought, having regard to the fact that it was through this valley the tramway was applied for, it was undesirable that one galee should have a railway to the prejudice of the interests of other galees, and stated that the Crown would be very happy to support an application to Parliament for a line through the valley. Since that time an application has been made for a line through the valley, and an Act obtained.

Q. 3477. You gave Mr. Brain the grounds why you should not advise his application to be agreed to? – Yes.

Q. 3478. Has Mr. Brain lately applied for any gale? – I understand that he has made applications for gales under the old customs.

Q. 3479. Just lately? – The 15th of June.

Q. 3480. Do you consider it of importance that barriers of gales set out by the award should be observed? – Yes; there is a special rule which provides that barriers are to be left, and these barriers are left to keep up water, and to prevent water flowing from one colliery to another. It becomes important that any breach of these barriers should be very closely and stringently dealt with in the interests of other galees and the Crown.

Q. 3481. Therefore, you consider that any breaking of a barrier should not be passed over without a substantial payment, such as would be likely to prevent the proceeding happening again? – Yes; I should say that there have been several breaches of barriers on the part of Mr. Crawshay, the Park End Colliery Company, and others, and they have all been dealt with upon the same principle.

Q. 3487. It has been a complaint before this Committee that the time during which deeds are sometimes kept at Coleford for registration has been excessive; is it not necessary sometimes to make searches and inquiries, and to obtain legal advice as to the propriety of registering deeds? – Yes; it is a matter of ordinary occurrence that searches have to be made, and I am not aware of any case in which any delay has arisen, except in consequence of searches being necessary.

Q. 3488. One of the witnesses, Mr. Tom Goold, stated that he has been required to take a lease of land on which an engine stood at the time of the passing of the Act of the 1 & 2 Vict., c. 43 [1838]? – I understand he refers to leases granted in 1862. Mr. Goold, who was then in partnership with Mr. Carter, applied, and I will read the correspondence. The leases were granted on the direct application of the galees, and this is the first letter on the subject, addressed to Mr. Howard, dated the 19th of March, 1862: "Sir – We are directed by Messrs. Aaron Goold and Company to apply to you for a lease of the pieces of land coloured red, and the ponds, or land covered with water, coloured blue on the plan sent herewith, for the purposes of the Bilson and Crump Meadow Collieries." Then this is the reply of the Commissioner, dated the 26th of May: "Gentlemen, – With reference to your letter of the 19th of March last, applying on behalf of Messrs. Aaron Goold and Company, for a lease of certain pieces of land and ponds, or lands covered with water, situated in Dean Forest, for use in connection with the Bilson and Crump Meadow Collieries, I have to inform you that I am willing to grant a lease to Messrs. Aaron Goold, William Philip Price, and John Hayworth, the registered owners of the collieries, and the premises shown in the plan which accompanied your letter—viz., in connection with the Bilson Colliery. Section B, the plots of land coloured red, and numbered 1 to 6, with the buildings erected thereon, and containing together 1 acre 22 perches. Section C, the plots of land coloured red, and numbered 1, 2, and 3, with the buildings thereon, containing together 13 perches, for a term of 31 years from the 25th of March, 1862, at an annual rent of £6. In connection with Crump Meadow Colliery – Section A on plan – the plot of land with the buildings thereon, coloured red, and numbered 1, containing half a perch. Section D, the ponds, or lands covered with water, numbered 1 and 2, and coloured blue, and the plots of land numbered 3 to 7, coloured red, with the building thereon, containing together 1 rood 38 perches, for a like term of 31 years at an annual rent of £4. The lease will contain such terms and conditions as are usually inserted in Crown deeds of a similar nature. The sum of £3 13s. 6d. on account of the expenses connected with the preparation and enrolment of the lease will have to be paid by your clients. On your informing me that Messrs. Goold and Company accept these terms, I will give directions for the preparation of a draft of the lease for your perusal." Then I have a letter dated the 27th of May, from Messrs. Carter and Goold, in these terms: "Our clients will accept a lease of the pieces of land and ponds, or lands covered with water, shown on the plan which accompanied our letter of the 19th day of March last, upon the terms mentioned in your letter of yesterday." Those are the leases referred to by Mr. Goold.

Q. 3489. Do you agree with a witness that has been examined here, that holders of gales only pay a nominal sum for surface occupied for any purposes connected with the working of the mines? – I do not see upon what principle of equity the galee has a right to take surface land for the purposes of his colliery without payment.

Q. 3490. Is such the case in regard to the workings under gales in private lands in the hundreds outside the Forest? – I should say outside the Forest of Dean, but still within the mineral field, and coming within the rules and regulations for working mines in Dean Forest, there are enclosed lands and minerals under those enclosed lands, and out of the royalties or galeages derivable from the minerals a moiety is to be paid to the owner of the land, and also there is a provision that the owner of the surface is to be compensated for surface damage, and the deputy gaveller is the person who has to ascertain the surface damage, and that is assessed as an annual payment, so that you have the Crown within the forest, who receives no remuneration for the spoil banks, and the owner of the land just outside being paid.

Q. 3491. You do not see any reason why the Crown, as landowner, should not receive the same compensation for the use of the surface that any other landowner, being also mine owner, would do, and as the owners of private lands in the Hundred of St. Briavels now do? – I think it is clear that the mine owners ought to pay for the surface land. As to whether they ought at once to be required to pay what would be fair and right is an open question, because this condition of things has existed for some years; and it might be estimated, say for a period, to allow them to continue to occupy the land at a lower rate, and then put up the full rent at a subsequent period. I think, in all probability, it would be considered a great hardship to at once call upon the mine owners to pay the full value of the surface, but I think it is quite clear they ought to pay a certain annual rent, and that they should fence in the land, because at present it is not fenced.

Q. 3492. You think that they have been rented under very favourable terms? – Yes. While I am upon the question of fencing, I think there ought to be provision that all the licenses for railways should be fenced off. I can see no reason why a railway passing through an open forest should be left exposed, and I also think that an annual rent should be paid for the land occupied.

Q. 3493. Do you produce a return of the royalties or tonnage duties for Bilson and Crump Meadow Collieries for 21 years, to the 31st of December, 1873? – Yes.

Q. 3494. What is the total amount for the 21 years? – From 1853 to 1873 inclusive, £25,821 1s. 5d.

Q. 3495. What is the annual average, assuming that the tonnage duties represented one-fifth of the profits? – That is to say the annual average to the Crown, £1,229; this would represent the annual one-fifth profit, assuming that the Crown had obtained its fifth of £6,145.

Q. 3496. If the profits of the collieries in the year ending the 31st of December 1873 were £38,192, would not that be about five times the amount of the average annual profits, assuming the tonnage royalties represent one-fifth of the profit? – For that particular year it would be something like six times; I have no means of knowing whether at the commencement of this period of 21 years the Crown did obtain their fifth, but I only know now it is their opinion that they do not get their fifth.

Q. 3497. From your knowledge of the Forest, do you consider that there would be any great difficulty in getting rid of the rights of free miners? – Yes.

Q. 3498. Are not nearly all the gales to which they would be entitled worked out, or claims for them already let? – All the coal practically is let out, though the iron ore is not; there is a considerable area of iron ore that is not galed; of course free miners' rights arise from time to time, because supposing from any cause a gale that has been galed out, before it is opened it becomes forfeited or lapses, then the free miners' rights arise again as regards the lapsed portion.

Q. 3499. Then you think that there would be great difficulty in getting rid of their rights? – Yes. I do; supposing the rights of the free miners were got rid of, the people who represent the free miners, I mean the now existing colliery and iron mine owners, would have to be dealt with, and you could not get rid of their interest. It has been suggested, and I think there is something in it, that where a property, or gale, or royalty falls in, it is just possible that an arrangement could be made by which the Crown would become the ordinary owner of that gale; I mean that in respect of that gale the free miners' rights could be got rid of.

Q. 3500. With regard to these barriers, would breaking through them tend to imperil life? – No, I do not think so; it might or might not; it would depend entirely upon the way in which they were pierced; no doubt if they were pierced without any regard to caution it would imperil life, but that is not the principle upon which barriers should be retained. I, perhaps, might explain it in this way: the middle series of the coal measures are those now chiefly worked; the gales or royalties are divided across the field and barriers are left, the drainage being originally from the surface, and if you have a barrier here and allow that to be removed, the whole of that drainage flows down to the next mine, and so on to the centre; If you allow all the barriers to be removed, ultimately there would be a lake of water all through this area, and the man who has to sink down to the gale below, instead of having only the drainage of a contracted area to pump, would have the drainage of the whole to deal with before he could get down to the lower measures.

Q. 3501. Would not such piercing of the barriers interrupt the whole ventilation of the mine? – It would depend upon circumstances; in one case it would, and in another case it would not.

Q. 3502. Would it not be well for the Crown to reserve certain portions of coal with a view of sinking to the lower beds? – That is one of the reasons, I take it, for leaving the barriers.

Q. 3503. What thickness are the barriers? – They range from 20 to 40 yards.

Q. 3504. With a thickness of 40 yards you would be able to get a shaft through safely? – It is rather little.

Q. 3505. The question, I believe, has arisen in some parts of the country where a piece of coal has been left; it is of great value as a block to sink through? – I think it would have been desirable to have some provision of the kind, but I think the opportunity is now gone.

Q. 3506. Supposing the opportunity to exist, what prospect would there be of what we call in Yorkshire "tubbing" the shafts? – Naturally they would "tub", but what I mean is this: if you have got to sink down to the lower measures before you put in the tubbing you have got to drain 7,000 acres instead of 400 acres, so that the difficulty is materially increased.

Q. 3507. What would be the depth in the centre of the field? – About 550 yards, I should say; there are rather unusual difficulties in sinking to these lower measures, because it is a very perfect coalfield, exposed all round its edges, and the rocks between the middle and lower series are porous. It is quite enough to have to deal with the drainage of the strata connected with the coal with which you are dealing, without having to deal with water belonging to measures that do not belong to you.

Q. 3508. In fact the getting of the lower measures would be very costly? – Very costly no doubt.

Q. 3509. What do you consider the average royalty got by the Crown as compared with the royalty that a private coalowner would get? – I should say the average royalty in the Forest at the present time would be under 3d. I have been acting for lessors who have let, I should think, 10,000 acres in the last three years, and the average royalty is from 8d. to 1s.

Q. 3510. Something less than half? – It would be between one-third and one-half.

Q. 3511. That is the same quality of coal? – I do not think it is the same quality; but I think, as far as regards the pecuniary value of it, it will probably be equal, though not of the same quality.

Q. 3512. You think the royalty got by the Crown is something less than half what a private owner under the same circumstances would get? – Yes. There was a prospectus shown to me of the Crump Meadow Colliery, and I think upon the face of it it is shown that that is the proportion.

Q. 3515. With regard to these rents, Mr. Goold, in his evidence here, stated that he thought he had a right to have the coal at as low a rate as 3d. a ton; do you know at all on what he bases that rate? – The only thing upon which he can base it is the Act, which says that the Crown is only to have a fifth of the profits.

Q. 3516. Have you any idea as to what is the ordinary calculation in the district with which you are acquainted of the relative proportion of rent to profit? – I was thinking of that; if you get a full fifth, it seems to me you get very nearly the ordinary royalty.

Q. 3517. Are you aware in the lead mines every fifth, or seventh, or eighth of ore worked goes to the landlord? – In the Teesdale district that is so, from a fifth to a seventh.

Q. 3518. Do you advise the Crown as to the rents they shall take? – With the chief mineral inspector.

Q. 3519. Who is the chief mineral inspector? – Mr. Warington Smyth.

Q. 3520. With regard to the late leases, what have you advised the Crown to ask? – We have endeavoured to get as near as we can what we think is a fifth.

Q. 3521. What rent have you advised the Crown to take? – The rent has varied in different cases, but it has been considerably in excess of many of the existing rents.

Q. 3522. A lease that was 3d. many years ago, what would you put upon it now? – That is rather a difficult thing; a good deal depends upon this, that we have got to assess the royalty for 21 years, and if it happens that the gale falls in at a very depressed time, the galee takes advantage of that, and says, "You must fix the royalty low"; but if it fell in at times when they were favourable to the Crown, we should get a higher royalty. Taking Crump Meadow, I should say to have a fair fifth there would be double what the present rent is.

Q. 3523. Does your engagement with the Crown prevent your taking any part in buying up gales? – My engagement with the Crown entirely prevents my taking up any professional work in the Forest of Dean.

Q. 3524. Or being a partner in any of the mines sunk there? – Yes.

Q. 3525. Even if they were limited liability ones? – Yes; I should say I have a large practice as a mineral adviser; and I am often asked in the forest to give advice, but I invariably refuse, and say it is not consistent with my duties.

Q. 3526. Even in inspecting the mines, or advising as to the laying of them out? – Yes; if I am called in as an arbitrator, or otherwise, I invariably communicate the circumstance to the Commissioner of Woods, and ask him for his opinion upon the subject.

Q. 3527. To your sole jurisdiction is confided the amount of surface damage on the enclosed lands? – Yes.

Q. 3528. Is not that often complained of? – No.

Q. 3529. There is no appeal by the man holding the enclosure from your verdict, as to the damages? – No.

Q. 3530. Have you not heard of any complaint upon that score? – No.

Q. 3531. Does it not strike you as being rather hard upon the owner of the enclosure to have the owner of the minerals' agent as the sole arbitrator of the damage done to the surface? – It is not quite in the way you put it; the galee obtains a gale; he opens a mine; I come in as between the galee and surface owner. The owner of the surface has a moiety of the minerals, and the owner of the surface is just as much interested as the Crown in the minerals, therefore it comes back to simply a question as between the surface owner and the galee.

Q. 3532. The lower the surface damages are the more rent he pays to the Crown? – There is that point no doubt, but I do not think it operates at all.

Q. 3533. No doubt it is infinitesimal; do you keep the gale book in which all the free miners are registered? – Yes; I register the free miners.

Q. 3534. Have you any idea what proportion of the free miners who have a right to register do register? – No; but I should think a great proportion.

Q. 3535. There was a witness here the other day, who said he had a right to register for 30 years, but he never took up his right; do you think there are many such cases? – There is a general impression that all the valuable gales are granted, and therefore there is a less disposition on the part of the free miners to register than there was years ago.

Q. 3536. Do you think the value of a free miner's right at the present moment is worth any consideration whatever? – I should not assess it at any very great sum. The people who really benefit are not the free miners, but the men who buy from the free miners.

Q. 3537. How many have you on your book? – I should think 1,200.

Q. 3538. How many are there holding gales of all sorts? – I should not think more than 20.

Q. 3539. And how many gales do you grant a year, as a rule? – From four to five.

Q. 3540. Then the chances of your 1,200 would be very small? – Yes, very. There is this explanation required, that the 1,200 represents all that have been registered, and of course a great many of those are dead.

Q. 3541. If your list were corrected, it would probably turn out that there were 700 or 800 living? – Yes, about that.

Q. 3542. Do you think any great hardship would be done by drawing a line at the end of your gale book and closing it? – I think the hardship would be more sentimental than real. I do not think there would be any great hardship at all; but from my experience of the free miners, I think any proposal of that kind would be calculated to meet with considerable opposition.

Q. 3543. With regard to those that might yet come on to the list? – Yes.

Q. 3544. In the district with which you are best acquainted, do the mine owners provide the houses, or do the masters provide them generally? – The miners generally provide them. Some parts are up on the hills, and you have to provide a population in those cases, and very often the lessees build a certain number of houses, and after that there are the ordinary operations of the miners, or individuals build houses and let them to the miners.

Q. 3545. Did you prepare the statistics that were given to the Coal Commission as to the quantity of coal in the Forest of Dean? – I supplied the bulk of the information.

Q. 3546. Was not the quantity you gave in your evidence of coal in the coalfield a very much smaller quantity than that which they reported? – They reported 265 millions, which is the figure I have given you; but that represents all the coal. The portion which is good coal, and which is likely to continue in development of the output, is about 150 millions.

Q. 3547. What do you consider the average duration of collieries now under lease? – Of open collieries?

Q. 3548. Yes? – I should think the open collieries would last from about 40 to 50 years.

Q. 3549. Why do you propose to grant 80 or 90 years' leases for the houses at those collieries? – I am not aware that I did.

Q. 3550. Did you hear Sir James Campbell's evidence? – Yes.

Q. 3551. That he thought 80 or 90 years' leases would be sufficient to induce colliers to build cottages? – My view is this, that the Crown ought to have power to grant leases for 99 years; and in the case of a colliery which will be exhausted in 40 or 50 years, they should have the power to grant a lease for that time.

Q. 3552. Is it not the common practice, in the coal trade, to grant a lease for building land, on moderate terms, for the same duration as the colliery? – Yes; in South Wales it is invariably done.

Q. 3553. Did you ever see a lease given for a longer term than the colliery lease? – No; never in the north of England; there are cases in South Wales, but that is where the colliery owner has not the lease, and where it has been granted to someone independently.

Q. 3554. The free miner has the recognised right of four-fifths, has he not, of the royalty? – No; the Crown has a recognised right to one-fifth.

Q. 3555. The remaining four-fifths, and what represents, under ordinary circumstances, the rent, belong to the free miner? – No, the profits.

Q. 3556. I will deal, first of all, with rent? – I do not understand how it is distinguished; we do not distinguish the two.

Q. 3557. The free miner finds all the plant and all the capital for the colliery? – Yes.

Q. 3558. Therefore he would be entitled to all the ordinary profits? – Yes; assuming he were the freeholder and held the fee of the property.

Q. 3559. The profits are irrespective of the freehold and ownership of the coal; finding all the plant and all the risk, as well as all the labour, he would be entitled to all the profits, would he not, and the Crown would be entitled to one-fifth of the profits if they put in their one-fifth man? – Yes.

Q. 3560. And, in addition to that, the free miner is entitled to what is the value of the coal in the ground before it is worked or developed? – I do not quite understand you.

Q. 3561. Does the Crown do anything for the purpose of getting a share in the profits; do they carry out any works or introduce any labour? – No.

Q. 3562. The Crown is not an adventurer in a colliery? – No, certainly not.

Q. 3563. The Crown is only the owner of the coal? – Yes.

Q. 3564. And that to the extent of one-fifth? – It is more than that.

Q. 3565. By the Forest right of free mining, has the Crown a right to more than one-fifth? – It has a right to more than one-fifth of the absolute coal, because it has a right to one-fifth of the coal after the colliery is opened.

Q. 3566. But is not that fifth liable to a deduction for all the cost of working the coal? – Yes, that is so; in fact, it comes back to one-fifth of the profits.

Q. 3567. You consider the Crown is entitled to one-fifth royalty and one-fifth of the profits? – To one-fifth of the profits.

Q. 3568. Although the Crown has not expended anything for the purpose of making those profits? – Yes.

Q. 3569. In that view you think 3d. would not sufficiently represent one-fifth of the rent and one-fifth of the profits, to which you hold the Crown entitled? – Yes, it is my opinion it is not one-fifth of the profits.

Q. 3570. If there is further legislation, would you require any further powers in reference to land for colliery purposes, or have you sufficient power now to regulate the use of land? – My own notion is that the Crown ought to have full facilities for leasing land in connection with collieries. My opinion is that there ought to be no restriction, and that it ought to be left to the commissioner for the time being to grant, in his discretion, what is necessary.

Q. 3571. The free miner claims the right to spoil banks, does he not? – Yes.

Q. 3572. And he enjoys that right generally? – Yes, he has exercised it.

Q. 3573. Invariably? – Yes.

Q. 3574. Not for other purposes than for spoil banks? – No.

Q. 3575. Have you sufficient power to regulate the use of land to enable the Crown to grant leases for other purposes than spoil banks? – Yes, except that it is limited to a certain area at the present time, and limited to a certain length of lease, and those are two restrictions which I think ought to be done away with.

Q. 3576. Would it be right or desirable that there should be a restriction by law in reference to land for spoil banks? – I have stated already that I certainly think the surface ought not to be taken possession of without some consideration.

Q. 3577. And for that legislation would be necessary? – Yes.

Q. 3578. A gale extends to the bottom of the basin? – No, not necessarily. A gale may apply to a certain number of seams.

Q. 3579. The bulk of the gales do go quite to the bottom of the basin? – No; one set of gales take the upper series, and another set take the lower series.

Q. 3580. Have you any reason to believe that the lower series consist of inferior coal? – No.

Q. 3581. From what part of the basin is the best coal got? – The upper series.

Q. 3582. Would that be about the Trafalgar Colliery? – Trafalgar, Crump Meadow, Fox's Bridge, and Lightmoor.

Q. 3586. You stated that you granted four or five gales a year of late? – Yes.

Q. 3587. Are those all of coal or mines that had been previously granted, and the right of gales to which had lapsed? – No; I should think on the whole they represent new gales. The last two years there have been several deep gales in the ironstone. Those have been the principal gales granted during the last two or three years, though there have been one or two cases in which coal gales have fallen in in consequence of the galee not paying the rent, so that the gale has been re-galed.

Q. 3588. If you confine yourself to coal, how many gales a year should you say you have granted? – I should think not more than one or two.

Q. 3589. And those were gales that had been previously granted, and which had fallen in? – Yes; the last of the important coal gales was granted, I think, about 1867.

Q. 3590. In re-granting those gales that have fallen in, are you altogether guided by priority of application? – Yes, entirely.

Q. 3591. Do you conceive there are still a considerable number of valuable iron gales that remain to be granted? – It is a very open question, and I hardly like to offer an opinion about it, though I am disposed to think the deeper iron ore gales are not so valuable as the upper; the iron ore is an uncertain deposit, found in the crevices of the limestone, and as it gets deeper my experience is it gets less in quantity, and the cost of producing it increases.

Q. 3592. As far as experience has gone, have the more recent gales of iron been profitable to those who have undertaken them? – They have not been opened.

Q. 3593. They have not been acted on? – They are taken, and the free miner who takes the gale goes to somebody else, and says, "I have got a gale, and I will sell it to you"; that man buys it, and pays £5,000 for it, and he sells it to somebody else for £10,000, so that it may be years before the gale is opened, a lot of money passing from one to the other, which does no possible benefit in any way to the development of the Forest.

Q. 3594. Is there any gale of iron actually at work? – Yes; but old gales mostly.

Q. 3595. What is the most modern gale of iron that has actually been acted on? – There is one that is now being opened by the Ebbw Vale Company; they are sinking a pit on a gale that has been granted, I should think, some 27 or 28 years.

Q. 3596. When was it begun to be worked? – They are only sinking the pit now; they have not reached the ore.

Q. 3597. One is justified in pronouncing the iron gales to be very speculative affairs? – The deep iron gales are more speculative than the others.

Q. 3598. Have the most recent re-grants of coal been acted on; has the working been resumed? – Some of the re-grants are for small gales of coal close to the surface, in some of the inferior seams, and during the late excitement in the coal trade there have been openings made.

Q. 3599. Were those re-grants? – Yes; but the grants of the deeper portions of the coalfield over a large area have not been opened.

Q. 3600. The iron is below the coal, is it not? – It is below where the coal is, but then the iron extends over a very much larger area than the coal; there is a large area of surface, where it is the only thing you get at.

Q. 3601. And in some parts it crops up? – Yes, all round. The coalfield occupies 20,000 acres, and the iron ore 25,000 acres, so that there are 5,000 acres outside the coalfields.

Q. 3602. You said that the working of iron gales was very speculative? – That is, the deep iron gales under coal are more speculative than the others.

Q. 3603. And not outside? – No; it is outside where we get 160,000 tons of iron ore now.

Q. 3604. Is that mixed with the lime? – Yes; it is a calcareous haematite.

Q. 3605. And makes a natural flux? – Yes.

Q. 3606. Which adds very much to its value? – Yes, undoubtedly.

Q. 3607. And facility of work? – Yes.

Q. 3608. Is it like the Northamptonshire iron-stone? – It is of a much higher quality.

Q. 3609. What percentage? – I should think from 40 to 50 per cent. It is calcareous.

Q. 3610. As regards your residence away from the Forest, has that been the subject of complaint? – I have never heard of a complaint till this inquiry; I give up one day a week, namely, Friday, and am always there, unless an exceptional thing like my being here prevents me; I should say that the matter was very fully discussed with Mr. Howard. There are, no doubt, several objections to an officer residing away, but, on the other hand, there are many advantages in the deputy gaveller residing out of the Forest; he is not subject to any local influences, and he gets a wider experience, and I can say, in my own case, the experience I have gained outside the Forest has been of material advantage to the Crown.'

The Hon. James K. Howard[1], a Commissioner of Woods, deposed:

'Q. 3614. It has been stated to the Committee that the general wish of the inhabitants of the Dean Forest and the neighbourhood is that the Forest should be disafforested and enclosed,

1 Pp. 152-9.

compensation in money being made for rights of common, and certain places being set out for public recreation and other public purposes. Assuming such to be the general desire in the locality, do you see any objection to the matter being dealt with in the way proposed? – As far as I can see at present I do not. If those persons who are locally interested wish it, there would be no objection to the bringing in of a Bill for the purpose of ascertaining and commuting for compensation rights of common. Much care would, however, be needed in framing and carrying out any such measure.

Q. 3618. It has been proposed that small plots of land near the centres of population and new works, should be sold for the erection of miners' cottages. Do you, so far as regards any part of the Forest other than the outskirts, think it would be desirable to sell? – I do not.

Q. 3619. Then I presume you would not assent to such a suggestion that the whole forest should be sold? – I do not.

Q. 3624. Are there some outlying or detached parts of the Forest the sale of which you think may properly be treated as a fit subject for consideration? – Yes; there are certain outlying parts, such, for instance, as about Coleford Meand, Joy's Green, Pope's Hill, and Breames Eaves, and other localities, the names of which I forget at present; but those are all in the outskirts.

Q. 3632. A complaint has been made of a charge for *nunc pro tunc* warrants for the entry of assignments of gales in the books of the deputy gaveller; is not the object of that charge as far as possible to prevent breaches of the 58th section of the Act 1 & 2 Vict. c. 43 [1838], which directs assignments to be entered within three months after such assignments are made? – Yes; that payment is required to prevent delay in complying with the provisions of the Act; they would be very loose in registering the assignments if they were not made to pay.

Q. 3705. I suppose you are acquainted with the Crown revenue from the mines as well as from the surface? – Yes.

Q. 3706. What has been the Crown revenue from mines, I do not mean accurately, but roughly, say for the last 10 years? – I think last year the revenue was about £15,000.

Q. 3707. Is that more than it has been, on an average, during the last 10 years? – Rather more I think.

Q. 3708. Not materially more? – No, not materially more.

Q. 3713. One or two questions about the free miners, if you have given that subject any consideration? – Yes, I have given the subject consideration.

Q. 3714. Do you think that their rights are detrimental to the interests of the Forest? – They are certainly detrimental to the interests of the Crown.

Q. 3715. If there were no free miners the minerals of the Forest would be worth more? – Yes, to be sure they would, to the Crown and to the public.

Q. 3716. Have you thought of any scheme of terminating the rights of free miners, so that they could be compensated for such rights as they have? – I have thought of it, but I think that it would be extremely difficult.

Q. 3717. Do you think it would be any hardship to draw a line, after the passing of an Act of Parliament, and say that no man born after the passing of that Act shall have any rights as a free miner? – They might consider it less of a hardship.

Q. 3718. Have you seen the evidence of Mr. Mountjoy, given before this Committee, where he states that he does not consider his rights as a free miner as worth 2½d.? – Yes, I have.

Q. 3719. Do you think that is a fair value of the chances of these free miners? – I can hardly say.

Q. 3720. Do you think that if a free miner could have the right of purchasing a small quantity of land as a freehold out of the Forest, at a price below the valuation figure, that that would not be a good way of extinguishing his rights as a free miner; making it a permissive power? – I think it is a question worth consideration.

Q. 3721. I mean the kind of arrangement as exists in many places with regard to foreshore, enclosed by river commissioners, where the frontager gets so much, the lord of the manor gets so much, and the party enclosing gets so much; I want to know whether you think such an arrangement as that might not be made so as to extinguish gradually the free miners' rights? – As I have already said, it is a question worth consideration.

Q. 3722. Has any other scheme occurred to you? – No; I think it might be desirable that the Crown should have the power to acquire free miners' rights when occasions occurred, but any question of dealing in one measure with the whole of the free miners' rights would be exceedingly difficult, and would probably entail such an expenditure of money to redeem their rights as that it would be hardly worth while to do it.

Q. 3723. The terms of all the mineral leases go through your hands? – Yes, I see them all.

Q. 3724. And you advise upon them? – Yes, I advise upon them.

Q. 3725. And therefore the free miner never obtains a lease upon less terms than the outside man (if there could be such a man) would obtain it. Let me put it in this way: Supposing a free miner gets a gale, does he get any other advantage as a Crown tenant? – No, he merely gets the gale.

Q. 3726. You can choke him with price? – No, not exactly, because there is the award, and the rights and royalties settled.

Q. 3727. Do you agree with the evidence given by Tom Goold, that the Crown has had one-fifth part of the produce of the coal net. Tom Goold stated that threepence a ton on the average of three years more than represented the fifth to which the Crown was entitled; do you think that is correct? – I have not read Mr. Goold's evidence, and I do not know upon what he grounds the assertion.

Q. 3728. He says that the profits of coal in the Forest would not come to 15d. a ton on the average of years, and that 3d. a ton has more than represented the Crown's fifth? – I could not say without investigation.

Q. 3729. Is it not the fact that the free miners have certain rights which other persons have not with whom the Crown would deal, and therefore a free miner claiming a gale can insist that the royalty shall be fixed at a sum not exceeding one-fifth of the estimated profits to be derived from the coal which he may work? – Yes.

Q. 3730. On the other hand, if it were possible for the Crown to deal with a person who is not a free miner, the Crown could let it to that person at the highest price he would be content to give? – Yes, clearly.

Q. 3731. Which might be very considerably more than this ideal fifth? – Yes.

Q. 3732. And therefore the Crown is at a disadvantage in dealing with a free miner as compared with any other person? – No doubt.

Q. 3733. That is if the market were open and free miners were done away with, the Crown minerals would let for a good deal more? – Yes, certainly.

Q. 3734. I think the deputy gaveller has stated that he estimates there would be a very considerable increase in the yield of the mines if the market were open? – I have no doubt he did.

Q. 3739. You said that you would object to sell land in the centre of the Forest; are there not large mining works springing up there, and would it not be desirable to have houses for the men, and so prevent them walking long distances? – Yes, certainly; but I would grant leases. You may grant as long leaseholds as you like.

Q. 3740. Would you say 99 years? – You might say 99 years; but I would leave it to the discretion of the Crown to grant a lesser term if it was thought advisable. I would not compel the Crown to grant a lease for 99 years in every case.

Q. 3741. It might be of the same duration as the lease of the mine? – Yes, quite so.'

Horace Watson[1], solicitor for the Commissioners of Woods, recalled, and further examined, deposed:

'Q. 3874. You have attended to the evidence all through this Committee, and I will ask you, generally, whether there is anything you wish to state? – The only observations I have to address to the Committee, I think, are in respect to the evidence of Tom Goold. He said that the position of the free miners is not so good in his opinion, by a great deal, as it was immediately after the passing of the Act of 1 & 2 Vict. c. 43 [1838], and he gave eight instances in support of his opinion. First, that the price of free miners' timber had been raised. Secondly, that free miners, or persons claiming from them, had been required to take leases of land for engine-houses where the engine-houses had existed at the time of the passing of the Act of 1 & 2 Vict. Thirdly, that charges were made for the *nunc pro tunc* warrant authorising the registration of assignment of gales. Fourthly, that in 1861 a Bill was brought in on behalf of the Government, in which a clause was contained, ultimately struck out owing to opposition. Fifthly, that a similar course was taken in 1871, in reference to a Bill brought in in that year. Sixthly, that payments were required by the Office of Woods for the breaking of a barrier in a case in which he was concerned. Seventhly, that the form of grant of gales had been altered from that which it was used to be; and, eighthly, that grants of gales had been refused by the Crown in the cases of the High Meadow Woods and Great Doward Woods. Those, I believe, are all the cases which Mr. Goold mentioned in support of his statement that, in his opinion, the position of free miners was not so good now, by a great deal, as it was immediately after the passing of the Act of 1 & 2 Vict. As regards the first point, miners' timber, I may say that any right or claim which the miners had to timber was directed to cease by the 30th section of the Act of 1 & 2 Vict. c. 43. Sir James Campbell, I believe, has explained to the Committee the circumstances under which the charge for timber used in the mines has been increased. He has explained to the Committee that, so far from the charge now made being too high, there is competition for the timber, and he believes, at the present rate, although the free miners have no legal right whatever to the timber, it is an advantage to them to obtain it at the rates at which they now obtain it in the Forest. The second point mentioned by Mr. Goold was as to leases of land which was used for the erection of engine-houses at the time of the passing of the Act 1 & 2 Vict. The case he instanced was a lease which he said he was made to take in 1862. The deputy gaveller has produced the correspondence which resulted in the granting of that lease, and the correspondence will have shown to the Committee that the lease was agreed for by Mr. Goold, and that the terms were proposed and accepted by him without objection, and the

[1] Pp. 165-7.

lease granted upon his own application. The third point as to the charge for registration of deeds under the *nunc pro tunc* warrants, I believe, had been explained by Mr. Howard today. Under the 58th section of the Act of 1 & 2 Victoria assignments of gales are directed to be registered within three months; but, by a subsequent section, the gaveller has power to authorise the entry of assignments afterwards, if he thinks fit, and in order to ensure that provision being complied with as far as possible a moderate charge is made for *nunc pro tunc* warrants. As to the facts that in 1861, and again in 1871, a Bill was brought in on behalf of the Government, which did not in all matters meet with the approval of the persons locally interested, and that an alteration was made in each case at the request of persons locally interested, and therefore that the Bill as passed was not exactly the Bill as introduced, and the allegation that therefore the Government are responsible for causing a diminution in the value of the interests of free miners, I think it is unnecessary for me to say a word. The sixth point is, that a charge was made for breaking a barrier, Mr. Brown, the deputy gaveller, has explained that it is very important that barriers should be preserved, and that if a breach of a barrier were passed over without payment serious consequences might result.

Q. 3875. Were the Crown acting under your advice when they told Mr. Goold that he had forfeited his lease? – I am really not able to answer the question without referring to the papers.

Q. 3876. Have you looked into the law upon the subject, because the observation against the Crown is, that unnecessary threats were held over him; threats which the Crown were unable to carry out; and so, in fact, going much beyond the province of the Crown? – Mr. Goold draws a distinction, as I understand, between gales that were granted by the award, and gales granted subsequently to the award, and he says that a particular rule, which is No. 18, as to the preservation of barriers, for the leaving of barriers, only applies to gales hereafter granted, and that as this gale was granted by the award the rule does not apply to that particular gale. The award itself says that barriers shall be left, and the Act of 1 & 2 Vict. c. 43, S. 29, says that the gales, after the making of the award, shall be held on condition of performing and abiding by the rules and regulations in all respects made by the Commissioners. The award itself said in this particular case a barrier should be left. With regard to the seventh point, which was the alteration in the form of grants of gales, I may say that the alteration was made in consequence of the passing of an Act of 24 & 25 Vict. c. 40, which defines the exact nature of the interest of a galee under the grant of a gale. The first section says, the grant of a gale of coal or iron, or a stone quarry, shall be deemed to confer upon the galee or his assigns the license to work the pit or gale therein comprised. Mr. Goold complains that it used to be a gale, and that now it is only a license to work; but I beg to say that the form of gale follows exactly the Act of Parliament.

Q. 3877. Do you think that that letter from the Crown, informing Mr. Goold that he had forfeited his lease, was correct? – I was referring to another point altogether without looking into the papers. That I believe, disposes of all the eight matters in regard to which Mr. Goold thinks he is justified in saying that the position of free miners is not so good as it was when the Act of 1 & 2 Vict. was passed. Perhaps I may be allowed to add one word as to the circumstance that no suits have been instituted against the Crown to enforce claims of free miners which Mr. Goold, and I think another gentleman, Mr. William Brain, suggested might not have been enforced owing either to the trouble or expense of enforcing them. The Committee are aware that under modern practice there is a remedy by petition of right open to any subject, which is not at all a more expensive proceeding than the proceeding by one subject against another. That is so in the case of Dean Forest I think may be taken to be pretty clear, because at the present moment there are three petitions of right pending with reference to grants of gales; two of them relate to an unopened iron mine, as to which one suit in Chancery is also pending and two others have been pending. There have been three suits by individuals against each other, and two petitions of right, with regard to some unopened iron mines. There is also another petition of right pending as to a coal mine. Therefore I do not think it probable that either the trouble or expense of instituting proceedings has prevented galees of mines in Dean Forest from taking proceedings they might be advised to take for enforcing legal rights, if such legal rights existed, and had been interfered with.

Q. 3879. Has any plan occurred to you by which the rights of free miners could be compromised? – I think that any commutation of the rights of free miners of a general and compulsory character would be found to be impracticable; I think if such a thing were ever possible it was before the Act of 1 & 2 Vict. passed; but now registered free miners are such a large body, and entertain such a high opinion of the value of their rights, not only as to the existing value of their rights but prospective value to their sons, that it will be practically impossible to induce them to concur in any arrangement which would be likely to be an advantageous one for the Crown to enter into.

Q. 3880. Is it not perfectly apparent that the larger the number of free miners the less the value of their rights? – Yes, that is perfectly true; and if the honourable Member were to ask any person competent to give an opinion upon the real value of free miners' rights, probably some sum might be named for which it might be desirable that the Crown should acquire the rights of the free miners; but you must remember there are a great number of persons born in the district, which has particular customs, who have from their birth probably had an exaggerated notion of the value of their rights, and it would be extremely difficult to propose any arrangement to give them satisfaction, and which it would be worth the while of the Crown to enter into.

Q. 3881. Is it not perfectly apparent, also, that the population very much increases in that district, and that the number of people who will have the power many years hence of receiving these rights will be much greater than at present? – That is also true; and if the free miners were as well imbued with principles of political economy as the honourable Member for South Durham, the probability is they might conceive it was their interest to accept moderate compensation; but they look to the possibility of their getting hereafter a grant of some forfeited gale, or of some value attaching to the rights of their sons.

Q. 3882. You heard Mr. Howard state that the value of the free miners' rights was very nominal? – I daresay it may convey an accurate representation of the fact, but you must also bear in mind that those free miners' rights have been confirmed by Parliament, and, inasmuch as they have now a Parliamentary basis, it would not be desirable to get rid of those rights without making compensation.

Q. 3883. Is it not the case with every landowner on a railway that Parliament puts aside his private rights for public consideration? – He gets, or is supposed to get, full compensation.

Q. 3887. Does your opinion as to the impracticability of compensating on reasonable terms the free miners for their rights apply to persons who have mere possible claims in the event of gales becoming vacant? – I understood the question only to apply to free miners' rights, and not to the rights of galees, such as Mr. Crawshay or any other proprietor.

Q. 3888. Confining it even to the free miners' rights, you think it would be impracticable to effect an arrangement? – I am afraid it would not be practicable to do so, but the other question opens a much larger subject; Mr. Brain told you he is himself a free miner, and also largely engaged in working a coal mine, and you would have to distinguish between compensation to him as working the mines, and compensation to him as a free miner. In the majority of the large works, probably the interest has gone into other persons' hands, as well as free miners.

Q. 3889. Confining ourselves to the cases which are the most numerous, where there is only the possible chance of a future gale, is it not the fact that that really is practically worth nothing? – I am afraid if you had any of the free miners before you that had made any applications, and asked them the same question, they would certainly give you an answer to the effect that they considered their rights of very great value, and I should have the same answer made to me if I had to negotiate with them for the purchase of their interests.

Q. 3890. In giving these answers, do you bear in mind that two or three of the free miners used such phrases as that their rights were worth nothing, or they were not worth 2½d.? – Since Mr. Brain has been examined before the Committee, he has applied for a grant of some of the largest ironstone mines in the Forest, those now worked by Mr. Crawshay. It has not been the practice hitherto to accept applications for gales as long as those gales were actually in grant, but the question has been raised in one of the petitions of right, whether such applications can be made during an existing grant. If you asked Mr. Brain what he would sell his contingent interest in Mr. Crawshay's mines for, I daresay he would not name a small sum, and would say he would not have taken the trouble to apply if he had not supposed the application would ensure to him some property of value, or a right of some value.

Q. 3891. I think you say that that application has been made during the sitting of this Committee? – Yes, by a witness.

Q. 3892. And probably since he was examined here? – Yes.

Q. 3893. Do I understand that is an application for a grant of a gale which is already in occupation, and is being worked by a galee? – Yes, by Mr. Crawshay, and it may be by other persons; however, he is one of the persons. They consider there is a possibility that these gales, or some of them, may some day lapse to the Crown, and therefore they apply for a grant in the event of the gale falling in.

Q. 3894. Is the Crown bound to receive and record an application? – It is entirely contrary to past practice to do so. The applicant has been or will be informed that that is the case, but as I have already mentioned in the case of a petition of right now pending, that point is raised, namely, that the gaveller is bound to entertain applications during the existence of a grant.

Q. 3895. I think the Committee understand you to state that you see no objection to the Crown taking powers to acquire the interest of a galee who may not have worked his gale? – I am not aware that I have expressed an opinion upon that subject, but I think it is at all events a matter well worthy of consideration. There are some difficulties about it, but I think it is a matter well worthy of consideration. So far as I can at present see, I think that is the only case where it would be expedient for the Crown to attempt to acquire the interests of free miners or galees.

Q. 3896. It would really be in the nature of purchasing a reversion, would it not? – That is not the purchase of a reversion, because in the case which I put the galee has the right to work at once if he pleases.

Q. 3897. And for a given number of years? – He has the right to work at once and in perpetuity, provided he observes the conditions of the award and the rules made under it. The fact that the Crown is also the recipient of the royalty and the grantor of the gale might raise difficulties, no doubt.

Q. 3899. The free miners' rights run over Abbot's Wood? – Yes, of course; but I should mention there is only a small part of Abbot's Wood, that on the western side, which is within the mineral field. The outcrop of the coal comes almost close to the margin of Abbot's Wood, and the outcrop of the ironstone comes a little way inside. In Abbot's Wood at the present moment may be seen some of the surface works of the ironstone, and excavations which have been made in the course of those workings.'

The following also appeared before the Committee: A. Stephens, relieving officer, of Coleford, Arnold Taylor, one of the Inspectors of the Local Government Board, Edmund Probyn, a verderer, William Phillip Price, MP for Gloucester from 1852 to 1873, and John Clutton, crown receiver. The Select Committee of 1874 reported, *inter alia*:

'5. The mines in the Forest have been extensively worked, and a considerable quantity of the surface (estimated at about 1,000 acres) is occupied by the mines, and by spoil banks, quarries, railways, tramways and other works. The present income to the Crown from the iron mines is from £4,000 to £5,000 per annum, and from coal mines from £11,000 to £12,000 per annum.

8. The rights of the free miners as they existed previous to the passing of the Act 1 & 2 Vict. c. 43 [1838] form the subject of the 4th Report (dated 25 August 1835) of the Commissioners under the Act 1 & 2 Will. 4, c. 12, but such rights are now regulated by the first-mentioned Act, and awards made by the Dean Forest Mining Commissioners appointed thereunder. Every male person born and abiding in the Hundred of St. Briavels, who is 21 years of age, and who has worked for a year and a day in a coal or iron mine within the hundred, is entitled to be registered as a free miner. The registered free miners have the exclusive right of having grants from the Crown of what are called "gales", which confer licences to work the mines. Such gales or grants confer an interest of the nature of real estate, and are perpetual subject to conditions for the payment of certain rents and tonnage royalties to the Crown, and for the observance of certain statutory provisions, and certain rules and regulations in the Dean Forest Mining Awards. The tonnage royalty payable to the Crown for each gale is fixed on the assumption that after the coal or ironstone has been won or reached by the grantee (called a "galee"), the Crown is entitled to one-fifth of the net profit of working the mine. In case of dispute, the royalty on the above basis is settled by arbitration. When once fixed, the royalty continues unaltered for 21 years; but at the end of that period it may be determined by the Crown or by the galee, and is then readjusted on the basis above mentioned, and so continues for a further term of 21 years. A free miner can sell his interest in a gale, and a large part of the mines in the Forest are not now held by free miners, but by persons who have purchased up the interests of free miners in their "gales". Nearly the whole of the coalfield in the Forest is included in existing gales.

9. From the judgment of Mr. Justice Byles, when assisting Vice-Chancellor Sir W. P. Wood (now Lord Hatherley) in a suit "The Attorney General *v.* Matthias", it appears that but for the statutory confirmation of the claims of the free miners which was given by the Act 1 & 2 Vict. c. 43, those claims could not have been maintained against the Crown in a court of

justice, and your Committee are of opinion that the rights of the free miners which now rest on the basis of the Act of 1838, tend to obstruct the advantageous development of the Dean Forest Mineral Field, and are detrimental to the interests of the Crown and of the public at large. Those rights so far as the free miners are concerned are almost valueless to those who do not already hold gales, as not more than four or five gales are granted annually amongst the long list of registered free miners.

10. The number of free miners who have been registered for having grants of gales of mines under the Act of 1838 is about 1,200, but of these many are dead. The number of existing gales of coal and iron in the Forest is about 260 of which about 80 are in work. The output of the coal mines is about 900,000 tons per annum, and of the iron mines about 160,000 tons per annum, and there is reason to believe that a large increase may take place in the produce of the coal mines. The quantity of coal reported by the Royal Commission in 1871 as existing in this field was 265 millions of tons. The portion which is good coal, and which is likely to continue in development of the output is about 150 millions of tons. There are also many stone quarries in the Forest which are worked under the authority of leases from the Crown.

13. It has been strongly urged upon your Committee, that great inconvenience is caused to the mining population in the Forest by the want of dwellings near to some of the large mining works, and that many miners have now to walk long distances to and from their daily labour, and that the houses are overcrowded to a degree which has a prejudicial effect upon the morality of the inhabitants:– Further, that Crown land is much wanted in connection with the mining works to an extent which, under existing circumstances, might possibly abridge the rights of commoners, and for terms which cannot be granted under the present limited powers of the Commissioners of Woods. Those powers do not warrant the granting of leases of land in Dean Forest for a longer term than 31 years, or except for certain restricted purposes. It was proved before your Committee that in a part of the Forest called Abbot's Wood, which (under grants from the Crown) belongs to Mr. Crawshay, the rights of common had been ascertained and commuted for money payments under an Act of Parliament passed in 1870 (33 Vict. cap. 8), and in a manner which gave satisfaction to the persons interested. It was suggested that a similar course of proceeding might be advantageously pursued with respect to the residue of the Forest.

14. The want of sufficient roads in the Forest has been strongly brought under the notice of your Committee by several witnesses.'

The foregoing Select Committee of 1874 recommended the Government to bring a Bill in the next session of Parliament for the appointment of a Commission to go further into the matter; the Bill to contain provisions to the effect:

'2(*b*) That the powers of sale, and of granting leases for terms exceeding 31 years, which the Commissioners of Woods possess as regards Crown land not being part of a Royal Forest, be extended to the Crown lands in Dean Forest, and that in any sales or leases of land for building purposes provision be made for adherence to a well-considered building plan, and for sanitary arrangements.

2(*c*) That the verderers be elected by the freeholders who are electors on the Parliamentary Registers, instead of by the freeholders of the two divisions of the county generally as at present.

2(*d*) That no person to be born after the passing of the proposed Act shall be entitled to be registered as a free miner. But where the purchaser of any Crown land is a free miner, a drawback may be allowed on the price of the purchase, in consideration of the surrender of the purchasers' rights as a free miner.

4. That it is expedient that provision be made, that the interests of the holders of gales which can be from time to time obtained on reasonable terms should be bought up and assigned to a trustee for the Crown, in order that the mines may be let and worked on leases under the terms which would be usually secured by a mineral owner.'

A Parliamentary Bill embodying the provisions of these recommendations was introduced in 1875.[1] It soon appeared, however, that the Committee of 1874 had been entirely misled as to the feeling of the people of the district. Indignation meetings were held in the district to protest against the Bill. Petitions were presented against it by the free miners and commoners, and the Commons Preservation Society[2] assisted in defeating the measure. Much Union and political action was involved. The Bill was withdrawn in 1875. The inhabitants' rights and privileges remained intact, at least for the time being.

Timothy Mountjoy,[3] one of the witnesses before the Select Committee of 1874, writing in 1887 recorded:

'Another word about these committees. What good has come to the Foresters from that enquiry? I believe, for one, that a lot of expenses have been put upon us that might have been avoided. I went, as I thought, to tell the committee the young men of the Forest wanted to buy the waste Crown land for 5s. per perch, the same as it was in Mr. Machen's time; but the third part of the questions put to me were foreign to the great question at issue – this is one of the things our legislators have missed their way in.

I have just found the blue book (1874) with my examination in. I was examined Friday, 12 June 1874, Col. Kingscote in the chair. I went before this committee a poor collier with little education; but I did not tell them so; I got as far as multiplication at school but never did much before I left for the pit. I knew the Lord's Prayer and the ten commandments, and the vulgar tongue. So I spoke to these gentlemen in my Forest tongue; they all asked me 398 questions, and they tried several of them, to hem me in like the Foresters do the sheep with a three-corner hurdle; but when they dodged me, I did the same to them. I did not feel at all afraid of their great advantage over me as it regards their great learning. All who read my evidence, ordered by the House of Commons to be printed 10 July 1874, will see how I answered all the questions put in an honest straightforward manner, hoping some good would be the result; but the good has not come yet. ...'

Meanwhile in 1874, a case[4] was decided relating to forfeiture to the Crown of a gale for non-performance of the conditions upon which the grant was made. This was a

---

1 A Bill to ascertain and commute Commonable Rights in H.M. Forest of Dean, and for other purposes relating thereto, and to Mines and Quarries in the Hundred of St. Briavels (Ordered by the House of Commons to be printed 1 March 1875).

2 Later 'The Commons, Open Spaces, and Footpaths Preservation Society', 71 Eccleston Square, Westminster, SW1.

3 Mountjoy, *op. cit.*, p. 34.

4 In *re* Brain (Law Reports: 18 Equity, 1874, pp. 389-410).

Petition of Right presented to Her Majesty by Ephraim Brain and others, claiming under John Brain, a free miner. The petition stated that John Brain, having applied to the deputy gaveller of the Forest for the grant of a gale or colliery known as the Alexandra Colliery, the gale was granted to him on 8 August 1864, and the certificate of the grant, after describing the boundaries of the gale, continued in these terms:

> 'Rendering and paying therefor to Her Majesty, her heirs and successors, for all such coal as shall be brought out, the sum of 2d. per ton as tonnage, such tonnage to be paid on 24 June and 25 December in every year; and, further, so working the said colliery as that there shall be wrought and gained in every year, from Midsummer, 1866, a quantity of not less than 24,000 tons: Provided that if by any reason whatsoever, in any one year, no coal shall be got in respect of the said colliery, or the tonnage rent to be paid for coal got within the year under the aforesaid reservation shall not amount to £200, then either the full sum of £200, or such other sums as, together with the amount paid or to be paid for tonnage rent in respect of coal got within the year (as the case may be), will make up the full sum of £200, shall be made up and paid to Her Majesty, her heirs and successors, on 24 day of June in every year: Provided also, and this grant is made upon this further condition, that the veins of coal hereby granted or galed shall be so worked as not to impede or injure the workings of the tracts already allotted or galed.'

In August 1864 one moiety of the Alexandra Colliery was granted by J. Brain to the suppliant, Ephraim Brain, his heirs and assigns for ever, and another moiety was granted by J. Brain to the suppliant, Richard Cook, his heirs and assigns for ever. Ephraim Brain and R. Cook afterwards made a grant of their respective moieties of the collieries to other persons, who were also suppliants upon this Petition of Right. J. Brain had since died. On 24 June 1867 the first year's rent of the colliery became due, and the sum of £200 was then paid by the suppliants. The next two years' rent becoming due on 24 June 1868 and 24 June 1869 were also paid; but as the colliery had not then been worked, correspondence took place upon the subject between the deputy gaveller and the suppliants, which resulted in the deputy gaveller extending the period for working the colliery for five years longer. The rent after this period, however, was not paid, and in the months of April, May, and June 1871 applications were made by the deputy gaveller to the suppliants for payment of the rent which had become due in respect of the colliery, and further correspondence passed between them. Ultimately, on 17 July 1871 the following declaration was addressed to the suppliants:

> 'Whereas there was due to Her Majesty the Queen, at Midsummer, 1870, for rent in respect of the Alexandra gale, the sum of £200, which still remains due and unpaid. Now, I, the Honourable James Kenneth Howard, the Commissioner of Her Majesty's Woods, Forests, and Land Revenues, having the management and direction of Her Majesty's Forest of Dean, and gaveller of the Forest, do hereby give you, and every of you, notice that the said gale has become, and I do hereby declare the same to be, forfeited to Her Majesty.'

This declaration was sent to the suppliants on 24 July 1871 by Horace Watson, solicitor to the Honourable J. K. Howard, Commissioner of Woods, accompanied by the following letter: 'Sir, – I send you herewith a notice declaring the forfeiture of the gale of the Alexandra Colliery, under which possession has been taken by the deputy gaveller.' Immediately after the date of this notice, possession of the Alexandra Colliery was taken by the deputy gaveller, who still retained possession thereof under the alleged forfeiture. In the meantime, and on 22 July 1871, an application was put in at the office of the gaveller at Coleford, by Benjamin Gwilliam, a free miner, to have a gale regranted to him of the Alexandra Colliery. On 24 May 1872 a notice was inserted in *The Forester*, a newspaper circulating in the neighbourhood, that the Alexandra gale so applied for by Gwilliam, was intended to be granted to him on 14 June. On 13 June, the day before the gale would have been granted to Gwilliam, the suppliants tendered to the gaveller the sum of £500, being the amount of the rent then due in respect of the said colliery up to 25 December 1871, but the gaveller refused to accept the sum, and insisted that the suppliants had forfeited all right to the colliery. On 14 June the suppliants appeared by their solicitor at the gaveller's office, and protested against the proposed grant of the gale to Gwilliam, on the ground that the alleged forfeiture was void in law, and that even if it were not, the tender of the rent in arrear was sufficient to relieve the suppliants against such forfeiture, and thereupon the gaveller postponed all further proceedings till 26 July instant. The suppliants therefore submitted that the declaration of forfeiture was illegal and void, inasmuch as no power to re-enter, or right of eviction for non-payment of rent, was given by or existed under the Acts of Parliament, but other and sufficient remedies for enforcing payment of the rents and royalties, and other dues payable in respect thereof, were provided by the Acts; but that even if they had legally incurred a forfeiture of the gale by reason of non-payment of rent, yet in equity and justice they ought to be relieved therefrom upon payment of all arrears of rent due, with all interest thereon, which they were willing to make. The petition then alleged that the gaveller still intended to enforce the grant of the gale to Gwilliam, and it prayed a declaration that the forfeiture of 17 July 1871 was illegal and of no effect; or if it should appear to the Court that the forfeiture was valid, then, upon payment of all arrears of rent due in respect thereof, with interest thereon, the suppliants might be relieved from the effect of such forfeiture, and might be restored to the possession of the gale; and that in the meantime the gaveller might be restrained by injunction from granting the gale to Gwilliam or any other person without the consent of the suppliants. Sir R. Malins, Vice-Chancellor, in giving judgement stated:

> 'It appears that J. Brain had not himself the capital to work the gale, which it was stated would require as much as £30,000, as it extends over an area of about 900 acres, and probably is of great value. Then J. Brain, having no capital, conferred a grant of one moiety thereof upon the suppliant, Ephraim Brain, and another moiety upon other persons, who are now represented by the other suppliants; and after these grants J. Brain died. Up to the end of the first five years, that is 1869, the minimum rent of £200 per annum was paid to the Crown; but the colliery was never worked, and the Crown thereupon extended the period within which the gale should be worked for five years longer – that is, up to the present year. After 1869 the rent fell in arrear, and in the early part of 1871 a correspondence took place between the gaveller and the suppliants, when applications were made for payment of the arrears of rent. This correspondence ended by the gaveller making a declaration, on 17 July 1871, that in consequence of non-payment of the rent for the previous year the gale had become forfeited, and possession thereof had been taken on behalf of the Crown. Immediately after the

suppliants had been served with notice of this forfeiture, possession was in fact taken by the deputy gaveller; and on the 22nd of July an application for a grant of this gale was made to the gaveller by Benjamin Gwilliam, also a free miner. The effect of this application for a gale, as I decided in *James* v. *The Queen,* is to give the free miner first applying a priority. I am assuming now that this was a perfectly vacant possession, and that all the rights of Brain were gone the day after the Crown resumed possession. It would seem, therefore, that Gwilliam, in making this application would stand the first, and that others making subsequent applications would stand behind him; and if Brain was out of the way, and Gwilliam was out of the way, the next person standing behind him would be entitled, and so on.

Now the Crown seems, after 21 July to have done nothing for some months, and I think it is perfectly clear that the suppliants did nothing, for there is no evidence of any letter of complaint having been written, or any offer by the suppliants to pay the rent due. Accordingly the Crown, having been in possession since July, and there being other applications made for the gale, was warranted in assuming that there was an end of Brain and those associated with him, for they allowed from July, 1871, to May, 1872, to elapse without taking any step the whole time. I am satisfied that if the suppliants had tendered the rent during the interim, the Crown would have been willing to accept it and to restore the suppliants to their previous position.

Under these circumstances the next step taken by the gaveller was to issue a notice on 24 May, 1872, in the newspaper called *The Forester*, according to the usual course adopted in such cases, than an application for a grant of the Alexandra Gale had been made by Benjamin Gwilliam, and that it was intended to grant the gale to him on 14 June 1872, at the gaveller's office. This notice seems to have startled the suppliants into activity, and then, finding their rights would be finally gone unless something was done, they found means to procure the rent, and offered the whole rent in arrear, together with interest, to the gaveller. That offer was refused, and the gaveller – very properly, I think – desiring to ascertain what rights the parties had, and whether the Crown had a right to resume possession or not on non-payment of rent, suspended the grant to Gwilliam; in consequence of which this Petition of Right was presented on the 14th of July, 1872, and the question having gone before the Law Officers of the Crown, the usual fiat that right should be done was made, and on the 4th of September the matter was set down for hearing, and now comes on for decision.'

Held, upon a Petition of Right by the representatives of the galee to be re-instated in the gale, that the grant was properly made upon conditions, one of which was the payment of rent, that upon breach of that condition by nonpayment, there had been a legal forfeiture and a right of the Crown to re-enter; and that the arrears not having been tendered, nor any proceedings taken within six months, there was no power in the Court to relieve against the forfeiture.

Quaera, whether the Court could have relieved if the Petition of Right had been presented within six months of the forfeiture.

Another case[1] of interest was one in 1876, in which it was held that the specific remedy provided by S.29 of the Act 1 & 2 Vict. c. 43 [1838] for enforcing rules, does not exclude the right of action for injuries caused by breach of such rules. The plaintiffs were owners of the Princess Royal Colliery and the defendants of the Flour Mill Colliery

---

1 Ross and Another *v.* Rugge-Price (Law Reports: 1 Exchequer Division. 1875-6, pp. 269-76).

which was on the land side of the former colliery and was drained by steam pumping engines. For some time previous to December 1874 both the collieries had been worked and drained by the plaintiffs and the defendant respectively according to the statute and rules and regulations, but in that month the defendant stopped the steam-engines by which the Flour Mill Colliery was drained, by reason whereof the water accumulated in the land gale of the Flour Mill Colliery, and flowed down into the deep gale of the Princess Royal Colliery, and flooded the same, and injured and destroyed the plaintiffs' underground works, plant, and machinery, and the plaintiffs were for a long time prevented from further working and lost the profits which they would otherwise have obtained. Huddleston, B.:

> 'By rule 19 there is a duty imposed upon the galees of the land gales, and the galees of the deep gales. The galees of the land gales are divided into two classes, those who use steam-engines and those who do not. The duty imposed on a man who uses a steam-engine is this, that if he uses the steam-engine he must continue to use it as long as he holds possession of those land gales. By the same rule, if he does not use a steam-engine, he is only liable where he wilfully or negligently suffers the water to fall down into the deep gale, and the duty imposed on the deep galee is to take care that his water does not rise to such a height as would injure the property of the land galee. Those are the duties laid down, and there is no provision with reference to compensation, or to the power of obtaining damages.
>
> I find in the case of *Gorris* v. *Scott* the rule applicable to this case very clearly explained by the Lord Chief Baron in his judgment thus: "Although, when penalties are imposed for the violation of a statutory duty, a person aggrieved by its violation may sometimes maintain an action for the damage so caused, that must be in cases where the object of the statute is to confer a benefit on individuals, and to protect them against the evil consequences which the statute was designed to prevent, and which have in fact ensued; if, therefore, by reason of the precautions in question not having been taken, the plaintiffs have sustained that damage against which it was intended to secure them, an action would lie."
>
> This rule would entitle the plaintiffs in this case to maintain their action. I am therefore of opinion that the plaintiffs are entitled to judgement.'

In 1877 it was held[1] that if a free miner who has made an application for a gale, dies before the gale has been actually granted, the grant cannot be made to his devisees if they are not free miners. James Davis, a free miner, on 4 November 1868 lodged with the deputy gaveller an application for a gale at Yorkley. One William Ellway made an objection to the grant, and nothing further appeared to have been done in the matter until 2 August 1872, when two other free miners, Adams and Jordan, made an objection to the grant, and claimed the gale on the ground that one John Beddis had, in 1844, applied for a grant of a gale of these mines, which had, on 7 January 1856, been granted to him; that this gale was, in 1868, forfeited under the provisions of the Acts, and that, therefore, a gale ought to be granted to Adams and Jordan under an application made by them in 1846. Davis thereupon filed a bill, in a suit called *Davis* v. *Howard,* against the gaveller, the deputy gaveller, Adams, Jordan, and the attorney general, to restrain the grant of the gale to Adams and Jordan. To this bill the gaveller

1 James *v.* The Queen (Law Reports: 5 Chancery Division, 1877, pp. 153-62).

and deputy gaveller demurred, and the demurrer was allowed on 14 November 1872. A further objection to Davis's grant was raised, that under sect. 61 no free miner could hold more than three gales, and that Davis was already the holder of three gales. As to this it appeared that Davis had been the holder of a third gale, called the Speedwell Mine, which had become so far worked out as to be unprofitable, and it was therefore surrendered to the deputy gaveller, who accepted the surrender, the free miners having power to surrender exhausted gales. One John Ellway, who had also applied, on 20 July 1871, for a gale of the Yorkley Mine, disputed the validity of this surrender on the ground that a mine was not necessarily exhausted because it had become unprofitable; but the Court held, in *Ellway* v. *Davis,* that the Speedwell Mine was properly surrendered, and that therefore Davis was not the holder of three gales. In consequence of these objections and of the litigation, the granting of the gale was postponed, and on 19 November 1873, Davis died, having by his will devised to A. James and T. Morse, all his interest in the gale. James and Morse then presented a petition of right, asking for a grant of a gale. A demurrer was filed on behalf of the Queen, on the ground that the suppliants were not free miners, which demurrer was overruled. The three suits, *Davis* v. *Howard, Davis* v. *Adams,* and *James* v. *The Queen,* came on for hearing before Vice-Chancellor Malins on 14 June 1876, when all the questions were again raised. Higgins, Q.C., and J. G. Wood, for the devisees of Davis stated:

'It has been established that Davis had a clear right to this gale under sect. 23 of 1 & 2 Vict. c. 43 [1838] and his devisees ought not to lose anything because the deputy gaveller was deterred by the notices and the litigation from granting the gale during Davis's lifetime. If the devisees had been free miners there could be no question about it.'

Glasse, Q.C., and W. W. Karslake, for the Crown:

'None but free miners can have gales, and if an applicant dies before the grant, the Crown has no right to grant a gale to his devisees, not being free miners. The 56th section assumes that none but a free miner can have a gale granted to him.'

Renshaw, for Adams and Jordan:

'We applied in 1846, no doubt, after Beddis, but if there is more than one application for a gale the deputy gaveller ought to keep a list, and if a previous application fails, or the grant has been forfeited, the next on the list ought to have the gale.'

Cozens-Hardy, for John Ellway:

'Davis had three gales, and therefore he could not take a fourth. It is not true that one gale was forfeited; no doubt it had been surrendered, but the surrender would not be valid unless the gale had been exhausted, and that has not been proved.'

Vice-Chancellor Malins, after referring to the facts of the case and the statutes, said that considering the question as if Davis had been now alive and had been an applicant in 1848, then it would be between him and Adams and Jordan, as John Ellway did not apply until 1871. The deputy gaveller had taken a very reasonable view of the case, that when there were several applicants, and a grant had been made to one, all the others were considered as out of the way. Beddis's grant came to an end by his forfeiture in 1868, and it would be very inconvenient to treat the application of Adams and Jordan as one subsisting after that grant, which in fact was, under 24 & 25 Vict. c. 40, a grant of the fee simple of the gale, leaving nothing in the Crown but a right of re-entry for forfeiture. It was admitted that Davis was the first applicant after the forfeiture, and there was no obstacle to the grant to him. As to John Ellway's claim on the ground that Davis had three gales and could not take a fourth, his Honour had in *Ellway* v. *Davis* decided that he was not the holder of three gales, and was therefore not disqualified from taking a gale, and his Honour adhered to that decision. His Lordship then continued:

> 'Having, therefore, on these grounds disposed of Adams and Jordan, and also of John Ellway, as between Davis and the Crown, if Davis were not alive, he would stand as the only applicant, and be entitled to the grant. But, on behalf of the Crown, it is contended, not now for the first time, but also on the demurrer in *James* v. *The Queen,* that the grant can only be made to a free miner. Davis, a free miner, died on 19 November 1873, and has devised to trustees who are not free miners: and the prayer of the present petition is that the gale should be granted to persons who are not free miners. Now this case came before me, and was argued very elaborately on the demurrer, when my reasons were very fully stated for coming to the conclusion which I did; and I must say that, having looked at the case, and at those reasons, I entirely adhere to the decision. It appears to me now, as it did then, that when a free miner does all that within him lies, namely, makes an application, and that application has been acceded to, and having then proceeded to endeavour to have his title perfected, he does all that is requisite. The deputy gaveller acceded to the application, and took the necessary steps to perfect it, and did what it was a part of his duty to do, namely, laid out the boundaries of what the gale was to be.'

His Lordship then read a notice issued by the deputy gaveller, and continued:

> 'Nothing then remained but the formal act of making the grant. Now that was proposed to be done by the gaveller on 2 August 1872, and it was owing to no default of Davis that it was not done. The disputes caused by Adams and Jordan and John Ellway led to all these difficulties, and occasioned the postponement of the grant of this gale from 2 August 1872, when the gaveller would have perfected it, to the present day. It is admitted on all hands that if, on 2 August 1872, when this duty was imposed on the gaveller, the grant had been made to James Davis, the title would have been perfect. The Act of Parliament makes it positive that, if he had obtained the grant on that day, he might forthwith have sold the gale to any person whatever.'

His Lordship after reading the 23rd section of 1 & 2 Vict. c. 43 [1838] continued:

> 'The day after the gale is actually granted, the Crown of course must deal with other persons than free miners, namely, anybody to whom the grantee thinks fit to sell or devise. Now it has been argued that the only other thing of any importance on the question is the 56th section of the Act, and that it was not cited before me on the former occasions. It is true that it does not appear either by my notes or by the report to have been read upon that occasion. But the question is whether it makes any difference. That section provides that in every grant of a gale the metes, bounds, limits, and extent of such gale, and the galeage rent, royalty or tonnage duty to be paid to Her Majesty, shall be specified in the grant thereof. It further provides that if any free miner claiming to be entitled to a gale shall not agree with

the gaveller or deputy gaveller as to the amount of such galeage rent, royalty, or tonnage duty to be paid for the same and to be specified in the grant thereof, then it shall be referred to an arbitrator to determine the galeage rent, royalty, or tonnage duty which ought to be paid. I take it that what will be done is this: The gaveller, having already settled the boundaries, will now fix the amount of the rent to be paid, and the conditions of the lease, which, I presume, will be precisely the same to Davis's devisees as they would have been to Davis himself. If either party is dissatisfied, Davis's devisees, by the petition of right, have offered to submit the whole thing. It appears to me, therefore, that the words "free miners" in section 56 merely mean the Crown on one side and the free miner or the grantee on the other, who may be either the free miner or the grantee himself, or persons claiming lawfully under him.

On the whole case, therefore, it appears to me that Davis's devisees have made out most clearly their title to have the grant of this gale perfected to them, and the order will, in pursuance of the prayer of the petition, be that the gale may be granted to them.'

From this order the Crown appealed. The appeal was heard on 26 March 1877, and the decision of Vice-Chancellor Malins was reversed. The opinions of the three Judges were:

James, L. J.:

'With all respect for the judgement of the Vice-Chancellor, and also with a full sense of what may be called the hardship upon the Respondents, I have come to the conclusion that the order of the Vice-Chancellor cannot be affirmed. There is really no question of what may be called justice or injustice. There is no question of contract. There is no question of equity of any kind. The rights are ancient legal rights which existed more or less imperfectly in the old class of free miners from, I believe, the time of the Romans, and were afterwards settled, and to a certain extent codified; the Acts of 1 & 2 Vict. c. 43, and 24 & 25 Vict. c. 40, establishing the rights of the free miners as between themselves, and as between themselves and the Crown. It was then established that nobody but a registered free miner had a right to a gale, that there should be a register of the free miners, and that whenever there was a gale required to be granted, the first of the free miners who made application for it should have the gale granted to him. The sole merit and the sole consideration and price which he has paid for the grant is that he is the first man who has run to the office to ask for it. He has given no consideration to the Crown, and no consideration to the public whatever, but he is entitled to have whatever the Act of Parliament says he is to have as the consequence of the first application. Then the Act of Parliament provides that when the gale has been so granted to him it shall be descendable as his real estate, and shall be capable of being assigned by him. That is all, and there is nothing to give him any estate or interest, legal or equitable, in the matter before the grant of the gale. The whole of the provisions of the Act of Parliament are inconsistent with the notion of his having any right whatever to touch the property or to do anything till the gale is granted to him. If he dies before the gale is granted to him, that is a misfortune which may occur to any person. As under the Act he got the right by being the first to run to the office and ask for the gale, so he lost the right by dying before the grant was made to him, and any other free miner would be let in. Would the devisees of a man who died the day after he made the application be entitled or would they be entitled if he died after the advertisement, or after the rent had been fixed? When is the right to be acquired as an equitable right, and can any right be acquired before the actual sealing of the grant by which the Crown is authorised to create the estate? It was not seriously contended that, unless there had been some default in some officer or other, there would be anything in the nature of the equity which is suggested, but it was said that there had been some delay and some misconduct on the part of the officers of the Crown. It appears to me that the officers of the Crown could hardly have done otherwise under the circumstances; and probably the accident has mainly arisen from the fact that the applicant, who was the predecessor in title of the present suppliants allowed an interval to elapse from 1868 to 1872 after making his application. That might, however, be ground of complaint against the officer, or there might have been an application for a mandamus; but those considerations cannot enable us to enlarge the Act of Parliament, or enable us to give an equitable right where the Act has merely given a legal right, in favour of a person who has nothing but a mere statutory right. The Act of Parliament must be taken as it stands, in favour of each free miner who has made an application, and in favour of the other free miners if an accident deprives the first applicant of the power of obtaining the gale. I am of opinion, therefore, that the order of the Vice-Chancellor should be discharged.'

Mellish, L. J.:

'I am of the same opinion. There are two questions: first, whether, according to the true construction of the Act of Parliament, there is a legal right in the heir or devisee of a free miner who has made the first application to obtain the grant; and, secondly, if there is no such legal right, whether there are any equitable considerations upon which the Court can give equitable relief, although there is no legal relief? Now, with respect to the first question, if a Court of law had to construe this Act of Parliament upon an application for a mandamus, they must clearly come to the conclusion that nobody except the free miner who has made the first application could obtain a mandamus.'

His Lordship then read sections 23 and 60 of the 1838 Act, commenting:

'It seems that, with the exception that the gaveller is not to grant a gale to a man who has already got three gales, and is not to grant a gale which will interfere with previous gales, he is to grant a gale to any free miner who makes the first application. But my opinion is that if a free miner dies after applying for a gale, then the first free miner who makes an application has the right to a grant of the gale, and the estate of the man who dies is deprived of a right which the Act of Parliament had given, the heir or devisee not being recognised in the Act. The Act says that the grant is to be made to a free miner, and therefore a person who is not a free miner, but only the heir or devisee of a free miner, has no *locus standi* to compel the gaveller to make a grant.

That being so, are there any equitable considerations on which the Court can say that equitable relief must be granted? If there was anything in the nature of contract, possibly the equitable doctrine would apply, that where a contract is made the Court considers that what is agreed to be done is to be treated as if it was done. But there is no contract between the Crown and the free miner, for the simple reason that there is nothing in the Act to compel a free miner to accept the grant after he has made his application for a grant. As far as I can see, at any time before the grant is actually made he can withdraw his application, and not insist upon it. The free miner is not bound by it, and it is contrary to the nature of contract to say that if one party is not bound the other party can be bound. Therefore the obligation on the Crown is not by way of contract, but it as a simple duty on the gaveller imposed by Act of Parliament, and there is no ground upon which, on equitable considerations, that right can be extended beyond its legal limit. On any other construction, and if death does not put an end to it, no one can tell how long an application may continue in legal force. I am of opinion, therefore, that, upon the true construction of the Act, in order to obtain a grant, the applicant must continue to be alive, and be a free miner at the time of the grant.'

Baggallay, J. A.:

'It appears to me that the single question involved in this appeal is, whether, at the time when the suppliants presented their petition of right, the gaveller or deputy gaveller had any power or authority to grant them the gale in question, and whether that question is to be answered in the affirmative or the negative must be decided upon the terms of the two Acts of Parliament. The duties of the gaveller and deputy gaveller are ministerial only, and they are not to act according to what they may think right or just in particular cases, but to obey the provisions of the Act of Parliament.'

His Lordship then referred to sections 14, 21, 23, 50, 57, and 60 of the 1838 Act, adding:

'Now, from the beginning to the end of this Act there is no provision for the grant of the gale to any other person than to a free miner. We have heard an ingenious argument on the 38th and 39th sections, that the Act of Parliament draws a distinction between the actual grant of a gale and the right to have a gale, but it is perfectly clear that those sections deal merely with a particular state of circumstances at the time when the Act passed, when there had been for some time a general suspension of grants of gales. This appeal has been properly brought and the order must be discharged.'

James, L. J.:

'We discharge the order of the Court below, and give no costs either in the Court below or here. It was worth while for the Crown to have our decision on this point.'

* * *

Mention has been made in Chapter VI of the informative Annual Reports of the Commissioners of Woods.[1] Among many items of interest is a receipt in 1861 of £100 'For damage to Parkend Barrier',[2] others are for expenditure on 'filling up old pits'.[3] Details are also given of free grants of land for ecclesiastical buildings. The Crown has frequently shown its wish to contribute to the social and other needs of the Forest

1 A report was issued for every year covered by this Chapter.

2 39th Rpt. (1861), p. 166. App. AA. No. 36.

3 *E.g.* £34 6s. 2d. in 36th Rpt. (1858) and £5 6s. in 37th Rpt. (1859). Some of the expenditure was also debited to the forestry account.

population and the Reports contain many instances of free grants of land for ecclesiastical buildings and for schools. They also include many large contributions to schools and other organisations. As to schools, the Commissioners stated in 1856:[1] 'The Crown contributes largely towards the support of these Schools ... ; and little assistance is derived in this respect from the Coalowners and Ironmasters, who have made, and still continue to make, considerable profits from their mines, and ought, therefore, to aid in the work of educating those who are employed in their service.' Mr. Protheroe, however, set a fine example. A school was erected by him at Cinderford and remained in his control until 1843, when he surrendered it absolutely with other property in part discharge of certain arrears of tonnage duties and other debts due by him to the Crown. He continued to take an interest in its welfare.[2] Proof is also available in the Reports of the desire of the Crown to be as helpful as possible in overcoming difficulties as regards the working of the mines and minerals. Many examples are given of licences granted for sinking air shafts in inclosures for ventilating mines.[3] In almost all cases the charge was a nominal 5s. Similarly, licences were granted to allow tramways to run through inclosures; in these cases the charge was £1 per annum plus the value of any trees that were damaged, sometimes amounting to such figures as £20, £30, £60, and £64.[4]

James G. Wood [Plate IX] included as an appendix to his book (1878)[5] a description of all the gales of coal and iron (but not the leases of quarries) granted subsequently to the Awards of 1841. The rents and royalties noted by him are the revised ones; should the old ones require consulting they may be found in the Annual Reports of the Commissioners of Woods. As regards coal gales, the revised rents varied from 10s. to £200 and the royalties from 1d. to 6d. per ton. In the case of iron gales the figures were £3 to £250, and 3d. to 1s. Gales granted from 1878 to the present day are recorded elsewhere[6] as well as statements of the Crown's receipts and expenditure regarding Dean's mines and minerals and of the yield of coal and iron ore.[7]

1 34th Rpt (1861), p. 91.

2 *Ibid.*, pp. 92-3.

3 *E.g.*, see 32nd Rpt. (1854), App. 18 (p. 78) and 35th Rpt. (1857), App. 16 (p. 99).

4 33rd Rpt. (1855), App. 17 (p. 107).

5 Wood, *op. cit.*, Appendix A, pp. 371-432.

6 Many gales are available in Annual Reports; for the remainder application should be made to the Gaveller's Office at Coleford.

7 See Returns to Orders of House of Commons, 4 November 1884 etc.

CHAPTER X

1884-1937: Bills of 1884 and 1889; Acts of 1904, 1906, and 1919

DURING the 1880s, the free miners were still in active opposition to the Government when the latter organised an attempt to at least curtail freemining in relation to developing the deep coal gales.

The Committee and Bill of 1884. In 1884 a Parliamentary Bill[1] drawn up by Sir Henry Loch, one of the Commissioners of Woods, was brought into the House of Commons by Mr. Courtney and Herbert Gladstone 'to facilitate the opening and working of certain of the lower series of coal seams in the Forest of Dean and Hundred of St. Briavels'. The Memorandum to the Bill states: 'All the underlying seams of coal are divided into separate portions called gales, and amounting in number to about 200. The gales which include the crowns of the (inverted) arches of the deepest seams are 45 in number. The number of free miners varies from 1,000 to 1,200. The Bill deals with the 45 gales above-mentioned, and does not in any way affect the remaining 155.' The object of the Bill was to provide for the working of the 45 deep seam gales. It was estimated that the three deep seam coal measures contained 97,900,000 tons of coal, and that its raising would generate employment for a population of several thousand miners and others; in effect, that it would create an almost new industry in the Forest. The promoters of the Bill stated:

> 'It cannot be doubted, that the general public would be benefited by any Bill which would carry such an object into effect; and that a numerous population in the district, who are not free miners, would be altogether in favour of such a Bill being passed.
>
> The obstacles at present to the working of the deep seam coalfield are as follows: In order to relieve the coalfield from water, it is necessary that very expensive pumping operations should be set in motion, and large sums of money expended in sinking pits and ventilating the collieries.
>
> To meet the expenditure necessary for such operations, it is essential that the deep seam galees should have a certain fixity of tenure. The Bill, therefore, is in the first place directed to secure fixity of tenure to the deep seam galees. This it is proposed to do by enabling the Crown [i.e. gaveller] to grant leases for sixty-three years with less onerous conditions than those which can be granted under the custom.
>
> The conditions which weigh so heavily against the power of the Crown to grant fixity of tenure are amongst others the customary rule that every galee should forfeit his gale unless he begins his work within five years, and continues it without any interval exceeding five years.
>
> Another onerous customary condition is the necessity for the Crown to revise every twenty-one years its scale of royalties, a condition which disables the Crown from fixing the royalties

1 Ordered by the House of Commons to be printed 30 April 1884. See Glos.R.O. D9096 F26/19, 20, 21, 23, 24.

Plate IX. *James G. Wood, a 19th century distinguished barrister, often consulted on freemining.*

for more than twenty-one years.

A further reason for bringing in the Bill is the necessity for a general co-operation of the deep seam galees in some general system of drainage, and working with a view to raise profitably the deep seam coal.

Dealing with the second of these causes as being the least difficult to resolve, the Bill proposes to make the gaveller an arbiter between the 45 galees, and to empower him to compel them to assent to a common system of drainage and working.

The Bill is brought in with the assent of the greater number of the deep seam galees, the clause, therefore, making the gavellers the arbiter is introduced with the assent of the persons on whom its obligations are imposed.

With respect to the first of the causes above-mentioned for bringing in the Bill, the necessity for altering the customary rules of working, a different case arises. The free miners, a body consisting of from 1,000 to 1,200 men, are interested in the forfeiture of any gale, inasmuch as on such forfeiture any free miner can claim to have made to him a grant in perpetuity (subject to defeasance on non-performance of its then conditions) of the forfeited gale. The whole interest that the free miners have in the 45 deep seam gales amounts to this, namely, that in the event of some three or four such gales being forfeited (probably the largest proportion likely to be forfeited) 3 or 4 men out of 1,000 or 1,200 would be entitled to a chance of benefiting by the forfeiture. The right of the free miners is an unsubstantial one; indeed it involves an element of chance amounting to at least 1,000 to 4 against any particular member benefiting by it.

The Bill proposes, as compensation for the discharge of the rights of the free miners in the deep seam coalfield, that a sum of £5,000 should be paid, half by the Crown and half by the deep seam galees, and that the sum so paid should be applied for the benefit of the body of free miners by a representative committee.

The free miners have been consulted, at first locally, and afterwards by means of a deputation from their number who were invited to come to London and discuss the question with the Commissioners of Woods. On these occasions the nature of the scheme, the great benefits which it would confer upon the district, and the way in which it would affect their class in particular, have been fully explained to them.'

The Bill was intended to be placed on the Statute Book as 'The Dean Forest (Lower Coal Seams) Act, 1884'. The forty-five gales in question were: Newcastle, Durham, Northumberland, Central, Alexandria, St. Low, East Dean Deep, New Bowson, Royal Colliery, High Delf Engine, Prince Albert, Beaufort Engine, Skinner's Garden, Morgan's Folly No. 2, Morgan's Folly No. 3, Emperor Colliery, Favourite, Extension Colliery, Cousin's Engine, Holly Hill, Princess Royal, Serridge, Venus and Jupiter, Arthur and Edward, Mirey Stock, All Profit, Pillowell Engine, Morgan's Folly No. 1, Prince of Wales, Rising Sun Engine, Union, Union and Cannop, Britannia, Small Profit, Richard White, Howbeach Engine, Blackpool Engine, Rudge Colliery, Flour Mill, Old Furnace, Birchen Grove, Pluds, Woodside, Newham Bottom, and East Slade. The whole covered about 11,800 acres.

In opposition to the Bill the following Statement was delivered in 1884 on behalf of the free miners[1]:

---

1 Glos.R.O. D9096 F26/19 [1884]

'1. – The Crown is the Owner of the Forest of Dean, but only of a portion of the Hundred of St. Briavels.

2. – The 200 gales referred to in the Memorandum to this Bill comprise, as there stated, 45 Deep gales, and 155 others. Of the last-mentioned the greater portion are worked out, or are not worth working, and the remainder are being worked or in the hands of private individuals. Of the 45 Deep gales, 4 are in work, 36 unopened, 1 is worked out, and 4 have been forfeited. The Freeminers' interest in the 45 gales is far more valuable than in the whole of the other gales: there are about 1,200 Freeminers interested in these gales.

3. – The Grant to the Freeminer, when made, is in fee simple, and he is able to dispose of the gale in fee to capitalists, who work the minerals. The interest proposed to be created under this Bill is to be a leasehold interest, and therefore the inducement to the capitalist to invest his money will not be so great as when he got the fee simple.

4. – The proposed dealings with the 45 Deep gales under this Bill would not, as suggested by the Memorandum attached thereto, increase the industry of raising coal in the Forest of Dean, there not being sufficient sale for the coal already raised under the existing system.

5. – The demand for coal in the Forest of Dean is not up to the power of supply: it consequently follows that the introduction of further population would cause a fall in wages, and more poverty, as the present miners would not be required to work nearly full time.

6. – The present population of the district, who are not freeminers, are wholly opposed to the Bill, and it is considered that, should it become law, great damage will be done in the Forest.

7. – The Freeminers consider that there is no necessity whatever for this Bill, but that what is required is that the Crown officials should be compelled to carry out the Acts of Parliament now regulating the Working of Mines in the Forest of Dean and Hundred of St. Briavels, and the Rules prepared in accordance with such Acts, especially Rule 4.

8. – The Freeminers submit that such Acts of Parliament have not been fairly carried out by the Government Officers, for that of the 45 Deep gales dealt with by this Bill, at the present time 36 have been, and still are, liable to forfeiture, and ought to be re-granted to Freeminers.

9. – The Coal in the 45 Deep gales is estimated to be 97,900,000 Tons: this at 2d. per Ton, gives £815,883. (The Crown Royalty averages 2$^{1}/_{4}$d. per Ton.) 36 of these gales are liable to forfeiture, and to be re-granted to the Freeminers. Thus at the present time, and at the sum per Ton as above, which is the Crown's charge as their one-fifth share (the Freeminers' share being four-fifths, or four times this amount) the Freeminers are entitled to gales containing coal of the value of £670,837 2s. 8d. The Act of 1838 recognises the Freeminers' Rights as four-fifths. Of the 45 gales, the subject of this Bill,–

28	have	been	granted	for	over	40	years
3	"	"	"	"	"	35	"
2	"	"	"	"	"	25	"
4	"	"	"	"	"	15	"
1	"	"	"	"	"	5	"
2	"	"	"	"	"	3	"
4	forfeited and not at present granted.						
1	worked out.						
45							

This statement shows the manifest unfairness of the Bill in its proposed treatment of the Freeminers' Rights.

10. – The present Regulations as regards the forfeiture of gales have not been found to work

prejudicially to the Forest generally, the only injury that has resulted from them being the loss sustained by the Freeminers in consequence of the Crown officials not carrying out the Act of Parliament strictly in enforcing the forfeitures and making the regrants of the forfeited gales.

11. – The Bill is conceived entirely upon wrong principles, being, as it now stands, merely a Bill to confiscate the Freeminers' Rights, and is thoroughly misleading as to the value of such Rights; and in the event of its passing all the gales would ultimately revert to the Crown.

12. – The Compensation proposed to be paid to the Freeminers is out of all proportion, as shown by the fact that two of the Deep gales which were forfeited some two or three years since, and subsequently regranted to Freeminers, were alone sold for £9,000.

13. – The statement in the Memorandum to the Bill as to the right of the Freeminers is an unsubstantiated one, is misleading, and quite contrary to the fact, as shown by the foregoing observations.

14. – The working of the scheme proposed by the Bill as to the compensation to be paid to the Freeminers is impracticable, and would result in a sum of about 3d. per year being paid to each Freeminer.

15. – The Bill does not meet with the approval of the inhabitants of the Forest of Dean and Hundred of St. Briavels, or that of the Freeminers.

16. – The Bill, if passed, would have the opposite effect to that suggested in the Memorandum to it, for on a regrant the Freeminer is always willing to sell to capitalists at a low price, whereas the Crown always imposed the highest price, which is a deterrent to purchasers, and causes the gales to remain long unworked.

17. – The Deep gales remain unworked because they are chiefly in the hands of persons at present working other gales in the Forest, who will not open them, there not being sufficient customers for the coal already raised. The present Bill would not alter this state of things.

18. – The Bill is not required for the reasons mentioned in the foregoing objections.

19. – For the above reasons it is respectfully hoped that the House of Commons will see fit to negative the Second Reading of the Bill.

These Objections are prepared by John Leonard Piddocke, of Ross, in the County of Hereford, solicitor, on behalf of the Freeminers of the Forest of Dean.'

In their renewed resistance, the free miners contradicted the testimony of those who thought their rights were useless. Much of the opposition was dominated by Union interests and local politics.[1] The weight of local opinion was too great. Eventually the Bill was withdrawn but the subject was reopened in 1889.

The Select Committee of 1889. Giving evidence to this Committee, George Culley, a Commissioner of Woods, on 21 June 1889 stated when questioned:

'Q. 557. It would require an Act of Parliament would it not (for the free miners to dispose of their rights to the Crown)? – A Bill was actually introduced into Parliament [in 1884] to do the thing with regard to a certain number of deep gales by my predecessor, Sir Henry Loch. It was exceedingly badly received by the free miners and their friends.

Q. 558. Was that after the report of the Committee in 1854? – Yes, but it was 1884. Sir

1 At this time, 1884, two Petitions of Right concerning freemining were proceeding:-
(a) T. Gwilliam & ors. *v*. G. T. Stephens (*re* Prince Albert Colliery); and
(b) N. Howells & ors *v*. G. T. Stephens (*re* Prince of Wales Colliery)
Ref. H.O. 45/9648/A 37325 C and B.

Henry Loch merely proposed to get rid of the free miners' rights in 42 [45] of the deep gales, because it seemed impossible under the then existing arrangement that the coal would ever be worked without this process being gone through; this proposal was that a certain compensation should be given to the free miners on account of the loss of their rights in those deep gales, that half of that should be paid by the Crown and half by the galees.

Q. 559. The colliery owners? – The colliery owners, as it were; but the colliery owners after agreeing to that and offering all the support in their power did not, I believe, move one little finger to help him when the thing came to discussion.'

Arnold Thomas, when questioned, deposed on behalf of free miners (19 July 1889):

'Q. 3877. But you also appear on behalf of the present galees and holders of the minerals in the Forest? – Yes.

Q. 3878. You desire on their behalf, I understand, to make a statement in reply to an answer made by Mr. Culley as to Sir Henry Loch's Bill, which was brought into the House of Commons in 1884? – Yes.

Q. 3879. I will refer to Questions 558 and 559, in which Mr. Culley mentioned that Bill. He then said that the colliery owners after agreeing to the Bill, and offering all the support in their power did not move one little finger to help him when the thing came to discussion. Can you give us a very short history of what the objects of that Bill were? – The objects of the Bill were something that the galees themselves had asked for. We asked for an interview with Sir Henry Loch, in order that we might consult with him as to the better means of developing the deep seams and we came to a substantial agreement as to the draft of a Bill. There were some things in it that we did not quite agree with; but generally the advantages of the Bill were that there were provisions for compensation in cases of benefits conferred in the matter of pumping: and, although we did not as galees attach very great importance to that, a longer period of tenure –

Q. 3880. Compensation to whom? – To other galees. In the case of the owner of a gale draining another gale by means of his pumps there were provisions in the new Bill for compensation for the benefit conferred thereby, which does not exist at the present time.

Q. 3881. The compensation would be from whom to whom? – The compensation would be from the gale owner who obtained advantage from the pumps put down by another gale-owner. There was a clause to that effect in the Bill.

Q. 3882. That would have been paid to those who put down pumps? – To those who put down the pumps, by those who had benefit conferred upon them thereby, the difficulty being that the quantity of water is too great for a single gale-owner to cope with.

Q. 3883. In what form was the compensation to be levied? – There was the provision in the Bill.

Q. 3884. Was it by means of a rate to be levied? – It simply says "entitled to compensation"; I think those are the words.

Q. 3885. It was not to be a general rate levied upon the district? – No, not necessarily a general rate levied upon it; "shall be entitled to compensation" I think are the only words; the compensation to be ascertained in some way or other. This is the section: "In all cases where any specified gale is drained by the working of any other specified gale, then and in every such case the lessee of the gale so drained shall be liable to pay compensation to the lessee of the gale by means of which such drainage is effected, or other person holding through or under him, and the amount of such compensation, in case the parties fail to agree about the same, shall be such as may be settled by arbitration", and so on.

Q. 3886. You wish, I think, to explain how it was that you ceased to back up Sir Henry Loch? – I do not think the galees did cease to back up Sir Henry Loch; that is the part of the answer which I complain of. As a matter of fact, I believe, the Office of Woods and Forests abandoned the Bill because of the opposition offered on the part of the free miners. We heard no more about it as galees.

Q. 3887. You were perfectly willing to proceed? – We were perfectly willing to proceed because we thought there was a sufficient foundation in the Bill for an agreement which would have been advantageous all round.

Q. 3888. Subject to certain alterations? – Subject to certain alterations. We said, "Subject to such alterations as may be found necessary", before we did agree. There was one clause in the Bill which we said at first we could not possibly agree with; that was Clause 47. We asked I should say for the power of amalgamation for the purposes of joint working.

Q. 3889. Amalgamation of gales? – Of any gales that may be conveniently amalgamated for joint working; and we said that, in the event of the amalgamation, we thought that the certain rent of all the gales should be recouped from the working of either of them. We also thought that such amalgamation should form one whole gale. We understood, however, that the Office of Woods was not prepared to give up its right to charge a wayleave for passing from one gale to another. That is a point upon which we were not agreed; but we thought that, if the Bill came in, that might be discussed and possibly got over; and I should say that since then the Office of Woods have practically conceded the reasonableness of that which we asked for, because they have, as a matter of fact, combined four large gales, and regarded them as one whole one.

Q. 3890. And in this case have they given up their wayleave? – By making one whole gale of it, there ceases to be any wayleave.

Q. 3891. What is the suggestion that you wish to offer to the Committee, as to the way in which the Crown under existing circumstances might treat you more favourably, and might make it more easy for you to develop the deep measures that you are dealing with? – I think that if there were powers of amalgamation for the purposes of joint working, and if the Crown were prepared to concede to persons who acquired a number of gales that which they have practically conceded in forming one gale out of four, a great deal of the difficulty would be got over, especially as provisions are made here for compensation in the case of pumping.

Q. 3892. You mean to say that you are in favour of consolidation of gales? – I am in favour of the consolidation of gales, but not if we are to have, with the consolidation of the gales, a charge for wayleaves over imaginary boundaries. They will be boundaries, then, which do not exist.

Q. 3893. But in the case to which you refer the free miners were consenting parties, were they not? – Oh, yes, I take it they would be.

Q. 3894. Could the assent of the free miners be obtained to an amalgamation of gales in which they had no interest? – I do not think their consent would be required at all.

Q. 3895. I thought you said that Sir Henry Loch abandoned the Bill in consequence of the opposition of the free miners? – The opposition of the free miners was a very sound one. It was proposed by the Bill to abolish the free miners, and to give the free miner, £5,000 to divide amongst them in exchange for their rights, which consist, in fact, of the practical ownership of four-fifths of the gales.

Q. 3896. They prepared a petition to Parliament, did they not? – They prepared a petition to Parliament.

Q. 3897. And I think they made no objection to the amalgamation of gales for the purposes of working the property? – Oh, no; they only insisted upon their rights, and objected to the terms of compensation.

Q. 3898. And you do not think the free miners would raise any difficulty about your being allowed to amalgamate your gales in what way suited yourselves? – I think not, the galees have never objected to the free miners at all. They have never found any difficulty in the existence of the free mines.

Q. 3899. But you say the free miners did object before? – They objected to being bought out and practically abolished under the Bill.

Q. 3900. Is there any other way of consolidation than that which has been adopted, and which Mr. Culley is trying, as he explained to us; where he has got a large number of free miners to consent that their rights should be dealt with by one man on behalf of the whole; I think he said they consolidated four gales together, and then made one colliery. Do you approve or disapprove of what Mr. Culley is now trying to accomplish? – I entirely approve of the manner in which Mr. Culley has amalgamated them; but in the case of the owners of four or five other gales agreeing among themselves to an amalgamation, what we ask for is that we should be allowed to amalgamate on the same terms as have been given in the case of the amalgamation of those four.

Q. 3901. Have they refused to allow you to amalgamate on those terms? – Oh, no; but they have no power yet, in the case of any other gales.

Q. 3902. I quite understand your point now. What you state to the Committee on that point is, that it is desirable that further Parliamentary powers should be granted to the Commissioners to enable them to carry out this process, so to speak, by agreement? – Certainly, and I say further, that in my view there is no need to interfere with the free miner's right in going to Parliament for that. The free miner, in my view, has nothing to do with it.

Q. 3903. Then, in your opinion, and in the opinion of those whom you represent, and as an owner of mineral property in the Forest, and having practical knowledge in the Forest, you do not think that the rights of the free miner need bar the working of the deep coal? – No; I have never known them any bar at all. I say the real bar consists in the present rules and regulations, which are inapplicable to the deep series of seams; and without an application to Parliament it cannot be done, because there must be an amalgamation, and there must be some provision made for the joint pumping.

Q. 3904. May I go a step further, and say that, in your opinion and in the opinion of those whom you represent, so far from having been a bar the free miners' rights have enabled you to stand on very favourable terms in the Forest? – I think we do. I think there are a great many privileges that we have in working which are due to the free miners' rights. You see under this Bill we should have ceased to be the owners of the gales, and we should become lessees. The 47th clause was this (which we never could have agreed to): "Subject to the provisions of this Act, the lessees of any two or more specified gales may from time to time enter into agreements for the amalgamation and joint working of such gales upon such terms and conditions as may be set forth in such agreement and the gaveller may approve." It put us entirely in the hands of the gaveller, whoever he may be at the time. We have not in that clause, as we have under the Dean Forest Mines Act [1838], the protection of arbitration.

Q. 3905. It got rid of the arbitration altogether? – Altogether; so that if we did not agree to the terms the gaveller thought proper, the safeguard of arbitration, and the free miner having gone, we should have the alternative of surrendering that which is now our property or submitting to terms which we did not agree with.

Q. 3906. You accepted those terms in order to get the advantage of being able to combine your gales? – No, we never agreed to the 47th clause. That we could not possibly agree to. We stated that.

Q. 3907. As a matter of fact, if you do not begin to work your gale within five years, do you forfeit, or do you not? – No; that has not happened. At the end of five years the Office of Woods says to us: "If we can see our way to give you another period of five years will you abandon half the accrued certain rents."

Q. 3908. And, as a rule, is that what actually occurs? – That is what actually occurs, because the alternative is to abandon the whole of it.

Q. 3909. You are in the position that you must either forfeit half or you must forfeit the whole? – Yes.

Q. 3910. The custom is to forfeit the half, is it not? – That we have done in the case of myself and others that I am associated with.

Q. 3911. And you know other cases in which it is continually happening? – I know other cases.

Q. 3912. So that at the end of the five years, in the case of the gales which are not worked, the Crown, so to speak, pockets half the over-paid dead rent and begins all over again? – Yes.

Q. 3913. Then do not you think that to that extent it is rather to the advantage of the Crown that the coal should not be worked, but that they should keep on in that way? – Yes. I think it is a very good business indeed to pocket half the certain rents every five years. If you can only get the gales into the hands of people who can pay, and every five years take half of that which has accumulated, that can go on for ever and the corpus remain untouched.

Q. 3914. The man is not bound to go on with the gale, is he? – No; the alternative is to give up all.

Q. 3915. He can either forfeit half at the end of the five years or forfeit the whole of the gale? – Or forfeit the whole of the gale. It is not to the advantage of the Crown to get the gale forfeited then, because if it is absolutely forfeited at the end of the five years in comes a free miner who gets a grant of it and pays no certain rent at all for two years.

Q. 3916. Then it is the interest of the free miner at the end of the five years, whenever you are unable to work your gale, that the gale should be forfeited to the Crown? – Yes, because he can get it granted again.

Q. 3917. And sell it again? – Yes.

Q. 3918. That is *qua* free miner? – Yes.

Q. 3919. But *qua* collier it is rather to his interest that the thing should be worked, and for the prosperity of the neighbourhood? – Yes; and I think the general feeling of the neighbourhood and of the free miners is in favour of some scheme by which it should be opened, because their interest as colliers is very much wider and broader than that of their interest as free miners.

Q. 3920. And in the meantime the coal is to a certain extent increasing in value, so that in that way the Crown is not suffering? – I do not think the Crown suffers by the gales not being opened, so long as they are in the hands of people who can pay the certain rents.

Q. 3921. You say there are other charges imposed upon you by the Crown besides the royalties? – The wayleaves.

Q. 3922. The wayleaves? – Yes; but we have no amalgamation at present. If there was a power of amalgamation we say we ought not to be called upon to pay wayleaves, because the grants of gales are not at all scientific. They were granted because they were applied for in all shapes and sizes, and in the event of an amalgamation (which could only be done under the terms of an Act of Parliament) we think it would be improper to charge the wayleaves, which we have been told by the Office of Woods they are not prepared to abandon.

Q. 3923. In what way are the wayleaves fixed? – The wayleave is fixed by the gaveller. There is nothing to prevent the gaveller demanding any amount that I know of, as a wayleave for passing through a barrier.

Q. 3924. Have you no appeal to arbitration in that case against a wayleave? – I think the power does not exist to amalgamate now.

Q. 3925. As to the rate of the wayleave, have you any appeal? – No.

Q. 3926. The gaveller fixes it at what he thinks right? – I do not think there is any mention of it in the Act.

Q. 3927. What is the actual amount of the wayleaves; does it vary in different cases or is it uniform? – I am not able to speak of any positively, but I have heard of a penny and twopence a ton; I think that would be about the minimum. In the event of four or five gales being joined together it would be a very heavy tax, 5d. a ton, if it were even a penny, in passing through every barrier.

Q. 3928. Do you know any instance on which as much as 5d. a ton is paid? – No, not of my own knowledge. I think in the case of one small gale a penny was paid.

Q. 3929. In each separate wayleave a penny, or what does it amount to? – As a matter of fact I believe only one barrier has been passed through at a time, and it has only been a penny. I say if we are to pay for passing through barriers, as many barriers as we pass through there would be so many pennies to pay.

Q. 3930. But there is no grievance of that kind at present, as I understand? – No, there is no power to deal with the thing. If powers are taken by the Office of Woods for amalgamation, we should like a provision made that would guard us against an arbitrary wayleave.

Q. 3931. Is timber growing ever made an obstacle to the development of your mines. Have you ever found that to be the case? – Well, we have to pay a very heavy price for such trees as we use for tip-room. Sometimes a part in which trees are grown is in the way of the tip-room; then we have to pay a very heavy price for the trees.

Q. 3932. The trees which you damage? – Yes; ten times as much as they are worth.

Q. 3933. Do you mean ten times as much as they are worth in the market? – Yes; 10s. to 15s. for small oak trees, or 7s. 6d., according to size. They are in no sense timber.

Q. 3934. Do you prevent them growing when you cut them down? – Yes, we bury the place on which they grow. It is to make the tip-room that the trees are destroyed.

Q. 3935. You do not have to pay for tip-room, do you? – No; we are entitled to sufficient tip-room under the Act.

Q. 3936. Unless you inclose? – Inclose the land on which the tip is?

Q. 3937. Yes? – That is never done. If we want inclosed space we have to pay rent for it.

Q. 3938. What sort of a rent do you pay. Do you pay the actual value of the land or do you pay a fancy price? – It is a fancy price. I do not think I ever calculated how much per acre. It is generally a few pounds. We do not use much; so that there is not much in that.

Q. 3939. Do you think that this custom in the Forest, this liability to forfeiture at the end of five years if not worked, has been a great impediment to the development of the trade of the Forest generally? – No, I think not.

Q. 3940. Do not you think it has kept speculators and investors from investing their money in collieries in the Forest? – That is possible; but so far as the purchase of a colliery is concerned it does not matter much who the owner is. Somebody is the owner every five years. I think the liability to forfeiture might prevent an outsider from buying.

Q. 3941. Generally speaking, you do not think that the complicated tenure has stood in the way of the development of the coal? – Not generally. I should think the five years is the worse clause; certainly the 21 years is no objection, to my mind.

Q. 3942. Do you think it would be a very great advantage if you could get that period extended, as Mr. Culley suggested, to 63 years? – No, I do not. I think at is an advantage to go to arbitration at the end of the 21 years.

Q. 3943. For fear of a fall in the price of coal? – Yes; and besides if you go to arbitration you presumably get what is reasonable, and if you were entitled to a reduction you would probably get it; if you were able to pay an increase you would not object to it I suppose.

Q. 3944. If a man is going to spend a great deal in sinking a shaft to get at the deep coal, is it not more advantageous for him that he should have a longer time on certain conditions to recoup himself? – I think not, because it may cut two ways. He may find when he gets to his coal that the royalty is too high a one. Then 21 years would be an advantage to him. That is my own view.

Q. 3945. Generally speaking, at the end of 21 years, when a fresh royalty has had to be assessed, has it been raised or lowered? – Some have been raised and some lowered. There has never been much difficulty about it; it has been generally a matter of agreement. There have been very few arbitrations.

Q. 3946. On the whole you think that rule acts very well, and you would be sorry to see the time extended to 63 years? – I do not see the good of it. It has never been the subject of complaint at all.

Q. 3947. Is there anything else you would like to say in reference to the collieries in the Forest? – I only wish to say this: that unless some further power is taken by the Office of Woods to deal with these deep seams I do not see how they are to be worked at all; and upon the lines I have suggested, it seems to me, without any interference whatever with the free miners' rights, that a Bill might be brought in which would give all that any reasonable man would desire for the purpose of developing these seams. If we had sufficient power of amalgamation to obtain such an area as would justify the outlay, and if we had also the provision which this Bill gives for compensation in the case of benefits conferred in pumping, I do not think that anything else practically is required. I do not care about the extension of the time beyond 21 years, for the reason I have given, that at the end of the 21 years it may be of advantage to the gale owner himself to have his royalties readjusted.

Q. 3948. Your local experience leads you, does it, to agree with what Mr. Forster Brown said, that if the deep measures were increased in number the water would be inconsiderable? – I have no doubt of it. It is a small area, and the water is a measurable quantity, at least by the ordinary rules that engineers adopt; and the misfortune is that whoever puts down the first set of pumps will probably have more water than he can manage; whereas if the coal could be approached at several points it would not be a very serious matter, because the water would be divided.'

The attitude adopted by the Crown towards the free miners over the period covered by this chapter is so well illustrated by the Report and Minutes of Evidence[1] of the Select Committee of 1889, that further relevant portions are here included. George Culley,[2] gaveller and a Commissioner of Woods since 3 June 1884, deposed that about two years ago, there were three chief officers in the Forest – a deputy surveyor, a deputy gaveller ('who is practically the viewer of the mining property') and a registrar and receiver; but on the retirement of the registrar and receiver he proposed to the Treasury and the Treasury accepted the proposal, to do away with that as a separate office, and to make the deputy surveyor the receiver of the surface rents and the deputy gaveller the receiver of the mine rents. This effected a saving of something like £400 per annum. The deputy surveyor received £137 12s. 8d. per annum as receiver of surface and quarry rents. Further relevant information was disclosed by the following Questions and Answers:

'Q. 145. What was the income from the minerals – year ended 31st March 1888? – In the Forest of Dean, from coal rents and royalties, £12,954 10s. 0d.; from iron, £1,374 3s. 9d.; from stone, £524 8s. 8d.; and a miscellaneous income of £4 2s.

Q. 189. Now let us come to the mines. The mines in the Forest of Dean last year, the coal and the ironstone (the stone is of no importance) would produce £14,328, I think? – Yes. You are deducting High Meadow, are you not?

Q. 190. No, I am not. I want to include it? – £15,220 16s. 2d., I have.

Q. 191. We did not get the figure for High Meadow. We got £12,954 from coal in the Forest of Dean? – £12,954 19s. 9d.

Q. 192. Never mind the shillings and pence? – I mean if you put the £12,955, coal rents and royalties; the £1,374 ironstone, £524; miscellaneous, £4; High Meadow, £363, together it will come to that.

Q. 193. £15,220 is the actual sum paid as royalty? – Yes, there are royalties upon the coal and upon the iron.

Q. 194. And the stone? – It is partly a royalty and partly rents of quarries. We are rather adopting of late the royalty system with stone also.

Q. 195. You do not work any of those mines yourselves? – None.

Q. 196. Those are all let on lease, I suppose ? – There is a peculiar custom which applies to Dean Forest; I cannot grant a gale of coal upon lease. I cannot grant a gale of coal in Dean Forest to anybody, except a free miner, and it becomes his absolute property so long as he fulfils the condition of that grant.

Q. 197. The Crown grants the mineral to the miner? – Yes, over a certain area.

Q. 198. Over a certain area, the miner paying a certain royalty? – The miner paying a certain royalty.

Q. 199. Your area is limited to the miner; a man cannot go as a stranger from another part of England and take a grant? – I can only grant to a free miner, a man born and bred, and who has lived 21 years in the Hundred of St. Briavels.

Q. 200. Is there any question as to the term of the lease? – No, the royalty is subject to revision every 21 years.

Q. 201. It is a lease then practically renewable at the expiration of 21 years on terms? –

[1] Ordered by the House of Commons, to be printed, 26 July 1889.

[2] Pp. 1-29.

Yes, subject to arbitration, if the Crown and the lessee disagree.

Q. 202. Do you remember what your royalties are just now on coal? – They vary very much, from a penny up to sixpence. They are very low.

Q. 203. Sixpence is your highest, and a penny the lowest? – Yes, in Dean Forest. In High Meadow, I think we have one case of 1s.

Q. 204. Is that 1s. per ton do you mean? – Yes, that is where the free miners do not exist, where the coal is absolutely the property of the Crown, and lying near the surface, I think.

Q. 205. What are your ironstone royalties? – They are threepence, fourpence, and sixpence. I have got it somewhere in a document.

Q. 206. Never mind, I see they are moderate. What are your staff for the mineral property? – Only the deputy gaveller who receives a salary of £550, an allowance for clerks of £202 10s.; allowance for travelling expenses in the Forest, £50; a commission of five per cent, upon the High Meadow minerals (£26 3s. last year); and as receiver of the rents of coal and iron mines, £353 5s. 4d.; total, £1,179 1s. 8d.

Q. 207. That is the deputy gaveller? – That is the deputy gaveller.

Q. 208. Now what does that gentleman do for that money? – He is practically the viewer of the Forest mines. He examines all the works, advises me in fixing royalties, and sees that the mines are worked in accordance with the rules of the Dean Forest, which are very peculiar.

Q. 209. Does he go down the pits? – Yes.

Q. 210. He is what I suppose would be called elsewhere a mining surveyor? – A mining surveyor, or what in the north of England would be called a viewer.

Q. 211. In Durham he would be called a viewer; but in Staffordshire we should call him a mine surveyor; he gets £1,180 a year? – All told; part being an allowance for clerks. He receives altogether £1,179 1s. 8d.

Q. 212. Taking the clerks off, he practically gets £1,000 a year ? – Something like it.

Q. 213. Who has he got to assist him? – He finds any assistants he requires for himself.

Q. 214. You have no other? – We have no other charge.

Q. 215. And he receives the rent for that? – He receives the rent and royalties for that.

Q. 216. And pays it over to you? – Yes.

Q. 217. I will just ask this question now: to whom do the two officials in the Forest, the one who inspects the woods, and the other who inspects the mines, pay the rents? – They remit the rents to the Receiver General.

Q. 218. In London? – Yes.

Q. 219. Just to put this matter quite clear; do I understand that the total cost involved in obtaining £15,220 from the mines in the Forest of Dean is £1,179 1s. 11d.; is that quite clear? – No; that is not the whole expense. That is the whole expenditure on officers.

Q. 220. What other expenses are there? – There are a certain number of men who are employed to make mineral surveys.

Q. 221. I want all those? – I have not got them stated in a separate sum at all. I could give you the gross sum.

Q. 222. I want the gross sum? – Including salaries and emoluments of the deputy surveyor, the whole cost was £2,533 11s.

Q. 223. If we subtract from that the deputy gaveller, there is another £1,354? – Yes.

Q. 224. Am I right? – Yes.

Q. 225. What is the bulk of that expenditure for? – For property tax, superannuation allowances out of tonnage duties, making surveys of the mines, and plans of the workings, and so on.

Q. 226. That is mineral surveyor's work? – Yes; but these men assist him in making the measurements.

Q. 227. In other words they do the work; they really go down and do the surveying? – I cannot of my own knowledge say to what extent he does or does not go down. I know that he does go down, and reports to me upon the condition of the mines.

Q. 228. Are the royalties paid by measurement, or are they paid by weight? – They are paid by tonnage; by weight.

Q. 229. Who checks the tonnage? – The deputy gaveller.

Q. 230. He does not do it himself you know; who does it. The returns are checked; now I want to know who checks them? – That I cannot of my own knowledge tell you. I should be very glad if you would examine the deputy gaveller.

Q. 231. We will do that. I do not for a moment suppose you would understand all that. But at all events, for completing the work of the Crown; the lessor; there is another expenditure of £1,350 a year? – Yes.

Q. 232. Does that cover everything? – That covers everything.

Q. 233. Then we have a total expenditure on minerals, the income of which is £15,220, of £2,533? – That is so.

Q. 234. You allow nothing else but these sums? – No, nothing else.

Q. 316. What are your views with reference to the holding of that description of property, as to whether it would be more advantageous to the Crown; to the public; if that property was sold or kept in its present condition? – The Forest of Dean would be a very difficult subject for sale, because you have the peculiar rights of the free miner which entitle the free miner to the grant of every gale; in fact, it prevents the Crown granting to anybody else, other than a free miner. Then you have, as is usual in all such cases, the commoners' interest. I do not know what advantage would arise from disafforesting the Forest of Dean.

Q. 317. You think if power were obtained to sell, that the produce of a sale would not be commensurate to the income which is at present derived? – No, I do not say that at all; I think if you could free the Forest of Dean; that is to say if you could disafforest and sell, you would probably benefit yourself pecuniarily, "*you*" being in the position of the Crown as the owner.

Q. 318. Do you extend that remark also to the mines as well as to the woods? – No one would be subject to the present rights, I think, of either commoners or free miners. You would have to get rid of the rights in both cases, otherwise you could not sell.

Q. 319. Can you tell us what a free miner is; how do you define a man who has these vested rights in the Forest of Dean? – He is a man who has been born in the Hundred of St. Briavels, twenty-one years of age, and has worked a year and a day in a mine. Those are the qualifications. Then he is put upon the register.

Q. 320. Is there any register? – Yes, there is a register kept.

Q. 321. Who keeps that register? – The deputy gaveller. That is one of the duties of the deputy gaveller.

Q. 322. What is the extent of this "Hundred" in which these free miners must be born; is it a series of parishes? – Yes, it is a series of parishes; but I believe the boundaries are not very well defined. It is much larger, for example, than the Forest of Dean itself. The acreage of the Forest of Dean is about 18,000 acres, and I believe the other is more like 30,000 or 40,000 acres.

Q. 323. Then the people born in this area of 40,000 acres, having served a year in a mine, and being 21 years of age, constitute the class of free miners? – They constitute the class of free miners.

Q. 324. And the Crown can grant no mining lease except to one of these free miners in the Forest of Dean? – That is so.

Q. 325. How do they manage with reference to master miners; are there any large colliery miners, or are they all small? – The free miner makes haste to sell his grant to some mining speculator or some practical miner.

Q. 326. Then the free miner having got the grant from the Crown can sell it? – Yes; it is in the nature of a freehold at once.

Q. 327. What area do you grant ordinarily to a man; what extent? – The areas were laid down by what are called the Dean Forest Commissioners in 1841. There were three Commissioners appointed. They settled the metes and bounds of these gales, which, up to that time, had been very uncertain. There was a tremendous quantity of litigation going on for years and years connected with the working of these gales and the boundaries, and so on. The object of this Commission was to settle these, and to lay down certain rules, which were practically adopted, in an Act of Parliament [1838] for working the mines. There are great peculiarities connected with it.

Q. 328. Are all those rules embodied in legislation? – They are in an Act [Award] of about the same time, 1841.

Q. 329. Just give us the reference to that Act? – 1st & 2nd Vict. c. 43 [1838].

Q. 330. Who settles the choice or priority of applicant for these gales? – That is in the order of application; but if more than one person applies upon a particular day, the first day of application, they draw lots for it. That is the old practice.

Q. 331. Is it the practice of to-day? – Well, it is the practice of to-day generally; but in a peculiar case lately, practically, I may say, I did what I could to defeat that system of lottery and uncertainty upon the forfeiture of four adjoining gales in the deep seams of the Forest. After consulting the Law Officer of the Crown to see that I had power to do so, I united these four gales to make a large area; one difficulty always represented to the office being that the areas are too small to tempt people to work the deep seams. In that way we got an area of about 2,000 acres. To defeat this, or to throw it open to more free miners than would probably be the case if the forfeiture had been advertised in the ordinary way, I advertised that the forfeiture would take place unless the dead rents were paid at a certain hour, five o'clock in the evening of a certain day. The result of that was that everybody knew that the next day that if they put their names down they would have as good a chance as anybody else for the large gale. The consequence was that 174 free miners put their names down.

Q. 332. For one gale? – For one gale. That is now called the "Deep United Gale". It covers an area of 2,000 acres for two or three seams. There is that peculiarity in the Dean Forest, that you do not let everything in one gale. A gale may have two or three seams; and another gale may have the seams below those. The whole of the seams below a certain surface are not let under one gale. This having happened, 174 men having put their names down, all of whom were entitled to draw lots under the ordinary rules of the Dean Forest for the gale, so that only one out of the 174 free miners could have got this grant. I met a body of the free miners, including nearly the whole of those people at the Speech House in the Forest of Dean, and after a time they agreed, all of them, to withdraw their names in favour of one to whom I could grant the gale as a trustee for the remainder; so that there are 170 I think it is, or 174, I forget which, free miners now interested in that one gale, instead of only one, as would have been the case if they had drawn lots, because I can only grant to one free miner.

Q. 333. I suppose this forms a sort of company then? – This man is entitled, as trustee of the others, to dispose of this deep gale to a company.

Q. 334. He will dispose of it at a profit? – If he can obtain any money for it, that will be shared amongst these 174 free miners.

Q. 335. He has paid you nothing for it? – He has paid us nothing for it.

Q. 336. He sells it to a company for a sum of money? – Yes, if he can.

Q. 337. This sum of money he divides amongst the 174 people who put their names down for it? – That is so.

Q. 338. He sells it subject to the royalty that has to be paid? – Yes; subject to the royalty that has to be paid.

Q. 339. Have you no power to accept tenders? – We have no power. We have done with the thing altogether so long as they fulfil the conditions.

Q. 340. If 174 people want the same article, of course according to the ordinary rules of commercial transactions in this country, the question would be which man will give the most for it, and the man who would give the most would have it? – No; I have no power to do that; they are all equal.

Q. 341. Then are the terms on which this property is let settled by you, or how do you settle them? – We settle the terms on which we make the grants. We settle the dead rent, and the royalty, the basis of the whole arrangement being the old right of the Crown to put in a fifth man after the coal is won.

Q. 342. You put it up at a certain dead rent, to begin with, and a certain mine rent on the coal got; that is the basis of the grant, is it not? – Yes.

Q. 343. You can put that dead rent and mine rent at a higher rate, if you think proper, can you not? – The royalty is limited by the old right of the Crown to what I said just now. It is supposed to represent one-fifth after the coal is actually won.

Q. 344. You mean one-fifth of the selling price? – One-fifth of the full royalty; one-fifth of the full royalty after the coal is actually won.

Q. 345. What do you mean by royalty ? – The full tonnage royalty. Suppose 1s. a ton is the royalty, it is one-fifth of that.

Q. 346. How do you get at the royalty, apart from the selling price? – Perhaps we are working from different ends, sir.

Q. 347. Yes, I am sure we are? – The position of the Crown is that these gales can only be granted by the Crown to a free miner.

Q. 348. Yes, that is first, the person. Your "person" is limited; you can only grant to a free miner. Now I want to know what limitation affects terms upon which you can grant to a free miner; you have 174 free miners all coming and asking for the same thing? – Yes.

Q. 349. Now I want to know whether you cannot raise your terms as anybody else would raise their terms if 174 people all wanted to buy the same article? – No, not at all.

Q. 350. That is what I want you to explain? – It is not fixed with reference to that at all. I am obliged to grant the gale to one of those 174. I have an application made, and I have no right to choose, or anything of that sort.

Q. 351. I want to know; are you bound, in originally fixing your terms, by any rules of the Forest, by say rules of the Act of Parliament, or by any rules of the Crown; if I were letting a mine in Staffordshire to-morrow I should fix my royalty according to the market price of the day? – What I am trying to explain is this: the royalty we fix depends upon that old right of the Crown, the one-fifth full royalty when the coal is won. If that was 1s. 3d., say, we would fix our royalty at 3d.

Q. 352. What I want to get at is how you fix the royalty? – I am trying to tell you.

Q. 353. Is it not one-fifth the value on the profit of the coal when won? – No.

Q. 354. Cannot you give us a concrete example? – I am trying to do that.

Q. 355. Take actual facts. What happened with regard to the last one which you granted? – The deputy gaveller, who, I explained some time ago, is actually the viewer, acting as our viewer or mining agent, advised me as to what the full royalty would be upon coal in that position, that is to say, in the position of the particular coal. He says: That would be worth (as I said just now) 1s. 3d. to you, the Crown; hampered by this condition it is worth 2½d. or 3d.

Q. 356. I quite understand that. Assuming the royalty for a certain description of coal, and that A B, if he was the absolute unfettered owner, would get 1s. 3d. a ton, the Crown are only entitled to get 3d.? – No, I do not explain myself well. I had said before that that was the full royalty after the coal was won. You must take what is the worth of that royalty, putting aside the expenditure incurred in winning the coal, which becomes a very serious thing in the deep gales.

Q. 357. All this is a variable figure. I want to see how you arrive at that. As I understand the matter, in dealing with the coal you get its selling price, that is the ultimate value of the coal, what the coal is worth in the market. There are three items which must be defrayed out of that selling price in an ordinary colliery. First there must be the cost of getting it, winning it as you call it, or, as we should call it in Staffordshire the "Charter". You have the cost of getting the coal. Secondly, you have to pay the mine owner his royalty, which represents his ownership of that specific mineral; and, thirdly, you have got to get the profit which the worker of the coal must have for having found the capital to work the mine. You have to get those three things, and of course if it is 10s. a ton it is one set of figures; if it is 15s. a ton it is another set of figures; if 20s. a ton it is another set of figures? – Yes, that is so.

Q. 358. Is there a customary royalty? – The royalties vary in each gale. I am advised by the deputy gaveller what the Crown's claim of one-fifth, after the coal is won, is worth in each case.

Q. 359. Worth as a royalty? – Worth as a royalty. Take for example where coal is lying on the surface, the winning of coal there costs nothing practically. We say it costs nothing; therefore the Crown is only entitled to one-fifth of whatever royalty you pay; but if the coal is lying 500 feet deep the Crown is entitled to more than one-fifth of the royalties.

Q. 360. One-fifth of what? – One-fifth of a full royalty.

Q. 361. What is that? – Suppose that the royalty was 1s. in the case of lying on the surface; suppose it was 1s. below the surface; supposing it to be the same coal, your royalty below would be reduced in consequence of the cost of sinking that 500 feet. That cost of sinking is not taken into consideration in fixing the Crown royalty, so that the interest of the free miner may be almost swallowed up by a 2,000 feet sinking, whereas the interest of the Crown remains pretty even, not of course quite even, because you would to bring the coal to the surface, and that cost would reduce the Crown royalty; but it is the duty of the deputy gaveller to advise me what the one-fifth share of the Crown is when the coal is won in any particular case. He takes into consideration the cost of winning.

Q. 362. Does not the value of that royalty depend upon the selling price of the coal? –

No doubt the selling price of the coal eventually fixes the royalty.

Q. 363. What do you put the royalty at in this case? – Two-pence, I think, or 2½d.

Q. 364. Why did not you put it higher? – Because we had no right to do so. The deputy gaveller advised me that that was the full value of the one-fifth share of the Crown.

Q. 365. What the deputy gaveller advised you is a division sum which any one can work out for you, what is one-fifth of a specific figure. We want to know how to arrive at that unknown quantity of the royalty. You know as well as I do that coal now, I suppose, in the Forest of Dean is 2s. a ton more than it was 12 months ago? – We must take it at the time the operation goes on; the time that the grant is made.

Q. 366. Then the deputy gaveller fixes his royalty at the time according to the price of the article in the market. Let us put it in this way: your deputy gaveller, for some reasons which you consider satisfactory, fixes what he considers is the proper royalty, and then one-fifth of that is calculated to be the Crown's share of it, and upon that you offer? – I cannot admit that last part, because there is a qualification "after the coal is won".

Q. 367. After the coal is won; you fix the royalty, then you deduct the cost of winning the coal, and the Crown gets one-fifth? – Yes.

Q. 368. That being so, you tell us as a matter of fact that these lessees, to whom you grant these gales, do not work them themselves; they sell them? – Generally speaking.

Q. 369. As a rule? – Where they are small ones they work them themselves.

Q. 370. Can you give us any idea of the profit they make? – No, I do not know how one could get at that.

Q. 371. Is it a considerable profit? – I think it has been. No doubt it has been in some gales. I do not know of any large profit lately on any one.

Q. 372. Say that the cost of sinking pits and opening the mine would be something like £100,000? – That is an extreme case.

Q. 373. A very large outlay of capital would be required, which not one of those free miners, who have been occupied a year in the pits, has the means of raising? – There is no doubt about that.

Q. 374. To one person, on behalf of those 174 people, you grant, with the consent of the 173, this mining lease so to speak? – Yes.

Q. 375. He then sells it to a promoter or speculator? – Yes.

Q. 376. Then the promoter forms a public company? – Yes, or works it himself.

Q. 377. Or a private company for the purpose of working the mines; and a large sum of money passes into the pockets of the first promoter who does the work; and, secondly, to the 174 people who have surrendered their rights? – Whatever sum is obtained for the gale will be divided amongst the 174.

Q. 378. What I want to ask you now, as the Senior Commissioner of Woods and Forests, is, whether you consider that is a satisfactory mode of dealing with the Crown property? – It is the mode in which I am obliged to deal with it.

Q. 379. Never mind the mode in which you are obliged to deal with it; we will come to that afterwards; do you think it is a satisfactory mode of dealing with it, or that it would be if you were not obliged to deal with it in that particular way? – I think all divided interests in property are bad, and cause great difficulties.

Q. 380. That is not my point; my point is not as a divided interest; do you think, if you were advising a nobleman or private owner to make the best of his property, that any nobleman or private owner in the Queen's Dominions would adopt such a mode of dealing with his property? – Certainly not, but there we are. This is the custom of Dean Forest, under certain Acts of Parliament, and the rules of Forest, and I must act accordingly. I think the position is a disastrous one myself.

Q. 381. You think the position is a disastrous one, and that the only justification for it is the actual wording of the Act of Parliament? – The justification of it is that these free miners have acquired a certain property, a certain right, which they greatly value. I do not know that there is any reason why we should deprive them of it. We are now experimenting in this way to see whether we can get the deep seams worked without having recourse to what was proposed some years ago, that is to abolish the free miners' interests so far as regards those deep gales.

Q. 382. Their rights are confirmed by Act of Parliament? – Their rights are confirmed by Act of Parliament. They have come down from time immemorial, I suppose.

Q. 383. And defined by Act of Parliament? – And are now defined by Act of Parliament [1838].

Q. 384. But outside that Act of Parliament you think it is a very disastrous method of dealing with Crown property? – I do not think I should explain myself perfectly well if I said so. Considering what the position is, the present arrangements are all you can make. I do not know how you could improve upon them without getting rid of the free miner. I have tried to improve the position to the extent I have mentioned. I waited until I had the chance of putting a large area together; and the free miners were very much pleased with it; 174 of them were in favour of one man who is well known in the Forest of Dean, a very capable man; and he is now doing his best to turn this property of theirs into money, perhaps into shares if he cannot get actual money for it. Beyond that there is only one peculiarity which struck me that we had no chance of getting over, but which perhaps a recommendation of this Committee might get over, and that is the necessity of revising the royalty every 21 years. That is to my mind objectionable. I do not know whether it will turn out so in this particular case. I am not an expert in mining; but my notion is that that capability of revision every 21 years might be a bar to a speculator taking up that which he would probably be willing to do if he had an assured royalty for 63 years. I think it would be well to extend the power of fixing the royalty practically to 63 years, instead of retaining the limit of 21 years.

Q. 385. Is that the term your leases are granted for, 63 years? – They are not leases at all. The thing becomes a freehold. It is granted to this free miner, and he sells it to whom he likes, but the royalty fixed is subject to revision every 21 years. I think that is rather a bar to the speculator.

Q. 386. You think it would be better if the royalty were fixed for a longer period? – I think it would get over that difficulty.

Q. 387. Have you any authority for that? – I think the thing is pretty evident. I only say it is qualified in this way: that the royalty itself every 21 years, if the Crown does not agree with the lessee, is subject to arbitration in the ordinary way. Arbitrators are appointed and the question of the royalty is actually fixed by them. We have had one arbitration just lately; so that the difficulty is not so great as it would be if there was not that provision for arbitration. I do not think capitalists like advancing their money even with a guard of that kind. They say, "It is all very well, but we do not know what arbitrators might do". I think it would be desirable to extend the royalty to 63 years. As I say, I am not an expert.

Q. 388. Do you not think it would be a disaster to the Crown supposing the price of coal went up? – It would be an advantage to the free miners, no doubt, if coal went up. Free miners would benefit by the greater security and the greater price they would get for their gale. At the same time the benefit to the Crown would be this, that if we cannot get the deep gales, the lower seams, developed without yielding, to that extent the Crown is losing. Certainly it would be to the advantage of the Crown to do something to have those deep gales worked.

Q. 389. Has the deputy gaveller reported that to you? – No. We have discussed the thing. I was not aware the Committee were likely to touch the Dean Forest, or the deputy gaveller would have been here.

Q. 390. We are going to have the deputy gaveller? – I think it would be better to have him.

Q. 391. How does a man become a free miner, can anyone being born in the district, and who comes in there, be a free miner, or must the parent be a free miner? – He must be born in the "hundred".

Q. 392. Accidentally born in the "hundred"; would that do? – Yes.[1]

Q. 393. Must his father be a free miner, or if his parents came to reside there for a week, and he happened to be born there, would he when he came of age be entitled to be a free miner? – He must be born in the "hundred", but it is not necessary to be the son of a free miner. He must work the day and a year in a mine, and be 21 years of age; but it does not follow that he need be the son of a free miner.

Q. 394. Then it is a vested right of a subject of Her Majesty, supposing he happens to be born there? – It is.

Q. 395. Supposing you repeated the operation of putting together a number of gales in another part of the Forest, and went through exactly the same process, would the 174 men who were applicants in the case to which you have referred be eligible to be applicants again? – A galee cannot hold more than three gales. All those that hold less than three would be eligible.

Q. 396. And there is no limit as to the extent of a gale? – They were all strictly limited by the Award. But when the gales come back into the hands of the Crown we claim to be able to unite them.

Q. 397. Therefore, supposing you united two or three other gales in another part of the Forest, would the men who would be applicants in the former case, and who presumably will reap a benefit supposing the company to be formed and the money acquired, be eligible again to repeat the operation with your freshly-united gales? – Yes, I consider so. I think distinctly that when I have united a number of gales they become one gale, and they are treated then as having only one gale.

Q. 398. You do not know how many of those free miners there are, do you? – About 1,200.

Q. 399. Is that the number on the register or the actual number you reckon there to be? – The number on the register.

Q. 400. The number who had taken the trouble to register themselves? – Yes, I daresay there are men who do not register themselves. I do not suppose there are very many who do not, because they are proud of their privileges.

Q. 441. I think you want to make one or two explanations, do you not? – Yes; if you would allow me I should like to do so. First as to the expenditure on account of mines in the Dean Forest. The figures which I have given, or rather the answers I have given, as to the payments to local officials, and so on, in the other places leading up to this one of Dean

---

1 A rather astonishing statement (C.H.).

Forest, do cover the whole expenditure; that is to say, in the case of Wales, for instance, and Scotland, and Ireland. When we get to the Dean Forest, say to this particular item of the mines, the payments to the local officials do not cover the whole expenditure. I have not seen my evidence, and I rather fancy the Committee might have been misled by a reference to a higher figure than that which covered these expenses. I should like to repeat what are the expenses of local management. The salary, including payment of clerk in registrar's and receiver's office through the deputy gaveller, was altogether for that year £903.

Q. 442. The answer is that you make the total cost of the Dean Forest £2,613? – That is not quite the figure. The figure is £2,533. However that is not important. I was only anxious to know whether that figure had been mentioned, and that being the case I had better give an explanation.

Q. 443. If you please? – I was going to say the payment to the deputy gaveller altogether, including his clerk in the registrar's and receiver's office was £903. Out of that the deputy gaveller pays £100 a year, I know, to a clerk, since he accepted the office of receiver as well as deputy gaveller.

Q. 444. What does that reduce his net income to? – I think his net income is reduced by one thing and another to something under £800. On the abolition of the separate office of receiver and registrar, Mr. Forster Brown, the deputy gaveller, undertook to collect the mining rents and his salary for that was £353 for that year. It was not quite a complete year; and out of that, as I say, he pays £100 a year to a clerk to help him in that capacity. Then mention was made from the notes I was then reading of an allowance of clerks of £202 10s. Those are actually the men who chiefly help him in the surveys under ground, and that is the payment made to them. There are the payment of £903 to the deputy gaveller, his commission on High Meadow Wood, £23; allowance for horse, £50; the clerks I mentioned just now £202 10s., and the cost of a mineral survey in addition to that, £61 12s. Then there come incidental expenses; I do not know whether I need read them all.

Q. 445. No, no; give us the total? – The total is £248 5s. I may mention one item there; for example, the cost of the repairs (gaveller's and receiver's office) is £55; then there come other things, poor rates, £1 19s. 5d., say £2.

Q. 446. Do not give us all these small items? – "Property tax allowed" is another, which is not even received; that is £3,665. It is not a receipt, yet that swells the apparent expenditure upon the property ; "moiety of tonnage paid to freeholders"; that is a thing I want to explain; it amounts to £298 in round figures; that is a mere incident of tenure. That is paid to owners of enclosed land outside the Forest of Dean, but within the Hundred of St. Briavels.

Q. 449. Do you say that the £2,600 includes £300 of income tax? – It includes £366 of income tax, and it includes this peculiar payment, which I would like to explain. It is a peculiar thing; the "moiety of tonnage paid to free-holders". The freeholders are the owners of enclosed land outside the forest boundary, but inside the Hundred of St. Briavels, still subject to the free miners' rights; they are entitled from the Crown to the payment of one-half the royalty received. The royalty, as I explained, was small, on account of the free miners' rights. In that case the freeholders are entitled to one-half the royalty; so that on one side of the expenditure appears this item, £298, which ought to have been really a deduction from the receipts. It appears on the expenditure side, and of course the expenditure on that item is 100 per cent.

Q. 550. I should like to ask one or two questions about the free miners. The free miners' rights are very ancient indeed, are they not? – Yes, and when their history begins is unknown.

Q. 551. Could you tell us very shortly how far they go back? – To one of the Edwards. I forget at this moment which it is, but it is either Edward the First or Edward the Third. Certainly it is as far back as Edward the First, because the free miners supplied a contingent for the siege of Berwick I think in the reign of Edward the First, so it must go back as far as that.

Q. 552. At any rate from time immemorial the free miners seem to have had the right of getting coal and ironstone? – From the time of the English kings. The grant was a grant from an English king.

Q. 553. And they are confirmed by Act of Parliament, are they not? – "Regulated" perhaps would better express it; by an Act of Parliament, since 1838.

Q. 554. They attach very great importance to these rights, do they not? – The free miners have a very strong attachment to their rights.

Q. 555. Do you think they also regard these rights as having some business value attached to them, as well as viewing them as sentimental rights? – They have I am afraid rather an exaggerated idea of their pecuniary value, but beyond that pecuniary value they have a very great attachment even to the mere name of "free miner", that is to say, the right to hold it.

Q. 556. You have never heard of any willingness on their part to dispose of their rights to the Crown for a sum of money out and out? – I have never heard of it except at an extravagant price; and not even then the whole of the right. With regard to a portion of the gales which would not have put an end to the right of the free miners, they might be willing to sell to the Crown, but at an exorbitant price.

Q. 560. Was any figures or sum named? – £5,000.

Q. 561. Is it not possible that the free miners from the sale of the lease of a single gale (as they are held now), might get as large a sum as that? – I should like to hear that they were going to get it; but that would be a very different thing to what existed at that time. What you are speaking of now is a combination of four different gales in the Forest. The position is altered altogether with regard to that one gale.

Q. 562. You do not think that at present the idea of the free miners would be at all favourable to receiving compensation for their rights from the Crown? – As far as I know, it would not be.

Q. 563. Are the Woods and Forest Office anxious at present to keep on those terms, or are they perfectly satisfied with the present state of affairs? – We are endeavouring at this moment to get over the difficulties that the position and rights of the free miners cause or have hitherto caused. We think that we have an opportunity just now (it may turn out good or it may turn out bad) to get the coal worked without infringing the rights of the free miners. I explained to the Committee at the last meeting of the Committee what had been done in the way of uniting four large gales, the smallness of the areas being one of the difficulties, no capitalist being willing to undertake such an expense as is necessary there except over a largish area. I took advantage of being able to forfeit four of the largest deep gales to unite them; and these have been galed to one man, representing 174 free miners, under the circumstances I explained to the Committee at the last meeting. There it remains. If the free miners who are now interested in that gale can persuade financiers to work the thing for them, the free miners' rights need not be interfered with at all.

Q. 564. Do you think that the free miners' rights act in the restriction of actual output of coal in the Forest at the present time? – I would rather you would ask that question of the deputy gaveller.

Mr. Culley then handed in the following statement[1]:

				£	s.	d.
'T. F. Brown [deputy gaveller] –						
Salary, including Payment to Clerks in Registry and Receiver's Office				903	5	4
Highmeadow Commission. 5 per cent. on mineral rents collected in the year 1886-7[2]				23	6	4
Allowance for Horse				50	0	0
Clerks				202	10	0
Mineral Survey				61	12	3
Incidental Expenses	£	s.	d.			
Cleaning Offices	13	17	11			
Postage	15	3	3			
Stationery, Advertising	101	4	9			
Coal, Gas, &c.	11	11	9			
Mineral Returns	6	6	0			
Filling up old Pits	6	0	0			
Gale Dinners	35	5	6			
Repairs, Gaveller's and Receiver's Office	55	0	0			
Rates and Taxes on Gaveller's and Receiver's Office	3	16	8			
				248	5	10
Poor Rates				1	19	5
				£1,490	19	2
G. E. Francis [receiver][3] –						
Salary and Expenses				81	9	10
Superannuation				271	3	10
Sir J. Campbell, Bart. –						
Salary				25	10	6
				£1,869	3	4'

Thomas Forster Brown,[4] deputy gaveller since March 1865, then gave evidence as follows:

'Q. 736. You are the deputy gaveller of the Forest of Dean? – I am.

Q. 737. Technically, the gaveller of the Forest of Dean is the First Commission of the Woods? – He is; and by the Act of Parliament his deputy must be some person skilled in mining.

Q. 738. How long have you held the office of deputy gaveller? – Since March 1865.

Q. 739. You have held the office then and been in the Forest of Dean 24 years? – Yes.

1 21 June 1889: App. No. 1.

2 This allowance ceased the next year being merged in Mr. Brown's salary, as Receiver.

3 Crown Receiver of Rents and Royalties for Dean Forest, Highmeadow Woods and the Manors of Staunton, English Bicknor, Newland and St. Briavels.

4 Pp. 31-41.

Q. 740. Were you employed previously under the Crown? – No.

Q. 741. You were a mining agent? – I was a mining agent at the time I was appointed.

Q. 742. Then you have practically under your control the whole of the mining interests of the Crown in the Dean Forest? – Yes, with the exception that the rents and royalties are reassessable every 21 years; and when they are reassessed Sir Warrington Smyth, the Crown inspector, joins me in a report on that subject.

Q. 743. Will you just explain to the Committee (that is what we have sent to you for) what are the mining rights and how the system of granting licences is carried out in the Forest; first tell us who are the free miners? – The free miners are all men over 21 years of age, who have been born within the Hundred of St. Briavels, which is considerably larger, and its outer boundary extends considerably beyond the boundaries of the Forest of Dean. They must have been born in the Hundred of St. Briavels, and they must have worked a year and a day in a mine. When, they have complied with that regulation they are entitled to come to the deputy gaveller and be registered as free miners. Being registered they have to produce a signed form stating the facts (which has to be witnessed by some one), and they produce their certificate of baptism. This being all in order in each case, I have no alternative but to register the man as a free miner.

Q. 744. You mean a certificate of "birth", I suppose? – A certificate of baptism.

Q. 745. The point is where the man is born, not where he is baptised, is it not? – Yes, the form which is witnessed states where he is born; but it has been considered and I have always insisted upon having also, as corroborative proof, the certificate of baptism.

Q. 746. But the certificate of birth is the legal register of where a man is born? – Yes, no doubt.

Q. 747. Then you enter him on your register? – Yes.

Q. 748. I will read this one sentence and ask you whether it is correct, then we shall have it on our notes. "Every free miner, duly qualified, claims the right to demand of the King's gaveller a gale, that is, a spot of ground chosen by himself for sinking a mine, and then, provided it does not interfere with the working of any other mine, the gaveller considers himself obliged to go, receiving a fee of 5s., and insert the name of the free miner in the gale book"? – Yes, that is according to the old customs, and subject to the modifications introduced by Act 1 & 2 Vict. c. 43 [1838] continues to be the custom.

Q. 749. That is the law? – Then I may add, the free miner cannot have more than three of those gales granted to him (any one free miner), and the grant must be to the first applicant of those free miners.

Q. 750. Then what size is the gale? – That is in the discretion of the gaveller and deputy gaveller. It has to be regulated by the conditions. For instance, the depth at which the minerals lie, the probable capital required to be expended, and so forth.

Q. 751. What is your average size? – It varies, because the coal-field is a complete basin. It crops out all round, and near the outcrop where the coal is shallow a very small area is sufficient to meet the requirements of the Act, whilst where the coal is deep and involves large expenditure the gale has to be a large area. I think Mr. Culley explained that one of the deepest gales which has lately been granted is about 2,000 acres in extent.

Q. 752. Is a gale ordinarily of such size as would justify the erection of a plant and the expenditure of capital to work what would be called the mine? – Yes, that is the intention. It is really a royalty area.

Q. 753. To such an extent that a man with only one gale could carry on a colliery? – Yes.

Q. 754. Now will you explain to us what the royalties are, and how they are fixed? – To begin with, the maximum of the royalties is the right of the Crown to put in a fifth man to work for the Crown's profit after the mine has been opened. That is the maximum.

Q. 755. How do you reduce that to cash value? – That is a very difficult and complicated operation, because the Crown mineral inspector and I have to advise the Commissioner as to what in our judgment that royalty would be, based on that maximum; and it is open to the free miner to say, if he likes, "That is too much"; and he can go to arbitration with the Crown to fix it at some amount that the arbitrator might decide; and, further, whatever royalty is fixed it is only fixed for 21 years in each gale, and it is open either to the gaveller on the one hand, or the free miner, or the person who has succeeded to the interest of the free miner on the other, to object or to wish to alter the rent at the end of every 21 years; and if they cannot agree, then that has to be referred to arbitration; and it very often happens that when an arbitration does occur, the Crown, in order to establish their interest, in an unopened mine for example, have to prove to the arbitrator first what in their judgment it will cost to sink the pits, the plant, and so forth; what then will be the quantity that will be worked; what then will be the profit realised, so as to get at the Crown's fifth proportion, and all that in case of dispute has to be gone into. Of course with experience and one's intimate knowledge of the mines and district it does not often happen that the galees go to that extreme course; but, for example, I had a case only this last year of that kind; and this bulky document which I hold in my hand contains the evidence and arguments, and it means a very complicated business.

Q. 756. What do you mean by a "complicated" case of that kind, is it an arbitration? – It is an arbitration to fix the new rents and royalties at the end of 21 years in two gales, but involves unusual assumption in the evidence.

Q. 757. That is at the expiration of 21 years? – Yes.

Q. 758. Now what I want to get at is, in the first instance, how the royalty is fixed; if I understand you aright what you mean is this: that assuming that this gale was a partnership property the Crown would have the right to put in one partner to four? – Yes.

Q. 759. The Crown make the fifth partner? – That is so.

Q. 760. The ascertaining what the cost of winning the mine would be the Crown's share of the profit is to be the gross profit and not the net profit? – Well, it would be the gross profit.

Q. 761. I want to understand whether that is so? – Yes, that is so, subject to this explanation: that the Crown are entitled to put in a fifth man after the free miner or his representative has opened the mine. Therefore, I mean the Crown have nothing to do with the expenditure involved in winning the mines, and as a result it turns out in this way, that if the mine is very shallow, which involves very little plant and very little expenditure, the free miner's interest might be very nearly really to the four-fifths, but if the mine is very deep, say it is 500 or 600 yards deep, the free miner will have to give away the whole of his interest in order to induce any capitalist to find the money to sink.

Q. 762. In an ordinary partnership of course every one of the five partners would have had to have paid his share of winning the mine? – Yes.

Q. 763. In this peculiar partnership the Crown pays no share of winning, but is entitled to one-fifth after it is won? – Yes, that is it.

Q. 764. Now I understand it; in the first instance, is there a power of arbitration as between the Crown and the free miner to fix what that sum should be the first time? – Yes, that is so; when the Commissioner says, "I am prepared to grant you a gale, and the royalty is so-and-so", it is open to the free miner to object, and to say, "That is too much", and go to arbitration if he wishes.

Q. 765. Does he ever go to arbitration? – No, he does not, because he wants to have his gale granted, and he thinks that this might interfere with his grant. I mean it is a kind of idea that he entertains.

Q. 766. We were told by Mr. Culley of a case in which 174 people applied for the same gale. How would the arbitration clause have worked there? – The 174 as a body of 174, through the representative who represented them, were in this position: it was open to them to go to arbitration and say that the royalty Mr. Culley fixed was too much.

Q. 767. Supposing half of them thought it was not too much, and the other half thought it was too much? – That is a matter they would have to work out. Mr. Culley would not take any proceedings to go into an arbitration unless the people that were wishing the arbitration were either in a majority, or at all events in a position to enforce the opposition.

Q. 768. Let us take two free miners; one man says, I am prepared to give 2d.; the other man says, I am prepared to give $2^1/_2$d. a ton? – It could only be granted to one in the name of both.

Q. 769. That I know; but I want to see whether the principle of competition comes in? – Well, I do not think it does very much in the first grant.

Q. 770. You yourself fix the first grant without competition? – Practically without competition.

Q. 771. Subject to the man saying you have fixed it at too high a figure? – Yes. The ground is let to one man, and it is open to him of course to object, but practically there is no objection. That is partly due to the fact, I presume, that the Crown exercise a sound judgment in fixing the rents at the beginning, and there are not many cases now of arbitrations at the end of 21 years, although as a matter of fact, the royalty has been increased. For instance, in 1842 the royalty averaged on coal under 2d.; now it is a little over 3d. On iron ore in 1842, I think it was about 2d.; if I remember correctly, and now it is $5^1/_2$d. nearly; that is to say, it is now 5.4d. on the iron and 3.1d. on the coal.

Q. 772. How long does the licence last? – It is granted in perpetuity, subject to the limitations I have mentioned.

Q. 773. Is it transmissible by will? – Oh, yes. Subject to what Mr. Gorst says, it is in the nature of a freehold, I think.

Q. 774. That is, a man who once having got a grant as a free miner, can devise that by his will to a man who is not a free miner? – Yes; the day he gets a grant he can sell it to someone else; and that is one of the bad features of the tenure. The tenure is about as bad as it can be really; but there it is, and I think Mr. Culley is very wise in trying to make the most of the present tenure, because there have been several attempts during my tenure of office to make some arrangement with the free mining interest, but there always have been so many difficulties, that it has been found impossible; for example, all the free miners have votes, and political interests arise in which I do not think the Crown's interest is always put to the front as it should be.

Q. 775. How many free miners are there now on the register? – 2,262 in the case of coal and iron mines, and 270 in the case of quarries. Of these there are probably 1,389 living of coal and iron free miners, and 103 of quarry free miners; that makes nearly 1,500.

Q. 776. Do you mean that the rights of those who are dead have lapsed? – Yes.

Q. 777. Then practically what you have to deal with now is with about 1,400 free miners who have the right to claim from the Crown a lease or license to get mines or minerals in this district on their paying what is equivalent to one-fifth of the gross profit to the Crown, and having got that they could sell it, and do what they like with it? – That is so.

Q. 778. I suppose as a matter of practical experience they do not work these mines themselves? – No, they are all men of no means; of course with a few exceptions. Mr. Samuelson will confirm that, that with few exceptions they are all men of no means, and their profit is to be derived from selling this concession to somebody else. The next person probably is a man who thinks he will make some money out of it, and simply buys it as a speculation; he does not open the mine but tries to retain it without spending any money, hoping to get some next man in who will find the money to develop it.

Q. 779. Having due regard to the vested interests of those 1,400 people, do you think it would be desirable in the interests of the public that this extraordinary tenure should be brought to an end? – I think as an abstract question there is no doubt that that would be a proper course, but then that is what ought to have been done in 1838 when these very rights were fixed and arranged and the rules and regulations prepared. If then the Government of the day had said, these men have a certain interest, and we will confine that to a belt round near the outcrop, it would have been the reasonable thing to do, because these men could have dealt with the shallow mine, and worked it themselves, or it would have involved very little money to have done it. Instead of that the Government thought proper to include in these regulations, which were only suitable for the shallower workings, the deep workings of the Forest involving a very large expenditure in order to develop them. That is the unsound part of the policy, but I do not quite see how the difficulty is to be got over.

Q. 780. It is now a pure money question to buy out the free miners' rights? – Yes; it is a pure money question. As Mr. Culley reminds me, it is not quite a money question altogether, because mixed up with it is a great deal of sentiment. These men for generations have had these interests; and people unborn of course are coming on.

Q. 781. Of course that is another question, and the same remark may be made as to all enclosures, that there is a sentiment, in the same way. Can you give us any idea what the value per acre is of one of these gales? – I do not think I ought to attempt to answer that question; it would vary entirely with the circumstances. I have drawn up an illustration which will show the point pretty well. If you will not mind looking at this I think you will at a glance see the point of it [handing in a document]. That is an illustration of two gales under different circumstances, showing what ultimately the free miners' position would be [the document is handed in].

Q. 782. I will read this to the Committee, "Dean Forest, Number 1; a shallow gale, area, say 100 acres". Is that an ordinary average area? – That is the ordinary area for a shallow gale.

Q. 783. The cost you put of winning coal is £4,000; machinery and appliances for raising is put at £1,000; annual produce, 30,000 tons, selling price 6s. per ton, that would be £9,000. You deduct first the cost of raising which you put at 5s. per ton, amounting to £7,500; then you put the interest and sinking fund on £1,000 at 5 per cent., £50, and trade risk and profit at 5 per cent., £50. You put another £100 on for that; you make the cost of getting and the interest upon the capital which gets the 30,000 tons, £7,600. That would leave a profit of £1,400 on that year's working. Then the Crown's one fifth of that is £280, which would be equivalent to the figure you gave us just now of 2¼d. per ton? – Yes.

Q. 784. Then the free miners' share who own the four-fifths, represents £1,120. Out of that £1,120 they find the whole of the machinery, and they have gone to the whole of the expense of sinking? – Yes.

Q. 785. You would deduct from that their interest and their sinking fund, at 5 per cent., you put it. Do you think that is sufficient in your district? – I think you will find I have added another 5 per cent.

Q. 786. You put the trade profit and risk at 5 per cent.; you have taken 10 per cent., all round. Do you think that that is enough? – I think it is.

Q. 787. Do you think that a man should be content with 10 per cent., out of which he is to replace his capital? – Well, of course I have rather a wide experience, and I question very much whether the colliery people, people who spend their money in mining, do on the average get more than 10 per cent.

Q. 788. That would leave a balance of £720? – Yes.

Q. 789. That would represent the value of what we may call the lessee's interest? – Yes, I wish to add to that, that therefore, practically, in that case the ultimate result is that the free miners' interest is about two-thirds, and the Crown's one-third.

Q. 790. It is £720; it is worth £7 per annum per acre? – Yes.

Q. 791. That is what it is? – Yes.

Q. 792. Mind you, the free miner finding all that work? – Yes.

Q. 793. Now we come to the case of the deep gale, of which the area is 1,000 acres? – Yes.

Q. 794. There you put the cost of winning the coal at £80,000; the cost of machinery and appliances for raising, £20,000; that makes a total of £100,000. Upon that £100,000 being spent, you say you may raise 200,000 tons a year, which would sell for £60,000; the cost of getting that £60,000, with interest and sinking fund and this moderate trading profit which you put on, is £52,000; that leaves a net profit of £8,000. The Crown's fifth of that you would put at £1,600, and the free miner's four-fifths you would put at £6,400. Of course from the free miner's profit has to be deducted the interest and sinking fund, and the trade profit, and the risk, which you put at £8,000; and there you make a balance against the free miner of £1,600 per annum? – Yes.

Q. 795. Of course an operation of that sort would kill itself. A man could not afford to pay you upon these figures a royalty of £1,600 a year? – No; therefore the opening would be deferred until profit per ton was higher.

Q. 796. He is losing by it ? – The practical effect of that would be, that if the free miner was not able to sell to someone who did not understand it, that the mine would not be open until the relative position was altered, and profit larger than 1s. per ton.

Q. 797. Yes 2d. a ton is not a very high royalty, is it? – It is the true position there, really.

Q. 798. According to these figures, you show that this would only produce a profit of 2d. a ton? – But you see in that case there might be no working until profit per ton increased.

Q. 799. Do you mean the "measure" could not be worked? – In that case it is too early to work the deep measures; that is to say, in that particular example.

Q. 800. These figures show that a capitalist spending £100,000 and managing the whole of the colliery himself, and only charging the concern with £8,000 in respect of that £100,000 as interest and sinking fund, at the end of the year has not one sixpence for himself? – Yes. I use that illustration only for the purpose of showing that the free miner's rights, although he may consider them valuable to him, may be worth less than nothing in the deeper portion of the mineral field.

Q. 801. Does that apply also to the Crown royalty? – No; for this reason, that the Crown have the right to put in their fifth man after the mine is opened. They have nothing to do with the expenditure in opening it.

Q. 802. I quite see your argument. Your argument is this, as I understand you; that in the case of the deep mine, practically the free miner is at a very great disadvantage compared with the Crown? – Yes.

Q. 803. In the shallow mine he has a valuable property. In the deep mine he has practically no property? – That is so. The Crown are practically the only people interested in the deep mine, in fact.

Q. 804. You are not prepared to suggest to the Committee any mode of dealing with these free miners' rights, are you? – I do not think so. I think that at all events I should prefer, so far as my judgment goes, to wait the result of the important experiment which Mr. Culley is now carrying out by way of giving the free miners as a body the opportunity of showing what they can do with these deep gales. I do not think I should like to commit myself to an opinion as to what ought to be done until we see the result of that important experiment.

Q. 805. That is the experiment of vesting in a trustee all the interests of a large number? – Yes; of course, it is quite clear the tenure is very unsound altogether; but the question is, how you are to get out of it. There have been several attempts in past years in various ways to meet the difficulty; and always when it came to a push it failed, because (very likely the sentiment, perhaps more than the reality, affected the free miners) they naturally, having votes, brought influence to bear on their various representatives; and whether from want of backbone or not, no Government seems to have been able to back up the Crown's position.

Q. 806. Are these free miners working miners? – Most of them.

Q. 807. Are they colliers? – Most of them.

Q. 808. Really working colliers? – Really working colliers.

Q. 809. And do not include capitalists in any sense of the word? – There are two or three exceptions, men who have made money, and obtained a position; but practically, taking the body of free miners, they are respectable working men.

Q. 810. And do they work as servants in pits in the Forest themselves? – Yes.

Q. 811. They obtain these licenses and then they at once proceed to sell them? – If they can.

Q. 812. No free miner can have more than three gales, I understand you to say? – That is so.

Q. 813. But I suppose anybody can buy more than three gales? – Oh, yes, there is no limit to that, of course.

Q. 814. The capitalist comes into the mining market and he buys as many gales as he can? – Yes.

Q. 815. Do you mean that the free miner cannot have more than three allotted, or that he cannot hold more than three? – One free miner cannot have more than three gales allotted to him. If one or more allotted are forfeited, the number may be made up again to three, supposing, of course, he is otherwise entitled.

Q. 816. But any capitalist can buy any number? – Yes.

Q. 817. Can you give us any idea of the number of real colliery owners, colliery lessees we will call them, in the Forest? – I think the best guide to that would be to give you the number of working collieries.

Q. 818. Yes? – I can give you that. There are 44 working coal mines, collieries, and 16 working iron mines.

Q. 819. That means separate concerns, does it not? – Separate concerns.

Q. 820. That is a diminishing number, is it not, the 44 and the 16? – More or less, I suppose it is. It is diminishing in this way, that some of the crop gales are working out; but, of course, as regards the deep gales it is rather increasing, because, as the deep coal is worked, the number of working gales is increased; the number of coal gales is 176. I have only given you the working gales.

Q. 821. If you consolidate them and put four gales together, as has been done, as I understand, in that last case, the consolidated gale would only count as one colliery? – Yes, but that is not working, and that, of course, is only with the deepest part of the field.

Q. 822. But that would tend to diminish the number, although not to diminish the area that is being worked? – It would in that particular case. There are 132 gales not working. I should explain that there are two series of coal seams.

Q. 823. Just one question on that point. When you say that there are 132 gales not working, does that mean that they have been opened and ceased to be worked, or partly one and partly the other? – Chiefly that they have not been opened, or that they have ceased to work, not been opened chiefly.

Q. 824. You have upwards of 1,400 free miners? – Yes.

Q. 825. You have 176 gales, I understand? – Yes, and 44 making 220.

Q. 826. You have 220 gales, of which 176 are not working, and 44 are working? – We have 60 working out of the 220, that is, including iron mines.

Q. 827. And the 60 gales are vested in 44 concerns; there are 44 collieries going, as I understand? – No, they are vested in 60, because the 60 includes the iron mines. The 44 are the collieries working, and the 16 are the iron mines working.

Q. 828. According to that each gale represents a colliery? – That is practically what it is.

Q. 829. Are there not several collieries in one hand? – Yes; do you mean pits? You are now referring to pits, I understand?

Q. 830. Yes? – Yes, there are cases in which the pits work more than one gale.

Q. 831. A gale may have a great many pits? – A gale may have a great many pits, and "pits" may have several gales.

Q. 832. I do not know what the phrase would be in your part of the world; but a colliery may extend over 1,000, 2,000, or 3,000 acres, may it not? – Yes, it might, but it does not, except in this case of Mr. Culley's consolidation.

Q. 833. You have only practically 44 collieries, and, including the ironstone, 60? – Yes.

Q. 834. Are the collieries getting both measures? – They are separate measures; separate gales.

Q. 835. I mean separate gales? – Yes.

Q. 836. You do not give a gale of coal and iron to the same man? – No, nor upper and lower series. We divide those.

Q. 837. Although you divide them. I suppose they frequently consolidate them before they work them? – No, not necessarily. The lower series extend over more than twice the area of the upper series. The upper series crop out in a lesser area about 6,500 acres than the lower. We have 16,200 acres of the lower series; 21,000 acres is the extreme extent of the iron ore field. Therefore the upper series were naturally opened first, and they have been pretty extensively worked, and the bulk of the coal is got from the upper series even now; the lower series being very much deeper, and the area of outcrop being very much wider, very much more encumbered with water; and there have been practical difficulties in getting the lower seams developed, and that no doubt influenced Mr. Culley in making the area so large in the particular case referred to, to justify the expenditure that would be necessary to develop so large an area of deep coal.

Q. 838. A fifth of the profit, not deducting the cost of sinking the colliery and the working plant, is a very large royalty, is it not, as royalties go generally throughout the kingdom? – No; I should think it is only about half the ordinary royalty.

Q. 839. Just reduce it to figures, how would that be? – My experience of an ordinary royalty is from 6d. to 9d. a ton.

Q. 840. But what I want you to make clear to my mind is this: whether you in fixing what you call the royalty are not fixing a very low sum in the first instance. If it was what you say it should be, it would give you an enormous royalty? – Take 2d. or $2^1/_2$d.; that would represent about 1s. per ton profit. Well, I doubt very much whether in the average of years collieries do produce more than 1s. a ton profit.

Q. 841. Including royalty? – Including the $2^1/_2$d. at all events; it is only $2^1/_2$d.; I doubt very much whether they do.

Q. 842. Do you think that is so in the case of collieries in Staffordshire and Yorkshire? – I should certainly think it is the case in Yorkshire. I do not know that it is so in Staffordshire.

Q. 843. What is the average royalty in the Barnsley district? – About 6d. to 8d., I should think.

Q. 844. What is the selling price? – The selling price, until just lately, has been exceedingly low. Very few of the collieries in Yorkshire, until the last 18 months, have been making any profits. Except one or two of the large ones they have not been making any money at all. Such collieries as Manvers Main, and some of those big mines that are working very large quantities and that have no faults or interruptions to trouble them seriously, have made a little money. I know one colliery (I do not know that I should name it) which was producing about 400,000 tons a year, and I do not think they made for years more than £10,000 or £12,000 a year. That is a good example of a good colliery in Yorkshire.

Q. 845. Sixpence a ton? – Yes.

Q. 846. Then they have paid a sixpenny royalty, and paid their outlay? – Yes, no doubt; that is 1s., but then that is an exceptional colliery. Our royalties in South Wales run from 6d. to 9d.

Q. 847. Is that steam coal? – That is steam coal, but then that is for the best coal; it is the first letting, and directly the best seams are worked out, the lessees go to their landlords and say "We cannot go on paying this 9d. royalty, we must have a reduction". The result is they have the reduction, and, practically, it is a sliding scale which only slides in one way, that is, against the landlords. He gets his maximum to begin with, but when the times become troublesome, the lessee goes for a reduction. In Cumberland, on the other hand, and, of course, in some other parts the royalties are on a pure sliding scale, which works very fairly, I think, and I have endeavoured to introduce it in some other districts. I have made several lettings lately on the sliding scale in South Wales, I think.

Q. 848. Not in the Forest? – No, you cannot, because there you are hit by this tenure.

Q. 849. You are fixed with the 21 years? – Yes.

Q. 850. Then as a practical mining surveyor, you think that the Crown is getting its fair royalty in this district? – I think it is. It is getting as full a royalty as the tenure; the condition under which they hold the minerals entitles them to, because the average royalty they get is about 3d. on coal and 5d. on iron, and after that what has been discussed here that would appear to be quite the full fifth.

Q. 851. What machinery have you for checking the output? – I get from the railway companies that take the whole of the traffic from the Forest half-yearly returns. My assistant checks the accounts with the books of the different gales, and in some cases I do it myself; then I myself check the whole of the returns with the railway returns from each colliery. Every half-year, therefore, in that way I get the accurate results, because if there is any discrepancy I follow it up until it is cleared up, with the exception of the few land sale collieries. There I inspect the books. I generally have the books brought to the office, inspect the books, and compare them with their returns; and the only difficulties I ever have in getting accurate returns are in the case of those very small land sales where the men are working men, and not over particular about the returns: and the way I manage to get them into order is by surcharging them if I find their books are not clear. I say "Very well, if you do not like to keep proper books, as you are bound by the rules and regulations to do, I shall charge you an extra quantity in this half-year's accounts, and if you want to get out of this kind of thing you must keep your books properly".

Q. 852. Mr. Culley was asked in question 195, "Do you work any of those mines yourselves?" and he said "None"; that is to say, you could not; you have not the right to work coal yourself except through the fifth man, have you? – No.

Q. 853. In fact you could not have any coal worked in the district at all except by granting first to the free miner? – At present that is so.

Q. 854. Talking about the sentiment attached to the free miners' rights, are not there some men who actually have worked a day and a year in a mine for the purpose of getting admitted later on as a free miner? – For the purpose of becoming registered, you mean?

Q. 855. Yes? – Oh, yes, there have been such. I only know of about two cases of that kind. I think one of the Brain's did that, if I remember rightly.

Q. 856. Do you think that the free miners' rights now in the pits which are at present working act as a restriction on the output of coal? – In this way, that a bad tenure always does retard and interfere with the development of a mineral field; and there is a very strong example here, I think. Of course it is impossible to particularise it, but for years and years the gale in the Forest of Dean, although not working, were in the hands either of speculators, or of a bank, as security, and it so went on. These people were not able to deal with it, and ultimately they found they were lending money on what appeared to be a sound investment, but which was not; it re-acted upon the Forest, and we have been suffering in the Forest of Dean for the last 10 or 15 years from the fact of the tenure being bad; and the money lent on those properties, instead of being lent to develop the property, being applied simply as a speculation and a loan.

Q. 857. But all that time the Crown were getting their dead rent? – Yes.

Q. 858. Their income was not suffering, was it? – Yes, it was suffering to the extent of not getting any surplus working on the working of the coal.

Q. 859. That is to say, not getting an income above the dead rent? – Yes.

Q. 860. Is it your opinion that the free miner's rights at present are preventing the deep coal from being worked? – I would not like to go so far as that. I would rather defer giving any opinion about the free miners until this experiment has been tested, because it is a *bonâ fide* attempt on the part of Mr. Culley to make the most of the Forest under the present rules and regulations in relation to the free miners. I would prefer not to express an opinion until we know the result of that experiment; I mean that I should rather like my mind to be open and myself at liberty to give such advice as I think the circumstances may justify at the time.

Q. 861. Has anybody ever succeeded in working these deep measures to a profit? – The Lightmoor and Foxes Bridge pits are 300 deep, and they are working. You refer to the lower measures?

Q. 862. I refer to the lower series? – They have been worked round the outcrop. It is only a question of tackling them properly, because the quantity of water, which is alleged to be the difficulty, is only the water due to percolation from the outcrop of that particular series. If it was tackled in one or two places, the quantity would be reduced at each opening. If, instead of as at present, having only one place where the drainage comes through, there were two or three, it would be reduced to one-third, and so on.

Q. 863. Which do you think is the greatest impediment to work the deep measures which cannot at present be worked; is it the free miners' rights or is it the water? – Well, I should think, in the first instance, it is the free miners' rights having affected the reputation of the Forest; that is one thing. Then, beyond that, no doubt the water has been a difficulty, because in one case, where an attempt to sink was carried out more or less, they had great difficulties with the water. There is no doubt that that operates; I mean that I think both circumstances operate. To what extent, or how much one operates more than the other, it is impossible to say, I think.

Q. 864. Has the Crown, or have you ever considered the propriety or the possibility of erecting pumping engines, and pumping the whole of the water from that deep coal, and charging an additional royalty to those who benefit by it? – I went into that very carefully some years ago, and came to the conclusion that it was not a practicable scheme at all. I took a lot of trouble, and, I think, I reported to Mr. Culley's predecessor, Mr. Howard. I came decidedly to the opinion that it was quite impracticable, and that the only way to deal with the lower measures was by individual speculators dealing with them. To begin with, if the Crown attempted to drain these lower measures they would have to sink one or two or more pits, establish pumping engines, then to make communications all round to get the water, then there would be all kinds of provisions as to how the rates were to be apportioned and divided among the various gales, so that the whole thing is totally impracticable, I am satisfied; and, I think, that the experience of South Staffordshire is not encouraging in that respect.

Q. 865. I suppose we have a good deal more water in Staffordshire than you have in the Forest of Dean? – Yes, no doubt. Still, this is a suggestion that the Crown should sink pits to drain a series of measures in a coal field. I do not think it is practicable, nor would it be judicious on the part of any public body to attempt to spend the public money in that kind of speculation.

Q. 866. Mr. Culley said something on Tuesday, and I could not quite understand what it referred to, with reference to an expenditure of about £1,300 a year for surveying or something of that sort in connection with these mines. Have you got a staff under you which does this surveying work? – I have one surveyor, and he has got a boy who carries the chain. They do the surveys, and they do the planning, and keep up the surveys of every one of the collieries and iron mines.

Q. 867. And make periodical visits down the mines? – Yes; these inspections are done every year. All round the Forest every mine has to be done every year, and if any question arises I go and inspect myself; for instance, if there is any point as to breach of barrier, or any question of that kind arising; and I may say that I personally surveyed every mine in the Forest during the earlier years of my appointment, and know the ins-and-outs pretty well of every mine, and by means of these surveys I keep up the knowledge in the gaveller's office, and the position of every gale is kept close up.

Q. 868. And the extent to which the coal is got? – That is the staff I have for surveying; that is really the deputy gaveller's staff. Beyond that two or three years ago Mr. Culley kindly advised the Treasury that I should take over the receiving of the rents. Well, I pay a clerk for assisting me in that out of my own salary.

Q. 869. When you say the "rents", do you mean the receipts for the royalties? – All the mineral rents; that is to say, all the rents except the quarries and the land rents.

Q. 870. Are they paid yearly or half-yearly? – Half-yearly. Then I hold an audit, and we have to dine these galees, and that is part of the expenditure which Mr. Culley put before you.

Q. 871. Then the quantity got is checked each half-year, is it? – Each half-year.

Q. 872. And the railway returns and other figures to which you refer are half-yearly accounts? – Yes.

Q. 873. You check the colliery returns by the railway returns? – First I check the colliery returns by the galee's books, and then afterwards by the railway returns.

Q. 874. Then we may take it from you that you do not feel able to make any practical suggestions for the improvement of the management of this colliery property, because the whole question is so entangled and complicated with these free miners' rights that unless you had a free hand you could not alter the present situation? – That is exactly the position. I am satisfied that the income of the Crown would have been very much larger years and years ago, but for the fact that their hands are tied and they cannot move.

Q. 875. But having regard to the free miners' rights and position, you think the public is getting as much as can be got under existing circumstances? – Yes, they are getting full value.'

Thomas Forster Brown, deputy gaveller, handed in the following statement[1]:

'No. 1 – A shallow Gale – Area 100 acres.

							£	s.	d.
Cost of winning coal							4,000	0	0
Machinery and appliances for raising coal							1,000	0	0
Annual produce – 30,000 tons.									
				£	s.	d.			
30,000 tons, selling price 6s. per ton				9,000	0	0			
Deduct –	£	s.	d.						
Cost of raising, 5s. per ton....................	7,500	0	0						
Interest and sinking fund on £1,000, at 5 per cent...	50	0	0						
Trade profit and risk on £1,000, at 5 per cent. ...	50	0	0						
				7,600	0	0			
				1,400	0	0			
Crown's one-fifth (About $2\frac{1}{4}$d. per ton.)				280	0	0			
Free miner's four-fifths				1,120	0	0			
Deduct –	£	s.	d.						
Interest and sinking fund on £4,000, at 5 per cent....	200	0	0						
Trade Profit and risk on £4,000, at 5 per cent.	200	0	0						
				400	0	0			
Balance for Free miner (Per annum.)				£720	0	0			

[1] 21 June 1889: App. No. III.

No. 2 – A deep Gale – Area 1,000 acres.

	£	s.	d.
Cost of winning coal	80,000	0	0
Machinery and appliances for raising coal	20,000	0	0

Annual produce – 200,000 tons.

	£	s.	d.	£	s.	d.
200,000 tons, selling price 6s. per ton				60,000	0	0
Deduct –	£	s.	d.			
Cost of raising, 5s. per ton	50,000	0	0			
Interest and sinking fund on £20,000, at 5 per cent.	1,000	0	0			
Trade profit and risk on £20,000, at 5 per cent.	1,000	0	0			
				52,000	0	0
				8,000	0	0
Crown's one-fifth (About 2d. per ton.)				1,600	0	0
Free miner's four-fifths				6,420	0	0
Deduct –	£	s.	d.			
Interest and sinking fund on £80,000, at 5 per cent.	4,000	0	0			
Trade Profit and risk on £80,000, at 5 per cent.	4,000	0	0			
				8,000	0	0
Balance against Free miner (Per annum.)				£1,600	0	0

If the cost of winning and machinery is greater, the loss would be increased; if less, the loss would be diminished.'

Sir James Campbell[1], deputy surveyor, answered:

'Q. 625. You have nothing to do, then, with the mines; your responsibility and duty is entirely with the Forest? – No, I have nothing to do with the mines as mines. I have to do with the letting of mines, for the better working of mines, that is, more, perhaps, with regard to the timber. The deputy gaveller decides whether it is proper to let land for a certain purpose; then I have to see that it does not interfere with anybody else, and that the timber, if there happens to be any on it, should be properly measured and the value paid for it.

Q. 626. The only power to let the land, as I understand, in the Dean Forest, is land for colliery purposes? – Colliery and mineral purposes generally.'

Sir Warrington W. Smyth, F.R.S.[2] chief mineral inspector to the Commissioners of Woods, deposed:

'Q. 3043. You do not interfere at all with the Forest of Dean, do you? – Yes, most of the questions are referred to me in conjunction with the deputy gaveller; and I have at times visited underground all the iron works, and a great portion of the collieries which are working; so that in the event of any difficulties arising I feel pretty familiar with the nature of the ground, and discuss the matter with the deputy gaveller, so that we may form joint conclusions on the subject.'

1 Pp. 29-33.

2 P. 129.

Sydney Elsom[1], free miner, of Yorkley, followed:

'Q. 4024. You are also a freeminer? – I am.

Q. 4025. And you appear here on behalf of the free miners? – Yes.

Q. 4026. In consequence of a public meeting held by them? – Yes.

Q. 4027. And also you appear as trustee for the Deep Amalgamated Gale, which the free miners as a body hold? – I do.

Q. 4028. You represent those 174 individuals, do you not? – Yes.

Q. 4029. You represent their interest? – Yes.

Q. 4030. Are you a free miner yourself? – I am.

Q. 4031. Are you qualified in the usual manner? – I qualified by working a year and a day in a mine; and I was born in the Hundred of St. Briavels.

Q. 4032. Then you can speak for the free miner as to the great value they attach to their rights? – They set a very high value upon their rights.

Q. 4033. Do you think that that value is not merely sentimental? – I do.

Q. 4034. That in the past they have made considerable profits from their rights? – Yes, they have.

Q. 4035. And that they believe that they are able to do so in the future? – Yes, and might I say further that they believe that the existence of the rights tends to the development of the hidden resources of the Forest.

Q. 4036. Do you say that they derive practical benefit, at present, from their rights? – Yes.

Q. 4037. In what way is that? – They derive practical benefit, or they have in the past, by having grants made to them which they have been able to sell to a capitalist or, if the grant has been a land seam, they have been able to work it themselves to a profit. If they have had to sell to capitalists they have benefited themselves, and also done something towards developing the trade of the district.

Q. 4038. That applies to the upper seams, does it not? – That applies to the upper seams.

Q. 4039. Are those upper seams nearly worked out? – Very nearly. Practical men say they may possibly last 12 or 15 years longer.

Q. 4040. But you believe that the free miners have still got a great interest in those deep seams? – Yes.

Q. 4041. As well as their past benefit? – Yes.

Q. 4042. It was for the benefit of those whom you represent, that Mr. Culley amalgamated several deep gales lately, was it not? – It was.

Q. 4043. And the free miners were very much pleased with his action in the matter were they not? – They were.

Q. 4044. A large body of the free miners, applied for a gale? – Yes; about 170 or 180.

Q. 4045. And they were induced to forego their separate rights in order, as a corporation, to have the gale granted to them? – Yes.

Q. 4046. And they chose you as their trustee to negotiate for them? – They did.

Q. 4047. How long is it since that grant was made? – Two years next September.

Q. 4048. Have you made any attempt to work the property? – Yes; ever since we have had the grant we have been attempting to do something.

Q. 4049. To work it? – No, not that.

---

[1] Pp. 168-74.

Q. 4050. But you have tried to dispose of it? – We have.

Q. 4051. Have you had negotiations with anybody concerning your property? – Oh, yes.

Q. 4052. Do you believe that you are going to bring them to a good issue? – The prospects now are very bright and we are very hopeful.

Q. 4053. Then it is not correct, in your experience, to say that capitalists or others who have wished to open up negotiations with you, have been prevented by the fact that you were a body of men instead of one individual owner? – Oh, no; for all correspondence has been carried on by myself.

Q. 4054. You have not found anybody who was shy of the thing, because it belonged to a great number of persons instead of one individual? – No.

Q. 4055. Of course you cannot speak as an engineer, or anything of that sort, but do you think the existence of the free miners' rights has impeded the development of the resources of the Forest? – I do not. I quite agree with what a practical man like Mr. Thomas has said, that is, that they do not impede but rather help the development of the trade of the district.

Q. 4056. And you do not think that they restrict the output at the present time? – Not in any way.

Q. 4057. Mr. Forster Brown handed in a statement showing that the free miners' right is very considerable in the shallow gales, but that in his opinion the free miners' right was practically swamped by the expenses in the deep gale. As free miners do you agree with that? – Among the applicants interested in the United Deep Colliery gale, we have several very practical men; one or two who are managers of some of the largest collieries in the Forest of Dean; and they have taken considerable trouble to estimate what will be the probable cost of putting down a pair of pits, putting up the engine house, erecting the necessary machinery, putting in sidings; and then upon a given out-put they have come to the conclusion that the profit would be from 1s. to 1s. 6d. a ton.

Q. 4058. So you think that in those particular cases, certainly, the free miners have a large interest? – Certainly.

Q. 4059. Have you got any suggestions that you would like to make to the Committee on behalf of the free miners? – No; we are very pleased with the action taken by the Commissioner of Woods and Forest in amalgamating the gales, thinking that was a necessary step towards the development of the lower seams.

Q. 4060. You would not have any objection to Mr. Culley, if he had the right to do so, amalgamating other gales which are not the property of the free miners, but which are the property of other holders at present, in order that they might be worked? – It is a question I have not considered. I may point out to the Committee that the free miners are interested in any forfeiture of a gale, and if there was a probability of gales being forfeited, then it would be for their benefit that such forfeiture should take place.

Q. 4061. But the forfeiture at present, as Mr. Thomas has shown, do not take place as a rule; but a re-grant is made for another five years as a rule? – I may say that forfeitures preceded the action of the First Commissioner; when he amalgamated the gales, the gales were forfeited; then he amalgamated them together into one, and if either of the deep seams, now held by capitalists and not worked, were forfeited, then it would be for the benefit of the free miner.

Q. 4062. But in the existing state of affairs the free miner does not wish to see these gales continually forfeited. What he would wish would be to see them worked, would he not? – Yes.

Q. 4063. There is no selfish policy of the other kind on their part? – No.

Q. 4064. But they desire what is for the good of the district? – The good of the district is really the good of the free miner.

Q. 4065. Their feeling as colliers is stronger than their feeling as free miners in that respect, is it not? – Certainly.

Q. 4066. At the same time they would view with dissatisfaction any recommendation by this or any other Committee to get rid of them altogether? – Yes; they believe that the existence of the free miners' rights, as I have intimated before, tends rather to the development of the coal measures of the Forest; because experience has shown that the capitalist can get better terms from the working free miner than from a person who is in independent circumstances.

Q. 4067. Do you know any case in which valuable tracts of coal have been sold by the miners for a very small sum? – I may say as regards the present grant, which is a very expensive grant, we are not asking anything like its worth. We are most desirous to see the measures developed and we are asking a very small sum indeed.

Q. 4068. Your principal idea is to see the measures developed? – Yes; and to get some recognition of our rights.

Q. 4069. That is to say, of the commercial value of your rights? – Yes.

Q. 4084. You do not want your rights interfered with; you consider that Mr. Culley's present policy of uniting the gales, and of dealing with the free miners through a representative of a large number (as you have been yourself of that 174) a wise policy, and you are anxious that it should be persevered in? – Yes.

Q. 4169. You spoke about the very high value which the free miners put upon their rights; have you any idea what the value is estimated at? – It is impossible to assess the value of the rights.

Q. 4170. Then it would be impossible to express any opinion as to the value? – I think so; we think (and we are of opinion that history justified us in thinking) that they have assisted materially in the past in opening up the mineral resources of the Forest.

Q. 4171. Yes; but that was not exactly my question; my question was as to whether it would be possible to estimate the value of the free miners' rights in the coal? – I quite see what you mean.

Q. 4172. You have never yourself made any estimate? – No.

Q. 4173. You have never put it as high as £3,671,000? – Oh, well, if you put it in that way, I understand what you mean; that has reference only to the present grant; I went upon the basis of the Crown's one-fifth claim in a speech I made at the Speech House. I say that if the Crown claimed as their one-fifth share 2½d. a ton then the interest of the free miners, considering that they were entitled to four-fifths, would be very large indeed; that is the ground I went upon.

Q. 4174. You did make that statement then in a speech which you made, that you estimated the value of their rights at £3,760,000? – Taking as a basis the claim of the Crown.

Q. 4175. I do not mind about the "basis", or whether you work that out correctly, but as a matter of fact you did state that in your opinion the free miners' rights were worth £3,760,000? – Yes; but if you please I must ask the Committee to remember that I took as a basis for that the one-fifth claimed by the Crown.

Q. 4176. Then you do not think the free miners' rights are worth £3,760,000? – No.

Q. 4177. You think it would be impossible, I suppose, to reduce them to a sum of money? – Yes, I do think it is impossible.

Q. 4178. And that any attempt to reduce them to cash value would meet with considerable opposition on behalf of the free miners? – Yes.

Q. 4179. They would prefer the present state of things to any attempt to reduce it to a money value, you think? – Yes.

Appendix No. 16 of the Minutes of Evidence of 1889 included a Return of Receipts and Expenditure in Dean Forest for the years 1850 to 1888 inclusive, from which the Receipts from Mines Department (but not the Expenditure on Mines Department) can be deduced. On 26 July 1889, the Select Committee reported the Minutes of Evidence, but owing to the impossibility of concluding their investigations in that Session they recommended that a Committee on the same subject should be appointed in the next Session of Parliament. Consequently a new Committee was appointed on 26 February 1890. Mr. Culley was the only person who put forward relevant information before the Committee:

'Q. 53. There has been a great deal of evidence about this division of gales; without going into any discussion of the question now, just tell the Committee shortly what you would ask? – We speak now of Section 21 of the Act 24 & 25 Vict. c. 40. The marginal note to that section says, "Gaveller or deputy gaveller with consent of owners, may unite or divide two or more gales, or parts of gales, and re-grant them to the persons entitled after surrender duly made"; but the text of the section itself omits the power to add; it only gives power to divide. This section only authorises the division of gales, not their union. It should be amended so as to agree with the rubric or marginal reference, as it is of great importance to the future prosperity of the Forest mining industry that the gaveller should have power to unite the deep gales so as to encourage galees to incur the expense of sinking to the deep coal. The area of coal comprised in some of the deep gales may not be found large enough to warrant the outlay necessary to win the coal. If you will remember, Sir, there was a good deal of evidence given about the uniting of a large area over the deep seams which came about, because four gales became subject to forfeiture. Under those conditions I was enabled to amalgamate all the gales together, and to re-grant them as one gale. I believe the thing has been a success. I am not so much in the secrets of the Forest, perhaps, as Mr. Samuelson, but I believe that that has succeeded; that, however, can only take place under forfeiture. What we ask for here is this: Suppose a man happens to have purchased two gales adjoining each other, and wants to work them as one concern, we want the power, on surrender, to amalgamate them; so that there would be first of all no necessity for a wayleave for example; there would be one set of books; there would not be a separate account to be kept for each gale.

Q. 54. That was all to be done by consent. You are simply asking for power if the parties consent? – That is so.

Q. 55. I think, with reference to what you call "the rubric", the marginal note of this Act of Parliament, I should think the real history of the clause would be this: that the Bill, as originally brought in, did give them power to unite, that that was struck out, and that the marginal note was left as it was before? – Possibly; I do not know.

Q. 82. About the amalgamation of the gales; as I understand you, you recommend that at any time owners may surrender any two or more adjoining gales, and that you should then have the power to re-grant; and you say that by this means wayleaves are avoided? – I do not say that that is the object, but that would be one of the consequences. The object is to simplify the title, for example; let a man start with a clear title for one work which had formerly been two to prevent two separate accounts being kept.

Q. 83. Will surrender be necessary for the purpose? – Yes, I think a surrender would be necessary; there would be no difficulty about that. If there are two holdings you surrender both and unite them in the re-grant.

Q. 84. Would it be necessary to wait until the end of the term of the lease? – No; it might be done at any time. We have power under that section that has been referred to to divide, but we have not power to amalgamate.

Q. 85. But I suppose the amalgamated properties would be for the same period of years as the original lease? – These grants are really in the nature of a freehold. As long as the conditions of the grant are fulfilled they are really in the nature of a freehold'

The Select Committee of 1889 finally reported on 30 July 1890 as follows[1]:

'The Committee are of the opinion, that, having proper regard to the rights of commoners and the convenience of those engaged in mining industries, the best available income is obtained from the surface whilst, as in the New Forest, regard is paid to the preservation of the natural beauty of the woods.

Possibly a larger income might be obtained by the sale of the surface and the reinvestment of the proceeds; but a difficult question would have to be dealt with in the purchase of the rights of commonage enjoyed by tenants and freeholders of certain parishes. This would be detrimental to the welfare of, and repugnant to the feelings of, the inhabitants of the district; whilst the destruction of the Forest would be most regrettable.

It is doubtful whether an "Assistant to the deputy surveyor" is required for the surface of Dean Forest, considering the large number of wood foremen and keepers.

The Committee have taken evidence as to the peculiar conditions under which, by customs confirmed by Acts of Parliament the mineral properties in the Dean Forest (both coal, ironstone, and quarry stone) are "galed" (leased) to free miners only on perpetuity leases, which are in almost all cases alienated by the original "galees".

They have not considered it within the scope of their inquiry to examine to what extent these peculiar conditions are, or are not, conducive to the further development of the mineral field, nor as to the desirability or feasibility of purchasing or extinguishing the interest of free miners in the undeveloped properties. Evidence was, however, taken as to some modification under existing conditions, which ought to be made in the laws which direct the conduct of the Commissioners.

In the Forest of Dean sites have been granted by the Crown for Churches and Church schools, whilst Nonconformist bodies for their places of worship, and the ratepayers for their board schools, have been compelled to pay a full competition price for their sites. Contributions in money also have been made towards the purposes of the Church of England. The Commissioners are advised that they are entitled only to make such grants or contributions to the Established Churches of England and Scotland … The Act of 24 & 25 Vict. c. 40 only authorises the division of gales in the Forest of Dean, not their union. It is of great importance to the future prosperity of the mining industry that the gaveller should have power to unite the deep gales so as to encourage galees to incur the expense of sinking to the deep coal. The

1 Report from Select Committee on Woods, Forest and Land Revenues of the Crown with Minutes of Evidence (Ordered to be printed 30 July 1890), pp. 7, 8 and 12.

area of coal comprised in some of the deep gales may not be found large enough to warrant the outlay necessary to win the coal. In such cases of amalgamation wayleaves and tolls should be avoided.

At the request of the galee or galees, the Commissioner, in granting a gale, should have power to fix the period of revision of the royalty at a longer term than 21 years. In some cases this would be an inducement to purchase and develop a deep gale. In cases where timber is destroyed or cut down by the necessary operations of mining (as, for instance, in the case of uninclosed "tipping ground"), only the value of the timber as growing timber should be charged.'

On 19 March 1891, the deputy gaveller, Thomas Forster Brown, gave evidence[1] before the Royal Commission on Royalties. The following has been extracted as of interest for this present volume:

Q. 14,079. I think you said that you were now mineral adviser to the office of Woods and Forests? – I am.

Q. 14,080. That is to say, in respect to those mineral properties which are in the hands of the Government, and are managed for the Government? – That is so. I also act specially, and have done for 25 years, for the Crown in the Forest of Dean.

Q. 14,081. I believe the customs of the Forest of Dean are totally different to any other customs almost in the world? – They are very peculiar; the tenure is an exceedingly peculiar one.

Q. 14,082. Is it not in the nature of a privilege, giving mineral rights to persons born within a certain area? – Yes. Working men born within a certain hundred have power, if they have worked a year and a day in a mine to come to me to be registered, and then they become what are called free miners, and they are entitled to apply for a grant of an area or a royalty of coal or iron, the first applicant being entitled to the grant. The area of the grant is within the control of the gaveller, and deputy gaveller; but the royalties, in case of dispute, can be settled by arbitration. The royalties only remain in existence for 21 years, when they can be re-adjusted either on the application of the Crown or on the application of the galee; and in case of dispute it may be referred to arbitration.

Q. 14,083. What is the principle on which the royalty is assessed? – The basis of the maximum of the royalty is the right which the Crown has to put in a fifth man to work after the mineral has been won. The effect of that is, that as regards a shallow mine or a shallow colliery, the free miner secures a considerable interest; but as regards a deep mine where the capital outlay is great, he has to give up or will have to give up the whole of his interest to compensate the person who sinks.

Q. 14,084. What happens with regard to those rights which the free miners obtain; do they work them themselves? – No.

Q. 14,085. What do they do? – Immediately a free miner acquires a right over an area, he goes into the market and endeavours to sell on the best terms he can get to a man who may be either a speculator or a man of capital who is going to open; if he is a speculator, he holds it with the hope of being able to sell to someone else at an improved price; if he is a person who puts his own money in and is going to work the mine, of course he proceeds at

1 2nd Report, of 1891.

once to work.

Q. 14,086. In point of fact, he is in very much the same position as a concessionaire would be in Spain, or in any of those countries in which the minerals belong to the Crown, and are given to concessionaires on application? – Yes, that is the simple operation; the result has been most fatal to the development of the Forest of Dean.

Q. 14,087. Will you explain how it has been so injurious to the development of the Forest of Dean? – To begin with minerals were sold to speculators; the speculators went to the Banks for loans on the security of these properties; the Banks, I suppose, had not appreciated the unsoundness of the properties, but the time came when those minerals had to be opened, under the rules and regulations, or they had to continue to pay rents without any result. As time went on the banks became aware of the unsound nature of the property, and they of course brought pressure to bear, and the result was a general collapse of the whole thing.

Q. 14,088. You gave some evidence, I think, on this subject a year or two ago, before the Committee of the House of Commons upon Woods and Forests? – I did.[1]

Q. 14,089. Have you looked into that evidence lately? – Yes.

Q. 14,090. Would you wish to add anything more to what you said upon this matter then? – I do not think so, except this: That although Royalties are very low, I do not suppose that in the Forest of Dean we have increased our output more than from 5 per cent. to 10 per cent. over the last twenty years.

Q. 14,092. Can you compare the development of the Forest of Dean, under this system, with the development of any similar properties, with similar coal, in the hands of private individuals in the neighbourhood? – I do not think so. There are so many other conditions entering into consideration, that I do not think I would be in a position to compare them. There is only the broad fact that although the Forest of Dean is well inland, and ought to have geographically, a position for supplying a great many markets, it seems to be successfully competed against, by the Midlands on the one side, and by South Wales on the other, so that in the Forest of Dean they have not been able to increase their output materially.

Q. 14,168. Difficulties arise frequently, I presume, between lessees and the Ecclesiastical Commissioners in relation to their property, and the lessees make applications frequently for reductions in the royalty charges? – I do not know that I can speak to that. I do not represent the Ecclesiastical Commissioners in the principal part of their property.

Q. 14,169. In that part of the country where you do represent them, have you had any difficulties? – It is a very small matter: I never had any difficulties.

Q. 14,170. You have had none? – No.

Q. 14,171. Have you had any in that part of the country which is owned by the Commissioners of Woods and Forests? – I have only held that appointment under the Woods and Forests a few months.

Q. 14,172. Have you had any such difficulties in the Crown lands of the Forest of Dean? – Yes, I have had to do with them, but there they are under this particular tenure which I have described.

Q. 14,173. You say that the power of arbitration exists there? – Yes.

Q. 14,174. They can appeal to arbitration as differences arise? – Yes, and a most complicated and most difficult business it is.

---

1 Appendix LII (p. 416 of this Rpt.). His evidence has already been included in this Chapter, taken from the Report of 1889.

Q. 14,175. It does not work well? – No.

Q. 14,176. Neither to the satisfaction to the lessee nor that of the Crown? – I do not think the Crown can complain.

Q. 14,177. The difficulties are all on the side of the lessees? – I think it is worse for the lessees; but still it is a very cumbrous and unsound mode of assessing the royalty.

Q. 14,178. Do the lessees often appeal to arbitration? – Not very often. I think they have got tired of it

By S.3 of the Crown Lands Act, 1894 (57 & 58 Vict. c. 43) a moiety of the gross rents and royalties received by the Commissioners of Woods was ordered to be credited to the Capital Account and likewise the expenditure on mines to be debited. The remaining half was to be credited and debited respectively to the Income Account. However, there has been some difficulty in this connection, for the expenditure applicable to minerals as opposed to timber etc. cannot be accurately distinguished, as the annual contributions etc. to, and repairs of, schools, churches, etc., as well as the gratuities in lieu of poor etc. rates, to which the plantations were not legally liable, is borne by the Crown, in consideration of the necessities of the mining population. These expenses, together with a portion of the cost of the roads, should properly form a charge upon the revenue from the minerals. As examples of such expenditure, under the Act of 5 & 6 Vict. c. 65, £10,347 8s. 5d. was expended in 1845-6 for the endowment and increased stipends of the ministers of the Forest churches, and in 1848-9 the sum of £333 6s. 8d. for a fund for the repairs of Cinderford Church. However, the Crown's accountants have not always been consistent in the charging of such expenditure for we find in some cases that donations to schools and hospitals have been debited to the Mines Account.

It is of interest to include at this stage the following remarks made in a book of 1887 by a free miner – Timothy Mountjoy[1]:

> 'The original free miners' rights was not confined to the Forest of Dean, but extended to all the parishes of the Hundred of St. Briavels; the whole of the parishes were subject to the rights of free miners. I had understood that the recent sales to the Foresters would put the new purchases upon the same footing as the old freeholds, but since I have looked at several of the conveyances, I am apprehensive that they are not put on the same footing, though I think they ought to be; the new sales ought to be put on the same footing as the old freeholds that were legalised some years ago by Act of Parliament. The right of a free miner is this, to have a gale granted to him that has not been already to him, granted the whole of the gales, so far as the coals are concerned, are taken, there may be here and there a spot of coal or tract of coal not taken. Our Forest collieries are now in the hands of purchasers from the miners, and in the hands of a few individuals; the free miners are not very many in number, and their rights now are practically of little value, I speak now as to coal gales; there may be some iron gales of some value, but it would be almost impossible to say whether they will be of any money value at all to the free miner; the actual value at present is not great, because most of the mines have been awarded or applied for twelve years ago. The number of registered free miners stood at 1,200 then, but by today they have decreased; very few

[1] *Op. cit.*, pp. 47-8.

think that the value of free miners at present is worth any consideration; I should not assess it at any great sum. The people who have been really benefited are not the free miners, but the men who purchased them from the free miner. I have heard there is not now more than 30 gale-holders on the gale list book. I have been asked how many coal gales are applied for in a year. On enquiry, I am told only one or two, and it so happens that some of them are gales that have been forfeited to the Crown. It is a fact that free miners have certain rights which others have not, therefore the Crown is at a disadvantage in dealing with a free miner, as appeared with another person. I hope and trust that we who have these rights will not stand in the way of progress and of opening out a way to our deep measures.'

The problem of working the deep coal gales was unresolved by the end of the century.[1] As and when they were forfeited from time to time, the deputy gaveller held them in reserve. After the turn of the century the Commissioners of Woods as gavellers, had no real difficulty in framing and carrying through legislation to permit working of united deep gales. On 5 July 1904 Westgarth Forster Brown,[2] deputy gaveller, and Frank Brain, colliery proprietor,[3] gave evidence before the Royal Commission on Coal Supplies. Mr. Brown, in explaining his duties as deputy gaveller, said that the gales varied in size from a few acres up to 800 acres. The total number of gales was 246, of which 123 were in hand – 67 of these being worked out. He recommended, for the future working of the deeper measures, the division into sufficiently large areas to entice people with capital to come forward with the purpose of development; also, that revision of royalties should be made after a period of up to 63 years instead of the present 21 years. Mr. Brain explained the great difficulty of obtaining the interest of people with capital for working the deep gales particularly in view of the water menace. There was also the possibility of this becoming even more serious when the pumping of the middle series was discontinued after exhaustion of those seams. He referred to the case of the amalgamated United Deep galeage area of almost 2,000 acres which he said was 'well suited and included all the lower series intact', containing some ten million tons of Coleford High Delph coal. 'Although favourably reported on by well-known engineers and extensively advertised and offered at a nominal price (he believed £1,000) and with a royalty of but 3d. per ton, these attempts were continued for several years but no buyer was ever found.' However, matters soon progressed.

The Dean Forest (Mines) Act 1904. A Parliamentary Bill was promoted in 1904 by the Commissioners of Woods with the sanction of the Treasury 'to facilitate the opening and working of certain of the lower series of coal seams in His Majesty's Forest of Dean and in the Hundred of St. Briavels and for certain other purposes connected with

---

1 An extract from a Foresters Election song of 1892 runs:
'.... and when we ask about Deep Gales,
Sir Charles will open wide his sails,
And steer right through, with merry crew,
A Bill that will our hopes renew.'
The above refers to Sir Charles Dilke, then Member of Parliament for the Dean Division.

2 Final Rpt. of the Roy. Com. on Coal Supplies, Pt. II (Rpt. of Sir Wm. T. Lewis), 1905 (Cd. 2354), pp. 362-8.

3 *Ibid.*, pp. 369-72.

the mines in the said Forest and hundred'. Sir Stafford Howard, gaveller and Commissioner of Woods, had taken a very active part by communicating with parties interested in the Forest's minerals. There was no petition against the Bill but various individuals or representatives of interested parties appeared before a Select Committee of the House of Commons on 29 June 1904 to object to certain of the clauses. The free miners' representatives attended with divergent views and without a considered and totally agreed case for presentation.[1]

According to the relevant Minutes of Evidence, at a meeting held at the Speech House, out of approximately 600 free miners present, about 550 had voted approval of the Bill as drafted. It appears, however, that those present had been largely from the eastern side of the Forest, and the leaders of those from the western side asserted that the result of the meeting had not represented the views of the free miners as a whole. In addition, certain witnesses before the Committee held divergent views as to each other's claims to represent the body of free miners. S. J. Thomas said he represented a considerable number of free miners and was president of the Free Miners' Association, started in 1882, but did not embrace all free miners, its membership being between 400 and 500 out of a total of 1,100 free miners. S. J. Elsom claimed that he represented the majority of the free miners and was president of a separate Association – the Forest of Dean Free Miners' Association. He did not know of any other Association. It seems that both Associations were inadequately run, there being no register of members, etc. Among those who gave evidence, in addition to the above, were the deputy gaveller, Westgarth Forster Brown, Sir Charles Dilke, MP for the Forest, and free miners J. J. Joynes,[2] W. D. Meredith,[3] H. Fox, J. Nicholls, and M. H. Perkins.

The representatives of the free miners succeeded in obtaining amendments to certain clauses of the Bill. They did not, however, succeed in getting accepted a proposal that the costs of arbitration should be paid by the Crown out of 'forfeited dead rents'. Regarding the latter, Mr. Joynes said: 'A large sum of money has been paid as dead rents, and has been forfeited, that neither the present galee, nor a subsequent galee can recoup himself of any part of this sum, and I consider that the costs of any arbitration under this Act might well be paid for out of such moneys, otherwise it is believed that the expected costs of arbitration might deter galees from claiming justice, whereas the gaveller in any case has power to compel him to part with his private property, or take the risk of arbitration, in which he might be mulcted [*sic*] in the total costs.' The deputy gaveller pointed out that no such 'Dead Rent Fund' existed, adding: 'I do not see why people in the Forest should not come under the same Act as regards that as everybody else in the kingdom. ... Besides it would be possible for any man who wanted to make himself unreasonable to fight at the expense of the general revenue for an unlimited time'. S. J. Thomas commented: 'Before the year 1869, I think, a free miner had the right to work back

1 In 1904 Sydney John Thomas claimed that he 'represented a very considerable number of free miners and the Free Miners' Association'; and that he was President of that Association, founded in 1882. However, on the same day Sydney J. Elsom claimed to be President of 'the Forest of Dean Free Miners' Association'; and that he had been their leader for 28 years; and he was unaware that there were two associations!'

2 J. J. Joynes was later well known as manager of Cannop Colliery.

3 W. D. Meredith was secretary of the Free Miners' Association and manager of Lightmoor Colliery.

for what are called "short-workings" – the dead rents which he had paid – they were not liable to forfeiture at the time, but it was always an asset to the colliery, and when he offered the colliery for sale he had got these short-workings to work off as a royalty – the dead rents. It amounts to this: there was forfeited in 1901 £36,444 11s. 6d., and we as free miners think that a sufficient amount out of that sum of forfeited dead rents should be taken to pay the costs of any arbitration that we were forced into by the gaveller'. However, after much discussion the Committee decided not to agree to this proposal. In subsequent evidence it was also stated that there were 5,796 applications at the gaveller's office for the following gales which were in hand:

Gale	*Year of Forfeiture*	*No of Applicants*
Central Colliery	1890	581
Holly Hill	1893	238
Emperor and Extension		400
All Profit	1896	538
Cousins Engine	1898	659
Skinners' Gardens	"	591
Small Profit	1899	519
Pillowell United	1903	756
Alexandra	"	670
United Deep	"	844

Some representatives of the free miners objected to that portion of the Bill which intended to sweep away these applications and start afresh. They thought those free miners who had not taken the trouble to apply for the gales should not be on an equal footing with those that had. When the gales had been forfeited the deputy gaveller had given due notice of the same and all free miners had had an equal chance of applying if they wished to do so. Other witnesses had opposing views, and the Bill was in this respect passed without amendment. H. Fox gave an account of the United Deep gale of which he and other free miners had obtained a grant sometime previously. They had held it without working it but paying the usual dead rent each year. A committee had been formed, of which he was a member, to hold the gale which they subsequently sold for £1,000. Although it was stated in 1889 that there were 174 applicants, another source asserts that the number was 901 and that the gale was granted to 800 of these.

The provisions of the resultant Dean Forest (Mines) Act 1904[1] in summary are[2]:

- gaveller empowered to amalgamate, sub-divide and re-arrange coal gales.
- consent of galees necessary except in certain stated cases.
- gaveller to advertise notice of any order respecting gales in hand so that

1 Copy in Hart, *Laws of Dean,* pp. 8-12.

2 Currently available from H.M.S.O. is an Official Revised Edition of the 1904 Act to 1 February 1978 omitting spent and repealed Sections. See also Appendix I.

application may be made by free miners for the grant of the new gales. All previous applications to be null and void.

- extension of period from 21 to 63 years for revision of rents and royalties.[1]
- *ad hoc* committees to receive the grant of any new coal gale whenever two or more free miners make applications on the same day for that gale.

The Act facilitated the amalgamation of 41 named coal gales (see Appendix B) in the deeper areas of the coalfield basin into multiple coal mining units to be devised at the discretion of the gaveller, who was given plenary powers to amalgamate, sub-divide and re-arrange those gales. However, S.10 [repealed in 1969] stipulated that the Act only applies to the 41 gales scheduled in it; and provided that any gales so divided and amalgamated should be new gales. It facilitated the regrouping of five major central mining areas (see Appendix B), which subsequently became significant collieries by the sinking of new accesses to the deep coal seams. The Act also facilitated the input of capital funds (mainly from outside the hundred, i.e. by so-called 'foreigners') to sink the vertical shafts and install the water pumping and winding equipment necessary to exploit the deeper coal seams.

The free miners were still a divided body. At a meeting held at the Speech House on 17 September 1904,[2] their president, S. J. Elsom, announced his resignation. Several hundred free miners attended and opposing parties arranged themselves on either side. Finally Mr. Elsom was re-elected and given a vote of confidence. Martin Perkins was elected vice-president and a committee was voted (see Plate X.). Mr. Elsom said he believed the Act would be a blessing to the Forest of Dean, and he was already in correspondence with people with capital for the development of the deep seams of coal. At a meeting held in February of the following year[3] W. D. Meredith said: 'the working of the deep gales was of paramount importance to the Foresters seeing that the middle series of gales were rapidly becoming exhausted. With the view to doing all they could to induce capitalists to come into the district to develop the coal in the deep gales, the free miners, instead of charging a lump sum on a given area, had resolved to go upon the royalty principle, and to charge a penny per ton.' The free miners had in the end to be satisfied with a payment of ½d. per ton. Referring to the proposed working of the new gales, H.M. Inspector of Mines for the district expressed his opinion that[4] 'unless the matter is started under favourable auspices of management and capital (in cash, and not in shares) it would be likely to prove detrimental rather than

1 The Act altered the 1838 Act's 21 year rent review period to 63 years. This qualification has caused misunderstandings even to the present day, for there is an incorrect argument promulgated by some free miners that the 63 year rent review period applies to all gales. It does not, and the correct period for all gales, other than those recited in the 1904 Act is 21 years. It appears that during the last three decades, rent reviews have not been made on those gales with a 21 year review period. [This is a matter which may require regularising in relation to the apparent statutory obligations of the Coal Authority under the 1994 Act, *infra*, for neither British Coal nor the Forestry Commission appear to have pursued this point latterly because nowadays the cost of collecting gale rents is considerably higher than the rental income.]

2 Reported in *Western Mail*, 19 September 1904 – 'Dean Forest Free Miners at Loggerheads'.

3 Reported in *Gloucester Journal*, 18 February 1905.

4 1905 Report (published in 1906), p. 743.

advantageous', and that in fact 'it would be better for the responsible authorities to disallow any transfer of the gales to fresh owners, unless they were guaranteed efficient management and ample available capital to provide for the difficulties and eventualities to be expected.'[1]

In consolidating the plethora of small deep gales into some five deep units, the newly formed mining companies involved did not wish to expend large sums of money by way of outright (capital) purchase of the individual gale licences, because they were already committed to separate large capital outlay for shaft sinking, pumping equipment, winding equipment, surface facilities and railways. They therefore elected to value the coal in the consolidated gale licences being assigned to them, and thence discharge their indebtedness over the years by dividing that sum by the total estimated tonnage, and thence paying it off at an estimated rate per ton. [It was not a royalty, which is a separate rate per ton (i.e. a production related rent) which had (and has) separately to be paid to a new nationalised coal owner (i.e. the State organisation concerned) or, previously to the Coal Act 1938, *infra,* the Commissioners/Crown.] The 'capital payment' per ton amount locally known in the Forest of Dean as 'Gale money', was paid annually (see Plate XI) to the heirs and assigns of the original multiple gales via their Trustees until the original purchase sums were discharged.

The Dean Forest Act 1906. In 1906 it was thought advisable to make provision for succession on the Committees appointed under the Act of 1904. The need would arise when committee members died or left the district. A Parliamentary Bill to legalise this and other points regarding enclosures, was drawn up in April 1906. S. J. Elsom and Mr. Westmacott gave evidence on the matter before a Select Committee of the House of Commons on 7 May 1906. The resultant Act was the Dean Forest (Mines) Act 1906.[2] The development of the lower measures continued, and each year the free miners received their shares of the gale money, the amounts depending, of course, upon output. Before the annual distribution was made an advertisement was inserted in the local press; an example in 1952 being[3]:

---

1 Some of the 41 gales mentioned in the 1904 Act (see Appendix B) were not included in the subsequent grouping the remainder were grouped as follows and transferred to various large companies on a basis of $^1/_2$d. ton royalty:

	Date of Grant
Northern United (Holly Hill United)	18 Nov. 1907
Eastern United	
Alexandra	10 June 1911
Western United	10 June 1907
Southern United	31 May 1907
South-Eastern United	20 Oct. 1913
Pillowell United	"
Cousins Engine	31 July 1911

A large percentage of the free miners were applicants for the above groups and consequently share, or their beneficiaries share, in the proceeds which are distributed annually. See Plate XI.

2 Copy in Hart, *Laws of Dean*, pp. 12-13. The 1906 Act has since been repealed.

3 Dean Forest *Guardian*, 4 July 1952.

NOTICE TO FREEMINERS

DEAN FOREST (MINES) ACT, 1904

HOLLY HILL UNITED
WESTERN UNITED
EASTERN UNITED
ALEXANDRA
SOUTHERN UNITED
SOUTH-EASTERN UNITED

A Meeting of the beneficiaries of the above mentioned Gales will be held at the Speech House on Saturday, July 12, 1952, at 5.30 p.m. , when a distribution of 1/4 per Gale will be made.

W. D. MEREDITH,
Hon. Secretary.

Following the Acts of 1904 and 1906, technical advances, mining machinery and scientific practices brought the economic extraction of coal to a fine art. Yet after much expert investigation of the lie of the strata and the coal seams, and the location of 'faults', sinking of trial shafts and adits was first resorted to in order to 'prove' coal. Exploratory tunnels called 'dipples' driven from the deep shafts, were also tried, and not all were successful. The favourable features that the coalfield possessed, of freedom from fire-damp (enabling work by naked lights) and from too many major 'faults', were unfortunately spoiled by the varying thickness within the coal seams, and the quantity of water encountered in relation to the coal output necessitating extensive pumping plant. Mine ventilation – another problem common to all other coalfields – was overcome in various ways so as to accord with the statutory provisions on mine air quality and quantity.

The Forestry Act 1919. The Forestry Commission was established by virtue of the Forestry Act 1919. The Forest of Dean was transferred to it under the Forestry (Transfer of Woods) Act 1923 by Orders in 1924 and 1926, whereby the Forestry Commissioners became the gaveller, their local representative, as now, being the deputy gaveller. Under the 1924 No. 386 Order, S.5,[1] the office of Keeper of the Gawle-Above-the-Wood within the Forest and also the office of Keeper of the Gawle-Under-the-Wood within the Forest which by S.13 of the Dean Forest (Mines) Act 1838 were vested in the First Commissioner of Woods and were therein and thereinafter referred to as the office of gaveller. On 1 April 1924 the office was transferred to and vested in the Forestry Commissioners together with all the powers, rights and authorities belonging or appertaining to the office of gaveller (including the power to appoint a deputy gaveller) and all such powers, rights and authorities after the transfer were exercised either by

1 S.5 of the 1838 Act was repealed in 1969.

Plate X. *Trustees of the Free Miners for the 'Deep Coal Gales'*; c. *1906.*
Top, left to right: F. Jones, R. Brown, C. Hirst, B. Dobbs, J. Hawkins;
middle: A. Sadler (auditor), T. Morse, G. Barnard, J. J. Joynes, T. Wright, C. Lees, J. Nicholls;
bottom: M. Perkins (vice-president), S. J. Elsom (president), W. D. Meredith (hon. sec.), G. T. Stephens (hon. treas.), C. Jenkins.

the Forestry Commissioners or by the deputy gaveller appointed by them. Any instrument required by any Act to be made under the hand or under the hand and seal of the gaveller may be made under the seal of the Forestry Commissioners.[1]

The Commissioners, as gaveller, have distinct connection with the free miners particularly through their deputy gaveller. (In 1997 the Forestry Commission had an important relevant Agreement with the Coal Authority under the Coal Industry Act 1994. This will be evident in Chapter XI)

It has been pointed out[2] that 'in days gone by a free miner has been able to dispose of his gale for many thousands of pounds at no cost to himself apart from the initial fee of 5s.' This presumably referred to grouped gales shared by a large number of free miners. There were so many applicants for the larger and more valuable gales or groups of gales that a free miner who had taken the trouble to apply for them has had to be content to share the proceeds of sale or lease with many hundreds of other free miners. Thus, when W. D. Meredith (see Plate X) the secretary of the Dean Forest Free Miners' Association, was asked in 1924[3]: 'Taking a period of five years, how much has been distributed to free miners and how many received a share?' his reply was: 'Between £5,000 and £6,000 has been divided amongst about 1,200 free miners from Grouped Gales.' The individual amounts vary, of course, with the number of free miners who have applied for each particular gale. However, it is correct to say that a free miner who has applied for and been granted a share in each of the six main Grouped Gales has benefited, or his beneficiaries have benefited, to the extent of 8s. to £2 per year. In the case of the distribution referred to in the above advertisement a free miner owning a share in each of the six gales received 8s. The value of each share in any one of the six gales, for the years 1937 to 1951 inclusive, has been 6s. 8d., 6s., 5s., 5s., 4s. 6d., 4s., 3s. 6d., 3s., 3s., 2s. 6d., 2s. 6d., 2s., 1s. 8d., 1s. 4d. and 1s. 4d. respectively. This indicates that the tonnage pulled is reducing each year. The share issue on the Cousins Engine Gale is not made yearly as the amounts would be too small. The amounts paid per share in respect of this gale have been 4s. in 1934, 4s. in 1937, 4s. in 1942 and 2s. 6d. in 1944. Distribution is made at the Speech House, when a meeting of free miners is usually addressed by the Chairman, Charles Jenkins. Beneficiaries not present have to apply to their local Committee Members[4] within one month. In some cases the Committee Members are good enough to remit amounts by post to beneficiaries living far away, even abroad.

In addition to the larger Grouped Deep gales, all of which are leased to colliery proprietors at a royalty of ½d. per ton, other gales have been sold or leased by groups of free miners through Committees appointed by them. For example, some eighty years ago [*c.* 1920] the Pillowell United gale was sold for about £1,100, and

1 26 February 1997 the Forestry Commission abrogated part of its rights as gaveller to the Coal Authority, appointed by the Coal Industry Act 1994. See copy in Appendix D.

2 R. I. Treharne Rees, deputy gaveller: Presidential Address to South Wales Inst. of Engineers (18 January 1945)

3 Dean Forest *Guardian,* 22 August 1924.

4 There were Committee Members for each of the seven following districts, Drybrook and Lydbrook, Berry Hill, Broadwell, Bream, Yorkley, Cinderford and Ruspidge. A Will Book was held for each district so that a free miner may, if he wished, state to whom he desired his shares paid after his death. Of course a will over-rides this.

approximately 550 free miners received £2 each; a smaller gale, The Speculation, was sold in 1944 for about £95. In the early 1950s small gales fetched as little as £10, but the average price for a normal gale was in the region of £50.

The First World War was responsible for the discontinuance of the ancient custom of the Gale Audit. For many years until that time, half-yearly Gale Audits were held at the Speech House. After the free miners had paid their rents and royalties to the deputy gaveller, they were invited to a dinner in the Court Room, at the conclusion of which leading colliery proprietors and representatives of other interests made speeches on the state of local trade in the coal and other industries.[1] Details of the costs of some of the nineteenth-century gale dinners were in an account book at the Gaveller's Office, Coleford.

Here it may be of interest to record that it has been suggested that many years ago miners on occasion went outside the limit of their gales, unknown to the crown officials, hiding their deception by 'gobbing up'. The only recorded mention is found in the 1905 Report[2] of the Inspector of Mines, who was informed by a collier in Hopewell Engine Colliery that he 'remembers 40 or 50 years ago, how, in dry summers it was the practice to drive "dipples" down on the lower side of the deep adit (which formed the body of the gale) as far as they could!' No doubt this was a rare occurrence, for, although being a convenient place to deposit waste earth, there must have been few free miners that would thus illegally take coal, and in any case they would realise the danger to adjoining gales. Later, improvements in mine surveying instruments and techniques disposed of any like 'suspicion'.

1 Unpublished memoirs of A. T. Bright (kindly put at my disposal by one of his sons, H. S. Bright).
2 For 1904 (p. 680).

CHAPTER XI

1938-2001: Acts of 1938, 1946, 1969 and 1994

THE *Coal Act 1938*. The deep coal mine gales consolidated by the 1904 Act and the related provisions for dealing with new applications for any coal gale (via an *ad hoc* Committee of free miners and appropriate advertisements placed in two local newspapers) continued to be mined until the Coal Act 1938, which in Part I, S.43 contains the following (abbreviated) in respect of the Forest of Dean[1]:

- 'This Part of this Act shall have effect in its application to land in the Forest of Dean or in any other part of the Hundred of Saint Briavels in the county of Gloucester, being land in respect of which the privileges of the free miners are exercisable, subject to the following modifications.
- The provisions of subsections (2) to (3) of S.3, and Ss. 4 and 5, of this Act, and the Second Schedule to this Act; shall not have effect, but this Part of this Act shall have effect as if for the said provisions there had been substituted the following provision, that is to say, on the vesting date the interest of the Forestry Commissioners in the coal and mines of coal comprised in the said land shall vest in the Coal Commission, subject to and in accordance with the provisions of the Dean Forest (Mines) Act, 1838, and of any other enactment relating to the said land (in this section referred to as "The Dean Forest enactments") and to all interests subsisting or to be created under or by virtue thereof.
- In the application of Ss. 6 and 7 of this Act; and of the Third Schedule to this Act, to the coal and mines of coal comprised in the said land, the interest therein subsisting in the Forestry Commissioners at the valuation date, and no other interest shall be treated as an acquired interest, and provision shall be made by rules made by the Board of Trade under the power in that behalf conferred upon them by the Third Schedule to this Act for treating the said interest as constituting a unit for compensation purposes and (in substitution for the provisions of that Schedule relating to registration under the Registration Act and the notification to the Regional Valuation Board of such registration) for the notification to that Board by the Forestry Commissioners of particulars thereof, and the Forestry Commissioners shall be the persons entitled to the compensation therefor.
- Ss. 8 and 13, subsections (1) to (3) of S.14 and S.19 of this Act, and the Fourth and Fifth schedules to this Act; shall not have effect.
- References to coal shall not be construed as including references to minerals or substances that are subsidiary coal hereditaments within the meaning of S.6 of this Act.

1 Some of the many subsequently repealed sections of the 1938 Act are noted in Appendix I.

- All powers conferred by the Dean Forest enactments that were vested in the Forestry Commissioners immediately before the vesting date shall continue to be exercisable by them notwithstanding the vesting in the Coal Commission of the said interest, and accordingly –
  - (a) rent attributable to the said interest shall continue to be coverable by the Forestry Commissioners until other provision in that behalf is made under the next succeeding subsection, but they shall pay to the Coal Commission all such rent recovered by them that accrues after the vesting date; and
  - (b) the Coal Commission shall pay to the Forestry Commission sums equal to such part of the expenses incurred by them in exercising the said powers after the vesting date as are attributable to the management of the said interest.
- Any difference arising between the Coal Commission and the Forestry Commissioners as to the amount of the rent, or of the expenses, to be paid under this subsection shall be determined by the Treasury.
- His Majesty may by Order in Council make provision for vesting in the Coal Commission any of the powers conferred by the Dean Forest enactments that were vested in the Forestry Commissioners immediately before the vesting date in so far as they relate to coal or mines of coal, and any such order may make provision for any requisite modification of the Dean Forest enactments. The Board of Trade shall lay before Parliament the draft of any Order which it is proposed to recommend His Majesty in Council to make under this subsection, and no further proceedings shall be taken in relation thereto except in pursuance of an Address presented to His Majesty by both Houses of Parliament praying that the Order may be made in the terms of the draft'

The 1938 Act in effect transferred the property in all unworked coal in Great Britain into the hands of a single public body – the Coal Commission. It nationalised unworked coal *but not the mining companies working it,* including that of the Forest of Dean, with the reservation in S.43 that, as regards coal, the interests of the Forestry Commission (on 1 July 1942) was to become vested in the then Coal Commission,[1] but subject to the rights of the free miners, their heirs and assigns. Thus in 1938 the Forest was the only coalfield in Great Britain in which the Coal Commission could not grant or refuse a lease of coal entirely at its discretion. The Act of 1938 is now mainly of academic interest, but at that time it preserved the right of freemining.

---

1 Named in Appendix D. The Coal Act 1938 provided for the unification of coal royalties under the ownership and control of the Coal Commission and for that purpose vested in that Commission, subject to compensation, the property in all unworked coal and mines of coal in Great Britain with certain exceptions. [Minerals other than coal remain vested in the holders of the fee simple.] The valuations had to be based on the evidence available on 1 January 1939 (called 'the valuation date') as to the income to be anticipated as and from 1 July 1942 (called 'the vesting date', i.e. the date on which the coal became vested in the Coal Commission, and as and from which date the incomes accruing would pass to the Coal Commission). The compensation was to be paid from a central UK Global Fund by the Coal Commission to the then holders of the consolidated deep gale mining licences who had acquired them earlier from the original gale owners per the provisions of the 1904 Act; i.e. in exactly the same way as other coal owners were compensated in other coalfields throughout the UK. Pursuant to para. 2(2) of the Third Schedule to the 1938 Act [under the Coal Commission (Dean Forest) Rules, 1939], the Coal Commission compensated the Forestry Commission. The final valuation of £137,239 was scaled down (by 14s. 5½d. in the £1) to £99,099. 1s. 5d.

The Coal Industry Nationalisation Act 1946. This nationalised (from 1 January 1947) the UK coal *operating companies and colliery concerns* which fell into the class of 'operating concerns' as defined in the Act, and created the National Coal Board (NCB).[1] However, S.63(2) provided that the working of coal by *individuals* by virtue of a gale granted in the Forest of Dean or the Hundred of St. Briavels should not constitute a 'colliery concern'. Thus the rights of freeminers were preserved. As from 1 January 1947, the Act transferred the 41 deep gales of the 1904 Act (by that time having become 52 + 2 gales) to the NCB (see Appendix C).[2] In effect, the large colliery companies working the consolidated deep gales (6 to 8 gales in each) were nationalised and financially compensated[3] and these were run and managed by the NCB. However, the separate gales run by *individual free miners,* their heirs and assigns remained outside the nationalisation regime; their rents and royalties were collected by the deputy gaveller and then paid to the NCB. Following the 1946 Act, the free miners' Trustees under their Committee Scheme (dating from 1904) continued annually to receive 'Gale money' (equivalent to half a penny a ton), where the commuted capital sums for the consolidated deep gales by the large colliery companies had not been fully paid up.[4]

Commentating on the 1946 Act, the then Minister of Fuel and Power, the Rt Hon. Emmanuel Shinwell, stated in the House of Commons at the time: 'The rights of free

1 Some of the many subsequently repealed sections of the 1946 Act are noted in Appendix I.

2 It appears that those 52+2 gales could have been surrendered and theoretically made available for regrant to free miners by the deputy gaveller after 5 years. They were not – for practical and financial reasons. The majority of the Coleford High Delph seam below the water table had been mined out, and the small remaining coal barriers in it can only be mined safely within existing Health & Safety legislation by initially lowering the mine water table to satisfactory safety levels, and thence continuously maintaining it at those levels by pumping, the costs of which, with current pit head coal prices, would be prohibitive. In any event; such pumping on a large enough scale to justify any significant sustainable output; would be likely to cause extensive surface subsidence because of disturbances to the present equilibrium.

3 The 1946 Act set up, under its S.12, a Central Valuation Board, District Valuation Boards and Valuation Districts to value the mining interests. A Valuation District Office was set up in Cinderford (covering East Wales, Dean Forest, Somerset and Bristol) and Major H. P. Herdman (sometime deputy gaveller) was head of it and was actively involved in the valuation process of the coal holdings in the Forest of Dean. The sanction of these Boards was to value the shares of the Colliery Companies which constituted 'colliery concerns' as defined by the 1946 Act. When these individual valuations were collected at a central office in London a 'Global Sum' was devised which came to £164.66 million for the whole country, as noted on the Schedule accompanying the Statutory Instrument dated 1949, Number 176 (Coal Industry: The Central Valuation Board Apportionment Certificate: 1 Feb. 1949). The value of the shares at the stipulated valuation date of the collieries in the Forest of Dean which constituted 'colliery concerns' for the purpose of the Act (free miners' gales did not constitute 'colliery concerns') amounted to £676,000. In simple terms, therefore, the shares of the holding companies in the Forest of Dean amounted to £676,000; this had to be distributed out of the national 'Global Sum' to the operating coal companies to pay off their shareholders, because the mines working the coal became vested in the State. The £676,000 figure must not be confused with any purchase money paid by the original mining companies to free miners earlier than the 1938 Act by virtue of the Dean Forest (Mines) Act 1904. At that time, the Colliery companies sinking and developing the deep mines made their own separate arrangements with the individual free miners within the Trusteeship set up under the 1904 Act.

4 In 1951 the dividend was 1s. 4d. on each share (compared with 1s. 8d. the previous year and with the peak dividend of 6s.). Every beneficiary holding a share in all six relevant gales received 8s. The total of shares was over 6,000, held by about 1,000 beneficiaries – mainly free miners but with some widows, sons, daughters, or other assignees.

Plate XI. *Distribution of 'Gale Money' in 1951. In front on right Charles Jenkins (chairman), standing on right W. D. Meredith (secretary).*

miners will be adequately safeguarded. It must be kept in mind that the right to work coal is vested in the NCB; subject to that exclusive right being exercised and accepted, the galees will be entitled, as individuals, to operate their gales or, if they are so disposed, to let or sell them to other parties. It will be understood that these parties can operate these gales subject to a licence being granted by the Board.' He added: 'There are freeminers in the Forest of Dean who work their own gales; that is to say, they operate the gales and do not lease them to other persons. These gales are of no practical importance, but if on the other hand there are gales worked by companies they will not come within the scope of the proposed amendment.' From this it appears that what the Minister had in mind was to exclude only the individual who worked the gale himself, and that where the workings were by a partnership or company these should not come within the scope of the exception.

However, S.36 of the 1946 Act did not state that it was lawful for the 'individual' to go on working his gale, as outlined by the Minister, and as an exception to the exclusive right conferred on the NCB by S.1(1)(a) of the Act. To deal with this anomaly it became necessary therefore to grant a short unconditional token 'bare licence' to these galees. However, this was not at all similar to the usual S.36(2)(a) licence under the 1946 Act; it was merely a simple grant without conditions, known as an 'individual' licence. The dual system of licences, unique to the Forest, operated from 1946 to 1993 and is the system by which the then free miners operated their mines either by virtue of an 'individual' licence accompanying a grant under the Dean Forest Mines enactments or by the grant of a NCB S.36(2)(a) licence. The grant of individual S.36(2)(a) licences could also be made to non-free miners who had purchased a gale or by licence from the NCB. [The numbers of small-scale mines operating in the dual manner declined from 36 with an output of 39,000 tons in 1948 to 13 working mines at March 1986 with an output of 3,500 tons.]

At nationalisation in 1946, the interests of the Forest's *colliery concerns* vested in the NCB comprised the six main collieries operating and the smaller colliery company ventures. In total, the interests of the NCB comprised: (a) 52+2 gales or part-gales; and (b) the interests of the earlier Coal Commission in unworked coal and mines of coal in or under land outside the Hundred of St. Briavels and thus outside the provisions of the Dean Forest Mines enactments. The NCB either worked the gales themselves in the case of the existing mines or licensed them to others.

Under the Act five large colliery undertakings were directly operated by the NCB. In addition, seventeen small colliery concerns vested their interests, which included forty-three coal gales, in the NCB. As these latter areas were not suitable for direct operations the Board invited applications for licences to work these gales, and thirty-seven S.36(2)(a) licences were granted, the remaining six gales having become exhausted and unprofitable to mine. (By the end of 1956 twenty-three gales were in production under S.36(2)(a) of the 1946 Act; the interests of eight other galees were excluded from vesting in the Board and these gales were working under Individual and S.36(2)(a) licences. The total number of small mines working in 1958 was thirty-one. The output from gales worked under licence from the NCB was about 27,000 tons annually, while the annual output from gales held by free miners under grant from the deputy gaveller amounted to about 5,000 tons.) The free miners urged that gales, unless operated by the NCB itself, should be forfeited and returned to the general pool of gales available for grant to free miners by the deputy gaveller. The NCB refused no application for a licence to work a gale which it did not require for its own working.[1] The deputy gaveller, on application being made, extended the period of grant, in respect of unworked gales, whether by the Board or by free miners.[2]

Under the NCB, the nationalised deep mines of the Forest struggled to compete in the 'national scene' because of rising costs, difficult mining conditions, exhaustion of reserves and the substantial quantity of water requiring to be pumped in relation to coal production. The NCB 'Revised Plan for Coal' in 1959 referred to the Forest as follows: 'This small isolated coalfield has a restricted market and most of the readily accessible coal has been worked. It is unlikely that more than one colliery will be in existence by 1965 and even this is dependent on demand.' The deep mines closed as each became economically exhausted with increasing pumping costs; and the coalfield was eventually abandoned by the NCB in December 1965. At that time the 52+2 gales involved could have been surrendered by the NCB as, in effect, collective galee. However, because the lowest thick seam – the Coleford High Delph – was mainly worked out below the ground water table, and the workings waterlogged, all the lower abandoned mine workings became flooded when pumping was discontinued.[3] In 1987, the NCB changed its trading name to British Coal Corporation. The 1946 Act is now mainly of academic interest, but nevertheless preserved the rights of free miners. (The 'bare licences' thereunder are currently recognised by the Coal Authority appointed by the Act of 1994 *infra.)*

Stone Quarries in the Statutory Forest. S.23 of the Dean Forest (Mines) Act 1838 entitled free miners in stone quarries to have leases granted to them. There is no provision for quarries corresponding to the rights of free miners of coal or iron ore to require a gale to be granted to them, but they are given preference. S.29 of the same Act required lessees working quarries to observe certain general rules and regulations. S.34 of the Dean Forest (Mines) Act 1871 allowed renewals of quarry leases to be to a person not a free miner. Leases may be assigned if approved by the Forestry Commission. The deputy gaveller has certain statutory responsibility for quarries under the Dean Forest Mines enactments and advises on quarry matters. However, since 1991, the leasing of and attending to stone quarries, including the collection of rents and royalties, is dealt with by the Forestry Commission's area land agent (currently, from 1994, Richard Davies, a chartered surveyor and land agent) [Plate XIII] based in Coleford.

---

1 On 15 October 1982, the chairman of the NCB, Norman Siddell, wrote to Paul Marland MP stating that the Board had no powers to dispose of the 43 gales vested in it under the 1946 Act; adding: 'This should not; however, inhibit any individual or groups of individuals from taking the necessary steps to work any parcel of coal that may remain in the Forest. We have always allowed mining in the Forest to take its own course and have never been obstructive when sent applications for new licences to work our gales. ... Today there are only some 13 mines in operation, employing together less than 30 men.'

2 *Report of the Forest of Dean Committee 1958*, p. 36.

3 Incidentally, in the early 1960s, Roy Piggott (then Regional Chief Surveyor and Minerals Estates Manager for the NCB) was a party to a mine planning scheme at Norchard to drive a special mine drainage underground system some 67 feet A.O.D. (below the now Steam Railway Engine Museum) to drain the lower abandoned mine waters into the River Lyd (an extension of the Cannop Brook). It worked to plan, and the waters commenced to flow out in 1967, and continues today.

The Crown Lands Act 1873 empowered the Commissioners of Woods (since 1924, the Forestry Commission) to grant leases for stone quarries for up to 21 years, apart from the rights of free miners. The Act specifically excludes gold and silver, now the responsibility of the separate Crown Estate Commissioners. There are three large scale roadstone quarries at Stowfield, Drybrook and Stowe Hill,[1] (all outside the statutory Forest but within the hundred, and about 12 small active dressed-stone quarries in the statutory Forest. The demand for stone from the small quarries is increasing as Local Planning Authorities are now insisting on greater use of local stone for new buildings. This may lead to the re-opening of further small dormant quarries. Normally the quarries are leased for a small base rent plus a royalty per tonne for the stone removed. All new quarries or extension of existing quarries require planning permission from Gloucestershire County Council, as the Mineral Planning Authority.

The Report of the Forest of Dean Committee, 1958.[2] This Committee, known as 'the Creed Committee' was appointed in June 1955 'to review the situation in the Forest of Dean, and having regard to all existing rights and interests to recommend such measures as they consider desirable, and necessary to secure that the administration of the Forest ...may be adjusted to modern requirements.' It gave relatively little attention to freemining, but under the heading of 'Freeminers and Quarrymen'[3] it made two recommendations as to 'Mines and Quarries'.[4]

(1) Any future proposal to carry out opencast coal working should be rejected in view of the grave effect such operations would have on the amenities of the Forest.

(2) The deputy surveyor should invariably be consulted when an application is made to the deputy gaveller for the grant of land for mining or quarrying or for the extension of the period of existing grants.

[Recommendation No. (1) was not followed: there have been several workings of coal by opencast. Recommendation No. (2) was followed.]

The Forestry Act 1981. The free miners, along with all persons having at heart the interests of the Forest, were grateful that the Act, whereby the Minister 'may dispose for any purpose' Forestry Commission land, this, uniquely, does not include land in the Forest of Dean, but may sell any such land if in his opinion it is not needed, or ought not to be used, for the purpose of afforestation or any purpose connected with forestry. The Minister may exchange any such land for other land more suitable for either of the said purposes.[5]

---

1 The extraction of tonnes, per year, respectively, are about 400,000 (Private), 500,000 (Hanson), and 800,000 (Tarmac).

2 Published in March 1959, Cmnd. 686, H.M.S.O.

3 Section VII: Freeminers and Quarrymen, pp. 35-7.

4 *Ibid*., p. 45.

5 Notes of the present author's modest contribution with Lord McNair and the Forest of Dean District Council to obtain the 1981 concession are deposited in Glos.R.O., Hart Dean Collection, D3921, II, 25, 26 (Access. 7366). To commemorate Lord McNair's services, three oaks were planted in 1981 in the northwest corner of the Speech House field.

Plate XII. *Typical mid-twentieth century free miners and their coal 'Level'.*

The Statute Law (Repeals) Act 1969. This Act by Sch. Pt. VII repealed certain sections of the Acts of 1838, 1861, 1871, 1904, 1938, and 1946 as noted throughout the text. Additional repeals of the last two Acts were made by the Coal Industry Act 1994 *infra,* see Appendix I.

[As at 18 June 1986 the number of registered free miners since 1 September 1838 was 4,271; the total number of gales that had been awarded since 1841 was around 450; the gales granted numbered 58; and the gales developing/working was 11. The remainder of the gales were held 'in trust' for the then free miners. A 2.5 hectare opencast site was operating at Edge End with the benefit of planning consent; eventually to be re-established with woodland that had previously been affected by shallow coal-mining.]

The Coal Industry Act 1994. This important Act provided for the UK coal industry to return to the private sector, operating under a licensing system. Until the appearance late in 1993 of a Parliamentary Bill relating to the nation's coal industry, the free miners' rights remained intact, secured by the Dean Forest Mines enactments (1838-1906 as amended), and unchallenged except particularly by serious alarms from Parliamentary Bills in 1874 and 1884, both of which were opposed and withdrawn. However, as a precursor to the 1993 Bill and 1994 Act, British Coal Corporation had already made arrangements with all S.36(2)(a) licensees that their licences would expire in March 1995. The new Act repealed *inter alia* parts of the Acts of 1938 and 1946.[1] At first, apparently it was hardly noticed by the free miners or by anyone likely to have wanted to safeguard their rights,[2] but shortly afterwards, it at first caused relatively modest but increasing alarm for freemining in the Forest and hundred.

The 1994 Act formulated a new Coal Authority, in which the fee simple of any coal is now vested, and set a deadline at 31 March 1995 for all coal mine operators, whether previously operating under licence or under nationalisation by British Coal, to cease mining by making available for bids in the open market all coal operations, including opencast. This, in effect, was a reversion to the scenario in 1938 under the then Coal Act, with the State (i.e. the Coal Authority) becoming the fee simple owner of the coal, and the coal mine operators of both deep and opencast operating under licence from the Coal Authority as a privatised industry. This aspect caused increasing alarm in the Forest because it meant that anyone could make a highest bid for a S.36(2)(a) licensed mine (e.g. Hayners Bailey) over the head of the licensee who had meticulously developed it throughout many years. Fortunately, however, this did not occur.

---

1 See Appendix I.

2 Previous to the 1994 Act, because there had been no rent and royalty reviews within the statutory period there were 50 galees paying rents ranging from 25p a year to £60 a year depending on how long ago the gale was granted. Some aged galees owned gales hoping they would benefit financially by being 'bought out'. One prospective opencast operator owned or had options on 19 'Lightmoor gales'. In addition there were local authorities licensed to extract coal but holding (and paying dead rent) on gales to prevent others working them; Gloucestershire County Council held two under Berry Hill School (Society 4 Part Gale and 5 Part Gale) and the Forest of Dean District Council two – Valletts Level (re sewage disposal from Broadwell Housing Estate) and Victoria No. 3 (re Coleford Town Water Supply), recently relinquished. Although the issue has not been tested in law, it is debateable whether or not these are *bonâ fide* mining prospects under the Dean Forest Mines enactments or, indeed, under the 1994 Act.

In effect the 1994 Act privatised the UK coal mining industry, the coal remaining vested in the State. It purports, *inter alia,* at the insistence of the Coal Authority, for the first time in the history of freemining, to impose on the grant of a gale by the deputy gaveller under the Dean Forest Mines enactments, a second licence and code of regulations. The Authority is precluded from itself producing coal for commercial purposes, and it is rather a facilitator than a competitor to those interested in coal mining. The Bill (and later the Act) made only two coincidental mentions of the Forest and hundred:

> Schedule 10(5) refers to the continuation of collection of coal gale rents (including royalty) by the Forestry Commission for the Coal Authority, at the latter's expense.
>
> S.40(4) relates: 'Nothing in S.38 above shall confer any entitlement to withdraw support in connection with the working of any coal or coal mines comprised in land in the Forest of Dean or any other part of the area of what was the Hundred of St. Briavel's, being land in respect of which the privileges of free miners are exercisable.'[1]

The stages of the Bill started 2 December 1993, with no indication of any unacceptable mention of the Forest of Dean. The Free Miners' Association during the Bill's passage through both Houses of Parliament showed little concern as to effect on the Forest and hundred. However, the relationship of freemining with the proposed Coal Authority was unclear. The threat of dual licensing and regulation virtually took the free miners by surprise. They set about refusing to recognise the potential licensing imposition; claiming that it would be contrary to the hitherto 'free' mining. They asserted that a gale itself is a licence; that dual regulation would be highly burdensome, especially in the current economic circumstances, also that substantial insurance cover regarding subsidence would be required. They maintained that reasons why they failed to lobby Parliament were, first, their legitimate expectation as previously, of conventional provision made for consultation re freemining *(vide,* especially, as to the Coal Act 1938 and the Coal Industry Nationalisation Act 1946); second, apparently an oral general assurance given in March 1994 by the then deputy gaveller, Albert Howell (who had followed J. R. Tallis in 1973), to their chairman and secretary to the effect that the free miners' rights would be protected and the Forest coalfield treated as 'special' as it had been in previous Acts. However, in January 1994, the few members of the Dean Forest Branch of the UK Small Mines Association, through Brian James secretary and Bert Hinton chairman, enquired of Paul Marland, the then Forest constituency MP, as to some relevant parts of the Bill. The M.P. then questioned the Rt. Hon. Tim Eggar MP, Minister for Energy, who on 25 January 1994 wrote assuring him that the forthcoming

---

1 Throughout time and even today, whilst gales grant the right to mine, they do not grant the right to withdraw support, i.e. to cause subsidence. Thus, in the event of surface subsidence caused by mining, the Common Law obtains, and an aggrieved surface owner/occupier has placed upon him the burden of proof that under-mining has caused damage by withdrawal of lateral or vertical support. This caused difficulty with the application of the Coal Mining (Subsidence) Acts of 1950 and 1957 in the Forest and hundred. As a result, in these and of the subsequent Acts dealing with coal mining subsidence (the Coal Industry Act 1975 and the Coal Mining Subsidence Act 1991) the Forest and hundred were specifically excluded so as to retain the Common Law position.

Explanatory Notes to the Bill 'makes reference to the fact that special arrangements will need to be made for licensing coal-mines in the Forest of Dean, where it is envisaged that the Coal Authority will grant galees a separate form of licence with a few conditions attached, a copy of which will follow as soon as it is available'.[1] This assurance was passed to the Small Mines Association. On 2 January 1995 the Association wrote informing Mr Marland that they were still awaiting information. Copies of the above correspondence were supplied to the Free Miners Association, but no precise action appears to have been taken upon it. Meanwhile the succeeding deputy gaveller, Roy Piggott, (Plate XIV) a Chartered Mining Engineer and a Chartered Minerals Surveyor, appointed in September 1994, soon appreciated that so far as the Forest and hundred were concerned, the 1994 Act was incompatible with the Dean Forest Mines enactments.

The Coal Authority has to pay the Forestry Commission the cost of managing their interest (in particular the deputy gaveller's costs); but matters became complicated. The Authority asserts that a gale plus a licence sit side by side in accordance with the Minister's note of 25 January 1994; and that they do not replace one another but fall under different regimes.

From 1994 onwards the free miners increasingly reasoned their case with the Coal Authority and with the deputy gaveller acting on behalf of the Forestry Commission as gaveller. Much written and oral debate ensued, notably against dual licensing, and as to interpretation of various sections of relevant Acts. Representatives of the free miners, along with the then constituency MP (Paul Marland till mid-1997, and Diana Organ thereafter) occasionally met succeeding Ministers of State for Energy and the Forestry Commission and Coal Authority officials either in the Forest or in London, receiving an open and co-operative reception, but without achieving anything positive.

Individual free miners, including Eric Morris, Don Johns, Jonathan Wright, Michael Howell, Mike Jones, Ray Wright (a galee and secretary of their Association), and John Hine, a galee, repeatedly argued the freemining case. Brian James (not a free miner but a galee), as secretary of the local branch of the Small Mines Association, with the chairman Bert Hinton, also pursued *its* interests.

On 26 March 1996, in reply to the submission of a question to the European Commission by a Member of the European Parliament, the Commission stated: 'it understands that the Free Miners in the Forest of Dean have been treated in the same way as other companies and individuals seeking licences to extract coal. It further understands that the Coal Authority is considering whether special arrangements could be made for the free miners in view of the extremely small quantities of coal they produce. There appears to be no grounds to conclude that there is any discrimination against the free miners or any other breach of the Community's competition rules'.

1 Not until 3 March 1997 was forthcoming from the Coal Authority a suggested type of simplified licence for the Forest. The free miners were daunted by its 18-page length. Some working free miners agreed to the licence, but without prejudice; others did not. The three elements to the general licence fees for mines are believed to be: (i) an application fee of between £500 and £12,000 payable depending on the size of the mine (most of the Dean mines being on or near the minimum); (ii) a fee of £1,000 on grant of the licence; and (iii) an annual fee of £1,000 for supervision and monitoring smaller mines. In 1997, the first fee above was reduced for Dean to £50. In July 2001 the following further concessions were made: tiered royalties, reducing to aid development (e.g. 40p to 20p per tonne); and the annual tonnage extraction limit increased from 500 to 1,500 tonnes per annum.

In October 1996 at the request of Paul Marland MP, Lord Lindsay the Forestry Minister, accompanied by David Bills, Director General of the Forestry Commission, Paul Marland, and Roy Piggott the deputy gaveller met representatives of the free miners in the Forest who advanced comments and claims.

The free miners gradually prepared their written case, again basically against dual licensing, asserting that if, besides obtaining a gale from the deputy gaveller, they had to obtain a licence to mine from the Coal Authority, their statutory rights would no longer be 'free'. Their case was comprehensively improved in successive years and in various ways was made known orally and by correspondence particularly to the Coal Authority, the MP, and the deputy gaveller.

Meanwhile, some free miners continued to perform work to preserve their gales. However, enforcement procedures were considered by the Coal Authority against some working free miners, particularly in respect of Morses Level Colliery gale (upper and lower working) and Hamblin Yorkley Mine – virtually injunctions against allegedly illegal working their gales as they were not dual-licensed in accordance with the statutory provisions of the 1994 Act. Other galees, however, accepted the situation under protest.

In 1996, under the 1994 Act, the old 52+2 coal gales related to the 1938 and 1946 Acts were formally transferred to the Coal Authority by Roy Piggott, [Plate XIV] then deputy gaveller. They were prominently the deep gales but there were others (e.g. Oakenhill bought by British Coal in the 1980s because of the opencast potential) and others which were bought by the NCB, mostly shortly after nationalisation in 1946, and licensed back under S.36(2)(a) bare licences to certain free miners who then sold them. (The licences came free of charge but were not assignable.) With the odd exception, most of these gales had stood dormant and abandoned for a considerable time; consequently they were held in contravention of the Rules and Regulations governing freemining and theoretically could be forfeited. Some free miners, as hitherto, consider that the Coal Authority should have surrendered them to the gaveller's office thereby making them available for application. Why they were not, was for the same valid practices and financial reasons noted earlier. The hydrological regime underground is presently within balancing equilibrium, with the higher elevation Coleford High Delph outcrop at Ruardean some 800 feet A.O.D. with the southern outflow at the 'River' Lyd near Norchard, some 67 feet A.O.D. (In consequence, the discharge of waste into the mine workings from the water treatment works north-east of Drybrook was stopped.) Any regrant of the 52+2 gales other than under a complete feasibility study to competent and financially secure grantees could be folly if the underground water equilibrium were to be disturbed, notably against the background of the common law position relating to subsidence damage. Thus the *status quo* is currently retained by the Forestry Commission and the Coal Authority.

In 1997 the Forestry Commission and the Coal Authority wished to bring the free miners and galees under modern mining and planning regulations, not least those relating to environment, pollution, Health & Safety, and subsidence. The Coal Authority was concerned that coal mining in the Forest was not properly controlled, mapped or secured, and therefore there were safety and legal implications, posing a threat to public safety (unmapped shafts, etc.). An Agreement between the two departments dated 26 February 1997 (see Appendix D) facilitated a workable way forward having regard to the duties of the Authority and of the deputy gaveller. It attempted to reconcile the characteristics of the free miners with the Coal Authority's statutory obligations. The Agreement offered a practical working solution, without legislation change, to enable the deputy gaveller to discharge his duties under the Dean Forest Mines enactments and the Coal Authority to discharge its licensing duties, taking into account the special circumstances of the Forest. The Forestry Commission thereby apparently accepted the responsibility for surface subsidence matters, for safety and mining information, and the treatment of mine entries, whilst the Coal Authority accepted simplified licence terms with a nominal fee. All was with the objective of allowing freemining to continue in the traditional manner. The Authority apparently were anxious to ensure that: (a) anyone carrying out a coal mining operation could satisfy his liabilities to any third party in respect of subsidence; (b) on cessation of mining, all mine entries and its shafts, etc. should be put into a proper and safe condition (increasingly important as public access to the Forest grows); and (c) adequate information (plans, maps, etc.) was available as to the position and extent of mine workings as well as to the treatment of mine entries. Following the retirement of Roy Piggott, from late 1997 the deputy gaveller has been John Harvey [Plate XV] a Chartered Mining Engineer.

Following a meeting in June 2000 with Government officials in the Forest, in August 2000 the Free Miners Association, at the invitation of the Rt. Hon. Helen Liddell, then Minister of Energy and Competitiveness in Europe, made to her their comprehensive 'Submission of the Free Miners'. Its contents are evident in the following pages. During a Parliamentary Private Member's debate in October 2000, Minister Liddell reported that the position of the free miners and the Forest had been recognised at an early stage by those who developed the licensing policy. The policy for the Forest was for the Coal Authority to follow the pattern established under the 1946 Act, and to issue simple, reduced fee licences to free miners. That had been made clear in Explanatory Notes on the Act published in 1994 and in correspondence with the Forestry Commission. However, with hindsight, it was a pity there had been no direct dialogue with the free miners, but certainly their position in relation to the new legislation was anticipated and the legislation prepared accordingly. The policy had always been that the Forest would fall within the ambit of the new licensing system. This information was passed on to the succeeding Minister of State for Energy, the Rt. Hon. Peter Hain MP, who on 17 May 2001 unofficially and very briefly met representatives of the free miners in the Forest. The succeeding Minister of State for Energy and Industry was the Rt. Hon. Brian Wilson MP who, on 17 July, responded to the free miners' 'Submission', as noted below.

The free miners' main submissions, supporting and enlarging their earlier assertions were in brief:

(1) They mine as or on behalf of the Crown, and that, on that basis, they are exempt from the Coal Authority's licensing regime, as set out in the 1994 Act. Furthermore that S.7 of the Dean Forest (Reafforestation) Act 1668 [incidentally, now repealed] preserves the Forest in Crown ownership.

(2) Contrary to the Coal Authority's claim of ownership of the coal and coal mines of the Forest, these did not pass from the Crown to the Coal Authority via the Coal Commission,

Plate XIII. *Richard Davies, a Chartered Land Agent/Surveyor, area land agent for the Forestry Commission, who attends to stone quarries in the statutory Forest.*

Plate XIV. *Roy Piggott, deputy gaveller 1994-1997, a Chartered Mining Engineer and Chartered Minerals Surveyor, who took an important balanced view of the 1994 Act.*

Plate XV. *John Harvey, deputy gaveller 1997- , a Chartered Mining Engineer, who administers freemining on behalf of the Forestry Commission per the Dean Forest Mines enactments.*

the NCB and the BCC but have remained the property of the Crown. Furthermore that the Crown's ownership of the coal and coal mines of the Forest and the issuing of gales by the deputy gaveller both point towards their coal-mining operations taking place by or on behalf of the Crown.

(3) The gale issued by the deputy gaveller on behalf of the Crown, is the only licence required for their coal-mining operations; and the fact that the gale is issued on behalf of the Crown establishes the fact that they mine as or on behalf of the Crown.

The Minister and his department (DTI) in response first pointed out that there are, *inter alia,* three legal pre-requisites to mining coal: a lease conferring the ownership of the coal; the possession of rights to a piece of land above the coal through which to gain access to the coal; and a regulatory licence to carry out mining activity. An examination had been made of how these three pre-requisites apply to the free miners, and were commented upon as in A, B, C, and D hereafter.

A. To the free miners' argument that the Crown owns the coal and coal mines of the Forest, the DTI contend that the ownership is now vested in the Coal Authority. They trace the ownership of the coal and coal mines of the Forest from the Act of 1668, at which time, the free miners claim, the coal and coal mines of the Forest were made inalienable. S.7 which falls within the part of the Act dealing with the increase and preservation of timber within the Forest, states that '... to the end the said Forest and Premises may be perpetually preserved and estated in the Crown for public use, and may not be granted or disposed to any private use or benefit ... in case any person or persons whatsoever shall presume to take, or shall obtain any gift, grant, estate or interest, of or in the said inclosures or wastes, or any wood or trees growing thereon, or of or in any part of the mines or quarries of or within the said inclosures or any part thereof, every such gift, grant, estate and interest shall, *ipso facto*, be null and void, and the person or persons so taking or obtaining the same, shall be, and is hereby made and declared utterly disabled and incapable to have, hold or enjoy any such gift, grant, estate or interest'. The Crown Lands Act 1829 consolidated various Acts which had made provision for the management and improvement of Crown estates, including the Forest. By virtue of these Acts, Crown woods, forests and parks had been placed under the management of the Commissioners of Woods, Forests and Land Revenues. S.2 of the 1829 Act re-affirmed the role of the Commissioners. In 1832 these Commissioners were replaced by the Commissioners of Woods, Forests, Land Revenues, Works and Buildings. Nearly 20 years later, by virtue of the Crown Lands Act 1851, the duties of the Commissioners in relation to the direction of Works and Public Buildings were passed to the First Commissioner of Works and Public Buildings. The greater part of the control of the royal forests was handed over to the Commissioners of Woods, Forests and Land Revenues (later the Commissioners of Crown Lands) and now the Crown Estate Commissioners.

In 1919, the Forestry Commission was established by virtue of the Forestry Act 1919. Between 1924 and 1926, '... all the estate, interest, rights, powers, and liabilities of the Crown and of the Commissioners of Woods in or in connection with any property under the management or control of the Commissioners of Woods ...' were transferred to and vested in the Forestry Commissioners, a Crown body. This expressly includes the coal and coal mines under the Forest.

The Coal Act 1938 transferred the property in all unworked coal in Great Britain into the hands of a single public body – the Coal Commission. However, S.43 made the following specific provision with respect to the Forest:

> (1) This Part of this Act [Part 1] shall have effect in its application to land in the Forest of Dean ... being land in respect of which the privileges of the free miners are exercisable, subject to the following modifications:
>
> (2) '... on the vesting date, the interest of the Forestry Commissioners in the coal and mines of coal comprised in the said land shall vest in the Commission, subject to and in accordance with the provisions of the Dean Forest (Mines) Act 1838, and of any other enactment relating to the said land and to all interests subsisting or to be created under or by virtue thereof.'

The free miners argue that S.7 of the 1668 Act renders the coal and coal mines of the Forest inalienable – that although S.43(2) of the 1938 Act vests the interests of the Forestry Commission in the Forest mines in the Coal Commission, this is subject, *inter alia,* to S.7 of the 1668 Act. The Dean Forest Mines enactments include the 1838 Act and any other enactment relating to the Forest. The free miners are of the view that this includes S.7 of the 1668 Act and that, if this is the case, the vesting of the interests of the Forestry Commission in the Coal Authority of 1994 was something less than full ownership. However, S.43(2) of the 1938 Act expressly transfers the interest of the Forestry Commissioners in the coal and coal mines to the Coal Commission. It would be wholly contradictory, therefore, to interpret the reference to the provisions to which this transfer is subject in the term '... *any other enactment* ...' as including S.7 of the 1668 Act. This would have precluded the transfer of the interests of the Forestry Commissioners to the Coal Commission. The free miners' argument would lead to the illogical conclusion that S.43 of the 1938 Act purports to transfer the Forestry Commissioners' interests in the coal and coal mines of the Forest to the Coal Commission, subject to the fact that these interests could not be transferred as a result of the provisions of the 1668 Act. It is clear that S.43 of the 1938 Act effected the transfer of the coal and coal mines in the Forest, but it also preserves those provisions of the Dean Forest Mines enactments that are not inconsistent with S.43. It is apparent that the Coal Commission transfer was made subject to the preservation of the ancient customs and regulations of the free miners, as set out in the 19th century Dean Forest Mines Acts, rather than S.7 of the 1668 Act.

The free miners argue that, because the 1668 Act had not been repealed or modified when the 1938 Act was enacted, it continued to apply to the Forest. However (at least in this context) Parliament is sovereign and a new law can repeal any existing law either expressly or by implication. The provision in the 1668 Act making the Forest inalienable was inconsistent with the transfer of the coal to the

Coal Commission, therefore it was by implication repealed. The clear wording of the 1938 Act on this point is conclusive that the coal was transferred out of Crown ownership in 1938.

Two other points, which demonstrate that the free miners' arguments in relation to S.7 are, in any event, inconsistent with the intention of S.43 of the 1938 Act, should be noted. Firstly, S.7 is clearly aimed at the protection of the Forest, for the purpose of re-establishing tree growth. Secondly, the preclusion in relation to the grant or disposal of Forest land was specifically tied to a grant or disposal for private use or benefit. As the 1938 Act transfer of the interests of the Forestry Commission to the Coal Commission was a transfer to a public body, the transfer could not be described as being for any private use or benefit. Thus, on 1 July 1942 (the vesting date), there vested in the Coal Commission all the interests of the Crown in all coal and coal mines as existing at that date together with all other interests, apart from retained interests (not relevant here). The vesting of all coal and coal mines included Crown lands, such as the Forest. Despite the transfer of the Forestry Commissioners' interests their powers under the Dean Forest Mines enactments continued to be exercisable by them by reason of the exception in S.43.

The Coal Authority's ownership of coal and coal mines under the Forest is demonstrated by the fact that the rents payable under a gale are passed to the Authority. Although the Authority makes payments from the rents to the deputy gaveller, these are payments for his work in managing the Authority's interests – a system established by S.43(6) of the 1938 Act.

The Coal Industry Nationalisation Act 1946 effected the nationalisation of the coal-mining industry as from 1 January 1947. By S.5 and Schedule 1, the Coal Commission's interests in all unworked coal and of the coal mining companies ('colliery concerns') and certain interests which were retained interests under the 1938 Act, passed to the NCB (renamed the BCC by virtue of S.1 of the Coal Industry Act 1987). The Coal Industry Act 1994 provided for the coal industry to return to the private sector, operating under a licensing system. S.1 established the Coal Authority, which, on 31 October 1994, succeeded to the interests of the BCC in unworked coal and coal mines, per S.7(3) of the Act. The system whereby the deputy gaveller collected the rent from the gales and passed them on to the Coal Commission was preserved by the 1994 Act, in paragraph 5 of Schedule 10. Thus the ownership of the coal by the Coal Authority is further confirmed. Although the Crown continues to own the surface of the Forest through the Forestry Commission, ownership of the coal under the Forest rests with the Coal Authority.

B. The free miners claim that they carry out coal-mining operations by or on behalf of the Crown, asserting that they are exempt from the licensing provisions of the 1994 Act as a result, because there is a specific exemption for coal-mining operations by or on behalf of the Crown in S.66(3) of the Act. The DTI contend that the 1994 Act introduced a prohibition on the carrying on of coal-mining operations otherwise than in accordance with the licensing provisions of the Act. The Coal Authority were given the power to license all coal-mining activities. This licensing regime is in the nature of a regulatory regime dealing with matters such as ensuring operators are able to deal with obligations associated with their mining activity. S.25 states that coal-mining operations shall not be carried on by any person except under and in accordance with a Part II licence. S.26 gives the Coal Authority the sole power to grant such a licence. The BCC granted licences to mine coal in the Forest under S.36 of the 1946 Act. Under the 1994 Act, the Coal Authority, in any case not covered by a continuing S.36 licence, exercises its licensing powers under Ss. 2 and 26. The same Act therefore empowers the Coal Authority to license coal-mining operations carried on in any part of Great Britain; it contains no exemption for licensing coal-mining in the Forest. S.66(3) states that 'Nothing in this section shall be taken as requiring a licence under Part II of this Act for the carrying on by or on behalf of the Crown of any coal-mining operations'. The free miners' arguments as to how they fall within S.66(3) are noted below.

B1. The free miners contend that the Crown owns the unworked coal in the Forest and, consequently, they mine as or on behalf of the Crown. The DTI's conclusion is that the law is quite clear that the ownership of the unworked coal, both within the Forest and elsewhere in Great Britain, is now vested in the Coal Authority. Consequently the free miners cannot be mining as or on behalf of the Crown, simply on the basis of Crown ownership of the coal. The Crown does have an interest in the Forest, in that it owns the land (but not the coal beneath it), but this does not mean that the 1994 Act does not apply in the Forest – S.66(1). Even if it were the case that the Crown owned the coal and coal mines under the Forest, S.66(l) would have the effect of obliging the free miners to obtain a Coal Authority licence in any event, unless they could establish that their coal mining activities take place by or on behalf of the Crown – the Coal Authority licence being a licence designed to regulate coal mining activities and has nothing to do with its ownership.

B2. The free miners suggest that they work in partnership with the deputy gaveller and that this indicates that they mine by or on behalf of the Crown. The DTI point out that the free miners' activities are regulated by the Crown through its appointed deputy gaveller. He is the officer who represents the Crown in its dealings with the free miners and this office is now vested in the Forestry Commissioners, by virtue of the Forestry (Transfer of Woods) Order 1924, which did not affect the duties and powers of the deputy gaveller. As a result of the 1938 Act the powers, conferred by the Dean Forest Mines enactments, that were vested in the Forestry Commissioners immediately before the 1938 Act, continued to be exercisable by them; for example, the deputy gaveller's power to demand a gale rent continued; however, the rents are paid to the Coal Authority, as the owner of the coal. The deputy gaveller continues to grant gales and has certain duties for regulating compliance with the provisions of the Dean Forest Mines enactments. The second Schedule of the Award of Coal Mines, 1841, identifies rules and regulations associated with the working of the gales and might be considered as relating to the policing of the proprietary interests. These are, in the main, distinct from the licensing issues covered under the 1994 Act. The relationship between the deputy gaveller, who represents the Crown and the free miners is that of the regulator and regulated. The free miners' relationship with the deputy gaveller does not provide further evidence of the free miners' activity on behalf of the Crown, as they suggest.

To the contrary, the deputy gaveller's regulation of the free miners suggests that their activities are subject to the control of the Crown.

B3. The free miners argue that it was accepted by Gloucestershire County Council that, under past planning legislation (the Town and Country Planning Acts 1947 and 1971) they fell within a corresponding exemption of 'by or on behalf of the Crown', quoting Halsbury's Laws, Volume 8. The free miners claim that they have not had to apply for planning permission for their developments by reason of the Crown exemption and claim that, as a result, they should be viewed as mining as or on behalf of the Crown for 1994 Act purposes. The DTI agree that there used to be a Crown exemption under planning legislation until this was revoked under the Town and Country Planning Act 1990. However, the DTI is not in a position to confirm whether it is factually correct that free miners were not and are not expected to apply for planning permission for their coal-mining activities – this being a matter for the County Council – and even if the County Council have not in practice required the free miners to obtain planning permission, it does not necessarily follow that this is because they are of the view that the free miners are acting on behalf of the Crown. The DTI's legal analysis is that the free miners do not carry on coal-mining by or on behalf of the Crown (in the guise of the Forestry Commission), as they assert, rather, the free miners' coal-mining activities are carried out on their own behalf subject to the control of the Crown. The provisions requiring them to be licensed by the Coal Authority clearly apply to them.

C. The free miners claim that an award of a gale by the deputy gaveller of itself is a sufficient statutory licence for their coal-mining activities. The DTI point out that coal operators need to secure a property interest in the coal as well as a licence to work the coal. In all areas of the country, apart from the Forest, the property interest is secured via a coal-mining lease from the Coal Authority, whereas, in the Forest, a free miner secures the property interest from the deputy gaveller via the grant of a gale. Modern legislation such as the 1946 Act and the 1994 Act do not alter this position, although the free miners do have to obtain a licence and pay the appropriate fee. The free miners contend that there is no need for them to have a licence, as the gale is a licence, according to S.1 of the Dean Forest (Amendment) Act 1861. Although S.l refers to the gale as a licence, it is clear from case law that the gale also confers a proprietary interest in the coal mines of the Forest – the leasing element required for coal-mining, as described above, as well as the right to mine in the Forest. Whenever a gale is mentioned in case law, there is little debate as to its nature. Gales are discussed in terms of a proprietary interest in the coal and coal mines of the Forest, similar to a lease [see Morgan and Others *v*. Crawshay (1871) LR 5HL 304; and The Great Western (Forest of Dean) Collieries Company *v*. The Trafalgar Company Limited (1887) 3 TLR 724]. The cases show that a gale confers the required proprietary interest in the coal and coal mines of the Forest and is the equivalent of the lease required in all other parts of Great Britain. The Coal Authority's ownership of the coal and coal mines under the Forest is reflected in the fact that the rents payable in relation to gales are passed to the Coal Authority. The

1994 Act left intact the legislation governing the grant of gales and the provisions for payment between the owner of the coal and the Forestry Commissioners in respect of their particular rights. It does, however, continue the system of regulation by licence of coal-mining that applies to the free miners as well as to every other coal operator in the country. Freemining was allowed to continue by virtue of specific exemptions in both the 1938 and 1946 Acts; indeed, S.63(2) of the 1946 Act makes it clear that the working of coal by a free miner did not constitute, for the purposes of the 1946 Act, a 'colliery concern'. But after 1946, the NCB, later the BCC, issued licences to the free miners under S.36 of the 1946 Act. Those developing the policy of licensing for the 1994 Act specifically considered the position of the free miners. The policy for the Forest was that the Coal Authority would continue to follow the BCC practice and issue simplified licences to free miners.

D. The free miners argue that the Secretary of State can and should give a direction to the Coal Authority exempting them from the 1994 Act licensing regime. The DTI point out that the Coal Authority must comply with such directions of a general character as may be given to it by the Secretary of State with respect to the carrying out of any of its functions, or to its activities generally, by virtue of S.6(1) of the 1994 Act. Under S.6(2), the Coal Authority must also comply with such specific directions as may be given to it by the Secretary of State with respect to: (a) whether or not it exercises any of its powers and the manner in which any of its powers is to be exercised; (b) the manner in which any of its duties is to be performed; or (c) any other conduct by the Coal Authority in connection with the carrying out of any of its functions or with its activities generally. However, these powers do not enable the Secretary of State to give a direction to the Coal Authority to exempt free miners from the licensing provisions of the 1994 Act. It is not in the power of the Authority to grant such an exemption, therefore there is no power for the Secretary of State to direct such a power to be exercised. Such an exemption would conflict with the clear prohibition on coal-mining without a Part II licence in S.25.

The DTI's summary of its conclusions is:

(a) The Coal Authority owns the coal and coal mines of the Forest.

(b) The free miners do not carry on coal-mining as the Crown or on behalf of the Forestry Commission. Rather, the free miners' coal-mining activities are carried out on their own behalf.

(c) The grant of a gale by the deputy gaveller is the grant of a proprietary interest in coal owned by the Coal Authority; this shown by statutory provisions for the rental income from gales to be paid, via the deputy gaveller, to the Authority. The gale is, in part, a licence to mine the coal. Although this might suggest that there could be some overlap between the Authority's licensing regime and the regulation of the free miners by the deputy gaveller under the Dean Forest Mines enactments, in practice, there is little crossover between the two regimes.

(d) The Secretary of State cannot direct the Coal Authority to exempt free miners from the licensing provisions of the 1994 Act.

The Minister and his DTI added that there are two regulatory systems impacting on freemining, and explained that both systems stem from primary legislation and therefore changes could only be made by primary legislation. Furthermore, their opinion is that, in practice, there is little duplication of the coverage of the two systems – that being especially so since the 1997 Agreement between the Coal Authority and the Forestry Commission [see Appendix D] gave responsibility for subsidence, safety and mining information to the Commission. It reconciled the characteristics of the free miners with the Coal Authority's duties and provided a simplified licence for a reduced fee. The Minister emphasised that the DTI conclusion on licensing did not in any way reduce the Government's respect for freemining. He recognised the value of freemining to the economy of the Forest both historically and today. It had done much to create the character and individuality of the region and added cultural interest to the beauty of the natural environment. The laws governing its operation were largely still extant and the Government had no wish to see these ancient customs disappear. However, it was clear that these laws are subject to more modern legislation which applies to the free miners just as much as it does to other parts of the country's coal mining community.

Hence, it appears that the fundamental outcome at present is that the free miners must continue to obtain not only a gale from the deputy gaveller but also a simple, reduced fee licence from the Coal Authority for any mining operations they wish to carry out in the coalfield. However, the free miners still argue that, as a matter of law, they are not subject to the Coal Authority's licensing regime and that, if they were, they ought, as a matter of policy, to be exempt from it.

The current (April 2002) relevant situation in regard to the 1994 Act is noted in Chapter XII.

TOWN AND COUNTRY PLANNING INCIDENCE

Planning incidence was hardly anywhere until the 20th century on any development, mining or otherwise. However, for freemining in the Forest and hundred, there were early Orders of the Mine Law Court as to the distance required between any workings, and as to 'filling-in' or fencing of abandoned pits; but usually they were ineffective. The 1841 Awards (Rule 12) of coal and iron ore gales and stone quarries, provided for the tidying of surface sites after working. In the mid-19th century, deputy gavellers (e.g. Edward Machen acting jointly with John Atkinson) awarded compensation against free miners for damage by subsidence.[1]

The Town & Country Planning (General Development) Order 1948 excluded then existing colliery concerns under Clause 19 so long as they continued to work; but planning consent for regrants or for new mines or extensions became statutorily necessary, including within the Forest.

1 Glos.R.O. D9096, F26/5 in 1843, /6 in 1848, /8 in 1854-56, /9 in 1855, and /11 in 1858.

The Town & Country Planning Act 1971 made it necessary for free miners or galees, i.e. heirs or assigns, to obtain planning permission if they wished to carry out development as defined in S.22. This particular incidence was debated during 1973 at a public local inquiry held into Enforcement Notices served by the Gloucestershire County Council on six galees: the Secretary of State for the Environment's decision 7 May 1974 agreed with the Council's view that there was a necessity to obtain planning permission before mining was permitted.

All coal mining requires planning consent under the Planning Acts but in recent decades in Dean it has not been obtained. Currently, a Coal Authority licence under the 1994 Act covenants that planning consent must be obtained; and it is a condition of a free miner's gale that the grantee 'observes the laws for the time being in force'. This is, of course, a matter for the Gloucestershire County Planning Department to enforce under the Town & Country Planning Acts. The deputy gaveller is in a difficult position regarding this, because, in any event, the 1995 Environment Act requires that all mining developments granted (or deemed) before March 1982 must be renewed. [As a test case, in 1996 the deputy gaveller, Roy Piggott, was engaged with Jonathan Wright, a free miner, in regard to his Drybrook iron ore gale, so as to keep separate coal gale issues with the Coal Authority.]

In 1996 Gerald Haynes, a free miner, applied for planning permission in respect of his Hayners Bailey Coal Licence of the Yorkley (Bailey) seam (part of the Union Gale of 1904). He had previously obtained from British Coal a S.36(2)(a) licence which had expired on 31 March 1995. He was granted a renewal by the Coal Authority, subject to planning conditions imposed by the Gloucestershire County Council, as required by covenant under the Authority's licensing regime.

The Dean Forest Mines enactments (1838 to 1906, as amended) and the associated licensing regimes, statutorily oblige galees to conform with all other Acts and regulations 'for the time being in force'. Thus, free miners, galees, their heirs and assigns are obliged to conform with all related statutory provisions as they are enacted, e.g. those relating to Health & Safety in mines and quarries, environmental control, pollution control, and all the Town & Country Planning Acts. Subsidence is a patent problem following the 1994 Act. During recent years the latter appears to cause some difficulty with coal and iron ore operations. Subsequently, Quidchurch, Addis Hill, Hayners, Hopewell in Wimberry and New Road Level (near Hopewell) have obtained planning consent. This, of course, having regard to geology, is a matter for Gloucestershire County Council as Mineral Planning Authority, for whilst its current Structure Plan (First Alteration) is silent in relation to iron ore mining, it does set out the following general policies with regard to both opencast and underground coal mining:

- Opencast coal mining is dealt with under County General Policy M 13[1] to the effect that it will not normally be permitted unless it can be demonstrated that there is no significant

[1] General Policy M 13 states: 'The extraction of coal by opencast methods will not normally be permitted unless it can be demonstrated that the proposal will not have a significant detrimental effect on the recreation and tourism role of the Forest of Dean, on environmental or traffic conditions or on settlements. In considering any proposals particular regard will be paid to the method of working and restoration, and to whether the proposals will lead to an improvement in the landscape or environment in areas of old mineral workings or to better conditions for agriculture and forestry.'

detrimental effect on the Dean Forest role relating to recreation, tourism, environmental and traffic conditions, and settlements (communities). Particular regard will be paid to working methods, restoration, landscape and environmental improvements in old mineral workings, as well as better conditions for agriculture and forestry.

- Underground coal mining is dealt with in County General Policy M 14[1] which provides that it will also be dealt with on its merits having regard to the 'free miner' background and history and the likely impact on the environment. There are no collateral rights to withdraw (physical) support.

For both opencast and underground coal mining, Annex E of Mineral Planning Guidance (MPG 3) sets out the Department of Environment Guidelines.

Two other Acts which must be borne in mind are: the Environmental Protection Act 1990, and the Water Resources Act 1991, where both Acts relate to mines drainage issues.

In July 1996 Ray Ashley, a free miner, and Nick Bull (agents acting for Mrs Jennifer Thomas – a galee by assignment) applied for, and were granted planning permission for the Quidchurch coal gale, near Ruspidge.

As to Health & Safety, the main relevant Act is the Health and Safety at Work etc. 1974 under which were made the Management and Administration of Safety and Health in Mines Regulations 1993 (MASHAM) – a matter for H.M. Mines Inspectorate. It had a profound effect on the perception of the coal mining because not one of the mines was in accordance with it. For instance, it led to an Enforcement Notice, apparently as an example to others, on New Road Level (Hopewell), galee Robin Morgan. [Incidentally, it should be noted that whereas the Dean Forest Mines enactments are civil law the MASHAM regulations are criminal law.]

Since 1 January 1999, where a mine or part of a mine is abandoned (ceased working) notice must be given to H.M. Mines Inspectorate under the Mines (Notice of Abandonment Regulations) 1998, at least six months before the abandonment takes place. However, in the Forest, the conditions of the licences of mines awarded by the Coal Authority or gales granted by the deputy gaveller, could require a mine operator to surrender a mine in a shorter time period than the regulations require.

As to planning incidence regarding mining, the free miners argue that it was accepted by Gloucestershire County Council that, under past planning legislation (the Town and Country Planning Acts 1947 and 1971), they fall within an exemption of 'by or on behalf of the Crown', quoting Halsbury's Laws, Volume 8. The free miners claim that they have not had to apply for planning permission for their developments by reason of the Crown exemption and further claim that as a result, they should be viewed as mining as or on behalf of the Crown for the 1994 Coal Industry Act purposes. There used to be a Crown exemption under planning legislation until this was revoked under the Town and Country Planning Act 1990.

---

1 General Policy M 14 states. 'Proposals for underground mining of coal will be considered on their merits bearing in mind both the history of freemining in the Forest of Dean and the likely impact of the activity upon the environment.'

However, it has not been tested in law whether it is factually correct that free miners were not and are not expected to apply for planning permission for their coal-mining activities – this being a matter for the County Council. Even if that Council has not in practice required free miners to obtain planning permission, it does not necessarily follow that this is because it is of the view that the free miners are acting on behalf of the Crown, notwithstanding that, as discussed earlier, the DTI position is that the free miners do not act on behalf of the Crown.

CHAPTER XII

THE PRESENT DAY (AD 2002)

THE present day situation of freemining is still dominated by the incidence of the Coal Industry Act 1994, as discussed in Chapter XI. The compatibility or otherwise of that Act and the Dean Forest Mines enactments (1838 to 1906, as modified), has caused considerable concern – to the Forestry Commission, as gaveller, the Coal Authority, and particularly to the free miners who are now involved in a dual licensing scenario (i.e. gale and licence) with all the implications and financial costs thereof. The incongruity between the two sets of legislation has for almost a decade been actively pursued by the free miners with the relative Government departments. The Coal Authority stance appears to be that whilst acknowledging the freemining rights under the amended enactments, the 1994 Act is equally cogent, with its relationship with the Forestry Commission being that set out in their Agreement of 1997 (see Appendix D). This scenario appears to have induced much frustration to the few working, and some politically motivated, free miners, thereby making the prospects of active freemining seemingly unnecessarily uncertain, fragile and speculative. Acting under a strong sense of principle, and alarmed at what they consider an impingement of their rights, the situation has generated in the free miners a resurgence, reinvigoration and strengthening of their endeavours to safeguard their ancient customs and heritage. Already the Coal Authority has made some concessions, chiefly by reducing its licence fee to £50 and increasing the licensing limit of extraction from 500 to 1,500 tonnes per annum.[1] The outcome of the long debate on the 1994 Act may not appear conclusive to the Free Miners Association themselves, but does provide a scenario wherein the relatively few qualified miners (and their successors) who desire to carry on traditional freemining of coal may do so, within existing legislation.

Two uncertainties relate to the resolution of two separate factors. First, the achievement of the essential qualification of birth within the Hundred of St. Briavels, there now being no Maternity Hospital therein. Second, obtaining the qualification of working for a year and a day in a local mine, there now being relatively few active operations.

The ancient customs and privileges of the free miners have been modified through the ages, but the principle that the exclusive right to work is in them, subject to certain rights of the Crown or State, has been maintained to the present time. In important features, rights of mining for coal and iron ore in the Forest and hundred is that formerly claimed in the miners' ancient 'Laws and Privileges' and in the Orders of their Mine Law Court, although now not statutorily binding. It differs in many respects from what is or has been applicable elsewhere in the United Kingdom. In simple terms, the

1 The DTI on 16 March 2002 informed the Free Miners Association that 'they see no reason why freemining cannot continue to exist and, hopefully, thrive within the existing regime while retaining the majority of that which makes it unique'. (The Rt. Hon. Brian Wilson, MP, Minister of State for Energy and Industry.)

qualifications necessary to become a free miner in accordance with the Dean Forest (Mines) Act 1838, as amended by the Statute Law (Repeals) Act 1969, Sch Pt. VIII are:

As to coal and iron ore mining

- born and abiding in the *hundred*[1]
- be male[2], and over 21 years of age
- worked a year and a day in a coal or iron ore mine[3] within the *hundred* (larger than the statutory Forest)

  A registered coal or iron ore free miner can be granted a gale or lease of a stone quarry.

As to stone quarrying

- born and abiding in the *hundred*
- be male, and over 21 years of age
- worked [no period stated] in a stone quarry within the *statutory Forest* (smaller than the hundred)

  A registered stone quarry free miner can *not* be granted a gale of coal or iron ore

Every registered free miner has the exclusive right to claim from the Crown, i.e. the State per the Forestry Commission, a gale to enable him to mine for his own profit (subject to payment of dead rents and royalties), iron ore and coal within the hundred or stone within the Forest perambulation. He may apply for and work the gale himself, or he may do so in partnership with other free miners; or he may lease, sell or gift his right in the gale, to 'galees', usually for a lump sum or on a royalty basis. No free miner may be granted more than three gales at any one time, though he may hold additional acquired gales; and a gale must not interfere with the working of any other gale. In return for his rights the free miner must comply with certain conditions, explained in earlier chapters. Since the Dean Forest (Mines) Act 1838 the area over which his rights extend has been curtailed, and any coal or iron ore gale applied for must be within the Hundred of St. Briavels, and even then must not include 'Excepted Lands' *infra*[4] and certain Forestry Commission afforested areas

1 The one-time qualification of 'free parentage' no longer applies.

2 Whilst the primary essential for the initial grant of a gale is that to a male free miner, his heirs and assigns can be female – notwithstanding they cannot qualify as free miners in any event, and, except in certain circumstances nowadays, cannot be employed underground.

3 Working in a mine was taken to mean *underground*, until from 1996 working in *opencast* coal mining also was clarified to be 'working in a mine' [Jones *v*. Piggott, 1996. No free miner formally objected.] Michael John Jones, an Upper Redbrook local entrepreneur in 1985 undertook and worked in a 2.5 hectare area of opencast coal mining at Edge End in the Forest, under the gales of part Hopewell in Wimberry and part of the Thatch, purchased from a free miner. Following the Coal Industry Act 1994, he decided in 1995 to apply for registration as a free miner. This was refused by the deputy gaveller Roy Piggott who considered that, *inter alia*, working in opencast was not 'working in a mine' but in a quarry under the 1838 Act. Jones took the deputy gaveller to Gloucester Crown Court in March 1996 under Ss. 14 and 19 of the Dean Forest (Mines) Act 1838. He was successful and the deputy gaveller by order of the Court was obliged to register him as a free miner on 19 April 1996 in accordance with S.20. Since 1942 there have been 14 local opencast coal sites, not all within the statutory Forest.

4 The free miners' rights have been disputed in some private properties within the hundred, especially in the 'Excepted Lands' referred to in the Act of 1838; subsequently the miners have not questioned the matter, except in a single case – Grindell's Petition of Right, 1870. See Appendix A. Particularly Noxon Park, Kidnalls and Sneyd Woods, and Mailscot. These areas were among those excepted from the operations of the Dean Forest (Mines) Act 1838. Since 1838 deputy gavellers have in many instances galed minerals under freehold lands other than 'Excepted Lands'. In these cases in compliance with S.67 of the Act of 1838, they have collected the royalty and handed over a moiety, less 2½ per cent., to the freeholders.

so long as they remain inclosed but, occasionally, under special conditions. The mineral district covers only about one-third of the land delimited. Gales granted have had surface areas ranging from a few acres to as much as 800 acres; in one case several forfeited gales were regranted to a large number of free miners as a combined gale of about 2,000 acres.

A local popular misconception concerns the consolidation/amalgamation of gales per the 1904 Act (see Appendix B). These gales were actually granted initially to free miners. The Act facilitated their amalgamation to suitably large coal areas so as to allow interested colliery companies sufficiently large areas to justify the capital expense of sinking the necessary deep shafts, carrying out the surface development and infrastructure etc. The colliery companies which eventually evolved were those listed in the third paragraph of Appendix B. The original amalgamated coal operators *bought* the gales as assignees from the galees listed at the top of that Appendix. The gales were not therefore initially granted to colliery companies; they became vested *in toto* in the individual companies concerned. The colliery companies who purchased the listed gales, agreed a sort of mortgage arrangement with the many galees instead of an outright capital sum. Thus the purchase money was paid piecemeal to the initial galees, or their heirs and assigns, at the Speech House. These payments were, therefore, purchase monies and not galeage rents and/or royalties as such, made until the purchase debt was extinguished in accordance with the trust arrangements. This was a 'private' bargain between the galees and the colliery companies and not the concern of the then Crown, or later the Forestry Commission. Some heirs of free miners are still confused by this background. That was the position up to the closure of the last deep mine, Northern United in 1965, with, paradoxically the NCB itself the amalgamated galee – naturally not paying rent to itself.

Following the Act of 1838 the coal and iron ore has been managed in accordance with its provisions as amended by subsequent Acts, and since 1841, boundaries of gales have been accurately described in writing and by means of plans and maps; and suitable boundary stones (some now missing) were set on the surface. In most cases barriers of coal, usually forty-four yards in width, were reserved between adjoining gales; the deputy gaveller has power to grant the coal in these barriers as and when he considers it advisable. The payment by the free miners, known as dead rents and royalties, are subject to adjustment every sixty-three years for deep gales and twenty-one for other gales, or such other times as the deputy gaveller might see justifiable. Grants of gales may be declared void, forfeited, and made available to other free miners, for breach of conditions of working, non-payment of rents and royalties, or failure to work within a stipulated period.

From the mid-nineteenth century up to about 1904 the mines were almost exclusively of coal and not of iron ore.[1] Some of the free miners are, as one would expect, very knowledgeable as to the geological structure of their underground neighbourhood, especially as regards outcrops, faults, successions, dips, inclines, and water difficulties: hence their advice has often been eagerly sought.

Many inhabitants of the district who possess the necessary qualifications for applying

1 In 1953 the only iron ore mine in production was the New Dunn Mine (owner, Fred. Watkins). Only a little ochre is latterly worked there.

for registration as free miners have never done so.[1] The rights are well appreciated by the majority of free miners and great excitement in the past has been displayed on occasions when the deputy gaveller, having regained possession of a potentially valuable gale, has given notice to the free miners that on a stated day applications could be made for the same.

To become a registered free miner the applicant must complete the following form:

Application for Registration

N.B.—This declaration must be supported by documentary evidence as to the date and place of applicant's birth, and as to his having worked a year and a day in a Mine (or Quarry).

Certificate of........................produced.
Nature of evidence produced that Applicant has worked a year and a day in a Mine (or Quarry).
....
....

THE
ROYAL FOREST OF DEAN
AND
HUNDRED OF ST. BRIAVELS
IN THE COUNTY OF GLOUCESTER

APPLICATION FOR REGISTRATION

To the Gaveller and Deputy Gaveller of Dean Forest

PURSUANT to an Act passed in the First and Second Years of the Reign of HER MAJESTY QUEEN VICTORIA, intituled " An Act for Regulating the opening and working of Mines and Quarries, in the Forest of Dean and Hundred of St. Briavels, in the County of Gloucester,"

I(a)

of(a) do hereby declare that I was born at in the said Hundred of Saint Briavels, on the day of in the Year of our Lord One Thousand Hundred and and that I have worked a year and a day in a(b) Mine that is to say in the(c) Mine within the said Hundred, that I am now abiding at within the said Hundred, and following the trade or business of and I hereby claim to be Registered as a Free Miner, pursuant to the provisions of the above-mentioned Act.

As witness my hand this day of Two Thousand and

(d)

Witness to the signature and above declaration of the above-named Applicant(e)

(a) Name and residence of Applicant to be here inserted in words at length.

(b) Here describe whether a Coal or Iron Mine, or a Stone Quarry, (c) and also the particular Mine or Quarry.

(d) Signature of Applicant.

(e) Signature and Address of Witness.

---

1 Of the average number of free miners in existence at various times in the past, it is known that there were 662 in 1788, 1,080 in 1835, and 829 in 1841 [R. J. Treharne Rees (a deputy gaveller); Presidential Address, South Wales Inst. of Engineers (18 Jan. 1945)]. From the year 1838 up to 17 May 1944, 4,035 free miners were registered [*ibid.*], but of these all but about 1,300 had since died.

The signature must be witnessed, and the form supported by documentary evidence as to (*a*) date and place of birth (where a birth certificate is not procurable, a certificate of baptism is usually accepted) and (*b*) having worked a year and a day in a mine or quarry within the hundred. The form when completed has to be submitted to the deputy gaveller at Coleford, and if all the conditions are complied with the applicant is duly registered as a free miner and his name entered in 'The Register of Free Miners of the Hundred of St. Briavels'. He is then supplied with an extract from the Register in the following form:

"EXTRACT FROM THE REGISTER OF FREE MINERS OF THE HUNDRED OF SAINT BRIAVELS

Pursuant to the Act of 1 and 2 Vic., Cap. 43, Sec. 22 [1838]

NO.	NAME	RESIDENCE	AGE	WHEN REGISTERED

.................*Deputy Gaveller*"

When a free miner wishes to apply for a gale he completes a form of which the following is a copy:

THE

FOREST OF DEAN

AND

HUNDRED OF ST. BRIAVELS

IN THE COUNTY OF GLOUCESTER

APPLICATION FOR A GALE

To the Gaveller and Deputy Gaveller of Dean Forest

I

of([a])

a Free Miner duly registered as such in the register kept by the Gaveller or Deputy Gaveller of Dean Forest in pursuance of the Act of the First and Second of the Queen hereinafter referred to, hereby signify my request to have a Gale for a([b])

made to me at([c])

to get the Coal from the Vein or Seam called([d])

(a) Fill up these blanks with the Christian and Surname and place of Residence of the Applicant, in words at length.

(b) Fill up this blank with Pit or Level as the case may be.

(c) Fill up this blank with the exact situation of the proposed Gale.

(d) Fill up this blank with the name of the particular vein of Coal intended to be worked: or in case of Iron Ore, strike out the words from "Coal" to "called" inclusive, and state the Ore intended to be got.

And if the Gale hereby applied for shall be granted to me, I hereby undertake and agree to open and work, and to use and enjoy the said Gale when so granted, subject in all respects to the provisions contained in and to the Award,

continued

continued

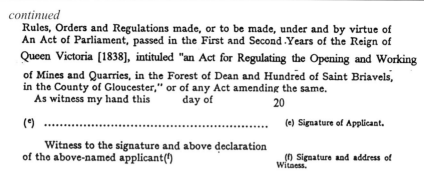

Rules, Orders and Regulations made, or to be made, under and by virtue of An Act of Parliament, passed in the First and Second Years of the Reign of Queen Victoria [1838], intituled "an Act for Regulating the Opening and Working of Mines and Quarries, in the Forest of Dean and Hundred of Saint Briavels, in the County of Gloucester," or of any Act amending the same.

As witness my hand this day of 20

(e) .... (e) Signature of Applicant.

Witness to the signature and above declaration of the above-named applicant(f) (f) Signature and address of Witness.

...

This form must be submitted to the deputy gaveller who enters the details in the Application Book and searches previous applications to ensure that the present applicant is the first to apply for the gale in question. If there are no previous living applicants, an Application Paper and draft grant are prepared by the deputy gaveller setting out the proposed boundaries of the gale, the dead rent, tonnage royalty and any special conditions deemed necessary. These documents if approved, are signed and sealed by him. The latter then inserts an advertisement in local newspapers, setting out the name of the free miner, the boundaries of the proposed gale and stating that a grant is to be made to the free miner at a certain stated date and hour at the deputy gaveller's office. An example in 1944 of such an advertisement is given below:

FOREST OF DEAN
AND HUNDRED OF ST. BRIAVELS

COUNTY OF GLOUCESTER

Act 1st and 2nd Vic., cap. 43 [1838]

NOTICE IS HEREBY GIVEN, that His Majesty's Gaveller of and for the Forest of Dean has received an application from Sydney Jones, Crow Ash, Berry Hill, Coleford, to have a gale granted to him of a certain work or intended work, or Coal Mine, situate or intended to be situate at or near Clements End, near Coleford, within the Forest of Dean and Hundred of Saint Briavels, in the County of Gloucester; that the Gale so applied for is intended to be worked by means of a Level or Slope and that the Trenchard veins are the veins or seams of Coal proposed to be got by means thereof; and that the said Sydney Jones, being a Freeminer duly registered for the purposes of the Act of Parliament 1st and 2nd Victoria, cap. 43, and entitled to have a Gale granted to him under the authority of the said Act of Coal and Iron Mines, within the Said Forest and Hundred:

NOTICE IS HEREBY FURTHER GIVEN that the Gale so applied for as above mentioned is intended to be granted on Wednesday, the 28th day of June, 1944, at 11 o'clock in the forenoon, in a certain building or place of business usually called or known as the Gaveller's Office, situate in the Town of Coleford, in the Hundred of St. Briavels and County of Gloucester aforesaid: and the said Gale so applied for and intended to be granted is bounded as follows:—Co-extensive with the boundaries of the Lass of the Mill No. 2 Colliery Gale in the Coleford High Delf seam. On the deep side by a level to be driven from a point extending 50 yards down Latham's Slope, in a north-westerly direction to the line of boundary stones Nos. 65 and 66 in a south easterly direction to the northern fence of Noxon Park Wood and on the land side by the cropping out of the coals, to be called, GREEN'S TRENCHARD COLLIERY GALE.

Dated this 6th day of June, 1944.

R. I. TREHARNE-REES,
Deputy Gaveller.

The advertisement must give at least fourteen days' clear notice of such proposed grant to enable all the other free miners to be aware of the grant and to enable them to lodge an objection if they think they have grounds for doing so. On the day of the grant the free miner attends at the deputy gaveller's office, and, if all is in order and no objections have been made, the deputy gaveller reads aloud the whole of the deed or grant, which is then signed by himself and the free miner. A fee of 25p. is paid by the free miner for the deed, this being the only cost incurred by him. He is then entitled to either work the gale himself or to dispose of it to other miners or colliery owners for any agreed sum or consideration. No one except a free miner may obtain any mining rights in the district unless it is galed in the first instance to a free miner. The free miner may sell, transfer, assign, or dispose of gales and works, either by deed or will, to another free miner or to any other person or persons, but such sale or assignment must be recorded in the books of the deputy gaveller within three calendar months after the making thereof. The deputy gaveller will then endorse and sign a memorandum of such entry and the date thereof on such transfer or on the original certificate of grant. The *nunc pro tunc* procedure is possible.

To enable a free miner, or his assignee, to develop his gale, which may entail some considerable cost, one of the clauses in the deed of grant stipulates that in the case of a coal gale he shall be exempt from paying the dead rent for a period of two years, and in the case of an iron mine for four years. However, as soon as he develops his gale and wins any coal or iron ore, the tonnage royalty has to be paid by half-yearly instalments on 30 June and 31 December of every year. After the expiration of the rent-free period the dead rent merges into the royalties. If, however, the tonnage royalty does not amount to the dead rent in any one year, then the full amount of the rent has to be paid and the ensuing shortages are carried forward to the credit of the galee. Returns of tonnages are supplied by the free miner and checked by the deputy gaveller by means of haulage accounts, etc.

A free miner holding three gales cannot have a fourth granted to him until one or more of his three gales are exhausted or forfeited. If a free miner or his assignee wishes to do so he may surrender his gale on giving six months' notice in writing, such notice to expire on the date of the grant. Likewise, if he commits a breach of the Rules and Regulations for working his gale or fails to pay his dead rent or tonnage royalty, the deputy gaveller has power to forfeit his gale. In the case of forfeiture on account of non-payment an advertisement, of which an example in 1947 is given below is inserted in the local press:

FOREST OF DEAN

AND HUNDRED OF ST. BRIAVELS

NOTICE TO FREEMINERS

I, the Deputy Gaveller of the Forest of Dean, HEREBY GIVE NOTICE that unless the arrears of Rent due on the 31st December last, in respect of the GENTLEMEN COLLIERS COLLIERY GALE are paid to me at Coleford before 5 o'clock p.m. on TUESDAY, the 5th day of AUGUST, 1947, it is the intention of the Gaveller soon after 5 o'clock on that day to declare the Gale to be forfeited.

In the event of such forfeiture taking place, applications for the Grant of the Gale or License to get the coal comprised in the said Gale, will be received at my Office, Coleford, at and after ten o'clock on WEDNESDAY, the 6th day of AUGUST, 1947.

(Signed) A. R. THOMLINSON,

Deputy Gaveller of the Forest of Dean.

After a gale has been forfeited or surrendered,[1] a notice is displayed in the local press stating the day on which forfeiture or surrender is taking place, and that applications will be received on the following day between the hours of ten and five o'clock for the regrant of the gale. This notice gives an equal chance to all free miners residing in the district to put in their applications on the same day and to have an equal share in the gale. When a valuable gale is surrendered as many as 800 or 1,000 free miners may put in their applications on the same day, and so all have an equal interest in the gale. As it would be impossible to incorporate such a large number of names and also their signatures on the certificate of grant, a notice is inserted in the local press. An example in 1952 is given below:

FOREST OF DEAN AND HUNDRED
OF ST. BRIAVELS
Dean Forest (Mines) Act, 1904

NOTICE to the FREEMINERS who made application on the 9th day of February, 1934, for a Grant of a Gale known as the LITTLE BROCK-HOLLANDS No. 2 COLLIERY GALE.

Pursuant to Section 7 of the above Act and Regulations made thereunder the Forestry Commissioners as Gaveller of the said Forest DO HEREBY summon a Meeting of the above mentioned Applicants for the purpose of nominating a Committee to receive the Grant of the above mentioned Gale, such Meeting to be held at the Speech House in the Forest of Dean on SATURDAY, the 9th day of AUGUST, 1952, at 6 p.m.

(Signed) H. P. HERDMAN.
Deputy Gaveller of the Forest of Dean.

Crown Offices, Coleford, Glos.
July, 1952.

A committee consists of four free miners, and the gale is granted to it on behalf of all the applicants concerned. The four of them sign the certificate of grant, the same procedure being carried out as previously described in the case of a grant to a single free miner. Thereafter the committee act as trustees for the whole of the applicants, and if the gale is later disposed of to any outside purchaser they carry through the sale and transfer and sign all the necessary deeds. In some cases the trustees in disposing of the gale have reserved an improved royalty. The free miners had a secretary and treasurer, and the proceeds of the gale were distributed to the various applicants by calling annual meetings at the Speech House by a notice in the local press. The distribution of the proceeds has no connection with the gaveller, and is a private arrangement concerning the free miners. Some free miners have advertised their holdings for sale in the local press, of which five typical examples have appeared in the years indicated:

1 An example in 1945 of a relevant advertisement is: 'Barnhill No. 3 Colliery Gale. The Deputy Gaveller of the Forest of Dean gives notice that unless unforeseen circumstances occur this Gale will be surrendered, and that applications for the Re-grant of the same will be received at the Deputy Gaveller's Office, Coleford, at and after 10 o'clock on Friday, the 21st day of December, 1945. (Signed) R. I. Treharne Rees, deputy gaveller. Crown Offices, Coleford, Glos. December, 1945.'

'Brazilly and No Coal Gale for sale, less than cost price.' [1944]
'Coal Company registration for sale with Crown Rights to 65 acres; good quality coal.' [1944]
'Coal Gale for sale, Brazilly and No Coal Seams, selling because of full-time occupation.' [1944]
'Coal Gale for sale, No Coal and Brazilly; partly opened.' [1944]
'For Sale, a number of small Colliery Gales in the Upper Series.' [1945]

The future of freemining. The deep coal resources have been virtually exhausted and the bottom of the coalfield basin is flooded in the Coleford High Delph seam, with its outlet near the Norchard Drift under the Steam Railway Museum, running via the Newerne or Lyd stream to the River Severn. The geology throughout the coalfield is not too difficult but coal mining is hindered by some faulting and steep inclinations. Plans of 'old workings' and 'barriers' are often incomplete – not until 1841 was the keeping of plans of workings essential, and not until 1872 were plans required to be deposited.

There are no significant reserves of mineable iron ore remaining, hence the prospect of any further mining of it is virtually nil, though there are some not fully proved resources on the western flanks of the ore-field at or below oscillating ground water table.[1] [Incidentally, past iron ore mining has left large void chambers which are creating serious current or potential subsidence, giving much concern under built-up areas especially in the village of Bream; and many old workings have required much fencing for safety – a notable example being in Noxon Park.]

As regards coal, there are still prospects of outcrop or shallow mining on a small scale, under strict regulations. However, the prospect of any future large-scale or labour intensive *underground* coal mining is highly unlikely, either on a nationalised or private basis, in view of the uncertainty or lack of workable or commercially valuable resources of coal, the strata control problems, and the massive extent of waterlogging existing or likely to exist in the past workings of the coalfield. Likewise, the prospect of future, large-scale *opencast* coal extraction is minimal in the known several site reserves. In any case, currently (AD 2002) the market demand for and price of coal is extremely low; while projected costs of production and transportation are costly and rising.[2]

Furthermore, a very important factor is the 'environmental' restriction that coal mining of any scale would have to operate within. The utility, charm and character of the Forest must be safeguarded. Hence among major factors which must influence decisions likely to affect the Forest's environment are (i) its landscape, and (ii) its amenity value. Its heritage aspect likewise stands highly in the minds of conservationists and of many inhabitants; and tourism as a result of amenity and heritage factors is an important 'industry'. Coal mining therefore has to conform to the environmental framework of heritage, amenity, landscape and the everyday working of a highly successful immense forest enterprise. However, coal mining, so far as small-scale underground mining is concerned, is not totally ignored in the Gloucestershire County Structure Plan policies. There is still potential for

1 Piggott, R. J., 'The Forest of Dean Free Miners: A.D. 2000', Feb. 1996. Dissertation presented to the R.I.C.S. South Wales Branch, Minerals Division, 7 March 1996.
2 *Ibid.*

Plate XVI. *Free Miners Association officials, 2002. Left to right: Eric Morris (president), Don Johns (chairman), Ray Wright (secretary), and Phillip Schwarz (treasurer). Behind them stands the monument erected in memory of those killed in the Union Pit Disaster of 1902.*
photo: Jonathan Wright

modest-scale operation by individual free miners, or galees through them, subject to stringent regulations and environmental, Health & Safety, subsidence, and other constraints.

Opencast mining in the Forest, is heavily weighted against by the General and Mineral Policies of the County's Structure Plan. Successful opencast mining, followed by appropriate rehabilitation of the site, was permitted on 67 hectares of Woorgreen in 1980-2. However, in 1986-8 an application was granted (but became expired and refused) for 20 hectares at Oakenhill Wood (several seams with an estimated potential recovery of 540,000 tonnes); and likewise, application was made in 1983-4 and 1995-6, for 70 hectares at Lightmoor and Middleridge (thirteen seams of 400,000 tonnes). Both applications claimed to potentially provide positive benefit to the locality and communities through consequent reclamation of land affected and scarred by former coal mining. It is difficult to envisage what measures of environmental 'gain' are likely to be constituted and qualifying for the case of 'exception' under the Policy M 13 of the Structure Plan, although it has to be acknowledged that the instability problems associated with many abandoned adits, shafts and shallow mining would be removed. In any case the current and expected financial costs and returns do not justify opencast mining. It is estimated that there are up to 8 million tonnes of workable opencast coal in Dean (e.g. Lightmoor – 70 hectares, and Addis Hill – about 20 hectares). Meanwhile such gales are held out of the true freemining system and out of the reach of the majority of free miners. Successful development thereof would of course financially benefit the galees and the Forestry Commission. Opencast coal mining in the Forest today is an extremely risky business financially and, except in a national emergency, is likely to remain so for the foreseeable future, quite possibly for ever.

There are four main reasons for gales, dormant or otherwise, held by free miners, or their heirs and assigns: (i) the few active gales currently being mined on whatever scale; (ii) those dormant held for sentimental reasons (i.e. by widows, daughters, sons, and families, by will or assignment); (iii) those dormant gales held by free miners or their assigns with potential opencast hopefully in mind; and (iv) gales held by the Forest of Dean District Council, Gloucestershire County Council, and a few private landlords needing support for their dwellings, with no intention of mining. Some free miners or galees retain their gales, paying only the annual dead rent on them, apparently awaiting what they would consider beneficial financial conditions. Some expectations are likely to be classed as pipe dreams. *Bonâ fide* mining is sometimes abused or is at least questionable, because, as concerns the Coal Authority, there is an obligation that the coal should be worked.

A gradual yet definite harm has arisen to the traditional and statutory right of freemining, as a result of the decline of the industry and its dwindling importance to the local and national economy which consequently has reduced and is reducing the number of males eligible for registration. Furthermore, the closure of the only maternity unit (Dilke Memorial Hospital) within the Hundred of St. Briavels, means that only a male baby born at home would ever become eligible; also with only a few extant workings available there is little facility for 'the year and a day' apprenticeship to be obtained.[1] The free miners are perusing the situation.

A coincidental separate but relevant problem of possible conflict has arisen between two pieces of legislation concerning the conservation of the habitat of two species of horseshoe bats. European legislation requires that hibernation sites are to be protected, whereas the Dean Forest Mines enactments ostensibly require the continuation of mining in such circumstances. English Nature are likely to be involved in this matter.

Throughout the centuries, following the gradual dwindling of 'protection' by the reigning monarchies, and later under the Crown, the great drawback until recently in the presentation of the free miners' case and the guarding of their customary privileges has been certain imperfections on their own part. Often they lacked substantial backing when it would have been helpful, yet occasionally attempted to rectify this by illegally appointing many local influential persons as 'Honorary Free Miners' – a great abuse of their traditions. In later years they had no option than to urge and encourage wealthy entrepreneurs (which earlier they had termed 'foreigners') to purchase or lease gales from free miners and to provide the capital required to work the deep seams (receiving a modest annual 'share-out' by way of a payment per ton of the capital cost of the original multi-gale purchases, and, more importantly at the time, valued employment). Often they were inadequate in stating their case. They discarded their Mine Law Court in 1777. Sometimes they lacked unity: there were numerous cases of 'miner against miner'; at times they had dual Associations and dual presidents. As late as 1904, their representatives appeared before a select Committee of the House of Commons holding somewhat opposing views.

Even in more recent years, some galees, perhaps unintentionally or inadvertently, occasionally exaggerated or embroidered their 'case': making unauthenticated claims to a charter; and sometimes advancing 'folklore' as facts. In quite recent years, some may have had undisclosed hopes for their dormant gales. Free miners have never been treated or accepted by Government as a 'statutory body' or 'corporation'. Even today it appears that the present Forest of Dean Free Miners Association (formed, as now constituted, in 1965) has no legal status as such. Membership is in the region of 40-50; few today are actively engaged in the safeguarding and furthering of freemining rights. The Small Mines Association in Dean has less than a dozen members not all being free miners; and few are actively safeguarding their own interests, although the national

1 On 15 March 1984, The Rt. Hon. Lord Hailsham wrote to Paul Marland MP: 'I do not think I can advise your constituents [the free miners]. My office have made extensive enquiries of other Government Departments, all of whom are unable to help because the Dean Forest (Mines) Act 1838 was a private Bill, [It is a public Act.] not promoted by any Government Department. Having said that, I think the advice given to you by the Research Division of the House of Commons Library may not be correct. I do not know how old the maternity unit [at Dilke Hospital] is whose closure is impending, but I doubt that it dates back to 1838. When the Act was passed the persons who qualified as free miners were undoubtedly born at home, no doubt with the assistance of a midwife, and the fact that a maternity unit was subsequently set up locally does not mean that, if the maternity unit is subsequently closed, that is an act of god which must result in a different construction of the statute. No doubt the vast majority of people are today born in an hospital maternity unit, but there is no reason why they should not be born at home, and this does still happen. It seems to me therefore that the closure of this maternity unit will simply drastically reduce the numbers of persons born within the Hundred of St. Briavels, and hence eligible to become free miners, but, short of amending the statute, there is nothing that Mr. [John] Hodges [Press Officer of the Free Miners Association] can in my opinion do.'

body is formally recognised by the Coal Authority and the Department of Trade and Industry.

Today, the mining era[1] is rarely mentioned by the local general public, and almost unknown to the young. The total number of free miners on the Register is 4,345. Some 250 are alive today. Only a few dozen are profoundly interested in their rights and participate in appropriate lobbying and the like, and few follow their calling, operating small coal mines under various licences. Three partners are extracting a small amount of ochre. Four galees are operating small coal mines under licence.[2]

All that remains to remind the visitor of the past history of mining in Dean are the abandoned workings previously described, and the disused pit shafts now surrounded for safety by either a squat round tower or wall of stone, or by fencing. Shallow holes and 'flattened' mounds are also to be seen where coal has been mined from the outcrop; some being the work of miners during strikes in the twentieth century. The Dean Heritage Museum holds much local coal miners' memorabilia; and a Dean miner's lamp is deposited in the National Coal mining Museum at Caphouse Colliery, Wakefield. The small Hopewell Colliery (proprietor, Robin Morgan) on 'Cannop Hill' provides an opportunity to view small scale underground coal mining.

Of past iron ore mining,[3] the only evident remnants are the 'scowles', hollows and crevices, usually covered by moss, fern, bramble and other plants – all shaded by gnarled yews whose bared roots entwine the rocks – and a few mine heads and adit entrances disintegrating and constricting, sealed for public safety. Occasionally, there is evidence on or near the surface, of the slag, termed cinders, the result of earlier smelting of iron ore. Underground repose the abandoned caverns, chambers, and other workings. Most of the deeper mines are flooded – the water often of a green hue, appearing worse by gloom, shadow, and silence. A few caverns, when authorised and regulated, offer adventure to cavers. Exploratory caving of the old workings bring to light abandoned clay pipes, 'nellies' (candle holders), lamps, ropes, ladders, trucks, and items of pumping equipment. Photographs taken underground show bats, also calcite straws of many shapes, sizes and colours festooned from roofs and draping the walls with curtain-like formations, as well as paving the floors – all developed after the workings were abandoned. From three mines, water supplies are extracted. Some of the old workings can be reached – where authorised – through almost unnoticed surface holes. Some chambers currently are giving anxiety to occupiers of surface dwellings and other buildings inadvertently built above them. Some of the vast worked

---

1 For the general history of Dean's mining, see Hart, *Industrial History* (1971), pp. 216-52 (iron ore), 253-95 (coal), and 296-315 (stone quarrying).

2 Free miners currently working coal gales are: Ray Ashley (Monument and Quidchurch), David Tuffley (Hamblins Yorkley), Mervyn Bradley (Monument), Robin Morgan (New Road Level and Hopewell); and galees: John Sibley (Hamblins Yorkley and Worcester), Nick Bull (Quidchurch), John Hine (Hamblins Yorkley), Mark Bradley (Monument), Daniel Howell (Worcester), and Andrew Loucher (Hamblins Yorkley). Other free miners very occasionally working are: Michael Howell, David Coates and Phillip Schwarz. Free miners infrequently working the iron ore gales of Clearwell Meend are: Jonathan Wright, David Harvey and Michael Grindle; also a galee, Ray Wright.

3 Hart, *Industrial History* (1971), pp. 242-3.

complexes are far below the surface. Occasionally in the past it had been possible to penetrate extensively through one mine system to another. The Clearwell Caves in the west of the Forest, run commercially by Ray and Jonathan Wright, are based in the old iron ore workings of the Old Ham Mine (originally galed to Jack Smith deceased) and associated with the New Dun Mine. A small quantity of ochre is being mined there. The caves are open to the public at a charge.

Of past coal mining,[1] the abandoned shafts and levels are required by law to be sealed for safety, and most of the spoil tips[2] have been levelled or clothed by nature by birch, hawthorn, bramble and grass or afforested with Scots and Corsican pines. In places the shallow hollows of one-time bell pits are evident. Most evidence – lost to sight – is underground. The workings – the deep collieries and some of the host of smaller enterprises – now flooded with often gouty, chill water, lie silent and weird – the abode of bats, and often enveloped by poisonous air. Tens of thousands of wooden pitprops lie broken, splayed or rotten, and covered with the fructifications and strands of various fungi whose luminosity was familiar to those who toiled among them. The now constricted 'road ways' with their escape 'manholes' intertwine the gobbed-up workings; and many high 'roads' have sunk to impenetrable passages and falls creating chaos. The whole workings are sepulchres of industry – cities of flooded roads and byways, unlikely again to be seen by man. Yet a few people consider that some of the water may one day be pumped out and channelled for domestic and industrial usages.

The one-time prosperous coalfield (relinquished except for the operation of a few free miners and galees, and the rather remote possibility of opencast mining – a controversial subject) has now recovered from its dying pains. Underground, the water-filled abyss, along with the awesome stone quarries, should be forgotten or avoided. Well remembered are the human tragedies, the gallantries, and the comradeship; and the part once played underground by valiant and usually well-treated, ponies and horses.

Thus terminates for the present the chronicle of mining in Dean, century upon century of activity sheltered beneath a verdant canopy which survives it all, to triumph anew. What was the sum of it? In physical terms, it involved the extraction and marketing of perhaps some ten million tons of iron ore, and a hundred million or more of coal, and much stone – to reach which, perhaps half a billion tons of spoil and rock had to be moved.

What of the participants – the men who toiled in, planned and financed this great and grimy bustle? To the miner, the work provided a livelihood – often a precarious and meagre one – exchanged for sweat and risk, sometimes for mangled limbs, and occasionally for life itself. The initiators of mining ranged from those who ran the 'one-man' or family concerns – the free miners – to the great industrialist. In recent times the Government has granted £3 million to Dean within The Coalfield's

1 Hart, *Industrial History* (1971), pp. 253-95.

2 A few coal spoil tips have been subjected to coal-washing, for example Northern United (not fully successful), Eastern United, and Hawkwell. Such tips have or will be restored following extraction. At Eastern United some 100,000 tonnes are expected to be reclaimed from a two hectare coal tip. Two brick making firms are using colliery shale and clay.

Plate XVII. *A free miner in 2001: Gerald Haynes at his Hayners Bailey coal mine (now renamed Monument mine, of Ray Ashley and Mark Bradley, free miners). This 'dipple' lies near the old Union Pit at Bixslade, which was disastrously flooded on 4 September 1902 claiming four lives.*

Regeneration Fund in recognition of the Forest's former coal workings – to be used to renovate derelict sites of five former mines (e.g. Princess Royal and Northern United); and the grant is likely to be increased in various ways. Furthermore, compensation is being arranged for miners now living for the damage sustained to their health as a result of mining – under the Coalfield Communities Campaign.

The Rev. F. W. Potto-Hicks, MA, kindly wrote in his Foreword to the First Edition (1953): '... your work will be a memorial to the folly of the free miners! What a fine bit of socialism in the best sense they blew to smithereens!' He believed his words 'though hasty not harsh', and added: 'Our old mining communities of Dean are more than fossils in the social strata, and the Forest is the home of many industrious people quite capable of seeing that, as long as coal remains under their feet, they do not become mere relics of a defunct industrial organisation. Many, but by no means all, of these inhabitants have besides their mining, ancient privileges which they wish to continue enjoying. Almost without exception they have an unbounded affection for a corner of England which has to a peculiar degree kept its gracious greenness and quietude.'

The free miners' exclusive rights still continue, though modified, and are jealously guarded. Today one hears such local assertions as: 'freemining has been our national emblem – it has given us our heritage', and 'freemining is part of the entire Forest community and the identity of the traditional inhabitants; an attraction for visitors; and the rights are an embodiment of the uniqueness and heritage of the Forest.' The present free miners remember with a certain amount of pride the hard struggles that their predecessors experienced in retaining their privileges and hold tenaciously to them. Though their rights are now of much reduced monetary value, their history is of unusual interest, and they have played a great part in the economic development of the district – not least during two world wars.

APPENDICES TO PART TWO : 1831-2002

Appendix A

FREE MINERS' RIGHTS IN PRIVATE PROPERTY ('EXCEPTED LANDS')

[Lands within the Hundred of St. Briavels, beyond the Statutory Forest, excepted from the operation of the Dean Forest (Mines) Act 1838]

> 'Important questions have been mooted, and may some day call for decision, as to the rights in the mines and of the free miners within those excepted portions of the hundred.'[1]

> 'If it should hereafter be determined that the lands within the hundred excepted from the operation of the Dean Forest (Mines) Act, 1838, are still subject to the ancient customs, then this evidence will be required to show the extent of those customs.[2]

The miners of Dean have from time immemorial claimed that their customs extended not only to crown land within the Forest and the Hundred of St. Briavels but also to all private land therein 'except gardens, orchards and curtilages'. Clause 4 of the miners' 'Laws and Privileges' claims 'that the said Myners may myne in any place that they will as well without the bounds as within, without the Forbodement of any man.' Again, Clause 13 states: 'If any bee that denyeth any soyle whatsoever hit bee, bee hit sowed or noe or what degree hit be named, then the gaveller by the strength of the King shall deliver the soyle to the Myners with a convenient way next stretching to the King's highway.' Their claims, as will have been seen in early chapters have been disputed throughout the centuries. As early as *c.* 1244 and 1282 the mineral rights of foresters-of-fee of bailiwicks in Dean were more or less recognised by the Crown. Later centuries saw the granting away of certain portions of the Forest, the minerals in almost all cases being reserved. In 1287 the Abbot of Flaxley objected to the miners' activities on lands belonging to the Abbey. In 1611-13 the miners' claims were opposed by William, Earl of Pembroke, and again by Sir Richard Catchmaye in 1622. Later in the same century legal clashes occurred between the miners and private landowners, the most notable being in connection with the lands of the Throckmorton family at Clearwell, in 1623-4, and regarding grants held by the Terringham family in 1635, 1637; and 1667-8. The depositions arising from these cases afford the following general relevant information: In 1623-4 Whittington deposed that 'since the time of his knowledge the miners and pioneers had used and still do use to come into the grounds of any of the freeholders to dig iron mine and iron ore, and to take, carry away, and dispose thereof to their best advantage at their pleasure, without taking any leave of the owners of the ground.' Hooper confirmed this custom saying that they 'do usually enter into any such lands, without the leave or consent of the owners.' Callowe and Keere deposed on similar lines, as did also Tucker, the 'deputy gailor Beneath the Wood', who added that the miners had exercised their custom in 'several grounds and

1 Wood, *op. cit.*, p. 8.

2 *Ibid.*, p. 103. Wood did not, however, include the Minutes of Evidence.

freehold lands of William Callowe and Mr. Aileway and other grounds'. His evidence was confirmed by the other deputy gaveller, Worgan. As to whether these customs applied to Noxon Park, on Clearwell Estate, Callowe and Keere thought so but were uncertain. Worgan deposed that the customs applied to Noxon Park adding that the King received the same from mines there as from other lands in the Forest. In 1675 Hawkins and West confirmed the custom as applying also to freehold lands, the latter adding that the miners had exercised the same in his own lands 'which he would not willingly have suffered could he have found any legal way to hinder them'.

In 1788 the then gaveller, G. C. Hopkinson, said[1] that he had 'always understood, and believed, that the crown is entitled to all the mines of iron and coal within the whole perambulation of the Forest, whether the lands in which such mines are found be freehold, and in cultivation or otherwise; and that there are at this time in working two pits, called True Blue and Windrells, not within the lands belonging to the crown in the said Forest, but within the perambulation thereof; for which pits he received the customary gale duty or composition'.

The first attempt to clarify the position as regards freehold lands was made by the Commissioners of 1831. Evidence placed before them in this connection in 1832 and 1833 included the following:

William Morgan, of Worrall Hill, free miner aged 70:[2]

> 'I consider the right of free miners extends to any lands within the Forest, whether private land or Forest, whether inclosed or uninclosed. I know of no exception within the Hundred of St. Briavels.'

Peter Teague, of Coleford, free miner aged 45:[3]

> 'I have never known the gaveller refuse an application, unless in inclosed lands, if it did not interfere with other gales. I have worked mines in private lands in Wilshill for one. I consider the Landlord's share to be a ninth. Where I worked I paid £20 a year by agreement; and to the King, I think, I paid £5 for his share, but I do not recollect exactly what it was.'

George Stephens, of Coleford, free miner:[4]

> 'I have opened works in the private land, in the Highlands belonging to Mr. Church, and the Rev. Mr. Poole's, in Lord Gage's lands [Highmeadow Estate], and many other places. I consider the free miners have a right to open any mines in private lands within the Hundred of St. Briavels; but then he has two to pay, the landlord and the King; but we tell the landlord to work his share, and he generally has in my case declined to take anything, whatever his share be; if he takes it he must bear his share of the expense.'

John Lewis, of Lydbrook, free miner aged 50:[5]

> 'I have understood that in working private lands the landlord is entitled to a fifth and the King to the next, that is, the sixth man. I think the miner has a right to work in any land,

1 Third Rpt. of 1788, App. No. 25. p. 91.
2 Fourth Rpt. (dated 25 August 1835), p. 12.
3 *Ibid.*, pp. 14-15.
4 *Ibid.*, p. 15.
5 *Ibid.*, p. 16.

public or private, in the Hundred of St. Briavels, except gardens, orchards and such like.'

James Machen, aged 90:[1]

'I always understood that a free miner had a right to apply to the gaveller for a gale anywhere that he pleases within the Hundred of St. Briavels, except in Kidnalls, and Noxon Park, and Mailscot, in which I understood the owners of the property claimed the mines. The miners always claimed a right to go into private as well as other lands in the hundred, but in the above excepted lands such right was disputed by the proprietors. My predecessor in the estate I now hold [Eastbach] told me he had put in a fifth man in his own private lands, but recommended me never to do so, for the miners always made the expense so great that I had better have nothing to do with it. They come into my land and are now working it; I get nothing from them.'

Thomas Davis, of Five Acres, free miner aged 80:[2]

'I never knew the King's man put in [but] I have known the lord put in his man. The lord's tenant put in a sixth man on me in the Five Acres. Free miners certainly have a right to go into any man's land within the hundred; I have been in several myself.'

Additional relevant evidence consists of information given in 1831-35 regarding (A) Lydney Park Estate, owned by Charles Bathurst, (B) Clearwell Estate, owned by Lord Dunraven, and (C) the Manor of Breckness Court and certain property at Clearwell, owned by the Symond family These estates are treated of separately below.

(A) LYDNEY PARK ESTATE.[3] Charles Bathurst produced four documents, viz.: (*a*) a copy of the grant to Sir John Winter, dated 20 February 15 Charles I [1640] of various woods and premises in the Forest of Dean, including two woods called Snead and Kidnalls on the now Lydney Park Estate; (*b*) a copy of a Surrender, dated 28 July 1662, whereby Winter surrendered all the lands contained in the last grant except Snead and Kidnalls; (*c*) the counterpart of a lease, dated 8 April 1778, from Thomas Bathurst to David Tanner, granting the latter 'the right to dig any quantity of iron-stone and ore, sand, clay and stone', in lands belonging to the Lessor in the parishes of Lydney, Newland and St. Briavels, for 99 years; (*d*) an indenture, dated 29 November 1813: 'whereby, after reciting, amongst other things, that the said lease had been assigned to John Thomas and John Pidcock for the remainder of the said term of 99 years', all the privileges thereby granted were assigned to a trustee for the Rt. Hon. Charles Bathurst,[4] then owner of the estate, 'save and except the privilege of digging for any coal, and digging, making and working any level and levels, gutter, trench or pit for raising coal'. John Ducker, who had been acting as steward on Lydney Park

1 Fourth Rpt. (dated 25 August 1835), p. 16.

2 *Ibid*., pp. 17-18.

3 Large quantities of ore have been won on this estate particularly from Tufts Mine in Lydney Park Wood, some 750 yards south-east of Chelfridge, and from the numerous surface workings described in Chapter I. Coal has also been worked, particularly from the 'Norchard' and other scattered workings.

4 One of the Commissioners. At the commencement, he expressed his determination to abstain from taking any part in the inquiries relating to the rights of the free miners to open mines, and receive timber, on the grounds that such rights were and had been by some persons claimed as extending to that part of the lands of which he was owner.

Estate for 19 years, deposed:[1]

'I remember that sometime ago Messrs. Pidcock worked coal in the Kidnalls for some years. There are stone quarries in the Kidnalls; since I have known the estate no quarries have been opened there without the consent of the proprietor; but for those which have been opened a rent has been paid, which has been done in more than one instance. In a part of the wood, called Old Park, belonging to Mr. Bathurst, situated in the Hundred of St. Briavels, iron ore has been raised within my recollection, but never by free miners, by means of a gale from the Crown. It has been done by the permission of the proprietor; several times leave has been asked, but not granted.

Where leave was granted, the mine, when opened, was paid for. I believe the person who raised the mine was a forester but I do not know whether he was a free miner or not. One of the persons who applied for leave, and to whom it was granted, was Mr. Moses Teague a free miner. The price paid for the ore was what was supposed to be the value.

In one instance a person named Priest living on the Forest having taken some spar, Mr. Bathurst insisted on his paying 2s. 6d. as an acknowledgement of the trespass to which he submitted. About four or five years ago a man worked without consent but only for a day or two and upon being told it could not be permitted he desisted.'

Thomas Tovey, one of the deputy gavellers, deposed:[2]

'About 35 or 36 years ago, a man named Wear had been working in the Kidnalls Wood; he was, I understood, a free miner of Dean Forest; I, as deputy gaveller, applied for payment of his gale-rent, and upon that the question as to the right of miners to enter Mrs. Bathurst's wood, called Kidnalls, to open mines was brought into discussion at Lydney Park. I attended there as deputy gaveller. Upon its being made to appear that a grant had been made by the Crown of Snead and Kidnalls Woods, without any reservation of the mines, I considered that the Crown had parted with all right in these woods; that I, as deputy gaveller, could not support any claim for gale-rent in respect of these mines, and therefore I did not persist in any claim for such rent against Wear on behalf of the Crown. Soon after I heard that Messrs. Pidcock had got possession of the collieries which Wear has been working, as lessees, or assignees of leases, under the Bathurst family of Lydney Park and I believe they have occupied it ever since.'

(B) CLEARWELL ESTATE.[3] Henry Davis appeared as agent on behalf of Lord Dunraven, and produced three documents,[4] viz: (*a*) a grant of 10 Edw. I to John de Wisham of Noxon Park and 200 acres adjoining; (*b*) an agreement, dated 2 August

---

1 Fourth Rpt. (dated 25 August 1835), pp. 31-2.

2 Fourth Rpt. *op. cit.*

3 Iron ore has been worked extensively from this estate by Noxon Park Mine, China Mine and by numerous smaller pits and outcrop workings. Out-crop mining was continued until at least 1885. An old level at the north-west corner of Noxon Park was reopened in 1922.

4 The case of 1623-4, the depositions connected with which have been given in Chapter V, concerned Noxon Park and other lands ('Thraves', 'Kingsmore', 'Chelfridge' and 'Lanquire') on this estate. The depositions at that time made it appear that the free miners' customs applied to this estate as to the whole Forest.

1798, between Charles Edwin and John Ellsmere and others, whereby Mr. Edwin allowed the parties of the second part to work the mines in Noxon Park at 2d. per ton; (*c*) a similar agreement, dated 2 October 1798, between the same Charles Edwin, of the first part, and Simon Bannister, Edward Mousell, and Betty Collins who signed, and others who did not sign, of the second part. Mr. Davis deposed that he had during the last two years let to Nash Elsmere and other free miners the privilege of mining ore in Noxon Park; that the mines had been worked, and rent paid accordingly. John Constant, a tenant of Lord Dunraven's, confirmed that rents had been paid in this way for ten years past. David Mushet prepared a case in order to attempt to prove that the free miners' customs still applied to this estate. He first handed in a copy of the following Memorial he had presented to the Commissioners of Woods on 27 October 1830:[1]

'The Memorial of David Mushet of Coleford,

Sheweth.

That the mines of coal, iron ore and ochre in the Forest of Dean, and in the freehold lands in the Hundred of St. Briavel's, have from time immemorial been deemed to belong to the Crown, and have accordingly been worked to the present time under its authority.

That it has frequently happened that mines begun in the Forest have been followed into, and worked in the adjoining freeholds within the hundred, and air and other pits sunk for the benefit of the original undertaking.

That when any dispute arose between the miners and the owners of the freehold, the gaveller was called in to give possession, and enable the miner to proceed with his operations unmolested; that such a practice is of old standing, and fully recognised in the Digest of the Miners' Laws and Customs, published in 1663, section 13, as will appear by the following extract: "And also, if any be that denieth any soil, whatsoever it be, be it sowed or no, or of what degree it may be named, then the gaveller, by the strength of the King, shall deliver the soil to the miners, with a convenient way stretching to the King's highway, by which mine may be carried to all places and waters that be convenient to the said mine, without withsaying of any man."

That your memorialist, on or about the 14th day of December 1820, purchased from one John Hawkins, a free miner of the Forest of Dean, a gale for a mine level near to Oakwood Mill, in the said Forest; that in the year 1825 your memorialist had the gale extended to a vein of iron ore, called the Sandstone vein, and has paid gale money for the same accordingly.

That your memorialist at the same time began to drive two levels for the purpose of working both the veins of iron ore, and forming a communication through the different parts of the intended workings for air, that after expending considerable sums of money, and finding that the iron ore lay at a much greater distance than had been expected, one of the levels was discontinued for a time, and the other carried to the extent of nearly 600 yards before any iron ore was found passing under the Noxon Park estate.

That in carrying forward the said level your memorialist found it necessary, either to sink an air pit in a field belonging to the Noxon Park estate, or to make a communication with one of the numerous old mine pits in Noxon Park; that your memorialist determined upon the latter, and employed workmen to enter an old air pit, and hasten the communication by cutting in the direction of the miners employed in the level.

---

1 Pp. 40-3

That soon after your memorialist had commenced his operations as above stated, he was interrupted for the first time by Mr. Henry Davies, acting on behalf of Lord Dunraven (the proprietor of the Noxon Park Estate), on the ground that the mines in the Noxon Park Estate belonged to Lord Dunraven, and were not the property of the Crown, as your memorialist contends they are.

That the said Mr. Henry Davies threatened to fill up the communication for thus making air, should your memorialist persist in carrying it on; but at the same time signified his consent that the work should be continued, on condition that your memorialist would submit the question, whether the Crown or Lord Dunraven was entitled to the mines, to the determination of a barrister; but this your memorialist, for obvious reasons, declined doing.

That your memorialist, in consequence of the above-mentioned threat, stopped his workmen from going on with the air pit in Noxon Park, and in compliance with the custom long established in similar cases, applied to Mr. Edward Machen, one of the gavellers of the Forest, to gale the pit in question, and enable your memorialist to proceed under the lawful authority of the Crown.

That your memorialist begs leave to annex a copy of his application to Mr. Machen, dated the 7th of August last, and also a copy of the answer to it received from Mr. Tovey (the other gaveller), dated the 30th of the same month, and your memorialist submits that this answer does not meet the important point at issue.

That under these circumstances your memorialist has no alternative but to state his case and apply to your honourable Board for assistance and relief.

That your memorialist believes the claim now made by Lord Dunraven was for the first time raised by the late Charles Edwin, about 30 years ago, who was at that time owner of the Noxon Park Estate.

That your memorialist has seen extracts from a grant made in the reign of Edward the Second to William de Wischam, of the Vineyard of Noxon, "with liberty to enclose 200 acres of the waste soil of Dean Forest."

That upon this grant, as your memorialist believes, Lord Dunraven founds his claim to the mines in Noxon Park; but your memorialist submits that a grant in terms like these cannot be construed to pass a right to mines and minerals.

That your memorialist further submits, that it does not appear that those ancestors of the late Mr. Edwin and of Lord Dunraven, who lived nearer to the time of the grant, ever considered that the Crown had conveyed a right to the mines, when it simply gave an authority to enclose a portion of the waste soil. In proof of this your memorialist begs leave to refer your Honourable Board to volume No. 4,850 of the Harleian MSS. now in the British Museum, which contains the particulars of a justice-seat held in the Forest of Dean, under commission from the Earl of Holland, the lord-justice of the Forests on this side of the Trent. This Commission was held in the 10th Charles the First [1634], for the purpose of enquiring into the rights and property belonging to the King in Dean Forest.

That among many other presentments of mines belonging to the Crown, the following are described as being situate in Noxon Park; namely:

Scarre Pit	Ash Pit
Wyche Wylder's Pit	Lady's Pit
Browne's Pit	Little Pit

with many others, the names of which were unknown.

That from this document your memorialist submits that it is evident that in the 10th of

Charles the First [1634], the Crown had the right to the Mines in Noxon Park, and that it rests with Lord Dunraven to produce some subsequent grant before he can establish his claim.

That your memorialist has within the last 20 years conversed with many old miners who from their boyhood worked in the Noxon Park mines and who, with their fathers and grandfathers, possessed and worked (amongst others) under the authority of the Crown, those identical pits mentioned in the presentment of the 10th of Charles the First, before referred to, leaving no doubt in the mind of your memorialist that there never did exist a shadow of a well-grounded claim against the rights of the Crown in those mines.

That your memorialist believes, as already stated, that Charles Edwin, the late proprietor of the Noxon Park Estate, was the first person who laid claim to the mines, under the pretence of having discovered a long-neglected grant from the Crown, which conveyed to him the woods, land and mines of Noxon, and thereupon gave notice to all the miners in Noxon Park, that they were no longer to work the mines under the authority of the Crown, but under a special agreement with him, otherwise not to work at all.

That the miners were greatly disturbed at this notice, and held many meetings to concert in what way they could best support their rights, and those of the Crown; but finding no one inclined to protect them against Mr. Edwin's demand, several of them agreed to work the mines, and pay Mr. Edwin 2d. a ton galeage.

That several of these agreements, in writing and stamped, have been seen by your memorialist, and one is now in his possession, a copy of which will be found amongst the papers belonging to this memorial.

That your memorialist begs leave to point out to your Honourable Board the following clause contained in these agreements, whereby Mr. Edwin engages to protect the miners "from all claims, and damage and demands whatsoever to be made and recovered by the King's Majesty, his gaveller, or any other of his officers of the Forest of Dean, upon or against either of them, for digging, raising or taking the said ore from out of the said mines hereby granted." And your memorialist submits that this clause is evidence of the superiority of the Crown in the mines until the year 1798, the date of these agreements.

That your memorialist might now let the matter of right in these mines rest, as being unquestionably vested in the Crown; but as it is a question of deep importance to your memorialist, he takes the liberty of subjoining the testimony of the only four surviving miners who worked and paid gale to the Crown for iron ore in Noxon Park previous to the claim made by Mr. Edwin in 1798.

John Morse, in his 92nd year, the oldest living miner in the Forest, says that he and his father had shares in several mines in Noxon Park, and that shares in Ash Pit and Wyche Wylder's Pit (being two of the pits described in the presentment of the 10th Charles the First, already referred to) descended to him by inheritance. That he and his father regularly paid gale to the Crown for these and other pits which they worked in Noxon Park, and that he continued to do so after his father's death till the time when Mr. Edwin set up his claim and obliged the miners to enter into agreements with him. He recollects the King's gavellers, Philip Eley, Messrs. Cooke and Robinson; has seen the two former acting as gavellers in Noxon Park; paid gale to all three, which he always considered paying gale to the Crown.

Richard Jones, aged 72 years, now confined to his bed, worked in Ashe Pit, Lady Pit, Knock Pit, Wyche Pit, Lord Pit and Little Pit, all situate in Noxon Park, and paid the rent to the gavellers till Mr. Edwin's papers came out. Recollects paying gale to Messrs. Ely,

Robinson, Cooke, and Tovey, whom he considered the gavellers appointed by the Crown. Recollects seeing Messrs. Ely and Cooke exercising the Crown's right as gavellers in Noxon Park. Never heard of any one besides the Crown claiming the mines in Noxon Park till Mr. Edwin served him with a notice to stop working, and to agree with him.

Thomas Skin, aged 68, worked for many years before Mr. Edwin's papers came out, and paid his gale to the Crown; worked in Lord Pit, Ashe Pit, Wyche Pit and Little Pit and Evans Pit; paid gale to Messrs. Cooke, Hopkinson, Robinson and Tovey. The gale-money for many years was 4s. per share per annum for each pit; but in Mr. Robinson's time it was raised to 10s., 20s. and ultimately to two guineas. Recollects receiving a notice from Mr. Edwin not to proceed with getting mine unless he agreed with him instead of the Crown. That all the park miners were disturbed on the occasion, and held meetings to take steps to protect themselves. That he and one Benjamin Jones were appointed to go to Mr. Tovey to learn whether he would assist them in maintaining their rights under the Crown. They went to Mr. Tovey's at Newnham, but not finding him at home, they went to Lydney and saw him there the next day. That Mr. Tovey declined interfering in the matter, and some time after the miners agreed to Mr. Edwin's terms to pay 2d. a ton on the mine got in Noxon Park, and to receive timber.

Benjamin Jones, aged 60 (alluded to in Thomas Skin's testimony), worked in the Noxon Park mines from the age of 10 years. Had shares in several pits, for which he paid gale to the Crown. Remembers Mr. Edwin's notice and the meeting of the miners on that occasion, but has no recollections of going with Skin to see Mr. Tovey, although he thinks it very probable he did, particularly as Skin says so. Complains of loss of memory of late years.

Jones afterwards came and acknowledged his having been with Skin to Newnham, and of his having seen Mr. Tovey at Lydney, and gave as a reason why he did not state this at first, that being then overheard by one John Nash, he was afraid to speak his mind before him.

Upon a review of the whole evidence, your memorialist trusts that your Honourable Board will be of opinion that he has made out a case in favour of the right of the Crown to the mines in Noxon Park; and he is at the present time subjected to a heavy extra expense, and has to contend with difficulties almost insurmountable, in consequence of his being denied his just and necessary privilege, as tenant to the Crown, to sink an air-pit, under the authority of the gaveller, in freehold land, your memorialist prays that your Honourable Board will speedily take his case into consideration, and direct that the gavellers, or one of them, shall immediately put him in possession of the soil in Noxon Park, that he may proceed with his air pit and be enabled to carry on his mine-works to the best advantage.

Coleford, 27 October 1830. (Signed) David Mushet.'

Previously, on 4 August 1830, Mushet had written to Edward Machen, one of the deputy gavellers, as follows:

'I understood that Henry Davies, on the part of Lord Dunraven, has given notice to stop some miners employed by me in sinking an air-pit in Noxon Park to communicate with my mine-level near Oakwood Mill.

My son, in my absence, has in consequence withdrawn the man until the authority of the gaveller has been obtained.

I have therefore to request that you will consider this as an application on my part to you, as gaveller, to gale an air-pit in Noxon Park for the benefit of my level as aforesaid, and on as early a day as may be most convenient to you.'

Thomas Tovey, the other deputy gaveller, replied on 30 August:

'Mr. Machen has sent your letter to me respecting our galing an air-pit to your mine-works, near Oakwood Mill. When levels have been galed, and air-pits are wanted to them, upon the levels being carried up to the parts where the air-pits are intended to be made, the air-pits are made by the miner under the authority of the first galing, and in respect of them no new galing is necessary, as I have understood. With respect to the claim made by Mr. Davis for Lord Dunraven, if any question arises on that head, of course you will get legal advice upon it.'

Mushet then presented the following agreement dated 2 August 1798 between Charles Edwin, of Clearwell, and Joseph Elsmore, John Preece, Richard Jones, John Symonds and Samuel Beach:

'The said Charles Edwin doth hereby agree to lett unto the said Joseph Elsmore, John Preece, Richard Jones, John Symonds and Samuel Beach, the pitt called Lord Pitt, in Noxon Park, in the Forest of Dean, in the county of Gloucester, now and for some time past used for raising iron ore by the said Joseph Elsmore, John Preece, Richard Jones, John Symonds and Samuel Beach, with full and free liberty to dig, raise and take all iron and other ore which can be found therein, and also to carry away the same along the roads and ways hereinafter mentioned, from the 29th day of September last, for so long a time as the said parties may please; and the said Joseph Elsmore, John Preece, Richard Jones, John Symonds and Samuel Beach do hereby severally promise and agree with the said Charles Edwin, his heirs and assigns, that they the said Joseph Elsmore, John Preece, Richard Jones, John Symonds and Samuel Beach shall and will, pay unto the said Charles Edwin, his heirs and assigns, the sum of 2d. for each customary ton of mine or iron ore, and in that proportion for every less quantity than a ton which shall be raised by them in the said mines during the term hereby granted; and if the present price of ore, which is 6s. a ton shall be increased, the said Joseph Elsmore, John Preece, Richard Jones, John Symonds and Samuel Beach do hereby promise and agree to pay the sum of 1d. in addition to the said sum of 2d. for every 1s. which the said ore shall be sold for by the ton above 6s., and shall and will give and deliver a ticket or memorandum in writing, signed by the stockholder of the iron works to which the said mine shall be carried, on the first day of every month during the term, or as often as the mine shall be weighed at the iron work, unto the said Charles Edwin, his heirs or assigns, or his or their agent, of all mine or iron ore which shall be raised in the said mines, and sold by them; and shall not nor will use any other road or way into or out of the said park unto the said mines than those which shall be assigned and appointed by the said Charles Edwin as hereinafter is mentioned, nor permit any horned cattle to be used therein, nor fall, cut down, crop, or in any manner do damage to any tree or part of the coppice wood in Noxon Park aforesaid, or to the fences, gates or rails thereof, nor dig or sink any new level therein without the consent in writing of the said Charles Edwin, his heirs or assigns, nor lett, sell or assign over to any other person or persons whomsoever any part of the right they enjoy by this agreement of getting and carrying away the mine, nor shall take in any partner, nor in any way participate the benefit thereof with any other person or persons whomsoever, without the consent in writing of the said Charles Edwin, his heirs or assigns, under the penalty of £10 to be paid by each of them the said Joseph Elsmore, John Preece, Richard Jones, John Symonds and Samuel Beach, making default in the premises aforesaid for every offence. And the said Charles Edwin doth hereby promise and agree with the said Joseph Elsmore, John Preece, Richard Jones, John Symonds and Samuel Beach, that he the said Charles Edwin, his heirs or assigns, shall and will within 10 days next after request made to him, for that purpose, as occasion shall require, assign and deliver sufficient wood and timber for working the said pits, and the levels of the same, and shall and will also permit the said Joseph Elsmore, John Preece, Richard Jones, John Symonds and Samuel Beach to use the levels to the said pits, and will also mark out and assign fit and convenient roads and ways, and give free liberty of ingress, egress and regress through and along the same with servants, horses and other cattle, except horned cattle, to take and carry away the ore from the said pits within one week from the date hereof, and shall and will at all times hereafter save harmless and indemnify the said Joseph Elsmore, John Preece, Richard Jones, John Symonds and Samuel Beach of and from all claims, damages and demands whatsoever to be made and recovered by the King's Majesty, his gaveller, or any other of his officers of the Forest of Dean, upon or against either of them, for digging, raising or taking the said ore from and out of the said mines hereby granted; provided always, that it shall be lawful for either of the said parties to determine this agreement on giving unto the other 12 months' notice in writing for that purpose, when the same shall determine accordingly; and the said Joseph Elsmore, Richard Jones, John Symonds and Samuel Beach shall and will yield and deliver up the possession of the said pits unto the said Charles Edwin pursuant to such notice.

(signed) Charles Edwin.

Signed by Charles Edwin in the presence of The mark of Richard Jones.
The mark of John Symonds.
The mark of Samuel Beach.'

With the above Mushet handed in the following documents:

'No.1. An original Conveyance. James Tingle to Messrs. Pyrke & James, dated 18 October 1771, of the Oiling Gin, otherwise the Water-wheel Engine Level.

No. 2. A Declaration of Trust, dated 20 March 1772. Joseph Blanch to same Pyrke & James, relative to a share of the same works, stating that the vendor was a free miner; the purchasers foreigners.

No. 3. An Agreement, 15 April 1776, whereby Pyrke and others sold back to free miners, Hobbs and others. Mr. Pyrke was an attorney, he signed the agreement for himself and the others.'

On 25 August 1832 Mushet appeared on behalf of himself, and of the free miners, to oppose the claim made by Henry Davis on the part of Lord Dunraven. He claimed under a lease for 500 years of a mine level, purchased from one John Hawkins, free miner; the progress of which level as will have been seen by his Memorial, was interrupted by Davis on behalf of Lord Dunraven, claiming a right on the mines of Noxon Park as against the Crown. He produced certain witnesses whose depositions are given below:

James Morse, of Clavering's End Green, aged 48, deposed[1]:

'My father, John Morse, had a share and worked in Witch Pit. I produce the gale book in which is the following entry (p. 333) showing that he was charged with gale in 1769: "Witch Pitt Mine works – John Morse, Edward Mousell. Received of John Morse 3s. 4d. ... 3s. 4d. Jan 17th, 1769 – Received, John Morse, one year. 8s." I worked with my father in Witch Pit, Ash Pit and the Coal Floor; they are in Noxon Park. I have heard my father say he paid gale to Philip Ely, the King's gaveller. I recollect an agreement being drawn about 34 years ago, between Charles Edwin and some miners. The meaning of that agreement was, that the miners should pay to Mr. Edwin, the owner of the Park, 2d. per ton for all the mines worked in the park. My father paid this for some time, and after this he paid no gale to the Crown.'

Thomas Skin, of Clavering's End Green, aged nearly 70[2]:

'I have worked in many pits in Noxon Park – Nock Pit, Witch Pit, Lady Pit, Lord Pit, and others. I had shares in them; some came by my father. Scarr Pit, Lady Pit, Hurl Pit, and the Coal Floor, descended to me from my father. These pits are in Noxon Park. I recollect the agreement between Mr. Edwin and the miners; before that I paid to the Crown 4s. annually for working these pits and others out of the park. I signed the agreement with Mr. Edwin; after that I paid no gale to the Crown for the works in the park, but I paid 2d. a ton to Mr. Edwin. Before this I had some timber from the Forest for making stakes; after, we did not look for any timber. When Mr. Edwin proposed the agreement, I and another person [Benjamin Jones] were deputed to go to Mr. Tovey [deputy gaveller], at Newnham, to ask if he would give us authority and support us in going to the mines in Noxon Park. He was not at home. The next day we went to him at Lydney, and he told us he would have nothing at all to do with it.'

Benjamin Jones, of Clavering's End Green, aged 62.[3]

'I have worked in Noxon Park mines before Mr. Edwin's agreement came out, in Witch, Nock and Lord's Pit, and others. I had no shares. I paid gale to the Crown; I never had a new gale in the park, but I worked in the old pits. I went with Thos. Skin to Mr. Tovey [deputy gaveller] and he would not protect us to gale in Noxon Park, and we therefore went to Mr. Edwin, and agreed to his terms."[4]

Thomas Tovey, deputy gaveller, deposed[5]:

'That he was deputy gaveller in 1797; that he received gale rent from John Kear, Thomas Kear, Israel Constance and William Allen, for a mine-work or coal-level, called Dog Kennell Level, and Merry Way, under Noxon Park; that he received it from June 1797 up to 1800. That he also received gale rent in 1809, and to June 1812, for a work called Quab, under Noxon Park.'

---

1 Fourth Rpt. *op. cit.*, p. 34.
2 *Ibid.*, p. 35.
3 *Ibid.*, p. 35.
4 *Ibid.*, p. 35. Mushet refers to this witness as Benjamin Brown.
5 *Ibid.*, p. 39.

John Constant, aged 62, deposed[1]:

'That he lived at Noxon; that he knew the pits in Noxon Park with mines in them. His father married there, and lived in the house now occupied by himself; his name was Israel, He had an uncle named John; he did not know anything of a gale standing in their names in the gale book. Mr. Edwin was proprietor of Noxon Park when his father lived there. His father was tenant to Mr. Edwin and has heard him say that he worked the lord's share. Mr. Edwin died in June 1801. About 35 years ago or more Mr. Edwin had told his father that he had discovered what he had long looked for – the grant of Noxon Park. He was going to mark out a great many acres of land; he sent to the men who worked the mines, asked them if they paid gales; they said they did. He said they should pay no more, they had no right to pay, and they paid none after to the Crown, but 2d. a ton to Mr. Edwin.'

On being examined by Mr. Davis, Lord Dunraven's agent, Constant said that 'he knew they never paid gale after. He had spoken to Mr. Tovey since but could not say that Mr. Tovey exactly acknowledged this, but when he stated the fact, Mr. Tovey did not deny it.' Philip Robinson,[2] assistant to the deputy gaveller, Mr. Tovey, produced an old gale book from which the following entries were taken:

(I) 'Sackfield, in Noxon Park, Mine-work; Thomas Skin.
Received of Thomas Skin .... 3/4d.
17 January, Thomas Skin, 1 year .... 4/-.'

(II) 'New work, mine pit in Noxon Park; Israel Constance and Joseph Constance, the partners, 11 June 1779, agreed with Israel Constance for 40/-, paid for the above works, from Midsummer-day next.

John Robinson [deputy gaveller], entered to Mr. Matthews:

To one year, due Midsummer	1780	£2.
– do –	1781	£2.
– do –	1782	£2.
– do –	1783	£3.
		£9.

24 March 1784. Received of Mr. Israel Constance. And he throws up the work.'

(C) MANOR OF BRECKNESS COURT AND CERTAIN PROPERTY AT CLEARWELL. On behalf of the Symons family the following letter was delivered to the Commissioners on 22 August 1832, from John Cooke of Ross-on-Wye:[3]

'My Clerk, Mr. Thomas Edwards, waits upon you for the purpose of ascertaining whether, under your commission, the manor of Breckness Court, and estates at Clearwell, belonging to the family of the late Thomas Symons, Esq., of the Mynde Park, Herefordshire, are in any

1 Fourth Rpt. *op cit.*. p. 39.
2 Pp. 39-40
3 P. 35

way connected with the subject of your enquiry under the Forest of Dean Commission, either as regards the Crown or the free miners. I have been led to suppose that your investigation could have no reference to this property; but as the agent of the family, I now feel it right to trouble you with this, to beg to be informed in what respects, if any, you have to hear and determine, and on what rights touching this property. With regard to the manor, I ought perhaps to say that it had been held with the estate by the ancestors of Mr. Symons' family for about 130 years; that, by reference to some old documents, it appears that in the reign of Henry 3 the King granted this manor to Hugh Kinnersley in fee, by the name of Wellington; that in the 5th of Edward I the Bishop of St. David's granted the Manor to Thomas Aubrey; in the 48th Edward III, a feoffment of it in fee was made from Richard Aubrey to Walter Ocle; in the 3rd of Edward 6, a feoffment was made from Ocle to Thomas Jones, under whose family the Symons purchased. There are, I believe, with the Mynde papers court rolls of the manor; but from the deaths in the Symons family these papers have been considerably disarranged. I have one of 1680, which the bearer brings with him. Now with regard to the estates, within the last three or four years a man of the name of Nash has, under the pretence or plea of right as a free miner, erected a cottage under the hedge of one of the fields belonging to this property, and lying within the manor, adjoining the road to Clearwell, which Mr. Machen is aware of, and likewise broken into the land in several places, as he states, in search of ore. It is the intention of the family whom I represent to resist this man's encroachments, and to bring the subject before a jury of the county, if it should not come within your province to hear, and set at rest these assumed rights; and I shall feel much obliged by your informing me how far your commission extends towards these matters.'

There is no evidence that any action was taken. In their 4th Report, dated 25 August 1835,[1] the Commissioners stated:

'The free miners claim a right to have land galed to them for opening mines not only in the open lands of the forest but also in all enclosed lands within the Hundred of St. Briavels, except churchyards, gardens and orchards, and excepting also such inclosures as have been made by the Crown under the Statute 48th Geo. 3 [1808], for the time they shall continue inclosed ....The free miners have fully exercised this right from time to time, except in Noxon Park, the property of Lord Dunraven, Kidnalls and Sneyd Woods, the property of Mr. Bathurst, and Mailscot now the property of the Crown, in which their rights have been more or less disputed.'

In the Dean Forest (Mines) Act, 1838, which followed the Commissioners' Report, the following reservation was made by S. 68:

'Provided nevertheless, that if the owner or owners of any of the inclosed lands within the said hundred shall at any time within six calendar months[2] from the passing of this act give notice in writing to the said commissioners hereby appointed of his or their desire that the provisions of this act should not extend to such lands, then and thereupon this act shall be

---

1 P. 7

2 The final date was 27 January 1839.

taken not to extend to such lands, so as the same be specified in such notice; but all and every rights, customs, and privileges existing at the passing of this act, so far as regards such lands, or the mines and minerals thereunder, and the rights to the same, shall continue in force in all respects as if this act had not been passed.'

Under the power given by this S. 68, the following owners of inclosed lands of the hundred (without the Forest perambulation), including the Commissioners of Woods on behalf of the Crown, gave notices to exempt their lands from the operation of this Act:

Name of Owner	*Description of Lands*			
Charles Bathurst, Esq., of Lydney Park, by notice dated 3 December, 1838.	The Kidnolls, The Snead, Tomkin's Land, Maple Hills, and Old Furnace Yard, and an inclosed piece or pieces of ground lying between the Kidnolls on the one side, the boundary of the Parish of Lydney on the opposite side, and the two pools called the Upper Forge Pool and the New Pool at the two ends thereof.			
Thomas Kear, of St. Briavels, yeoman, by notice dated 16 January, 1839.	All his inclosed lands in the Tything of Bream, in the parish of Newland, then in the occupation of William James.			
Sir Thomas Crawley Boevey, of Flaxley Abbey, baronet, by notice dated 15 January, 1839.	'Divers inclosed lands and estates, situate within the Parish of Flaxley.'			
The Earl of Dunraven, by several notices dated respectively 15 January, 1839, 16 January, 1839, and 19 January, 1839; the first two relating to Noxon Park only.	The Clearwell Estate, situate in the several Parishes of Newland, St. Briavels, and Hewelsfield, namely:			
		A.	*R.*	*P.*
	The Clearwell Court mansion house and demesne lands belonging thereto, and Wood lands (including Noxon Park and Ashtree Grove containing together 100A. 2R. 8P.)	394	0	16
	Longney Farm	266	1	19
	Trowgreen Farm	222	2	7
	Noxon Farm	212	2	22
	Cadwell Farm	97	0	23
	Shophouse Farm	42	0	26
	Gatewell Farm	4	3	13
	Bream Farm	18	2	25
	Beasthouse Farm	211	2	32
	Great House Farm	106	1	39
	Hartley's Court Farm	177	3	30

continued

The Commissioners of Woods by notice dated 25 January, 1839.	The High Meadow Estate, including: Mailscot Wood, Braceland Farm, Hadnock Wood, Bunjup's Grove, Knockall Grove, Blackmoor Grove, Birchin Grove, The Hoods, The Sheep Pasture, The Reddings, Broomhall Farm and any other lands then belonging to Her Majesty in right of her crown situate within the Parishes of Staunton, English Bicknor and Newland.

The notices given on behalf of the Earl of Dunraven claimed that he was the owner of the mines and the minerals under the lands mentioned the same having been granted by the Crown to a subject under whom the earl derived title. Also that the lands were not subject to the customary rights of the free miners intended to be regulated by the Dean Forest (Mines) Act, 1838. The Commissioners of 1838 did not, however, acquiesce in this claim, for the following saving words introduced into three of the gales under the Award of Iron Mines 1841 show that they considered that the title of the Crown to the minerals under the earl's lands, Mr. Kear's lands and other freehold lands, was an open question:

'and excepting out of this allotment so much of the said ore as is under the lands of .... and other proprietors of freehold lands (if any) who have given notice that the Act 1st and 2nd Vic., cap. 43. shall not apply to their lands, until the ore under the last-named lands shall be decreed or admitted to be the property of the Crown.'[1]

J. G. Wood[2] submits that S. 68 of the Act of 1838

'did not apply and was not intended to apply to the crown or to crown lands. The owners of the lands so withdrawn (including the crown), have since that time considered themselves as owners of the mines discharged from the customary rights of the free miners, notwithstanding the saving words of this section; but this is at least doubtful, for the customs may have been, in fact, valid and binding before the act, although most inconvenient, even if the same be not expressly and in terms confirmed by the very words of this section.'

He adds:[3]

'The power to withdraw lands from the operation of the Act occurring in a section relating in other respect to surface damage only, and the crown, by passing the Act, acquiescing in the claims of the free miners as thereby sanctioned, it would seem *primâ facie* that the

1 See the Oakwood Mill, Park Hill, and China Engine Iron Mine Gales. See also the reservation of coal under Kidnall's Wood in the granting of the Pillowell Engine Colliery (1843) and Rudge Colliery (1844) Gales. In the granting of the gale of the High Meadow Iron Mine in 1857 the Crown reserved out of the grant 'the land called "Birchamp", the property of the Crown, and any other land which may have been withdrawn from the operation of the Mining Act'.

2 Wood, *op. cit.*, p. 171.

3 Pp. 460-1.

power was not intended to apply to crown lands or crown mines, and that the notice given by the Commissioners of Woods ... was *ultrà vires*; and, consequently, that the mines under the lands specified in such notice are still liable to be galed. It is observed that neither the Crown nor the Commissioners of Woods and Forests are mentioned in the 68th section; whereas, in the provisions as to appeal against the Awards of 1841 (sect. 34-37 of the Act) when the rights of the crown were in contemplation, express power is given to the Commissioners of Woods and Forests to appeal on behalf of her Majesty. In any case, if this notice was binding, the mines remain subject to the old customs; ... Having regard to the words "so as the same be specified in such notice" in the 68th section, the validity of the notices given by Mr. Kear and Sir Thomas Crawley Boevey, as not complying with this condition, seems very doubtful; and the same consideration, apart from the question above referred to, applies to the general words at the end of the parcels described in the notice given by the Commissioners of Woods and Forest.'

The special cases of Abbotswood and the High Meadow Estate, are as below:

(I) ABBOTS WOOD.[1] The history of this wood has been dealt with in Chapter V, whence it will have been seen that the rights in the mines and minerals were by the Abbots Wood Act, 1870 (33 Vict. c.8) declared to remain unaffected by the disafforestation and sale. Thus, so far as regards mining and the free miners' rights, and for the purpose of the Act of 1838, Abbots Wood is still to be considered as part of the Forest, being therefore subject to free miners' rights.

(II) THE HIGH MEADOW ESTATE[2] (within the hundred, but not within the present Forest perambulation) was purchased by the Crown in 1817 who later claimed that free miners' rights do not extend over the estate. These are the only lands in regard to which the free miners have, since the Act of 1838, attempted to dispute the right of an owner to prohibit the operation of their customs. In 1870 a person not a free miner made an application to the gaveller, The Hon. J. K. Howard, for the grant of a lease of an iron mine on the above estate. A free miner, James Grindell, of Coleford, through his attorney, John Hullett, objected to the grant of any gale, lease, licence or other disposition to any person not a free miner, and himself applied for ten iron ore gales in or near 'Marians', 'Whippington's Brook' and 'The Slaughter', all on the above estate. Another free miner, W. B. Brain, also lodged applications. On the gaveller refusing to grant the gales applied for, Grindel tendered a Petition of Right to her Majesty submitting that the gaveller should be restrained by the injunction of the High Court of Chancery from granting a gale to anyone not a free miner.

1 Contains iron ore deposits adjoining the eastern edge of the Forest.

2 Coal has been worked on this estate from shafts and levels at High Meadow Colliery near Hillersland, and from Mailscot Colliery. The outcrop of the Trenchard Measures extends southwards from Symonds Yat through Mailscot Wood to Marian's Inclosure east of Staunton. Several trials for both Upper and Lower Trenchard Seams are said to have been made in Mailscot Wood and although the positions of both seams are reputed to have been located, there has been no working of consequence (Trotter. *Geology of the Forest of Dean Coal and Iron-Ore Field*, p. 31: note by W. C. C. Rose). Iron ore has been won from Robin Hood Mine, from a level in Whippington Brook and from various outcrop workings. Many shallow workings cover the outcrop of the Crease Limestone between Staunton Mine and Crowsnest Mine.

Nothing appears to have resulted but when evidence was given before the Select Committee in June, 1874, the matter was mentioned as follows by T. Goold:

'Q. 2811. Is there any other instance you wish to give? – Yes; we think in the matter of the Highmeadow and Great Doward Woods, the same thing has been attempted by the Crown indeed successfully there, because I believe they will not grant a gale to go under those woods to any free miner. The Great Doward Woods and the Highmeadow Woods were subject to the old free miners' customs and rights; by a section in the first Act, any person giving notice to that effect, might exempt their inclosed property from the operation of the Act, and the Crown with several others did give notice; but those properties remained subject to the old miners' customs and rights just the same as before the Act was passed, but notwithstanding that the Crown have positively refused to grant any gales under the Great Doward and Highmeadow Woods.

Q. 2812. Do you consider they have no power to grant gales there? – We think they have no right to refuse to grant them; we think the woods remain just the same as they did before the passing of the 1st and 2nd Victoria.

Q. 2813. As a matter of fact, they have not granted the gales? – No; in Mr. Brain's case, they positively refused to grant it, without giving any reason.

Q. 2814. That was property that had been bought by the Crown itself? – Yes, from Lord Gage, I believe; but the property was still subject to all freemen's rights, whoever held it, if within the Hundred of St. Briavels.

Q. 2815. Is that the general opinion, or your own opinion? – I believe there is no doubt about it; I have the letter here where the Crown declined to grant, simply saying, "I am directed by Mr. Howard to acknowledge the receipt of your notice, dated the 28th ultimo, relative to minerals in certain land, part of the Highmeadow estate, which was acquired by the Crown by purchase, and I am to acquaint you that your notice cannot be entertained".

Q. 2816. You know nothing more? – No; so that really Highmeadow Woods and Great Doward Woods have been withdrawn from the miners' rights altogether.

Q. 3024. You stated there were other proprietors than the Crown in the Hundred of St. Briavels? – Yes.

Q. 3025. Do the rights of free miners extend over the whole of that property? – I think the rights of free miners extend under the whole of that property in the Hundred of St. Briavels.

Q. 3026. Are you aware of many cases where those rights are exercised; and are you acquainted with the facts under which they are exercised? – I do not state it positively, because I have not any absolute personal knowledge as to it, but I have no doubt they are exercised.

Q. 3027. You spoke of the High Meadow Woods and Great Doward Woods; are they within the Hundred of St. Briavels? – I believe the High Meadow Woods are.

Q. 3028. Are they not in Herefordshire? – I believe there is no doubt about the High Meadow Woods being in the Hundred of St. Briavels, and I think also the Great Doward Woods are. The Crown, however, have a more perfect knowledge upon that subject than I have.'

Thomas Forster Brown, deputy gaveller, deposed:

Q. 3482. It has been stated by Mr. Tom Goold that the rights or claims of the free miners extend over Great Doward Woods; are those woods in Gloucestershire? – No; Herefordshire.

Q. 3483. Have you heard that the rights of free miners exist in Herefordshire? – No.

Q. 3484. It has been stated that the Crown has refused to grant gales in High Meadow Woods, is that so? – High Meadow Woods were excepted from the operation of the Act of the 1st & 2nd of Victoria, in the same way that Mr. Bathurst's property and the Dunraven property were excepted, and there has been no grant of a gale in High Meadow Wood since the Act, though there have been applications. There was an application made by Mr. Grindell for a grant of a gale in High Meadow, and I think, if I remember correctly, he presented a petition of right demanding a grant; that was in 1870, I think, but I believe no further proceedings have been taken; the Crown has granted ordinary leases as in the case of ordinary property.

Q. 3485. Were they excepted before the passing of the first Act of the 1st & 2nd of Victoria? – They were excepted under that Act.

Q. 3486. What has been done as to the ironstone in those woods? – It was in respect of the iron ore that ordinary leases have been granted, the same as would be granted in respect of ordinary property.

Q. 3513. I understand you to say the High Meadow Woods are exempted from the operation of 1 & 2 Vict., c. 43? – Yes; by 1 & 2 Vict., c. 43, the owner of lands out of the Forest had the option of giving notice of exemption from the operation of the Act; notice was given by the High Meadow Woods, Countess Dunraven, and other private owners, and these private owners have leased in the ordinary way since the passing of that Act, and the Crown has also leased just as a private landowner.

Q. 3514. Are High Meadow Woods and Great Doward Woods in the Hundred of St. Briavels? – The Great Doward Woods are in Herefordshire, but the High Meadows are in the Hundred of St. Briavels.

Q. 3583. You spoke of the Doward Rocks; those are at the very edge of the basin? – Yes; they are in the mountain limestone.

Q. 3584. Almost abutting on the Old Red? – Yes, immediately on the Old Red.

Q. 3585. There is no reason to suppose that there is any coal under the Doward Rocks? – There is iron ore, but not coal.'

On 23 June 1874 Horace Watson, solicitor to the Commissioners of Woods, deposed [1]:

'The eighth point was that grants had been refused in High Meadow Woods and Great Doward Woods, and the gist of Mr. Goold's evidence was that those woods were still subject to rights of free miners. It has been explained to the Committee that the Great Doward Woods are in Herefordshire, and not in Gloucestershire; whereas the customs of free miners only extend to the Hundred of St. Briavels, which is in Gloucestershire; and, therefore, cannot extend to the Great Doward Woods, which are in Herefordshire. As to the High Meadow Woods, it has also been stated that they were acquired by purchase from Lord Gage, and notices were given, taking them out of the operation of the Act of 1 & 2 Vict. under the 68th section of that Act, which enables owners of enclosed lands to give notices by which the lands mentioned in those notices are excepted altogether from the operation of the Act. The

1 Q. 3877.

Commissioners of Woods, as regards the High Meadow Woods, as well also as several other private owners, gave notice exempting the lands which belonged to them from the operation of the Act. A claim was made to the grant of a gale by a free miner named Grindell, in the High Meadow Woods, which was declined. Mr. Grindell presented a petition of right. He obtained a fiat from the Home Office, but has never, to my knowledge, filed the petition in Chancery, and certainly no copy has ever been served on the Office of Woods; and no further proceedings have been taken upon it. On the other hand, the Crown has leased in the ordinary course its own property, part of the iron mines in the High Meadow Woods, and I believe they are now being worked under that lease.'

It appears unlikely that the free miners will in the future claim to exercise their privileges in the freehold lands dealt with in this Appendix. Nevertheless it has been of interest to show that there is at least an element of doubt as to whether they should have ever been denied rights in any land lying within the area of their original privileges.

Postscript. In respect to the 'Excepted Lands' of Noxon Park, Philip Robinson, deputy gaveller, wrote on 9 September 1840 to David Mushet[1]:

'Herewith I send you exact copies of Mine Gales in Noxon Park, which the Crown absolutely received Gawle-Rents for. I have also sent copies of several Mines in private lands to show you there was no distinctions as to gawling on private property. I have no doubt many other Mine Gales, on the Books, were in Noxon Park although not described on the Gale Books as being there. Shall be happy to render you any further information in my power. I went through every Book yesterday, leaf by leaf, which took me nearly the whole of the day.'

1 Hart MSS. 1840, and see PRO F432:1902.

Appendix B

GALES OF COAL AMALGAMATED, SUB-DIVIDED, OR REARRANGED BY THE DEAN FOREST (MINES) ACT 1904

1 Birchen Grove
2 Pluds
3 Arthur and Edward
4 Mirey Stock No. 2
5 Serridge No. 2
6 Woodside
7 New True Blue and Newham Bottom
8 East Slade
9 Britannia
10 Favourite
11 Small Profit
12 All Profit
13 New Bowson
14 East Dean Deep
15 Holly Hill
16 Richard Whites
17 Old Furnace No. 2 (Cannop)
18 Union and Cannop
19 Prince Albert
20 Alexandra
21 Central
22 Extension
23 Emperor
24 Union
25 Flour Mill
26 Rising Sun Engine
27 Venus and Jupiter No. 2
28 Princess Royal
29 Prince of Wales
30 Royal
31 High Delf Engine
32 Skinner's Gardens
33 Beaufort Engine
34 New United Deep No. 1
35 New United Deep No. 2
36 New United Deep No. 3
37 Morgan's Folly No. 3
38 Morgan's Folly No. 2
39 Morgan's Folly No. 1
40 Cousins Engine
41 Pillowell United

Some of the gales mentioned in the 1904 Act were not included in the subsequent grouping. The remainder were grouped as follows and transferred to various large companies on a basis of half a penny a ton royalty: Northern United (Holly Hill United), Eastern United, Alexandra, Western United, Southern United, South-Eastern United, Pillowell United, Cousins Engine.

The resultant deep collieries were: Arthur and Edward or Waterloo (1909), Northern United (1933), Cannop (1909), Eastern United (1910), Princess Royal (Flour Mill and Park Gutter Pits). In 1938 there was the following slight alteration in the groups of gales worked by certain collieries:

Northern United Colliery:
- New Bowson
- East Dean Deep
- Holly Hill United No. 1
- Holly Hill United No. 2 [Small Profit]

Cannop Colliery:
- Union and Cannop Engine
- Prince Albert
- Old Furnace No. 2
- Western United

North Western United:
- Arthur and Edward
- Favourite
- Mirey Stock No. 2
- Serridge No. 2
- Alexandra No. 3

Eastern United:
- New United Deep No. 2 [Part]
- Emperor
- Extension

Southern [?Morgans Utd] United Colliery:

- Royal
- High Delf Engine
- Flour Mill
- Princess Royal
- Beaufort Engine
- Union
- Rising Sun Engine
- Prince of Wales
- Venus and Jupiter No. 2
- Southern United

Central (part of)

Pillowell United:

- Howbeach Engine
- Blackpool Engine
- Unity
- New Rudge
- Pillowell Engine
- Pillowell Level
- Yorkley
- Nagshead
- New Whitecroft

Appendix C

GALES OF COAL VESTED IN THE NCB: 9 SEPTEMBER 1948

Gale	Late Galees
1. New Speedwell 2. Thatch or Independent (part)	S. and T. Adams
3. Tile Quarry	B. Ellis and W. J. Brown
4. Farmers Folly 5. Mapleford Engine No. 3	Farmers Folly Colliery Co. Ltd
6. Arles Level	C. T. H. and S. Gwilliam
7. Hillersland No. 2	J. H. and S. Gwilliam
8 Society No. 4 (part) 9. Nine Wells	E. R and H. H. Gwilliam
10. Worrall Hill No. 2 11. Jones Yorkley No. 2	Hale & Wintle
12. Prosper on Harrow Hill No. 2	M. H. & R. Hamblin & Meek
13. Gorbrook No. 4 [Added: 53. Harrow Hill Green No. 3]	M. H. & R. Hamblin
14. Lonk Level 15. Patches No. 2	S. J. & A. Hawkins
16. Cross Knave (part) 17. Bailey Hill	B. H. James & Sons
18. Hopewell Engine 19. St. Vincent 20. Dark Hill Endeavour No. 2 21. Ellesmore No. 2 (part) 22. Mapleford Engine No. 4	Mapleford Collieries Limited
23. Fancy No. 3	Peter and Basil Morgan
24. Valletts Level No. 2 (part)	E. J. & H. V. Smith
25. Birchen Grove 26. True Blue & Newham Bottom 27. Reddings Level No. 2	True Blue Colliery Co. Ltd.
28. Gorsty Knoll No. 3	F. Nash & Sons & Powles
29. Milkwall No. 3	-do- (no licence)
30. Old Strip and At It No. 2	L. Lewis and Reps of late J. Powell
31. New Found Out No. 2 32. Thatch or Independent (part)	T. H. Teague, decd.
33. Mansfield Trenchard	B. H. James & Sons
34. Poolway Trenchard 35. Smiths Trenchard No. 2 36. Slopes Trenchard No. 2	B. H. James & Sons – lessees: Trenchard Collieries Ltd
37. Cannop (4 Gales) 38. New Mill Engine No. 2	Cannop Colliery Co. Ltd

39. Eastern United 40. Northern United (4 Gales) [Added: 54 Findall (part)]	Henry Crawshay & Co. Ltd
41. North Western United (5 gales) 42. Old Engine No. 2 43. Worrall Hill No. 3 44. Lydbrook Colliery No. 3	Lydney & Crump Meadow Collieries Ltd
45. Pillowell United (part) 46. Cousins Engine No. 2 (part)	Park Colliery Co. Ltd
47. Parkend Deep Level 48. Ellwood 49. Diamond No. 2 50. Whitemead 51. Midsummer Level No. 2 52. Southern & Morgans United (14 gales)	Princess Royal Colliery Co. Ltd

The above named Gales are hereby registered in the Records of the Deputy Gaveller of the Forest of Dean in the name of the National Coal Board as Registered Galees as from 1st January 1947, the interests in the Gales having vested in the National Coal Board by virtue of the provisions of the Coal Industry Nationalisation Act, 1946, Section 5 (1) and Part 1 of the First Schedule to the Act.

A. R. Thomlinson, deputy gaveller
9 September 1948

[To the original 52 gales were added No. 53 and 54, hence the whole is referred to as 52+2.]

Appendix D

AGREEMENT BETWEEN THE FORESTRY COMMISSION AND THE COAL AUTHORITY: 26 FEBRUARY 1997

THIS AGREEMENT [Between the Forestry Commission as Gaveller and the Coal Authority, 26 February 1997] witnesseth as follows:

1. In this Agreement:

   (a) "Dean Forest Enactments" means the Dean Forest Act 1819, Dean Forest (Mines) Act 1838, Dean Forest Act 1861, Dean Forest (Mines) Act 1871 and Dean Forest (Mines) Act 1904 and all Awards, Orders, Rules and Regulations made thereunder,

   (b) "Gale" means a gale of coal in accordance with the Forest of Dean Enactments;

   (c) "Licensee" means a person to whom the Authority, in exercise of its powers under Part II of the Coal Industry Act 1994, may grant a licence to carry on underground coal-mining operations within the Forest;

   (d) "Forest" means the Forest of Dean or any other part of the Hundred of St. Briavels in the County of Gloucester in respect of which the Dean Forest Enactments apply;

   (e) "subsidence damage" means damage occurring to any land or property as a consequence of subsidence resulting from the carrying on by a Licensee of any coal-mining operations in a licensed area;

   (f) "Mines and Quarries Legislation" means the Mines & Quarries Act 1954 and any Regulations made thereunder; and

   (g) "licensed area" means an area in respect of which a licence under Part II of the Coal Industry Act 1994 shall have been granted.

2. Any licence granted by the Authority in respect of underground coal-mining operations within the Forest shall be substantially in the form [not included hereto] set out in the Schedule hereto, with such modifications only as the circumstances in each case shall require.

Whereas

1. the Commission is entitled by virtue of *inter alia* the Dean Forest Enactments to exercise the powers and duties of Gaveller in the Forest of Dean or any other part of the Hundred of St. Briavels in the County of Gloucester (hereinafter called "the Forest") including the right to grant Gales.

2. By virtue of Section 25 of the Coal Industry Act 1994 (hereinafter called "the 1994 Act") a licence or other authorisation under Part II of the 1994 Act is required for the carrying on of any underground coal-mining operation within the Forest to which that Section applies, and by virtue of Section 26 of the 1994 Act, it is the Authority which has the power to grant such a licence.

3. This agreement is entered into for the purpose of settling, as between the

Commission and the Authority

(a) the form of licences which the Authority may grant in respect of such coal-mining operations carried on or to be carried on within the Forest,
(b) the manner in which subsidence matters and the treatment of mine entries shall be dealt with, and
(c) the acquisition by the Authority of information relating to coal-mining operations.

To the extent that they shall not be discharged by the appropriate Licensee, the Commission shall discharge all claims relating to coal-mining subsidence in any area which may reasonably be expected to have been influenced by mining operations carried on by a Licensee.

4. The Commission shall notify the Authority immediately upon receipt of any such claim and, as soon as practicable after the discharge of each such claim, shall notify the Authority of the manner of such discharge.

5. In exercising their powers under the Dean Forest Enactments as Gaveller or Deputy Gaveller to grant any Gale or to control the working of any Gale, the Commission shall have regard, in cases where it appears that subsidence damage might occur to the extent of such damage which is likely to occur and to the character of the land or other property in question and to the uses to which it is or is likely to be put. Where it appears that subsidence damage may occur to any listed buildings, or other sensitive features of whatever nature, the Commission shall take such steps as may be open to it in exercise of its powers under the Dean Forest Enactments as may be necessary to protect such buildings or other features from severe subsidence damage.

6. The Commission shall henceforth be responsible to the exoneration of the Authority for the proper back-filling, sealing or plugging (whether by itself or by the holder of any Gale) of all mine entries which form or may form part of any coal-mining operation that is carried on within the Forest in pursuit of a licence under Part II of the Coal Industry Act 1994.

7. The Commission shall exercise its powers under the Dean Forest Enactments to require all persons to whom any Gale or Gales may be granted to supply it with plans, sections and other information relating to their respective mines in accordance with the Dean Forest Enactments at such times as the Authority may reasonably require but in any event not less frequently than would be required in order to comply with the Mines and Quarries Legislation and will without delay pass copies of such plans sections and other information to the Authority.

IN WITNESS whereof the parties have set their respective hands the day and year first before written

SIGNED on behalf of the Coal Authority
by NEVILLE JAMES CAMERON WASHINGTON

SIGNED on behalf of the Forestry Commission
by DAVID JAMES BILLS [Director General]

Appendix E

THE GAVELLER AND DEPUTY GAVELLER

The office of gaveller arose from the thirteenth century, then representing the Crown in its dealings with the miners. There is evidence of the derivation of gaveller from a person entitled by the king to receive the revenues from the mines to an official of that title [confirmed in PRO F20(1)17, p. 10 (1662)]. The cycle of events has been:

- From at least *c. 1244,* and confirmed in 1282, the gaveller was a person appointed or authorised by the king to collect the dues from the miners of iron ore and coal, usually paid to the king's receiver or to his assigns, or to his nine or ten foresters-of-fee of the bailiwicks.
- The first record of the sinecure/financial benefit office of gaveller (then termed 'Custodian of the Gawle') is in 1435-36 (Henry VI reign). The perquisites included the revenue from 'the Gawle' (i.e. gawle dues from the miners). The appointment was usually supplemented by the sinecure offices of aleconner of the Forest as well as custodian of Whitemead Park. The beneficiary delegated the gale collection and administration to two deputies one 'Above the Wood' and the other 'Below the Wood' (see Glossary). Sometimes the deputy gavellers were recruited from miners.
- From the eighteenth century the custodianship or gavellership devolved to an official of the Crown who appointed either one or two deputy gavellers.
- In 1808 the office of gaveller was vested in the Surveyor-General of Woods and in 1838 in the First Commissioner of Woods and Forests.
- In 1924 the office of gaveller was vested in the Forestry Commission. Today, because there is no First Commissioner of Forestry, the gaveller is a collective noun for all the Commissioners of the Forestry Commission, and is represented *de facto* by the Director General. Policy is the Commissioners' prerogative exercised via the gaveller and his deputy.

Deputy gaveller. From 1838 the deputy gaveller was a person skilled in mining (S.13 of the Dean Forest (Mines) Act 1838, now repealed by the 1969 Act). His duties now extend geographically beyond the Statutory Forest of Dean (Plate V) to the boundary of the Hundred of St. Briavels (Plate VI).

The Coal Act 1938 and the Coal Industry Nationalisation Act 1946 virtually confirmed the office and duties of deputy gaveller except for gales vested in the National Coal Board under the 1946 Act. Nowadays the post is on a part time basis, but the role is far reaching, particularly following the Coal Industry Act 1994 and other statutes, e.g., the Environment Act 1995. The work relates to:[1]

---

1 Piggott, R. J., 'The Forest of Dean Free Miners: AD 2000', Feb. 1996. Dissertation presented to the R.I.C.S. South Wales Branch, Minerals Division, 7 March 1996.

- investigating applications from men wishing to be registered as free miners, and, as appropriate, enrolling and registering them in accordance with Ss.14-17 and 19-22 of the Dean Forest (Mines) Act 1838;
- dealing with all matters under S.13 of that Act and others of the Dean Forest Mines enactments, relating to gale licences, rents and royalties; he is empowered to divide and amalgamate certain licence areas under the Dean Forest (Mines) Act 1904 and under S.52 of the 1838 Act to make special Rules;
- advice on mining searches in the iron ore field (coalfield searches since 1994 are referred to the Coal Authority on examination of a request per the Law Society CON 29 Procedure);
- stability aspects of abandoned coal and iron ore mine workings, shafts, adits, and opencast coal mining;
- pollution in abandoned mine workings and stone quarries;
- liaison with the Crown Mineral Agent, Mineral Planning Authority and Forest of Dean District Council relating to mining matters;
- liaison with the Coal Authority;
- liaison with the Forestry Commission Land Agency and Civil Engineering Departments;
- advising the Forestry Commission Land Agency on quarrying matters;
- liaison with the Treasury Solicitor on litigious issues relating to Dean mines and miners;
- liaison with H.M. Inspectorate of Mines;
- providing information for school children, students and the public on free miner related matters, geology, and mining history.

In brief, the duties of the deputy gaveller, based in Coleford (from late 1996 John Harvey, a chartered mining engineer), include: registration of free miners, granting gales to them only, assessment and collection of tonnage royalties and dead rents based on the availability and accessibility of the mineral resources, and maintenance of plans, books and records.

As noted in the text, the requirement that the deputy gaveller should be 'skilled in mining' by the Dean Forest (Mines) Act 1838 was repealed in 1969 and did not replace this requirement with other qualifications – but in view of the complexity of the role, he should in all prudence be an appropriately qualified chartered mining or surveying (or both) person.

The deputy gaveller does not carry out mine surveys himself – this is now the direct statutory responsibility of the underground mine operator whether galee or licensee, in accordance with comprehensively described rules in MASHAM 1993 regarding the safety and health of the mine employees. This has to be done in accordance with the statutory provisions of that Act, and notified to H.M. Mines Inspectorate by the mine operator. They have similar obligations under the Coal Authority parallel licences. The deputy gaveller can inspect mines at will, on reasonable notice, under the Dean Forest Mines enactments, as amended. He inspects and monitors the mine scenario, in accordance with the statutory provisions, including the Coal Authority licensing regime per its Agreement in 1997 with the Forestry Commission.

Appendix F

GALES OF IRON ORE AND COAL

Nature of a gale. A free miner has the right to require a grant to himself[1] of specified seams of coal or deposits of iron ore or stone in a specified situation.[2] The grant, as also the subject matter of the grant, is known as a 'gale'.[3] No gale may be made of any inclosed land belonging to the Crown.[4] Grants of gales are made in accordance with the order of application.[5] The deputy gaveller is not bound to grant a gale if he is of opinion that it would interfere with an existing gale[6] or that, from its proposed situation or extent, it is not adapted for winning the mineral in the best manner.[7]

Extent of the gale. The extent of the gale is determined by the deputy gaveller, and in setting out the metes and bounds he must have regard to the probable cost of winning the mineral and the quantity of mineral likely to be obtained.[8] Every grant of a gale must specify the extent of the gale.[9]

Grant of a gale. The grant is made subject to any special rules and regulations thought necessary by the deputy gaveller,[10] and provides for the working of a minimum quantity of mineral in each year,[11] with liberty to make up short workings in any subsequent year.[12] An underlying seam may be galed even if an upper seam has been previously galed, and the upper seam may be sunk through by the galee of the lower seam.[13] A free miner is not entitled to the grant of more than three gales at any one time, or to a fresh grant, until one or more of the three existing gales is exhausted,[14] unless he surrenders a gale as not containing sufficient mineral to be workable.[15] To be effectual, the grant must be enrolled in the books of the deputy gaveller, and a copy is given to the free miner.[16]

1 Dean Forest (Mines) Act 1838, S.23. Only the Crown has the right to make such grants: *A-G* v. *Mathias* (1858), 4 K & J 579.
2 Awards of Coal and Iron Ore Mines 1841, Sch. 2, r.11, and 1871 Act.
3 See *Great Western, (Forest of Dean) Collieries Co. Ltd* v. *Trafalgar Colliery Co. Ltd* (1887) 3 TLR 724 at 725, per Kekewich, J.
4 Dean Forest (Mines) Act 1838, S.64.
5 *Ibid.*, S.60; Dean Forest (Mines) Act 1904, S.7; Dean Forest Act 1906, S.2.
6 A valid application for a gale cannot be made unless the gale is available at the time: *James* v. *Young* (1884) 27 Ch.D 652.
7 Dean Forest (Mines) Act 1838, S.62.
8 *Ibid.*, S.56; Award of Coal and Iron Ore Mines 1841, Sch. 2, r.11.
9 Dean Forest (Mines) Act 1838, S.56.
10 *Ibid.*, S.56.
11 Awards of Coal and Iron Ore Mines 1841, Sch. 2, r.13.
12 *Ibid.*, Sch. 2, r.14; Award of 1871, para. 3.
13 *Goold* v. *Great Western Deep Coal Co.* (1865) 2 De GJ & Sm. 600.
14 Dean Forest (Mines) Act 1838, S.61.
15 *Ellway* v. *Davis* (1873) LR 16 Eq 294; and see *James* v. *R* (1877) 3 Ch.D 153, CA.
16 Dean Forest (Mines) Act 1838, S.57.

Effect of grant of a gale. The right granted by a gale of coal or iron ore mine is of the nature of real estate limited to the galee, his heirs and assigns, but conditional upon the due payment of the rents, royalties and dues reserved, and due performance and observance of the rules and regulations for the time being in force,[1] and contained in the Awards[2] and any special rules and regulations contained in the grant.[3] Non-compliance by the miner in any of these respects will render the gale liable to forfeiture[4] although the specific remedy of forfeiture does not bar an action for damages.[5] Forfeiture is complete on service of notice, without actual entry by the deputy gaveller.[6]

Transfer of gales. Gales may be transferred either *inter vivos* or by will to any person or persons.[7] A memorial in statutory form[8] of every transfer by deed must be registered in the books of the deputy gaveller within three months from its date,[9] or such extended period as the Forestry Commissioner, as gaveller, for reasonable cause allow,[10] and if not so registered is void.[11] Registration may be refused if dead rent is unpaid[12] or if the deed effecting a transfer subsequent to one which took place by will or descent does not contain a recital of the circumstances under which devolution by will or descent took place.[13] A memorandum of the entry is inclosed on the original certificate of the grant of the gale[14] or on the last preceding transfer.[15]

Inclosed land. Where mines situated under inclosed land outside the statutory Forest belonging to private persons are galed, the surface owner is entitled to half the profits,[16] and any owner of closed land is entitled to compensation assessed by the deputy gaveller for surface damage.[17] The compensation may consist of a gross or an annual sum.[18] The statutory provisions do not extend to damage by subsidence, as a galee has no power to let down the surface.[19] No steam engine or dwelling house may be erected on inclosed land without the consent of the owner.[20]

---

1 Dean Forest (Amendment) Act 1861, S.1. It seems that galees are liable to the general rate in respect of their occupation: see *Morgan* v. *Crawshay* (1871) LR 5 HL 304.

2 Dean Forest (Mines) Act 1838, S.29.

3 *Ibid*., S.56.

4 *Ibid*., S.29. As to relief by the court, which cannot be granted after the expiration of 6 months, see *Re Brain* (1874) LR 18 Eq 389.

5 *Ross* v. *Rugge-Price* (1876) 1 Ex D 269; *Brain* v. *Thomas* (1881) 50 LJQB 662, CA.

6 *Ex parte Young and Grindell* (1880) 50 LJ Ch 221; *James* v. *Young* (1884) 27 Ch.D 652.

7 Dean Forest (Mines) Act 1838, S.23.

8 Dean Forest (Amendment) Act 1861, S.10, Schedule.

9 Dean Forest (Mines) Act 1838, S.58; see also the Dean Forest (Amendment) Act 1861, S.11.

10 Dean Forest (Mines) Act 1838, S.59.

11 Dean Forest (Amendment) Act 1861, S.14.

12 *Ibid*., S.9.

13 *Ibid*., S.11.

14 Dean Forest (Mines) Act 1838, S.58.

15 Dean Forest (Amendment) Act 1861, S.12.

16 Dean Forest (Mines) Act 1838, S.67.

17 *Ibid*., S.68

18 Dean Forest (Amendment) Act 1861, S.16.

19 *Allaway* v. *Wagstaff* (1859) 4 H & N 681.

20 Dean Forest (Mines) Act 1838, S.69.

Working of gales. A galee must commence to open the mine within five years of the date of the grant of the gale, but in case of accident or other unforeseen impediment the deputy gaveller may give an extension of time.[1] In working a gale general regulations must be complied with.[2] The mine must be worked in a workmanlike manner;[3] proper accounts and plans must be kept, which the gaveller or deputy gaveller is at liberty to inspect;[4] pits and level mounds must be in situations determined by the deputy gaveller;[5] the deputy gaveller and their agent have power to enter and inspect the mine;[6] and the person working coal must leave such barriers as may be directed by the deputy gaveller.[7] In one respect the obligations of a person working a gale are more onerous than those imposed by the general law: a person working a gale drained by a steam engine and situate near and to the rise of another must pump so as to prevent water flowing from one mine into the other.[8] On the abandonment or disuse of a gale the surface must be restored.[9] The duty of performing and observing the rules and regulations is a personal obligation on the person for the time being in possession or receipt of the proceeds of the gale, whether as owner, lessee or underlessee.[10]

Surrender of gales. A gale or part of a gale may be surrendered on giving notice to the gaveller,[11] he has power to accept a surrender of part only of a gale and, on such terms as he thinks fit, a surrender other than by notice.[12] A galee whose gale is drained by a steam engine or other machinery, and lies to the rise of another, must give to the gaveller or deputy gaveller, and also the owner of the gale lying to the deep, three months' notice of his intention to discontinue working his engine.[13]

Amalgamation, subdivision and rearrangement of gales. Whenever the deputy gaveller thinks it desirable so to do, having regard to the proper opening or working of any gale and to any representation made by any galee, he may by order in writing under his hand amalgamate, subdivide or otherwise rearrange the area of either any gales in hand or any existing gales. This is empowered by the Dean Forest (Mines) Act 1904 S.1(1), which applies only to the gales in the Schedule to the Act, S.10(1). Such an order may not be made in respect of any existing gales without the consent of the galees, except where the gale is so situated that it cannot be separately worked without great injury or detriment to any adjoining or contiguous gale, or without greatly impeding the proper and effectual working of any of the seams of coal within the

1 Award of 1871, para. 2.
2 Dean Forest (Mines) Act 1838, S.29.
3 Awards of Coal and Iron Ore Mines 1841, Sch. 2, r.9.
4 *Ibid.*, Sch. 2, r.16.
5 *Ibid.*, Sch. 2, r.10.
6 Dean Forest (Mines) Act 1838, S.53; Awards of Coal and Iron Ore Mines, 1841, Sch. 2, r.17.
7 Award of Coal Mines 1841, Sch. 2, r.18, The deputy gaveller may permit the working of any barrier directed to be left on such terms as he thinks fit: Dean Forest Act 1861, S.24.
8 Award of Coal Mines 1841, Sch. 2, r.19; Award of Iron Ore Mines 1841, Sch. 2, r.18.
9 Awards of Coal and Iron Ore Mines 1841, Sch. 2, r.12.
10 Dean Forest (Amendment) Act 1861, S.4.
11 Awards of Coal and Iron Ore Mines 1841, Sch. 2, r.6; Dean Forest (Amendment) Act 1861, S.19.
12 Dean Forest (Mines) Act, 1871, S.33; Dean Forest (Amendment) Act 1861, S.20.
13 Awards of Coal and Iron Ore Mines 1841, Sch. 2, r.8. See also The Mines (Notices of Abandonment) Regulations, 1998.

Hundred of St. Briavels which require the use of expensive pits, engines or machinery, or where the gale is so small or otherwise of such a character that it cannot properly or economically be developed and worked as a separate mine (S.1(3)). Any such order must be advertised in at least two local newspapers (S.2), and the order takes effect, in respect of existing gales, as if it were a grant of new gales and must be enrolled accordingly (S.3(1)). In addition to any terms and conditions which may be specified in the grant, the order may contain such terms and conditions, including a provision requiring the payment of any sum or compensation by one galee to another, as the gaveller may think proper and as may be agreed to by the galees concerned or, in specified circumstances, determined by arbitration (S.3(2)).

Galeage rents and royalties. These are usually due to the Crown in respect of each gale. Galeage rents include dead rents which the Commissioners under the Dean Forest (Mines) Act 1838 had power to award.[1] Dead rents and royalties may also be reserved on making subsequent grants.[2] Galeage rents are payable on 31 December and royalties on 30 June and 31 December in each year.[3] No galeage rent is payable, in the case of coal mines, for the first two years, and in the case of iron ore mines for the first four years, after the grant of the gale, unless the minerals are actually wrought.[4] Royalties, per ton, are based on the ancient rights of the Crown to share in the profits of a gale.[5]

Rules relating to payment. Galeage rents and royalties are payable by the person in possession or receipt of the proceeds of the gale, whether as owner, lessee or otherwise.[6] Every grant of a gale must specify the dead rents and royalties,[7] and in case of dispute the amount is determined by arbitration.[8] The rents and royalties of any gale may be revised every twenty-one years (or, in the case of gales to which the Dean Forest (Mines) Act 1904 applies, sixty-three years), reckoning from 24 June next following the grant[9] and in of dispute the amount of the revised rents and royalties must be fix by arbitration.[10] The rents and royalties are recoverable by distress[11] or in an action[12] by the deputy gaveller.[13]

Some of the sections mentioned in the foregoing footnotes of this Appendix F have been amended by the Statute Law (Repeal) Act 1969 and the Coal Industry Act 1994 – see Appendix I.

1 *Lord Seymour* v. *Morrell* (1851) 17 LTOS 139.

2 Dean Forest (Mines) Act 1838, S.56.

3 Dean Forest (Mines) Act 1871, S.35.

4 Awards of Coal and Iron Ore Mines 1841, Sch. 2, r.5.

5 See Fourth Report of the Dean Forest Commissioners 1831 (published 1835).

6 Dean Forest (Amendment) Act 1861, S.4.

7 Dean Forest (Mines) Act 1838, S.56.

8 *Ibid.*, S.56; as to arbitration, see Ss. 47.49; Dean Forest (Amendment) Act 1861, S.8; and Dean Forest (Mines) Act 1871, S.37.

9 Dean Forest (Mines) Act 1838, Ss.27, 46; Dean Forest (Amendment) Act 1861, S.7.

10 Dean Forest (Mines) Act 1838, Ss.27, 47, 48; Dean Forest (Amendment) Act 1861, S.8; Dean Forest (Mines) Act 1871, S.37.

11 59 Geo. III c.86 (Dean Forest) (1819), S.7; Dean Forest (Mines) Act 1838, S.52; Dean Forest (Amendment) Act 1861, S.4; Dean Forest (Mines) Act 1871, S.36.

12 59 Geo. III c.86 (Dean Forest) (1819), S.8.

13 *Lord Seymour* v. *Morrell* (1851) 17 LTOS 139.

Appendix G

DEPOSITS OF MINING RECORDS IN GLOS.R.O. BY THE FORESTRY COMMISSION 1989-98: D5947 AND D7920

(1) Gloucestershire Record Office D5947:
Deposits made 1989-1997 of Forest of Dean documents by the Forestry Commission, Coleford, per the deputy surveyor and the deputy gaveller:

i Free Miners, 1838-1997
1838-1956: original applications to be registered (1-4,102)
1838-to date (ongoing): photocopy of register of applications

ii 1841: Awards of coal and iron ore gales within the hundred of St. Briavels, and of stone quarries within the Forest of Dean perambulation.

iii Gales: Applications
Grants: 1811-1838 Gale Books
1842-(ongoing) Gales
Transfers: 1839-*c.*1958

iv Licences: 1847-1905

v Gale Rent Ledgers (Accounts): 1789-1841
Accounts of coal and iron ore raised from under freehold land of private estates (who received 50% of the royalties).
Coal raised: 1851-1873
Iron ore raised: 1851-1875

vi Correspondence: 1911-1933 Surface damage award books

vii Maps and plans: 1835-1904

viii Reports: 1861-1954

ix Highmeadow estate: 1871-1942

x Other records (1668)-1900.

(2) Glos.R.O. D5947: Additional deposits made 1992 of Forest of Dean documents by the Forestry Commission, Coleford, per the deputy surveyor:
Plans of coal and iron ore workings: 1830-*c.*1960. Includes plans by Thomas Sopwith, John Roper, W. Wood, John Atkinson, Joseph Hale, Jeremiah Head, R. Woolford, James Buffry, B. J. Lyddon, James Harris, F. W. Brain, and A. L. B. Brain.

(3) Glos.R.O. D7920: Deposits made 1998 of Records of, and inherited by, the former National Coal Board relating to the Forest of Dean:
These records have several particular points of interest which predate the nationalisation of the coal industry in 1947, and many of the reports were produced during World War II. Much of the deposit comprises reports by the Coal Survey Laboratories in Birmingham and Cardiff. Although these are very technical in nature, some files contain more generalised material, such as notes on individual collieries. The coal output statistics down to colliery level are particularly noteworthy. Collieries mentioned include – Northern United, Eastern United, Cannop, Princess Royal, Arthur and Edward, New Fancy, Parkend Royal, Lightmoor, Speech House, and Wynols Hill. Various other items include the great 'fault' called 'The Horse' and reserves in the coalfield.

Appendix H

PUBLIC RECORD OFFICE: ADDITIONAL MINING RECORDS RELATING TO THE FOREST OF DEAN

F20/6: 1838-1840:	Minute Book of the proceedings of the Dean Forest Mining Commissioners, Thomas Sopwith, John Buddle and John Probyn, in pursuance of the 1838 Act; marked 'No. 1'. Indexed.
F20/7:1839-1841:	Depositions and other evidences as to rights of mines laid before the Commissioners at their meetings; marked 'A/B'.
F20/8:April 1839:	Claims to gales and mine workings inquired into by the Commissioners, and evidence heard by them, marked 'D'. Indexed.
F20/9:1839-1841:	Depositions and other evidences as to rights of mines laid before the Commissioners at their meetings; marked 'F'. Indexed.
F20/10: 1839-1840:	Depositions and other evidences as to rights of mines laid before the Commissioners at their meetings; marked 'Q'. Indexed.
F20/1 1:1842:	'Observations on the Mineral Produce of Dean Forest and on its present and proposed means of distribution': Original Report of Sir Henry de la Beche, FRS, Director of the Ordnance Geological Survey of Great Britain, on his examination of the proposal for a railway in the Forest
F17/426: 1835:	Plans of the coal and iron ore Mine Districts of the Forest, and sections of coal seams. T. Sopwith, engrossed and coloured, 8 chains to an inch, 27 sheets in one volume, which also contain a MS copy of the Mining Commissioners' Award of Coal Mines within the Forest dated 8 March 1841 (100 pages).
F430:Early 20th C:	Ordnance Survey of part of the Forest showing boundaries, quarries, etc. Printed, MS additions, coloured, one mile to 25 inches, 38 sheets in one volume.
F431 :Early 20th C:	Ordnance Survey of the Forest showing lands held with gales. Printed, MS additions, coloured, one mile to 25 inches, 31 sheets in one volume.
F432: 1902:	Ordnance Survey of the Forest showing boundaries of lands exempted from the Dean Forest (Mines) Act 1838. Printed, coloured, one mile to 25 inches, 15 sheets in one volume.
F20/36: 1842-1876 /37:1877-1907 /38:1908-1923 /39:1923-1930	Grants of gales made to free miners pursuant to the Dean Forest (Mines) Act 1838. Indexed.
/40:1841-1873 /41:1874-1897 /42:1898-1906 /43:1907-1924	Grants of gales: approbations by the Commissioners of Woods, etc. Indexed.
F20/44:: 1852-1872:	Disputes over mines; copies of Case Papers and Law Officers' opinions. Indexed.
F20/45: 1904:	Register of free miners 1838-1904. List of names taken therefrom.
F20/46: 1917:	'Report of William Forster Brown, deputy gaveller, on the iron ore deposits of the Forest of Dean'. With maps appended, O.S. sheets and some MS sections.

Appendix I

FOREWORD BY CYRIL HART TO THE REPRINT[1] IN 2000 OF JAMES G. WOOD'S *THE LAWS OF THE DEAN FOREST AND HUNDRED OF ST. BRIAVELS* (1878)

James G. Wood's book of 1878 (478 pp.) was based largely on a publication by Thomas Sopwith in 1841 (under the direction of the Commissioners of Woods and Forests on the completion of the work of the Dean Forest Mining Commission of 1838, of which Sopwith was one of the three Commissioners). Sopwith included copies of much of the Commissioners' five Reports of 1832-35; the important Dean Forest (Mines) Act 1838; and the Awards of Gales of Coal and Iron Ore Mines, and Stone Quarries in Dean Forest up to 1841. Wood added the Gales awarded in 1871. His volume has been of considerable value and interest to a large public. Since its publication in 1878, much of relevance has occurred, in particular:

- Numerous other gales have been awarded by the deputy gaveller,
- Numerous free miners have been registered, the conditions of qualification slightly amended, and some of the Rules of Working changed;
- Deep mines of coal were worked during the period 1904 to 1965;
- The functions of gaveller since 1924 have been exercised by the Forestry Commissioners. The office of deputy gaveller has hardly changed (it is currently held by John Harvey, a chartered mining engineer, in the Coleford Office of the Forestry Commission);
- Much new Case Law has arisen, chiefly:

1880	Young and Grindell: re Action of Right
1881	Brain *v.* Thomas
1884	James *v.* Young
1887	G.W. (F. of D) Colliery Co. Ltd *v.* The Trafalgar Colliery Co.
1898	The Queen *v.* The Gaveller and Deputy Gaveller
1929	Elsmore *v.* Morgan: re Commoning and Pound breach
1986/7	Matthews *v.* Wicks: re Commoning
1996	M. J. Jones *v.* R. L. Piggott, deputy gaveller: re clarification of qualification for Registration

To Wood's own Addenda (his p. xii) should be added:

p. 10, line 23, for 'culling' read 'cutting'
p. 17, line 13, for '1635' read '1634'
p. 26, line 2, delete comma
p. 124, line 12: for '20' read '26'
p. 134, the note to S.13 is incorrect
p. 165, line 15 from bottom for '62' read '61'
p. 314, line 16: read 're-entry'

[1] A limited number of reprints of Wood's *Laws* was published in 2000 by 'Ross Old Books' (Ross-on-Wye) and 'Past and Present Books' (Coleford).

- The Dean Forest (Reafforestation) Act 1668 has been wholly repealed.
- *Parts* of some Statutes have been amended, chiefly:
  - Dean Forest (Timber) Act 1808 (By, e.g. the Crown Estate Act 1961 and the Wild Creatures and Forest Laws Act 1971)
  - Dean Forest (Encroachments) Act 1828
  - Woods and Forests (General Purposes) Act 1829
  - Dean Forest (Mines) Act 1838 (Ss. repealed: 1-13, 18, 24-26, 28, 30-44, 49-51, 55, 63, 66, 70-82, 84-89, 91; Ss. part repealed or amended: 16, 17, 19, 20, 22, 27, 29, 48, 53, 56-68, 60-61, 65, 68, 83. S.14 is now clarified – *vide* Lawsuit of 1996)
  - Dean Forest (Amendment) Act 1861 (Ss. repealed: 2, 5, 6, 17, 22, 25, 27; S. part amended: 13)
  - Dean Forest (Mines) Act 1871 (Ss. repealed: 5-32; Sections part repealed or amended: 2, 34, 37)
- Many new relevant Statutes have been enacted since 1878, namely:
  - Dean Forest (Mines) Act 1904 (Ss. repealed: 5, 8; Ss. part repealed or amended 3(2a), 7 (7)
  - Dean Forest Act 1906 (Repealed)
  - The Coal Mines Act 1911
  - Forestry (Transfer of Woods) Act 1923 (Parts now repealed)
  - The Mining Industry Acts of 1920 and 1926
  - Forestry Act 1927 (Parts now repealed)
  - The Crown Lands Acts of 1885, 1894, 1906, and 1927
  - The Coal Act 1938 (Ss. repealed: 2, 3(2) and (4), 5, 6, 11, 14, 15, 17, 19, 22-34, 41-45, 52, 55, 58
  - The Coal Acts of 1943, 1949, and 1965
  - The Coal Industry Nationalisation Act 1946 (mostly repealed)
  - Mines and Quarries Act 1954
  - Coal-Mining (Subsidence) Acts 1950 and 1957
  - Opencast Coal Act 1958
  - The Statute Law (Repeals) Act 1969. (This repealed in the 1938 Act Ss. 1-13, 18, 24-26, 28, 30-44, 49-51, 55, 63, 66, 70-82; and in the 1861 Act Ss. 5, 6, 17, 25, 27.
  - Mines & Quarries (Tips) Acts 1969 and 1971
  - Coal-Mining (Subsidence) Act 1991 (Forest of Dean and Hundred of St. Briavels excluded)
  - The Crown Estate Act 1961
  - Wild Creatures and Forest Laws Act 1971
  - Health & Safety at Work etc. Act 1974 (and Regulations made thereunder, e.g. Management and Administration of Safety & Health at Mines Regulations 1993)
  - The Coal Industry Acts 1975, 1977, 1990, and 1994.
- Some Statutes relating to other than coal and iron ore mines and quarries are now patently obsolete.

The Coal Industry Act 1994 privatised the UK coal mining industry and set up the Coal Authority whose role is as a facilitator rather than a coal producer and which is statutorily obliged to license all coal mining operations in Great Britain. The relationship between the free miners and the Coal Authority is not clear, but the Dean Forest Mine enactments and the 1994 Act appear incompatible and at present neither one can be said to take clear precedence over the other. The relationship is subject to much debate.

In 1952, I updated some of J. G. Wood's information in my modest *Laws of Dean* (25 pp.). I was partly inspired to do this by having purchased Wood's personal copy of his book (which he had interleaved with blank sheets, hence its overall size is twice that of his published volume; on these pages he had from time to time until his death in 1928, noted many addenda and inserted extra notes, cuttings of his letters to the press, etc.) [This invaluable copy has been donated to the Forestry Commission in The Cyril Hart Dean Mining Collection, 2002.]

In 1952 I approached the publishers of J. G. Wood's book, Sweet & Maxwell Ltd., who unhesitatingly gave permission for my writing of a Supplement. Difficulty was experienced in tracing Wood's representatives, but eventually I was fortunate to get in touch with his daughter-in-law, Mrs M. L. Wood of Victoria, British Columbia, who most kindly gave my intention her blessing and posted to me the photograph of her father-in-law which I used in my book. The following year, 1953, I was pleased to meet Mrs Wood during a forestry visit to the West coast of America; she was a nun in Vancouver City; one of her many talents was making small pottery.

My *Laws of Dean* included copies of the Dean Forest (Mines) Acts 1904 and 1906 (authorising deep coal mining in Dean), and briefly touched upon the Coal Act 1938 and the Coal Industry Nationalisation Act 1946. It also included a map of the Forest of Dean and of the Hundred of St. Briavels; and added much Case Law, but did not include any Awards of gales since 1877 (the list is available in the records of the deputy gaveller).

In 1953, after further extensive research, the First Edition of my *The Free Miners of the Royal Forest of Dean and Hundred of St. Briavels* (527 pp.) provided much additional information on the history of freemining.

Postscript: James George Wood MA, LLB, FSA, FGS (see Plate VIII), was born on 11th December 1843. He was the second son of Edmund Fowle Wood of Chepstow, Mon., Land Agent. He married on 13 May 1873, Marian Cordelia, third daughter of George Watkins, MRCS of Gwy House, Chepstow.

Wood was a Fellow of Emmanual College, and Chancellor's Legal Medallist and Whewell Law Scholar in the University of Cambridge. He rowed in the Cambridge boat in 1868. He was called to the Bar at Lincoln's Inn on 17 November 1869 and acquired a large junior practice at the Chancery Bar and as a conveyancer. He was subsequently elected a bencher of his Inn.

Wood took a very great interest in the Forest of Dean, both in its history and in the legal aspects of the rights, customs and privileges of the district. His advice was eagerly sought after by both the Crown and the public. He published many papers in historical and archaeological journals. A list of most of Wood's other books and articles is given on p. 23 and 24 of my *Laws of Dean* (1952). The majority of his notes and papers are available in bound volumes at The Central Library, Dock Street, Newport, Mon.

James G. Wood died on 11 January 1928 at the age of eighty-four. (He had a son George Llewellyn and a daughter Grace Edith. His brother, the Reverend Edmund Gough de Sales Wood, was Vicar of St. Clements, Cambridge, and Canon of Ely.)

Appendix J

THE CYRIL HART DEAN MINING COLLECTION DONATED IN 2002 TO THE FORESTRY COMMISSION, COLEFORD

(A) *RECORDS. SOURCES, etc., re FREE MINERS*

1. Copy of J. G. Wood's *The Laws of the Dean Forest and Hundred of Saint Briavels*, 1878, 478 pp. This copy was Wood's own, interleaved and annotated by him, including his extra notes (donor purchased it in the 1880s, Updated by donor in his *Laws of Dean* (1952 including Acts of 1904 and 1906, photograph of J. G. Wood; also many Lawsuits).

2. *Another copy of J. G. Wood's Book as above*. This copy was presented by Wood to Thomas Sopwith, and contains his letter to him dated 19th October 1878; also Sopwith's note of acknowledgement dated 8 November 1878. Updated by donor in his *Laws of Dean* (1952 including Acts of 1904 and 1906, photograph of J. G. Wood; also many Lawsuits).

3. *Photograph of J. G. Wood*: Given to donor (1953) by Wood's then known sole surviving relative – a Nun in a Convent in Vancouver – visited by donor during his first forestry tour of USA and Canada, 1953. The photograph was used in donor's *Laws of Dean* (1952).

4. *Acts of Parliament, etc.*
   (a) List of 19th C. Acts (photocopied by donor from the Report of the 'Duncan Select Committee' App. Aa. 1848 (PRO, Kew), 1 page.
   (b) *Coal Industry Nationalisation Act 1946*. (As to Dean Forest, see p. 54.)
   (c) *Coal-mining (Subsidence) Act 1950*, 16 pages.
   (d) Copy of *Coal Industry Act 1994*, 171 pages. (As to Dean Forest, see pp. 36, 160-171.)

5. *Sundry Documents (some are photocopies)*

   (i) Sundry Notes of Mine Law Court Records, abstracted by donor at PRO, Kew, Ref. F26/1. [F26 files moved to Glos.R.O. in 2002]
   (ii) Sundry Notes re Deep Gales, etc., abstracted by donor at PRO, Kew (Ref. F26/19 and F26/261). [F26 files moved to Glos.R.O. in 2002]
   (iii) Photocopy of Article by J. J. Joynes (Manager, Cannop Colliery); also letter and Report from his widow to donor.
   (iv) Photocopies of Records 1841 (originals in Glos.R.O.).
   (v) Photocopy of *Mining Journal* by Insole and Bunning, 1881 (re Dean Forest).
   (vi) Photo and correspondence re Free Miner's sword, 1679.

(vii) Printed Petition to Parliament by Owners of Coal Mines in Dean, *c.*1840.
(viii) A Gawle Rent demand by Edward Machen (as Joint Dep. Gav.) 1838; also George Jenkins (re Gale) to T. Tovey (Dep. Gav.) 1833; also Copy Notice to H. V. Gwilliam from R. J. Piggott when working for NCB, 1965.
(ix) Various Notes re Free Miners, 1975.
(x) Free Miners prevent dumping of Atomic Waste in Dean mines, 1954 (Sir John Cockcroft suggested, but did not succeed).
(xi) Photocopy of PRO, Kew (F16/53) of List of Coal raised in West Dean 1846-56. [F16 files moved to Glos.R.O. in 2002]
(xii) Little booklet 'Fine Forest of Dean Coal', 36 pp. *c.*1930s.
(xiii) HMSO: 'Forest of Dean Coalfield: Regional Survey Report', 1946.
(xiv) Photocopy of Abstract of Records (ref: donor's MSS. (p. 22), brief 'historical summary' used by donor in his earlier books.
(xv) Notes by donor re Ochre in Dean Forest: 1857-8.
(xvi) Notes by donor re 'Exempted Lands', particularly Noxon Park, 1854.
(xvii) Photocopy of Colliery rents, Arrears, etc. 1849.
(xviii) Photocopy of Dean Forest (Dead Rents) 1854/6. Includes Thos. Sopwith's unpublished letter of 9 Nov. 1847.
(xix) Copy of Thos. Sopwith's 'Observations' speech, Coleford, 5 Sept. 1838.

(B) Copy of 2nd Edition, *The Free Miners,* (2002) by the donor (author).

(C) *SUNDRY*

Copy of donor's *Laws of Dean* (1952): see Contents page of the volume.
Copies of 10 Lawsuit Reports re Dean Mines.
Copy of Thos. Sopwith's *The Awards. . . of Coal and Iron Mines,* 1841. Inserted in this copy are:

1. Letter from Thos. Sopwith to Rev. H. G. Nicholls, 17 March 1857.
2. Letter from Thos. Sopwith to Rev. H. G. Nicholls, 18 March 1861.
3. Letter from Thos. Sopwith to Rev. H. G. Nicholls, 8 Feb. 1861.
4. 'Observations' (as in xix above) by Thos. Sopwith, Coleford, 1838.

Copy of Robert Sopwith: *Thomas Sopwith, Surveyor: An Exercise in Self-Help,* 1994 (contains a few errors). (T. S. was Robert's great-great-grandfather). Included in my copy are letters from the author to donor, May 1973 and 1996.

Copy of Tony Oldham 'The Mines of the Forest of Dean …', 1997. Incomplete, and contains some errors. Typewritten booklet.

(D) *TO FOLLOW*

1. 1848: Framed, coloured Map of Dean in *Report of the Select Committee on the Woods, Forests, and Land Revenues of the Crown* – relating to the 'Duncan Committee of 1848/9.

2. 1848: Framed, coloured Geological Map of Dean Coalfield relevant to (1) above.

GLOSSARY

IN PARTICULAR

The forest — The royal *forest* throughout the realm. Not necessarily woodland. Originally named 'King's hunting grounds'.

The Forest — The Statutory Forest of Dean (*q.v.*) (named from *c.*1080. See Plate V. Now covers about 35 square miles.

The castle — The castle of St. Briavels, the administrative centre of the Forest of Dean from *c.*1130 to *c.*1800.

The hundred — The Hundred of St. Briavels (named from *c. 1244,* See Plate VI.

The Statutory Forest — See 'The Forest' *supra* and Plate V.

IN GENERAL

'Above the Wood' and 'Below the Wood' — The ancient, and pre-1838, divide of the Forest and hundred for mining regulations and other relevant purposes was the Lydbrook-Mirey Stock-Cannop valley running north to south. To the east was called 'Below the Wood', including Ruardean, Mitcheldean, Littledean, and Flaxley; to the west was called 'Above the Wood', including Newland, St. Briavels, Staunton, and Bicknor. Certain mining regulations applied to 'Below' and not to 'Above', and *vice versa.* Usually there was a gaveller and deputy gaveller for each of the two divisions. The ancient mining divide became obsolete after the 1838 Act, and subsequently all coal and iron ore below the land surface of the Forest and hundred has been under the jurisdiction of the gaveller per the deputy gaveller.

Attachment Court — The verderers' court for preliminary hearing of forest offences. Sitting usually every sixth week, it was chiefly concerned in adjudicating cases of small trespasses to the vert. In the case of venison, the offences were recorded for presentation to the Justice in Eyre of the Forest. On some occasions the

	Attachment Court was called a Swanimote, or the two merged. In Dean, the Attachment Court became known as the Speech Court, where the local populace appeared to solicit wood and timber (estovers) for their needs. It still functions.
Bailiwick	An ancient forest divide to facilitate organisation and management. The nine in Dean were each in the charge of a forester-in-fee (*q.v.*). The difference between bailiwick and woodwardship is somewhat uncertain; they tended to merge, and are no longer extant.
'Bare licence'	A free but not assignable licence supplied by the former NCB for then extant freemining under the Coal Industry Nationalisation Act 1946. Except for any of them not issued for a period which has now expired, the present Coal Authority accepts that, without prejudice, they still remain in force, and no miner who has such a licence needs a new one under the 1994 Act, although its legality has yet to be tested.
'Barriers'	Intact areas of unworked coal which separate one gale from another so as to keep the ventilation and working system of one mine distinct from another [Dean Forest (Mines) Act 1861, S.24]. In certain circumstances, these areas of coal are specifically excluded from grants so that any miner working into them is guilty of trespass. The deputy gaveller has authority to permit their working.
Bonâ fide working	The Dean Forest (Mines) enactments set out the criteria for genuine intentions to work a gale. If these are not met the galee is liable to forfeiture. This has not latterly been tested in the Courts. There are some instances of gales being held where the galee has no intention of mining – which may need to be redressed.
Cabbiners	Often from afar (with their temporary cabins), formed most of the labour force of the iron industry, especially in cutting, cording and charcoaling. Exceptions were the miners - they were local and more permanent.
Cinders (Slag)	Partly-smelted iron ore, usually from the bloomery period, used for re-smelting in blast furnaces. They contained much iron, and acted as a flux in smelting. Sometimes used for road making.

Coal	Mineral coal; termed 'Seacole' in early times.
Cole	Charcoal.
Collier	Originally a charcoal burner. From the eighteenth century, a miner of mineral coal. See Free Miner.
Common, 'Right' of	'Right' (by Crown sufferance) of an individual or community to exercise 'Herbage' and 'Pannage'.
Commoners	Local populace claiming 'Rights' of common or 'turn-out'. Often referred to as 'sheep badgers'.
'Concession', ('Concessionaire, 'Patentee'; Farmer)	Referred in Dean to the 'King's Ironworks' and the cordwood necessary therefor. There was no reluctance to accept the 'concession'; for all the unpleasantness and rivalries generated, it remained a desirable and presumably profitable undertaking. It generated almost constant conflicts between conservative and positive administrators as well as between the local populace and the new industrial interests. The commoners, miners and other local populace maintained a stream of complaints, accusations, petitions and informations usually leading to litigation. From 1611 to 1642, at least twelve special Exchequer investigations were issued and returned to investigate the alleged misdemeanours of 'Concessionaries' and their employees, as well as of the forest officials engaged with them.
Constable-Warden	The earlier chief administrator in Dean, using St. Briavels castle as headquarters. An office of some honour but little labour, with many perquisites. Sometimes the appointments did not include both offices. Most administration was by deputies.
Country, The	The local populace.
'Crown Freehold Land'	Parcels of Crown freehold land within the statutory Forest. They are exempt from freemining rights and commoning privileges. Generally arisen where Crown land after sale or lease was later re-acquired by the Crown.
Dead rent	A minimum rent (currently ranging from £1 to £80) payable annually on a gale whether coal or iron ore is

	produced. A free miner after the grant of a coal gale is exempt from paying a dead rent for a period of two years and, in the case of an iron ore gale, of four years. As soon as any mineral is won, the tonnage royalty has to be paid each half-year. After the expiration of the free period the royalty merges into the dead rent, however, if the royalty does not amount to the dead rent in any one year, the full amount of the dead rent has to be paid and the ensuing short workings are carried forward to the credit of the galee. See 'Unworked gales'.
Dean Forest Mines enactments	The Acts of 1838 to 1906. They have been considerably modified, in particular by the Statute Law (Repeals) Act 1969 and by the Coal Industry Act 1994.
Deforest, Deforestation	Releasing all or part of a *forest* from forest law. (Not to be confused with its meaning from the eighteenth century – to remove the tree crop from woodland without the intention of reforesting.)
Delivery	Release, e.g. of estovers (botes) and pitwood, by the Attachment Court; or of cordwood by forest officials to 'farmers' of the 'King's Ironworks'.
Demesne	Land held by the sovereign for his own use.
Dole	A vernacular term for a free miner partner's share of the profits of working a gale.
Encroachment	Encroachment on forest land; usually an illegal enclosure.
Estover (Bote)	An allowance of firewood, poles, timber and other necessaries released by the court of attachment as a privilege to the local populace. Included firebote, housebote, hedgebote and ploughbote. Not exercised in Dean since the Act of 1668.
'Excepted Land'	Subject to the mineral ownership facts, where coal or iron ore was raised from private freehold land, 50% of the tonnage royalty was paid by the deputy gaveller to the owner. See Appendix A. In some areas, e.g. Noxon Park, the deputy gaveller was not involved, financial terms being solely between the landowner and the operator.

Eyre, Forest	(*a*) Judge's tour, (*b*) session of an Itinerant Judge's Court; (*c*) the principal forest court, due to be held every three years. See Justice Seat. Chiefly concerned with fines and amerciaments for breaches of forest law. Called into being by the sovereign's letters patent, appointing the justices to hear and determine pleas of the forest. The last held for Dean was in 1656.
Farm, Ferm	A right granted or leased in *forest.*
Farmer	A holder or patentee of a farm/ferm/'concession' significantly in the Dean iron industry.
Forest	Territory designated by a perambulation and used by the sovereign for his, or his assigned, hunting, and subject to his will by *forest law* (*q.v.*). The protection of deer and their habitat was paramount.
Forest law	Took precedence over common law and partly excluded it. It punished and restricted, but also maintained a system of husbandry well suited to the exploitation of woodland and waste.
Forester-of-fee	A feudal holder of a forest bailiwick (*q.v.*). There were usually nine. By 1637, 1676, and 1713 it is possible that not all the holders of the office were hereditary, in which case the method of appointment is not evident. Sometimes the office was purchased from the previous holder. The office was valued for its prestige and perquisites, and undertaken by a deputy. The difference between a forester-of-fee and a woodward is somewhat uncertain. The office, which had the entitlement of several perquisites, has long been extinct.
'Forfeiture'	If a free miner or other galee commits a breach of the statutory Rules and Regulations or fails to pay his dead rent or tonnage royalty, or does not mine within five years, the deputy gaveller can at his discretion forfeit the gale and make it available for application by other free miners.
Free Miner	A registered miner with rights of mining coal, iron ore and stone.
Gale	A defined area granted for the working of coal or iron

	ore within the Hundred of St. Briavels; or stone within the now statutory Forest. A free miner cannot have granted more than three gales at any time but can acquire others. A free miner can sell, lease, or gift his gale. If for any reason a free miner or other galee wishes to surrender a gale, he may do so on giving six months notice to the deputy gaveller, and it can then be available for application by other free miners. Can be forfeited if not mined within five years of grant. See Appendix F.
'Galeage money'	Payments once made by the consolidated deep miners to the trustees of the original galees for purchase of those gales needed to sink the deep shafts.
Hundred of St. Briavels	Substantially larger than and not coterminous with the now statutory Forest (named from *c.*1154). Only a portion is owned by the Crown. See Plate VI.
Ironmaking	(*a*) the 'direct process', a bloomery made decarbonised iron straight from the ore. (*b*) the 'indirect process' (from *c.*1540) employed a blast furnace to smelt iron ore, and a fining forge to decarbonise the iron.
Ironmaster	See 'Concessionaire' and Farmer. Sometimes they were 'financiers' and/or 'enterprising landowners' (with some financial backing) attempting to make profit from ironmaking, or at least to obtain an outlet for their woods and coppices which otherwise were virtually unsaleable.
Iron ore	Originally termed 'ore-myne'.
Justice Seat	The location where the Chief Justice of the Forest or Justice-in-Eyre held his enquiries and administered forest law. The principal forest court. See Eyre.
Keeper	A forester or woodman in charge of a walk (*q.v.*).
'King's fifth man'	The King's early right to put in a fifth man to share the mining profit with four other men after the mine had been opened. See (*a*) 'Laws and Privileges', and (*b*) Mine Law Court Orders. Royalty in lieu thereof was later provided by S.44 of the Dean Forest (Mines) Act 1838.
'Law ore'	Anciently part of the dues from the miners to the king.

Leases	(*a*) For quarries, and (*b*) for surface (*q.v.*).
Licence	(*a*) 'Bare licence' from NCB; (*b*) S. 36(2)(a) licence from NCB as galee; (*c*) Forestry Commission grant of a surface licence to sink air-shafts, make roads or tramways, and other matters affecting the surface; and (*d*) a mining licence granted by the Coal Authority in accordance with the Coal Industry Act 1994 for the mining of coal (see Appendix D, Agreement between the Forestry Commission and the Coal Authority 1997). Currently the Coal Authority hold 62 licences.
'Lord's fifth man'	The holder of private freehold land early right to put in a fifth man to share the mining under his land with four other miners, after the mine has been opened.
Metes	The bounds or perambulation of *forest.*
Mine, Myne	Iron ore.
Miner, Myner	A digger of iron ore. See Free miner.
Perambulation	Delimitation of a forest by metes and bounds. Undertaken by walking/riding, but sometimes by consultation, enquiry and perusal of documents. Usually undertaken by a number of regarders, generally twelve.
'Private Freehold Land'	Land not within the Statutory Forest; and see 'Excepted Land'.
Regard, The	A periodical inspection of *forest* made by regarders, usually knights. Once in every three years an inspection of the woods within the metes and bounds of the forest was or ought to have been made by twelve regarders chosen for the purpose. They were not 'full-time'. The inspection was known as The Regard. The duty of the twelve regarders was to find answers to a set of interrogatories entitled the Chapters of the Regard which included: herbage in the king's demesne, eyries of hawks and falcons, forges, mines, honey, assarts, purprestures, waste of woods, and other offences. Documents of 1637, 1676, and 1713 show that regarders were no longer knights but simply esquires or gentlemen of the Forest neighbourhood.

Region, Dean — All or part of the land lying between the Severn and the Wye and bounded in the north by an approximate line Monmouth-Ross-Newent-Gloucester (outskirts). Not into Monmouthshire or Herefordshire.

Royalty — A sum (currently a minimum of about 10p per tonne) payable by a free miner or galee on the tonnage of iron ore, coal, or stone extracted. From at least *c.* 1244, and confirmed in 1282, miners of iron ore and coal rendered to the king acknowledgements for their privileges. Usually these were: ½d. or 1d. weekly for each miner, also a 'seam' (a measure) of the minerals won, sometimes called 'law ore'; as well as permitting the king (or his nominee) 'to put a fifth man' (*q.v.*) into each partnership of four, termed 'the king's man', without his having to bear any of the expense of sinking and maintaining the mine. Similar acknowledgements were rendered either to the forester-of-fee of each of the king's bailiwicks or, in later times, to the owner of private freehold land – thereby admitting 'the lord's man' (*q.v.*). The foregoing 'one man in five working', in later years, virtually formed the basis of the rent and royalty paid by the miners to the Crown, per S.44 of the Dean Forest (Mines) Act 1838. In 1841 the royalty was 4d. per ton; in later years 1d. to 6d.
Royalty for ordinary gales is fixed by the deputy gaveller (and reviewed every 21 years, for deep gales every 63 years). The deputy gaveller can also revise the royalty and the scope of the grant on transfer of a gale. Royalty under Coal Authority licences is fixed by that Authority and can be tiered-reducing, e.g. 40p to 20p per tonne.

Scowle — Irregular shallow open cavities, the result of surface iron ore extraction from the Roman period (and possibly earlier) until at least the eighteenth century. Some scowles between Coleford and Staunton were scheduled in October 2000 as ancient monuments.

Statutory Forest — Substantially smaller than and not coterminous with the Hundred of St. Briavels. See Plate V. Owned by the Crown. Now covers about 35 square miles. The boundaries are as defined in 1835 by Commissioners appointed in 1831. Includes Abbot's Wood but not Highmeadow Wood.

Stone quarries	All leases within the Statutory Forest are now made by the Forestry Commission through its area land agent. See Appendix F.
Subsidence (surface)	See the 1994 Act. The general regime as to subsidence is expressly excluded in the Hundred of St. Briavels – under the Coal Mining Subsidence Act 1991 S.2. Section 1(4)(a)(ii) 'does not apply where the coal was worked or gotten by virtue of the grant of a gale in the Forest or any other part of the hundred'. The coal galee is liable in Common Law for subsidence damage. The coal galee has no power to let down the surface (Allaway *v.* Wagstaff, 1859 4 H & N 681). Further, the right to withdraw support contained in S.38(1) of the 1994 Act does not extend to free mining: see S.40(4). The galee is liable in tort to pay compensation to the surface owner. It is noteworthy that in the Agreement of 1997 between the Forestry Commission and the Coal Authority (see Appendix D) a dual licence obliges a coal licensee to take out insurance against surface subsidence damage, though the Forestry Commission accepts the relevant management responsibility for it, but no financial or legal responsibility, the latter resting with the mine operator.
Surface damage	Payment to private landowners in compensation for damage incurred by the opening of a coal or iron ore mine, as distinct from subsidence damage (*q.v.*).
Surface leases	Forestry Commission lease for land above gales, necessary for soil-tipping, buildings, etc. – under the jurisdiction of the Forestry Enterprise area land agent in liaison with the deputy gaveller. Leases for spoil-heaps were free, but trees destroyed were charged for.
Swanimote	The forest court of presentment. One of the two lesser courts of the forest (the other being the Attachment Court – in Dean the Speech Court). The Swanimote merged with the Attachment Court, significantly in Dean. Often the Swanimote was a vague word used both of the Attachment Court and Forest inquisitions. The latest relevant references found for Dean are in 1713.
'unopened' 'Unworked' gales	After two years, galees of coal pay a dead rent via the deputy gaveller to the Coal Authority; of iron ore after

	four years, to the Forestry Commission.
Verderer	A forest official with limited judicial power. Usually held the office for life. Four to each forest. Main duty to guard the venison and the vert. Elected under the sheriff by the freeholders of the county and appointed by the Sovereign. See Attachment Court.
Vern	A partner in working a gale.
'Walk'	A forest division to facilitate organisation and management. Usually in the charge of a keeper (*q.v.*). There were six Walks in Dean.
Warden	See Constable-Warden.
Waste of the *forest*	General term for unenclosed and uncultivated wooded *forest*. Now part of the Statutory Forest.

BIBLIOGRAPHY

(1) MAIN MANUSCRIPT SOURCE[1]

PUBLIC RECORD OFFICE

Chancery
- C53 Charter Rolls
- C54 Close Rolls, Elizabeth I to Charles I
- C60 Fine Rolls
- C62 Liberate Rolls
- C66 Patent Rolls, Elizabeth I to Charles II
- C99 Forest Proceedings, Modern

Exchequer, King's Remembrancer
- E134 Accounts various
- E134 Bills and Answers, Elizabeth I to Commonwealth and Protectorate
- E124/125/126 Decrees and Orders
- E134 Depositions by Commission, Elizabeth I to Charles II
- E134 Estreats of Fines
- E134 Forest Proceedings
- E134 Memoranda Rolls, Elizabeth I to James I
- E134 Special Commissions and Returns, Elizabeth I to Charles II
- E134 Pipe Rolls

Various
- E32/31 The Regard of 1282
- E32/30 The Eyre of 1282

State Paper Office
- SP12 State Papers Domestic, Elizabeth I
- SP14/15 State Papers Domestic, James I
- SP16 State Papers Domestic, Charles I
- SP18 State Papers Domestic, Interregnum
- SP25 Council of State

1 The Calendars have been used extensively, and occasionally the actual documents have been inspected.

Office of Woods and Forestry Commission

F3/14/16*	Dean Forest, Records [F3 & F16 moved to Glos.R.O. D9096 in 2002]
F16/17*	Dean Forest, Deputy Surveyor's Office
F20 F26* F261 F430 F431 F432	Dean Forest; Records [F26 moved to Glos.R.O. D9096 in 2002]

* *The present author's original studies of the PRO documents, especially F3, F16 and 26 were in the PRO Chancery Lane, London. After they were removed to the PRO Kew, the study of them was renewed there. Early in January 2002 the three series of documents were removed to Gloucestershire Record Office, under Ref. D9096.*

Annual Reports of the Commissioners of Woods, Forests and Land Revenues of the Crown, 19th C. and to 1923

PRO Maps See end of this Bibliography

BRITISH LIBRARY

Harleian Manuscripts
4850 Copy of Proceedings at the Forest of Dean Justice Seat, 1634

Lansdowne Manuscripts: various

BODLEIAN LIBRARY MANUSCRIPTS

Rawlinson
D119 Forest of Dean Justice Seat, 1634

GLOUCESTER LIBRARY MANUSCRIPTS

L.F.1.1 Copies of records relating to the Forest of Dean
L.F.6.2 Copy of Proceedings at the Forest of Dean Justice Seat, 1634

GLOUCESTERSHIRE RECORD OFFICE

D3921 Hart Forest of Dean Collection
D2026 Bond Papers
D23 Probyn Papers

D4431	Phillipps Papers
D5942 D5947 D7920	Various
D9096	F3, F16 and F26 Records moved from PRO in 2002.

(2) MAIN PRINTED SOURCES

Calendar of State Papers Domestic, Edward VI- 1660

Calendar of Treasury Papers, I, 1557-1696

Calendar of Treasury Books, I-IV, 1660-1675

HISTORICAL MANUSCRIPTS COMMISSION

Various Reports and Papers

RECORDS

The Third Report of the Commissioners appointed to enquire into the State and Condition of the Woods, Forests, and Land Revenues of the Crown ... (London) 3 June 1788 (cf. *Commons Journal,* 1787-8, XLIII, pp. 559-632)

Commissioners of Woods, Forests, &c of 1831: 5 Reports

Report of The Forest of Dean Committee, 1958

GENERAL

M. L. Bazeley	The Forest of Dean in its Relation with the Crown during the 12th and 13th Centuries', *Trans. B.&G.A.S.,* 33 (1910), pp. 153 *et seq.*
Chris Fisher	'The Independent Collier' (London, 1978)
	Custom, Work and Market Capitalism: The Forest of Dean Colliers, 1788-1888 (London, 1981)
Edward Machen (deputy surveyor)	The *Machen Notes, 1818,* written in two 'exercise books' were studied by the present author, who took copies of many of the pages. The two books were then returned to H. A. Machen of English Bicknor. He was assumed to have deposited them in the Gloucestershire Record Office; this was not done, and their present location is unknown.

J. Manwood — *The Forest of Dean,* 1858
Treatise and Discourse of the Lawes of the Forest (London, 1605)

Rev. H. G. Nicholls — *The Personalities of the Forest of Dean*, 1863

Iron Making in the Olden times, 1866

R. J. Piggott — 'The Forest of Dean Free Miners: AD 2000', Feb. 1996. Dissertation presented to the RI.C.S. South Wales Branch, Minerals Division, 7 March 1996.

James G. Wood — *The Laws of the Dean Forest and Hundred of St. Briavels* (1878)

Victoria County History of Gloucestershire, vols II and V

MAPS

1608: PRO F17/1, MR 879, Glos.
1608: PRO MPC 108, Mon.
c. 1244, PRO F17/7
1782: T. Pinnell: PRO F17/14
1787: Drivers': Glos.R.O. F16/47 MR 415; F16/59; F17/5 and 6 (copy in Glos.R.O., Hart Forest of Dean Collection D3921)
1842: J. Atkinson (copy in Glos.R.O., Hart Forest of Dean Collection D3921)
1847: J. Atkinson (copy held by the present author)
1848: Map in *Report of the Select Committee on the Woods, Forests, and Land Revenues of the Crown* – relating to the 'Duncan Committee of 1848/9. (Incidentally, the map held by the present author was produced for the debates in the House of Lords relevant to 'the saving of the Forest from sale' resulting by the Forestry Act 1981.)

INDEX OF SUBJECTS

The main group-headings include: Acts; Coal; Coal Gales; Collieries; Deputy Gaveller; Forestry Commission; Forest of Dean; Free Miners; Gale; Gaveller; Hundred of St. Briavels; Iron Ore; Lawsuits; Measures and Weights; Mine Law Court; Mining Techniques and Workings; Occupations; Quarries; and 'Words'.

Abbot's Wood .... 145, 309, 316, 353, 371, 372, 407, 528, *and* Abbot's Wood (Dean Forest) Act 1870.
'Above the Wood' an ancient mining district (the west of the Hundred of St. Briavels) ..... xv, 4, 45, 46, 47, 48, 50, 51, 57, 63, 71, 89, 107, 113, 119, 121, 122, 123, 125, 213, 225, 226, 227, 235, 237, 238, *and* Glossary
explanation 119
extent 46, 47, 119
occasional alterations 47, 119, 122, 123, 125
disused after 1838 Act 306
prices of minerals, and detail of regulations, occasionally different to 'Below the Wood' (*q.v.*) 9, 38, 47, 119, 121
ACTS (in date order)
Charter of the Forest 1217 xxii
Charter of the Forest 1225 xxii
Act to mitigate forest law in Dean, 1657 .... 183, 184
declared void in 1660 186
Dean Forest (Reafforestation) Act, 1668 .... xvi, 5, 8, 194, 195, 204, 205, 206, 207, 222, 239, 255, 258, 293, 486
Dean Forest (Timber) Act, 1808 .... 223, 257
Dean Forest (Gale Rents) Act, 1819 .... 225, 248, 345,534
1825 225
Woods and Forests (General Powers) Act, 1829 .... 225, 345, 547
Dean Forest Commission Act, 1831 .... 251, 252
Dean Forest (Mines) Act, 1838 (defined and confirmed rights of free miners) ... xix, 8, 73, 306-12, 313, 314, 321,323, 476, 495, 496, 513, 525, 527, 528, 536
need for 312,313
Dean Forest &c. (Leases) Act, 1855 345
Dean Forest (Amendment) Act, 1861 .... 311, 319, 348, 349, 536, 547
Dean Forest (Mines) Act, 1871 .... 310, 354, 476, 536, 547
Crown Lands Act, 1873 (Leases of Stone Quarries) 358, 476, 477
Crown Lands Act, 1894 461
Dean Forest (Mines) Act, 1904 .... 462, 471, 532, 536, 547
Dean Forest Act, 1906 .... 466, 547
Forestry Act, 1919 467
1981 .... xix, 477, 550
Forestry (Transfer of Woods) Act, 1923 .... xxiv, 467, 547
1924 Order thereunder 467
1926 Order thereunder 467
Coal Act, 1938 .... xiv, xv, xvi, xviii, 4, 8, 195, 471, 472, 476, 547
Coal Industry Nationalisation Act, 1946 .... xiii, xvii xviii, 473, 475, 535, 547
Coal Mining (Subsidence) Acts, 1950, 1957 .... 480, 547
Mines & Quarries Act, 1954 .... App. D
Statute Law (Repeals) Act, 1969 .... 310, 479, 495, 496, 547
Wild Creatures and Forest Laws Act, 1971 .... xix, xxxiii, 225
Coal Industry Act, 1994 .... xv, xvi, xvii, xviii, xxvi, 465-469, 479-91, 495, 536, 547, 548
Town and Country Planning Act, 1947 493
1971 .... 492, 493
1990 493

Environmental Protection Act, 1990 . . . 493
Coal Industry Subsidence Act, 1991 . . . 480
Water Resources Act, 1991 . . . 493
Environment Act 1995 . . . 492, 538
see also Dean Forest Mines enactments (as modified) 1838-1904 . . . xviii, 476, 479, 480, 483, 492, 493, 486, 495, 536 *and* Glossary
Admiralty Commissioners . . . 176, 185, 196, *and see* Ship building
aleconner of the Forest . . . 49, 52, 53, 54, 57, 213, 235, 236
Amalgamated Association of Miners (1871) . . . 355, 375
'ancient instruments in writing' . . . 31, 102, 106, 108, 111, 113, 117, 118, 127, 135, 245, 270, 297
chest (wooden) for same . . . 43, 44, 106, 108, 113, 128, 297
'ancient miners' equipment, sword, tools, workings . . . 21, 22, 23, 24-30, 59, 68, Plate II
arbitration, by deputy constable . . . 130
by deputy gaveller . . . 338
by the 1838 Act . . . 309
Awards of Gales (1841) . . . 312-20, 326, 527
boundary stones . . . 318
coal . . . 118, 319
iron ore . . . 318, 319
need for . . . 312, 313
Preface to . . . 136-40
stone quarries . . . 319
Awards of Gales (1862) . . . 348, 349
Attachment Court . . . 207 and Glossary; *and see* Speech Court and Verderer
steward of . . . 277, 361

'Below the Wood' an ancient mining district (the east of the Hundred of St. Briavels) . . . xv, 4, 9, 38, 45, 46, 47, 48, 50, 51, 57, 63, 69, 70, 76, 80, 107, 112, 113, 115, 119, 120, 121, 122, 123, 124, 125, 130, 165, 183, 213, 216, 226, 236 *and* Glossary
explanation . . . 119
extent . . . 38, 46, 47, 119
occasional alterations . . . 47, 119, 122, 123, 125
disused after 1838 Act . . . 306
prices of minerals, and detail of regulations, occasionally different to 'Above the Wood' (*q.v.*) . . . 9, 38, 47, 119, 121
bailiff . . . 36
bailiwicks . . . 6, 8, 11, 12 *and* Glossary *and see* forester-of-fee
Abenhall . . . 11, 12
Bearse . . . 12, 13
Bicknor, English . . . 13
Blakeney . . . 12, 13
Bleyth's . . . 14
Lea . . . 12
Littledean . . . 6, 13, 14
Mitcheldean . . . 6, 13, 14
Staunton . . . 12, 13
'bare licence' see National Coal Board (NCB) *and* Glossary
Bats, Horseshoe, in mines . . . 506
Bible, use of . . . 68 *and see* oath
'Blue Book, The' (1874 Report) . . . 359
'Book of Dennis' (so-called) . . . xvi, 16, 34, 251, 242, 254, App. 5
boys in mines . . . 215
British Coal Corporation (BCC) from 1987 . . . 476, 479

cabins, cabbiners . . . 74, 161, 188, 205, 222 *and* Glossary
carrier of minerals . . . 5, 9, 36, 73, 74, 77, 78, 81, 82, 83, 85, 88, 93, 95, 101, 107, 108, 112, 115, 116, 117, 118, 120, 122, 137, 138 *and see* horses, donkeys and mules
caves (iron ore), Clearwell . . . 507, 508
other . . . 507
charcoal for smelting iron ore . . . 149, 168
charter, none found . . . xv, 17, 245, 247
chiminage . . . 146
Christianity references . . . 7, 18, 38, 46, 60, 149, 461, *and see* Bible and 'Words'

churches . . . 461
cinders (slag) . . . 146, 152, 153, 154, 156, 168, 205, 207, 210, 254 *and* Glossary
Civil Wars . . . 179, 180, 239, 292 *and see* Commonwealth *and* Cromwell.
COAL . . . 146, 147, 169, 187, and *passim*
coalfield extent . . . xiv, and Plate V
estimated life of . . . 362
geology . . . 250, and Plate VII
fire cole . . . 74, 86, 89, 112, 113, 122
lime coal . . . 74, 89, 95, 101, 107, 112, 119
sea cole . . . 11, 12, 14, 40, 164, 155
smith cole . . . 82, 85, 86, 93, 113, 121, 122
stone coal charks . . . 122
'colliery concerns' under 1946 Act . . . 473, 475
opencast mining . . . xvii, 479, 496, 505
Edge End . . . 479, 496
Woorgreen . . . xvii, 505
elsewhere . . . xii
potential, Lightmoor and Middleridge . . . 505
colliers in 1608 . . . 151
coal pits in 1788 . . . 215
coal output in 1800-1818 . . . 247
Coal Board, National (from 1946) *see* National Coal Board
barriers of coal between gales, . . . 349, 384, 394, 417 *and* Glossary
deaths in coal mines (1871-73) . . . 361
prices of . . . 76, 89, 93, 94, 95, 97, 101, 104, 107, 113, 119, 120, 121, 122, 221, 325, 335
bargainers for prices/sales, *see* Mine Law Court
Coal Authority (from 1994) . . . 476, 479-91, 495
Agreement with the Forestry Commission (1997) . . . 469, 482, 483, 536, 537, 538, App. D
debate with Free Miners Association regarding the 1994 Act . . . 295
licence under . . . 481, 482, 483, 490, 492, 495, 536, *and* Glossary
Coal Companies
B. H. James & Sons . . . 534
Bullo Pill Co. . . . 276
Cannop Bridge Co. . . . 274
Cannop Colliery Co. Ltd. . . . 534
Cheltenham Protector Coal Co. (1841) . . . 318
Cinderford Iron Co. . . . 287
Farmers Folly Colliery Co. Ltd. . . . 534
Forest of Dean Iron Co., Parkend . . . 287
Great Western Coal Consumers' Company . . . 372
Great Western Deep Coal Co. . . . 351-2
Har(t)ford, Partridge & Co. . . . 266
Henry Crawshay & Co. Ltd. . . . 535
Lydney & Crump Meadow Collieries Ltd. . . . 535
Mapleford Collieries Ltd. . . . 534
Montague and Church, Gloucester . . . 287
Morrell. Messrs., of Oxford . . . 328, 342, 343
Park Colliery Co. Ltd. . . . 535
Partridge, Platt & Co., coalmasters . . . 271
Princess Royal Colliery Co. Ltd. . . . 535
Trenchard Collieries Ltd. . . . 534
True Blue Colliery Co. Ltd. . . . 534
Coal Seams: named . . . 326, 344, 366, 462
'Church coal' . . . 304
'Churchway High Delph' . . . 318, 326, 351
'Coleford High Delph' . . . 318, 326, 351, 462, 473, 476, 482
'Lowery' . . . 326
'Nags Head' . . . 326
'Parkend High Delph' . . . 326
'Rocky' . . . 326
'Trenchard' . . . 326
'Whittington's Delph' . . . 326
'Woorgreen' . . . 326

Coalfield Regeneration Fund ... 508
Collieries, Deep (Northern United last to close, 1965) ... 497
Arthur & Edward or Waterloo (1909) ... 532
Northern United (1933) ... 532
Eastern United (1910) ... 532
Cannop (1905) ... 532
Princess Royal (Flour Mill and Parkgutter) ... 532, 533
Regrouping: Northern United ... 532
Eastern United ... 532
Southern United ... 533
Central ... 533
Collieries: named including Levels and 'Dipples' (sometimes may refer to the relevant gale and not to the working thereof).
Addis Hill ... 505
Alexandra Colliery (1884, 1904) ... 409, 410, 466, 532
All Profit (1884, 1904) ... 421, 464, 532
Arthur and Edward (1884, 1904) ... 421, 532
'Arthur's Folly' (1774) ... 271
Aywood (1661) 'Oake Pit' ... 70, 189, 239, 240
Barnhill No. 3 Gale (1945) ... 502
Beaufort Engine (1884, 1904) ... 421, 532
Bilson Colliery (1848, 1865, 1874) ... 280, 282, 327, 351, 361, 363, 389, 393
Birchen Grove (1884, 1904) ... 421, 532
Blackpool Engine (1884) ... 421
Bowson, New (1904) ... 532
Britannia (1884, 1904) ... 421, 532
'Broadmoor Engine' (1754) ... 134-135
'Brown's Green Colliery' (1792) ... 266, 271
Brunswick Colliery (1849) ... 325
Cannop Colliery (1909) ... 532
'Cannop Bridge Level' (1832) ... 271, 275
Central Colliery (1904) ... 464, 532, 533
'Churchway Coal Work, otherwise Turnbrooke' (1748) ... 124, 277, 282, 286
Cinderford Bridge Colliery (1859) ... 318
'Coal Level called The Windmill' (1751) ... 130
'Coal mine in Coleford' (1637) ... 174
Cousin's Engine (1884, 1904) ... 421, 464, 466, 469, 532
Crabtree Pit (1656) ... 70
Crumpmeadow Colliery (1848, 1874) ... 335, 362, 363, 389, 393
'Dog Kennel Level', Noxon (1797-1800) ... 523
'Dowler's Chambers' (1741) ... 47, 119
East Dean Deep (1904) ... 532
Eastern United (1907) ... 466, 532
East Slade (1884) ... 421, 532
Edge End (opencast) ... 479, 496
Emperor Colliery (1884, 1904) ... 421, 464, 532
Extension Colliery (1884, 1904) ... 421, 464, 532
Favourite (1884, 1904) ... 421, 532
Fire Engine Coalpit (1780) ... 126, 216, 217, 225
Flourmill Colliery (1876, 1904) ... 411, 412, 421, 532
Foxes Bridge Colliery (1830) ... 318, 325
'Gentlemen Colliers Coal Work' (1753) ... 128, 258, 269, 270, 271, 272
'Great Bilson Coal-works' ... 276
Hayners Bailey ... 479, 492
'Hill Works' near Ruardean (1741) ... 121
High Meadow Colliery near Hillersland ... 528
Holly Hill (1884, 1904) ... 421, 464, 466, 532
Hopewell (1656, 1906) ... 90, 470
currently open for inspection (Robin Morgan) ... 80, 90
Howbeach (1884) ... 325, 421
'Howler's Slade (Vallets Level)' (1832) ... 274
'Howler Slade Deep Engine' (*c.*1827) ... 268
'Inging Coal Work, near Nailbridge' (1754) ... 129

Lass of the Mill (1944) . . . 500
Lightmoor . . . 318, 384
Little Rockey (1777) . . . 244
'Lydbrook Water Engine' (1792) . . . 266
Mailscot Coal Colliery . . . 528
'Major [Wade's] Suff' (1766) . . . 270, 286
'Major's Suff Level Gutter' [Major John Wade's] (1775) . . . 129
'Mendall Level' near Coleford (1818) . . . 269
'Merry Way', Noxon (1797-1800) . . . 523
Mirey Stock (1884, 1904) . . . 421, 532
'Monument' . . . 504, 507, 509, Plate XVII
'Moorwood Coal-works' (1773) . . . 271
Morgan's Folly No. 2 (1884, 1904) . . . 421, 532
No. 3 (1884, 1904) . . . 421, 532
New Fancy Colliery . . . 324
Newham Bottom Colliery (1841, 1904) . . . 318, 421, 532
New United (1904) . . . 532
Norchard . . . 515
Northern United (1906) . . . 466, 496, 532
'Oake Pit in Aywood' (1656) . . . 70, 189, 239, 240
'Oakwood Mill Level' (1820) . . . 517, 520, 521
Old Forester Colliery (1843) . . . 356
'Oiling Gin (Fire Engine)' (1776) (Water-Wheel Engine Level) . . . 257, 268, 270, 284, 522
'Old Furnace Level' (*c.*1827, 1904) . . . 421, 532
'Parkend Coal Works' . . . 280, 324, 335
Park Gutter (1904, 1906) . . . 532
Pillowell Engine Colliery (1843, 1904) . . . 421, 464, 466, 527, 532
Pluckpenny Colliery (1843) . . . 310, 356
Pluds (1884, 1904) . . . 421, 532
Prince Albert (1904) . . . 532
Prince of Wales (1884, 1904) . . . 423, 532
Princess Royal Colliery (1884, 1904) . . . 421, 423, 532
'Pulwell Level' (1805) . . . 269
Quab (1797) Noxon Park . . . 523
Resolution Colliery . . . 344
Richard Whites (1884, 1904) . . . 421, 532
Rising Sun Engine (1884, 1904) . . . 421, 532
Rose in Hand Colliery, near Speech House (1849) . . . 325
Royal (1904) . . . 532
Ruardean Hill (1873) . . . 310
Rudge Colliery (1844) . . . 421, 527
Safeguard Colliery . . . 344
'Serridge Works' (1741 and 1884, 1904) . . . 121, 421, 532
Skinner's Garden (1884, 1904) . . . 421, 464, 532
Small Profit (1884, 1904) . . . 421, 464, 532
South-Eastern United (1906) . . . 466
Southern United (1906) . . . 466, 532
Speculation Colliery (1944) . . . 470
'Speedwell Colliery near Tresser Mill' (1741, 1843) . . . 47, 119, 356, 413
'Strip-and-at-it Colliery' (1832) . . . 271, 275
Tail Level Coalwork' (1777) . . . 216
Trafalgar Colliery (1874) . . . 366, 391
'True Blue' (1777, 1788) . . . 217, 514
'Tyrringham's Surfe' (1675) . . . 175, 197, 239 *and see* Aywood
Union (1884, 1904) . . . 421, 532
Union and Cannop (1884, 1904) . . . 421, 504, 509, 532
United Deep (1904) . . . 464
'Upper Rockey Coal Work' (1754) . . . 129
Vellets Level . . . 479
Venus and Jupiter (1884, 1904) . . . 421, 532
Waterloo (1909) . . . 532
'Water Wheel Ingine at the Orling Green near Broadmoor' (1750) . . . 126, 139
Wellington Colliery (1874) . . . 325

Western United (1906) 466
'Windrels' (1777, 1788) 130, 217, 514
Woodside (1884, 1904) 421, 532
Woorgreen (opencast) 505
'Wyrall Hill' (1741) 47
Yorkley Mine (1871) 413
'Young Colliers (Level) in Ruardean Walk' (1784) 7, 129, 269, 274
Coal Commission (1938) 396, 472
Dean Forest, Rules, 1939 472
coal washing from pit-tips (Northern United, Eastern United, Hawkwell) 508
Commissioners of Woods (managers of Dean until 1919) . . . . . xxiv, 57, 277, 284, 306, 311, 312, 314, 318, 321, 327, 339, 341, 334, 348, 358, 359, 360, 395, 399, 402, 407, 409, 417, 419, 421, 430,446, 453, 459, 463, 467,485, 526, 527, 530, 531
Commissioners, Committees 1673 196
1691 207
1780 211-17
1788 . . . . . 15, 196
1838 306
1871 354
Commoners, commoning . . . . . xvii, xxi, xxv, 14, 155, 180, 182, 183, 185, 188, 191, 192, 193, 210, 217, 223, 408, 409
Commonwealth 60, 69, 179, 180, 182, 183
conservator 212
constable of St. Briavels Castle . . . . . 10, 36, 38, 39, 40, 73, 76, 77, 78, 80, 87, 88, 98, 100, 102, 103, 105,108, 111, 115, 116, 124, 144, 157, 160, 168, 178, 182, 183, 192, 212, 251, 253, *and see* Index of Personal Names *and* Glossary
deputy constable 62, 69, 73, 75, 77, 78, 79, 80, 89, 91, 97, 98, 100, 101, 102, 103, 104, 105, 107, 108, 109, 110, 111, 112, 115, 124, 127, 144
copper works, Redbrook 104, 122, 208, 258, 272
Courts of the forest . . . . . xxiii, 144 *and see* Attachment Court, Eyre, *and* Swanimote

Crown's (fifth) man; royalty in lieu363, 393, 397, 422, 435, 443, 445, 446, 452, 453, 456, *and see* King's (fifth) man
Crown Estate Commissioners 477
Crown Freehold lands . . . . . 240, *and see* Glossary
manors . . . . . xxv, 441
receiver 406, 430, 441
'Custodian of the Gawle (Gale)', later Gaveller . . . . . xv, 46, 48, 53, 54, 55, 144, 213, 225, 235, 236

dead rent . . . . . 323, 324, 328, 333, 334, 342, 343, 344, 501, 543 *and* Glossary
Dean Forest Mining Commissioners (1831) 137
Dean Forest National Park (1938) . . . . . xxv, xxvi
Dean Heritage Centre at Soudley 507
deer . . . . . xxiii, 191, 325
fence month restriction (cancelled in 1971) 191
poaching 325
winter heyning restriction (cancelled in 1971) 191
Department of Trade & Industry (DTI) 48, 485-91, 495
answer to Free Miners' submission 48, 485-91, 495
DEPUTY GAVELLERxv, xvi, xix, 4, 6, 7, 45, 47, 49, 50, 51, 52, 54, 55, 56, 57, 58, 60, 75,77, 78, 79, 80, 83, 94, 105, 107, 108, 109, 111, 112, 113, 115, 116, 124, 127, 129, 135, 181, 182, 212, 213, 214, 264, 265, 269, 273, 286, 306, 307, 321, 328, 349, 350, 412, 413, 417, 431, 432, 436, 438, 439, 441, 452, 462, 463, 467, 469, 519, 520, 523, 524, 538, 539, App. E *and see* Index of Personal Names *and passim*
qualifications 54
duties . . . . . 45, 46, 50, 321, 328, 539, App. E
miners often recruited as . . . . . *passim*
expected to reside in Dean Forest 362, 363
must be skilled in mining; repealed in 1969 . . . . . xxv, 306
anciently, one for 'Above the Wood', and one for 'Below the Wood'. (*q.v.*)
Deputy surveyor . . . . . xxv, 54, 167, 212, 213, 217, 218, 321, 388, 430, 441, 453, 462
first appointment in Dean, 1633 167
Dilke Memorial Hospital 495, 505, 506

'dipple' (a coal working) . . . 470
'dole' (mining partners share) . . . 8, 37
Domesday (1086) . . . xxiii, 17, 141, 146
drainage, pumping, of workings . . . 9, 76, 77, 88, 97, 100, 102, 124, 128, 129, 138, 187, 294, 302, 303, 304, 305, 412, 424, 473, 476, 482 *and see* 'surf'
Drummond Select Committee of the House of Commons (1854) . . . 344, 345
Duncan Select Committee of the House of Commons (1848) . . . 321, 340, 341, 550
Duchy of Lancaster . . . 112, 151

East Dean dispute with West Dean (1519-20) . . . 150
encroachments, land . . . 251, 320
engines, steam, for coalmines, *see* licences
estovers, botes (cancelled from 1668) . . . xxv, 155, 183, 191, 192, 207 *and* Glossary
'Excepted Lands': (exempt parts of Hundred of St. Briavels)
  inclosures, gardens, orchards, churchyards, and curtilages . . . 310, 340, 496, 513, App. A *and* Glossary
  moiety of minerals royalty payable to private land owner . . . 310
Enforcement Notices . . . 482, 492, 493
European Parliament . . . 481
Eyre, Forest Justice Seat . . . 168, *and see* Glossary
    1282 . . . 6, 11-14
    1634 . . . xv, xvi, 8, 168, 171, 196, 291
    1656 . . . 183

FORESTRY COMMISSION (appointed 1919) . . . xiv, xvii, xix, xxi, xxii, 467, 497
  Forestry Act, 1919 . . . 467
  Forestry (Transfer of Woods) Act, 1923 . . . 467, 485
    Order made in 1924 . . . 467, 485
    Order made in 1926 . . . 467, 485
  Forest of Dean transferrred to it in 1923 . . . 427
  Gavellership transferred to it in 1924 . . . 467
  appoints deputy gaveller (*q.v.*)
  appoints deputy surveyor (*q.v.*)
  Compensation for coalfield from Coal Commission under 1938 Act . . . 472
  responsible for stone quarries in Statutory Forest . . . 476, 477
  effect of 1971 Act . . . xix
  effect of 1981 Act . . . xix, 477
  effect of 1994 Act on freemining . . . 481, 482, 483, Chapters XI, XII, App. D
  Agreement with Coal Authority 1997 . . . 469, 482, App. D

FOREST OF DEAN (named from *c.* 1080) 141, 144, 146, 147, 148, 150, 152, *and* Glossary *and passim*
  extent, boundaries . . . xiii, xxi, 251, Plate V
  'Open Forest' . . . xxv, *and* Glossary
  'Waste' of . . . 560 *and* Glossary
  Statutory Forest . . . xiii, 307, Plate V, *and* Glossary
  Minerals (coal, iron ore, stone) *see* COAL, IRON ORE *and* stone
    (other) *see* gold and silver
  Commoning in *see* commoners
  Freemining in *see* Free Miners
  Conservation . . . xxvi
  Recreation . . . xxvi
  Timber production . . . xxiv, xxvi
  'farmers' (lessees) of . . . 32
  grants, *see* Pembroke (1611-12) *and* Winter (1640, 1662, 1667)
  'Creed Committee' Report (1958) . . . 476, 477
  effect of 1971 Act . . . xix
  effect of 1981 Act . . . xix, 477
  effect of 1994 Act on freemining . . . 481, 482, 483, App. D
Forestry Report by Hill (1897) . . . 246
Forestry School, Parkend . . . xxiv, xxv
Forester, The (19th C.) . . . 133, 351, 411
forest . . . *see* Glossary *and forest law*
forest law . . . xxi, xiv, xxii *and* Glossary
forester-of-fee . . . 6, 12, 13, 144, 212 *and* Glossary *and see* bailiwicks

'foreigners' (i.e. not a Free Miner) 4, 5, 39, 72, 73, 74, 75, 76, 85, 95, 105, 107, 112, 116, 117, 118, 120, 126, 127, 133, 134, 137, 140, 150, 160, 174, 198, 251, 256, 257, 258, 261, 263, 264, 266, 271, 272, 274-87, 298-301, 315, 318
'Memorial' against other miners (1834) 288-98
(1884) 423
forges, bloomeries 12, 13, 119, 146, 147, 151, 254, 281
FREE MINERS (relates to iron ore and coal, but less to stone) Frontispiece, 3, 11-17, 141, 157 *and passim*, *and see* Index of Personal Names
customs, privileges and rights (from 1838) 3, 4, 11, 12, 137, 138, 157, 158
'saved' by Act of 1668 but not defined . . . . xvi, 195, 251, 352, 254, 255
defined and confirmed by Act of 1838 306-10
'Laws and Privileges' 4
earliest transcript (1612) 31
next transcript (1673) . . . . 32 and Plate III
printed copies (1687) 32, 273, 321
The miners' 'Inquisition' . . . . xv, 18, 32, 42, 87
no rights in Lydney Park and Highmeadow Estates . . . . App. A, 513-31
extent of rights (Hundred of St. Briavels for iron ore and coal; the Statutory Forest for stone) 4, 15, 307
freemining cycle of events . . . . xvi, 538
self-regulating Mine Law Court (*q.v.*)
qualifications 4, 257, 298-301, 306-7, 496, 498
'born and abiding in the Hundred of St. Briavels' 4, 306
'mining for a year and a day' 4, 73, 120, 255, 256, 307
opencast mining as qualification 496
application (Form) for registration 498
application (Form) for gale 499
apprenticeship (no longer required) 4, 73, 95, 97, 118, 138, 140, 255, 256, 300
grant of a gale (Form) 500
present difficulty over birth qualification . . . . xviii, 495, 505, 506
present difficulty in gaining experience . . . . xviii, 495, 505, 506
present qualifications as to stone 496
register of 307, 507
often recruited as deputy gavellers (*q.v.*)
rights of way to workings 4, 5, 46
power to sell or bequeath a gale 8, 39, 126, 127, 257, 262, 263, 278
dues to king . . . . 4, 6, 7, 12, 13, 37, 38, 46 and see king's (fifth) man; later royalties in lieu
dues to Crown, royalty in lieu of Crown's (fifth) man *see* Crown
dues to private landowners . . . . 37; *and see* Lord's (fifth) man, *and* moiety of royalty
power to mine in any place except (a) timber inclosures, (b) gardens, churchyards, orchards and curtiliges 18, 257
Military services 19-21, 148, 150, 259
'miner v. miner' . . . . 43, 50, 59, 65, 70, 80, 93, 128, 129, 130, 237, 244, Apps. 3 and 6
'Memorials', 1825 . . . . 255-8, 261
1832 266
1834 288-98
'Resolution' in 1832 252
Lawsuits relating to, *see* LAWSUITS
Warrants and Orders against (1612-13, 1636, 1661) 170, 171, 189, 291
Levies made by, *see* Mine Law Court
miners in 1608 151
1818 . . . . 247, 248
'Submissions' made to DTI and Coal Authority following the 1994 Act 483, 485, 486, 487, 489, 490, 495
effect of the 1994 Act on freemining . . . . Chapters XI and XII
Free Miners Association (current) 481, 483, 495, 506
Legal appeal connection with Verderers *see* Act of 1838
Honorary Free Miners 10, 54, 76, 81, 88, 106, 110, 113, 115, 118, 123, 125, 130, 131, 132, 133, 138, 258, 271, 306, 506
reasons for (to gain support and backing; out of the due respect which they have for them) . . 10, 11, 50, 110
adverse effects of; break with tradition 10, 506
illegal since the Act of 1838 . . . . 133, 306
furnaces 81, 93, 94, 95, 101, 281
Bishopswood 93, 94, 95

Blakeney ... 94
Flaxley ... 93,94, 95, 114, 145, 147, 148
Gunsmills ... 93, 268
Linton ... 93, 94
Longhope ... 93
Lydney ... 94
Redbrook ... 94
St. Weonards ... 81, 93, 96
Tintern ... 94
Whitchurch ... 93

GALES ... 8, 46, 307, 308, 309, 418, 448, App. F. *and* Glossary *and passim*
gale, nature ... 500
extent ... 540
effect ... 541
transfer ... 541
working ... 542
surrender, abandonment ... 542
rents, royalties ... 543
rules relating to payment ... 543
gavelling ... 37, 130, 256, 257, 264
using a holly stick ... 36, 38, 67, 68, 134
gales (52+2) vested in NCB (1948) ... 534, 535, App. C
3 gales maximum (but others can be acquired) ... 356, 501, 540
amalgamated, sub-divided, or rearranged (1904) ... 532, 533, App. B
Awards of Minerals, 1841, *see* Awards
1862, *see* Awards
boundary stones ... 318, 330
barriers, coal, between gales, *see* COAL
deep gales ... 419, 430, 453, 471, 482
45 deep gales (1884) covering 11,800 acres ... 419-22
41 deep gales under the Act of 1904 ... App. B
galee, by gift or purchase ... 271, and *passim*
female as galees ... xviii
'forfeiture' of gale ... 349, 408, and Glossary
'Unopened', unworked' gale ... 355, and Glossary
bonâ fide working ... 479 , and Glossary
'Gale Money' under Act of 1906 (1/2d. per ton) ... 466, 469, 473, 532, Plate XI, and Glossary
Trustees for ... 468, 473, 496, Plates X and XI
Gales (coal): named [No evidence that names used until mid 17th century]
(Sometimes may refer to the actual coal working (mine, level and dipple) and not to the actual gale.)
Addis Hill ... 492
Alexandra (1884, 1904, 1938) ... 421
All Profit (1884, 19040 ... 421
Arles Level (1948) ... 534
Arthur and Edward (1884, 1904, 1938) ... 421
Bailey Hill (1948) ... 534
Beaufort Engine (1884, 1904, 1938) ... 421
Birchen Grove (1884, 1904, 1948) ... 421, 534
Blackpool Engine (1884, 1938) ... 421
Brittania (1884, 1904) ... 421
Cannop, 4 gales (1948) ... 534
Central (1884, 1904, 1938) ... 421
Cousins Engine (1884, 1904, 1911, 1948) ... 421, 535
Churchway High Delph Colliery (1841) ... 351
Cross Knave (1948) ... 534
Dark Hill Endeavour No. 2 (1948) ... 534
Deep United (1889) (174 applicants) ... 433, 455, 462
Diamond No. 2 (1948) ... 535
Durham (1884) ... 421
East Dean Deep (1884, 1904, 1938) ... 421
Eastern United (1948) ... 535
East Slade (1884, 1904) ... 421

Ellesmore No.2 (1948) . . . 534
Ellwood (1948) . . . 535
Emperor (1884, 1904, 1938) . . . 421
Extension (1884, 1904, 1938) . . . 421
Fancy No.3 (1948) . . . 534
Farmers Folly (1948) . . . 534
Favourite (1884, 1904, 1939) . . . 421
Findall (1948) . . . 533
Flour Mill (1884, 1904, 1938) . . . 421
Gorbrook No.4 (1948) . . . 534
Gorsty Knoll No. 3 (1948) . . . 534
Green's Trenchard Colliery Gale (1944) . . . 500
Hamblin Yorkley (1996) . . . 482, 507
Harrow Hill Green No.3 (1948) . . . 534
Hayners Bailey . . . 492, Plate XVII
High Delph Engine (1904, 1938) . . . 421
Hillersland No. 2 (1948) . . . 534
Holly Hill (1884, 1904, 1938) . . . 421
Hopewell Engine (1948) . . . 534
Hopewell in Wimberry . . . 492, 507
Howbeach Engine (1884, 1938) . . . 421
Jones Yorkley No. 2 (1948) . . . 534
Lass of the Mill No. 2 (1944) . . . 500
Little Brockhollands No. 2 Colliery (1952) . . . 502
Lonk Level (1948) . . . 534
Lydbrook Colliery No. 3 (1948) . . . 535
Mansfield Trenchard (1948) . . . 534
Mapleford Engine No. 3 (1948) . . . 534
Mapleford Engine No.4 (1949) . . . 534
Midsummer Level No. 2 (1948) . . . 535
Milkwall No. 3 (1948) . . . 534
Mirey Stock No. 2 (1884, 1904, 1938) . . . 421
'Monument' (1998) . . . Plate XVII
Morgan's Folly No. 1 (1884, 1904, 1948) . . . 421
Morgan's Folly No. 2 (1884, 1904, 1948) . . . 421
Morgan's Folly No. 3 (1884, 1904, 1948) . . . 421
Morses Level (1996) . . . 482
Nagshead (1938) . . . 533
New Bowson (1884, 1904, 1938) . . . 421
Newcastle (1884) . . . 308, 421
Newfoundout No. 2 (1948) . . . 534
Newham Bottom (1884, 1904) . . . 421, 534
New Mill Engine No. 2 (1948) . . . 534
New Speedwell (1948) . . . 534
New True Blue (1904, 1906) . . . 534
New United Deep No. 2 (1904, 1938) . . . 532
New United Deep No. 1 (1904) . . . 532
New United Deep No. 3 (1904) . . . 532
New Road Level . . . 492, 493, 507
Nine Wells (1948) . . . 534
Northumberland (1884) . . . 421
Northern United (1949) . . . 535
North Western United (1948) . . . 535
Old Engine No. 2 (1948) . . . 535
Old Furnace No. 2 (Cannop) (1884, 1904, 1938) . . . 421
Old Strip And At It No. 2 (1948) . . . 534
Parkend Deep Level (1948) . . . 535
Patches No. 2 (1948) . . . 534
Pillowell Engine (1884, 1904, 1913, 1938) . . . 421
Pillowell Level (1904, 1938) . . . 464, 535
Pillowell United (1904, 1948) . . . 464, 535
Pluds (1884, 1904) . . . 42
Poolway Trenchard No. 2 (1948) . . . 534

Prince Albert (1884, 1904, 1938) 421
Prince of Wales (1884, 1904, 1938) 421
Princess Royal (1884, 1904, 1938) 421
Prosper on Harrow Hill No. 2 (1948) 534
Quab (1797) (Noxon Park) 523
Quidchurch 492, 493, 507
Reddings Level No. 2 (1948) 534
Richard Whites (1884, 1904) 421
Rising Sun Engine (1884, 1904, 1938) 421
Royal Colliery (1904, 1938) 421
Rudge Colliery (1884, 1938) 421
Serridge No. 2 (1884, 1904, 1938) 421
Skinner's Garden (1884, 1904) 421
Slopes Trenchard No. 2 (1948) 534
Small Profit (1884, 1904) 421
Smiths Trenchard No. 2 (1948) 534
Society No.4 (1948) 534
Southern & Morgans United (1948) 535
Southern United (1938, 1946) 466, 532
St. Low (1884) 421
St. Vincent (1948) 534
Thatch or Independent (1948) 534
Tile Quarry (1948) 534
True Blue & Newham Bottom (1904, 1948) 514, 534
Union (1884, 1904, 1938) 421, 492
Union & Cannop (1884, 1904, 1938) 421
United Deep, New, No. 1 (1904) 464
United Deep, New, No. 2 (1904) 464
United Deep, New, No. 3 (1904) 464
Unity (1938) 533
Vallets Level No. 2 (1948) 534
Venus & Juniper (1884, 1904, 1938) 421
Western United (1938) 466
Whiteccroft, New (1938) 533
Whitemead (1948) 535
Woodside (1884, 1904) 421
Worcester 507
Worrall Hill No. 2 (1948) 534
Worrall Hill No. 3 (1948) 535
Yorkley (Bailey) (1938) 492
gales consolidated in 1906 .... 496, App. B
gales owned by Forest of Dean District Council and Gloucestershire County Council 479
gales of coal .... 540-43, App. F
gales of iron ore .... 540, 543, App. F
nunc pro tunc ('then for now') 349, 508
GAVELLER ..... xv, xvi, xix, 36, 38, 39, 40, 45, 46, 47, 48, 52, 53, 54, 55, 56, 57, 58, 63, 73, 75, 77, 79, ... 124, 127, 128, 157, 213, 235, 236, 238, 255, 306, 307, 350, 467, 538, 539, App. E *and passim*
no *active* participation with the miners 58, 538
originally 'custodian of the Gawle (Gale)' 538
appointed by the King's Letters Patent 538
a sinecure – an office requiring little or no work but yielding a net income (after paying deputies to collect dues etc. from the miners) .... xv, 59, 539
sometimes appointed for 'Above the Wood' or 'Below the Wood', or for both 4, 57, 538
office often granted with the office of aleconner of the Forest, riding forester, and custodian of Whitemead Park *see* aleconner, riding forester, *and* Whitemead Park
In 1808, office vested in the surveyor-general of woods 58
later in a Commissioner of Woods 467
in 1924 in the Forestry Commissioners 58, 467
'Gaveller's Office', Coleford .... 7, 43, 56, 57, 319, 418, 464, 470, 500, *and see* deputy gaveller
gold mining 208, 358, 477
'goutwater', 'goutway' 9, 97, 100, 102
grants of the Forest to, Earl of Pembroke (1611-1612) 152, 290
Sir John Winter (1640, 1662, 1667) 186, 188, 515

Health & Safety factors . . . 310, 473, *and see* MASHAM
High Meadow Estate and Woods . . . xxiv, 224, 225, 345, 402, 528, 529, 530, 531
no free miners rights therein . . . App. A
see Index of Place Names, and App. A
Holly sticks, use of in oath . . . 36, 38, 67, 68, 134
Honorary Free Miners, *see* Free Miners
horses, donkeys, mares, mules, for carrying minerals . . . 74, 78, 81, 83, 97, 100, 105, 120, 121
House of Commons . . . 179, 185, 190, 247, 321, 340, 341, 344, 359, 418, 419, 423, 430 *and see* 'Duncan' *and* 'Drummond'
Select Committees, 1874 . . . 359, 407
1884 . . . 419
houses, cottages . . . 168, 180, 222, 325, 419, *and see* Cabins, and Lodges
Hundred of Bledisloe . . . 112, 149, 151
Hundred of Botloe . . . 112
HUNDRED OF ST. BRIAVELS (named from *c.* 1154) xiii, xxi, 4, 112, 151, 307, 328, 423, 496, 529, and *passim*, and Glossary
extent, boundaries . . . Plate VI
application to Free Miners' customs . . . *passim*
'Excepted Lands' within . . . App. A
query as to northern boundary . . . 92
Hundred of Westbury . . . 112, 149, 151

inclosures (timber) . . . xxv, 191, 192, 195, 196, 206, 208, 251, 294, 309, 323, 339, 340, 541
mining not in (but under) . . . 195, 206
Inclosure Commissioners (from 1668) . . . 195
Inhabitants, 'Petition' by (1661) . . . 293
(1869) . . . 353
'Inquisition', a summary collection of the miners' customs . . . xv, 18, 42, 87
IRON ORE . xiv, 12, 13, 14, 18, 146, 147, 161, *and passim, and see* cinders (slag), forges *and* furnaces
geology of iron ore field . . . 250, Plate VII
miners ('diggers') of . . . 13, 153, 155, 156, 158, 161, 162, 165, 237, 238
caves (iron ore), Clearwell . . . 508
churns, deposits of . . . 28, 29
output (1800-1816) . . . 247
exports of iron ore to Ireland . . . 102, 103, 104, 106, 154, 158, 159
to Wales . . . 147, 158
imports of iron from Ireland . . . 158
prices of . . . 70, 73, 94, 95, 96, 101, 102, 104
bargainers for prices/sales, *see* Mine Law Court
ironmasters . . . 73, 77, 93, 94, 149, 152, 153, 156, 161, 208, 267, 318
iron ore mine owners . . . 251
smytholders v. miners (1375), (1590-20) . . . 144, 150
tithes of iron ore granted to Bishop of Llandaff . . . 148
iron mines in 1788 . . . 215
iron mines: named (Some entries may refer to the gale and not to the working thereof.)
Ash Pit, Noxon (1634) . . . 518, 523
Browne's Pit, Noxon (1634) . . . 518
Buckshraft . . . 181
'Chelfridge' in Noxon Park . . . 516
'China Mine' . . . 516, 527
Crowsnest Mine . . . 528
Coal Floor, Noxon . . . 523
Evans Pit, Noxon (1634) . . . 518, 523
Highmeadow Iron Mine (1857) . . . 527
'Hill pitt' (1469, 1470) . . . 237, 238, App. 3
Hurl Pit, Noxon . . . 523
'Kingsmore' in Noxon Park . . . 516
Knock Pit, Noxon (1634) . . . 518, 523
'Lanquire' in Noxon Park . . . 516
Le Dene Iron Mine (1469) . . . 237, 238, App. 3
Little Pit, Noxon (1634) . . . 518, 523
Lord Pit, Noxon (1634) . . . 518
New Dunn . . . 497

Noxon Park 516
Oakwood Mill 527
'Okerpitt called Maplepitt or Yellowshroft' (1652) 508
Maple Iron Mine (1841) 508
Park Hill 527
Robin Hood Mine 528
Sackfield, Noxon (1780) 524
Scarre Pit, Noxon (1634) 518
'Seynt Colas pytt' (1469, 1470) 237, App. 3
Staunton Mine 528
'Thraves' 516
True Blue Colliery Co. Ltd 514
Tufts Iron Mine, Lydney Park 515
Wyche Wylder's Pit, Noxon (1634) 518, 523
Yellowshroft (ochre) (1652) 508
Ironworks 178, 181, 188, 189, and see forges, furnaces *and* Glossary
King's, demolished (1674) 196
iron workers sent to Glamorgan (1531) 150

Justice of forest 144, 146
Justice Seat, *see* Eyre, Forest *and* Glossary
Justices of the Peace 172, 182

keeper, forest 129, 130, 135, 168, 196, 207, 214, 215, 257, 301, 302
King's (fifth) man 5, 6, 37, 157, 176, 200, 256, 258, 264, 265, 269, 308, 312, 321, 325
developed to Crown's (fifth) man, and replaced by royalties, *see* Glossary
'Kingscote Committee', (1874) 359

LAWSUITS 52, 78, 89, 94, 97, 100, 102, 106, 108, 109, 128, 130, 138, 152, 153, 161, 239, 240, 241, 245, 263, 308, 351, 352, 353, 356, 406, 408, 411, 412, 413, 416, 417, 423
Allaway *v*. Wagstaff (1859) *re* surface damage 309, 347, 541
Attorney General *v*. Mathias (1858) 310,345, 346, 406, 540
Beck(e) *v*. Cowles etc. *re* Terringham (1683) *re* quarryman 205, 206, 240, 241, App. 4 and 5
Brain *v*. Thomas (1881) 541
Brayne *v*. Tucker (deputy gaveller) *et al*. (1652) 181, 182
East Dean *v*. West Dean (1519-20) 150
Ellway *v*. Davis (1873) 356, 540
In *re* Brain (1874) *re* forfeiture of gales 408
Goold *v*. Great Western Deep Coal Co. (1865) *re* impeding working 351, 352, 540
Great Western Collieries Co. *v*. Trafalgar Co. Ltd. (1887) 489, 540
Grindell's Petition of Right (1870) 496, 531, 541
Humphries *v*. Brogdon re subsidence 309
James *v*. The Queen (1877) *re* limit of 3 gales 412, 413, 416, 417, 540
James *v*. Young (1884) 540, 541
Jones, M. J. *v*. Piggott, R. J. (deputy gaveller), (1996) 496
Jones, Francis *v*. Governor and The Company of Copper Mines in England (1752) 208, 258
v. Earl of Pembroke (1612-13) 152-5
Philips, Thomas *v*. Governor and The Company of Copper Mines in England (1752) 208, 209, 258
Morgan, George & ors. v. Henry Crawshay (1874) *re* rateability of mines 356, 489, 541
N. Howells and ors. v. G. T. Shephens (1884) *re* Prince of Wales Colliery 423
Ross *v*. Rugge-Price (1876) *re* breach of regulations 411, 541
Seymour, Lord *v*. Morrell (1850) 342, 343, 543
T. Gwilliam and ors. v. G. T. Shephens (1884) *re* Prince Albert Colliery 308, 423
Terringham *v*. Yarworth and others1635, 1637, 1675, 1683 60, 64, 169-73, 177, 196-200, *and* App. 4
v. Throckmorton (1625) 161-7
Thomas and ors. *v*. Pearce (1812) 223, 224
Trotter, J. & ors. *v*. Gwynne (1829-30) 263
Young and Grindell (1878) *re* 'unopened gales' 355
Law Commission xix
'Law(e) ore' 6, 7, 13, 38, 157, 165
Levels, coal 122, 124, 125, 126, 128, 139, 226, 256, 258, 269, 302, 303, 304, 305, 517, 522, 523
lime burners 106, 107, 207
in 1608 151, 207

lime kilns . . . 74, 107, 113, 119, 122, 125
Lord's fifth man . . . 5, 6, 37, 165, 176, 202, 257, 264, 265, 269
later, moiety of royalty in lieu . . . 496
lodges, keepers' . . . 168, 196, 206 *and see* keeper
Lydney Park Estate; no Free Miners' rights therein . . . 174, App. A

MASHAM, The Management and Administration of Safety and Health in Mines Regulation . . 493, 538
MEASURES AND WEIGHTS . . . 9, 38, 74, 76, 94, 102, 104, 107, 121, 122
'barrel' . . . 76, 95, 113
'belleyes' (a weight) . . . 8, 9, 40
'bushel' . . . 9, 94, 104, 122
'dozen' . . . 9
'seame' one seaminage or man's bearing on land of iron ore or coal . . . 6, 38, 121
'Winchester bushel' (3 to a 'barrel') . . . 9, 76, 95, 104, 122
MINE LAW COURT (self-regulated; relates to iron ore and coal, not stone) . . . . . Chapter IV, xv, xvi, 4, 5,
. . . 7, 8, 10, 38, 39, 46, 65, 90, 157, 168, 182, 209, 212, 226, 227, 245, 255,
. . . 256, 257, 259, 261, 265, 285, 288, 289, 296, 495, 506
earliest known session (1469) . . . 59, 69, 237, 254, App. 3
second known session (1656) . . . 69-72
last session (1777) . . . 127, 128, 140, 244, 256, 257, 288, 289, 296
reason for discontinuance . . . 132, 133, 134, 135, 136, 140, 270
revival urged . . . 135, 136, 262, 266, 267, 274, 297
Orders of . . . 137, 140, *et seq.*, Plate IV
bargainers for mineral prices/sales . . . 71, 72, 73, 74, 77, 88, 89, 94, 95, 97,
. . . 101, 103, 104, 106, 107, 113, 119, 128, 138
judge of . . . 61, 62, 123
constable's role . . . 132, 133
deputy constable's role . . . 132, 133
deputy gaveller's role . . . 132, 133
clerk . . . 133
crier . . . 133
beadle . . . 62, 144
steward . . . 63, 66, 109, 129, 301
no sueing in any other court . . . 65, 74, 110, 138
widow attending . . . 71
disturbances in . . . 71, 83, 86, 91, 111, 244
miner v. miner . . . 70, 80-93, 128, 129, 130
miner v. deputy gaveller . . . 93
distrainings . . . 36, 37
pleading . . . 39
verdicts . . . 104
'forbids', 'forebodement' . . . 35, 36, 41, 115, 127, 129, 250, 259, 513
penalties for non-compliance with rules and regulations . . . 138
fines and forfeits (usually '100 dozen of good and sufficient iron ore or coal,
one half to the king, and one half to the miner who will sue for the same') 9, 65, 67, 120,
. . . 121, 122, 138
perjury, expulsion for . . . 10, 100, 103, 104
trespasses, prevention of . . . 35, 37
witnesses to be paid . . . 104
imprisonment threatened (in St. Briavels Castle) . . . 117
levies for legal defence . . . 9, 78, 79, 89, 94, 95, 97, 98, 99, 100, 102, 105, 106, 108,
. . . 110, 117, 138, 239, 241, 242, 245, 246
collectors of . . . 10, 79, 94, 97, 99, 100, 102, 106, 108, 109, 110, 246
levies to aid miners maimed or hurt underground . . . 10, 78, 79, 89, 138
collectors of . . . 78, 79, 246
jury, jurors (12, 24, or 48) . . . 39, 69, 73, 76, 78, 79, 80, 81, 84, 85, 86, 87, 88, 92, 93, 94, 95, 96,
. . . 97, 98, 99, 100, 102, 103, 104, 105, 106, 109, 111, 112, 113, 114, 115, 116,
. . . 122, 123, 124, 126, 128, 130, 134, 136, 237, 238, 243, 245, 246
failing to serve . . . 83
occasionally half from 'Above the Wood', and half from 'Below the Wood' . . . 119
Mineowners' 'Petition' (1832) . . . 252
Mine and Battery Works,Tintern . . . 152, 153
mining techniques and workings, *see* WORKING (MINING) TECHNIQUES

musters, military . . . 150
minerals, value to the Crown (1848) . . . 327,335
Minerals Exhibition (1863) . . . 350
Miners' Union and 'Lodges' . . . 255, 355, 375
Mines Inspectorate, H.M. . . . 493, 538, *and see* MASHAM
Mining records, deposited in Gloucestershire Record Office by Forestry Commission, Coleford 544, App. G
  retained by PRO, Kew . . . 543, App. H
  donated in 2002 by present author to Forestry Commission, Coleford . . . 349, 500, App. J

nailers, in 1608 . . . 151
nationalisation of coal (1938, 1946) . . . 472, 473, *and see* Acts
National Coal Board (British Coal Corporation from 1987) . . . 473, 475, 476, 534, 535
  'bare licence' of . . . 476, 482
    recognised by Coal Authority . . . 476, *and* Glossary
National Coal Museum, Wakefield . . . 507

oath, swearing of (and use of holly) . . . 36, 68, 103, 134
OCCUPATIONS (See also Index of Personal Names)
  attorney . . . 528
  attorney-general . . . 173, 161, 164
  baker . . . 268
  basketmaker . . . 204
  blacksmith . . . 204
  caskmaker . . . 212
  clerk . . . 302, 524, 306
  clerk, deputy clerk, of St. Briavels castle . . . 109, 118, 124
  clerk, of Mine Law Court . . . 63, 64
  coalmaster, colliery proprietor . . . 318, 328, 365, 362, 371, *and passim*
  coal miner, collier . . . *passim*
  counsel . . . 153
  crier . . . 54, 109, 118
  crown receiver . . . 406, 150
  deputy surveyor . . . xxv, 54, 55, 56, 167, 255, 388, 441, 453
  deputy gaveller . . . *passim*
  dyer . . . 151
  engineer . . . 269, 305
  gun founder . . . 179
  house-carpenter . . . 203
  inn keeper . . . 238
  ironmaster . . . 124, 160, 161, 162, 181, 189, 190, 194, 208, 382, 513
  iron ore miner . . . *passim*
  iron workman . . . *passim*
  keeper . . . 130, 215, 301
  land agent . . . 476
  lime burner . . . 107, 151
  merchant . . . 158, 159
  metalman . . . 151
  minerals valuer . . . 326
  minerals surveyor . . . 325
  mining engineer . . . 136, 306
  nailer . . . 151
  ochre merchant . . . 181
  overseer . . . 194, 195, 196
  printer . . . 251, 254
  publisher . . . 32, 34
  purveyor of timber . . . 211
  quarryman . . . 246, *passim*
  relieving officer . . . 406
  sergeant at law . . . 251
  serjeant-at-arms . . . 191
  shoemaker . . . 46
  shipwright . . . 183, 194
  solicitor . . . 251, 261, 262, 263, 271, 275, 277, 301, 306, 350, 360, 361, 524

steward ... 301, 515, 516
steward of Attachment Court ... 129, 214
steward of Mine Law Court ... 18, 31, 50
smith ... 151
smytholder ... 237, 238
surveyor ... 305
town clerk ... 68
weaver ... 7, 203
narrow weaver ... 203
wharfinger ... 271
wiredrawer ... 151, 153
woodward ... 144, 192, 207, 212
Ochre ... xviii, 3, 49, 67, 164, 166, 181, 182, 245, 255, 310, 508
Office of Woods ... xxiv, 137, 247, 248, 251, 263, 265, 325, 428, *and see* Commissioners of Woods
'Return' made (1818) ... 247, 248, App. 8
opencast coal mining *see* COAL

Parliamentary Bills, (1831) ... 251, 252, 254, 255
(1832), railways ... 252
(1874) ... 359-408
withdrawn ... 359, 360
(1884) ... 419, 421-3, 479
withdrawn ... 423, 425
(1889) ... 423, 430, 458
withdrawn ... 458
pasture lands of the King ... 14
pills, landing places (Severn) ... 122, 252, 254
pits, mines, *see* COAL, IRON ORE and Bats, Horseshoe
domestic water extracted ... 507, 508
planning incidence ... 482, 503
The Town and Country Planning (General Development) Order, 1948 ... 491
plans of workings required from Free Miners and galees ... 503, 537
private lands, minerals in ... 5, 257
'Excepted Lands' ... 261, App. A
Protectorate (Oliver Cromwell) ... 69, 70, 71
'Proposals' by inhabitants (1663) ... 190, 191, 195
prison in St. Briavels Castle ... 252
politics and Union, (local) factors ... 355, 423, *and passim*
Public Record Office, Kew, additional Dean mining records maintained ... App. H

QUARRIES (STONE) QUARRYMEN ... 4, 5, 7, 55, 57, 64, 86, 161, 188, 205, 206, 207, 239,
... 240, 307, 318, 319, 345, 358, 430, 476, 477, 496
not dealt with by Mine Law Court (*q.v.*)
Award in 1841 ... 318, 319
quarrymen in 1608 ... 151
'rights' apply only to Statutory Forest, not to the Hundred of St. Briavels ... 307, 476, 496
leases now under Forestry Commission's area land agent in
liaison with deputy gaveller ... 57, 310, 311, 312, 358, 476, 538
planning incidence ... 477, 491
sole remaining Award quarry, No. 114 (Bream) ... 318, 476, 477
'free quarries' ... 318, 476, 477
named:
Drybrook ... 477
Stowe Hill ... 477
Stowfield ... 477
Bixhead ... 161, 309
'Blakeney' ... 55, 345
qualification ... 496

rail roads ... 227, 252, 254, 265, 309, 324, 325, 327, 334, 335, 337, 339
ranger ... 21
receiver, King's ... xvi, 47, 48, 150, 235, 238
regarder, The Regard ... 92, 144, 177, 190, *and* Glossary

roads and turnpike trusts . . . 361, 362
roadways, ancient . . . 27
riding forester . . . 49, 52, 53, 54, 57, 144, 213, 235, 238
riots, outrages, disturbances, spoils, wastes, abuses . . . 133, 152, 153, 155, 185, 186, 190, 196, 206, 210, 211
in 1631 . . . 167
in 1831 . . . 133, 251
rents, rules relating to payment . . . 543
Restoration of the Monarchy (1660) . . . 166
'Robin Hoods' . . . 152
Roman Period, mining . . . xiv, 11, 22, 24, 26, 30, 141, 254
pre-Roman . . . 254
Report of Commissioners (1788) . . . 212-23
(1831) . . . 254-61
(1835, 4th) . . . 254-61, 306
Rules and Regulations . . . 139, 319, 350, 354, 355, *and passim*
royalties, coal308, 309, 321, 325, 326, 332, 335, 406, 418, 422, 434, 435, 436, 437, 459, 501, *and* Glossary
fixed by Coal Authority (tiered reducing) . . . 481
maximum of 4d. per ton . . . 308
other minerals than iron ore or coal (maximum of 10% of market value) . . . 308
revision every 21 years . . . 479
rules relating to payment . . . 543
rateability of mines . . . 360

Safety & Health *see* Health and Safety factors
St. Briavels Castle . . . 144, 148, 154, 157, 168, 216, *and see* constable
clerk to . . . 36, 39, 75
St. Briavels court . . . 46, 135, 185, 252, 264, 265
'scowles' (old iron ore workings) . . . 28, 29, 258 *and see* Glossary
'seasoames' (? Severn) . . . 4, 25, 35
sergeant-of-fee . . . 12, 144
serjeant-at-law . . . 103
Severn custom charged on minerals . . . 146, 147
ship building, ship timber . . . 151, 152, 174, 178, 183, 186, 187, 189, 190, 193, 194, 196
silver mining . . . 358, 477
Small Mines Association (Dean Forest Branch) . . . 480, 481, 495, 506
smith, smithman, smytholder . . . 20, 36, 40, 144, 146, 150, 208
smiths in 1608 . . . 151
smytholder in Coleford . . . 238
tools . . . 23, Plate II
Spanish Armada . . . xxiv, 151
Speech Court (Attachment Court) . . . 39, 43, 60, 182, 196, 266, *and see* Verderers.
steward to . . . 277, 361
Statutory Forest . . . xiii, 307, Plate V, *and* Glossary
strikes, workers' (1871) . . . 363
(1874) . . . 356
stone *see* Quarries
storms (wind and rain) . . . 190
subsidence damage . . . 480, 482, 491, 492, 493, 503, 536, *and* Glossary
awards by deputy gaveller . . . 347, *and* Glossary
supervisor of the Forest . . . 196
'surf', for drainage . . . 76, 77, 88, 97, 102, 138, 187, 189, 197, 226, 239
surface damage . . . 347, 348, *and* Glossary
surveyor-general of Woods . . . xxiv, 211, 212, 321
Swanimote . . . xxiii, 221, *and* Glossary

thegns (Saxon) . . . 141
timber, free for early mining . . . 5, 8, 39, 40, 89, 129, 130, 158, 194, 195, 205, 207, 209, 215, 216,
. . . 217, 218, 219, 220, 221, 257, 266, 292, 301, 302, 341, 368, 371, 388
'boothes', bothels, bothes . . . 40
opposition to . . . 89, 195
cancelled by 1668 and 1838 Acts . . . 195, 308, 323, 324, 341
tramroad . . . 8, 223, 251, 287, 309, 326, 327

Union and political local factors . . . . 408, 423, *and passim*

vehicles: carts, waines 40
ventilation underground 41, 121, 129
air gutter 129
verderer . . . . xix, xxiii, 8, 39, 144, 182, 189, 207, 210, 212, 307, 325, 361, 406, *and* Glossary
court (Attachment Court) . . . . xxiii, 8, 207, 277, *and* Glossary
legal appeal connected with Dean Forest Mines enactments *see* Act of 1838
vern (mining partner) 8, 70, 80, 90, 91, 117, 122, 124, 128, 129, 134, 244, 255
vessels: barge, boat, piccard, trowe 33, 35, 36, 119, 120, 121

'walk' (Forest management division) . . 8, 119, 129, 130, 196, 215, 257, 301, 302 *and see* keeper *and* lodges
Blakeney 215
Latimer 215
Parkend 215
Ruardean (Herbert) 215
Speech House 215, 302
Worcester 215, 301
Warden of the Forest . . . 75, 78, 87, 89, 113, 144, 145, 146, 148, 168, 212, *and see* Index of Personal Names
water problems in mines *see* drainage
water pits, engine pits, water wheels 22, 139, 226, 227, 256, 258, 282, 302, 304, 313, 314
water (domestic) extracted from mines 507, 508
West Dean dispute with East Dean (1519-20) 150
Whitemead Park, custodianship 57, 235
wiredrawers, in 1608 151
wireworks, Tintern 152, 154
WORKING (MINING) TECHNIQUES 22, 138, 255, 269, 302-6,
distance apart of workings 9, 40, 41, 77, 88, 102, 115, 125, 138, 139, 140, 226, 227, 256,
. . . . 269, 300, 302, 303, 304, 305, 311, 313, 314
fencing of . . . . 9, 97, 100, 109, 138, 507, and App. D and F
filling-in of . . . . 109, 417, 537, App. D and F, *and see* drainage, ventilation *and* subsidence
woodward 144, 192, 207, 212
women as galees . . . . xviii, 39, 496, 505
women in mines 215
WORDS
'Between Matins and Mass' 7, 18, 38, 46
'Burned our light' 128
'Blast of a horn' 35, 38
'Descent of three steps' 6, 165
'Horn or the cry' 4, 35
'old men's workings' 503
'Until mattocks meet' 206
'Year and a day' 4, 73, 120, 255, 256, 307

INDEX OF PERSONAL NAMES

[* denotes a Free Miner; some were recruited as deputy gavellers]

Abenhall, Ralph of, forester-of-fee 12, 14
* William of 147
* Adams, James 111
* John 96
* S 534
* Stephen.......................... 105
* T............................... 534
* Thomas.......................... 105
* William, deputy gaveller 52, 73, 75, 76,
.. 77, 79, 80, 82, 83, 84, 86, 87, 88, 89, 93, 94,
.. 96, 97, 98, 99, 101, 102, 103, 112, 124, 237
W. D., of Office of Woods 248
* Addis, Adys, John 42
Adeane, John, of Awre, a regarder 64, 177
Agar, Thomas, surveyor-general of woods 191-6, 206
Aileway, -, of Mitcheldean 165, 514
Albermarle, John de...................... 144
Robert de.......................... 144
Aldridge, Augustus, shipwright............ 183
Alford, John 324
Allaway, ,-,............................. 251
Allen, William 523
* Amb(u)rey, John, of Staunton ... 199, 202, 203
* William.................. 77, 120, 126
* Ambrose, George 116, 118, 243
*Martin 103
William, lord of the manor of Blakeney 310, 345
Andover, Charles, Viscount............... 167
* Andrews, Anthony 80, 96, 99, 105
* John 83, 90, 101
,-, purveyor of timber 211
* Annesley, William....................... 83
* Annetts, James 116
* Nicholas 103, 107, 270
* Arminger, John 41
Arundel(l), George, deputy gaveller ... 52, 75, 77,
.. 78, 79, 80, 82, 84, 87, 89, 90, 93, 94, 96, 112
Susan, of Clearwell.................. 86
Arnold, Thomas 424
Ashley, Evelyn, a Mining Commissioner of 1871 354
* Ray 493, 507, 509
Aston, Walter of, forester-of-fee 12, 13
Atherton, Nathan, of Calne (Wilts) 287
Athewy, Thomas 149
Atkins, Sir Robert 68, 222
Atkinson, John, joint deputy gaveller 32, 43,
.... 55, 56, 321, 328
Aubrey, Thomas, of Breckness Court 525
Richard 525
* William.......................... 118
Aust, John of 13
Avenant, Richard, ironmaster 208

Babin, Ambrose 184
* Backstar, John 42
Bacon, Sir Francis 152
* Baddam, Badham, Christopher 72
* James 71, 72
* Robert............................ 107
Baggalley, J.A., Justice 417
* Baker, John 41, 42
* William......................... 41, 42
* Bangham, William 107
Bankes, Sir John, attorney-general 173
* Bannister, Edmond 75, 77, 83, 86, 96, 109
* George, of Clearwell 79, 84, 86, 96,
.... 98, 99, 101, 103
* junior 99, 104, 105, 106, 109, 115, 116, 243
* John 101, 105, 126
* Henry 105, 109, 116, 246
* Richard......................... 79, 98
* Simon 124, 126, 517
* Bar(r)on, Barton, John 41
Thomas, clerk of St. Briavels Castle 118, 124
the younger, of Coleford 124
* Barrow, John 99
Laurence, of Bream Lodge............ 124
* Thomas...................... 118, 126
Bassh, Thomas, gaveller 49, 57
Basset, Gilbert 20
* Baster, Thomas 41
Bathurst, Charles, of Lydney Park 251, 257,
.... 260, 515, 516, 526
Lawrence.......................... 194
Thomas 515
Baynham, Thomas, of Clearwell, gaveller49, 51, 57
Bazeley, Miss M.L., historian ..... xxii, 144, 146
* Beach, John 101, 105, 109
Richard 103
* Samuel 521
* Thomas.......................... 123
* William.......................... 118
Beane, Henry 150
Beauchamp, Henry, Duke of Warwick 150
Beaufort, Henry Somerset, Duke of,
constable and warden 98, 100, 102,
.... 103, 223, 251, 253
Beck(e), Thomas 42, 98, 240, 241
* Beddis, John 412, 413
Thomas, of Littledean Hill 266
Bedford, Jacquetta, Duchess of............ 149
Henry, Duke of, warden 206
John, Duke of, gaveller . 18, 21, 31, 47, 149, 150
* Bele, Henry 237
Bell, William 160
Bellamey, Thomas, of Hadnock 115, 117
Bellows, John, of Gloucester 34
* Bennett, Emanuel 105

* James 118, 123, 124, 126, 129
* Jonathan 79
* Jonathan, of Ruardean 75, 79, 94, 124
* John 98, 109, 118, 124, 126
* Richard 109, 113
Richard, keeper of Worcester walk 215
* Thomas 111, 116, 246
* William 126
William 271
Bennys, George, deputy gaveller 52
Berkeley, Augustus, Earl of, constable and warden 53, 54, 125
Charles, Earl of, constable and warden . 53, 54, 105, 108, 109, 128
Frederick Augustus, Earl of, constable and warden 116, 124, 128, 209, 211, 212
James, Earl of, constable and warden 109, 111, 115, 131
Berow, Thomas, preservator 180
* Berowe, Thomas 237
Berrow, Edmund of Blakeney, 'chief forester' 64, 168
* John 98
Bills, David J., Director-General, Forestry Commission 482, 537
Binding, Doris Elizabeth, of Mile End *see* Hart
Bird, William, printer of Newnham 231
Birt, *see* Byrt
Biby, William 123
Bishop, Capt. George 181
William, of Cinderford 287
Blakeney, Thomas of, forester-of-fee 12
* Blanch, Joseph 268, 270, 522
Blunt, John 81
Thomas, deputy surveyor 217, 218
Boevey, William 207
Mrs., ironmaster, of Flaxley 208
Bond, Christopher, deputy gaveller 54, 69, 110, 118, 124
George, of Redbrook, deputy constable . 102, 103, 105, 108, 109, 243, 271
* Philip 238
* Richard 77, 80, 86, 92
* Thomas 80, 107
* William 107
* Borrowe, Thomas, of St. Briavels 162
* Boseley, William 77, 80, 85, 90, 91
* Boughton, Richard 98
* Bound, Richard 118
* Bradley, George 244, 274
John, keeper of Ruardean walk 130
* Mark, galee 507, 509
Mervyn 507
Richard 115, 118
Richard, keeper of Ruardean (Herbert) walk 215
Brain(e), Captain, ironmaster 181
Ephraim 409, 410
Frank, coalmaster 462
* John 409, 410
J. B. 310
* W. B., coalmaster of Cinderford and Trafalgar Colliery 365, 366, 367, 528, 529
* Bray, Edward 99
* Peter 83
* Brayne, Edward 77, 79
* George, of Littledean 197, 198, 203
* Giles 113
Henry, an early gaveller 49, 57, 235, 236
* John 85
John 181, 182
John, esquire, a lessee from free miners . 181
Kettford 192
Richard 178
* William, of Littledean 198
Bret, Nicholas 19
Brett, John, keeper of Latimer walk 215
John, ochre merchant, of London 181
Bridgeman, Charles 172
Bridges, Giles 152
Brien(ne), Guy de, warden 20, 148, 149
Bright,Tom, of Coleford xix
* Brin(k)worth, John 181
John, weaver, of Littledean 7, 203
* Samuel 123
* Thomas 93
Brooke, Sir Basil, ironmaster 161
Brooks, James, of Bream 325
Broughton, John, first deputy surveyor of Dean (1633) 167
* Brown, Benjamin 523
J. Riley, chairman of Free Miners' Committee . 234
Thomas Forster, deputy gaveller . 22, 56, 388, 441, 452, 455, 459, 529, 530
Westgarth Forster, deputy gaveller56, 462, 463
William 90
* W. J. 534
Browne, John, gun-founder 179
* Thomas, of Clearwell 50, 61, 175, 176
* William, of English Bicknor 92
* Brownrick, Nicholas, of Coleford 5, 7, 52
Brownwick, Col. J. 181
* Brute, John 41
Buckley, Alfred, a Mining Commissioner of 1871 354
Buddle, John, a Mining Commissioner, of Wall's End 306, 312
* Bufford, James 237
Bule, Richard 144
Bull, Nick 493, 507
* Burgeis, Alexander 148
Byles, Mr Justice 345
* Byrley, Henry 237
* Byrt(e), Burt, Birt, Henry 111
* James 155, 156, 238
* John 155, 156
* Richard 155
* Thomas 90, 91
* William 80, 83, 85, 90, 91, 115, 514

Callowe, Anthony, of Mitcheldean 5, 60, 164, 165
* William 41, 77, 165, 166
* Calnoe, William 42
* Cameron, Gilbert 148
Campbell, Sir James, Bt., deputy surveyor . 55, 56, 388, 441, 453
* Care, Edward 71
Carpenter, William 63, 64
Carpynter, John, of Coleford, smytholder 237, 238
* Philip 237, 238
Carter, M.F., solicitor, of Newnham 360
* Cassel, Giles 156
* Thomas 79

* Casway, Thomas ... 96
Catchmay(e), Cachmay(e), Thomas, gaveller 49, 57
John ... 161
Philip, an early gaveller ... 57, 235
Sir Richard, ironmaster ... 161, 513
Thomas, gaveller ... 51, 53, 164
Tracy, of Bigsweir, deputy constable ... 102
Cecil, Sir William ... 150
Challenor, -, ironmaster ... 160
Chandos, Lord ... 152
* Chapman, Jonathan ... 111, 113
Charles I ... 293
Charles II ... 75, 186, 194, 290, 293, 297
Charnock, Sir George, sergeant-at-arms ... 191
Charval, William, of London, merchant . 158, 159
Chinn, John ... 149
* Chrisham, John ... 75
* Church, Churchay, George 71, 72, 77, 80, 85, 118
,-, ... 514
Clare, Thomas, warden ... 147
Clarence, George, Duke of ... 150
Clark(e), -, solicitor, of Newnham 274, 288, 298, 301
Abraham, of Flaxley ... 187
* John ... 41, 42
John, of The Hill, Herefordshire ... 124
Richard, Judge of Mine Law Court ... 123
* Thomas ... 41, 42
Clayton, Robert, ironmaster ... 189, 190, 194
* Clement, James, alias Soop ... 69, 72, 92
* William alias Sopor ... 90
Clifford, Henry, of Over Ross ... 251
Clutton, John, Crown receiver ... 406
Coke, Sir Robert ... 172
Colchester, Sir Duncombe, deputy constable .. 90, ... 91, 191
Maynard, deputy constable, of Westbury-on-Severn 115, 116, 124, 126, 128, 130, 131, 243
the younger ... 124, 126
William, deputy constable ... 246
Cole, Robert ... 149
Collins, Betty ... 517
* William ... 126
William ... 272
* Constant, Constance, Israel ... 523, 524
* John ... 517
* Joseph ... 524
Cook(e), -, deputy gaveller ... 54, 519, 520
John, solicitor, of Ross-on-Wye ... 524
* John ... 111, 118
* Jonathan ... 103
Richard ... 409
* Samuel ... 107
William, J.P. ... 207
* William, of Whitecroft ... 77, 84, 85, 262
Cookson, -, ... 357
* Coole, Robert ... 71, 72
* Cooper, Henry ... 86
* Griffith ... 111
* Jonathan ... 116
* Joseph ... 124
* William ... 85, 90, 92, 96
* Corry, James ... 118
* Coster, John ... 90, 93
Cotton, -, QC ... 357
* Court, John ... 54, 126
Courtney, -, ... 419
Coventry, Sir Thomas, attorney-general . 161, 164
Cowles, -, quarryman ... 240
* Cowley, William ... 82, 90
Cowmeadow, James ... 318
* Robert ... 123
* William ... 105, 118
Cox, Richard, of Oxford ... 287
* Cradock, John ... 126
Crawley, Thomas ... 118
E. of Cinderford, coalmaster .. 362, 365, 371
Crawley-Boevey, Sir Thomas, of Flaxley 145, 211, ... 237, 268, 269, 270, 526
S. M. ... ; xxi, *and see* Boevey
Crawshay, Henry ... 145
William, coalmaster, of Cyfarthfa Castle, Glam. ... 145, 328, 353
Creed(e), Thomas, gent., of Ruardean .. 192, 204
Cromhall, Crumhall, Cromehale, Hugh, receiver 150
John, gaveller ... 47, 48, 49, 57, 156
Thomas ... 41, 42
Cromwell, Oliver, 'Protector' ... 57, 69, 182, ... 183, 184, 222, 292
Crosse, William, yeoman, of Mitcheldean ... 203
Crowdey, William, of Highworth (Wilts.) ... 287
Crowe, Sir Sackville ... 169
Culley, George, gaveller and a Commissioner of Woods ... 423, 430, 441

* Daniell, Thomas, of Coleford ... 79
* Dau, Dull, Walter ... 41, 42
* Davies, David, of Lydney ... 287
John ... 118
* Richard alias Evans ... 90
Richard, area land agent, Forestry Commission .... xiv, 476, App.F, Plate XIII
Thomas, deputy clerk of St. Briavels Castle . 32, 41, 44, 89, 98, 99, 100, 102, 103, 105, 108, 109
Thomas, gent., of Clearwell ... 203, 243
* Walter ... 42
* William, clerk of St. Briavels Castle .. 109, ... 111, 113, 118
* William ... 43
* Davis, Christopher . 96, 101, 103, 109, 115, 126
Henry, narrow-weaver, of Newland ... 203
Henry, steward of Clearwell Estate .. 516, 518, ... 520, 521, 522
* James ... 356, 412, 413
* John 80, 82, 90, 91, 103, 111, 118, 126, 253, 271
* Matthew ... 71
Rev. -, ... 271
Richard, alias Evans ... 91
* Thomas, of Five Acres 134, 262, 300, 302, 515
* Davy, John ... 105
* Daw, John ... 84
* Day, Dey, Thomas ... 237, 238
Daykin, Vernon ... xix
* De(a)ne, George ... 123
Henry, gaveller ... 47, 57
William of *Dene* ... 141
* Den, George ... 118, 120
Dennis, -, ... xvi, 16, 34, 239, 240, 241, 242
Desborow, Lord ... 85
Dew, George, of Huntsome ... 124
Mrs. ... 272

Mr. -, ... 270, 272
* Dey, Thomas 237, 238
Dilke, Sir Charles, MP 68, 462, 463
* Dolett, Walter 41
* Dolwy, Dolwyre, Phillip 41, 42
Doler, Henry 41
Dorrett, Harry 42
Dovye, Stephen, innkeeper, of Coleford 238
* Dowle, Christopher 107, 155
* Henry 155
* John 77, 83, 199, 201, 203
* Richard 155
Downes, William, minerals valuer 326
* Drew, James 123
* John, of Littledean 197, 198
Drinkwater, Thomas 123
Drummond, , -, *see* 'Drummond Committee'.
* Drutt, John 42
* Dubberley, Henry 109
Ducker, John, steward of Lydney Park Estate515, 516
* Dukes, John 105, 123
* Joseph 107
* William 126, 128
Duncan, Lord334, 340 *and see* 'Duncan Committee'
Duncannon, Lord, a Commissioner of Woods 328
* Duninge, Dunninge, Thomas 52
Dunraven, Countess, of Clearwell 376
Lord, of Clearwell Estate . . 11, 257, 515, 517,
. . . . 518, 519, 520, 521, 527
Dursley, Lord George Augustus 125
* Dutheridge , Francis 124
Dutton, -, ... 270, 272
Dykin, S., of Cinderford 310

East, Robert, keeper of Parkend walk 215
* Eddy, George 108
* Henry, of Ruardean 70, 109, 111
* John 126
Edward I 16, 17, 18, 19, 21
Edward II 16, 17, 18, 19, 21, 31, 148, 166
Edward III . . . 16, 17, 18, 19, 21, 31, 32, 87, 157,
. . . . 255, 289, 292, 293, 295, 298
Edward IV 47, 235, 237, 238
Edwin, Charles, of Clearwell Estate . 11, 517, 518,
. . . . 519, 520, 521, 522
Eggar, Rt. Hon. Tim 480
Elley, Elly, George 96, 99
* James 56
* Phillip, deputy gaveller and crier of
Mine Law Court 54, 109, 113,
. . 116, 118, 124, 126, 246, 286, 519, 520, 523
* Richard 77, 81, 91, 104, 123, 161
* Thomas 80, 98
* Ellis, B 534
Thomas 70, 72, 92
Ellway, John 356
* William 412, 413, 414
Elric, a thegn of *Dene* 141
Ellsmere, Elsmere, John 517
Nash 517
* Elsmore, Daniel 109, 111
* James 126, 129
* John 118, 123, 517
* Joseph 521-522
* William 109, 111
* Elsom(e), Richard 96
* Sydney J., president of Forest of Dean Miners' Association 1882 . . . . 463, 465, 466, Plate X
Elsworth, Henry, clerk 306
Embray, Henry 101
Ernle, Sir John, junior, supervisor and
conservator 206
Ernui, a thegn of *Dene* 141
Escourte, -, counsel 152
Evans, Mary 92
* Phillip 90, 92
* Thomas 99, 123
Everett, John, deputy clerk of St.
Briavels Castle 111, 113
Evelyn, John . . . . xxiv, 190

Finch, Francis, ironmaster 189, 190
Fisher, Thomas, of Newnham 266
FitzArthur, Nigel 141
FitzHerbert, Herbert 141
FitzMilo, Roger 141
FitzNorman, Hugh of *Dene* 141
William of Taynton 141
FitzWalter 141
Flower, Tristram 178
Foley, Paul, ironmaster 196, 208
Thomas, the elder, ironmaster, of
Stoke Edith 124, 208
Thomas, the younger, ironmaster, of
Stoke Edith 124, 208
* Forden, Foden, John 107
* Henry 107
* Forthy, Fortey, Robert 237
* Thomas 42
Foule, Richard, of Lydney 175
* Fox, George 71, 86
* H, ... 463, 464
* John 155
* William 123
Francis, G. E., Crown receiver of rents and
royalties 441
Fraser, James, of Gloucester 287
Freysil, James 146
Frobisher, Martin, Captain 121, 150
Fryer, -, ... 271
* John 153
* Thomas 155
Kedwyn, H., town clerk of Gloucester . . . 68
W. H., of Coleford, solicitor 28, 206
Furzer, Daniel, shipwright 183, 194

Gage, Viscount 115, 224, 514, 529
Hon. Thomas 110, 118
Sir Thomas 223
William Hall, of Highmeadow 115
* Gagg, William alias Smith 124
* Gardner, William, of English Bicknor . . . 90, 92
George 110
* Garon, Garren, John 41, 42
Gaunt, John of 21
George, John 178
George I 246
* Gething, Gethin(s), James 79, 83, 90, 93,
. . . . 96, 98, 99, 111, 116, 118
* Samuel 118, 123, 126

* Thomas 126
Gernoun, Thomas 21
* Gibbon(s), Charles 274
John, gaveller 51, 52, 53, 57
Gifford, Captain, ironmaster 181
* Gilbert, Thomas 82, 118
Gladstone, Herbert, Prime Minister 419
Gloucester, John, Duke of 149, 150
Richard, Duke of 150
Thomas, Duke of 149, 150
* Godding, Charles 123
* Christopher 80
* Jonathon 79
* William 99, 101
Godric, a thegn of *Dene* 141
* Godwin, Godwyn, Goodwin, Charles 90, 91, 110,111, 115, 128
* Christopher 90, 98
Earl of Staunton 141
George, of English Bicknor 92
* John 84, 118, 123
* Richard 113
* Thomas 111
* William 85, 91
* Good, James 82, 90, 99
Goode, George, of Readings 355
Goold, Alfred, coal and iron master, of Newnham 362, 363
Aaron 392
Messrs. 351
Thomas, coal and iron master, of Newnham 382, 385, 529
Gordon, Robert, MP, of Kemble 251
Gore, Hon. Charles, a Commissioner of Woods 56
Gough, -, Capt., deputy gaveller 54
Warren, of Hewelsfield, a regarder 177
Gowstanne, Richard, of Westbury 69
Graham, Thomas, solicitor 251, 306
Green & Co., solicitors 263
Grenehill, John, gaveller 48, 57
Greyndour, Robert, 'chief forester[-of-fee]' 168
Griffin, K. P., steward to verderers xxiii
* Griffith(s), Christopher 111, 113
* David 77, 81, 116
* Edward 80
* Edmond 90, 91, 101
* Giles 268
* Henry, of Coleford 79, 83, 86, 107, 113, 115, 116
* John 111, 113, 115
* Jonathon 99
* Richard 79, 85, 96, 99
* Symon 156
* Thomas 96
* Grindell, James, of Coleford 528
* Grindle, Michael 507
Grundy, Dr G. B. 14
Guest, Rob, deputy surveyor xxv
Sir Josiah, coalmaster, of Dowlais House, Glam. 318
Guise, Sir Christopher, JP, of Brockworth 183, 191
Sir John 206
* Gwilliam, Benjamin 410, 411
* C. T. H. 534
* E. R. 534
* H. H. 534
* J. H. 534
* T. 423
* T. H. 534
* S. 534
* Gwyllm, John 153
Gwynne, George 263

Hackett, Thomas, ironmaster 161
* Hadd, Hynd, William 42
Hailsham, Lord 506
Hain, Rt. Hon Peter, MP 483
* Hale, Aaron 109
* -, 534
* John atte 20
Thomas, of Littledean 268, 270
* Hall, Henry 238
Henry 191
William 153
Halliday, Thomas 355
* Hamblin, M. H. 534
*R. 534
* Ham(m)ond, Richard 237, 238
* Hanys, William 237
Harbord, Sir Charles, surveyor-general of woods 169, 180, 186, 187, 189, 190, 192
William 206
Hardwick(e), Eustace, gent., deputy gaveller, of Littledean 52, 59, 203, 204, 205, 206
* Harper, John 155
Ralph, of Coleford xix
* Simon 116
* Harries, G. 96
Harris, Frank H., of Lydney, local archaeologist 26, 27, 28, 29, 161
,-, ironmaster 160
Hart, C. E., OBE, a Verderer xiv, xix, xxiii, 477
Doris Elizabeth (neé Binding) *see* Dedication
* Joseph 99
Hartford, Partridge & Co. 255, 266
Hartland, Miles, assistant to deputy surveyor 218
Harvey, John, deputy gaveller xix, xxv, 58, 493, 546, Plate XV, App. E
David 507
Thomas, keeper of Speech House walk 215
William, keeper of Worcester walk 301
* Hathen, Heth, Richard 41
* Hathley, Hathewy, Hathway, John 41, 42
Hatton, Philip, deputy gaveller 53, 105, 129
William, deputy gaveller 147, 148
* Hawkins, -, 268
A. 534
Henry, of Office of Woods 248
* John 270, 272, 517, 522
* Richard 85, 109, 116, 123, 124, 126
S. J. 534
William, of Coleford 200, 202, 203
William, of Coleford, shoemaker 46, 199
* Hawkyns, John 237
* Haynes, Edmond 189
Gerald 492, 509, Plate XVII
* Richard 41, 42, 82, 103
* Thomas 84, 93, 103, 189, 246
* Haywood, Hayward, Henry 111, 118
* John 113, 116
* Jonathon 118

* Richard . . . 83, 98, 99, 101
Hayworth, John . . . 392
Head, Jeremiah . . . 544
* Heane, Henry . . . 123
* James . . . 69, 72
* John . . . 70
Heath, Charles, publisher, of Monmouth . . . 34
Henry I . . . xxiii, 144
Henry II . . . xxii, 141, 145, 147
Henry III . . . xxii, 145, 146
Henry IV . . . 149
Henry V . . . 149
Henry VI . . . 538
Henry VII . . . 48
Henry VIII . . . 235, 236
Henry, Lord, Marquis of Worcester, constable and warden . . . 78, 80, 81, 83
Herbert, Henry, Lord, of Raglan, constable and warden . . . 73, 182
Herdman, Major H. P., deputy gaveller56, 473, 502
Hereford, Roger, Earl of . . . 145
* Heth, Richard . . . 42
* Hewett, William . . . 80
* Hewlett, Richard, of Bream . . . 243, 380
Samuel, of Ayleford . . . 287
Hicks, Arthur, of Coleford . . . 27
Higford, John, of Alvington, deputy constable . . . 102, 103
* Higgins, Jeremiah . 105, 106, 107, 108, 109, 113, 115
* Thomas . . . 123
Hill, Anthony, coalmaster . . . 318
H. C., forestry consultant . . . 240
* John . . . 152
Hine, J. . . . 480
* Hinton, Bert, . . . 480
* Hobbs, -, . . . 522
* Daniel . . . 111
* Paul . . . 101
Robert, of Gloucester . . . 85
* Thomas . . . 129
Thomas, of Littledean . . . 268, 270
Hodges, Thomas, deputy constable . . . 69, 183
Hodge, John . . . 506
* Hok, Alexander . . . 148
* Philip . . . 20
* Hold, Holte, Richard . . . 41, 42
Walter . . . 148
* Holder, William . . . 41, 42
Holland, Henry, Earl of, Justice . . . 169, 187
Holt, Arabella, of Gloucester . . . 287
Hooley, Henry, of Lydney . . . 175
* Hoop, Edward . . . 69, 72, 75
* Henry . . . 75
Hooper, -, . . . 71
,-, solicitor, of Ross-on-Wye . . . 275
* Edward . . . 80, 86
* Henry . . . 43, 64, 77, 82
junior 82, 83, 85, 98, 99, 101, 105, 107, 108,109
Thomas, deputy gaveller . . . 52
* Thomas . . . 107, 116, 246
* Thomas, of Clearwell . . . 162
* Hop', William, of 'Hanford' . . . 237
* Hopkin, John . . . 42
John, of Monmouth, lime burner . . . 107
* Richard . . . 41
Hopkinson, Col., deputy gaveller . 135, 265, 514, 520
A. D., deputy surveyor . . . 72
George, Caesar, gaveller 44, 54, 58, 127, 213
Horne, A., preservator . . . 180
Horne, -, woodward . . . 192
* Hoskin(s), Kedgwin . . . 98, 155
the Elder of Clearwell . . . 124
the Younger of Clearwell . . . 124
Hosmer, John, map surveyor . . . 251
Houghton, Thomas, *The Compleat Miner* . . . 32
Howard, Hon, J.K., a Commissioner of Woods . . . 350, 363, 399, 409, 528, 529
Sir Stafford, gaveller and a Commissioner of Woods . . . 463
Howe, John, gaveller . . . 53, 58
Thomas deputy gaveller . . . 82
Howell, Albert, MBE, deputy gaveller . . . 58, 480
Daniel, galee . . . 507
* Michael . . . 481
* Walter . . . 80, 85
* William, of Littledean . . 126, 265, 268, 270
Hughes, William . . . 85
* Humphries, Humphreys, John . . . 70
* Richard . . . 70
* William . . . 77, 80, 96, 99
* Hutton, John . . . 272
Hyett, Robert, early gaveller . . . 47, 48, 49, 57
* Hynam, Arthur . . . 80
* Gyles, alias Symons . . . 82
* William . . . 82

Jackson, George, Elwell, ironmaster, of Birmingham . . . 318
James I, King . . . xv, 178, 290-3, 299
James, A. . . . 413
Brian, galee . . . 480
B. H. . . . 534
* George, deputy gaveller . 53, 110, 113, 115, 116, 123, 131, 246
* John . . . 82, 98, 111
John, ironmaster and coalmaster, of Lydney 267
* John, solicitor, of Newnham . . . 261, 262
L. J., Justice . . . 415, 417
* Peter . . . 118
* Richard . . . 77, 111, 115, 126, 128, 302
Richard . . . 69
* Richard, of Whitecroft . . . 134, 262
Robert, of Soylewell . . . 115
Thomas, deputy constable . . . 118, 126
Warren . . . 133, 251
William . . . 243
William, deputy constable . 43, 111, 113, 115, 131, 246
Jane, John . . . 80
* Jelf(e), Richard, deputy gaveller . . . 52, 101
William . . . 105, 107, 109
William, deputy constable . . . 111, 113, 116
William, gaveller . . . 58
William, of Bream . . . 526
* Jenkins, Charles, chairman of Free Miners' Committee . . . 469, Plate XI
Elizabeth, of English Bicknor . . . 92
* John . . . 129
R. W., a Verderer . . . xxiii
* Thomas . . . 118, 356

W. D. . . . xix
Joce, John . . . 149
* William, of Bearse . . . 12
John, James . . . 243
Sir Robert, gaveller . . . 48, 57, 236
* William . . . 83, 86
Johns, Donald . . . 504, Plate XVI
Jonathan . . . 21
Johnson, Ralph, an early gaveller . . . 49, 57, 236
* Jones, Andrew . . . 105, 109, 111
* Anthony . . . 118, 126
Benjamin, of Clavering's End Green 520, 523
* Charles . . . 99
* Enoch . . . 111
Francis . . . 116
*James . . . 80
James . . . 208, 258
* John . . . 84, 90, 103, 107, 109
* John alias Philips, of Ruardean . . . 199
* Michael J., of Upper Redbrook . . . 479, 482, 496, 546
* Richard . . . 126, 519, 521
Rev. Roynon, deputy constable, of Monmouth . . . 108, 109, 124, 131, 243
Roynon the younger, of Nass . . 112, 113, 124, 131, 243
Selwyn, of Chepstow . . . 268, 270
* Stephen, of Hawthorns . . . 136, 274, 300
* Sydney, of Crow Ash, Berry Hill . . . 500
* Thomas . . . 77, 79
Thomas . . . 85, 525
William, of Nass . . . 115, 130, 131
William, deputy constable, of Soylewell . 115, 116, 118, 130, 131
* Jordan, Edrean . . . 109
* Henry . . . 103
* John . . . 105, 107, 148
la Ware, deputy constable . . . 147
* William . . . 268
* Jows, John . . . 111
* Joynes, J. J., colliery manager, of Lydbrook . . . 463, Plate X

Kear(e), -, . . . 527
Edward, deputy gaveller . . 52, 77, 80, 96, 155
* Francis . . . 101, 109
* George . . . 156
* Henry . . . 105
* James, of Newland31, 32, 107, 156, 164, 165
* John, of Clearwell . . . 237, 523
* Jonathan . . . 80, 98
* Richard . . . 85, 86, 94, 96, 98, 99, 101, 106, 107, 108, 109, 155, 243
* Thomas . . . 98, 99, 103, 156, 523
Thomas, yeoman, of St. Briavels . . . 526
* William . . . 77, 83, 101, 107, 128, 237, 238
* Kedg(w)in, John . . . 155, 159
* Nicholas, deputy gaveller 52, 69, 72, 73, 75, 77, 88, 112
* Sturl(e)y, deputy gaveller . . . 7, 52, 69, 84, 86, 92, 103, 104, 107, 109, 177
* Thomas . . . 77, 85, 90, 91, 96, 155, 159
* Thomas, of Clearwell . . . 99, 101, 103, 105, 106, 107, 162
* junior . . . 107
* William . . . 111
* Kedwellen, John . . . 85
Kennedy, T. F., a Commissioner of Woods . 56, 141, 344
Kerle, Col., ironmaster . . . 181
* Kerr, Samuel . . . 124
* William . . . 124
King John . . . xxii
King Stephen . . . 141, 144
* Kinggot, John . . . 148
Kingscote, Col. Robert, MP . . . 353, 369
Kingston, Sir William . . . 145
Kinnersley, Hugh, of Breckness Court . . . 525
Kirle, Kyrle, James, of Walford, deputy constable . . . 62, 178
Jonathan . . . 207
Knight, Knyght, John, deputy gaveller . 52, 101, 126
* Richard . . . 93
* William . . . 238
* Korb, Thomas . . . 70
* Kyn, Edward . . . 156

* Lambard, Lambert, John . . . 41, 42
Lane, Robert . . . 115
William, deputy clerk of St. Briavels Castle . . . 115, 116, 118, 246
William, of King Stanley . . . 124
Langham, John, assistant deputy surveyor 321, 324
* Laurence, John . . . 41, 42
Lea, Nicholas of, forester-of-fee . . . 14
Levingston, James . . . 167
* Lewellen, John . . . 90, 93
*Lewis, John . . . 105, 303
* John, of Lydbrook . . . 263, 513, 514
John . . . 275
* Henry . . . 246
L. . . . 534
* Richard . . . 77, 80, 98, 103, 105, 109, 111
* Thomas . . . 123
Liddell, Rt. Hon. Helen, MP . . . 483
Lilly, Thomas, of Huntsham . . . 118
Limesi, Ralph de, of Wyegate . . . 141
* Linch, Richard . . . 99
Lisle, Lord . . . 152
Llandaff, J. Bishop of . . . 145, 148
Llewellyn, T., of Coleford . . . 54
William, King's Receiver . . . 48
Lloyd, Joseph, of Guns Mills . . . 268, 270
Loch, Sir Henry, a Commissioner of Woods . 419, 424, 425
* Lockyer, Giles . . . 108, 109
* Lodge, George . . . 80, 84, 86
* Thomas . . . 103
Long(e), Richard, an early gaveller . 49, 57, 235, 236
* Loofe, John . . . 42
Lougher, Andrew, galee . . . 507
Lough, Jonathan, of 'The Sign of the King's Head', Ross on Wye . . . 240
* Lowe, John, alias Watkins . . . 91
Lowther, Lord, a Chief Commissioner . . . 277
Lucas, John, solicitor, steward to Attachment Court . . . 277, 301
Ludlow, Ebenezer, sergeant-at-law . . . 251
Luke, John, of Gloucester . . . 65

Machen, C. E., landowner, of Staunton 381
Edward, deputy surveyor and joint deputy .. gaveller ...... 225, 251, 252, 253, 263, 322, . 326, 331, 344, 518, 520, 525, 563, Plate VIII
Edward Tomkins, deputy constable, as judge of Mine Law Court........ 54, 123, 130
Edward Tomkins, deputy surveyor and joint deputy gaveller........... 54, 55, 133
James (Davies), deputy gaveller, of Eastbach 54, 515
* James 134
Richard, of English Bicknor, deputy constable 54, 109, 110, 111, 113, 243
Maclean, Sir John xiii
Maddock, John, of Mitcheldean, clerk of Mine Law Court.................. 63, 64
* Thomas...................... 153, 155
* Malden, George 85
Malins, Sir R., Vice-Chancellor 357, 410, 413, 415
Mallore, Lawrence...................... 146
* Manning, Thomas...................... 77
* William......................... 126
Manny, Sir Edward 19
Mansel, John 184
* Thomas...................... 116, 126
Mare, Peter de la 148
* Marks, Randell 154, 155
Marland, Paul, MP...... 476, 480, 481, 482, 506
Marling, Samuel, MP, of Stroud 353, 386
Marshall, George 107, 159
* George 246
* Joseph......................... 116
Thomas, of English Bicknor 118
William 144
Martin, George......................... 217
Richard 107
* Mason, George 108, 109
Masters, Sir William 178
Matilda (Maud), Empress 141
Massy, Major-General................... 179
* Mathon, Henry, of Howle........... 197, 198
* Matthew(s), Jonathan, steward of Attachment Court................ 129, 214
* James 111, 118
* Richard.................... 79, 83, 98
* William...... 107, 108, 109, 111, 116, 243
William 270
* Mawswell, Thomas, of English Bicknor ... 177
May, Adrian 178
John, overseer 194, 195, 196
McNair, Lord...................... xix, 477
Meek(e), -, ... 534
* Francis 103, 109, 274
* Jeremiah.................... 109, 115
* John 101, 103, 118
* Thomas, of Ruardean .. 109, 134, 262, 263
* Walter......................... 115
* William........................ 124
Mellish, L.J., Justice 416
* Meredith, Henry 79
Robert 149
* W. D., secretary of the Dean Forest Free Miners' Association .... xix, 463, 467, 469, Plate XI
* Michill, John 41
* Thomas......................... 41
Milbourne, Henry, deputy constable ... 89, 97, 98
* Miles, John, of Berry Hill 381
* Miller, William 41, 42
Milne, Alexander, a Commissioner of Woods 54, 327
Milo, Earl of Gloucester 141
Roger, son of....................... 144
* Milson, William 82, 104, 105
* Miner, John the 19, 21
Maciame, widow of 21
* Mitchill, John 41, 42
* Thomas........................ 41, 42
* Monjoy, Montjoy, Joseph 99, 111
* Thomas........... 83, 92, 101, 103, 132
* Thomas the elder 90
* Thomas the younger 152
Monmouth, John of 12
* Monsell, Thomas 109, 118, 126, 155
* Mo(o)re, John 77, 85, 126
* Richard, alias Portyngale 237
* William......................... 126
* Moorfield, Morefield, John 110, 111
* Richard 107
* William.......................... 98
* Morgan, Basil 534
Christopher, of Clearwell, deputy gaveller 165, 166
David, an early gaveller 49, 57, 87, 236
* Evan 96
George....................... 101, 356
* Henry 77, 98, 99, 105
* Isaac 113
* James 123, 135
James, of Littledean Woodside 274, 275
John, steward of Mine Law Court, of Bream 18
John, of Bream 61, 85, 116, 155, 243
Jonathan 105
* Peter 534
Richard of Esbach 79, 99
*Robin (of current Hopewell Colliery)493, 507
Thomas, of Hurst, deputy constable 61
Thomas 149
* Thomas................. 118, 302, 303
* William, of Coleford 118, 237, 238, 272, 303
* William, of Chappell Hill (Mon.)61, 173, 176
William, of Reddings 355
* William, of Worrall Hill ..... 6, 7, 8, 50, 71, ... 133, 178, 262, 514
Morpeth, Viscount, a Commissioner of Woods 340
* Morris, Eric, chairman of Free Miners' Association .... 481, Plate XVI
Richard, deputy gaveller 112
* Morse, Clifford 246
George........................... 266
James, of Clavering's End Green....... 523
* John, of Clearwell . 110, 111, 243, 519, 523
the younger 111, 126
* John 115, 126
* Jonathan 79
* Matthew 155
* Richard, deputy gaveller, of Clearwell 41, 43, ... 73, 75, 77, 79, 85, 88, 111, 115, 116, 118, 246
* Samuel 115
T. 413
* Thomas.......................... 156
Thomas, deputy gaveller, of Clearwell 32, 46

* William........ 96, 98, 101, 103, 155, 159
* Morton, Henry 155
The Hon. Matthew Ducie 110
Moton, Motten, Motton, John, gaveller 57
Thomas, gaveller 57
* Mountjoy, Anthony, of Littledean 268, 270
* Thomas........ 77, 86, 105, 123, 126, 246
* Timothy, of Bilson Green 353, 355, 375, 408
* Mowsell, Mowsall, Mousall, Edward . 110, 111, ... 115, 116, 523
* Edwin junior 126
* John 81
* Nicholas 77, 80, 85, 103
* Richard........................ 101
* Thomas.................. 96, 99, 111
* William.......................... 123
Muchegros, Cecilia of, forester-of-fee 13, 14
* Mulle, William de 19, 20
* Mullen, James 123
Mungey, Thomas, deputy gaveller 52
Mushet, David, coalmaster and ironmaster, of.....
Coleford . 6, 11, 34, 44, 126, 241, 251, 258, 259, .. 268, 274, 282, 284-87, 303, 318, 517-22, 531
* Robert Forester, of Coleford 11, 14
* Mutley, Mutloe, James 113, 116
* Myll(e)(r), John, of Clearwell 237
* Myllyng, Robert 238
* Myning, John 42
Mynne, George, ironmaster.............. 161

Nash, Fred 534
John 520
* Thomas............. 101, 105, 109, 116
Neale, Thomas 237
Neele, Thomas, engineer, of
Westerley, Gloucester................ 269
* Nelmes, Richard . 77, 79, 82, 85, 96, 98, 99, 101
* Thomas..................... 105, 107
Nelson, Lord 223
Neville, William de 144
* Nicholas, Thomas 244
* William.......................... 85
Nicholls, Rev H.G., local historian .. xiv, 29, 241, ... 311, 564
* John 274, 463
* Thomas.......................... 274
* William................. 7, 69, 72, 181
Nicholson, Rev. Thomas, coalmaster, of
Yorkley 324, 325, 327, 370
Northampton, Earl of.................... 152
* Norton, Harry 42
* Richard, of Staunton 237, 238
* Thomas.......................... 42

* Ocle, Richard 238
Walter, of Brecknock Court 525
Okey, Col. John 185
* Orle, Nicholas 41, 42
Organ, Diana, MP 481
Ow, William de, of Wyegate 141
Oxford, Aubrey, Earl of.................. 187

* Page, Elys 147
* Walter.......................... 148
* William.......................... 147

Palmer, Sir John, Bt., of Newland........... 59
* Edward.......................... 103
* Thomas.......... 103, 105, 109, 111, 118
Thomas, blacksmith, of Coleford 204
* William....................... 96, 98
* Parish, James.......................... 80
* Parler, William 85
* Parry, James 172, 173
Joan, widow of free miner (in
Mine Law Court) 71
* Matthew 93, 111
* William......................... 209
* Parsons, John 41, 42, 238
* Partridge, Edward 155, 156
,-, ... 155
Patteson, Mr. Justice 308
Paul, Matthew, solicitor, Newent 271
Pauncefot, Grimbald, warden 147, 148
Payn, -, of Lydney 146
Pembroke, Philip, Earl of, constable and gaveller 178
William, Earl of, constable and gaveller . xv, 32, ... 52, 53, 54, 57, 61, 152, 155, 156, 159, ... 160, 161, 167, 168, 290, 291, 513
Pepys, Samuel 188, 196
Percy, Henry, Lord 189
* Perkins, Martin H. .... 463, 465, Plate X
* Phelpotte, Philpott, Henry 69, 72, 80
* John 77, 80, 83, 86, 92
* Johnathan 96, 98, 101
* Thomas, of Goodrich, steward of
Mine Law Court 50, 63, 175, 176
Phil(l)ips, -, ... 208, 258
* Alexander 243
Captain, ironmaster 181
* John 70, 123
Thomas 7, 32, 55, 155, 272
* Thomas.......................... 135
* William, of the Lea 123, 124, 126, 130
* Phipps, Thomas....................... 356
Pidcock, John, ironmaster 515, 516
Piggott, Roy, deputy gaveller xix, 58, 349, 476, 481, .. 482, 483, 492, 503, 538, 546, 564, Plate XIV
* Pitchard, William 77
* Pitcher, William 90, 93, 93, 99
* Plummer, George 155
Poole, Rev. 514
* Portyngale, Portimer.................. 118
* Richard, alias More 237
Richard 271
Potto-Hicks, Rev F. W. .... vii, xiv, 510
* Powell, Giles....................... 77, 79
Hugh 115
J. 534
* Matthew 115
* Richard................. 105, 124, 129
William, sergeant-at-law and deputy constable
Powis, Roger of 41
Powles, -, ... 534
Powlett, William, sergeant-at-law 105, 107
* Preece, James 99
John 521
* Thomas....................... 71, 72
* Price, Thomas, the elder 155
* Thomas, the younger 155
* William Phillip, MP............ 392, 406

* Pritchett, Anthony 243
* Priest, Preest, -, of Bream 325
  * George 118
  * James 77, 92, 105, 116
  * John 103
  * Jonatha 101
  * Joseph 118
  * Richard, of Bream, deputy gaveller . 53, 77, ... 85, 96, 98, 99, 101, 103, 104, 105, ... 106, 108, 109, 243
  * Stephen 41, 42
Probert, Sir George, deputy constable78, 80, 83, 84, 89
  * Richard 101, 111, 115, 116, 118, 126
Probyn, Edmund, the younger, a verderer, of Newland 113, 124, 130, 138, 406
  Edward 306
  John, a Mining Commissioner, of Longhope Manor House . 64, 113, 124, 138, 306, 312
  William, of Newland 43, 64, 124
  the younger 124, 191
Proctor, Rev. P. M. 149
* Prosser, Christopher 172, 173
Protheroe, Edward, coal and iron master, of Newnham . . . . . 251, 258, 259, 260, 268, ... 274, 276, 318, 324, 418
  junior 318
Pury, Captain, ironmaster 181
Pye, Sir Walter 178
Pyndar, R. 207
Pyrke,-, attorney 522
  Joseph 211
  Robert, gent., of Newnham 270
  Thomas, of Huntsham 268
  Thomas, of Littledean, deputy constable . 110, ... 115, 246

Queen Anne 209
Queen Mary 53

* Ranell(s), Edward 172, 173
  * John, of Berry Hill 69, 72, 126
  * Thomas 75, 79, 81, 90, 91
* Raulyns, John, of Clearwell 238
* Reynolds, Anthony 99, 103, 105
  * George 113
  * John 123, 209
  * Richard 123
  * Thomas, of Lydney 99, 105, 236, 237
Richard I 144
* Robert, William 21
* Roberts, John 41, 42
  * Henry 111, 116, 124
  * Thomas 110, 111
* Robins, Robyns, Richard 77, 92, 101
Robinson, John, deputy gaveller, of Littledean Hill . . . . . 11, 44, 54, ... 129, 268, 270, 519, 520, 524
  Philip, deputy gaveller, of Littledean Hill 44, 55
  junior 44, 55
  Thomas, deputy gaveller 264, 266, 268
Rochester, Earl of 152
Rock(e), Thomas, deputy gaveller 52
  * Edward 101
  * Joseph 93
  * William 77, 80, 105
Rogers, -, of Usk 271
  * Walter 41, 42
Rooke, James 118
  * Joseph 101
  * William 96
* Ross, John 272
Rowles, William, steward of Mine Law Court, and clerk of St. Briavels Castle . . . . 64, 73, 75, 77, ... 78, 80, 83, 84, 87, 88, 93, 111, 112
  Arthur, preservator 180
  William, gent., of Newnham 203
Rudder, Samuel 9, 48
* Rudge, Thomas 111, 118
  Thomas, of Ross-on-Wye 287
  * William 111
Rupert, Prince 179, 180
Ryder, Dr T. A. 29
Ryley, Philip, surveyor general of woods, and gaveller . . . 53, 58, 206, 207, 208

Salisbury, Earl of 180
Sandwich, Ralph of 13
Sapy, Robert de, warden 148
Sargent, Thomas, baker, of Mitcheldean 268
Scott-Garrett, Dr C., MBE, local archaeologist 26
Seise, Serjeant 185
Seymour, Lord 342, 343
Sheyare, Joan 237
Shinwell, Rt. Hon. Emmanuel 473
Sibley, John, galee 507
Singleton, William 178
* Skiffington, William 246
* Skin, Skyn(n)e, Christopher 155
  * Edward, of Clearwell 162
  * Robert 238
  * Thomas senior 77, 79, 80, 85, 109
  junior . . 77, 85, 86, 93, 96, 101, 243, 520, 523
  * Thomas, of Clavering's End Green 523, 524
  * William 126
* Skinner, Roger 42, 90
Slade, Benjamin, timber purveyor 211
* Sladen, John 123
  John 270, 272
  Richard 270, 271, 272
* Slye, Philip, of Lydney 237, 238
* Smart, Andrew 79
  * Anthony 83, 96, 98, 99, 103
  * Edward 79, 96
Smirke, E., Judge of the Stannaries of Cornwall 37
Smith, D. J., assistant overseer to West Dean . 361
  E. J. 534
  James, clerk, of Coleford 266, 302
  * John 41, 52, 92, 96
  John 151, 178
  John, of North Nibley 151
  * Henry 96
  H. V. 534
  * Walter 41, 42
  * William 172, 173
* Smyth(e), John 80, 83, 86, 98, 156
  * Henry 107
  * Richard 77, 79, 96, 98
  Sir Warringtton, W., chief mineral inspector to Commissioners of Woods 453
  W. W., deputy gaveller 55

* Sopor, Soop, *see* Clement
Sopwith, Thomas, a Mining Commissioner and mining engineer, of Newcastle-upon-Tyne . . . 136, 140, ... 149, 260, 306, 310, 311, 312, 318, 344
Robert . . . 306
Southampton, Lord Treasurer . . . 189
Stallard, -, . . . 185
* Standon, John de . . . 19
* William, of Coleford . . . 64
Staunton, Richard of . . . 12
* Staure, William of . . . 147
* Steel(e), John . . . 116, 118, 246
* Samuel . . . 116, 118, 126
* Thomas . . . 269
Stern(e)hold, Thomas, of Dixton . . . 5, 52, 63
Stevens, Stephens, A., relieving officer, of Coleford . . . 406
* George . . . 105, 514
G. T. . . . 423, Plate X
* Henry . . . 111, 115
Henry . . . 178
* John . . . 126
John, J. P. . . . 183
John, basketmaker, of Ruardean . . . 204
Nathaniel . . . 178
* Ralph . . . 92
* Thomas . . . 105
* William . . . 113
William, keeper of Blakeney walk . . . 215
Stinton, -, printer, of Coleford . . . 254
* Stock, Thomas . . . 116
* Sutton, Richard, of Lydney . . . 236, 237
* Schwarz, Phillip . . . 504, Plate XVI
* Sybrance, Siberance, Sibrance, Edward77, 85, 98
* Henry . . . 98
* John . . . 116
* Thomas, of Coleford . . . 83, 84, 85
* Thomas . . . 75, 96, 101
* William . . . 154, 155, 159
Symms, Soloman, of Newnham . . . 69
* Symon(d)s, Anthony . . . 105, 110
* Arthur . . . 107, 109, 111, 115
Arthur . . . 271
* Edmond . . . 98, 101, 109
* John, of Clearwell . . . 63, 64, 115, 118, 521
John, of The Mean, Mine, Mynde, Herefordshire (re Breckness Court) . . . 124, 515
* Richard . . . 107
Thomas, of The Mean, Mine, Mynde, Herefordshire (re Breckness Court) 515, 524, 525
* William . . . 109

Talbot, Gilbert, forester-of-fee . . . 12
Talebatt, Sir Richard, of Goodrich Castle . . . 13
Tallis, J. R., deputy gaveller . . . 58, 480
* Tallowe, William . . . 41, 42
Tanner, David . . . 515
Taylor, Arnold . . . 406
* George, of Lydney . . . 175
* John . . . 70, 81
John, a Mining Commissioner of 1871 . . 354
* Teague, Edward . . . 262
Isaiah, mineral surveyor, of Blakeney . . . 325
* James, of Littledean Woodside . . . 124, 262
* Moses, coal surveyor and engineer305, 318, 516
* Peter, of Coleford . . . 134, 514
Peter . . . 275
T. H. . . . 534
* Thomas . . . 98
* Teckoll, John, of Littledean . . . 174, 177
* Tench, Christopher . . . 93
Terrett, Thomas, of Ruardean . . . 123
Terringham, Katherine . . . 196, 197, 198, . . . 239, 240, 241, App. 5
Edward . . . 94, 169, 170, 172, 173, 177, . . . 196, 197, 198, 199, 203, 239, App. 5.
Francis, Captain . . . 195, 197, 239, App. 5.
Thomas, Arnold . . . 424
* George . . . 124
James, of Winnall's Hill, near Coleford . 287
* John . . . 107
* Jonathan . . . 105
J. T., coalmaster, of Coleford . . . 366, 515
* Owen . . . 90, 91, 92, 101
* Richard . . . 107
S. J., president of Free Miners' Association (1882) . . . 463
* William . . . 118, 126, 128
Thomlinson, A.R., deputy gaveller . . 56, 501, 535
Thomsett, Thomas . . . 237, 238
Throckmorton, Sir Baynham (d. 1664), of Clearwell . . . 53, 58, 73, 75, 76, 77, . . . 81, 87, 88, 93, 96, 111, 112, 513
Sir Baynharn, Bt. (d. *c.*1680), ironmaster, of . . Clearwell . . 161,164, 168, 172, 177, 178, 179, . . . 189, 190, 191, 193, 196, 205, 513,
junior, gaveller . . . 52
Sir William, Bt. (d. 1628) of Clearwell . . . 160, 161, 164, 166
* Tingle, James . . . 216, 522
James, of Littledean . . . 268, 270
* Richard . . . 124
* Robert . . . 128
* Tristram . . . 116, 118
* William . . . 118, 123, 126
William . . . 270
* Tinker, Richard . . . 41, 42
* Tombe, Richard . . . 107
* Tomlyne, William . . . 155
Tovey, H., of Coleford . . . 87
Thomas, solicitor and deputy gaveller, of Newnham 44, 55, 127, 135, 225, 261, 262, 264, 286, 296, 297, 516, 518, 520, 521, 523, 524
Treharne-Rees, R. I., deputy gaveller 56, 469, 498, 500
* Treste(e)d, -, . . . 271
* Charles . . . 107
* Edward . . . 107, 111
Joan . . . 91
* John . . . 91, 103, 113
* Richard . . . 86
* Thomas . . . 123
* Trestram, of Newland 43, 92, 206, 240, 246
* Trig(g)e, James, of Littledean . . . 134, 262
John . . . 101, 111, 263, 270
* Samuel . . . 123
* Stephen . . . 101
* William . . . 77, 85, 86, 96, 98, 101, 118
Trotter, Arthur W., of Coleford, engineer . . . 27
John, of Coleford . . . 263
Thomas . . . 274

* Tucker, Christopher, of Littledean, deputy gaveller 164, 167, 174, 181, 197
Tudor, O., publisher, of Monmouth 32
Tuffley, David 507
* Turner, Robert 274
* William 126
* Twety, John 237
* Tyler, Edward 80, 98, 243
* Henry 126, 155, 156
* Jonathan 99
* John 81, 98, 101, 105, 126
Mary 92
* Thomas 41, 42
Typer, John, of Aylburton, deputy gaveller 52, 177

Vaughan, John, of Courtfield 117, 124
* William 69, 72, 80, 90
* Ve(a)re, John 7, 181
Vick, William 161
Villiers, Sir Edward, of Mailscot 167
Lady, of Mailscot 177
Viney, J. 207
Vowell, Peter, ochre merchant, of London . . . 181
* Vowle, Christopher 98
* Voyce, John 70
* Richard 105

* Wade, James 80, 90, 93
* John, of Clearwell 98, 118
Major John, administrator of Dean for the Commonwealth . . . . 129, 181, 183, 185, 186, ... 188, 189, 205, 239, 270
* Walden, Thomas . . 93, 96, 98, 99, 103, 111, 116
* Waldin(g), Charles 111, 115, 116
* Henry 107
John, of Staunton 225
Thomas, of Staunton 12, 110
* Walter 19
* Wallon, Walden, Thomas 77
Walerond, Robert 146
*Walter, son of Nicholas 148
Walwin, Hugh son of 19
Ward, James, coal merchant and wharfinger, of Bishops Wood 271
* John 101, 126
* Thomas 116
Thomas 276
* Warre, Walter 41, 42
Washington, N.J.C., of the Coal Authority . . . 537
Warwick, Earl of *and see* Beauchamp 13, 14
* Wath, With, Witt, Wytt, Thomas 41
Watkins, Baden F., of Flaxley Abbey . 28, 29, 144
Fred 497
* John 71, 77, 82, 96, 101, 108, 109, 111, 113, 243
* Jonathan 116
* Richard 103
* William 126
Watson, Horace, solicitor to Commissioners of Woods 360, 402, 530
* Watten, Thomas 80
Watts, A. M. R., OBE, a Verderer xxiii
* Way, John 98
Weale, Thomas 71
Wear, -, ... 516
* John 69, 70, 72
Weaver, Thomas, of Gloucester 268, 270
* Webb, William 123
Webley, Kedgwin, of London 124
William, JP 183
* Wellington, John alias Francis 70
Thomas, of Littledean 7, 45, 52, 64
* Thomas 181
* West, John, steward of Mine Law Court . . 31, 32, ... 64, 98
John, gent., a regarder 199, 200
Westbury, Lord Chancellor 352
* Westerd, Westwood, Jonathan 79
* Thomas 99
Westmacott, -, ... 466
Westphaling, Westfaling, Herbert, of Rudhall 116, 124
Weymouth, Viscount, warden 53
Weyson, James, deputy gaveller 52
Wheatstone, William 216
* Wheeler, Edward, alias Partridge 155
John, ironmaster 208
R. E. M. and T. V., archaeologists xxiii, 24, 25, 29
* Whetson, Whetston(e), Whitson, George . . 80, 85, ... 96, 103
* Nicholas 111, 116, 243
* Richard 118
* Thomas, of Clearwell 7, 64
* Thomas 155, 156, 177
* William 77, 80, 93, 98, 116, 270
White, Col. 185
* Edward 103
* Edwin 109, 118
* George 107, 116, 123
* Henry 65
* James 113
* John 156, 172, 193
* John, keeper 134, 262, 301
Jonathan 191
* Richard 20
Thomas 65
* William 110, 111, 123
Whitefoote, William, wiredrawer, of Chappell Hill, Mon. 153
Whitehouse, Edwin, of Lower Redbrook 287
Sarah, widow of free miner 318
* Whittington, -, ... 45
Richard, of Newland 162
* Who(o)per, Richard 156
* Thomas 156
* Wilce, Jonathan 99
* Thomas 126
* Wilcocks, Henry 159
* Wilcox, Edward 113, 116
* Henry 77, 103, 123, 155
Henry 270
* Jonathan 98
Mr., -, surveyor general of woods 209
* Richard 126
Richard 270, 272
Stephen, merchants' agent 182
* Thomas 243
* Wilk(e)s, Thomas 116
* Walter 42
William the Conqueror . . . . xxii, xxiii, 87
* Williams, George 123
* James 274

John, deputy gaveller 52, 92
* John 156
John, yeoman, of Clearwell 204
* Josiah 123
* Richard 115, 116
* Walter 107
* William, of Coleford . 111, 135, 262, 273, 274
Wilson, Rt. Hon. Brian, MP, Minister of DTI 483, 495
Windebank, -, ... 171, 172
Winter, Sir Edward, of Lydney, constable . . . . . .
. . . . 152, 153, 175
Christopher, of Lydney 175
Sir John, of Lydney, ironmaster etc. 161, 167,
. 174, 177, 178, 179, 184, 186, 188, 189, 190,
. . . . . . 191, 192, 193, 194, 197, 199, 239, 515
William 160
* Wintle, George 126
* ,-, ... 534
James, solicitor, and steward of Verderers, of
Newnham 361
* Wisham, James 172, 173
John de, of Noxon Park 516
* Thomas 99, 101, 103
William de, of Noxon Park 96, 518
Witt(s), John 189
Thomas 41, 42
Thomas, keeper of Speech House walk . . 301
Wodeward, Thomas, an early gaveller . . . 57, 235
Wolesley, William, deputy constable and
gaveller 53, 58, 97, 98, 100, 101
* Wood, Fortune 181
James G., barrister, historian, . . . xiv, 46, 195,
. . . . . . 346, 348, 413, 418, 420, 513, 527, 528,
. . . . 546-8, 564, Plate IX, App. I.
* Jonathan 105
Silvanus, JP 183
* Wood(s), Francis 101, 103
* Richard 85, 118, 123
Robert, deputy gaveller 52, 53, 73, 75, 88,
. . . . 108, 109, 112, 243
* Thomas 77, 103
Woodward, Mr., of The Hill (Mon.) 126
Worcester, Charles, Marquis of constable and
warden 53, 75, 76, 88, 89, 97, 192,
. . . . 193, 196, 205, 222, 292, 299
Henry, Marquis of, constable and warden . . 80
* Worgan, Anthony 118, 123
Charles, of St, Briavels 173, 176
Charles, preservator 180
Christopher, of St. Briavels, deputy gaveller . .
. . . . 7, 48, 49, 51, 52
Edward, of Woolaston 50, 61, 116, 173
* Henry 69, 72, 92, 99, 103, 107, 109
* James 106, 107, 113
* John, of Five Acres 135, 266
* John 83, 86, 96, 99, 101, 109, 111, 113, 159
* Jonathan 99, 107
* Oliver 69, 72, 80, 92
* Richard, of Clearwell, deputy gaveller
. . . . 52, 53, 70, 79, 80, 96, 97, 98, 99, 102,
. . . . 103, 105, 106, 107, 118, 514
* Thomas 98, 99, 101, 116, 123
* William . . . 81, 83, 90, 92, 99, 116, 123, 156
William, attorney 91
* Workman, Anthony 83
* Wright, Jonathan . . . . . 481, 492, 508, Plate XVI
Ray, a verderer, galee, secretary of Free Miners
Association . . . . xxiii, 481, 508, Plate XVI
* Wulewy, John son of 21
* Wyeham, Thomas 77, 93, 105, 109, 115
Wykeham, William de, warden 148
* Wysham, Wysam, Wisham, Richard, of
English Bicknor 96, 105, 109, 113
* Thomas, of Staunton 96, 104, 109
* William 74, 79
Wyndham, Charles, of Clearwell 124
Francis [of SPCK], of Clearwell 43, 106, 108, 243
John 110
Thomas, the Hon. 131
* Thomas junior, deputy gaveller, of
Clearwell 115, 131
Thomas, gaveller 58
Wyrall, George, of English Bicknor Court 28
* Wy(e)sham, Richard, of English Bicknor . 107, 108
* Thomas 103, 107
* William 107

* Yarsley, Yearesley, Christopher 172, 173
Yate, John, of Arlingham 124
* Yeame, William 155, 159
Thomas 172, 173
* Ye(a)rworth, James 77
Richard, deputy gaveller 52
William, of Newland 52
Yemm, Yem(e), James, house-carpenter, of
Staunton 203
* John 77, 103
* Jonathan 98, 99
* Stephen 90
* Thomas 92
* William 69, 70, 99, 107
Ye(a)rworth, Henry 239, 240, 270
* Gyles 77, 96
* James 94, 96, 103, 199, 202, 203
* William, of Newland 106, 108, 176
* Yorke, Richard 96
* Youre, Philip 113

INDEX OF PLACE NAMES

Abenhall 12, 14, 151
Church 36
Adset 151
Abbots Wood . . . . . 14, 145, 309, 341, 353, 371, ... 372, 417, 528
Allaston 151
Ardland, Edland, Erland 145, 147, 235
Arlingham 124
Awre 64, 177
Aylburton 151, 177
Aylloe Hill in Aywood 70
Aywood (Haywood) 70, 189, 191

Bearse 12, 13, 351
Berry Hill 69, 72, 381, 479
Berkeley 36
Castle 110
Bicknor, *see* English Bicknor.
Bicslade 509
quarry 161
Bigsweir 102
Bilson Green 372
Bircham Grove 527
Birchin Grove 527
Birmingham 318
Bishopswood 93, 94, 95, 113, 271
Blackpool bridge 47
brook 47, 119
Blackstones 74
Blakeney . . . . 47, 55, 94, 119, 151, 168, ... 246, 310, 325, 345
bailiwick 168
'Blakes, The' 91
Bledisloe, Hundred of 112, 149, 151
'Bleyth's' bailiwick 14
Botloe, Hundred of 112
Braceland 527
Bream . . . 29, 104, 110, 151, 246, 325, 380, 503, 526
'Devil's Chapel' 29
lodge 124
tithing 526
Breckness Court (manor) 515, 524
Broadmoor 126
Broadwell 479
Brockweir 81, 83, 94, 104
Brockworth 191
Buckshraft 181
Bullo Pill (on Severn) 253, 254, 327, 330
railway 327

Caerleon 36
Cannop . . . . 14 *and see* 'Newernhay'
bridge 47, 119, 122
brook 119, 476
wayn way 119
Castiard, Vale of . . . . 145 *and see* Chestnut Wood
Chappell Hill, Mon. 173
Chelfridge, Noxon Park 164, 165, 515, 516
Chepstow 268, 270
bridge 35
'Chesters, The', Woolaston 26
'Chestnut Wood' . 178, *and see* Castiard, Vale of
Churchends, Beame 151
Cinderford 240, 365, 371, 418, 461
Clavering's End Green 520, 523, 524
Clearwell 17, 32, 41, 43, 66, 73, 75, 78, 79, 83, 86, 87, 88, 89, 93, 97, 98, 100, 102, 103, 104, 105, 110, 111, 115, 118, 156, 162, 164, 175, 177, 180, 203, 204, 237, 242, 246, 525
Ashtree Grove 526
Beasthouse Farm 526
Bream Farm 526
Cadwell Farm 526
caves (iron ore) 508
Court Mansion House 526
Estate 514, 516
Gatewell Farm 526
Great House Farm 526
Hartley's Court Farm 526
Longley Farm 526
Noxon Farm 526
Shophouse Farm 526
tithing 526
Trowgreen Farm 526
Clements End 500
Coldwall 46
Coleford 27, 57, 66, 79, 80, 84, 85, 87, 89, 110, 113, 118, 130, 133, 135, 151, 174, 199, 204, 237, 238, 239, 243, 246, 254, 262, 266, 268, 272, 276, 312, 337, 362, 363, 366, 406, 479
Angel Hotel 267
Chapel 149
Market-house 243, 225
Conpill (on Severn) 83
Courtfield (Mon.) 117, 120, 125
Crabtree Hill 28
Crow Ash, Berry Hill 500

Deadman's Cross, Viney Hill 47
Dean Pool 28
'Dean Road, The' 27
'*Dene*' 6, 141 *and see* Mitcheldean *and* Littledean
Magna 6, 48, 49
Doward 28, 29, 529, 530
Great 28, 29, 529, 530
Little 74, 529, 530
Drybrook 122, 482, 492

Edge End 479, 496
English Bicknor . . . . 7, 28, 92, 110, 113, ... 118, 151, 177, 246, 322
court 28
Eastbatch 79, 515
Etloe 151

Five Acres 134, 135, 263, 266, 300, 515
'Five Meadows' 272
Flaxley 93, 95, 144, 145, 147, 151, 187, 268
Abbey 526
Lynnards Coppice 187
Forest of Dean . . . . *passim*
Foxes Bridge 47, 119, 252, 318

Gannerew (Mon.), Baddhams Lays in 119
Gatcombe Pill (on Severn) 122, 210
Gattles Cross at Scar 67
Glamorgan 150
Gloucester 85, 268, 269
Goodrich 63, 175
castle 13, 168
Grass Moor near Broadmoor 126
Gunsmills furnace 93, 268
Gun(s)pill 81, 94

Hadnock (Mon.) 115, 117
Haye of Ross, The 141
Hereford, Herefordshire 119, 120, 121, 141
Hewelsfield 177
Highmeadow Estate, Woods . . . . xxiv, 224, 225, ... 257, 265, 339, 345, 430, 441, 514, ... 527, 528, 529, 530, 531
Birchin Grove 527
Blackmoor Grove 527
Braceland Farm 527
Broom Hall Farm 527
Bunjups Grove 527
Hadnock Wood 527
Hoods, The 527
Knockall Grove 527
Mailscot Wood 527
Reddings, The 527
Sheep Pasture, The 527
Hillersland 528
Hoarthorns 273
Howbeach 325, 421
Howle, Herefordshire 197
Howler's Slade 268, 274
Hudnalls xxv
Huntley 151
Huntsham 118, 125
ferry 95, 96

Ireland 102, 103, 104, 106, 156, 188

Kensley 196
house 39, 196
Kidnalls Wood, north of Lydney . . 178, 189, 257, ... 496, 515, 516, 526, 527
Kingsmore, Noxon Park 164
Knockall 527

Lambsquay 237
'Lanquire', Noxon Park 164
Latham's Slope 500
Latimer walk 261
Lea, The 125, 151
Bailey 178, 190, 196
Lining Hill wood 29
Linton Furnace, Herefordshire 93, 94, 95
Little Cross Hill 271
Littledean ('Little Dene') *Dene Parva* . 7, 38, 48, 49, 60 74, 110, 115, 119, 134, 151, 164, 174, 177, 180, 197, 203, 246, 261, 266, 268, 269
Woodside 262, 265, 274
Llandaff 148
Longhope 71, 93, 94, 151
Manor house 306
Lydbrook . . . . 47, 74, 113, 119, 120, 121, ... 123, 210, 239, 243, 263
Boxbush near 74
Lydney 13, 27, 29, 70, 71, 72, 94
Pill . . . . . . 122, 146, 151, 152, 161, 175, 178, ... 237, 238, 267, 526
Lydney Park 22, 29, 251, 252, 515, 526
Old Park 516
Lydney Park Woods 13
Maple Hills 526
New Pool 526
Old Furnace Yard 526
Tomkin's Land 526
Upper Forge Pool 526
. . . . *and see* Kidnalls, *and* Sneade
'Lynnards Coppice' 187

Mailscot, ('Lymeslades') . 74, 95, 167, 257, 265, 496, 515, 528
Marians 528
Meen, Mine, Mynde, The (Herefordshire)524, 525
Milkwall 77, 295
Minsterworth 151
Mirey, Moyery, Stock 47, 119
Mitcheldean ('Great Dene') *Dene Magna* 34, 48, 49, 67, 74, 90, 91, 108, 110, 151, 164, 165, 68, 183, 246, 268
Monmouth, Monmouthshire . . . . 32, 34, 36, 108, ... 119, 120, 122
bridge 35, 74, 95, 107, 113
'The Hill' 126
Moseley Green 14

Nailbridge 129
Nass, Naas 115, 130
Newent 35
'Newernhay' (Cannop) 14
New Forest xxii
Newham Bottom 14
Newland . . 43, 48, 113, 149, 162, 164, 176, 178, ... 203, 204, 205, 208, 240, 246
church 22
. . . . *and see* Welington.
stanck 177
Newnham-on-Severn 69, 74, 133, 151, 203, 221, 261, 264, 266, 268, 271, 288, 301, 360, 361, 362, 382
Bear Inn 276
Newport 36
New Weir Ford 115, 119
Norchard, north of Lydney174, 177, 476, 482, 503
Northwood 151
Noxon Park, ('Thraves', 'Kingsmore', 'Chelfridge', Lanquire') . . . 28, 161, 164, 166, 257, 496, 503, 514, 515, 516, 517, 518, 519, 520, 523, 524, 526, 531
(Vineyard of) 518

Oakenhill Wood 505
Oakwood 520
'Oldefolde' 14
Orling Green, near Broadmoor 126

Overley 151
Oxford 328

Parkend . . . . . . 69 *and see* Whitemead Park
'Pain's Wood' 30
Perrygrove Wood 28, 30
Pluds 421, 532
Purton, Pill (on Severn) 122, 252, 253, 254
'Puzzle Wood' 30

Raglan 152
Readings, Reddings 527
Redbrook 21, 74, 81, 94, 208
Copper Works 104, 122
Rodley 151
Ross-on-Wye 240, 524
Ross Ash 35
Over Ross 251
Ruardean 38, 70, 105, 106, 110, 119, 121, 122, 123, 124, 129, 130, 134, 151, 202, 204, 246, 262, 482
Rudhall (Herefordshire) 117
Ruspidge 34

St. Briavels 18, 82, 135, 144, 146, 162, 173
Castle . . . . 18, 36, 37, 40, 47, 67, 75, 78, 89, ... 105, 111, 117, 124, 141, 144, 148, 178
St. Weonards (Herefordshire) 93, 96
Saintlow, St. Low 14
Sally, Sallow, Vallet 47, 114, 421
Scar near Milkwall 67
Scowles, The 28
Serridge 121, 122
Severn, River 77, 102, 149, 334
'Sitegrave' 19
'Slad called the Lyme Slad' 74
'Slads at Wyeside' 72
Slaughter, The 528
Soylewell 115, 132
Sneade, Sneyd Wood, north of Lydney . 178, 189, ... 257, 496, 515, 516, 526
Speech House43, 44, 47, 66, 93, 96, 109, 111, 113, 115,
116, 119, 123, 124, 127, 128, 130, 134, 135, 136, 266,
267, 272, 297, 361, 324, 353, 372, 462, 465, 469, 470
. . . . . . *and see* Lodges *and* Walks.
Stapledge inclosure 217
Staunton12, 81, 104, 110, 113, 141, 151, 202, 203, ... 237, 238, 246, 381
Staure 147
Stowe, quarry 447
Stowfield, quarry 417
Symons Yat(e) 92

Taynton 141
Tewkesbury 149
'Thraves', Noxon Park 164
Tibberton 151
Tidenham 151
Tintern 94, 145, 152, 157
furnace 94, 115
wireworks 152, 154
Trellick 36
'Tresser Mill' 119
Trowgreen 526
'Turner's Wood' 30

Usk 271

Viney Hill 37
Deadman's Cross 47

Wales 12, 21, 147, 158
Walford 64
Wallstringers Coppice 187
Walmore Common 149, 351
'Wartokesay' 14
'Watkins' Wood' 30
Welington Manor (old name for Newland) . . 525
Welsh Bicknor 47, 105, 107
parish church 113
Westbury-on-Severn 74, 112, 115, 149, 151
Whippington Brook 528
Whitchurch Furnace 93
Whitebrook (Mon.) 152
Whitecroft 134, 262
Whiteley Green 14
Whitemead Park45, 48, 49, 57, 72, 178, 182, 189, 235, 253
Wilshill 514
Wilton Bridge (Ross-on-Wye) 94, 96
Winnall's Hill, Coleford 544
Woolaston 26, 173
Worcester lodge 206
Wyaston Leys near Monmouth
Wye, River 47, 74, 77, 95, 96, 102, 105, 107, 113, ... 119, 120, 121, 126, 158, 159
New Weir Ford 115, 119
Wyes Green 164
Wyeside 72
Wygate 141
Wyrrall, Worrall, Hill 47, 119, 132, 262
Yorkley 174, 253, 412